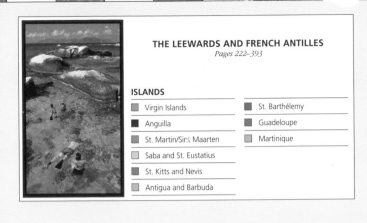

THE LEEWARDS AND FRENCH ANTILLES
Pages 222–393

ISLANDS

- Virgin Islands
- Anguilla
- St. Martin/Sint Maarten
- Saba and St. Eustatius
- St. Kitts and Nevis
- Antigua and Barbuda
- St. Barthélemy
- Guadeloupe
- Martinique

DOMINICAN REPUBLIC

PUERTO RICO

ANGUILLA

ST. MARTIN/SINT MAARTEN

ST. BARTHÉLEMY

VIRGIN ISLANDS

ANTIGUA AND BARBUDA

SABA AND ST. EUSTATIUS

ST. KITTS AND NEVIS

GUADELOUPE

MONTSERRAT

DOMINICA

MARTINIQUE

ST. LUCIA

BARBADOS

ST. VINCENT AND THE GRENADINES

GRENADA

ABC ISLANDS

TRINIDAD AND TOBAGO

THE WINDWARDS
Pages 394–481

ISLANDS

- Dominica
- St. Lucia
- St. Vincent and the Grenadines

D0274637

EYEWITNESS TRAVEL
CARIBBEAN

EYEWITNESS TRAVEL

CARIBBEAN

LONDON, NEW YORK,
MELBOURNE, MUNICH AND DELHI
www.dk.com

MANAGING EDITOR Aruna Ghose
EDITORIAL MANAGER Ankita Awasthi
DESIGN MANAGERS Sunita Gahir, Kavita Saha
PROJECT EDITOR Shikha Kulkarni
PROJECT DESIGNER Anchal Kaushal
EDITORS Divya Chowfin, Jayashree Menon, Souvik Mukherjee
DESIGNERS Sonal Bhatt, Neha Gupta, Kaberi Hazarika
SENIOR CARTOGRAPHIC MANAGER Uma Bhattacharya
CARTOGRAPHER Zafar-ul-Islam Khan
DTP COORDINATOR Azeem Siddiqui
SENIOR PICTURE RESEARCHER Taiyaba Khatoon
PICTURE RESEARCHER Sumita Khatwani

CONTRIBUTORS
Christopher Baker, James Henderson, Skye Hernandez,
Lynda Lohr, KC Nash, Don Philpott, Theresa Storm,
Lynne Morgan Sullivan, Polly Thomas

PHOTOGRAPHERS
Demetrio Carrasco, Nigel Hicks, Linda Whitwam

ILLUSTRATORS
Chapel Design & Marketing Ltd., Chinglemba Chingtham,
Aurgho Jyoti, Arun Pottirayil, Mark Arjun Warner

Reproduced in Singapore by Colourscan
Printed in Malaysia by Vivar Printing Sdn. Bhd.

First published in Great Britain in 2009
Dorling Kindersley Limited
80 Strand, London WC2R 0RL

11 12 13 14 10 9 8 7 6 5 4 3 2 1

Reprinted with revisions 2011

Copyright © 2009, 2011 Dorling Kindersley Limited, London
A Penguin Company

ISBN 978-1-4053-6069-2

FLOORS ARE REFERRED TO THROUGHOUT IN ACCORDANCE WITH
AMERICAN USAGE; IE THE "FIRST FLOOR" IS AT GROUND LEVEL.

Front cover main image: Palm trees on beach, Grenadines

MIX
Paper from
responsible sources
FSC
www.fsc.org   FSC™ C018179

**The information in this
DK Eyewitness Travel Guide is checked regularly.**
Every effort has been made to ensure that this book is as up-to-date
as possible at the time of going to press. Some details, however,
such as telephone numbers, opening hours, prices, gallery hanging
arrangements and travel information are liable to change. The
publishers cannot accept responsibility for any consequences arising
from the use of this book, nor for any material on third party
websites, and cannot guarantee that any website address in this
book will be a suitable source of travel information. We value the
views and suggestions of our readers very highly. Please write to:
Publisher, DK Eyewitness Travel Guides, Dorling Kindersley,
80 Strand, London WC2R 0RL, Great Britain, or email: travelguides@dk.com.

◁ School of scalefin anthias at a coral reef, Dominican Republic

CONTENTS

Souvenir mask, Puerto Rico

VISITING THE
CARIBBEAN

THE CARIBBEAN
AT A GLANCE

Yachts in Christiansted harbor,
St. Croix, US Virgin Islands

Palm Beach in Grand Anse Bay, Grenada

Musée Victor Schoelcher in Pointe-
à-Pitre, Guadeloupe

HOW TO USE THIS GUIDE

This guide helps you get the most from your visit to the Caribbean. It provides detailed practical information and expert recommendations. *Visiting the Caribbean* maps the area and provides tips on practical considerations and travel. The *At a Glance* section introduces the region's history and culture, with an overview of the best activities available. The isles are divided into four main groups, each broken down into individual island chapters. These begin with a map, followed by descriptions of local sights and top beaches. Information about outdoor activities, hotels, restaurants, nightlife, and practical details is found at the end of each chapter.

ISLAND BY ISLAND
The map on the inside front cover shows the four main divisions and the 22 different Caribbean island entities dealt with in this guide.

1 At a Glance Map
Each section starts with a map color coding the various islands covered in separate chapters.

2 Introduction to an Island
Some isles with particular characteristics get a more in-depth introduction to their geography, history, and culture.

Captions briefly describe some of the important sights on the island.

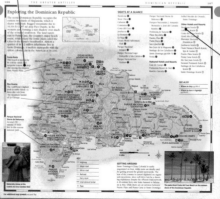

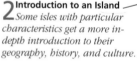

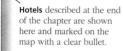

Hotels described at the end of the chapter are shown here and marked on the map with a clear bullet.

3 Area Map
For easy reference, sights in each island nation are numbered on the map, in the same order that they are described in the chapter.

Thumb tabs are color coded to make it easier to locate different islands.

4 **Street-by-Street Map**
This illustration gives a bird's-eye view of the important streets and buildings of the sightseeing area in a town.

Stars indicate the sights that no visitor should miss.

A **suggested route** covers some of the more interesting and attractive streets in the area.

5 **Detailed information**
Towns, nature attractions, and beach areas are described individually, some with their own maps and icons.

Numbers refer to a sight's position on the area map.

6 **Outdoor Activities**
Detailed information of the different kinds of outdoor activities available in each island is given here, along with a directory.

Special features provide in-depth pictorial depiction of an aspect or sport.

Color bars make it easy to locate the practical spread.

7 **Practical Information**
This spread deals with subjects such as when to go, visas, security, transport, and language.

Directory boxes give contact details for the services mentioned in the text.

VISITING THE CARIBBEAN

DISCOVERING THE CARIBBEAN

Despite similarities in their history and geographical location, the 7,000 and more islands that make up the Caribbean are each distinct in cultural and physical character. Ruled by feuding European powers for centuries, infused with the African cultures of those brought

Souvenir at a craft market

here as slaves, this potpourri is also known as the West Indies and offers many distinctions. The islands are organized into sovereign states, overseas departments, and dependencies. Below is an overview of the main subgroups, highlighting their top resorts and attractions.

The Capitolio in Havana, Cuba

THE GREATER ANTILLES

- Majestic colonial cities
- Challenging diverse terrains
- Exciting wildlife

Comprising the large islands of the northwest Caribbean, this group of four major islands and one tiny subgroup is closely associated with Columbus's arrival in the New World in 1492. Together they offer a great diversity of terrain, with fabulous coral reefs, rolling plains, and even desert-dry regions in the shadow of looming mountains. The colonial cities of the Spanish-speaking islands hold special attraction. The **Dominican Republic** (see pp164–93), which takes up the eastern half of Hispaniola, is steeped in Columbus lore. Santo Domingo, the oldest city in

the New World, boasts the Americas' oldest cathedral among its colonial treasures. More than four million visitors a year flock to the stunning white sands, turquoise waters, and an unrivaled choice of hotels. It is possible to visualize pre-Columbian myths in the once-sacred caverns, play golf on the Caribbean's best courses, or hike to the summit of Pico Duarte, the highest point in the Caribbean. Spanish-speaking **Cuba** (pp68–99), to the west, is by far the largest island in this group and has the most fascinating colonial cities, as well as white-sand beaches, and superb diving sites. The island's complex culture is an amalgamation of vastly different traditions. Visitors can explore Havana, where the lively nightlife is topped by glamorous cabarets, or hire a classic 1950s American auto to see the rest of the island, including the

18th-century "suspended in time" town of Trinidad, a UNESCO World Heritage Site.

The easternmost island of the Greater Antilles, mountainous **Puerto Rico** (pp194–221) draws many cruise ships to San Juan with its historic core of well-preserved colonial structures. Modern San Juan is known for its fine dining restaurants and ritzy nightclubs. Thrilling activities include hiking in El Yunque rainforest and taking the spectacular drive on the Ruta Panorámica along the island's mountain spine.

Jamaica (pp132–63), south of Cuba, is renowned for reggae and its Rastafarian culture. The island's flatlands are studded with former plantation homes, strangely picturesque reminders of a brutal era. Rugged mountains beckon visitors to explore beyond the lovely beaches. West of Jamaica, the trio of **Cayman Islands** (pp100–15) are pancake flat. Divers rave about the coral reefs and the crystal waters lapping pristine-white beaches of these three English-speaking islands.

Hiking and canyoning in the Toro Negro mountains, Puerto Rico

◁ Beach at Great Harbor, Jost Van Dyke, Virgin Islands

A view of Deadman's Beach on Peter Island, British Virgin Islands

Turks and Caicos *(pp116–31)*, comprising eight main islands, lie outside the Caribbean Sea, north of Hispaniola. Flat and semiarid, they are known for superlative sands: Grace Bay is perhaps the most beautiful beach in the Caribbean. Highlights include whale-watching off Salt Cay, diving the HMS *Endymion* wreck, and angling for bonefish.

THE LEEWARDS AND FRENCH ANTILLES

- BVI's frost-white beaches
- St. Barth's chic bars and nightclubs
- Dramatic active volcanos

Beginning east of Puerto Rico, this northern group of the Lesser Antilles reflects the amazing diversity of the Caribbean geography and cultures. The group of some 20 islands arching southeast are rich in natural beauty, superb beaches, and cosmopolitan life.

In the **Virgin Islands** archipelago *(pp226–57)*, the US Virgin Islands (St. Thomas, St. John, and St. Croix) are frequented by cruise ships and are replete with architectural reminders of their past as Dutch, Danish, and French colonies. The more easterly and serene British Virgin isles (Tortola, Virgin Gorda, and the Outer Islands), are a sailing mecca clinging to a laid-back lifestyle.

Tiny **Anguilla** *(pp258–69)* is a flat limestone plateau with talcum-fine beaches that lure sophisticated travelers to its boutique hotels. Nearby **St. Martin/Sint Maarten** *(pp270–85)* has a split personality. Hedonists flock to the nudist beaches of the northerly French half; Philipsburg, on the southern Dutch half, has forts and duty-free shopping. French **St. Barths** *(pp344–57)* is a haven for wealthy sybarites, with Paris-style bistros and boutiques.

The twin Dutch-speaking isles of **Saba and St. Eustatius** *(pp286–301)*, formed of dormant volcanos, rise steeply from the sea and offer excellent hiking and scuba diving. The main draw of French-speaking **Guadeloupe** *(pp358–75)* is its colorful Creole culture.

The magnificient frigate bird, Barbuda

St. Kitts and Nevis *(pp302–19)* trace a British colonial legacy to 1624. Brightly painted fishing boats line lovely beaches backed by sugarcane fields and green mountains. Lively festivals culminate in the Carnival each December. For colonial history, visit **Antigua and Barbuda** *(pp320–41)*, famed for Nelson's Dockyard at English Harbour as well as its many beaches. Barbuda's Frigate Bird Sanctuary is a spectacle not to be missed. Nearby, Montserrat is the perfect place to view an active volcano.

The southernmost Leeward island, **Martinique** *(pp376–93)*, features an appealing blend of French and Creole culture, architecture, and cuisine, as well as great physical beauty epitomized by an active volcano, Mont Pelée.

Crafts and souvenir stalls in St. Martin/Sint Maarten

The twin peaks of Petit Piton and Gros Piton, St. Lucia

THE WINDWARDS

- **Hiking in Dominica**
- **St. Lucia's twin peaks**
- **Sailing in the Grenadines**

Named for the fact that they face east into the trade winds, these lush, rugged islands are among the most beautiful and green in all of the Caribbean. With the exception of Barbados, this group comprises a series of volcanic peaks that rise from a submarine mountain chain, most lying within sight of one another.

Dominica (pp398–413) is known as the "Nature Isle" for its rainforests – a hiker's delight – and the large numbers of whales that gather offshore in winter. So mountainous is this island that it has its own micro-climate, with rains feeding abundant vegetation. It is also home to the region's only reserve of indigenous Carib people. Tourism here is focused on nature, and includes attractions such as an aerial tram through the forests, while Morne Trois Pitons National Park offers some excellent and challenging mountain hiking.

Tear-drop-shaped **St. Lucia** (pp414–31) is equal in beauty, with its twin Pitons, and a drive-in volcano at Soufrière adds to the adventure. As the most developed of the Windward Islands, it offers some of the best hotels, from all-inclusive resorts spread out along golden beaches to charming bed-and-breakfasts tucked into intimate coves.

To the south, the dozen or so islands comprising **St. Vincent and the Grenadines** (pp432–47) are a sailor's and hiker's delight. The islands are steeped in history and this is where travelers can still meet the descendants of the "Black Caribs" (see p434) and get a glimpse of their life-style. St. Vincent also has some of the Caribbean's most luxurious accommodations, popular with international celebrities. Bequia, Mustique, and Petit St. Vincent are among the tiny and exclusive gems of the Grenadines renowned for their exclusive hotels overlooking super-lative beaches.

Grenada, known as the "Spice Island" (pp448–63), has gorgeous beaches but also lures hikers into its dense mountainous wilds. The island's capital, St. George's, is set in a massive volcanic bowl scalloped into a dramatic bay – one of the prettiest settings in the Caribbean, enhanced by forts and venerable mercantile buildings.

Nutmeg and mace, grown in Grenada

Barbados (pp464–81), far out to the southeast, is still carpeted with sugar-cane and steeped in old English traditions and colonial architecture. Atlantic rollers crash ashore along its rugged east coast, providing some of the best surfing in the Caribbean, although most exclusive hotels face west onto soft white beaches and calm turquoise shallows protected by pristine coral reefs.

Sailing yachts anchored in the port of Kingstown, St. Vincent

Locals dressed up for the annual Carnival, Trinidad

THE SOUTHERN CARIBBEAN

- **Carnival in Trinidad**
- **Traditional Dutch architecture**
- **Surfing on Aruba**

Just north of the Venezuelan coast is a medley of much fought-over isles divided into easterly and westerly groups as distinct as thumbprints.

The islands of **Trinidad and Tobago** *(pp486–507)* are well known for calypso and soca music. Their rich and diverse cultures, infused with Hindu, Muslim, and Chinese elements, explode into life during the Carnival, a sensual whirligig extravaganza held each year just before Lent. Although industrialized, populous, and cosmopolitan, Trinidad also boasts a remarkable variety of flora and fauna, from coastal swamps to montane rainforest. Tobago, a tiny isle to the northeast of the much larger Trinidad, is diminutive and low-key. It moves at a slower pace and boasts some picturesque beaches, many tucked into intimate coves. The island offers drives along back roads that snake through the hills and the forest reserves have excellent hiking trails through the deep-green jungles. Compact islands off Tobago such as Little Tobago offer a range of watersports including

diving and scuba diving among the varied and colorful marine life.

Although **Aruba**, **Bonaire**, and **Curaçao** *(pp508–535)* are geographically located as "ACB", the three isles are popularly known as "the ABCs". They are distinct for their Dutch architecture and relatively barren low-slung terrain comprising ancient lava fringed by limestone brittle, called *klips* by the locals. Whipped by winds that take the edge off the relentless sun, these isles are studded with cactus and thorny scrub, such as the native divi-divi trees. The largest island, Aruba, a mere 15 miles (25 km) off the coast of Venezuela, has been a Dutch possession since 1636. Oranjestad, the capital, is graced by classically Dutch architecture. Huge high-rise resort hotels line stunning beaches, and many have lively casinos and glitzy floorshows – a thoroughly modern form of tourism that distinguishes this island from all its neighbors. Constant 15-knot trade winds spell nirvana for kite- and windsurfers, while divers rave about the coral reefs that run the length of the protected leeward shore.

Curaçao, largest of the ABCs, is a favorite of cruise ship passengers who come to see its charming traditional Dutch architecture in Willemstad, resembling a mini-Amsterdam in the tropical sun. For long a trading center, the island changed

Scuba diver swimming past corals and sponges, Salt Pier, Bonaire

hands many times in colonial days. It has a diverse ethnic population and its towns are graced by façades painted in pretty ice-cream pastels. The island makes up for its lack of beaches by its excellent duty-free shopping, diving, windsurfing, kitesurfing, and sailing.

Boomerang-shaped Bonaire, second largest of the ABCs, also has fantastic diving, plus kayaking in Bonaire National Marine Park. Salt is the island's main industry and the isle is the least developed among the trio, with none of the glitz of Aruba. Nonetheless, it has plenty of wealth when it comes to its flora and fauna: many visitors come to see flamingos – the island's signature bird. Other than birding, it is the diving that truly astounds visitors and most hotels here cater to scuba enthusiasts.

Dutch-style buildings on the Handels Kade, Willemstad, Curaçao

Putting the Caribbean on the Map

Sweeping in a great arc some 2,000 miles (3,218 km) long, from the western tip of Cuba to the Leewards in the east, then south to the top of South America, and westward along Venezuela's north coast, the chain of island nations comprising the Caribbean wrap around the Caribbean Sea like a shepherd's crook. The Greater Antilles to the northwest include the larger islands: Cuba, Jamaica, Hispaniola, and Puerto Rico. To their east, the smaller islands of the Lesser Antilles form a barrier against the Atlantic Ocean. Together they encompass a dazzling diversity, from semiarid deserts to fern-choked rainforests; limestone plateaus to soaring volcanos; and coral reefs to mountains.

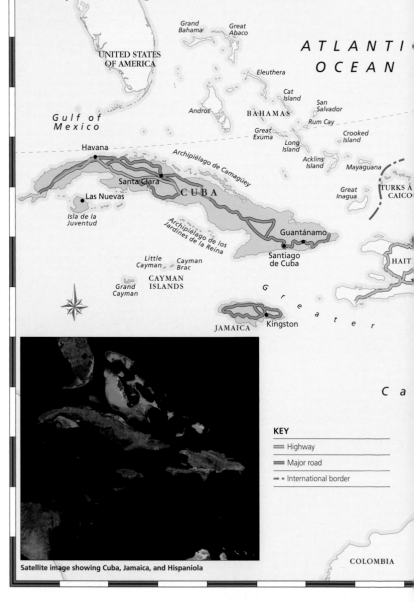

Grand Bahama

Great Abaco

UNITED STATES OF AMERICA

ATLANTIC OCEAN

Eleuthera

Cat Island

San Salvador

Gulf of Mexico

Andros

BAHAMAS

Rum Cay

Great Exuma

Crooked Island

Long Island

Havana

Archipiélago de Camagüey

Acklins Island

Mayaguana

Santa Clara

CUBA

Great Inagua

TURKS & CAICO

Las Nuevas

Isla de la Juventud

Archipiélago de los Jardines de la Reina

Guantánamo

Santiago de Cuba

HAIT

Little Cayman

Cayman Brac

CAYMAN ISLANDS

Grand Cayman

Greater

JAMAICA

Kingston

Ca

KEY

▬ Highway

▬ Major road

– – International border

Satellite image showing Cuba, Jamaica, and Hispaniola

COLOMBIA

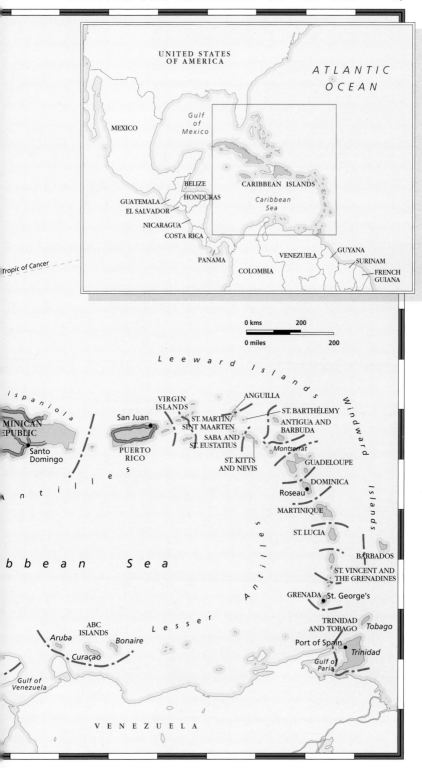

Climate of the Caribbean

All the Caribbean islands lie within the tropics and the climate is like an endless summer, although the weather patterns vary from isle to isle. Temperatures are fairly constant year-round, but seasonal temperatures in the Greater Antilles vary more than in the Lesser Antilles. The trade winds blow throughout the year and keep temperatures within tolerable levels, especially on east-facing shores. Variations in altitude affect the climates of the islands: temperatures decline with increasing elevation, and higher mountains form rain shadows on their leeward sides, eastern shores thus receiving more rain than the western sides. Rainfall varies from about 10 inches (25 cm) per year on Bonaire to 350 inches (900 cm) in parts of Dominica.

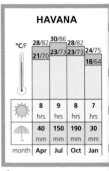

HAVANA

°C/F	Apr	Jul	Oct	Jan
	28/82	30/86	28/82	24/75
	21/70	23/73	23/73	18/64
☀	8 hrs	9 hrs	8 hrs	7 hrs
☂	40 mm	150 mm	190 mm	30 mm
month	Apr	Jul	Oct	Jan

Turks and Caicos has an average of 350 days of sunshine a year.

Cuba's summers can be torrid, especially in the eastern provinces.

Jamaica can be cold atop the highest peaks of the Blue Mountains.

HURRICANES

The Caribbean islands are located within a hurricane belt. These tropical storms, which evolve over warm ocean water and revolve around a low-pressure center, are characterized by very high winds and rainfall and can cause huge devastation. The hurricane season lasts from June to November, with a peak in September, but this does not at all mean that all islands are affected every year. The southernmost islands rarely get hit by forceful hurricanes.

KINGSTON

°C/F	Apr	Jul	Oct	Jan
	31/88	33/91	32/90	30/86
	24/75	24/75	23/73	21/70
☀	09 hrs	09 hrs	07 hrs	08 hrs
☂	64 mm	74 mm	188 mm	69 mm
Month	Apr	Jul	Oct	Jan

Cienfuegos in Cuba struck by a powerful hurricane

0 km		100
0 miles		100

Large boulders in the arid landscape of Aruba

SANTO DOMINGO

°C/F				
	30/86	31/88	31/88	29/84
	21/70	23/73	22/72	20/68
☀	07 hrs	06 hrs	06 hrs	06 hrs
☂	99 mm	163 mm	152 mm	61 mm
Month	Apr	Jul	Oct	Jan

Puerto Rico's wettest part is El Yunque, with an average of over 200 inches (508 cm) of rain annually.

The Dominican Republic has several distinct climates and a pronounced rainy season in the summer months.

ROSEAU

°C/F				
	29/84	31/88	32/90	32/90
	20/68	20/68	22/72	22/72
☀	08 hrs	08 hrs	07 hrs	08 hrs
☂	61 mm	274 mm	198 mm	132 mm
Month	Apr	Jul	Oct	Jan

ST. THOMAS

°C/F				
	30/87	32/89	32/89	29/85
	23/74	26/78	24/76	22/72
☀	07 hrs	08 hrs	08 hrs	09 hrs
☂	70 mm	62 mm	136 mm	47 mm
Month	Apr	Jul	Oct	Jan

Average monthly maximum temperature

Average monthly minimum temperature

Average daily hours of sunshine

Average monthly rainfall

Aruba is arid but the temperature stays moderate thanks to a constant ocean breeze.

WILLEMSTAD

°C/F				
	30/86	31/88	31/88	28/82
	24/75	25/77	26/79	24/76
☀	08 hrs	09 hrs	08 hrs	08 hrs
☂	23 mm	20 mm	81 mm	53 mm
Month	Apr	Jul	Oct	Jan

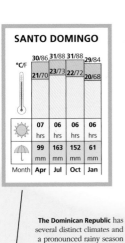

PRACTICAL INFORMATION

Virtually every Caribbean isle relies on tourism and provides visitors with a broad range of amenities up to international par. However, in more remote areas tourist facilities may be limited. It is relatively easy to island hop, although advance planning is essential. Most islands have their own tourist offices, which can assist in itinerary planning and give information on hotels, restaurants, attractions, and other activities. There are plenty of travel and tour agencies in the islands, and an effective approach is to book local excursions using their offices, usually based in the major hotels.

Signage at a hotel, Canouan, Grenadines

WHEN TO GO

Any time of year is good for visiting the Caribbean. However, June through November is hurricane season, and July and August are torrid months that can make touring away from the beach quite tiring. December to April is the best period to visit, when the climate is warm without being unbearable, and there are cultural events on most isles.

GETTING THERE

The best way to get to the Caribbean is by air, although cruises can be a leisurely way to explore the area. Prices soar during the peak season from December to April. The ferry is also an option between some islands. Refer to the respective islands for more details.

DOCUMENTATION

Entry requirements vary widely among the island nations, so always check before you travel. For most countries, visitors need to have a valid passport and a return ticket, as well as a tourist visa (typically good for 30- to 90-day stays), usually issued by the travel agency. Trinidad and a few other islands require that visas be issued in advance. Canadian citizens can enter the Turks and Caicos without a passport, although valid ID together with a birth certificate is mandatory. Special restrictions apply to US citizens wishing to visit Cuba. Most islands require those who visit for business or as a journalist to apply for a special visa in advance. All US citizens returning to the United States by air are required to present a valid passport for re-entry, and since 1 June 2009 those re-entering the country by land or sea must have a passport book (full passport), passport card (credit-card-sized mini passport), or a Global Entry Trusted Traveler Program card, issued to pre-vetted frequent border crossers. The only exception to these new Western Hemisphere Travel Initiative requirements is travelers on closed-loop cruises, who do not require a passport. For further details of WHTI-compliant documents, contact the **US Customs and Border Protection Agency**, the **US Department of Homeland Security** or the **US Department of State**.

CUSTOMS AND DUTY-FREE

Besides personal belongings, tourists are allowed to carry up to 2 liters (67 fl.oz) of alcohol and two cigarette cartons to most Caribbean isles. Certain drugs require a prescription. Local and Caribbean customs are on guard for drug trafficking.

US Customs allows $800 worth of goods duty-free, including 1 liter (33 fl.oz) of alcohol, 200 cigarettes, and 100 non-Cuban cigars, plus an unlimited amount of original art. Visitors who travel to the US Virgin Islands plus another Caribbean island may bring back $1,600 worth of goods duty-free. No Customs declaration is required when traveling between Puerto Rico and the US. The UK permits ±390 worth of goods, plus 200 cigarettes or 50 cigars, plus 4 liters (144 fl.oz) of wine, and 1 liter (36 fl.oz) of spirits.

Avoid buying items made from endangered species such as tortoise shell, black coral, or reptile skin. These are covered under the Convention on International Trade in Endangered Species (CITES) and anyone in possession can be fined.

VISITOR INFORMATION

The **Caribbean Tourism Organization** represents the entire region and has headquarters in London and New York. All the island nations have official tourism promotion boards that provide maps, literature, and other information. Most have offices in the UK and North America, as well as local offices on the respective islands.

HEALTH AND SECURITY

The islands vary greatly in terms of safety and medical facilities. Private clinics are preferable to public hospitals. Malaria is prevalent on many islands, and the region has experienced an epidemic of dengue fever in recent years; check for recommended inoculations before traveling.

Visitors need to guard against pickpockets and mugging in most large Caribbean cities. Traffic is one of the biggest dangers as locals often drive without due regard for the law. Riptides (dangerous undertows) claim many lives among inattentive swimmers. On beaches, avoid seeking shade under coconut palms, as falling fruit is a real hazard. Women should avoid lonely beaches. Due to security concerns, Haiti has not been covered in this guide.

BANKING AND CURRENCY

A wide variety of currencies are in use throughout the Caribbean. Many English-speaking islands use the Eastern Caribbean dollar; the French-speaking isles use the euro; and the Netherlands Antilles use the florin. The US dollar is accepted almost everywhere and many businesses also accept euros. Banks are ubiquitous, although ATMs often run out of cash. Most hotels are also happy to change foreign currency.

COMMUNICATIONS

Hotels usually charge high fees for phone calls. It is wise to buy a phone card for use with public phones. Every island has them and the cards can be bought in stores and gas stations. If you plan to use your cellphone, check that your carrier network is compatible with the island(s) you wish to visit. Internet is available throughout the Caribbean and there is no shortage of Internet cafés. Many hotels have Wi-Fi access, either complimentary or available for a fee.

TRANSPORT

Getting around can be a challenge, depending on the island. Bus service on most small islands is by crowded minivans. Tourist taxis offer efficient, albeit pricey service from major hotels in big cities; elsewhere locals prefer cheaper shared taxis. For details on car rentals, refer to the Practical Information pages for each island.

SHOPPING

The Caribbean is a cornucopia of crafts and every island has its own distinct style. Cuba, especially, has some of the most profound art, while the Dominican Republic is a great place to pick up Haitian art. Beautiful wood carvings are a specialty on every isle, as are jewelry, straw hats and baskets, sold at beach stalls and markets and where haggling over the price is half the fun. Cigars and rum, hammocks, and *guayaberas* (on Spanish-speaking isles) are other local treasures. Cruise ports specialize in duty-free items such as perfumes and watches. It is advisable not to buy items made from animals, or coral and seashells.

LANGUAGES

The official language of each island reflects its colonial heritage. Cuba, Puerto Rico, and the Dominican Republic speak Spanish; English is spoken on Britain's former colonies; while French and Dutch are the *lingua franca* of the islands with ties to those nations. Virtually every island also has its own local patois, vernacular Creole languages, that creatively merge a form of the colonial "mother tongue" with words adopted from African languages.

ELECTRICITY

Most islands of the Greater Antilles operate on 110 volts, as in the US, but even here many outlets use 220 volts. In the Lesser Antilles, 220 volts is common, as in Europe, and North American travelers may need adaptors for their appliances. Power outages are common throughout the region; take a flashlight.

TIME

The Caribbean islands span two time zones. The Dominican Republic and islands to the east are in the Atlantic Standard Time Zone, 4 hours behind Greenwich Mean Time. Islands to the west are on Eastern Standard Time, 5 hours behind GMT. Some islands use Daylight Saving Time, with beginning and ending times varying for each nation.

ETIQUETTE

Most islands are conservative and nudism and topless bathing are not permitted. However, the French islands are renowned for being more liberal and even other conservative islands have all-inclusive naturalist resorts. Bathing suits should not be worn away from the beach.

The Spanish-speaking islands especially retain macho traditions and, except in Cuba, the taboo against homosexuality remains ingrained in most island cultures. Caribbean men feel virtually obliged to pay compliments to women passing by, although it is not always expressed in good taste. No reaction is seriously expected, and women would be wise to totally disregard such comments. The best way to put an end to unwanted flirtation is to say that you are married.

Barring business meetings, fine-dining restaurants and nightclubs, a jacket or formal evening dress is not needed. Many resort restaurants demand proper shoes (no toes showing and no trainers), especially for men.

DIRECTORY

VISITOR INFORMATION

Caribbean Tourism Organization
80 Broad Street, Suite 3200, New York, NY 10004.
Tel 212 635 9530.
22 The Quadrant, Richmond, London TW9 1BP. *Tel* 020 8948 0057. **www**.caribbeantravel.com

DOCUMENTATION

US Customs and Border Protection Agency
www.cbp.gov

US Department of Homeland Security
www.dhs.gov/files/crossingborders

US Department of State
travel.state.gov
www.getyouhome.gov

TRAVEL INFORMATION

The Caribbean covers a huge region and trying to explore the many diverse islands in one go is a challenge. Most islands have airports served by direct or non-stop international flights while many smaller islands are served by smaller planes from regional hubs. There are many luxurious Caribbean cruises which stop at several islands. Apart from cruises, traveling between many of the islands by sea is difficult, as only a few are linked by ferry. Bus services vary. Modern air-conditioned buses link major tourist destinations on larger islands, but most islanders rely on crowded minibuses. Driving offers the most flexibility in terms of speed and accessibility, but it can be hair-raising with bad road conditions.

Runway at the small airport of St. Barthélemy

ARRIVING BY AIR

Taking a plane to the Caribbean islands is the best way to get here. International long-haul flights from North America and Europe serve most of the islands, although visitors may need to connect in major regional hubs such as San Juan or St. Thomas. The major North American carriers with Caribbean service include **Air Canada**, **American Airlines**, **Delta**, **JetBlue**, **Spirit Airlines**, **United Airlines**, and **US Airways**. Three Caribbean airlines are **Air Jamaica**, **Caribbean Airlines**, and **LIAT** also have international service to the region, while **Cubana** serves Cuba from Canada and Europe. From Europe, some international airlines fly via the US, although Air France, **British Airways**, Iberia, **KLM**, and **Virgin Atlantic** operate direct flights, as do LIAT and Air Jamaica. Many charter airlines also fly to the Caribbean.

Small passenger planes are a staple form of getting around within the islands.

American Eagle links major airports within Puerto Rico, and Cubana and **AeroDomca** provide domestic service within Cuba and the Dominican Republic, respectively. Dozens of charter companies offer scheduled flights aboard 4- to 16-passenger aircraft linking key tourist destinations within individual islands or island groups.

Visitors can also island-hop between the small isles of the Lesser Antilles by one of several small Caribbean carriers. For more details, refer to specific islands.

AIRPORTS

There are some 30 major Caribbean airports that receive international flights, plus dozens of other airports and airstrips for domestic flights. Most Caribbean airports are small and the aircrafts are not connected directly to a terminal. Hence, visitors will have to walk on the tarmac from the plane to the terminal.

CRUISES

The Caribbean is a top year-round destination for cruise ships. More than 20 cruise lines offer a vast range of ships and itineraries. The ships sail at night and berth at their next port of call before dawn, permitting visitors to explore ashore by day. Cruise companies sell a wide range of group-oriented shore excursions, but it is often cheaper and more fun to make your own arrangements ashore. Special theme cruises are a popular option. More details are available from **Cruise Line International Association**.

A huge cruise liner moored at Pointe-à-Pitre, Guadeloupe

Passengers getting off a ferry boat in Puerto Rico

FERRIES AND SAILBOATS

Ferries link Puerto Rico to both the Dominican Republic and the US Virgin Islands, which are connected by ferry to the British Virgin Islands. Trinidad and Tobago are also connected by ferry. Sailboat charters are a popular way of exploring the islands. Yachts can be chartered with or without crews on virtually every island, although it is wise to book your sailing vacation in advance from a reputable company such as the **Caribbean Yacht Rental** or **Ed Hamilton**.

DRIVING

Traveling by car is the most practical and flexible way of exploring all but the smallest isles. Car rentals are widely available, and major international rental companies have franchises on most islands. Driving in the Caribbean can be challenging. Hazards include poorly paved and pot-holed roads, stray animals on the road, and local drivers who have no concern for the safety of other road users. It is advisable not to drive at night. Cars drive on the left side of the road on most Caribbean islands except Bonaire, St. Eustatius, Aruba, the Dominican Republic, Guadeloupe,

Curaçao, Cuba, Martinique, Puerto Rico, St. Martin/Sint Maarten, and Saba.

PACKAGE DEALS AND ORGANIZED TOURS

Air fares can vary greatly from season to season, between airlines and ticket wholesalers, and according to time of year. The further in advance you buy your ticket, the cheaper it usually is. Air-hotel packages are available for every island. These inclusive vacations tend to be cheaper than independent travel. Most major airlines offer inclusive packages, as do many companies in Europe and North America.

If you are interested in a beach vacation, there are special tours that may appeal

to visitors. Most islands offer a variety of watersports and there are several package deals. Popular themed vacations include birding, hiking, cycling, scuba diving, and sportfishing. For more details, refer to specific islands.

Driving through the rainforest, Puerto Rico

DIRECTORY

ARRIVING BY AIR

AeroDomca
www.aerodomca.com

Air Canada
www.aircanada.com

Air Jamaica
www.airjamaica.com

American Airlines
www.aa.com

British Airways
www.ba.com

Caribbean Airlines
www.caribbean-airlines.com

Cubana
www.cubana.cu

Delta
www.delta.com

Jet Blue
www.jetblue.com

KLM
www.klm.com

LIAT
www.liat.com

Spirit Airlines
www.spiritair.com

United Airlines
www.united.com

US Airways
www.usairways.com

Virgin Atlantic
www.virginatlantic.com

CRUISES

Cruise Line International Association
910 SE 17th Street., Suite 400
Fort Lauderdale, FL 33316.
Tel 754 224 2200.
www.cruising.org

The Cruise Line Ltd.
Softech House, London Road,
Albourne, West Sussex, UK.
Tel 0800 008 6677.
www.cruiseline.co.uk

FERRIES AND SAILBOATS

Caribbean Yacht Rental
Tel 800 581 7130.
www.caribbeanyachtsrental.com

Ed Hamilton
Tel 800 621 7855.
www.ed-hamilton.com

THE CARIBBEAN AT A GLANCE

Best Beaches

The Caribbean's greatest appeal is the unequaled beauty of its beaches. While it is almost impossible to make a mistake when choosing a sun-and-sand destination, there are distinct differences among the islands and their beaches. The Atlantic Ocean batters the eastern shores of most of the 7,000 islands and cays between North and South America, making their windward coasts rugged with huge breaking waves and a surfer's dream. The leeward coasts are washed by the gentle Caribbean Sea and are favored by swimmers, snorkelers, and divers. The sand too varies from soft and white to black and coarse.

Punta Cana *is part of the 21-mile (34-km) Coconut Coast on the eastern end of the Dominican Republic. Hundreds of swaying palms tower over fine white sand and dozens of all-inclusive resorts provide all comforts and offer a variety of activities.*

Grace Bay *(see p118)* on Turks and Caicos has 12 miles (19 km) of uninterrupted beach scattered with upscale resorts.

BAHAMAS

CUBA

TURKS AND CAICOS

Playa Ancón

CAYMAN ISLANDS

HAITI   DOMINICAN REPUBLIC

JAMAICA

Seven Mile Beach in Negril, Jamaica, has been one of the Caribbean's most popular stretches of sand since the 1960s, when hippies discovered it. Though over-developed, it is innately beautiful.

C a r i b b e a n

ISL

Seven Mile Beach *in Grand Cayman is a well-groomed beach on the island's west coast. Although lined with busy shops, restaurants, and resorts, this stretch of sand gives an impression of spaciousness and unspoiled nature.*

BEST OF THE REST

Good beaches line both sides of virtually every island but top ratings go to beaches with the best water conditions, sand quality, availability of shade, facilities, and ease of access.

Playa Ancón (see p84), *Cuba, is a lovely white strip of sand on the secluded stretch of Caribbean Sea facing Ancón peninsula.*

Great Bay Beach *in Sint Maarten is a white sand beach along the bay, with Philipsburg's main shopping street running parallel to it.*

Luquillo (see p208) *in Puerto Rico offers light golden sand, calm waters, and ample amenities making it a popular beach for families. As a certified Blue Flag Beach, the area adheres to strict environmental standards, guarantees good water quality, and provides facilities for disabled travelers.*

Honeymoon Beach, St. John, USVI, is among Caneel Bay's seven spectacular beaches. Its powdery soft sands can only be reached by foot or boat.

Pink Beach in Barbuda is an 8-mile (13-km) strip of pink-hued sand along an isolated stretch of the island's coast.

Great Bay Beach

ST. MARTIN/
SINT MAARTEN

ANGUILLA

ST. BARTHÉLEMY

ANTIGUA AND

TO
O

VIRGIN
ISLANDS

BARBUDA

SABA AND
ST. EUSTATIUS

MONTSERRAT

ST. KITTS
AND NEVIS

GUADELOUPE

The Baths (see p240), *Virgin Gorda, has some bizarre-shaped natural features, with giant boulders scattered along the water's edge, creating tranquil pools and striking grottos.*

DOMINICA

MARTINIQUE

Shoal Bay in Antigua has visitors lounging on its shaded shimmery-white sand and snorkeling in the calm waters.

ST. LUCIA

BARBADOS

e a

ST. VINCENT AND
THE GRENADINES

Man O' War Bay

Grand Anse Beach

GRENADA

Pigeon Point

TRINIDAD
AND TOBAGO

0 km   300

0 miles   300

ZUELA

Anse Chastanet *on St. Lucia is one of the world's most popular beaches, especially among divers, for its excellent diving sites.*

The beaches of Tobago *offer a near Robinson Crusoe-type holiday. Pigeon Point is a long coral beach. Man O' War Bay is known for its beautiful natural harbor and long stretch of sand.*

Grand Anse *in Grenada stretches over 2 miles (3 km) in length. Its powdery white sands extend far offshore making it broad as well. Most of the island's best hotels are within walking distance of this beach strip.*

Beachlife

Each island enjoys a unique heritage, yet all Caribbean residents share a common modern-day culture based on year-round sunshine and close proximity to the sea. Daily life revolves around the beach, which becomes livelier at night and during special events, and visitors pick up this tropical rhythm with ease. By law, most beaches are public up to the high-water mark, and beachfront property owners allow access. Lifeguards keep watch at popular spots, but in other areas, swimmers are responsible for their personal safety. Police often patrol and signs warn of strong water currents.

Catamaran, Saline Bay, St. Vincent and the Grenadines

SPORT ACTIVITIES

Volleyball, scuba diving, surfing, yachting, and other watersports dominate the tourist activities during the day. Calm water on leeward beaches is ideal for swimming and snorkeling, while the windward coasts are best for surfing. Scuba divers favor islands with offshore reefs.

Horse-riding *along the beach and into the nearby countryside is a popular and relaxing way to tour the coasts of many islands. Riders of all skill levels can participate in beach rides and most include a cooling canter into the surf. Several tour operators also offer romantic sunset rides along the shore.*

Beach volleyball *is one of the most popular sports in the islands. The annual Caribbean Beach Volleyball Championships are held each fall on different islands, drawing players and fans from around the world.*

Parasailing *is a fun activity available on many beaches. Participants sit in a sling seat attached to a specially-designed parachute, which is hoisted skyward by a boat. Paragliding is also popular on islands with mountains and steady trade winds, such as the Dominican Republic.*

Naturalist resorts exist on some islands but in general nudity is outlawed on most public beaches and topless sunbathing is not common. Wearing wet or uncovered swimsuits in restaurants and shops is unacceptable, even near the beach.

LEISURE ACTIVITIES

The highlight of a vacation is an early morning leisurely stroll along the beach with long afternoons spent in the shade napping, reading, and picnicking on soft white sand or exploring rocky coastlines. Beachfront resorts supply towels, umbrellas, and lounge chairs for guests while waterside huts have rentals for day visitors.

Children's packages *at all-inclusive resorts usually include building sand castles, treasure hunts on the beach, or going for nature walks.*

The Caribbean Sea is known for its turquoise color and crystal-clear visibility.

Typical thatched umbrellas, found on most beaches, provide welcome shade from the tropical sun.

Shopping *on the beach is a fine way to spend the day. Vendors set up shop on the busiest beaches to sell sarongs, towels, and souvenirs, as well as swimsuits. Whether locally produced or imported, these will all bring back a flavor of the Caribbean.*

Beach food, *beach bars, and snack shacks specialize in rum-based drinks, ice-cold beer, and seafood sandwiches. On many islands, roti is a popular light meal made of fish, shrimp, chicken or mutton wrapped in flat bread, thinner than naan or pita.*

Beach parties *take place on most weekends. Except for small private gatherings, visitors are almost always welcome to join the fun. Full-moon parties are often hosted at beachfront bars, especially during festive events.*

Popular Diving and Snorkeling Spots

With long stretches of spectacular coral reefs and scores of diverse sites, the Caribbean offers superlative diving and snorkeling. The remarkable marine habitats are a trove of underwater treasures where crystal-clear waters allow visitors to experience profuse marine life viewing combined with the thrill of exploring mysterious Spanish galleons and the wrecks of World War II vessels. Visitors can also island-hop to mix and match a range of incredibly varied and exciting activities, from mingling with stingrays off Grand Cayman to exploring underwater volcanic craters off Dominica.

An outlet renting diving and snorkeling equipment, Curaçao

WRECK DIVING

Sunken ships hold a special allure for divers as they attract a wealth of marine life. Often, cannons and other artifacts can still be seen, while World War II warships are fascinating to explore. Wrecks are scattered all along the Caribbean island chain.

Superior Producer, *an overloaded freighter that sank in 1977, rests at a depth of 107 ft (32 m), off Curaçao's southwest coast. Divers can also view this artificial reef at night, lit by the glow of cup corals and tiny hunters.*

Hilma Hooker *wreck, lying 98 ft (30 m) below the waters off Bonaire, was seized in 1984 with marijuana on board. It sank after lying unclaimed for months and now hosts plenty of marine life such as sea anemones.*

SNORKELING

Snorkeling is a great way to experience the underwater world without leaving the water surface and all that is needed is a face mask, breathing tube, and flippers for propulsion. It is perfect for exploring coral reefs that lie close to the surface. Unlike scuba diving, snorkeling requires no training. Several islands have good snorkeling sites, including Antigua, Bonaire, the Grenadines, and the Virgin Islands.

Stingray City (see p102), *located in the waters off the northwest corner of Grand Cayman, is shallow enough for snorkelers to enjoy feeding and swimming with stingrays.*

The Baths (see p240), *in the British Virgin Islands, is a great place for snorkelers to glimpse exotic marine life in pools and grottoes amid enormous boulders. It is important to exercise caution during a north swell, which can be tumultuous.*

For more details on specific diving and snorkeling spots, refer to the Outdoor Activities pages for each island

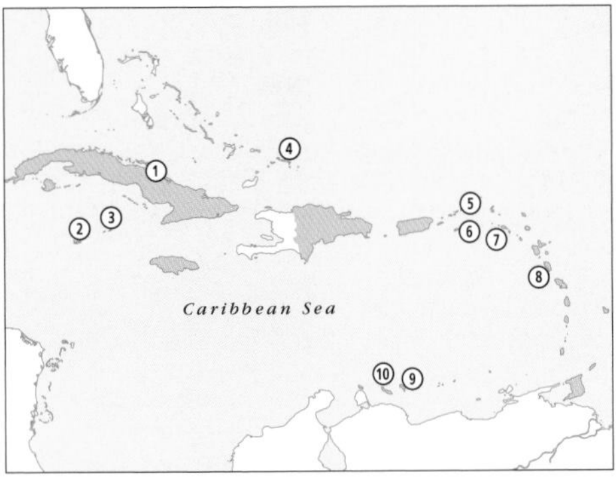

BEST SITES

The Baths, Virgin Islands [5]
Bloody Bay Marine Park, Cayman Islands [3]
Buck Island Reef National Monument, Virgin Islands [6]
Hilma Hooker wreck, Bonaire [9]
HMS *Endymion*, Turks and Caicos [4]
Jardines del Rey, Cuba [1]
M/V Talata wreck, St. Kitts [7]
Soufrière Marine Reserve, Dominica [8]
Stingray City, Cayman Islands [2]
Superior Producer wreck, Curaçao [10]

SCUBA AND SNUBA

Scuba diving lets divers explore far below the surface, but requires special training and the use of specialized gear, including canisters of compressed air for breathing. Snuba (SNorkel + scUBA) tethers the canisters to floating rafts, connecting swimmers by air lines without heavy restrictive gear.

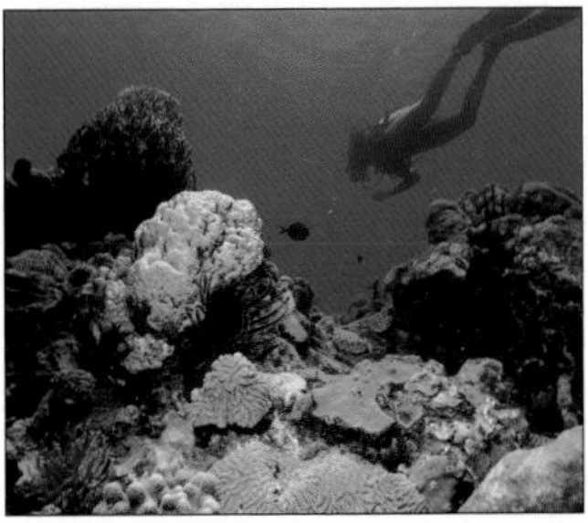

Dominica *has a number of dive sites along its west coast. With an abundance of marine creatures, the Scott's Head and Soufrière Bay areas are popular diving sites.*

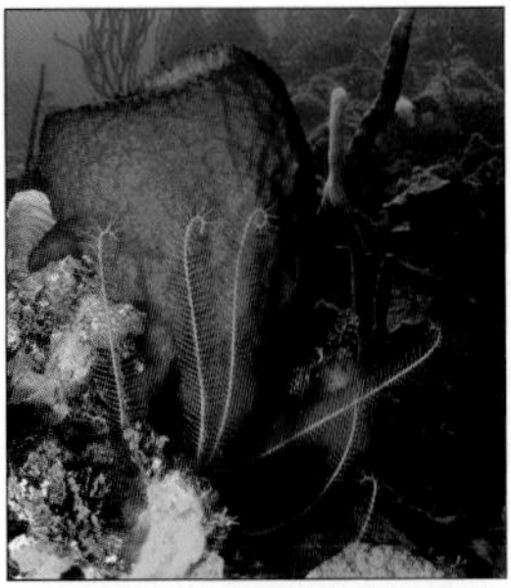

Bloody Bay Marine Park (see p107) *in the Cayman Islands combines dozens of dive sites ranging from those at a mere 6 ft (2 m) depth to others along a wall that plummets to more than 1,640 ft (500 m).*

Snuba diving *is the best way to explore Aruba's coral-laden wrecks. At Antilla divers can encounter exquisite marine life around a partially submerged German World War II freighter and a Lockheed Lodestar plane teeming with sea fans and sponges.*

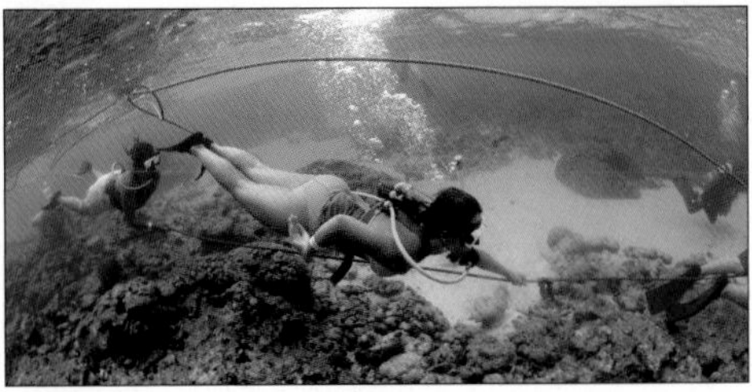

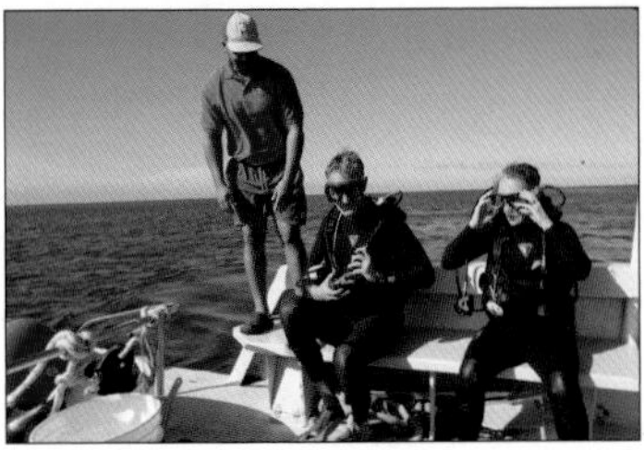

Divers preparing to go into the water

WHO CAN DIVE?

A PADI (Professional Association of Diving Instructors) or NAUI (National Association of Underwater Instructors) certificate is required for most dives. Dive operators offer both one- and two-tank dives and certification courses. Experienced divers can take night dives, plus advanced courses that include rescue diving. Novices can take "resort courses" – introductory lessons usually followed by a dive. Many all-inclusive resorts have their own dive shops.

Top Sailing Islands

Antigua Sailing Week logo

Antigua, the Grenadines, the British Virgin Islands (and the USVI) top the list of islands with the best conditions for sailing and numerous beautiful islets to visit. The Virgin Islands are blessed with dramatic scenery and are also more developed, while the Grenadines have the quiet charm of an earlier era. Antigua is a base for both small and large-crewed yachts, while St. Martin/Sint Maarten and Guadeloupe are also popular sailing destinations.

Sightseeing catamaran at Heritage Quay, St. John's, Antigua

ANTIGUA

Antigua has a centuries-long sailing history, ever since it was the center of British maritime power in the region during the colonial era. The annual Antigua Sailing Week is one of the world's top five regattas and is the highlight of the Caribbean yachting calendar. Five days of tough international competitions attract sailors from all over the world as well as boats of every type.

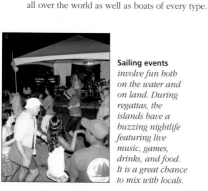

Sailing events *involve fun both on the water and on land. During regattas, the islands have a buzzing nightlife featuring live music, games, drinks, and food. It is a great chance to mix with locals.*

SAILING REGATTAS

Carriacou Regatta Festival, an important summer sailing event

Grenadines: Carriacou Regatta Festival (Jul/Aug) Boats from all over take part in the biggest sailing festival of the Southern Caribbean, which began as a local boat race.

Antigua: Sailing Week (Apr/May) A top sailing event with local and international participation.

Grenadines: Bequia Easter Regatta (Mar/Apr) First run in 1967, it includes races for all classes of boats.

Sint Maarten: Heineken Regatta (Mar) This sailing event strives for a "Clean Regatta".

Historic Redcliffe Quay *in St. John's, Antigua, was once home to warehouses storing supplies for the British navy and local merchant ships.*

For more on sailing see pp244–5, p329, p441, and p523

The Tobago Cays, *a collection of tiny isles surrounded by stunning coral reefs, is a popular destination for day sailing trips from the other Grenadine islands.*

THE GRENADINES

The sailing here is preferred by sailors who find the British Virgin Islands a little overdeveloped. The isles are known for their superb sailing conditions with constant trade winds, island-hopping opportunities, and many regattas.

Sailors *often drop anchor in one of the natural anchorages provided to protect the coral reefs surrounding the isles. They use their own dinghies or take watertaxis to come ashore to explore the islands.*

THE VIRGIN ISLANDS

The British and the US Virgin Islands, separated by the Sir Francis Drake Passage, have the most developed marina facilities. Owing to the layout of the islands, the anchorages are closer and the isles offer sheltered sailing as well as great island-hopping opportunities.

Monohull yachts *are perfect for cruising and are typically used when sailing long distances. A variety of well-maintained yachts, including catamarans, motor yachts, crewed yachts, and bareboats are available for hire.*

Bars and restaurants, *at most anchorages, offer a place for sailors to relax with cool refreshing drinks and barbecued dishes. Popular hangouts in the British Virgin Islands include Foxy's bar at Jost Van Dyke, Rhymers' Restaurant at Cane Garden Bay on Tortola, and the Bath and Turtle on Virgin Gorda.*

Tortola, *the largest of the British Virgin Islands, is considered a major sailing hub in the Caribbean. Yachts for day trips to the offshore cays of Anegada, and the Baths at Virgin Gorda, depart from the island's several marinas.*

Popular Watersports

The Caribbean is a paradise for vacationers who enjoy watersports ranging from exhilarating Jet Ski rides over the waves to tranquil kayaking trips into coastal lagoons. Many individual islands are renowned for certain specific sports, such as Barbados for surfing and the Dominican Republic for kiteboarding. Every all-inclusive hotel offers non-motorized equipment, usually with instructions, while commercial vendors have outlets for motorized watersports on most beaches.

Snapper, Bonaire

Water boats for hire lined up on Palm Beach, Aruba

RIDING THE WATERS

Active vacationers are spoilt for choice when it comes to watersports, with specific activities varying according to local weather conditions and facilities. Although surfing is restricted to certain areas where high waves roll ashore, easier lessons for beginners are also available. Placid aqua-bikes and thrilling banana-boat rides are great family activities, while kayaking is a good way to get close to wildlife.

Surfing *is a popular sport, and many islands offer world-class surfing. Rincón, on the west coast of Puerto Rico, is the setting for many world championship competitions.*

Banana boats, *inflatable pontoons towed at high speed, offer a bumpy ride and are lots of fun, though passengers can expect the "banana" to tip over.*

Aqua-bikes *are available at many popular beach resorts. These tricycles are kept afloat by huge tires, and steered by a pair of riders who constantly work the pedals.*

Jet Skis, *powerful scooters that skim across the water at high speed, are a potential risk to nearby swimmers and many resorts have banned or confined them to special areas.*

Kayaking *through mangroves and lagoons is a great way to explore the indigenous flora and fauna of the Caribbean islands.*

For more details on watersports, refer to the Outdoor Activities pages for each island

SPORTFISHING

The Caribbean and Atlantic waters teem with game fish such as sailfish, marlin, tuna, wahoo, and barracuda. Almost every island offers excellent sportfishing opportunities.

Bottom fishing *for snapper, grouper, and jack is a popular sport. Visitors can try fly-fishing for bonefish in the inshore shallows.*

Charters, *catering to sportfishers, are available for half- and one-day trips. Most islands offer deep-sea fishing, with the types of fish varying according to season.*

WIND POWERED

The year-round trade winds, usually on the windward side of the Caribbean islands, create ideal wind and wave conditions for kiteboarding, sailing, and windsurfing, drawing a number of experts. With a bit of tuition, amateurs can also easily enjoy these sports.

Windsurfing *is a favorite activity at almost every beach resort and many hotels include this sport in their charges.*

Hobie Cats *are relatively small and easy-to-maneuver sailcrafts preferred by most resort-goers with limited sailing experience.*

Paragliding *involves flying either solo or in tandem, tethered by harness to a parachute towed by a speedboat. It offers a bird's-eye view of the coastline.*

Kiteboarding *is essentially a form of surfing where the rider's feet are strapped to a mini surfboard, while a waist harness is attached to a giant kite. Sweeping above the waves, aficionados perform exhilarating aerial acrobatics.*

RIPTIDES

Dangerous undertows or riptides claim many lives each year. They can occur on beaches where incoming waves bring ashore more water than the backwash can drain. The excess water pours back to sea via narrow, fast-moving channels that can pull unwary swimmers out to sea. Riptide locations change unpredictably. If caught, it is vital to swim parallel to the shore.

Crashing waves at Bathsheba, Barbados.

Hiking in the Caribbean

Geology differs throughout the Caribbean chain, with the terrain varying from flat and barren to mountainous and forested, depending on whether the island is a coral formation or the result of a volcanic eruption. Hikers are treated to spectacular vistas with a vast range of foliage, wildlife, and archaeological sites. There are numerous nature reserves and national parks with well-maintained trails. Tour operators on the islands arrange guided hikes for visitors at all levels of fitness, though experienced hikers may prefer self-guided excursions.

Waterfall at Asa Wright Nature Centre, Trinidad

HIKING OPTIONS

Most islands have trails with a gradual incline that are suitable for hikes of 2 hours or less. Nearly all trails passing through national parks are paved, beginning at a visitors' center, and meander among labeled native plants or historic sites. However, experienced hikers can enjoy the more challenging treks such as the one leading to Guadeloupe's La Soufrière summit.

Pico Duarte, Dominican Republic, *is the highest mountain in the Caribbean (see p177). Experienced climbers can cover the distance to the top in about a 3-day round-trip, accompanied by mules that carry their gear.*

BEST HIKING TRAILS

EASY TRAILS

1. Arikok National Park, Aruba,
   21 miles (33.8 km) of marked trails
2. Barre de l'Isle Forest Reserve, St. Lucia,
   1 mile (1.6 km)
3. The Baths, Virgin Gorda, BVI,
   0.5 mile (0.8 km)
4. Lake Trail, Grand Etang National Park, Grenada,
   2.5 miles (4 km)
5. Reef Bay Trail, St. John, USVI,
   2 miles (3.2 km)

MODERATE TRAILS

1. Blue Mountains hike, Jamaica,
   7 miles (11 km)
2. Chaconia Trail, Asa Wright Nature Centre, Trinidad
   2 miles (3.2 km)
3. El Yunque trails, Puerto Rico
   36 miles (58 km)

4. Hooiberg (Haystack), Aruba,
   562 steps at 541 ft (164 m)
5. Parc Naturel, Basse-Terre, Guadeloupe,
   180 miles (290 km) of marked trails
6. Pic du Paradise, St. Martin
   4 miles (6.4 km)

CHALLENGING TRAILS

1. Adventure Trail, Asa Wright Nature Centre, Trinidad
   19 miles (31 km)
2. Edmund Forest Trail, St. Lucia
   7 miles (11 km)
3. La Soufrière summit, Guadeloupe
   5 miles (8 km)
4. Mount Qua Qua, Grenada
   3 miles (4.8 km)
5. Pico Duarte, Dominican Republic
   14.5 miles (23.3 km)
6. Valley of Desolation, Dominica
   5.5 miles (8.9 km)

Morne Trois Pitons National Park, Dominica, *has many hikes from the easy Trafalgar Falls to the more difficult Valley of Desolation trail. Some trails are not as well maintained, so a guide is recommended.*

Blue Mountains, Jamaica, *covering 28 miles (45 km) east to west, offer some of the best hiking on the island (see pp144–5). The most rewarding is the 6-hour hike to the Blue Mountain Peak.*

El Yunque National Forest, Puerto Rico, *has various dirt and paved trails (see p208). The El Yunque Trail reaches a peak overlooking the Atlantic Ocean from 3,500 ft (1,067 m).*

Arikok National Park, Aruba, *has a number of easy to moderate marked trails (see p513). The trek up the 620-ft (188-m) Mount Jamanota is steep but short, and offers fantastic views from the summit.*

The Baths, Virgin Gorda, BVI, *is more of a rock scramble than a hike (see p240). It provides an afternoon of exploration through dramatic landscapes riddled with caves, tunnels, and giant boulders along the sea.*

Reef Bay Trail, St. John, USVI, *is one of the most popular in the Caribbean. The trail runs downhill from Centerline Road to Genti Bay Beach, past a natural pool inscribed with petroglyphs.*

Golf in the Caribbean

Golf has been a popular sport in the Caribbean for the past century. A new hybrid grass has eliminated many problems related to maintaining greens in the tropics, as a result of which more courses are being laid out and many of the older ones have been updated to meet the expectations of today's player. Year-round sunshine guarantees an ideal vacation for golfers of all levels; while international championships draw big-name players to the best courses. Vacation packages are widely available, but independent travelers can schedule their own tee times through most pro shops. Professional coaching is available to beginners.

Fidel Castro at a golf course in Havana, Cuba, in 1961

Tryall Club, Jamaica, *offers a demanding 18-hole golf course tempered by breathtaking views. Designed by Ralph Plummer, the championship course incorporates the natural challenges of the Caribbean Sea and Flint River. It also hosts various international tournaments.*

Sandy Lane, Barbados (see p475), *has three courses with a total of 45 holes. Known by the quirky names Green Monkey, Old Nine, and the Country Club, each course has tropical landscaping, perfectly accentuated by natural seascapes.*

Casa de Campo, Dominican Republic (see p181), *has three renowned courses designed by Pete Dye. The seven-hole Teeth of the Dog is considered one of the best in the Caribbean.*

OTHER COURSES

The Manchester Country Club in Jamaica was built more than one hundred years ago, with magnificient views from the course's 2,200 ft (660 m) elevation. Recent favorites include Raffles, St. Lucia, an 18-hole, members-only Jack Nicklaus Signature Course, Royal St. Kitts Golf Club, and Temenos Golf Club, Anguilla, designed by Greg Norman.

Coamo Springs, Puerto Rico, *an 18-hole course with amazing mountain views, is designed by Ferdinand Garbin.*

Provo Golf Club, Turks and Caicos, *is known for its 18-hole course that blends with the limestone outcroppings.*

For more details on golf courses, refer to the Outdoor Activities pages for each island

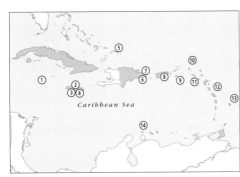

TOP GOLF COURSES

BEST GOLF COURSES

The Caribbean golf courses often have panoramic views of the sea, intriguing landscaping, and natural water hazards such as creeks, streams, and gullies. The larger islands offer a selection of celebrity-designed courses, with more being built.

Tierra del Sol Golf Course, Aruba, *is designed by Robert Trent Jones II. Gallons of desalinated water are used to keep the grass lush on the 18-hole course on this arid island.*

Water bodies on island courses come in the form of lakes, ponds, rivers, and the ocean lending a scenic appeal to the Caribbean courses.

The greens are usually well maintained and the grass is cut very short to allow the ball to roll a longer distance.

Carambola Golf & Country Club, USVI, *has an outstanding 18-hole golf course designed by Robert Trent Jones Sr. for philanthropist Laurence Rockefeller. It has a tropical forest in the backdrop.*

The North Sound Club, Grand Cayman, *located at Crystal Harbor, was designed by Roy Case to complement the terrain.*

Empress Josephine Golf Course, Martinique, *is an 18-hole course designed by Robert Trent Jones Sr. on an exceptional location.*

White Witch Golf Course, Jamaica, *named after Rose Hall Plantation's owner, is a Ritz-Carlton property.*

Sport Culture

The Caribbean's diverse heritage is reflected in the wide variety of sports played here, though the popularity of each game varies between islands. Vibrant passions range from the love of cricket among the English-speaking isles to the frenzied craze for baseball in Spanish-speaking Cuba and the Dominican Republic. However, almost all residents adore soccer, while dominoes is practically a national pastime. Many of the islands have produced world-class athletes who have found international success at the Olympics.

Children playing cricket in a local park, Jamaica

CRICKET

The popularity of cricket extends from St. Kitts and Nevis to powerhouse nations Jamaica and Trinidad. Although each isle has its own team, the region is represented in international Test cricket as the West Indies team. The game has inspired art, music, and endless debate and made players such as Sir Garfield Sobers and Brian Lara iconic figures.

Kensington Oval *in Bridgetown, Barbados, was built in 1882 and is known as the Caribbean mecca of cricket. The stadium also hosted the final match of the ICC Cricket World Cup in 2007.*

Cheering fans, *drinking, dancing, and singing, are the highlights of any Caribbean sporting event. The atmosphere is similar to that of a carnival, with families setting up picnics in the viewing galleries.*

Regional cricket teams, *such as Antigua's Stanford Superstars, play with local and international sides in tournaments that have corporate sponsors and offer big amounts in prize money.*

Cricket on the beach *clearly indicates the islands' obsession with cricket. Often playing scratch matches with makeshift bats, balls, and wickets, youngsters hone their skills in less than perfect, albeit lovely settings. Locals happily welcome strangers into their game.*

BASEBALL

US marines introduced baseball to the Spanish-speaking islands in the 19th century. Although Cuba and the Dominican Republic vie with each other to be the best in the world, Puerto Rico also has well-known players. The islands supply US league clubs with talented players.

Cuba beat USA *in the semifinal of men's baseball in the 2008 Olympics. Traditionally Cubans take great pride in every victory over the USA. However, Cuba lost to South Korea in the Beijing finals, winning the silver medal.*

Tigres de Licey, *a professional baseball team of the Dominican Republic, celebrates victory over Aguilas de Cibao. The team was founded in 1907 and has won many titles since then.*

OTHER SPORTS

Along with cricket, golf, and baseball, dozens of other sports are played in the Caribbean. These range from cycling to soccer and Jamaica even has a bobsled team, despite the lack of snow or ice. Almost every island nation has a Ministry of Sports and visitors can participate in many of the events.

Soccer *is a universal favorite throughout the Caribbean and it is easy to find a game being played somewhere. Although national competitions take place in stadiums, less serious games are played on the sands and soccer fields in the villages.*

Boxing *is part of the school curriculum in countries such as Barbados and Trinidad. Cuba has produced dozens of Olympic medal winners, but smaller isles have had their own successes too.*

DOMINOES

The most popular non-active pastime in the Caribbean is dominoes. Played with gusto, it is a source of competition among all the islands. Usually limited to men, this game is generally played in the open under the shade of trees or on the street, and accompanied by shots of rum. On most islands, players slam down their pieces with a loud crack.

Playing dominoes, Cuba

Athletics *is where Caribbeans have made a big impact on the international arena. Usain Bolt, Melanie Walker, and Dayron Robles are the latest to join the long star-list.*

Family-Friendly Islands

The natural attractions of the Caribbean make it a perfect destination for children. There are sand castles to be built, waves to be surfed, reefs to be snorkeled, and rainforests to be explored. Each island offers its own unique set of experiences, with a variety of family-oriented activities ranging from water parks, dolphin encounters, and whale-watching to zip lines and animal habitats. Anguilla, Jamaica, Curaçao, Dominica, Turks and Caicos, St. Martin/Sint Maarten, and the Dominican Republic are the islands with the best child-friendly resorts and destinations.

Turks and Caicos *are the first choice for families looking for the ultimate island adventure. Children particularly enjoy the dune buggy excursions and the action-packed water park.*

BAHAMAS

CUBA

CAYMAN ISLANDS

HAITI

Jamaica *has many attractions for families, such as Dolphin Cove, Caliche Rainforest, Luminous Lagoon, Island Village, and Dunn's River Falls, although children might need a hand negotiating these.*

ACTIVITIES AT THE RESORTS

Many resorts have created environments where families can enjoy a wide range of activities without ever leaving the property. Large chains such as Beaches, Breezes, and Club Med even create special programs just for little ones, older children, and teens. It is worth doing some research before booking, as some resorts have no special facilities for children or are more aimed towards adults.

Playgrounds *for children incorporate many special features, such as the pirate ship at Malliouhana Hotel and Spa in Anguilla.*

Pools, *such as the one at Beaches Resort and Spa in Turks and Caicos, make many resorts ideal places for family vacations.*

The Beach *is a big draw, so the easiest is to opt for a resort right on the sands, such as Sol de Plata in the Dominican Republic.*

Party venue *at Sonesta Maho Beach Resort, Sint Maarten, is ideal for great family outings as well as private parties.*

The Dominican Republic's *Cabarete Beach on the north coast attracts families with all types of watersports. Also popular are the Manati Park dolphin and sea lion shows, the Ocean World Adventure Park, as well as the Punta Cana Ecological Park petting zoo.*

Anguilla's *Dolphin Discovery invites families to swim with dolphins and learn about their habitat and behavior. Children of all ages can enjoy exploring the "hands-on" coral tide pool as well as a jungle bird exhibit.*

St. Martin/Sint Maarten *have many highlights, including the Sint Maarten Park and Zoo and Butterfly Farm. Other entertainment venues are movie theaters, bowling alleys, and skating rinks.*

ST. BARTHÉLEMY

VIRGIN ISLANDS

PUERTO RICO

ANTIGUA AND BARBUDA

SABA AND ST. EUSTATIUS

MONTSERRAT

GUADELOUPE

ST. KITTS AND NEVIS

MARTINIQUE

C a r i b b e a n   S e a

ST. LUCIA

BARBADOS

ST. VINCENT AND THE GRENADINES

GRENADA

ABC ISLANDS

TRINIDAD AND TOBAGO

0 km 200

0 miles 200

Dominica's *Rainforest Aerial Tram soars over the treetops, while more airborne adventures can be found on the Wacky Rollers Adventure Park's zip lines. River tubing on the Layou River is another popular activity.*

Curaçao's *Sea Aquarium allows visitors to swim with stingrays. Other attractions are Seaworld Explorer semi-submarine, Dolphin Academy, and Christoffel National Park.*

Flora and Fauna

Purple honey-creeper

The biologically-rich Caribbean is sculpted to show off the full potential of the tropics with a potpourri of terrains and ecosystems. Most of the major islands are mountainous and buried in tropical forests cut through by rivers that slowly snake across coastal wetlands. Others are desert-dry plateaus studded with cacti. Almost every isle is ringed by coral reefs. Birds and butterflies are prolific, as are reptiles, although mammal species are relatively few – just 90 species, of which 60 are endemic, such as the endangered solenodon, a giant shrew found in Cuba.

Limestone mogotes dominating Valle de Viñales, Cuba

MONTANE FORESTS

The densest tropical forests occur on the windward slopes, which receive moisture-laden trade winds. Mists enshroud cloud forest at higher elevations, above which pine forests thrive in cool alpine air. Mosses and epiphytes adorn the branches.

The Hispaniolan woodpecker *is endemic to Hispaniola, comprising Haiti and the Dominican Republic. Like all woodpecker species, it nests in tree trunks.*

Puerto Rico's coquí frog *is among the tiniest of the 162 Caribbean frog species.*

Montane cloud forest *has endemic trees such as mountain mahogany, a member of the tea family unique to Saba. The trees are usually covered with epiphytes.*

LOWLAND FORESTS

Rainforests cloak many of the plains and lower mountain slopes. These complex ecosystems harbor much of the region's wildlife. *Jutias*, an endangered rodent, and iguanas inhabit the understory, while parrots cavort in the treetops. Various palms rise from the plains, including coconut palms.

The streamer tail hummingbird *of Jamaica is one of the 18 hummingbird species found here.*

Leafcutter ants *chew leaves into mulch that is used to fertilize fungi, whose spores the ants eat.*

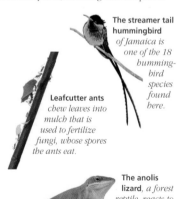

The anolis lizard, *a forest reptile, reacts to disturbance by extending the white fan under its throat.*

ENVIRONMENT UNDER THREAT

Pollution of the air, soil, and waterways threatens many of the Caribbean's delicate environments and endemic species of flora and fauna. Deforestation has been a great concern on many islands, although countries such as the Dominican Republic have legislated in favor of protecting their forests, including mangrove systems of vital importance. Most islands have established special reserves aimed at protecting environments critical to the survival of specific endemic species, but coral reefs are increasingly threatened by global warming.

Deforestation, a major threat to the environment of the Caribbean islands

WETLANDS AND COASTS

Wetlands are some of the area's most diverse ecosystems. Lakes and coastal lagoons are vital staging posts for migrating birds, notably waterfowl. Mangrove swamps are particularly rich in bird and endemic species such as arboreal crabs and crab-eating raccoons.

Raccoons, *an endangered species, have official conservation status throughout the Caribbean.*

Roseate spoonbills, *egrets, flamingos, herons, and other wading birds and waterfowl inhabit the water bodies.*

Mangroves, *which thrive in alluvial silt, form a vital nursery for marine creatures and birds, such as the frigate bird.*

DRY FORESTS

Dry forests cover the terrain in the rain shadow – usually the southwestern lee of mountains. Deciduous flora sheds its leaves during seasonal drought, making wildlife easier to spot. Some areas are so arid that the predominant flora is cacti and scrub.

Iguanas *are camouflaged green for a life in the trees, or brown when living on the ground. Males turn orange during the mating season.*

Royal poincianas *or* flamboyáns *burst into vermilion bloom in spring. This drought-resistant tree is common on almost every isle.*

Bats, *comprising more than half of Caribbean mammal species, play a vital role in sustaining the ecosystem.*

Marine Wildlife

From starfish and stingrays in turquoise shallows to swordfish and manta rays cruising the ocean deep, the Caribbean is a cornucopia of marine life. The coral reef environment is especially rich, where scuba divers can admire an ever-changing kaleidoscope of creatures varied in size and color. The wildlife includes many species unique to the Caribbean's marine habitats. Dolphins are ubiquitous, as are sharks, while migrating whales add an extra thrill in warm-water bays and the passages between many islands.

Scuba diver exploring a coral reef in Bonaire

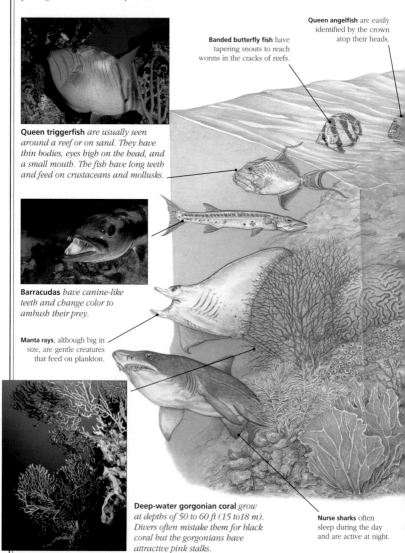

Queen angelfish are easily identified by the crown atop their heads.

Banded butterfly fish have tapering snouts to reach worms in the cracks of reefs.

Queen triggerfish *are usually seen around a reef or on sand. They have thin bodies, eyes high on the head, and a small mouth. The fish have long teeth and feed on crustaceans and mollusks.*

Barracudas *have canine-like teeth and change color to ambush their prey.*

Manta rays, although big in size, are gentle creatures that feed on plankton.

Deep-water gorgonian coral *grow at depths of 50 to 60 ft (15 to 18 m). Divers often mistake them for black coral but the gorgonians have attractive pink stalks.*

Nurse sharks often sleep during the day and are active at night.

Green moray eel *is the largest of the Caribbean eels and grows up to 6 ft (2 m). It has big powerful jaws and feeds on small fish and mollusks. It lives in crevices in the reef, and is reclusive during the day but active at night.*

Queen parrotfish *are spotted easily but tend to shy away from divers. They grow up to 15 inches (38 cm) and feed on algae.*

Octopuses have an excellent sense of vision, smell, and touch. They can change color instantly.

Nassau groupers *are found near the entrances of caves or behind sea fans between 40 and 100 ft (12 and 30 m) deep. They like to ambush their prey.*

Sharknose gobys are small, active fish cleaners found near the ocean floor.

Spiny lobsters are nocturnal feeders, lurking at the back of caves during the day.

ENDANGERED MARINE TURTLES

Six species of marine turtles inhabit the Caribbean waters – from the tiny loggerhead to the massive leatherback. Although protected by law, marine turtles are threatened by ocean pollution, illegal hunting, stealing of eggs, and loss of beach habitat. Females nest on the beaches but only a fraction of their eggs survive to adulthood.

Loggerhead sea turtles

CORAL REEFS

Coral reefs form a habitat for both animal and plant life. They support several species, from anemones and sponges to sea urchins and fish. These fragile ecosystems are threatened by pollution and global warming; Caribbean reefs have diminished by 80 percent in the past decade.

Top Spots for Wildlife

While tourism in the region depends on resort-based vacations, visitors can readily explore the magnificent wildlife, ranging from manatees and curly-tailed lizards to the ivory-billed woodpecker – the Holy Grail of Caribbean birds. Most islands have taken vigorous steps to safeguard their beaches, reefs, and forests, and the varied national parks, reserves, and wildlife centers are ideal for visitors who appreciate nature and are keen to contribute to its conservation. Every isle has its own endemic species. The wide spectrum of birds provides for spectacular photography. Whale sightings are virtually assured in the winter months.

Humpback whale leaping out of the water, not an uncommon sight

CUBA: GRAN PARQUE NATURAL DE MONTEMAR ①

Cuba's most important wetland area *(see p80)* is known for its large flocks of flamingos. It protects 171 species of birds, 31 of reptiles, and 12 of mammals, a primitive fish called the *manjuarí*, as well as crocodiles, caimans, and the world's smallest bird, the *zunzuncito*.

Cuba's Zapata Biosphere Reserve displaying a diversity of ecosystems and habitats

Zunzuncito, *the smallest warm-blooded vertebrate, has been nicknamed bee hummer owing to its tiny size.*

Land crabs *typically inhabit the marshes. Every spring, millions emerge from the swamps surrounding the Bay of Pigs to breed in the nearby sea.*

Flamingos *inhabit the salt water lagoons of Península de Zapata. Their pink color is believed to be obtained from a particular insect's larvae that they consume.*

DOMINICAN REPUBLIC: LAGO ENRIQUILLO ③

This lake *(see p179)* has the Caribbean's largest population of American crocodiles, which bask in cool marshy waters along the north shore, and on the salty mudbanks of Isla Cabritos. Rhinoceros iguanas can also be spotted.

American crocodiles *belong to the same family as the endemic Cuban crocodile, but are considered to be less aggressive.*

Iguanas *are found crawling about the island. These leathery giant lizards live in both wet and dry ecosystems and like to bask in the sun.*

BARBUDA: FRIGATE BIRD SANCTUARY ⑧

Amid the mangroves of tiny Man O'War Island in Codrington Lagoon *(see p326)* can be found one of the Caribbean's largest frigate bird colonies. During the mating season which lasts from September to April, the males inflate their vermilion chests as the females soar overhead. These birds obtain much of their food by stealing it from other sea birds, a habit which lends them their nickname: man o'war. Their nests are just above the water's edge and can be observed from close.

A pair of frigate birds during mating season

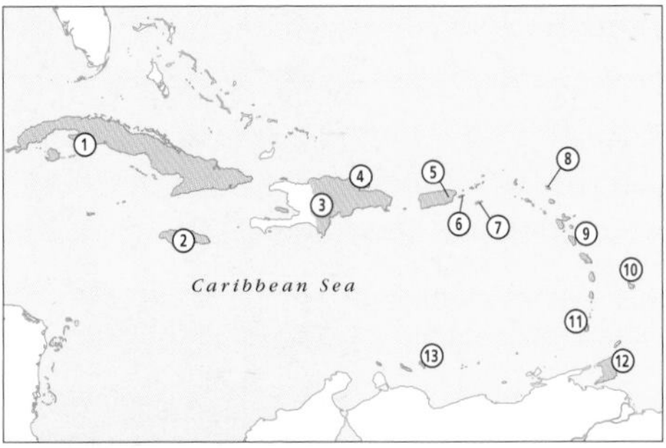

TOP NATIONAL PARKS

Asa Wright Nature Centre [12]
Bahía Fosforente [6]
Bahía Samaná [4]
Barbados Wildlife Reserve [10]
El Yunque National Forest [5]
Frigate Bird Sanctuary [8]
Gran Parque Natural de Montemar [1]
Grand Etang National Park [11]
Lago Enriquillo [3]
Marshall's Pen Great House [2]
The Parrot Research Centre [9]
Sandy Point [7]
Washington Slagbaai National Park [13]

A pair of green monkeys in the Barbados Wildlife Reserve

BARBADOS: BARBADOS WILDLIFE RESERVE [10]

This reserve *(see p470)* protects a Noah's Ark-load of endemic and exotic species, including brocket deer and green monkeys.

The caiman *can tolerate both salt and fresh water, and is therefore the most common of all crocodile species.*

Agoutis *are forest-dwelling, rabbit-sized rodents related to the guinea pig. They live mostly on fallen fruits and nuts.*

Brocket deer *are shy creatures who live either alone or in pairs. Due to their small size and nocturnal behavior, they are not easily observed.*

TRINIDAD: ASA WRIGHT NATURE CENTRE [12]

Covered by rainforest, this reserve *(see p491)* provides habitat to a wide variety of birds including at least 13 species of hummingbirds. From a comfortable balcony, visitors may observe endemic as well as exotic birds such as the chestnut woodpecker and the white-bearded manakin.

Conservation *is promoted through education and research. The center also provides expertly guided trails and tours.*

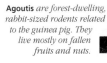

Hummingbirds *are little nectar-drinking birds. Exotic varieties include this white-chested emerald and blue-chinned sapphire.*

NATIONAL PARKS WITH ENDANGERED SPECIES

The Caribbean islands have set up a wide range of national parks and wildlife centers that protect the habitat of endangered species of birds, mammals, amphibians, and reptiles.

Washington Slagbaai National Park *in Bonaire* (see p517) *has endemic bird species like the endangered yellow-shouldered parrot and the Caribbean or brown-throated parakeet.*

The Parrot Research Center *in the Botanical Gardens of Roseau* (see p400), *Dominica, educates visitors about the endangered sisserou and jaco parrots that are bred here.*

Sandy Point on St. Croix *is a nesting site for rare leatherback turtles, one of the world's six marine turtle species.*

Music of the Caribbean

Music is everywhere in the Caribbean. Pouring out of buses, shops, and bars, Jamaican reggae is a constant soundtrack, while soca provides the pulsing backbeat to the many annual carnivals. Sunsets too, would not be the same without the tinkling tones of that quintessential Caribbean sound, the steel pan. And like the islands themselves, the various musical genres here vary enormously. Whilst everyone can hum along to a Bob Marley classic, discovering lesser-known styles such as zouk or merengue provides an insight into the heart of Caribbean culture.

Cuban swing music cover from 1937 for a rumba dance tune

Salsa to merengue, most Caribbean music is tuned for dancing.

Soca *is an evolution of calypso, credited to the late Ras Shorty I by most people. A faster, syncopated version of calypso, suitable for dancing rather than listening, it is the ultimate sound of the Caribbean carnivals.*

Reggae *evolved from a slowing of the ska beat in the 1970s and its best-known exponent is Bob Marley, with a string of albums with the Wailers. Reggae crooners have been eclipsed by the faster dancehall.*

DIVERSE CARIBBEAN MUSIC
Each island is represented by different genres of music. Cuba's popular dance music, *son*, combines Spanish and African rhythms.

SINGERS AND MUSICIANS
Caribbean music has spawned countless stars over the years and the musicians constitute some of the most talented names in the world. Calypso stalwarts include Mighty Sparrow and the late Lord Kitchener (Trinidad and Tobago), while reggae singers and DJs from Jamaica, such as Sean Paul and Damian Marley, have scored international hits. Ricky Martin and Marc Antony (Puerto Rico) are the superstars of Latino music, while Cuba has produced the Buena Vista Social Club (*son*) and the late Damaso Perez Prado (mambo).

Bob Marley, *Jamaica's king of reggae, is still celebrated as a master singer and songwriter and as a musical ambassador.*

Monty Alexander, *a virtuoso pianist, is at the forefront of the Caribbean's burgeoning jazz scene.*

Calypso *lyrics with their lilting tunes may sound a bit laid-back. However, they uncover a biting social commentary, humor, and some very mischievous double entendre. Trinidad and Tobago's Mighty Sparrow is a very well-known calypso artiste.*

Merengue, *hailing from the Dominican Republic, is as much a dance style as it is a musical genre. Fast and lively, its Latin-style two-step beat is ideal for dancing with a partner and the twirls and dips are integral.*

Percussion ranges from goatskin drums to conventional drumkits.

Steel Pan, *said to be the only "new" instrument of the 20th century, was invented in oil-rich Trinidad after World War II. The top panels of barrels once used to store crude oil are shaped to form notes, which are beaten by players, known as pannists, to create a distinctive metallic sound.*

The guitar is an essential accompaniment providing the all-important bassline.

Zouk, *the music of the French Caribbean, particularly Martinique and Guadeloupe, is a derivative of the Haitian cadence genre and sounds like an African version of Trinidadian soca. It is mainly party music.*

Machel Montano *is the biggest name in the Caribbean soca. His live shows are legendary high-energy affairs.*

Celia Cruz *was the Caribbean's most successful salsa singer. She is credited with taking Cuban music to the world.*

Beenie Man's *combination of humor and lyrical skill has ensured his place as one of Jamaica's top dancehall DJs.*

Festivals and Events

The Carnival, an elaborate spectacle celebrated in most of the Caribbean, was originally portrayed by African slaves as an irreverent parody of their masters' pre-Lenten masquerade balls. Some events are traditionally still held before Lent, while others take place in July, August, or December. Sailing festivals bring visitors from all over the world for exciting activities and parties. There are also events unique to particular isles, like Tobago's Heritage Festival, or Carriacou's Big Drum festival, and a number of music festivals.

Masked dancers at the Dominican Republic Carnival

CARNIVAL

Carnival is the mother of all Caribbean celebrations. The Trinidad festival, an exuberant blend of music, costumed parades, and massive fêtes, has inspired other carnivals.

Costumes are elaborate as various groups flaunt their leaders for the Carnival King and Queen titles.

Trinidad Carnival, *following Caribbean traditons, features Jouvert, a pre-dawn jump-up.*

Blue Devils *(Jab Jabs) take over the Paramin area of Trinidad, dancing and demanding payment from onlookers.*

Moko Jumbies, *as these towering stilt-dancers are known, stride through the streets on Carnival days. They have their origins in traditional African rituals.*

Grenada Carnival *is celebrated differently in each parish. Various versions of the traditional characters, including Short Knees, Wild Indians, and Jab Jabs, come out on the streets on Carnival days.*

Crop Over Festival, Barbados, *was originally a harvest festival that celebrated the reaping of the sugarcane crop after a long season of hard work by the plantation slaves. It is now one of the most popular summer highlights.*

MUSIC FESTIVALS

Music festivals have sprung up in many islands and performances by well-known local and international stars have made them extremely popular.

St. Lucia Jazz Festival, *established in 1992, is one of the best music festivals in the Caribbean.*

Merengue Festival, *held in the Dominican Republic during late July or early August, features merengue dance and music.*

Reggae Sumfest, *held in Montego Bay, Jamaica, highlights the best of reggae and dancehall entertainers with new stars and veterans.*

BEST OF THE REST

Many islands have opted for summer carnivals such as Vincy Mas of St. Vincent and the Grenadines. Jamaica's Carnival, breaking all religious ties, is held during Lent and culminates at Easter. St. Kitts, St. Croix, and Montserrat have lively Carnival celebrations at the year end.

Fête des Cuisinières *is held in early August, in Point-à-Pitre on Grande-Terre. The festival celebrates the masters of Creole cuisine with a 5-hour banquet that is open to the public.*

Antigua Sailing Week *hosts international and local sailing enthusiasts. The keenly contested races on the ocean are coupled by fun, food, and partying on land during the week-long celebrations.*

Buccoo Goat Races *are held on the island of Tobago on Easter Tuesday. This is part of a tradition dating back to 1925. People place bets on the rigorously trained and well-groomed animals.*

MAJOR FESTIVALS

Some of the important Caribbean festivals are given below:

Barbados Jazz Festival (January)

Mustique Blues Festival (January/February)

Bob Marley Week, Jamaica (early February)

Festival Casals, Puerto Rico (mid-February to early March)

Trinidad Carnival (Monday and Tuesday before Ash Wednesday)

Holders' Opera Season, Barbados (March/April)

Antigua Sailing Week (April)

St. Lucia Jazz Festival (May)

Reggae Sumfest, Jamaica (July)

Crop Over Festival, Barbados (late July–early August)

Merengue Festival, Dominican Republic (late July–early August)

Grenada Carnival (August)

World Creole Music Festival, Dominica (October)

Diwali, Trinidad and Tobago (October/November)

Flavors of the Caribbean

The Caribbean owes its varied cuisine to the diverse groups of people who settled in the area over the centuries, combining ingredients they found here with those they brought from elsewhere. First the Europeans and their African slaves, then people from India, China, and the Middle East, contributed to the region's cultural mix. Each island's cuisine differs according to its ethnic make-up and colonial history, but they have much in common, such as assorted rice-and-pea combinations, seafood, okra dishes, and stews.

Nutmeg, cinnamon, and allspice

EUROPEAN TASTES

Many islands were fought over by European powers, and some had a succession of colonial rulers. The French brought delicate pastries and rich sauces, as well as dishes like stuffed crab back, snails in garlic, and frogs' legs. The British influence is strongest in Barbados – one Christmas specialty is Scottish Jug Jug, made with pigeon peas, cornflour, and salted meat, supposedly based on haggis. From Spain came *pastelles*, *empanadas* (spicy patties), and *escovitch* (pickled and fried fish), while Trinidad's *bacalhau* and *buljol*, both made with salt cod, are Portuguese in origin. Pastries and desserts often combine European culinary styles and local ingredients, such as Christmas rum cake and coconut crème pie.

Preparing conch for a beachside restaurant, Turks and Caicos

AMERINDIAN HERITAGE

Native Amerindians gave the world their staples of corn, beans, squash, and potatoes. The Taínos of the Greater Antilles smoked and grilled their meat and fish over wood and fragrant leaves. Such grills were known as *barbacoas*, which is the root of the word we now use for the same process – barbecue.

Custard apple   Banana   Grapefruit   Pineapple
Watermelon   Coconut   Mango
Papaya

Selection of luscious, ripe tropical fruits of the Caribbean

CARIBBEAN DISHES AND SPECIALTIES

Rice-and-peas is one of the staples on every island, but the ingredients and tastes differ – in Cuba for example, *moros y cristianos* is made with black beans and white rice, and gets much of its flavor from pork; in Trinidad and Tobago, pigeon peas or red beans are used and the dish is flavored with several kinds of herbs and often with coconut milk; the same dish has added hints of nutmeg and other spices in Grenada. Every island has several must-taste dishes, but a sampling of the best known would include curry crab and dumpling in Tobago; jerk chicken or pork in Jamaica; roasted breadfruit and fish in St. Vincent and the Grenadines; *farci* (stuffed crab) in Guadeloupe and *stoba di cabritu* (goat stew) in Curaçao.

Raw giant shrimps

Pastelles *are made of cornmeal stuffed with a spicy meat or vegetable filling and steamed in banana leaves.*

Colorful, bustling street market in St. George's, Grenada

MEMORIES OF AFRICA

During the time of the slave trade, many new dishes arrived along with the millions of people who were forcibly brought to the Caribbean from West Africa. Produce included okra, plantains, fufu, yams, and ackee. Dishes from Africa included spicy stews like *callaloo*. Jamaica's "jerk" has become popular all over the world, and is believed to have its roots in a fusion of Amerindian barbecue methods with African and Spanish herbs and spices: allspice (also known as Jamaican spice or pimento) is a key ingredient. Cheap and plentiful produce that was used to feed the slaves, such as salt fish and breadfruit, has also become part of the repertoire of island cuisine.

ASIAN FLAVORS

Indentured servants from India, and immigrants from China, added Asian spices and methods of cooking to the mix. Among the well-known dishes is Trinidad's roti – curried meat and vegetables wrapped in a soft

Hot peppers for sale at a market in Pointe-à-Pitre, Guadeloupe

flatbread and often accompanied by hot mango or golden apple chutney. Many Indo-Caribbean dishes are vegetarian: split pea *daal*, curried potato and garbanzos, eggplant and tomato *choka* (roasted with garlic). There are also divine sweets made of flour or milk and flavored with rosewater, cardamom or ginger. Chinese food is widely available, but is particularly good in Trinidad, and considered a special treat by many locals, who do not know how to cook it.

ON THE MENU

Ackee and salt fish (Jamaica)
Delicate yellow ackee fruit looks like scrambled egg and blends well with tasty salt fish for this breakfast specialty.

Bake and Shark (Trinidad)
Popular beachside treat of deep-fried shark wrapped in a fried (not baked) flatbread.

Callaloo (Most islands)
Thick soup made with okra, spinach, crab or salted meat.

Coo coo (Barbados)
Seasoned cornmeal dish eaten with fried or stewed flying fish.

Feroce (Guadeloupe and Martinique)
Mashed, spiced avocados with cassava flour and salt fish.

Pepperpot (Most islands)
A fiery stew of vegetables and meat. An Amerindian seasoning, casareep, gives this long-simmered dish its distinctive dark color and exotic taste.

Sancocho *is a hearty, festive dish from the Dominican Republic, combining seven types of meat and vegetables.*

Arroz con Gandules, *Puerto Rico's national dish, is made with rice and pigeon peas and seasoned with saffron.*

Majarete, *a rich and creamy corn dessert, is flavored with coconut milk, vanilla essence, and cinnamon.*

Best Wedding and Honeymoon Islands

Romance is synonymous with the Caribbean, and its dazzling beaches, lush tropical gardens, historic plantations and forts, and beautiful vistas with a backdrop of mountains sloping into a turquoise sea are all desirable settings for destination weddings. Resorts and local governments are happy to oblige with an impressive array of locations and services for elegant or casual ceremonies and receptions. Even better, couples do not have to travel far to enjoy a perfect honeymoon at one of the many romantic resorts. Top islands for weddings and honeymoons include Antigua, Barbados, Jamaica, St. Kitts, and St. Lucia.

A wedding gazebo with floral decorations in Antigua

ANTIGUA

With a number of ideal romantic settings, Antigua would certainly feature in a top-10 list of wedding destinations. June has been designated the Month of Romance on the island, which hosts a Celebrity Destination Wedding each year. From beaches and hilltop vistas to intimate, posh five-star hotels, the island's exotic locales create indelible memories.

Blue Waters *resort's trademark is the wedding gazebo placed on a narrow strip of land jutting into the sea. Their five-bedroom Rock Cottage Villa provides the perfect spot for an intimate reception.*

Sandals Grande Antigua *is one of the leading honeymoon resorts in the world. The lush tropical grounds and beautiful Dickenson Bay Beach provide the ideal backdrop to a luxurious honeymoon at a* rondavel *(traditional African-style house).*

BARBADOS

On this island, couples have a wide choice of venues, from beaches, botanical gardens, clifftops to plantation great houses, private yachts, and elegant resort settings. For something unique, there are wedding safaris into the forests, a submarine for ceremonies, and a high-flying helicopter wedding.

The Flower Forest, St. Joseph, *has a picturesque hillside setting overlooking the island's east coast, amid 50 acres (20 ha) of colorful tropical plants.*

Sandy Lane Resort *allows for great ceremonies and receptions, but this resort is better known for its honeymoon packages that include luxury ocean view rooms, spa treatments, candlelight dinners, champagne, and excellent service.*

Almond Beach Village Resort's *old sugar mill and grounds host wedding ceremonies, adding a touch of history to the proceedings.*

JAMAICA

The north coast locations of Negril, Ocho Rios, Port Antonio, and Montego Bay have almost perfect weather and outstanding world-renowned resorts, making it easy to plan a wedding. Among the top resorts known for this are the Ritz-Carlton, the Caves, Strawberry Hill, Tryall Club, and Royal Plantation.

Strawberry Hill Resort, *perched on the Blue Mountains, features a main house and 12 Georgian-style cottages surrounded by botanical gardens that are perfect for relaxed honeymoons.*

Sandals Montego Bay Resort, *on the longest private white-sand beach on the island, has its own wedding chapel, while the Bay Roc Estate Beachfront Villas are perfect for honeymoons.*

ST. KITTS

This island is ideal for weddings and honeymoons mainly because many former plantations have been converted into inns and hotels, which give it a unique flavor. Historic sites, such as Brimstone Hill Fortress and Romney Manor, and natural wonders, such as Black Rocks and Mount Liamuiga, offer scenic marriage locales.

Ottley's Plantation Inn *is a popular site for weddings. The stone-walled restaurant and pool area and the great house with its lawn sloping down to the sea create a lovely backdrop for elegant ceremonies.*

Golden Lemon, *a beautifully restored, atmospheric 17th-century great house, also boasts a restaurant known as one of the best on the island and among the most romantic in the Caribbean.*

ST. LUCIA

Designated as the world's leading honeymoon destination during the World Travel Awards, this island has both natural beauty as well as high-end resorts that attract newlyweds. One of the favorite wedding locations is Jalousie Plantation.

Gros Piton and Petit Piton, *the towering volcanic cones on the southwest coast, are among the most distinguished landmarks in the Caribbean, giving an unusual wedding backdrop.*

Anse Chastanet *resort provides intimate wedding experiences in a spectacular scenic location. Among the setting choices are a treehouse, a colonial plantation, a waterfall, and even a coral reef.*

Getting Married

With spectacular features ranging from tropical beaches, waterfalls, and gardens to historic locations, the Caribbean is, for many, the dream destination for a wedding. While it may seem like a simple affair, a wedding still involves a legal ceremony as well as arranging various suppliers for photography, wedding cakes, flowers, and entertainment. So it is best to plan well in advance and study the chosen location's rules and regulations, or hire the services of a wedding planner, before enjoying an exotic wedding experience on a beautiful Caribbean island.

A wedding on one of the beaches of St. Lucia

A wedding ceremony at Ottley Plantation Inn, St. Kitts

LEGALITIES

The Caribbean is a polyglot collection of island nations and protectorates, each with its own regulations and requirements regarding marriage. Every island has different residency requirements ranging from over a month in the French islands of Martinique, St. Barths, Guadeloupe, and St. Martin, to none in Antigua, Barbados, the Cayman Islands, and the Dominican Republic. When going for the license, expect to produce passports and birth certificates of the couple getting married, as well as any divorce decrees or death certificates if there were previous spouses. Most documents must be either originals or certified copies. The Spanish-language islands, including Cuba and the Dominican Republic, as well as the French islands, expect documents to be translated to their native languages. St. Eustatius and Sint Maarten require that documents be translated into Dutch, and offer local contacts who can handle the documents. Two companies that offer translations are **Spanish Wedding Translations** and **DESS (Diplôme d'études supérieures spécialisées)**.

Other requirements vary from island to island, for example, the number and type of witnesses needed.

TYPES OF WEDDINGS

The Caribbean offers an idyllic setting for a tropical wedding, with colorful flowers, lush vegetation, superlative beaches, and turquoise seas. Couples can choose from an incredible array of locales to create their picture-perfect ceremony and reception.

Beach weddings are popular with couples seeking a casual atmosphere, as well as the beautiful backdrop of the aquamarine sea and azure sky. Some splendid beaches include Magens Bay in the US Virgin Islands, Jalousie Plantation in St. Lucia, Grace Bay Beach in Turks and Caicos, and Jumby Bay in Antigua.

Historic-site weddings use painstakingly restored plantation great houses, museums, sugar mills, and military sites as dramatic backdrops for ceremonies and receptions. Antigua, St. Kitts and Nevis, Barbados, and St. Lucia offer some of the best sites.

Nature weddings are set against backdrops of spectacular waterfalls or vistas, or are located in gorgeous botanical gardens. St. Lucia, Nevis, and Dominica are among those offering unique sites.

Villa weddings held in luxurious private villas offer the advantages of having a home-like setting, often with either a spectacular view or private beach.

Exchanging vows at the historic site of Brimstone Hill, St. Kitts

An unusual way to celebrate a wedding is a cruise ceremony that takes place either on the ship or on a beach in one of the ports. Some wedding planners specialize in making arrangements in ports and offer an array of special services.

Nautical weddings are another unique way to get married, and are popular with boating enthusiasts who charter one of the luxury yachts or catamarans available throughout the islands. Antigua, Sint Maarten, the US and British Virgin Islands, and Barbados have the best selections due to their extensive marinas and facilities catering to the yachting crowd.

Websites with detailed information on planning a Caribbean wedding include **Isledo Caribbean Wedding Resource**, **Island Hideaways**, **No Frills Wedding**, **Caribbean Weddings**, **Islandbrides.com The Beach Wedding Guide**, **Luxe Destination Weddings**, and **The Wedding Experience**.

Music bands are arranged by hotels

also offer some of the best reception options since spacious restaurants are located right on-site. The Sandals chain is the "wedding hotel," offering packages from designers such as Preston Bailey. Other luxury favorites include Anse Chastenet in St. Lucia, Rose Hall Resort in Jamaica, and Carenage Bay in the Grenadines.

WEDDING INSURANCE

Weddings, especially in a foreign land, often require significant outlays for

deposits and lots of uncertainties. Many couples opt for wedding insurances, which cover the loss of deposits because of severe weather, vendor no-shows, and transportation cancellations, as well as providing reimbursement if the wedding dress, tuxedo or rings are lost in travel or for non-recoverable costs should sudden illness strike the bride, groom or close family members. Among such insurance companies are **Wed Safe** and **Wedding Protector Plan**.

Waterfall wedding arranged by Tropic Isle Weddings

HOTEL PACKAGES

One of the easiest and often most cost-effective ways to arrange a wedding in the Caribbean is by using the special packages offered by many hotels and resorts. Packages include a room for the couple and the services of the hotel's wedding planner, and extras such as cakes, decorations, musicians, and a photographer. These

WEDDING GUIDE

Caribbean Weddings
www.caribbeanweddings.com

DESS (Diplôme d'études supérieures spécialisées)
Tel 713 589 6496 (US).
www.desss.com

Islandbrides.com The Beach Wedding Guide
www.islandbrides.com

Island Hideaways
Tel 800 832 2302 (US).
0808 234 5122 (UK).
703 378 7840 (International).
www.islandhideaways.com

Isledo Caribbean Wedding Resource
www.isledo.com

Luxe Destination Weddings
www.luxedestination
weddings.com

No Frills Wedding
Tel 866 460 2545 (St. Kitts).
www.nofrillswedding.com.

Spanish Wedding Translations
Tel 0845 130 4547 (UK).
www.spanishweddingtranslations.
co.uk

The Wedding Experience
Tel 877 580 3556 (US).
www.theweddingexperience.
com

Wed Safe
Tel 877 723 3933 (US).
www.wedsafe.com

Wedding Protector Plan
Tel 888 342 5977 (US).
www.protectmywedding.com

Architecture

The Caribbean pre-Columbian architecture is limited to ceremonial plazas, best seen in Puerto Rico. During their rule, the Spanish built massive fortresses, ornate colonial churches and mansions that still dominate the Greater Antilles' urban centers. The greatest architectural legacy of the Dutch-, English-, and French-speaking isles is in plantation homes and simple, quaint urban dwellings influenced by European trends of the time. In recent years, the major cityscapes have changed significantly due to the growth of contemporary architecture, especially in the financial districts.

The courtyard – a typical feature of Spanish colonial architecture

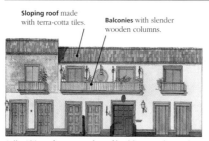

Sloping roof made with terra-cotta tiles.

Balconies with slender wooden columns.

Calle Obispo *has a number of buildings with wooden balconies and courtyards, reflecting Spanish influence.*

Bohíos *are quintessential rural dwellings, with thatched roofs and timber or adobe walls.*

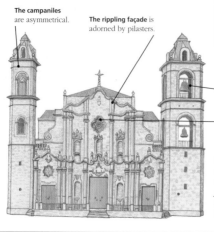

The campaniles are asymmetrical.

The rippling façade is adorned by pilasters.

The bells are said to have been cast with a dash of gold to enhance their musical tone.

The vitral over the main entrance resembles a rose.

Catedral de la Habana *shows the Baroque style imported from Europe in the late 17th century, and is remarkable for its grandiose façade, famously described by Cuban writer Alejo Carpentier as "music set in stone".*

CUBA

Cuba has a spectacular amalgam of architectural styles spanning Mudéjar-style palaces and 19th-century French Rococo structures, while Art Deco and Art Nouveau exteriors from the 1920s fuse with the 1950s Modernist style.

Mediopunto, *or stained-glass windows, evolved in the mid-18th century as protection against the tropical sun.*

Edificio Bacardí *(1930) is a superb example of the Art Deco style. Its pink granite and limestone façade is embellished with terra-cotta motifs.*

PUERTO RICO

Enclosed by massive walls, colonial Old San Juan has more than 800 historic structures, while modern San Juan teems with Art Deco and contemporary buildings.

Tibes Indigenous Ceremonial Center (see p206) *features pre-Hispanic* bateyes *(ceremonial plazas) that were used for games and are ringed by granite boulders etched with petroglyphs.*

Castillo San Cristóbal (see p200) *was completed in 1771. It is one of the largest Spanish fortresses of its day and exemplifies colonial military architecture featuring multiple lines of defense.*

TRINIDAD

The English-speaking island of Trinidad has a rich architectural legacy. The island's somber 19th-century colonial buildings are in sharp contrast to the crop of towering contemporary structures, and religious shrines reflecting the island's eclectic potpourri of cultures.

Nicholas Towers *(2003), a 21-story blue glass tower, is one of Port of Spain's tallest buildings.*

Two minarets, 80 ft (25 m) tall, flank the mosque.

The dome is 40 ft (12 m) in diameter and is typical of Muslim architecture.

Jinnah Memorial Mosque, *St. Joseph, built in 1954, is named after Pakistan's first governor-general. The hexagonal mosque, can accommodate up to 1,000 worshippers.*

MARTINIQUE

Martinique shows off its French roots with a cosmopolitan flavor enhanced by numerous late 19th-century buildings of pre-cast metal. Chic contemporary structures contrast with colonial forts, stone churches, and quaint humble cottages.

The Bibliothèque Schoelcher (see p378), *by architect Henri Pick, was built in Paris for the 1889 World Exposition before being dismantled and moved to Fort-de-France to serve as a library.*

Roofs are slanting and made from brick tiles.

Façades are painted in bright colors.

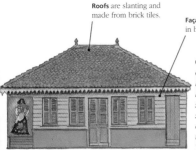

Cases cimentées, *or humble homes made in local vernacular style, are best seen in the charming village of Trois-Îlets.*

HISTORY OF
THE CARIBBEAN

Firstirst inhabited by Amerindian tribes, the islands of the Caribbean were later conquered by the Spanish, English, French, and Dutch, who all competed for control of the isles. Once slaves were introduced, the decimated civilizations blended with the African and European cultures. After independence many islands forged their own paths but still maintain ties with their former colonizing nations._

The Caribbean islands began to be inhabited around 7,000 years ago when various Arawak tribal communities started migrating north from South America's Orinoco basin region. Island-hopping in giant _canoas_ (dugout canoes), they eventually settled on all the islands.

Arawak communities lived in clan villages led by _caciques_ (chieftains). They gathered shellfish, hunted wild animals, and lived well off the sea. They were also skilled slash-and-burn farmers who grew _maíz_ (corn) and yuca, a starchy edible root used to make flour for cassava bread. They wove _henequen_ (sisal) and wild cotton into _hamacas_ (hammocks), and inhaled the smoke of a plant called _cohiba_ through a _tabaco_ (hollow tube) to induce hallucinations. The Arawaks worshiped _zemís_ (spirit gods), which were depicted in rock paintings and carvings in sacred caverns, and on ceremonial ball-courts called _bateyes_.

By the time Christopher Columbus (Cristóbal Colón) arrived in 1492, the

Engraving of an Indian tribal leader of Cuba greeting Christopher Columbus

larger westerly islands of the Caribbean were inhabited by the Taíno, who had achieved a high degree of social organization. By the 15th century, these relatively peaceful farmers and hunter-gatherers, living on today's Puerto Rico and Hispaniola, were being harassed and enslaved by the more warlike Caribs, who were now migrating north through the islands.

TIMELINE

5000 BC First Arawak tribes begin moving north from Orinoco Basin, South America

AD 1000 Caribs start driving out the Taíno

1493 On his second voyage, Columbus establishes Nueva Isabela, the first settlement in the New World, on Hispaniola

1530 First African slaves transported to Hispaniola

5000 BC

AD 1460

1520

1000 BC Taíno tribes settle in the Greater Antilles

The Caribs, a fierce warlike tribe

1492 Christopher Columbus sets out on his first voyage of exploration

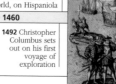

Etching showing Christopher Columbus landing on Hispaniola

THE CONQUISTADORES

Columbus's arrival on his first voyage to the New World spelled doom for the native population. Between 1492 and 1504, he made four voyages and mapped the Caribbean islands from Trinidad to Cuba. He died in Valladolid in 1506 clinging to his belief that these were the islands of Japan and the East Indies. In his wake came gold-hungry Spanish conquistadores who settled the major islands, enslaving the natives to mine gold. Within a few decades, the indigenous peoples were almost entirely wiped out by overwork, brutal massacres, and European diseases; the Spanish began importing African slaves in the 1520s to supply the need for forced labor. The Spanish also used Hispaniola, Puerto Rico, and Cuba as bases for exploring the New World. Hernán Cortés conquered Mexico in 1520 and Aztec gold treasures began to be plundered by the Spanish. Soon Colombian emeralds and Inca wealth were added to Europe-bound fleets and led to the development of Santo Domingo, Havana, and San Juan.

Engraving showing the city of Santo Domingo being attacked by Francis Drake

THE AGE OF PIRATES

The wealth lured pirates, who began to prey upon Spanish ships and ports by the mid-16th century. Sailing with large fleets, these swashbuckling sea captains blazed a terror trail. In 1555, French pirate Jacque de Sores sacked Havana, and in 1586 privateer Francis Drake led a 20-ship fleet against

Portrait of Francis Drake

Santo Domingo in a month-long raid. This led to the construction of impressive forts, such as Havana's Castillo de la Real Fuerza and St. Kitts' Brimstone Hill, to guard against future attacks.

Pirate attacks increased in the 17th century as Spain attempted to enforce a trade monopoly. The restrictions fostered resentment in France, England, and the Netherlands, leading to wars with Spain and each other for control of the region. European nations issued licenses to privateers for state-sanctioned piracy against the Spanish. The infamous "buccaneers" began life hunting wild boar on a tiny island off Hispaniola. Driven off by the Spaniards, they turned to piracy, captured Spanish ships, and grew powerful. They were officially welcomed to Jamaica's Port Royal, and under Henry Morgan they wreaked havoc throughout the Caribbean and Central America. In 1697, Spain and England signed the Treaty of Ryswyck and committed to ending privateering and piracy.

1623 The English establish their first Caribbean colony, on St. Kitts

1634 The Dutch colonize the southwest Caribbean islands

1697 Spain and England sign the treaty of Ryswyck to end piracy

580   1640   1700

1635 Guadeloupe and Martinique are colonized by the French

1655 English Admiral Penn seizes Jamaica from the Spanish

Welsh pirate, Henry Morgan (1635–88)

African slaves laboring on a sugar plantation, an engraving by Theodore de Bry, 1596

SUGAR AND SLAVERY

During the early 17th century, the rest of the Lesser Antilles' islands were colonized by England, France, and the Netherlands. The Dutch dominated early colonization, founding the Dutch West India Company in 1621. They promoted Caribbean trade in defiance of a Spanish monopoly. Constant wars for possession ensued and some islands changed hands more than 20 times. Spain encouraged tobacco and sugar cultivation, fostering a booming economy to satisfy Europe's growing demand for sugar. Other European nations followed suit, and sugar dominated the islands' economy.

The phenomenal growth of the sugar industry was made possible by African slave labor. African men, women, and children were captured and packed aboard ships for the harrowing Middle Passage to the New World, where most were auctioned to planters. Many slaves fell sick and died en route. Britain alone shipped more than three million Africans to the Caribbean between 1662 and 1807. By the late 18th century, slaves outnumbered the white population by ten to one. The slave trade was so lucrative that rival European powers warred for control.

Plantation slaves toiled in the cane fields with little respite from flogging or worse punishments. Slave masters suppressed rebellions with force. By the end of the 18th century, slave uprisings grew in size and frequency – in 1804, a rebellion in France's Saint-Domingue led to the creation of the world's first black republic, Haiti. Plantations were in decline, however, and in 1834 Britain abolished slavery (but introduced Indian indentured labor to Jamaica and Trinidad); the French did so in 1848. Slavery on the Spanish islands continued until 1886, and contributed to Cuba's brutal wars of independence.

INDEPENDENCE

Each Caribbean island evolved its distinct Creole culture that crystallized into nationalist independence movements. The United States, concerned by the violent events in Cuba and Puerto Rico (the Dominican Republic, the third major Spanish possession, had won independence in 1844), declared war on Spain in 1898. The short Spanish-American War ended with Spain's defeat and Cuba and Puerto Rico were ceded to the US. Puerto Rico was retained by the US as a "Commonwealth." In 1903, the

TIMELINE

Slave rebellion led by Toussaint L'Ouverture in 1794

1775 Trade embargo on British West Indies enforced by the US till 1783

1845 Indentured labore from India begin arrivin in British colonies

| 1755 | | 1820 |

1784 France cedes St. Barthélemy to Sweden

1807 England bans slave trading

1834 Britain grants emancipation to slaves in its colonies

US granted freedom to Cuba, which witnessed a boom-and-bust economy under a series of corrupt US-backed governments that ended in 1959, when Fidel Castro toppled dictator General Batista and the island became a Communist nation.

The Danes sold their Virgin Islands to the US in 1917, while Aruba, Curaçao, Bonaire, St. Eustatius, Saba, and Sint Maarten were incorporated as autonomous constituents of the Netherlands. The French possessions were also integrated as full departments of France, with the citizens having the same rights as the French.

In 1958, an attempt to forge the British-ruled islands into an independent Federation of the West Indies foundered. Jamaica and Trinidad and Tobago became independent states within the British Commonwealth in 1962, followed by Barbados in 1966. Next came independence for Dominica (1978), St. Lucia (1979), St. Vincent (1979), Antigua and Barbuda (1981), and St. Kitts and Nevis (1983). Anguilla, Montserrat, Cayman Islands, British Virgin Islands, and the Turks and Caicos still remain dependencies or British Overseas Territories.

Demonstrators in the US protesting against the regime of Rafael Trujillo in the Dominican Republic

scene in the Dominican Republic today. The Dominican Republic has now emerged from three decades of brutal dictatorship (1930–61) under Rafael Trujillo, and is one of the leading Caribbean destinations for tourism.

In Cuba, Fidel Castro handed power to his brother Raúl in 2008. However, the nation continues to chart a unique socialist path in the face of a US trade embargo. In January 2010 a devastating earthquake struck Haiti, killing more that 230,000 people. Jamaica's capital, Kingston, was rocked when an anti-drug offensive led to gunfights that claimed dozens of lives in May 2010. Nevertheless, the trend today is towards greater political stability and development with each island presenting its unique culture, blending African, European, and other influences into a fascinating combination.

THE CARIBBEAN TODAY

Most islands have overcome their colonial legacy and have evolved as major tourist destinations. Jamaica was the birthplace of the all-inclusive resorts, which dominate the

Poster of Fidel Castro and "Che" Guevara

| 1898 US intervenes in Cuba's independence war; seizes Puerto Rico | 1961 US imposes trade embargo on Cuba | 1962 Trinidad and Tobago gain independence | |
| 1902 Mont Pelée erupts on Martinique; St. Pierre is destroyed | | 1965 25,000 US Marines quell labor unrest in the Dominican Republic | Hurricane George (1998), Greater Antilles |

1950   2015

| 1958 Federation of British West Indies established but fails four years later | 1959 Fidel Castro seizes power in Cuba and begins a Communist revolution | 1983 US Marines invade Grenada to topple a leftist government | 2010 A huge earthquake hits Haiti, leveling Port-au-Prince and killing 230,000 people |
| Cyparis, sole survivor of Mont Pelée eruption | | | 2008 Hurricane Ike devastates Grand Turk, Haiti, and Cuba |

THE GREATER ANTILLES

THE GREATER ANTILLES AT A GLANCE

The larger nation states of the Greater Antilles offer the greatest diversity in the Caribbean due to their size. Spanish-speaking Cuba, the Dominican Republic, and Puerto Rico each boast remarkable early-colonial cities crammed with cathedrals and castles; of these Havana is particularly enthralling. All three islands have sensational beaches, rugged mountains, and world-class hotels, as does English-speaking Jamaica. The relatively tiny Cayman Islands and Turks and Caicos have splendid beaches, fantastic diving, and unique wildlife.

LOCATOR MAP

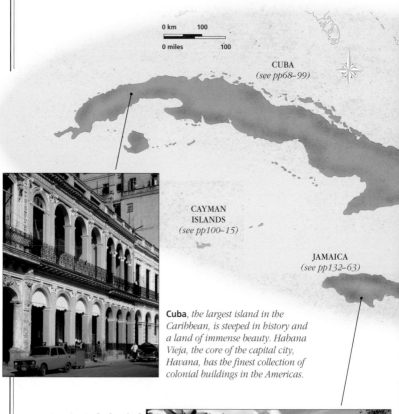

0 km   100

0 miles   100

CUBA
(see pp68–99)

CAYMAN ISLANDS
(see pp100–15)

JAMAICA
(see pp132–63)

Cuba, *the largest island in the Caribbean, is steeped in history and a land of immense beauty. Habana Vieja, the core of the capital city, Havana, has the finest collection of colonial buildings in the Americas.*

Jamaica *is the land of reggae music and spectacular beaches. The craggy Blue Mountains, fabulous Blue Lagoon, famous resorts, sandy beaches, and vibrant towns with festive nightlife make it one of the most popular islands with visitors.*

◁ Bicitaxi outside a colorful old building in Havana, Cuba

The Turks and Caicos *sit atop an underwater plateau with walls that plunge to the bottom, making it a world-class diving and snorkeling destination. Rich marine life, nature reserves that protect scores of bird species, historic buildings, lively nightlife, and excellent hotels make these islands a major tourist attraction.*

Puerto Rico *is a unique island fusing Latin and American cultures with dramatic landscapes, boutique hotels, and exciting activities ranging from golf to surfing. The capital, San Juan, boasts cobbled streets lined with magnificent colonial buildings.*

TURKS AND
CAICOS
(see pp116–31)

HAITI

DOMINICAN
REPUBLIC
(see pp164–93)

PUERTO RICO
(see pp194–221)

The Dominican Republic, *one of the most geographically diverse islands in the region, provides innumerable opportunities for adventure and eco-tourism. Mangrove swamps, alpine wilderness, cascading waterfalls, spectacular beaches, and colonial buildings add to the charm of the island.*

A PORTRAIT OF CUBA

*C*uba is typified by images of the hot sun, sugarcane fields, tall palms, and clear blue sea. This largest Antillean island is indeed all these things, but it is also a nation with a deep-rooted, complex culture where old traditions and modernism co-exist. Dance and music are the soul of this exhilarating and vital island.

Tourism in this Caribbean nation has boomed and attracts more than two million visitors annually, mainly from Europe and Canada. Despite setbacks since the collapse of the Soviet Union in 1991, Cuba has developed its hotel and tourist infrastructure in keeping with international standards. While most travelers come to relax on the spectacular beaches and swim in the jade-colored seas, the real Cuba is to be found in the centuries-old cities and countryside, where peasant farmers still live in simple thatched houses shaded by royal palms. Creaking ox-drawn carts trundle past tobacco plantations, and lime green sugarcane fields sway in the lee of dramatic limestone formations, epitomized by the

Painting in typical Cuban style

knoll-like *mogotes* of Valle de Viñales. Forested mountains and the largest Caribbean swamps teem with exotic wildlife, drawing both birders and hikers. Cuba's coral reefs are extremely beautiful, earning accolades from divers.

LIFESTYLE

Cubans are gregarious and sociable, a blend of ethnic diversity – part Asian, part Spanish, and part African. Life is lived on streets as women pull their *sillones* (rocking chairs) onto the sidewalks to gossip, while men play dominoes, smoke cigars, and share shots of aguardiente (cheap white rum). They have a passion for music and dance – the sensual undercurrent of daily life. The streets are abuzz with the sounds of *son* and salsa, reflecting their

A rhumba singer entertaining passersby on Havana's Callejón de Hammel, a street with colorful murals

Classic Cuban car in front of El Capitolio, Havana

traumatic history, and monuments to the wars of Independence and the Revolution that swept away the corrupt US-backed regime of Fulgencio Batista, take pride of place in every city. For five decades Cuba has been Communist under the leadership of Fidel Castro, who stepped down in 2008 in favor of his brother Raúl Castro. Fidel Castro's larger-than-life presence is everywhere – along with that of Che Guevara – in billboards and media exhortations. Cubans are divided between those who support the socialist system and those who chaff at the restrictions on liberty. Nationalist pride that derives from the nation's freedom from US control is tempered by the dictates of a paternalistic government on which they are entirely dependent.

instinct for gaiety despite material hardship. Santería, the mix of Catholicism and African beliefs, plays a significant part in many people's lives and it is common to wear beads in the color of one's personal *orisha* (god).

Vibrant, bustling Havana, a city of two million people, is filled with nightclubs simmering with sentimental allure. The modern city is adorned with buildings spanning Art Deco to Art Nouveau, while in Habana Vieja (Old Havana) the previously crumbling but now restored Baroque and Neo-Classical cathedrals and cobbled plazas are made even more surreal by the omnipresent 1950s automobiles trundling down the narrow streets to radios blaring rhumba. UNESCO has recognized the cultural and architectural importance of Old Havana, which is one of Cuba's nine World Heritage Sites.

HISTORY AND POLITICS

Cuban heritage is steeped in struggle. The people take profound pride in their rich, often

CULTURE AND THE ARTS

Part of Cuba's appeal is its unique blend of Communism and Caribbean culture. Cabarets recall the Mafia heyday of the 1950s, while *casas de la trova* (clubs showcasing live music) keep alive traditional forms of music, such as the *son*. The Ballet Nacional de Cuba, managed by reputed ballerina Alicia Alonso, is one of the top ballet companies of the world.

Varadero, one of Cuba's most popular beaches

Exploring Cuba

Cuba's north coast bustles with thriving resorts edged by white sands and coral reefs. Its southern coast is less developed and is a haven for crocodiles and other wildlife. Two mountain ranges dominate the west and east, while the Sierra Escambray rises over the center. In the lowlands, ox-drawn carts trundle past sugar-cane fields, and dramatic limestone formations loom over lush tobacco fields. Havana, the capital city, is full of bustle and entertainment, teeming with architectural gems. Trinidad is caught in a time-warp, while Santiago de Cuba is a center for Afro-Cuban rhythms.

Varadero
All-inclusive hotels line the spectacular beach running the length of the long peninsula.

Habana Vieja
The castles, palaces, cathedrals, museums, and cultural venues of the capital's colonial core have been restored to their former splendor.

SEE ALSO

Trinidad
Set on a hill, with a fine beach close by, Trinidad has a restored, fully pedestrian center.

SIGHTS AT A GLANCE

KEY

═══ Highway

──── Major road

═ ═ ═ Minor road

▪▪▪ Railroad

- - - Ferry route

▬▬▬ International border

0 km   75

0 miles   75

Jardines del Rey
This series of offshore cays
is fringed by snow-white
sands and surrounded by
turquoise waters. Cayo Coco
is the major beach resort.

Iglesia y Convento de San Francisco, Trinidad

GETTING AROUND

Cuba is a large island and the easiest way of exploring end to
end is by rental car. All major cities are linked by air and train.
Air-conditioned tourist buses connect important cities and
beach resorts, but inter-city buses serving locals no longer
accept tourists. High-speed hydrofoils run from Isla de la
Juventud to Batabanó in Havana province. Tourist taxis
operate throughout Havana, in the beach resorts, and at
other tourist centers. Buses in and around towns are generally
uncomfortable; locals also tend to rely on *bicitaxis* (bicycle
rickshaws) and horse-drawn carts.

Baracoa
The oldest city in Cuba,
Baracoa is famous for its cocoa.
Located on a curved bay, it
provides beautiful views.

Archipiélago de

NTA MARÍA   JARDINES DEL REY

San Rafael   Camagüey

Morón   Esmeralda

Ciego de Ávila

Florida   Nuevitas

CAMAGÜEY   Minas

Vertientes   Cascorro   Manati   Puerto Padre   Gibara   GUARDALAVACA

Guáimaro   PLAYA SANTA LUCÍA   Santa Lucía

Amancio   Jobabo   Las Tunas   HOLGUÍN   Moa

Santa Cruz del Sur   Cueto   Mayarí   Sagua de Tánamo

Media Luna   BAYAMO   Jiguaní   La Maya   BARACOA

Niquero   Yara   Palma Soriano   Guantánamo   San Antonio del Sur

Pilón   El Cobre   SANTIAGO DE CUBA   US Naval Base, Guantánamo Bay

Archipiélago de los nes de la Reina

Green tobacco fields in Valle de Viñales, Pinar del Río province

Havana ➊

The Fuente de los Leones

One of the great historical cities of the world, Havana is a lively, vibrant capital full of architectural jewels in a medley of styles. The city is worth the trip to Cuba in its own right. Encompassing the colonial city that lay within the now largely demolished, original city walls, Habana Vieja (Old Havana) was declared a UNESCO World Heritage Site in 1982. This historic heart has regained its splendor after ongoing restoration; its castles, convents, museums, and cobbled plazas mesmerize visitors. Mementos of Havana's 20th-century heyday are concentrated in Vedado, the municipal center, and the residential Centro Habana.

View of the Catedral de San Cristóbal from Plaza de la Catedral

🏛 Plaza de la Catedral
Calles San Ignacio & Empedrado. 🚻 **Museo de Arte Colonial** Calle San Ignacio 61. **Tel** *(7) 862 6440.* ⬜ *9am–5:30pm daily.* 📷 🎥 🚻 🚫 *without a fee.*
This exquisite and intimate square was once a terminus for the Zanja Real, the royal aqueduct constructed to supply water to ships in the adjoining harbor. A plaque marks the spot now. The cobbled plaza is dominated by the Baroque profile of the **Catedral de San Cristóbal**, completed by Jesuits in 1777, with asymmetrical bell towers to each side. The Neo-Classical nave with eight side chapels is austere, as is the simple altar.
In the 18th century, Spanish nobles built their palaces around the square. Most noteworthy is the Casa del Conde de Bayona, today housing the **Museo de Arte Colonial**, full of period furnishings. Mulatta women, dressed in colorful colonial costume, stroll the plaza and pose for photos beneath the shaded arcades. Just off the northwest corner, is La Bodeguita del Medio *(see p96)* bar-restaurant, where Ernest Hemingway was once a regular visitor.

🏛 Calle Mercaderes
Linking Plaza de Armas to Plaza Vieja. **Maqueta de la Habana** Calle Mercaderes 114. **Tel** *(7) 866 4425.* ⬜ *9:30am–6:30pm daily.* 📷 🎥 🚫 *without a fee.*
This narrow cobblestoned street is lined with restored colonial structures and boasts

The tree-shaded Calle Mercaderes

a mix of museums, restaurants, and boutiques. Not to be missed, the **Maqueta de la Habana**, housed in one of the buildings here, is a 1:500 scale model of Habana Vieja. The 17th-century Casa de la Obra Pía is a fine example of colonial architecture.

🏛 Calle Obispo
🚻 **Farmacia Taquechel** Calle Obispo 155. **Tel** *(7) 862 9286.* ⬜ *9am–6pm daily.* 🚻
Habana Vieja's liveliest street, sloping west from Plaza de Armas *(see pp74–5)* to Parque Central, is the pedestrianized Calle Obispo, which bustles with commercial activity just as it did in colonial days. At its west end, El Floridita is where Ernest Hemingway famously downed daiquiris; today his bronze likeness rests an elbow at the bar. His room (No. 511) at Hotel Ambos Mundos *(see p74)* is preserved as a museum. Another interesting site is **Farmacia Taquechel**, an old pharmacy with apothecary jars lining the shelves.

🏛 Plaza San Francisco
Calle Oficios. 🚻 **Basílica Menor de San Francisco de Asís** Calles Oficios y Amargura. **Tel** *(7) 862 9683.* ⬜ *9am–5:30pm Mon–Fri, 11:30am–7pm Sat.* 📷 🎥 🚻 🚫 *without a fee.*
Next to the modern cruise-ship terminal, this airy cobbled square once opened onto the colonial waterfront. At its heart, the marble Fuente de los Leones, guarded by lions, is modeled on a fountain in the Alhambra in Spain. To the north is the restored Neo-Classical Lonja del Comercio, the commerce exchange, crowned by a winged statue of Mercury. Dominating the square, the **Basílica Menor de San Francisco de Asís** dates back to the 1580s, although it was rebuilt in 1730. In 1762, the British seized Havana and began worshipping in the church. Today it is a concert hall and the adjoining convent is a museum of religious art.

Façade of the colonial Casa del Conde Jaruco, Plaza Vieja

VISITORS' CHECKLIST

N coast of Cuba. 🏠 60,000.
✈ 🚌 🚉 🚢 ℹ *Calle Obispo
524, Habana Vieja, (7) 866 3333.*
🎭 *Festival Internacional del
Nuevo Cine Latinoamericano
(Dec).* www.infotur.cu

Plaza Vieja

Calles Mercaderes & Brasil. ♿
"Old Square" began as Plaza
Nueva (New Square) in 1587
and served as Havana's main
market place and bullfight
arena. Buildings from four
centuries surround the plaza,
which has been restored,
complete with a fountain replicating the original. **Casa del
Conde Jaruco**, built between
1733 and 37 on the southeast
corner, features colonial
details, including *mediopun-
tos* (half-moon stained-glass
windows). The Palacio Cueto
is an astonishing Art Nouveau
building, currently being
converted into a hotel.

Ecclesiastical Quarter

S of Plaza Vieja. **Convento de Santa
Clara** Calle Cuba 610. **Tel** (7) 866
9327. ⬜ 9am–5pm Mon–Fri. 🎫 ♿
**Iglesia de Nuestra Señora de la
Merced** Calle Cuba 806. **Tel** (7) 863
8873. ⬜ 8am–noon & 3–6pm daily.
♿ **Casa-Museo José Martí** Calle
Leonor Pérez 314. **Tel** (7) 861 3778.
⬜ 9am–5pm Tue–Sat. 🎫 ♿
Southern Habana Vieja was in
colonial days a major ecclesi-
astical center and has many

convents and churches.
The charming 17th-century
Convento de Santa Clara is
an outstanding example of
colonial architecture. A part
of it is today a *posada*-style
hotel. The **Iglesia de Nuestra
Señora de la Merced**, with a
lavish interior and frescoed
dome ceiling, is popular
with followers of both
the Catholic and Santería
(Afro-Cuban) religions.

Casa-Museo José Martí,
almost a religious shrine to
Cubans, is the birthplace of
Cuba's foremost national figure, José Martí *(see p76)*. The
simple home of the hero is
now a museum. Visitors can
view paintings, furniture, and
some of his written works.

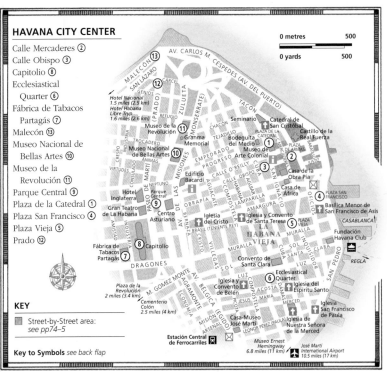

HAVANA CITY CENTER

0 metres 500
0 yards 500

AV. CARLOS M. CESPEDES (AV. DEL PUERTO)
MALECÓN
SAN LÁZARO
CÁRCEL
GENIOS
(PRADO)
ZULUETA
MONSERRATE)
TACÓN
Hotel Nacional
1.5 miles (2.5 km)
Hotel Habana
Libre Tryp
1.6 miles (2.6 km)
REFUGIO
CHACÓN
Seminario
Catedral de
San Cristóbal
Museo de la
Revolución ⑪
PLAZA DE
LA CATEDRAL
Castillo de la
Real Fuerza
TROCADERO
TEJADILLO
Gramma
Memorial
Bodeguita
del Medio
Museo de
Arte Colonial
PLAZA DE
ARMAS
CRESPO
INDUSTRIA
Museo Nacional
de Bellas Artes ⑩
ÁNIMAS
EMPEDRADO
PROGRESO
O'REILLY
Casa de la
Obra Pia
VIRTUDES
CONSULADO
MISIONES
CALLE OBISPO
AGUIAR
HABANA
COMPOSTELA
Casa de
África
OFICIOS
PLAZA SAN
FRANCISCO
Edificio
Bacardí
CALLE O'REILLY
AGUACATE
Casa de
África
Basílica Menor de
San Francisco de Asis
NEPTUNO
Parque
Central
OBRAPIA
LAMPARILLA
AMARGURA
PLAZA
VIEJA
CASABLANCA
Hotel
Inglaterra
PASEO DE MARTÍ
Gran Teatro
de La Habana
Centro
Asturiano
BERNAZA
Iglesia
del Cristo
BRASIL (TENIENTE REY)
Iglesia y Convento
de Santa Teresa
LA
HABANA
VIEJA
MURALLA
Fundación
Havana Club
AMISTAD
Fábrica de
Tabacos
Partagás ⑦
⑧ Capitolio
VILLEGAS
CRISTO
MURALLA
SOL
Convento de
Santa Clara
SOL
CUBA
SANTA CLARA
LUZ
SAN PEDRO
REGLA
DRAGONES
M. GOMEZ MONTE
AV. BÉLGICA
COLONIA
Plaza de la
Revolución
2 miles (3.4 km)
Iglesia y
Convento
de Belén
LUZ
ACOSTA
Ecclesiastical
Quarter ⑥
Iglesia del
Espíritu Santo
Cementerio
Colón
2.5 miles (4 km)
MISIÓN (EGIDO)
JESÚS MARÍA
MERCED
Iglesia
San Francisco
de Paula
ARSENAL
Casa-Museo
José Martí
LEONOR PÉREZ (PAULA)
Iglesia de
Nuestra Señora
de la Merced
Estación Central
de Ferrocarriles
Museo Ernest
Hemingway
6.8 miles (11 km)
José Martí
International Airport
10.5 miles (17 km)

Street-by-Street: Plaza de Armas

This elegant cobbled plaza was laid out in its current guise during the 1600s, when it served as a military parade ground (Plaza de Armas) and the center of government. At its heart, a small leafy park is ringed on most days by stalls selling secondhand books. The square is framed by Baroque and Neo-Classical buildings, which have been painstakingly restored in recent years. Benches and cafés provide relaxing spots to sit and absorb the colonial atmosphere.

★ Palacio de los Capitanes Generales
A grand Baroque palace, this building served as the governor's mansion. Now the Museo de la Ciudad, it provides an insight into Havana's history with exhibits ranging from the remains of the Espada Cemetery to mementos from the independence wars.

Palacio del Segundo Cabo (1776)
The former residence of the Spanish lieutenant-governor is now the home of the Cuban Book Institute.

Hotel Ambos Mundo
The typewriter and desk of Ernest Hemingway are preserved in the bedroom at this hotel. It is here that he wrote the famous novel, For Whom the Bell Tolls *(1940).*

Plaza de la Catedral
(see p72)

CALLE TACÓN

CALLE O'REILLY

CALLE MERCADERES

CALLE

Former Ministerio de Educación

Farmacia Taquechel

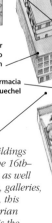

Calle Obispo
Lined with buildings dating from the 16th–19th centuries as well as cafés, shops, galleries, and museums, this cobbled pedestrian thoroughfare is the district's liveliest.

CALLE OBRAPÍA

★ Castillo de la Real Fuerza
Completed in 1582, this is the oldest fortress in Havana. It features a broad moat and angular ramparts. In 1634, a weathervane known as La Giraldilla was placed on a lookout tower over the western rampart and soon became a symbol of the city. Today, the Castillo houses a ceramics museum.

0 metres 60
0 yards 60

The statue of Carlos Manuel de Céspedes depicts the national hero who launched the War of Independence.

★ El Templete
The Neo-Classical temple stands on the site of the city's first mass, depicted on a wall-to-wall triptych. A sacred ceiba stands outside.

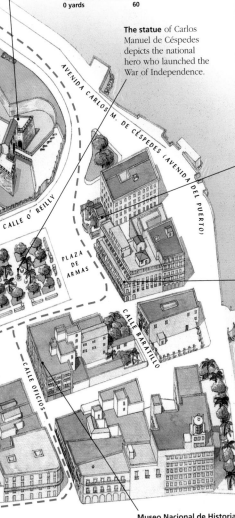

AVENIDA CARLOS M. DE CÉSPEDES (AVENIDA DEL PUERTO)

CALLE O´REILLY

PLAZA DE ARMAS

CALLE BARATILLO

CALLE OFICIOS

Hotel Santa Isabel
Former home of the Count of Santovenia, this Neo-Classical structure was built during the 18th century.

Museo Nacional de Historia Natural has excellent exhibits on Cuba's flora and fauna.

KEY

– – – Suggested route

STAR SIGHTS

★ Palacio de los Capitanes Generales

★ Castillo de la Real Fuerza

★ El Templete

🏭 Fábrica de Tabacos Partagás

Calle Industria 520. **Tel** *(7) 863 5766.* 🕐 *9–11am & noon–3pm Mon–Fri.* ⊘ *public hols.* 📷 *for a fee.* 🛍

This four-story, 19th-century cigar factory has a Spanish-style industrial façade with pilasters and a Baroque roofline. It was founded by Jaime Partagás Ravelo, a Catalan businessman. Visitors can take in aromatic tobacco scents and witness the hand-rolling of premium cigars for export.

🏛 Capitolio

See p77.

🍁 Parque Central

Paseo de Martí at Calle Neptuno. ♿

This spacious park, the informal center of the city, serves as the major gateway between Habana Vieja and the modern districts to the west. Designed in 1877, the park has a statue of José Martí in its center. Gracious structures surround the park, including the Hotel Inglaterra and Hotel Plaza, notable for their elegant 19th-century façades. Most striking is the Gran Teatro de la Habana, a Baroque confection adorned with statues.

🏛 Museo Nacional de Bellas Artes

Palacio de Bellas Artes, Trocadero e/ Zulueta y Monserrate. **Centro Asturiano**, San Rafael y Zulueta. **Tel** *(7) 863 9484.* 🕐 *10am–6pm Tue–Sat, 10am–2pm Sun.* ⊘ *public hols.* 🎧 📷 ♿ 🚫📸 🛍 **www**.museonacional.cult.cu

Havana's National Fine Arts Museum displays an astonishingly rich trove in two buildings. The **Palacio de Bellas Artes** is given over to Cuban art, with sections that are devoted to colonial and 20th-century works. The **Centro Asturiano**, on the other hand, houses international works, including those of European masters, plus a collection of Egyptian, Greek, and Roman antiquities.

JOSÉ MARTÍ (1853–95)

Born in Havana in 1853, José Martí became a nationalist in his youth and was imprisoned by the Spanish for treason at 16. He was later exiled and, after settling in New York, led the campaign for Cuban independence. A prodigious writer and philosopher, he also championed the cause of social justice. In 1895 he returned to Cuba with General Máximo Gómez to lead the War of Independence. On May 19 the same year, he was killed in action at Dos Ríos.

Statue of José Martí

Granma Memorial inside the Museo de la Revolución

🏛 Museo de la Revolución

Calle Refugio 1 e/ Zulueta y Monserrate. **Tel** *(7) 862 4091.* 🕐 *10am–5pm daily.* 🎧 📷 🚫📸 *without payment.* ☕ 🛍

Housed in the extravagantly eclectic former presidential palace inaugurated in 1920, the Museo de la Revolución dramatizes the Cuban struggle for independence, from the colonial era to the current day. Most exhibits depict the revolution that toppled dictator Fulgencio Batista. To the rear, the Granma Memorial displays military hardware related to the Bay of Pigs invasion in 1961 *(see p81)*.

🏛 Prado

Between Parque Central and Malecón. ♿

Officially named Paseo de Martí, this tree-shaded boulevard was redesigned in 1927 by French architect Forestier and features a raised walkway adorned with bronze lions, wrought-iron lampposts, and marble benches. The many Neo-Moorish buildings include the Hotel Sevilla, from 1908. Nearby, Havana's main wedding venue, the beautiful Neo-Baroque Palacio de los Matrimonios, has an ornately stuccoed interior.

🏛 Malecón

Between Prado and Río Almenderes. ☕

The sinuous seafront Malecón boulevard is Havana's main thoroughfare. It is lined with fanciful buildings and, in the Vedado district, high-rise hotels. Highlights include the Monumento al Maine, a memorial to sailors killed when the USS *Maine* exploded in the Havana harbor on February 15, 1898.

🛏 Hotel Nacional

Calles O & 21. **Tel** *(7) 836 3564.* **Fax** *(7) 873 5054.* [$][$][$] *475 rooms* 🍴 ≡ [W] **www.**hotelnacionaldecuba.com

Overlooking the Malecón, this gem of an Art Deco building opened in 1930. It features a lavish Moorish interior, while cannons stud the lawns. Considered Havana's finest hotel, its illustrious guest list includes Churchill, Sinatra, Ava Gardner, and Hemingway.

The tree-lined Prado, also known as Paseo de Martí

🏨 Hotel Habana Libre Tryp

Calles L & 23. ***Tel*** *(7) 834 6100.* ***Fax*** *53 7834 6365.* $$ *533 rooms.* 🍴 ♿ [W] **www**.solmeliacuba.com

A Havana landmark, this modernist high-rise hotel atop La Rampa opened as the Havana Hilton in 1958. A spectacular mural, *Carro de la Revolución,* adorns the *porte cochère* entrance, and the atrium lobby features modernist art pieces.

🏛 Cementerio Colón

Zapata y Calle 12. ***Tel*** *(7) 830 4517.* 🕐 *8am–5pm daily.* 📷 🎥 *for a fee.* ♿ 🚫 *without payment.*

Havana's vast cemetery covers 135 acres (56 ha) and was arranged in a strict grid in the 1870s. It has been named a National Historic Monument for its spectacular mausoleums in eclectic styles, from Neo-Classical to Avant-Garde. At its core is the Capilla Central, a chapel with lavish frescoes.

🏛 Plaza de la Revolución

Paseo between Av. Carlos M. de Céspedes & Av. Rancho Boyeros. ♿

This monumental plaza has been Cuba's political and administrative center since it was laid out in the 1950s as Plaza Cívica. It is the main center for political rallies. The façade of the Ministerio del Interior is adorned with a seven-story high steel sculpture of Che Guevara.

Dominating the plaza, the Memorial José Martí features a marble statue of the national hero backed by a star-shaped tower with the Museo de José Martí at its base. Behind the memorial are the main government headquarters.

🏛 Museo Ernest Hemingway

Calle Vigía y Steinhart, San Francisco de Paula. ***Tel*** *(7) 691 0809.* 🕐 *10am–5pm Mon–Sat, 10am–1pm Sun.* 📷 🎥 🚫 *without payment.* 🛍

Ernest Hemingway's former home, Finca Vigía, is maintained as the author left it, with his possessions in situ. Visitors, not allowed to enter inside, can look through the open windows and door.

Capitolio

The most imposing Neo-Classical structure in Havana, the Capitolio was inaugurated in 1929 by the dictator General Gerardo Machado. An imitation of the Washington DC Capitol, Cuba's former congressional building served as seat of government until 1959. A section today houses the Ministry of Science, Technology, and Environment. Maintained in perfect condition, it is open for guided as well as self-guided tours of the government chambers and the magnificent library.

VISITORS' CHECKLIST

Paseo de Martí esq. San José. ***Tel*** *(7) 861 5519.* 🕐 *9am–7pm daily.* 📷 🎥 *for a fee.* 🚫 *without payment.* 💻

The Dome
At 300 ft (92 m), the dome is higher than the Capitol in Washington DC.

Staircase of Honor
This flight of steps was formerly reserved for MPs.

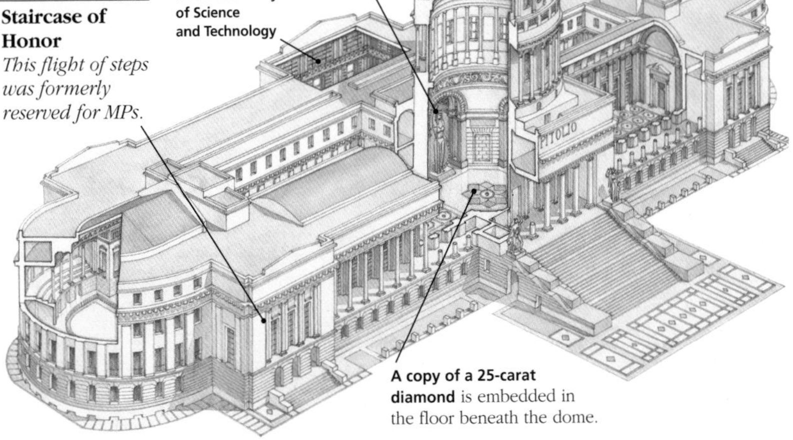

Statue of the Republic
The 56 ft (17.4 m) tall bronze statue was made by the Italian sculptor Angelo Zanelli.

National Library of Science and Technology

A copy of a 25-carat diamond is embedded in the floor beneath the dome.

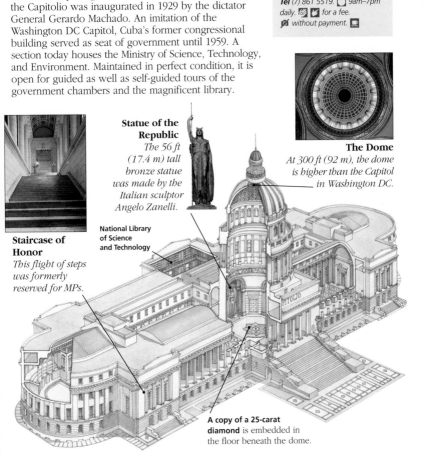

White sandy beach of Cayo Largo

Cayo Largo ❷

112 miles (180 km) S of Havana.

This narrow isle, with its white sands shelving into turquoise waters, is a long-established holiday destination. Sailing, watersports, and horse-riding are offered by all-inclusive resorts served by charter flights and overnight excursions from Havana. Visitors can spend time swimming or relaxing on a beach. Iguanas patrol the craggy shoreline, and marine turtles are often seen by divers.

Isla de la Juventud ❸

94 miles (150 km) S of Havana. ✈
🚢 daily from Batabanó.

The "Isle of Youth" has few major tourist draws, and hence offers a genuine Cuban experience. Sleepy Nueva Gerona is the main town with colonial homes. The isle's main draw is

Presidio Modelo, a former prison, now a museum, where Fidel Castro and his men were jailed after they attacked the Moncada barracks in July 1953.

On the southwest shore, Hotel Colony Siguanea (*see p94*) is a base for diving to amazing coral formations and shipwrecks. To the south, **Parque Nacional del Sur** offers good viewing, with a crocodile farm and pre-Columbian petroglyphs at Cuevas de Punta del Este.

🏛 Presidio Modelo
3 miles (5 km) E of Nueva Gerona. *Tel* (46) 32 5112. ◯ 8am–4pm Mon–Sat, 8am–noon Sun. 🗏 ✔ ✔

🐾 Parque Nacional del Sur
25 miles (40 km) S of Nueva Gerona. *Tel* (46) 32 7101. 🏋 Ecotur, Calles 24 & 31, Nueva Gerona. 🚗 from Ecotur.

KEY

━━━	Highway
━━━	Major road
━━━	Minor road
━━━	Unpaved road

Sierra del Rosario ❹

54 miles (87 km) W of Havana. 🚗

Covered with tropical forests, this rugged mountain chain delights birders and hikers. At its eastern end, the lovely rural community of **Las Terrazas** is Cuba's premier ecological center. Nearby Soroa is known for its **Orquideario** (orchid garden) and the **Saltón** waterfall.

🐾 Las Terrazas
Autopista Habana-Pinar del Río Km51. *Tel* (48) 57 8700. ◯ 8am–5pm daily. 🍴 ◻ ◻ ⟡ ◭

🌸 Orquideario
Carretera de Soroa Km8. *Tel* (48) 52 3871. ◯ 8:30am–4:30pm daily. 📷 ✔ compulsory. ♿ ∅ without payment. ◻

Façade of the Palacio de Guasch, Pinar del Río

Pinar del Río ❺

109 miles (175 km) SW of Havana. 🏃 125,000. 🚌 🚆

Founded in 1669, the orderly provincial capital is graced by Classical and Art Nouveau columns. Most buildings of note line Calle Martí. The Museo de Ciencias Naturales, in the **Palacio de Guasch**, displays native flora and fauna. The Neo-Classical Teatro Milanés dates back to 1835. Visitors can watch cigars being hand-rolled at the **Fábrica de Tabacos Francisco Donatién**.

Fábrica de Tabacos Francisco Donatién
Calle Maceo Oeste 157. *Tel* (48) 77 3069. ◯ 9am–noon & 1–4pm Mon–Fri, 9am–noon Sat–Sun. 🗏 ♿ ◻

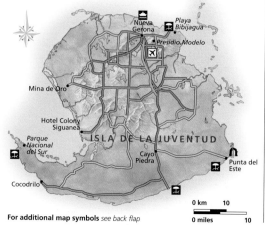

Nueva Gerona
Playa Bibijagua
Presidio Modelo
Mina de Oro
Hotel Colony Siguanea
Parque Nacional del Sur
ISLA DE LA JUVENTUD
Cayo Piedra
Punta del Este
Cocodrilo

0 km	10
0 miles	10

For additional map symbols *see back flap*

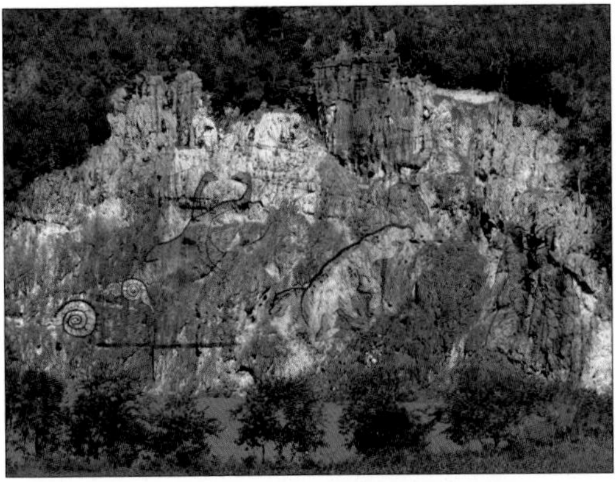

Mural de la Prehistoria by Leovigildo González, Valle de Viñales

Valle de Viñales [6]

127 miles (205 km) W of Havana. 🚌

The lyrical landscapes of the broad Viñales Valley are the most quintessential in Cuba. Giant *mogotes*, karst formations resembling beehives, stand over this and adjoining valleys that comprise a quiltwork of thatched peasants' huts and tobacco fields shaded by royal palms.

Caves riddle the *mogotes*. The **Cueva del Indio** has an underground lake and river, and can be explored by boat excursions. There is even a nightclub that features a cabaret show in Cueva de San Miguel. Between 1959 and 1962, Mogote Dos Hermanos was brightly painted with the **Mural de la Prehistoria**, a modern depiction of evolution.

The village of Viñales is a rural charmer. Its main street, Calle Salvador Cisneros, is lined with beautiful red-tile-roofed colonial homes fronted by columned arcades. Parque Martí, the village square, has a lovely church – the Iglesia del Sagrado Corazón de Jesús – as well as the Casa de la Cultura, where many cultural events are held.

Cueva del Indio
3 miles (5 km) N of Viñales.
Tel *(48) 79 6280.* 🕒 *9am–5pm daily.* 🎫 🍴 🛍

Mural de la Prehistoria
3 miles (5 km) W of Viñales.
Tel *(48) 79 6260.* 🕒 *8am–7pm daily.* 🎫 ♿ 🍴

Hotel Los Jazmines [7]

Carretera de Viñales Km25.
Tel *(48) 79 6205.* ***Fax*** *(48) 79 6215.*
$$ *78 rooms.* 🍴 ≡ ♿
www.cubanacan.cu

Enjoying a superb location atop the southern flank of the magnificent Viñales Valley, Hotel Los Jazmines is popular for the unsurpassed views it offers. The pool sundeck hovers over the cliff-face. The main building, dating from the 1930s, features classic colonial elements such as *mediopuntos*.

Cayo Levisa [8]

🏖 155 miles (250 km) W of Havana.
Tel *(48) 75 6501.* ⛴ 🚻 🍸 🐬 🏊 ⛵ 🤿 www.cubanacan.cu

This tiny island off the north coast, ringed by white sands and mangroves, has a namesake hotel, the only one in the Los Colorados archipelago. The isle is geared for diving and has spectacular coral reefs. Sportfishing is also good, notably for marlin.

María la Gorda [9]

🏖 193 miles (310 km) SW of Havana. ***Tel*** *(48) 77 8131.* 🚻 🍸 🐬 ⛴ 🤿 www.gaviota-grupo.com

Sunbathers can enjoy the fine sands of this renowned bathing-spot at the far west end of Cuba. The crystal-clear waters teem with extraordinarily beautiful coral reefs and marine life that includes whale sharks.

Environs
The Bahía de Corrientes forms the underbelly of the Península de Guanahacabibes, a rare tropical dry deciduous forest protected within the **Reserva de la Biosfera Península de Guanahacabibes**.

MOGOTES

Mogotes are the remains of an ancient limestone plateau. Over eons, underground rivers eroded the soft limestone, forming vast caverns whose ceilings eventually collapsed. The pillars left standing, the present-day *mogotes*, have become covered with protective vegetation that includes endemic plants and even some reptile species found only here.

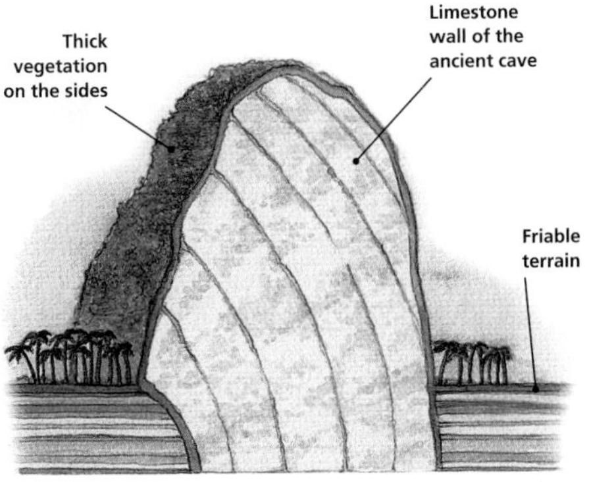
Thick vegetation on the sides
Limestone wall of the ancient cave
Friable terrain

Aerial view of some of Varadero's resorts

Varadero ⑩

�︎ 90 miles (145 km) E of Havana.
🛕 ⛵ 🍸 🏤 ⛴ ♨

One of Cuba's top resort areas occupies the 12-mile (19-km) pencil-thin Península de Hicacos, lined by stunning white beaches along its Atlantic seaboard. Once a private playground for Cuba's elite, today Varadero is the island's main tourist destination; still off-limits to the majority of Cubans. The dozens of all-inclusive hotels here all offer watersports, with scuba diving being the main draw. The Varadero Golf Club (see p91) is Cuba's only 18-hole course. Visitors can enjoy swimming with dolphins at the **Delfinario**.

Environs
Most visitors to Varadero take excursions to nearby sites, including **Matanzas**, a historic port city with a cathedral, plaza, and theater, and the **Cuevas de Bellamar**, which feature fascinating dripstone formations. The **Museo Municipal Oscar María de Rojas**, in the town of Cárdenas, dates back to 1900 and is among the oldest museums on the island. It has an eclectic collection of shells, butterflies, colonial weapons, and stuffed animals.

> ### 🐬 Delfinario
> Autopista Sur Km11. **Tel** (45) 66 8031. ⏱ 9am–5pm daily.
> 🏊 extra charge to swim with dolphins. 🚫 without payment.

Mansión Xanadú ⑪

🍽 Carretera Las Morlas. **Tel** (45) 66 8482. **Fax** (45) 66 8481.
💲💲💲 6 rooms. 🚗 🍴 📶
www.varaderogolfclub.com

US billionaire Alfred Irénée DuPont owned much of Varadero in the 1920s, and built this grand marble-and-mahogany villa atop the cliffs. It is now a deluxe hotel with an elegant restaurant and bar.

Península de Zapata ⑫

125 miles (202 km) SE of Havana.
🚍 ⛵

This vast peninsula, with the Caribbean's largest swamp, is protected in the Gran Parque Natural de Montemar. Crocodiles and flamingos are among the wildlife that can be seen here. **Boca de Guamá**, the main tourist center of the area, has a crocodile farm. Playa Larga has a good beach and its namesake hotel makes a good base for exploration.

Environs
North of the Boca de Guamá is Central Australia, former sugar factory and Fidel Castro's headquarters during the 1961 Bay of Pigs invasion. It now houses the intriguing **Museo Memorial Comandancia FAR**, the displays of which recall the invasion. The main landing of the CIA-backed counter-revolutionaries occurred at Playa Girón, a beach where the **Museo Playa Girón** exhibits military hardware.

> ### 🐊 Boca de Guamá
> Carretera Playa Larga Km16.
> **Tel** (45) 91 5551. ⏱ 7am–7pm daily. 🚻 🍴 📷 🔲
>
> ### 🏛 Museo Memorial Comandancia FAR
> Australia. **Tel** (45) 91 2504. ⏱ 9am–5pm Tue–Sat, 8am–noon Sun.
> 📷 📹 🚻 🚫 without payment.

Boat ride through a lake, Boca de Guamá, Península de Zapata

For hotels and restaurants in this island see pp92–5 and pp96–7

Statue of Sleeping Beauty at La Reina cemetery, Cienfuegos

Caridad and the **Museo de Artes Decorativas**, with its period furnishings from the 17th–20th centuries.

Environs
North of the city, the **Vuelta Abajo** region is a scenic center of tobacco production. In its midst, **Remedios** is a sleepy colonial town that bursts to life during Christmas festivities, when competing teams host a fireworks battle.

Monumento Tren Blindado
Carretera Camujuani. **Tel** (42) 20 2758. ☐ 9am–5:30pm Mon–Sat.

Monumento Ernesto Che Guevara
Av. de los Desfiles. **Tel** (42) 20 5878.
☐ **Museo de Che** 9:30am–5pm Tue–Sun.

Museo de Artes Decorativas
Calle Martha Abreu y Luis Estévez. **Tel** (42) 20 5368. ☐ 8am–6pm Mon, Wed & Thu, 1–10pm Fri–Sat, 6–10pm Sun.

Cienfuegos ⑬

150 miles (242 km) E of Havana.
🏘 105,000. ✈ 🚉 🚌

This provincial capital, in a bay on Cuba's south coast, was founded in 1819. Its well-preserved historic core is replete with buildings of note, centered around spacious Parque Martí. The Neo-Classical Teatro Tomás Terry and the Catedral de la Purísima Concepción, dating from 1870, are not to be missed. Nearby, the **Cementerio La Reina**'s Neo-Classical marble tombs are fascinating. The graceful Paseo del Prado crosses the historic center and leads to the Punta Gorda district, tipped by the **Palacio de Valle** – a Mughal-inspired mansion built in 1817, that now houses a restaurant.

Environs
The **Jardín Botánico Soledad**, located 9 miles (15 km) from Cienfuegos, is one of Latin America's foremost botanical gardens with a special area dedicated to cacti. Just southeast of here rises the Sierra Escambray with several trails leading to waterfalls and coffee estates.

Palacio de Valle
Calle 37 Y2. **Tel** (43) 55 1003.
☐ 10am–11pm daily.

Jardín Botánico Soledad
Calle Central 136, Pepito Tey.
Tel (43) 54 5115. ☐ 8am–4:30pm daily. ☐ public hols.

Santa Clara ⑭

170 miles (274 km) E of Havana.
🏘 175,000. 🚌

A sprawling industrial and university city, Santa Clara is famous for a single historical event: in 1958 it was here that the final battle that led to dictator Batista's ouster took place. The **Monumento Tren Blindado**, a re-creation of a troop train derailed by Che Guevara's guerrillas on December 28, 1958, is worth a visit. At the **Monumento Ernesto Che Guevara**, a bronze statue of the "heroic guerrilla" stands atop a plinth featuring bas-reliefs and inscriptions. Below the plinth is the Museo de Che, with displays of his life and role in the revolution.

Vase, Museo de Artes Decorativas

The main square, Parque Leoncio Vidal, has some fine colonial buildings, including the Neo-Classical Teatro de la

Cayo Santa María ⑮

🚌 220 miles (354 km) E of Havana.

This beach-fringed isle off the coast of Villa Clara province, at the western end of the Jardines del Rey (see p85), is accessed by a 30-mile (48-km) long *pedraplen* (causeway). Several deluxe hotels have been built, and more are planned here and on neighboring Cayo Las Brujas. Fishing and scuba diving are prime draws while the mangroves lining the inner shore are good for bird-watching.

POWs captured by Castro's men board a plane for Miami

BAY OF PIGS INVASION
The long narrow Bahía de Cochinos (Bay of Pigs) was the setting for the landing of 1,400 CIA-trained anti-Castro Cuban exiles on April 16, 1961. Fidel Castro took charge of the defense. After three days of intense fighting that involved US and Soviet tanks, the US withdrew its air support and the abandoned invaders were defeated. After 20 months in prison, the captured exiles were exchanged for medicines.

Trinidad ⑯

Founded by Diego Velázquez in 1514, this city was declared a UNESCO World Heritage Site in 1988. From the 1600s to the 1800s, Trinidad was a major center for the sugar and slave trades, and the fine buildings in the heart of the city reflect the wealth of the leading landowners of the time. A long period of isolation from the 1850s until the 1950s protected the city from any radical change. The historic center has been restored, and the original cobblestone streets and pastel-colored houses give the impression that time and life here have scarcely moved on since colonial times.

★ Museo Romántico
Formerly the Palacio Brunet, this mansion is now a museum exhibiting colonial furnishings of the wealthy.

Nuestra Señora de la Popa

★ Iglesia y Convento de San Francisco
The church bell tower offers fine views, while the monastery houses the Museo de la Lucha Contra Bandidos (Museum of the Fight Against Counter-Revolutionaries).

KEY

- - - Suggested route

CALLE HERNÁNDEZ ECH

CALLE PIRO GUINART

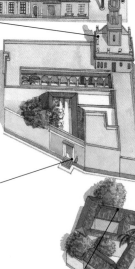

Canchánchara
This typical casa de infusiones, *housed in an 18th-century building, is known for its namesake cocktail* canchánchara, *made from rum, lime, water, and honey. Live music is played here.*

STAR SIGHTS

★ Museo Romántico

★ Iglesia y Convento de San Francisco

★ Palacio Cantero

Plazuela del Jigüe, named for its acacia tree *(jigüe)*, was the site of the first mass in Trinidad, in 1514.

Ayuntamiento y Cárcel, the old town hall and jail, has a portion of wall exposed to show the original stone-and-lime masonry.

Iglesia Parroquial de la Santísima Trinidad

With an austere façade, the church of the Holy Trinity was built in 1894 replacing another church. The interior has an impressive carved wooden altar with inlaid wood.

VISITORS' CHECKLIST

230 miles (370 km) SE of Havana. 🏠 *75,000.* ✈ 🚉 🚌 🚏 *Cubatur, Calle Maceo 352, (41) 99 6314.* 🎭 *El Recorrido del Via Cruz (Apr).*

0 meters   100

0 yards   100

Casa de la Música

The Casa de los Conspiradores, today an Italian-run art gallery, was the meeting place of the secret society, La Rosa de Cuba.

CALLE LUMUMBA

La Casa de la Trova

Located on Plazuela de Segarte, this is a popular venue for traditional live music and hosts music sessions in the afternoon and evening.

PLAZA MAYOR

CALLE JAVIER

Museo de Arquitectura Colonial

Housed in the restored Casa de los Sánchez Iznaga, this museum displays Trinidadian architecture.

CALLE MARTÍNEZ VILLENA

Casa de la Cultura

CALLE SIMÓN BOLÍVAR

★ Palacio Cantero

This early 19th-century Neo-Classical gem houses the Museo Histórico Munipical which recounts local history. Its tower has fine views over the city.

Valle de los Ingenios against the backdrop of the Sierra Escambray

Valle de los Ingenios ⓱

6 miles (10 km) E of Trinidad.
🚂 tourist steam train at 9:30am daily. 🍴 daily at Hacienda Iznaga.

This broad fertile valley is named for the numerous *ingenios* (sugar mills) located here during the late 18th and 19th centuries. The sweeping cane fields still remain but the sugar mills are mostly relics. **Hacienda Iznaga** is an exception where the estate owner's mansion is now a restaurant. The 147-ft (45-m) high seven-story tower allows great views. Nearby, Sitio Histórico Guaímaro is being restored as a museum; the estate house boasts splendid murals. The best way to see Valle de los Ingenios, a UNESCO World Heritage Site, is by the steam train departing from Trinidad.

🏚 **Hacienda Iznaga**
Iznaga, 9 miles (14 km) E of Trinidad. *Tel (41) 99 7241.*
🕐 9am–5pm daily. 🎫 🚻 🍴

Topes de Collantes ⓲

14 miles (21 km) NW of Trinidad. 🛈
Hotel Los Helenchos, (42) 54 0117.
🎫 through Gaviotatours. 🍴 🛍

The pristine alpine forests of the Sierra Escambray can best be experienced at the Topes de Collantes mountain retreat, 2,625 ft (800 m) above sea level. The Kurhotel solarium here is used as a recuperative clinic. Hikes lead to Salto de Caburní and its 250-ft (75-m) waterfall, and to the Hacienda Codina coffee estate, with an orchid garden and medicinal mud pools. The **Museo de Arte Cubano Contemporáneo** displays modern works by famous artists.

🏛 **Museo de Arte Cubano Contemporáneo**
Topes de Collantes. 🕐 8am–8pm daily. 🎫

Playa Ancón ⓳

🚩 6 miles (10 km) S of Trinidad.
🍷 🏖 🚤 ⛱ 🏊

Lining the tendril-thin Ancón peninsula, this lovely white beach is lapped by warm turquoise waters. Gorgeous coral reefs tempt divers, most notably at Cayo Blanco, a 20-minute boat ride away. La Boca, a village with a rocky beach at the neck of the peninsula, is popular with Cubans.

Camagüey ⓴

165 miles (265 km) E of Trinidad.
🚶 275,000. ✈ 🚂 🚌 🛈 Infotur, Ignacio Agramonte International Airport, (32) 26 5807. 🎭 Jornadas de la Cultura Camagüeyana (early Feb).

Surrounded by pastures, Cuba's third-largest city is known for its *tinajones* – large earthenware jars once used for collecting and storing water. The large historic center was laid out in an irregular fashion – an apparent attempt to confuse pirates – and is rich in colonial plazas.

Palm-shaded Parque Ignacio Agramonte is pinned by an equestrian statue of Ignacio Agramonte, a local independence hero, and by the Catedral de Nuestra Señora de la Candelaria, built in 1757.

The cobbled and colorful Plaza San Juan de Díos is ringed by quaint examples of vernacular architecture, plus the Iglesia de San Juan de Díos. Life-size figures of real-life residents adorn the restored **Plaza del Carmen**. The triangular Plaza de los Trabajadores draws visitors to the Casa Natal de Ignacio Agramonte (birthplace of Agramonte) and the Baroque Iglesia de la Merced, which contains a Holy Sepulcher, cast from silver coins. The acclaimed Ballet de Camagüey performs at the **Teatro Principal**, built in Neo-Classical style.

Teatro Principal
Calle Pedro Valencia 64. *Tel (32) 29 3048.* 🕐 9am–5pm daily. 🎫 🚻

Ceramic statue alongside real-life resident at the Plaza del Carmen, Camagüey

Jardines del Rey ㉑

Sprinkled like diamonds off the north coast of Ciego de Ávila and Camagüey provinces, the 400 or so isles of the Archipiélago del Jardines del Rey (King's Garden) stretch for almost 300 miles (500 km). Covered in mangroves and scrub, almost all are uninhabited except by wild pigs, iguanas, and waterfowl, while flamingos, spoonbills, and ibis dot the shallows that separate the cays from the mainland. Lovely beaches line the Atlantic shores and are slated to receive dozens of new hotels in the future. Current development is limited to Cayo Coco and Cayo Guillermo, served by their own international airport.

VISITORS' CHECKLIST

133 miles (215 km) NE of Trinidad. ✈ 🛈 *Cubanacan, Hotel Tryp Club Cayo Coco, (33) 30 1300; Cubatur Cayo Coco, (33) 30 1436.*

Cayo Coco
With 14 miles (22 km) of fine sugary beaches, the water-sports here are a major attraction and the diving on offer is superb.

Cayo Guillermo
This small cay has several hotels plus a marina. The inshore mangroves serve as a nesting site for seabirds. Playa Pilar has huge sand dunes.

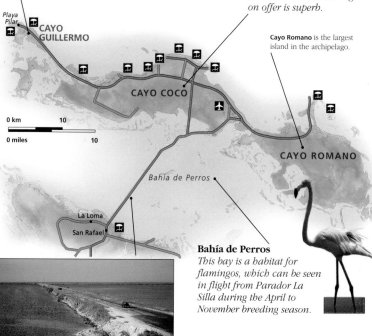

Cayo Romano is the largest island in the archipelago.

Playa Pilar
CAYO GUILLERMO

CAYO COCO

0 km   10
0 miles   10

CAYO ROMANO

Bahía de Perros

La Loma
San Rafael

Bahía de Perros
This bay is a habitat for flamingos, which can be seen in flight from Parador La Silla during the April to November breeding season.

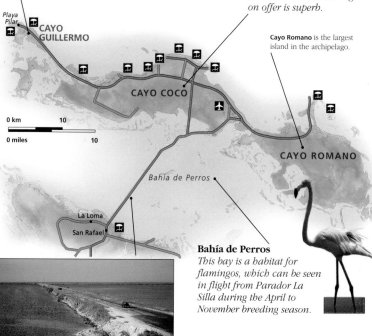

The Pedraplen
This causeway connects Cayo Coco to the mainland. It stretches over 16 miles (27 km) as it unfurls across Bahía de Perros.

KEY

🏖	Recommended beach
✈	Airport
▬	Major road
▬	Minor road

Playa Santa Lucía ㉒

✈ 338 miles (544 km) E of Havana.

🍴 🚲 🏄 🏊 ⛵ 🛶 🏇

This gorgeous beach resort stretches along 13 miles (21 km) of barren shoreline. Turquoise waters feature beautiful coral reefs and scuba diving is the main draw. Playa Los Cocos, at the western end of Santa Lucía, is a ramshackle fishing village with the most spectacular beach.

Green and tranquil Parque Céspedes in Bayamo

Guardalavaca ㉓

✈ 450 miles (724 km) E from Havana. 🍴 🚲 🏄 🏇 ⛵

Cuba's third largest beach resort area is being expanded; with new all-inclusive hotels appearing at the western end while the original mid-1980s resort overlooks Playa Guardalavaca. Separating them, Bahía de Naranjo has wildlife-rich nature trails plus an aquarium with dolphin and sea lion shows. Not far away, **Chorro de Maíta** is the largest pre-Columbian necropolis unearthed in the Caribbean. It has skeletons in situ, and an *aldea taína* – a reconstructed pre-Columbian village.

Artifact, Museo
Provincial de
Historia

🏠 Chorro de Maíta
3 miles (5 km) E of Guardalavaca. **Tel** (24) 43 0421. ⏰ 9am–5pm daily. 🈲 🔇 🚫 without payment.

Holguín ㉔

460 miles (740 km) SE of Havana. 🏛 200,000. 🚌 🚉 🚍 🎭 Romerías de Mayo (May 3).

Full of leafy colonial squares, this large city is an industrial center. Holguín was freed from Spanish rule in 1872 by General Calixto García, whose birthplace is east of Parque Calixto García. To the plaza's north, the **Museo Provincial de Historia** features pre-Columbian exhibits. Catedral de San Isidro, completed in 1720, stands over Parque Peralta, and Plaza San José boasts a fine church and colonial houses. About 458 stairs lead to the top of Loma de la Cruz, which has great views.

Environs
An hour's drive east of Holguín is **Sitio Histórico Birán**, Fidel Castro's birthplace at Finca Manacas, which is open to visitors. Gorgeous valley views can be enjoyed from **Mirador del Mayabe**, 6 miles (10 km) southeast of town, which has an *aldea campesino* (re-created farmer's village).

🏛 Museo Provincial de Historia
Calle Frexes 198. **Tel** (24) 46 3395. ⏰ 8am–4pm Tue–Sat, 8am–noon Sun. 🔴 public hols. 🈲 🔇 🚫 without payment.

🏛 Sitio Histórico Birán
Finca Manacas. **Tel** (24) 28 6114. ⏰ 8am–4pm Tue–Sat, 8am–noon Sun. 🔴 public hols. 🈲 🔇 🚫

Bayamo ㉕

423 miles (680 km) SE from Havana. 🏛 130,000. 🚌 🚍

Founded in 1513, Cuba's second oldest city was devastated by fire in 1876, during the Ten Years' War. Parque Céspedes, the main square, is overlooked by interesting buildings, including **Casa Natal de Carlos Manuel de Céspedes**, birthplace of the man behind Cuba's quest for independence, and the lovely church, Iglesia Parroquial Mayor de San Salvador.

Environs
To the south lies the rugged **Sierra Maestra** mountain chain, and hikes to the 6,476-ft (1,974-m) Pico Turquino are possible from San Rafael.

Casa Natal de Carlos Manuel de Céspedes
Calle Maceo 57. **Tel** (23) 42 3864. ⏰ 9am–5pm Tue–Sat, 9am–3pm Sun. 🈲 🔇 🦽

Blue waters and sandy beach, Guardalavaca

For hotels and restaurants on this island see pp92–5 and see pp96–7

Santiago de Cuba ㉖

535 miles (862 km) SE from Havana. 🏘 375,000. ✈ 🚢 🚌 ℹ *Infotur, (22) 66 9401.* 🎭 *Carnival (Jul 26).*

Santiago, the most African of Cuban cities, and the second largest, is lively and exciting: Santiagueros are passionate about music and dance, especially during Carnival. Founded by Diego Velázquez in 1514, it has a gently sloping historic core, over-looking a huge flask-shaped bay. At its heart, the bustling Parque Céspedes is surrounded by fine buildings: the Ayuntamiento (town hall); the mostly 20th-century Neo-Classical Catedral de la Asunción; and the Casa de Diego Velázquez, the original governor's 1516 mansion superbly maintained as the **Museo de Ambiente Histórico Cubano**. Hotel Casagrande's patio *(see p95)* is a marvelous spot for a mojito and has fine views over the plaza.

Calle Heredia is lined with historic buildings. Not to be missed are the Casa de la Trova for traditional music, the Museo del Carnaval, and the **Museo Provincial Bacardí**, with vast, eclectic displays ranging from Egyptian mummies to modern art.

Sprawling in a half-moon around the historic core, Santiago's 20th-century districts are full of sites that honor the city's title of the "Cradle of the Revolution." The Museo Histórico 26 de Julio, in Cuartel Moncada, where Fidel Castro launched the revolution on July 26, 1953, is near the massive equestrian statue of indepen-dence hero Antonio Maceo that towers over Plaza de la Revolución. The Avenue Juan Gilberto Gómez connects the plaza to Cementerio de Santa Ifigenia, a monumental ceme-tery with José Martí's *(see p76)* tomb.

Detail of Maceo's statue, Plaza de la Revolución

Environs

Basilica El Cobre, a hilltop basilica with a statue of the Virgen del Cobre, draws pil-grims from all over. East of the city, **Parque Baconao** spans 310 sq miles (800 sq km) with quiet beaches, artists' commu-nities, and an aquarium. Santiago bay is guarded by the imposing 1637 **Castillo del Morro**. Soldiers dressed in period costumes fire a cannon at sunset.

🏛 **Museo de Ambiente Histórico Cubano**
Calle Felix Peña. **Tel** *(22) 65 2652.* ⬜ *9am–4:45pm Mon–Thu & Sat; 2–4:45pm Fri; 9am–12:45pm Sun.* 🎫 ♿ 📷 *without payment.*

🏛 **Museo Provincial Bacardí**
Calle Pío Rosado. **Tel** *(22) 62 8402.* ⬜ *9am–9pm Tue–Sat; 9am–1pm Sun.* 🎫

POLYMITES

Endemic to the Baracoa region, the *polymita* is a snail with a colorful shell. Each snail's shell is as distinct as a thumbprint, with whorled patterns in various combinations of reds, yellows, blues, greens, blacks, and white.

Patterned polymita shells

Baracoa ㉗

98 miles (157 km) E from Santiago de Cuba. 🏘 65,000. ✈ 🚌 🎭 *Semana de la Cultura (Apr).*

Cuba's first settlement was founded in 1511 and is unusual for its rickety, cen-turies-old wooden homes. It is set on a broad bay framed by lush mountains. The best view over town is from Hotel El Castillo *(see p92)*, in the 18th-century Castillo de Seboruco fortress. The Catedral de Nuestra Señora de la Asunción, on Parque Independencia, exhibits a cross said to have been left by Christopher Columbus in 1492.

Environs

West of Baracoa is the 1,885-ft (575-m) high **El Yunque** (the Anvil). This flat-topped for-mation lures birders and hikers with spectacular views. Its lush rainforests are part of a UNESCO Biosphere Reserve protected within Parque Nacional Alejandro Humboldt.

Panoramic view of the city of Baracoa with El Yunque in the background

Outdoor Activities and Specialized Holidays

Guided excursions are the best way of discovering Cuba's extraordinary wilderness areas and wildlife. Mountains offer rainforest hikes, including to the summit of Pico Turquino, Cuba's highest peak, while lowland ecosystems include mangroves, swamplands, and dry forest. Beach resorts provide a spectrum of watersports, including scuba diving, which is a major draw.

The palm-shaded Playas del Este, Havana

BEACHES

Cuba has endless stretches of superb beaches ranging from taupe to gold and snow-white. Most beach resorts are on the north coast, with the heaviest concentration of hotels at Varadero; and at Cayo Santa

María, Cayo Coco, and Cayo Guillermo in the Jardines del Rey, where the spectacular white sands of Cayo Sabinal await development. Farther east, Playa Santa Lucía and Guardalavaca's Playa Mayor appeal to budget travelers, while deluxe all-inclusive

resorts are the forte of Guardalavaca's Esmeralda, Yuraguanal, and Pesquero beaches. Marea del Portillo in the far east serves budget

Scuba Diving

Cuba is a paradise for scuba divers, thanks to crystal-clear waters, with temperatures ranging from 70–85° F (23–30° C), and spectacular coral reefs, Spanish galleons and other sunken wrecks, including Soviet vessels and aircrafts. There is an abundance of premium dive sites along both the north and south coasts, and all beach resorts have dive centers. Many all-inclusive tourist hotels have their own dive facilities with professional staff.

Cueva de los Peces *is a cenote or "blue hole" full of different kinds of fish.*

María la Gorda is a good venue for spotting whale sharks in the Bahía de Corrientes, which also has many dolphins and a garden of black corals.

La Costa de las Piratas has tranquil waters and 56 dive sites off Punta Francés.

Isla de la Juventud *offers a variety of sites for both beginners and experienced divers. Huge coral parapets, sponges, and wrecks of the Spanish galleons are highlights of the area.*

Punta Perdiz, in the Bay of Pigs, is a spectacular wall dive.

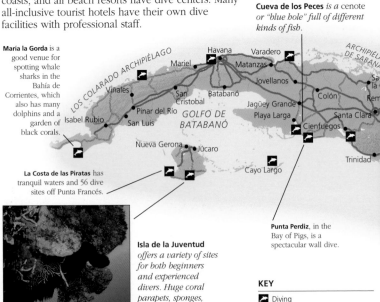

KEY

Diving
Major road
Minor road

travelers with two all-inclusive hotels, while Playa Siboney is a big lure for families from nearby Santiago de Cuba.

The south coast is mostly swampy and has fewer beaches. Exceptions include Playa Ancón and undeveloped Playas del Este and Playa Blanca on Isla de la Juventud. Playa Sirena stands out among Cayo Largo's sublime beaches. In the far west, Cayo Levisa has some excellent sands. Havana has lovely beaches at Playas del Este, which is a great place to meet locals.

FISHING

Fishing enthusiasts will be in their element in Cuba. Most beach resorts have marinas from where sportfishing vessels set out to catch tuna, swordfish, and marlin. In Havana, the Marina Hemingway is the venue for the Ernest Hemingway International Marlin Fishing Tournament. Cuba's freshwater lakes are stocked with prize-winning sized bass: try Embalse Zaza, in Sancti Spíritus province. Tarpon and bonefish draw anglers to Las Salinas (Gran Parque Natural de Montemar) and the Jardines de la Reina, off the south coast of Ciego de Ávila and Camagüey, where specialized live-aboard boats cater to package tours. On Cayo Largo, the **Villa Gran Caribe Ecolodge** has a lodge which overlooks flats that are good for bonefishing.

Fly-fishing at Cayo Santa María

Scuba diving in the Caribbean Sea is one of the most rewarding activities with the coral reef scenery providing the most exciting backdrop to the spectacular fish varieties found here.

DIVE CENTERS

Avalon Dive Center
Tel (72) 04 7422.
http://cubandivingcenters.com
Barracuda Scuba Cuba
Tel (45) 66 7072.
**Centro Internacional
de Buceo**
Tel (48) 77 8131.
www.gaviota-grupo.com
Club Octopus
Tel (45) 91 7294.
El Colony
Tel (46) 39 8181.
Scuba Diving Center Acua
Tel (45) 66 8063.

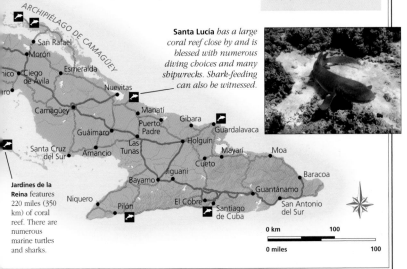

Santa Lucía has a large coral reef close by and is blessed with numerous diving choices and many shipwrecks. Shark-feeding can also be witnessed.

ARCHIPIÉLAGO DE CAMAGÜEY

San Rafael
Morón
Ciego
de Ávila
Esmeralda
Nuevitas
Camagüey
Manatí
Guáimaro
Puerto
Padre
Gibara
Guardalavaca
Las
Tunas
Holguín
Santa Cruz
del Sur
Amancio
Mayarí
Moa
Cueto
Jiguaní
Baracoa
Bayamo
Guantánamo
Niquero
Pilón
El Cobre
Santiago
de Cuba
San Antonio
del Sur

Jardines de la Reina features 220 miles (350 km) of coral reef. There are numerous marine turtles and sharks.

0 km 100

0 miles 100

Boats on the beach of Cayo Coco, Jardines del Rey

WATERSPORTS

All the tourist beach resorts offer a range of watersports including parasailing and rent sailcrafts such as Hobie Cats, Jet Skis, and banana boats. Larger sailcraft can be hired from almost 20 **Marlin Marinas** nationwide. Visitors wishing to charter their own yacht or catamaran for cruising the Jardines de la Reina can do so through **Charter Partner** and **Plattensail** in Cienfuegos. All the best resorts have windsurfing, a popular option, especially at large all-inclusive hotels, where the activity and tuition are usually included in the price.

BOAT EXCURSIONS

Almost all the holiday resorts have boat excursions, with Varadero providing the most options. Seafari Cayo

Hikers on a trail, accompanied by a guide

Blanco uses state-of-the-art catamarans to take visitors to nearby cays. Sunset sailing trips are also available at Varadero, Cayo Largo, Cayo Santa Maria, Playa Ancón, Cayo Coco, and Playa Santa Lucía, as well as Guardalavaca. Several venues have a "Jungle Tour" exploration of the mangrove ecosystems, but the speedboats used are potentially damaging to the local ecology.

HIKING AND BIRDING

Until recently, organized hiking trails were limited to the Sierra del Rosario, around Topes de Collantes, and the Sierra Maestra, where the arduous 2-day ascent to the summit of Pico Turquino rewards intrepid hikers with vast views and the ultimate high. More trails are being developed, along with programs for birders and other ecotourists.

Cuba offers fabulous bird-watching. The Península de Zapata, with its bird-rich wetlands and *salinas*, is a particularly good area for birders. Guided trips are available here and in the Reserva Guanahacabibes, Sierra Escambray, and Refugio Ecológico Los Indios on Isla de la Juventud. In the east, Parque Nacional Alejandro Humboldt, and El Saltón, in the eastern foothills of the Sierra Maestra, are good for birding. Flamingos can be seen at Cayo Coco. For more information contact **Gaviota Tours** and **EcoTur**.

CAVING

Cuba is riddled with caverns, although the Valle de Viñales area is the only region currently promoting caving. Boat trips are offered inside Cueva del Indio, but the adventurous guided explorations of Cuevas de Santo Tomás, with 28 miles (45 km) of chambers, are more thrilling. Pre-Columbian petroglyphs can be seen in Cuevas de Punta del Este in Isla de la Juventud, and in caves that stipple Parque Nacional Cuguanas in Sancti Spíritus province. To visit either, you will need to join a guided excursion through EcoTur.

Tour boat exploring the cave at Cueva del Indio

CYCLING

Bicycles are the main form of transport for millions of Cubans, and cycling is an excellent way to meet locals and enjoy the landscapes at a leisurely pace. Many visitors bring their own bicycles, but bikes can also be bought at **El Orbe** in Havana. Puncture repair shops are numerous, but it is advisable to bring plenty of spare parts as they may be hard to source locally. Extreme care should be taken on Cuba's dangerous roads; always wear a helmet. Bikes should always be left in supervised places and locked. **Club Nacional de Cicloturismo** offers guided bicycle tours. **WowCuba**, based in Canada, specializes

For hotels and restaurants on this island see pp92–5 and 96–7

in organized group bicycle tours to Cuba, as does **KE Adventure Travel** in the UK.

GOLF

Cuba currently has only two golf courses, although several others are planned in key beach resort areas such as Guardalavaca and Cayo Coco. The **Club de Golf Habana** is a 9-hole course. The 18-hole **Varadero Golf Club** has oceanfront fairways and greens, plus a pro shop.

Signage of Varadero Golf Club

HORSE-RIDING

Trekking on horseback is a delightful way to explore the countryside, where many Cubans still rely on horses to get around. In Havana, horse-riding is available at Parque Lenin and Playas del Este.

Most resorts and hotels in Cuba offer organized horse-riding excursions along the beach and into the nearby mountains. **Sitio La Güira** is a basic equestrian center on Cayo Coco. Other popular

sites for horse-riding include the **Hacienda La Vega** and the nearby **Casa Guachinango**.

SPAS

Many beach resorts and upscale urban tourist hotels have spa facilities offering massage as well as various other treatments. Spa facilities in Cuba tend to be relatively sparse by Western standards and are focused on recuperative health treatments rather than pampered enjoyment. The

country's two main spas are **San Diego de los Baños Spa** in Pinar del Río province, and **Baños de Elguea** in the province of Santa Clara.

TENNIS

There are no dedicated tennis centers in Cuba, but many hotels in the beach resorts have their own courts for guests' use, and non-guests can often use the facilities for a fee. In Havana, **Club Habana** has squash and tennis courts exclusively for foreigners, as does the Hotel Occidental Miramar *(see p94)*.

Horse-riding along a sandy white beach, Jardines del Rey

DIRECTORY

FISHING

Villa Gran Caribe Ecolodge
El Pueblo, Cayo Largo.
Tel (45) 24 8385.

WATERSPORTS

Charter Partner
www.charterpartner.com

Marlin Marinas
Marina Darsena,
Carretera de las Morlas
Km31, Varadero.
Tel (45) 66 7550.
Marina Hemingway,
Av. 5 y 248,
Santa Fe, Havana.
Tel (7) 204 5088.
Marina Tarará,
Via Blanca Km18,
Tarará, Havana.
Tel (7) 796 0242.
Marina Trinidad,
Playa Ancón.
Tel (41) 99 6205.
www.nauticamarlin.com

Plattensail
www.platten-sailing.de

HIKING AND BIRDING

EcoTur
Av. Boyeros 116 esq,
Havana. *Tel (7) 641 0306.*
www.ecoturcuba.co.cu

Gaviota Tours
Av. del Puerto 102 e/ Justiz
y Obrapia, Havana.
Tel (7) 204 5708.
www.gaviota-grupo.com

CYCLING

Club Nacional de Cicloturismo
Plaza San Francisco,
Habana Vieja.
Tel (7) 96 9193.

El Orbe
Calle Monserrate 304,
Habana Vieja.
Tel (7) 860 2617.

KE Adventure Travel
Keswick, England.
www.keadventure.com

WowCuba
Prince Edward Island,
Canada.
www.wowcuba.com

GOLF

Club de Golf Habana
Carretera de Vento Km8,
Capdevila, Havana.
Tel (7) 649 8918.

Varadero Golf Club
Carretera Las Morlas,
Varadero.
Tel (45) 66 7788. **www.**
varaderogolfclub.com

HORSE-RIDING

Casa Guachinango
2 miles N of Iznaga, Valle
de los Ingenios.

Hacienda La Vega
Playa Ingles, Cienfuegos.
Tel (43) 55 1126.

Sitio La Güira
Cayo Coco.
Tel (33) 30 1208.

SPAS

Baños de Elguea
Villa Clara.
Tel (42) 68 6298.

San Diego de los Baños Spa
San Diego de los Baños.
Tel (48) 54 8880.

TENNIS

Club Habana
5ta Av. 188 y 192, Flores,
Havana.
Tel (7) 204 5700.

Choosing a Hotel

Cuba has a wide range of accommodations, from small moderately priced hotels to expensive luxury resorts. All rooms have basic facilities such as private bath, TV, and air-conditioning unless otherwise indicated. In addition, every town except Varadero and other key beach resorts offers *casas particulares* (private room rentals), ideal for those wishing to stay with Cuban families.

PRICE CATEGORIES
The following price ranges are for a standard double room per night and all taxes included.

$ under \$100
$$ \$100–200
$$$ \$200–300
$$$$ \$300–400
$$$$$ over \$400

CUBA

Hotel Nacional – *p76*
Havana's flagship grande dame Hotel Nacional exudes 1930s elegance. It boasts a spa/fitness center, tennis courts, and a cabaret nightclub.

Hotel Habana Libre Tryp – *p77*
The striking 1950s Modernist Hotel Habana Libre Tryp comes with a rooftop pool and sizzling nightclub.

Hotel Los Jazmines – *p79*
Perched atop a *mogote*, Hotel Los Jazmines has spectacular views. Modern blocks house comfortable rooms.

Mansión Xanadú – *p80*
The Baroque Mansión Xanadú, overhanging the ocean, has rooms with marble floors and wrought-iron beds. Guests have golf privileges.

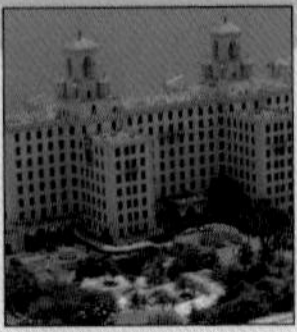
Hotel Nacional

BARACOA Hostal La Habanera
🍴 ☰ [W] — $

Calle Maceo 68 **Tel** *(21) 64 5273* **Rooms** *10*

Located in the town square, the enchanting Hostal La Habanera was converted from a colonial mansion in 2003. Amenities here include a pharmacy and a restaurant. Massages and mud treatments are also offered. Guest rooms feature simple rattan furnishings, twin beds, lofty ceilings, and modern bathrooms. **www.cubanacan.com**

BARACOA Hotel El Castillo
🍴 ☰ [W] — $

Calle Calixto García, Loma el Paraíso **Tel** *(21) 64 5106* **Fax** *(21) 64 5339* **Rooms** *62*

Occupying a former fortress with magnificent vistas towards El Yunque and over town, Hotel El Castillo has spacious rooms, modestly furnished in colonial fashion. The restaurant offers inventive fare and the pool bar is a pleasant place for cocktails alfresco. It provides car and scooter rental services. **www.gaviota-grupo.com**

BAYAMO Hotel Royalton
🍴 ☰ — $

Calle Maceo 53 **Tel** *(23) 42 2290* **Fax** *(23) 42 4792* **Rooms** *33*

A pleasant 1940s hotel in Neo-Classical style, Hotel Islazul Royalton has been restored to serve international visitors. Gleaming hardwood and marble adorn public arenas. Comfortable guest rooms are sparsely furnished and have modern bathrooms. The hotel's main draw is its location overlooking Parque Céspedes. **www.cubanacan.cu**

CAMAGÜEY Hotel Islazul Colón
🍴 ☰ [W] — $

Calle República 472 **Tel** *(32) 25 4878* **Fax** *(32) 28 1188* **Rooms** *48*

This charming hotel is a bargain and offers comfortable guest rooms following a restoration. Full of shiny hardwoods and marble and antique reproduction furnishings, the hotel also has its own boutique. One of the city's finest restaurants is here, and the atmospheric bar is a great place to enjoy a mojito and cigar. **www.islazul.cu**

CAYO COCO Hotel Tryp Cayo Coco
🏖 🍴 ☰ 🏋 ♿ [W] — $$$

Ciego de Ávila **Tel** *(33) 30 1300* **Fax** *(33) 30 1386* **Rooms** *508*

With 4 serpentine pools and a magnificent beachfront setting, the sprawling Hotel Tryp Cayo Coco is a perfect mid-priced option. Tropical decor adorns tile-floored guest rooms with modern amenities. Eight restaurants, bars, spa facilities, family rooms, and plenty of options for active vacationers. **www.solmeliacuba.com**

CAYO COCO Meliá Cayo Coco
🏖 🍴 ☰ 🏋 ♿ [W] — $$$$

Ciego de Ávila **Tel** *(33) 30 1180* **Fax** *(33) 30 1381* **Rooms** *266*

Spanish hotel chain Sol Meliá's top-ranked resort on Cayo Coco, Meliá Cayo Coco comes with superb facilities and handsome decor. Some accommodations are built over a lagoon; others have beach views. A choice of restaurants, nightly entertainment, plenty of watersports, tennis, and spa services are on offer. **www.solmeliacuba.com**

CAYO GUILLERMO Iberostar Daiquirí
🏖 🍴 ☰ 🏋 ♿ [W] — $$$

Ciego de Ávila **Tel** *(33) 30 1560* **Fax** *(33) 30 1645* **Rooms** *312*

The elegant Iberostar Daiquirí offers a great seaside location and impresses with its landscaped grounds and nicely-appointed rooms with balconies and modern comforts. The watersports center offers scuba diving and a splendid kids' club makes this a good choice for families. Spa and tennis courts on-site. **www.iberostar.com**

CAYO LARGO Sol Cayo Largo
🏖 🍴 ☰ 🏋 ♿ [W] — $$$$

Cayo Largo del Sur **Tel** *(45) 24 8260* **Fax** *(45) 24 8265* **Rooms** *296*

The most impressive of the hotels on Cayo Largo, the colorful Spanish-run Sol Cayo Largo is set back from a stunning beach. It has watersports, tennis, 3 restaurants, bars, spa, and a beautiful pool complex. Romantic and spacious guest quarters have four-poster beds and pastel color schemes. **www.solmeliacuba.com**

Key to Symbols *see back cover flap*

CAYO LAS BRUJAS Villas Las Brujas

Villa Clara **Tel** *(42) 35 0025* **Fax** *(42) 35 0505* **Rooms** *24*

Enjoying a clifftop position overlooking a scintillating beach, Villas Las Brujas features wooden cabins with simple bamboo furnishings plus telephones, satellite TVs, mini bars, and safes. The airy seafood restaurant perches over the beach. Sportfishing, sailboarding, and scuba diving facilities are available. **www.gaviota-grupo.cu**

CAYO SANTA MARÍA Meliá Cayo Santa María

Villa Clara **Tel** *(42) 35 0200* **Fax** *(42) 35 0505* **Rooms** *360*

The deluxe Meliá Cayo Santa María is one of Cuba's premier beachfront resorts, combining lavish accommodations with a complete range of facilities. Guest rooms combine white and turquoise schemes, with canopied king beds, although only 32 rooms have beach views. Several watersport options are available. **www.solmeliacuba.com**

CIENFUEGOS Hotel Unión

Calle 31 & Av. 54 **Tel** *(43) 55 1020* **Fax** *(43) 55 1686* **Rooms** *49*

A small, colonial-era hotel dating back to the 19th century, the Hotel Unión is located in the heart of the old city. It is adorned with antiques and stained-glass windows. While not quite gourmet, the Restaurante 1898 *(see p96)* is perhaps the city's finest. Facilities include a gym, spa, open-air pool, and beauty parlor. **www.cubanacan.cu**

CIENFUEGOS Hotel Jagua

Calle 27 between 0 & 2 **Tel** *(43) 55 1003* **Fax** *(43) 55 1245* **Rooms** *140*

Dating back to the 1950s, the remodeled seven-story Hotel Jagua now has 21st-century styling, including in the guest rooms. It overlooks the bay at the south end of town, adjacent to Palacio del Valle. The handsome open-air pool and a vivacious cabaret are highlights. Good bar and excellent service. **www.gran-caribe.com**

GUARDALAVACA Blau Costa Verde Beach

Playa Pesquero **Tel** *(24) 43 3510* **Fax** *(24) 43 3515* **Rooms** *307*

The modern Blau Costa Verde Beach features lush landscaping and a huge pool. The guest rooms have rattan furnishings and lively color schemes. Children's facilities, family rooms, spa services, archery, badminton, and volleyball, along with plentiful watersports, are on offer. **www.blau-hotels.com**

GUARDALAVACA Club Amigo Guardalavaca

Playa Guardalavaca **Tel** *(24) 43 0180* **Fax** *(24) 43 0200* **Rooms** *747*

An amalgam of 4 separate hotels now under the Cubanacan banner, the modest Club Amigo Guardalavaca offers a choice of accommodations, from hotel rooms to self-catering bungalows. Modest furnishings combine with modern amenities. Wide choice of restaurants, bars, family rooms, and sports facilities. **www.cubanacan.cu**

GUARDALAVACA Occidental Grand Playa Turquesa

Playa Yaraguanal **Tel** *(24) 43 3540* **Fax** *(24) 43 3545* **Rooms** *520*

The spectacular beach is a major draw for the Occidental Grand Playa Turquesa, as are the 7 inviting pools linked by water cascades. Stylish contemporary furnishings highlight spacious guest rooms. Multiple restaurants and bars, and the wide choice of activities meet international standards. **www.occidental-hoteles.com**

HAVANA Hostal Valencia

Calle Oficios 53, Habana Vieja **Tel** *(7) 857 1037* **Fax** *(7) 860 5628* **Rooms** *12*

Located in the heart of Habana Vieja, Hostal Valencia has no frills but is in a great location just steps from Plaza San Francisco. The colonial-era mansion is run like a Spanish *posada* and has comfortable rooms. The highlight is the atmospheric La Paella restaurant *(see p96)*, adorned with bullfighting paraphernalia. **www.habaguanexhotels.com**

HAVANA Hotel Florida

Calle Obispo 252, Habana Vieja **Tel** *(7) 862 4127* **Fax** *(7) 862 4117* **Rooms** *25*

Housed in a stately 19th-century mansion, Hotel Florida is one of Havana's best bargains. Rooms on three levels wrap around a palm-filled atrium lobby lit by a stained-glass ceiling. Checkerboard marble floors and reproduction furnishings create a nostalgic atmosphere. The Continental restaurant echoes the theme. **www.habaguanexhotels.com**

HAVANA Hotel Habana Riviera

Paseo y Malecón, Vedado **Tel** *(7) 836 4051* **Fax** *(7) 833 3739* **Rooms** *352*

A famous 1950s high-rise, Hotel Habana Riviera overlooks the waterfront boulevard. The sensational lobby retains its original Modernist sculptures. Cigar lovers get their own lounge here, and the Salón Internacional nightclub is a popular party spot. Facilities include a spa, bar, family rooms, and Internet access. **www.gran-caribe.com**

HAVANA Hotel Meliá Cohiba

Av. Paseo between 1ra & 3ra, Vedado **Tel** *(7) 833 3636* **Fax** *(7) 834 4555* **Rooms** *462*

A modern high-rise close to the Malecón, the Hotel Meliá Cohiba is one of Havana's finest. Five restaurants, a fun nightclub, 2 swimming pools, spa facilities, and upscale boutiques are major draws. Spacious guest rooms feature contemporary furnishings plus modern appointments. **www.solmeliacuba.com**

HAVANA Hotel NH Parque Central

Calle Neptuno e/ Zulueta & Paseo de Martí, Habana Vieja **Tel** *(7) 866 6627* **Fax** *(7) 866 6630* **Rooms** *281*

A contemporary conversion of a colonial building, the Hotel NH Parque Central has stylishly appointed rooms with antique reproductions and most modern facilities. Its 2 restaurants are first-class, the cigar lounge impresses, and the palm-filled lobby lounge tempts guests to linger over mojitos. **www.nh-hotels.cu**

HAVANA Hotel Raquel

🍴 📋 ♿ ⓦ　　　$$$

Calle Amargura 103, Habana Vieja **Tel** *(7) 860 8280* **Fax** *(7) 860 8275* **Rooms** *25*

A renovated Art Nouveau stunner, this popular hotel, located close to Plaza Vieja, exudes style and charm. Honey-hued rooms feature faux antique brass beds and modern accoutrements, such as cordless phones. The lounge bar beneath a stained-glass atrium ceiling is the place to see and be seen. **www.habaguanexhotels.com**

HAVANA Hotel Santa Isabel

🍴 📋 ♿ ⓦ　　　$$$

Calle Baratillo 9, Habana Vieja **Tel** *(7) 860 8201* **Fax** *(7) 860 8391* **Rooms** *27*

Facing the Plaza de Armas, the glamorous colonial-themed Hotel Santa Isabel has tradition and elegance combined with stylish 19th-century furnishings and an inviting marble-floored lobby lounge. Facilities include 2 restaurants, plus patio and rooftop bars. **www.habaguanexhotels.com**

HAVANA Occidental Miramar

🍴 📋 ♿ ⓦ　　$$$$

5ta Av. between Calles 72 & 76, Miramar **Tel** *(7) 204 3584* **Fax** *(7) 204 9227* **Rooms** *427*

A large and stylish modern option on Miramar's main boulevard, the sprawling Occidental Miramar combines colonial and modern elements. Rooms are cavernous and decorated in regal blues and golds. Fitness facilities include a vast pool, spa services, plus tennis and squash courts. **www.occidental-hoteles.com**

HAVANA Hotel Saratoga

🍴 📋 ♿ ⓦ　$$$$$

Paseo de Martí 603, Habana Vieja **Tel** *(7) 868 1000* **Fax** *(7) 868 1001* **Rooms** *96*

A 19th-century Neo-Classical gem, Hotel Saratoga is decorated with stylish contemporary furniture and tasteful color schemes bringing in a new level of sophistication. Other draws include a Moroccan-themed restaurant and bar, rooftop gym, spa, and pool. Service is excellent. **www.habaguanexhotels.com**

HOLGUÍN Villa Mirador de Mayabe

🍴 📋 ♿ ⓦ　　　$

Alturas de Mayabe Km8 **Tel** *(24) 42 2160* **Fax** *(24) 42 5498* **Rooms** *24*

With a superb clifftop perch overlooking the Mayabe Valley, the Villa Mirador de Mayabe is a clean, simple and endearing option. The thatched restaurant has live music. Most bungalows have splendid vistas; all have satellite TVs, handsome furnishings, and modern marble bathrooms. There is a swimming pool too. **www.islazul.cu**

ISLA DE LA JUVENTUD Hotel Colony Siguanea

🏖 🍴 📋 🎣 ♿ ⓦ　$$

Carretera de Siguanea Km42 **Tel** *(46) 39 8181* **Fax** *(46) 39 8420* **Rooms** *77*

The somewhat faded, off-the-beaten-track 1950s Hotel Colony Siguanea is today a dedicated dive resort. Choose from hotel rooms or bungalows set in gardens. It has a desultory beach and offers watersports, including sportfishing. The thatched bar overhanging the ocean is inviting.

LAS TERRAZAS La Moka

🍴 ⓦ　　　$$

Autopista Habana-Pinar Km51, Pinar del Río **Tel** *(48) 57 8600* **Fax** *(48) 57 8603* **Rooms** *26*

Overlooking the community of Las Terrazas, in the Sierra del Rosario Biosphere Reserve, the modern, ecologically-minded La Moka is inspired by colonial architecture. Large, bright rooms have delightful rustic elements, and the lush grounds feature a pool and tennis courts. Guided birding, hiking, and horseback trips offered. **www.lasterrazas.com**

MARÍA LA GORDA CIB María de la Gorda

🏖 🍴 📋 🚤 🎣 ♿　$$

Pinar del Río **Tel** *(48) 77 8131* **Fax** *(48) 77 8077* **Rooms** *55*

Facing turquoise waters, the CIB María de la Gorda is associated with the dive center Centro Internacional de Buceo. Choose from simply appointed beachfront rooms or wooden cabins, with satellite TVs and telephones. A second restaurant improves on the basic buffets. Reservations essential. **www.gaviota-grupo.cu**

PLAYA ANCÓN Brisas Trinidad del Mar

🏖 🍴 📋 🎣 ♿ ⓦ　$$$

Trinidad **Tel** *(41) 99 6500* **Fax** *(41) 99 6565* **Rooms** *241*

Sitting on one of the finest beaches in Cuba, the modern Brisas Trinidad del Mar adopts quasi-colonial architecture. Activities center on the vast pool complex, but plenty of watersports are offered. Spacious guest rooms are colorful and offer satellite TVs, telephones, safes, modern bathrooms. Spa services are available. **www.cubanacan.com**

PLAYA SANTA LUCÍA Oasis Brisas Santa Lucía

🏖 🍴 📋 🎣 ♿ ⓦ　$$$

Camagüey **Tel** *(32) 33 6317* **Fax** *(32) 36 5142* **Rooms** *412*

The best option available at Playa Santa Lucía, Hotel Brisas Santa Lucía is set in tropical gardens and has plenty of watersports, reasonable entertainment, a splendid swimming pool, and several other sports facilities including tennis. Guest rooms have modern bathrooms, satellite TVs, telephones, and safes. **www.cubanacan.cu**

REMEDIOS Hotel E Mascotte

🍴 📋 ⓦ　　　$

Calle Máximo Gómez 114 **Tel** *(42) 39 5341* **Fax** *(42) 39 5327* **Rooms** *14*

The pleasant 19th-century Hotel E Mascotte faces Plaza Mayor and has been restored to international standards, with modern bathrooms, telephones, and satellite TVs in guest rooms. Louvered French doors open to breeze-swept verandas, many overlooking the plaza. The best restaurant in town is here. **www.cubanacan.cu**

SANCTI SPÍRITUS Hostal del Rijo

📋 ⓦ　　　　$

Calle Honorato del Castillo 12 **Tel** *(41) 32 8588* **Fax** *(41) 32 8577* **Rooms** *16*

Housed in a restored Neo-Classical colonial mansion, Hostal del Rijo is today the city's most endearing hotel. Rooms feature beamed ceilings and wrought-iron details. There is a bar and humidor. Breakfast is served, and the Mesón de la Plaza *(see p97)* restaurant is across the street. **www.cubanacan.cu**

Key to Price Guide *see p92* **Key to Symbols** *see back cover flap*

SANTA CLARA Villa Los Caneyes
🗐 ♿ Ⓦ $$

Av. Eucaliptos y Circunvalación **Tel** *(42) 21 8140* **Fax** *(42) 21 8140* **Rooms** *96*

On the western outskirts of town, the sprawling Villa Los Caneyes features octagonal bungalows supposedly inspired by Taíno architecture, but with satellite TV, refrigerators, and modern bathrooms. The pool deck is a setting for entertainment. Buffet meals are served, and it has a nightclub. **www.cubanacan.cu**

SANTIAGO DE CUBA Hotel E San Basilio
🍴 🗐 $$

Calle San Basilio 403 **Tel** *(22) 65 1702* **Fax** *(22) 68 7039* **Rooms** *8*

The tiny Hotel E San Basilio in the heart of the old city has been converted from a townhouse mansion. Antiques and antique reproductions add to the colonial ambience. Guest rooms are simply yet nicely furnished and have satellite TVs and modern bathrooms. It has a small restaurant and bar. **www.cubanacan.cu**

SANTIAGO DE CUBA Hotel Casagranda
🍴 🗐 ♿ Ⓦ $$$

Calle Heredia 201 **Tel** *(22) 68 6600* **Fax** *(22) 68 6035* **Rooms** *58*

Since opening in 1912, the Neo-Classical Hotel Casagranda has been considered the city's finest. Its location is unbeatable, the Restaurante Casagranda *(see p97)* impressive. Guest rooms are comfortable; suites have sumptuous furnishings. The patio snack bar overlooking the plaza is a buzzing social scene. **www.gran-caribe.com**

SANTIAGO DE CUBA Meliá Santiago de Cuba
🍴 🗐 ♿ Ⓦ $$$

Av. de Las Américas & Calle M **Tel** *(22) 68 7070* **Fax** *(22) 68 7170* **Rooms** *270*

The deluxe high-rise Meliá Santiago de Cuba features striking post-Modernist architecture. Its facilities include two fine restaurants, boutiques, a humidor, spa, a nightclub, and a splendid open-air swimming pool. Stylish decor in guest rooms features mahogany furnishings. **www.solmeliacuba.com**

SOROA Hotel & Villa Horizontes Soroa
🍴 🗐 ♿ Ⓦ $$

Carretera Soroa, Km8, Candelaria, Pinar del Río **Tel** *(48) 52 3534* **Fax** *(48) 52 3861* **Rooms** *78*

This pleasant hotel appeals to nature lovers with renovated, simply appointed bungalows around an Olympic pool complex. Hillside family villas are another option. The rates are a bargain, although it has only modest facilities, including a spa, and a tiny bar plus a simple restaurant where musicians entertain. **www.cubanacan.cu**

TRINIDAD Iberostar Gran Trinidad
🍴 🗐 ♿ Ⓦ $$$

Calle José Martí 262 **Tel** *(41) 99 6070* **Fax** *(41) 99 6077* **Rooms** *40*

Offering true luxury, the spectacular colonial Iberostar Gran Trinidad is Cuba's finest hotel outside Havana. Lavishly appointed throughout, it has a pricey but superb restaurant, bar, a games room, Internet service, and a cigar lounge. **www.iberostar.com**

VARADERO Mercure Cuatro Palmas
🎦 🍴 🗐 🏊 ♿ Ⓦ $$

Av. 1ra between 61 & 62 **Tel** *(45) 66 7040* **Fax** *(45) 66 7208* **Rooms** *282*

The perennially popular Mercure Cuatro Palmas in Varadero is built around General Fulgencio Batista's former Spanish-colonial-themed summer palace. The guest rooms, some of which are separated from the hotel by Avenue 1ra, are modest yet pleasantly furnished. Entertainment is offered around the pool complex. **www.mercure.com**

VARADERO Hotel Varadero Internacional
🎦 🍴 🗐 🏊 ♿ Ⓦ $$$

Av. Las Américas **Tel** *(45) 66 7038* **Fax** *(45) 66 7246* **Rooms** *163*

The remodeled 1950s-era Hotel Varadero Internacional has an advantageous location close to the town. The main restaurant is acclaimed, and it hosts Varadero's key cabaret. Rooms are comfortable and spacious, with modern conveniences. Spa facilities, tennis courts, and watersports are available. **www.gran-caribe.cu**

VARADERO Barceló Marina Palace Resort
🎦 🍴 🗐 🏊 ♿ Ⓦ $$$$

Punta Hicacos Final **Tel** *(45) 66 9966* **Fax** *(45) 66 7022* **Rooms** *296*

The all-suite Barceló Marina Palace Resort at the tip of the peninsula is the top act in Varadero. The handsome nautical-themed contemporary styling features lots of blues, golds, and calming pastels. It has 4 restaurants, 6 bars, a disco, and hosts live shows. Watersports and spa facilities available. **www.barcelo.com**

VARADERO Blau Varadero Hotel
🎦 🍴 🏊 ♿ Ⓦ $$$$

Carretera Las Morlas Km15 **Tel** *(45) 66 7545* **Fax** *53 (45) 66 7494* **Rooms** *395*

Inspired by Maya architecture, Blau Varadero Hotel has a vast pyramidal atrium lobby, a spectacular pool complex, a state-of-the-art theater, several watersports, and tennis. Guest rooms feature stylish contemporary furnishings in subdued colors, king-sized beds, and marble-clad bathrooms. **www.blauhotels.com**

VARADERO Sandals Royal Hicacos Resort & Spa
🎦 🍴 🗐 🏊 ♿ Ⓦ $$$$

Carretera Las Morlas Km14 **Tel** *(45) 66 8844* **Fax** *(45) 66 8851* **Rooms** *404*

This spectacular resort comes with sophisticated tropical decor and a full panoply of watersports, activities, and entertainment that includes a disco. All guest rooms are junior suites or suites, with king-sized beds, lively color schemes, and modern amenities including safes and coffee-makers. **www.sandalshicacos.com**

VIÑALES Hotel Horizontes Rancho San Vicente
🍴 🗐 ♿ $$

Carretera P. Esperanza Km33, Pinar del Rio **Tel** *(48) 79 6201* **Fax** *(48) 79 6265* **Rooms** *53*

The Horizontes Rancho San Vicente on the edge of a forest, just north of Viñales, has pleasantly furnished, albeit rustic cabins on lawns encircling a pool and sundeck. The cabins have TVs, telephones, and hot water. There is an appealing restaurant. A small on-site spa offers mud treatments. **www.cubanacan.cu**

Where to Eat & Nightlife

Eateries in Cuba vary from state-run restaurants to informal private residences that offer inexpensive home cooking. Although many quality restaurants have opened, many towns still have only very basic options. In contrast, Cuba's vivacious nightlife ranges from jazz, *son*, and salsa *(see pp48–9)* clubs to sensational cabarets. A 10 percent service charge is usually added to your bill.

PRICE CATEGORIES
The price ranges are for a two-course meal for one, including tax and service charges and half a bottle of wine.

$ under $10
$$ $10–15
$$$ $15–25
$$$$ $25–35
$$$$$ over $35

RESTAURANTS

Choosing a restaurant
Many of the best restaurants found in Cuba are associated with tourist hotels, outside which breakfasts are hard to come by. Most beach hotels rely on buffet meals, called *mesa sueca* (Swedish table). Havana has some excellent restaurants, including *paladares* (private restaurants in homes).

Restaurante 1869

La Paella

CIENFUEGOS Restaurante 1869 $$
Calle 31 & Av. 54 **Tel** *(43) 55 1020*

The elegant colonial-themed Restaurante 1869 in the Hotel Unión *(see p93)* is the nicest of the few restaurants in town. The ambience delights, service is willing and friendly, and the menu has some intriguing, although not always satisfying, dishes. Try the calamari in tomato sauce. Take a sweater against the excessive air-conditioning.

GUARDALAVACA El Ancla $$$$
Playa Mayor **Tel** *(24) 43 0381*

Squatting atop a coral outcrop overlooking Guardalavaca's main beach, El Ancla's setting is a perfect complement to its seafood menu. Most dishes are fairly priced. The *corvina al ajillo* (garlic sea bass) is consistently good. There is a large wine list. The main restaurant has walls of glass and a breeze-swept veranda.

HAVANA La Bodeguita del Medio $$
Calle Empedrado 207, Habana Vieja **Tel** *(7) 862 1374*

A cramped and atmospheric tourist favorite for its excellent *criollo* cuisine and Ernest Hemingway associations, La Bodeguita del Medio serves excellent roast pork with black beans, succulent plantains, and garlic yucca, washed down by mojitos. The mood is endearing, thanks to the performances hosted here.

HAVANA La Paella $$
Calle Oficios 53, Habana Vieja **Tel** *(7) 857 1037*

The menu at La Paella, a welcoming Spanish-bodega-style eatery at Hostal Valencia *(see p93)*, has classical Iberian dishes, including paella (minimum two people). Also serves seafood and *criollo* dishes. Posters of matadors and bulls-heads adorn the walls. Steps away from Plaza San Francisco and Plaza de Armas, it is a handy lunch stop.

HAVANA Los Nardos $$
Paseo de Martí 563 **Tel** *(7) 863 2985*

Hidden upstairs in a seemingly tumbledown building one block south of Parque Central, Los Nardos packs in tourists and locals alike to enjoy huge plates of garlic shrimp, *bistec* and paella. A dramatic atmosphere adds extra flavor; for less ambience but quicker service, there are other restaurants situated on the two upper floors.

HAVANA Cocina de Lilliam $$$
Calle 48 1311, Miramar **Tel** *(7) 209 6514*

Catapulting to international fame when US President Carter dined here in 2002, Cocina de Lilliam delivers some of the most creative and well-served dishes in town. Guests can choose to dine indoors or in the leafy garden. Try the traditional and savory *ropa vieja* made with lamb. Closed Aug 1–15.

HAVANA El Aljibe $$$
Av. 7ma between Calles 24 & 26, Miramar **Tel** *(7) 204 1583*

Perhaps Havana's most popular restaurant, the constantly expanding, thatched open-air El Aljibe draws diplomats and business folk as well as tour groups. While it offers an à la carte menu, the all-you-can-eat *prix fixe* house special – succulent roast chicken with yucca, black beans, plantain, and rice – is the way to go.

HAVANA La Casa $$$
Calle 30 865 **Tel** *(7) 881 7000*

This is one of the few upscale *paladares* still remaianing in Havana, housed in a 1950s Modernist mansion in Nuevo Vedado. The owners deliver consistently tasty and creative fare such as octopus with onions. Members of the Kennedy family and actor Matt Dillon are among the many famous people to have dined here.

Key to Symbols *see back cover flap*

HAVANA La Terraza de Cojímar 🍽️🎵♿♿ $$$

Calle Real 161, Cojímar **Tel** *(7) 766 5151*

One of Ernest Hemingway's favorite haunts, the seafront La Terraza plays up the associations heartily. The bargain prices are a major draw, as is the quality seafood that includes oyster cocktail, sautéed calamari, and paella. The Gregorio Fuentes cocktail is named for Hemingway's skipper, a now-deceased Cojímar local.

HAVANA Don Cangrejo 🍽️🏠♿ $$$$

Av. 1ra between 16 & 18, Miramar **Tel** *(7) 204 3837*

Havana's preeminent seafood restaurant, Don Cangrejo, is run by the Ministry of Fisheries. Housed in a Modernist 1950s mansion overlooking the Atlantic Ocean, it even has a swimming pool. The menu ranges from crab cocktail and crab-filled wontons to garlic shrimp and seafood paella. An extensive wine list spans the globe.

HAVANA Comedor de Aguiar 🍷🍽️🍽️🎵♿♿ $$$$$

Calle O & 21, Vedado **Tel** *(7) 873 5054*

Inside the Hotel Nacional *(see p76)*, the elegant Comedor de Aguiar offers an expensive dining option. Glittering chandeliers and silverware, and waiters in vests and bow-ties combine to create a hushed, reverential mood. The international menu offers outlandishly priced steak and lobster dishes, but other dishes are fairly priced.

HOLGUÍN Taberna Pancho 🍽️♿♿ $

Av. Dimitrov & Plaza de la Revolución **Tel** *(24) 48 1868*

Popular with locals, the lively Taberna Pancho serves budget-priced set meals. Choose from chicken, pork, and shrimp, although some days only limited items are available. The price includes two locally brewed beers – hand-drawn and served in steins. It is named for the famous beer-swilling donkey whose stuffed head now hangs over the bar.

SANCTI SPÍRITUS Mesón de la Plaza 🍷♿♿ $

Calle Máximo Gómez 34, Sancti Spíritus **Tel** *(41) 32 8546*

One of the favored provincial restaurants in Cuba, the bargain-priced Mesón de la Plaza is themed as a Spanish bodega with cowhide chairs and rough-hewn tables. The house special, *garbanzo mesonero*, with bacon, pork, and sausage, is delicious, as is the roast chicken in orange sauce. Try the sangría.

SANTIAGO DE CUBA Restaurante El Morro 🏠🎵♿♿ $$$

Parque Histórico El Morro **Tel** *(22) 69 1576*

Out of the way, but well worth the effort, the simple, laid-back rustic Restaurante El Morro is spectacularly perched atop the cliffs at the mouth of Santiago de Cuba bay. Dine inside at rough-hewn tables with goat-hide seats, or beneath an arbor on the patio. There are simple *criollo* dishes, such as bean soup and *ropa vieja*.

SANTIAGO DE CUBA Restaurante Zunzún 🍽️🏠🎵♿ $$$

Av. Manduley 159 **Tel** *(22) 64 1528*

Set in a charming colonial mansion in the peaceful Vista Alegre district, Restaurante Zunzún offers romantic patio dining. Despite the traditional ambience, this sophisticated restaurant offers an elaborate menu of Cuban and international dishes, including tapas, and seafood. The garlic shrimp is a good bet. Prices are reasonable.

SANTIAGO DE CUBA Restaurante Casagranda 🍷🍽️🎵♿♿ $$$$

Calle Heredia 201 **Tel** *(22) 68 6600*

Named for the eponymous host hotel *(see p95)*, the elegant Restaurante Casagranda applies a dress code. Stylishly done up with antiques, antique reproductions, and gilt chandeliers, it offers an ambitious international menu at fair prices. The patio bar adjoining is a great place to enjoy a postprandial cigar and cocktail.

BARS AND CLUBS

Cubans adore music and dance and there is no shortage of venues where visitors can enjoy world-class renditions from *son* and salsa to jazz, rock, and even rap. Every town has a *casa de la trova* – a traditional "music house" – where *son* and *boleros* can be heard. Las Vegas-style cabarets add color and flair to the nightlife in every city and beach resort. The bar scene is not quite so exciting, although Havana has plenty of lively venues. Most beach resorts have discos independent of hotels.

Jazz Café in Havana

RECOMMENDED PLACES TO GO

Café Parisien
Hotel Nacional, Calle 0 & 21, Havana. (Dazzling cabaret revue.)

Casa de la Trova
Calle Echerri 29, Trinidad. (Dancing to *son* bands.)

Casa de la Trova
Calle Heredia 208, Santiago de Cuba. (The best place for *son*.)

Disco Ayala
Motel Las Cuevas, Trinidad. (Disco inside a huge cave.)

Gato Tuerto
Calle 0 & 17, Havana. (1950s redux.)

Jazz Café
Av. 1ra & Paseo, Havana. (Cuba's premier jazz club.)

La Comparsita
Calle 60 & 3ra, Varadero. (Open-air cabaret & nightclub.)

Mambo Club
Autopista Sur, Varadero. (Hip nightclub with salsa bands.)

Tropicana
Calle 72 4504, Marianao, Havana. (Cuba's largest cabaret.)

Practical Information

Following a boom in tourism over the past decade, Cuba now has modern services on par with most of the other Caribbean destinations. There are some weak links, however, and advance planning is essential. Visitors need to be flexible, and patience is required to deal with Cuba's all-encompassing bureaucracy. Refunds are rarely given when things go wrong, and state-run tourism entities and individual tourism workers are adept at extracting extra money from visitors.

Relaxing in the sun at Guadalavaca beach, Cuba

WHEN TO GO

Any time of year is good for visiting Cuba, although July and August have torrid rainfall and September to November are prime hurricane months. The best period to visit is from December to April, when it is pleasant. Rain can occur year-round, but is concentrated from June to November, when hotel and car rental rates drop. Many key festivals are held in Havana from November to December, including the Festival Internacional del Nuevo Cine Latinoamericano and the jazz festival.

GETTING THERE

Charter and regular scheduled flights arrive from Europe, Canada, and Central and South America. Cuba has nine international airports, but most visitors land at either Havana's José Martí International Airport (HAV) or the Juan Gualberto Gómez Airport at Varadero (VRA).

Virgin Atlantic has two weekly flights from Gatwick to Havana. **Cubana** flies from London and Europe. **Air Canada** serves Cuba from gateways in Canada. **Grupo Taca**, **Mexicana**, and **Copa** fly from Central America, and **Air Jamaica** links Jamaica with Cuba. There are special flights from USA for eligible licensed travelers. There is no ferry service to Cuba.

DOCUMENTATION

Visitors must have a valid passport, onward ticket, proof of travel insurance, and a tourist visa *(tarjeta de turista)*, issued by your airline upon airport check-in. Visas are valid for 30 days (Canadians receive 90 days), and can be extended. Individuals subject to US law are barred from visiting Cuba and significant penalties apply for transgressions. Certain US residents (such as journalists and Cuban-American families) can get permission from the **US Treasury Department**.

VISITOR INFORMATION

Official **Cubatur** offices in the United Kingdom and Canada provide brochures. Travel agencies and websites are good for details on specific activities. **Infotur** has offices in major cities and Cuban tour companies have information desks in all hotels and sell organized excursions. A huge amount of information about Cuba is available on the Internet. All websites originating in Cuba are state-run and care should be taken if making bookings online. The US websites are barred from accepting online bookings relating to Cuba travel.

HEALTH AND SECURITY

All hotels have a doctor or nurse on duty, or on call 24 hours a day. Special clinics treat visitors, while **Asistur** provides varied assistance to travelers in distress. Cuba is generally a safe place to visit. However, petty theft is endemic. Snatching and mugging are frequent in run-down Havana areas. Keep valuables in hotel safes.

BANKING AND CURRENCY

Cuba's currency is the *peso*, but all tourist transactions are in *convertible pesos* (designated as CUC$), which can be exchanged for foreign currency at Cadeca exchange bureaux (a surcharge applies for converting US dollars), often located near shops.

Tourist information office on a Havana street

Colorful papier-mâché dolls on display in a Cuba stall

Euros can be used in Cayo Coco, Varadero, and Cayo Largo. Non-US credit cards are accepted for most tourist transactions. All beach resorts and major cities have state-owned banks serving foreigners.

COMMUNICATIONS

Public phones are plentiful and reliable, and work with prepaid phone cards that can be purchased at hotels and post offices. Calls from hotels are expensive. **Cubacel** provides cellular service, but activating your personal phone is expensive. To call outside Cuba, dial 0, then 9 followed by the country code. To call Cuba from abroad, dial the international access number, then 53 and the local number. All laptops must be declared on entry. Most hotels have Internet access and there are cybercafés in most cities.

TRANSPORT

The state-owned car rental companies, such as **Rex**, have desks at all hotels. Cars are not well maintained and customer service is not very efficient. Reservations are essential in high season. Tourist taxis are available at all hotels and resorts. Many drivers prefer to negotiate a fare rather than use meters. **Víazul** runs air-conditioned coaches between Havana, key cities, and tourist destinations. Inter-city buses cater only for locals and not tourists. Cuba's railway system links Havana to Pinar del Río and Santiago de Cuba. Visitors can opt for bicycle rickshaws, popular in Havana.

SHOPPING

All tourist hotels and ARTex shops sell cigars, rum, and other typical Cuban souvenirs. Many of the best bargains are found at street crafts markets, where you can buy from the artisans. Look out for wooden statues, papier-mâché dolls, paintings, and antique model cars. Havana's Fería de la Artesanía market and Trinidad are great places to shop.

LANGUAGE

Spanish, the official language of Cuba, is spoken with a local inflection, which can be difficult to understand. Tour guides and most service staff in hotels speak English.

ELECTRICITY

Electric current is 110-volt, but 220-volt current is also found (and usually marked as such). Most outlets use the US two-prong plugs. The system is unreliable and blackouts (*apagones*) are common.

TIME

Cuba is on Eastern Standard Time, 5 hours behind Greenwich Mean Time. Daylight saving is in effect from May to October.

GETTING MARRIED

Getting married in Cuba is bureaucratic and requires that all necessary documents be translated into Spanish and notarized. Contact the **Consultoria Jurídica** in Cuba for more information.

A bicitaxi (bicycle rickshaw) in Havana

DIRECTORY

GETTING THERE

Air Canada
www.aircanada.com

Air Jamaica
www.airjamaica.com

Copa
www.copaair.com

Cubana
www.cubana.cu

Grupo Taca
www.grupotaca.com

Mexicana
www.mexicana.com

Virgin Atlantic
www.virgin-atlantic.com

DOCUMENTATION

US Treasury Department
Tel 202 622 2480 (USA).
www.treas.gov

VISITOR INFORMATION

Cubatur
Tel 416 362 0700 (Canada),
020 7240 6655 (UK).
www.cubatravel.cu

Infotur
Tel (7) 866 3333.
www.infotur.cu

Useful Websites:
www.cubaabsolutely.com
www.cubalinda.com
www.dtcuba.com
www.cubatravel.cu

HEALTH AND SECURITY

Ambulance
Tel 105 nationwide.

Asistur
Tel (7) 866 4499.

Police and Fire
Tel 106 and 105.

COMMUNICATIONS

Cubacel
Tel (7) 264 2266.
www.cubacel.com

TRANSPORT

Rex
Tel (7) 273 9166.
www.rex.cu

Víazul
Tel (7) 881 1413.
www.viazul.cu

GETTING MARRIED

Consultoria Jurídica
Havana. *Tel (7) 33 2490.*

Exploring the Cayman Islands

This British overseas territory comprises three tiny islands – Grand Cayman and its sister islands, Little Cayman and Cayman Brac. Located in the western Caribbean, they cover a total land mass of 100 sq miles (259 sq km). The islands are actually coral-encrusted summits of a submarine mountain range. Deservedly, the trio is world-renowned for its stunning beaches and scuba diving. Unspoilt and unhurried, lying 90 miles (145 km) northeast from the busier Grand Cayman, the sister islands are ideal for divers, nature lovers, and those seeking tranquility.

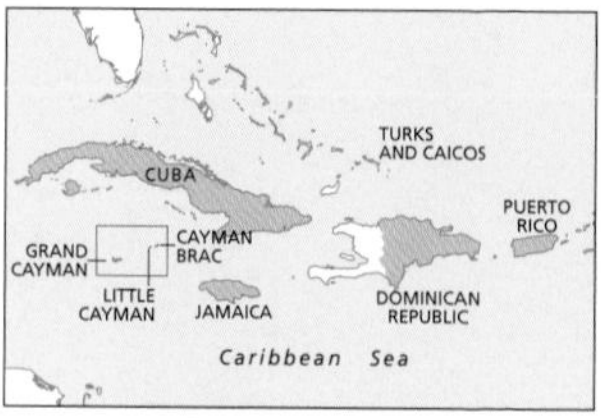
TURKS AND CAICOS
CUBA
PUERTO RICO
GRAND CAYMAN
CAYMAN BRAC
LITTLE CAYMAN
JAMAICA
DOMINICAN REPUBLIC
Caribbean Sea

SEE ALSO

- ***Where to Stay*** pp110–11
- ***Where to Eat & Nightlife*** pp112–13

Grand Cayman
The largest of the three islands, Grand Cayman is also the most developed, particularly its western districts. The eastern districts serve good Cayman cuisine.

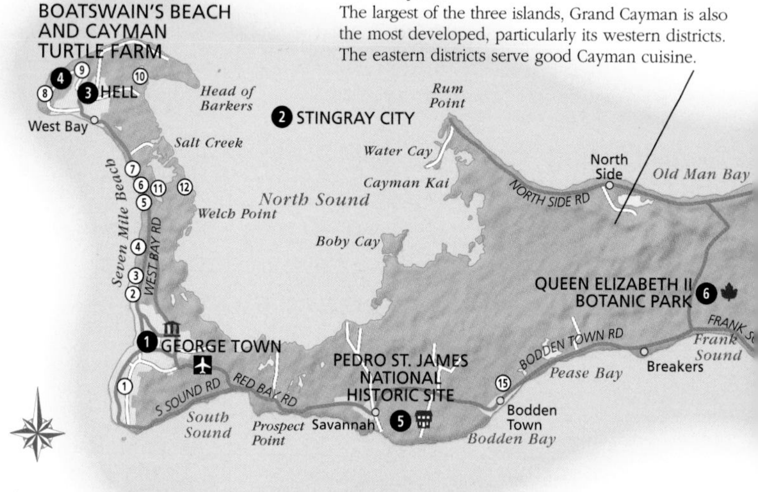
BOATSWAIN'S BEACH AND CAYMAN TURTLE FARM
HELL
West Bay
Head of Barkers
STINGRAY CITY
Rum Point
Salt Creek
Water Cay
Seven Mile Beach
WEST BAY RD
Cayman Kai
North Side
Old Man Bay
NORTH SIDE RD
North Sound
Welch Point
Boby Cay
QUEEN ELIZABETH II BOTANIC PARK
GEORGE TOWN
FRANK SOUND RD
Frank Sound
BODDEN TOWN RD
Breakers
PEDRO ST. JAMES NATIONAL HISTORIC SITE
Pease Bay
S SOUND RD
RED BAY RD
South Sound
Prospect Point
Savannah
Bodden Town
Bodden Bay
0 km 5
0 miles 5

SIGHTS AT A GLANCE

Boatswain's Beach and Cayman Turtle Farm p103 4
Cayman Brac 8
George Town 1
Hell 3
Little Cayman 7
Pedro St. James National Historic Site 5
Queen Elizabeth II Botanic Park 6
Stingray City 2

Hotels and Resorts
Brac Caribbean Beach Village 19
Brac Reef Beach Resort 20
Cobalt Coast Resort & Suites 9
Comfort Suites 3
Compass Point Dive Resort 14
Coral Stone Club 7
Grand Cayman Beach Suites 4
Grand Cayman Marriott Beach Resort 2
Little Cayman Beach Resort 16
Paradise Villas 17
Pirate's Point Resort 18
Ramada Grand Caymanian Resort 12
The Reef Resort 13
Ritz-Carlton, Grand Cayman 6
Rocky Shore Guest House and Villas 8
Shangri-La B&B 10
Sunset House 1
Sunshine Suites Resorts 11
Turtle Nest Inn & Condos 15
Westin Casuarina Resort and Spa 5

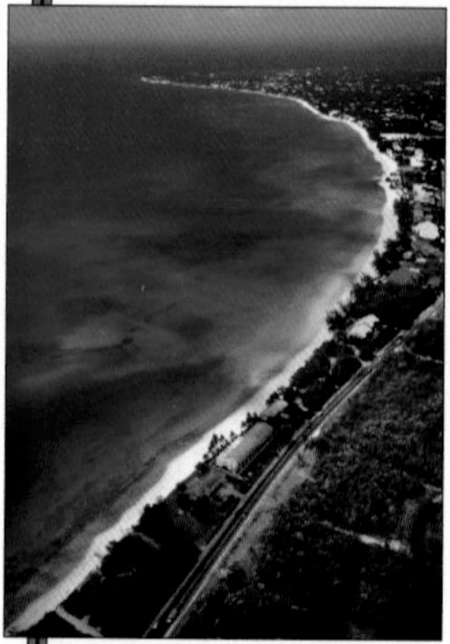

Aerial view of the coastline, Grand Cayman

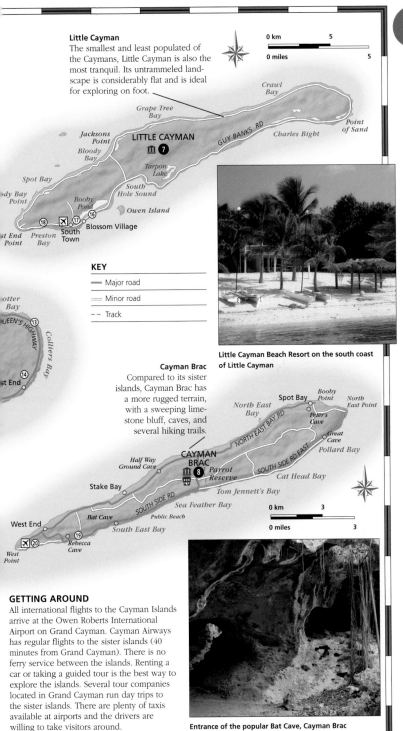

Little Cayman

The smallest and least populated of the Caymans, Little Cayman is also the most tranquil. Its untrammeled landscape is considerably flat and is ideal for exploring on foot.

0 km   5
0 miles   5

Crawl Bay

Grape Tree Bay

LITTLE CAYMAN 🏛 **7**

GUY BANKS RD

Charles Bight

Point of Sand

Jacksons Point

Bloody Bay

Spot Bay

Tarpon Lake

dy Bay Point

South Hole Sound

Booby Pond

Owen Island

18 ✈ **17** **16**

Blossom Village

st End Point

Preston Bay

South Town

KEY

— Major road

⎓ Minor road

-- Track

Little Cayman Beach Resort on the south coast of Little Cayman

otter Bay

UEEN'S HIGHWAY **13**

Colliers Bay

st End **14**

Cayman Brac

Compared to its sister islands, Cayman Brac has a more rugged terrain, with a sweeping limestone bluff, caves, and several hiking trails.

North East Bay

Spot Bay

Booby Point

North East Point

NORTH EAST BAY RD

Peter's Cave

Great Cave

Pollard Bay

Half Way Ground Cave

CAYMAN BRAC 🏛 **8**

Parrot Reserve

SOUTH SIDE RD EAST

Cat Head Bay

Stake Bay

SOUTH SIDE RD

Tom Jennett's Bay

Sea Feather Bay

Bat Cave

Public Beach

0 km   3
0 miles   3

West End ✈ **20** **19**

Rebecca Cave

South East Bay

West Point

GETTING AROUND

All international flights to the Cayman Islands arrive at the Owen Roberts International Airport on Grand Cayman. Cayman Airways has regular flights to the sister islands (40 minutes from Grand Cayman). There is no ferry service between the islands. Renting a car or taking a guided tour is the best way to explore the islands. Several tour companies located in Grand Cayman run day trips to the sister islands. There are plenty of taxis available at airports and the drivers are willing to take visitors around.

Entrance of the popular Bat Cave, Cayman Brac

George Town ❶

West coast of Grand Cayman.
🏠 21,000. ✈ ℹ *PO Box 67, Grand
Cayman, 345 949 0623.* 🎭 *Pirates'
Week (Nov).*

With a steady stream of cruise
ships docking at the port,
George Town, the capital of
the Cayman Islands, is a busy
place all year round. It takes
about an hour to casually stroll
the streets lined with duty-free
shops and restaurants – the
city's major attractions. The
**Cayman Islands National
Museum**, located in the Old
Courts Building, one of the
few surviving 19th-century
structures, has exhibits that
document the islands' past,
including the replica of a
hand-made catboat from the
1920s. Nearby, on Harbour
Place, is the National Gallery
of the Cayman Islands displaying local art. Not to be missed
is Cayman Craft market –
located in the heart of town.

**Cayman Islands National Museum
in George Town**

Stingray City ❷

5 miles (8 km) NE of George Town,
Grand Cayman. 🤿 🚤 *nearly all dive
and watersports operators offer
guided trips.*

A 12-ft (4-m) dive site in the
clear, turquoise waters of
North Sound, Stingray City is
world-famous for its Atlantic
southern stingrays. A perfect
paradise for snorkelers and
divers, this is the only place
in the world where they can
swim with, touch, and hand
feed wild stingrays. The rays
were first spotted here in the

Visitors enjoying the shallow waters of Stingray City, Grand Cayman

early 1980s by fishermen
cleaning their catches in the
shallow, protected sound.
Dive operators saw this as an
economic opportunity and
began to offer trips to divers.
Nearby is "The Sandbar," a
shallow sandbank, where non-
divers can also experience
close encounters of the marine
kind. On disembarking the
boat into the waist-deep
waters of the Sandbar, visitors
are surrounded by rays and
yellowtail snappers.
Rays are gentle and it is
possible to touch their velvety
white underbelly, but the tail
should be avoided because of
its barb. Dive operators show
how to shuffle along the sea
bed to avoid stepping on a
barb and feed the rays chunks
of squid by making a fist with
the thumb tucked in. The rays
have no teeth, but visitors will
feel quite a strong suction as
the ray hoovers the tidbit.
There have been concerns
that some operators mishandle
the rays in the name of photo

opportunities. It is best to just
enjoy the beauty of their
movement and the tickle of
their fins as they swim past.

Hell ❸

7 miles (11 km) N of George Town,
Grand Cayman. ℹ *Post Office, 345
949 6999.* ♿ **www**.tab.ky

In the village of the same
name in West Bay, Hell is a
small site featuring 1.5-million-
year-old jagged shards of
jet-black ironshore (limestone
coral and dolomite). Many
theories abound about how
the place got its name. It is
popularly believed that the
name originated after a local
official exclaimed, "This is
what hell must look like."
The name stuck and the site
is now a great tourist attraction, with a hell-themed
post office where visitors can
send postcards from Hell. The
place can be crowded as it is
a stop for cruise ship tours.

**ATLANTIC SOUTHERN
STINGRAYS**

These massive creatures
are broad, flattish, carti-
laginous fish closely
related to sharks. They
are the most common of
the stingray family and
are frequent visitors to
Stingray City. Female
southern stingrays can

**An Atlantic southern stingray
foraging for food along the sea floor**

grow up to 6 ft (2 m) across while males are smaller. Rays
are constantly on the prowl for food – crabs, shellfish, and
worms – and they hunt by smell, not sight, and suck the
food into their mouth where it is crushed by hard cartilage
plates. In the wild, they find their food by flapping their
wing-shaped fins over the sea bed so that sand moves
around and any small creatures hiding there are revealed.

Boatswain's Beach and Cayman Turtle Farm ❹

Turtle hatchling

This 23-acre (9-ha) marine theme park is a great place to spend at least half a day. Pronounced "Bo-suns" Beach, the marine park offers a wonderful opportunity to learn about the unique flora and fauna of the Cayman Islands. The highlight is snorkeling with fish and other marine life in the huge saltwater lagoon. Boatswain's Beach is also the home of the Cayman Turtle Farm, which breeds the rare green sea turtles.

VISITORS' CHECKLIST

825 Northwest Point Road, West Bay, Grand Cayman. **Tel** 345 949 3894. 🚌 🅿 8:30am–5pm daily. 🌐 📷 📖 ⛑ 🍴 🚻 🛍
www.boatswainsbeach.ky

Caribbean Bird Aviary
This free-flight aviary houses many colorful bird species indigenous to the Cayman Islands and the greater Caribbean.

Breaker's Lagoon
This swimming pool is the largest in the Cayman Islands and is perfect for relaxing and cooling off.

Shoreline Nursery is a protected reef and a safe-haven for disabled fish that cannot survive in the wild.

Turtle Tank

Entrance

Education Center

Boatswain's Lagoon
Visitors can wade into this saltwater lagoon to see the marine life or watch through the underwater viewing panel.

Touch Tanks
Under staff supervision, visitors can get to hold one of the sea turtle yearlings and also get a photograph taken.

Breeding Pond
Huge green sea turtles breed in this large artificial pond rimmed by a sandy beach.

Everyday items on display at Pedro St. James National Historic Site

Pedro St. James National Historic Site ❺

5 miles (8 km) E of George Town, Grand Cayman. 🚌 🛈 *Pedro Castle Road, Savannah, 345 947 3329.* ⏰ *9am–5pm daily.* ⬤ *Christmas Day.* 📷 📽 ♿ *not on upper floors of the Great House.* 🖥 📱 **www**.pedrostjames.ky

Located high above Pedro Bluff, Pedro St. James is the oldest building on the Cayman Islands. William Eden, a wealthy Englishman, used Jamaican slave labor to construct this magnificent three-story stone building in 1780. In 1831, the first Cayman government was formed in this building. The building later suffered damage from hurricanes, fire, and even lightning, but in 1992 the government decided to restore it. Guides are dressed in period costumes and a tour of the house shows a display of its period furniture with mahogany floors and staircases, timber beams, and gabled framework. The visitors' center features an excellent 3-D multi-sensory theater, where, in 20 minutes, visitors can experience 200 years of Cayman history. There are breathtaking views from the house and the site is also a popular location for weddings, concerts, and parties. A memorial commemorates the devastating Hurricane Ivan of 2004.

Queen Elizabeth II Botanic Park ❻

15 miles (24 km) E of George Town, Grand Cayman. 🚗 🛈 *345 947 3558.* ⏰ *9am–5:30pm Oct–Mar; 9am–6:30pm Apr–Sep daily.* ⬤ *Christmas and Good Friday.* 📷 ♿ *golf carts to assist people with limited mobility are available with advance reservation.* 🖥 📱 **www**.botanic-park.ky

This 65-acre (26-ha) park showcases more than half of the plant species native to the Cayman Islands, as well as birds and wildlife, including the rare, endemic blue iguanas. The park offers visitors a short walk through the lovely 3-acre (1-ha) Floral Color Garden, which features hundreds of species of tropical and subtropical plants laid out colorfully. Adjoining the garden is a picturesque lake that attracts aquatic birds including the rare West Indian whistling duck. Located nearby is the Heritage Garden with its traditional ornamental and medicinal plants, which Caymanians used for various ailments. The garden also has a pretty traditional Cayman house dating back to 1900 and a collection of fruit trees.

A path near the entrance, Woodland Trail, gives people the opportunity to view the natural landscape, which

"Iguana right of way" sign

covers almost 40 acres (16 ha) of the park. Visitors get a chance to see the blue iguana roaming freely in this stretch. The park is also home to 56 species of butterflies and a garden of orchids.

Little Cayman ❼

89 miles (143 km) NE of Grand Cayman. 🚤 *200.* ✈

A mere 10-sq-mile (25-sq-km) island, Little Cayman is the smallest of the three Cayman islands and is inhabited by only a few residents. Nature rules this laid-back, one-road island, where iguanas and birds outnumber humans. The island is a popular day trip from Grand Cayman for travelers who mainly come here for solitude or exceptional diving. Bloody Bay Wall Marine Park *(see p107)* offers the Caribbean's finest drop-offs and is known all over the world.

East of the tiny airport sits Blossom Village, the only town on the island, where visitors can stop at a restaurant. Close by is the Booby Pond Nature Reserve, a 206-acre (83-ha) RAMSAR site, a nesting ground for 20,000 red-footed boobies as well as the magnificent frigatebirds and waterbirds. The **National Trust House** at Blossom Village offers viewing platforms with

The traditional Cayman house inside Queen Elizabeth II Botanic Park

For hotels and restaurants on these islands see pp110–11 and pp112–13

Corals and seafans growing on Bloody Bay Wall, Little Cayman

telescopes to observe the birdlife. Just across the reserve is **Little Cayman Museum** that has displays of the island's history. Tarpon fishing and bird-watching is great at Tarpon Lake. Point of Sand, at the eastern tip, has a pretty little beach. The East End Point Lighthouse here overlooks Cayman Brac. Offshore lies Owen Island, a tiny white beach cay, which is ideal for picnics and kayaking.

National Trust House
Blossom Village. *Tel* 345 749 1121.
🕐 9am–noon & 2–6pm Mon–Fri.
🖥 www.nationaltrust.org.ky
🏛 **Little Cayman Museum**
Blossom Village. *Tel* 345 948 1033.
🕐 3–5pm Mon & Fri.

Cayman Brac **8**

90 miles (144 km) NE of Grand Cayman. 👥 *1,800.* ✈ 🏢 *Cayman Islands Department of Tourism, Brac Office, West End Community Park, 345 948 1649; District Administration, Stake Bay, 345 948 2222.* www.itsyourstoexplore.com

Brac, the Gaelic word for bluff, is a suitable name for this Cayman isle which has the most dramatic topography of the group, dominated by a limestone cliff reaching up to 146 ft (44 m) on its eastern tip. The island has several caves and many trails to explore. A 3-hour hike from Spot Bay leads to an old lighthouse from where

there are splendid views of the ocean. Halfway down the trail is Little Cayman Brac Outlook (a large rock), where bird enthusiasts can see nesting brown boobies.

Another interesting hike is off Bight Road south to the 310-acre (125-ha) National Trust Parrot Reserve and Nature Trail, which protects the endemic Cayman Brac parrot, other birds, plants, and native trees. On South Side Road is the Bat Cave, which is home to fruit bats. Farther down the same road, visitors can also see Rebecca's Cave, the historic site where the islanders took shelter during the worst hurricane ever in 1932. It contains the grave of Rebecca Bodden, a baby girl who died in the cave during the storm. Just beside the cave starts the challenging Salt Water Pond trail, which takes hikers from the south to north coast.

At the end of the hike is Salt Water Pond, a sanctuary for a tern colony. Apart from bird-watching, hikers can visit the beautiful **Cayman Brac Heritage House** on North East Bay Road. Local artisans display their work here. Nearby, at Stake Bay is the island's first museum, **Cayman Brac Museum**, opened in 1983. It has exhibits on ship-building and displays on the islanders' lifestyles during the 1930s. The island is undergoing serious reconstruction after being severely damaged in Hurricane Paloma that struck the island in 2008.

Cayman Brac Heritage House
North East Bay. *Tel* 345 948 0563.
🕐 9:30am–1pm, 2–5pm Mon–Fri, 10am–3pm Sat. 🖥 ♿ 🚻
🏛 **Cayman Brac Museum**
Stake Bay. *Tel* 345 948 2222.
🕐 9am–noon, 1–4pm Mon–Fri; 9am–noon Sat. 🖥 🚫 🚻

Brown boobies at Little Cayman Brac Outlook on the way to the lighthouse

BLUE IGUANAS

The Queen Elizabeth II Botanic Park is home to the Blue Iguana Habitat, the center for the National Trust's Blue Iguana Recovery Program. Just two decades ago, the endemic Grand Cayman blue iguana was facing extinction. With an ultimate repopulation goal of 1,000, the Habitat, along the park's Woodland Trail, is the captive breeding ground for these critically endangered reptiles. The blue iguana grows up to 5 ft (2 m) long and can live up to 69 years. Males and females differ in colors. While the coloration of male iguanas can vary from dark grey to turquoise blue, females are olive green to pale blue. They are primarily herbivorous and their diet mainly consists of fruits, plants, and flowers. The National Trust runs daily blue iguana safaris with a 2-hour guided tour that takes visitors behind the scenes of the breeding facility.

The unique blue iguana

Outdoor Activities and Specialized Holidays

The Cayman Islands are renowned for activities that focus on the sea, particularly scuba diving and snorkeling. All three islands have scores of superb diving and snorkeling sites. Non-divers can also experience marine wonders from a submarine with a glass viewing chamber. All the different types of watersports are available in Grand Cayman, as are day-sails aboard a variety of boats. The islands also offer excellent bird-watching opportunities with seven bird sanctuaries on Grand Cayman, as well as great hiking and fishing.

The exquisite Seven Mile Beach, Grand Cayman

BEACHES

This tri-island nation is blessed with plenty of white-sand beaches, all of which are public. The crown jewel is Grand Cayman's Seven Mile Beach, a spectacular beach. The crescent of white sand is lined with high-end hotels and condos, beachside restaurants, and watersport operators who offer plenty of activities. On the north tip of Grand Cayman, Cayman Kai has huts, hammocks, beach volleyball, and a good bar and grill. Rum Point's Beach, with calm, shallow water, is a bevy of action and the week-end favorite with the locals. Little Cayman's secluded Point of Sand on the eastern tip is a great picnicking spot and offers sweeping views of Cayman Brac. The wide beach at Little Cayman Beach Resort (see p111) is excellent. On the northern shore, Jacksons Point provides a perfect setting for shore diving and snorkeling.

Although Cayman Brac's shoreline is predominantly limestone, there are a few good beaches including Public Beach and the beach in front of Brac Reef Beach Resort (see p110) on West End Point.

WATERSPORTS

A large number of the islands' watersports centers are located at major hotels and on the most popular beaches. On Grand Cayman, they offer

Tour boat leaving the beach, Grand Cayman

a full array of watersports and rentals that include ocean kayaks, waverunners, Hobie Cats, aqua bikes, parasailing, water skiing, banana boat rides, and paddleboats.

The reef-protected shallows, stretching for 4 miles (7 km) off East End, are the best location for windsurfing of all levels. Other good spots are found at North Sound and along the west coast. **Red Sail Sports** at Morritt's Tortuga Resort rents equipment, and is the only operator that offers lessons to beginners.

Watersports on Little Cayman and Cayman Brac are primarily non-motorized. Most resorts provide kayaks, wind-surfing boards, and other gear.

DAY-SAILS AND BOAT TRIPS

For a day out on the Caribbean Sea, there are a gamut of options available in Grand Cayman. Sailing tours aboard the *Santa Clara* (also known as the *Nina II*), a 115-ft (35-m) replica of Christopher Columbus's ship, are operated by **The Columbus Foundation**.

Visitors can party with the **Pirates of the Caymans** on the *Jolly Roger*, a two-thirds-size replica of Columbus's *Nina*. The afternoon pirate adventure and sunset cruises include an open bar. Sailing excursions on a luxury cata-maran are available with Red Sail Sports. **Sail Cayman Ltd.** offers a range of sailing options. Travelers can paddle through tranquil lagoons and protected mangroves on a guided eco-adventure expedition organized by **Cayman Kayaks**. The unique **Oculus** is a 30-ft (9-m) glass-bottom speedboat with a huge window at its base that helps occu-pants view a larger area. Located in George Town, the National Trust orga-nizes guided boat tours through the Central Mangrove Wetlands that cover a large part of Grand Cayman.

For hotels and restaurants on these islands see pp110–11 and pp112–13

Diving off the Cayman Islands

Home to some of the best dive sites in the Caribbean, the Cayman Islands have been continually named among the world's top-five dive and snorkel destinations. The three islands feature pristine walls, shallow reefs, several shipwrecks, a variety of

Hawksbill turtle, Little Cayman

marine life, and more than 250 dive sites. Bloody Bay Wall, offshore Little Cayman, is a diver's mecca. Stingray City, off Grand Cayman, provides the rare opportunity to get up close and personal with dozens of Atlantic southern stingrays.

The wall is thick with bright sponges, hard and soft corals, and swaying sea fans.

DIVING BLOODY BAY WALL

Bloody Bay Marine Park is just a short swim from Little Cayman's north shore. The sheer vertical wall beginning at 18 ft (5 m), plunges to more than 6,000 ft (1,828 m). The wall boasts many formations, such as chimneys, canyons, and coral arches.

The visibility level is good down to 196 ft (60 m).

Schoolmaster snappers, *with distinctly yellow fins, are found just above the reefs. These fish are usually wary of divers.*

Yellow tube sponges *are common in the Cayman Islands, as are red rope, strawberry, and orange vase sponges.*

DIVING OFF THE OTHER TWO ISLANDS

Grand Cayman has around 130 dive sites, some just a short distance from the shore. Cayman Brac's 50-plus dive sites include four wrecks, the most famous being the 330-ft (100-m) Russian-built warship, *M/V Captain Keith Tibbetts*, sunk in 1996.

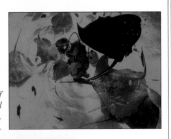

Stingray City (see p102), *in North Sound off Grand Cayman, offers a wonderful opportunity to swim with, or wade among, stingrays flocking here to feed.*

DIVE OPERATORS

Diving Spots
www.divecayman.ky
Ocean Frontiers
www.oceanfrontiers.com
Pirates Point
www.piratespointresort.com
Reef Divers
www.bracreef.com

Lost world of Atlantis, *off Cayman Brac, is an underwater attraction created by local sculptor J. Foots. This replica of the mythological city, with more than 100 sculptures, is popular with divers.*

Visitors looking out of Atlantis XI submarine, Grand Cayman

SUBMARINE RIDES

A great way to explore Grand Cayman's renowned coral reef and marine life, including tropical fish, is a trip on one of the island's submarines.

Atlantis Adventures offers rides aboard the *Atlantis XI* to depths of 100 ft (30 m). Their *Seaworld Observatory* semi-submarine is a floating observatory just 5 ft (2 m) below the ocean's surface. Its wall-to-wall glass viewing chamber offers spectacular views of the reefs and wrecks.

Another shallow option on Grand Cayman is the glass-hulled **Nautilus**, which takes visitors around the Caymans' waters to see the marine life.

BIRD-WATCHING

In peak season, up to 200 native and wintering bird species can be seen on the Cayman Islands. Grand Cayman has seven protected bird sanctuaries, including the Queen Elizabeth II Botanic Park *(see p104)*, Colliers Pond, and the Majestic Reserve. The National Trust's Governor Michael Gore Bird Sanctuary in Bodden Town is home to about one-third of the islands' recorded avian species. It also features an elevated walkway over a freshwater pond. A bird blind and interpretive signs make sighting the 60 species of water and wading birds easy. The **National Trust** offers weekly bird-watching tours to various sites. There are five seabird colonies on the sister islands. These are home to

the red-footed booby, brown booby, the magnificent frigate bird, white-tailed tropicbird, and summer visitor – the least tern. Nature Cayman arranges free bird-watching tours with nature guides.

Booby Pond Nature Reserve in Little Cayman is home to the largest breeding colony of red-footed boobies in the Western Hemisphere and the only breeding colony of frigate birds on the Cayman Islands.

Cayman Brac has a 180-acre (73-ha) parrot reserve where visitors may get a glimpse of one of the 350 endangered Brac parrots. Other good birding sites include the East Point bluff, with nesting brown boobies. The Westerly Ponds, Salt Water Pond, and the marshes are inhabited by waterbirds and other seasonal birds. Visitors can also see fruit bats hanging upside down in the Bat Cave *(see p105)*.

Brown boobies, Lighthouse Footpath, Cayman Brac

HIKING

Grand Cayman's most popular hike is the 2-mile (3-km) long Mastic Deep Forest Trail. The woodland has a variety of habitats ranging from wetland to dry forest, including trees that are unique to the Cayman Islands. Wildlife here also includes indigenous species as well as other animals such as butterflies, frogs, lizards, and hermit crabs. Guides for independent hikers are available at the National Trust, which also organizes weekly guided hikes. The trail is not suitable for children under six, the elderly, and the infirm.

Hiking trails are mapped in the Nature Tourism brochures, available at the airport. Hikers will come across ceramic interpretive signs and ecology panels on beach walks, woodland trails, and flora and fauna. Free guided hikes are also offered on the island.

On Cayman Brac, people enjoy walking along the 146-ft (44-m) bluff *(see p105)* from where a variety of birds can be spotted. The isle is peppered with trails including the Salt Water Pond hike and the well trodden Lighthouse Footpath on the eastern tip.

On Little Cayman, there are more than a dozen secluded beaches perfect for strolling, lagoons, mangrove forests, salt ponds, and wetlands to explore. The West End is home to the historic Salt Rock

View from a rugged limestone bluff, Cayman Brac

Nature Trail that once linked Blossom Village to the Salt Rock dock.

FISHING

Prized gamefish such as blue marlin, tuna, wahoo, and mahimahi can be caught year-round. Light tackle and fly-fishing for bonefish and tarpon challenge anglers, especially in the flats off Little Cayman. The **Cayman Islands Angling Club** arranges fishing tournaments and welcomes visitors. The islands have plenty of guides that offer half- and full-day deep-sea, bone, tarpon, and reef fishing. On Grand Cayman, Captain

Fishing in a lagoon, Cayman Brac

Ronald Ebanks of **Fly Fish Grand Cayman** organizes flyfishing and light tackle trips, as does **Fish Bones Guided Fly Fishing**. **Bayside Watersports** provide all types of fishing, from casting for bonefish and tarpon in the flats to wrestling marlin out at sea. Robin Walton's **Comfish** is a reputed fishing concessionaire on Cayman Brac.

GOLF

The 9-hole championship **Britannia Golf Club**, which can also be played as an 18-hole executive course, is one of only three Caribbean golf courses designed by golf legend Jack Nicklaus. The links-style course has all the natural challenges of a traditional seaside layout, including grassy mounds, rolling dunes, carries over water, and oversized bunkers. The other golf course on Grand Cayman is the 9-hole **Blue Tip** at the Ritz-Carlton (*see p111*). Designed by

Landscaped grounds, Britannia Golf Club, Grand Cayman

well-known golf course designer Greg Norman, it is only open to guests of the Ritz-Carlton. There are no golf courses on the sister islands.

HORSE-RIDING

Guided horse-rides along scenic trails or on one of Grand Cayman's many beautiful beaches are offered by **Pampered Ponies** or **Spirit of the West**. Private rides are also available. To make the ride more memorable, visitors can canter into the surf on horseback or sign up for an early morning or sunset ride.

DIRECTORY

WATERSPORTS

Red Sail Sports
Grand Cayman.
Tel 345 949 8745.
www.redsailcayman.com

DAY SAILS AND BOAT TRIPS

Cayman Kayaks
Grand Cayman.
Tel 345 926 4467.
www.caymankayaks.com

The Columbus Foundation
British Virgin Islands.
Tel 284 495 4618.
www.thenina.com

Oculus
c/o Blue Tip Watersports.
Tel 345 525 0668. www.
bluetipwatersports.com

Pirates of the Caymans
Grand Cayman. *Tel 345 945 7245.* www.pirates ofthecaymans.com

Sail Cayman Ltd.
Grand Cayman.
Tel 345 916 4333.
www.sailcayman.com

SUBMARINE RIDES

Atlantis Adventures
South Church St.,
George Town, Grand Cayman.
Tel 800 887 8571.
www.atlantis adventures.com

Nautilus
George Town,
Grand Cayman.
Tel 345 945 1355.
www.nautilus.ky

BIRD-WATCHING

National Trust
George Town,
Grand Cayman.
Tel 345 949 0121.
www.nationaltrust. org.ky

FISHING

Bayside Watersports
Morgans Harbor,
West Bay,
Grand Cayman.
Tel 345 949 3200.
www.bayside watersports.com

Cayman Islands Angling Club
Grand Cayman.
Tel 345 945 3131. www. fishcayman.com

Comfish
Cayman Brac.
Tel 345 948 2382.

Fish Bones Guided Fly Fishing
www.fish-bones.com

Fly Fish Grand Cayman
Coconut Place, West Bay Road, Grand Cayman.
Tel 345 947 3146. www. flyfishgrandcayman.com

GOLF

Blue Tip
The Ritz-Carlton,
Grand Cayman.
Tel 345 815 6500.

Britannia Golf Club
Grand Cayman.
Tel 345 745 4653. www. britannia-golf.com

HORSE-RIDING

Pampered Ponies
Grand Cayman.
Tel 345 945 2262.
www.ponies.ky

Spirit of the West
Grand Cayman.
Tel 345 916 6488.
www. cayman-horse-rides.com

Choosing a Hotel

Although Grand Cayman is reputed to be high-end, there are hotels and lodges to fit most budgets. Accommodations on the sister islands are smaller, with an easygoing tropical flavor. High season runs mid-December to mid-April, with rates dropping during the low season. Government tax is 10 percent and most hotels charge 10–15 percent gratuity in lieu of tipping.

PRICE CATEGORIES
The following price ranges are for a standard double room per night and all taxes included.

$ under $100
$$ $100–200
$$$ $200–300
$$$$ $300–400
$$$$$ over $400

CAYMAN ISLANDS

Villas and Condos of Cayman Islands
For those who prefer a home away from home with a little self-catering, the Cayman Islands have a broad range of condominiums and villas for every taste and budget. They are more private and have most basic facilities, with some facing the beach. Villa rental agencies are scattered around the isle and villas can be rented on a weekly basis. Prices are variable. Consult the Cayman's Department of Tourism's website *(see p115)* for further information.

Ritz-Carlton

Tropical Sunshine Suites

CAYMAN BRAC Brac Caribbean Beach Village $$
Tel 345 948 2265 **Rooms** 16

On a sandy beach in a quiet lagoon on the Brac's south shore sits this luxury condominium resort managed by Brac Vacations. Units are oceanfront, featuring two bedrooms, and two or three baths, with separate entries to each bedroom and family rooms. The hotel has an on-site restaurant, bar, Captain's Table. **www.866thebrac.com**

CAYMAN BRAC Brac Reef Beach Resort $$
Southside Road **Tel** 345 948 1323 **Fax** 345 948 1207 **Rooms** 40

Set on 4.5 acres (1.8 ha) of white-sand beach, this iconic resort is perfect for relaxing or a romantic dinner *(see p112)*. Rooms are painted in warm tropical colors and have basic facilities. Hammocks, pool, spa, Jacuzzi, bicycles, tennis facilities, fitness room, and boutique on-site. **www.bracreef.com**

GRAND CAYMAN Rocky Shore Guest House and Villas $$
30 Grass Piece Lane, West Bay **Tel** 345 926 0119 **Fax** 345 946 0118 **Rooms** 4

Chris and Trina Christian, owners of this cozy guesthouse, live on-site and attend to the guests. Three units have one bed, one bath and one has three beds, two baths. Includes Queen beds and family rooms. Massage treatments and traditional Cayman craft lessons, such as weaving, are also available. **www.getaway.ky**

GRAND CAYMAN Shangri-La B&B $$
1 Sticky Toffee Lane, West Bay **Tel** 345 526 1170 **Rooms** 8

This affordable, yet luxurious, bed-and-breakfast was twice voted the island's best B&B. Located beside a lake, it is a short distance from George Town and a 3-minute drive from Seven Mile Beach. Beautiful furniture and elegant decor. No children under 12. **www.shangrilabandb.com**

GRAND CAYMAN Turtle Nest Inn & Condos $$
166 Bodden Town Road, Bodden Town **Tel** 345 947 8665 **Fax** 345 947 6379 **Rooms** 7

This intimate, off-the-beaten-path beachfront inn with fully-furnished apartments and condos is a good alternative to a large hotel. Pleasing Spanish-style architecture, fresh water pool and sandy beach with superb snorkeling offshore. All except one unit has a full kitchen. **www.turtlenestinn.com**

GRAND CAYMAN Cobalt Coast Resort & Suites $$$
18 Sea Fan Drive, West Bay **Tel** 345 946 5656 **Fax** 345 946 5657 **Rooms** 18

With a secluded setting on the northwest shore near Boatswain's Beach, this small off-the-beaten-track hotel offers spectacular views over the Caribbean Sea. Breakfast included, meal plan available for lunch and dinner. Family rooms and 24-hour service. Dive shop and bar on-site. No private beach, but an ocean dock. **www.cobaltcoast.com**

GRAND CAYMAN Comfort Suites $$$
22 Piper Way, West Bay Road, Seven Mile Beach **Tel** 345 945 7300 **Fax** 345 945 7400 **Rooms** 108

The hotel has lovely one- and two-bedroom suites and family rooms with a kitchenette. The restaurant is open only during lunch and dinner and there is a bar on-site. Pool and Jacuzzi, fitness room, spa, and laundry facilities are available. There is also a dive shop on-site. **www.caymancomfort.com**

GRAND CAYMAN Ramada Grand Caymanian Resort $$$
278 Crighton Drive, Safehaven Crystal Harbor **Tel** 345 949 3100 **Fax** 345 949 3161 **Rooms** 88

With a cozy welcoming atmosphere, this beautiful villas-only resort is the only resort on the shores of Grand Cayman's North Sound Lagoon, next to the North Sound Golf Course. Includes family rooms, a full-service restaurant, tennis facilities, and kids club. 24-hour service available. **www.grandcaymanian.ky**

Key to Symbols *see back cover flap*

GRAND CAYMAN Sunset House
390 South Church Street, George Town **Tel** *345 949 7111* **Fax** *345 949 7101* **Rooms** *54*

This full-service, family-owned dive resort is a veteran of Grand Cayman tourism. Thatched-roof My Bar, the isle's largest outdoor bar, and SeaHarvest restaurant overlook the Caribbean Sea. Excellent shore diving right off the property, and custom boats. **www.sunsethouse.com**

GRAND CAYMAN Sunshine Suites Resort
West Bay Road, Seven Mile Beach **Tel** *345 949 3000* **Fax** *345 949 1200* **Rooms** *128*

Located across West Bay Road from the beach, this resort is next to the Ritz-Carlton and the North Sound Golf Course. All suites have full kitchens; family rooms available. Continental breakfast available at the restaurant/bar. Pool and beautiful manicured gardens. **www.sunshinesuites.com**

GRAND CAYMAN Compass Point Dive Resort
346 Austin Connolly Drive, East End **Tel** *345 947 7500* **Fax** *345 947 7600* **Rooms** *18*

One- and two-bedroom fully-equipped condominiums with ocean view, patio or balcony in secluded East End. There is a fresh water pool, beach with BBQ pit, kayaks, and kite-boarding instruction. On-site Ocean Frontiers Dive Shop has custom-built dive boats. **www.compasspoint.ky**

GRAND CAYMAN Grand Cayman Marriott Beach Resort
389 West Bay Road, Seven Mile Beach **Tel** *345 949 0088* **Fax** *345 949 0288* **Rooms** *295*

Centrally located on Seven Mile Beach, this hotel has a lovely oceanfront pool, Jacuzzi, 4 restaurants including oceanfront dining, family rooms, and spa. The lush gardens feature a turtle lagoon while the spacious rooms are painted in tropical hues, accented with dark woods. Includes 24-hour service. **www.marriottgrandcayman.com**

GRAND CAYMAN The Reef Resort
1 Queens Highway, East End **Tel** *345 947 0100* **Fax** *345 947 9920* **Rooms** *152*

Located in tranquil East End, Grand Cayman's only all beachfront-suite resort fronts a short stretch of white sand. Guaranteed great view and no crowds. Two freshwater pools, spa, tennis facilities, and diving with Ocean Frontiers. Includes meals and drinks. Family rooms available. **www.thereef.com**

GRAND CAYMAN Westin Casuarina Resort and Spa
Seven Mile Beach **Tel** *345 945 3800* **Fax** *345 949 5825* **Rooms** *343*

This resort features lush tropical gardens with waterfalls and fountains, large freshwater pools with a swim-up pool bar, whirlpools, spa, water activities stand, and dive shop. It has both indoor and outdoor restaurants, including Casa Havana, one of the best on the Caymans. Family rooms and 24-hour service available. **www.westincasuarina.com**

GRAND CAYMAN Coral Stone Club
West Bay Road, Seven Mile Beach **Tel** *345 945 5820* **Fax** *345 945 5917* **Rooms** *37*

This oceanfront vacation condo delivers luxury and tranquility in the heart of Seven Mile Beach. Both the three-story buildings have three bedrooms with attached baths, gourmet kitchens, and oceanfront terraces. No two condos are alike. Family rooms available. Includes tennis facilities. **www.coralstoneclub.com**

GRAND CAYMAN Grand Cayman Beach Suites
747 West Bay Road, Seven Mile Beach **Tel** *345 949 1234* **Fax** *345 949 8528* **Rooms** *53*

Rooms have seaview, beach, and two swimming pools, one with a swim-up bar, the other with whirlpool. Includes a 24/7 fitness center, European boutique spa, watersports facilities, on-site tennis and dive center and catamaran trips, and the Britannia golf course designed by Jack Nicklaus. 24-hour service. **www.grand-cayman-beach-suites.com**

GRAND CAYMAN Ritz-Carlton
West Bay Road, Seven Mile Beach **Tel** *345 943 9000* **Fax** *345 943 9001* **Rooms** *365*

With a prime location on Seven Mile Beach, the Ritz-Carlton delivers the luxury and service for which the brand is renowned. Five restaurants *(see p112)*, several bars, family rooms and 24-hour room service. Also includes a spa, Silver Rain, a tennis program designed by Nick Bollettieri, and a Greg Norman golf course. **www.ritzcarlton.com**

LITTLE CAYMAN Paradise Villas
Guy Banks Road **Tel** *345 948 0001* **Fax** *345 948 0002* **Rooms** *12*

One-bedroom oceanfront villas with pullout couch in the living area. Each unit has a large front and back porch, and a well-equipped kitchenette. The grocery store is a short walk away. On-site bar. Bicycles are available for rent. Hammocks are located at the water's edge. **www.paradisevillas.com**

LITTLE CAYMAN Little Cayman Beach Resort
Blossom Village **Tel** *345 948 1033* **Fax** *345 948 1024* **Rooms** *40*

This lovely south-shore resort is located on a private white-sand beach with shaded hammocks. Bar, pool, Jacuzzi, floodlit tennis court, beach volleyball, basketball, darts, and a fitness room. Rentals of sailboats, kayaks, windsurfers and bicycles. Reef Divers, on-site, offers valet dive service. **www.littlecayman.com**

LITTLE CAYMAN Pirate's Point Resort
Guy Banks Road **Tel** *345 948 1010* **Fax** *345 948 1011* **Rooms** *11*

A simple and relaxing dive resort *(see p113)*. Former Texan owner, Gladys Howard, is a delight and enjoys interacting with her guests, as does her long-time staff. Personal attention from the top-notch dive crew. Freshwater pool, Jacuzzi, bar, and hammocks. All inclusive option. No children under 5. **www.piratespointresort.com**

Where to Eat & Nightlife

Grand Cayman is the hub for fine dining and its restaurants, most of which are on the popular western half, serve a wide variety of cuisines. This is also where the best nightlife is, although it never gets as hectic as on the larger Caribbean islands. Cayman Brac and Little Cayman are usually quieter and some of the restaurants here serve traditional Caymanian dishes.

PRICE CATEGORIES
Prices are per person for two courses and a half-bottle of wine (where available), including 15% service charge (there is no tax).

$ under $10
$$ $10–15
$$$ $15–25
$$$$ $25–35
$$$$$ over $35

RESTAURANTS

Seafood Specialty
Fresh fish and seafood dominate Cayman menus, including lobster, conch, wahoo, and tuna. Fish is served baked or stewed with tomatoes, onions, and peppers, but fish 'n fritters, seasoned and fried with dough balls in coconut oil, is the favorite. The islands' national dish is green sea turtle (meat from the turtle farm, not wild), often cooked in a stew.

Abacus Restaurant

Deckers Grille & Lounge

CAYMAN BRAC The Grand Palm Restaurant　🅥 🔳 ▦ 🗇 ✎ 🅱　$$$$$

Brac Reef Beach Resort, West End **Tel** *345 948 1323*

This restaurant largely caters to divers staying at the resort *(see p110)* and offers buffet-style dining with a different menu daily. The food is fresh, including home-made soups, entrées, and gourmet desserts. The resort also has the lively Tipsy Turtle Pub with a large selection including wraps, salads, steak, burgers, and pasta.

GRAND CAYMAN Vivine's Kitchen　▦ ✎ 🅱　$$

Gun Bay area, East End **Tel** *345 947 7435*

Run by Ms. Vivine Watler, this budget restaurant sells excellent local food in the quiet East End. Favorites include the stew beef and fresh catch-of-the-day. There is a fantastic view of the sea from the restaurant's outdoor dining area, perched on a hilltop high above the shore, and there are hammocks to relax in after the meal.

GRAND CAYMAN Icoa Fine Foods　🅥 🍴 🔳 ▦ ✎ 🅱　$$$

10–11 Seven Mile Shops, West Bay Road, Seven Mile Beach **Tel** *345 945 1915*

The hallmark of this bakery, deli, and restaurant is fresh, quality food in a modern, casual setting. Everything is made from scratch, including decadent pastries, cakes, and breads. Specialties are local fish and *aglio e olio* (traditional Italian pasta) with local produce. Open for breakfast and lunch. Reservations advisable.

GRAND CAYMAN Abacus Restaurant, Bar & Lounge　🅥 🍴 🔳 ▦ 🅱　$$$$$

Camana Bay **Tel** *345 623 8282*

This chic restaurant is the newest offering by the owners of Deckers and Prime and the first restaurant to open in Camana Bay. Sip a perfect Bellini at the trendy bar or outdoor lounge or watch the chefs' theatrical performance in the open kitchen. Open for lunch and dinner (except Sundays). Reserve beforehand.

GRAND CAYMAN Blue by Eric Ripert　🅥 🍴 🔳 ▦ ✎ 🅱　$$$$$

The Ritz-Carlton, West Bay Road, Seven Mile Beach **Tel** *345 943 9000*

Set in the Ritz-Carlton *(see p111)* and created by three-Michelin-starred chef Eric Ripert, Blue is rated by the American Automobile Association as one of the Caribbean's three Five Diamond restaurants. Conch *ceviche* and snapper baked in a Puerto Rican stew are signature dishes. There is a three-course prix fixe or six-course tasting menu. Book in advance.

GRAND CAYMAN Copper Falls Steak House　🅥 🍴 🔳 ✎ 🅱　$$$$$

43 Canal Point Drive, Seven Mile Beach **Tel** *345 945 4755*

This restaurant is known for steaks, topped with a choice of six sauces. Entrées also include a martini or beer. Copper-clad waterfalls, earth tone colors, and hand-painted, three-dimensional metal art adorn the walls and there are comfortable chairs and booths. Reservations advisable.

GRAND CAYMAN Deckers Grille & Lounge　🅥 🍴 🔳 ▦ 🅱　$$$$$

West Bay Road, Seven Mile Beach **Tel** *345 945 6600*

This restaurant with its authentic red British phone booth and double-decker bus out front cannot be missed. It is a good place to relax with a mojito and listen to live music Thursday through Saturday evenings. Dine outdoors on the terrace or indoors on Caribbean/Mediterranean fusion cuisine. Reservations recommended.

GRAND CAYMAN Edoardo's　🅥 🍴 🔳 🅱　$$$$$

Coconut Plaza, West Bay Road, Seven Mile Beach **Tel** *345 945 4408*

A long-time local favorite, this Italian restaurant has a warm and friendly ambience. Delicious dishes include fresh mussels, linguine *ai frutti di mare* (mixed seafood), and *filet cambozola* (cheese). For dessert, try the banana toffee pie. Excellent wine list. Lunch is Monday to Saturday, while dinner is daily. Reserve beforehand.

Key to Symbols *see back cover flap*

GRAND CAYMAN Grand Old House

South Church Street, George Town **Tel** *345 949 9333*

This classy restaurant and its seaside veranda is perfect for a leisurely lunch or romantic dinner, complete with piano music. Originally a Caribbean great house, the Grand Old House was built in 1908. Today it is one of the island's finest restaurants, with an award-winning wine list. Book in advance.

GRAND CAYMAN Luca

871 West Bay Road, at Caribbean Club, Seven Mile Beach **Tel** *345 623 4550*

Casual fine dining featuring contemporary Italian dishes and over 400 wines, some available nowhere else on Cayman. This upscale restaurant overlooks the Caribbean Club's infinity pool and Seven Mile Beach. Open Monday to Saturday for lunch and daily for dinner. Reservations highly recommended.

GRAND CAYMAN Mezza Restaurant & Bar

233 West Bay Road, Seven Mile Beach **Tel** *345 946 3992*

Popular for its chic atmosphere, this restaurant and bar offers Mediterranean cuisine. An extensive wine list complements specialties such as tuna roulade, hoisin ribs, and steak. All you can eat "Ocean Harvest" menu on Wednesday and à la carte brunch on Sundays. Book in advance.

GRAND CAYMAN Prime, Brazilian Churrascaria Steak House

Governors Square, West Bay Road, Seven Mile Beach **Tel** *345 623 7272*

Eat all you can at this authentic Brazilian *churrascaria*. Dining begins with a two-level appetizer buffet, followed by succulent and perfectly carved Brazilian grilled meats and fresh fish and seafood. Exceptional wine list with a Sunday champagne brunch. Child-friendly. Reservations advisable.

GRAND CAYMAN Ragazzi Ristorante & Pizzeria

Buckingham Square, West Bay Road, Seven Mile Beach **Tel** *345 945 3484*

Recommended by locals as "tried and true", Ragazzi is the spot for relaxed Italian dining and great cuisine including seafood. Cayman's only wood-burning brick oven turns out delicious thin-crust pizzas. The wine list offers a broad range of vintages at good prices. Open for lunch and dinner daily. Reserve in advance.

GRAND CAYMAN Ristorante Pappagallo

444b Conch Point Road, Seven Mile Beach, West Bay **Tel** *345 949 1119*

Nestled on the shore of a secluded private lagoon, the thatched building, with a Mexican palapa-style roof, sets the perfect tone of tropical elegance. Excellent Italian food with a Caribbean flair, like fresh pastas and seafood, and delicious steaks. The wine list is excellent. Open only for dinner. Reservations required.

GRAND CAYMAN The Wharf Restaurant and Bar

West Bay Road # 43, Seven Mile Beach **Tel** *345 949 2231*

Visitors flock to the seaside Wharf not only for fresh fish and seafood, but for Tarpon Fish Feeding at 9pm. Help feed the showy big fish, and then dine on the terrace with a beautiful ocean view. Try the signature basil and pistachio Chilean sea bass. Free salsa lessons Tuesday 9pm, followed by Salsa Night. Book early.

LITTLE CAYMAN Hungry Iguana Restaurant

Guy Banks Road, Blossom Village **Tel** *345 948 0000*

The only à la carte restaurant on Little Cayman is also the only one with oceanfront dining. It is the place locals go to, either for drinks in the large bar area with big screen TV, or dining inside or out on the patio. There is also a non-smoking dining room. It is also the only restaurant where reservations are not required.

LITTLE CAYMAN Pirate's Point

Guy Banks Road, Pirate's Point Resort **Tel** *345 948 1010*

With owner Gladys Howard a Cordon Bleu-trained chef, it is no surprise that this kitchen serves the isle's tastiest food. Non-guests are welcome for the fixed-price buffet dinner, including wine, hosted by Gladys *(see p111)*, but booking must be done at least the day before. Includes home-made Cayman dishes and international cuisine.

BARS AND CLUBS

Grand Cayman has several late-night spots. Most major hotels offer high season entertainment including live music and dancing, or take to the sea for a dinner/dance cruise. There are many nightclubs playing good music as well. The sister island bars are fun, casual affairs, where both visitors and locals go to "lime" (hang out).

Bar at Deckers Grille & Lounge

RECOMMENDED PLACES TO GO

Beach Nuts Bar
Little Cayman Beach Resort. (Friday night karaoke.)

Coral Isle
South Side, Cayman Brac. (Outdoor bar, pool table, jukebox.)

Deckers Grille & Lounge
Seven Mile Beach, Grand Cayman. (Live bands.)

Matrix
Seven Mile Beach, Grand Cayman. (Dance floor, loud music.)

Reef Grill at Royal Palms
Seven Mile Beach, Grand Cayman. (Dancing on the beach.)

The Wharf
Seven Mile Beach, Grand Cayman. (Free salsa lessons, live bands.)

Practical Information

Thanks to a flourishing tourism industry and an equally prosperous banking sector, Caymanians enjoy one of the highest standards of living in the world. With the Cayman Island dollar (CI$) worth more than the US dollar, the islands are an expensive destination. The largest and most developed of the islands, Grand Cayman attracts the maximum number of visitors. Though Hurricanes Ivan (2004) and Paloma (2008) dealt a severe blow, the islands are being rebuilt rapidly.

Taxis outside Owen Roberts International Airport, Grand Cayman

WHEN TO GO

December to April is when most people visit the Cayman Islands. The year-round temperature ranges between 70–90° F (21–32° C). The dry season lasts from November to April, while the rainy season runs mid-May through October. August to October are prime hurricane months. The islands' unique Hurricane Guarantee covers any cancellations made prior to arrival and offers compensation if vacation time is cut short because of inclement weather.

GETTING THERE

All international flights arrive at Grand Cayman's Owen Roberts International Airport. Scheduled flights to Grand Cayman are available on **Air Canada**, **Air Jamaica**, **American Airlines**, **British Airways**, **Delta**, **United Airlines**, **US Airways**, and **Spirit Airlines**. **Cayman Airways** is the national flag carrier, offering flights from the US. A host of charters also provide non-stop flights from US cities.

Inter-island daily service from Grand Cayman to the sister islands is provided by Cayman Airways and its affiliate Cayman Airways Express. Charter flights can be booked with **Island Air**. There is no ferry service.

DOCUMENTATION

A valid passport is required, along with a return ticket. British, Canadian and US nationals do not need a visa to enter the Caymans, but many other countries, including several Caribbean states, do. The **Immigration Department** website has details of countries requiring and those exempted from visas. A departure tax is included in the airline ticket.

VISITOR INFORMATION

The **Cayman Islands Department of Tourism** has its head office in Grand Cayman and a branch in Cayman Brac. **District Administration** has information on the sister islands. The **Tourism Attraction**

Board and **Sister Islands Tourism Association** also provide useful information.

HEALTH AND SECURITY

The Caymans are one of the Caribbean's safest destinations, with a low crime rate. However, petty theft and pickpocketing does occur, and it is advisable to keep valuables in the hotel safe. The islands are hassle-free, with no street or beach vendors.

The **Cayman Islands' Health Services Complex** has modern facilities, and is well-equipped to deal with emergencies. The state-run **Faith Hospital** is in Cayman Brac, while Little Cayman has the **Little Cayman Clinic**. Medical insurance is mandatory. In serious cases, patients are often sent to larger islands with better facilities.

BANKING AND CURRENCY

The Cayman Islands has its own currency, the CI dollar (CI$), but the US dollar is accepted everywhere and there is a fixed rate of exchange. Major credit cards and traveler's checks are widely accepted. ATM machines are available all over Grand Cayman. There is only one on Cayman Brac and none on Little Cayman. The latter has just one bank that opens only on Mondays and Thursdays from 9am–2:30pm.

COMMUNICATIONS

International Direct Dialing is available from most hotels on the Cayman Islands. The area code is 345, followed by a seven-digit local number. Public phones are available throughout the islands. Prepaid calling cards and mobiles for hire can be found at **Lime Cable & Wireless** offices. **Digicel** also provides

A fully equipped fire engine, Grand Cayman

mobile service. Internet access is available at airports, most hotels, and some restaurants. Cyber cafés are found in most larger towns.

TRANSPORT

Visitors must be at least 21 years to drive and have a temporary driving permit issued at any car rental firm. Vehicles can be hired from **Coconut Car Rentals** on Grand Cayman; **CB Rent-A-Car** at the Cayman Brac airport; and from **McLaughlin Car & Moped Rentals**, the only car rental firm in Little Cayman, although scooters can also be rented from **Scooten! Scooters!**. Driving is on the left. Main roads are paved and in good condition.

Taxis are readily available at all resorts and airports. There is a taxi stand in George Town.

Daily public bus service on Grand Cayman runs from 6am until midnight depending on the route and the day.

Duty-free shop, George Town, Grand Cayman

SHOPPING

Shops selling duty-free goods are found on all the islands. Traditional crafts made of leather, thatch, wood, and shell are the best locally-made buys, as are the local art and food products. Look out for Caymanite (an indigenous semi-precious stone) art and jewelry. The **Cayman Craft Market** is a good place to buy local products.

LANGUAGE

English is the official language of the Cayman Islands.

ELECTRICITY

The electrical system on the Cayman Islands delivers 110 volts at 60 cycles. US-style plugs are used. European appliances will require adaptors and transformers.

TIME

The Cayman Islands are on Eastern Standard Time (EST), 5 hours behind Greenwich Mean Time (GMT). The islands do not observe daylight savings.

GETTING MARRIED

Visiting couples can marry the day they arrive. It is possible to arrange for a marriage official and apply for a non-resident's marriage license, granted by the Governor, in advance. Contact the **District Commissioner's Office**.

DIRECTORY

GETTING THERE

Air Canada
www.aircanada.com

Air Jamaica
www.airjamaica.com

American Airlines
www.aa.com

British Airways
www.ba.com

Cayman Airways
Tel 345 949 8200.
www.cayman
airways.com

Delta
www.delta.com

Island Air
www.islandair.ky

Spirit Airlines
www.spiritair.com

United Airlines
www.united.com

US Airways
www.usairways.com

DOCUMENTATION

Immigration Department
Tel 345 949 8344.
www.immigration.gov.ky

VISITOR INFORMATION

Cayman Islands Department of Tourism
Tel 345 949 0623
(Grand Cayman).
Tel 345 948 1649
(Cayman Brac).
www.caymanislands.ky

District Administration
Cayman Brac.
Tel 345 948 2222.
www.itsyoursto
explore.com

Sister Islands Tourism Association
www.sisterislands.com

Tourism Attraction Board
Tel 345 949 6999.
www.tab.ky

HEALTH AND SECURITY

Cayman Islands' Health Services Complex
Grand Cayman.
Tel 345 949 8600.

Faith Hospital
Cayman Brac.
Tel 345 948 2243.

Little Cayman Clinic
Little Cayman.
Tel 345 948 0072.

Police and Fire
Tel 911.

COMMUNICATIONS

Digicel
www.digicelcayman.com

Lime Cable & Wireless
www.time4lime.com

TRANSPORT

CB Rent-A-Car
www.cbrentacar.com

Coconut Car Rentals
www.coconutcarrentals.
com

McLaughlin Car & Moped Rentals
Little Cayman.
Tel 345 948 1000.

Scooten! Scooters!
www.scooten
scooters.com

SHOPPING

Cayman Craft Market
George Town,
Grand Cayman.

GETTING MARRIED

District Commissioner's Office
George Town,
Grand Cayman.
Tel 345 948 2222.

Exploring Turks and Caicos

A group of islands, Turks and Caicos lie southeast of The Bahamas and northeast of Cuba. Providenciales, the westernmost isle, has the lion's share of beach resorts, spread along Grace Bay. Most of the island's 22,000 inhabitants live on Providenciales. The capital, Cockburn Town, is located on Grand Turk, the easternmost isle. Lightly-populated North, Middle, East, and tiny South Caicos are mostly scrub-covered and teem with birds. Flat as pancakes, the isles sit atop an underwater plateau with walls that plunge to the bottom of near fathomless ocean trenches.

West Caicos Marine National Park
This park protects iguanas and birdlife. It is also a world-renowned scuba diving venue with great wall dives, tunnels, and pelagic sealife.

Three Mary Cays Sanctuary
Parrot Cay
Dellis Cay
Fort George Cay
Pine Cay
Little Water Cay
Wheeland Beach
Northwest Point
Pigeon Pond
Blue Hills
GRACE BAY
Princess Alexandra Land and Sea National Park
Downtown
PROVIDENCIALES
Chalk Sound National Park
Discovery Bay
Conch Farm
Caicos
Long Bay Beach

Whitby
Whitby Beach
Cottage Pond
Kew *Flamingo Pond*
Bottle Creek
NORTH CAICOS
East Ba Nation

North, Middle And East Caicos

MID CAI

West Caicos Lake Catherine
Yankee Town
WEST CAICOS MARINE NATIONAL PARK

North, Middle and East Caicos Nature Reserve
Spanning three Caicos islands, this nature reserve protects the habitat of manatees, iguanas, flamingos, and scores of other bird species.

The luxurious Grace Bay Club, Providenciales

SEE ALSO

• *Where to Stay* pp126–7

• *Where to Eat & Nightlife* pp128–9

GETTING AROUND
The Turks and Caicos have a total land area of 166 sq miles (430 sq km) scattered across 10,000 sq miles (26,000 sq km) of ocean. The isles are connected by a few ferry services and scheduled, small plane charters. A new bridge connects North and Middle Caicos. Providenciales is served by tourist taxis and cars. Minivans offer communal taxi service on Grand Turk and on the smaller isles, where scooter and bicycle rentals are offered, although Grand Turk is small enough to walk around town.

Hobie Cats lined up on the cottony sands of Providenciales

SIGHTS AT A GLANCE

Grace Bay 2
Grand Turk 7
North Caicos 4
Middle Caicos 5
Providenciales 1
Salt Cay 10
South Caicos 6
West Caicos Marine National Park 3

Featured Hotels and Resorts

Grand Turk Inn 8
Salt Raker Inn 9

Other Hotels and Resorts

Amanyara 1
Blue Horizon Resort 8
Gansevoort 3
Grace Bay hotels 4
The Meridian Club 5
Miramar Resort 2
North Caicos hotels 7
Osprey Beach Hotel 10
Parrot Cay 6
South Caicos Ocean & Beach Resort 9

Quiet Blue Horizon Resort in Middle Caicos

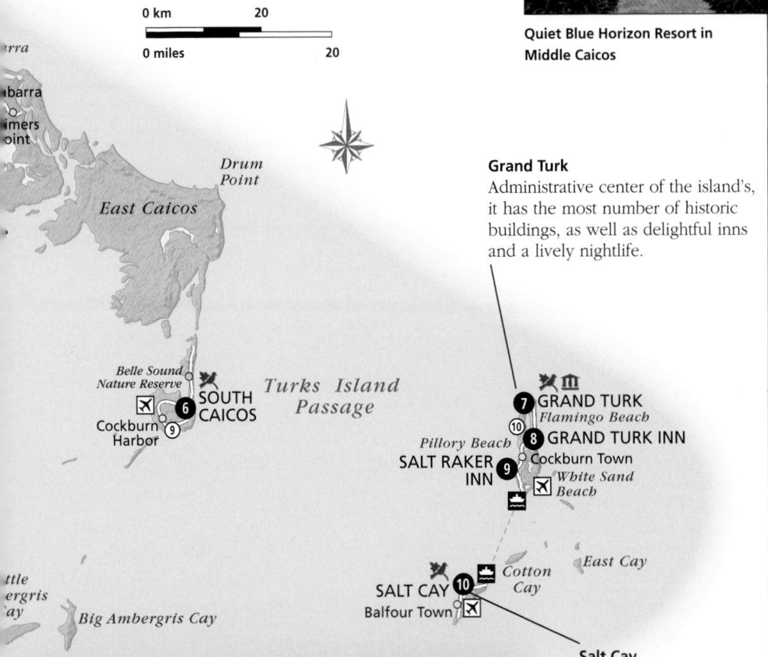
0 km 20
0 miles 20
Drum Point
East Caicos
Belle Sound Nature Reserve
6 SOUTH CAICOS
Cockburn Harbor
9
Turks Island Passage
7 GRAND TURK
Flamingo Beach
10
8 GRAND TURK INN
Pillory Beach
Cockburn Town
SALT RAKER INN 9
White Sand Beach
East Cay
Cotton Cay
SALT CAY 10
Balfour Town
Big Ambergris Cay

Grand Turk
Administrative center of the island's, it has the most number of historic buildings, as well as delightful inns and a lively nightlife.

Salt Cay
The saltpans here offer tremendous birding. Humpback whales frolic off the north shore, and can be seen from a close distance.

Colorful houses along the seafront of Cockburn Town, Grand Turk

KEY

Minor road

Ferry route

The sprawling Caicos Conch Farm, eastern Providenciales

Providenciales ❶

Second westernmost isle of Turks and Caicos. 🏛 15,000. ✈ 🚢
🛈 Stubbs Diamond Plaza, 649 946 4970. 🌐 Big Blue Unlimited, 649 946 4970. 🎏 Kite Flying Competition (Mar); Music and Cultural Festival (Jul–Aug).

This ox-jaw-shaped isle is renowned for the crescent of never-ending beach at Grace Bay. "Downtown" is the island's business center and has a few shops and offices.

The isle tapers east from Northwest Point, that is pinned by a lighthouse and reached by rough sandy trails. The entire west shore is protected within Northwest Point Marine National Park and Pigeon Pond and Frenchman's Creek Nature Reserve, sheltering wetlands, mangroves, tidal flats, and offshore reefs. Chalk Sound National Park, along the south shore, has beautiful blue waters. For a fine view, head to South Rock, where rock slabs are carved with mariner's markings from the 18th and 19th centuries. At the island's eastern tip, **Caicos Conch Farm** raises edible mollusks and introduces visitors to the life-cycle of the queen conch.

Excursion boats depart from near the farm for snorkeling and party cruises, and to a string of tiny cays off the east coast, including Little Water Cay, crawling with iguanas. Pine Cay is a private jewel and setting for The Meridian Club (see p127), an all-inclusive family resort with sports facilities that range

from Hobie Cats to the resort's own yacht. Wrapped in snowy sands and turquoise waters, Parrot Cay, to the northeast of Providenciales, hosts an eponymous resort (see p127) with deluxe rooms decked out in minimalist decor, and a fine-dining restaurant. Guest quarters are a blaze of whites and feature romantic canopy beds. Its luxurious COMO Shambhala spa, on a 2-mile (3-km) long beach, is a perfect place to relax.

Caicos Conch Farm
Leeward Hwy.
Tel 649 946 5330.
⏰ 9am–4pm Mon–Fri, 9am–2pm Sat & hols. 🈲 🚻

Grace Bay ❷

🏖 N coast of Providenciales. 🏄 🚤 🚣 ⛱

This stupendously beautiful bay, curling along the north shore for 12 miles (19 km), is

Watersports at the excellent Grace Bay

lined with talcum-white sands shelving into shallows and some of the best snorkeling spots on the island. This is all protected within the 6,500-acre (2,630-ha) Princess Alexandra Land and Sea National Park, along with iguanas, ospreys, and a variety of marine life.

The beach, tufted with wispy grasses peeping up from sand dunes, is lined with upscale hotels and has plenty of watersports, but there are a lot of quiet spots too.

Among the most deluxe hotel options on Grace Bay, the Andalusian-style Grace Bay Club (see p127) is acclaimed for its Anacaona restaurant (see p128). Sprawling over 11 acres (4 ha), the all-suite resort offers tennis and watersports among many other facilities.

West Caicos Marine National Park ❸

15 miles (24 km) SW of Providenciales. 🚤 hire a boat in Providenciales, or join an excursion.

A tiny island of 9 sq miles (23 sq km), West Caicos is inhabited by iguanas, lizards, and birds. In the 1890s, the isle's Yankee Town was the center for salt extraction. Its ruins, including railroads and old buildings, still stand. Near the town, at Lake Catherine Nature Reserve, bird-watchers can spot flamingos while divers can explore the West Caicos wall that plunges to a 7,000 ft (2,133 m) abyss.

An angler with a bonefish, a popular catch

BONEFISH

An easily spooked, bottom-feeding habitué of shallow inshore waters, this relative of the herring has silvery flanks, well-camouflaged against the sandy bottoms. It grows to 10 pounds (4 kg) and is one of the most feisty of an angler's quarries. Once hooked, bonefish typically race off and put up an uncanny fight. It is also known as the phantom and can be caught year-round without a license.

unpopulated **East Caicos**, a habitat for several species of birds, including flamingos.

Fishing boats docked at Cockburn Harbor, South Caicos

North Caicos ❹

12 miles (19 km) NE of Providenciales. 👥 1,900. ✈
🚤 between Providenciales and North Caicos, 6:30am–5:45pm Mon–Sat, 9am–4:30pm Sun, 649 946 5406.
🎉 North Caicos Extravaganza (Jun), Festarama Festival (Jul).

With its dense and lush vegetation, North Caicos is the most beautiful of all the Turks and Caicos islands. A short distance from Kew village in the north, Wades Green Plantation recalls the days when sisal and cotton were grown, and ancient cannons still stand sentinel on Fort George Cay nearby. Hotels are concentrated at Whitby Beach, the best of several ultra-white sands, while a boat ride delivers visitors to East Bay Islands National Park, where iguanas and marine turtles can be seen.
   Birders flock to Cottage Pond (see p121), a sinkhole with jade waters, to see ducks and grebes; and to the appropriately named Flamingo Pond to observe flamingos. Just offshore is Three Mary Cays Sanctuary (see p121), which is a habitat for ospreys.

Middle Caicos ❺

15 miles (24 km) E of North Caicos. 👥 300. ✈

This sparsely populated isle was once a major center of the Lucayan Amerindian civilization, remains of which can be seen at the Armstrong Pond Village Historical Site, one of the many pre-Columbian sites here. This, and some plantation ruins, are accessible via the well-signed Middle Caicos Reserve and Trail System. Stalactites and stalagmites can be admired in **Conch Bar Caves National Park**, a haven for bats. The remote Vine Point and Ocean Hole Nature Reserve, on the south coast, is named in part for its massive blue hole and thrills divers and birders. Mudjin Harbor Beach, near the main settlement of Conch Bar, is framed by dramatic cliffs cusping sheltered coves. Bambarra Beach offers superb snorkeling and hosts the annual Valentine's Day Cup, a sailboat race using scale models handcrafted by local artisans.

Environs

Located about 2 miles (3 km) east of Middle Caicos is the

South Caicos ❻

15 miles (24 km) SE of Middle Caicos. 👥 1,200. ✈ 🚤
🎉 South Caicos Regatta (May).

This diminutive and arid isle, almost entirely lacking in resorts, combines superb wall dives and excellent bonefishing in the jade-blue Belle Sound Nature Reserve and Admiral Cockburn Nature Reserve. Pink flamingos flock around the briny salinas ponds, within sight of the down-at-heels town of **Cockburn Harbor**. The town was severely damaged by Hurricane Ike in 2008. Every May, the streets of Cockburn Harbor burst into life for the South Caicos Regatta, which includes speedboat races, beauty pageants, float parades, and donkey races.

Entrance of the Conch Bar Caves National Park, Middle Caicos

Post office building in Cockburn Town, Grand Turk

Grand Turk [7]

120 miles (195 km) E of Providenciales. 👥 *3,700.* ✈ ⛴ ℹ *Front Street, 649 946 2321.* 🎉 *Grand Turk Heineken Game Fishing Tournament (Jul).*

The small, semi-arid Grand Turk is an unlikely outpost for Turks and Caicos' capital, **Cockburn Town**. Strolling the streets of its charming historic center casts a time-warp spell. Bermudan-style limestone-and-clapboard structures line the sand-blown streets. Built of ships' timber, 19th-century Guinep House hosts the **Turks and Caicos National Museum**, with especially fine exhibits from the Molasses Reef shipwreck dating from 1513.

The town overlooks coral-tinged Pillory Beach, one of a string of beaches lining the windward shore. Locals believe that Christopher Columbus made his first New World landfall here on October 12, 1492. The offshore reef is protected within Columbus Landfall Marine National Park. The leeward shore is also sprinkled with long, lonesome beaches with soft powdery sands. Two of the most beautiful beaches are Flamingo Beach, in the north, and White Sand Beach, in the south. Between them, South Creek National Park protects precious mangroves.

🏛 **Turks and Caicos National Museum**
Front Street. ***Tel*** *649 946 2160.*
🕐 *9am–4pm Mon–Fri, 9am–1pm Sat.* 📷 ♿ *ground floor only.* 🛍
www.tcmuseum.org

Grand Turk Inn [8]

✉ Cockburn Town, Grand Turk. ***Tel*** *649 946 2827.* ***Fax*** *649 946 2827.* $$$ *5 rooms.* 💳 ⛱ [W]
www.grandturkinn.com

Tucked behind a white picket fence, this lovingly restored former Methodist manse in traditional vernacular style is an architectural charmer. The suites of this adults-only inn are accessed by a wrought-iron staircase and are furnished with a combination of antique and contemporary pieces, all with stunning views.

Salt Raker Inn [9]

✉ Cockburn Town, Grand Turk. ***Tel*** *649 946 2260.* ***Fax*** *649 946 2263.* $$$ *13 rooms.* 🍴 💳 ⛱
www.hotelsaltraker.com

Originating in the 1850s as a shipwright's home, this two-story, white-and-blue structure in Bermudan style has a marvelous oceanfront setting. It is a tempting place to relax over lunch in the garden restaurant and to listen to live music on Friday evening.

Salt Cay [10]

8 miles (13 km) SW of Grand Turk. 👥 *200.* ✈ ⛴ *bi-weekly ferry between Grand Turk and Salt Cay.*
www.saltcay.org

An arid, arrow-shaped speck of an isle, Salt Cay is named for the salt ponds initiated in the 17th century with windmills to pump water from the sea. Many of the warehouses, homes, and other limestone structures built by Bermudan salt traders have been restored, making tiny Balfour Town an adorable capsule of vernacular industrial architecture. Most locals get around by bicycle or golf cart; cars are virtually unknown.

The salt ponds are one of the Caribbean's premier sites for spotting ospreys and wading birds. In winter, humpback whales gather in the warm waters southeast of Salt Cay and are easily seen close to shore.

Environs

In 1790 a storm claimed HMS *Endymion*, a British man-o'-war that sank south of Salt Cay. Today, the wreck of the 44-gun frigate is a world-renowned diving site *(see p123)* and draws divers keen to explore among its remains and the unspoilt habitat that surrounds it.

HUMPBACK WHALES

These gentle leviathans of the deep gather every January to March to breed and give birth in the warm, shallow waters of the Silver and Mouchoir Banks, southeast of Salt Cay. Despite their massive bulk, up to 50 ft (15 m) long, they often leap clear of the water. Calves are fully functional at birth and feed on up to 150 gallons (570 liters) of protein-rich milk a day. By April the whales migrate north to their feeding grounds in the North Atlantic.

Humpback whale calf with its mother in the ocean waters

For hotels and restaurants on these islands see pp126–7 and pp128–9

Birding in the Turks and Caicos

These islands are renowned for their waterfowl and seabirds, and more than 190 bird species can be seen, including cuckoos, doves, and warblers. About 275 sq miles (712 sq km) of habitat are protected, notably within the North, Middle and East Caicos

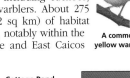

A common yellow warbler

Nature Reserve, designated an International Ramsar Site and spanning scrub forests, 12 types of wetland, mangroves, and intertidal flats on the southern halves of North, Middle, and East Caicos islands. This site is home to about 61 waterfowl species.

Cottage Pond Nature Reserve *is a magnet for waterfowl such as West Indian whistling ducks, which are resident birds year-round.*

Three Mary Cays Sanctuary, *on North Caicos, is a nesting site for ospreys.*

North, Middle and East Caicos Nature Reserve *is a habitat for brown pelicans, West Indian flamingos, common terns, and lesser yellowlegs.*

South Creek National Park is an important habitat for wading birds such as dowitchers and sandpipers.

Vine Point and Ocean Hole Nature Reserve has Turks and Caicos' largest breeding colony of frigate birds.

0 km — 15
0 miles — 15

Caicos Passage

Whitby
Kew
North Caicos — Bottle Creek
Providenciales — Grace Bay
Downtown
Discovery Bay
West Caicos
Conch Bar
Middle Caicos
Lorimers
East Caicos
South Caicos
Cockburn Harbor
Turks Island Passage
Grand Turk
Cockburn Town
East Cay
Salt Cay
Balfour Town

Grand Turk Cays Land and Sea National Park encompasses several cays. Frigate birds nest on Penniston Cay. Brown boobies roost on Pinzon Cay.

Lake Catherine Nature Reserve *protects a breeding habitat for flamingos and other wading birds. The flamingos thrive on brine shrimp which inhabit this lagoon, once used as a salt pan.*

KEY

✘ Wildlife reserve

—— Minor road

TOUR COMPANIES

Big Blue Unlimited
Tel 649 946 5034.
www.bigblue.tc

Salt Cay Tours
Tel 649 244 1407.
www.saltcaytours.com

A male frigate bird inflating its gular sac

FRIGATE BIRDS

Frigate birds are gregarious sea-going birds that roost atop mangroves. Extremely light birds with huge wing-spans, these kleptoparasites harry other seabirds to steal their food with the aid of their long, hooked bills. They also hunt fish from the ocean surface. Their iridescent black-green feathers lack waterproof oils and the birds risk drowning if they land in the sea.

Outdoor Activities and Specialized Holidays

Snorkeling and scuba diving are the big draws, offering an exhilarating way to explore the Turks and Caicos' phenomenal underwater life. In winter, whale-watching is excellent, and almost every isle offers a rich birdlife, easily seen along the many hiking trails that lace the islands. Many beaches have watersports such as windsurfing, Hobie Cats, and kayaking. Apart from these activities, visitors also have a choice of a relaxed pampering session in any of the islands' luxurious spas.

Grace Bay, one of the best beaches in Turks and Caicos

BEACHES

Most visitors to the Turks and Caicos come to feel the soft sun-soaked sand between their toes. All the isles have lovely beaches, but by far the best is Grace Bay (see p118), on Providenciales. Curving gently along 12 miles (19 km) of shore, it has plenty of hotels, cafés, and watersport outlets, as well as sections where visitors can stroll in solitude and peace. Farther west, Wheeland Beach is more remote, with fewer hotels. Locals like to head to the otherwise deserted Malcolm Road. For a Robinson Crusoe-type escape, rent a boat and seek a secluded beach on Pine Cay or Dellis Cay.

Whitby Beach runs along the northern shore of North Caicos and shelves gently into reef-protected jade-colored shallows. It runs west to Pumpkin Bluff Beach, where snorkelers can explore an ancient wreck. Seemingly endless Long Bay Beach, on South Caicos, is virtually deserted, with rough surf often pounding ashore. Grand Turk is blessed with options. On the leeward side, Governor's Beach fringes Cockburn Town and extends north to Pillory Beach, but outshining both are intimate White Sands Beach and the never-ending Flamingo Beach, on the windward shore. Tiny Salt Cay also boasts the lovely North Beach.

SPAS

The Turks and Caicos islands, especially Providenciales, are a spa lover's mecca. Most of the top spas are associated with deluxe hotels. Anani Spa, at Grace Bay Club (see p127), specializes in Euro-Asian spa treatments. Parrot Cay's COMO Shambhala Spa (see p127) offers Asian-inspired holistic therapies, plus yoga on an Oriental pavilion overhanging the island's wetlands. Thalasso Spa, at Point Grace (see p127), is a European-style spa with treatment rooms that have lovely ocean views. **Spa Anani**, at Grand Turk Cruise Center, is handy for cruise passengers seeking a beach-front massage.

BOAT EXCURSIONS

Taking to sea on a sailboat is a great way to break the routine of lazing on Grace Bay Beach. Some catamarans can be boarded right off the beach; others depart from Leeward Marina. **Sail Provo** offers a broad menu of half-day snorkeling and sunset cruises, plus the joy of an overnight luxury charter. The romance of the past comes alive aboard the *Atabeyra*, a traditionally rigged trading schooner opera-ted by **Sun Charters**, which offers a pirate cruise plus a nocturnal cruise.

Sail Provo catamaran, Phoenix, on an excursion off Providenciales

WHALE-WATCHING

The arrival, each January, of humpback whales to the Mouchier Banks, south of Grand Turk, provides for spectacular close-up encounters. Whale-watching trips take place in the Turks Island Passage (between South Caicos and Grand Turk) and in the warm, shallow waters off Salt Cay. **Oasis Divers** offers whale-watching excursions, from January to April, as do **Salt Cay Divers**, which let participants actually swim with the whales.

The luxurious Anani Spa at Grace Bay Club, Providenciales

For hotels and restaurants on these islands see pp126–7 and pp128–9

Diving Sites in the Turks and Caicos

Turks and Caicos offers some of the best diving in the world for walls, whales, and wrecks. The crystal clear waters are warm with average temperatures of 73–84° F (23–29° C). There are plenty of shallow dives, but the isles excel for breathtaking wall

Diver with a Nassau grouper

dives and for wrecks, such as the HMS *Endymion*. Providenciales is blessed with great diving sites, while Grand Turk and Salt Cay have a wall that begins from the shallow waters close to the shore with magnificent corals and marine life.

Shark Hotel *is a good place to swim with sharks who live among the coral reef. It is also home to many species including spotted moray and southern stingrays.*

Black Forest *is a wall dive with overhangs adorned with black coral. Turtles and groupers abound and smaller fry form a kaleidoscope against the chromatic corals.*

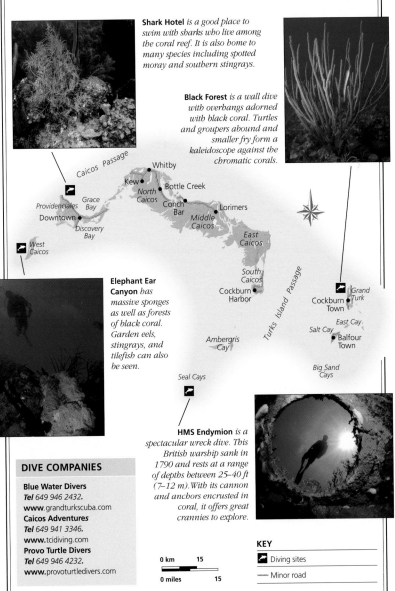

Caicos Passage

Whitby
Kew
North Caicos
Bottle Creek
Providenciales
Grace Bay
Downtown
Conch Bar
Lorimers
Discovery Bay
Middle Caicos
West Caicos
East Caicos
South Caicos
Cockburn Harbor
Turks Island Passage
Cockburn Town
Grand Turk
East Cay
Salt Cay
Balfour Town
Ambergris Cay
Big Sand Cays
Seal Cays

Elephant Ear Canyon *has massive sponges as well as forests of black coral. Garden eels, stingrays, and tilefish can also be seen.*

HMS Endymion *is a spectacular wreck dive. This British warship sank in 1790 and rests at a range of depths between 25–40 ft (7–12 m). With its cannon and anchors encrusted in coral, it offers great crannies to explore.*

DIVE COMPANIES

Blue Water Divers
Tel 649 946 2432.
www.grandturkscuba.com

Caicos Adventures
Tel 649 941 3346.
www.tcidiving.com

Provo Turtle Divers
Tel 649 946 4232.
www.provoturtledivers.com

0 km 15
0 miles 15

KEY

⬈ Diving sites

▬ Minor road

Hikers on one of the popular trails in Grand Turk

HIKING

Several islands have trails that wind through mangroves and wetland ecosystems, with fabulous birding opportunities. On Little Water Cay off Providenciales, the 509-ft (155-m) North Shore Trail and the South Shore Trail, a 675-ft (206-m) long route, provide good access to both habitats. Iguanas can often be spotted during the hikes.

Middle Caicos has the best hiking, thanks to the 10-mile (16-km) long Middle Caicos Reserve and Trail system, that runs along the scenic north shore and passes colonial plantations and lagoons with flamingos. Stay on the trails, and bring plenty of water and insect repellent. For more information, contact **Turks and Caicos National Trust**.

HORSE-RIDING

Wild horses roam several islands, but opportunities for horseback riding are limited. **Provo Ponies** will take visitors cantering along Grace Bay. On Grand Turk, **Chukka Caribbean** also offers a "Horseback Ride 'n' Swim".

GOLF

Provo Golf Club, the only one in Providenciales, is a par-72 course designed by well-known golf course architect, Karl Litten. It is acclaimed as one of the top Caribbean courses. Its rugged layout features fairways that ripple through limestone formations framed by Caribbean pine and studded by palm-shaded lakes. The

18-hole **Turks and Caicos Miniature Golf Club** in Long Bay is fun for the entire family. Visitors can take a break with cool drinks and snacks at the club's restaurant.

TENNIS

Most resort hotels in Providenciales have tennis courts, and non-guests are usually welcome for a fee. The Provo Golf Club has two tennis courts open to the public but only by reservation. Club Med Turkoise *(see p126)* has noteworthy facilities for its guests. There are four hard courts and private instructors as well. Options for tennis on other islands are limited.

CAVING

The islands are filled with limestone outcrops and are riddled with caves, although few are accessible and most are underwater. The most extensive system open for viewing is Conch Bar Caves National Park on Middle Caicos *(see p119)*. Guides are available for exploring the winding caverns stippled with stalagmites and stalactites and etched with pre-Columbian petroglyphs. Nearby, the less extensive Indian Cave has a vast cavern crawling with strangler fig roots. This cave also has many legends that local guides love to tell. Both caves are partially paved.

Visitors on a horse-riding trip along with guides, Grand Turk

For hotels and restaurants on these islands see pp126–7 and pp128–9

Boats waiting for fishing tours in Providenciales harbor

FISHING

The shallow waters of the Caicos Banks form a 2,000-sq-mile (5,179-sq-km) habitat for the elusive, hard-fighting bonefish *(see p119)*, an ultimate test of anglers' patience and skill. Tarpon can also be caught in the mangrove lagoons and are known as "silver rockets" for a good reason. Local guides are available on all the isles to punt visitors across the clear waters to the best fishing spots. Reputable operators for bonefish trips include **Bonefish Unlimited** and **Silver Deep**. Visitors can also wade off the beach into fish-full flats on most isles, sometimes right in front of the hotels.

The streaming currents beyond the fringing reefs are virtual highways for migrating sailfish, tuna, wahoo, and marlin. The summer months are the best time to fish for marlin. Providenciales and Grand Turk have the best spots and facilities for deep-sea fishing. Half- and full-day charters are also provided by Silver Deep. Prices vary depending on the size of the group. All equipment, food, and drinks are included in the packages that are offered by most fishing operators on the islands.

WATERSPORTS

Non-motorized watersports, such as windsurfing and aqua-bikes, are free for guests at most resort hotels. Scudding across Grace Bay, one of Providenciales' few beaches that offers water-sports, is a special thrill. Private beach concessionaires, such as **Dive Provo** and Sail Provo also rent kayaks, boards, and Hobie Cats. For more information, contact **Abuv-It-All Ltd.** and **Ocean Vibes** for snorkeling. **Captain Marvin's** provides an exhilarating birds'-eye view of the isles by parasail. **Snuba Turks & Caicos** offers snuba, a cross between scuba and snorkeling.

Children on an aqua-bike ride in shallow beach waters

DIRECTORY

SPAS

Spa Anani
Tel 649 232 1503.
www.spaanani.com

BOAT EXCURSIONS

Sail Provo
Tel 649 946 4783.
www.sailprovo.com

Sun Charters
Tel 649 231 0624.
www.suncharters.tc

WHALE-WATCHING

Oasis Divers
Tel 649 946 1128.
www.oasisdivers.com

Salt Cay Divers
Tel 649 241 1009.
www.saltcaydivers.tc

HIKING

Turks and Caicos National Trust
Tel 649 941 5710.
www.nationaltrust.tc

HORSE-RIDING

Chukka Caribbean
Tel 649 332 1339.
www.chukka caribbean.com

Provo Ponies
Tel 649 946 5252.
www.provoponies.com

GOLF

Provo Golf Club
Tel 649 046 5991.
www.provogolfclub.com

Turks and Caicos Miniature Golf Club
Tel 649 231 4653.

FISHING

Bonefish Unlimited
Tel 649 946 4874.
www.provo.net/
Bonefish

Silver Deep
Tel 649 946 5612.
www.silverdeep.com

WATERSPORTS

Abuv-It-All Ltd.
Tel 649 241 1687.
www.windsurfingprovo.tc

Captain Marvin's
Tel 649 231 0643.

Dive Provo
Tel 649 946 5040.
www.diveprovo.com

Ocean Vibes
Tel 649 331 1104.
www.oceanvibes.com

Snuba Turks & Caicos
Tel 649 332 7333.
www.snubaturksand caicos.com

Choosing a Hotel

Most hotels in Turks and Caicos are beachfront. The island of Providenciales has the majority of places to stay. The hotels here, particularly in Grace Bay, are generally all five-star properties. More intimate historic hotels are typical on Grand Turk. All the rooms have basic facilities such as a private bath, TV, and air-conditioning unless otherwise indicated.

TURKS AND CAICOS

Grand Turk Inn – *p120*
The intimate and historic Grand Turk Inn features spacious and comfortable suites with kitchens; two have king-sized beds. There is an airy sundeck as well.

Salt Raker Inn – *p120*
A casual restaurant and its historic charm adds to the appeal of the quaint Salt Raker Inn. All rooms are spacious. Upstairs, two suites have a shared balcony with views.

Grand Turk Inn

Salt Raker Inn

GRAND TURK Osprey Beach Hotel $$$
Duke Street   **Tel** 649 946 2666   **Fax** 649 946 2817   **Rooms** 37

This modern hotel has a beach setting but also offers additional accommodations in town houses, plus some units in an older building off the beach. Rooms have ceiling fans and plantation-style furnishings. On Wednesday and Sunday nights the local rake-n-scrape band plays at the pool bar. **www.ospreybeachhotel.com**

MIDDLE CAICOS Blue Horizon Resort $$$$
Mudjin Harbor   **Tel** 649 946 6141   **Fax** 649 941 6139   **Rooms** 7

A reclusive breeze-swept perch, the family-friendly Blue Horizon Resort guarantees spectacular vistas over glistening sands cusped by limestone cliffs. The modestly furnished, self-catering, Caribbean-style cottages are airy and have kitchenettes, screened porches, and blue tin roofs. Makes a good base for hiking. **www.bhresort.com**

NORTH CAICOS Ocean Beach Hotel Condominiums $$$
Whitby Beach   **Tel** 649 946 7113   **Fax** 649 946 7386   **Rooms** 10

A quiet and peaceful condominium-hotel with a gorgeous beachfront setting and views over warm turquoise waters. Rooms are simply furnished, but clean and comfortable. The Silver Palm Restaurant (*see p128*) has live music and draws locals for good food, drinks, and fun. There is an on-site pool. **www.turksandcaicos.tc/oceanbeach**

NORTH CAICOS Pelican Beach Hotel $$$
Whitby Beach   **Tel** 649 946 7112   **Fax** 649 946 7139   **Rooms** 14

Enclosed by a picket fence, the intimate and adults-only beachfront Pelican Beach Hotel, without telephones and TVs, but with excellent room service, is a calming retreat. The hotel features an unremarkable yet comfortable decor. Use of bicycles is included in room rates. Closed mid-Aug to mid-Sep. **www.pelicanbeach.tc**

PROVIDENCIALES, GRACE BAY Caribbean Paradise Inn $$
Grace Bay Road   **Tel** 649 946 5020   **Fax** 649 946 5022   **Rooms** 17

The Caribbean Paradise Inn is a five-minute stroll from the beach. It offers a homey intimacy rare for Grace Bay. Decor includes terra-cotta tile floors, rattan furnishings, and also an option for a canopied four-poster bed. The Coyaba Restaurante (*see p128*) has won much acclaim. There is a good bar as well. **www.caribbean-paradise-inn.com**

PROVIDENCIALES, GRACE BAY Sibonné Beach Hotel $$$
Grace Bay Road   **Tel** 649 946 5547   **Fax** 649 946 5770   **Rooms** 30

The oldest hotel on Grace Bay, the lovely, casual, beachfront Sibonné Beach Hotel is popular with divers. The garden quadrangle has a circular pool just steps from the powdery sands. Rooms are no-frills with conservative decor. A bistro restaurant and bar overhangs the sands, drawing guests from neighboring hotels. **www.sibonne.com**

PROVIDENCIALES, GRACE BAY Club Med Turkoise $$$$
Grace Bay Road   **Tel** 649 946 5500   **Fax** 649 946 5497   **Rooms** 290

Popular with Europeans, Club Med Turkoise is an adults-only resort offering a panoply of activities including scuba diving, tennis, casino, spa, and theater, plus a circus workshop and sailing academy. King-sized beds are an option in the contemporary-style accommodations, painted in lively tropical colors. **www.clubmed.com**

PROVIDENCIALES, GRACE BAY Beaches Resort & Spa $$$$$
Lower Bright Road   **Tel** 649 946 8000   **Fax** 649 946 8001   **Rooms** 615

The vast, Neo-Classically themed family-focused, fun-filled Beaches Resort & Spa has superb children's programs in addition to the various activities offered to adults. Seven room categories include villas, all with king-sized beds. There are 6 restaurants, spa facilities, 5 pools, tennis, and watersports. **www.beaches.com**

Key to Symbols *see back cover flap*

PROVIDENCIALES, GRACE BAY Gansevoort   🏠 🍴 📋 �

Grace Bay Road **Tel** 649 941 7555 **Fax** 309 210 9091 **Rooms** 91

The Gansevoort has elevated Provo's hip trend to new heights with its urban-chic color scheme that blends chocolate, turquoise, and white. Walls of glass permit vast views of the beach and bay. It has a spa, yoga classes, and a trendy beachfront bistro and lounge. **www.gansevoortturksandcaicos.com**

PROVIDENCIALES, GRACE BAY Grace Bay Club

Grace Bay Road **Tel** 649 946 5050 **Fax** 649 946 5758 **Rooms** 81

The sprawling deluxe, all-suite, Andalusian-style Grace Bay Club is acclaimed for its beachfront Anacaona restaurant (see p128), but has plenty of other irresistible draws. The rooms are painted in white, cream, and chocolate colors with gleaming marble floors. There is a huge clover-shaped pool, a spa, and tennis courts. **www.gracebayclub.com**

PROVIDENCIALES, GRACE BAY Point Grace

Grace Bay Road **Tel** 649 946 5096 **Fax** 649 946 5097 **Rooms** 28

The exclusive Point Grace resort, with classical plantation-styling, draws the wealthy for its soothing decor and pampering service. Sumptuous suites and penthouses in three-story units enfold a beachfront pool. Fine dining at Grace's Cottage (see p128), family rooms, spa facilities, and watersports are available. **www.pointgrace.com**

PROVIDENCIALES, GRACE BAY The Regent Palms

Grace Bay Road **Tel** 649 946 8666 **Fax** 649 946 5188 **Rooms** 72

The all-suite, luxurious The Regent Palms replicates the Neo-Classical plantation look and ambience. It has marble floors, vaulted ceilings, and mahogany furnishings, including king-sized beds and bathrooms with hydro massage bathtubs. There is a good restaurant, Parallel 23 (see p129), bar, and a spectacular pool. **www.regenthotels.com**

PROVIDENCIALES, GRACE BAY The Sands at Grace Bay

Grace Bay Road **Tel** 649 946 5199 **Fax** 649 941 3433 **Rooms** 148

This four-star, all-suite hotel gleams with granite and marble. Choose from studios with kitchenettes, or one-, two-, and three-bedroom suites. There are 3 swimming pools, the delightful open-air Hemingway's On the Beach restaurant (see p129), spa services, and an on-site wedding planner. **www.thesandsresort.com**

PROVIDENCIALES, GRACE BAY Seven Stars Resort

Grace Bay Road **Tel** 649 941 7777 **Fax** 649 941 8601 **Rooms** 200

The deluxe, all-suite, beachfront Seven Stars Resort features four six-story structures overlooking Grace Bay. The studios and suites have contemporary plantation-style furnishings, and bedded beach pavilions guarantee comfort. The resort includes 2 fine-dining restaurants, bar, tennis courts, and spa services. **www.sevenstarsresort.com**

PROVIDENCIALES, GRACE BAY The Tuscany

Grace Bay Road **Tel** 649 941 4667 **Fax** 649 941 4619 **Rooms** 30

Designed with multigenerational families in mind, The Tuscany features two- and three-bedroom suites all facing the cotton white sands with dining and living rooms plus half-moon ocean-view verandas. The decor combines a medley of styles. There is a restaurant and bar and private chefs can be arranged. **www.thetuscanyresort.com**

PROVIDENCIALES, NORTHWEST POINT Amanyara

Northwest Point **Tel** 649 941 8133 **Fax** 649 941 8132 **Rooms** 58

The Balinese-inspired deluxe resort Amanyara has a spectacular beach setting atop a limestone headland on the secluded west coast of Provo. Guests sleep in elevated pavilions and villas fitted with elegant teak furnishings. Facilities include a beach club, infinity pool, spa facilities, and 2 tennis courts. **www.amanresorts.com**

PROVIDENCIALES, PARROT CAY Parrot Cay

Providenciales Island **Tel** 649 946 7788 **Fax** 649 946 7789 **Rooms** 71

On its own isle, Parrot Cay fronts a gorgeous 2-mile (3-km) long beach and attracts millionaires and Hollywood stars. Deluxe guest quarters are a blaze of whites and teak hardwoods with minimalist decor. Fine-dining restaurant and bar, the luxurious COMO Shambhala spa, tennis, and an array of watersports. **www.parrotcay.como.bz**

PROVIDENCIALES, PINE CAY The Meridian Club

Providenciales Island **Tel** 649 941 7011 **Fax** 649 941 7010 **Rooms** 13

An unpretentious, old-world, all-inclusive family resort shunning TVs and telephones, The Meridian Club is nestled among pines and sand dunes. Guest rooms and private cottages in whites and pastels offer a soothing ambience. Bicycles, Hobie Cats, the resort's own yacht, tennis, and spa facilities are available. **www.meridianclub.com**

PROVIDENCIALES, TURTLE COVE Miramar Resort

Turtle Cove **Tel** 649 946 4240 **Fax** 649 946 4704 **Rooms** 22

Inland of Turtle Cove Marina, the Miramar Resort is perfect for sailing enthusiasts who want a break from the sea. It has tennis courts and in-room massage. Decor is a bit basic, but some rooms have comfortable romantic canopied beds. The Magnolia Wine Bar & Restaurant offers alfresco dining with a view. **www.miramar.tc**

SOUTH CAICOS South Caicos Ocean & Beach Resort

Cockburn Town **Tel** 649 946 3219 **Fax** 649 941 3508 **Rooms** 26

This hideaway resort sits on a ledge overlooking azure waters. It is an excellent base for scuba dives, whale-watching, and bonefishing. Furnishings are fairly ascetic and amenities are limited. The resort has self-catering condominiums and a pool. **http://southcaicos.oceanandbeachresort.com**

Where to Eat & Nightlife

Turks and Caicos has a wide spectrum of restaurants. Fine-dining establishments are mostly found in the deluxe beach resorts while unpretentious restaurants and beach shacks provide for casual dining. Some of the big hotels have discos, and Providenciales has a few lively stand-alone bars and dance spots. Elsewhere, nightspots are limited mostly to beachfront restaurants and hotel bars.

PRICE CATEGORIES
The price ranges are for a two course meal for one, including tax and service charges and half a bottle of wine.

$ under $10
$$ $10–15
$$$ $15–25
$$$$ $25–35
$$$$$ over $35

RESTAURANTS

Seafood Special
The more expensive the hotel, the more upscale the restaurant. However, there are restaurants that suit almost everybody's budget. Also, there is no shortage of beach shacks. Most restaurants specialize in freshly-caught seafood. The main specialty here is conch, which is put raw in salads and cooked in other dishes. Snapper and grouper feature on most menus.

Osprey Beach Hotel's café

Da Conch Shack

GRAND TURK The Sand Bar 🍴 ♿ $$

Duke Street ***Tel*** *649 946 1111*

A small and casual beachfront restaurant, The Sand Bar is run by two Canadian sisters and offers shaded deck dining. It is a popular hub for locals. Grilled grouper sandwiches, fish and chips, cracked conch, lobster *quesadillas*, and burgers typify the menu. Happy hour draws a huge party crowd. Closed on Saturdays.

GRAND TURK Secret Garden Restaurant 🍴 ♫ ♿ $$$

Duke Street ***Tel*** *649 946 2260*

The no-frills Secret Garden Restaurant is tucked in the shady courtyard of the Salt Raker Inn *(see p120)*. On the menu are Continental dishes such as spaghetti Bolognese and island specialties such as conch, grilled lobster, and curried mutton with rice-and-peas. For lunch, try the grouper sandwich. The cocktails here excel.

GRAND TURK Guanahani 🍴 ♿ $$$$

Pillory Beach ***Tel*** *649 946 2135*

Located within the Bohio Dive Resort & Spa, Guanahani has a lovely beach setting and serves sensational international dishes using local ingredients, including crispy sushi rolls, pad thai, and a delicious pecan-encrusted mahimahi. Typical Caribbean dishes are generally served for lunch.

NORTH CAICOS Silver Palm Restaurant 🍴 ♫ ♿ $$

Whitby Beach ***Tel*** *649 946 7113*

This beachfront restaurant is set in Ocean Beach Hotel Condominiums *(see p126)*. Owner serves delicious local seafood, such as conch *quesadillas*, and nouvelle Caribbean dishes such as Oriental breast of chicken. It has theme nights, where local talent, Lovey Forbes, entertains. Leave room for the West Indian rum cake.

PROVIDENCIALES, BLUE HILLS BEACH Da Conch Shack 🍴 ♫ ♿ $

Blue Hills Beach ***Tel*** *649 946 8877*

Da Conch Shack's beautiful location on the Blue Hills Beach and casual ambience adds to its appeal. It is known for its fresh seafood such as grilled snapper. Conch is a specialty and guests can choose to have their conch cooked, cracked, fried, or spiced. There is live music on Friday nights.

PROVIDENCIALES, GRACE BAY Caicos Café 🍴 ≡ ♿ $$$

Grace Bay Road ***Tel*** *649 946 5278*

A favorite with locals for its romantic ambience, this restaurant is in a quaint Caribbean cottage lit at night by flaming torches. Chef Pierrik Marziou prepares delicious seafood recipes such as gumbo, plus Mediterranean dishes. Try the spicy jumbo shrimp served with a seafood risotto.

PROVIDENCIALES, GRACE BAY Anacaona [V] 🍷 ≡ 🍴 ♫ 🚭 ♿ $$$$$

Grace Bay Road ***Tel*** *649 946 5050*

The signature restaurant at the Grace Bay Club *(see p127)*, Anacaona sits over the sands, with alfresco tables tiered beneath open-sided thatched *palapas*. The interior space has glistening wooden floors and black chandeliers. Fine Euro-Caribbean fusion cuisine is served. A dress code applies, and no children are allowed.

PROVIDENCIALES, GRACE BAY Coyaba Restaurante 🍷 ≡ 🍴 🚭 ♿ $$$$$

Grace Bay Road ***Tel*** *649 946 5186*

The smart Coyaba Restaurante in the Caribbean Paradise Inn *(see p126)* is a Chaine des Rôtisseurs member and delivers consistently superb fusion dishes. The extensive menu changes daily and includes island and international favorites with a twist. The desserts are reason enough to visit; try the chocolate fondant.

PROVIDENCIALES, GRACE BAY Grace's Cottage

Grace Bay Road **Tel** 649 946 5096

A sublimely romantic indulgence, Grace's Cottage at Point Grace *(see p127)* is one of Providenciales's finest restaurants. The Victorian gingerbread cottage provides an inviting ambience, aided by candlelit tables and a choice of softly-lit, tree-shaded patios. Their specialty is exquisite, fresh seafood dishes.

PROVIDENCIALES, GRACE BAY Hemingway's On the Beach

Grace Bay Road **Tel** 649 941 8408

Housed inside The Sands at Grace Bay *(see p127)*, this peaceful poolside restaurant, lit by torches at night, is ideal for enjoying lobster and coconut shrimp dishes. More typical fare includes burgers and Caribbean jerk chicken breast. Tuesday is Barbeque Night, and live jazz is the Friday night highlight.

PROVIDENCIALES, GRACE BAY O'Soleil

Princess Dr. **Tel** 649 946 5900

A sophisticated restaurant within The Somerset Resort on Grace Bay, O'Soleil oozes contemporary chic with its chocolate-and-white minimalist decor. A patio has canopied Bali beds, good to relax on after a meal. The menu infuses Caribbean influences into creative meat and seafood dishes. Live music on Friday nights.

PROVIDENCIALES, GRACE BAY Parallel 23

Grace Bay Road **Tel** 649 946 8666

White upon white elegance welcomes the guests at the ritzy Parallel 23 in The Regent Palms *(see p127)*. The restaurant has options for indoor as well as outdoor seafront dining, perfect for viewing the sunset. The exciting tropical fusion menu spans the globe and is complemented by an extensive wine list. Dress code for dinner.

PROVIDENCIALES, TURTLE COVE, Jimmy's Dive Bar

Turtle Cove **Tel** 649 946 5282

The bustling indoor-outdoor Jimmy's Dive Bar in the Ports of Call shopping plaza has a laid-back ambience. The owners, Jimmy and Darlene, serve generous helpings of local cuisine as well as typical American fare including scrumptious steaks, burgers, salads, and pasta. Also serves hearty breakfasts and seafood platters. Great mojitos.

PROVIDENCIALES, TURTLE COVE Aqua Bar & Terrace

Turtle Cove Marina **Tel** 649 946 4203

Overlooking the marina, the Aqua Bar & Terrace is an airy seafood restaurant drawing a loyal clientele for its nightly specials, which include mussels on Thursdays and sushi on Saturdays, and the popular Peking duck dinner on Mondays. The restaurant and its palm-shaded circular bar with fairy-lights is the place to be for a good nightlife.

PROVIDENCIALES, TURTLE COVE Baci Ristorante

Turtle Cove Marina **Tel** 649 941 3044

The elegant Italian Baci Ristorante right on Turtle Cove Marina offers outside dining on a waterfront terrace. The menu features staples such as fettuccine Alfredo and lasagne, in filling portions. Sailors gather at the massive bar. A mermaid fountain tinkles in the entrance courtyard.

SALT CAY Island Thyme Bistro

North District **Tel** 649 242 0325

A colorful fun-lovers' hang-out, Island Thyme Bistro looks over the *salinas* and is a great venue for birders. It serves bargain-priced seafood and international classics, including steamed snapper in pepper wine sauce, steaks, and a searingly hot chicken curry. Friday is pizza night. A great place for breakfast too.

BARS AND CLUBS

Several upscale resorts have discos and a few of the larger all-inclusives have cabarets, most of which are open to non-guests. Away from the main hotels, nightlife focuses on beachfront bars, where happy hour draws crowds to view the sunset green-flash phenomenon. The island music scene is dominated by local rake-n-scrape bands armed with banjos, drums, maracas, a concertina, and the trademark carpenter's saw. Bars range from thatched, sand-floored holes-in-the-wall to chic minimalist dens.

Infiniti Bar in Grace Bay

RECOMMENDED PLACES TO GO

Bambooz Bar & Grill
Saltmills Plaza, Grace Bay Road,
Providenciales.
(Sports bar.)

BET Soundstage & Gaming Lounge
Leeward Highway, Providenciales.
(Video casino, live music, late-night disco.)

Club Sodax Sports Bar
Leeward Highway, Providenciales.
(Pool, dominoes.)

Danny Buoy's
Grace Bay Road, Providenciales.
(Darts, pool tables, and sports TV.)

Infiniti Bar
Grace Bay Club, Providenciales.
(For the martini crowd.)

The Lounge
Grace Bay Club, Providenciales.
(Lounge beds on the beach.)

Police Canteen
Police headquarters, Grand Turk.
(Drinking and dancing on weekends.)

The Tiki Hut
Turtle Cove Marina, Providenciales.
(Sailors' hang-out.)

Practical Information

Providenciales has witnessed an investment boom during the past decade, and its tourist infrastructure is world class, with a focus on deep-pocket vacationers, while budget travelers prefer Grand Turk for its laid-back charm. North, Middle, East, and South Caicos have relatively limited tourist infrastructure and hotel options, and advance planning is essential. Hurricane Ike, in 2008, devastated Grand Turk, South Caicos, and Salt Cay, affecting a number of services.

One of the banks at Cockburn Town, Grand Turk

WHEN TO GO

These breeze-swept isles are pleasant year-round, although the best weather is from December to April, when there is hardly any rain and the temperatures are near perfect. The mid-summer months can be torrid, while the weather can get sticky during the hurricane season that runs from June to November. Cultural events are mostly in winter, but rates are also higher than in summer.

Grand Turk International Airport, near Cockburn Town

GETTING THERE

Charter and regular scheduled flights arrive at Providenciales International Airport from North America. There are a few direct flights from North America to Grand Turk International Airport. Private charter planes connect all the other islands to Grand Turk and Providenciales. **US Airways**, **Delta**, and **American Airlines** fly to Providenciales from six US gateways. **British Airways** serves Providenciales once a week via the Bahamas, which is also served by **Bahamas Air**. **Air Canada** has

direct flights from Montreal and Toronto to Providenciales. Charter flights from Canada are also provided by **Air Transat** and **Sky Service**.

DOCUMENTATION

No visas are required for stays of up to 30 days. All visitors must have a valid passport and a ticket for onward travel.

VISITOR INFORMATION

The **Turks and Caicos Islands Tourist Board** has offices in the US, Canada, and the UK that provide information. Within the Turks and Caicos, it has offices on Grand Turk and on Providenciales (at the airport and at Turtle Cove Marina). Hotel tour desks can also give advice on organized excursions and entertainment. Most companies have websites that give more specific details.

HEALTH AND SECURITY

There are public clinics on each island, and a general hospital on Grand Turk, but many may not meet the standards that most people are used to. Private clinics such as **Grace Bay Medical Center** and **Grand Turk Hospital** are preferred. Some all-inclusive resorts have a nurse on staff. Providenciales also has a hyperbaric chamber. Theft and crime affecting tourists is rare in Turks and Caicos, but it is best to keep valuables in a hotel safe, and to avoid wearing expensive jewelry when out and about.

BANKING AND CURRENCY

The US dollar is the official currency of Turks and Caicos, which also issues its own crown and quarter. Traveler's checks in US dollars are accepted in most hotels, taxi services, and restaurants in Providenciales, and can be cashed at local banks. However, cash and credit cards are preferred on other islands, where banks may be fewer. Most major credit cards are accepted. There is no limit on the amount of money that visitors may bring to the islands.

COMMUNICATIONS

The Turks and Caicos has an efficient telephone system operated by **Cable & Wireless**, which has public phones throughout the islands. Prepaid phone cards can be bought at many stores. Calls from hotels incur a hefty surcharge. To call abroad from the Turks and Caicos, dial 011 and the country code, then the area code and number. To call Turks and Caicos from North America, dial 1, then 649 and the local number; from the UK, dial 00 for international access, then 649 and the local number. Calls within the islands require only the seven digit number. Most hotels offer Internet access. There are Internet cafés on all the islands.

Public phone, on the islands

TRANSPORT

Holders of an International Drivers license and citizens of the UK, USA, and Canada can drive on their own license. Others need a Visitors' Permit, which can be obtained from the **Road Safety Department**. Reputable rental companies are **AVIS**, **Hertz**, and **Grace Bay Car Rentals**. Hotels can also arrange for car rentals. Scooters can be rented from companies such as **Tony's Car Rental** on Grand Turk. It is advisable to wear helmets.

Minivans operate taxi services on all islands and can be used for touring. Rates can be expensive so be sure to negotiate an agreed fare before setting off. The concierge or front desk staff of most hotels will help visitors call for a taxi.

SHOPPING

Most hotels have boutiques selling swimwear, cigars, rum, and local craft items such as conch shell jewelry and the island's trademark rag dolls. Select locations, including the airport departure lounge and downtown plazas on Providenciales, sell duty-free cameras, china, crystal, liquor, and perfumes. The Turks and

Colorful souvenir shops in Grand Turk

Caicos has no sales tax. A receipt is needed for conch shell items; the Turks and Caicos is one of the few countries in the world where conch shells can legally be purchased and exported.

TIME

Turks and Caicos is on Eastern Standard Time (EST), 5 hours behind Greenwich Mean Time (GMT). Daylight Savings is in effect the first Sunday of April through the last Sunday of October.

LANGUAGE

English is the official language in the Turks and Caicos, spoken by everyone, although many locals speak with a distinct dialect. Many speak a patois version, while the

many Haitians working here speak their own French-derived Creole patois.

ELECTRICITY

Turks and Caicos operates on 110 volts. Outlets use US two-prong plugs. Most large hotels have their back-up generators to supply power during occasional outages.

GETTING MARRIED

A 24-hour minimum residency on the island is required and visitors need to apply for a marriage license in person through the **Registrar of Marriages**. A nominal fee is charged. Documents such as passport, birth certificate, and proof of single status is mandatory. Licenses are issued at the **Registrar Office** in Provo.

DIRECTORY

GETTING THERE

Air Canada
www.aircanada.com

Air Transat
www.airtransat.com

American Airlines
www.aa.com

Bahamas Air
www.bahamasair.com

British Airways
www.ba.com

Delta
www.delta.com

Sky Service
www.skyserviceairlines.com

US Airways
www.usairways.com

VISITOR INFORMATION

Turks and Caicos Islands Tourist Board
Tel 649 946 4970 (Providenciales), 649 946 2321 (Grand Turk).
www.turksandcaicostourism.com
www.turksandcaicos.tc
http://turksandcaicoshta.com

HEALTH AND SECURITY

Emergencies
Tel 911.

Police
Tel 649 946 4259 (Providenciales), 649 946 2299 (Grand Turk).

Grace Bay Medical Center
Neptune Plaza, Providenciales. Tel 649 941 5252, 649 231 0525 (emergencies).

Grand Turk Hospital
Hospital Road, Grand Turk. Tel 649 946 2040.

COMMUNICATIONS

Cable & Wireless
www.time4lime.com

TRANSPORT

AVIS
Tel 649 946 4705.
www.avis.com

Grace Bay Car Rentals
Tel 649 941 8500. www.gracebaycarrentals.com

Hertz
Tel 649 941 3910.
www.hertz.com

Road Safety Department
Good Street, Providenciales; Old Airport Road, Grand Turk.

Tony's Car Rental
Tel 649 946 1879.

GETTING MARRIED

Registrar Office
Providenciales.
Tel 649 946 2800.

Registrar of Marriages
Front Street, Grand Turk.
Tel 649 946 2801.

A PORTRAIT OF JAMAICA

*J**amaica is the quintessential Caribbean island. Its extraordinary
natural beauty encompasses white sand beaches, tumbling
cascades, and the misty Blue Mountain range with its terraced
plantations of premium coffee. The electrifying music scene provides
a cultural depth and has helped in making Jamaica famous.***

Jamaica has an amazing natural abundance – a reality that did not escape the island's various colonizers. First to settle were the Amerindians from the South American mainland, who farmed and fished here until the arrival of Christopher Columbus in 1494. He claimed the island on behalf of Spain, setting in motion the establishment of the plantation economy which the British made more efficient when they captured Jamaica in 1655. The parting gift of the Spanish was to release the slaves working in the plantations. Heading into the uncharted terrain of Cockpit Country, the freed slaves, known as Maroons, became a thorn in the side of the plantocracy, using guerrilla tactics to win two armed campaigns against British forces. A peace treaty was

Mural with a parrot, Margaritaville Restaurant

eventually signed and Maroon villages still exist as separate enclaves to this day. For the rest of the island's African population, however, life remained unimaginably harsh. Uprisings against the British continued to be brutally suppressed and matters only slowly started to improve after the Emancipation Act of 1833.

POLITICS

After Jamaica became independent in 1962, two main political parties emerged, the largely right-wing Jamaica Labour Party (JLP), and the more left-wing People's National Party (PNP). The former was the first party to lead an independent Jamaica. The PNP came to power under the radical Michael Manley during the turbulent 1970s, an era characterized

Ocho Rios beach with a cruise ship in the background

A Rastafarian at his stall of local arts and crafts, Ocho Rios

to US$40 per pound. Tourism is the main economic earner, however, with the industry fetching US$2 billion in 2009. The tourist infrastructure is mainly concentrated along the north coast, with the three big resorts of Montego Bay, Negril and Ocho Rios receiving most visitors.

by violent clashes between party supporters during elections. The 1980s were dominated by the JLP but by 1992, the PNP returned led by P.J. Patterson, the country's first black prime minister. The PNP remained in power until 2007 (with a short stint by Portia Simpson, Jamaica's first female prime minister), when Bruce Golding and the JLP won back the reins.

ECONOMY

During the early 20th century, the economy was given a boost by the nascent banana and tourism industries. Agriculture now accounts for just seven percent of the GDP, with key crops including sugar and bananas. Though sugar production is steadily declining due to competition from South American mechanized farms and the banana industry has been practically crippled by the World Trade Organization's removal of preferential tariffs to European Union markets, the island still earns US$20 million from banana exports. Coffee is another important export, with the annual average production of green beans worth US$32 million; about 85 percent of Jamaica's coffee is shipped to Japan, with the other 15 percent going to the UK, USA, and other countries, where it often sells for up

JAMAICA TODAY

The nation's capital city, Kingston, best encapsulates Jamaica's edgy reputation and life is undeniably harsh in the impoverished ghettos here. However, Kingston also has brilliant restaurants and nightlife. Music in Jamaica is vibrant and exciting. Besides the inimitable Bob Marley, there are innumerable international stars in the field of dancehall and reggae in Jamaica. In 2008, the island received a massive boost when its athletics team dominated the Beijing Olympics, bringing home six gold medals, with Usain Bolt winning both the 100m and 200m races and becoming the fastest man in the world. In 2010 a crackdown on drug lords resulted in mayhem in Kingston, and 72 deaths.

Plantations of premium coffee on the slopes of the Blue Mountains

Exploring Jamaica

Jamaica's ample proportions allow for a varied landscape. To the west are the lavish beaches and grand limestone cliffs of Negril. Popular ports of call for cruise ships, Montego Bay and Ocho Rios in the north are also the island's nightlife hubs, while Port Antonio in the east has an old-world charm. For a taste of the "real Jamaica", head to Kingston, a fascinating city overlooked by the Blue Mountains, and within easy driving distance of great hiking.

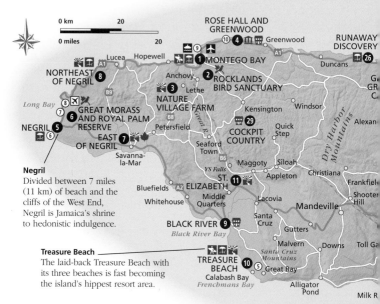

Negril
Divided between 7 miles (11 km) of beach and the cliffs of the West End, Negril is Jamaica's shrine to hedonistic indulgence.

Treasure Beach
The laid-back Treasure Beach with its three beaches is fast becoming the island's hippest resort area.

SIGHTS AT A GLANCE

Black River **9**

Blue Mountains Tour pp144–5 **15**

Bob Marley Centre & Mausoleum **28**

Cockpit Country **29**

Cranbrook Flower Forest **25**

Dolphin Cove and Dunn's River Falls **24**

East of Negril **7**

Firefly **21**

Frenchman's Cove and the Blue Lagoon **17**

Great Morass and Royal Palm Reserve **6**

Green Grotto Caves **27**

Hellshire **13**

Kingston p142 **12**

Long Bay **19**

Montego Bay **1**

Nature Village Farm **3**

Negril **5**

Northeast of Negril **8**

Ocho Rios **23**

Oracabessa **22**

Port Antonio **16**

Port Royal **14**

Reach Falls **20**

Rocklands Bird Sanctuary **2**

Rose Hall and Greenwood **4**

Runaway and Discovery Bays **26**

St. Elizabeth **11**

Treasure Beach **10**

Winnifred Beach **18**

Hotels and Resorts

Breezes Runaway Bay **11**

Coyaba Beach Resort **10**

Forres Park **3**

Idle Awhile **8**

Jamaica Inn **13**

Kingston hotels **4**

Mockingbird Hill **15**

Montego Bay hotels **9**

Negril hotels **7**

Negril, West End Road hotels **6**

Ocho Rios hotels **12**

Port Antonio hotels **14**

Starlight Chalets **1**

Strawberry Hill **2**

Treasure Beach hotels **5**

For additional map symbols *see back flap*

Boats lined along the edge of a lagoon in Ocho Rios

KEY

▬▬ Highway

▬▬ Major road

═══ Minor road

⌐┐⌐┐ Railroad

SEE ALSO

• *Where to Stay* pp156–9

• *Where to Eat & Nightlife*
  pp160–61

Blue Mountains
Shrouded in mist, the cool and
craggy Blue Mountain peaks are
dotted with farms growing some of
the best coffee in the world.

Kingston
With plenty in the way of culture
and nightlife, Kingston also
offers days out to the former
pirate capital of Port Royal and
Hellshire Beach, for fresh fish.

GETTING AROUND

Most flights tend to land in Montego Bay, which
has easy access to Negril and Ocho Rios. To go
to Port Antonio or Treasure Beach, it is easier
to fly to Kingston. Internal flights are restricted
to the odd service between Montego Bay and
Kingston/Negril by charter airlines, though the
new highway which runs the length of the
north coast makes driving to Ocho Rios or
Negril from Montego Bay far easier than flying.
The best option for getting around the island is
to hire a car or a local driver, as buses can be
chaotic with no set schedules.

Display of exquisite Jamaican wood carvings
at a roadside craft stall

Montego Bay ❶

NW Coast. 🏛 *83,000.* ✈ 🚌 ⛴
🛈 *Cornwall Beach Complex off Gloucester Av.; 876 952 4425.*
www.montego-bay-jamaica.com

Enclosed by a cradle of hills with stunning views of the western coastline, Montego Bay's lovely beaches are the main reason for its enduring popularity. A favorite stopover for cruise ships and the destination for most international flights to Jamaica, it is a busy place, with the center of activity concentrated along the length of Gloucester Avenue, rechristened the Hip Strip. Working south to north, the first point of interest along the Strip is **Walter Fletcher Beach**, a handsome crescent popular with locals, with a go-kart track, excellent watersports facilities, and tennis courts.

Bars, restaurants, and gift shops line most of the avenue between Aquasol and the Strip's only green space, a grassy park with great views down the coast. Past the tacky façades of the Margaritaville and Coral Cliff bars is the entrance to the famed white sand and crystal-clear water of **Doctor's Cave Beach** and, some 720 ft (220 m) beyond, Cornwall Beach.

The Strip tails off where Gloucester Avenue becomes Kent Avenue, and the seafront is once again visible; there is a fine slip of beach and great snorkeling offshore. Downtown Montego Bay provides a refreshing antidote to the schmaltz of Gloucester Avenue, and though most visitors do not venture past the southern end of the avenue, there are a couple of sights to look out for. Across the road at the end of the Strip is Fort Street, which threads past the chaotic Gully fruit and vegetable market to Sam Sharpe Square, named after one of Jamaica's national heroes and distinguished by its central fountain. In the northwest corner, next to the cutstone Cage built by the British as a lock-up for runaway slaves, is a sculpture of Sam Sharpe preaching to his followers. Just around the corner the **Montego Bay Civic Centre** houses a small museum on local history, which has more information about Sam Sharpe.

Doctor bird, Rocklands Bird Sanctuary

🏖 **Walter Fletcher Beach**
Gloucester Av. **Tel** *876 979 9447.*
🕐 *9am–7pm daily.* 🏄 ♿ 🍴 🚻

🏖 **Doctor's Cave Beach**
Gloucester Av. **Tel** *876 952 2566.*
🕐 *8:30am–sunset daily.* 🏄 🍴 🚻
www.doctorscavebathingclub.com

🏛 **Montego Bay Civic Centre**
St. James Street. **Tel** *876 952 5500.*
🕐 *9am–5pm Tue–Fri, 10am–3pm Sat, noon–5pm Sun.* 🏄

Rocklands Bird Sanctuary ❷

Anchovy, 5 miles (8 km) SW of Montego Bay. **Tel** *876 952 2009.*
🚌 🅿 *8am–5pm daily.* 🏄 🅿

Just off the B8 Highway and past the Lethe turnoff at Anchovy, Rocklands Bird Sanctuary is a low-key attraction that offers bird-lovers one of Jamaica's most unforgettable experiences. The former home of the celebrated ornithologist Lisa Salmon (d. 2000), it is a favored spot for a multitude of birds that come here to feed each day. Buses from Montego Bay to Savanna-la-Mar run past the approach road, but it is a steep and difficult walk up to the sanctuary. No direct route taxis to Rocklands are available and it is advisable to charter one from Montego Bay.

On arrival, visitors are given a feeder of sugar-water. The objective is to entice the diners – mostly different kinds of hummingbirds, including the doctor bird – to descend and perch on the people's hands to drink the water, the whirr of their wings vibrating musically in the air. Other species of birds can also be spotted here, including banaquits, the greater Antillean bullfinch, and the gorgeous black-throated blue warbler. To get so close to these elusive and beautiful creatures is an incredible experience. An interesting nature walk through thick vegetation is also included in the entry fee.

Nature Village Farm ❸

6 miles (10 km) SW of Montego Bay. **Tel** *876 912 0172.* 🚌 *from Montego Bay (no route taxi service to Lethe).*
🕐 *10am–6pm Mon–Fri, 10am–7pm Sat, 11am–7pm Sun.*

From the main coast road, the B8 Highway threads into the hills southwest of Montego Bay – a lush, green, and

Sailing on the crystal-clear waters of Montego Bay

For hotels and restaurants on this island see pp156–9 and pp160–61

SAM SHARPE AND THE CHRISTMAS REBELLION

The Christmas Rebellion of December 1831 was perhaps the most significant uprising of African slaves in Jamaica's history. Though the slave trade had been outlawed in 1807, plantation culture still held sway here, with thousands of Africans working in the sugar estates quite unaware of the legislation. It was in the planters' interests to maintain this ignorance and they made great efforts to suppress the inevitability of emancipation. However, Sam Sharpe, a house slave working in Montego Bay who had taught himself to read by way of his position as deacon

Sam Sharpe monument, Montego Bay

of a Baptist church, learned of the activities of abolitionists in Britain, and preached in his sermons that freedom was close. The news spread like wildfire, and talk of insurrection intensified as Christmas approached. By December 27, non-violent protests had developed into full-scale rebellion, with western Jamaica ablaze as some 160 estates were razed to the ground. The British response was brutal, with 1,000 slaves shot dead and another 300 – including Sharpe – hanged by the neck. The death-knell of slavery had been sounded, however, and the uprising was the first step on the road to complete abolition in 1838.

Antique piano on display at Greenwood Great House

Great River on the outskirts of Lethe, near Nature Village Farm

peaceful alternative to the sun-bleached glare of the coast. To make the best of the surroundings, it is a good idea to turn off for **Lethe** and follow the signs to the secluded and serene Nature Village Farm. Inside the property, sweeping lawns and football pitches lead down a hillside to the banks of the Great River, overhung by lianas and towering stands of bamboo. There are several places to take a dip and it is also possible to go on a relaxing tube ride down the river on huge rubber rings. Visitors can enjoy a meal or drink at the open-air restaurant overlooking the water.

Rose Hall and Greenwood ❹

Rose Hall 10 miles (16 km) E of Montego Bay. **Tel** 876 953 2323. 🚍 ⬜ 9am–5pm daily. 🈺 📷 📺 ⬜ **www.**rosehall.com
Greenwood 12 miles (19 km) E of Montego Bay. **Tel** 876 953 1077. 🚍 ⬜ 9am–6pm daily. 🈺 📺 **www.**greenwoodgreathouse.com

Understandably, Jamaica does not make too much of an issue about its colonial past, but the era of plantation slavery comes to the fore east of Montego Bay in the form of two palatial great houses that have been opened up as tourist attractions, both of which are signposted from the main coastal highway.

Buses along the highway pass the entrances to Rose Hall and Greenwood.

Closest to Montego Bay is Rose Hall Great House, the former home of the "White Witch" Annie Palmer. She came to Rose Hall as the wife of its owner, John Rose Palmer, and soon unleashed a reign of terror. Her wicked deeds are made much of by the tour guides. The supposedly haunted house has been slickly refurbished in period style, with lavish furnishings and antiques. The tours start from the gift shop which has displays of old photographs.

Far more atmospheric, Greenwood Great House is also a more handsome structure, commanding amazing coastal views and filled with original fittings and curiosities. The house once belonged to relatives of the renowned British poet, Elizabeth Barrett Browning. Today it has a large and rare collection of musical instruments as well as a library.

Austere façade of the infamous Rose Hall Great House

Hotels and restaurants lining the beach at Negril, a popular resort area

Negril **5**

52 miles (83 km) SW of Montego Bay. 🚶 4,200. ✈️ 🚌 from Montego Bay along Norman Manley Boulevard, and from Savanna-la-Mar along Sheffield Road. 🚐 **www**.negril.com

Perhaps the most popular of Jamaica's three main resort areas, Negril is split between its 7 miles (12 km) of picture-perfect white sand, backed by the wide Norman Manley Boulevard, and the limestone cliffs that make up the island's extreme western tip. Both cliffs and beach are lined with hotels, restaurants, and the ever-busy bars that have helped to give the area its reputation for nightlife and loud music; rarely a high-season weekend goes by without a huge stageshow taking place, and visitors can dance in the sand to live reggae most nights of the week.

With its clear warm waters, sheltered by a reef and almost mirror calm, the beach is one of the Caribbean's best. However, the beauty of the place also means crowds of people, including vendors selling everything from hair braids or glass-bottom boat rides to ganja (cannabis). Hotels set up loungers and umbrellas on the sand for the use of their guests, but there are plenty of bars and restaurants that also offer beach facilities.

For a quieter environment, it is best to head east along the sand toward Long Bay beach park, where the buildings thin out and the hustle also diminishes accordingly.

Ranged along pockmarked limestone cliffs that sheer off into 13-ft (4-m) deep, crystal-clear waters studded with lovely reefs, the **West End**, south of downtown Negril, is a world away from the beach. It is relatively quieter, although still home to some seriously upscale hotels, as well as a multitude of places geared towards budget travelers. The swimming on offer is fantastic, and restaurants and hotels have stairs down the cliffs and ladders to get in and out – but it should be borne in mind that exiting can be challenging when the water is choppy.

The West End also provides the perfect spot for watching the sun set, with bars offering happy hour, live music, and cliff-diving displays, during which divers plunge into the sea from amazingly high cliffs.

Great Morass and Royal Palm Reserve **6**

Sheffield Road, 2 miles (5 km) E of Negril. **Tel** 876 364 7407. 🚌 🕐 9am–6pm daily. 🎫 📷 🚻 🚻

Running inland from Norman Manley Boulevard and covering some 9 sq miles (24 sq km), the Great Morass is Jamaica's second-largest wetland. It can be accessed by bus or route taxi from Negril to Savanna-la-Mar, but is a long walk away from the nearest stop. It is best to take a chartered taxi.

The Great Morass is a peaty, reed-covered expanse that provides a habitat to a number

Boardwalk across the wetlands at Royal Palm Reserve

For hotels and restaurants on this island see pp156–9 and pp160–61

of rare animals and plants, including the many trees around which the Royal Palm Reserve has been created. With wooden boardwalks that lead right out onto the morass, the air alive with the chirping of crickets, cicadas, frogs, and with every inch of surface covered in thick greenery, it is a great place for a walk. Also a good spot for bird-watching, the reserve has a couple of observation towers and more than 50 species of birds to look out for. Visitors can try their luck at fishing as well.

Horse-riding at Rhodes Hall Plantation, northeast of Negril

East of Negril

Sheffield Road trundles inland from Negril's main round-about toward the dusty market town and parish capital of Savanna-la-Mar. There is not much to see in the town, so it is best to turn off the main road before getting into "Sav" proper. Signposts lead visitors to **Roaring River Park**, just outside the small community of Petersfield. Set in a former plantation, the park has a deep cave to explore.

However, the real draw is the **Blue Hole Garden**, just a 5-minute drive farther down the road, where a deep blue spring-water pool overhung with greenery makes it a magical place for a swim.

🏵 **Roaring River Park**
5 miles (8 km) N of Savanna-la-Mar.
Note: take a guided tour from Negril; it is advisable to ignore unofficial guides.

🏵 **Blue Hole Garden**
5 miles (8 km) N of Savanna-la-Mar.
Tel 876 401 5312.
⬜ 8am–6pm daily. 💷 🍴 🚻
http://fatheresauproductions.com

Northeast of Negril

Northeast of Negril, the coastal highway swings past a few diverting attractions. The first is **Rhodes Hall Plantation**, a 550-acre (220-ha) coconut and vegetable plantation that offers horse-riding both inland and along the beach. There is a crocodile reserve and bird sanctuary on-site. Visitors also have the opportunity to snorkel or enjoy a dip in the mineral spring infinity pool. Just beyond is **Half Moon Beach**, the polar opposite of Negril with no motorized watersports or hassle, just a calm cove, hammocks to swing in, and a good restaurant. Both destinations can be reached either by bus or shared taxi.

Inland from the coast, in the heart of the Dolphin Head Mountains, lies another tour-company staple – **Mayfield Falls**. There are 22 mini-cascades along a greenery shrouded river. It is a good idea to take a guided walk up the river, which has lots of deep swimming pools, and get a snack or drink, or change into swimwear at the base. At the end of the tour, visitors are led back through pastures lined with fruit trees and clusters of bamboo. The falls can be hard to find, but all the local taxi drivers know the way.

Rhodes Hall Plantation
8 miles (13 km) NE of Negril.
Tel 876 957 6422. 💷 🚻
www.rhodesresort.com

🏵 **Half Moon Beach**
10 miles (15 km) NE of Negril.
Tel 876 531 4508. ⬜ 8am–late daily. 💷 🍴

🌿 **Mayfield Falls**
Glenbrook, 15 miles (24 km) northeast of Negril. **Tel** 876 792 2074. 💷 🚻 🍴
www.mayfieldfalls.com

HEDONISTIC NEGRIL

First "discovered" in the 1970s, hippies descended on Negril to laze on the beaches in a ganja-wreathed haze. Many are still drawn here by Negril's reputation, which has been built around intemperance. In fact, one of the biggest hotels here goes all out to advertize its deliberately risqué ethos of raunchy pool parties and skinny dips under the stars. The place certainly has a debauched quality to it, and hordes of people come here for the wild partying. Drugs, too, remain part of the fabric, with "special" (magic mushroom) tea on the menu at the occasional restaurant and more than a whiff of marijuana in the evening air. These days, though, the area's most bacchanalian aspect is its nightlife, with a string of lively bars along the beach offering dancing on the sand any day of the week.

A party in one of Negril's hotels

A Jamaican crocodile soaking in the sun on the banks of Black River

Black River ❾

46 miles (73 km) S of Montego Bay.
👥 *4,100.* 🚌 🚉 *between Savanna-la-Mar and Treasure Beach.*
🛒 *Fri & Sat.*

Weatherbeaten Black River may be the largest town in the parish of St. Elizabeth, but that is not saying much given the region's bucolic feel. Spreading back from the coastline and centered around its bustling market and commercial main street, it is certainly not a tourist hotspot, though it does have a couple of interesting buildings along the waterfront. The most notable among these is the elaborate Invercauld Hotel, built in 1889 during Black River's heyday as one of the island's main ports.

The main reason people come here, though, is to take a boat safari up the Black River, the island's longest

river, populated by Jamaican crocodiles. Boats leave from the depot at both sides of the main town bridge, and meander upstream through the peaty, water-hyacinth-dotted river, passing thick clumps of twisted mangrove that provide a habitat for many bird and marine species. The crocodiles are used to visitors, and many of them have been named by the boat captains; nonetheless, at up to 12 ft (4 m) long, they look fairly menacing up close.

For those who are looking for an even quieter retreat, there is the option is to head west of Black River to **Font Hill Beach Park**, a privately-owned beach with a good strip of white sand.

🏞 Font Hill Beach Park
Main Road, 2 miles (3 km) W of Black River. **Tel** 876 462 9011.
🕐 *9am–5pm daily.* 🅿 🚻
Note: *lockers are available for hire.*

Treasure Beach ❿

56 miles (90 km) SE of Montego Bay. 🚌 *from Mandeville and Black River.* 🏨 *hotels can arrange taxi transfers from Montego Bay or Kingston airports.*
www.treasurebeach.net

In direct contrast to the glitz and concrete of the north coast, the string of peaceful fishing villages that make up the relaxed and laid-back Treasure Beach offer a more authentic island experience than the resorts. Tourism has developed sustainably here, with the community getting tangible benefits from the industry, both by being directly involved – most of the hotels and restaurants are owned by locals – and by way of initiatives such as the BREDS foundation. A non-profitmaking organization funded largely by visitor donations, BREDS has, among many other things, created an emergency medical response unit for the community and purchased an ambulance. They have also equipped schools with computers and fishermen with much-needed radios.

Beautifully situated between the sea and the arid flatlands that spread out below the Santa Cruz Mountains, Calabash Bay is the heart of the community. Here, the very hip Jake's hotel *(see p159)* provides a focus for most of

Colorful fishing boats on the sands at Treasure Beach

For hotels and restaurants on this island see pp156–9 and pp160–61

the activities, with a smattering of places to eat and stay close by. To the north, Frenchman's Bay offers great opportunities for swimming and body-surfing. The scenic beach is ideal for sunbathing too. This place is home to more accommodations, and eating, and drinking options. South of Calabash and Frenchman's bays; and separated from them by pastureland and the Great Pedro Pond, is Great Bay, with another fine beach and a thriving fishing industry. Though the sand here is brown rather than white, the waters are clear and extremely clean, and the odd wave makes a refreshing change to the millpond-like northern shore.

It is easy to while away an entire holiday dividing time between the beaches, but it is well worth arranging for a boat trip along the coast to the unique **Floyd's Pelican Bar**. Built on stilts stuck into a sandspit offshore of Parrottee Point near Black River, this ramshackle wooden, thatch-roofed bar is a one-of-a-kind experience. Guests can paddle around the shallows, snorkel in the surrounding waters, or just sit in the bar and have a meal or a beer, enjoying the sunset, which is especially atmospheric here.

St. Elizabeth ⓫

60 miles (100 km) SE of Montego Bay.

Characterized by bauxite-rich deep red earth and rolling cattle pastures, St. Elizabeth is one of Jamaica's most beautiful parishes. It is not swamped with tourist attractions, but there are a few places worth visiting by way of a driving tour from Treasure Beach.

From Black River, a signposted road threads north, affording lovely views across the plains toward the Santa Cruz Mountains. After about 12 miles (20 km), the quaint little village of **Middle Quarters** announces itself through a crowd of women selling bags of the spicy and

The tunnel of bamboos in the Bamboo Avenue, parish of St. Elizabeth

delicious pepper shrimp that the area is known for. Just past here, the signposted road to the left leads towards YS, a huge cattle farm that is also home to the lovely **YS Falls**, surrounded by lush pastures and jungle-covered hills. Reached via a short tractor-trailer ride through the fields, the falls – seven cascades of varying sizes tumbling out of the greenery – are an absolute delight. Several of these end in deep pools which are great for swimming, although some are too rocky. There is a spring-water swimming pool near the snack shop, which is ideal for kids. When water levels allow, tubing along the river is a lot of fun, and there are also three zipwires that allow visitors to whoosh through the tree canopy and over the water.

The seven cascades at YS Falls, St. Elizabeth

Beyond YS, the road gets even narrower. Once through the tiny community of Maggotty, the route turns onto Highway B6 for the **Appleton Rum Estate**, which is surrounded by endless fields of sugarcane. Appleton is the oldest producer of rum in Jamaica; the estate dates back to 1655 although distilling began only in 1749. Its rums are considered by many to be the island's best. The tour inside the factory complex takes guests through the whole production process, from the selection of the sugarcane to the bottling of the rum, and ends with a chance to sample all 17 of their brands, so it is worth noting that the estate offers transportation for its visitors from their hotels.

The scenic route back follows the B6 Highway south of Maggotty, and turns right at Lacovia along **Bamboo Avenue**, where thick overhanging strands of bamboo create a tunnel-like effect. Just a short distance from here, the route ends at Middle Quarters.

🎣 YS Falls
3 miles (5 km) N of Middle Quarters. **Tel** 876 997 6360.
🕒 9:30am–3:30pm Tue–Sun. 🏊 🛶 tubing and canopy tour on payment. 📷 **www**.ysfalls.com

Appleton Rum Estate
8 miles (13 km) NE of Middle Quarters. **Tel** 876 963 9215. 🕒 9am–4pm Mon–Sat. 🏊 📷 🍴 🛍 **www**.appletonrumtour.com

Visitors enjoying ice cream at Devon House, Kingston

Kingston ⑫

119 miles (190 km) SW of Montego Bay. 🏙 660,000. ✈ 🚢 🛈 Jamaica Tourist Board, 64 Knutsford Boulevard; 9am–4:30pm Mon–Fri; 876 929 9200. 🎭 Kingston on the Edge Urban Art Festival (Jun).

Spreading inland from a large natural harbor and cradled to the north by the peaks of the Blue Mountain range, Kingston is Jamaica's cultural and commercial center. The city is loosely divided into New Kingston and Downtown. At the heart of New Kingston is Knutsford Boulevard, which holds the manicured **Emancipation Park** at its southern end, with fountains, a jogging track, and Laura Facey-Cooper's *Redemption Song* sculpture. Roughly parallel to Knutsford, Hope Road swings past some of the classic Kingston sights. Shady gardens surround the splendid **Devon House**, built by the nation's first black millionaire. The complex is a popular place to head for an ice cream or a snack, a tour of the house, or just to relax on the park benches. Farther along Hope Road, Rasta flags and mural-painted walls enclose the **Bob Marley Museum**. Set in his former home, it is a surprisingly low-key tribute to Jamaica's most famous son, with displays of gold and platinum discs, stage clothing, and a wall papered with newspaper reports of his exploits.

His kitchen and bedroom remain as he left them, while in a room at the back, bullet-holes testify to a failed assassination attempt in 1980. At the northern end of Hope Road, it is worth making time for a stroll around **Hope Botanical Gardens**, set in a former sugar estate and filled with rare trees and plants.

Downtown is home to banks, offices and, on its fringes, some of the country's roughest ghettos. Right on the waterfront, behind the grassy lawns and swaying palms of Ocean Boulevard, the **National Gallery** houses the best collection of home-grown art in the country.

⚓ Devon House
26 Hope Road. **Tel** 876 929 6602.
🕙 9:30am–5pm Mon–Sat. 🎟 🅿 garden only. 🍴 🛍 🎦 📷
www.devonhousejamaica.com

🏛 Bob Marley Museum
56 Hope Road. **Tel** 876 978 2929.
🕙 9:30am–4pm Mon–Sat. 🎟 🅿 🍴 🛍 🎦 📷
www.bobmarleymuseum.com

🌿 Hope Botanical Gardens
Hope Road. **Tel** 876 927 1257.
🕙 6am–6pm daily. 🅿 🍴

🏛 National Gallery
12 Ocean Boulevard. **Tel** 876 922 1561. 🕙 10am–4:30pm Tue–Thu, 10am–4pm Fri, 10am–3pm Sat.
🎟 🅿 🛍 📷

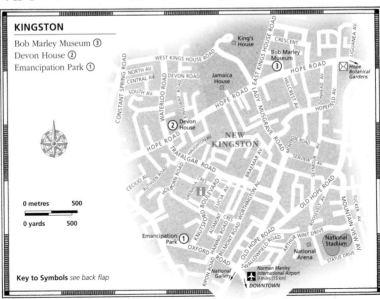

KINGSTON
Bob Marley Museum ③
Devon House ②
Emancipation Park ①

0 metres   500
0 yards   500

Key to Symbols see back flap

For hotels and restaurants on this island see pp156–9 and 160–161

Hellshire

10 miles (16 km) SW of New
Kingston. 🏃 85,000. 🚌

On the other side of the
harbor from Kingston, and
reached by the toll highway
to the huge dormitory suburb
of Portmore, the Hellshire
Hills are an arid, cactus-
strewn expanse jutting down
into the Caribbean Sea. The
main reason to come here is
for a swim at **Fort Clarence
Beach**, a stretch of white sand
that is popular with
Kingstonians, or to have a
plate of fried fish at the
neighboring fishing village
of Hellshire, known islandwide for its outstandingly
good seafood. Here, ram-
shackle restaurants line the
sand, selling fried fish served
with vinegary pepper sauce
and bammy or festival breads.
It is a thoroughly Jamaican
scene during the weekends
when huge speakers blast
out reggae and local families
descend on the beach.

Past Hellshire, the **Two
Sisters Caves** are a series of
deep caverns in the limestone
made accessible by wooden
walkways and stairs. Guides
explain the caves' history and
point out an Amerindian petro-
glyph on one of the walls.

🚻 **Fort Clarence Beach**
Main Road, Hellshire.
🕐 10am–6pm Mon–Fri, 9am–6pm
Sat–Sun. 🎫 🍴 🅿 **Note:** showers
and changing rooms on-site.

🏞 **Two Sisters Caves**
Main Road, Hellshire.
Tel 876 999 2283. 🕐 9am–6pm
Wed–Sun. 🎫 🅿

**Interior of a restaurant with
brightly colored murals, Hellshire**

Cannons in the courtyard of Fort Charles

Port Royal ⑭

5 miles (8 km) S of New Kingston.
🏃 4,300. 🚌

A series of small cays joined
together to form a breakwater
between Kingston's harbor
and the open ocean, the thin
strip of road running along the
Palisadoes takes visitors to
Port Royal. This atmospheric
fishing village, with a colorful
past of piracy and naval might,
was scarred by a catastrophic
natural disaster. A thriving
town under the British, it
suffered a massive
earthquake in 1692 that
destroyed most of the
place and killed
thousands of people,
effectively putting an
end to its importance
as a trading post.

Port Royal still holds
several of the original
British-built fortifica-
tions, the largest of
which is **Fort Charles**,
the first of five bas-
tions built here from
bricks that had served
as ballast on British
ships. The Maritime
Museum in the court-
yard has a small but
fascinating collection
of artifacts dredged up from
the ruins of the original town.
Back toward the main square,
visit the graveyard of St. Peter's
Church; one of the tombs is
of Lewis Galdy, who was swal-
lowed by the earth during the
earthquake, and miraculously
regurgitated seconds later.
Another activity here is to
take a boat to Lime Cay, a
tiny island with white
sands and clear waters.

⚓ **Fort Charles**
Tel 876 967 8438. 🕐 9am–4:45pm
daily. 🎫 🅿

PIRATES OF PORT ROYAL

When the British took Jamaica
from Spain in 1655, they established a huge fort at the tip of the
Port Royal peninsula to guard
Kingston's harbor – Nelson himself was stationed here – and set
about employing the services of
pirates to help their meager forces
defend Jamaica. More palatably
referred to as privateers, the
pirates enthusiastically went
about the business of plundering
treasure-laden Spanish ships sail-
ing between Europe and their New World colonies. The huge
profits they made saw Port Royal boom. Notorious as a
haven for piracy and debauchery, it was condemned by the
church as the "wickedest city in Christendom". However,
the pirates' days ended when Britain signed a peace treaty
with Spain in 1670. Having made his name plundering the
Spanish colony of Panama in the name of the British king, Sir
Henry Morgan was chosen as the Crown's lieutenant-
governor to persuade his fellow privateers into a life of
peace. His most famous captures were that of "Calico" Jack
Rackham and his female accomplices, Mary Read and Ann
Bonney. Rackham was executed, his body packed into a
cage and left on a cay as warning to others.

**Sir Henry Morgan, pirate and
later lieutenant-governor**

Blue Mountains Tour ⓯

With its highest peak reaching 7,402 ft (2,256 m), Jamaica's largest range – the Blue Mountains – stretches for 28 miles (45 km) from east to west, its lower canopy of soapwood, dogwood, and Caribbean cedar interspersed with coffee plantations and its upper slopes covered with stunted montane rainforest. From Papine and Kingston, there are two main tour routes. The road divides at The Cooperage, with one fork heading towards Holywell Recreational Park, taking in coffee plantations and a glitzy hotel en route, and the other to Gordon Town and Mavis Bank, where jeeps can be hired to get to the start of the hiking trail to Blue Mountain Peak.

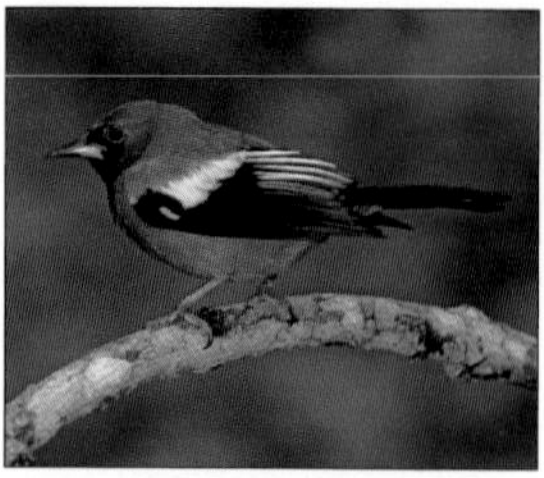

Jamaican oriole, one of the many birds found in the Blue Mountains region

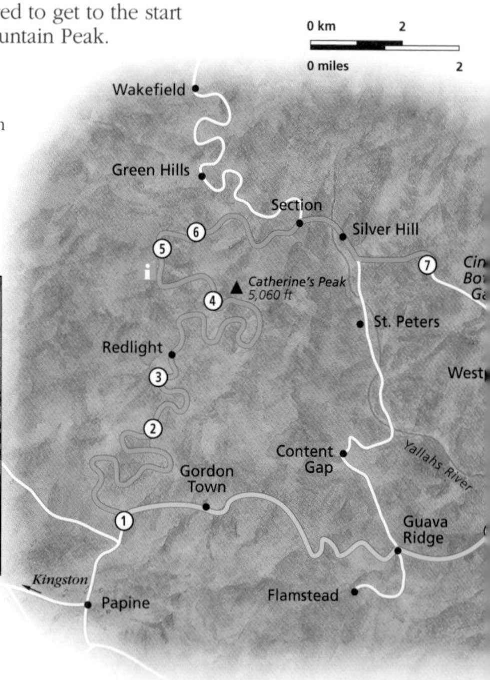
0 km 2
0 miles 2
Wakefield
Green Hills
Section
Silver Hill
Catherine's Peak
5,060 ft
St. Peters
Redlight
Content
Gap
Yallahs River
Gordon
Town
Guava
Ridge
Kingston
Papine
Flamstead

The Cooperage ①
This nondescript junction is named for the Irish coopers who made rum barrels here in the 19th century.

Irish Town ②
Home to the famed Strawberry Hill Hotel, where Bob Marley convalesced after being shot in 1976.

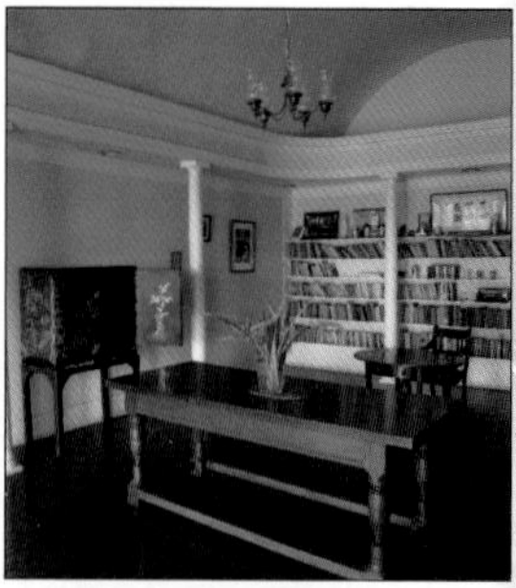

Craighton Coffee Estate ③
This Japanese-owned coffee plantation is centered around the pretty Great House, where guided tours are available.

Newcastle ④
This colonial-era former British military base, now a training ground of the Jamaica Defence Force, is closed to visitors.

TIPS FOR DRIVERS

Starting point: *Papine.*
Length: *A full day to see both the Holywell and Mavis Bank sides of the mountains.*
Driving conditions: *Drive slowly, use the horn on hairpin bends, and avoid the hills if it is raining, as landslides are fairly common.*

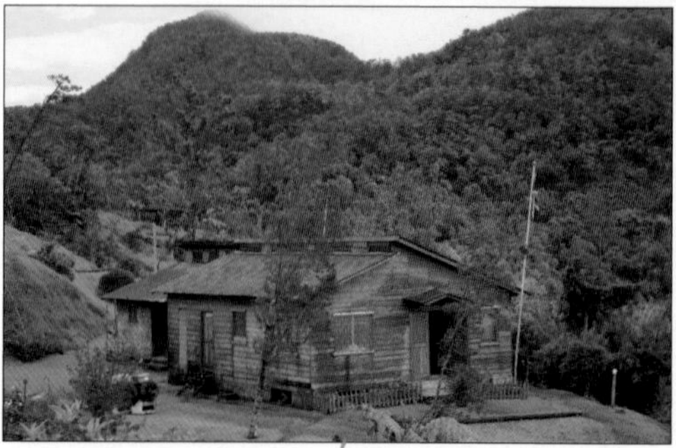

Holywell Recreational Park ⑤
The main visitor center for the Blue and John Crow Mountains National Park, with designated trails through the cloud forest, cabins to stay in, and spectacular views down to Kingston.

Abbey Green ⑨
With whispering eucalyptus trees usually shrouded in mist, Abbey Green is the start of the trail to Blue Mountain Peak. It is home to lodges that serve as bases for the peak climb.

Mavis Bank ⑧
This tiny mountain town is home to the tourable Blue Mountain Coffee Processing Plant and has fabulous views.

Clydesdale and Cinchona ⑦
The former coffee plantation of Clydesdale is the starting point for the hike to the dilapidated but beautiful botanical gardens at Cinchona.

KEY

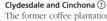

▲	Peak
i	Visitor information
▬	Route 1
▬	Route 2
═	Other road

*Johns Peak
? ft*

*Peak
12 ft* ▲

GRAND RIDGE OF THE BLUE MOUNTAINS

*Blue and John
Crow Mountains
National Park*

*Mossman's Peak
6,703 ft* ▲

i

⑨

▲
*rm Hill
,062 ft*

▲ *Blue
Mountain Peak
7,402 ft*

● *Hagley
Gap*

Old Tavern Coffee Estate ⑥
This is the only estate in the mountains to roast and process its own coffee.

Picking coffee berries

Sorting the beans

Drying in the sun

Roasting in processors

BLUE MOUNTAIN COFFEE
Widely acknowledged as one of the best in the world, Blue Mountain coffee is grown at 2,000–5,000 ft (609–1,524 m). The unique climate and rich soil produces the distinctively delicious beans. Once ripe, beans are hand-picked and transported to the processing factory at Mavis Bank. They are first floated to remove inferior beans, then washed in holding tanks to remove the outer section. After being dried in the open air, or in drums if it is raining, the beans are rested for ten weeks before finally being hulled, sorted into grades, roasted, and packed.

Port Antonio 🔟

61 miles (98 km) NE of Kingston.
🏙 *13,000.* 🚌 ⛴ ℹ️ *City Center
Plaza, Harbor Street; 876 995 3051.*
🎣 *Port Antonio International Marlin
Tournament (Oct).*

A quiet little town that grew
around its deep twin harbors,
Port Antonio owes its origins
as a tourist spot to actor Errol
Flynn (1909–59). Having run
aground here aboard his
private yacht, Flynn took a
liking to the Portland area,
buying Navy Island just
offshore that used to stand on the Titchfield
peninsula – the western tip
of Port Antonio's East harbor.
By the 1950s, he was well-
known for inviting a string
of celebrities, including Bette
Davis and Ginger Rogers to
Jamaica to stay and go rafting
on the Rio Grande.

Although little remains to
be seen of the Flynn legacy
today, the area does retain a
sense of faded glamor, especially in the palatial resorts
east of town. Port Antonio
still has a certain shabby
charm, with a few colonial-
era buildings with typical
overhanging verandas
along its main street. There
is a bustling fruit and
vegetable market and the
Port Antonio Court House,
housed in a grand old
Georgian building.

Facing Navy Island is the
new Port Antonio Marina,
now known as the Errol
Flynn Marina. The marina
offers world-class facilities,
including waterfront paths for

Frenchman's Cove, one of Jamaica's best beaches

promenading, manicured
lawns, a slip of white-sand
beach, and an upscale restaurant. Unfortunately, Navy
Island is officially closed to
visitors, though local fishermen still take people to its
lovely beaches for a swim
and to snorkel.

Frenchman's Cove and the Blue Lagoon 🔟

5 miles (8 km) E of Port Antonio.
Tel *876 993 7270.* 🚌 🕐 *9am–5pm
daily.* 🅿️

The coastline east of Port
Antonio is one of the most
beautiful in the country.
Watered by frequent rain
showers that bounce off the
Blue Mountains, the jungle-
like tangle of ferns, flowers,
and palms cascade down the
inland side of the coast road.
The turquoise waters offshore

are spectacular, with the
odd palm-covered island
just adding to the perfection.
Local hoteliers have long
tried to capitalize on the
Portland area's natural
attractions by developing it
as a tourist resort. However,
the lack of decent roads
means it is still relatively
unspoilt, with just a couple of
hotels, including the turreted
Trident Castle, and a sprinkling of beautiful guesthouses.

Just a short distance from
Port Antonio, a weatherbeaten
sign marks the entrance to
Frenchman's Cove, easily the
most beautiful of Jamaica's
beaches, a perfect horseshoe
of sand enclosed by jungle-
clad hills and with a refresh-
ingly cool, sandy-floored
river running into the bay.

A short way farther east
along the main road, past
the sadly dilapidated San San
Beach, signposts indicate the
turnoff for the Blue Lagoon.
At this almost circular pool of

The twin harbors of Port Antonio on Jamaica's northeast coast

For hotels and restaurants on this island see pp156–9 and pp160–61

unknown depth, chilly springwater mixes with the warm seawater to amazing effect, making the pretty lagoon an unforgettable place to swim. The location was also made famous by the 1980 movie, *The Blue Lagoon*, starring Brooke Shields and Christopher Atkins. The lagoon is slated for redevelopment, with plans for a luxury spa on the banks, but for the time being it is open to all. Visitors are, however, advised to be wary of the local "guides" who may ask for non-existent entrance fees.

Water cascading into the clear pool of Reach Falls

Peaceful blue waters lapping Winnifred Beach

Winnifred Beach ⑱

🚌 5 miles (8 km) E of Port Antonio at Fairy Hill. 🍴 ⛱

Laid-back Winnifred Beach is a rarity in Jamaica. This spectacular white-sand cove has still not fallen victim to development and thus retains its pristine quality. At the moment, only forested cliffs border this curve of soft, powdery sand.

People can walk down to the beach from the main road, just opposite the Jamaica Crest Resort. The only buildings breaking the view are the odd shacks selling food and drink alongside the not-so-functional changing facilities. There is a small reef, which is ideal for snorkeling but visitors need to bring their own equipment.

This lovely place is as popular with locals as it is with visitors. However, the regulars are in the midst of a dispute with the government, whose redevelopment plans could irrevocably alter the character of Winnifred Beach.

Long Bay ⑲

12 miles (19 km) E of Port Antonio. 🚌

The wide beach of Long Bay, a glorious 1-mile (2-km) stretch of yellow sand and crashing waves, has only a few hotels and restaurants overlooking the water. Tourism has developed over the years with young Europeans coming here to relax and go surfing. Currents can be dangerous, so take local guidance before swimming. It is usually safe though, and the waves make an invigorating change to most of Jamaica's beaches. This windswept shore has also become popular in recent years for kiteboarding, thanks to its consistent swells and dependable trade wind. Visitors can negotiate sea trips with the local fishermen who draw their small craft up onto the sands.

Reach Falls ⑳

6 miles (9 km) E of Long Bay. 🚌 🕗 8:30am–4:30pm Wed–Sun. 🚫 ♿ 🅿 🛍 📷 www.reachfalls.com

Beyond Long Bay, the coast road sweeps spectacularly below cliffs and around the calm reaches of Manchioneal Bay before turning inland again. A signposted road to the right winds upwards through the rainforest to the beautiful Reach Falls that cascade from Drivers River. The green pools at the bottom of the fall are at least 4 ft (1.2 m) deep with crystal-clear water and pebbled floor.

The surrounding area has been developed by the government and now has changing facilities, a visitors' center, and refreshment outlets. However, the falls have suffered a little from development, losing their unspoilt quality. Still, the deep main pool is beautiful and visitors can also follow the river upstream to seek out underground caves and more swimming spots nearby.

Palm trees and the inviting sea at Long Bay

Firefly ㉑

43 miles (69 km) NW of Kingston.
Tel *876 725 0920.* 🚌 ⬜ *9am–5pm
Mon–Thu & Sat.* 📷 ⬜

Sitting pretty above the village
of Port Maria, Firefly was the
Jamaican home of the well-
known English playwright,
actor, and songwriter Noel
Coward (1899–1973) and his
partner, Graham Payn (1918–
2005), who both lived here
until Coward's death. The
simple 1950s house, a retreat
from his first Jamaican home
Blue Harbour which became
overrun with houseguests,
has been left as it was.
Photographs on the walls
show the famous visitors to
his residence, from Sophia
Loren and Audrey Hepburn to
Queen Elizabeth II. Perhaps
best known for such quintessentially English ditties as
"Mad Dogs and Englishmen",
Coward also wrote many
plays, some of them in this
house. However, the main
attraction is the fabulous
view that Firefly affords of the
coastline below, with Cabarita
Island in the foreground.

The privately-owned James Bond Beach, Oracabessa

**Statue of English novelist and
songwriter Noel Coward at Firefly**

Oracabessa ㉒

60 miles (95 km) NW of Kingston.
🏠 *4,300.* 🚌

A nondescript little place,
Oracabessa was the center of
banana export until the 1900s.
However, the town's claim to
fame is that it drew the attention of author Ian Fleming,
who built a house and wrote
most of his James Bond novels

here. Today, the house is part
of the exclusive Goldeneye
hotel *(see p158)* and is closed
to non-guests. However, the
007 connection remains with
the **James Bond Beach Club**,
just down the coast from
Goldeneye. It was opened in
the mid-1990s by Jamaican-
born impresario Chris
Blackwell, who produced
most of Bob Marley's albums
and also owns 70 acres (28
ha) of Oracabessa beachfront.

🏖 **James Bond Beach Club**
Old Wharf Road. ⬜ *9am–6pm Tue–
Sun.* 📷 🍴 **Note:** *changing rooms,
toilets, and watersports on-site.*

THE 007 CONNECTION

The tiny town of Oracabessa
may seem an unlikely
inspiration for a fictional
world of spies, villains, and
fantastical gadgets, but that
is just what it offered to Ian
Fleming. He fell in love with
the place during a visit to
Jamaica in 1943. Following
the footsteps of his friend,
Noel Coward, who built two
homes just down the coast,
Fleming created Goldeneye

**Ian Fleming's former home is now
part of the Goldeneye hotel**

as a retreat from the bleak English winter and visited
Jamaica regularly. Friends such as Graham Greene, Truman
Capote, and Evelyn Waugh came to stay and lap up the
sybaritic routine of sundowners and snorkeling. It was not
until his wife became pregnant in 1952 that Fleming settled
down to writing. Naming his hero after an author of a book
on birds of the West Indies, and using Jamaica as the
setting for *Doctor No* and *The Man with the Golden Gun*
(both were eventually filmed here), Fleming was entranced
by the island that inspired him to write, "Would these
books have been born if I had not been living in the
gorgeous vacuum of a Jamaican holiday? I doubt it".

Ocho Rios ㉓

54 miles (86 km) N of Kingston.
🏠 *16,300.* ✈ 🚌 ⛴ ℹ *TPDCO
Information Office, Ocean Village
Plaza, Main Street; 876 974 7705.*

Very much on the beaten
track, Ocho Rios has grown
up around the tourist industry
and these days its principal
sources of income are the
cruise ships whose massive
bulk overshadows the harbor
most days of the week. Built
around a wide bay with a
sweeping arc of hotel-lined
beach, Ocho Rios is well-
geared to meet the limited

time constraints of cruise passengers, with several attractions that can easily be seen in half a day. Buses and minibuses arrive and depart at the terminal on Main Street and route taxis cover all the main local roads.

The chief attraction is Island Village, at the far west end of Main Street. It is a slick collection of shops, restaurants, and bars with a private beach and the **Reggae Xplosion**, the only museum in Jamaica dedicated to the island's best-known export. The exhibits take visitors from the early days of ska and rocksteady via roots reggae, Bob Marley, and right up to dancehall. The museum also includes a nightclub where guides will demonstrate the latest moves.

Other than **UDC Beach**, the main attractions overlook the town at Murphy Hill, where the restful **Shaw Park Botanical Gardens** sit some 550 ft (167 m) above sea level. The gardens have beautiful views of the town, and are home to rare plants and trees, as well as a pretty waterfall. Just down the road is **Coyaba River Garden**, offering equally striking views. It is more compact, with paths threading past pools and streams. It also has a small museum dedicated to

local history. The garden has a waterfall in which visitors can take a quick splash.

Reggae Xplosion
Island Village. *Tel* 876 675 8895.
9am–5pm Mon–Fri, 10am–5pm Sat.

UDC Beach
Main Street. 9am–5pm daily. *Note: changing facilities, lifeguards, and watersports on-site.*

Shaw Park Botanical Gardens
Shaw Park Road. *Tel* 876 974 2723.
8am–5pm daily.
www.shawparkgardens.com

Coyaba River Garden
Shaw Park Road. *Tel* 876 974 6235.
8am–5pm daily.
www.coyabagardens.com

Dolphin Cove and Dunn's River Falls ㉔

Dolphin Cove 2 miles (3 km) W of Ocho Rios. *Tel* 876 974 5335.
8:30am–5:30pm daily. for Dolphin Cove. limited.
Dunn's River Falls *Tel* 876 974 2857. 8:30am–4pm daily. limited.
www.dolphincovejamaica.com
www.dunnsriverfallsja.com

Practically opposite one another on the coast road west of Ocho Rios, are the

Preparing for a dolphin encounter at Dolphin Cove

well-known Dunn's River Falls and Dolphin Cove, the latter a kind of mini-theme park which provides the opportunity to swim with dolphins, stingrays (with barbs removed), and nurse sharks.

The entrance fee charged at Dolphin Cove gives visitors a run of the complex, including a walking trail where handlers let people get up close to macaws, snakes, iguanas, and goats. It also covers snorkeling in the bay and the use of glass-bottom kayaks. Dolphin, shark, and stingray encounters, of varying degrees, take place throughout the day but cost extra.

Just up the road is Dunn's River Falls, a magnificent cascade of multiple tiers pouring over smooth limestone rocks, encircled by interesting ferns and foliage, and ending in the sea. Guides lead easy and invigorating climbs up the falls, with everyone holding hands daisy-chain style. While the surrounding land has undergone extensive development, with plenty of car parks and an abundance of concrete, the falls themselves remain spectacular, as does the white-sand beach at their base. There is also a lively reef offshore and it is possible to rent snorkel gear. Snack outlets abound on-site and there is a local craft market on the way to the exit.

Both Dunn's River and Dolphin Cove can get a little crowded on cruise ship days, (mostly late in the afternoons).

The serene Shaw Park Botanical Gardens, Ocho Rios

Footbridge leading into the lush green Cranbrook Flower Forest

Cranbrook Flower Forest **㉕**

18 miles (29 km) W of Ocho Rios.
Tel 876 770 8071. ▦ ◯ 9am–5pm
daily. ▦ ▦ ▦ ▦ ▦ **www.**
cranbrookff.com

The perfect antidote to Ocho
Rios, the Cranbrook Flower
Forest offers 130 acres (53 ha)
of beautifully landscaped
gardens and a thriving forest,
all threaded with paths.
Shaded by palms and planted
with all kinds of beautiful
tropical blooms, from heli-
conias, philodendrons, birds
of paradise, hibiscus, and
begonias to an amazing
display of orchids, the flower
gardens are exquisite.
    The other highlight is the
River Head Adventure Tour
which begins at the entrance
lawns. It is a lovely walk
through the unspoilt tropical
forest along the bank of the
Little River. The trail leads up
to where the river rises from a
spring to form a 20-ft (6-m)
wide intensely blue natural
pool. Elsewhere on-site, visitors can fish for tilapia, picnic
on the lawns surrounding the
central building, a restored
sugar mill, or go bird-
watching or take part in an
adrenaline-filled canopy tour.
    The lush grounds makes
this a popular place for
weddings and it is possible to
rent just the location or have
Cranbrook make all the
arrangements. There is also a
small gift and snack shop
near the entrance.

Runaway and Discovery Bays **㉖**

25 miles (40 km) W of Ocho Rios.
▦

Unlike Ocho Rios or Montego
Bay, the neighboring towns of
Runaway Bay and Discovery
Bay are made up of a string of
huge all-inclusive resorts that
line the coast, interspersed
with a few roadside restaurants and a couple of good
beaches. Runaway Bay has
the Cardiff Hall Public Beach,
a handsome strip of white
sand that is popular with the
locals. There is no entry fee,
nor are there any facilities to
speak of except for a small
bar and a snackshop. Located
on Discovery Bay is the
Puerto Seco Beach, which
has a strip of pristine white
sand and all the facilities.
It is relatively deserted
on weekdays.

▣ **Puerto Seco Beach**
Main Road, Discovery Bay.
◯ 9am–5pm daily. ▦ ▦ ▣
Note: lifeguards and changing
facilities on-site.

Green Grotto Caves **㉗**

22 miles (35km) W of Ocho Rios.
Tel 876 973 2841. ▦ ◯ 9am–4pm
daily. ▦ **www**.greengrotto
cavesja.com

On the main road between
the Runaway and Discovery
Bays, Green Grotto Caves is
an extensive network of limestone caverns with a subterranean lake and plenty of
impressive stalactites and
stalagmites. Guided tours take
visitors through the history of
the caves, which were used
by Amerindians as a place
of worship and later as a
hideout by Spanish troops.
    Although it makes a great
half-hour trip, the entry fee
is rather inflated. There is a
pond outside where visitors
can fish for tilapia.

One of the limestone caverns in the vast Green Grotto Caves

The Rasta-colored meditation rock at the Bob Marley Mausoleum in Nine Mile

Bob Marley Centre & Mausoleum ②⑧

25 miles (40 km) SW of Ocho Rios.
Tel 876 843 0498. ▭ *infrequent rural buses run to Nine Mile.* ▭
◯ *9am–4pm daily.* ▭▭▭▭
▭ www.bobmarleymovement.com

High in the St. Ann hills amid a gorgeous landscape of rich red earth and grassy cattle pastures, the Bob Marley Mausoleum is located in the hamlet of Nine Mile, where Marley was born and spent his early childhood before moving to Kingston at the age of 13. Encircled by a high fence and with Rasta red, gold, and green flags flapping in the wind, the compound is centered around the tiny wooden shack where the Marleys once lived, complete with the single bed that guides will say featured in the song "Is This Love". The mausoleum itself is a simple whitewashed building holding Marley's marble tomb. Incense burns and the stained-glass windows filter colors on to the stone, creating a moving atmosphere.

Located on the property is a vegetarian restaurant as well as a gift shop which sells CDs and various Marley memorabilia. There is also a Rasta-colored "meditation stone" where Marley used to rest his head while contemplating.

Chukka Adventures *(see p155)* takes visitors to the mausoleum on an old-time country bus. Each year on February 6, Marley's birth anniversary, the village comes alive with a huge concert in tribute to Jamaica's best-known musician.

Cockpit Country ②⑨

36 miles (58 km) E of Montego Bay.
▭ *minibuses run to Windsor but services are very infrequent.*
ℹ *Windsor Great House, 876 997 3832; Southern Trelawny Environmental Agency, 876 610 0818.*
www.stea.net

A vast wilderness covering some 500 square miles (1,294 sq km), the largely uninhabited Cockpit Country is one of Jamaica's most ecologically important areas. Home to innumerable rare plants and animals, it is characterized by the bizarre karst topography of conical hillocks separated by deep sinkholes in the limestone. The best place to appreciate the Cockpit's serene remoteness is **Windsor**, a tiny hamlet on the northern fringes of the area, where visitors can have a "Meet the Biologists" dinner with the owners of Windsor Great House and learn about the ecology of the area. They have rooms to rent adjacent to the great house and also arrange tours to the nearby Windsor Caves, a bat colony carpeted with pungent guano.

There are also hiking trails into the Cockpit's fringes from Albert Town, some 10 miles (16 km) south of Windsor, where the Southern Trelawny Environmental Agency offers walks and bush picnics.

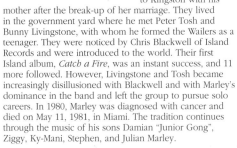

Bob Marley performing at a concert

BOB MARLEY

Born on February 6, 1945, to Cedella Malcom, a 17-year-old farmer's daughter, and 51-year-old Norval Marley, a white Jamaican former soldier, Bob Marley remains the biggest reggae star in the world. Having grown up in the country, Marley moved to Kingston with his mother after the break-up of her marriage. They lived in the government yard where he met Peter Tosh and Bunny Livingstone, with whom he formed the Wailers as a teenager. They were noticed by Chris Blackwell of Island Records and were introduced to the world. Their first Island album, *Catch a Fire*, was an instant success, and 11 more followed. However, Livingstone and Tosh became increasingly disillusioned with Blackwell and with Marley's dominance in the band and left the group to pursue solo careers. In 1980, Marley was diagnosed with cancer and died on May 11, 1981, in Miami. The tradition continues through the music of his sons Damian "Junior Gong", Ziggy, Ky-Mani, Stephen, and Julian Marley.

Ruins on the grounds of Windsor Great House, Cockpit Country

Outdoor Activities and Specialized Holidays

Jamaica has an excellent tourist infrastructure and offers a large variety of outdoor activities to its visitors. Besides the obvious pursuits, from world-class golf courses and fantastic beaches to spas and watersports, there are also some unusual options. To give the island an edge over its neighbors, many activities have been designed especially for cruise ship passengers. Alongside boat tours and Jet Skis, horseback rides, and hikes, visitors can also glide down a river on a bamboo raft, swing through treetops, and take a ride on a dogsled.

Visitors at the Mahogany Beach, Ocho Rios

BEACHES

Jamaica's top beaches are located along the island's north coast. Sheltered by reefs and boasting powdery white sands straight out of the brochures, they are everything visitors would expect from a Caribbean shoreline. The finest of these beaches, however, have been snapped up by developers and are either incorporated into hotel complexes (therefore off-limits for non-guests) or are privately owned attractions with showers, changing rooms, and an entrance fee.

Along the south coast, owing to past volcanic eruptions, the shore features brown and sometimes decidedly black beaches rather than splendid white sands. Although the movement of the water may give it a murky appearance at the shoreline, a little farther out it is possible to find a perfectly clear blue sea that provides excellent swimming.

DIVING AND SNORKELING

While Jamaica's reefs may not be the best in the Caribbean, having suffered damage from storms and human carelessness by way of dropped anchors and coastal pollution, there are still some lovely spots for diving and snorkeling. The best snorkeling and diving is along the north coast between Negril and Ocho Rios, where visibility is at a peak, and an almost continuous reef runs parallel to the coast. On these excursions, visitors can observe the fire, elkhorn, and brain corals, and a host of colorful marine life. Several wreck dives are also available, including submerged planes used in ill-fated ganja smuggling operations. All the main resorts have dive sites and operators who rent out snorkeling equipment. The latter is also available from the several watersports outlets on the beaches. Some of the main operators in Jamaica include the **Negril Scuba Centre**, **Resort Divers**, and **Lady G'Diver**.

RIVER RAFTING

Gliding along calm waters surrounded by riverbanks swathed in greenery remains a spectacular way to see the island. River rafting was first popularized by Errol Flynn (*see p146*), who noticed farmers transporting their goods along the Rio Grande by bamboo raft and thought it might make a pleasurable jaunt. Although there is no organized rafting center in Port Antonio, raft captains offer trips to interested visitors. The Martha Brae River, west of Montego Bay, is the next best spot. While lacking the towering mountain scenery of the Rio Grande, it is a beautiful trip

Rafting on the Martha Brae River

For hotels and restaurants on this island see pp156–9 and pp160–61

Horse-riding in the water at Chukka Cove, near Ocho Rios

through the lush Trelawny countryside. **Rafting on the Martha Brae** offers tours on a 30-ft (9-m) bamboo raft, with a trained raft captain. Whitewater rafting can be done on the Great River – when water levels allow. Rafting trips are provided by **Caliche River Rafting Tours**.

BOAT CRUISES

From Negril, Ocho Rios, and Montego Bay, boats offering day trips for visitors cruise up and down the coastline. Most are catamarans, complete with bathrooms, bars, and nets over the hulls for sunbathing. The trips tend to include an open bar, as well as a stop for snorkeling. Some boats also offer shorter sunset cruises or evening trips that include dinner. These could be the party-hard booze cruise type, so do check before booking. **Cool Runnings Boat Tours**, **Wild Thing Watersports**, and **Dreamer Catamarans** offer boat cruises.

WATERSPORTS

All of the main beaches in Ocho Rios, Montego Bay, and Negril have watersports outlets offering everything from rental of scuba equipment to non-motorized options such as kayaking and sailing in Sunfish boats. The motorized activities include Jet Skiing, parasailing, waterskiing, glass-bottom boats, and banana boat rides. The **Garfield Diving Station** offers Jet Skiing and glass-bottom boat rides.

HORSE-RIDING

Alongside gentle horse-rides through the countryside, Jamaica's stables have also developed beach rides. Visitors may take a short amble through the bush to the seashore, de-saddle their mount, change into swimming gear, and climb back on for an exhilarating trot through the water. The rides offered by Chukka Caribbean Adventures (*see p155*) and **Hooves** have the horses walking through deep water, but Montego Bay's **Half Moon Equestrian Centre** takes it a step further and has the horses swim, a magical experience. The latter also offer riding lessons.

HIKING

Jamaica's thick forests offer many pleasant hikes through spectacular scenery. The best of the walks are located in the misty Blue Mountains (*see pp144–5*), where visitors can amble along the easy trails within Holywell Recreational Park or go for more challenging routes such as the uphill trek to Cinchona Botanical Gardens. The island's ultimate hike, however, is the Blue Mountains Peak trail, a 6-hour walk through forest that changes from montane rainforest to stunted elfin growth, overhung with ferns and surrounded by miniature orchids and epiphytic plants.

BIRD-WATCHING

Jamaica provides for some great bird-watching, most notably in the Blue Mountains, Cockpit Country (*see p151*), the Royal Palm Reserve near Negril (*see p138*), and the Black River (*see p140*). Of the 280-odd species recorded on the island, 21 birds are found nowhere else in the world, a level of endemism not found on any other Caribbean island. Spectacular hummingbirds can be seen up close at Rocklands Bird Sanctuary in St. James (*see p136*). Jamaica's national bird, the streamertail hummingbird, the Jamaican woodpecker, and the 2-inch (5-cm) long vervain hummingbird, the second-smallest bird in the world, are a few species to look out for. Tour companies such as the **Sun Venture Tours** provide birding trips. Hotels, including the Forres Park (*see p156*) and Mockingbird Hill (*see p159*), offer packages.

Hiking through the spectacular forests of the Blue Mountains

CAVING

Much of Jamaica is covered with soft sedimentary limestone, eroded by water over centuries to create thousands of caves. Many of these, such as the Roaring River and Two Sisters, are open to the public as show caves, with electric lights and walkways. However, most caves remain untouched. Of these undeveloped ones, Windsor Caves in Cockpit Country *(see p151)* are the easiest to access. Cockpit Country also has the deepest of the island's sinkholes – deep pits with sheer edges that are descended by way of ropes and pulleys. Guided tours and trips are provided by **Cockpit Country Adventure Tours** and **Jamaican Caves Organization**.

GOLF

Jamaica has 12 golf courses, which host local and international tournaments all year round. Recognized as some of the best courses in the world, and designed by some well-known golf course architects,

Golf course at the Half Moon Club, Montego Bay

including Robert Trent Jones Sr. and Jr., Jamaica's links boast spectacular locations by the sea. Montego Bay has no less than five premier courses around town. Ocho Rios is second best. Smaller courses are found in both Negril and Kingston. Useful information is available from the **Jamaica Golf Association**.

SPAS

No high-class resort in Jamaica is complete without its spa, and several smaller places

also offer massages and beauty treatments. Many spas are beautifully located, with massage rooms right on the water, cooled by sea breezes, and with a soundtrack of waves. Alongside massages, larger spas such as **Charlie's Spa**, the Aveda Concept Spa at The Caves hotel *(see p158)*, Half Moon Hotel's Fern Tree Spa *(see p157)*, and the Driftwood Spa at Jake's hotel *(see p159)*, offer the full range of beauty, body, and facial treatments, as well as manicures and pedicures.

DIRECTORY

DIVING AND SNORKELING

Lady G'Diver
Port Antonio,
Portland.
Tel 876 995 0246.
www.ladygdiver.com

Negril Scuba Centre
Negril Escape Hotel,
West End Road,
Negril.
Tel 876 383 9533.
www.negrilscuba.com

Resort Divers
Hotel Royal Decameron,
Montego Bay.
Tel 876 973 6131.
www.resort
divers.com

RIVER RAFTING

Caliche River Rafting Tours
Montego Bay.
Tel 876 940 1745.
www.whitewater
raftingmontegobay.com

Rafting on the Martha Brae
Gloucester Avenue,
Montego Bay.
Tel 876 952 0889.
www.jamaica
rafting.com

BOAT CRUISES

Cool Runnings Boat Tours
121 Main Street, Ocho
Rios. *Tel 876 974 4593.*
www.fivestar
watersports.com

Dreamer Catamarans
Montego Bay.
Tel 876 979 0102.
www.dreamer
catamarans.com

Wild Thing Watersports
Norman Manley
Boulevard, Negril.
Tel 876 957 9930.
www.wildthingwater
sportsnegril.com

WATERSPORTS

Garfield Diving Station
Ocho Rios, St. Ann.
Tel 876 544 4354.
www.garfielddiving.com

HORSE-RIDING

Half Moon Equestrian Centre
Half Moon Hotel,
Ironshore, Montego Bay.
Tel 876 953 2286.
www.horsebackriding
jamaica.com

Hooves
61 Windsor Road,
St Ann's Bay.
Tel 876 972 0905.
www.hoovesjamaica.com

BIRD-WATCHING

Sun Venture Tours
Kingston 10.
Tel 876 960 6685.
www.sunventure
tours.com

CAVING

Cockpit Country Adventure Tours
Albert Town, Trelawny.
Tel 876 610 0818.
www.stea.net/ccat.net

Jamaican Caves Organization
www.jamaicancaves.org

GOLF

Jamaica Golf Association
80 Knutsford Boulevard,
Kingston 5.
Tel 876 906 7636.
www.jamaicagolf
association.com

SPAS

Charlie's Spa
Couples Sans Souci Hotel,
Ocho Rios.
Tel 876 994 1206.
www.couples.com

For hotels and restaurants on this island see pp156–9 and pp160–61

"Soft" Adventure Tours

Jamaica provides a variety of alternatives to spending a day on a beach. Popularly known as "soft" adventures, these refer to fun but safe activities and range from river tubing to horseback rides in the sea. More unusual adventures include a swing through the treetops

A horse-riding trip in the countryside

attached to a harness and a zipwire, an aerial bobsleigh run, open gondola rides up the hillside, or a dogsled tour. Most of these activities take place at sites along the north coast and the trips include pickups and drop-offs at hotels in Montego Bay, Ocho Rios, and Negril.

LAND ADVENTURES

Popular land-based tours include safaris aboard zebra-striped, open-top jeeps or old-time country buses into the heart of Jamaica's rugged interior, or up to the Bob Marley Museum. Downhill mountain-bike rides are also offered by different agencies.

Dogsled tours *involve riding in modified buggies on wheels, pulled by an enthusiastic team made up of mostly rescue dogs.*

Canopy tours *provide for an exciting adventure. From a series of wooden platforms built into the rainforest canopy, soar through the trees by way of an intricate system of harnesses, pulleys and carabiners attached to horizontal traverses.*

ATV safaris *include a lesson on handling these rugged four-wheel buggies or all-terrain vehicles, after which visitors can meander through the countryside, negotiating a few gullies and hills.*

WATER ADVENTURES

Visitors are never far from the sea in Jamaica, and even horseback rides here involve a dip in the ocean. Rafting down the island's rivers is a pleasant way to spend half a day. Guided ocean safaris aboard dinghies weave around the coast, stopping for swimming or snorkeling.

Sea Trek *is a great way to get up close to the reefs and marine life. Walk on the seabed, breathing through a spaceman-like helmet.*

TOUR OPERATORS

Chukka Caribbean Adventures
Montego Bay.
Tel 876 953 6699.
www.chukkacaribbean.com
Rain Forest Aerial Trams
Ocho Rios.
Tel 876 974 3990.
www.rainforestrams.com

River tubing and kayaking *are exhilarating ways to see Jamaica's rivers. Paddle downstream sitting in a huge rubber ring, or tackle gentle whitewater in a kayak. Sections of tame rapids keep things lively.*

Choosing a Hotel

Despite being the home of many sanitized and exclusive enclaves, Jamaica offers great diversity in its accommodation options. As well as its beach resorts, often with private areas of sand, watersports, and all the usual facilities of a holiday hotel, the island also has some unique places, from misty mountain retreats to hip boutique hotels and inexpensive boltholes.

PRICE CATEGORIES
The following price ranges are for a standard double room per night and all taxes included.

$ under $100
$$ $100–200
$$$ $200–300
$$$$ $300–400
$$$$$ over $400

JAMAICA

All-Inclusive Hotels of Jamaica
Jamaica is the birthplace of the all-inclusive hotel, where everything from food and drinks to watersports and tips is included in the price. All-inclusives are a popular choice for honeymooners, and many places in Jamaica cater to couples only. Some resorts even have minimum age requirements ranging from 12 to 18. Others specialize in family holidays, with lots of amenities for children, from kids' clubs to waterparks.

Half Moon

Jake's

BLUE MOUNTAINS Starlight Chalets $

Silver Hill Gap **Tel** 876 907 3070 **Fax** 876 906 3075 **Rooms** 17

Fantastically remote and deep in the hills close to Cinchona Botanical Gardens, this is a magical spot, often wreathed in mist and usually quite cold at night. The rooms are cozy and facilities include a spa, yoga classes, and meeting and conference rooms. **www.starlightchalet.com**

BLUE MOUNTAINS Forres Park $$

Main Street, Mavis Bank **Tel** 876 927 8275 **Fax** 876 978 6942 **Rooms** 14

In the shadow of Blue Mountains Peak, this peaceful retreat offers comfortable, rustic rooms and cottages dotted around pretty gardens. The owners have 8 sq miles (20 sq km) of coffee plantations in the mountains, so tours can be arranged, as can the climb to the peak and birding trips. Excellent food and drinks. **www.forrespark.com**

BLUE MOUNTAINS Strawberry Hill $$$$$

Irish Town **Tel** 876 944 8400 **Fax** 876 844 8408 **Rooms** 12

One of Jamaica's best hotels, this place has beautifully designed wooden cottages spread over a hillside with spectacular Kingston views. Each cottage offers the height of comfort, and the infinity pool is a photographer's dream. There is also an Aveda spa, sauna, and a great restaurant *(see p160)* and bar. **www.islandoutpost.com**

KINGSTON Altamont Court $$

1 Altamont Terrace, New Kingston **Tel** 876 929 4498 **Fax** 876 929 2118 **Rooms** 58

This friendly place in the heart of New Kingston is perfectly placed for the area's restaurants, bars, and clubs. Rooms are smart and appealing, with balcony or deck. Family rooms are available. Rates include breakfast. There is a pool on-site, as well as a bar, Jacuzzi, and sundeck. **www.altamontcourt.com**

KINGSTON Courtleigh $$

85 Knutsford Boulevard, New Kingston **Tel** 876 929 9000 **Fax** 876 926 7744 **Rooms** 127

This family-owned place is the best of the large hotels along Knutsford Boulevard; upmarket and efficient but still friendly and accommodating. Rooms range from plush doubles to luxury suites, and all feature mahogany furniture and have views over Kingston. There is a large pool on-site and a popular bar. **www.courtleigh.com**

KINGSTON Knutsford Court Hotel $$

16 Chelsea Avenue, New Kingston 5 **Tel** 876 929 1000 **Fax** 876 960 7373 **Rooms** 143

Centrally located, this clean, well-run hotel focuses on business travelers but its elegant, Georgian-themed decor will suit leisure vacationers too. Its swimming pool helps beat the heat, and it has a gym plus a restaurant serving choice Jamaican dishes and continental favorites. **www.knutsfordcourt.com**

KINGSTON Mikuzi $$

5 Upper Montrose Road, New Kingston **Tel** 876 978 4859 **Rooms** 11

A good little budget option, built around a lovely old great house and with a collection of individually-styled rooms that range from compact backpacker units to elegant apartments with kitchenette and handsome wooden furniture. Friendly and helpful staff, and the location is convenient for local sights. **www.mikuzijamaica.com**

KINGSTON Christar $$$

99a Hope Road, New Kingston **Tel** 876 978 3393 **Fax** 876 978 8068 **Rooms** 24

Conveniently located on Hope Road, just up from the Bob Marley Museum, this compact, efficiently run little place offers a collection of well-appointed rooms and studios, the latter with kitchen, bar, and dining area, as well as more luxurious suites. There is a gym on-site, and a small pool and Jacuzzi. **www.christarvillashotel.com**

Key to Symbols *see back cover flap*

KINGSTON Pegasus

81 Knutsford Boulevard, New Kingston **Tel** *876 926 3961* **Fax** *876 929 0593* **Rooms** *300*

This 17-story hotel towers over New Kingston. Facilities include a gym, spa, jogging track, tennis court, and an Olympic-sized pool, while smartly refurbished rooms range from commodious doubles to luxury suites. All have private balconies affording fabulous views of the city below. **www.jamaicapegasus.com**

MONTEGO BAY Hotel Gloriana

1–2 Sunset Boulevard, Hip Strip **Tel** *876 979 0669* **Fax** *976 979 0698* **Rooms** *75*

Good budget option, just back from the Hip Strip but within walking distance of the beaches, bars, and restaurants. Rooms in the new block, with tiled floors and more natural light, are the best choice, and there is a pool, Jacuzzi, gym, games room, and spa on-site. Family rooms are available. **www.hotelgloriana.com**

MONTEGO BAY Altamont West

33 Gloucester Ave, Hip Strip **Tel** *876 620 4540* **Fax** *876 971 7337* **Rooms** *32*

A chic little place opposite Aquasol Beach, furnished with a Jamaican theme. Offers good service, and appealing rooms and suites equipped with hair dryer, iron and board, and wireless Internet. There is a spa, bar, pool, and grassy sundeck. **www.altamontwesthotel.com**

MONTEGO BAY Doctor's Cave Beach Hotel

Gloucester Avenue, Hip Strip **Tel** *876 952 4355* **Fax** *876 952 5204* **Rooms** *90*

In an excellent location directly opposite Doctor's Cave Beach, this is a busy little place, friendly and popular throughout the year. Rooms, though basic, are adequate and clean. There is a pool, Jacuzzi, ping-pong and pool tables, and a good restaurant and bar. **www.doctorscave.com**

MONTEGO BAY El Greco

11 Queen's Drive **Tel** *876 940 6116* **Fax** *876 940 6115* **Rooms** *96*

High above the Hip Strip overlooking Doctor's Cave, but with access to the beach via an elevator down the cliffside, the villa apartments at this appealing resort have full kitchens and are a great choice for families. The place offers a pool, floodlit tennis courts, and plenty of peace and quiet. **www.elgrecojamaica.com**

MONTEGO BAY Coyaba Beach Resort

Main Road, Ironshore **Tel** *876 953 9150* **Fax** *876 953 2244* **Rooms** *50*

One of the better resort hotels east of town, Coyaba Beach Resort is small enough to feel quite intimate yet is professionally run and offers ample degrees of luxury. It has a pleasant private beach and facilities throughout the resort are excellent, as is the service. **www.coyabaresortjamaica.com**

MONTEGO BAY Half Moon

Main Road, Rose Hall **Tel** *876 953 2211* **Fax** *876 953 2731* **Rooms** *398*

This stalwart resort exudes all the class of old-time Jamaica. Fantastic private beaches with watersports, tennis courts, a world-renowned golf course, a dolphin lagoon, spa, and restaurants and bars are ranged around the spacious landscaped grounds. The rooms and villas are appropriately sumptuous. **www.halfmoon.com**

NEGRIL Yellow Bird

Norman Manley Boulevard **Tel** *876 957 4252* **Fax** *876 957 3692* **Rooms** *22*

Great budget accommodation with rooms and cottages around a grassy lawn at the edge of the beach, and a very friendly and helpful staff. The cottages have two bedrooms (but you can rent just the one). The rooms are simple, pleasant, and clean; some with shared bathrooms. **www.theyellowbird.com**

NEGRIL Citronella

West End Road **Tel** *876 460 8369* **Fax** *876 460 8369* **Rooms** *10*

Set amid lovely clifftop gardens and grassy lawns, these two- to three-bedroom cottages are simply built, but offer comfortable beds and plenty of space. Some have thatched roofs and hammocks on the veranda. Carved cliffside steps lead to the sea. **www.citronellajamaica.com**

NEGRIL Country Country

Norman Manley Boulevard **Tel** *876 957 4273* **Fax** *876 957 4342* **Rooms** *20*

This appealing place is in a busy part of the beach, and is painted in a palette of pastels with rooms set just back from the sand. All the rooms are spacious and comfortable, and are equipped with hair dryer, refrigerator, and kettle. The restaurant-bar is beautifully situated right on the water. **www.countryjamaica.com**

NEGRIL Idle Awhile

Norman Manley Boulevard **Tel** *876 957 3302* **Fax** *876 957 9567* **Rooms** *14*

Classy and upscale place right on the beach and offering gorgeous rooms with private verandas, refrigerators, and all mod cons; the suites have a kitchen. Guests have access to the excellent sports facilities at nearby Swept Away resort including gym, yoga, tennis, squash courts, sauna, Jacuzzi, and of course a pool. **www.idleawhile.com**

NEGRIL Charela Inn

Norman Manley Boulevard **Tel** *876 957 4277* **Fax** *876 957 4414* **Rooms** *54*

This long-established beach hotel has an enduring appeal owing to its location, amenities (including a pool and conference facilities) and, more especially, the service it provides. The rooms are tasteful, with wireless Internet and all the usual comforts. The on-site restaurant is excellent. **www.charela.com**

NEGRIL Nirvana on the Beach
🅿 🍴 📄 ♿ Ⓦ $$$

Norman Manley Boulevard **Tel** *941 708 0203 (Nov–May); 716 789 5955 (Jun–Oct)* **Rooms** *8*

This collection of beautiful wooden cottages in shaded gardens dotted with hammocks makes for a very secluded place to stay. Creatively decorated, each unit has screened windows to keep out insects, and the services of a cook/housekeeper are included in the rates. There is a private section of beach as well. **www.nirvananegril.com**

NEGRIL Tensing Pen
🅿 🍴 📄 Ⓦ $$$

West End Road **Tel** *876 957 0387* **Fax** *876 957 0161* **Rooms** *22*

Networked by little paths and with a hair-raising suspension bridge between the cliffs, this is a truly beautiful place to stay, with a range of cabins and cottages nicely spaced around the grounds. Each has been fitted out to a very high standard, and the food is excellent; there is a yoga studio too. **www.tensingpen.com**

NEGRIL The Caves
🅿 🍴 📄 ♨ Ⓦ $$$$$

West End Road **Tel** *876 957 0270* **Fax** *876 957 4930* **Rooms** *12*

Perhaps the most exclusive choice in Negril, and certainly the most romantic. Individually designed and stylishly furnished, the rooms and villas have everything one could ask of a tropical hideaway, as well as an Aveda spa. The food is great, the highlight being dining in a cave at the waters' edge. **www.thecavesresort.com**

NEGRIL Rockhouse
🅿 🍴 📄 Ⓦ $$$$$

West End Road **Tel** *876 957 4373* **Fax** *876 957 0557* **Rooms** *34*

A ravishing cliffside setting and plenty of designer touches make this one of the West End's most stylish options. The thatched cabins are a lot less rustic than they appear from the outside and there is a gorgeous "horizon" pool. Its namesake restaurant *(see p161)* is built over the water, and there is a spa too. **www.rockhousehotel.com**

OCHO RIOS Fisherman's Point
🅿 🍴 📄 Ⓦ $$

Cruise Ship Pier, Turtle Beach Road **Tel** *876 350 9162* **Fax** *876 974 4147* **Rooms** *78*

In a location adjacent to both the beach and Island Village, this complex of self-contained condos is ideal for someone looking for a bit of freedom. Each condo has a fully equipped kitchen and balcony, and there is a playground, a pool, restaurant *(see p161)*, bar, spa facilities, and family rooms. **www.fishermanspoint.net**

OCHO RIOS Hibiscus Lodge
🅿 🍴 📄 ♿ Ⓦ $$

83–87 Main Street **Tel** *876 974 2676* **Fax** *876 974 1874* **Rooms** *26*

Up on the cliffs past the manic part of Main Street, the lodge has peaceful gardens, a pool, and access to the shallow, clear ocean waters via a deck. Rooms are comfortable and functional, some with balconies that offer views of the mirror-calm sea, protected by the huge offshore reef. **www.hibiscusjamaica.com**

OCHO RIOS High Hope Estate
🍴 Ⓦ $$

PO Box 11, St. Ann's Bay **Tel** *876 972 2277* **Fax** *876 972 1607* **Rooms** *5*

Beautiful old great house, high in the St. Ann's hills and just a short distance from Ocho Rios, offering a selection of elegant, individually decorated rooms with beautiful antique furniture. Meals at the restaurant, featuring local (often organic) ingredients, are memorable, as are the views down to the sea. **www.highhopeestate.com**

OCHO RIOS Rooms
🅿 🍴 📄 ♿ Ⓦ $$

Turtle Beach, Main Street **Tel** *876 974 6632* **Fax** *876 516 1544* **Rooms** *97*

Right on the main town beach, this functional SuperClubs property offers clean, spacious rooms with all amenities for those who want resort-style ambience without the all-inclusive rate. There is a pool and fitness center on-site, and guests are within walking distance of the town's shops and bars. **www.roomsresorts.com**

OCHO RIOS Shaw Park Beach Hotel and Spa
🍴 📄 ♿ Ⓦ $$

Shaw Park Road **Tel** *876 974 2552* **Fax** *876 674 5042* **Rooms** *94*

Within the beautiful Shaw Park botanical gardens (guests have free access), this delightful retreat offers spacious rooms and suites with spectacular views down over the bay from the balconies and picture windows. The waterfront Palm Room Gourmet Restaurant is a romantic spot for enjoying choice seafood. **www.shawparkbeachhotel.com**

OCHO RIOS Goldeneye
🅿 🍴 📄 ♨ Ⓦ $$$$$

Oracabessa, Main Street **Tel** *876 975 3354* **Fax** *876 975 3620* **Rooms** *17*

Built around the Jamaican home of James Bond author Ian Fleming *(see p148)*, this exclusive hotel oozes style, with a collection of unique villas set around a headland. Excellent service and fine food, spa facilities and a great pool. Celebrities are fond of this place. **www.goldeneyehotel.com**

OCHO RIOS Jamaica Inn
🅿 ♨ Ⓦ $$$$$

White River, Main Street **Tel** *876 974 2514* **Fax** *876 974 2449* **Rooms** *47*

One of Jamaica's classiest hotels, and certainly among the most upmarket, this elegant, sedate place is set around a gorgeous private beach and sweeping greens that include a croquet lawn. The tastefully decorated suites have every degree of luxury, and there is a pool, fitness center, and a blissful seaside spa. **www.jamaicainn.com**

PORT ANTONIO Drapers San
🅿 🍴 $

Main Road, Drapers **Tel** *876 993 7118* **Rooms** *6*

Friendly budget option owned by an Italian lady who cooks up delicious Jamaican and Italian dinners. Rooms in the two eclectically decorated cottages range in size and facilities – some have shared bathrooms – but all are clean and comfortable, and there is a path to the tiny beach below. **www.go-jam.com**

Key to Symbols *see back cover flap*

PORT ANTONIO Mikuzi

Winnifred Beach, Fairy Hill **Tel** 876 978 4859 **Rooms** 8

Just 2 minutes' walk from the sublime Winnifred Beach, these simple yet appealing rooms and cottages make for a lovely low-key stay. Some are more basic, with shared facilities, while the cottages have kitchens and cable TV. The gardens have hammocks to laze around in, and meals are available. **www.mikuzijamaica.com**

PORT ANTONIO Goblin Hill Villas

San San **Tel** 876 993 7443 **Fax** 876 993 7716 **Rooms** 20

A slice of old Jamaica overlooking San San Bay. Decorated in cool modern style, the 28 one- and two-bedroom villas are staffed by a housekeeper who cooks good Jamaican meals. There is a large pool on-site, tennis courts, family rooms, and guests get a pass to Frenchman's Cove Beach. **www.goblinhillvillas.com**

PORT ANTONIO Mockingbird Hill

Main Road, Drapers **Tel** 876 993 7627 **Fax** 876 993 7133 **Rooms** 10

In the foothills of the John Crow Mountains, this eco-oriented place has a restful, relaxed feel. Rooms are airy and spacious, with hammocks on the balcony, and there is a pool and the fantastic Mille Fleurs restaurant on-site *(see p161)*. Birding tours can be arranged. **www.hotelmockingbirdhill.com**

PORT ANTONIO Geejam

San San **Tel** 876 993 7000 **Fax** 876 993 7156 **Rooms** 7

A 10-minute drive from Port Antonio, this luxury hotel has a state-of-the art recording studio where international artistes such as Gwen Stefani and the Gorillaz have written and recorded their songs. Villas and deluxe cabins are set in tropical gardens. Each room has the latest sound system. Spa and fitness facilities.**www.geejamhotel.com**

RUNAWAY BAY Breezes Runaway Bay

Main Street **Tel** 876 973 4820 **Fax** 876 516 4153 **Rooms** 266

Huge "super all-inclusive" on a lovely strip of beach with all watersports available, tennis courts, and with its own 18-hole PGA golf course just across the road. Rooms are attractively designed with all the trappings of a chain resort, and there are several restaurants. **www.superclubs.com**

TREASURE BEACH Golden Sands

Frenchman's Bay **Tel** 876 965 0167 **Fax** 876 965 0167 **Rooms** 20

A budget option whose main draw is its location right on Treasure Beach's best stretch, perfect for swimming and chilling out. The rooms are basic, but clean and serviceable, with fans or air-conditioning, private bathrooms, screened windows, a bar, and shared communal kitchens. **www.goldensandstreasurebeach.com**

TREASURE BEACH Ital Rest

Great Bay **Tel** 876 421 8909 **Rooms** 4

The two wooden, thatch-roofed cottages set in lovely gardens have two comfortable bedrooms each that are simply decorated, with fans and mosquito nets. They offer complete peace and quiet and a real sense of getting away from it all. The hosts are very friendly. **www.italrest.com**

TREASURE BEACH Mar Blue Villa Suites

Old Wharf, Calabash Bay **Tel** 876 965 3408 **Rooms** 8

In a quiet location right on the seafront, these villas and suites benefit from exacting attention to detail, from the huge bath towels to the light, open design. A pool overlooks the ocean, and the excellent restaurant and bar on-site has won several awards. **www.marblue.com**

TREASURE BEACH Treasure Beach Hotel

Frenchman's Bay **Tel** 876 965 2305 **Fax** 876 965 2544 **Rooms** 32

Though it has seen better days, this remains the only full-blown resort hotel in the area, with room blocks dotted around spacious gardens, and two pools overlooking one of Treasure Beach's best stretches of sand. It can feel a bit deserted, but that somehow adds to the charm. **www.treasurebeachjamaica.com**

TREASURE BEACH Treasure Cot

Calabash Bay **Tel** 876 965 3000 **Fax** 876 965 0552 **Rooms** 2

An intensely atmospheric and very private villa, Treasure Cot is enclosed by its gardens. A veranda overlooks the beach just out front. The chic decor includes lots of artwork on the walls, and it is a great place to just get away from it all. The villa has a full kitchen, and two bathrooms.**www.islandoutpost.com/jakes**

TREASURE BEACH Blue Marlin

Great Bay **Tel** 876 855 1122 **Rooms** 7

Two gorgeous villas set in sweeping gardens that go right up to the sands of Great Bay, a marvelous swimming spot. With three and four bedrooms respectively, each villa is furnished with a mix of modern and antique furniture, and there is a full housekeeping staff on hand. **www.bluemarlinvillas.com**

TREASURE BEACH Jake's

Calabash Bay **Tel** 876 965 3000 **Fax** 876 965 0552 **Rooms** 29

Perhaps the coolest place to stay in all of Jamaica, this is the island's ultimate boutique hotel, and hub of the local tourist scene. The eclectic and very individual rooms and cottages feature beautiful design touches; there is a saltwater pool, great restaurants *(see p161)*, spa, and an extremely convivial bar. **www.jakeshotel.com**

Where to Eat & Nightlife

Jamaica's resorts overflow with restaurants serving local cuisine as well as Italian, Chinese, and American-style burger meals, and there is always a hole-in-the wall café doling out plates of filling food to local workers, too. The island's fantastic music scene is showcased in its many bars and clubs, where DJs play classic reggae and dancehall, and live acts belt out Bob Marley standards.

PRICE CATEGORIES
The price ranges are for a two-course meal for one, including tax and service charges and half a bottle of wine.

Ⓢ under $10
ⓈⓈ $10–15
ⓈⓈⓈ $15–25
ⓈⓈⓈⓈ $25–35
ⓈⓈⓈⓈⓈ over $35

RESTAURANTS

Boston Jerk Shacks
Jerk cooking – seasoned meat slowly barbecued over pimento wood – was invented in Boston Bay (between Port Antonio and Long Bay). There is nowhere better in the whole country to taste this smoky and spicy specialty than in the Boston jerk shacks which line the Main Road of Boston Bay. Pork, chicken, fish, and seafood are sold by weight here.

Jerk chicken shack

Rockhouse

KINGSTON Ashanti Oasis 🆅 🖾 ⓈⓈ
Hope Gardens, Hope Road, Mona **Tel** *876 920 2079*

Wonderful location in a wooden house in the heart of Kingston's botanical gardens, this vegetarian restaurant is a great retreat, with a soothing tinkle of water from the central waterfall and delicious daily specials, from ratatouille to soya and vegetable balls with pumpkin and rice, or curried ackee. Some interesting local wines are on sale, too.

KINGSTON Gloria's 🖾 🖾 ♿ ⓈⓈ
Port Royal, 5 Queen Street **Tel** *876 967 8066*

Just up from Port Royal's square, with tables under awnings on the pavement, the ever casual Gloria's is a legendary stop-off for seafood. Bought fresh from local boats, the fish comes steamed, fried, or brown-stewed, and there is also curried shrimps and lobster. It is all served with festival bread or rice and peas.

KINGSTON Red Bones 🆅 🍷 🍽 🖾 🎵 ⓈⓈⓈ
21 Braemar Av., Uptown **Tel** *876 978 6091*

Enduringly popular, with tables indoors or in the garden courtyard, where there is often live jazz or blues. Starters might consist of *callaloo* strudel with cream cheese and chives, or smoked marlin with salad, while main courses range from grilled smoked pork chops in a ginger sauce to chicken and shrimp linguine with basil and tomato.

KINGSTON Strawberry Hill 🍷 🖾 ♿ ⓈⓈⓈⓈⓈ
Irish Town Blue Mountains **Tel** *876 944 8400*

Set in the eponymous resort *(see p156)* with views of Kingston and Port Royal below, the location is as much of a draw as the food. Sunday brunch includes curried plantain, smoked salmon and marlin, rack of lamb, jerk chicken, fish washed in lime juice and cooked in a vinegar-based marinade, and pork in red-wine sauce, plus an array of desserts.

MONTEGO BAY The Native 🆅 🖾 ⓈⓈⓈ
29 Gloucester Av., Hip Strip **Tel** *876 979 2769*

One of the best places in town for a sit-down Jamaican meal, with tables laid out on the veranda and excellent service. Local staples include oxtail, ackee and saltfish, jerk chicken, or *escoveitched* fish (or a "Boonoonoonoos" platter featuring them all) alongside seafood and vegetarian fare such as green curry or jerked ackee and tofu.

MONTEGO BAY Houseboat Bar and Grill 🍷 🍽 🖾 ⓈⓈⓈⓈ
Freeport Peninsula, Bogue Lagoon **Tel** *876 979 8845*

Unusual location in a refurbished floating houseboat, with tables inside and on the decks. Making imaginative use of local ingredients, the cooking is fantastic, with offerings such as conch fritters with remoulade sauce, or mahimahi fillet with caper and lime *beurre blanc*. Live lobsters can be chosen from a tank. Divine desserts.

NEGRIL Three Dives 🖾 ⓈⓈ
West End Road **Tel** *876 782 9990*

This is an eternally popular place in a tree-filled garden on the cliffs, with a nightly bonfire creating some atmosphere. Many people swear by the quality of the jerk chicken and pork, but they are also good with lobster. A very casual place so one should not expect five-star service and linen tablecloths, but it is pleasantly laid-back.

NEGRIL Kuyaba 🆅 🖾 ⓈⓈⓈ
Norman Manley Boulevard **Tel** *876 957 4318*

Among the best places to enjoy a delectable breakfast, Kuyaba is located in its namesake hotel on Long Beach. The excellent dinner menu features freshly prepared king-sized shrimps and crayfish (during season). The restaurant is known for its brown stew conch dish. Free shuttle service for guests from other hotels.

Key to Symbols *see back cover flap*

NEGRIL Sunrise Club

Norman Manley Boulevard **Tel** *876 957 4293*

Excellent Italian restarant, serving authentic cuisine that includes pizzas baked in a wood-fired brick oven. Grilled meats and seafood are also good, with plenty of inventive dishes on the dedicated "Lobster House" menu. Pasta highlights include the beetroot gnocchi in creamy parmesan sauce. Wines are excellent.

NEGRIL Rockhouse

West End Road **Tel** *876 957 4373*

The in-house restarant of Rockhouse hotel *(see p158)*, this beautifully styled restaurant on the cliffs is as notable for its location as its cooking. Great for lunch or dinner, with mains such as crab quesadillas with black bean and papaya salsa, char-grilled tuna with green bananas, or jerk chicken fajitas.

OCHO RIOS Coconuts on the Bay

Fisherman's Point, Cruise Ship Pier, off Main Street **Tel** *876 795 0064*

Set in the Fisherman's Point *(see p158)*, this place features Caribbean and international food, all well executed and reasonably priced. Everything from salads, wraps, and burgers to quesadillas and nachos, Thai-style snapper fillet, and Bombay chicken curry is served. Excellent cocktails and desserts such as pina colada cheesecake, and tiramisu.

OCHO RIOS Toscanini

Main Road, Harmony Hall, Tower Isle **Tel** *876 975 4785*

Set under the verandas of a gorgeous old great house, and serving some of the best Italian food in Jamaica. All of the pasta is handmade on the premises, and delicious; other specialities include beef *carpaccio*, veal escalope with prosciutto and parmesan, and delectable lobster spaghetti. A worthy wine list and great service.

PORT ANTONIO Dickie's

Coast Road, Port Antonio **Tel** *876 809 6276*

Offering an extremely unusual dining option, this restaurant is set in a private home on a cliffside and a short drive from Port Antonio. Cooked by the entertaining Dickie, three-course dinners (advance order required) might consist of ackee on toast, steamed fish or garlic lobster, and a fruity dessert. Breakfast, lunch, and afternoon tea available.

PORT ANTONIO Mille Fleurs

Mockingbird Hill, Drapers **Tel** *876 993 7267*

Wonderful hotel *(see p159)* restaurant serving consistently mouthwatering food for breakfast (try the corn pancakes with goat's cheese, or great omelets), lunch, and dinner. The menu changes daily, but highlights include cinnamon-dusted chicken breast with coconut sauce and vanilla carrots and jerk-spiced snapper with wafer-thin potatoes.

TREASURE BEACH Jack Sprat Pizza and Seafood Restaurant

Calabash Bay **Tel** *876 965 3583*

A perfect beachside restaurant set in Jake's *(see p159)*, this is adorned with battered Appleton rum signs, black and white photos, and an old jukebox. Pizzas – huge and generously topped – are a specialty, and there is also seafood and lovely soups. The delicious local Devon House ice cream is available too.

TREASURE BEACH Jake's

Calabash Bay **Tel** *876 965 3000*

Located in its namesake hotel *(see p159)*, it has tables under shade trees and is a laid-back spot for some really good food. Ingredients are sourced locally. Dishes might include smoked marlin dip or mains such as curried goat and scrumptious cooked fresh fish and lobster. Desserts are also excellent, especially the lemon curd tart.

BARS AND CLUBS

Whether it's for some entertainment over cocktails or a quiet drink overlooking the ocean, Jamaica's bar scene is second to none, with many places serving regular and some outstanding drinks. Unsurprisingly, given the island's fabulous musical heritage, the nightlife scene in the resorts features plenty of live music, from no-name reggae bands to full-fledged stageshows featuring the cream of the island's performers. Though reggae and dancehall dominate, the clubs also play hip-hop and R&B.

Margaritaville

RECOMMENDED PLACES TO GO

Asylum
69 Knutsford Boulevard, Kingston.
(Essential clubbing stop-off.)

Bourbon Beach
Norman Manley Boulevard, Negril.
(Busy bar, live music twice a week.)

The Brewery
Gloucester Av., Montego Bay.
(Friendly bar with a dance floor.)

The Jungle
Norman Manley Boulevard, Negril.
(Nightclub extending outdoors.)

Margaritaville
Gloucester Av., Montego Bay.
(Popular bar and club.)

Margaritaville
Island Village, Ocho Rios. (Eternally busy tourist-oriented nightspot.)

Pier One
Howard Cook Boulevard, Montego Bay. (Open-air club.)

Quad
20–22, Trinidad Terrace, Kingston.
(Kingston's flashiest nightclub.)

Roof Club
11 West Street, Portland.
(Portland's best nightclub.)

Practical Information

With its excellent tourist infrastructure, Jamaica is an easy destination to visit. The resorts are bursting with places to eat, drink, and sleep, as well as shops and currency changers, and even out-of-the-way towns and villages have a few hotels. The public transportation system is somewhat ad-hoc, being privately run outside of Kingston, but buses and minibuses are very cheap, taxis are plentiful, and car rental companies abound.

Holidaymakers climbing Dunn's River Falls near Ocho Rios

WHEN TO GO

Jamaica is at its best from mid-December to mid-April, when there is less rainfall and the heat is tempered by cooling trade winds. June through November is hurricane season, with the threat reaching its peak in September. The summer months can get uncomfortably hot.

GETTING THERE

Jamaica is well served by direct charter and scheduled flights from Europe, the US and Canada, which land at Donald Sangster International Airport in Montego Bay, or Norman Manley International Airport in Kingston. **Air Jamaica** flies from six US cities to Kingston and Montego Bay, and **American Airlines**, **Delta**, **JetBlue**, **Spirit Airlines**, **United Airlines**, and **US Airways** also offer direct services from various US hubs. There are direct flights from Toronto with Air Jamaica and **Air Canada**. From the UK, **British Airways** and Air Jamaica fly to both Montego Bay and Kingston, as do several charter operators.

DOCUMENTATION

Citizens of the European Union, US, Canada, Australia, New Zealand, Japan, and Israel have no visa requirements for a stay of less than three or six months depending on the country of origin. All visitors need a valid passport and an onward ticket. Citizens of other countries require a visa, which can often be obtained on arrival in Jamaica with production of a valid onward ticket.

VISITOR INFORMATION

Jamaica Tourist Board has offices in Montego Bay, Port Antonio, and Kingston, as well as booths at cruise ship ports and at the airports. Their website also provides detailed information.

HEALTH AND SECURITY

Jamaica is generally safe health-wise. Water is filtered and chlorinated at most places. Visitors may bring their own prescription medicines. No vaccinations are required to enter the island unless visitors have been to an infected area.

The island is not altogether crime-free and there are incidents of drug-related violence especially in Kingston. It is best to avoid the town during any tension. Keep to the main streets and avoid lonely areas. Do not walk alone late at night in the cities or along beaches. Women travelers can expect to receive very graphic and forward comments. These tend to be directed at all women in Jamaica though such attention is generally harmless. It is best to brush off comments with humor.

Visitors are advised to avoid carrying and using drugs even if easily available. The penalties for possession are severe.

BANKING AND CURRENCY

The local currency is the Jamaican dollar (J$), with notes available in the denomination of J$1,000, J$500, J$100, and J$50. Bureaux de change are widespread in the resorts, generally offering better rates than the banks. There are ATMs at all banks and also scattered around the big resorts; in the latter, some dispense US dollars rather than local currency.

COMMUNICATIONS

Card phones proliferate throughout the island, but the popularity of cell phones has made most of them obsolete. Supermarkets and small stores sell calling cards and cheap-rate international calling cards that can be used from any landline connections. Tri-band mobiles function in Jamaica. Local pay-as-you-go SIM cards are available all over Jamaica.

TRANSPORT

In terms of public transport, with the exception of Kingston, where city buses are government-run and quite efficient, all buses (usually minibuses) are owned and run by private individuals.

A police patrol car in Jamaica

Routes are painted on the front or the side of the bus. Knutsford Express offers a regular shuttle bus service from Kingston to Montego Bay and Ocho Rios.

Route taxis running set routes are great for short trips. Taxis are freely available in all the resorts; the national association of drivers is **JUTA**.

Renting a car is the easiest way to get around, and there are rental outlets in all the resorts. **AVIS** and **Island Car Rental** are the major players.

Jamaica's tour companies range from one-man shows to huge outfits with fleets of buses that ferry visitors between the island's most popular attractions. There are plenty of outfits in the middle of these two extremes. Some of the renowned ones are **Barrett Adventures**, **Caribic Vacations**, **Sun Venture**, and **Treasure Tours**.

SHOPPING

Most tourist centers in Jamaica have craft markets selling souvenirs ranging from wood carvings to jewelry, straw goods and sculptures. Haggling in these markets is common unlike in stores. Jamaicans start all exchanges with a polite greeting, so it is best to greet people before asking for goods in shops. There are specialist shops that sell indigenous art, rum, cigars, and Jamaican flags. Rasta fans can also buy T-shirts, bandanas, reggae music, and red-gold-green tassels for cars in most markets. It is well worth picking up the jerk sauce and gauva jelly that are available in any super-market. Blue Mountain coffee,

sold all over the island, also makes a good souvenir. On the north coast, there may be products made from coral and tortoiseshell. These are illegal as they are made from the endangered hawksbill turtle.

Most shops are open between Monday and Friday from around 8am to 5:30pm, and on Saturday from 8am to 5pm. Supermarkets stay open very late, even on Sunday.

LANGUAGE

Jamaica's official language is English, but everyone also speaks the patios version, heavily accented and sprinkled with local slang.

ELECTRICITY

The electric current is 110 volt but some hotels may have 220 volt, 60 cycles. Plug sockets usually take two flat prongs.

TIME

Jamaica runs on Eastern Standard Time, and is 5 hours behind GMT. It does not observe daylight savings.

GETTING MARRIED

To get married in Jamaica, the couple must have been on the island for at least 24 hours (not including week-ends) before they can apply for a marriage license. They will need their passports, birth certificates with their father's name, Decree Absolute or death certificate if divorced or widowed, and proof of any name change. There are many companies, such as **White Sand Weddings**, who can take care of all the formalities.

A wedding ceremony on the beach, Negril, Jamaica

A PORTRAIT OF THE DOMINICAN REPUBLIC

*S*pectacular beaches, lush valleys, rich flora and fauna, and the region's highest mountain are what make this a nation with extraordinary natural beauty. Historically, its capital city boasts the oldest cathedral and fortress in the New World, among other colonial treasures lining cobbled streets laid out five centuries ago.

Much of the country is mountainous, particularly in the west where the Cordillera Central dominates the landscape. Rising to 10,164 ft (3,097 m), the mist-shrouded Pico Duarte is its highest peak. Carpeted with thick forests, the slopes of the Cordillera, and to the south, those of the Sierra de Neiba and Sierra de Baoruco, are the habitat of many of the republic's endemic birds. Between the two sierras, Lago Enriquillo shimmers at 131 ft (39 m) below sea level – the Caribbean's lowest point. This saline lake, lying in a broad, semiarid vale in the cactus-studded southwest, attracts more than 60 species of birds, including flamingos that gather here in large numbers at dawn and dusk. Other wildlife found here includes the American crocodile and the endangered rock iguana. In all, there are 16 national parks and other protected areas that conserve the country's rich flora and fauna.

Small stalls selling local art and craft on the beach in Bayahibe

HISTORY

The country's colorful history dates back to pre-Columbian days, when Taíno Indians adorned caverns with the area's largest galleries of rupestrine art, many of which can still be seen today. Richer still is the colonial legacy predating any in the Western

Detail of Columbus's statue, Santo Domingo

Hemisphere. In 1492, Christopher Columbus landed on the island of Hispaniola (which the republic shares with Haiti today) and the Americas' first permanent settlement was established at La Isabela a year later, marking the start of Spanish rule. In 1498, Santo Domingo, the capital, was founded. The golden age of the Spanish colony ended when the English privateer Francis Drake vandalized Santo Domingo in 1586. The French invaded the island in the 17th century and the Treaty of Ryswyck (1697) divided Hispaniola between French Saint-Domingue to the west and

Clear blue waters and white sand at Cayo Levantado, Samaná

Spanish Santo Domingo to the east. The French colony prospered until the late 18th century, when civil war broke out, culminating in a revolt by former slaves who drove the French out, declaring Haitian independence in 1804. Continued hostilities between Santo Domingo and Haiti led to war and a 23-year occupation by the latter from 1821 to 1844, when a separate, independent Dominican Republic was created after an uprising led by Juan Pablo Duarte. Continuing unrest in the area led to a US occupation which lasted until 1924. By 1930 Rafael Trujillo had emerged as the most brutal dictator who unleashed 30 years of authoritarian rule. He was assassinated in 1961.

THE REPUBLIC TODAY

The Dominican Republic is a modern nation with high-rise hotels and casinos glittering on Santo Domingo's shorefront. Most other cities have a definite cosmopolitan, 21st-century buzz as well.

The republic now has a stable democratic government. Its economy is dependent on tourism and many all-inclusive resorts have sprung up along Costa del Coco and the Atlantic shore. Inland, the

Cibao region is quilted with estates producing fine coffee, sugar, and tobacco, the basis for a flourishing cigar industry. Despite the evolved middle-class, there is no escaping the poverty – many rural families live in shacks and urban wages are often at subsistence level.

PEOPLE AND CULTURE

The culture is a mix of Taíno, African, and Spanish, which is reflected in the ethnically diverse population. Spanish is the official language. Fun-loving Dominicans swing to the fast-paced merengue and the nation's own bachata. Although a Catholic nation, many people worship spirits – a legacy of the Taíno and African heritage.

Rural landscape with green fields and thatched houses, typical of the Dominican Republic

Exploring the Dominican Republic

The scenic Dominican Republic occupies the eastern two-thirds of Hispaniola, which it shares with Haiti. Rugged mountains rise to 10,164 ft (3,097 m) atop Pico Duarte, in the western part, forming a rain shadow over much of the semiarid southwest. The land tapers east to Punta Cana, the country's major beach resort, while inland the fertile plain called the Cibao is the island's breadbasket. Almost a quarter of its 9.2 million inhabitants live in Santo Domingo, a modern metropolis with the oldest colonial city in the Americas at its core.

Punta Rucia
This beach is known for its cottony sands and turquoise waters. It is popular among day-trippers from Puerto Plata.

Pico Duarte
The Caribbean's highest peak is easily hiked – a three-day trek from the mountain hamlet of La Ciénaga.

Parque Nacional Sierra de Bahoruco
Around 150 species of birds live in this remote national park.

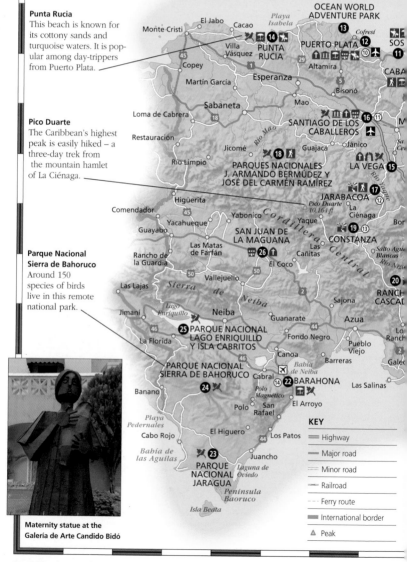

KEY

- Highway
- Major road
- Minor road
- Railroad
- - - - Ferry route
- International border
- △ Peak

Maternity statue at the
Galería de Arte Candido Bidó

SIGHTS AT A GLANCE

SEE ALSO

• *Where to Stay* pp186–9

• *Where to Eat & Nightlife*
  pp190–91

GETTING AROUND
Santo Domingo's Zona Colonial is easily
negotiated on foot, while taxis are ideally used
for getting around the greater metropolis. The
rest of the country is easiest explored on organized excursions, since self-drive can be a daunt-
ing experience despite the efficient road network.
A 20-minute ferry ride links Samaná to Sabana
de la Mar, while there are air services between
Puerto Plata and Punta Cana to Santo Domingo.

**The palm-lined Costa del Coco Beach on the eastern
shore of the Dominican Republic**

Santo Domingo ❶

Santo Domingo's main sites concentrate in the Zona Colonial, the historic heart of the city. This once-walled enclave of cobbled streets and leafy plazas boasts some of the oldest colonial buildings in the Western Hemisphere. Calle Las Damas echoes to the bootsteps of the first Spanish *conquistadores*, who set sail from Santo Domingo to conquer Latin America. Many colonial structures today house hotels, restaurants, and nightclubs, while the district also bustles with neighborhood life. Beyond the colonial core, the modern metropolis of three million people radiates inland in a quiltwork of districts.

Exterior of the fashionable Hotel Sofitel Nicholás de Ovando

🏛 Plaza España

N end of Calle Las Damas. ♿ **Museo de las Casas Reales** Calle Damas cnr Calle Mercedes. *Tel* 809 682 4202. ◯ 9am–5pm Tue–Sun. ♿ **Museo Alcázar de Colón** Plaza de España. *Tel* 809 682 4750. ◯ 9am–5pm Tue–Sat, 9am–4pm Sun. **Museo Mundo de Ambar** Calle Arzobispo Meriño 452. *Tel* 809 682 3309. ◯ 9am–6pm Mon–Sat, 9am–2pm Sun. www.amberworldmuseum.com

This broad, virtually treeless plaza is the setting for two preeminent museums. The **Museo de las Casas Reales**, in the Renaissance-style former chamber of the Royal Court, showcases colonial artifacts from antique weaponry and suits of armor to exhibits on Columbus's voyages. A massive Reloj del Sol (sundial) stands outside the entrance, which dates back to 1753.

The former home of Christopher Columbus's son Diego, a Mudejar-style two-story building dating from 1517, has been magnificently restored to house **Museo Alcázar de Colón**. It re-creates

the Columbus household with many original pieces such as carpets, silverware, and mahogany furniture, that once belonged to the family.

At night, the plaza comes alive as its numerous bars and restaurants fill up.

Located two blocks west, the impressive ruins of the Monasterio de San Francisco, dating from 1508, form a backdrop for occasional concerts. Nearby, the **Museo Mundo de Ambar** displays splendid examples of the semi-precious gem, amber.

⚓ Hostal Nicolás de Ovando

Calle Las Damas. *Tel* 809 685 9955. *Fax* 809 686 6590. $$$$ 104 rooms. 🍴 📶 ♿ ⓦ www.accorhotels.com

The class act in the Zona Colonial, this hotel occupies the former home of Nicolás de Ovando, who founded the city in 1502. The stylish conversion combines

contemporary sophistication with comfortable furnishings while retaining original, well-worn stone floors and walls. A superb restaurant, plus cigar lounge, swimming pool, gymnasiums, and meeting rooms are other bonuses at this atmospheric hotel.

🏛 Calle Las Damas

Between Fortaleza Ozama and Plaza España ♿ **Panteón de la Patria** Calle Las Damas & Plazoleta de María Toledo. *Tel* 809 689 6010. ◯ 9am–5pm Tue–Sun. **Museo Infantil Trampolín** Calle Las Damas. *Tel* 809 685 5551. ◯ 9am–5pm Tue–Fri, 9am–7pm Sat & Sun. ♿ www.trampolin.org.do

The first cobbled colonial street laid out in the New World is named for Doña María de Toledo (wife of Diego Columbus) and other ladies of the nobility. It is lined with beautifully restored historic buildings, including the **Panteón de la Patria**, completed in 1743 as a Neo-Classical Jesuit church, and today a somber mausoleum for national heroes, guarded by a uniformed soldier. It has a stone dome and extravagant chandelier, which was presented to President Rafael Trujillo from the Spanish dictator Francisco Franco.

Children enjoy the **Museo Infantil Trampolín**, a fun-filled educational forum covering earth sciences to social affairs.

🏛 Fortaleza Ozama

Calle Las Damas. *Tel* 809 686 0222. ◯ 9:30am–6pm Mon–Sat, 9am–3pm Sun. ♿ Overlooking the mouth of the Río Ozama, this fortress begun in 1502 is the oldest colonial military edifice in the Americas. At its heart, the Torre del Homenaje

Coral rock exterior of Fortaleza Ozama

For hotels and restaurants on this island see pp186–9 and 190–91

Statue of Christopher Columbus overlooking Parque Colón

(Tower of Homage) stands tall over a surrounding green swathe. Originally a watch-tower, Fortaleza Ozama later served as a prison. Rusting cannons stand atop the river-front wall and armaments are displayed in the esplanade, pinned by a statue of Spanish military commander, Gonzalo Fernández de Oviedo, who died in 1557.

✿ Parque Colón

Calle El Conde & Calle Arzobispo Meriño. ♿ **Larimar Museum** Calle Isabel la Católica 54. *Tel 809 689 6605.* ⏲ *8am–6pm Mon–Sat, 8am–2pm Sun.* 🌐 www.larimar museum.com

Named after Christopher Columbus, whose larger-than-life statue dominates the square, this wide, tree-shaded plaza is a center for social life. The park is surrounded by colonial and 19th-century buildings. Looming over the southern half of Parque Colón is the grandiose Catedral Primada de América.

One block south, the **Museo de Larimar** has educational exhibits on larimar, a semi-precious blue stone, which is mined solely in the Dominican Republic. On the plaza's northwest corner, Antiguo Palacio Consistorial, built in Neo-Classical style, is the former town hall.

Nearby, Plazoleta Padre Billini is named after a 19th-century priest who founded a hospital for the poor. It is the setting for the Museo de la Familia Dominicana del Siglo XIX, which is furnished to replicate a typical middle-class 19th-century home. Visitors can also stop by at many souvenir and cigar shops, located north of the park.

🏛 Catedral Primada de América

See p171.

🏛 Parque Duarte

Calle Padre Billini & Calle Hostos. The most intimate of Santo Domingo's colonial plazas, this small square shaded by *flamboyán* trees is a gathering spot for locals to gossip beneath the statue of the island's independence hero, Juan Pablo Duarte. On the eastern side, Iglesia y Convento de los Padres Dominicos is famous for its stone zodiac wheel in the chapel. Nearby, the tiny Capilla de la Tercera Orden Dominicana is a Baroque chapel erected in 1759.

SANTO DOMINGO

0 meters 200
0 yards 200

Key to Symbols *see back flap*

Altar de la Patria, dedicated to the island's heroes

🏛 Parque Independencia

Calle Palo Hincado & Av. Bolívar.
This bustling plaza is located at the western end of the Zona Colonial. The plaza has beautiful landscaped lawns, dotted with fountains, and is a popular meeting place. One of its entrances is via the 17th-century Puerta del Conde gate where the Dominican flag was first raised in 1844. The Republic's three principal heroes – Juan Pablo Duarte, Francisco del Rosario Sánchez, and Ramón Marías Mella – rest within the **Altar de la Patria**, a marble mausoleum where an eternal flame burns in their honor. The tomb is guarded by a soldier in uniform.

🏛 Palacio Nacional

Calle Dr. Delgado Báez. **Tel** 809 695 8000. ☐ by appointment Mon, Wed, & Fri. 📷 **Galería de Arte Candido Bidó** Calle Dr. Báez 5. **Tel** 809 685 5310. ☐ 9am–5pm Mon–Fri.
www.grupointeractivo.com/bido
Museo Bellapart Edificio Honda, Av. John F. Kennedy. **Tel** 809 541 7721 (ext 296). ☐ 9am–6pm Mon–Fri, 9am–12:30pm Sat.
www.museobellapart.com
The Palacio Nacional was completed in 1947 as an ostentatious palace for dictator-president Rafael Trujillo. This Neo-Classical structure, made of pink roseate Samaná marble, was designed with a domed roof and grandiose imperial staircases by renowned Italian architect Guido D'Alessandro. Prior permission is required to view the exquisite interior full of glistening mahogany furniture, crystal chandeliers,

and gilt mirrors. The Salón de las Cariátides, featuring walls lined with 44 elegant caryatids (draped female figures), is a highlight. The Salón now houses government departments. A formal dress code (shirt or blouse with full sleeves) is enforced for visitors. Shorts, sandals, and tennis shoes are not allowed.

A short stroll southwest of the Palacio Nacional will bring visitors to **Galería de Arte Candido Bidó**, the studio-home of the republic's most famous living artist, Candido Bido, with his colorful art-works displayed in a 1950s mansion. Perhaps the city's most impressive art gallery, the **Museo Bellapart** exhibits a magnificent private collection of art by leading Dominican artists from the mid-19th century onwards, and includes some stunning sculptures.

🏛 Faro a Colón

Av. Estados Unidos, Parque Mirador del Este. **Tel** 809 591 1492.
☐ 9am–5:30pm Tue–Sun. 📷
Acuario Nacional Av. España 75.
Tel 809 766 1709. ☐ 9:30am–5:30pm Tue–Sun. 📷 ♿
This massive monument in honor of Christopher Columbus was initiated in 1929 and only completed

in 1992, when it was dedicated for the quin-centennial celebration of the explorer's arrival. The "Columbus Lighthouse" was designed in the shape of a cross by neophyte British architect Joseph Lea Gleave. Soaring ten stories high over Parque Mirador del Este, the 680-ft (207-m) long concrete structure is stepped in tiered layers. Hollow within, it houses a Gothic marble sepulcher by Spanish sculptor Pere Carbonell I Huguet.

This contains a bronze urn, filled, supposedly, with Columbus's ashes, which were transferred from the Catedral Primada de América. A uniformed soldier and four bronze lions guard the explorer's remains. On special occasions, high-power beams are turned on to cast a cross-shaped light in the sky.

Stretching near the Río Ozama, woody and pretty Parque Mirador del Este is the city's chief recreational area, with various sports arenas and centers. At its far eastern end, Cueva Los Tres Ojos (Three Eyes Cave) is named for three water-filled limestone sinkholes, a pop-ular visiting spot for families on weekends.

The **Acuario Nacional** or National Aquarium over-looks the Atlantic Ocean and has displays of marine life such as sharks, rays, and eels. Opposite the aquarium, the Agua Splash, a water-based theme park, has pools and slides.

Neo-Classical-style façade of the stately Palacio Nacional

For hotels and restaurants on this island see pp186–9 and pp190–91

Catedral Primada de América

Diego Columbus laid the foundation stone of this cathedral in 1514. The New World's oldest cathedral was designed by architect Alonso de Rodríguez, who was inspired by the cathedral in Seville, Spain. It was revised by Luis de Moya and Rodrigo de Liendo and completed in 1541, but was added to through the 18th century. In 1920, Pope Benedict XV elevated it to the status of Basílica Menor de la Virgen de la Anunciación. Visitors should take care to avoid wearing shorts or short skirts to the cathedral.

VISITORS' CHECKLIST

Parque Colón, Calle Arzobispo Nouel & Arzobispo Meriño.
🕐 8am–4:30pm daily. ♿

Bell Tower
The cathedral combines classical, Baroque, and Gothic styles. The red-brick bell tower was added in 1625, after the original architect sailed for Mexico with the designs.

Rib-Vaulted Ceiling
Supported by 14 columns, the ceiling soars above a floor of black-and-white-checkered marble.

The stained glass was destroyed by Francis Drake's pirates in 1586.

Twin pillars topped by pointed turrets are adorned with fanciful friezes.

Main Façade
The Plateresque, west-facing main façade was built of limestone, with Romanesque archways topped by double Gothic windows unique in the Americas, and flanked by Renaissance pillars.

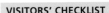

Double-Headed Eagle
The eagle bears the Spanish imperial coat of arms.

A busy street with bars and restaurants in Boca Chica

Boca Chica ➋

🚆 20 miles (32 km) E of Santo Domingo. 🏙👫🍸🛶🎣🏖⛵🚤

A darling of Santo Domingo's masses, this compact beach area, a 30-minute drive from the capital, gets packed on weekends and holidays, when people spill out of the bars on to the narrow streets. The palm-fringed sands dissolve into peacock-blue shallows, good for snorkeling as it is protected by a reef. Wade out to the Isla La Mastica and Isla Los Pinos, where mangroves harbor a wealth of birdlife.

Environs
Divers are delirious about **Parque Nacional Submarino La Caleta**, where 28 dive sites

MAMAJUANA
Bottle of Mamajuana
Dominicans attribute all manner of cures and medicinal qualities to their favorite home-made drink, a concoction of rum, red wine and honey steeped for weeks on end with herbs, bark, and secret ingredients. A variation is made of rum with seafood but there is no single recipe for it. This drink is considered to be an aphrodisiac and is drunk as shots in neighborhood bars.

include the wrecks of the *Hickory*, *El Limón*, and *Captain Alsina*.

🌿 **Parque Nacional Submarino La Caleta**
5 miles (8 km) W of Boca Chica. 🎟 free. 🐟 *Treasure Divers, 809 523 5320.* **www**.treasure-divers.eu

La Romana ➌

80 miles (129 km) E of Santo Domingo. 🏙 250,000. ✈ 🛈 *Av. Libertad 7, 809 550 6922.*

This coastal port town is the republic's principal center for sugar production. Although modern, it retains many colonial structures centered on Parque Central, studded with wrought-iron sculptures in the shade of Iglesia Santa Rosa de Lima. El Obelisco, at the juncture of Avenida Libertad at Calle Francisco del Castillo, shows the nation's history. The main draw is Altos de Chavón, a fantastical 1970s re-creation of a Tuscan hill town complete with a "Roman amphitheater" used as a music venue by its owners, the nearby Casa de Campo resort (*see right*). Its **St. Stanislaus Church** is named after Poland's patron saint, whose ashes were brought here by Pope John Paul II during his visit in 1979. It also houses the Regional Museum of Archaeology, displaying pre-Columbian Taíno artifacts.

Environs
About 5 miles (8 km) to the southwest of La Romana is Isla Catalina, a small island that serves day-trippers with

great beaches. On the main road to San Pedro de Macorís is an underground cave with natural dripstone formations, **Cueva de las Maravillas**.

🔦 **Cueva de las Maravillas**
Tel 809 951 9009. ☐ *9am–5pm Tue–Sun.*

Casa de Campo ➍

🏌 81 miles (130 km) E of Santo Domingo. *Tel 809 523 8171.* 💲💲💲 279 rooms. 🍴🏊♿🖥 **www**.casadecampo.com.do

This exclusive resort's rooms are luxuriously furnished in plantation style by fashion designer Oscar de la Renta, as are many of the villas, favored by such guests as the Bushes, Clintons, and Hollywood stars.

Playa Bayahibe ➎

🚆 89 miles (142 km) SE of Santo Domingo. 🏙👫🍸🛶🎣🏖⛵🚤

Considered one of the best places to dive in the country, the Bayahibe area has endless white-sand beaches, notably Playa Dominicus and Playa Bayahibe. The original fishing village is diminishing with the spread of all-inclusive resorts. Local tour operators offer boat excursions to Isla Saona, with its own beaches plus a lake with flamingos.

Environs
A short distance from Bayahibe is **Parque Nacional del Este**, which protects a rare

St. Stanislaus Church, La Romana

stand of dry forest atop a limestone plateau pockmarked with *cenotes* (sinkholes) and caverns. A good access point is the fishing village of Boca de Yuma. Nearby, the fortified **Casa Ponce de León**, built in 1505, is furnished in early colonial fashion. The house is kept locked but a guard will open the doors for visitors.

⚞ Parque Nacional del Este
Guaragua, 3 miles S of Bayahibe.
Tel 809 833 0022. ◯ 8am–5pm daily. 📷

🏛 Casa Ponce de León
Calle los Jobitos, San Rafael del Yuma. ◯ 9am–3pm Tue–Sun.
📷 ♿

Costa del Coco ➏

🚗 150 miles (241 km) E of Santo Domingo. 🏖 🎿 🍴 🚤 🎣 🏊 🚵 🚶

This coastal zone is the setting for the majority of all-inclusive resorts. The country's most beautiful beaches, from snow white to gold, unspool along a picture-perfect coconut palm-lined coast. Resort development concentrates around Punta Cana and Playa Bávaro, but new resorts such as Uvero Alto are evolving to

Palm-fringed Playa Bávaro lined with resorts, Costa del Coco

the north, where the virginal Playa Lavacama and Playa Los Muertos are great places to escape the crowds. Jeep safaris offer excellent diversions, as do marine theme parks such as the **Manatí Park**.

Environs
A short distance inland is the regional capital city, Higüey, renowned for its Modernist cathedral, **Basílica de Nuestra Señora de la Altagracia**, designed in 1950 by French architects André Dunoyer de Segonzac and Pierre Dupré.

✈ Manatí Park
Tel 809 221 9444.
www.manatipark.com

⛪ Basílica de Nuestra Señora de la Altagracia
◯ 5am–7pm daily. ♿
Note: *no shorts or bare shoulders permitted.*

Puntacana Resort & Club ➐

🚗 2 miles (3 km) S of Punta Cana airport. *Tel* 809 959 2262.
Ⓢ Ⓢ Ⓢ Ⓢ 400 rooms. 📶
🍴 🚵 ♿ **www**.puntacana.com

Launched in 1971 as the first property in Punta Cana, the original club has metamorphosed into a deluxe resort with an all-inclusive hotel and villas with superb facilities. Its seven restaurants include two top eateries *(see p191)*. The resort's ecological park has guided trails and organizes bird-watching tours. The resort also offers horseback riding and has two golf courses.

Parque Nacional los Haitises ➑

47 miles (75 km) NE of Santo Domingo. ◯ 8am–5pm daily. 📷
📋 *arranged by local tour operators.*

This national park protects a region of rugged limestone terrain studded with *mogotes* (ancient limestone plateau, *see p79*) and riddled with caverns. The dense forests are home to at least 112 bird species, including seabirds nesting on Isla de los Pájaros and swallows that swarm Cueva de las Golondrinas. The easiest access is on guided boat trips arranged by **Paraíso Caño Hondo**, an activity center with accommodations.

🚤 Paraíso Caño Hondo
7 miles (11 km) W of Sabana de la Mar. *Tel* 809 248 5995.
www.paraisocanohondo.com

Laguna del Limón
Playa Los Muertos
Nisibón
Playa Lavacama
COSTA DEL COCO
Uvero Alto
Playa del Macao
El Macao
104
El Cortesito
Playa Bávaro
Bávaro
Charca de Bávaro
Manatí Park
Higüey
Borrachón
KEY
🛬 Airport
🏖 Beach
⛪ Church
▬▬ Major road
▭▭ Minor road
LA ALTAGRACIA
Punta Cana
Playa Punta Cana
Juanillo
Playa Juanillo

0 km   10
0 miles 10

Península de Samaná ❾

110 miles (177 km) NE of Santo Domingo. ✈ ✕ ⓘ *Calle Santa Barbara 4, 809 538 2332.* 🎏 *Día de Santa Bárbara (Dec 4).*

Jutting into the Atlantic Ocean, this slender peninsula is lined by white-sand beaches along its north and east shores. On the southern shore, rivers cascade down from a thickly forested mountain spine sloping down to the Bahía de Samaná, a favored wintering spot for humpback whales. Every year, whales mate and give birth in the warm sheltered waters protected within the beautiful Santuario de las Ballenas Jorobadas.

The regional capital, Santa Bárbara de Samaná, has fine restaurants and is a good base for exploring, including boat trips to Cayo Levantado. Just 7 miles (11 km) north of town is **El Salto de Limón** waterfall, which makes for a favorite day-trip on horseback.

There are many all-inclusive hotels but the peninsula is known for its boutique hotels in the two small beach resorts: Las Terrenas on the north coast and Las Galeras in the east. While Las Terrenas is popular for its nightlife, Las Galeras is known for its gorgeous long beaches.

Bars and restaurants next to the beach in Cabarete

Cabarete ❿

119 miles (190 km) NW of Santo Domingo. 🚌 ⓘ *Calle Principal, 809 571 0962.* 🎏 *Kiteboard World Cup (Jun).*

With a vibrant nightlife, Cabarete is the Republic's party beach resort as well as its watersports capital. The wind-whipped beaches are among the very best in the Caribbean for kiteboarding and windsurfing. Small hotels and colorful restaurant-bars edge up to the sands of this beach village. The watersport action centers on Kite Beach.

Environs
Just 3 miles (5 km) east of Cabarete is one entrance to the **Parque Nacional El Choco**, which has trails and a lagoon

with waterfall. Another popular excursion from Cabarete is to **27 Charcos De Demajagua Natural Monument**, 2 miles (3 km) to the south. Visitors can hike along a riverbed to a series of 27 cascades and natural waterslides.

🏄 Parque Nacional El Choco
Callejón de la Loma, Cabarete. **Tel** 809 472 4204. ⏱ *9am–4:30pm daily.* 🈺 🅿

🌿 27 Charcos De Demajagua Natural Monument
Imbert. ⏱ *8:30am–4pm daily.* 🈺 www.27charcos.com

Sosúa ⓫

110 miles (175 km) NW of Santo Domingo. 🚌 ⓘ *Calle Duarte 1, 809 571 3433.* 🏙 *45,000.*

This clifftop beach town is laid out on either side of the long Playa Sosúa. The beach has watersports and is backed by a sandy path lined with bars, restaurants, and souvenir stores. Sosúa is divided into two areas – Los Charamicos to the west and El Batey to the east, where German and Austrian Jewish refugees settled during the 1940s. Fine wooden architecture, including the synagogue and adjoining **Museo Judío Sosúa**, can be seen here. A coral reef nearby offers fabulous scuba diving, and local dive operators offer trips that include the wreck of the *Zingara*, scuttled in 1993.

🏛 Museo Judío Sosúa
Calle Dr. Alejo Martínez. **Tel** 809 571 1386. ⏱ *9am–1pm & 2–4pm Mon–Fri.* 🅿

El Salto de Limón plunging over 131 ft (40 m) down, Península de Samaná

For hotels and restaurants on this island see pp186–9 and pp190–91

Puerto Plata ⑫

145 miles (233 km) NW of Santo Domingo. 🏘 *147,000*. ✈ ℹ *Calle José del Carmen Arizo 45, 809 586 5059*. 🎭 *Fiesta Patronal de San Felipe (May 3), Merengue Festival (Oct), International Film Festival (Nov).*

Founded in 1502, this lively port town is replete with historic buildings, notably in the Zona Victoriana with its cluster of 19th-century wooden gingerbread houses inspired by the Victorian style then fashionable in Britain. At its heart lies Parque Independencia, which has the steepled Catedral San Felipe Apostól on the south side and, two blocks east, the popular **Museo del Ambar** with its amber-related exhibits in a 1919 wooden galleried mansion. Also worth visiting is the four-square **Fortaleza San Felipe**, the oldest colonial fortress of the New World, completed in 1557. The Malecón Boulevard lines Playa Long Beach, stretching for almost 2 miles (3 km) along the city shoreline.

Beyond the historic core, the modern city is an ungainly sprawl. Fine beaches extend along the coast east and west of Puerto Plata. More than a dozen all-inclusive and boutique hotels congregate on Playa Dorada, named for its palm-shaded golden sands. It has a world-class golf course and plentiful watersports. Locals gather at Playa Cofresí, a laid-back beach with few watersports but some restaurants. The 2,565-ft (781-m) **Monte Isabel De Torre**, soaring over Puerto Plata, lures visitors to its cool summit, where a botanical garden and forest have trails. A cable car accessed from Avenida Teleférico, west of town, to the summit provides stupendous views of the city.

AMBER

Considered a semi-precious gem, amber is actually a fossilized resin of an extinct tree species, *Hymenaea protera*, and dates back as much as 40 million years. The translucent gem comes in colors ranging from gold to purple and blue, found solely in the Cordillera Septentrional, south of Puerto Plata. The Dominican Republic is renowned for amber fossils, known as "inclusions", containing insects that were trapped in the oozing sap. An export license is required to leave the Republic with rough amber with an "inclusion."

Insect inside amber, Museo del Ambar

Monument at San Felipe, Puerto Plata

🏛 **Museo del Ambar**
Calle Duarte 61. **Tel** 809 586 2848.
⏰ 9am–6pm Mon–Sat. 📷 www. ambermuseum.com

🏰 **Fortaleza San Felipe**
Av. Gregorio Luperón. ⏰ 9am–5pm daily. 📷

⛰ **Monte Isabel De Torre**
Av. Manuel Tavárez Justo.
Tel 809 970 0501. ⏰ 8am–5pm Thu–Tue. 📷

Ocean World Adventure Park ⑬

3 miles (5 km) W of Puerto Plata.
Tel 809 291 1000. ⏰ 8:30am–6pm daily. 📷 www.oceanworld.net

Located in the small tourist enclave of Cofresí, this interactive marine theme park is an exciting all-day experience for adults and children. A highlight is the option to swim with dolphins up close and personal, in addition to viewing dolphin and sea lion shows. The place also has a snorkeling reef aquarium teeming with exotic fish, sharks and stingrays, as well as tropical birds that swoop around an aviary.

Punta Rucia ⑭

🚤 20 miles (32 km) W of Puerto Plata. 🏖🍴🛥🌴🚣🛶

Graced by cottony sands shelving gently into turquoise waters, this remote beach is a favorite of day-trippers who arrive on boat excursions from Puerto Plata. Banana boat rides and other watersports add excitement. Most excursions include a visit to Cayo Paraíso, an idyllic horseshoe-shaped cay with talcum-fine sand and crystal waters colored by a kaleidoscopic palette of fish.

Environs
A dirt track leads east from Playa Rucia to Refugio de Manatís Estero Hondo, a huge mangrove-fringed lagoon protecting manatees. Farther east is **Parque Nacional La Isabela**, which preserves the scant ruins of the first permanent settlement in the New World, established by Christopher Columbus in 1492.

⛏ **Parque Nacional La Isabela**
El Castillo. ⏰ 9am–5:30pm daily.
📷📹♿

One of Puerto Plata's many traditional houses

La Vega ⑮

70 miles (113 km) NW of Santo Domingo. 🏢 220,000. 🚻 *Calle Mella cnr Durangé, 809 242 3231.* 🎭 *Carnival (Feb).*

Founded in 1562, La Vega is a sprawling, chaotic city on the banks of Río Camú in the heart of El Cibao Valley. It is renowned for its lively Carnival and for its Catedral de la Concepción de la Vega, a controversial post-Modernist, industrial-style design that visitors either love or hate. The dramatic exterior, with Gothic elements, offers a garish counterpoint to the sparse interior with a simple altar. The city's other sights of interest surround the main square and include the Neo-Classical Palacio Municipal and Palacio de Justicia.

Northeast of La Vega, atop a steep hill, lies the Santo Cerro (Holy Hill), where an annual pilgrimage is made every September 24 to Iglesia Las Mercedes. The simple church is considered to be the site of a miracle during the colonial days. Nearby is the original settlement of La Concepción de la Vega, founded in 1494 as a base for gold-mining but destroyed by an earthquake in 1562. The ruins are preserved within **Parque Nacional Arqueológico Histórico La Vega Vieja**.

⛰ Parque Nacional Arqueológico Histórico La Vega Vieja
Carretera Moca, Santo Cerro.
🕐 *8am–3pm Mon–Fri, 9am–4pm Sat.* 🎟

Santiago de los Caballeros ⑯

88 miles (138 km) NW of Santo Domingo. ✈ 🏢 650,000.
🚻 *Gobernación, Parque Duarte & Calle del Sol; 809 582 5885.*
🎭 *Carnival (Feb).*

Built on the banks of the Río Yaque in the center of El Cibao Valley, Santiago de los Caballeros, the Republic's second largest city, thrums with energy and traffic, having several exceptional hotels and a lively nightlife.

The colonial Catedral Santiago Apóstol, Santiago de los Caballeros

The hub of agriculture and commerce outside Santo Domingo, this wealthy city also boasts fine attractions, including an easily walked colonial core and numerous monuments that recall its past status as a tobacco boom town. Cigar manufacture remains its most important industry; deft hands can be seen rolling fine cigars at Fábrica de Cigarros La Aurora, part of Centro León, a cultural institute with a contemporary art gallery and an anthropology museum.

Any tour should begin at Parque Duarte, surrounded by an eclectic assemblage of colonial structures, including **Catedral Santiago Apóstol**. Nearby, Fortaleza San Luís has been restored and displays pre-Columbian artifacts.

The Monumento a los Héroes de la Restauración, a soaring monument capped by a 230-ft (70-m) tall column, was erected in 1940 by the dictator Rafael Trujillo (1891–1961). The Museo Folklórico Don Tomás Morel offers an introduction to the city's vibrant Carnival culture.

Environs
Around 45 miles (72 km) east of Santiago, **Reserva Científica Quita Espuela** has trails into montane rainforest, where the Hispaniola parrot and other endemic birds can be spotted. Another interesting place to visit is **Casa Museo Hermanas Mirabal**, in Salcedo, 30 miles (48 km) east of Santiago. It is where the sisters María Teresa, Minerva, and Patria Mirabal, who opposed Trujillo, grew up in a middle-class home, now maintained as a shrine.

🦋 Reserva Científica Quita Espuela
Tel 809 588 4156. 🕐 *8am–5pm Mon–Fri.* ❗ **Note:** *call to reserve a guide and for access on Sat & Sun.*

🏛 Casa Museo Hermanas Mirabal
Conuco Salcedo. *Tel 809 577 2704.*
🕐 *9am–6:30pm (mid-Jun–Aug), 9am–5pm (Aug –Dec).* 🎟
📷 *compulsory.* ♿

Jarabacoa ⑰

96 miles (154 km) NW of Santo Domingo. 🏢 155,000. 🚻 *Plaza Ramírez, Calle Mario Nelsón Galán between Duarte and Calle del Carmen, 809 574 7287.*

Deep in the Cordillera Central, at a height of 1,750 ft (533 m) and surrounded by forest, this wealthy agricultural town draws those escaping the heat of the lowlands for a crisp alpine climate. Parque Mario Nelsón Galán, the small town square, is a

A rugged wooden bridge on the hike to Pico Duarte

For hotels and restaurants on this island see pp186–9 and pp190–91

good spot to watch life go by. The town nestles in the valley of the Río Yaque del Norte and is a base for whitewater rafting as well as horseback riding and for hiking, including to three local waterfalls: Salto de Baiguate, **Salto de Jimenoa**, 3 miles (5 km) southeast of Jarabacoa, and Salto de Jimenoa Alto, best reached through the **Proyecto Ecoturístico Comunitario El Gran Salto**.

Jarabacoa is also the gateway for Pico Duarte which is the tallest mountain in the Caribbean.

Salto de Jimenoa
Sabanete. ◷ 8am–5pm daily. 🎟
Proyecto Ecoturístico Comunitario El Gran Salto
El Salto de Jimenoa. **Tel** 809 541 1430. ◷ 9am–6pm. 🎟 📷

Parques Nacionales J. Armando Bermúdez y José del Carmén Ramírez ⑱

16 miles (26 km) NW of Jarabacoa. **Tel** 809 472 4204. 🎟 📷 for a fee, Asociación de Guías de Montaña, La Ciénaga. 🅰

The Cordillera Central forms a rugged backbone rising to 10,164 ft (3,097 m) atop Pico Duarte, accessed from the mountain hamlet of La Ciénaga. The hulking mass is a popular, albeit challenging three-day round-trip hike to the summit, where the Dominican flag flutters over a bust of Juan Pablo Duarte (1813–73), father of the nation. This mountain terrain of razorback ridges and plunging gorges is known as the "Dominican Alps," and is enshrined within the Armando Bermúdez and José del Carmén Ramírez national parks. Rainforest smothers the lower flanks, while trails lead up through the mist-shrouded cloud forest and then pine forest above. Birding is superb here.

Fields surrounding the farming town of Constanza

Bust of Juan Duarte, Pico Duarte

Constanza ⑲

16 miles (26 km) NW of Santo Domingo. 🏘 90,000. 🛈 Calle Matilda Viña 18, cnr Miguel Andrés Abreu, 809 539 2900.
www.constanza.net

With an exquisite location surrounded by mountains at 4,000 ft (1,219 m), this town is set in a broad valley that is the breadbasket of the nation. A quiltwork of fields produce much of the nation's fruit and a variety of flowers. With splendid scenery and crisp mountain air, Constanza is a good starting point for hikes, though it has been bypassed by tourism. Mountain drives by jeep guarantee great scenery. Colonia Japonesa, a hamlet on the northern outskirts of Constanza, was founded in the 1950s by Japanese farmers lured here by dictator Trujillo. Several structures here are in traditional Japanese style.

Environs
A challenging yet extremely beautiful drive south of

Constanza leads to **Salto Aguas Blancas**, a trio of waterfalls cascading 285 ft (87 m) into a chilly pool. The highest free waterfall in the Caribbean is fringed by pretty ferns and other vegetation that clings to the sheer rock faces of the canyons.

Rancho Cascada ⑳

🛏 65 miles (104 km) NW of Santo Domingo. **Tel** 809 343 2575. Ⓢ 5 rooms. 🍽 🏊
www.ranchocascada.com

Nestled on the Río Nizao (crossed by fording or by hand-winched funicular) in the foothills of the Cordillera Central, this German-run ecolodge is perfect for activity-minded travelers. Kayaking, mountain biking, horseback rides, and canoe trekking are among the organized excursion options.

Individually-styled bungalows and apartments are sparsely furnished; riverstone floors add ambience. The open-air restaurant overhangs the river, and a stream feeds several plunge pools in the hilly grounds.

FACELESS DOLLS

The towns of El Cibao, and specifically Moca, are known for making ceramic *muñecas sin rostros* (faceless dolls) meant to symbolize the nation's multi-ethnic make-up in which no racial group is favored. The tiny, brightly painted dolls usually portray country women wearing headscarves or straw hats and holding flowers or *tinajones* (earthenware jars).

The commonly found faceless dolls in Cibao

San Cristóbal ㉑

17 miles (27 km) W of Santo Domingo. 🏘 221,000. 🚌
🛈 Gobernación, Av. Constitución 25, 809 528 1844. 🎉 Fiesta Patronal (mid-Jun).

Founded in the late 16th century, San Cristóbal is steeped in historical significance. Capital of the province of the same name, this sprawling, busy city was originally named Trujillo after the dictator, Rafael Leonidas Trujillo. The name, however, was changed after he was gunned down in 1961. During his dictatorship, he built many monuments in the town to honor himself. One of them is the domed, mustard-colored **Iglesia Nuestra Señora de la Consolación**. This church also had a tomb intended for Trujillo, but he was eventually buried in Paris. The interior is decorated with murals by Spanish artist José Vela Zanetti. His work also adorns Trujillo's hilltop mansion, Castillo del Cerro, which was once embellished with gold leaf and murals. It is now a police academy and is closed to the public. Other noteworthy buildings include **Casa de la Cultura**, on the south side of Parque Colón, the main square. The Casa hosts local art exhibitions. On Parque Duarte is Iglesia Parroquial, a pretty church, built in 1946 to honor Trujillo's hometown.

Located just 2 miles (3 km) northwest of the city is Reserva Antropológica El Pomier, which protects 11 of the 54 caves adorned with pre-Columbian pictographs. More than 6,500 ancient pictographs and petroglyphs have been identified, most being spiritual symbols and animal figures. Paved paths lead through the major caverns, populated by harmless bats. There is a museum, shop, and café at the reserve.

🛈 **Iglesia Nuestra Señora de la Consolación**
Av. Constitución & Calle Padre Brown. ◐ 8am–5pm daily.

🏛 **Casa de la Cultura**
Calle Mella. ◐ 9am–noon Mon–Fri.

The long and scenic coastline near Barahona

Barahona ㉒

120 miles (193 km) SW of Santo Domingo. 🏘 34,000. ✈ 🚌
🛈 Oficina de Turismo, Av. Enriquillo, 809 524 3650. 🎉 Carnival Cimarrón (Easter).

Founded in 1802 by the Haitian general, Toussaint L'Ouverture, Barahona, at the head of Bahía de Neiba, evolved as a center for sugar production in the 20th century and is today a port city. The city is the gateway to a little-visited region of enormous natural beauty. Palm-fringed beaches unfurl south along a roller-coaster road named Vía Panorámica, a scenic drive framed by the turquoise ocean.

Environs
Just 12 miles (20 km) south of the city, Playa San Rafael is a popular beach for its cool pools fed by natural spring waters. Only 25 miles (40 km) west of Barahona is Polo Magnético, an optical illusion in which the road, sloping in one direction, appears to

slope the other way. Also worth visiting is **Reserva Científica Laguna de Cabral**, 12 miles (20 km) northwest of the city. It has boardwalk trails for spotting waterfowl and wading birds.

🛈 **Reserva Científica Laguna de Cabral**
Cabral. **Tel** 809 835 3919. ◐ 8am– 6pm daily. 🎫 🚻

Parque Nacional Jaragua ㉓

124 miles (200 km) SW of Santo Domingo. 🚌 🛈 Grupo Jaragua, 809 472 1036. 🎫 🚻 ♿
www.grupojaragua.org.do

The nation's largest national park, Jaragua offers great wildlife viewing, although most of this semiarid terrain, lying in a rain shadow at the extreme southwest of the country, is off-limits. Endangered Ricord's and rhinoceros iguanas inhabit the park, accessed by trails from Fondo Paradí. Flamingos and roseate spoonbills can be

Flamingos flocking around Laguna Oviedo, Parque Nacional Jaragua

seen in Laguna Oviedo, where the visitor center has a lookout tower. Marine turtles nest at Bahía de las Águilas, accessible by boat or jeep.

Parque Nacional Sierra de Bahoruco ㉔

116 miles (186 km) SW of Santo Domingo. ◯ 9am–4:40pm Tue–Sun. ▮ Grupo Jaragua, 809 472 1036. ▨ Ⓐ

Dry shrub on the sandy Isla Cabritos, center of Lago Enriquillo

One of the least visited in the country due to its remoteness and rugged terrain, this park is a must for bird enthusiasts. Protecting 310 sq miles (803 sq km) of forests that range from dry deciduous lowland forests to cloud forests and pines at higher altitudes, the park has 150 species of birds. White-necked crows and narrow-billed todies can be seen around Laguna La Charca and along trails from the visitor center at Hoyo Pelempito. Vía Panorámica El Aceitillar, the sole access, offers magnificent scenery.

The endangered rock iguana, Isla Cabritos

Parque Nacional Lago Enriquillo y Isla Cabritos ㉕

112 miles (180 km) W of Santo Domingo. ▮ Asociación de Guías del Lago Enriquillo, 809 816 7441. ◯ 7am–5pm daily. ▨ boat trips 7:30am–1pm.

Encircled by mountains, super-saline Lago Enriquillo is the Caribbean's largest lake as well as its lowest point, at 131 ft (39 m) below sea level. The lake is a remnant of the Caribbean Sea left land-locked by ancient tectonic movements. About 5,000 American crocodiles inhabit the lake and are easily seen on Isla Cabritos. Flamingos tip-toe about the waters, home to more than 60 other bird species, including roseate spoonbills. Visitors will find plenty of rhinoceros iguanas around the ranger station at La Azufrada, from where boats leave on guided tours.

Environs
Nearby **Las Caritas**, outside the hamlet of Postrer Río, has rocks etched with pre-Columbian petroglyphs showing human faces. At the western end of the lake is Jimaní, a border town abutting Haiti, known for its bustling market and brightly painted Haitian buses called *tap-taps*.

San Juan de la Maguana ㉖

140 miles (225 km) W of Santo Domingo. ▨ 130,000. ▨ Festival de Espíritu Santo (Jun), El Día de San Juan (Jun 24).

Founded in 1508, this city is now the capital of San Juan province. Although most of the early colonial structures were destroyed during the 19th-century Haitian invasions, it still boasts some intriguing sites, centered on Parque Central. The domed, eclectic-style Catedral San Juan Bautista, dating from 1958, features Baroque and Rococo ornamentation and an exterior spiral metal staircase. On the east side of town, Parque Duarte has the Neo-Classical Palacio Ayuntamiento and Modernist Palacio de Justicia.

Also worth visiting is the pre-Columbian site, El Corral de los Indios, just 4 miles (6 km) north of town. It has a wide stone circle used as a *bateyes* (ball courts).

Environs
Against the backdrop of the magnificent mountain range of Cordillera Central lies the **Presa de Sebana Yegua**, a popular man-made lake known for its bass and tilapia.

🎣 **Presa de Sebana Yegua**
15 miles (24 km) E of San Juan de la Maguana. **Note:** ask at the military guardpost for entry.

Ancient pre-Columbian petroglyphs in Las Caritas

Outdoor Activities and Specialized Holidays

The Dominican Republic is the Caribbean's most physically diverse nation and offers plenty of exciting activities and watersports. Cordillera Central is the only place in the Caribbean with whitewater rafting while Cabarete is considered the top spot for watersports. Diving is excellent as well, with incredible wreck-diving close to the shores. On land, the island is the region's golf capital. Other thrilling outdoor activities include jeep safaris, ATV excursions, and horse-riding, and the many national parks offer exceptional birding and hiking, especially Pico Duarte, the Caribbean's highest peak.

A kiteboarder enjoying the azure waters of the Dominican Republic

BEACHES

The Dominican Republic has some of the most spectacular and varied beaches in the Caribbean, with something for every taste and interest. To escape the crowds, visitors should take their tents and camping gear and head to Bahía de las Aguilas in the southwest of the island. Choice options along the south coast include Punta Cana and Playa Bayahibe *(see p172)*, where all-inclusive hotels line snow-white sands. The windswept Kite Beach at Cabarete on the north coast, is renowned for kiteboarding; nearby Playa Sosúa is a good base for scuba diving; and Playa Dorada, outside Puerto Plata, has a golf course amid all-inclusives. Cayo Levantado, Playa Rincón, Las Terrenas, and Cosón are the highlights of the Samaná Peninsula.

BIRDING AND WILDLIFE VIEWING

The Dominican Republic astounds with its wealth of birds. There are around 300 species, including 30 endemic ones. Parque Nacional Sierra de Bahoruco *(see p179)* and the Cordillera Central offer the largest diversity, and have well-developed trails. **Tody Tours** offers birding excursions to Sierra de Bahoruco. For those who are interested in seabirds and waterfowl, the best places to head to would be Parque Nacional Jaragua and Parque Nacional los Haitises

(see p173) with **Paraíso Caño Hondo**. Flamingos color Lago Enriquillo, where crocodiles and iguanas can be easily viewed. Spotting manatees is virtually guaranteed at Refugio de Manatís Estero Hondo.

However, the crown jewel of wildlife-viewing experiences in the Dominican Republic is to see humpback whales, which can be encountered close-up in winter in Bahía de Samaná. **Whale Samana** offers trips. **Excursiones Guariquén** organizes ecotours of the Samaná Peninsula.

DIVING

The Dominican Republic holds its own when it comes to diving, with some of the best wreck dives in the Caribbean. A 30-minute drive from Santo Domingo, Parque Nacional Submarino La Caleta has three wrecks; Bayahibes Bay features the wreck of the *St. George*, plus the underwater museum, 1724 Guadalupe Underwater Archaeological Preserve; and the world-renowned wreck *Zingara* can be explored off Sosúa, also known for the Airport Wall. In Samaná, divers rave about Cabo Cabrón and Islas las Ballenas. Off the far north-west, Monte Cristi is a remote spot with sensational coral formations and a fine wreck dive. Visitors can book through **Scubafun** in Bayahibe, **Las Terrenas Divers** in Samaná, and **Dolphin Dive Center** in Sosúa.

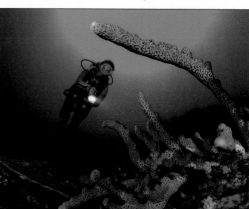

A scuba diver examining a colony of colorful sponges

For hotels and restaurants on this island see pp186–9 and pp190–91

Golf in the Dominican Republic

The Dominican Republic has some 40 championship golf courses – a major forte of the island – and more are being added by the leading names in golf design. All the major beach resorts have golf courses. Casa de Campo is the setting for three leading courses, and the Punta Cana-Playa Bávaro area has half a dozen, and many of them host a number of international tournaments.

DYE FORE

Signage of one of the three golf courses in Casa de Campo

Playa Dorada Golf Course, *designed by Robert Trent Jones, offers exceptional greens and serves the all-inclusive Playa Dorada Resort in Puerto Plata.*

KEY

🏌 Golf course

— Major road

— Minor road

LOCATOR MAP

☐ Area illustrated

Cocotal Golf & Country Club has an 18-hole championship course and a 9-hole regular one. It is designed by six-times Spanish champion Jose Gancedo.

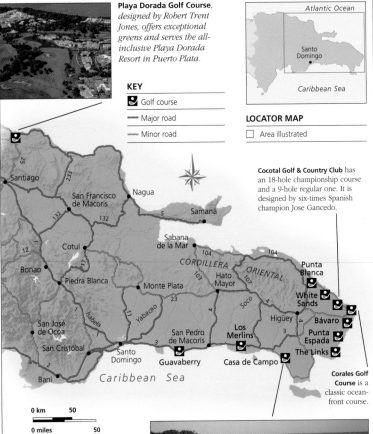

Corales Golf Course is a classic ocean-front course.

0 km   50

0 miles   50

TOP COURSES

Casa de Campo
www.casadecampo.com.do
**Cocotal Golf &
  Country Club**
www.cocotalgolf.com
Corales Golf Course
www.puntacana.com
**Playa Dorada
  Golf Course**
www.playadoradagolf.com

Teeth of the Dog Golf Course, *rated the best course in the Caribbean, is one of the three world-renowned courses located at the Casa de Campo resort.*

Windsurfer setting off from one of the beaches

KITEBOARDING AND WINDSURFING

Cabarete is considered the Caribbean epicenter for kite-boarding and windsurfing, with perfect conditions for both novices and experts. The beaches of Cabarete face directly into the Atlantic trade winds, which whip up whitecaps good for surfing while giving lift to kiteboards. **Kite Excite** and **Carib Wind Center** are among the many outfitters that offer tuition. For surfers, tuition and board rentals are available from **Ali's Surf Camp**. **Laurel Eastman Kiteboarding** offers kiteboarding tuition at Playa Punta Popy, at Las Terrenas.

FISHING

The Mona Passage, separating Hispaniola from Puerto Rico, teems with gamefish, as do the deep waters off the north shore. The main venues are **Casa de Campo Marina**, Punta Cana, and Puerto Plata.

Typical half-day charters cost about $375 for up to four people. Leading charter companies include **Punta Cana Fishing** and Puerto Plata's **Gone Fishing**. Inland lakes offer fishing for bass and tilapia; anglers require no license.

BOAT EXCURSIONS

Boat trips are a great way of viewing the coast and having fun. Catamarans and yachts depart on scheduled day and sunset excursions from every beach resort. Most of these excursions are party-hearty, with free-flowing rum cocktails. Glass-bottom boat rides reveal the fascinating beauty of the underwater world. A self-drive speedboat excursion with **Bávaro Splash** is thrilling. **Cayo Arena Tours** offers speedboat and catamaran excursions to Punta Rucia and Cayo Paraíso, the only coral island in the Dominican Republic.

WATERSPORTS

Visitors to the main beach resorts are spoilt for choice with all manner of water-sports, including Hobi Cats, banana-boat rides, Jet Skis, and speedboat safaris, which are a favorite with holiday-makers. All-inclusive resorts also do their bit in providing their guests with free use of non-motorized equipment. Enthusiasts of motorized watersports, however, have to mostly rely on the numerous private outfitters.

Rafters negotiating the rapids on a whitewater rafting trip

WHITEWATER RAFTING

Cascading out of the Cordillera Central, the Río Yaque del Norte guarantees plenty of thrills on whitewater trips offered by **Rancho Baiguate**, in the mountain-city of Jarabacoa.

TENNIS

Most resort hotels have tennis courts and most grant non-guests use of their facilities for a fee. Casa de Campo (see p172) has a large and modern tennis academy.

HORSE-RIDING

Horseback rides are available at all the beach resorts. Not to be missed is a ride to El Salto de Limón waterfall; visitors can book through **Santí Rancho**. The specialist facilities at **Casa de Campo Equestrian Center** and **Sea Horse Ranch Equestrian Center** are exceptional.

Yachts and motor boats docked at the marina of Casa de Campo

For hotels and restaurants on this island see pp186–9 and pp190–91

MOUNTAIN BIKING

The Republic's rugged terrain is perfect for energetic cyclists. Mountain biking is offered by outfitters at most beach resorts, including **Iguana Mama** in Cabarete, with trips for beginners and hard-core cycling junkies. Rancho Cascada *(see p177)* is

Mountain bikers close to Cabarete

a great base for adventures in the Cordillera Central. Many of the major cities in the Dominican Republic have clubs for mountain biking who arrange for weekly rides.

ATV AND JEEP TOURS

ATV and jeep excursions are popular at many beach resort areas. Often, the "jeep" will be an open-top truck fitted to carry passengers in comfort. Some companies let visitors drive their own jeep in convoy through sugarcane fields, rainforest, and local communities. **Bavaro Runners** and **Outback Safari** have trips from Punta Cana and north coast resorts. **Auceen Raid Aventure** offers ATV tours in Las Terrenas, Samaná.

HIKING

Hiking up Pico Duarte, the Caribbean's highest peak, which stands at a height of 10,164 ft (3,097 m) is the

Hiker on the trail of Pico Duarte, the highest peak of the Caribbean

ultimate challenge for hikers in these islands. Guided three-day round-trip hikes depart La Ciénaga *(see p177)*. Rancho Cascada is a good base for exploring other parts of the Cordillera Central. Reserva Científica Quita Espuela *(see p176)* and **Parque Nacional del Este** offer less demanding hikes.

DIRECTORY

BIRDING AND WILDLIFE VIEWING

Excursiones Guariquén
http://guariquen.
adventourspr.com

Paraíso Caño Hondo
Tel 809 248 5995. www.
paraisocanohondo.com

Tody Tours
Tel 809 686 0882.
www.todytours.com

Whale Samana
Calle Mella corner Av.,
La Marina, Samaná.
Tel 809 538 2494.
www.whalesamana.com

DIVING

Dolphin Dive Center
Tel 809 571 3589.
www.dolphindivecenter.
com

Las Terrenas Divers
Playa Bonita, Las Terrenas.
Tel 809 889 2422.
www.lt-divers.com

Scubafun
Calle Principal, Bayahibe.
Tel 809 833 0003.
www.scubafun.info

KITEBOARDING AND WINDSURFING

Ali's Surf Camp
Tel 809 571 0733.
www.alissurfcamp.com

Carib Wind Center
Calle Principal, Cabarete.
Tel 809 571 0640.
www.caribwind.com

Kite Excite
Kitebeach Hotel, Cabarete.
Tel 829 962 4556.
www.kiteexcite.com

Laurel Eastman Kiteboarding
Tel 809 571 0564.
www.laureleastman.com

FISHING

Casa de Campo Marina
Tel 809 523 8646.
www.marinacasade
campo.com.do

Gone Fishing
Plaza Tourisol,
Puerto Plata.
Tel 809 261 4141.

Punta Cana Fishing
Tel 809 867 0381.
www.firstclassfishing.com

BOAT EXCURSIONS

Bávaro Splash
Tel 809 688 1615.
www.bavarosplash.com

Cayo Arena Tours
Tel 809 656 0020.

WHITEWATER RAFTING

Rancho Baiguate
www.ranchbaiguate.com

HORSE-RIDING

Casa de Campo Equestrian Center
Tel 809 523 3333. www.
casadecampo.com.do

Santí Rancho
El Limón, Samaná.
Tel 809 956 5526.
www.saltolimon.com

Sea Horse Ranch Equestrian Center
Tel 809 571 3880.
www.sea-horse-ranch.
com

MOUNTAIN BIKING

Iguana Mama
Tel 809 571 0908.
www.iguanamama.com

ATV AND JEEP TOURS

Auceen Raid Aventure
Tel 809 240 6784.
www.samana.net/fun-
rental.html

Bavaro Runners
Tel 809 455 1135.
www.bavarorunners.com

Outback Safari
Tel 809 455 1573. www.
outbacksafari.com.do

HIKING

Parque Nacional del Este
Between Bayahibe and
Boca de Yuma.

Plunging waterfalls of El Salto de Limón, near Samaná ▷

Choosing a Hotel

Santo Domingo has splendid boutique hotels converted from old colonial mansions, as well as modern high-rise chain hotels, while the island's beach resorts are dominated by all-inclusives. The Samaná Peninsula and north coast resorts also offer fine boutique hotels and budget accommodations. Hotel rates are lower during the off-season between September and November.

PRICE CATEGORIES
The following price ranges are for a standard double room per night and all taxes included.

$ under $100
$$ $100–200
$$$ $200–300
$$$$ $300–400
$$$$$ over $400

DOMINICAN REPUBLIC

Hostal Nicolás de Ovando – *see p168*
A stone's throw from the major plazas and museums, this hotel occupies one of the oldest buildings in Santo Domingo.

Casa de Campo – *see p172*
The epitome of upscale living, this swank and sprawling resort is renowned for its golf and other activities, plus fine dining.

Puntacana Resort & Club – *see p173*
The resort has been recently restored and the new Tortuga Bay villas are among the most genteel in the country.

Rancho Cascada – *see p177*
This mountain retreat and activity center is loved by mountain bikers, hikers, and kayakers, despite barebone accommodations.

Sofitel Nicolás

BARAHONA Playazul Hotel-Restaurante 🏊 🍴 ≡ 🧒 ♿ [W] $
Carretera Barahona-Paraíso Km7, Punta Prieta ***Tel*** *809 204 8010* ***Rooms*** *18*

A lovely minimal option on the up-and-coming Barahona coastline, this clifftop hotel sits over a cove with a pink-sand beach and peacock-blue waters. Tasteful pastel decor adorns the well-lit rooms. A breeze-swept thatched restaurant offers alfresco dining. The hotel also offers massage treatments.

BARAHONA Casa Bonita Tropical Lodge 🍴 ≡ [W] $$
Carretera de la Costa Km17, Barahona ***Tel*** *809 476 5059* ***Fax*** *809 565 7310* ***Rooms*** *12*

Hanging on a mountainside, with magnificent ocean and rainforest vistas, this chic eco-lodge offers sublime comfort. Spacious bungalows of coral stone and thatch boast designer furnishings. Celebrated chef Carlos Estevez oversees the gourmet restaurant. The lodge offers birding tours, hikes, and coffee plantation tours. **www.casabonitadr.com**

BOCA CHICA Don Juan Beach Resort 🏊 🍴 ≡ ♿ $$$
Av. Abraham Nuñez 8 ***Tel*** *809 687 9157* ***Fax*** *809 688 5271* ***Rooms*** *224*

A handsome beachfront resort with a handy heart-of-town location, this hotel has been a mid-price staple for many years. Its lively tropical decor, large freeform swimming pool, and excellent children's facilities keep families coming back year after year. Scuba diving classes and trips are available. **www.donjuanbeachresort.com**

CABARETE Agualina 🏊 🍴 ≡ 🧒 ♿ [W] $
Carretera Principal, Kite Beach ***Tel*** *809 571 0805* ***Fax*** *809 571 0856* ***Rooms*** *22*

A favorite with kiteboarders, Agualina is a great beachside bargain. Small, intimate and well run, it has a marvelous modern aesthetic. An invitingly airy restaurant serves healthy fare, and the on-site kite school is popular. The delightful swimming pool is surrounded by a palm-shaded lawn. **www.agualina.com**

CABARETE Hotel Villa Taína 🏊 🍴 ≡ 🧒 ♿ [W] $
Carretera Principal ***Tel*** *809 571 0722* ***Fax*** *809 571 0883* ***Rooms*** *57*

A rambling, laid-back beachfront option in the thick of Cabarete's bar and restaurant strip, this place is good for everyone – from surfers to families. Attractions include an alfresco bar and dining on the sands, a palm-shaded swimming pool, and a spa. There is also an on-site kiteboarding school and rentals. **www.villataina.com**

CABARETE Kite Beach Hotel 🏊 🍴 ≡ 🧒 ♿ [W] $
Carretera Principal, Punta Goleta ***Tel*** *809 571 0878* ***Fax*** *809 571 0278* ***Rooms*** *43*

This popular Cabarete hotel has a thatched atrium lobby and offers modestly furnished one- and two-bedroom apartments and penthouse suites with cable TV and in-room safes. A colorful open-air restaurant serves buffets and international dishes. Kiteboarding lessons are also offered. **www.kitebeachhotel.com**

CABARETE Natura Cabañas 🏊 🍴 ≡ ♿ $$
Paseo del Sol 5, Perla Marina ***Tel*** *809 571 1507* ***Fax*** *809 571 1056* ***Rooms*** *11*

This eco-sensitive resort at Playa Encuentro, midway between Cabarete and Sosúa, exudes charm in its thatched bungalows of natural stone and rough-hewn furniture. Some of the bungalows have kitchenettes. The swimming pool is shaded by palms, the spa offers soothing treatments, and it has a dojo for yoga. **www.naturacabana.com**

CONSTANZA Hotel Alto Cerro 🍴 ≡ ♿ $
East of Constanza, Colonia Kennedy ***Tel*** *809 539 1553* ***Fax*** *809 530 6193* ***Rooms*** *40*

One of few options around Constanza, this hillside hotel is a 20-minute walk from town. Guests can choose from sparsely furnished rooms and self-catering apartments. The hotel also provides tents for camping on tree-shaded lawns. The restaurant has a terrace and fresh trout is a specialty. **www.altocerro.com**

COSTA DEL COCO Sivory Punta Cana 🎫 🍴 📋 ♿ ⓦ $$$$

Playa Uvero Alto **Tel** *809 330 0500* **Fax** *809 334 0500* **Rooms** *55*

A boutique resort for sophisticates, this all-suite hotel fuses fashionable minimalist decor with a Zen-inspired motif plus plenty of Taíno-style thatch. Suites feature contemporary furniture and state-of-the-art amenities. There are three superb restaurants, plus a vast wine cellar, and a world-class spa. **www.sivorypuntacana.com**

COSTA DEL COCO Zoetry Agua Resort & Spa 🎫 🍴 📋 🌴 ♿ $$$$$

Playa Uvero Alto **Tel** *809 468 0000* **Fax** *809 468 0001* **Rooms** *53*

A deluxe resort hotel on the golden sands of Uvero Alto, the hotel's decor is inspired by traditional Taíno architecture, with plenty of thatch, coral stone floors, and natural hardwoods. Cavernous accommodations with stylish appointments. Amenities include spa facilities and a chauffeured jeep for touring. **www.zoetryresorts.com**

JARABACOA Hotel Gran Jimenoa 🍴 📋 ♿ $

Av. La Confluencia **Tel** *809 574 6304* **Fax** *809 574 4177* **Rooms** *28*

In a lush, forest-enclosed setting on the banks of the Río Yagua del Norte, this hotel has a lovely riverside restaurant and is popular for its business facilities. No-frills bedrooms with simple bathrooms are comfortable enough and have cable TV. Horseback riding is a specialty here. Renovation is ongoing.

JARABACOA Rancho Baiguate 🍴 📋 🌴 ♿ $

Barrio La Joya, 2 miles (3 km) SE of Jarabacoa **Tel** *809 574 6890* **Rooms** *27*

Doubling as an activity center specializing in river rafting and horseback riding, this riverside option has a lush garden setting. Rooms and suites are comfortable and homely. Backpackers can opt for dorms. The place has an airy thatched buffet restaurant plus a games room and basketball, volleyball, and softball courts. **www.ranchobaiguate.com**

PLAYA BAYAHIBE Iberostar Hacienda Dominicus 🎫 🍴 📋 🌴 ♿ $$$$

Playa Dominicus, 3 miles (5 km) S of Bayahibe **Tel** *809 688 3600* **Rooms** *501*

Fronted by sand and reef-protected waters with a wreck close to shore, this all-inclusive resort has a Spanish hacienda-style decor with eclectic furnishings. The extensive amenities include four restaurants, a kids' club and pool, diving, as well as thatch beach umbrellas. **www.iberostar.com**

PUERTO PLATA BlueBay Villas Doradas 🎫 🍴 📋 🌴 ♿ ⓦ $$$

Playa Dorada **Tel** *809 320 3000* **Fax** *809 320 4790* **Rooms** *245*

This adults-only all-inclusive is nestled between the Playa Dorado Golf Course and sparkling white sands. Suites with minimalist furnishings and Balinese beds have whirlpool tubs. Facilities include four classy restaurants, each with its own mood, a golf-pro shop, and volleyball court. Watersports cost extra. **www.bluebayresorts.com**

PUERTO PLATA Victoria Golf & Beach Resort 🎫 🍴 🍸 📋 ♿ ⓦ $$$

Playa Dorada **Tel** *809 320 1200* **Fax** *809 320 4862* **Rooms** *190*

A short walk (or horse-drawn carriage ride) from the beach, the Victoria faces the Playa Dorado Golf Course. Most of the rooms, suites, and villas are painted in blazing whites with soft pastel decor. All have balconies and fairway views. It has four restaurants, plus a beach club. **www.vhhr.com**

PUERTO PLATA Casa Colonial Beach & Spa 🎫 🍴 📋 ♿ ⓦ $$$$

Playa Dorada **Tel** *809 320 3232* **Fax** *809 320 3131* **Rooms** *50*

Exuding class, this intimate deluxe boutique hotel resembling a coral stone colonial mansion draws international celebrities for its contemporary sophistication. Highlights include a lovely rooftop spa and pool, two restaurants, a hip bar, and cavernous rooms with irresistibly tasteful decor and furnishings. **www.casacolonialhotel.com**

PUERTO PLATA Iberostar Costa Dorada 🎫 🍴 📋 🌴 ♿ $$$$

Carretera Luperón Km4, Costa Dorada **Tel** *809 320 1000* **Fax** *809 320 2023* **Rooms** *516*

This all-inclusive hotel has attractive public arenas including a thatched atrium lobby blending with Neo-Classical motifs. Colorful accommodations offer contemporary wicker furnishings. Activities revolve around a vast free-form swimming pool and separate kids' pool. There are four restaurants and a full-service spa. **www.iberostar.com**

PUNTA CANA Blau Naturapark Beach Ecoresort & Spa 🎫 🍴 📋 🌴 ♿ $$

Cabeza de Toro **Tel** *809 221 2626* **Fax** *809 221 6060* **Rooms** *520*

On the sands at Cabeza de Toro, this handsome all-inclusive is named for the wetlands and palm plantations that envelop it on three sides. Spacious accommodations boast gorgeous decor using bamboo and rattan; ceiling fans complement air-conditioning. A spa and heaps of activities and sports are on offer. **www.blauhotels.com**

PUNTA CANA Barceló Dominican Beach 🎫 🍴 🌴 ♿ $$$

Playa Cortecito **Tel** *809 221 0714* **Fax** *809 221 0814* **Rooms** *600*

One of five sister hotels in the sprawling Barceló Bávaro mega-resort along 3 miles (5 km) of shore, this four-star option shares facilities with the other four hotels, including a casino, disco, 14 restaurants, and the most extensive watersports and activities program in the area. **www.barcelobavaro.com**

PUNTA CANA Iberostar Bávaro 🎫 🍴 📋 🌴 ♿ $$$

Playa Arena Gorda **Tel** *809 221 6500* **Fax** *809 688 6186* **Rooms** *588*

A distinguished all-inclusive, this low-rise, all-suite resort has an ideal location close to the center of beach action. The open-air atrium lobby offers a lovely welcome. Guest rooms in 74 eight-unit "bungalows" have lively contemporary decor. Restaurants include Japanese and Mediterranean. **www.iberostar.com**

PUNTA CANA Hard Rock Café Hotel & Casino $$$$

Boulevard Turistico del Este, Playa Macao **Tel** *809 687 0000* **Rooms** *1,791*

This mammoth resort may not be to all tastes due to its overwhelming size, but its facilities are world-class. Eleven restaurants deliver sensational service and cuisine, and bedrooms feature dramatic rock-themed designs that will appeal to youthful sophisticates. **www.hardrockhotels.com/puntacana**

PUNTA CANA NH Real Arena $$$$

Carretera El Cortecito, Playa Bávaro **Tel** *809 221 4646* **Fax** *809 552 6851* **Rooms** *658*

The NH Real Arena is a classy all-inclusive hotel with a sensational contemporary style. Flat-screen TVs, Wi-Fi service, and colorful furnishings are standard in lavish guest rooms. Facilities include six restaurants, eight bars, five pools, an upscale shopping mall, and complete watersports and entertainment. **www.nh-hotels.com**

PUNTA CANA Grand Palladium Palace Resort, Spa & Casino $$$$

Playa Bávaro **Tel** *809 221 0719* **Fax** *809 221 0819* **Rooms** *409*

One of the most elegant family-friendly all-inclusive hotels at Playa Bávaro, this Neo-Classical-styled resort shares facilities with two neighboring siblings. It offers sumptuous accommodations. Eleven restaurants span the globe, and nightlife includes a disco and casino. Activities range from basketball to scuba diving. **www.fiestahotelgroup.com**

PUNTA CANA Paradisus Punta Cana $$$$

Playa Arena Gorda **Tel** *809 687 9923* **Fax** *809 687 0752* **Rooms** *500*

This large, all-inclusive resort stands out by its huge lake-like swimming pool, framed by lush landscaping. The colorful guest rooms have colonial-style hardwood furnishings and separate lounge area. There are ten restaurants, and plenty of entertainment and activities including a 27-hole golf course. **www.paradisuspuntacana.travel**

PUNTA CANA Secrets Sanctuary Cap Cana Golf & Spa $$$$$

Cap Cana **Tel** *809 544 4343* **Rooms** *176*

Intended for high-end travelers, this sumptuous all-suite hotel is situated within a charming village setting. It has a mega-yacht marina, casino, gourmet restaurants, and a championship golf course. Furnished with plantation-style decor, rooms feature glazed hardwood floors and coral stone walls. **www.secretsresorts.com**

RÍO SAN JUAN Hotel La Catalina $

3 miles (5 km) W of Cabrera **Tel** *809 589 7700* **Fax** *809 589 7550* **Rooms** *36*

This handsome, breeze-cooled hillside hotel offers awesome coastal views. The airy guest rooms and apartments are furnished in tropical style with bamboo and floral prints, and have bougainvillea-clad balconies. There is a swimming pool with a thatched bar and also a billiard room. **www.lacatalina.com**

RÍO SAN JUAN Caliente Caribe $$

2 miles (3 km) E of Playa Grande **Tel** *813 996 3700* **Fax** *813 949 3616* **Rooms** *126*

An upscale, clothing-optional resort occupying its own white-sand beach cusped by cliffs, the hotel has a superbly scenic setting. The beachfront one- and two-bedroom bungalows are preferred to average clifftop rooms. Amenities include three pools, a TV lounge, live entertainment, and a disco. **www.calienteresorts.com**

RÍO SAN JUAN Bahía Principe San Juan $$$

5 miles (8 km) W of Río San Juan **Tel** *809 226 1590* **Fax** *809 226 1994* **Rooms** *941*

One of the country's most impressive mid-priced beachfront all-inclusives, this sprawling, low-rise option is self-contained, with many amenities and facilities. A good option for families. Bedrooms have wicker furnishings and lively tropical fabrics. The place has a casino and offers plenty of entertainment. **www.bahia-principe.com**

SAMANÁ PENINSULA Alisei Hotel, Restaurant & Spa $$

Calle Francisco Caamaño Deño, Las Terrenas **Tel** *809 240 5555* **Fax** *809 240 5556* **Rooms** *48*

Enjoying a lovely beachfront setting, this exciting and intimate boutique hotel centered on a gorgeous pool is a short stroll from key bars and galleries. The hip self-catering apartments gleam with mahogany furniture. There is a gourmet restaurant and a fashionable cocktail bar. **www.aliseihotel.com**

SAMANÁ PENINSULA Grand Paradise Samaná $$

Las Galeras **Tel** *809 538 0020* **Fax** *809 538 0040* **Rooms** *334*

Budget all-inclusive with a lovely beach setting, this low-rise resort caters mainly to Dominican families and package tourists. Accommodations are spacious but somewhat spartan. Restaurants provide buffet and Chinese options. Activities include plenty of watersports, the highlight being free scuba diving. **www.amhsamarina.com**

SAMANÁ PENINSULA Villa Eva Luna $$

Calle Marico, Las Terrenas **Tel** *809 978 5611* **Fax** *809 240 6600* **Rooms** *5 villas*

Mexico meets the Dominican Republic in this endearing boutique hotel. Kiwi, mango, and papaya colors adorn the self-catering villas which have contemporary furnishings, king-sized beds, and private terraces. The gourmet fusion restaurant is the region's finest. Services include yoga classes and baby-sitting. **www.villa-evaluna.com**

SAMANÁ PENINSULA Villa Serena $$

Las Galeras **Tel** *809 538 0000* **Fax** *809 538 0009* **Rooms** *21*

A gem with lush gardens and a sandy cove, this plantation-themed mansion is close to the heart of Las Galeras. There is an airy lounge and individually themed romantic and spacious guest rooms; some have four-posters. The candlelit, cross-ventilated garden restaurant serves set three-course dinners. **www.villaserena.com**

Key to Symbols *see back cover flap*

SAMANÁ PENINSULA Gran Bahía Principe Cayacoa
Loma Puerto Escondido, Samaná **Tel** 809 538 3131 **Fax** 809 538 3056 **Rooms** 295

This hotel with a private beach has a sensational clifftop setting with dramatic views of the bay. It is furnished in plantation style with shiny marble and hardwoods. A kidney-shaped pool studs the headland. The restaurant offers good views as well. An elevator leads down to the beach. **www.bahia-principe.com**

SAMANÁ PENINSULA Gran Bahía Principe Cayo Levantado
Cayo Levantado **Tel** 809 538 3232 **Fax** 809 538 2425 **Rooms** 193

Guests are delivered by private launch to this all-inclusive hotel that commands the view of a spectacularly beautiful and eponymous cay. A vast pool and sundeck complement two private beaches with sheltered waters. Accommodations combine luxurious fittings and modern amenities. **www.bahia-principe.com**

SAMANÁ PENINSULA Viva Wyndham Samaná
Playa Cosón, Las Terrenas **Tel** 809 240 5050 **Fax** 809 240 5536 **Rooms** 218

A great family option, this sprawling mid-priced all-inclusive resort fronts a gorgeous beach with a choice of rooms and bungalows. The mood is lively and there is an excellent children's camp, plus three restaurants and plenty of entertainment. **www.vivawyndhamresorts.com**

SANTIAGO DE LOS CABALLEROS Hodelpa Centro Plaza
Calle Mella 54 **Tel** 809 581 7000 **Fax** 809 582 4566 **Rooms** 85

Colorful and trendy minimalist furnishings combine with a superb location to make this inner-city hotel great value. The well-lit lobby sets the cheerful contemporary tone. Accommodations are fresh and airy, with handsome chocolate-and-white color schemes. Facilities include a business center and a casino. **www.hodelpa.com**

SANTIAGO DE LOS CABALLEROS Hodelpa Gran Almirante
Av. Salvador Estrella Sadhala **Tel** 809 580 1992 **Fax** 809 241 1492 **Rooms** 156

Blazing white linen, rich hardwoods, and cream leather furnishings make this mid-sized property on the outskirts of the city the classiest hotel. The casino, cigar lounge, and rooftop pool are major draws, and the restaurants, bars, and nightclub are all among the city's best. **www.hodelpa.com**

SANTO DOMINGO Hodelpa Caribe Colonial
Isabel La Católica 159 **Tel** 809 688 7799 **Fax** 809 685 8128 **Rooms** 49

A stone's throw from Parque Colón, this hotel occupies a mid-20th-century, five-story structure. The decor is a little gauche and many guest rooms are on the small side, but the price is great for its location and the staff are friendly. It has a tiny restaurant and bar, and limited parking space. **www.hodelpa.com**

SANTO DOMINGO Hostal Duque de Wellington
Av. Independencia 304 **Tel** 809 682 4525 **Fax** 809 688 2844 **Rooms** 29

In the Gazcue district, within walking distance of the Zona Colonial, this well-run, no-frills hotel is a great bargain. The small but handsome reception lounge offers a warm welcome, reflected in clean and cozy, modestly appointed rooms. The plunge pool is welcome on hot days. It also has a travel agency. **www.hotelduque.com**

SANTO DOMINGO Hotel Conde de Peñalba
Calle El Conde and Arzobispo Meriño **Tel** 809 688 7121 **Fax** 809 688 7375 **Rooms** 20

This three-story hotel with gracious Mediterranean-style façade is recommended for its great position on Parque Colón, and for its lively open-air restaurant and café – a hub of local social life. Colonial-style rooms are comfortable albeit simply appointed; request a south-facing room overlooking the plaza. **www.condepenalba.com**

SANTO DOMINGO Hotel Doña Elvira
Padre Billini 207 **Tel** 809 221 7415 **Fax** 809 221 7369 **Rooms** 15

Run by a friendly Belgian and American couple, this charming bed-and-breakfast in tropical mango and papaya pastels is a thoughtful conversion of an 18th-century town home in the heart of the Zona Colonial. Rooms on two levels face a shady courtyard with a small swimming pool; all have cable TV and Wi-Fi. **www.dona-elvira.com**

SANTO DOMINGO Meliá Santo Domingo
Av. George Washington 365 **Tel** 809 221 6666 **Fax** 809 687 8150 **Rooms** 245

Despite its garish Las Vegas-style frontage with an overbearing casino entrance, this modern high-rise has spacious and inviting guest rooms with upscale modern furnishings plus balconies. There are two elegant restaurants, a rooftop swimming pool, and sauna. Live music is played in the lobby. **www.solmelia.com**

SANTO DOMINGO Renaissance Jaragua Hotel & Casino
Av. George Washington 367 **Tel** 809 221 2222 **Fax** 809 686 0528 **Rooms** 300

Soaring over the Malecón seafront boulevard this hotel has extensive convention facilities, a big swimming pool amid expansive grounds, a large casino, and hip, 21st-century decor. Spacious guest rooms are chocolate and cream colored with elegant contemporary furnishings and lavish bathrooms. **www.renaissancehotels.com**

SANTO DOMINGO Hilton Santo Domingo
Av. George Washington 500 **Tel** 809 685 0000 **Fax** 809 685 0202 **Rooms** 228

A remodel has graced this shorefront high-rise with a dynamic futuristic decor and bold color schemes. The oceanfront rooms are preferred for views through glass walls. Amenities include the city's largest casino, a gym, and a large business center. **www.hiltoncaribbean.com/santodomingo**

Where to Eat & Nightlife

Dining in the Dominican Republic is cosmopolitan, especially in the main tourist centers, though tasty local criollo dishes are widely available. Santo Domingo has a night scene hot enough to cook the pork, with everything from traditional music venues to sizzling nightclubs. Punta Cana caters mainly to tourists, with discos and bars in major hotels.

PRICE CATEGORIES
The price ranges are for a two-course meal for one, including tax and service charges and half a bottle of wine.

$ under $10
$$ $10–15
$$$ $15–25
$$$$ $25–35
$$$$$ over $35

RESTAURANTS

Choice of Restaurants
All-inclusive hotels provide meals as part of the room rate and most of the hotels have several restaurants to choose from. Some resort restaurants are open to non-guests also, though only by reservation. Santo Domingo has many world-class restaurants. Apart from these, all the main beaches here also have unpretentious shacks and restaurants that serve freshly-caught seafood.

Sam's Bar & Grill

El Mesón de la Cava

BOCA CHICA Restaurante Boca Marina   🔲🍴🎵♨️♿ $$$
Calle Duarte 12-A **Tel** *809 688 6810*

This trendy open-air restaurant overhangs the turquoise waters, with steps luring patrons to swim. Gleaming hardwood furniture occupies a coral stone floor beneath a soaring thatch roof. The globe-spanning menu ranges from salads and pasta dinners to steaks, and fresh seafood. Service is efficient and friendly.

CABARETE La Casita de Papi   🍴 $$$$
Calle Principal **Tel** *809 986 3750*

The two-story restaurant in a former Dominican home on the beach is famous for its freshly prepared seafood. Specially popular is the garlic-shrimps-pan as well as crayfish cooked in coconut and anise sauce. The French owner Don Papi also prepares a delicious paella. Open only at night and reservations are not essential.

CONSTANZA Exquisites Dilenia   🍴♨️ $$
Calle Gaston F. Feligne 7 **Tel** *809 539 2213*

Built of rustic timbers in true country fashion, this is one of the most charming, authentically Dominican restaurants in the country, with an irresistible ambience plus delicious local fare at unbeatable prices. Owner-chef Dilenia de la Rosa Durán delivers satisfying rabbit, guinea fowl, and goat dishes. The stewed goat in red wine is highly recommended.

LA ROMANA La Piazzetta   🍷📋🍴 $$$$
Altos de Chavón **Tel** *809 523 3333 ext. 5339*

Of the several Italianate restaurants at Altos de Chavón, this one stands out for its authentic Tuscan decor replicating a wood-beamed farmhouse, and for its exceptional Italian cuisine. Try the gnocchi stuffed with cheeses, or the superb porcini mushroom risotto. Leave room for the divine profiteroles. Open only at night.

PUERTO PLATA Sam's Bar & Grill   📋♿ $$
Calle José del Carmen Ariza 34 **Tel** *809 586 7267*

A local institution among expatriate gringos for three decades, this charmingly unpretentious and off-beat downtown diner in a creaky wooden colonial mansion delivers US favorites, such as filling pancakes, steak and eggs, and Mexican scramble for breakfast, plus tuna salads, and meatloafs.

PUERTO PLATA Embocca   🍴♨️📋🎵♿ $$$$
Carretera Cabarete a Sabaneta 3 km **Tel** *809 571 0173*

This chic beachfront restaurant is a short ride from downtown. Its stylish contemporary decor and deck with lounge chairs on the sands are key draws, as is an acclaimed tapas menu and superb paella. It offers salsa lessons on Fridays, and has live music.

PUNTA CANA Captain Cook   🍴📋 $$$$
Playa El Cortesito **Tel** *809 552 0645*

At this beachfront restaurant, diners are served freshly caught fish. Visitors can ask the cook to prepare the fish the way they like it. Fresh-water crabs, shrimps, calamari, and crayfish are specialties as well as paella. Enjoy the beautiful views of the ocean.

PUNTA CANA Jellyfish   🍴🎵♿ $$$$
Playa Bávaro **Tel** *809 840 7684*

Sitting atop the sands, this open-walled restaurant with dramatic architecture doubles as a lively beach bar. A Mediterranean influence infuses the nouvelle menu, heavy on seafood, such as spicy lobster bisque and garlic shrimp. Deep-cushion sofas invite lounging on the mezzanine. Offers free hotel transfers.

Key to Symbols *see back cover flap*

PUNTA CANA Cocoloba

🍴 🍷 🚗 ♿ $$$$$

Punta Cana Resort & Club **Tel** *809 959 2262*

A highlight of the Punta Cana Resort & Club *(see p173)*, this classy restaurant with tall shuttered windows was decorated by Oscar de la Renta. Mouthwatering nouvelle dishes include the likes of crab cakes with a mango chutney appetizer, and lobster tempura over glazed pumpkin. Reservation required.

PUNTA CANA La Yola

🍴 🍷 $$$$$

Punta Cana Marina, Punta Cana Resort & Club **Tel** *809 959 2262*

Beautifully situated on a pier above the ocean, this first-class restaurant in the Punta Cana Resort & Club *(see p173)* is shaped like a fisherman's boat. The restaurant has fresh Mediterranean and Caribbean cuisine and specializes in seafood. The appetizers are especially good. Reservations are recommended. Closed Tuesdays.

SAMANÁ Restaurante Xamana

🍴 📋 🚗 ♿ $$$$$

Av. Malecón **Tel** *809 538 2129*

A stunning, Italian-run restaurant on the seafront boulevard at the east end of town, Xamana's fusion menu melds Italian techniques with fresh Dominican ingredients in creative pasta and seafood dishes. The black bean soup is the specialty here. Minimalist in style, it offers great marina views through a glass wall.

SANTIAGO DE LOS CABALLEROS Pez Dorado

🍴 📋 🚗 ♿ $$$

Calle del Sol 43 **Tel** *809 582 4051*

A tremendous bargain, this heart-of-downtown institution is renowned islandwide. Decor is in slightly gloomy Spanish bodega fashion. Dishes include Chinese as well as local and international staples, all superbly prepared and filling. Stuffed sea bass is recommended. It also has an excellent wine selection.

SANTO DOMINGO El Mesón de la Cava

🎵 🚗 $$$

Av. Mirador del Sur 1 **Tel** *809 533 2818*

Occupying a real cave (actually multiple caverns) with dramatic limestone formations, and entered via a rickety staircase, this rambling underground restaurant delivers gourmet cuisine in addition to its romantic ambience. The creative international menu includes seafood, plus steaks and succulent lamb chops.

SANTO DOMINGO Mesón de Barí

📋 🎵 ♿ $$$$

Calle Hostos 302 **Tel** *809 687 4091*

A bohemian gem in the heart of the Zona Colonial, this eatery occupies a colonial mansion festooned with original art made by famous patrons. It serves traditional criollo dishes, including *empenada lambi* (conch-stuffed pastries) and the popular stewed crab house special, *cangrejo guisado*. Reservations are recommended.

SANTO DOMINGO Pat'e Palo

🍷 🚗 🎵 🚗 ♿ $$$$

Calle La Atarazana 25 **Tel** *809 687 8089*

The wonderful setting overlooking Plaza España is reason enough to dine here. Quality Continental and local dishes include beef *carpaccio*, sautéed shrimp in coconut-curry sauce, and sea bass in white wine. Wait staff dress as pirates – an allusion to Peg-Leg (Paté Palo), a buccaneer who ran a tavern centuries ago.

SANTO DOMINGO Vesuvio del Malecón

🍴 📋 🍷 🚗 ♿ $$$$$

Av. George Washington 521 **Tel** *809 221 1954*

This popular Italian restaurant offers alfresco dining on its seafront terrace. Known for its fresh seafoods, such as garlic crayfish and delicious porcini mushroom risotto in squid ink, it is a must for visiting gourmets. Scrumptious desserts include profiteroles. The air-conditioned interior offers classical elegance.

BARS AND CLUBS

Many of Santo Domingo's high-rise hotels and the major all-inclusive beach resorts have discos and casinos, some of which also host cabarets open to non-guests. Punta Cana has a few bars beyond the hotel confines, while at Cabarete visitors jive on the sands at lively oceanfront bars, many of which do not get in the groove until almost midnight. Dominicans' favorite music is hip-swiveling merengue and plaintive, home-grown bachata, played on a banjo-like acoustic guitar.

Signage of Atarazana 9

RECOMMENDED PLACES TO GO

Atarazana 9
Calle Atarazana 9, Santo Domingo.
(Lively dance club.)

Bambú
Calle Principal, Cabarete. (Disco-bar
also shows movies alfresco.)

Disco Club Mangu
Occidental Gran Flamenco Hotel,
Bávaro. (Sophisticated disco.)

El Mambo Social Club
Av. 27 de Febrero, Las Terrenas.
(Stylish lounge bar.)

Guácara Taína
Paseo de los Indios, Santo Domingo.
(Nightclub in a cave.)

Lax
Calle Principal, Cabarete. (Crowded
beach bar with disco.)

Loft Lounge & Dance Club
Calle Tiradentes 44, Santo
Domingo. (Live merengue.)

Ocean Club Disco
Ocean Sands Casino, Cabarete.
(Hip air-conditioned disco.)

Tropicalissimo
Barceló Bávaro Beach Resort, Punta
Cana. (Cabaret revue.)

Practical Information

The Dominican Republic's tourist infrastructure is concentrated around Punta Cana-Bávaro, where the expansion of deluxe all-inclusives is spreading along Costa del Coco. Samaná is also rapidly growing in popularity, with new construction, but retains its laid-back ambience. Tourist offices are scattered across the island with the main offices situated in Santo Domingo, and the staff are generally helpful. Bear in mind that things often get accomplished at a slower pace here.

A sign at the Punta Cana International Airport

WHEN TO GO

The best time for visiting the Dominican Republic is November to April, the dry season, when temperatures are pleasantly moderate. Summers can be exceedingly hot, although hotels and car rental companies offer discounts. Temperatures vary with elevation; Cordillera Central is delightfully cool year-round. Cultural events occur throughout the year, but much of the country comes to a halt for Semana Santa (holy week).

GETTING THERE

Although Santo Domingo's Las Américas International Airport (SDQ) is the main airport, most international flights serving beach resorts land at Punta Cana International Airport (PUJ), while other flights also arrive and depart from regional airports such as Aeropuerto Internacional Gregorio Luperón (POP), in Puerto Plata. **American Airlines, Delta, JetBlue, Spirit Airlines, United Airlines,** and **US Airways** offer service to the

Dominican Republic, as do many charter airlines. Several European airlines connect through Miami.

DOCUMENTATION

All foreign citizens need a passport plus proof of onward travel to visit the Dominican Republic, where a tourist card ($10) valid for 30 days is issued upon arrival. Extensions for an additional 90 days cost $25 from the **Dirección General de Migración**.

VISITOR INFORMATION

The Dominican Republic's **Ministry of Tourism** has offices in the US, Canada, and UK, as well as in major tourist centers in the Republic. The key local offices include one on Santo Domingo's Parque Colón, in Bávaro, and Puerto Plata. The ministry publishes a series of pocket-sized guides to the major regions. Hotel tour desks can also provide information about organized excursions, and other activities. Many tour companies and travel suppliers have websites that provide more specific information.

HEALTH AND SECURITY

Most destinations in the Dominican Republic are safe, and endemic tropical diseases are limited to dengue, and malaria, a rare occurrence primarily along the Caribbean coast. Additional threats include sunburn, dehydration,

and rip tides; check conditions with locals before swimming. Private doctors and clinics are found in every town, and basic government-run *centros de salud* (health centers) serve most communities. **Hospiten** operates medical clinics and ambulance service in major resorts. A few safety precautions are advisable as petty theft and crime is endemic in visitor venues and remote and unlit places at night. Leave all valuables in the hotel safe when exploring on foot. Driving on isolated rural roads at night is risky due to poor lighting, so use extreme caution.

BANKING AND CURRENCY

The Dominican currency is the peso (RD$), but the US dollar is accepted everywhere. Euros and pounds Sterling can be exchanged at banks, including **BanReservas**, and foreign-exchange booths. Most shops and tourist outlets accept major credit cards. Traveler's checks in US dollars are accepted in very few places. Most banks have ATMs, but they often run out of cash.

COMMUNICATIONS

Ubiquitous public phones use prepaid phone cards, which can be purchased at stores and call centers. Calls from hotels incur a hefty surcharge. The Republic's area code is 809. Calls within Santo Domingo require the ten-digit number including 809, which should be preceded by 1 when dialing beyond Santo Domingo. Most hotels have Internet service; many have Wi-Fi. The main service providers are **Claro**

Policeman patrolling the beach in Punta Cana

Stalls selling colorful native Haitian art, Costa del Coco

Codetel, Orange, and Tricom. There are Internet cafés in every town and tourist center.

TRANSPORT

Taxis are the best means of getting around within cities. Tourist taxis await visitors outside most hotels. Locals rely on *carros públicos* (private unmetered cars) that operate as communal taxis, but are best avoided as drivers tend to overcharge. *Motoconchos* (motorcycle taxis) form the main transport only for locals outside Santo Domingo and are best avoided as well. Air-conditioned buses link most destinations nationwide.

SHOPPING

The country is a veritable Aladdin's Cave of crafts, including amber and larimar jewelry unique to the isle. Museo del Ambar *(see p175)* and **Harrison's Fine Caribbean Jewelers** have outlets in tourist venues. Native Haitian art is ubiquitous, but Santo Domingo also has fine galleries selling more contemporary pieces by local artists. All beaches host souvenir stalls and artisan markets spilling their art, linen blouses, and hardwood sculptures onto the sands. Most large hotels also have souvenir stores. The island is renowned for the quality of its cigars, available throughout the country.

LANGUAGE

Spanish is the official language, spoken by everyone, although some locals also speak English, as do most people working in the tourism industry.

ELECTRICITY

The Dominican Republic operates on 110 volts, but 220 volts is sometimes found in hotels and is usually marked as such. Outlets use US two-prong or three-prong plugs.

Visitors from Europe should bring transformers or adapters. Most large hotels have their own back-up generators to supply power during frequent outages. A surge protector or transformer is good protection against power surges.

TIME

The Dominican Republic is on Atlantic Standard Time (AST), 4 hours behind Greenwich Mean Time (GMT) and 1 hour ahead of New York and Miami.

GETTING MARRIED

Getting married in the country is easily arranged. If the visitor is staying in a resort hotel, the easiest way is to have the hotel make the arrangements. Couples will need to provide passports, birth certificates, and single-status affidavits, which must be translated into Spanish and certified by a Dominican Republic Consulate.

Marriage applications are made through the local *oficialia del estado civil* (city clerk).

DIRECTORY

GETTING THERE

American Airlines
Tel 800 433 7300.
www.aa.com

Delta
Tel 800 221 1212.
www.delta.com

JetBlue
Tel 800 538 2583.
www.jetblue.com

Spirit Airlines
Tel 800 772 7117.
www.spiritair.com

United Airlines
www.united.com

US Airways
Tel 800 428 4322.
www.usairways.com

DOCUMENTATION

Dirección General de Migración
Av. George Washington, cnr of Héroes de Luperón.
Tel 809 508 2555.

VISITOR INFORMATION

Ministry of Tourism
Tel 809 221 4660.
www.godominican republic.com

HEALTH AND SECURITY

Hospiten
Tel 809 541 3000 ext. 2500.
www.hospiten.com

Police, Fire, Ambulance
Tel 911.

BANKING AND CURRENCY

BanReservas
Tel 809 472 5000.
www.banreservas.com

COMMUNICATIONS

Claro Codetel
Tel 809 220 1111.
www.codetel.net.do

Orange
Tel 809 859 6555.
www.orange.com.do

Tricom
Tel 809 476 6000.
www.tricom.net

SHOPPING

Harrison's Fine Caribbean Jewelers
Tel 809 586 3933.
www.harrisons.com

A PORTRAIT OF PUERTO RICO

The smallest and easternmost of the Greater Antilles, Puerto Rico is as much American as Latin in flavor and mood. By far the wealthiest of the Caribbean nations, thanks to its status as a US Commonwealth, this bullet-shaped island abounds in physical beauty, offers world-class activities, and has the finest hotels and resorts.

Called Borinquén (Land of the Brave Lord) by the native Taínos, Puerto Rico lies between Hispaniola, to the west and the Virgin Islands, to the east. It is exceedingly mountainous inland of the coastal plain and dense forests cover a rugged backbone sweeping down to the Atlantic and Caribbean shores, edged with pristine blues and greens. The sea is lined with coral reefs and beaded with beach-fringed cays, plus Vieques and Culebra – the Spanish Virgin Islands – floating off the northeast shore of the mainland. Home to two-thirds of Puertorriqueños, San Juan is the political and cultural capital. It is a contemporary city with a well-preserved colonial core.

Girafo sculpture, San Juan

HISTORY

The Taínos had evolved a modestly advanced culture when Christopher Columbus arrived here on November 19, 1493. As elsewhere in the Caribbean, the indigenous people were rapidly decimated by the Spaniards. The first settlement was founded in 1508 by the conquistador Juan Ponce de León, the island's first governor, who christened the isle Puerto Rico (Rich Port). In 1521, San Juan was founded and became the capital, with a flask-shaped harbor well protected by forts. However, under the Earl of Cumberland, the English invaded and seized San Juan. In 1598, an epidemic swiftly forced

Cobbled street lined with restored buildings, Old San Juan

People in colorful costumes at the Three Kings festival celebrations, Ponce

ECONOMY

Puerto Rico is the Caribbean's most industrialized island, and its citizens are by far the region's wealthiest. Today, less than 3 percent work in agriculture. The pharmaceutical industry is well developed as is the tourism industry. More than 5 million visitors arrive here annually and the opening of the Caribbean's largest convention center in 2007 has further boosted the island's stature.

LIFESTYLE AND CULTURE

Puerto Rico's 3.9 million Spanish-speaking people are proud of their rich cultural heritage – a mixture of Hispanic, African, and Taíno. Following more than a century of US domination, the lifestyle and culture today lie on the cusp between cultures: part Hispanic and part American. The march of modernity has been so thorough, however, that the *jíbaro* (country peasant) now belongs to the distant past, and folkloric music has faded in favor of merengue and salsa.

the occupation army to flee. The Spanish finally reoccupied the island after a brief invasion by the Dutch in 1625. The 18th century witnessed a coffee boom, and many of the island's towns date from this period. Although Spain granted autonomy to Puerto Rico in 1897, the island was captured by US troops during the Spanish-American War in 1898 and it became a US Protectorate.

GOVERNMENT AND POLITICS

The Commonwealth of Puerto Rico is a self-governing US territory – a controversial status dating back to 1898. Ever since, the islanders have been torn between a minority who long for independence, some who hope to become a US state, and a majority happy with the current status as a "Free Associated State," granted in 1952. Puerto Ricans were given US citizenship in 1917, prompting mass migration to the US mainland. Currently, more people of Puerto Rican ancestry live in the US than on the island itself. However, the island is not represented in the US Congress, and Puerto Ricans may not vote during the US presidential election.

Lush foliage, including bromeliads flourishing in the rainforests of Puerto Rico

Exploring Puerto Rico

Oblong-shaped Puerto Rico is a mountainous, beach-fringed depiction of virtually everything the Caribbean offers. Old San Juan's colonial treasures gleam after restoration, while the modern capital city hops to a hip *vida loca* beat. The rugged interior is at its best along the mountain-crest Ruta Panorámica, linking historic towns. Beaches range from cottony whites to black and are most glorious on Vieques and Culebra. Rincón offers excellent surfing while Playa Dorado has top-end golfing.

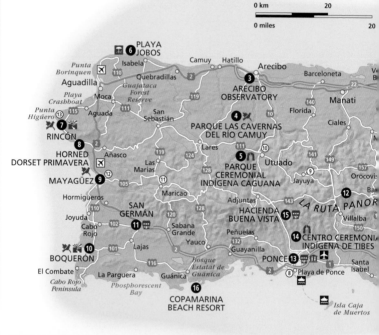

Souvenirs on display near Parque Ceremonial Indígena Caguana

GETTING AROUND

The easiest way of discovering the island is to hire a rental car or to stitch together a series of island excursions. These can be taxi tours, day trips offered by tour companies, plus hiking and caving outings, and even sailing trips. Domestic flights connect San Juan to Vieques and Culebra – the Spanish Virgins – but the most pleasant way to visit these outlying islands is by ferry from Fajardo, which takes about an hour. Crowded minivans provide public transportation between towns. Driving in Puerto Rico has its own challenges and traffic jams are ubiquitous in urban centers.

View from Mirador on Route 143, La Ruta Panorámica

Vieques
One of the Spanish Virgin Islands, Vieques's chief appeals are its boutique hotels, gorgeous white-sand beaches, and its phosphorescent bay.

El Yunque National Forest
The Caribbean National Forest protects the only tropical rainforest in the US National Park System.

San Juan ❶

Cockerel, Museo de San Juan

Founded in 1521, San Juan was laid out in a grid on a headland protecting a large, flask-shaped bay. Known as San Juan Viejo ("old"), this historic core has been restored, with beautiful 17th- and 18th-century buildings painted in tropical fruit pastels lining the narrow, cobblestoned streets. Some of the houses have been converted into charming boutique hotels. Two castles guard the colonial city, a port-of-call for cruise ships which dock alongside the ancient harbor. Inland, modern San Juan has an altogether different feel *(see p201)*.

Interior courtyard of Museo de San Juan

Plaza del Quinto Centenario

Calle Norzagaray and Calle del Cristo. ♿ **Museo de las Américas** Calle del Morro. ***Tel*** *787 724 5052.* ◯ *10am–4pm Tue–Wed & Sat–Sun, 9am–4pm Thu–Fri.* **Casa Blanca** Calle San Sebastián 1. ***Tel*** *787 725 1454.* ◯ *9am–noon & 1–4pm Wed–Sun.* 🎟 **www**.icp.gobierno.pr

This triple-tiered plaza, laid out in 1992 for the 500th anniversary of Columbus's arrival, is pinned by Totem Telúrico, a granite totem representing the island's peoples. The plaza is surrounded by the Ballajá barracks, now housing **Museo de las Américas**, with exhibits on New World culture, and the 16th-century Convento de los Dominicos. Nearby is Parque de Beneficencia, a peaceful setting for the Neo-Classical Instituto de la Cultural Puertorriqueña, displaying historical artifacts from art to religious icons. Built in 1521, **Casa Blanca** now serves as a museum depicting early colonial life.

Plaza de San José

Calle del Cristo and Calle San Sebastián. ♿ **Museo de Pablo Casals** Calle San Sebastián 101. ***Tel*** *787 723 9185.* ◯ *9:30am–4:30pm Tue–Sat.* 🎟 ♿

The most intimate of San Juan's colonial plazas has at its heart a bronze statue of the conquistador Ponce de León (1474–1521), the island's first governor. Along Calle San Sebastián, quaint colonial mansions come alive at night as lively bars and trendy restaurants. Step inside Iglesia San José to view the magnificent muraled ceiling, then browse through **Museo de Pablo Casals**, celebrating the life of Spanish-born cellist Pablo Casals (1876–1973), who lived his last two decades in San Juan. Also worth stopping by is the **Museo de San Juan** on Norzagaray which has an excellent art collection and displays on local history.

Displays in Museo de San Juan

El Convento

Calle del Cristo 100. ***Tel*** *787 723 9020.* $$$$$ *58 rooms.* 🍴 ▤ ♿ [W] **www**.elconvento.com

This charming boutique hotel *(see p214)* was once a convent, built in 1651. It has gracious period furnishings, an excellent restaurant and a tapas bar. The upstairs terrace looks over the cathedral.

Calle del Cristo

Between Calle Norzagaray and Calle Tetuán. ♿

Sloping downhill from Plaza de San José, the Calle del Cristo is paved with blue-tiled cobblestones and to each side, charming two-story townhouses graced by wooden balustrades double as art galleries, boutiques, and cafés. A good time to explore is on a Tuesday night, during Noche de Galerías, when the galleries remain open late. The Neo-Classical Catedral de San Juan Bautista was completed in 1852 atop the site of the city's first cathedral. Admire the *trompe-l'oeil* ceiling and the marble mausoleum containing the remains of Ponce de León. The street ends at the tiny Capilla del Cristo (Christ Chapel), adjoining the Parque de las Palomas named after the pigeons that flock here.

Stained glass at Catedral de San Juan Bautista

Plaza de Armas

Calle San José and Calle San Francisco. ♿

San Juan Viejo's central plaza originated as a 16th-century parade ground and later became the administrative center. Open and airy, it has lost much of its early charm to fast-food outlets. Still, the Alcaldía (City Hall), dating from 1789, impresses, as do the Neo-Classical Diputación (Provincial Delegation) and Intendencia, now the State Department offices.

For hotels and restaurants on this island see pp214–16 and pp217–19

Headquarters of Puerto Rico Tourism Company

🏛 Paseo de la Princesa

Between Calle La Marina and El Morro headland. [i] *Puerto Rico Tourism Company, 787 721 2400.* ♿ 🚌 *Sat & Sun.*

This waterfront promenade begins at the dock-front and leads west, tracing the course of the towering city walls and ending beneath Fortaleza San Felipe del Morro, at the tip of the headland. The 1.5-mile (2.4-km) long walkway of the Princess esplanade is lined with wrought-iron street lamps. Tree-shaded Plaza del Inmigrante hosts several fascinating buildings and soaring over the north side, the Art Deco Banco Popular. Walking west, visitors will pass the former La Princesa prison, now the **Puerto Rico Tourism Company**'s headquarters.

🏛 Plazuela de la Rogativa

Caleta de las Monjas and Calle Recinto del Oeste. ♿

The tiny Plaza of the Divine Intervention features a monument celebrating the delivery of San Juan from a British siege in 1797. The Modernist bronze statue shows a bishop leading a torch-lit procession that fooled the invaders into believing that the civilian torch-bearers were a large garrison of Spanish troops.

To the south, the plaza offers fine views of La Fortaleza, the governor's mansion built in 1533, as well as the Puerta de San Juan, at the end of Paseo de la Princesa, which was the main entrance to the walled city in colonial days and still bears its heavy wooden gates.

VISITORS' CHECKLIST

N coast of Puerto Rico. 👥 *435,000.* ✈ ✈ ⛴ *San Juan-Cataño.* [i] *La Casita, Calle Tanca, 787 721 2400.* 🎉 *Casals Fest (Feb–Mar); Heineken Jazzfest (May).* **www**.gotopuertorico.com

⛫ Fortaleza San Felipe del Morro

Calle del Morro. ***Tel*** *787 729 6960.* 🕘 *9am–6pm daily.* 💳 📷 ♿ 🍴 🛍 **www**.nps.gov/saju

Initiated in 1539 to guard the harbor entrance, the headland fortress was completed in 1786. A lighthouse offers fine perspectives of the castle and the green swathe toward the Campo del Morro.

The Main Battery looking south, Fortaleza San Felipe del Morro

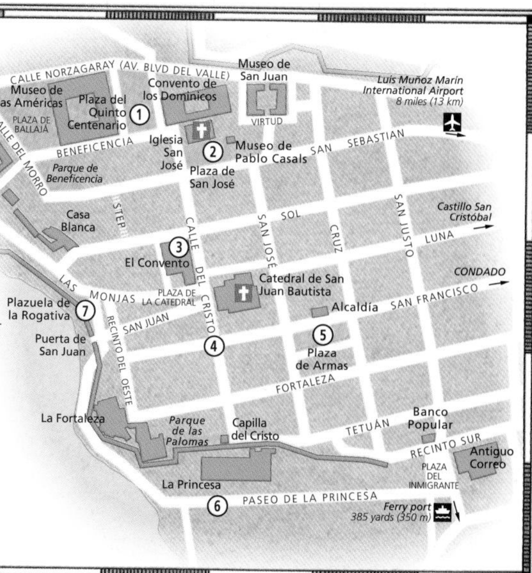

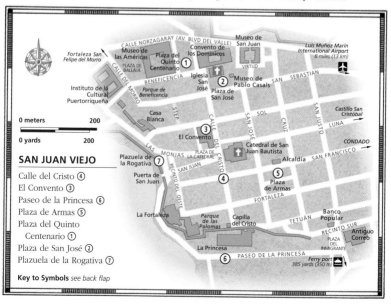

SAN JUAN VIEJO

Calle del Cristo [4]
El Convento [3]
Paseo de la Princesa [6]
Plaza de Armas [5]
Plaza del Quinto Centenario [1]
Plaza de San José [2]
Plazuela de la Rogativa [7]

Key to Symbols *see back flap*

Castillo San Cristóbal

Commanding the Atlantic clifftop at San Juan Viejo's eastern entrance, Castillo San Cristóbal was initiated in 1634 and completed in 1783. It was designed by military engineers Tornis O'Daly and Juan Mestre to prevent a land assault. It last saw action in 1898 during an artillery exchange with US warships but the US military occupied the fortress until 1961. Now a UNESCO World Heritage Site, it is administered by the US National Parks Service.

VISITORS' CHECKLIST

Calle Norzagaray.
Tel 787 729 6960.
San Juan National Historic Site, 787 729 6777.
9am–6pm daily.
10am & 2pm (in English).

Devil's Sentry Box
A lonely lookout post, this is the oldest surviving element of San Cristóbal. Sentries regularly shouted "Alerta!" to keep themselves awake during the long night watch.

Ordóñez Cannon
This is the north-facing battery which fired the first shots of the Spanish-American War in Puerto Rico on May 12, 1898.

The Great Moat, a wide-open space, was designed to trap enemy troops in a cross-fire.

Tunnels were used to move soldiers and supplies during battle. Portions could be destroyed by gunpowder to block an enemy's advance.

Plaza de Armas, the main parade ground, overlays massive cisterns.

The Chapel has an image of St. Barbara, patron saint of artillery men to whom gunners prayed before battle.

The imposing walls of Castillo San Cristóbal

Barracks
The barracks have eight vaulted rooms on two levels, with the one on Plaza de Armas furnished as it was 200 years ago.

For hotels and restaurants on this island see pp214–16 and pp217–19

Modern San Juan

The modern metropolis evolved around San Juan Viejo, the original colonial city. The area comprising Condado, Ocean Park, and Isla Verde is an upscale residential district teeming with Art Deco and Modernist structures. Southward, separated by the Marin Peña channel, lies the commercial zones of Santurce and Hato Rey, with the university and many of the city's cultural venues. Beyond, traffic-jammed thoroughfares fan out to the sprawling residential suburbs and industrial zones of Carolina, Trujillo Alto, Guaynabo, Cataño, and Bayamón, setting for the Bacardí rum company headquarters.

Works by local artists, Museo de Arte de Puerto Rico

Condado

Puerto Rico's first resort built in 1950s, Condado became popular with the tourists only after the 1980s. Lined with towering high-rise condominiums and hotels, this upscale district occupies a slender isthmus wedged between the Atlantic Ocean and Laguna Condado.

The main thoroughfare, Avenida Ashford, is a favored shopping district among the locals and visitors. Only 2 miles (3 km) from Avenida Ashford, Condado Beach, a talcum-white beach lining the seashore, draws sun-seeking locals on weekends. The place is also well-known for its great nightlife with plenty of bars and restaurants that come to life after sunset.

Connecting Condado eastward is the trendy residential neighborhood of Ocean Park, favored by beach-going youth and a great place to enjoy parasailing and other watersports. The good beaches extend east to Isla Verde, the setting of some of the city's finest hotels (*see pp214–16*).

Santurce

Museo de Arte de Puerto Rico

Av. De Diego 229. **Tel** 787 977 6277. ◯ 10am–5pm Tue & Thu–Sat, 10am–8pm Wed, 11am–6pm Sun. 🔲 📷 👤 🏢 💻 🚻 www. mapr.org **Fundación Luis Muñoz Marín** Carretera 877 Km0.4. **Tel** 787 755 4506. ◯ 10am–2pm Mon–Fri, 10:30am–1pm Sat–Sun. www.flmm.org

The heart of metropolitan San Juan lies inland of Condado, centered around Ponce de León. This formerly posh region had declined in recent decades, but has seen a rebound with the opening of Centro de Bellas Artes, the city's main performing arts venue; and **Museo de Arte de Puerto Rico**, boasting a superb collection by Puerto Rican artists spanning three centuries. The Plaza del Mercado de Santurce, a traditional market, is housed in a Renaissance-style structure erected in 1909. Santurce merges west into Miramar, the most desirable residential address in the city. The nation's premier university, Universidad de Puerto Rico, is located in Hato Rey district, southwest to Santurce, and hosts Museo História Antropología y Arte, displaying Puerto Rico's foremost collection of pre-Columbian exhibits. Nearby, **Fundación Luis Muñoz Marin** honors the legendary politician considered "father" of modern Puerto Rico.

🏭 Bacardi Rum Distillery

Carretera 888 Km2.6, Cataño. **Tel** 787 788 1500. ◯ 8:30am–5:30pm Mon–Sat, 10am–5pm Sun. 📷 compulsory. ♿ www.casabacardi.org

Luis A Ferré Science Park Carretera 167, Plaza del Sol Bayamón. **Tel** 787 740 6868. ◯ 9am–4pm Wed–Fri, 10am–6pm Sat–Sun. 🅿 ♿ 💻

Spanning 127 acres (51 ha) of landscaped grounds, the world's largest rum distillery, Bacardi, produces more than 100,000 gallons (378,540 liters) daily. Visitors are given a tour that traces the history of the company and of rum manufacture. Guests are offered a free tasting in the bar and can visit the nearby **Luis A Ferré Science Park**, which has an excellent zoo. The park is also home to a planetarium and an aerospace museum.

The world-famous Bacardí Rum Distillery

View of Arecibo Observatory, the world's largest radio telescope

Dorado ❷

15 miles (24 km) W of San Juan.
🏃 35,000. 🚍

Named for the golden sands stretching along the palm-shaded Atlantic shore, Dorado provides a gateway to the beaches for San Juan families and deluxe hotels command the best beachside turf. It became a fashionable sunspot in the 1950s, with the Dorado Beach Hotel attracting celebrities such as the Kennedys. The best public beaches include Cerro Gordo and Playa Sardinera. The town has a main square, Plaza de Recreo, and local history exhibits can be seen at **Museo La Casa del Rey**, built as a parador in 1823 and later a Spanish garrison.

Environs
West of Dorado, **Guajataca Forest Reserve** protects a vast tropical forest. Nearby is the Lago Guajataca which has picnic and fishing facilities.

🏛 **Museo La Casa del Rey**
Calle Méndez Vigo 292. **Tel** 787 796 1030. ◯ 8am–4:30pm Mon–Fri. 🈺

Arecibo Observatory ❸

55 miles (88 km) W of San Juan.
Tel 787 878 2612. 🚍 ◯ Noon–4pm Wed–Fri, 9am–4pm Sat–Sun.
🈺 www.naic.edu

The world's largest single-dish radio telescope is a bowl suspended between towering *mogotes* in the Gaurionex

Mountains. It opened in 1963 under the Department of Defense to study the upper atmosphere and outer space using radio frequency transmission. Officially known as the National Astronomy and Ionosphere Center, and operated by Cornell University and National Science Foundation, it is the headquarters of the Search for Extraterrestrial Intelligence. The observatory's Angel Ramos Foundation Visitor Center has good research facilities.

Parque Las Cavernas del Río Camuy ❹

57 miles (92 km) SW of San Juan.
Tel 787 898 3100. 🚍 ◯ 8am–4pm Wed–Sun. 🈺 🅿 🛉 🅰 for a fee.
www.parquesnacionalespr.com

Puerto Rico's largest cave system is also the world's third largest, with more than 220 caverns, of which only 16

can be visited on guided tours. These begin with a steep downhill trolley ride to the Cueva Clara de Enpalma, followed by an hour-long walk on concrete pathways that snake through the cool cavern, which soars 170-ft (52-m) high. Key dripstone formations are spot-lit. Bats flit about overhead and a blind endemic fish species swims in the black underground river. This is followed by a ride in the tram to Tres Pueblos Sinkhole, plunging 400 ft (122 m). In its depths, an underground river can be seen emerging from a cavern and entering another.

Parque Ceremonial Indígena Caguana ❺

65 miles (105 km) W of San Juan.
Tel 787 894 7325. 🚍 ◯ 9am–4:30pm daily. 🈺 🛉 **Note:** *trails can be muddy during the rains.*

Surrounded by lush montane forests, Parque Ceremonial Indígena Caguana provides an excellent overview of ancient Taíno culture. The archaeological site – excavated in 1915 – was once used for ceremonial and recreational purposes. It features 10 ceremonial *bateyes* (ball courts) surrounded by monolithic granite slabs that are etched with petroglyphs of human figures, most notably the Mujer de Caguana, a fertility figure showing a woman in childbirth. A small museum displays ancient artifacts, and a gift shop sells *zemis* (worshipped figures).

Stalactites in the spectacular caves of Cavernas del Río Camuy

For hotels and restaurants on this island pp214–16 and pp217–19

Playa Jobos ⑥

🚌 82 miles (132 km) W of San
Juan. 🍴 🏖 ⚓

Surfers ride the Atlantic
breakers that wash ashore at
this long beach which shines
like silver lamé. The sands
here have been pushed into
dunes by the winds. Beach
bars, restaurants, and hotels
line twin beaches separated
by a craggy headland of ironshore (limestone-coral formation). El Pozo de Jacinto is a
small blowhole that attracts
many visitors.

Environs
Punta Borinquen, southwest
of Playa Jobos, has some
spectacular beaches, including
Playa Crash Boat, which
offers great diving
just offshore, and is
popular with surfers.
The point served as
a former US air force
base. Visitors can
enjoy a round on the
old Base Ramey golf
course. Columbus
first set foot on the
island near the town
of Aguadilla, where
the Caribbean's
largest aquatic theme
park, **Parque Acuático
Las Cascadas**, is located.

**Ocean Front
Restaurant,
Playa Jobos**

Parque Acuático Las Cascadas
Carretera 126 Km2, Aguadilla.
Tel 787 819 0950. ⭘ Mar–Sep,
May–Jul 10am–5pm. 🎟 🅿 www.
parqueacuaticolascascadas.com

Rincón ⑦

Carretera 115, 88 miles (140 km)
W of San Juan. 🏙 17,000.
✈ Aquadilla Airport, 5 miles (8 km).
🚌 🎉 Whale Festival (Mar.)

Considered the premier surfing
spot in Puerto Rico, this beach
resort midway down the west
side of the island combines
rugged beauty, a laid-back
social scene, and a lively
nightlife. A network of roads
link several beaches and
rustic communities, including
Rincón, spread across the
pointy Punta Higuero peninsula. Tide-pooling here is fun,
while snorkeling is great in

Breakfast on the beach at the Horned Dorset Primavera

the protection of the scattered
reefs, and open waters offer
superb diving. Winds whip
up waves that can reach as
high as 40 ft (12 m), drawing
surfing aficionados in search
of the ultimate ride.
Sunsets are a blaze
of sensational color
and humpback
whales are often
sighted from shore as
they migrate through
the Mona Passage
during winter.

Environs
Rincón faces the
Mona Passage, stud-
ded by **Isla Mona**, a
rocky, uninhabited
outcrop populated by bird species, iguanas, and marine turtles. This wildlife refuge
requires a permit from
Departamento de Recursos
Naturales (see p212) to visit.
Moca, inland of Rincón, produces *mundillo* (lace) and
hosts the Mundillo Festival
each June.

Horned Dorset Primavera ⑧

🏨 Carretera 429 Km3, Rincon.
Tel 787 823 4030. Ⓢ Ⓢ Ⓢ Ⓢ
52 rooms. 🍴 open to public 7–
9:30pm. 📋 🏖 🅦 www.horned
dorset.com

Named after a breed of English
sheep, the Horned Dorset
Primavera is a Spanish
hacienda-style hotel which
sits right atop its own tiny
beach, where kayaks are
available for free use. A splendid experience awaits the
visitors who choose to stay
here. The restaurant (see p218)
is acclaimed for its gourmet
cuisine and draws diners
from as far afield as San Juan.
There is also a good bar.
The hotel's spacious suites
are decorated in a regal
fashion with gorgeous
plantation antiques. A dress
code is applicable in the
evenings. Horned Dorset
Primavera does not allow
children below 12.

KARST COUNTRY
Karst topography is
remarkable for its dramatic
limestone landscapes studded
with sinkholes, caverns,
canyons, and isolated cone-
shaped hillocks known as
mogotes. The features are remnants of a limestone plateau
that rose from the sea about
160 million years ago, after
which underground rivers
and rain gradually dissolved
the limestone, to form caverns
that finally collapsed, leaving
freestanding hummocks.

**Impressive topography, northern
Puerto Rico's karst region**

Mayagüez ❾

100 miles (150 km) SW of San Juan. 🏙 105,000. ✈ 🚢 Carnival (May); Festival de la Cocolia (Jul).

Puerto Rico's third largest city, Mayagüez, was founded in 1760. But it shows little sign of its early past following a series of devastating fires. Nonetheless, its spacious main square – Plaza Colón –

View of the Plaza Colón and the façade of the Town Hall, Mayagüez

is adorned with fine buildings, most notably the Neo-Classical Town Hall and behind it, the Teatro Yagüez. Also notable are the square's 16 bronze statues, and that of Christopher Columbus. Locals gather here to play dominoes beneath jacaranda trees.

Children love to visit the nation's main zoo, **Parque Zoológico Dr. Juan A. Rivero**, which has an excellent collection of animals from around the world, including gorillas, elephants, lions, and Bengal tigers.

Mayagüez is home to an important tuna-processing industry, and is also a departure point for sportfishing.

> 🐾 **Parque Zoológico Dr. Juan A. Rivero**
> Carretera 108, Barrio Miradero.
> **Tel** 787 834 8110. ⏲ 8:30am–5pm Wed–Sun. 🅿 ♿ 🏪 📷
> www.parquesnacionalespr.com

A clapboard house, Boquerón

Boquerón ❿

15 miles (24 km) S of Mayagüez.

Locals flock to this slightly rough-around-the edges beach town, with a lovely beach hidden behind old clapboard houses and a string of restaurants and bars. A special treat is to buy freshly caught oysters from street stands. Bosque Estatal de Boquerón protects a dry tropical and mangrove forest and offers tremendous birding, as does nearby **Refugio de Aves de Boquerón**,

La Ruta Panorámica ⓬

The panoramic route, officially known as La Ruta Panorámica, runs along the island's mountainous backbone from Yabucoa to Mayagüez. About 40 separate highways make up the clearly-marked, well-paved route. It passes Cerro de Punta, the island's highest peak, as well as a variety of dense montane forests. The route is best traversed with at least an overnight stay at a parador.

PUERTO RICO

Caribbean Sea

LOCATOR MAP

☐ Area illustrated

Cerro de Punta ⑧
A thread-thin spur road switchbacks to the summit of Puerto Rico's highest peak, at 4,390 ft (1,338 m).

0 km   15

0 miles   15

Jayuya ⑦
In the center of Puerto Rico lies this town with its Museo El Cemí, a fine museum of indigenous culture. It is designed like a giant *cemí*, an earthly representation of Taíno divinities.

Maricao ⑨
This town is a center of coffee production. From here, the road descends to Mayagüez.

which has blinds for close-up viewing of various waterfowl and manatees.

Environs
South of town lies the **Cabo Rojo Peninsula**, where a semi-derelict lighthouse pins a dramatic headland named for its red-hued rocks. Nearby, simple accommodations at **Playa El Combate** cater to island families who gather to sun, flirt, and party on this narrow beach. An hour's drive east of Boquerón, the south coast community of **La Parguera** is one of Puerto Rico's liveliest coastal resorts. The mangrove-fringed bay is despoiled by buzzing Jet Skis and excessive construction, including wharfs touting boat trips to Isla Magueyes and **Phosphorescent Bay**.

Refugio de Aves de Boquerón
Carretera 301 Km 5.1. ***Tel*** *787 851 4795.* 🕐 *7:30am–4pm daily.* 🎟 ♿

San Germán ⑪

30 miles (48 km) SE of Mayagüez.
👥 *38,000.* 🎉 *Fiesta Patronal (Jul 31).*

This quaint hillside town was founded in 1573 and is home to the most intact colonial core outside San Juan Viejo. Colorful reminders of the wealth generated by the 19th-century coffee boom adorn its leafy plazas: 249 buildings are listed on the National Register of Historic Places. The Iglesia Porta Coeli, dating from 1606, exhibits religious statuary and *santos* in the Museo de Arte Religioso. The church stands over Plaza Santo Domingo, which is noteworthy for the 19th-century gingerbread Casa Morales. A short walk west leads to the Plaza Francisco Mariano Quiñones, graced by the Neo-Classical Iglesia de San Germán de Auxerre, which was rebuilt in 1737 after an earthquake.

Historic buildings in the center of San Germán

Carite Forest Reserve ①
Sierra palms and bamboo are among the lush flora lining the road here.

Aibonito ②
The island's highest town enjoys a scenic mountain setting and spring-like climate year-round.

TIPS FOR DRIVERS

Starting point: *Yabucoa.*
Length: *166 miles (266 km).*
Stop-off points: *Roadside* lechonerías *at Guavate, for roast pork on the spit. For lodging: Hacienda Gripinas and Parador Hacienda Juanita (see p214).*

Barranquitas ③
The town has a pretty church and former homes of father-son politicians Luis Muñoz Rivera and Luis Muñoz Marin (exterior detail of their house above).

Hacienda Gripinas ⑥
This historic parador is a perfect place to rest your head *(see p214).*

Orocovis ④
This town is known for producing *santos* figurines.

Toro Negro Forest Reserve ⑤
Sodden with rains, this 11 sq mile (28 sq km) reserve has spectacular waterfalls.

KEY

✈ Airport

ℹ Visitor information

Driving route

Other road

Impressive façade of the Castillo Serallés, Ponce

Ponce ⑬

78 miles (125 km) S of San Juan. 🏛
187,000. ✈ 🚢 🚌 ℹ️ *Plaza las Delicias,
787 841 8044.* 🎭 *Carnival (Jan).*

Founded in 1692, Ponce still
remains an important port city
and abounds in cultural insti-
tutions reflecting its historical
preeminence as a center for
artists and political thinkers.
Architecturally distinct from
San Juan, its downtown area
reminds many visitors of New
Orleans, notably so during
its renowned Carnival, when
dancers parade through the
streets in extravagant *vejigante*
(horned) masks. The city
was a major slave-trading port
during the early colonial days
and African heritage is firmly
rooted in local culture.

The city witnessed a steady
decline in the 20th century.
Fortunately, the "Ponce en
marcha" restoration project
was initiated in the mid-
1980s, and most of the
city's notable historic buildings are once again gleaming. Tourist trolleys have made
exploring the colonial
center convenient.

At the heart of Ponce, the
spacious Plaza Las Delicias
goes by various other names
including Plaza Central. It
actually comprises two
squares – Plaza Luis Muñoz
Rivera and Plaza Federico
Degetau, to the north and
south, respectively, of the
Catedral Nuestra Señora de la
Guadalupe and the famous,
black-and-red striped **Parque**

de Bombas. This whimsical
fire station has an antique fire
truck and vintage cars on display. The twin squares have
several statues, and the Lion's
Fountain, bought at the 1939
World's Fair in New York,
which looks splendid when
floodlit at night. The buildings
around the square are a
medley of architectural styles
spanning three centuries and
ranging from Spanish colonial
to Neo-Classical and Art
Deco. The most commanding
building is the Neo-Classical
Teatro La Perla, which has
served as a performing arts
center since 1941. The surrounding streets, notably
Calle Cristina, are graced
by pretty homes fronted by
wrought-iron grills. Adjoining
the theater, the **Museo de la
Historia de Ponce** is the
nation's foremost history

museum. One block east,
Casa Serallés is an exemplar
of Art Nouveau styling. Today
it houses the **Museo de la
Música Puertorriqueña**, which
traces the evolution of music
on the island.

Towards the north, the
city is flanked by Loma Vigía
(Watchman's Hill), which is
dominated by La Cruceta de
Vigía, a huge cement cross
consisting of a hollow tower
with a horizontal sky bridge.
At its base, **Castillo Serallés**, a
Spanish Revival mansion built
in 1926 for the rum magnate
Don Juan Serallés, is furnished
with a few splendid colonial
pieces and also serves as a
Museum of Sugar & Rum. The
gardens in its complex are
exquisite. The **Museo de Arte
de Ponce**, a Modernist structure designed by Edward
Durrell Stone, has works of
artists such as Gainsborough,
Diego Rivera, and Delacroix,
as well as some avant-garde
Puerto Rican artists.

Parque de Bombas
Plaza Las Delicias. **Tel** *787
284 3338.* ⏰ *9am–5:30pm
Wed–Mon.*

🏛 **Museo de la Historia de
Ponce**
Calle Isabel 53. **Tel** *787 844 7042.*
⏰ *9am–5pm Tue–Sun.* 🎫 ♿

🏛 **Museo de la Música
Puertorriqueña**
Calle Isabel 45. **Tel** *787 848 7016.*
⏰ *8:30am–4:30pm Wed–Sun.* ♿

Castillo Serallés
Cruzeta El Vigía 17. **Tel** *787 259
1774.* ⏰ *9:30am–5pm Tue–Thu,
9:30am–5:30pm Fri–Sun.* 🎫 🚻
Note: *free tram from Plaza Las
Delicias.*

🏛 **Museo de Arte de Ponce**
Av. Las Américas 2325. **Tel** *787 848
0505.* ⏰ *10am–5pm daily.*
🚫 *pub hols.* 🎫 🚻
www.museoarteponce.org

Centro Ceremonial
Indígena de
Tibes ⑭

2 miles (3 km) N of Ponce. **Tel** *787
840 2255.* ⏰ *9am–4pm Tue–Sun.*
🎫 📷 *obligatory.* ♿ 🚻

Discovered after Hurricane
Eloise in 1975, Centro
Ceremonial Indígena de Tibes

Vintage car displayed at Parque de
Bombas fire station, Ponce

For hotels and restaurants on this island see pp214–16 and pp217–19

is a pre-Columbian site which is still being excavated. Today, it covers 5 acres (2 ha), and includes nine *bateyes (see p202)* plus burial grounds, all hemmed by granite boulders etched with petroglyphs. The site is unusual as it displays signs of two cultures: the Igneris, who settled on the island around AD 300, and the Taíno, who overran the Igneris around AD 1000. A small museum displays remarkable exhibits including pottery, axe-heads, and *cemi (see p204)* excavated at this site, along with an adult skeleton curled up in a fetal position. A reconstruction of a traditional Taíno village helps educate visitors on the lifestyle of the indigenous people. Visits are by guided tour only and it is advisable to make reservations in advance.

Souvenir mask

Hacienda Buena Vista 15

7 miles (11 km) N of Ponce. ***Tel*** *787 722 5882.* ☐ *two-hour guided tours Fri–Sun at 8:30am, 10:30am, 1:30pm (English only) and 3:30pm; reservations required.*

Deep in the mountains north of Ponce, this beautiful plantation can be traced to 1833. Although a primary producer of coffee, it also grew rice and maize. Original mill machinery shows how the maize was milled and the still working water-turbine can be seen alongside other hacienda memorabilia, the elegant two-story great house, warehouses, and slave quarters. It is administered by the Conservation Trust of Puerto Rico, which has resurrected the farm as a working coffee estate. The place is also used for educational purposes.

The great house of the plantation Hacienda Buena Vista

Copamarina Beach Resort 16

20 miles (32 km) SW of Ponce. ***Tel*** *787 821 0505.* ***Fax*** *787 821 0070.* $$$$ *106 rooms.* 🍴 [W]
www.copamarina.com

This lovely low-rise hotel opens onto palm-shaded lawns fringing a coral-colored beach with Bali beds for shaded lounging. All guest rooms and suites have an ocean view. The resort has plenty of options for water-sports, such as parasailing and scuba diving, and other activities including tennis. A spa offers massages and beauty treatments, and day visitors can also use the airy restaurant *(see p217)* and bar.

Environs

North of Copamarina Beach Resort is a great base for hikes in **Bosque Estatal de Guánica**, a dry forest reserve studded with cactus. Visitors on a day trip from Guánica can also enjoy picnicking on **Gilligan's Island**, a small cay fringed with talcum sands and turquoise waters, while divers will thrill to the exceptional coral formations along **The Wall** *(see p211)*, which is the island's foremost dive site stretching for 20 miles (32 km) parallel to the south coast.

Sprawling gardens and sandy beach, Copamarina Beach Resort

Cyclist on the Paseo Piñones Recreational Trail

Playa Piñones ⑰

🚋 19 miles (30 km) E of San Juan.
🚶🧍 🍴 🎣

This golden beach located on Carretera 187 is favored by the locals on weekends, when families set up picnics beneath the palms. Weekend traffic jams the roads, so it is ideal to visit the beach on weekdays. Roadside restaurants sell fried seafoods. **Paseo Piñones Recreational Trail** runs along the shore, providing a scenic thoroughfare for cyclists, joggers, and strollers.

Environs

The beach extends east to **Playa Vacia Talega**, known for its "cemented" sand dunes. **Bosque Estatal Piñones**, inland of the beaches, protects a prize wetland habitat for waterfowl and wading birds. Occupying the coastal flatlands east of Playa Vacia Talega, the small, relatively impoverished town of **Loíza Aldea** is a center for African culture. Every year in late July it plays host to the week-long Fiesta de Santo Apóstol, Puerto Rico's premier carnival.

Luquillo ⑱

🚋 45 miles (72 km) E of San Juan.
🚶🧍 🍴 ⛵ 🎣 ⛴

A string of golden-white beaches decorates the northeast shore between the towns of Río Grande and Luquillo. The beauty is enhanced by the brooding Sierra Luquillo in the backdrop. The sands

meld into warm, reef-protected waters of peacock blues and greens. Snorkeling and tidepooling is great in these shallows. Playa Luquillo is lined by a number of upscale resorts. To the west, Playa Río Mar is a relatively uncrowded setting for the mammoth Río Mar Beach Resort & Spa *(see p215)* and Río Mar Country Club. East of Playa Luquillo are the windwhipped Playa Azul and Playa La Selva, where breakers bring surfers ashore.

El Yunque National Forest ⑲

25 miles (40 km) SE of San Juan. **Tel** 787 888 1880. ⏱ 7:30am–6pm daily. 🎟 for El Portal Visitor Center only. 🎫 hourly 9am–5pm Sat–Mon. ♿ El Portal Visitor Center & some trails. 🖥 www.fs.fed.us/r8/caribbean/

The 44 sq-mile (114 sq-km) El Yunque National Forest, formerly the Caribbean National Forest, is the only tropical rainforest within the US National Park system. Ranging from an elevation of 30 ft (9 m) at its base to 3,533 ft

(1,077 m) at the top of Cerro El Toro, the rain-sodden park – named for a flat-topped mountain, "the anvil" – features various ecosystems, including high mountain cloud forest and dwarf forest atop the highest slopes. El Portal Rain Forest Center, the main visitors' center, offers splendid exhibits on local geology, geography, and ecosystems. The park has a number of hiking trails *(see p213)* from easy to strenuous amidst plunging waterfalls and steep ravines. This region offers hikers some of the best birding and wildlife viewing on the island.

Fajardo ⑳

36 miles (58 km) SE of San Juan.
🧗 40,000. ✈ 🚢 🎊 Fiesta Patronal (Jul).

The sprawling coastal town of Fajardo is a major maritime center for sportfishing and sailing charters, available at Marina Puerto Real and Puerto del Rey Marina. Scheduled ferries also depart here for Vieques and Culebra.

Environs

Las Cabezas de San Juan Nature Reserve, immediately north of Fajardo, protects a 440-acre (178-ha) mangrove forest where manatees paddle

Hikers at one of the trails in El Yunque National Forest

Municipal building in Isabel Segunda, Vieques

about in freshwater lagoons and dozens of waterfowl can be seen on the boardwalk trail. The El Faro lighthouse, built in 1882, is beautifully preserved. Nearby **Playa Seven Seas** offers good snorkeling in reef-protected shallows.

Las Cabezas de San Juan Nature Reserve

Carretera 987. *Tel* 787 722 5882. 🎦 🎫 *included in entrance fee; 8:30am, 9:30am, 10am, 10:30am and 2pm Wed–Sun (in English).* **Note:** *reservation required.*

El Conquistador Resort ㉑

🛥 1000 Conquistador Av., Fajardo. *Tel* 787 863 1000. $ $ $ $ 910 rooms. 🚐 🍴 🍽 🐾 ♿ Ⓦ www.elconresort.com

Puerto Rico's largest resort enjoys a sensational hilltop position overlooking Vieques Sound. The mega-resort includes a championship golf course and a children's waterpark, plus a casino, a full-service spa, and more than 20 restaurants *(see p217)*, bars, and lounges. Nine types of rooms and villas offer cosmopolitan contemporary decor and the latest amenities.

The resort has an exclusive lease on Isla Palomìnos, a beautiful cay wrapped in a cottony beach, in the calm waters off Fajardo. Various watersports are on offer to guests who are transported from the resort by funicular to a marina from where there is a boat shuttle.

Vieques ㉒

20 miles (32 km) SE of Fajardo. 🚶 9,500. ✈ 🛥 🎭 *Festival de Cultura (Apr).*

Largest of the 24 isles of the Spanish Virgin archipelago surrounding Puerto Rico, Vieques moves at a far more lackadaisical pace than Puerto Rico. Most of the inhabitants live in Isabel Segunda, a little town that remains charmingly old world, with little traffic. During World War II the US Navy began using the isle for gunnery practice – a deterrent to development during the next five decades. The bombardment ceased in 2003, when the navy pulled out. Today, Vieques is a chic spot for tourists seeking off-the-beaten-track charm to see deer, manatee, and four species of marine turtles at Vieques Wildlife Refuge. The isle is fringed by the sugary sands of Playa Sombé, Playa Media Luna, Green Beach, and Blue Beach. Hotels are small-scale and trendy, and found mostly around Esperanza, a sleepy village overlooking a gorgeous bay. Nearby Phosphorescent Bay literally comes alive at night, when bioluminescent microorganisms glow when disturbed: a kayak trip lets visitors slip into the waters to spark their own halo. Manatees also frequent the coastal lagoons. Vieques is also a major nesting site for marine turtles. The **Vieques Art and History Museum**, in the 19th-century Fort Conde Mirasol, has exhibits on island history.

🏛 **Vieques Art and History Museum**
Fuerte Conde de Mirasol, Rt. 989, Isabel II. *Tel* 787 741 1717. ◯ 8:30am–4:30pm Wed–Sun. 🎫 🅿

Culebra ㉓

27 miles (43 km) E of Fajardo. 🚶 2,000. ✈ 🛥 🎭 *Fiesta Patronal (Jul).*

Vieques' even more somnolent smaller sister is renowned for its scintillating beaches, including undisputably Puerto Rico's finest, Playa Flamenco, a broad, long scimitar of pure white sand and gorgeous ocean waters drawing daytrippers from Puerto Rico on weekends. Nearby Playa Carlos Rosario has a coral reef within a short distance of the shore, while Playas Resaca, Brava, and Flamenco are protected as marine turtle nesting sites within Culebra National Wildlife Refuge.

Powdery white sands of Playa Flamenco on the island of Culebra

Outdoor Activities and Specialized Holidays

Hiking is a great way to discover Puerto Rico's amazing diversity of terrains and ecosystems, including tropical lowland dry forest, montane rainforest, and mangrove wetlands. There are plenty of opportunities for scuba diving and snorkeling, as well as for surfing and numerous other watersports including sportfishing, windsurfing, parasailing, and kayaking. Cavers are spoilt for choice, and golfers will find some of the Caribbean's best courses here on this island.

Watersport enthusiast on the Ocean Park Beach

BEACHES

Visitors don't have to leave San Juan to enjoy Puerto Rico's gorgeous beaches. Playa Condado, Ocean Park, and Isla Verde line the shore of those eponymous districts and offer parasailing and a youthful social scene. On weekends many *sanjuaneros* escape the madding crowd (but add to a traffic melee) and head east to Playa Piñones and Playa Luquillo.

Surfers prefer Playa Jobos and Playa Crashboat, near Aguadillas, in the northwest, although their most preferred destination is Rincón, with its dozen or so wave-washed beaches such as Playa Barrero and Sandy Beach.

The south coast has a relative paucity of nice beaches. Notable exceptions are Playa El Combate and Playa Caña Gorda. The lion's share of white-sand beaches lies off the east shore of mainland Puerto Rico. One such is Isla Palominos, just one hour from Fajardo. The most beautiful beaches are found in the Spanish Virgin Islands. Visitors are spoilt for choice

on Vieques where Playa Sombé, Playa Media Luna, Playa Navío, Green Beach, Red Beach, and Blue Beach are prize-winning beaches. Culebra claims Playa Flamenco, by far the most spectacular beach of all.

BIRDING AND WILDLIFE VIEWING

The varied ecosystems of Puerto Rico are habitats for a veritable ark of colorful creatures, including 270 species of birds. Seeing them is easy along trails that wind through various forests. El Yunque National Forest *(see p208)* is acclaimed for sighting the Puerto Rican parrot. Waders and waterfowl are easily seen

in Bosque Estatal de Boquerón and Las Cabezas de San Juan Nature Reserve, both with boardwalks and blinds, while the open deciduous woodlands of Bosque Estatal de Guánica make viewing the endemic species such as Puerto Rican whippoorwills, easy.

To view marine turtles laying eggs, head to Vieques Wildlife Refuge and Culebra National Wildlife Refuge. Manatees can also be seen here, and in Reserva Natural Laguna Tortuguero. In winter, head to Rincón for whale-watching trips in the Mona Passage. The El Faro Lighthouse Park has a whale-viewing vantage point, and **Taino Divers** offers excursions **Adven Tours** also organizes birding trips to various Puerto Rico areas.

CAVING

Puerto Rico is riddled with caves, although spelunking is for experienced cavers only and is best done with an organized group. The preeminent cave system is Parque Las Cavernas del Río Camuy. Rappelling and caving in the Angels Sinkhole is offered through **Aventuras Tierra Adentro**.

SURFING

Puerto Rico offers some of the finest surfing in the Caribbean, centered on Rincón, where **Rincón Surf School** offers classes and **El Rincón Surf Shop** rents and sells boards. Other prime surfing sites include Boca de Cangrejos, off San Juan; Playa Jobos and Playa Crashboat, in the northwest; and La Pared, at Luquillo.

DIVING

The island is a paradise for divers, with fabulous coral reefs ringing almost three-quarters of the isle. The water temperatures range from 70° F (20° C) in winter to mid-80° F (25° C) in the summer. In

Enjoy a whale-watching tour

Divers exploring the magnificent underwater world of sponges

winter it is best to head to the south shore, as north coast diving is subject to rough seas and full wet suits are a must. The almost 300 species of fish include major pelagics, such as grouper, sharks, and large rays, and marine turtles are also common. The Isla Desecho dive site, off Aguada, has a wreck of a World War II PT boat to explore. The Wall, which parallels the south coast for 20 miles (32 km), is easily accessed from Copamarina Beach Resort *(see p207)* and Guánica. The waters off Fajardo are placid and good for beginners, as are the fringing reefs off Vieques and Culebra, where wreck sites include a tugboat. **Sea Ventures Dive Centers** has three outlets, in Fajardo, Humacao, and Guánica. In the Spanish Virgin Islands, **Culebra Divers** take visitors to the best diving sites.

FISHING

Puerto Rico offers splendid deep-sea fishing out of San Juan, Mayagüez, and most resort towns, including Fajardo. The north shore is known as Blue Marlin Alley. Sailfish, tuna, and wahoo are other game fish that give a prize fight, while anglers can cast for tarpon and bonefish in inshore waters and flats. Many world records have been set here, and the numerous fishing tournaments are highlighted by the **San Juan International Billfish Tournament** in August/

September. Winter is the best season for gamefishing, although blue marlin are more numerous in summer. Recommended outfitters for fishing include **Puerto Rico Angling**, **Puerto Rico Fishing Charters**, and **Tight Loop Tarpon**. Mountain lakes are good for peacock bass and tilapia. Among the best inland freshwater sites is Lago Guajataca. Visitors need to contact the **Departamento de Recursos Naturales** for information and a license.

BOAT EXCURSIONS

Few activities induce a sense of romance as the experience of a sunset cruise under sail. Several companies offer day and evening excursions by yacht or by catamaran, with most craft setting sail from Fajardo to the archipelago of tiny cays known as La Cordillera. Most cruises feature stops for snorkeling. Key options include **Erin Go Bragh Charters**, which uses a 50-ft (15-m) cutter, the **Spread Eagle II** catamaran, and **Ventajero Sailing Charters**. **Katarina Sail Excursions** in Rincón offers sunset cruises.

HIKING

With more than a dozen forest reserves,

Puerto Rico is a nirvana for hikers. The diverse habitats provide plenty of contrasts, too, so that on one day visitors can hike the El Yunque *(see p213)* cloud forests while on the next they can follow the coastal trails of Bosque Estatal de Guánica. For more scenic drama, Bosque Estatal de Cambalache and Bosque Estatal de Guajataca have a number of trails that slide between towering *mogotes* *(see p203)*. There are many more mountain reserves to choose from here, while on the island of Vieques, the easy trails of Refugio de Vida Silvestre de Vieques combine spectacular ocean views with the possibility of plentiful animal and bird sightings.

For detailed information on hiking within the individual reserves, visitors have to contact the **Departamento de Recreación y Deportes**. For organized hikes, visitors can also try the company Aventuras Tierra Adentro.

A few precautions need to be taken by visitors before heading for any hike. It is essential to carry plenty of water since none will be available along the route. It is also advisable to use an insect repellent.

Hiking through the Big Tree Trail, El Yunque

Kayaking at the Copamarina Beach Resort, Rincón

WATERSPORTS

The beach resorts have all manner of watersports, from windsurfing and parasailing to Jet Skis. Waterskiing is offered where the waters are placid. Large hotels usually offer free use of non-motorized equipment, while commercial concessionaires offering motorized sports have outlets on the most popular beaches. A good option is kayaking, which is available at Rincón, Copamarina Beach Resort, and Playa Jobos, and at Vieques' Phosphorescent Bay, where **Island Adventures Biobay Eco-tours** will take visitors out at night to swim in the bioluminescent waters. **Kayaking Puerto Rico** arranges guided excursions.

GOLF

Few Caribbean islands can outdo Puerto Rico, which has some 20 championship courses designed by renowned architects. Top clubs include the Río Mar Beach Resort & Country Club (*see p215*) and El Conquistador Resort (*see p209*). At the northwest tip of the island, the **Punta Borinquen Golf Club** occupies the former US Air Force Ramey Base. Visitors can call **Puerto Rico Golf Association** for information about tournaments.

TENNIS

Most major resort hotels have their own courts. For those looking for some fun workout on the courts it is best to head to the Río Mar Beach Resort & Country Club, which has 14 courts, or the El Conquistador Resort, with seven courts. **Puerto Rico Tennis Association** provides information on local tennis clubs and facilities.

The well-kept tennis courts at El Conquistador Resort

DIRECTORY

BIRDING AND WILDLIFE VIEWING

Adven Tours
Main Office, 1102 Uroyan, Alturas de Mayagüez.
Tel 787 530 8311.
www.adventourspr.com

Taino Divers
Black Eagle Marina, Rincón. *Tel* 787 823 6429.
www.tainodivers.com

CAVING

Aventuras Tierra Adentro
Av. Jesús Piñero 7268A, San Juan.
Tel 787 766 0470.
www.aventuraspr.com

SURFING

El Rincón Surf Shop
PO Box 250171, Aguadilla. *Tel* 787 890 3108. www.elrincon surfshop.com

Rincón Surf School
PO Box 1333.
Tel 787 823 0610.
www.rinconsurfschool.com

DIVING

Culebra Divers
Tel 787 742 0803.
http://culebradivers.com

Sea Ventures Dive Centers
Tel 787 863 3483.
www.divepuertorico.com

FISHING

Departamento de Recursos Naturales
Tel 787 999 2200.
www.drna.gobierno.pr

Puerto Rico Angling
Tel 787 724 2079.
www.puertoricofishing.com

Puerto Rico Fishing Charters
Tel 787 382 4698.
www.puertoricofishing charters.com

San Juan International Billfish Tournament
Club Nautico de San Juan, 482 Fernández Juncos Av., San Juan. *Tel* 787 722 0177. www.sanjuan international.com

Tight Loop Tarpon
Tel 787 383 1562.
www.nomoworks.com/fishing

BOAT EXCURSIONS

Erin Go Bragh Charters
Tel 787 860 4401.
www.egbc.net

Katarina Sail Excursions
Tel 787 823 7245.
http://sailrinconpuertorico.com

Spread Eagle II
Villa Marina, Fajardo.
Tel 787 887 8821.
www.snorkelpr.com

Ventajero Sailing Charters
Marina Puerto del Rey, Ceiba.
Tel 787 863 1871.
www.sailpuertorico.com

HIKING

Departamento de Recreación y Deportes
Tel 787 721 2800.
www.drd.gobierno.pr

WATERSPORTS

Island Adventures Biobay Eco-tours
Road 996, Puerto Real Sector, Vieques.
Tel 787 741 0720.
www.biobay.com

Kayaking Puerto Rico
HC-4, Río Grande.
Tel 787 435 1665.
www.kayakingpuertorico.com

GOLF

Puerto Rico Golf Association
264 Matadero St., Suite 11, San Juan.
Tel 787 793 3444.
www.prga.org

Punta Borinquen Golf Club
Golf St., Ramey, Aguadilla.
Tel 787 890 2987. www.puntaborinquengolf.com

TENNIS

Puerto Rico Tennis Association
Tel 787 726 8782.
www.caribbean.usta.com

For hotels and restaurants on this island see pp214–16 and pp217–19

Hiking in Puerto Rico

Puerto Rico's numerous forest reserves and its mountainous terrain provide ample trekking and climbing opportunities. Most visitors who choose to hike in Puerto Rico make El Yunque National Forest *(see p208)* their prime focus. This reserve alone has 23 trails that weave through the varied habitats. The Toro Negro

Hibiscus flower

Forest Reserve, Maricao State Forest, and Bosque Estatal de Guánica are among other areas that have several marked trails for hikers. Most are short and unidirectional, but intersect with other trails to make for easy loops. Some trails are strenuous and slippery. Waterproof clothing and footwear are essential.

EL YUNQUE TRAILS

El Yunque National Forest is the most popular trekking spot in Puerto Rico with 36 miles (60 km) of trails. Among them are the El Yunque Trail, Baño de Oro Trail, Los Picachos Trail, El Toro (Tradewinds) Trail which leads through four different habitats, and the moderately difficult Big Tree Trail, which is one of the best maintained.

La Mina Trail *is a moderately difficult 1-hour downhill hike that follows Río Mina and ends at La Mina Falls.*

Mount Britton Trail *leads to a mountaintop observatory; passing through sierra palms of the rainforest and dwarf cloud forests.*

The Puerto Rican parrot *is among the 50 species of birds found in the national forest. Apart from birds, a number of lizards and crabs can also be spotted.*

TRAILS IN OTHER RESERVES

Puerto Rico has 14 forest reserves besides El Yunque. Some of the best ones for hiking are the arid Bosque Estatal de Guánica, the Toro Negro Forest Reserve, and the Bosque Estatal de Maricao.

Bosque Estatal de Maricao *is located near Maricao on La Ruta Panorámica (see pp204–5). Trails pass through beautiful cloud forests, plantations, and up large hills.*

Bosque Estatal de Guánica *is home to the endangered bufo lemur toad, birds, and 700 plant species. The dry forest has marked trails.*

Toro Negro Forest Reserve, *along La Ruta Panorámica, has five trails. One leads to an observation tower that provides great views. Lago El Guineo, Lago de Matrullas, and the headwaters of several main rivers are located in the park.*

Choosing a Hotel

The accommodations available in Puerto Rico include inns, guesthouses, large hotels and resorts, as well as *paradores* (family-oriented hotels owned by local entrepreneurs). The parador system was created on this island during the 1970s to promote tourism in rural areas. Large hotels are located mainly in San Juan, Ponce, and Vieques.

PRICE CATEGORIES
The following price ranges are for a standard double room per night and are inclusive of all taxes.

ⓢ under $100
ⓢⓢ $100–200
ⓢⓢⓢ $200–300
ⓢⓢⓢⓢ $300–400
ⓢⓢⓢⓢⓢ over $400

PUERTO RICO

El Convento – *p198*
This former nunnery has deluxe accommodations, a superb restaurant, and a splendid location in the heart of Old San Juan.

El Conquistador Resort – *p209*
A mammoth hotel with a sensational clifftop perch, children's water-park, a casino, and a championship golf course.

Horned Dorset Primavera – *p203*
This hacienda-style beachfront hotel with gracious antique furnishings and gourmet dining is an oasis of luxury.

Copamarina Beach Resort – *p207*
A low-rise resort on the edge of Bosque Estatal de Guánica, this hotel has all ocean-view rooms, watersports, and scuba diving.

El Convento

CAGUAS Four Points by Sheraton Caguas Real Hotel and Casino 🍴📄♿🅦   ⓢⓢⓢ
500 Alhambra en Granada Blvd. **Tel** *787 653 1111* **Fax** *787 653 1700* **Rooms** *126*

Opened in 2005, this glitzy hotel mid-way between San Juan and Ponce aims at a business clientele but is a quiet stop for all travelers. The hotel has elegant styling in the spacious guest rooms with full amenities, including high-speed Internet. It has Puerto Rico's largest casino. Dining options include a sushi bar. **www.starwoodhotels.com**

CEIBA Ceiba Country Inn 🍴🅦   ⓢ
Rt. 977 Km1.2 **Tel** *787 885 0471* **Fax** *787 885 0475* **Rooms** *9*

Surrounded by lush countryside, this mountainside bed-and-breakfast is a good option for birders. The inn has comfortable rooms that have tropical motifs with floral murals and splendid ocean views as far as Isla Culebra from the terrace. It is run by a US couple. The Caribbean National Forest is a short drive away. **www.ceibacountryinn.com**

CULEBRA Club Seabourne 🍴📄♻♿🅦   ⓢⓢⓢ
Fulladoza Bay **Tel** *787 742 3169* **Fax** *787 742 0210* **Rooms** *12*

Set in lush gardens, this end-of-the-road hillside property located in Fulladoza Bay is peaceful. The pastel rooms, cottages, or larger villas, have colonial-style reproduction furnishings. There is a library-lounge, a wooden sundeck, and a restaurant serving modest meals. Kayaks are provided free of charge. **www.clubseabourne.com**

DORADO Embassy Suites Dorado del Mar 🏊🍴📄♿🅦   ⓢⓢⓢ
201 Dorado del Mar Blvd. **Tel** *787 796 6125* **Fax** *787 796 6145* **Rooms** *251*

This massive, eight-story hotel is popular with families. Most rooms have ocean views and are furnished in a Caribbean tropical style. Some units are self-catering condos. The Chi Chi Rodriguez signature golf course is top-rated. It also has a lovely lagoon pool, spa, and tennis court. **http://embassysuites1.hilton.com**

HUMACAO Four Points by Sheraton Palmas del Mar Resort 🏊🍴📄♿🅦   ⓢⓢⓢⓢ
170 Candelero Dr. **Tel** *787 850 6000* **Fax** *787 850 6001* **Rooms** *107*

Located within the Palmas del Mar community is this elegant beachfront hotel with classical European styling. Gracious accommodations have elegant upscale furnishings, and high-speed Internet. It has 4 restaurants, a good wine selection, tennis courts, 2 golf courses, and children's facilities. **www.starwoodhotels.com**

JAYUYA Hacienda Gripiñas 🍴   ⓢⓢ
Rt. 527 Km2.5 **Tel** *787 828 1717* **Fax** *787 828 1719* **Rooms** *20*

Historic charm pervades this 19th-century coffee estate in the shadow of Puerto Rico's highest peak. The rooms are simply furnished and comfortable. The hotel's restaurant serves local dishes. It is a good base for going on hikes and horseback rides to Cerro Punta. **www.haciendagripinas.com**

MARICAO Parador Hacienda Juanita 🍴🅦   ⓢⓢ
Rt. 105 Km23.5 **Tel** *787 828 2550* **Fax** *787 828 2551* **Rooms** *21*

This historic wooden plantation-turned-parador still functions as a coffee estate. It has a scenic mountain setting. Accommodations are functional but cozy and include four-poster beds and ceiling fans. The rustic restaurant serves tasty meals and has live folk music. There is also a tennis court. **www.haciendajuanita.com**

MAYAGÜEZ Howard Johnson Downtown Mayagüez 🍴📄♿🅦   ⓢⓢⓢ
9 Calle Méndez Vigo **Tel** *787 832 9191* **Rooms** *39*

Despite its uninspired downtown location, this chain hotel occupies a landmark building next to the cathedral that was formerly a monastery. Most rooms are small, but many boast original stained glass windows. Family rooms are more spacious. There is a small outdoor swimming pool. **www.hojo.com**

Key to Symbols *see back cover flap*

PATILLAS Caribe Playa Sea Beach Resort ⬛ 🍴 📋 ♿ Ⓦ Ⓢ

Rt 3 Km112.1 **Tel** *787 839 6339* **Rooms** *32*

This 1960s-era low-rise resort has a lovely, palm-shaded shorefront setting. The resort has a small library and a comfortable TV lounge. Studio rooms vary – choose a "Mamey" room for a king-sized bed and air-conditioning. The cozy restaurant offers romantic candlelit dinners alfresco. **www.caribeplaya.com**

PONCE Hotel Bélgica 🍴 📋 ♿ Ⓦ Ⓢ

122 Calle Villa **Tel** *787 844 3255* **Fax** *787 844 3470* **Rooms** *20*

Located in the historic center of Ponce, Hotel Bélgica was built in 1872 in colonial European Neo-Classical style. The rooms are simple but elegant and all have cathedral ceilings while some also have Spanish balconies with a charming view of the historical part of the city. Only breakfast served here. **www.hotelbelgica.com**

PONCE Hilton Ponce Golf and Casino Resort ⬛ 🍴 📋 ♿ Ⓦ Ⓢ Ⓢ Ⓢ

1150 Av. Caribe **Tel** *787 259 7676* **Fax** *787 259 7674* **Rooms** *255*

A massive and slightly ungainly resort on a gray-sand beach, this hotel has adequate amenities. Guest rooms have ocean views and balconies. The rooms have lively tropical motifs and ceiling fans. Facilities include tennis courts, 4 restaurants *(see pp217–18)*, a casino, spa, bar, and a pool complex. **www.hiltoncaribbean.com**

PONCE Hotel Meliá 📋 ♿ Ⓦ Ⓢ Ⓢ Ⓢ

Plaza Degetau y Calle Cristina **Tel** *787 842 0260* **Fax** *787 841 3602* **Rooms** *73*

An excellent position near Parque Degetau facing Plaza las Delicias is a bonus at this family-run centenary Art Deco hotel. Rooms are clean and comfortable. Period details add charm to the wood-paneled lounge and there is a rooftop pool and terrace. **www.hotelmeliapr.com**

RINCÓN Lazy Parrot 🍴 📋 Ⓦ Ⓢ Ⓢ

Road 413, Km4.1 **Tel** *787 823 5654* **Fax** *787 823 0224* **Rooms** *20*

While not on the beach, this inland hillside hotel offers a good bargain for travelers not too fussy about the Lazy Parrot's lack of sophistication. Rooms are functional yet cozy and have balconies. There is also a small gift shop. The snack bar downstairs and the restaurant upstairs serve quality dishes alfresco. **www.lazyparrot.com**

RÍO BLANCO Casa Cubuy Ecolodge Ⓦ Ⓢ Ⓢ

Río Blanco **Tel** *787 874 6221* **Rooms** *10*

A simple mountain lodge on the south side of the Caribbean National Forest, this hotel appeals to hikers and birders. It has its own trails with waterfalls. Rooms are spacious but sparsely furnished and airy and have balconies. Breakfast is served, otherwise good meals are available down the hill. **www.casacubuy.com**

RÍO GRANDE Río Mar Beach Resort & Spa ⬛ 🍴 📋 🎾 ♿ Ⓢ Ⓢ Ⓢ Ⓢ

6000 Río Mar Blvd. **Tel** *787 888 6000* **Fax** *787 888 6235* **Rooms** *672*

Formerly a Westin Resort, this Wyndham group high-rise sprawls across a former coconut plantation and beach. Guest quarters are furnished in contemporary tropical island fashion and all have balconies. Excellent watersports, an Oriental-themed spa, 11 restaurants, a casino, and its own golf courses. **www.wyndhamriomar.com**

SAN JUAN At Wind Chimes Inn ⬛ 🍴 📋 ♿ Ⓦ Ⓢ Ⓢ

1750 McLeary Av., Condado **Tel** *787 727 4153* **Fax** *787 728 0671* **Rooms** *22*

Located about 3 miles (5 km) from the airport, At Wind Chimes Inn is one of the best guesthouses in Condado. A restored Spanish manor, it has beautiful rooms with high ceilings while bathrooms are shower-only. There is an outdoor pool for guests to relax in. **www.atwindchimesinn.com**

SAN JUAN Hotel Milano 🍴 📋 ♿ Ⓢ Ⓢ

307 Fortaleza Street **Tel** *787 729 9050* **Fax** *787 722 3379* **Rooms** *30*

Hotel Milano is a renovated 19th-century warehouse in the heart of Old San Juan close to the cruise dock. It features modern decor in clean and comfortable non-smoking rooms. It has a lovely waterfront view from the top-floor open-air restaurant. Friendly staff. **www.hotelmilanopr.com**

SAN JUAN Caribe Hilton ⬛ 🍴 📋 ♿ Ⓦ Ⓢ Ⓢ Ⓢ

Calle Los Rosales, Condado **Tel** *787 721 0303* **Fax** *787 725 8849* **Rooms** *646*

On its own private beach adjoining Fort San Gerónimo, this historic hotel has been in the Hilton chain since opening in 1949. From studio rooms to deluxe villas with kitchens, the rooms are decorated in a contemporary style, with state-of-the-art amenities. It has a restaurant *(see p218)* and spa. **www.hiltoncaribbean.com**

SAN JUAN Condado Plaza Hotel and Casino ⬛ 🍴 📋 ♿ Ⓦ Ⓢ Ⓢ Ⓢ

999 Ashford Av., Condado **Tel** *787 721 1000* **Rooms** *577*

A short taxi ride from Old San Juan, this high-rise hotel has its own beach as well as good tennis courts and a well-equipped gym. Decorated in a modish minimalist style for an upmarket clientele, all its suave guest rooms are zingy with color. It has a restaurant *(see p219)*, spa, and a 24-hour casino. **www.condadoplaza.com**

SAN JUAN El San Juan Hotel and Casino ⬛ 🍴 📋 ♿ Ⓦ Ⓢ Ⓢ Ⓢ

6063 Isla Verde **Tel** *787 791 1000* **Fax** *787 791 6985* **Rooms** *382*

Considered San Juan's signature beachfront hotel, the facilities at this elegant high-rise include 3 swimming pools, a casino, a bar, a spa, and 9 restaurants. Guest rooms have lily-white contemporary styling. The opulent Palm Lobby is a great place for cocktails and hosts classical concerts. **www.elsanjuanhotel.com**

SAN JUAN Gallery Inn ▤ [W] $$$$

204 Calle Norzagaray ***Tel*** *787 722 1808* ***Rooms*** *23*

The quirkiest hotel in town is also among the most endearing, thanks to eccentric live-in owners Jan D'Esposo and Hernán "Manuco" Gandía. The couple have filled this rambling town house with curios, tapestries, and Jan's own art pieces. A courtyard swimming pool and deck are perfect for socializing over cocktails. **www.thegalleryinn.com**

SAN JUAN Ritz-Carlton, San Juan Hotel, Spa & Casino 🏊 🍴 ▤ ♿ [W] $$$$

6961 Av. Los Gobernadores, Isla Verde ***Tel*** *787 253 1700* ***Fax*** *787 253 1777* ***Rooms*** *416*

As the capital's premier deluxe hotel, this huge beachfront resort offers sumptuous accommodations with classical European styling and deluxe bathrooms. Non-guests have access to the ritzy casino and elegant spa. It also has tennis courts, a bar, and a business center. Executive rooms have concierge service. **www.ritzcarlton.com**

SAN JUAN Sheraton Old San Juan Hotel & Casino 🍴 ▤ ♿ [W] $$$$

100 Brumbaugh Street ***Tel*** *787 721 5100* ***Fax*** *787 721 1111* ***Rooms*** *240*

Steps from the cruise dock on the edge of Old San Juan, this high-rise hotel has a faux-colonial exterior but is thoroughly modern within. Guest rooms are stylish but have conservative furnishings in rust and brown. The choice of restaurants include an excellent Italian eatery *(see p218)*. **www.sheratonoldsanjuan.com**

SAN JUAN The Water and Beach Club 🏊 🍴 ▤ ♿ [W] $$$$

2 Tartak Street, Isla Verde ***Tel*** *787 728 3666* ***Fax*** *787 728 3610* ***Rooms*** *84*

This trendy, luxurious boutique hotel has a chic minimalist ambience aimed at a sophisticated clientele. The rooms have contemporary decor and floor to ceiling windows offering spectacular views of the Atlantic. The 2 gourmet restaurants *(see p219)* and a hip bar draw locals at night. **www.waterbeachclubhotel.com**

UTUADO Casa Grande Mountain Retreat 🍴 [W] $

Rt. 612 ***Tel*** *787 894 3939* ***Fax*** *787 894 3900* ***Rooms*** *20*

This bargain-priced mountain resort was once a coffee plantation. Surrounded by forest, its magnificent setting grants fabulous vistas as well as hiking trails. Its simply furnished wooden cabins on stilts rise over a lush tropical garden. A colorful and airy restaurant serves hearty and delicious meals. **www.hotelcasagrande.com**

VIEQUES Bananas Guesthouse 🏊 🍴 ▤ ♿ [W] $

Calle Flamboyan 142, Esperanza ***Tel*** *787 741 8700* ***Rooms*** *12*

This guesthouse is perfect for budget travelers seeking an unpretentious beachfront lodging. The small rooms have ceiling fans and louvered windows but do not offer phones or TVs. The popular open-air restaurant has board games and is always packed. The bar offers happy hours. **www.bananasguesthouse.com**

VIEQUES The Crow's Nest 🍴 ▤ ♿ [W] $$

Rt. 201 Km1.5, Barrio Florida ***Tel*** *787 741 0033* ***Fax*** *787 741 1294* ***Rooms*** *17*

Located on a forested hillside, this inn has spectacular views of the Atlantic. The rooms are well-decorated and some have their own cooking facilities. They offer activities such as snorkeling and horseback riding. The nearest beach is 10 minutes by car. **www.crowsnestvieques.com**

VIEQUES Hacienda Tamarindo 🍴 ▤ ♿ [W] $$$

Rt. 996 Km4.5, Esperanza ***Tel*** *787 741 8525* ***Fax*** *787 741 3215* ***Rooms*** *16*

Perched on a hilltop, this lovely Spanish-style, family-run plantation home with vast views is a short drive from the beach. Airy and well-lit rooms sport chic vibrant color schemes and Caribbean-style furnishings, including wicker. The hosts are amiable and there is a friendly house dog and a parrot. **www.haciendatamarindo.com**

VIEQUES Hix Island House 🍴 ▤ ♿ [W] $$$

Rt. 995 Km1.6 ***Tel*** *787 741 2302* ***Fax*** *787 741 2797* ***Rooms*** *13*

The Hix Island House is an avant-garde, eco-friendly, Zen-inspired boutique hotel with dramatic post-Modernist architecture. Colorful furnishings and luxurious fabrics characterize the loft apartments, which have private outdoor showers. The hotel specializes in yoga and spa treatments. **www.hixislandhouse.com**

VIEQUES Inn on the Blue Horizon 🍴 ▤ ♿ [W] $$$$

Rt. 996 Km4.2, Esperanza ***Tel*** *787 741 3318* ***Fax*** *787 741 0522* ***Rooms*** *10*

One of Puerto Rico's original boutique hotels, it has a spectacular hillside setting and ocean vistas. Intimate Mediterranean-themed villas are a relaxing retreat but lack phones and TVs. The rooms have elegant colonial style furnishings. It has a restaurant *(see p219)*, tennis courts, and bicycles. **www.innonthebluehorizon.com**

VIEQUES La Finca Caribe Guesthouses and Cottages 🏊 🍴 ▤ ✱ ♿ [W] $$$$

Rt. 995 Km1.2 ***Tel*** *787 741 0495* ***Fax*** *787 741 3584* ***Rooms*** *6*

Situated in a forested hillside near Sun Bay, La Finca is a perfect getaway for eco-sensitive travelers. There are 6 rooms and 2 private cottages with their own decks and kitchen space. The common lobby has a library and indoor board games while there is an outdoor pool and hammocks with a great view of the sea. **www.lafinca.com**

VIEQUES W Retreat and Spa 🏊 🍴 ▤ ✱ ♿ [W] $$$$$

Rt. 200 Km3.2 ***Tel*** *787 741 4100* ***Fax*** *787 741 4171* ***Rooms*** *138*

The former Martineau Bay Resort and Spa metamorphosed in 2010 as this trendy, avant-garde beachfront hotel blending contemporary aesthetics with luxurious Spanish-style villa living. Rooms are a blaze of whites and French doors open to ocean views. It has a deluxe full-service spa. **www.whotels.com/explore**

Key to Symbols *see back cover flap*

Where to Eat & Nightlife

San Juan is abuzz with stylish contemporary restaurants to complement Old San Juan's flavorful bistro-style options. The more expensive hotels have more upscale restaurants and the majority are open to non-guests. Some have a dress policy, so check in advance. The capital is world-famous for chic nightclubs and there are also jazz outlets and even classical music venues.

PRICE CATEGORIES
The price ranges are for a two-course meal for one, including tax and service charges and half a bottle of wine.

$ under $10
$$ $10–15
$$$ $15–25
$$$$ $25–35
$$$$$ over $35

RESTAURANTS

Island Specialities
Puerto Rico is a trend-setter in nouvelle Latin cuisine in addition to delicious local dishes such as *mofongo* (mashed yucca with garlic) and roast pork. Many of the Caribbean's finest chefs hail from here. The *lechonerías* and simple roadside *colmados* are great places to sample local fare.

Ajili Mójili

Lemongrass restaurant

CANA GORDA Alexandra 💳 🍴 ♿ $$$$$
Carretera 333 Km6.5 ***Tel*** *787 821 0505*

Located at the Copamarina Beach Resort *(see p207)*, this is one of the south coast's best eateries. Seafood staples, steaks, and creative adaptations of comfort food, such as grilled pork chops with pineapple chutney, and free-range chicken with cumin and thyme butter are popular here. Open for dinner only.

DORADO El Ladrillo 🍷 💳 ♿ $$$
Calle Mendez Vigo 334 ***Tel*** *787 796 2120*

For surf-and-turf, head to El Ladrillo ("The Brick"), a charming restaurant with brick walls festooned with historic prints and contemporary art. Non-vegetarians will find all their favorites – fresh US prime Angus beef, sirloin, T-bones and *filet mignon*. Lobster is the house specialty among seafood. The wine stock is good.

FAJARDO Blossoms [V] 💳 🍴 ♿ $$$$
1000 Conquistador Av. ***Tel*** *787 863 1000*

One of 13 restaurants in the El Conquistador Resort *(see p209)*, Blossoms takes you on a tour of the Orient with its elaborate lanterns, fish tank, teppanyaki tables serving *filet mignon*, lobster, and a menu ranging from Hunan and Szechuan specialties to a superb sushi bar. Decor is conservative. Dinner only. Reservations recommended.

FAJARDO La Piccola Fontana 🍷 💳 🍽 🍴 ♿ $$$$
1000 Conquistador Av. ***Tel*** *787 863 1000*

La Piccola Fontana is a contemporary and elegant restaurant at the El Conquistador Resort *(see p209)*. The minestrone soup is a winning starter, followed by the exceptional seafood pasta, risotti, meat, and poultry. The terrace offers a romantic setting beneath the stars. Reservations are required.

HUMACAO Chez Daniel 💳 🍽 🍴 ♿ $$$
Marina Palmas del Mar, Km86.4 ***Tel*** *787 850 3838*

A casual waterfront atmosphere for romantic alfresco dining. French couple Daniel and Lucette Vasse prepare French country-style dishes including *bouillabaisse*, escargots, onion soup, and coq au vin. The restaurant also has an extensive wine cellar. Reservations are required. Closed on Tuesdays.

LUQUILLO Brass Cactus 💳 ♿ $$
Carretera 3, Complejo Turístico Condominio ***Tel*** *787 889 5735*

A Tex-Mex eatery, Brass Cactus appeals to the North American tourists with its familiar menu in English. The burgers are succulent and come with generous portions of crispy fries. The spicy ribs are popular too. The TV usually plays American sports or Latin American soccer and there is a jukebox. Live bands also perform here.

PONCE La Terraza 💳 🍽 🍴 ♿ $$$
1150 Av. Caribe ***Tel*** *787 259 7676*

In the Hilton Ponce Golf and Casino Resort *(see p215)*, this casual atrium restaurant extends onto a terrace bordered by a koi pond with ducks. No gourmet fare here, but the international and local dishes are filling, and the all-you-can-eat buffets are a bargain; an à la carte menu is always available. Theme nights are offered.

PONCE Archipiélago [V] 💳 🍴 $$$$
76 Calle Cristina ***Tel*** *787 812 8822*

This chic restaurant fills the void as Ponce's foremost gourmet dining hotspot. Chef Alejandro Vélez Blasini conjures up mouthwatering nouvelle Puerto Rican dishes, such as corn-crusted mahimahi in beurre-blanc sauce. Live jazz is hosted on a terrace on weekends.

PONCE La Cava
1150 Av. Caribe **Tel** *787 259 7676*

This clubby restaurant in the Hilton Ponce Golf and Casino Resort *(see p215)* offers sleek contemporary styling. The seasonally changing menu highlights nouvelle Continental dishes, such as duck foie gras with toasted brioche and fricassee of lobster and mushrooms in a pastry shell. The restaurant has an excellent wine list. Closed Mondays

RINCÓN Horned Dorset Primavera
Carretera 429 Km3 **Tel** *787 823 4030 or 800 633 1857*

Drawing gourmands from as far as San Juan, the oceanfront restaurant at this strangely named hotel *(see p203)* has the island's strictest dress code, requiring jackets for men. Chandeliers reflect on the black and white marble floors. Owner-chef Aaron Wratten serves a five-course daily menu and a nine-course tasting menu of fusion dishes.

SAN JUAN La Bombonera
Calle San Francisco 259 **Tel** *787 722 0658*

This place is a marvelous option for authentic Puerto-Rican dishes such as seafood *asopao* (traditional Puerto Rican stew), plus stuffed sandwiches, delicious home-made pastries and pies. This local landmark with counter dining is a popular lunchtime spot for busy workers and for Sunday brunch, thanks to its bargain prices.

SAN JUAN Ajili Mójili
Av. Ashford 1052, Condado **Tel** *787 725 9195*

An evocative colonial plantation theme pervades this modern restaurant appropriately serving *cocina criolla* (Creole cooking) with a stylish twist. Faux-antique brick walls add to the ambience. Staple dishes such as *mofongo* (garlicky mashed plantain), or plantain crusted shrimp in a white wine herb sauce are worth a try.

SAN JUAN Amadeus
Av. Chardon 350, Hato Rey **Tel** *787 641 7450*

This fashionable restaurant boasts a stylish, contemporary look and banquet seating in the dining room. The menu features nouvelle Caribbean dishes, with appetizers such as spicy tuna tartare, and entrées including coconut shrimp.

SAN JUAN Barú
Calle San Sebastián 150 **Tel** *787 977 7107*

Regarded by local cognoscenti as one of the fashionable top spots in town, Barú's reputation draws a young, hip crowd. The eclectic and inventive fusion menu spans the globe, although most dishes are tapas sized. The dark interior of this lovingly restored colonial house guarantees a romantic ambience.

SAN JUAN Dragonfly
Calle Fortaleza 364 **Tel** *787 977 3886*

This place is popular with locals who appreciate the ambience and great food. The blood-red Asian-inspired decor is part bordello, part opium den. Chef Roberto Trevino's Latin Asian fusion menu comes in portions intended to be shared. Guests must arrive early to get a seat.

SAN JUAN Pamela's Caribbean Cuisine
Calle Santa Ana 1, Ocean Park **Tel** *787 726 5010*

Tucked away in the beachfront Numero Uno Guesthouse, Pamela's offers the ultimate alfresco experience. Chef Esteban Torres' Caribbean fusion menu features daily specials. The favorite dishes are the plantain encrusted crab cakes with spicy tomato herb emulsion or opt for coconut corn *arepas* with guava coulis.

SAN JUAN Parrot Club
Calle Fortaleza 363 **Tel** *787 725 7370*

The Parrot Club is a vivacious Old San Juan nightspot with bare crumbling walls and where the cocktails are strong, the music loud. The Nuevo Latino cuisine imbues old Puerto Rican specialties with recherché twists. Delicious crab cakes and pan-seared tuna with dark-rum sauce are favorites. Enjoy Sunday brunch in the leafy courtyard.

SAN JUAN Aguaviva
Calle Fortaleza 364 **Tel** *787 722 0665*

Delicious Latin nouvelle seafoods are the trademark of this ultra-hip restaurant. The name of the restaurant means jellyfish. The signature dish is the gravity defying *torre del mar* (sea tower) piled high with oysters, shrimp, and other delights from King Neptune's larder. Reservations are required. Closed Sundays.

SAN JUAN Lemongrass
Calle Los Rosales **Tel** *787 721 0303*

A highlight of the Caribe Hilton *(see p215)*, this airy, post-Modernist-style restaurant is a sleek fine-dining venue for enjoying Pan Asian Latino cuisine. Shrimp spring rolls and spare ribs in hoisin tamarind sauce with guava glaze are typical. They have an excellent sushi bar. Closed on Sundays (Jan–Nov). Only from 5:30–10:30pm.

SAN JUAN Palio
Calle Brumbaugh 100 **Tel** *787 289 1944*

In Sheraton Old San Juan Hotel and Casino *(see p216)*, which describes it as a Tuscan chop house, this restaurant serves delicious grilled meats in Italian style. Dishes range from lasagne to veal chops, Angus beef porterhouse, and *filet mignon* with rum peppercorn glaze. Blush-red walls and curtains, and fine views over San Juan harbor.

Key to Symbols *see back cover flap*

SAN JUAN Tangerine

José M. Tartak St. 2 **Tel** *787 728 3666*

On the ground floor of The Water and Beach Club *(see p216)*, this restaurant features a fantastic oceanfront view and a blazing white and neon-blue decor. The menu has a wide range of cuisines that please all the senses. Tangerine is suitable for all occasions, including romantic dinners.

SAN JUAN 311 Trois Cents Onze

Calle Fortaleza 311 **Tel** *787 725 7959*

In the heart of Old San Juan, this elegant restaurant serves delicate, artfully presented and always delectable French cuisine from the hands of highly respected local chef, Juan Peña. The elegant ambience draws guests, especially during special food-and-wine-pairing nights. They have a huge wine list. **www.311restaurantpr.com**

SAN JUAN Il Perugino

Calle Cristo 105 **Tel** *787 722 5481*

This well-respected Italian restaurant in the heart of Old San Juan exudes old world elegance. (Luciano Pavarotti was among its many famous patrons.) The kitchen delivers consistently satisfying dishes, such as ravioli stuffed with chicken liver, spinach, and black truffles, plus veal *entrecôte* with mushrooms. **www.ilperugino.com**

SAN JUAN Marmalade

317 Calle Fortaleza **Tel** *787 724 3969*

Dazzlingly inventive food and a stunning interior make this the in-place for San Juan sophisticates to dine. Owner-chef Peter Schintler has furnished Marmalade with minimalist decor, a white-and-orange color scheme, and a chic lounge bar. The fusion menu includes such treats as Colorado lamb shank with pomegranate and minted yogurt.

SAN JUAN Pikayo

Av. Ashford 999 **Tel** *787 721 1000*

This starkly minimalist restaurant is located in the San Juan Condado Plaza Hotel and Casino *(see p215)*. Owner-chef Wilo Benet serves artful award-winning, Cajun-inspired fusion dishes. Museum pieces adorn the walls. Crab cake with aioli, and *mofongo* topped with saffron shrimp exemplify the menu.

VIEQUES Bananas

Calle Flamboyan 142, Esperanza **Tel** *787 741 8700*

A favorite waterfront bar and alfresco dining spot for tourists and expatriate gringos, this unpretentious restaurant with concrete tables has a fabulous beachfront setting. The menu is geared to the predominantly US clientele, with babyback ribs, burgers, salads, jerk chicken, and red snapper sandwich, plus some local favorites.

VIEQUES Chez Shack

Carretera 995, Km1.8 **Tel** *787 741 2175*

A bohemian delight in the hills, ramshackle wooden Chez Shack is the most off-beat spot to dine in Vieques. Laid-back owner Hugh Duffy delivers what his loyal clients demand: wholesome favorites such as fish filets, baked crab, chicken, and steaks. Monday nights are lively with a live reggae band and popular barbecued ribs.

VIEQUES Carambola

Rt. 996 Km4.2, Esperanza, Vieques **Tel** *787 741 3318*

Located in the Inn on the Blue Horizon *(see p216)*, this room with a view is a total winner. Chef Xandra fuses Asian and Mediterranean cuisines to concoct mouth-watering signature dishes. You can also dine in the Blue Moon Bar and Grill, with a tapas menu and a bar adorned with magical motifs. It is closed on Mondays.

BARS AND CLUBS

San Juan has a sizzling night scene catering to a sophisticated and young crowd, who flock to hip bars and nightclubs to dance to exciting Latin sounds, such as the salsa and bomba. Traditional country folk music known as *décimas* can still be heard in countryside *colmados*, simple grocery stores that double as local bars and where dominoes is the pastime of choice. Some of the best bars are found in hotels.

Bar in Calle San Sebastián

RECOMMENDED PLACES TO GO

Al's Mar Azul
Calle Plinio Peterson, Isabela Segunda, Vieques. (Open-air bar.)

Akua
Plaza Nuevo Mundo, Ponce. (Wine bar/lounge with live music Thu–Sat.)

Calypso Café
Rt. 4413, Rincón. (Live rock.)

Club Brava
El San Juan Hotel & Casino, 6063 Av. Isla Verde. (Classy nightclub.)

El Patio de Sam
Calle San Sebastián 102, San Juan. (Fun bar with live entertainment.)

Eternal
Av. Ashford 999, San Juan. (Trendy lounge bar with live music.)

Liquid
The Water and Beach Club Hotel, Calle Tartak 2, San Juan. (Lush bar.)

Palm Court Bar
6063 Av. Isla Verde. (Live music.)

Parrot Club
Calle Fortaleza 363, San Juan. (Hip nightclub bar with great music.)

Practical Information

Puerto Rico is a modern and sophisticated society with a top-notch infrastructure. Much of it, such as the postal service, is shared with the US mainland. Tourist hotels are highly concentrated at specific beaches, and large sections of coastline, as well as the Cordillera Central, have few options. The densely populated island has horrendous traffic congestion in most towns, and many of the beach resorts popular with locals can get crowded and terribly littered.

WHEN TO GO

As in most of the Caribbean, the best weather here is from December to April. The other months get more rain and are hotter, although breezes help keep things cool year-round. Parts of the southwest are in a rain shadow and also receive few breezes. Accommodation rates are generally lower during summer months, but cultural events are spread through the year.

GETTING THERE

Most scheduled flights arrive at San Juan's Luis Muñoz Marin International Airport (SJU), with flights from more than 20 US cities. Some flights arrive at regional airports in Ponce, Mayagüez, and San Juan's Isla Grande Airport (SIG). **American Airlines**, **Delta**, **JetBlue**, **Spirit Airlines**, **United Airlines**, and **US Airways** offer services to Puerto Rico, as do **Air Canada** and numerous charter airlines. Several European airlines such as **British Airways** connect through Miami, while **Iberia** has direct flights.

The regional partner of American Airlines, American Eagle connects the provincial airports within Puerto Rico, including Vieques and Culebra, which can also be reached by ferry from Fajardo.

DOCUMENTATION

All visitors, including US citizens, must show a passport when visiting Puerto Rico. A passport is needed when re-entering the US by air. Visitors from Europe may enter for 90 days without a visa, but must register with **ESTA**. This can take up to 72 hours for approval and there is a charge. Travel requirements may change - check before travel. All visitors must have a ticket for onward travel.

VISITOR INFORMATION

The **Puerto Rico Tourism Company** has offices in the US, Canada, Germany, and Spain that provide brochures. Within Puerto Rico, it has offices on Paseo de la Princesa and by the cruise port in San Juan. Hotel tour desks also have details of organized tours and activities.

HEALTH AND SECURITY

Puerto Rico is safe and there are no endemic tropical diseases. Violent crime against visitors is rare, but carjackings and opportunistic snatch-and-grab theft are not uncommon in San Juan. Avoid wearing jewelry in public and keep valuables in a hotel safe. Puerto Rican drivers have little regard for traffic rules, so drive cautiously Check with locals about tidal conditions before swimming. Private medical clinics, such as **Clínica Las Américas**, are ubiquitous and all major towns have hospitals. Hotels can arrange for a doctor in any emergency.

BANKING AND CURRENCY

The US dollar is the official and sole currency of Puerto Rico, although locals still use the term "peso" or "billetes" for the dollar. Traveler's checks in US dollars are accepted in many hotels, restaurants, and stores, although credit cards are always preferable. There are banks with ATMs in almost every town.

An ATM machine at the town center in Fajardo

COMMUNICATIONS

Puerto Rico has a highly efficient telephone system currently operated by Mexico's América Móvil company under their international **Claro** brand. Public phones are present islandwide and prepaid phone cards can be purchased at many stores. Calls from hotels incur a hefty surcharge.

Puerto Rico's area code is 787. To call the island from North America, dial 1, then 787 and the local number; from the UK, dial 00 for international access, then 1 787 and the local number. Calls within Puerto Rico require 787 and the seven-digit number. Most hotels offer Internet access; many have Wi-Fi. There are Internet cafés on all the islands.

A small plane used for internal flights, Vieques airport

Taxis at the Plaza de Armas, Old San Juan

TRANSPORT

The island has an extensive road system, but traffic congestion is severe, and a frightening disregard for traffic regulations makes driving in Puerto Rico quite risky. Most major international car rental companies, such as **AVIS**, **Hertz**, and **Budget**, are represented. Renting a scooter is a good option for exploring Vieques and Culebra, but be sure to wear a helmet.

Taxis offer efficient service within San Juan. The hotel concierge or front desk can call for a taxi waiting outside most tourist hotels. Locals rely on *públicos* (private minivans) that operate communal taxi services for town-to-town travel. Puerto Rico Tourism Company can provide information on taxi companies.

SHOPPING

San Juan's historic center has many stores selling local crafts, including the island's trademark *santos* (saint figurines) as well as cigars, rum, and clothing items. Most tourist hotels also sell crafts, and have upscale boutiques, as does Avenue Ashford in San Juan's Condado district and Plaza Las Américas mall. Puerto Rican coffee and lace items make great souvenirs, as do hand-made crafts, such as *vejigante* masks, *santos*, and other wooden carvings that can be bought at source in studios around Orocovis and Utuado. There is no sales tax, and no duty is payable upon return to the US mainland.

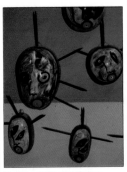
Masks on display in a shop on Calle de la Fortaleza, San Juan

LANGUAGE

Spanish is Puerto Rico's official language, spoken by everyone, although many locals also speak English, as do most Puerto Ricans working in tourism.

ELECTRICITY

Puerto Rico operates on 110 volts. Outlets use US two- or three-prong plugs. Visitors from Europe should bring transformers or adapters.

TIME

Puerto Rico is on Eastern Standard Time (EST), 5 hours behind Greenwich Mean Time (GMT), like New York and Miami. Daylight saving is not observed in Puerto Rico, which is therefore one hour behind EST from the last Sunday of March through the last Sunday of October.

GETTING MARRIED

At least two months' forward planning is needed to get married in Puerto Rico. Both parties' passport or identification card, plus original birth certificate, and divorce and spouse's death decrees, if applicable, are required. Blood tests within two weeks and a medical examination within 10 days of the wedding are also needed. Any couple wanting to go it alone will need to visit the Marriage License Bureau of the **Registro Demográfico**, or make arrangements through **Wed Affair**.

DIRECTORY

AIRLINES

Air Canada
www.aircanada.com

American Airlines
www.aa.com

British Airways
www.ba.com

Delta
www.delta.com

Iberia
www.iberia.com

JetBlue
www.jetblue.com

Spirit Airlines
www.spiritair.com

United Airlines
www.united.com

US Airways
www.usairways.com

DOCUMENTATION

ESTA
www.cbp.gov/esta

VISITOR INFORMATION

Puerto Rico Tourism Company
Tel 787 721 2400.
www.gotopuertorico.com

HEALTH AND SECURITY

Emergencies
Tel 911.

Clínica Las Américas
Tel 787 765 1919. www.clinicalasamericas.com

COMMUNICATIONS

Claro
Tel 787 775 0000.
www.claropr.com

TRANSPORT

AVIS
Tel 787 253 5926.
www.avis.com

Budget
Tel 787 791 0600.
www.budget.com

Hertz
Tel 787 791 0840.
www.hertz.com

GETTING MARRIED

Registro Demográfico
171 Calle Quisqueya, Hato Rey, San Juan.
Tel 787 767 9120.

Wed Affair
www.wedaffair.com

THE LEEWARDS
AND FRENCH
ANTILLES

THE LEEWARDS AND FRENCH ANTILLES AT A GLANCE

The Leeward Islands, comprising the Virgin Islands, Anguilla, Antigua and Barbuda, Saba and St. Eustatius, and St. Kitts and Nevis, are a paradise for tourists in search of adventure. From renowned sailing regattas in Antigua to strenuous hiking in Saba, all the islands offer exciting outdoor activities. On the other hand, the French Antilles, St. Martin/Sint Maarten, St. Barthélemy, Guadeloupe, and Martinique, have fantastic beaches, world-class hotels and restaurants, and great shopping.

LOCATOR MAP

ANGUILLA
(see pp258–69)

VIRGIN ISLANDS
(see pp226–57)

ST. MARTIN/ SINT MAARTEN
(see pp270–85)

ST. BARTHÉLEM
(see pp342–

SABA AND ST. EUSTATIUS
(see pp286–301)

ST. KITTS AND NEVIS
(see pp302–19)

The Virgin Islands, *with their spectacular beaches, emerald waters, stunning coral reefs, and amazing flora, leave most visitors breathless. The islands are popular among adventure tourists who come for snorkeling, hiking, and sailing.*

St. Martin/Sint Maarten *is almost divided equally between France and The Netherlands. Sint Maarten is more tourist oriented, while St. Martin is quieter and peaceful.*

Saba, *with its volcanic peak, rises steeply out of the sea. It presents to visitors an experience of peace and tranquility with its eco-lodges, unspoilt hiking trails, serene beaches, and dive sites, making it different from any other Caribbean island.*

Antigua and Barbuda *has long winding coastlines, azure waters, and a generally laid-back feel perfect for relaxation. Antigua offers plenty of activities including diving, sailing, and snorkeling to old shipwrecks and some of the best coral reefs anywhere. The small island of Barbuda, on the other hand, is a haven for birdwatchers and eco-tourists.*

**ANTIGUA
AND
BARBUDA**
(see pp320–41)

MONTSERRAT
(see pp332–35)

Guadeloupe, *a small archipelago and part of the French Republic, is highly urbanized. However, it is also known for its rugged mountains, waterfalls, thick rainforests, and great hiking trails. It is home to La Soufrière, an active volcano.*

| 0 km | 50 |
| 0 miles | 50 |

GUADELOUPE
(see pp358–75)

DOMINICA
(The Windwards,
see pp398–413)

MARTINIQUE
(see pp376–93)

Martinique's *landscape is dotted with sugarcane fields – the island's major crop. Its dense and lush green forests cover over one-third of the island.*

Exploring the Virgin Islands

Except for the flag flying overhead, the US and
British Virgin Islands share many similarities.
Visitors come for swimming, snorkeling,
and sailing as well as hiking, shopping,
and relaxing. St. Croix (USVI) to the south
is larger and flatter than most islands in the
north; except for Anegada, the BVI are peaks
jutting out of the clear waters. Anegada, far to
the east of the BVI chain, is a coral atoll
fringed with powdery white sands.

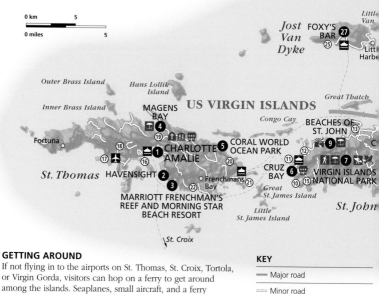

GETTING AROUND

If not flying in to the airports on St. Thomas, St. Croix, Tortola,
or Virgin Gorda, visitors can hop on a ferry to get around
among the islands. Seaplanes, small aircraft, and a ferry
connect St. Thomas and St. Croix. St. John and St. Thomas
are also linked by ferry service. To Tortola, a ferry is available
at Charlotte Amalie or Cruz Bay. Virgin Gorda is reached by
ferry from St. Thomas, St. John, and Tortola. Ferries also go
from Tortola to Jost Van Dyke and Anegada.

KEY

▬▬	Major road
══	Minor road
---	Ferry route
▬▬	International border
△	Peak

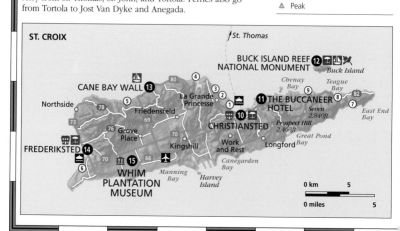

ANEGADA

Cow Wreck Bay · Windlass Bight · Jack Bay · Loblolly Bay · Table Bay · Flamingo Pond ㉓ ㉔ · *Caribbean Sea* · The Settlement ✈ · Lower Bay · White Bay · Tortola

0 km 3
0 miles 3

Great Camanoe · *Guana Island* · Scrub Island · West Dog · George Dog · Great Dog · Savannah Bay · Necker Island · Prickly Pear Island · Mosquito Island · Saba Rock · ㊱ ㊲ ㊳ ㊴ ㉕ · **GORDA PEAK NATIONAL PARK**

MARINA CAY ㉑ · **DRIVING TOUR OF VIRGIN GORDA** ㉔ · Spanish Town · ㉟ · *Virgin Gorda*

JR O'NEAL BOTANICAL GARDENS NATIONAL PARK · THE VALLEY ㉒ · ㉝ · Coppermine National Park · THE BATHS · ㉜

ROAD TOWN ㉖ ⑰ ⑯ · *Tortola* · Fallen Jerusalem ㉓ · Ginger Island · Round Rock

⑱ SAGE MOUNTAIN NATIONAL PARK · ㉗

BRITISH VIRGIN ISLANDS · Cooper Island · Salt Island · ㉖ ✈

RMS RHONE MARINE PARK · Peter Island · Pelican Island · Norman Island · *CARIBBEAN SEA*

SEE ALSO
- *Where to Stay* pp248–52
- *Where to Eat & Nightlife* pp253–5

SIGHTS AT A GLANCE

St. Thomas

While visitors can be as laid-back as they like on St. Thomas, the island offers plenty of watersports, good shopping, excellent restaurants, and some nightlife. The scenery is stunning, with lush mountains reaching skyward from turquoise bays fringed by white sandy crescents. St. Thomas, together with St. John and St. Croix, was under Danish control for centuries, a heritage clearly reflected in the busy town of Charlotte Amalie with its red roofs and many streets still carrying a Danish name.

Charlotte Amalie ❶

SW coast of St. Thomas. 👥 *19,000.*
✈ ⛴ 🚗 🎭 *Carnival (Apr).*

While there are ample stores filled with everything from T-shirts to crafts to luxury items that beckon, Charlotte Amalie, long the center of commerce, offers more than just shopping opportunities. The island's history reveals itself in stores that formerly served as warehouses or merchants' homes centuries ago. A short walk takes visitors to **Fort Christian**, a military construction begun in 1672 by the Danish, who controlled the island at the time. Today it has been converted into a museum that displays exhibits on the island's history and culture. Just across the Veterans Drive from Fort Christian, the big green building that now serves as home to the local **Legislature** was the site for the March 31, 1917, transfer of power from Denmark to the US of all three islands. The purchase cost the US government $25 million. Every year on the same day, residents observe the transfer anniversary in the Legislature's garden.

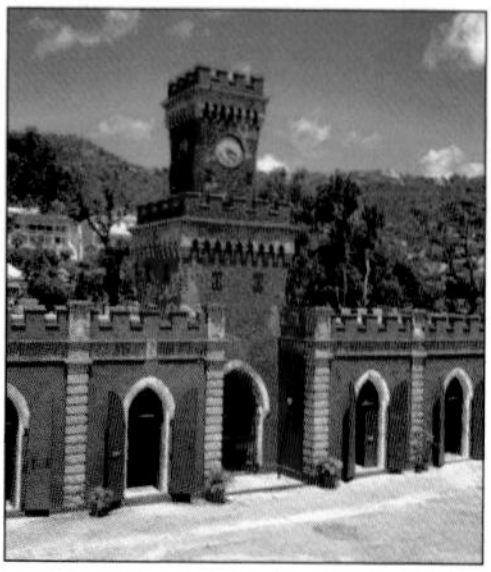

The magnificent façade of Fort Christian, Charlotte Amalie

History aside, Charlotte Amalie presents excellent shopping opportunities with the **Vendor's Plaza** offering great bargains. Various art galleries are scattered around the **Shopping District**.

Two streets inland from the Shopping District's Main Street, **St. Thomas Synagogue** has served as the spiritual home to the island's Jewish population since 1833. Other historic churches are scattered around Charlotte Amalie. The Neo-Classical white building, just uphill from the Shopping District, is the seat of the local government's administrative branch and is where the governor has his office.

Lunch can be enjoyed at any of the numerous restaurants that range from simple sandwich eateries to more formal ones, sitting along Main Street and on the streets and alleys that connect Main Street to the waterfront and the streets inland.

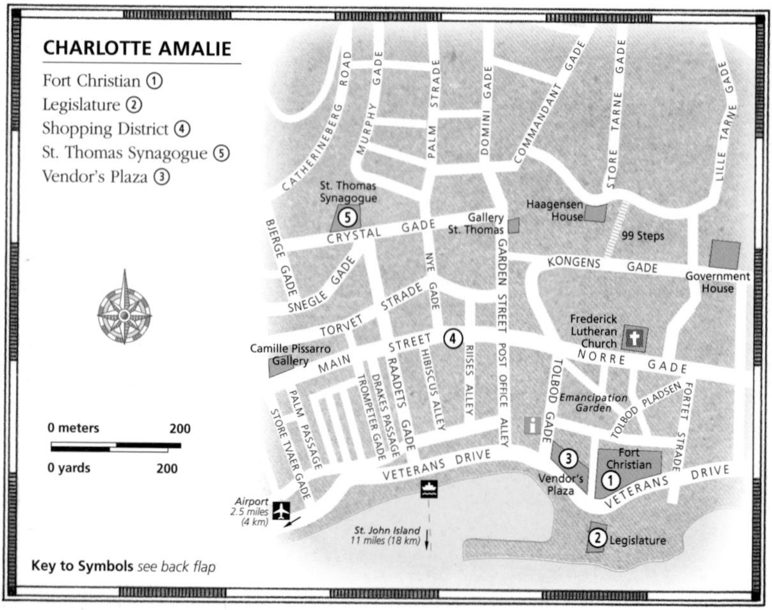
CHARLOTTE AMALIE
Fort Christian ①
Legislature ②
Shopping District ④
St. Thomas Synagogue ⑤
Vendor's Plaza ③
0 meters 200
0 yards 200
Key to Symbols see back flap
CATHERINEBERG ROAD
MURPHY GADE
PALM STRADE
DOMINI GADE
COMMANDANT GADE
STORE TARNE GADE
LILLE TARNE GADE
St. Thomas Synagogue
Haagensen House
Gallery St. Thomas
99 Steps
BJERGE GADE
CRYSTAL GADE
KONGENS GADE
Government House
SNEGLE GADE
STRADE
NYE GADE
GARDEN STREET
TORVET
Frederick Lutheran Church
Camille Pissarro Gallery
MAIN STREET
NORRE GADE
RISES ALLEY
POST OFFICE ALLEY
HIBISCUS ALLEY
RAADETS GADE
DRAKES PASSAGE
TROMPETER GADE
PALM PASSAGE
STORE TVAER GADE
TOLBOD GADE
Emancipation Garden
TOLBOD PLADSEN
FORTET STRADE
VETERANS DRIVE
Vendor's Plaza
Fort Christian
Airport 2.5 miles (4 km)
St. John Island 11 miles (18 km)
Legislature

Shoppers scanning through the displays, Havensight Mall

Havensight ❷

2 miles (3 km) SE of Charlotte Amalie. 🚢 🚍 ℹ️ *Havensight Mall, 340 774 8784. Dept. of Tourism, 340 777 5313.* **www**.havensightmall.com

Home to the island's largest cruise ship dock, Havensight bustles with activity. Those who arrive on a cruise ship can join their sailing, scuba, or exploring excursions at the dock. Many prefer a short stroll to the vast Havensight shopping area. It stretches from **Havensight Mall** to Port of Sale Mall and around the corner past Wendy's fast food restaurant to Yacht Haven Grande Mall. Several downtown Charlotte Amalie stores have branches here, but there are dozens of others as well. Many visitors buy liquor from here at much better prices than available anywhere else.

The area is home to many restaurants, so cruise ship passengers not eating on board will not go hungry.

Marriott Frenchman's Reef and Morning Star Beach Resort ❸

🛥️ Rt 315, 5 Estate Bakkeroe. **Tel** *340 776 8500.* **Fax** *340 715 6193*
💲💲💲💲 *506 rooms.* 🅿️ 🍴 📶
🏊 ♿ Ⓦ **www**.marriott.com

The vast Marriott Frenchman's Reef and Morning Star Beach Resort is the kind of place where guests can settle for more than a few days, but day visitors are also welcome. The resort is easily reached

by taxi, car or the Reefer, a small boat that ferries visitors to the resort from the Charlotte Amalie waterfront.

The beach, a white sandy confection, is one of the most popular on the island. Sailing and snorkeling trips depart from the dock, Jet Skis are available and the hotel's restaurants make a great spot for lunch or dinner.

Visitors can also make an appointment at the hotel's spa – the Reef Health Club and Spa – for a massage, manicure, or a session on the club's fitness equipment.

Magens Bay ❹

🚉 Rt 35. 🏊 👫 🎣
www.magensbayauthority.com

Ever popular Magens Bay beach stretches along a U-shaped bay. This beach has a snack bar, snorkel gear and small sailboat rentals, a beachwear shop, showers, and bathrooms. On cruise

ship days the beach can get crowded. Locals like to party on weekends and holidays when music gets very loud and the atmosphere more than lively. For some solitude, it is best to stroll down to either end of the beach away from the crowds.

Inland from the beach is the Magens Bay Arboretum, a botanical garden with native and imported plants.

Coral World Ocean Park ❺

4 miles (6 km) NE of Charlotte Amalie. **Tel** *340 775 1555.* 🚗
🕐 *9am–5pm Sat–Thu.* 🎫 ✓
♿ 🍴 🛍️ **www**.coralworldvi.com

A popular spot with families, Coral World Ocean Park appeals to anyone who is interested in marine life. The undersea observatory is reached by a bridge that takes visitors 100 ft (30 m) offshore and down 15 ft (5 m) to the briny depths in the middle of a coral reef. The round structure features huge windows for extensive views of colorful fish swimming by. Included in the admission price is a walk along a nature trail, a view of the 21 aquariums that feature a variety of sea life, and a chance to feed stingrays.

The 5-acre (2-ha) park offers various other guided attractions including an in-pool swim with sea lions, a swim with sharks and turtles, and Sea Trek, a scuba-like adventure. These activities have an extra charge.

Undersea observatory, Coral World Ocean Park

St. John

Wildflower, St. John

St. John is a jewel with the Virgin Islands National Park at its center. The island offers varied accommodations that lure visitors bent on sampling the park's white sandy beaches, hiking trails heading up verdant hillsides, and a variety of restaurants and shops. Most of the island remains untouched thanks to the park, but the eastern and western fringes serve as centers of commerce, with Cruz Bay, a bustling town, the main point of entry.

Families wandering around in Cruz Bay Park

Cruz Bay ⑥

W coast of St. John. 🚶 2,750. 🚌 🚕 ℹ *Henry Samuel Street, 340 776 6450.* **www.**usvitourism.vi

Most vacationers pass through Cruz Bay, St. John's main town: ferries from St. Thomas and the British Virgin Islands pull into the port, it has the widest choice of restaurants and shops, and many watersports excursions depart from here. Near the ferry dock, in Cruz Bay Park, taxi drivers wait to pick up visitors and people relax on the benches scattered around the

park. Shops and restaurants are anchored by Wharfside Village shopping center, sitting beachfront near the ferry dock, and the Mongoose Junction shopping center is located where the North Shore Road starts uphill and out of Cruz Bay.

The town is home to a few historical sites. The red-roofed Battery, on the north side of the harbor, dates back to 1825 and is currently the seat of the territorial government. Farther afield, at Tamarind Court, is the Elaine Ione Sprauve Library located in a restored 1757 plantation house.

Virgin Islands National Park ⑦

4 miles (6 km) E of Cruz Bay. 🚌 ℹ *Cruz Bay Visitors' Center, Cruz Bay, 340 776 6201.* ⏰ *24 hours a day.* 📷 🚻 ♿ ⛺ **www.**nps.gov/viis

Covering nearly two-thirds of St. John, Virgin Islands National Park encompasses 11 sq miles (29 sq km) above ground and 9 sq miles (23 sq km) of marine sanctuary. It was established in 1956, thanks to land donations by philanthropist Laurance S. Rockefeller. The Visitors' Center in Cruz Bay has exhibits, books for sale, and rangers on duty to answer questions and distribute brochures about various beach, watersports, and hiking opportunities. The park offers guided programs including beach walks and birding trips.

Coral Bay ⑧

6 miles (10 km) E of Cruz Bay. 🚌

About 200 years ago, Coral Bay was the only large settlement on St. John. Today, it is home to a handful of shops and restaurants along the main road. It is anchored by the Skinny Legs Bar and Grill complex (*see p253*) and the Cocoloba shopping center to the south. The Emmaus Moravian Church is an important historical site. The congregation dates to 1756, but the church was rebuilt after the 1916 hurricane.

The Visitors' Center of Virgin Islands National Park, near Cruz Bay

For hotels and restaurants on these islands see pp248–52 and pp253–5

View of the blue waters and white sand, Trunk Bay

Beaches of St. John ⑨

For those who want to venture beyond their hotel beach, St. John has a wealth of luscious sands to explore, with or without facilities. Many are on the north coast, easily accessible by car via the North Shore Road, but it is also worth heading down to the south coast where beachlife can be combined with a hike.

Northeast of Cruz Bay, in front of the upscale Caneel Bay Resort, is Caneel Bay, the only one of the resort's beaches that welcomes non-guests; it has a snorkeling point at the east end. Hawksnest Bay, a short distance away from Caneel Bay, is a local favorite with good snorkeling above the reef patches dotted around

the bay. The smallish Jumbie Bay, farther north from Hawksnest, has excellent snorkeling and is also popular with the locals. Jumbie is a common word for ghost and this beach has plenty of ghost stories. It is accessed via some stairs down from the road.

The ever popular **Trunk Bay** can be crowded with cruise ship visitors, but its far fringes offer some solitude. Alternatively, visitors could come early or late in the day to snorkel around the underwater trail, where the features are marked with explanatory signs. Trunk Bay has a snack bar, snorkel gear rentals, a gift shop, and picnic pavilions.

Cinnamon Bay, farther along North Shore Road, is a good bet for a day out although the white sandy beach can be windy in winter. There are restrooms and a small convenience store. A watersports

center rents snorkel gear and kayaks. The Cinnamon Nature Trail, across the road from the beach, takes visitors through interesting plantation-era ruins. The gorgeous Maho Bay is just a short drive away. However, there are no restroom facilities on the beach.

The south shore also has some excellent beaches. Salt Pond Bay is a scimitar of white sand with great snorkeling opportunities. It is also the starting point for hiking trails including the Drunk Bay Trail and the hike up to Ram's Head. A 15-minute drive down a mostly-paved road leads to the remote Lameshur Bay's small white sandy beach, which has good snorkeling along the east edge, a nice walk to Yawzi Point, and a restroom.

Kayaking in the warm waters of Cinnamon Bay

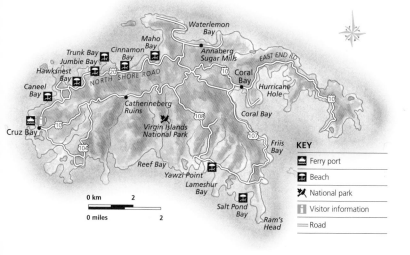

KEY

⛴ Ferry port

🏖 Beach

✕ National park

ℹ Visitor information

═ Road

St. Croix

St. Croix is an island of many facets. Plantation ruins sit side-by-side with suburban developments and a large oil refinery. The main town of Christiansted is filled with shops and restaurants, and reminders of the era when St. Croix, St. John, and St. Thomas were Danish. Frederiksted is a quiet place, occasionally a stop on the cruise ship route. Pretty beaches fringe the coasts, with small resorts and modest hotels in the two main towns.

Christiansted ❿

N coast of St. Croix. 🏃 3,000.
🛬 ⛴ 🚌 ℹ️ Government House, King Street, 340 773 1404.
www.usvitourism.vi

Home to Christiansted National Historic Site and its massive waterfront Fort Christiansvaern, this charming town is also the jumping-off point for trips to Buck Island Reef National Monument. Rangers at the fort offer information on the site's highlights. Christiansted was erected in the 18th century and most of the buildings date back to then. They have been restored, most now housing shops and restaurants. The Tourism Department office, in the 18th-century Government House, has maps and brochures about St. Croix. Tours of this historic structure, built as a home for a Danish merchant in 1747, are available.

Visitors can stroll on the Christiansted Boardwalk that passes along the harbor past Fort Christiansvaern. Benches are strategically placed for prime harbor viewing. The town is also home to a handful of small hotels, but the closest beach is at the Hotel on the Cay (see p248), located in the midst of the Christiansted Harbor.

The old Danish customs house in Christiansted

The Buccaneer Hotel ⓫

🛥️ Rt 82, Shoys. **Tel** 340 712 2100.
💲💲💲💲 138 rooms. 🅿️ 🍴 🖥️
🏊 ♿ 🅦 **www**.thebuccaneer.com

With a historic sugar mill as a centerpiece, The Buccaneer is one of the oldest St. Croix hotels. There has been a building at this site since 1653, but what is now the hotel grounds served as a cattle ranch earlier. The hotel has welcomed the rich, famous, and just plain folks since 1947. An array of activities and sports are available.

Whim Plantation Museum ⓯

This historical landmark is one of the oldest plantations on St. Croix. Its history dates back to 1743, when it started as a cotton plantation with slaves brought here from West Africa. After cotton, sugarcane was grown until 1952. The museum includes the restored great house, sugar factory ruins and mills, plots of sugarcane, and gardens.

Windmill
The plantation's windmill was built in the late 1700s and used until the 1880s. Cane grown in the surrounding fields was turned into juice when slaves fed it into rollers powered by the mill's wind-driven sails.

Animal Mill
These mills, pulled by draft animals, were used in the sugar factory to process the cane.

For hotels and restaurants on these islands see pp248–52 and pp253–5

Buck Island Reef National Monument ⑫

miles (1.6 km) NE of Christiansted. Tel 340 773 1460. ⬛ ⬜ daylight. 🔲 www.nps.gov/buis

Day-sail and power boats leave from Christiansted waterfront and Green Cay Marina to this 176-acre (70-ha) national park. The colorful reefs that make up the underwater trail at the eastern side of the monument offer some good snorkeling. After the snorkel stop, most boats head around to anchor off a gorgeous white sandy beach at the western end. Visitors can also hike uphill to the island's highest point, at 328 ft (99 m) above sea level.

Cane Bay Wall ⑬

7 miles (12 km) W of Christiansted. 🚗

Stretching along St. Croix's north side, the famous Cane Bay Wall attracts divers from around the world. Most prefer to go out on a boat with dive operators, but the wall is accessible from Cane Bay Beach and other locations along the island's north shore. It sits just 100 ft (30 m) to 200 ft (60 m) offshore. Canyons plummet over 2,000–3,000 ft (610–920 m) down, giving novice and experienced divers a view of colorful corals (including the rare black coral), sponges, and fish as well as the occasional shark.

Frederiksted ⑭

12 miles (19 km) SW of Christiansted. 🏛 3,800. ⬛ 🚌 ℹ️ Strand Street, 340 772 0357.

St. Croix's second town is a sleepy place. However, it is the site of the territory's most historic event. On July 3, 1848, about 8,000 slaves marched from nearby Estate LaGrange

Fort Frederik in Frederiksted

to Fort Frederik to demand their freedom. Standing in a carriage parked in front of the fort, Danish Governor-General Peter von Scholten announced that freedom was theirs. The Danish government recalled von Scholten home, while the former slaves continued to work the plantations. Frederiksted was later the scene of other labor uprisings by discontented workers.

The town does not have many shops and only a few restaurants and a small hotel in the downtown area, but when cruise ships pull in, this is where they arrive. A lovely white sandy beach stretches north from Fort Frederik.

Steam engines were used to crush cane.

The Research Library and Archives has a large collection of history books and photographs.

VISITORS' CHECKLIST

Centerline Rd, Rt 76. **Tel** 340 772 0598. ⬜ 10am–4pm Mon–Sat. 📷 **www**.stcroix landmarks.com

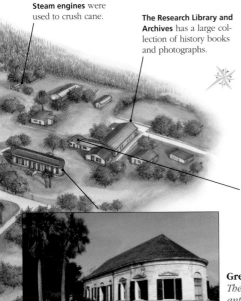

Cookhouse
The original cookhouse dates to around 1766. Its raised hearth helped keep the room cooler.

Great House
The oval great house is filled with antiques to show how planters lived a long time ago. It is a site for musical concerts in winter.

Outdoor Activities and Specialized Holidays

Activities in the US Virgin Islands mainly focus on the outdoors. Most involve the water in some form or other such as lounging at the pristine beaches, snorkeling, scuba diving, sailing excursions, fishing, and kayaking. However, some visitors come just to hike in the hills of Virgin Islands National Park or to play golf at one of the magnificent courses on St. Thomas and St. Croix. Vacationers will find plenty of outfitters ready to rent equipment and plan tours.

Pool and beach of Ritz-Carlton hotel, St. Thomas

BEACHES

Nearly everyone makes it to the beach at one time or the other during their vacation to the US Virgin Islands. Many hotels have their own beaches, just steps away from their rooms, while others have to rely on nearby public beaches. Whatever the case, since the islands are small, a good strip of sand is never more than a short drive away. Some beaches have numerous amenities while others just feature lovely white sand and clear blue sea. For safety's sake, it is best to stick to the more visited beaches on St. Thomas and St. Croix.

On St. John, the best beaches are strung out along the North Shore, but visitors will find a few in other locations. Trunk Bay *(see p231)*, the most popular, is equipped with all facilities.

St. Thomas' best beach is Magens Bay *(see p229)*, which gets lots of traffic and has the most amenities of any beach in the US Virgin Islands.

Brewer's Bay is popular with the locals. It sits right along Route 30 near the University of the Virgin Islands. Visitors might find vans selling sandwiches and the like parked along the road. Most of the other top beaches in St. Thomas are located mainly at the hotels.

On St. Croix, visitors will find lovely beaches north and south of Frederiksted. There are no safety issues at the beaches near the several restaurants tucked in between Frederiksted and Sprat Hall or near Sandcastle on the Beach, south of Frederiksted.

DIVING AND SNORKELING

It is possible to get up close and personal with the island's rich undersea life on either a snorkeling or diving tour. All gear, including a mask, snorkel, and fins, can be rented at the watersports shops located in most hotels or any of the others scattered across the territory. Among the established operators are **Aqua Action**, **Coki Beach Dive Club**, and **Cruz Bay Watersports**.

Diving is slightly more complicated but visitors can learn the ropes through a diving introductory course at most watersports shops. The instructor will go over the ins and outs of the equipment, show beginners

Snorkeling in the crystal-clear waters of the US Virgin Islands

For hotels and restaurants on these islands see pp248–52 and pp253–5

Golfers at the luxurious Mahogany Run Golf Course, St. Thomas

how to dive, and supervise closely. Visitors can get a certification card at their hometown dive shop. Some watersports centers such as **Cane Bay Dive Shop**, **St. Croix Ultimate Bluewater Adventures**, **Low Key Watersports** and **Dive Experience**, rent gear and take divers out to the top sites, if they already hold a certification card.

DAY SAILS

With the wind in your face and the good company of other sailors, set sail on any one of the charter boats that leave from various locations around the islands. After a few hours of sailing, the captain will drop the anchor for a snorkeling session and lunch, prepared by the crew and eaten under a canopy.

On St. John, day sail boats leave from Cruz Bay and the hotels for trips to offshore cays or one of the island's bays. More information can be provided by **St. John Concierge Service**. In St. Thomas, sail boats depart from the hotels, Red Hook, or Charlotte Amalie for trips to Buck Island Reef National Monument *(see p233)*, a small cay south of St. Thomas, and other offshore cays on St. John. **The Charter Boat Center** can be contacted for day sails.

St. Croix day sail boats leave from Christiansted or Green Cay for Buck Island

Reef National Monument. Tour operators here include **Big Beard's Adventure Tours** and **Teroro Charters**.

GOLF

The **Mahogany Run Golf Course** on St. Thomas is designed by acclaimed golf course designers, George and Tom Fazio. It is home to the Devil's Triangle, a wicked trio of holes that sits right above the ocean.

On St. Croix, **The Buccaneer Golf Course** vies for attention with **Carambola Golf Club**, which are both 18-hole gems. **The Reef Golf Course** is a 9-hole course and is definitely worth a try.

St. John only has an 18-hole mini-golf course at Pastory, especially popular with families looking for an hour of fun after dinner.

HIKING

St. John offers some good hiking. While the Reef Bay Trail *(see p237)* gets the most visitors, Virgin Islands National Park *(see p230)* has plenty of other trails. In the Cruz Bay area, follow the Lind Point Trail for about 1 mile (2 km) to Lind Point for great views of Cruz Bay. A taxi can be hired to the start of Cinnamon Bay Trail, which is a good hike downhill to Cinnamon Bay Campground. The Johnny Horn Trail is nearly 2 miles (3 km), stretching from Emmaus Moravian Church in Coral Bay to the secluded Brown Bay. A few trails such as Ram's Head Trail and Salt Pond Trail begin from the southern shore. It is possible to enjoy walks through estate ruins such as the Annaberg Plantation.

Hikers on the Reef Bay Trail, St. John

American yacht harbor at Red Hook, St. Thomas

FISHING

Most fishing boats head out to the sea from Red Hook, St. Thomas and Christiansted, St. Croix. Visitors can either fish on half-day or day-long excursions. The main operators are **Capt. Byron Oliver**, **Caribbean Sea Adventures**, **Gone Ketchin**, **Abigail III**, and **Marlin Prince**.

KAYAKING

There is kayaking off many beaches across the Virgin Islands, but Salt River in St. Croix is the prime destination. It is possible to kayak among mangroves and over reefs all the way to the ocean. Operators here are **Caribbean Adventure Tours** and **Virgin Kayak Tours**. On St. John, kayakers can head for any of the small cays that sit offshore. **Arawak Expeditions** and **Crabby's Watersports** are good operators here. In St. Thomas it is best to paddle along the fringes of various bays to view birds and other coastal inhabitants. **V.I. Ecotours** operates tours here.

DIRECTORY

DIVING AND SNORKELING

Aqua Action
Secret Harbor Beach Resort, Off Rt 332, St. Thomas.
Tel 340 775 6285.
www.aadivers.com

Cane Bay Dive Shop
Rt 80, Cane Bay, St. Croix.
Tel 340 718 9913.
www.canebayscuba.com

Coki Beach Dive Club
Coki Beach, Rt 388, St. Thomas.
Tel 340 775 4220.
www.cokidive.com

Cruz Bay Watersports
Lumberyard Shopping complex, Cruz Bay and the Westin Resort and Villas, St. John.
Tel 340 776 6234.
www.divestjohn.com

Dive Experience
1111 Strand Street, Christiansted, St. Croix.
Tel 340 773 3307.
www.divexp.com

Low Key Watersports
Cruz Bay, St. John.
Tel 340 693 8999.
www.divelowkey.com

St. Croix Ultimate Bluewater Adventures
Queen Cross Street, Christiansted, St. Croix.
Tel 340 773 5994.
www.stcroixscuba.com

DAY SAILS

Big Beard's Adventure Tours
Christiansted Waterfront, St. Croix.
Tel 340 773 4482.
www.bigbeards.com

The Charter Boat Center
Red Hook, Rt 38, St. Thomas.
Tel 340 775 7990.
www.charterboat.vi

St. John Concierge Service
Cruz Bay, St. John.
Tel 340 998 6975.
www.stjohnconcierge service.com

Teroro Charters
Green Cay Marina, St. Croix.
Tel 340 773 3161.

GOLF

The Buccaneer Golf Course
Rt 82, Shoys, St. Croix.
Tel 340 712 2144.
www.thebuccaneer.com

Carambola Golf Club
Rt 80, Davis Bay, St. Croix.
Tel 340 778 5638.
www.golfvi.com

Mahogany Run Golf Course
Rt 42, Mahogany Run, St. Thomas.
Tel 340 777 6250.
www.mahogany rungolf.com

The Reef Golf Course
Teague Bay, St. Croix.
Tel 340 773 8844.

FISHING

Abigail III
Sapphire Beach Marina, Rt 38, St. Thomas.
Tel 340 775 6024.
www.visportfish.com

Capt. Byron Oliver
St. John.
Tel 340 693 8339.

Caribbean Sea Adventures
59 Kings Wharf, Christiansted, St. Croix.
Tel 340 773 2628.
www.caribbeansea adventures.com

Gone Ketchin
St. Croix.
Tel 340 713 1175.
www.goneketchin.com

Marlin Prince
6100 Red Hook Quarters 2, St. Thomas.
Tel 340 693 5929.
www.marlinprince.com

KAYAKING

Arawak Expeditions
Wharfside Village, Cruz Bay, St. John.
Tel 340 693 8312.
www.arawakexp.com

Caribbean Adventure Tours
Rt 80, Salt River Marina, St. Croix.
Tel 340 778 1522.
www.stcroixkayak.com

Crabby's Watersports
Rt 107, South Coral Bay, St. John.
Tel 340 714 2415.
www.crabbys watersports.com

V.I. Ecotours
Mangrove Lagoon, Rt 32, St. Thomas.
Tel 877 845 2925.
www.viecotours.com

Virgin Kayak Tours
Rt 80, Cane Bay, St. Croix.
Tel 340 718 0071.
www.virginkayaktours. com

For hotels and restaurants on these islands see pp248–52 and pp253–5

Hiking in St. John

St. John is the US Virgin Islands' premier hiking destination and appeals to both the experienced hiker and the casual stroller. The Reef Bay guided hike is the most popular, with trips departing from the Virgin Islands National Park's Cruz Bay Visitors' Center several times

Signpost for start of trail

a week. The island also has other trails including the historic walk through the Annaberg Plantation and the Ram's Head Trail along the southern shore. A brochure available at the Visitors' Center describes nearly two dozen hikes ranging in length and difficulty.

REEF BAY TRAIL

The 2-miles (3-km) long Reef Bay Trail begins on Centerline Road, from where it heads downhill to a sandy beach. A boat picks up hikers for the return trip to Cruz Bay.

Reef Bay great house, *now in ruins, is a remnant of bygone days when plantations dotted St. John.*

Ancient petroglyphs, *possibly carved by Taínos, are found along the edges of rock pools.*

The Reef Bay sugar factory ruins *and beach mark the end of the Reef Bay Trail. The old mill has been partially restored. The grave of former owner Will Marsh is tucked back in the bushes.*

SHORTER HIKES

St. John has several fairly easy hiking trails that cut across flat terrain. Many of these, including the Salt Pond Trail and Francis Bay Trail, are no more than 1 mile (2 km) long.

The Annaberg Plantation path *leads visitors through a 518-acre (209-ha) sugar plantation. Now in ruins, the plantation's sugar mill, factory, and kitchen date back to the 18th century.*

Ram's Head Trail, *beginning at Salt Pond Bay, stretches across a rocky beach with a short climb uphill to an overlook with fantastic views of the Caribbean Sea.*

Salt Pond Trail *offers pleasant hiking through arid vegetation to the pretty Salt Pond Bay Beach. This easy hike takes less than 20 minutes to complete.*

Tortola

Tortola is a study in contrasts. Road Town, its main hub, is busy with travelers shopping and office workers heading to and from work, but a drive just five minutes out of the town brings visitors to the island's rural roots. On the north side this is even more evident – here it is common to have to wait a few minutes for a herd of goats or sheep to cross the road. A drive along the south coast offers views of sailboats bobbing in the breeze as they head up Drake's Passage.

A cruise liner at the port in Road Town

Road Town ⑯

SE coast of Tortola. 🏙 *9,400.*
🛬 🚤 🚌 ℹ️ *Akara Building, de Castro Street, 284 494 3134.*
www.*bvitourism.com* 🎫 *August Festival (Aug).*

Road Town bustles on days when cruise ships tie up, but even on days when no cruise ships are in port, the British territory's main town is active. It is the seat of BVI commerce and home to a large offshore banking industry, government offices, shops, and restaurants. Ferries from Virgin Gorda and St. Thomas in the US Virgin Islands tie up at the Road Town ferry dock, further adding to the town's traffic. It is a working town rather than just a tourist destination, visible in the even mix of locals and visitors having lunch in the many restaurants. Road Town sprawls along the Waterfront Highway. The very heart of the town runs from the waterfront inland one block to the narrow Main Street.

East of here, restaurants, shops, and banks overflow on Wickham's Cay I, that is also home to marinas. Farther east sits Wickham's Cay II, base of the huge Moorings charter operations, but with only a few shops and restaurants.

JR O'Neal Botanical Gardens National Park ⑰

Road Town, off Main Street.
Tel *284 494 3904.* ⏰ *9am–4:30pm Mon–Sat.* 🎫 **www**.*bvinational parkstrust.org*

Road Town's Botanical Gardens provide a pleasant respite from the commotion. Visitors can walk here from the heart of town, but on a hot day a taxi is a better bet. Once here, the gardens offer plenty of shade and benches for resting. The 3-acre (1-ha) gardens feature collections that represent the different plant habitats, exotic species, and a vast collection of palms. Orchids bloom in the gazebo, lilies float in the pond, and cacti grow in the tropical sun.

Sage Mountain National Park ⑱

3 miles (5 km) SW of Road Town.
Tel *284 494 3904.* 🖫
www.*bvinationalparktrust.org*

Established in 1964, the Sage Mountain National Park is BVI's first national park, founded through a donation from philanthropist Laurance S. Rockefeller. Stretching over 86 acres (35 ha), the park reaches a lofty 1,716 ft (523 m) and is the highest point on the entire Virgin Islands. It sits so high that Sage Mountain creates rain; as warm moist air rises from the east and south, it cools as it crosses the mountain, falling as rain on the park's northern side.

The park offers lovely panoramic views to hikers willing to spend some time walking its trails. It is home to many native and introduced species of trees and plants, including mahogany, white cedar, and mamey trees. Hikers on its dozen trails, including the popular Mahogany Forest Trail and the Rainforest Trail, might glimpse mountain doves and thrushes flitting among the trees. Much of the vegetation is second growth owing to clearing activity that was carried out by farmers for agricultural purposes, before the establishment of the park.

Plant along trail, Sage Mountain National Park

For hotels and restaurants on these islands see pp248–52 and pp253–5

Handicrafts on display at Apple Bay, North Shore

North Shore ⑲

Visitors can enjoy spending part of their day in Tortola driving the North Coast Road for some glorious ocean views and a glimpse into the island's local life.

The drive can be challenging in spots, with lots of twists, turns, and steep hills on the narrow roads. Those driving should remember to keep to the left and watch out for wandering livestock. The intersection of Zion Hill Road and North Coast Road, where Sebastian's on the Beach *(see pp251)* is located, is a good place to start the drive. The road west from here leads to Long Bay Beach Resort *(see p251)* where local dishes are served for lunch. Past the hotel a bumpy road snakes down to the lovely Smuggler's Cove Beach. The beach has no amenities, so it is best to carry snacks, water, sunblock, and other essentials.

Heading east, back to Sebastian's, visitors can make a stop at its beachfront restaurant *(see p255)* or spend some time on the lovely sands of **Apple Bay**. Here, just down the road, there is a gaggle of thrown-together boards that makes up Bomba's Shack, the site of legendary full moon parties and other similar events. Another particularly popular Apple

Bay Beach is the one in front of the Sugar Mill Hotel *(see p252)*. Farther ahead, visitors will reach the village of Carrot Bay, home to small restaurants and some more beaches. The trip ends in Cane Garden Bay.

Cane Garden Bay ⑳

4 miles (6 km) NW of Road Town. 🚌 🎵 *BVI Music Fest (May).* 🍴

Stretching along part of the North Coast Road, Cane Garden Bay is the destination of choice for many vacationers who wish to relax in a laid-back rural atmosphere

and walk barefoot to the beach, restaurants, and bars. Accommodations available here largely consist of small hotels and apartments. The bay provides the perfect opportunity for a swim at the white sandy beach and the casual restaurants that line the gorgeous beach make a good stop for lunch or drinks.

It is also a popular anchorage for the many boaters on week-long sails through the British Virgin Islands *(see pp244–5)*.

The beach, especially in front of the popular hotel Myett's *(see p251)*, can get very busy on cruise ship days, but once the passengers leave after a drink or two at the bar, the beach returns to its normal quiet self. In May, the annual BVI Music Fest brings out thousands of people for a weekend of fun.

Marina Cay ㉑

Off Tortola's NE coast. ⛴
***Tel** 284 494 2174.*

Home to Pusser's Marina Cay Hotel and a popular boating anchorage, the 8-acre (3-ha) Marina Cay makes an interesting day trip from Tortola. American newly-weds Robb and Rodie White set up house on the island in 1937 and lived here for three years. In his 1985 book, *Two on the Isle*, Robb White tells the story of their adventures. What is left of their home serves as part of the hotel, and guests can wander the grounds, take a dip in the ocean from the sandy beach, and enjoy the salty ambience of the bar and restaurant. Activities include strolling the nicely planted grounds and snorkeling colorful reefs sitting just off the island's white sandy beach. Those with a thirst for a bit more adventure can enjoy scuba diving from the beach or a boat.

Yachts lining the harbor at Marina Cay

Virgin Gorda and Outer Islands

With luscious white sandy beaches, Virgin Gorda and the outer islands beckon visitors who want to relax with a good book and a frosty drink in hand. Virgin Gorda has a handful of restaurants, a bit of nightlife, and some modest shopping, but the real draw is the beach and the chance to do nothing but gaze at the glorious sunrises and sunsets. It is the same with the outer islands, some of them home to just one resort and excellent sailing anchorages.

Wooden beach villas framed by palm trees, The Valley

The Valley **22**

SW coast of Virgin Gorda. 🏘 2,000.
🛬 🚢 🚌 🛈 Virgin Gorda Yacht Harbour, 284 495 5181.
www.bvitourism.com

Also called Spanish Town, The Valley on Virgin Gorda is the heart of the island's activity. Most of it is centered at Virgin Gorda Yacht Harbour, a smallish marina and the shopping area. A few restaurants are sprinkled along the main road of what is not much more than a village. The Yacht Harbour is home to Buck's Grocery where visitors can pick up essentials. The tourist office is in the same building and has maps and brochures. Ferries land at the jetty a short walk away, where visitors from the US Virgin Islands go through the routine customs checks.

The Baths **23**

S point of Virgin Gorda. **Tel** 284 494 3904. 🚌 🏊 **www**.bvinational parkstrust.org

The Baths National Park, a collection of massive granite boulders that form lovely pools, is on the must-do list for nearly every visitor to Virgin Gorda as well as parties of charter boat sailors plying these waters. Some of the boulders are 40 ft (12 m) in diameter. They were formed when molten rock seeped into existing volcanic rock layers. Erosion exposed them and they are weathered around the corners. Similar rocks are found in other areas near the Baths.

It is a bit of a walk down from the parking area but, in addition to the boulders, there are white sandy beaches and excellent snorkeling opportunities. Two restaurants and a few shops near the parking area provide lunch, drinks, and the obligatory T-shirt, as well as other souvenir items.

Driving Tour of Virgin Gorda **24**

Visitors to Virgin Gorda should rent a car for at least a day to get out and about. The 8-sq mile (21-sq km) island has one road running from 6 miles (10 km) from the Baths at the southwest end to North Sound at the northeast and a handful of side roads, so it is just about impossible to really get lost. Maps can be picked up at the tourism office at Virgin Gorda Yacht Harbour.

Farther west on Lee Road from The Valley, a side road heads off to the left to Coppermine Point, a ruin of a mine which was originally built in the 1800s by Cornish

Huge boulders dotting the crystal-clear waters of The Baths

For hotels and restaurants on these islands see pp248–52 and pp253–5

Ruins of an old copper mine in Coppermine Point, Virgin Gorda

miners. Back on Lee Road, vacationers can drive on to the Baths, the island's premier attraction. Spring Bay National Park, sitting seaside just before the Baths, sees far less people and is an ideal spot to relax for a few hours after snorkeling at the Baths. A short drive east from The Valley, an unpaved road leads to gorgeous Savannah Bay, which is great for sunbathing and swimming. Back on the main road, Gorda Peak National Park makes a good spot to stop for a hike. Lovely views abound in this hilltop area, and the BVI government has installed several viewing platforms. The drive can end at Gunn Creek, which is the jumping-off point for ferry trips to North Sound, and has a few small restaurants serving local cuisine.

Gorda Peak National Park 25

North Sound Road, Virgin Gorda. *Tel* 284 494 3904. **www.** bvinationalparkstrust.org

The Gorda Peak National Park covers 260 acres (105 ha) of land and is one of the last remaining examples of the Caribbean dry forest in the region. It is home to a couple of endangered and threatened plant species, as well as the world's smallest lizard – the Virgin Gorda gecko. Two trails lead up to the Gorda Peak, Virgin Gorda's highest point at 1,370 ft (417 m), where a lookout tower offers panoramic views of the BVI. On a clear day, it is possible to see Anegada to the north-east. A picnic table is placed under the shade of a mango tree where the two trails meet, and provides a pleasant place for lunch or snacks. During the hike uphill, the forest gets moister with increasing altitude and the vegetation changes from species that survive only in dry scrubby areas to those that thrive in slightly damp soil.

Signage, National Park Trust, BVI

RMS Rhone Marine Park 26

Off Salt Island. *Tel* 284 494 3904. **www**.bvinationalparkstrust.org

The Royal Mail Steamer *Rhone* went down in an 1867 hurricane. Today, it is the main dive destination in the British Virgin Islands. The 310-ft (95-m) vessel sits in two parts at depths ranging from 20 to 80 ft (6m to 25m). Much of the ship is intact, with parts such as the propeller, boilers, and more still identifiable. The *Rhone* is encrusted with marine growth and serves as a home to many types of fish and marine life. Dive trips depart from Tortola and other British Virgin Islands as well as St. Thomas and St. John in the US Virgin Islands. Those who wish to dive the site need a permit from the National Parks Trust.

Foxy's Bar 27

Great Bay, Jost Van Dyke *Tel* 284 495 9258. **www**.foxysbar.com

The legendary Foxy Callwood entertains at his eponymous Foxy's Bar, the number one draw on Jost Van Dyke. Day-sail and power boats as well as ferries from West End on Tortola also stop here, making it easy to reach. Visitors on a day trip can enjoy lunch and Foxy's own style of Caribbean music during the afternoon, plus a swim in the warm waters of Great Bay. The last ferry to West End leaves in the early evening, so visitors will have to sleep over or anchor in the harbor if they want to stay for dinner during the week and for barbecues on Friday and Saturday evenings.

A diver swimming through the wreck of the RMS Rhone

Outdoor Activities and Specialized Holidays

The sea is the star when it comes to activities in the British Virgin Islands. Visitors can spend time sunning at the beach, but most guests come here because they want to practise their sailing in small boats off the beach or set sail either for a day, a week, or more through the chain of small islands that make up the British Virgin Islands. At most anchorages, snorkeling over colorful reefs and wrecks beckons. Hiking in the national parks is also popular.

Boat rental sign in Cane Garden Bay, Tortola

One of the many beach bars on Tortola

BEACHES

The beaches in British Virgin Islands come in all shapes and sizes, from tiny pockets of soft sand at some small cay to the gorgeous stretch of white sand at Savannah Bay on Virgin Gorda. Many of the beaches have few facilities right on the sand and none are patrolled by lifeguards. Some do have restaurants and beach bars while others offer nothing but perfect sand and sea. If visitors prefer more amenities, a beachfront hotel is a good idea.

Every island has its share of beaches, but flat Anegada gets the prize for its talcum-powder beaches that nearly fringe the entire island.

Virgin Gorda does not lack when it comes to beaches either. In addition to Savannah Bay, the beaches in the area around the Baths offer good snorkeling spots. The island's resorts also have their share of white sandy strands.

Jost Van Dyke's beachy attitude lures folks who want to amble up to a local watering hole after having spent some time lounging at the beach.

Tortola's best beach treasures stretch along the north coast and include the ever popular Cane Garden Bay (see p239), but rough water can be a problem, particularly during the winter months when storms in the north stir up the water. When that is the case, it is a good idea to head to Beef Island, located off Tortola's eastern edge and home to the airport and the gorgeous Long Bay. The BVI Tourism website provides details (see p257).

SAILING

With numerous small islands and rocky outcrops that serve as anchorages and sit close to Tortola and Virgin Gorda, day-sails are easily accomplished. However, for those not keen on a boat with sails, plenty of motorized boats making the same trips are also available.

Tortola in particular has plenty of sail and power boats ready to depart from Road Town, West End, Nanny Cay, and other locations. If leaving from Virgin Gorda, a day trip aboard a motor boat can get people as far away as Anegada.

Some vocabulary to help pick the right sailboat – monohulls have one hull, catamarans have two, and trimarans have three. Boats with more than one hull tend to provide a more stable sail. Power boats may provide a smoother trip.

Most day-sail and motorboat trips provide lunch, snorkeling gear, and instructions on how to use it when the boat drops anchor one or more times during the day. The most popular tour operators offering day-sails are **Aristocat Charters** and **White Squall II**. For more information on boat rentals, visitors can contact **King Charters**.

Apart from day-sails, there are also week-long charters that take people on a longer tour around the islands. Some of the reputable charters are

Catamaran setting out on a cruise

Surfer at Apple Bay in Tortola

BVI Yacht Charters, The Moorings, Regency Yacht Vacations, Sunsail, Catamaran Charters, and Voyages.

OTHER ACTIVITIES

When the weather is good, the islands offers myriad watersports activities. It is possible to rent masks, snorkel and fins from hotels and watersports shops. For diving, if visitors are not certified to dive by one of the national agencies like NAUI or PADI, dive operators offer a learn-to-dive course. For a great diving experience in the islands, it is best to sign on with a charter to the wreck of the *Rhone*, near Salt Island. Main dive and snorkel operators are Blue Water Divers, Jost Van Dyke Scuba, Dive BVI and Sunchaser Scuba. Fishing boats leave from various spots around Tortola, Virgin Gorda, and Anegada. Caribbean Fly Fishing Outfitters offer guided fishing trips that include all equipment. Brisk winds blow across the islands, with Trellis Bay in Tortola a hotbed of windsurfing activity. Boards can be rented, while lessons are offered by the handful of watersports shops at Trellis Bay and other locations around the islands. The main operators include Boardsailing BVI, HiHo, and Bitter End Yacht Club.

Head inland for an easy hike at Sage Mountain National Park *(see p238)* on Tortola or Gorda Peak National Park *(see p241)* on Virgin Gorda. However, these parks do not have rangers leading guided tours. The island of Prickly Pear, in Virgin Gorda's North Sound, has a hiking trail but it takes a boat ride to get to the island. In Road Town, Tortola, the JR O'Neal Botanical Gardens National Park *(see p238)* is a relaxing place for a walk.

Hiking trail visible from Gorda Peak, Virgin Gorda

DIRECTORY

SAILING

Aristocat Charters
Soper's Hole,
Tortola.
Tel 284 499 1249.
www.aristocat
charters.com

BVI Yacht Charters
Road Town,
Tortola.
Tel 284 494 4289. www.
bviyachtcharters.com

Catamaran Charters
Village Cay Marina,
Tortola.
Tel 284 494 6661.
www.catamarans.com

King Charters
Nanny Cay Marina,
Tortola.
Tel 284 494 5820.
www.king
charters.com

The Moorings
Wickham's Cay II, Tortola.
Tel 284 494 2322.
www.moorings.com

Regency Yacht Vacations
Wickham's Cay I, Tortola.
Tel 284 495 1970.
www.regency
vacations.com

Sunsail
Wickham's Cay II,
Tortola.
Tel 284 495 4750.
www.sunsail.uk

Voyages
Tel 284 494 0740.
www.voyage
charters.com

White Squall II
Village Cay Marina,
Tortola.
Tel 284 494 2564.
www.whitesquall2.com

OTHER ACTIVITIES

Bitter End Yacht Club
North Sound,
Virgin Gorda.
Tel 284 494 2746.
www.beyc.com

Blue Water Divers
Nanny Cay and Soper's
Hole, Tortola.
Tel 284 494 2847.
www.bluewater
diversbvi.com

Boardsailing BVI
Trellis Bay, Tortola.
Tel 284 495 2447.
www.windsurfing.vi

Caribbean Fly Fishing Outfitters
Nanny Cay, Tortola.
Tel 284 494 4797.
www.caribflyfishing.com

Dive BVI
Virgin Gorda Yacht Harbor
and Leverick Bay Resort
and Marina, Virgin Gorda.
Tel 284 495 5513.
www.divebvi.com

HiHo
Trellis Bay, Tortola.
Tel 284 494 7694.
www.go-hiho.com

Jost Van Dyke Scuba
Great Harbour, Jost Van
Dyke. *Tel 284 495 0271.*
www.jostvandyke
scuba.com

Sunchaser Scuba
North Sound,
Virgin Gorda.
Tel 284 495 9638.
www.sunchaser
scuba.com

Sailing the British Virgin Islands

The British Virgin Islands is one of the premier destinations for sailing. Anchorages are just an easy sail apart, and range from deserted cays with not a single boat to busy bays known for their salty conviviality. Numerous charter companies rent bare boats, where visitors can serve as captain, or charter boats that come complete with captain and crew. Most boats are rented in Tortola, but charters to the British Virgin Islands also set sail from St. Thomas and St. John in the US Virgin Islands. Both St. Thomas and Tortola have large grocery stores with everything that sailors will need to provision their boats.

Boats at Wickhams Cay, Tortola

Cane Garden Bay *is a good anchorage on the north side of Tortola. The bay is a party spot with more than a handful of bars and restaurants perfect for whiling away a few hours and escaping from galley duties. Supplies are available at a couple of small markets situated along the main North Coast Road.*

Jost Van Dyke has several anchorages. It is mandatory to clear customs check at Great Harbour if coming from the US Virgin Islands. Vacationers can relax with a beer at Foxy's, pull up anchor, and motor around to White Bay for some peace and quiet.

West End *in Tortola is a busy marina during the day when ferries come and go. Sailors will have to clear customs here if they are coming from the US Virgin Islands and have not done so already. Travelers can take their dinghy ashore on the opposite side of the harbor for a browse around the shops.*

Marina Cay is home to Pusser's Bar and Restaurant, and the infamous painkiller rum drinks that lure sailors from far and wide. A small shop sells books, souvenirs, and more.

North Sound *has excellent sailing conditions given its location and facilities. The few restaurants, bars, and resorts cater primarily to sailors. Watersports outlets offer an entire gamut of activities.*

KEY

⚓ Anchorage

— Major road

— Minor road

0 km   5

0 miles   5

Necker Island

Mosquito Island

Prickly Pear Island

Saba Rock

Great Camanoe

West Dog

George Dog

Great Dog

The Dogs

Virgin Gorda

Scrub Island

Savannah Bay

Spanish Town

Beef Island

st End

CARIBBEAN SEA

Fallen Jerusalem Island

Round Rock

Ginger Island

Cooper Island

ter
and

The Baths *in Virgin Gorda is where nearly everyone stops to snorkel among the giant boulders. Visitors can also hike up the path to a small shopping area and have lunch at Bath and Turtle, replenish the larder at Buck's Shop, and buy souvenirs at a gift shop.*

Salt Island *has great diving opportunities, such as the RMS Rhone nearby. Cooper Island is an ideal stop for lunch for those sailing down the string of small islands that lie south of Tortola. Peter Island offers some fine dining, while Norman Island is home to several caves perfect for snorkeling.*

Choosing a Hotel

Accommodations in the US and British Virgin Islands range from bare campgrounds to posh resorts with all amenities. Both sets of islands have many family-owned properties, at or near the beach, and in the hills where a car is needed to get around. Prices vary, but better deals are available during the summer season. Some properties may shut down during the hurricane season.

PRICE CATEGORIES
The following price ranges are for a standard double room per night and are inclusive of all taxes.

$ under $100
$$ $100–$200
$$$ $200–$300
$$$$ $300–$400
$$$$$ over $400

US VIRGIN ISLANDS

Marriott Frenchman's Reef and Morning Star Beach Resort – p229
Sitting at the edge of the harbor on St. Thomas, the resort offers enough amenities for an entire vacation. A launch makes frequent trips to the downtown shopping district.

The Buccaneer Hotel – p232
The rooms of this luxurious hotel come in a variety of styles, and are all well-appointed and have lovely views of the sea.

Divi Carina Bay Resort

The Ritz-Carlton

ST. CROIX Carringtons Inn ▤ [W] $$

Off Rt 70, 56 Hermon Hill, outside Christiansted ***Tel*** *340 713 0508* ***Fax*** *340 719 0841* ***Rooms*** *5*

Owners Roger and Claudia Carrington provide stellar hospitality at this bed-and-breakfast tucked in the hills above Christiansted. Each room is different, and all are named after flowers and have good views. Breakfast is superb and served around the pool. A car is needed to get out and around. **www.carringtonsinn.com**

ST. CROIX Cottages by the Sea ⛱ ▤ 🏊 ♿ [W] $$

Rt 70 & 702, outside Frederiksted ***Tel*** *340 772 0495* ***Fax*** *340 772 0495* ***Rooms*** *21*

Guests step out their door and into the sea at the family-owned Cottages by the Sea. Modestly furnished but perfectly adequate, most units come with cooking facilities. It is the sort of place to relax in the chaise lounge with a good book since Frederiksted is on the quiet side. **www.caribbeancottages.com**

ST. CROIX Hotel on the Cay ⛱ 🍴 ▤ 🏊 [W] $$

Protestant Cay, Christiansted ***Tel*** *340 773 2035* ***Fax*** *340 773 7046* ***Rooms*** *53*

A complimentary 2-minute ferry ride across the Christiansted harbor brings guests to this hotel. Boasting the only beach in Christiansted, it is perfect for lazing on the sands or swimming, with shops and restaurants only a short walk away. Rooms are modest, but ideal for a tropical vacation. **www.hotelonthecay.com**

ST. CROIX Sandcastle on the Beach ⛱ 🍴 ▤ 🏊 [W] $$

Rt 71, outside Frederiksted ***Tel*** *340 772 1205* ***Fax*** *340 772 1757* ***Rooms*** *21*

St. Croix's only gay-oriented hotel sits right on the beach. Rooms at the Sandcastle on the Beach vary by style and price, but all are comfortable. Guests gather to socialize at the beach, the pool, and the restaurant and bar. Frederiksted, with its restaurants and bars is nearby. **www.sandcastleonthebeach.com**

ST. CROIX Villa Margarita ⛱ ▤ [W] $$

Off Rt 80, Salt River ***Tel*** *340 713 1930* ***Fax*** *340 719 3389* ***Rooms*** *3*

Villa Margarita is a home away from home. Located near remote Salt River Bay, the guesthouse units vary in size, but all have cooking facilities and gorgeous views of the windswept coast. A sandy beach is nearby. It is advisable to have a rental car at hand. **www.villamargarita.com**

ST. CROIX Carambola Beach Resort ⛱ 🍴 ▤ 🏊 ♿ [W] $$$

Off Rt 80, Davis Bay ***Tel*** *340 778 3800* ***Fax*** *340 718 1682* ***Rooms*** *157*

With a lovely beach, restaurants and bar, tennis, spa, and other amenities including golf nearby, this resort is perfect for a family vacation. The rooms are comfortable with neutral tones and pleasant views. The remote location means a car is required to venture out. **www.carambolabeach.com**

ST. CROIX Divi Carina Bay Resort ⛱ 🍴 ▤ 🏊 ♿ [W] $$$

Rt 60, Turner Hole ***Tel*** *340 773 9700* ***Fax*** *340 773 6802* ***Rooms*** *146*

Sitting by the seaside on the island's East End, the Divi Carina Bay Resort has stylish rooms with a crisp blue-toned decor, sea views, and kitchenettes. The hotel has many amenities with a focus on watersports, tennis, and swimming. Visitors can also enjoy gambling at the hotel's casino across the street *(see p255)*. **www.divicarinabay.com**

ST. CROIX Hotel Caravelle 🍴 ▤ ♿ [W] $$$

44A Queen Cross St, Christiansted ***Tel*** *340 773 0687* ***Fax*** *340 778 7004* ***Rooms*** *45*

A stay at Hotel Caravelle puts guests right on the Christiansted Boardwalk and steps from the town's restaurants, shopping, and sightseeing. Rooms are spacious with colorful bedspreads, draperies, and carpets. Many have views across the water. The hotel also provides parking. **www.hotelcaravelle.com**

Key to Symbols *see back cover flap*

ST. CROIX Palms at Pelican Cove

$$$

La Grande Princesse **Tel** 340 718 8920 **Fax** 340 718 9218 **Rooms** 40

With a lovely strand of white sand right at the doorstep, the Palms at Pelican Cove attracts vacationers who want to sun, snorkel, and swim. Facilities include tennis and yoga lessons. The staff is friendly and helpful. The hotel is only a 10-minute drive from Christiansted's boutiques and restaurants. **www.palmsatpelicancove.com**

ST. CROIX Sugar Beach Condominiums

$$$

Off Rt 74, Estate Golden Rock, outside Christiansted **Tel** 340 718 5345 **Fax** 340 718 1359 **Rooms** 46

With Christiansted's shopping, restaurants, and sightseeing just a short drive away, this family-friendly resort offers all the comforts of home right on a white sandy beach. The swimming pool is laid around an old sugar mill. A car will be needed to get out and move about. **www.sugarbeachstcroix.com**

ST. CROIX Tamarind Reef Hotel

$$$$

Off Rt 82, Green Cay **Tel** 340 773 4455 **Fax** 340 773 3989 **Rooms** 39

A sandy beach, good snorkeling, and an excellent restaurant makes Tamarind Reef Hotel a good spot to settle in. It is a casual place with a few amenities such as tennis, but the rooms are pleasant and guests will find themselves only a 10-minute drive away from Christiansted's activities. **www.tamarindreefhotel.com**

ST. CROIX Villa Greenleaf

$$$$

Island Center Road, Montpelier **Tel** 340 719 1958 **Fax** 207 221 1777 **Rooms** 6

With a sophisticated ambience and attention to every detail, a stay at this bed-and-breakfast is a delight. Rooms have four-poster beds and most come with splendid sea views. Guests like to gather around the pool when they are not out exploring. A car is included in the rates. **www.villagreenleaf.com**

ST. CROIX Villa Madeleine

$$$$$

Off Rt 82, Teague Bay **Tel** 800 533 6863 **Fax** 340 773 8989 **Rooms** 43

Sitting hillside with lovely sea views from most units and individual pools, Villa Madeleine provides a comfortable stay for those who want more than just a hotel room. Each condominium unit is individually decorated, but all have amenities such as wicker furniture, marble showers, and lots of privacy. **www.villamadeleine-stcroix.com**

ST. JOHN Cinnamon Bay Campground

$

Rt 20, Cinnamon Bay **Tel** 340 776 6330 **Fax** 340 776 6458 **Rooms** 126

A National Park service facility, Cinnamon Bay Campground is next to a lovely beach with good snorkeling. Hiking trails, ranger-led programs, a restaurant, and convenience store are nearby. Guests have a choice of cottages or tents or can bring their own tents. There are centrally located toilets and showers. **www.cinnamonbay.com**

ST. JOHN Inn at Tamarind Court

$$

Rt 10, Cruz Bay **Tel** 340 776 6378 **Fax** 340 776 6722 **Rooms** 20

For budget accommodations near the heart of Cruz Bay, the Inn at Tamarind Court is a good bet. Rooms are simple, but comfortable. Guests can walk to town, but need to take a taxi or car for the beach. The hotel's attractive courtyard features a popular restaurant and bar. **www.innattamarindcourt.com**

ST. JOHN Maho Bay Camps

$$

Off Rt 20, Maho Bay **Tel** 340 776 6226 **Fax** 340 776 6504 **Rooms** 114, plus 12 studios

Walkways connect the hillside Maho Bay Camps, which attracts guests who wish to enjoy nature in canvas tents with little comforts besides electricity, although there are a handful of basic studio rooms. There is a restaurant nearby. The toilets and cool showers are down the path. Activities offered focus on the sea. **www.maho.org**

ST. JOHN Estate Lindholm Bed-and-Breakfast

$$$

Rt 20, outside Cruz Bay **Tel** 340 776 6121 **Fax** 340 776 6141 **Rooms** 14

Perched hillside overlooking Cruz Bay, this bed-and-breakfast has attractive rooms with dark woods and crisp white accents. The views, gardens, and hospitality are all stellar. A pool provides a cooling respite, but a car or taxi is needed to sample St. John's beaches, hiking, restaurants, and shopping. **www.estatelindholm.com**

ST. JOHN Coconut Coast Villas

$$$$

Turner Bay, outside Cruz Bay **Tel** 340 693 9100 **Fax** 340 779 4157 **Rooms** 9

It takes about 10 minutes to walk to Coconut Coast Villas from Cruz Bay, which means a car is not required to dine and shop. This small condominium complex has a pool and offers good snorkeling off its rocky beach. Rooms come with full kitchens and local artwork. **www.coconutcoast.com**

ST. JOHN Estate Zootenvaal

$$$$

Rt 10, Hurricane Hole **Tel** 340 776 6321 **Rooms** 4

Peace and quiet are the hallmarks of Estate Zootenvaal. Units are both seaside and inland, but all are just steps away from a small sandy beach perfect for sunning, swimming, or snorkeling. The Estate is ideal for a family vacation. Coral Bay is just a 5-minute drive away. **www.estatezootenvaal.com**

ST. JOHN Caneel Bay Resort

$$$$$

North Shore Rd, Caneel Bay **Tel** 340 776 6111 **Fax** 340 693 8280 **Rooms** 166

This fashionable resort stretches along seven gorgeous beaches. With all amenities available, including fine dining, watersports, and tennis, many guests do not venture outside the grounds. The rooms, done in neutral tones, are very comfortable. Most are just steps from the palm-fringed beaches. **www.caneelbay.com**

ST. JOHN Gallows Point Resort $$$$$

Bay St, Cruz Bay **Tel** *340 776 6434* **Fax** *340 776 6520* **Rooms** *60*

Gallows Point Resort is an attractive condominium complex overlooking the harbor. The units are decorated in tropical brights with lots of wicker and rattan. The excellent Zozo's Ristorante *(see p253)*, above the reception area, offers close-to-home dining. Cruz Bay is nearby. **www.gallowspointresort.com**

ST. JOHN Westin Resort and Villas $$$$$

Rt 108, Great Cruz Bay **Tel** *340 693 8000* **Fax** *340 779 4985* **Rooms** *321*

A busy resort with lots of watersports, tennis, and good restaurants and bars, the Westin Resort and Villas provides varied accommodation options ranging from beachfront hotel rooms to hillside condominiums. The other beaches of Great Cruz Bay are easily accessible via car. **www.westinresortstjohn.com**

ST. THOMAS Island View Guest House $$

Scott Free Rd, Crown Mountain **Tel** *340 774 4270* **Fax** *340 774 6167* **Rooms** *12*

Budget travelers love the aptly-named Island View Guest House. The decor is a bit basic and guests will have to drive to the beaches. The nightly rate includes a Continental breakfast. All rooms come equipped with a fridge, while some have kitchenettes set in the balconies. **www.islandviewstthomas.com**

ST. THOMAS Villa Santana $$

2602 Bjerge Gade, Denmark Hill **Tel** *340 776 1311* **Rooms** *5*

The former home of exiled Mexican general, Antonio Lopez de Santa Ana, was built in the 1850s. The great house is gone, but the other buildings now serve as well-appointed guest rooms for visitors who want a location close to Charlotte Amalie. The decor varies by room, but all are comfortable. **www.villasantana.com**

ST. THOMAS Holiday Inn Windward Passage $$$

Waterfront Highway, Charlotte Amalie **Tel** *340 774 5200* **Fax** *340 774 1231* **Rooms** *150*

For a downtown Charlotte Amalie spot, the Holiday Inn St. Thomas is ideal. All rooms come with harbor or town views. While it is safe to walk to shops and restaurants during the day, it is advisable to take a taxi at night. The closest beach is a 10-minute drive. **www.windwardpassage.com**

ST. THOMAS Best Western Emerald Beach Hotel $$$$

Scott Free Rd, Lindbergh Bay **Tel** *340 777 8800* **Fax** *340 776 3426* **Rooms** *90*

With lovely white sand at the doorstep, the Best Western Emerald Beach Hotel offers well-kept accommodations with amenities including watersports and tennis. Room furnishings include travertine floors in the bathroom. The rooms are more than comfortable with balconies or patios and sea views. **www.bestwestern.com**

ST. THOMAS Bolongo Bay Beach Resort $$$$

Rt 30, Bolongo Bay **Tel** *340 775 1800* **Fax** *340 775 3208* **Rooms** *65*

Stretched out along a white sandy beach, Bolongo Bay Beach Resort offers complimentary watersports including snorkeling and kayaking. The resort's Iggies Beach Bar is a popular nightspot *(see p255)*. The decor is standard Caribbean with wicker furniture and tile floors. All rooms are beachfront. **www.bolongobay.com**

ST. THOMAS Point Pleasant Resort $$$$

Rt 38, Smith Bay **Tel** *340 775 7200* **Fax** *340 776 5694* **Rooms** *128*

The units of the Point Pleasant Resort range from smallish suites to two-bedroom villas, but all come equipped with kitchens and balconies that look out to the sea or gardens. Guests have easy access to the adjacent Pineapple Beach as well as the lovely Sugar Beach. **www.pointpleasantresort.com**

ST. THOMAS Wyndham Sugar Bay Resort and Spa $$$$

Rt 38, Smith Bay **Tel** *340 777 7100* **Fax** *340 777 7200* **Rooms** *294*

Wyndham Sugar Bay Resort and Spa comes with enough amenities to keep its guests occupied on its property. Tennis, a pool, watersports, spa services, fine and casual dining – the hotel has it all. It sits beachfront on the island's East End with sea views and balconies or patios. Children are welcome. **www.wyndham.com**

ST. THOMAS Anchorage Beach Resort $$$$$

Cowpet Bay, off Rt 322 **Tel** *340 775 6100* **Fax** *340 776 5694* **Rooms** *11*

Anchorage Beach Resort is set in the busy Cowpet Bay area. All suites are just steps from a white sandy beach, but beach proximity varies by location. Next to the St. Thomas Yacht Club, the units offer views of boats bobbing in the water. All are well-equipped with full kitchens. **www.antillesresorts.com**

ST. THOMAS The Ritz-Carlton $$$$$

Cowpet Bay, Off Rt 322 **Tel** *340 775 3333* **Fax** *340 775 4444* **Rooms** *358*

Sitting beachfront on the island's eastern end, the Ritz-Carlton provides attentive service with a gorgeous ambience. Sophisticated rooms are spacious with balconies or patios and great views. Even the spa has a great view. Plenty of watersports during the day and fine dining at night. **www.ritzcarlton.com**

ST. THOMAS Secret Harbour Beach Resort $$$$$

Off Rt 322, near Cowpet Bay **Tel** *340 775 6550* **Fax** *340 775 1501* **Rooms** *64*

With a white sandy beach and plenty of activities including tennis to keep one occupied, Secret Harbour Beach Resort is a good bet for families and couples. The suites are studio, one- and two-bedroom, and all have cooking facilities and nice views. The decor is typically tropical with colorful accents. **www.secretharbourvi.com**

Key to Symbols *see back cover flap*

BRITISH VIRGIN ISLANDS

Varied Accommodations

BVI has a range of options for staying apart from the island's several hotels and resorts. Many private houses, villas (see p257), as well as guesthouses provide ample options for a wide range of prices. Tortola, Anegada, and Jost Van Dyke also have campsites for those interested in being closer to nature. If staying in accommodations with a kitchen, it is best to stock up on groceries and other goods on Tortola, as there is limited fare available on the smaller islands.

Sugar Mill Hotel

Biras Creek Resort

ANEGADA Neptune's Treasure
$$

Bender's Bay **Tel** *284 4 95 9439* **Fax** *284 495 8060* **Rooms** *9 plus 2 cottages*

Rooms are modest, but squeaky clean at Neptune's Treasure. This family-owned guesthouse sits next to a stunning beach that stretches as far as the eye can see. The staff arranges watersports and serves up scrumptious lobster at the namesake restaurant and bar. **www.neptunestreasure.com**

ANEGADA Anegada Reef Hotel
$$$

Setting Point **Tel** *284 495 8002* **Fax** *284 495 9362* **Rooms** *20*

Sitting seaside on remote Anegada, the Anegada Reef Hotel is the sort of place visitors settle into for a few days or more to socialize with other guests, snorkel or walk the lovely stretches of white sand. The restaurant has great food. There is a bar as well. Rooms are modest but perfectly comfortable. **www.anegadareef.com**

JOST VAN DYKE Sandcastle
$$$$

White Bay **Tel** *284 495 9888* **Fax** *284 495 9999* **Rooms** *6*

Casual accommodations sit beachfront and in the garden, but both are just steps from Sandcastle's lovely white sandy beach. The allure of the place is in its laid-back character. Energetic guests can hike over to Great Harbour to eat at its handful of restaurants. **www.soggydollar.com/sandcastlehotel**

TORTOLA Fort Burt Hotel
$$

Waterfront Drive, Road Town **Tel** *284 494 2587* **Fax** *284 494 2002* **Rooms** *18*

For a stay within walking distance of downtown Road Town, it is a good idea to try this hotel. With the fort's ruins as its centerpiece, the rooms of varying sizes and styles sit hillside overlooking the harbor. Parking is tight on the narrow road snaking through the property. **www.fortburt.com**

TORTOLA Maria's Hotel by the Sea
$$

Waterfront Drive, Road Town **Tel** *284 494 2595* **Fax** *284 494 2420* **Rooms** *41*

Sitting seaside in the heart of Road Town, Maria's Hotel by the Sea provides basic but spacious rooms with colorful spreads and drapes as well as town or ocean views. The restaurants and shopping are nearby. The hotel has parking, but it can be tight during the day. **www.mariasbythesea.com**

TORTOLA Village Cay Resort and Marina
$$

Wickham's Cay 1, Road Town **Tel** *284 494 2771* **Fax** *284 494 2772* **Rooms** *22*

Village Cay Resort and Marina is set in the heart of Road Town and is a great location for visitors interested in the various boutiques and restaurants nearby. Rooms vary in size, but all have a tropical feel with rattan furniture and town or marina views. Spa services available. Parking is tight during the day. **www.igy-villagecay.com**

TORTOLA Moorings-Mariner Inn
$$$

Wickham's Cay 2, Road Town **Tel** *284 494 2333* **Fax** *284 494 1638* **Rooms** *40*

The Moorings-Mariner Inn is a good base for a Road Town vacation or if heading out on a charter boat. The rooms are spacious and comfortable and all suites are well-equipped with kitchenettes. The inn is just a quick drive away from the town's boutiques and restaurants. **www.bvimarinerinnhotel.com**

TORTOLA Myett's Garden Inn
$$$

North Coast Road, Cane Garden Bay **Tel** *284 495 9649* **Fax** *284 495 9579* **Rooms** *6*

This small hotel sits beachfront in busy Cane Garden Bay. Basic rooms, but with colorful accents. Plenty of dining options at its restaurant (see p255), which can get busy on cruise ship days, as numerous other eateries are only a short stroll away. Spa services and watersports are available. **www.myetts.com**

TORTOLA Nanny Cay Marina and Hotel
$$$

Off Waterfront Drive, Nanny Cay Marina **Tel** *284 494 2512* **Fax** *284 494 0555* **Rooms** *40*

Nanny Cay Marina and Hotel is a great spot to serve as a base when visiting Tortola. Rooms are attractive with bright colors. Guests can enjoy watching the boats sail in and out of the adjacent marina. There is a pool and tennis courts on-site. The complex has some shops and restaurants. **www.nannycay.com**

TORTOLA Fort Recovery Beachfront Villas
$$$$

Waterfront Drive, West End, The Towers **Tel** *284 495 4467* **Fax** *284 495 4036* **Rooms** *30*

A sandy beach with calm waters, great views of St. John, an old fort to explore, and comfortable rooms are the features at this villa complex. All rooms have kitchens and lots of space. The villa's staff can organize watersports activities; there is a spa, and yoga classes on the beach. **www.fortrecovery.com**

TORTOLA Long Bay Beach Resort
West End, Long Bay **Tel** *284 495 4252* **Fax** *284 495 4677* **Rooms** *157*

Tortola's biggest hotel, Long Bay Beach Resort spreads uphill from a beautiful beach. Accommodations range from beachfront hotel rooms to hillside condominiums and villas, but all are nicely decorated and overlook the sea. Guests enjoy watersports, tennis, spa, and fine dining. There is an on-site car rental. **www.longbay.com**

TORTOLA Sebastian's on the Beach
North Coast Road, Apple Bay **Tel** *284 495 4212* **Fax** *284 495 4466* **Rooms** *35*

With a sandy beach and a good restaurant *(see p255)*, this is a great spot for a Caribbean vacation. Rooms vary from basic to attractive seaside villas and comfortable beachfront hotel rooms in between. A wide range of activities such as watersports, tennis, and hiking can be organized by the staff. **www.sebastiansbvi.com**

TORTOLA Sugar Mill Hotel
North Coast Road, Apple Bay **Tel** *284 495 4355* **Fax** *284 495 4696* **Rooms** *23*

Sprawling uphill from the old sugar mill that houses its acclaimed restaurant *(see p255)*, the Sugar Mill Hotel is set right across from a narrow sandy beach. Rooms are attractive with kitchens or kitchenettes, comfortable furniture, floral accents, and sea views. A car is needed to explore more of the island. **www.sugarmillhotel.com**

TORTOLA Surfsong Villa Resort
Off Beef Island Road, Beef Island **Tel** *284 495 1864* **Fax** *284 495 0089* **Rooms** *8*

This resort is located at a remote beach near Tortola's airport. Each of the villas is different in size and style, but all are attractive. The owners are attentive and service is efficient. Guests are advised to hire a car to get out and move around. **www.surfsong.net**

VIRGIN GORDA Leverick Bay Resort
Leverick Bay Road, Leverick Bay **Tel** *284 495 7421* **Fax** *284 495 7367* **Rooms** *18*

With a small beach, a pool, tennis, restaurant *(see p255)* and bar, some shopping, and lots of watersports, this resort is a great spot for a Caribbean vacation without the glitz of a big resort. The units are modest with bright, colored accents and wicker furniture. A car is essential to tour the island. **www.leverickbay.com**

VIRGIN GORDA Saba Rock Resort
North Sound **Tel** *284 495 7711* **Fax** *284 495 7373* **Rooms** *9*

There is a complementary ferry to the tiny Saba Rock Resort. While there is not much to do but swim from the small beach and snorkel, the social scene here is usually great. Rooms vary in style, but all are clean and comfortable. Guests can also take the ferry to other nearby resorts. **www.sabarock.com**

VIRGIN GORDA Guavaberry Spring Bay
Tower Road, Spring Bay **Tel** *284 495 5227* **Fax** *284 495 5283* **Rooms** *35*

With one-, two-, and three-bedroom cottages (not all air-conditioned) near the beach and nestled in lush landscaping, Guavaberry Spring Bay is within walking distance of the Baths. The decor is modest and rooms comfortable. Spring Bay offers more peace and quiet than the Baths. **www.guavaberryspringbay.com**

VIRGIN GORDA Nail Bay Resort
Nail Bay **Tel** *284 494 8000* **Fax** *284 495 5875* **Rooms** *30*

Accommodations vary from smallish studios to villas, but all have kitchenettes. They stretch from the oceanfront to way up the hill, so a car is a necessity to get to the sandy beach. The hotel has a restaurant *(see p255)* and bar, and offers activities including tennis and several watersports. **www.nailbay.com**

VIRGIN GORDA Old Yarde Village
North Sound Rd, The Valley **Tel** *284 495 5544* **Fax** *284 495 5986* **Rooms** *34*

Old Yarde Village is located just a short drive out of The Valley. The condominium units vary in size and decor, but all have kitchens, tropical decor, splendid views, and ample space. Those located nearest to North Sound Road can be a little noisy. There are two tennis courts and a gym on-site. **www.virgingordavillage.com**

VIRGIN GORDA Mango Bay Resort
Mahoe Bay **Tel** *284 495 5672* **Fax** *284 495 5674* **Rooms** *17*

Duplex apartments at Mango Bay Resort are spacious and just right for enjoying the comforts of home with a beachfront ambience. Complimentary floats, kayaks, and snorkeling equipment give guests an alternative to sunning on the sandy beach. A car is needed to get beyond the resort. **www.mangobayresort.com**

VIRGIN GORDA Biras Creek
North Sound **Tel** *284 494 3555* **Fax** *284 494 3557* **Rooms** *31*

Reached only by the hotel's launch from Gunn Creek, Biras Creek Resort comes with every amenity and gracious staff. There are room-only and all-inclusive rates. Rooms have separate bedrooms and are decorated in neutral tones. Transportation to the restaurant, swimming beach, and spa is by bicycle. **www.biras.com**

VIRGIN GORDA Little Dix Bay
The Valley **Tel** *284 495 5555* **Fax** *284 495 5661* **Rooms** *98 plus 14 villas*

Little Dix Bay stretches out along a beach perfect for sunning and swimming. Guests enjoy watersports, tennis, spa, excellent dining *(see p255)*, and a comfortably casual ambience. Rooms are done in neutral tones with nice views. Walk to The Valley, but rent a car to explore the island. **www.littledixbay.com**

Key to Symbols *see back cover flap*

Where to Eat & Nightlife

Restaurants range from very fine dining to casual beachfront bistros, with international fast food outlets available on St. Thomas and St. Croix. Many chefs are graduates of prestigious schools, and their menu selections show off their considerable abilities. Seafood remains a popular item on the menus at many restaurants, with local lobster getting lots of kudos.

PRICE CATEGORIES
The price ranges are for a two-course meal for one, including tax and service charges and half a bottle of wine.

Ⓢ under $10
ⓈⓈ $10–15
ⓈⓈⓈ $15–25
ⓈⓈⓈⓈ $25–35
ⓈⓈⓈⓈⓈ over $35

US VIRGIN ISLANDS RESTAURANTS

Seafood in the USVI
Innovative preparations of seafood and fish are usually on the menu at hotels and upscale restaurants, but most of it is probably flown in from the US mainland. The small food stands lining the roadsides are popular with both locals and visitors. These sell freshly prepared and cooked local food, including fish caught daily on the islands.

Fish Trap Restaurant

Vie's Snack Shack

ST. CROIX Off the Wall
ⓈⓈⓈ

Rt 80, Cane Bay **Tel** *340 778 4771*

Sitting close to the sea at Cane Bay Beach, this restaurant makes for a great stop while on an island tour. Guests can experience eating alfresco in this restaurant, which is completely open to sea breezes. Serves sandwiches, pizzas, and salads for lunch and dinner. Look for music several nights a week.

ST. CROIX Restaurant Bacchus
ⓈⓈⓈⓈ

Queen Cross St, off King St, Christiansted **Tel** *340 692 9922*

Interesting fare and an extensive wine list are a hallmark at Restaurant Bacchus. Try the open-faced portobello mushroom stuffed with goat cheese, sautéed spinach, oven-roasted balsamic tomatoes, and grilled asparagus. Desserts are divine – the white-rum cake with a mango glaze is a big favorite.

ST. CROIX Savant
ⓈⓈⓈⓈ

Hospital St, Christiansted **Tel** *340 713 8666*

With an eclectic menu that blends Mexican, Thai, and Caribbean fare, Savant is a casual place with indoor and outdoor dining. It may feature chicken curry, fresh fish, or a beef dish dressed with an interesting sauce on the menu. It is a favorite with the locals, so it is advisable to make reservations to ensure a table.

ST. JOHN Skinny Legs Bar and Restaurant
ⓈⓈⓈ

Rt 10, Coral Bay **Tel** *340 779 4982*

With its boatyard ambience, despite a small menu, Skinny Legs Bars and Restaurant makes a great lunch spot on an island tour. A favorite with the locals, who stop by to catch the game of the day on the big screen TVs. The menu, both lunch and dinner, includes burgers and fish sandwiches.

ST. JOHN Vie's Snack Shack
ⓈⓈⓈ

Rt 10, Hansen Bay **Tel** *340 693 5033*

It is worth the drive to the East End to enjoy an alfresco lunch at Vie's Snack Shack by the side of the road. Vie's is famous for limeade, johnnycakes, tasty garlic chicken legs, delicious conch fritters, and for dessert – home-made fruit tart. For a small fee, Vie lets you use her lovely and quiet white sandy beach.

ST. JOHN Fish Trap Restaurant
ⓈⓈⓈⓈ

Bay and Strand Streets, Cruz Bay **Tel** *340 693 9994*

The Fish Trap Restaurant's extensive menu and casual ambience make it a good option for families. Kids can enjoy a fish sandwich, while parents usually prefer the lobster, New York strip steak, or both if they opt for the combo. The chef prepares some delicious appetizers, especially the popular conch fritters.

ST. JOHN Sweet Plantains
ⓈⓈⓈⓈ

Rt 107, Coral Bay **Tel** *340 777 4653*

Owners Rose and Prince Adams serve a range of delicious and sophisticated West Indian fare including dishes such as grouper with coconut and tomato sauce flavored with allspice. Try the sweet plantain custard for dessert. Ingredients are fresh; some grow behind the restaurant.

ST. JOHN Zozo's Ristorante
ⓈⓈⓈⓈ

Gallow's Point Resort, Cruz Bay **Tel** *340 693 9200*

Set in the Gallow's Point Resort (*see p250*) with the island's best sunset views, Zozo's Ristorante is a place to go for drinks before segueing into dinner. The food has its roots in northern Italy, but the chef adds his own touch. Serves filling dishes such as grilled pork chops with rosemary roasted potatoes.

ST. THOMAS Texas Pit Barbecue

$$

Waterfront Highway, Red Hook, Wheatley Center **Tel** *340 776 9579*

With locations around St. Thomas, this busy take-out truck sells the best barbecue ribs, chicken, and brisket on St. Thomas. Meals come with a roll and a choice of potato salad or coleslaw, all as delicious as the barbecue. Stop by Texas Pit Barbecue on the way home from the beach for an easy dinner at your condominium.

ST. THOMAS Greenhouse Restaurant and Bar

$$$$$

Waterfront Highway, Charlotte Amalie **Tel** *340 774 7998*

Head to the Greenhouse Restaurant and Bar for casual fare – burgers, salads, wraps, pasta, and chicken. This venerable St. Thomas restaurant is a good bet for lunch when on a Charlotte Amalie shopping trip. As expected, the ambience at this open-air eatery includes ample greenery. After dinner, it turns into a party place.

ST. THOMAS Herve Restaurant

$$$$$

Government Hill, Charlotte Amalie **Tel** *340 777 9703*

The stellar view matches the food at Herve, where the chef conjures up a wide variety of dishes. Many have a French flair, but the menu also features Herve's take on upscale Caribbean cuisine. The conch fritters with mango chutney are especially tasty and the fresh Caribbean lobster is always a treat.

ST. THOMAS Randy's Bistro

$$$$$

Al Cohen's Plaza, Weymouth Rhymer Highway **Tel** *340 775 5001*

Situated in a busy shopping center, Randy's Bistro is a local favorite. The sandwiches are generous and dinners include an ever-changing array of specials including the pasta of the day. If only passing by, visitors can pick up something to take out from the counter at the back of the restaurant.

ST. THOMAS Virgilio's

$$$$$

Off Main Street, Charlotte Amalie **Tel** *340 776 4920*

With a northern Italian menu featuring dishes such as home-made pasta, Virgilio's serves up some delightful fare. It is popular with the island's celebrities who enjoy the sophisticated ambience and personal attention, and it offers shoppers an air-conditioned break from Charlotte Amalie's busy streets.

BRITISH VIRGIN ISLANDS RESTAURANTS

Eating in the BVI

A wide range of options including simple restaurants, casual family eateries, and candle-lit dining spots fills out the BVI's dining choice. Seafood, especially locally caught lobster, remains a favorite. Service can be a little slow so guests should be prepared to spend a few hours at dinner. Reservations are usually necessary at the more remote spots.

Foxy's Tamarind Restaurant

Sugar Mill Restaurant

ANEGADA Cow Wreck Bar and Grill

$$$$$

Lower Cow Wreck Beach **Tel** *284 495 8047*

Dine with your feet practically in the sand at the Cow Wreck Bar and Grill. The conch fritters are legendary, but the restaurant also dishes up delightful fresh-caught Anegada lobster and fish as well as grilled steak, chicken, and ribs. Guests can enjoy themselves at the beach after dinner at this casual place. Live music on some nights.

JOST VAN DYKE Foxy's Tamarind Restaurant

$$$$$

Great Harbour **Tel** *284 495 9258*

While the open-air Foxy's Tamarind Restaurant made its name as a bar *(see p241)*, it is also a good restaurant with the specialty being freshly caught lobster. Come early to hear the legendary Foxy Callwood sing. The famed barbecue featuring chicken, ribs, and mahimahi is served on Friday and Saturday.

TORTOLA Roti Palace

$$$

Main Street, Road Town **Tel** *284 494 4196*

Jean Leonard's Roti Palace sports an unassuming and simple decor. It is well-known around the region for preparing some of the best roti, an Indian flatbread, filled with curried chicken, beef, conch, goat, or vegetables, and served along with potatoes and onions.

TORTOLA Capriccio di Mare

$$$$

Waterfront Drive, Road Town **Tel** *284 494 5369*

With its roots in Italy, the open-air Capriccio di Mare is a good breakfast or lunch stop when in Road Town (although it gets very busy during lunch). Try a sandwich on freshly baked bread or tomato and mozzarella pizza. The dinner menu features some pasta favorites.

TORTOLA Le Cabanon

$$$$$

Waterfront Drive, Road Town **Tel** *284 494 8660*

Open to the breeze, Le Cabanon is an alfresco oasis in busy Road Town. The fare has a decidedly French influence, with a traditional onion soup and grilled tuna with *foie gras* on the menu. This restaurant attracts a crowd of local office workers for lunch, so it tends to get busy.

Key to Symbols *see back cover flap*

TORTOLA Mountain View $$$$$

Sage Mountain **Tel** 284 495 9536

The appropriately named Mountain View restaurant sits just outside the entrance to Sage Mountain National Park. It is a bit out of the way, but a good lunch stop if touring. The grilled mahimahi in lime-onion sauce is delicious, as are the beef and chicken dishes.

TORTOLA Myett's Garden and Grille $$$$$

North Coast Road, Cane Garden Bay **Tel** 284 495 9649

Popular with cruise ship passengers, this seaside restaurant is part of the Myett's hotel *(see p251)* and is known for its delicious fare. The conch chowder is a house specialty, but guests will have a choice of seafood, beef, and chicken dishes at both lunch and dinner. Live entertainment some nights.

TORTOLA Sebastian's Seaside Grille $$$$$

North Coast Road, Apple Bay **Tel** 284 495 4212

Sitting seaside, Sebastian's Seaside Grille is part of its namesake hotel *(see p252)*. It serves delicious seafood and good beef and chicken. The Caribbean lobster comes fresh in its shell. Guests can finish with the popular rum coffee. It is a good lunch or breakfast stop, when touring the North Coast Road.

TORTOLA Sugar Mill Restaurant $$$$$

North Coast Road, Apple Bay **Tel** 284 495 4355

With a location inside an old sugar mill *(see p252)*, the aptly-named Sugar Mill Restaurant serves candlelit fine dining with a menu that changes daily. The owners are food writers Jeff and Jinx Morgan, and the food reflects this. Try the pan-roasted duck breast with Asian coleslaw and soba noodles.

VIRGIN GORDA The Pavilion Restaurant and Bar $$$$$

The Valley **Tel** 284 495 5555

Set in the Little Dix Bay Resort *(see p252)*, guests dine alfresco by candlelight with attentive staff bringing scrumptious dishes like a pan-seared red snapper served over linguine. The Monday night buffet has an extensive array ranging from oysters on the half shell and carved roast beef to delicious desserts.

VIRGIN GORDA The Restaurant at Leverick Bay $$$$$

Leverick Bay Resort, Leverick Bay **Tel** 284 495 7154

Located at a busy little marina and shopping area, the restaurant at Leverick Bay Resort *(see p252)* is a good bet if touring or staying in the area. The restaurant downstairs serves sandwiches, burgers, and pizzas day and night, while upstairs features finer dining with steaks and fish being the specialty.

VIRGIN GORDA Sugarcane $$$$$

Nail Bay Resort, Nail Bay Road **Tel** 284 494 8000

With an alfresco ambience, this Nail Bay Resort *(see p252)* restaurant serves basic fare such as burgers and chicken sandwiches for lunch and the catch of the day for dinner. Try the popular Rasta veggie burger or a roti sandwich filled with curried chicken, fish, or beef. Several innovative preparations of fresh seafood are served.

VIRGIN GORDA Top of the Baths $$$$$

The Baths **Tel** 284 495 5497

With gorgeous views over the sea, the Top of the Baths restaurant is a great spot for breakfast, lunch, or dinner on the way to or from the Baths. Lunch runs to fish and chips as well as sandwiches, but at dinner, fresh seafood reigns. Desserts like mango cheesecake are delicious.

BARS AND CLUBS

It is possible to party hard at the clubs across the US and British Virgin Islands. Ask at the hotels which club has the most popular band playing. Some of the bars are known for their happy hours when drinks come at a discounted rate. Others host performances by well-known reggae artistes and local musicians. On the third Friday of every month, local artistes perform Sunset Jazz on the Frederiksted waterfront with many people turning up for this free 2-hour entertainment.

Duffy's Love Shack

RECOMMENDED PLACES TO GO

The Bath and Turtle
Spanish town, Virgin Gorda. (Live music two nights a week.)

Divi Carina Bay Casino
Christiansted, St. Croix. (Island's only casino, music on the weekends.)

Duffy's Love Shack
Red Hook Plaza, St. Thomas. (Located in a parking lot.)

Epernay Bistro
Frenchtown, St. Thomas. (Popular with local celebrities.)

Fred's Bar and Restaurant
Cruz Bay, St. John. (Live music a couple of nights every week.)

Iggies Beach Bar & Grill
Bolongo Bay, St. Thomas. (Karaoke, live bands on weekends.)

Myett's
Cane Garden Bay, Tortola. (Local bands play nightly during the winter.)

Quito's Gazebo
North Coast Road, Tortola. (Owner Quito Rymer sings.)

Woody's Seafood Saloon
Cruz Bay, St. John. (Happy hours during late afternoon.)

Practical Information

The tourist infrastructure across the US and British Virgin Islands works fairly well. The islands are quite small, and traveling from one end to the other on St. Croix, the largest island, takes under an hour. That said, other than a highway on St. Croix, roads are narrow and winding. Drivers often stop to chat with passersby and so one needs to be patient while driving. Inter-island ferries and planes connect the islands.

WHEN TO GO

The Virgin Islands generally have good weather throughout the year. The hurricane season runs from June to November, reaching its peak in September. Rates tend to be low during this season, but some hotels may be closed in August and September.

GETTING THERE

Vistors can fly directly from the US mainland to St. Croix and St. Thomas, but will have to change planes in San Juan, Puerto Rico, for Tortola and Virgin Gorda destinations. Flights are offered by **American Airlines**, **Delta**, **Northwest Airlines**, **Spirit Airlines**, **United Airlines**, **US Airways**, **Air Sunshine**, **LIAT**, and **Seaborne Airlines**. It is also possible to reach St. John, St. Thomas, Jost Van Dyke, Anegada, Tortola, and Virgin Gorda by ferry.

DOCUMENTATION

Citizens of USA do not need a passport to visit the US Virgin Islands, though one is required for all visitors to the British Virgin Islands. More details regarding visa and passport regulations can be obtained from **US Department of State** and the tourism websites.

VISITOR INFORMATION

Visitors' centers provide information, brochures, and maps. Opening hours are usually 9am–5pm. More information on where to stay, restaurants, activities, and more can be obtained from the various **USVI Tourism** and **BVI Tourism** offices or their websites.

HEALTH AND SECURITY

Hospitals are located on the bigger islands including **Juan F. Luis Hospital**, **Myrah Keating Smith Community Health Center**, **Pebbles Hospital**, **Roy L. Schneider Hospital**, **Virgin Gorda Government Health Clinic**. The British Virgin Islands outer islands have their own health clinics.

Use normal precautions to ensure your safety. Avoid dark alleys and deserted beaches.

BANKING AND CURRENCY

Both the US and British Virgin Islands use American currency. Banks are located on St. John, St. Thomas, St. Croix, Tortola, and Virgin Gorda and the **Virgin Islands Bankers Association** website has information about some US Virgin Islands banks. All banks have ATMs, while independent ATMs are found in bars and restaurants. Most hotels, restaurants, and other tourist facilities accept credit cards.

Local phone booth in Tortola

COMMUNICATIONS

From the US Virgin Islands to the US mainland, calls are inexpensive, but calling the US mainland from the British Virgin Islands is considered an international call. The US-based carrier **AT&T** has the most cell coverage across the US Virgin Islands. In the British Virgin Islands, it can be accessed from the southeast coast of Tortola and near the ferry dock on Virgin Gorda. Phone cards are available at pharmacies and stores. Some hotels offer Internet access and major towns have cybercafés.

TRANSPORT

Renting a car is the best way to get around on the Virgin Islands. Car rental agencies have booths at airports and at ferry terminals. Driving is on the left. There are a number of global rental agencies such as **AVIS** and **Hertz** as well as local companies that operate in St. Croix, St. Thomas, Tortola, and Virgin Gorda. A valid driver's license is needed to rent a car on the Virgin Islands. It is advisable to make prior reservations during the high season. Rates are high, particularly on the smaller islands. Fuel is also more expensive than on the US mainland.

Taxis meet arriving planes and ferries and are stationed at major hotels. There is a bus service on the main US Virgin Islands, but none on the British Virgin Islands.

The Great Harbour ferry terminal and docks, Jost Van Dyke

SHOPPING

Duty-free shops in Charlotte Amalie in St. Thomas sell jewelry, spices, and local crafts. British Virgin Islands also has a few stores selling a variety of goods. Store timings are typically 9am–5pm, but shops tend to open till late when cruise ships are in port.

Market sign, Spanish Town in Virgin Gorda

LANGUAGE

English is the official language spoken on the Virgin Islands.

ELECTRICITY

The electrical system operates on 110 volts and 120 volts in the British Virgin Islands and US Virgin Islands respectively.

TIME

The Virgin Islands are on Atlantic Standard Time, 1 hour ahead of the Eastern Standard Time in the US and 4 hours behind Greenwich Mean Time. The islands do not observe daylight savings.

GETTING MARRIED

In the British Virgin Islands, couples must apply for a marriage license in person at the **Attorney General's Office**. Once ready, it also needs to be collected in person. In the US Virgin Islands, apply for a license at the **Superior Court** offices on St. Thomas and St. Croix. Here, applications need not be made in person, but

the people concerned need to pick the license up themseves. Wedding planners such as **Anne Marie Weddings** or **Weddings the Island Way** help couples through the legalities, and organize the ceremony.

VILLAS

Many people visiting the Virgin Islands stay in vacation villas. The villas range from small one-bedroom places to houses that are quite impressive. St. John alone has at least 400 villas available through **Catered To Vacation Homes**, **Vacation Vistas**, **Caribbean Villas**, and **Island Getaways** to name a few.

Other reputed rental agencies are **Island Villas**, **Smith's Gore**, **McLaughlin Anderson**, **Vacation St. Croix**, **Areana Villas**, and **Virgin Gorda Villa Rentals**.

DIRECTORY

Exploring Anguilla

A small but beguiling British Overseas
Territory, Anguilla is fairly flat and covered in
dry vegetation. Its coral base, however, gives
the island superb bright white sand and truly
spectacular blue sea dotted with coral reefs
and tiny cays. The island is overwhelmingly
modern in its appearance and has luxurious
accommodations with some of the most
impressive villas and resorts in the Caribbean,
second only to St. Barthélemy.

Prickly Pear Cays

The semicircular beach at Sandy Ground

Sandy Ground
A long, curved beach
lined with cliffs and a
rum factory are the high-
lights of Sandy Ground.

Black
Lime
Flat Cap

Katouche
Benzies Bay

Sandy
Island

Road Point   *Ro*
                       Po
SANDY ❷
GROUND   ❹
Long Bay   *South*
         ❸   *Village*
Meads Bay ② *Long Bay*
         Meads Bay *Village*   *Blowing*
Barnes Bay *Pond* *Rendezvous Bay* *Village*
West End ①   ⑨ *Salt Pond*
   Bay   *Cove*   *Rendezvous*
          Pond   *Bay*
WEST END ❸ ⑩   *Pel*
       West End *Cove*   *Bay*
Lower West *Salt Pond* *Bay* *Blowing*
End Point ⑫   ⑪ *Cap Juluca* *Point* *St. Marti*
         Shoal Bay *Maunday's*   *Sint Maa*
          (West)   *Bay*
   Anguillita *Blowing*
     Island   *Rock*

SIGHTS AT A GLANCE

SEE ALSO

• **Where to Stay** pp264–5

• **Where to Eat & Nightlife**
  pp266–7

For additional map symbols *see back flap*

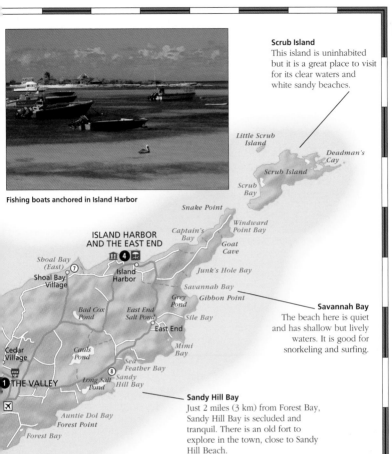

Fishing boats anchored in Island Harbor

Scrub Island
This island is uninhabited but it is a great place to visit for its clear waters and white sandy beaches.

Little Scrub Island

Deadman's Cay

Scrub Island

Scrub Bay

Snake Point

Windward Point Bay

Captain's Bay

ISLAND HARBOR AND THE EAST END

Goat Cave

Shoal Bay (East) ⑦

Shoal Bay Village

Island Harbor

Junk's Hole Bay

Savannah Bay

Bad Cox Pond

East End Salt Pond

Grey Pond

Gibbon Point

Savannah Bay
The beach here is quiet and has shallow but lively waters. It is good for snorkeling and surfing.

Sile Bay

East End

Cedar Village

Cauls Pond

Mimi Bay

Sea Feather Bay

⑧

THE VALLEY ❶

Long Salt Pond

Sandy Hill Bay

Auntie Dol Bay

Forest Point

Forest Bay

e Bay

Sandy Hill Bay
Just 2 miles (3 km) from Forest Bay, Sandy Hill Bay is secluded and tranquil. There is an old fort to explore in the town, close to Sandy Hill Beach.

0 km   3

0 miles   3

KEY
— Major road

═ Minor road

– – Tracks

- - - Ferry route

St. Gerard's Roman Catholic Church, The Valley

GETTING AROUND
Close to the island's capital, The Valley, is the small airport. There is no public transport in Anguilla and so the easiest way to get around the island is by taxi or a hired car. These can be ordered through the hotel front desk. Island tours are also possible and take just a couple of hours.

Wallblake House, one of the oldest buildings on the island

The Valley ❶

Center of Anguilla. 🏠 *1,200.* ✈️
🚗 ℹ️ *Anguilla Tourist Board,
Coronation Av., 8am–5pm Mon–Sat,
264 497 2759.* 🛒 *People's Market
(Mon–Sat).* 🎭 *Anguilla Summer
Festival (Aug).* **www**.anguilla-
vacation.com

The capital of Anguilla, The
Valley is so small it barely
seems like a town. Along
the broad Queen Elizabeth
Avenue, there are a few
civic buildings, including the
government offices, the post
office, the telecommuni-
cations office, and a couple
of shopping malls. At the foot
of the street is the open-sided
People's Market, where fruit
and vegetables are sold.

The oldest section of the
town is Coronation Avenue,
which runs north past the
Anguilla Tourist Board and up
the hill towards Crocus Bay.
A gentle climb up the hill
has a handful of the town's
original stone buildings,
including the Warden's Place,
a former sugar plantation
greathouse, which has an
excellent bakery.

Along Queen Elizabeth
Avenue, towards the airport,
is the brightly decorated St.
Gerard's Catholic Church with
its three pebble-dashed arches.
The adjoining building,
Wallblake House, is one of
the oldest buildings in
Anguilla. Built in 1787, this
old plantation house was
restored recently. It has a
stone foundation and a clap-

board upper set behind a
picket fence. The kitchens,
stables, and workers' quarters
are all intact. The house was
donated to a Catholic church
in 1959 but proved too small
to hold services.

Wallblake House
Wallblake Road. **Tel** *264 497 6613.*
🕐 *10am–2pm Mon, Wed, Fri.*
www.wallblake.ai/history.html

Sandy Ground ❷

2 miles (3 km) W of The Valley. 🚗

Road Bay is Anguilla's deep-
water port, but the sand still is
as good as some of the best
beaches on the other islands.
Set in a cliff-bound bay, the
west-facing harbor and its
small settlement, Sandy
Ground, are well protected.
The long stretch of sand is
magnificent, backed by beachfront restaurants and bars,

houses, and the pier. Offshore,
fishing and pleasure boats can
be seen anchored in the bay.
This is the home of Anguilla
sailing. Around the lagoon,
which was once used for the
cultivation of salt by evapora-
tion, the low mud walls that
sectioned the solar pans can
still be seen. Salt was once a
thriving Anguillan industry and
a major export until the 1980s.
On Thursday mornings you
can tour the **Old Salt Factory
and Pumphouse** in Sandy
Ground village, courtesy of
the splendidly named Sir
Emile Gumbs. A small
donation is appreciated.

🔩 **Old Salt Factory and
Pumphouse**
Sandy Ground. **Tel** *264 497 711.*
📷 *by appointment, 10am Thu.*

West End ❸

8 miles (13 km) W of The Valley. 🚗

All of Anguilla is rimmed with
excellent sand, but the West
End has the greatest concentration of beaches, and conse-
quently hotels. The West End
is fed by a central road along
the spine of the island, lined
with shops, some art galleries,
and mini-markets. An
interesting place to stop by
on the main road in West End
is **Cheddie's Carving Studio**,
where Cheddie, a local artist,
sculpts works of art from
driftwood. On the north side,
Meads Bay and Barnes Bay
are two fantastic beaches.

While Anguilla has little
visible architectural tradition
of its own, in the past 20

Tasting and souvenir shop at Pyrat Rum Factory, Sandy Ground

The modern-looking Covecastles resort on the beach at Shoal Bay, West End

years, the island has seen some extraordinary buildings in some of its villas and hotels. The most original and striking are the ultra modern Covecastles *(see p265)* on Shoal Bay (West), near the western tip of the island. Designed by architect Myron Goldfinger, these villas resemble storm-swept white faces buried to their necks in the sand, staring southwards to St. Martin.

Next door at Altamer *(see p265)*, Goldfinger has developed his distinctive white concrete design further, with triangular roofs that reflect the sails of Anguillian yachts. Meanwhile, Temenos *(see p264)* has introduced a stylish, almost geometrical theme, with clean-lined columns, cubes and crow-stepped walls, also in white concrete. Lastly, Cap Juluca *(see p264)* features 18 villas standing in a line in the stupendous Maunday's Bay, a compendium of Moorish arches and domes all dressed in white, standing stark against the spectacular blues of the sea and sky. The villas are the most alluring place to stay – more than anywhere else in the Caribbean.

Cheddie's Carving Studio
The Cove. **Tel** 264 497 6027.
⬜ *10am–6pm, Mon–Sat.*
www.cheddieonline.com

Island Harbor and the East End ❹

6 miles (10 km) E of The Valley. 🚗

The East End of the island has a slightly stronger Anguillian feel than the West End, with local houses, churches, and schools scattered in small settlements.

Two roads encircle the East End, starting at The Valley and meeting again at the only other town of any size, Island Harbor. The north road leads via Shoal Bay (East), the liveliest beach on the island and one which is ideal for independent travelers. The south road passes through occasional settlements and comes to East End. Here, opposite the East End Lagoon, seasonal home to some of Anguilla's birds, visitors will find the **Heritage Collection Museum**. The museum has an excellent, if eccentric, collection of artifacts illustrating Anguillian natural life and history through geology, Amerindian, and colonial times to recent days. Displays also include pottery, coins, old gramophone players, and plenty of photographs. A little farther ahead is Island Harbor, a fishing community, where brightly colored boats bob at anchor out in the bay. The Anguilla National Trust *(see p263)* arranges hikes to some of the island's few archaeological sites in this area. Beyond the settlement, towards the end of the island, are some remote beaches, including Captain's Bay and Savannah Bay.

🏛 Heritage Collection Museum
Liberty Road, East End. **Tel** 264 497 4092. ⬜ 10am–5pm Mon–Sat. 📷 ♿

An aerial view of Shoal Bay (West)

THE HISTORY OF ANGUILLA

Anguilla's early history is mostly clouded in mystery and legend. It is mainly a story of tenuous settlements and piracy. Originally called Malliouhana, which supposedly means sea serpent, it later took its current name from Spanish colonists, perhaps after its long, thin shape (Anguilla means "eel" in Spanish). It was never a successful plantation island and the slaves were encouraged to look after themselves by growing their own crops. Eventually the islanders took to traveling and trading, and as a result their descendants are scattered around the Caribbean. There is a large community of Anguillians in the Dominican Republic, some of whom have returned because of the island's recent development.

Brightly painted boats anchored in the bay at Island Harbor

Outdoor Activities and Specialized Holidays

Most of the activities in Anguilla are centered around the sea and its superb beaches, and the island promotes various watersports, including snorkeling, scuba diving, and sailing. There are relatively fewer activities on land, but hiking, biking, and horse-riding are popular pastimes. There are golf courses, while many of the hotels have spas and tennis courts.

Villa overlooking the stunning blue waters of the Atlantic Ocean, Shoal Bay

BEACHES

With powder-soft, bright, fluorescent white sand that sparkles at night in some places, the beaches in Anguilla are some of the finest in the Caribbean. There are lots of undeveloped stretches but not much natural shade, though hotels and beach bars have parasols and covered bars.

The most popular beach is Shoal Bay (East) which is liveliest on Sundays. It has several beach bars, an excellent snorkeling reef, and watersports operators. Sandy Ground, too, comes alive on Sundays with its string of bars and activities. Other beaches with great sand and easy access include Meads Bay, Barnes Bay, and Cove Bay. Among more secluded beaches are Little Bay, Captain's Bay, and the offshore Sandy Island and Prickly Pear Cays.

Anguilla's beach bars are among its finest features. They vary from classic West Indian shacks to sophisticated restaurants on the sand, and make an ideal base for the day (or a day trip to the offshore islands). Shoal Bay (East) is home to well-known

bars and restaurants such as Uncle Ernie's, Madeariman Reef, Elodia's, and Gwen's Reggae Grill. Sandy Ground is the setting for the popular bar, Johnno's *(see p267)*.

Elsewhere, classic West Indian bars are set on endless stretches of sand. Smokey's is another favorite on Cove Bay. The Dune Preserve located on Rendezvous Bay is an institution in itself. The classy Trattoria Tramonte on Shoal Bay (West) offers great Italian cuisine and Côté Mer in Island Harbor has an impressive menu featuring French fusion cuisine.

Johnno's brightly colored shack, Sandy Ground

SAILING

A sailing trip often promises to be the most memorable day of a Caribbean holiday and Anguilla has something unique to offer in this respect. Sailboats and motorboats sail regularly to the offshore islands, Sandy Island and Prickly Pear Cays, which are not much more than sandbars with a few palm trees and an excellent beach. Lunch, typically lobster and salad, is included in the trip, which can be arranged through the concerned hotel or through concessionaires such as **Shoal Bay Scuba**, **Sandy Island Enterprises**, or the independent catamaran, **Chocolat Sail**. For others who do not wish to spend a full day sailing, an interesting variation is the popular **Gorgeous Scilly Cay**, set on a tiny island just offshore in Island Harbor. Operators also organize glass-bottom boat trips. St. Martin/ Sint Maarten *(see pp270–85)*, which is popular for shopping, is just a 20-minutes ferry ride south of Blowing Point. The island, part French and part Dutch, is ideal for a day trip from Anguilla. The last ferry returns to Anguilla at 7pm, but water taxis are also available.

DEEP-SEA FISHING

Deep-sea fishing is a popular activity off Anguilla. Boats head off to the deep water beyond the smaller islands to the north and northeast. Here they trawl for wahoo, sailfish, and tuna among others. **Gotcha Sea Tours** is among the known fishing charters on the island. Deepsea fishing is also available through Shoal Bay Scuba and Sandy Island Enterprises.

WATERSPORTS

Anguilla offers reasonable opportunities for great watersports off some of its alluring beaches. Crocus Bay is well protected and ideal for watersports. Many of the hotels have some equipment including snorkeling gear, kayaks, surf boards, and small sailing

For hotels and restaurants on this island see pp264–5 and pp266–7

boats. Visitors who wish to set out on their own have the option of hiring equipment at Shoal Bay, either at Shoal Bay Scuba or at **Anguillan Divers**.

SCUBA DIVING

The clear water and excellent reefs make scuba diving in Anguilla worthwhile. With little freshwater run-off, the island has good corals, reef fish, and the occasional larger fish. But the main draws are the five wrecks that were intentionally sunk to provide remarkable dive sites, some of which are penetrable. Diving trips are arranged by operators such as Anguillian Divers and Shoal Bay Scuba.

SNORKELING

The word "shoal" means reef and considering that there are two Shoal Bays on the island, it might be expected that snorkeling in Anguilla would be good. The best reefs are in Shoal Bay (East), where there is a marked snorkeling trail, and Little Bay, a small cove backed by cliffs on the north shore, near The Valley. Road Bay, Maunday's Bay, and Barnes Bay also have excellent snorkeling. Equipment is available on most of the popular beaches.

HIKING

There are some unexpectedly remote areas around Anguilla's eastern end, which can be explored on foot. The **Anguilla National Trust** organizes a walk around Island Harbor that includes archaeological sites.

HORSE-RIDING AND BIKING

Horseback rides through the countryside and on the resplendent beaches are available through **Seaside Stables**. The land is relatively flat and therefore mountain biking is another great way to get acquainted with Anguilla's interior. Biking equipment can be hired from outlets such as **Exotic Plus**.

Golfer playing at the sprawling golf course, Temenos Golf Club

GOLF

The 18-hole, par 72 Temenos Golf Club was designed by famous golf course designer Greg Norman. The first golf course to be built in Anguilla, it was opened in Merrywing in 2006. Stretching for 4 miles (6 km), it has lush green gardens, flowing streams and sweeping views of the Caribbean Sea and nearby St. Martin/Sint Maarten.

SPAS

There are two excellent purpose-built spas attached to the Malliouhana Hotel and the Cuisinart Resort and Spa *(see p265)*. The Malliouhana Spa stands just above Meads Bay and has three treatment rooms, including a "his and hers" suite, and a gym. The Venus Spa at Cuisinart Resort has been redeveloped to include a hydrotherapy room and a well-equipped gym.

Divers set to explore the thriving marine life off Sandy Ground

DIRECTORY

SAILING

Chocolat Sail
Sandy Ground. *Tel* 264 497 3394.

Gorgeous Scilly Cay
Tel 264 497 5123.

Sandy Island Enterprises
Sandy Ground. *Tel* 264 476 6534.

Shoal Bay Scuba
Shoal Bay (East). *Tel* 264 235 1482. **www**.shoalbayscuba.com

DEEP-SEA FISHING

Gotcha Sea Tours
Tel 264 235 7902. **www**.gotcha-garfields-sea-tours-anguilla.com

WATERSPORTS

Anguillian Divers
Meads Bay. *Tel* 264 235 7742. **www**.anguilliandivers.com

HIKING

Anguilla National Trust
Albert Lake Drive, The Valley. *Tel* 264 497 5297. **www**.axanationaltrust.org

HORSE-RIDING AND BIKING

Exotic Plus
The Cove. *Tel* 264 497 8528.

Seaside Stables
Tel 264 235 3667. **www**. seaside-stables-anguilla.com

Choosing a Hotel

Anguilla has some excellent luxury hotels, as well as a few self-catered apartments and guesthouses for those who prefer being independent. Tour operators have ties with the main hotels and offer a reduced price on specialized packages. All independent travelers' hotel bills are supplemented by a 10 percent government room tax and by a 10 percent service charge.

PRICE CATEGORIES
The following price ranges are for a standard double room and taxes per night during the high season.

$ under $100
$$ $100–$200
$$$ $200–$300
$$$$ $300–$400
$$$$$ over $400

ANGUILLA

Private Villas
There are several villa rental agents that offer full service including reservations and providing service or private chefs. In an island that values privacy, "villa resorts" give guests their own space, often with staff and facilities such as a central dining room and beach service. Most villas are rented out for a minimum of three days to a week and prices reflect weekly rental.

Carimar Beach Club

Cuisinart Resort and Spa

BARNES BAY Cerulean Villa $$$$$

Barnes Bay **Tel** *264 497 8840* **Fax** *264 497 8841* **Rooms** *7*

The original Anguillian supervilla – a stunning modern design by architect Deborah Berke. Seven bedrooms in luxurious style are centered around a pool overlooking the soft sands of Barnes Bay. Spa services, fitness center, and private tennis courts are available. The staff includes a private chef. **www.cerulean-villa.com**

BARNES BAY Viceroy Resorts and Residences Anguilla $$$$$

Meads Bay **Tel** *264 497 7000* **Fax** *264 497 7001* **Rooms** *172*

A complete and stylish resort of "residences" – suites, town homes, and villas with private pools – set on the point between and on the truly spectacular sands of Meads Bay and Barnes Bay. Excellent facilities with fine dining, spa village, children's center, elegant beach clubs, and watersports. **www.viceroyhotelsandresorts.com/anguilla**

COVE BAY Paradise Cove Resort $$$$

PO Box 135, The Cove **Tel** *264 497 6603* **Fax** *264 497 6927* **Rooms** *29*

This modern, largely business-oriented hotel is set slightly inland on Cove Bay. The plush suites, well equipped with full kitchens, and ranging from studios to penthouses, stand in gardens around a central pool, deck, and bar. There are conference rooms, a business center, spa, and a golf course nearby. **www. paradise.ai**

CROCUS HILL Brooklands Island View Apartments $$

Crocus Hill, The Valley **Tel** *264 497 5078* **Fax** *264 497 7191* **Rooms** *3*

The three-bedroom apartments are set in a large impressive building with an amazing setting and stunning view over Crocus Bay and beach. Relatively simple, they are modern and spacious. The full kitchens and living rooms are ideal for families or visitors traveling in a group. **www.brooklandsislandview.com**

CROCUS HILL Lloyd's $$

PO Box 52, The Valley **Tel** *264 497 2351* **Fax** *264 497 3028* **Rooms** *9*

An authentic West Indian guesthouse, Lloyd's is located just above the Crocus Bay Beach. It has just nine rooms set around a traditional Caribbean home that has been restyled to suit the tastes of international travelers. Guests will find it welcoming and comfortable. **www.lloyds.ai**

LONG BAY Temenos $$$$$

Merrywing **Tel** *264 498 9000* **Fax** *264 498 9020* **Rooms** *3 villas*

Temenos means sanctuary in Greek. This upscale villa resort combines the best of Anguilla's geometrical architecture and Greek influences. The four-bedroom villas are spacious, stylish, and sit above the fantastic sand of Long Bay. It has an excellent restaurant (*see p266*). **www.temenosvillas.com**

MAUNDAY'S BAY Cap Juluca $$$$$

PO Box 240, Maunday's Bay **Tel** *264 497 6666* **Fax** *264 497 6617* **Rooms** *108*

Striking white luxury villas with Moorish domes and arches are set in a line on the magnificent beach of Maunday's Bay. Service is efficient and many activities including watersports, golf, and spa treatments are available right on the beach. **www.capjuluca.com**

MEADS BAY Sirena Resort and Villas $$$$

PO Box 200, Meads Bay **Tel** *264 497 6827* **Fax** *264 497 6829* **Rooms** *30*

This small resort hotel has 20 individual rooms, 6 suites, and 4 villas. The rooms are concentrated around a central garden and pool with an easy-going, sometimes lively atmosphere, with entertainment. The resort has a main restaurant and the villas have kitchens. **www.sirenaresort.com**

Key to Symbols *see back cover flap*

MEADS BAY Carimar Beach Club   📶🍴📺 $$$$$

PO Box 327, The Valley **Tel** *264 497 6881* **Fax** *264 497 6071* **Rooms** *24*

A horseshoe of one- and two-bedroom apartments set on the spectacular sands of Meads Bay, the Carimar is very attractive. The cottages are adorned with sprays of bright bougainvillea, and are informal and comfortable, with full kitchens. Central facilities include a games room and tennis court. **www.carimar.com**

MEADS BAY Malliouhana Hotel and Spa   📶🍴📺 $$$$$

PO Box 173, Meads Bay **Tel** *264 497 6111* **Fax** *264 497 6011* **Rooms** *53*

An impressive hotel set in lush grounds on a bluff above the superb Meads Bay, Malliouhana Hotel and Spa attracts an elegant, well-heeled crowd. It has an excellent French restaurant and full service spa. The hotel is also child-friendly and has a playground. Facilities include tennis courts. **www.malliouhana.com**

RENDEZVOUS BAY Cuisinart Resort and Spa   📶🍴📺 $$$$$

PO Box 2000, Rendezvous Bay **Tel** *264 498 2000* **Fax** *264 498 2010* **Rooms** *93*

A Greek-styled luxury resort hotel, Cuisinart is large and upbeat, with a young but affluent crowd. Its line of white, domed villas sits on the gorgeous Rendezvous Bay. It offers a full service spa, cookery classes, and hydroponic gardens. **www.cuisinartresort.com**

SANDY HILL Ocean Breeze Holiday Apartments   📺 $$

PO Box 187, Long Path, The Valley **Tel** *264 729 7376* **Fax** *264 497 3084* **Rooms** *7*

Ocean Breeze Holiday Apartments comprise a modern house with several one- and two-bedroom suites surrounding a central pool and overlooking the coast and the island of St. Martin in the distance. Comfortable and well-priced, they are equipped with full kitchens and for an extra charge there is a daily maid service.

SHOAL BAY (EAST) Kú Hotel   📶🍴📺 $$$$$

PO Box 51, Shoal Bay (East) **Tel** *264 497 2011* **Fax** *264 497 3355* **Rooms** *27*

The small and stylish Kú Hotel is set on the fantastic sands of Shoal Bay, Anguilla's liveliest beach. Self-catering suites in two- and three-story buildings are located directly on the sand. It also has a restaurant, spa, gym, and gift shop, and offers scuba and other watersports. **www.ku-anguilla.com**

SHOAL BAY (EAST) Serenity Cottages   📶🍴📺 $$$$$

PO Box 309, Shoal Bay (East) **Tel** *264 497 3328* **Fax** *264 497 3867* **Rooms** *10*

Tucked away in a quiet corner just down from the main activity of Shoal Bay, this small hotel of studios and suites is set in two modern buildings. The different kinds of suites each have a living room, outside space, and full kitchens and guests can enjoy their privacy. There is a small restaurant and beach bar. **www. serenity.ai**

SHOAL BAY (EAST) Shoal Bay Villas   📶🍴📺 $$$$$

PO Box 81, Shoal Bay (East) **Tel** *264 497 2051* **Fax** *264 497 3631* **Rooms** *12*

Homely one- and two-bedroom apartments are set around a central pool right on the superb sands of Shoal Bay (East). All apartments have a kitchen, but there is also a central restaurant, Le Beach. The service is friendly, and all the activity of the beach is available at hand. **www.sbvillas.ai**

SHOAL BAY (WEST) Altamer   📶🍴📺 $$$$$

PO Box 3001, West End **Tel** *264 498 4000* **Fax** *264 498 4010* **Rooms** *3*

This trio of extremely comfortable, ultra-modern villas, designed by award-winning Modernist architect Myron Goldfinger, are named Russian Amethyst, Brazilian Emerald, and African Sapphire, with matching colors. Guests enjoy privacy and service, of butlers and a chef. A restaurant *(see p267)* is also attached. **www.altamer.com**

SHOAL BAY (WEST) Covecastles   📶🍴📺 $$$$$

PO Box 248, Shoal Bay (West) **Tel** *264 497 6801* **Fax** *264 497 6051* **Rooms** *16*

This curve of extraordinary white concrete villas is designed by Myron Goldfinger. The white walls and hefty wicker furniture make it an elegant hideaway with stylish space and a fine view across to St. Martin/Sint Maarten. Villas have full service as well as a central restaurant. Facilities offered include a tennis court. **www.covecastles.com**

SOUTH HILL Ambia   📺 $$$$

Sandy Ground **Tel** *264 498 8686* **Rooms** *5*

An elegant private home, set on the ridge overlooking Sandy Ground, has been turned into an extremely stylish bed-and-breakfast with four rooms and a suite. Asian and Caribbean decor, including Shoji screens and contemporary furniture. Attentive and efficient service is provided. **www.ambia-anguilla.com**

THE VALLEY Island Dream Properties

PO Box 549, The Valley **Tel** *264 498 3200* **Fax** *264 498 3201*

A villa rental agency offering 55 of Anguilla's finest villas. It provides full service including reservations, transfers, provisioning a private chef, spa, and restaurant and trip reservations. They arrange for both short or long term rentals and real estate sales, from one to six or more bedrooms around the island. **www.islanddreamproperties.com**

THE VALLEY My Caribbean

PO Box 1488, The Valley **Tel** *1877 471 2733* **Fax** *1815 301 1771*

An online rental agency that calls on around 100 villas, apartments, and suites in all locations around Anguilla. They can make reservations for visitors and also offer a number of additional services including food, a chef, car rental, and organizing a wedding. **www.mycaribbean.com**

Where to Eat & Nightlife

Anguilla has some great restaurants with superb settings on the beaches and on bluffs above the sea. With little by way of local food tradition, the hotels brought in chefs from outside. Almost uniquely, hotel-trained Anguillian chefs have now branched out, offering their own Caribbean or international fusion cuisine. Restaurants are quite expensive and reservations are usually required.

PRICE CATEGORIES
The price ranges are for a two course meal for one, including tax and service charges, and half a bottle of wine.

$ under $10
$$ $10–15
$$$ $15–25
$$$$ $25–35
$$$$$ over $35

RESTAURANTS

Roadside Barbecues
There are quite a few evening barbecue plots and lunch wagons in simple roadside settings around Anguilla. They tend to serve grilled chicken, meat, and fish. Rafe's, in South Hill above Sandy Ground, built with driftwood and set under a tin lean-to, and DB's near Malliouhana are among the most popular barbecues.

Zurra

Ripples

BARNES BAY Mango's
$$$$$

Barnes Bay **Tel** *264 497 6479*

An extremely attractive setting on an open-fronted terrace on the spectacular sands of Barnes Bay gives Mango's a classic beachfront feel. They offer candle-lit contemporary Caribbean cuisine and seafood such as Anguillian lobster and crayfish, as well as classic steaks. Lively, informal atmosphere.

COVE BAY Zurra
$$$$$

Temenos resort, Merrywing **Tel** *264 222 8300*

Backed by long-time Anguilla restaurateurs, Bob and Melinda Blanchard, Zurra is a top-class Mediterranean restaurant located in the grounds of the Temenos resort complex *(see p264)*. Dishes are adapted classics from Morocco, Italy, and Spain, and include vegetarian options. Tables are also set under parasols on the patio.

ISLAND HARBOR Côté Mer Seaside Restaurant
$$$$$

Island Harbor **Tel** *264 498 2683*

Part elegant beach bar, part informal French restaurant, Côté Mer is set in a large and brightly decorated building with an impressive view out into the bay at Island Harbor. Excellent menu, mainly French cuisine adapted for the tropics, offering a light but sophisticated lunch and a good dinner. Closed on Sunday and Wednesday evening.

ISLAND HARBOR Hibernia
$$$$$

Island Harbor **Tel** *264 497 4290*

Outstanding French cuisine with an Asian touch served in a small dining room with a home-like setting just outside Island Harbor. Very intimate atmosphere, with always beautifully presented dishes. The owners have an art gallery where guests can browse as well. Vegetarian dishes are also served. A good wine list.

MEADS BAY Blanchards
$$$$$

Meads Bay **Tel** *264 497 6100*

The signature restaurant of Bob and Melinda Blanchard, Blanchards is set in a lovely open-fronted Caribbean-style dining room within walking distance of Meads Bay. Offers a grand international menu with tastes from around the globe – Cajun, Asian, and Caribbean. Fine wine list and vegetarian fare.

MEADS BAY Straw Hat
$$$$$

Meads Bay **Tel** *264 497 8300*

Located in the Frangipani Hotel, Straw Hat is set right on the sands of Meads Bay. A pleasant, informal atmosphere, efficient service, a fine wine list, and great mix of international and Caribbean dishes – even delicious variations on jerk and mutton curry. Vegetarian fare as well.

RENDEZVOUS BAY The Dune Preserve
$$$$$

Rendezvous Bay **Tel** *264 235 5734*

The well-known beach bar owned by local reggae star Bankie Banx has got Dale Carty, chef of Tasty's, onboard to create the exciting menu with Caribbean fusion dishes, served among boathulls and surfboards. Some of the dishes include marinated conch and snapper salad. In the evening it is a bar only. Closed on Monday.

SANDY GROUND Ripples
$$$$

Main Street **Tel** *264 497 3380*

A very attractive bar and restaurant at the heart of Sandy Ground, in a lilac and blue building with gingerbread trim. Headed by the chef Jackie Ruan, it offers wholesome and simple fare. It has a very lively atmosphere, particularly during the early evening happy hour. Popular with locals as well as visitors.

Key to Symbols *see back cover flap*

SANDY GROUND Barrel Stay [V] 🍸 🏡 ♿ $$$$$

Sandy Ground ***Tel*** *264 497 2831*

A classic wooden deck right on the beach at Sandy Ground, with hefty wooden beams, palm fronds, and fairy lights. This restaurant serves elegant cuisine, a blend of international and local flavors, accompanied by a good wine list. There are ample options for vegetarians. Gorgeous views over the sand, especially at sunset.

SANDY GROUND Veya [V] 🍸 🏡 $$$$$

Sandy Ground ***Tel*** *264 498 8392*

An extremely pretty traditional-looking Caribbean house off the road down into Sandy Ground, with a bar inside and tables on the large wraparound veranda overlooking beautiful gardens. They serve "cuisine of the sun", with tastes from the Caribbean, Southern Asia, Mexico, and Northern Africa. Closed in August.

SHOAL BAY (EAST) Elodia's 🏡 $$$

Upper Shoal Bay Beach ***Tel*** *264 497 3363*

A simple restaurant set on the outstanding sands of Shoal Bay, Elodia's is famous for its superb West Indian fare – jerk chicken, curry goat, and fish with rice-and-peas – particularly on Sundays, when it sees a lively addition of islanders who come down to join the visitors. Friendly and lots of fun.

SHOAL BAY (EAST) Gwen's Reggae Grill 🏡 $$$

Upper Shoal Bay Beach ***Tel*** *264 497 2120*

A very simple, brightly painted wooden shack set on Lower Shoal Bay, within walking distance from Shoal Bay (East). Very relaxed atmosphere, with parasols on the sand and a deck for shade. Guests are greeted by mouthwatering aromas of grilling chicken, fish, and lobster, with reggae music in the background.

SHOAL BAY (WEST) Altamer [V] 🍸 📋 ♿ $$$$$

The Valley, Shoal Bay (West) ***Tel*** *264 497 4040*

This restaurant, in the Altamer hotel *(see p265)*, is elegantly furnished with glass tables and glass-fronted façades. The kitchen, viewed through a glass pane, prepares outstanding French cuisine with local ingredients for tropical flavor. There are plenty of options for vegetarians.

SOUTH HILL Deon's Overlook [V] 🏡 $$$$$

Back Street ***Tel*** *264 497 4488*

A dining room set on the balcony of a modern house above Sandy Ground, with an unforgettable view over the boats in the bay and out west beyond. Overlook serves delicious international fare, including seafood. The menu here also offers vegetarian dishes. Reservation required.

SOUTH HILL Tasty's 📋 ♿ $$$$$

Main road ***Tel*** *264 497 2737*

The chef, Dale Carty, has been trained in top hotel kitchens and has brought a unique Anguillian interpretation to his international and French cuisine. Friendly service adds to the pleasant atmosphere at this very popular restaurant. Closed on Thursdays.

THE VALLEY English Rose 📋 $$$$

The Valley ***Tel*** *264 497 5353*

Simple setting in a brightly painted but otherwise unspectacular modern building in the capital, The Valley, the English Rose has a friendly casual atmosphere. It is popular with both Anguillians and visitors for its simple international fare, which include burgers, and fish and chips.

WEST END Picante [V] 📋 $$$$

West End Road ***Tel*** *264 498 1616*

A "Caribbean taqueria" or Mexican restaurant near the West End of Anguilla, Picante is set in a modern building painted in turquoise and canary yellow. Friendly reception with traditional Mexican dishes – enchiladas, burritos, quesadillas, tacos, and of course, margaritas to drink.

BARS AND CLUBS

Although fairly quiet after dark, Anguilla has a few stalwart bars which feature live music and dancing. The liveliest area is Sandy Ground, with a handful of bars, dotted around the beaches. Music is usually a mix of Caribbean rhythms and international music, but at local events there are often string bands and calypsonians too.

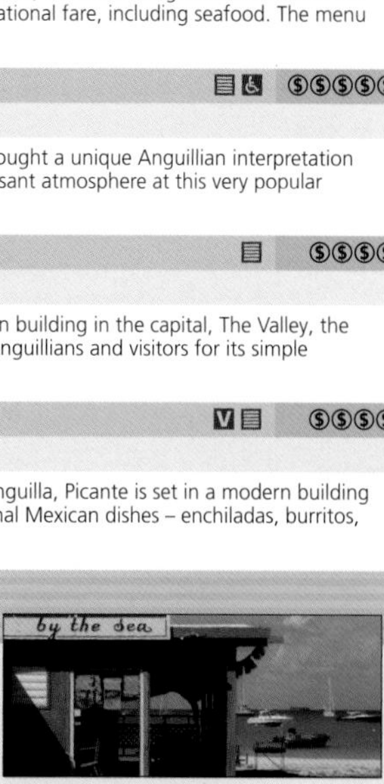

A beach bar in Sandy Ground

RECOMMENDED PLACES TO GO

The Dune Preserve
Rendezvous Bay. (Bar on the beach with reggae, often live.)

Elvis's Beach Bar
Sandy Ground. (A boat for a bar, old cable barrels for tables.)

Johnno's
Sandy Ground. (Lively on Sundays, dancing several nights a week.)

Madeariman Reef
Shoal Bay (East). (Lively on Sundays.)

The Pump House
Sandy Ground. (Mixed crowd, live music several nights a week.)

Uncle Ernie's
Shoal Bay (East). (Inexpensive drinks, splendid barbecue.)

Practical Information

Anguilla is one of the most exclusive and expensive destinations in the region. The island has seen an extraordinary building boom over recent years, but has retained its laid-back character and high standards in tourism. Its hotels and villas are top-notch and restaurants offer a world-class dining experience. A good time to visit Anguilla is during the island's festivals, generally held during July and August.

Ferry boat leaving from the Blowing Point terminal

WHEN TO GO

Anguilla's average annual temperature is around 80º F (27º C), with the hottest weather during the hurricane season that runs from July to October. The lightest rainfall occurs from February to April, and the heaviest from August to November. The island has mild weather from December to April.

GETTING THERE

No carriers fly directly from North America into Anguilla, so access is easiest via neighboring St. Martin/Sint Maarten or Puerto Rico, where visitors can transfer to **American Eagle** or a private charter. There are many carriers into St. Martin from where the crossing to Anguilla can be made by ferry or private water taxi which includes the **Link**, or by the local airline **Winair**. Europe is linked to St. Martin from France and Holland. Most UK visitors travel via Antigua, from where Caribbean flights (**LIAT** and Winair) run up the island chain to Anguilla.

DOCUMENTATION

Visitors to Anguilla require a valid passport with at least six months' validity remaining, as well as a return or onward ticket. Visas are not needed by US citizens, Canadians, or EU travelers, but citizens of some other countries do require them.

If in doubt, visitors should check with the closest British High Commission for details regarding entry visas. A departure tax and an airport security charge needs to be paid when leaving the island.

VISITOR INFORMATION

The **Anguilla Tourist Board** has its main office in The Valley. International offices of the board are located in the UK and the US. There is also an information booth at the Wallblake airport. Visitors can pick up maps, brochures, and magazines at the airport.

HEALTH AND SECURITY

Anguilla is a very safe island. There are hardly any problems concerning personal security and theft is extremely rare. However, it is advisable not to leave any valuables unattended. Sunburn is the main health hazard. Mosquitoes can be a problem after it rains. No vaccinations are necessary unless visitors are coming from a yellow-fever infected area. There is an accident and emergency department at **Princess Alexandra Hospital**.

BANKING AND CURRENCY

The currency of Anguilla is the Eastern Caribbean dollar (EC$), which is shared with current and former British territories as far south as Grenada. The US dollar is also widely accepted. Banks follow regular business hours, Monday to Thursday 8am to 3pm, and to 5pm on Fridays. Credit cards are accepted in almost all establishments except in the smallest shops. There are ATMs attached to several banks, and also free-standing in some malls. They give a choice of Eastern Caribbean and US dollars.

COMMUNICATIONS

The international dialling code for Anguilla is 1 264, followed by a seven digit island number. When calling out of Anguilla, dial 011 and the international code. When calling locally, all seven digits need to be dialled. The island

Anguilla Tourist Board office, The Valley

has complete cell coverage and visitors can use their personal phones, if on roaming. Handsets and SIM cards with local numbers are available at the **Digicel** and **Cable & Wireless** offices on the island. Almost all the hotels and villas have Wi-Fi, which is available to their guests.

TRANSPORT

Car hire companies are not officially permitted to deliver to the airport or ferry port, and will first take visitors to their office to complete formalities. However, they do drop passengers to hotels and villas. Driving is on the left side of the road, and a temporary Anguilla driver's license, in addition to a valid driving license, is mandatory. This can be purchased at any of the car-rental agencies such as **AVIS**, **Island Car Rentals**, and **Carib Rent A Car**. The airport and ferry terminals have taxi stands and usually the rate is fixed for two passengers and two pieces of luggage. There are no public buses in Anguilla. Hitch-hiking works sometimes, but as is the case anywhere, there is no guarantee of a ride.

SHOPPING

While Anguilla is not really known for its shopping, the island has a number of art galleries, which offer handicrafts, paintings, and sculptures by resident artists alongside imported works. The **Loblolly Art Gallery** and the **Savannah Gallery** in The Valley exhibit Caribbean art, while the **Devonish Art Gallery** displays the clay, stone, and wood creations of internationally known potter and sculptor Courtney Devonish. Similarly, **La Petite Art Gallery** showcases paintings by Susan Graff. **Albert's Market Place** is the largest supermarket in The Valley. **Irie Life** is a good place to shop for colorful beachwear and accessories.

LANGUAGE

The language of Anguilla is English, which the Anguillians speak with a slightly Irish-sounding lilt.

ELECTRICITY

The usual electricity supply in Anguilla is 110 volts AC (60 cycles). Most hotels have two-pin sockets in US style.

Savannah Gallery, displaying contemporary Caribbean art

TIME

Anguilla is on Atlantic Standard Time (AST), 4 hours behind Greenwich Mean Time (GMT) and 1 hour ahead of Eastern Time in the US.

GETTING MARRIED

A marriage license can be obtained once both parties have been on the island for 48 hours. Documents required include proof of identity, decree nisi if divorced, and spouse's death certificate if widowed. Visitors can contact any of the many hotels and tour companies, including **Malliouhana Travel and Tours**, which organize weddings.

DIRECTORY

Exploring St. Martin/Sint Maarten

St. Martin/Sint Maarten occupies the smallest land mass governed by two nations. This 37-sq m (96-sq km) island is divided almost equally between France and the Netherlands, making it one of the most diverse vacation destinations in the Caribbean. The Dutch side, Sint Maarten, is known for casinos, high-rise luxury resorts, and non-stop activity. St. Martin, the French side, is less developed but popular for its gourmet bistros, naturist beaches, chic boutiques, and hotels. Each side of the island is distinct in many ways and vacationers can sample the best of both, since there is no real border or document control between the two.

Marigot
St. Martin's charming capital is filled with Creole homes, boutiques, and tiny bistros surrounding a lively marina.

0 km 2

0 miles 2

Simpson Bay
The Simpson Bay area, with many shops, restaurants, and resorts, is the center for tourists on the Dutch side.

GETTING AROUND
A rental car is the best way to get around St. Martin/Sint Maarten. A two-lane highway encircles the coast and the secondary roads are in good condition. Public transport is limited to small daily buses between Philipsburg, Marigot, and Grand Case. Taxis are easily accessible at the airport, ship docks, and main towns. Rates are set by the government and posted in each cab. Commercial jets arrive at the international airport, located on the Dutch side. Small aircraft fly to nearby islands from L'Esperance Airport on the French side. Island-hopping is possible by high-speed ferry to St. Barts and by catamaran to Anguilla and Saba.

Anguilla

FALAISE DES OISEAUX
Saba
④
Baie aux Prunes
Terres Basses
Baie Rouge
MARIGO
Baie Nettlé
Sandy Ground
Baie Longue ⑬
Simpson Bay Lagoon
Cupecoy Bay ⑫
Mullet Bay
Maho Bay ⑪
Burgeaux Bay
SIMPSON BAY AND AROUND ③
⑩
Koo
Pelican Key ⑨

Cruise ship off the coast of Philipsburg, Sint Maarten

SIGHTS AT A GLANCE

Baie Orientale 10
Butterfly Farm 9
Colombier 6
Falaise des Oiseaux 4
Grand Case 8
Îlet Pinel and Île Tintamarre 11
Marigot 5
Old House 12
Philipsburg 1
Pic du Paradis 7
Simpson Bay and Around 3
Sint Maarten Park and Zoo 2

Hotels and Resorts

Anse Marcel hotels 3
Baie Orientale hotels 5
Captain Oliver's 6
Caravanserai Beach Resort 11
Cupecoy hotels 12
Divi Little Bay Beach Resort 8
Fantastic Guest House 1
Grand Case hotels 2
La Samanna 13
La Vista Resort 9
Philipsburg hotels 7
Simpson Bay hotels 10
Sol é Luna 4

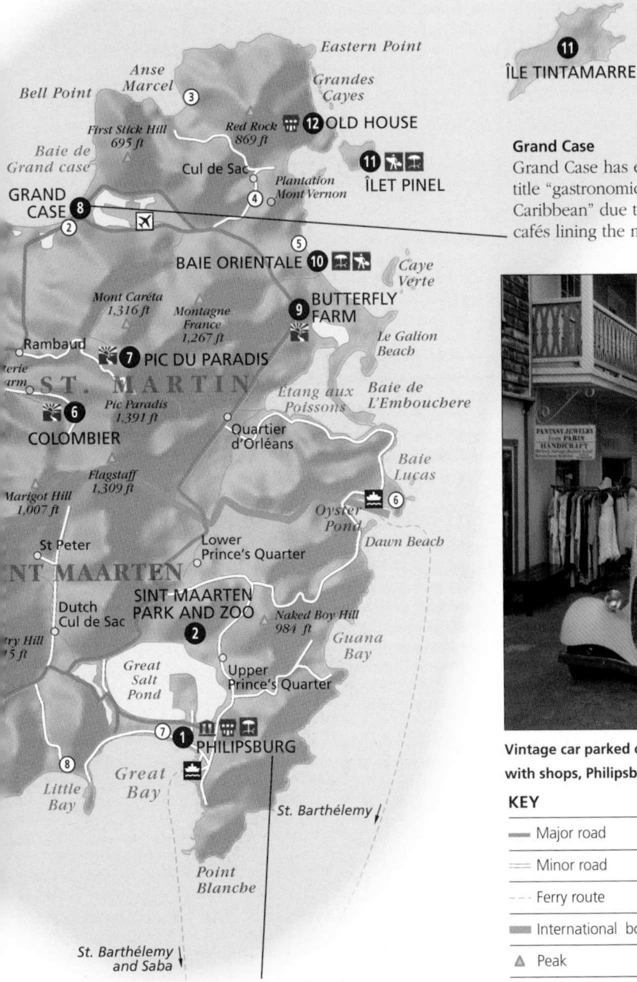

Grand Case
Grand Case has earned the title "gastronomic capital of the Caribbean" due to the many cafés lining the main road.

Philipsburg
The Dutch capital, Philipsburg, curves around the Great Bay. It is a major stop for cruise ships.

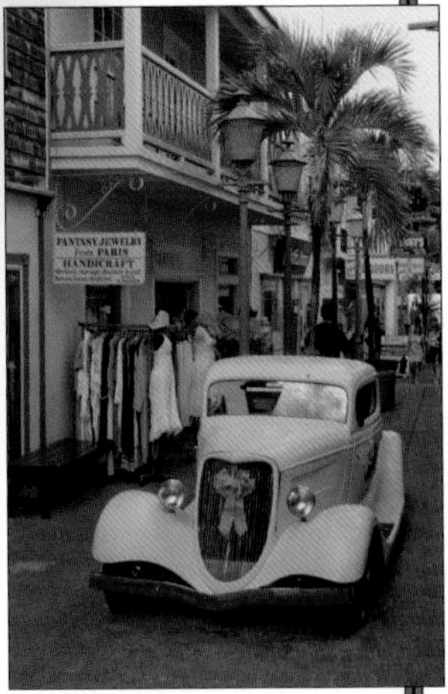

Vintage car parked on a street lined with shops, Philipsburg

KEY

- Major road
- Minor road
- Ferry route
- International border
- Peak

SEE ALSO

• ***Where to Stay*** pp280–81
• ***Where to Eat & Nightlife*** pp282–3

Philipsburg ●

S coast of Sint Maarten. 🏠 18,000.
✈ 🚌 ⛴ ℹ *Vineyard Office Park,
WG Buncamper Rd.* 🚢 *Carnival
(Apr–May).* **www**.st-maarten.com

The capital city of Dutch
Sint Maarten stretches a mile
(2 km) across a narrow strip
of land that separates the sea
from a marshy inland pond.
Of the four roads that run
from one end of the town to
the other, the popular Front
Street brims with waterfront
cafés, flashy casinos, and
duty-free shops. Town
beautification projects
have replaced aging brick
pavements and outfitted new
sidewalks with palm trees and
decorative lampposts. Sand,
dredged from the bottom of
the sea, was spread on Great
Bay Beach, which flaunts an
impressive new boardwalk.

Cyrus Wathey Square on
Front Street, across from
Captain Hodge Pier, has a
striking white courthouse
built in 1792 by the Dutch
commander Willem Hendrik
Rink. The square is an
excellent starting point for a
walking tour as it has a tourist
information booth and is at
the beginning of the shopping
district. Old Street and Sea
Street are pedestrian-only
walkways lined with flowers,
potted palms, and shops.

The **Guavaberry Emporium**
occupies a late 18th-century
cedar town house, once
home to a former governor.
Flavored liqueurs from the
local guavaberry fruit are the

shop's chief product alongside
other island-made goods. Set
in a restored 19th-century
two-story house, the **Sint
Maarten Museum** displays
local historic artifacts such as
the replica of a typical
Arawak *pirogue* (canoe),
which stands at the entrance,
a photo exhibit of daily island
life in the early 1900s, and
rescued articles from HMS
Proselyte, a frigate that sank
off Fort Amsterdam in 1801.

At the far east end of town,
locally known as the Head of
Town, Bobby's Marina and
Great Bay Marina have car
rental agencies, a dive shop,
and a marine supply store.

🍴 **Guavaberry Emporium**
8–10 Front Street. **Tel** 599 542
2965. ◯ 10am–6pm daily.

🏛 **Sint Maarten Museum**
7 Front Street. **Tel** 599 542 4917.
◯ 10am–4pm Mon–Fri; 10am–2pm
Sat. 🖼 🛗

Sint Maarten Park and Zoo ●

0.5 mile (1 km) N of Philipsburg, Sint
Maarten. **Tel** 599 543 2030. 🚌
◯ 9:30am–6pm daily. 🖼 🍴 🛗

Animal lovers and children
are fascinated by the 200 or
more species at the 3-acre
(1-ha) Sint Maarten Park and
Zoo, located in the residential
area of Madame Estate. More
than one hundred parrots
perch on trees above
numerous turtles and iguanas.
An interesting sight is the rare
golden lion tamarin, a monkey

Golden lion tamarin monkeys at
the Sint Maarten Park and Zoo

with a long tail and a lion-like
mane. The grounds also have
lovely tropical plants.

Simpson Bay and Around ●

2 miles (3 km) W of Philipsburg, Sint
Maarten. 🚌

The Simpson Bay area
includes the bay and beach
abutting Princess Juliana
International Airport on the
island's south coast, and the
Simpson Bay Lagoon, which
at 11 sq miles (29 sq km) is
the largest lagoon in the
eastern Caribbean. A narrow
strip of land circles it, separating it from the sea, and
several of the most popular
resorts, restaurants, and
activities are located here.
The invisible Dutch-French
border runs through the
lagoon, so everything on the
south shore including the

View of Philipsburg, with Great and Little Bay beaches

For hotels and restaurants on this island see pp280–81 and pp282–3

Maho Bay, Mullet Bay, and Cupecoy Bay areas with their great beaches, is Dutch. Marigot touches the lagoon on the north (French) side at the trendy Port La Royale.

Falaise des Oiseaux ❹

7 miles (11 km) W of Philipsburg, St. Martin. 🚗

The high ridge of cliffs which lies along the Simpson Bay Lagoon, overlooking the Caribbean Sea on the western edge of Terres Basses (Lowlands), is called Falaise des Oiseaux (Cliff of the Birds). Many indigenous and migrating bird species nest in the cliff's caves and bird-watchers gather here to observe great blue herons, ospreys, yellow warblers, and bullfinches. Pretty homes and villas are scattered along the *falaise* between Baie Rouge (Red Bay) and Baie aux Prunes (Plum Bay).

Marigot ❺

10 miles (16 km) NW from Philipsburg, St. Martin. 🏛 *12,700.* ✈ 🚌 ⛴ 🛈 *Route de Sandy Ground, 590 875 721.* 🎭 *Carnival (Feb–Mar).* **www**.st-martin.org

Marigot, the capital of French St. Martin, is a charming town built along the sandy curve of a yacht-filled bay. Contemporary boutiques have moved into colonial buildings and Creole-style houses, and the new blends pleasantly with the old in the center of town. A quaint public square near the harbor is the site of a daily market that offers fresh produce and several locally-made products. The largest markets are open on Wednesdays and Saturdays, and mornings are the best time to visit.

Nearby, Fort Saint-Louis overlooks the sea. Built between 1767 and 1789 by the French, the fort was captured and held for two years by the British from 1794 until 1796. The hilltop fortress offers a panoramic

Oyster Pond, meeting point of French and Dutch

THE GREAT DIVIDE

Between 1648, when the French and the Dutch signed the Treaty of Concordia, and 1817, when the borders of the island were officially set, St. Martin/Sint Maarten changed government 16 times. Legend says that the Dutch and French settlers decided to partition it by staging a march. A Frenchman began walking south from the north coast, while a Dutchman headed north from the south coast. The French and Dutch citizens cheered their representatives on by offering them cups of wine and shots of gin, respectively. While the drowsy Dutchman stopped for a nap, the Frenchman trudged on. When the two met near Oyster Pond, the French had claimed a larger portion by 4 sq miles (10 sq km).

view of Marigot and the island's western shore. **Sur les Traces des Arawaks** (On the Trail of the Arawaks) is a history and archaeology museum with exhibits such as tools, pottery, and jewelry crafted by the native tribes who lived on the island as early as 1800 BC. Experts, by comparing the design of these pieces, trace the history of the Arawaks to South American natives and follow their migration from the Orinoco River basin in Venezuela.

On the waterfront of Simpson Bay Lagoon, Port La Royale marina complex is lined with boutiques and small restaurants reminiscent of those on the French Riviera. During high season, carnival-like entertainment takes place on several evenings each week.

🏛 **Sur les Traces des Arawaks**
7 Rue Fichot. **Tel** 690 567 892. ◯ 9am–5pm Mon–Sat. ◉ pub hols. 🈺 🗂 🈺 🗂

Cattle grazing in the lush meadows, Colombier

Colombier ❻

3 miles (5 km) E of Marigot, St. Martin. 🚗

Just inland from Baie de Friar, this fertile hilly area at the foot of Pic du Paradis (Paradise Peak, *see p274*) provides the vegetables and fruit sold at the public market in Marigot. At one time, residents produced large crops of sugar-cane, mangoes, and coffee. The big plantations no longer exist, and goats now graze along the road that runs past scattered Creole houses.

Colorful displays at the market place, Boulevard de France, Marigot

A child taking the Fly Zone tour at Loterie Farm, Pic du Paradis

Pic du Paradis ❼

4 miles (6 km) E of Marigot, St. Martin. ℹ *Loterie Farm, 590 878 616.* ⏱ *9am–4pm daily.* 🌐🅿
🍴🛍 *www.loteriefarm.net*

The island's highest point at 1,391 ft (424 m) offers great views of Baie Orientale and neighboring islands, and is well worth the trouble of getting to the top. A steep, rutted secondary road, off the coastal highway to Colombier, leads inland up the west side of the mountain to within 1 mile (2 km) of the peak, but only a 4-wheel-drive vehicle can manage the drive.

Tours leave from trails beginning at Loterie Farm, 3 miles (5 km) east from Marigot. The farm is a private nature park covering more than 150 acres (61 ha) at the base of Pic du Paradis. Trails lead into the tropical forest, which is home to hundreds of species of plants that shelter a variety of birds and animals. Guides take individuals and small groups on nature walks and moderate to difficult hikes, including a 1-hour trek up Pic du Paradis. A popular attraction is the **Fly Zone** tour, where participants are strapped to a safety harness that is attached to sturdy cables, and zip along through the tree tops. Rope ladders and suspended swing bridges add to the excitement. The farm's Hidden Forest Café is a destination in itself. Its dining room is set in a reconstructed section of an 18th-century sugar mill. The menu has dishes made from produce grown in the farm's organic garden.

Grand Case ❽

4 miles (6 km) N of Marigot, St. Martin. 🏠 *2,500.* 🚌
🎭 *Harmony Nights Street Fest (Jan–Apr).* **www.grandcase.com**

Called the Gastronomic Capital of the Caribbean, the tiny town of Grand Case has one main road, a fine beach, and many excellent restaurants run by European-trained chefs. The gourmet restaurants are housed in quaint Creole-style houses that sit side by side, allowing prospective diners the opportunity to stroll from one to another comparing menus that are posted outside. In addition, local cooks serve island specialties from open-air lo-los (locally owned – locally operated) set up along the same street. Here, local cooks grill fresh seafood and meats over oil-drum barbecue pits, and patrons sit at picnic tables. Although the town is known for fine dining rather than swimming, the 1-mile (2-km) long sandy beach with gentle waters is perfect for swimming and has some great snorkeling spots. The bay also offers a spectacular view of neighboring Anguilla and Creole Rock.

On Tuesday nights in the winter the town hosts Harmony Nights Street Festival. Local bands play music on everything from home-made drums to fine brass instruments. Residents also sell traditional art and crafts, and cooks prepare favorite dishes that are local to the island.

Butterfly Farm ❾

5 miles (8 km) NE of Marigot, St. Martin. **Tel** *590 590 873 121.* ⏱ *9am–3:30pm daily.* 🌐
🌐 *9am–3pm.* ♿🛍📷
www.thebutterflyfarm.com

A butterfly in the Butterfly Farm

Hundreds of butterflies from all parts of the world swirl about in this mesh-enclosed garden, which features fish ponds and waterfalls. More than 40 species of butterflies are found in the farm. The best time to visit is early morning, when the butterflies are born. Displays here show the progression from egg to caterpillar to pupae.

The gift shop sells unusual butterfly art, books, and jewelry. Admission fees include return visits, so visitors can drop in several times during the vacation.

The beach at Grand Case, ideal for snorkeling

For hotels and restaurants on this island see pp280–81 and pp282–3

The beach at Baie Orientale, with different types of watersports available

Baie Orientale ⑩

4 miles (6 km) NE of Marigot, St. Martin.

Watersports operators, bars, and restaurants line the popular 4-mile (6-km) beach that spreads along this highly developed bay. Calm water and a protective reef make this an ideal spot for swimming and snorkeling, and motorized and wind-powered watercraft add to the fun.

Environs
Nearby, **Plantation Mont Vernon** is a park and interactive museum on more than 5 acres (2 ha) of landscaped land on a mountainside overlooking Baie Orientale. Walking paths and an audio handset guide visitors past labeled tropical plants, historical buildings, coffee museum, and a sugar and rum museum.

Plantation Mont Vernon
Route d'Orient Baie. **Tel** 590 295 062. 9am–5pm daily. **www**.plantationmont vernon.com

Îlet Pinel and Île Tintamarre ⑪

Îlet Pinel 0.5 miles (1 km) N of Baie Orientale, St. Martin. *French Cul de Sac (N of Baie Orientale).*
Île Tintamarre 1 mile (2 km) NE of Îlet Pinel, St. Martin. *day-sails to Tintamarre from Grand Case.* *on day excursions.*

These two undeveloped offshore islands are within the protected waters of the nature reserve, and their beaches are usually deserted. Both islands are difficult to reach when the wind is strong, due to high waves, but in fine weather, each makes an ideal day trip. Pinel is easier to reach by boat, and more likely to have visitors, but the north side is isolated and its shore is battered by crashing surf. Water taxis regularly shuttle passengers from the beach at French Cul de Sac, just north of Baie Orientale, to Îlet Pinel. The south coast beaches face St. Martin and have gentle waves, snack shacks, and equipment rentals for watersports.

Tintamarre is less visited, but day-sail excursions often make this a snorkeling stop. White-sand beaches ring the 200-acre (81-ha) island, which is nicknamed Flat Island, and underwater life is amazing. Mud from beaches here is said to have healing powers and visitors often slather it over their faces and bodies.

Old House ⑫

5 miles (8 km) NE of Marigot, St. Martin. **Tel** 590 873 267. 10am–4pm Tue–Sun.

Once the main house of a thriving plantation, this renovated Creole-style building has an interesting selection of antique tools and machines once used in cultivating sugarcane and producing rum. The manor house sits at the top of a hill overlooking the Spring Estate, which is still held by the Beauperthuy family, the original owners. The living room and master bedroom of the authentically restored home hold treasures collected by the family over six generations and include photographs, rare lithographs and ancient maps arranged among the period furniture as they might have been during the 1700s, when sugar and rum production drove the island's economy. There is a rum and coffee museum on-site.

Pretty houses overlooking Baie Orientale Beach

Outdoor Activities and Specialized Holidays

While many vacationers plan to just relax on a beach during their visit to St. Martin/Sint Maarten, there are also plenty of options for those seeking a bit of excitement. Watersports are the prime focus and range from snorkeling to kiteboarding. On land, activities offered include bird-watching and mountain biking. Several companies act as a one-stop outlet for both land and sea adventures, and there are also operators who specialize in specific activities.

Visitors basking in the sun on Dawn Beach, Sint Maarten

BEACHES

St. Martin/Sint Maarten has 36 named beaches, most with powdery white sands. Many of the best are highly developed, making them lively, crowded, and fun. However, it is still possible to find secluded stretches, usually on the French side. The Atlantic coast beaches have bigger waves, more wind, stronger currents, and are preferred by watersports enthusiasts. The Caribbean side is calmer and favored by swimmers, snorkelers, and families with children. All beaches are public, but resorts may reserve sands for registered guests.

Great Bay in Philipsburg has an amazing beach with white sand that was dredged up from the sea floor to deepen the harbor for large cruise ships. It tends to get crowded, especially when passengers disembark from the ships, but this adds to the festive ambience. West of town, gorgeous beaches lie along a narrow strip of land that separates the Caribbean Sea from Simpson Bay Lagoon. At Maho Bay Beach, a sign

warns of low-flying aircrafts, but it is always crowded and beachgoers cheer and snap pictures as jumbo jets drop close to the sand on final approach. The hotels, casinos, and restaurants at Maho are among the most popular on the island.

Cupecoy Bay Beach, westernmost on the Dutch side, is small and dramatic, with a clothing-optional end. It is backed by towering cliffs and the sand is constantly reshaped by the surf, so the place rarely looks the same from one day to the next. The drop-off between the beach

Game fishing boat at Marigot in St. Martin

and sea is sharp, and waves often top 2 ft (0.6 m). The French side of the west coast has a section called Terres Basses lined with an almost continuous stretch of white sand. Baie Longue is quiet with calm turquoise waters and Baie aux Prunes is popular with surfers when the waves are high. Baie Rouge has a few snack shacks and huts that rent umbrellas and chairs. Grand Case (see p274) has a popular beach for jogging, sunbathing, swimming, and snorkeling, with calm waters that lap onto nicely-packed white sand.

On the east coast, Baie Orientale (see p275) is home to Club Orient, a well-known naturist resort. This stunning 2-mile (3-km) long bay has five connecting beaches. The entire bay is dotted with open-air boutiques, bars, restaurants, massage huts, watersport shops, and live music.

Back on Dutch soil, Dawn Beach is popular with early risers who like to watch the sun rising on this east coast beach. A large, shallow reef protects it from crashing waves and provides excellent snorkeling and surfing.

FISHING

The sea around St. Martin/Sint Maarten teems with fish such as marlin, wahoo, tuna, and snapper. International tournaments include the Blue Marlin Tournament in June and the Anglers Big Fishing Tournament in March.

Visitors can charter boats at full- or half-day rates throughout the year, and captains structure the trips to meet the skills and interests of each group. Bait, gear, and refreshments are included in the rates. One of the best areas for wahoo and tuna is the drop-off at Baie Longue, where the fish feed at depths of 200 ft (60 m).

The Proselyte Reef off Great Bay is excellent for all types of reef fish that feed in depths of 8–12 ft (2.4–3.6 m). **Lee's Deep Sea Fishing, Taylor Made Charters and Deep Sea Fishing,** and **Rudy's Deep Sea Fishing** are popular operators.

For hotels and restaurants on this island see pp280–81 and pp282–3

Casinos on Sint Maarten

Dutch Sint Maarten has more than a dozen casinos, most in or near Philipsburg, where shoppers and cruise ship passengers come to enjoy refreshments and play their favorite slots and table games. Outside the capital, Casino Royal in Maho Bay, Princess Casino at Port de Plaisance, and Atlantis World in Cupecoy

Card Poker game sign, Diamond Casino

are the largest and offer the most entertainment and glamour. Smaller casinos are more basic and draw a relaxed crowd looking just for slot machines and icy rum punch. The mid-range casinos offer a good selection of games, live music or big-screen TVs tuned to sports events, and a variety of bar food.

Westin Dawn Beach Resort Casino is a Vegas-style casino that has several games from blackjack dealer to hit-the-slots.

Casino Royale *has well-dressed guests who come to see glamorous productions at the Showroom Royale, dance to music in the Q-Club, and win or lose at 200 slot machines and great games.*

The croupier spins the wheel and sends the ball rolling along the track in opposite directions.

Roulette is an extremely popular game in most of the casinos.

Diamond Casino *is popular and features an outstanding selection of table and card games, such as Caribbean stud poker, roulette, blackjack, and baccarat, as well as nickel to $5 slots.*

PRINCESS CASINO

The largest casino on the island, Princess Casino at Port de Plaisance is a glitzy, two-level venue for gaming tables including roulette, slots, private high-dollar salons, and nightly entertainment.

CASINOS

Casino Royale
www.playmaho.com
Diamond Casino
www.diamondcasinosxm.com
Jump Up Casino
www.jumpupcasino.com
Princess Casino
www.princessportdeplaisance.com/casino
Westin Dawn Beach Resort Casino
www.westinstmaarten.com

Jump Up Casino *has daily, dazzling parades in bright and colorful costumes and traditional Caribbean music reliving the carnival spirit of Sint Maarten.*

Children SNUBA diving in the waters of Sint Maarten

DIVING AND SNORKELING

Much of the water surrounding the island is protected by environmental agencies, such as the Dutch Nature Foundation and the French Réserve Naturelle, so coral reefs and sea creatures are thriving in most areas or recovering in others. Interesting marine life along the reefs include banded coral shrimps, blue crabs, queen conch, and fireworms. Green moray eels, yellow goatfish, stoplight parrotfish, barracuda, and nurse sharks are among the local fish found here. Visibility is typically clear for 100 ft (30 m), and often up to 150 ft (45 m). Shore diving and snorkeling are good at Dawn Beach, where the reef runs parallel to the shore directly out from the center of the beach, and Baie de Friar, where coral grows on rocks and a shallow reef runs out from the shore for about 100 ft (30 m). The best sites are off Îlet Pinel, Île Tintamarre, Caye Verte, and Anse Marcel. Most resorts and marinas are affiliated with dive shops, such as **Scuba Fun**, **The Scuba Shop**, and **Dive Safaris** that rent and sell equipment, provide discovery and certification classes, and run scheduled scuba trips for certified divers.

Blue Bubbles outlets offer SNUBA, a tank-free system that allows divers, including children and uncertified adults, to dive and stay underwater while breathing through a long hose that reaches the air at the surface.

BOATING AND SAILING

Many international regattas are held annually, the largest being the 3-day Heineken Regatta, drawing more than 200 boats from two dozen countries to compete in 20 categories. The **Sint Maarten 12-Metre Challenge** is a mini-race between 40-ft (12-m) yachts and tourists can also participate. This activity takes place daily, and all passengers are seen as working crew members and allowed to learn or display sailing skills. For those who prefer motor-boats, trips are organized through agencies based at marinas throughout the island. Charter companies, such as **The Moorings**, **Captain Alan's Boat Charters**, and **Captain Morgan**, arrange crewed and bareboat rentals for sailing vacations, and full- or half-day outings are offered through booking agencies while watersport kiosks on the beaches and resorts rent small boats. **Atlantis Adventures** offers the Seaworld Explorer,

a 49-ft (15-m) semi-submarine, that leaves Grand Case daily for an underwater exploration of reefs and marine life around Creole Rock.

WATERSPORTS

There are several watersports operators, such as **Aqua Mania** and **Tropical Wave and Chez Pat**, and resorts usually offer guests complimentary use of non-motorized equipment. Colorful Hobie Cats, Jet Skis, banana boats, kayaks, and parasail-toting speedboats fill the waters at Baie Orientale, Great Bay, and Simpson Bay Lagoon. Kiteboarding and windsurfing are popular at Le Galion Beach, and wake-boarding on Simpson Bay Lagoon, Nettle Bay, and Grand Case Bay. Boardsurfing is excellent from November through March on the island's north and west coasts, and from July through October, along the east coast.

HIKING

Trails on Pic du Paradis (see p274), are popular with hikers as it is cool here and the views are exceptional. **Loterie Farm**, at the base of the mountain, offers guided and self-guided hikes, but trails are accessible from back roads between Baie de Friar and the west side of Pic du Paradis. **National Heritage Foundation** organizes hikes geared to various fitness levels through other scenic parts of the island. **Tri-Sport** in Simpson Bay and **Authentic French Tours** in Marigot arrange group and private hikes with local guides.

Windsurfers off Le Galion Beach, St. Martin

For hotels and restaurants on this island see pp280–81 and pp282–3

Cyclist riding through the coastal region, Mullet Bay, St. Martin

BIKING

Mountain and biking off the road is a great way to explore the countryside and isolated coastal areas. Many biking routes are along hiking trails, others are little-used back roads in less populated areas. Tri-Sport and Authentic French Tours rent bikes and arrange guided rides for all skill levels.

HORSE-RIDING

Professional equestrian guides lead rides for all ages and skill levels through the countryside, along beaches, and into the surf. **Lucky Stables** takes riders through the Cape Bay area while **Bayside Riding Club** has a Pony Club for kids and offers vacation horse rentals.

GOLF

The 18-hole **Mullet Bay Golf Course** is still popular among golfers, even though Mullet Bay Resort and the golf club remain closed since Hurricane Luis in 1995. Players may rent a cart or walk the course, and all fees, including club rental, are based on games of either 9 or 18 holes.

TENNIS

Many of the large resorts like **Sonesta Maho Beach Resort**, **Pelican Resort**, and Divi Little Bay Beach Resort (see p281) have tennis courts and allow non-guests to play by reservation, and for a fee. The **American Tennis Academy** gives lessons to adults and children. Courts may be reserved for private play 24 hours in advance.

DIRECTORY

FISHING

Lee's Deep Sea Fishing
84 Welfare Road, Cole Bay, Sint Maarten. **Tel** 599 544 4233. www.leesfish.com

Rudy's Deep Sea Fishing
Airport Road, Simpson Bay, Sint Maarten. **Tel** 599 545 2177. www.rudysdeepseafishing.com

Taylor Made Charters and Deep Sea Fishing
Simpson Bay Lagoon, Sint Maarten. **Tel** 599 524 7510. www.taylormadecharters.shoreadventures.net

DIVING AND SNORKELING

Blue Bubbles
Dock Maarten, Philipsburg, Sint Maarten. **Tel** 599 554 2502. www.bluebubblessxm.com

Dive Safaris
Simpson Bay, Sint Maarten. **Tel** 599 545 2401. www.divestmaarten.com

Scuba Fun
Great Bay Marina, Philipsburg, Sint Maarten. **Tel** 599 542 3966. www.scubafun.com

The Scuba Shop
Tel 590 874 801 (Oyster Pond, St. Martin), 599 545 3213 (Simpson Bay, Sint Maarten). www.thescubashop.net

BOATING AND SAILING

Atlantis Adventures
15 Walter Nisbeth Road, Philipsburg, Sint Maarten. **Tel** 599 542 4078. www.atlantisadventures.com

Captain Alan's Boat Charters
Oyster Pond, Sint Maarten. **Tel** 599 524 1386. www.captainalan.com

Captain Morgan
Great Bay Marina, Philipsburg, Sint Maarten. **Tel** 590 690 498460. www.captainmorgandaycharters.com

The Moorings
Captain Oliver's Marina, Oyster Pond, St. Martin. **Tel** 590 873 255. www.moorings.com

Sint Maarten 12-Metre Challenge
Bobby's Marina, Philipsburg, Sint Maarten. **Tel** 599 542 0045. www.12metre.com

WATERSPORTS

Aqua Mania
Pelican Marina, Simpson Bay. **Tel** 599 544 2640. www.stmaarten-activities.com

Tropical Wave and Chez Pat
Le Galion Beach, St. Martin. **Tel** 590 873 725. www.sxm-orientbeach.com/chezpat

HIKING

Authentic French Tours
Rue de Hollande, Marigot, St. Martin. **Tel** 590 870 511.

Loterie Farm
Route Pic du Paradis, St. Martin. **Tel** 590 878 616. www.loteriefarm.net

National Heritage Foundation
Sint Maarten Museum, 7 Front Street, Philipsburg, Sint Maarten. **Tel** 599 542 4917. www.speetjens.com

Tri-Sport
14B Airport Boulevard, Simpson Bay, Sint Maarten. **Tel** 599 545 4384. www.trisport sxm.com

HORSE-RIDING

Bayside Riding Club
Le Galion Beach, St. Martin. **Tel** 590 873 664.

Lucky Stables
2 Traybay Drive, Cay Bay, Sint Maarten. **Tel** 599 544 5255.

GOLF

Mullet Bay Golf Course
Mullet Bay, Sint Maarten. **Tel** 599 545 2081.

TENNIS

American Tennis Academy
Cul de Sac, St. Martin. **Tel** 590 690 382217. www.americantennisacademy.net

Pelican Resort
Simpson Bay, Sint Maarten. **Tel** 599 544 2503. www.pelicanresort.com

Sonesta Maho Beach Resort
Maho Bay, Sint Maarten. **Tel** 599 545 2115. www.sonesta.com/MahoBeach

Choosing a Hotel

There are a wide variety of hotels, resorts, and
guesthouses on both the Dutch and the French side
of the island. The accommodations here offer a range
of prices, facilities, and amenities. Rates drop by
25–50 percent between mid-April and mid-December.
Discounts may be available year round if bookings
are made through agencies.

PRICE CATEGORIES
The following price ranges
are for a standard double
room per night and all
taxes included.

$ⓢ$ under $100
$ⓢⓢ$ $100–200
$ⓢⓢⓢ$ $200–300
$ⓢⓢⓢⓢ$ $300–400
$ⓢⓢⓢⓢⓢ$ over $400

ST. MARTIN/ SINT MAARTEN

Private villas, condos, and time-share units are also available
in St. Martin.

Jennifer's Vacation Villas
Tel 599 544 3107 **Fax** 599 544 3375
www.jennifersvacationvillas.com

Villa Lady
Tel 800 338 4552
www.villalady.com

Captain Oliver's

Pasanggrahan Royal

ST. MARTIN, ANSE MARCEL Radisson Blu Resort, Marina & Spa 🖥🍴📶♿Ⓦ $ⓢⓢⓢ$
Anse Marcel Beach Road **Tel** 590 876 700 **Fax** 590 873 038 **Rooms** 252

L'Habitation de Lonvilliers has been taken over and completely remodeled as this family-friendly resort. The
award-winning Le Spa is a popular accompaniment to the large marina and beach facilities. Rooms have Euro-Carib
furnishings, balconies, and flat-screen TVs. **www.radisson.com/stmartin**

ST. MARTIN, ANSE MARCEL Marquis Hotel, Resort and Spa 🖥🍴📶♿Ⓦ $ⓢⓢⓢⓢⓢ$
1 Pigeon Pea Road **Tel** 590 294 230 **Rooms** 17

This luxurious little boutique resort is done up in French-Caribbean style. The staff wears traditional West Indian
madras outfits. All rooms have king-sized beds and furnished terraces overlooking the sea. Fitness classes are
offered in the gym, and in-room spa services are available. **www.hotel-marquis.com**

ST. MARTIN, BAIE LONGUE La Samanna 🖥🍴📶♿Ⓦ $ⓢⓢⓢⓢⓢ$
Long Bay Beach Road **Tel** 590 876 400 **Fax** 590 878 786 **Rooms** 81

Deserving of its five-star rating, this French resort may seem too reserved to some. The highlights of the place
include elegant Mediterranean architecture, the fabulous infinity pool and the beachside deck with canopies. They
also have a spa and fitness center, and tennis courts. **www.lasamanna.com**

ST. MARTIN, BAIE ORIENTALE Club Orient 🖥🍴📶♿Ⓦ $ⓢⓢⓢ$
1 Baie Orientale **Tel** 590 873 385 **Fax** 590 873 376 **Rooms** 137

Most guests are repeat visitors at this popular, naturist resort set in an isolated area right on the beach. Each
roomy wooden chalet is rustically simple and has a furnished patio, outdoor shower, and an equipped kitchen.
The village-like complex is quiet and well run. Do not expect a party scene here. **www.cluborient.com**

ST. MARTIN, BAIE ORIENTALE Palm Court 🖥📶♿Ⓦ $ⓢⓢ$
Parc de la Baie Orientale **Tel** 590 874 194 **Fax** 590 294 130 **Rooms** 24

Just a short walk to the sand at Baie Orientale, these spacious rooms have a sitting area, balcony or patio, and
kitchenettes. The modern Moroccan style features relaxing touches, such as candles and herb-filled bowls. Rates
include Continental breakfast. Family rooms available. **www.sxm-palm-court.com**

ST. MARTIN, GRAND CASE Grand Case Beach Club 🖥🍴📶♿ $ⓢⓢⓢ$
Boulevard de Grand Case **Tel** 590 875 187 **Fax** 590 875 993 **Rooms** 73

Two beaches are just steps away from each large room at this relaxed resort located on landscaped grounds
at the end of town. Each unit is casually furnished and equipped with a kitchen or kitchenette and a patio.
On-site amenities include watersports, dive shop, and floodlit tennis court. **www.grandcasebeachclub.com**

ST. MARTIN, GRAND CASE Hotel L'Esplanade 📶♿Ⓦ $ⓢⓢⓢⓢ$
Hillside above Boulevard de Grand Case **Tel** 590 870 655 **Fax** 590 872 915 **Rooms** 24

On a hill above Grand Case, all units at this luxurious resort overlook the sea. Rooms are spacious and upscale
with a full kitchen and private furnished terrace. Upgrade to a loft unit for more space and a sleeper sofa. The
pool and adjacent bar are set in a Mediterranean-style garden. **www.lesplanade.com**

ST. MARTIN, GRAND CASE Le Petit Hotel 🖥📶♿ $ⓢⓢⓢⓢ$
248 Boulevard de Grand Case **Tel** 590 290 965 **Fax** 590 870 919 **Rooms** 10

Set right on the beach and restaurant row, this classy Mediterranean-style boutique hotel is run by friendly staff
offering excellent service and insider advice on activities and dining. Bathrooms are small, but all units have
balconies and kitchenettes. Guests enjoy a self-serve Continental breakfast. **www.lepetithotel.com**

Key to Symbols *see back cover flap*

ST. MARTIN, MARIGOT Fantastic Guest House

▤ $

Low Town **Tel** *590 877 109* **Fax** *590 877 351* **Rooms** *19*

Perfect for anyone on a budget, this small guesthouse overlooking Simpson Bay Lagoon in Marigot is within walking distance of shops and restaurants. Double rooms have cooking facilities. There is a small pool and some units accommodate families with children. **www.fantasticguesthouse.com**

ST. MARTIN, MONT VERNON Sol é Luna

🍴▤Ⓦ $$

Route de Mont Vernon **Tel** *590 290 856* **Rooms** *6*

Six guesthouses set in the hills above Baie Orientale make up this family-owned restaurant and inn. A lovely pool and landscaped grounds add to the Mediterranean ambience of the property. Each unit is uniquely decorated and features marble baths and patios with views of the sea. **www.solelunarestaurant.com**

ST. MARTIN, OYSTER POND Captain Oliver's

🛏🍴▤Ⓦ $$$

Oyster Pond Road **Tel** *590 874 026* **Fax** *590 874 084* **Rooms** *50*

This marina-front resort sits mostly on French soil facing Dutch waters. Luxury yachts fill the harbor and every type of water activity is available. Bungalows are scattered around tropical gardens filled with parrots, iguanas, and turtles. All units are spacious with balconies. **www.captainolivers.com**

SINT MAARTEN, BURGEAUX BAY Caravanserai Beach Resort

🛏🍴▤🏊 $$$

Beacon Hill Road **Tel** *599 545 4000* **Fax** *599 545 4101* **Rooms** *216*

Guests who stay here rarely leave the property. Just south of Maho Bay, the resort offers its guests everything – from the popular Sunset Beach Bar, where locals and visitors meet for drinks when the sun goes down, to a casino, four restaurants, and four pool tables. Upgrade to a suite for more room. **www.caravanseraibeachresort.net**

SINT MAARTEN, CUPECOY The Summit Resort Hotel

🍴▤Ⓦ $$

42 Jordan Road **Tel** *599 545 2150* **Fax** *599 545 2615* **Rooms** *32*

Standard garden-view rooms have a small sitting area, balcony, and a fridge, while the deluxe ones come with fully equipped kitchens, a living and dining area, and a tiled terrace. Accommodations for families available. The lush grounds are on a cliff that overlooks Simpson Bay Lagoon. **www.thesummitresort.com**

SINT MAARTEN, CUPECOY Wyndham Sapphire Beach Club

🛏🍴▤🏊 $$$

147 Lowlands **Tel** *599 545 2179* **Fax** *599 545 2178* **Rooms** *180*

Even the smallest units here have fully equipped kitchens, king-sized beds, living areas, sofa beds, and patio or terrace, making this ideal for families. Spa services on-site. Beachfront villas come with a private plunge pool. Activities, parties, and dinner specials are scheduled throughout the week. **www.sbcwi.com**

SINT MAARTEN, PELICAN KEY La Vista Resort

🛏🍴▤ $$

53 Billy Folly Road **Tel** *599 544 3005* **Fax** *599 544 3010* **Rooms** *50*

Accommodations are in a variety of rooms, suites, and cottages, all with kitchenettes. Facilities are limited, but include a large pool. Guests may use the beach facilities at the 18-unit La Vista Beach Resort, which is within walking distance. Watersports are available at the nearby Pelican Marina. **www.lavistaresort.com**

SINT MAARTEN, PHILIPSBURG Pasanggrahan Royal Guest House

🛏🍴▤ $$

19 Front Street **Tel** *599 542 3588* **Fax** *599 542 2885* **Rooms** *30*

This was once the Governor's residence and Dutch royalty has stayed here. It is quaint, historic, and in the middle of the town. All rooms have mosquito-netted beds, plantation-style furniture, and ceiling fans. Deluxe rooms have more space and better furnishings. The Queen's Room has an original four-poster bed. **www.pasanhotel.com**

SINT MAARTEN, PHILIPSBURG Holland House

🛏🍴▤ $$$

43 Front Street **Tel** *599 542 2572* **Fax** *599 542 4673* **Rooms** *54*

This mid-town boutique hotel has become quite trendy. Redesigned rooms feature chic colors, upscale bedding, and flat-screen TVs. Beach level suites offer more space and open onto oversized patios with water views. Step through the open lobby directly into Front Street action. **www.hhbh.com**

SINT MAARTEN, PHILIPSBURG Divi Little Bay Beach Resort

🛏🍴▤🏊 $$$$

Little Bay Road **Tel** *599 542 2333* **Fax** *599 542 4336* **Rooms** *265*

Built on the site of Fort Amsterdam, the hilltop Divi has great water views. The massive grounds invite strolling, and there are three pools, restaurants and a bar, a spa, tennis courts, and several watersports. Basic rooms open to a balcony; bathrooms are small. Upgrades are worthwhile. **www.divilittlebay.com**

SINT MAARTEN, SIMPSON BAY Mary's Boon Beach Plantation

🛏🍴▤ $$

117 Simpson Bay Road **Tel** *599 545 7000* **Fax** *599 545 3403* **Rooms** *31*

Small and well-run, this little beachfront inn is a throwback to simpler times. As well as colorful rooms there are bungalows with large verandas and up to two bedrooms and two baths. Guests tend to return because of the friendly staff and relaxed atmosphere. **www.marysboon.com**

SINT MAARTEN, SIMPSON BAY Horny Toad Guesthouse

🛏▤ $$$

2 Vlaun Drive **Tel** *599 545 4323* **Fax** *599 545 3316* **Rooms** *8*

This spotlessly clean inn, steps from the water's edge, does not have any restaurants, bars, or organized activities. With phones and smoking barred, guests here can shut out the rest of the world. Each unit has a kitchen and king-sized beds. Children under 7 not allowed. **www.thehornytoadguesthouse.com**

Where to Eat & Nightlife

Grand Case is the epicurean capital of St. Martin. Splurge on a gourmet meal at one of its bistros, or indulge in a low-cost dish at one of the locally owned-locally operated (lo-lo) stalls along the main road. Marigot's Port Royale and Simpson Bay have a large selection of excellent international restaurants. There is plenty of music and entertainment at the casinos and nightclubs.

PRICE CATEGORIES

The price ranges are for a two-course meal for one, including tax and service charges and half a bottle of wine.

$ under $10
$$ $10–15
$$$ $15–25
$$$$ $25–35
$$$$$ over $35

RESTAURANTS

Special Eateries

Open-air restaurants are quite popular, and the selection runs from fine food served at romantic candlelit waterfront tables to grilled meats served from a roadside "lo-lo". Good places for alfresco eating are the boardwalk in Philipsburg, on the lagoon side of Simpson Bay, at Port Royale in Marigot, and at beachfront resorts on both sides of the island.

A common open-air eatery

Le Pressoir

ST. MARTIN, BAIE ORIENTALE Paradise View   🖼️📶 $$$

Hope Hill, above Baie Orientale **Tel** *690 619 442*

Looking over Baie Orientale to St. Barthélemy, the views are the big draw here, but the food is good too. The menu focuses on burgers and sandwiches; Sunday buffet includes fish and Creole favorites. Open from 8am to 4pm, and for dinner Fri–Sun. Closed Tuesdays.

ST. MARTIN, FRENCH CUL DE SAC Sol é Luna   🛎️📋🖼️📶 $$$$$

61 Mont Vernon **Tel** *590 290 856*

Well worth the drive inland from Baie Orientale, this restaurant serves Italian pastas and French/Creole main dishes in a charming Provençal home tucked into the lush hillside. Menu choices change often. Dine on one of the terraces to enjoy the views. After dark, candlelight adds to the romantic ambience. Open daily for dinner.

ST. MARTIN, GRAND CASE Le Cottage   🛎️📋🖼️📶 $$$$$

97 Boulevard de Grand Case **Tel** *590 290 330*

Bruno, the owner, and Stephane, the sommelier, run this lovely place with friendly service, the best wines by the glass, and fabulous food. Try the *foie gras*, a fresh crab starter, and duck or sea bass for the main course. The Creole dishes are as excellent as the French meals. Dinner served daily.

ST. MARTIN, GRAND CASE Le Pressoir   🛎️📋📶 $$$$$

30 Boulevard de Grand Case **Tel** *590 877 662*

A restored cottage across the street from an antique salt press, this bistro-style eatery must not be missed. Owners Franck and Melanie inspire a friendly atmosphere, and the food is consistently excellent. Local seafood tops the menu. Open for dinner daily.

ST. MARTIN, MARIGOT La Belle Epoque   🖼️📶 $$$

Port La Royale **Tel** *590 878 770*

Open all day with breakfast standouts being pastry and terrific coffee. Lunch and dinner share the same menu that includes particularly good pizzas as well as freshly caught seafood dishes. The chef makes all desserts daily and the profiteroles are a best seller. The waterfront tables are perfect for lingering late into the night.

ST. MARTIN, MARIGOT Le Bistrot Nu   🖼️📶 $$$$

Allée de l'Ancienne Geôle **Tel** *590 879 709*

Worth hunting for, this little bistro is on a narrow back street that runs at right angles to Rue de Hollande, across from the stadium. Sit at one of the sidewalk tables and enjoy unpretentious French classics at lower prices than elsewhere in town. Open for dinner during weeknights.

ST. MARTIN, MARIGOT La Vie en Rose   🛎️📋🖼️📶 $$$$$

Boulevard de France **Tel** *590 875 442*

An institution, this popular restaurant overlooks the bay from its second-floor location and serves a delicious lunch featuring soup, salad, and grilled meats. Dinner is outstandingly French with excellent sauces to accompany main dishes. Tends to get overcrowded.

SINT MAARTEN, CUPECOY Temptation   🛎️📋🎵📶 $$$$$

Atlantis Casino **Tel** *599 545 2254*

Chef Dino oversees the kitchen at this upscale restaurant. Each dish is crafted in nouveau-Caribbean style featuring treats including crab-apple cake, tandoori duck, as well as scrumptious home-made cheesecake. Outstanding wine list. Open evenings only. Closed on Sundays.

Key to Symbols *see back cover flap*

SINT MAARTEN, DAWN BEACH Daniel's by the Sea · $$$$$

Oyster Pond **Tel** *599 543 6828*

Enjoy al fresco dining, with the sounds of the ocean in the background. During the day, this place is Mr. Busby's Beach Bar serving breakfast and lunch from 7:30am. At 6pm the name changes to Daniel's by the Sea and the menu switches to grilled meats. Deserves its popularity awards.

SINT MAARTEN, PHILIPSBURG Greenhouse · $$$$$

Bobby's Marina **Tel** *599 542 2941*

This landmark restaurant is as much about fun, such as theme parties, as about food. Lunch centers on hefty sandwich plates with fries and salad. Happy hour runs 4:30–7pm daily to get patrons in the mood for seafood or steak dinners. Every evening there are special food or drink offers. Big screen TVs add to the fun value.

SINT MAARTEN, SIMPSON BAY Lee's Road Side Grill · $$$

Airport Road **Tel** *599 544 4233*

Lee's has become a word-of-mouth legend on the island. His passion is fish and he has trophies to prove he's good. The grill is a casual gathering place for locals and visitors who like the fresh-catch meals, live music, excellent happy hour, and fair prices. Open 11am–midnight daily.

SINT MAARTEN, SIMPSON BAY Peg Leg Pub & Steakhouse · $$$$

Port de Plaisance **Tel** *599 544 5859*

Happy customers have voted Peg Leg's steaks the best on the island several years in a row. Casual atmosphere and pirate theme makes this a fun place for families. Lunch fare is huge sandwiches, soups, salads, and burgers. Live music several times per week.

SINT MAARTEN, SIMPSON BAY Bonita's Cantina · $$$

Airport Road, Lagoon Side **Tel** *599 545 3630*

This busy place serves casual meals, and is a sports bar with TVs tuned to live events. Breakfast starts at 7:30am with an outstanding burrito or American-style egg dishes. Lunch and dinner feature burgers, sandwiches, and Mexican specialties along with island-made ice cream. Separate kids' menu and large drink menu.

SINT MAARTEN, SIMPSON BAY Turtle Pier · $$$$

Airport Road, Lagoon Side **Tel** *599 545 2562*

Open-air and extending over the water, Turtle Pier serves a traditional full American breakfast. Lunch features sandwiches and burgers while seafood stars at dinner. There is a lobster night with live music on Wednesdays and a buffet on Sundays.

SINT MAARTEN, SIMPSON BAY Zee Best · $$$$

Plaza del Lago, Airport Road **Tel** *599 544 2477*

French pastries are made fresh every day in time for the café's 7:30am opening. Breakfast, including fabulous coffee, fresh juice, crêpes and eggs, is served until the 2pm closing. At noon, burgers, sandwiches, and salads join the menu. A second location is on the terrace at Port de Plaisance, across the lagoon.

SINT MAARTEN, SIMPSON BAY Saratoga · $$$$$

Yacht Club, Airport Road, Lagoon Side **Tel** *599 544 2421*

This well-known restaurant manages to be casual and elegant at the same time. Sit outside for a touch of island romance. Menu options change constantly. Wines include some of the best vintages, and the bar pours premium brands. Dinner only from Mondays to Saturdays.

BARS AND CLUBS

Resorts, casinos, and the main tourist areas in St. Martin have stylish clubs and casual open-air bars. Many of the best are in the Simpson Bay Lagoon area on the Dutch side and in the Baie Orientale beach on the French side. Dinner and party-boat cruises also provide evening entertainment and leave from several marinas on both sides of the island. Pick up a free copy of *K-Pasa*, a weekly publication that lists happy hours, public parties, and events.

Outdoors at Bliss

RECOMMENDED PLACES TO GO

Bamboo Bernies
Sonesta Maho Beach Resort, Sint Maarten. (Sushi bar.)

Bikini Beach
Baie Orientale, St. Martin. (Tapas, live music, and outdoor seating.)

Bliss
Beacon Hill Road, Maho Beach, Sint Maarten. (Two dance floors.)

Boo Boo Jam
Baie Orientale, St. Martin. (Beach bar, DJ plays dance music.)

Kali's Beach Bar
Baie de Friar, St. Martin. (Its full-moon parties are famous.)

Lady C Floating Bar
Simpson Bay Lagoon, Sint Maarten. (Open-air dance floor on a boat.)

Pineapple Pete
Simpson Bay, Sint Maarten. (Casual bar with a dance floor.)

Sopranos Piano Bar
Maho Bay, Sint Maarten. (Live jazz and rock.)

Sunset Beach Bar
Caravanserai Resort, Sint Maarten. (Cocktails at sunset.)

Practical Information

Both the French and Dutch sides of the island are tourist oriented and well set up to meet the needs and demands of international vacationers. The range of accommodations, dining venues, and leisure activities is wide, but focused on the upmarket. Government Tourist Boards have offices in Philipsburg and Marigot, as well as in Europe, the US, and Canada. Their websites have links to a number of businesses that cater to travelers. Maps and brochures are available from car rental agencies, hotels, and activity-booking agencies.

Visitors strolling down the esplanade, Philipsburg

WHEN TO GO

While the island of St. Martin and Sint Maarten enjoys sunshine all year round, the best time to visit is during the high season – December through to April. During this time, Carnival, a two-week fiesta, takes place. Humidity starts to build up in May and does not dissipate until late November. Tropical storms blow through and hurricanes can strike between June to November.

GETTING THERE

The island has frequent flights to and from North America and Europe, as well as other Caribbean islands. All international flights land at Princess (Queen) Juliana Airport (SXM) on the Dutch side. Regional carriers land at both the Dutch airport and the French airport, Aeroport de l'Esperance (SFG). Major carriers flying in include **Delta**, **United Airlines**, **US Airways**, **American Airlines**, **Air Canada**, **KLM**, **Air France**, **Air Caraïbes**, **Air Antilles**, **Winair**, and **LIAT**.

DOCUMENTATION

Citizens of the European Union may enter St. Martin and Sint Maarten by presenting a national ID or valid passport. Citizens of all other countries must show a valid passport.

All visitors must possess an onward or return ticket off the island. No visa is required for stays of up to three months. More information can be obtained from the **Embassy of France** in Washington DC, **Passport Canada**, and **UK Passport Services**.

Passengers boarding a Winair flight at Princess (Queen) Juliana Airport

VISITOR INFORMATION

Visitor information kiosks are located at the airports, main marinas, and cruise ship docks. **Sint Maarten Tourist Bureau** has its office in Philipsburg and **Office du Tourisme de Saint-Martin** has a branch in Marigot. Local weekly and monthly publications listing current events and activities are available free of cost throughout the island.

HEALTH AND SECURITY

Theft is a problem on the island, further complicated by the fact that the Dutch and French police do not readily exchange information. Rental cars are a prime target, as are the valuables left in them. Isolated beaches and hiking trails are other areas where theft is rampant. Report all crimes to the police, and get a report of the incident.

BANKING AND CURRENCY

Banks and ATMs are located at many locations throughout the island, with the majority in the capital cities, larger towns, and big resort areas. Most hotels, resorts, restaurants and shops accept major credit cards. The US dollar is widely accepted on both sides of the island, but officially the currency on the French side is the euro and on the Dutch side it is the Netherlands Antilles florin or guilder (NAF).

COMMUNICATIONS

To use a personal cell phone on the island, travelers must check with their service provider for instructions before leaving home. Hotel reception desks offer information regarding short-term cell phone rental outlets. Phone cards are available at major post offices. On St. Martin/Sint Maarten, the area code for the Dutch side is 599 and the area code for the French side is 590; calls between the two are considered international. Many resorts have wireless Internet service, and Wi-Fi hotspots are scattered around the island.

TRANSPORT

Most large international agencies such as **AVIS** and **Hertz** rent cars on the island, and many local companies such as **Paradise** meet or beat their rates. Book well ahead during the high season. Several agencies have booths at the airports and large resorts usually have rental cars on-site. Taxis are abundant and charges are government regulated. Rates increase in the evening, and drivers may charge extra for more than three passengers and any excess luggage.

Shop signages, Philipsburg

SHOPPING

Philipsburg is second only to Charlotte Amalie in the Virgin Islands for excellent duty-free bargains. Shops in Marigot are stocked with French merchandise at lower prices than those found in North America and some parts of Europe.

Visitors should check government duty-free exemptions before they leave home to determine the amount of goods they may bring back to their home country without paying a customs tax. Caribbean-specialist travel agencies and government websites provide further information.

Most shops on the Dutch side are open Monday to Saturday, from 9am to 6pm. On the French side, stores are open on the same days from 8:30am to 12:30pm and from 2pm to 7pm. Many shops on both sides keep longer hours when cruise ships are docked on the island.

Best buys include loose gemstones, local art and crafts, porcelain figurines, china and crystal, watches and island-made liqueurs and Caribbean rum.

LANGUAGE

The official language is Dutch on the Dutch side and French on the French side, but those who work in the tourism business can speak some English and maybe some Spanish. Among themselves, some locals speak in Papiamento (a Creole form of Spanish) or in a French patois.

ELECTRICITY

On the French side, electricity is 220 volts, and plugs must fit French outlets. On the Dutch side, electricity is 110 volts and appliances made for use in North America do not need a converter or plug adapter, however the ones made for use in Europe would require a converter and adapter.

TIME

Both sides of the island are on Atlantic Standard Time (AST), 4 hours behind Greenwich Mean Time (GMT). Neither the French nor the Dutch side observes daylight savings.

GETTING MARRIED

To get married in Sint Maarten allow at least two months to make plans and process documents. **Tropical Wedding and Honeymoon** help to save time and avoid confusion. To marry in St. Martin, requirements are far more complicated. It is possible to have the official ceremony on the Dutch side and have the reception on the French side. Many resorts make special arrangements for newlyweds as well.

DIRECTORY

GETTING THERE

Air Antilles
www.airantilles.com

Air Canada
www.aircanada.com

Air Caraïbes
www.aircaraibes.com

Air France
www.airfrance.com

American Airlines
www.aa.com

Delta
www.delta.com

KLM
www.klm.com

LIAT
www.liat.com

United Airlines
www.united.com

US Airways
www.usair.com

Winair
www.fly-winair.com

DOCUMENTATION

Passport Canada
Tel 800 567 6868.
www.pptc.gc.ca

UK Passport Services
Tel 0300 222 0000.
www.ukps.gov.uk

Embassy of France, Washington DC
Tel 120 294 46000 (USA).
www.info-france-nsa.org

VISITOR INFORMATION

Office du Tourisme de Saint-Martin
Tel 590 875 721.
www.st-martin.org

Sint Maarten Tourist Bureau
Tel 599 542 2337.
www.st-maarten.com

HEALTH AND SECURITY

Dutch Fire, Police, and Medical Assistance
Tel 911.

French Fire and Police
Tel 17.

French Medical Assistance
Tel 112.

TRANSPORT

AVIS
Tel 599 545 2847.
www.avis.com

Hertz
Tel 599 545 4541.
www.sxmrentacar.com

Paradise
Tel 599 545 3737. www.paradisecarrentalsxm.com

GETTING MARRIED

Tropical Wedding and Honeymoon
Tel 599 544 4143. www.sintmaarten-wedding.com

Exploring Saba and St. Eustatius

Many people have not even heard of these two small volcanic islands. Saba, only 5 sq miles (13 sq km) in size, has a rough coastline with few natural harbors. The interior is hilly, dominated by Mount Scenery, the extinct volcano now clad in tropical vegetation. St. Eustatius, or Statia, is more spread out and has The Quill – an extinct volcano with a deep crater that is home to a dense rainforest. The islanders have made an effort to preserve their history, making these two gems a must for those looking beyond all the glitz and glamour of the Caribbean.

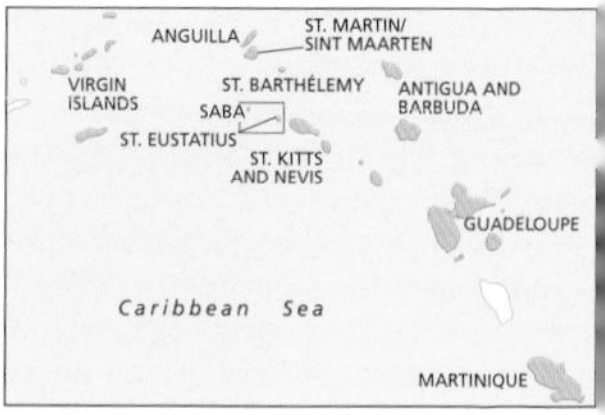

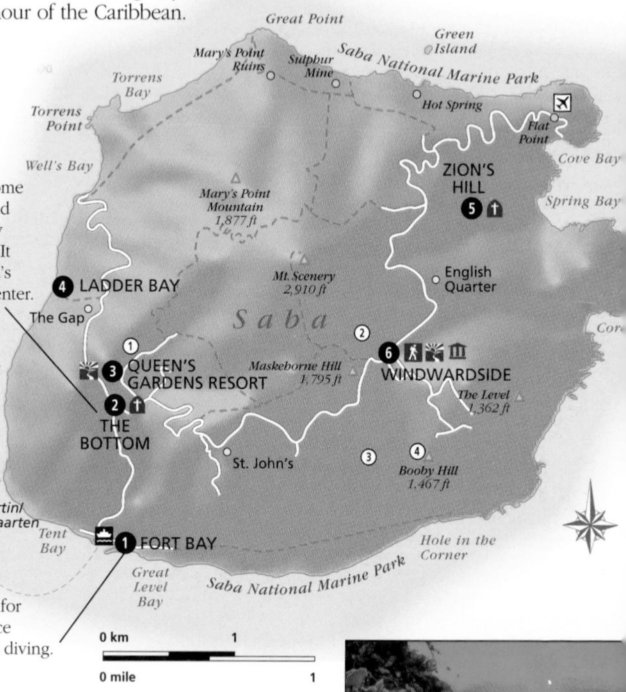

The Bottom
The town has some pretty houses and is surrounded by beautiful peaks. It is also the island's administrative center.

Fort Bay
An arrival point for visitors, this place also offers good diving.

SIGHTS AT A GLANCE

The Bottom 2
Fort Bay 1
Ladder Bay 4
Lynch Plantation Museum 10
Miriam Schmidt Botanical Gardens 11
National Park Visitors' Center 9
Oranjested 7
Windwardside 6
Zion's Hill 5

Featured Hotels and Resorts
The Old Gin House 8
Queen's Gardens Resort 3

Other Hotels and Resorts
The Anole House 4
Booby Hill hotels 3
Country Inn 6
Haiku House Villa 1
Oranjestad hotels 5
Windwardside hotels 2

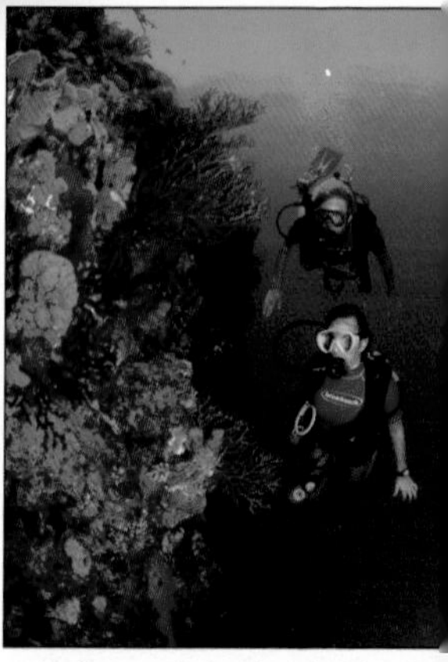

Scuba divers exploring the colorful reefs off Saba's coast

For additional map symbols *see back flap*

The small town of The Bottom, nestling beneath an extinct volcanic peak, Saba

KEY

=== Minor road

-- Track

--- Ferry route

▲ Peak

GETTING AROUND

The only way that Saba and St. Eustatius can be reached is by traveling through Sint Maarten. There are several flights each day from the Princess (Queen) Juliana Airport (SXM) to the islands, and between them. In addition, there are ferry services to Saba from St. Martin/ Sint Maarten. Once on the islands, the best way to get around is by taxi or rental car. It is easy to find your way as there is only one main road on Saba, and a limited amount of roads in St. Eustatius. Sometimes taxis can be scarce, so it is best to contact the tourism offices and make arrangements ahead of time.

Zeelandia Bay
The beach here is a nesting site for the endangered sea turtles.

SEE ALSO

• *Where to Stay* pp296–7

• *Where to Eat & Nightlife* pp298–9

The Quill
An area with a 1,968-ft (600-m) high volcanic cone and a deep crater, The Quill dominates St. Eustatius' topography.

0 km   1
0 mile   1

Boven Bay

*Boven
965 ft*   *Venus
Bay*

*Boven
National Park*

kins Bay

*Little Mount
656 ft*   Zeelandia

*Zeelandia
Bay*

Concordia Bay

⑥ *Lynch Bay*

Great Bay

Cultuurvlakte

*Berkel's
Family
Museum*   *Statia Marine
National Park*

*Compagnie
Bay*

*Tumble-
Down-
ick Bay*

*Signal Hill
768 ft*

Golden
Rock   Concordia

✈

*Interlopers
Point*

*Fort
Royal*

**LYNCH
PLANTATION
MUSEUM**   New Ground

*English
Quarter*

*Corre
Corre
Bay*

**Behind the
Mountain**

Oranje Beach ⑩ 🏛

THE OLD GIN HOUSE ⑧ ⑦ 🏛🏠🏛   *St. Eustatius*

⑤ **ORANJESTAD**

Oranjestad Bay

*Statia Marine
National Park*

⑨ **NATIONAL PARK
VISITORS' CENTER**

*Gallows
Bay*

*Mount Mazinga
1,968 ft*   ⑪ ⚔

**MIRIAM SCHMIDT
BOTANICAL GARDENS**

*Kay
Bay*

*Fort
de Windt*   *Buccaneers
Bay*

*Back-off
Bay*

Fort Bay ❶

SW coast of Saba.

Saba's main port, Fort Bay is also the starting point for diving excursions. With a harsh coastline and no sandy beaches or real harbors for boat docking, the island was hard to access. In 1972, the Dutch government built a 277-ft (84-m) deep-water pier at Fort Bay, making it easier for landing cargo and for ferry services. The only gas station on the island is located here, along with the office of Saba Deep Divers and the Saba Marine Park Visitor's Center and Hyperbaric Facility *(see pp290–91)*.

The adjacent In Two Deep café and Pop's Place are two relaxing places to enjoy a cool drink and their famous sandwiches with fantastic views of the sea.

The Bottom ❷

1 mile (1.6 km) N of Fort Bay, Saba. 👥 600. ✈ 🚌 🎷 Summer Festival

On the winding road up from Fort Bay, the first town is The Bottom – the largest on the island and the seat of

Heleen Cornet's mural at Sacred Heart Church

government. Before The Road was built, the main mode for transporting goods from the sea was walking up 200 steps from Fort Bay or 800 steps from Ladder Bay, and then onto 900 more steps into Windwardside.

Most buildings are in the typical Saban style with white clapboard houses with red roofs and trimmed lawns, all neatly kept with pride. Among the town's highlights are **Sacred Heart Church**'s sacristy adorned with original paintings done by local artist Heleen Cornet, and the **Saba Artisan Foundation** where Saban lace and other handwork are sold. Both are within walking distance from the center of the town. Other notable buildings here include the grand governor's house, and Saba University School of Medicine.

Lacework at Saba Foundation

🏠 **Saba Artisan Foundation**
The Bottom. **Tel** 599 416 3260.
🕐 8am–noon & 2:30–5pm Mon–Fri.

Queen's Gardens Resort ❸

🏨 Troy Hill, Drive 1, Saba. **Tel** 599 416 3494. **Fax** 599 416 3495.
$$$ 12 suites. 🍴 🅦
www.queensaba.com

High on the hill above The Bottom sits the Queen in all her splendor. Set amidst the hill's flora overlooking the Caribbean Sea, with 100-year-old mango trees and other tropical plants, this luxury hotel is cut off from the hustle-bustle of the town. The hotel features spacious one- and two-bedroom suites with full kitchens, dining and living areas, and private outdoor Jacuzzis facing the ocean. On the main deck below the rooms is the renowned King's

The luxurious Queen's Gardens Resort situated on Troy Hill

Crown restaurant *(see p298)*, a patio bar, and the largest swimming pool on Saba, with spectacular views of the sea. The Bottom is only a short walk down the pretty hill.

Ladder Bay ❹

1 mile (1.6 km) NW of The Bottom, Saba. 🚶 dawn–dusk daily. 🥾 hiking fee. 🌿 Saba Conservation Foundation. **www**.sabapark.org

Saba's first port, Ladder Bay served the island before the pier was constructed at Fort Bay in 1972. Steps leading from Ladder Bay up to The Bottom were the major mode of transportation for people and goods until as late as the 1970s.

Today, visitors can climb down to Ladder Bay through the Ladder Trail, which begins near The Bottom. The only route to reach the bay, this trail continues down a steep road through a residential area where the steps veer off to the left. Views from the steps to the ocean are impressive, but the hike is strenuous and takes about 40 minutes each way. Although the trail can be done without a guide, it is advisable not to stray off the track as it crosses private land. The highlight of this route is the remains of the old Customs House.

The bay has several areas ideal for diving, including Ladder Bay Deep, a sloping reef that resembles a pinnacle, dropping to a maximum depth of 110 ft (33 m).

Zion's Hill ❺

2 miles (3 km) NE of The Bottom, Saba. 👣 100. ✈ 🚕

Perched on the little Zion's Hill, Hell's Gate is a small town, closest to Juancho E Yrausquin Airport and can be reached only by The Road, a winding one-lane thoroughfare which rises up to 2,000 ft (609 m). Since many residents did not appreciate the negative name, the town is also known as Zion's Hill.

One of the main highlights in this town is the Holy Rosary Church. Made to resemble a structure from the medieval period, it was in fact built in 1962. Behind the church is **Saba Lace Boutique**, where some of the best lacemakers on the island exhibit and sell their delicate pieces of art. The town is also well-known for its locally produced and very potent spice rum called Saba Rum. The other important building here is the popular hotel, The Gate House (see p297).

Zion's Hill is the closest to the Saba National Marine Park (see p291) and the now-closed old sulphur mines.

🏠 **Saba Lace Boutique**
Zion's Hill. 🕐 9am–noon & 2:30–5pm Mon–Fri.

Windwardside ❻

1 mile (1.6 km) E of The Bottom, Saba. 👣 600. 🚕 ℹ Tourism Office, 599 416 2231. 🌐 www.saba tourism.com

Beyond Zion's Hill, The Road passes through thick forests offering fantastic views of the island before reaching

Artist JoBean in her Hot Glass Studio, Windwardside

THE ROAD THAT COULD NOT BE BUILT

Before the 1930s, Saba did not have a road, which made everyday activities, such as shopping, quite difficult. Goods arriving by sea had to be transported up steep steps to the towns. When the Sabans asked the Dutch government to build a road in the 1930s, both Dutch and Swiss engineers believed it was impossible for a road to be built because of the island's steep hills and valleys. Undaunted, a Saban named Josephus Lambert Hassell took up the challenge. He enrolled in a correspondence course in civil engineering, and convinced a crew of locals to start building a road in 1938. After five years the first section, from Fort Bay to The Bottom, was completed. The first motor vehicle arrived here in 1947. It took until 1951 to finish the section to Windwardside and St. Johns, and finally in 1958 the entire road to the airport, north of Zion's Hill, was constructed. It is aptly and simply called "The Road".

The long and winding Road of Saba

the charming town of Windwardside. A sleepy little place, this town is a step back in time, with its quaint shopping area and several restaurants. However, the real interest is the residential area that encircles the town center, with outstanding examples of typical Saban cottages, many historical in nature.

At the far end of the village, The Trail Shop offers a map that shows the name, location, and construction dates of these lovely houses. Windwardside is also known as the base for hiking trips and beyond the Trail Shop begins the hike to Mount Scenery (see p290). Other highlights are the **Harry L. Johnson Museum**, a sea

Glass artifact at JoBean's Studio

captain's 160-year-old cottage now used as a museum. The original furnishings of the Victorian era have been left as they were. In addition, a collection of Amerindian artifacts is displayed. Another interesting place to visit is **JoBean's Hot Glass Studio** at the southern end of town going toward Booby Hill. Visitors can learn to make glass beads or even watch JoBean at work.

Other opportunities for shopping are at El Momo Folk Art, which has interesting tapestries called Molas, and The Peanut Gallery (see p301), for local arts and crafts.

🏛 **Harry L. Johnson Museum**
Windwardside. **Tel** 599 416 2231. 🕐 10am–noon & 2–4pm Mon–Fri. 🌐 www.saba tourism.com/museums.html

JoBean's Hot Glass Studio
Windwardside. **Tel** 599 416 2490. 🕐 10am–5pm Mon–Sat, 10am–3pm Sun. 🌐 www.jobeanglassart.com

Outdoor Activities and Specialized Holidays

The combination of a hilly topography and volcanic origins makes Saba a prime choice for those who love hiking and diving. Through natural evolution and the lack of large-scale tourism, the island remains an eco-escape where visitors can explore rare elfin forests, winding trails robed in tropical plants, underwater pinnacles and chasms, and a host of other features.

Hiker on a trail on the extinct volcano, Mount Scenery

HIKING

Saba is quite simply a hiker's paradise with its many steep hills and deep valleys. The trails that crisscross the island were once the only means of travel and are still maintained in excellent condition.

Dominating the island's skyline is Mount Scenery, an extinct volcano. The Mount Scenery Trail begins from Windwardside *(see p289)*. It has 1,064 steps and takes up to two hours each way. At the lowest levels, cactus, red-woods, mountain fuchsia, and fruit trees can be found. The flora changes to palms, tree ferns, elephant ears, and wild plantain trees as the trail rises. At the top, climbers can view the elfin rainforest full of ferns, bromeliads, orchids, and mountain mahogany. Hikers are rewarded with sightings of Saba's rich bird species, totaling about 60.

Among other trails the Crispeen Track is the most accessible and least demanding trail, affording great views, and transporting hikers from Windwardside to The Bottom. The Sandy Cruz Trail through the valley between Mount Scenery and Mary's Point is not too demanding either. The Ladder Trail offers fantastic views of Ladder Bay *(see p288)*, while those looking for a longer hike with spectacular scenery will have to find a guide to take them along the North Coast Trail, running from Lower Zion's Hill to Wells Bay.

Another trail is the Sulphur Mine Track, which starts at Zion's Hill and winds through forests, before opening up to a meadow leading down to the sea. At the ocean's bluff, hikers descend the mine, which can be explored through flashlights. One of the best ways to ply the trails is with guide James "Crocodile" Johnson, who knows every trail. **Saba Conservation Foundation Trail Shop** can book tours with him. All hikers have to pay a fee.

DIVING AND SNORKELING

Saba is rapidly earning a reputation as a premier dive destination in the Caribbean. Because the influx of tourists has been low, the dive sites have not been heavily explored. No dive boats, except the licensed Saban dive operators, are allowed to moor at the dive sites in the marine park. This ensures that the reefs are protected and all diving is done in a safe environment. **Saba Deep Dive Center**, **Saba Divers**, and **Sea Saba** offer an upgrade to Nitrox air for free. Divers need to pay a park fee at the **Saba Marine Park Visitors' Center** or through their dive operators. Another important resource is the Hyperbaric Facility run by the Saba Conservation Foundation. This four-person decompression chamber at Fort Bay is designated to serve divers in the area from Puerto Rico to Barbados. Travelers can also visit Saba University Medical School that offers a program in hyperbaric medicine.

Sea and Learn, an annual month-long celebration in October, offers one of the best introductions of Saba to marine explorers. It includes workshops, lectures, and field projects relating to environmental awareness.

DIRECTORY

HIKING

Saba Conservation Foundation Trail Shop
Windwardside, Saba. **Tel** 599 416 2630. **www**.sabapark.org

DIVING AND SNORKELING

Saba Deep Dive Center
Fort Bay, Saba. **Tel** 599 416 3347, toll free USA: 1 866 416 3347. **www**.sabadeep.com

Saba Divers
Scout's Place Hotel, Windwardside, Saba. **Tel** 599 416 2740. **www**.sabadivers.com

Saba Marine Park Visitors' Center
Fort Bay, Saba. **Tel** 599 416 3295. **www**.sabapark.org

Sea and Learn
Tel 599 416 2246. **www**.seaandlearn.org

Sea Saba
Windwardside, Saba. **Tel** 599 416 2246. **www**.seasaba.com

Divers setting out on a dive off Saba

Saba National Marine Park and Saba Bank

Just offshore from this tiny volcanic island is a dramatic underwater world of deep chasms, sheer walls, 99-ft (30-m) pinnacles, and teeming coral reefs. This environment is protected by the Saba Conservation Foundation. They have designated the area from the high-water mark to a depth of 197 ft (60 m) all around the island as the Saba National Marine Park since 1987. In addition, 3 miles (5 km) southwest of the island lies a large submerged atoll known as the Saba Bank, a biodiversity hotspot which environmentalists are trying to protect from supertankers.

Blue-eyed goby barely visible amid the coral

Colorful corals in great abundance are protected by the marine park.

Pinnacles are suitable only for experienced divers.

LOCATOR MAP

▢	Yacht moorings
▢	Fishing and diving
▢	Recreational diving
▢	All-purpose area

ATLANTIC OCEAN

Well's Bay

SABA

Caribbean Sea

The pinnacles of Saba *rise from the deep-sea floor allowing for a "bottomless" dive, making it a popular diving site.*

Saba Bank *offers some of the most diverse marine life in the Caribbean. An expedition in 2006 located 200 species of fish, including two previously unidentified species.*

Dive sites, *totaling 29 in the marine park, offer a range of depths for divers of all experience levels. Most of the sites are along the Caribbean Sea on the western side of the island where the waters are not as rough as on the Atlantic side.*

The underwater marine park *is flush with numerous varieties of tropical fish as well as eels, sharks, and the occasional humpback whale or whale shark.*

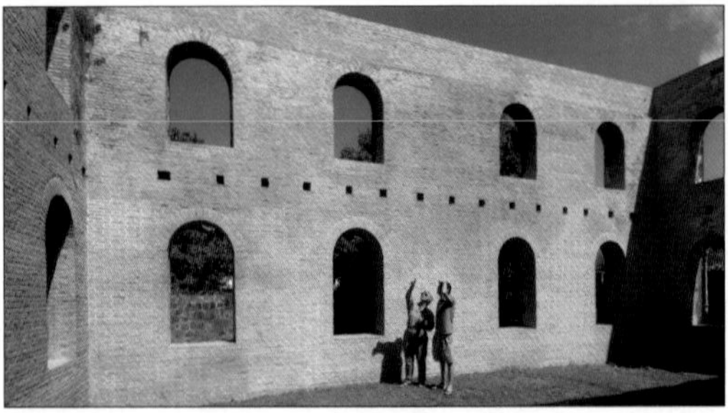

Visitors at the ruins of Honem Dalem Synagogue, Oranjestad

Oranjestad ❼

South coast of St. Eustatius. 👥 2,000. ✈ ℹ *in Fort Orange, 599 318 2433.* 📅 *Statia-America Day (Nov 16).* **www**.statiatourism.com

The island of St. Eustatius, or Statia, was known during the colonial period as the Golden Rock, because of its importance as a center for international trade. The population during the peak trading years jumped to over 20,000, and the main town of Oranjestad was a thriving, cosmopolitan place. Since 2000, a concerted effort has been made by the St. Eustatius Historical Foundation to restore much of the town area. Now, a stroll through the Upper Town is like stepping back in time, with graceful 17th- and 18th-century wood and stone structures lining the cobblestone streets.

Shops and restaurants are just steps away down the streets lined with traditional wooden cottages. The town offers the second largest collection of standing wooden 18th-century buildings in the Americas, exceeded only by Colonial Williamsburg in the US. The **St. Eustatius Historical Foundation** is housed in the 18th-century home of merchant Simon Doncker. On the main level are period rooms filled with authentic furnishings and many household goods from the 18th century. The museum staff coordinates guided walking tours of the town. The Government Guest House is an old stone structure that has been restored and is now in use as an office building. It first served as barracks for the troops at **Fort Oranje** which sits on a bluff overlooking Lower Town and Gallows Bay. Originally built by the French in 1629, the fort has been fully restored, with the Tourist Office occupying one of the buildings. One of the noted landmarks is the flagstaff, flying the flags of St. Eustatius and the US. Just to the south of the fort are the ruins of the **Dutch Reformed Church**, built in the 1750s, and the adjacent cemetery. The outer structure of the main church is occasionally used for weddings. The tower gives an overall view of the town. Another historic site is **Honem Dalem Synagogue**, one of the oldest synagogues in the Americas. Now in ruins, plans for its restoration are underway with support from St. Eustatius Center for Archeological Research (SECAR). Built in 1739, the structure and grounds include a cemetery, dating back to the same period, and a *mikvah*, a ritual bath, that was discovered during one of the SECAR excavations.

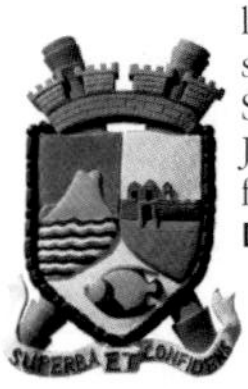

Detail, salute pillar, Fort Oranje

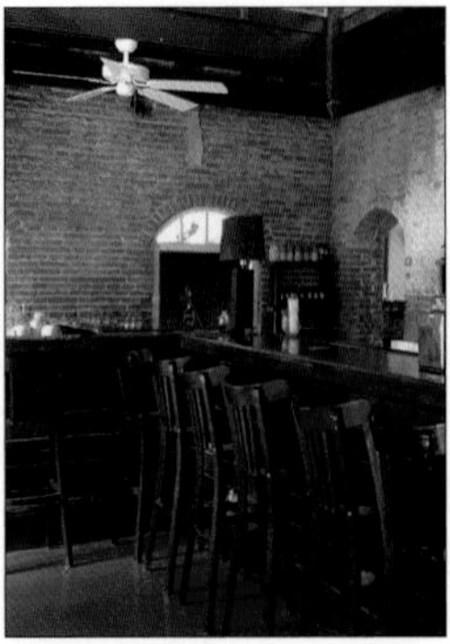

The interiors of the bar in the Old Gin House

🏛 **St. Eustatius Historical Foundation**
Wilhelminaweg 3. ***Tel*** *599 318 2288.* 🕘 *9am–5pm Mon–Fri.* **www**.steustatiushistory.org

🏰 **Fort Oranje**
Kerkweg. ℹ *599 318 2433.* 🕘 *sunrise–sunset.* ♿ **www**.statiatourism.com

⛪ **Dutch Reformed Church**
Kerkweg. 🕘 *sunrise–sunset.* ♿ **www**.steustatiushistory.com

⛪ **Honem Dalem Synagogue**
Breedeweg. 🕘 *sunrise–sunset.* ♿

The Old Gin House ❽

📍 Lower Town, Oranjestad, St. Eustatius. ***Tel*** *599 318 2319.* ***Fax*** *599 318 2135.* $$ *Rooms 18.* ❄ 🍴 ☰ [W] **www**.oldginhouse.com

Formerly a cotton processing unit, this historic structure has now been turned into the island's only luxury inn. The main building houses the lobby, the bar, the restaurant *(see p299)*, and the rooms; furnished with colonial reproduction furniture these face the manicured garden and pool behind it. Across the street, the hotel has a patio café overlooking the sea and serving breakfast and lunch. The hotel also houses a small but good bar. Oranje Beach and the National Park Visitors' Center are only a short distance down the road. A walkway, with steps leading up to Oranjestad's Upper Town, is adjacent to the property.

National Park Visitors' Center ❾

Gallows Bay, below Oranjestad, St. Eustatius. ***Tel*** *599 318 2884.* 🕘 *7am–6pm Mon–Fri.* ♿ 🛍 **www**.statiapark.org

The St. Eustatius National Park Foundation (STENAPA) oversees its many programs from the Visitors' Center in Gallows Bay. It offers exhibits, a small

Volunteers at work at Miriam Schmidt Botanical Gardens

souvenir shop, an Internet café, showers, public bathrooms, and a picnic area. Visitors can book tours, make taxi reservations, pay fees for park usage or diving, and even purchase plants from the botanical gardens.

Lynch Plantation Museum ⑩

1 mile (1.6 km) N of Oranjestad, St. Eustatius. *Tel* 599 318 2338. ⏰ on request. 🎥

This small domestic museum was constructed by the Berkel family on their homestead. The exhibition house, which was built by the family in 1916, is a replica of the original house and displays furniture, artifacts, and tools from the plantation. A private school also shares the plantation grounds, which are well maintained with fruit trees as well as the natural flora of the island. An area on the side with a bower is used for weddings and receptions.

Berkel Museum on the sprawling grounds of the Lynch Plantation

Miriam Schmidt Botanical Gardens ⑪

3 miles (5 km) E of Oranjestad, St. Eustatius. *Tel* 599 318 2884. 🚗
⏰ sunrise–sunset. 🎥 📷
www.statiapark.org

As one of the national parks under the direction of STENAPA, this developing site serves to educate locals and visitors about the varied plant life of the island, thus helping to protect and preserve the island's native and endangered flora. Development of the gardens began in 1998, and volunteers work daily on improving various areas. Already completed are the Sensory Garden, Palm Garden, Shade House, Lookout Garden (with views of St. Kitts and humpback whales), and the Jean Gemmill Bird Observation Trail. Guided tours are arranged by the National Park Visitors' Center in Gallows Bay.

STATIA IN AMERICAN HISTORY

November 16, 1776, was a day like any other in colonial St. Eustatius, when the American Brig-of-War *Andrew Doria* came sailing into Gallows Bay. The ship fired off a 13-gun salute, commemorating America's new independence from England. The troops at Fort Oranje fired back an 11-gun salute, thereby making St. Eustatius the first foreign nation to officially recognize the new nation of the United States of America.

Cannon pointing out to sea at Fort Oranje in St. Eustatius

The event was not overlooked by the British fleet in the Caribbean, which expended its wrath on Statia. Franklin D. Roosevelt, during his term as US President, presented the island with a plaque in commemoration of its support of the US in those early times. In return, the Statians named their airport after him. Each year, the island celebrates the American connection with the Statia-America Day, held on November 16. Usually, the week before the big day is filled with musical events and a carnival-like atmosphere. On the big day itself there is a flag-raising ceremony at Fort Oranje.

Outdoor Activities and Specialized Holidays

Just like Saba, the natural beauty of St. Eustatius attracts those looking for unspoiled forests and reefs to explore. But unlike Saba, St. Eustatius has a few beaches to add to the attractions, although their use is limited. The volcanic origin of the island makes for a variety of hikes and the dense concentration of colonial period artifacts offers a unique opportunity for excavating.

Snorkeling amidst a school of sergeant majors, off the coast of St. Eustatius

BEACHES

Most Caribbean islands are blessed with multitudes of beautiful beaches, but St. Eustatius is not one of them. While swimming is an option on some, Statia, as it is popularly known, has three beaches best used for sunbathing, playing in the sand, and flying kites.

Oranjestad Bay is the most accessible and swimmer-friendly beach on the Caribbean Sea side. Located in Oranjestad, it has patches of tan and black sand interrupted by rocks jutting into the sea. The water is shallow and calm. The renowned inn, The Old Gin House (*see p292*) is just down the road.

Lynch Bay is a stretch of brown sand midway down the island's Atlantic Coast. The water is shallow near the beach, but develops an undertow farther out so swimmers have to be careful. Visitors need to bring essentials since there are no amenities here.

Zeelandia Bay is a 2-mile (3-km) long Atlantic strand that looks inviting, but activities should be restricted to sunbathing and sand castle building. The water has a heavy undertow, so swimmers are warned to stay out of it.

HIKING

St. Eustatius offers hikers a variety of hiking trails in the national park that encompasses the Boven and The Quill peaks. The STENAPA was founded in 1988 to manage these two areas plus the marine park and botanical gardens. It maintains the hiking trails, posts signs, monitors animal and plant life, and conducts guided hikes. All hikers must pay a fee at the STENAPA Visitors' Center (*see p292*).

The Boven National Park area consists of five hills on the northern point of the island. Most of the trails are not maintained at this point because of unresolved property disputes. However, visitors can still follow four trails, including Boven, Venus Bay, Gilboa Hill, and Bergje. All trails start at the end of road in Zeelandia, and range in length from 60 to 120 minutes to complete.

DIVING, SNORKELING, AND KAYAKING

Diving is the reason why most visitors come to St. Eustatius. The Statia National Marine Park is considered one of the top five dive sites in the Caribbean. The park extends from the shore to a 99-ft (30-m) depth and around the entire coast. The park authority maintains 42 mooring sites.

Diving is allowed only through the three local dive operators, and divers must pay either annually or for each dive at the Gallows Bay Visitors' Center.

St. Eustatius has nearly 200 ship wrecks and other underwater structures such as coral reefs on volcanic substrates, including lava flows shaped like fingers and a spur and groove zone. These can be seen at Hangover, Five Fingers North and South, and the Ledges dive sites.

Among the 36 dive sites are historical areas such as Double and Triple Wreck, Stingray City, and Anchor Reef. Deep dive sites including Grand Canyon/Off the Wall, Coral Gardens, and Doobie's Crack range from 85–99 ft (26–30 m). **Golden Rock Dive Center** rents out underwater cameras and organizes guided dives.

The prime sites for snorkeling in Oranjestad Bay have an entire range of submerged sea walls, warehouses and old piers, which are accessible from Oranje Beach or the Golden Era hotel pier. An interesting way to snorkel is using the Sea-Doo underwater scooters that **Dive Statia** rents out. **Scubaqua** and Golden Rock Dive Center also offer snorkeling trips.

Some of the bays are inaccessible by road but can be reached by kayaks. Dive Statia has Malibu Two Xl ocean kayaks for hire.

Signages at the Quill Trail

For hotels and restaurants in this region see pp296–7 and pp298–9

Hiking The Quill

In Dutch, a "kuil" is a pit, and this is how the high mountain crater called The Quill got its name. This volcanic cone's topography ranges from rough slopes leading up to the edge of the crater to the broad inner floor, surrounded by a national park. Throughout The Quill National Park the vegetation zones vary from thorny woodland on the outer slopes of The Quill, to lush evergreen seasonal forest in the crater and a rare elfin forest on the rim at the highest point, called Mount Mazinga. Ten hiking trails surround The Quill.

LOCATOR MAP

☐ *Area illustrated*

Birds *of various kinds can be found in the area. The Bird Trail has posted signs indicating the species that can be seen at certain points.*

Oranjestad

Mount Mazinga
1,968 ft

Fort de Windt

```
0 km        1
0 miles      1
```

KEY

— Around the Mountain Trail

— Bird Trail

— Botanical Garden Trail

— Couchar Mountain Trail

— Crater Trail

— Mazinga Trail

— Panoramic Point Trail

— Quill Trail

— Rosemary Lane Trail

— Tompi Hill Trail

ℹ Visitors' center

The Quill Trail *leads to the rim of the crater. It is rated as one of the moderate hikes. The view from the rim shows the vast and varied vegetation zones.*

Hikers *can choose from the easy Bird Trail to the difficult Crater Trail, and from the longest Around the Mountain Trail to the relatively short and steep Panoramic Point Trail.*

EXCAVATING

Called "The Pompeii of the New World" by archaeologists, St. Eustatius has over 600 documented archaeology sites with artifacts dating from the slavery era. The **St. Eustatius Center for Archaeological Research** hosts digs where students and volunteers help uncover the remnants of household goods and tools from the ruins of slave houses, warehouses, and domestic buildings that existed during that time.

Choosing a Hotel

Relatively untouched by an onslaught of visitors and developers, Saba and St. Eustatius are ideal for those seeking a quieter, gentler Caribbean experience. The hotels are small and family-run, and guests are treated like visiting friends. While all the services might not be available, locals are very eager to share their islands' resources and interested in making their guests' stay special.

PRICE CATEGORIES
The following price ranges are for a standard double room per night and all taxes included.

§ under $100
§§ $100–200
§§§ $200–300
§§§§ $300–400
§§§§§ over $400

SABA AND ST. EUSTATIUS

Queen's Gardens Resort, Saba – *p288*
This all-suite hotel high on the hill above The Bottom offers luxury accommodations in a tropical garden, with panoramic views to the sea.

The Old Gin House, St. Eustatius – *p292*
The historical recreation of colonial times so prevalent throughout Oranjestad has produced this lovely, intimate hotel on the waterfront.

Queen's Gardens Resort

The Old Gin House

SABA, BOOBY HILL The Anole House ▢ §
Tel 599 416 2246/1800 833 7222 **Fax** 599 416 2362 *Rooms 2*

Tranquil and very secluded within beautiful tropical gardens, the Anole House is just 3 minutes' walk from Windwardside. This light and airy, high-ceilinged villa, a modern building in traditional style, has three terraces that offer breathtaking panoramic views. The pool is open-access, so unsuitable for children under 12. **www.theanolehouse-saba.com**

SABA, BOOBY HILL El Momo Cottages ▢ §
Tel 599 416 2265 **Fax** 599 416 2265 *Rooms 6*

A pleasant, short walk to JoBean Glass Studio and Windwardside, these simple "earth-kind" cottages offer a relaxing way to spend a vacation, sitting on the porch and gazing out over the scenery. Some units available with kitchen. The property includes a pool. Gourmet breakfast is available for a small fee. **www.elmomo.com**

SABA, BOOBY HILL Flamboyant Cottage ▤ ▢ §§
Tel 239 560 1330 (US) *Rooms 2*

This picture-perfect Saban cottage sits 1,500 ft (460 m) above sea level on Booby Hill, with great views. It has a modern kitchen, bathrooms, and furniture, separate living and dining rooms, dining gazebo, terraces, and a private pool. The shops and restaurants of Windwardside are just 10 minute's walk away. **www.oursabacottage.com**

SABA, BOOBY HILL Shearwater Resort ▯ §§
Tel 599 416 2498 **Fax** 599 416 2482 *Rooms 10*

This luxury hotel sits 2,000 ft (610 m) above sea level with incredible views of St. Eustatius, St. Kitts, and beyond. The property includes a pool, a hot tub, an exercise room, tennis court, putting green, and restaurant *(see p298).* Diving and honeymoon packages are available. **www.shearwater-resort.com**

SABA, TROY HILL Haiku House Villa ▤ §§§§§
Drive 1 **Tel** 599 416 3494 **Fax** 599 416 3495 *Rooms 3*

This striking three-bedroom villa high on Troy Hill has commanding views of the Caribbean Sea. Done in natural woods with luxury appointments and a Siematic kitchenette, it has a spacious living room and an office. The master bedroom is air-conditioned. Also a pool and Jacuzzi on the wide wooden deck. **www.sabavillas.com**

SABA, WINDWARDSIDE Ecolodge Rendezvous ▯ §
Crispean Track **Tel** 599 416 3348 *Rooms 12*

The ecologically sensitive will love this place. The quaint wooden cottages – brightly decorated by resident artist-owner Heleen Cornet – are set in the rainforest, equipped with solar panels and showers, low-flush composting toilets and kitchenettes. Includes a restaurant *(see p298),* pool, and sweat lodge. **www.ecolodge-saba.com**

SABA, WINDWARDSIDE Althea Cottage §§
Tel 540 885 3345 (US) *Rooms 2*

A 150-year old Saban cottage has been renovated into a perfect accommodation for a small family. Living room has a sofabed, kitchen is fully equipped and CD and DVD players are available in the family room. There is an outdoor dining area with stunning views of Mount Scenery. **www.saba-cottage.com**

SABA, WINDWARDSIDE The Cottage Club ▢ §§
Tel 599 416 2486 **Fax** 599 416 2476 *Rooms 10*

The 10 charming cottages in this small resort are stairstepped up the hill, with a view out to the sea. All cottages have full kitchens, dining and living areas as well as cable TV. The resort has a pool and an Internet café. Dive packages with Sea Saba and cookery classes are available. **www.cottage-club.com**

Key to Symbols *see back cover flap*

SABA, WINDWARDSIDE Daphne's Cottage $$

Tel 603 782 4569 *Rooms 2*

Built in 1850, this cottage has been lovingly restored and updated. Situated 1,450 ft (440 m) up on a hill in a tropical garden in Windwardside, Daphne's Cottage has two bedrooms, one bath, American kitchen, dining patio, and an area for sunbathing. Excellent views of Mount Scenery and the ocean. **www.sabadaphnecottage.com**

SABA, WINDWARDSIDE House on the Path $$

Tel 599 580 9188 *Fax 599 542 6300* *Rooms 2*

This charmingly restored cottage sits above Windwardside, just adjacent to the steps leading up to Mount Scenery. Surrounded by a lush forest, the cottage is cooled by mountain breezes and offers guests a full kitchen, DVD player, laundry facilities, and a cell phone for use while there. **www.houseonthepath.com**

SABA, WINDWARDSIDE Island View Villa $$

Tel 599 416 2954/1877 952 8899 (US) *Rooms 2*

Delivering a genuine Saban experience, this typical white-shingled, green-shuttered house has a full kitchen, dining and living room, two bedrooms, and a bath. Balconies on all sides, with views of the sea and Mount Scenery, are an added highlight. TV, DVD, and CD players are provided. **www.sabaislandrealty.com**

SABA, WINDWARDSIDE Juliana's $$

Tel 599 416 2269 *Fax 599 416 2389* *Rooms 12*

This small hotel is centrally located and has nice views of the ocean from some rooms, the restaurant *(see p298)*, and the pool deck. Other rooms have a garden view. Breakfast is included in the room charges. The place is affiliated with Sea Saba for dive packages. **www.julianas-hotel.com**

SABA, WINDWARDSIDE Scout's Place Hotel $$

Tel 599 416 2740/2205/2213 *Fax 599 416 2741* *Rooms 15*

A diver's delight, the hotel is centrally located with views to the sea and the town. Options for rooms include standard, deluxe and cottage rooms with balconies, refrigerators, TVs, and Internet access. Also available is the two-bedroom Pirates Cottage with full kitchen. There is a pool and a restaurant. **www.scoutsplace.com**

SABA, WINDWARDSIDE The Pilot House $$$

Park Lane *Tel 440 323 8926 (US)* *Fax 440 323 0213* *Rooms 2*

This beautiful two-bedroom Saban cottage features luxury accommodations for four people. It has a fully equipped kitchen and a large room with flat screen TV and DVD player, along with gorgeous views of the Atlantic Ocean. Guests get pool privileges at Juliana's, and there is a lovely outdoor patio. **www.pilothousesaba.com**

SABA, WINDWARDSIDE Hibiscus Cottage $$$$

Park Lane *Tel 599 544 3056* *Rooms 2*

Newly built in traditional Saban style, this two-bedroom cottage offers an open floorplan, full kitchen, en-suite bathrooms, an oversized patio for entertaining, and a private picnic area. Furnishings are mahogany and rattan. Excellent views of Mount Scenery and adjacent gardens. Restaurants and shops nearby. **www.sabahibiscus.com**

SABA, WINDWARDSIDE Villa Fairview $$$$$

Tel 316 2955 1223 (US) *Rooms 3*

This comfortable villa has a full kitchen, living room, two air-conditioned bedrooms, and a bath on one level, and a separate en-suite bedroom on the second level along with laundry facilities. There is also a wraparound veranda for views overlooking Windwardside. **www.villasaba.nl**

ST. EUSTATIUS, CONCORDIA Country Inn $

Tel 599 318 2484 *Rooms 6*

This intimate guesthouse is located at Concordia with pretty views of Zeelandia Bay, nestled in a tropical garden. The air-conditioned rooms include TV, and meals are served on request at an additional fee. Oranjestad is a very short taxi ride, or a 15-minute walk from the hotel. **www.statiatourism.com/countryinn**

ST. EUSTATIUS, ORANJESTAD Golden Era Hotel $$

Lower Town *Tel 599 318 2455* *Fax 599 318 2445* *Rooms 20*

This waterfront hotel in the Lower Town offers basic accommodations and a convenient location. Choice of rooms includes singles, doubles, suites, and efficiency suites; rooms feature cable TV and refrigerators. Rates include breakfast. There is also a pool, restaurant *(see p299)*, and pool bar on-site. **www.goldenerahotel.com**

ST. EUSTATIUS, ORANJESTAD King's Well Resort $$

Tel 599 318 2538 *Fax 599 318 2538* *Rooms 12*

This hotel has one of the best locations on the island, between Oranjestad and Lower Town, with beautiful views to the beach and sunset. Owners Win and Laura keep a menagerie of pets to add color. Some rooms have air-conditioning. Restaurant *(see p299)*, pool and Jacuzzi facilities are offered on-site. **www.kingswellstatia.com**

ST. EUSTATIUS, ORANJESTAD The Villa $$

Tel 316 2955 1223 *Rooms 2*

This private two-bedroom villa is perfect for families. Contains full kitchen, laundry facilities, and a living area with TV, DVD, and CD players, plus a porch with views of the ocean and Mount Scenery. Extra beds are provided to accommodate a total of up to six guests. Minimum stay is for 3 nights. **www.vrbo.com/144811**

Where to Eat & Nightlife

Since Saba and St. Eustatius are small islands the choices for dining and nightlife are limited. But what is there is good, keeping up to the standards expected by the repeat visitors. Most of the restaurants and bars in Saba are concentrated either in Windwardside or at hotels scattered around the island. In St. Eustatius the biggest concentration of both establishments is in Oranjestad.

PRICE CATEGORIES
The price ranges are for a two-course meal for one, including tax and service charges and half a bottle of wine.

[$] under $10
[$][$] $10–15
[$][$][$] $15–25
[$][$][$][$] $25–35
[$][$][$][$][$] over $35

RESTAURANTS

Special Cuisines
With the largest influx of visitors coming from the US and Canada, these islands offer a lot of American food. However, there are also some West Indian Creole dishes and many seafood options. Most restaurants in Saba generally offer standard international fare, though there are some Chinese/Asian and German eateries in Oranjestad as well.

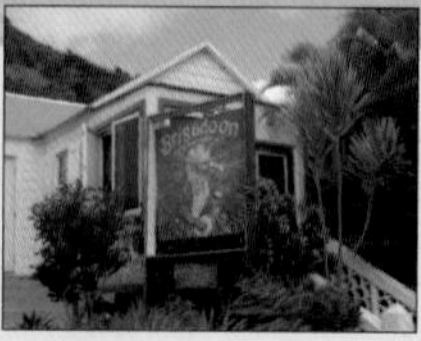

Brigadoon

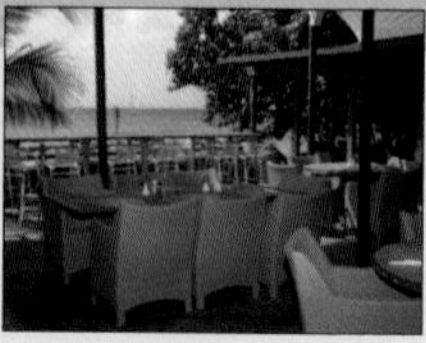

The Old Gin House

SABA, BOOBY HILL Bistro del Mare Restaurant 🍸 ▤ ⛱ ♿ [$][$][$][$][$]
Shearwater Resort ***Tel*** *599 416 2498*

FIne fresh local seafood and produce is given a northern Italian flavor here, and the wine list is showcased with a "taster menu". The airy dining room is ideal for dinner (served Tue–Sat), but for Sunday brunch try to bag one of the poolside tables, which provide a spectacular panorama of St. Eustatius, St. Kitts, and on a clear day, Nevis.

SABA, THE BOTTOM Family Deli [V] ⛱ [$][$][$]
Troy Hill Drive 1 ***Tel*** *599 416 3858*

This friendly, casual place is open for breakfast, lunch, and dinner, and also offers food to go. Specialties include pizza, burgers, sandwiches, and regular dinner entrées, in addition to smoothies, milkshakes, ice cream, and baked goods. The walls are covered with local art and there is a small veranda for outdoor dining.

SABA, THE BOTTOM King's Crown [V] ⛱ [$][$][$][$][$]
Queen's Gardens Resort ***Tel*** *599 416 3494*

One of the most elegant on Saba, King's Crown excels in seafood and international cuisine. Outdoor tables have commanding views of the sea, and there is a European feel indoors. Check out the live lobster tank just outside the doors from the stone patio. The patio bar is a favorite of hotel guests and visitors alike.

SABA, FORT BAY In Two Deep ▤ [$][$][$][$][$]
Tel *599 416 3438*

Divers flock to this bar-cum-café right near the docks in Fort Bay. The atmosphere is casual and colorful, with a New England motif, including a mahogany bar and stained-glass windows. The fare, including sandwiches, eggs Benedict, omelets, chowder, and salads, is well prepared. Open for breakfast and lunch only.

SABA, WINDWARDSIDE Saba's Treasure ⛱ [V] 🚸 [$][$][$][$]
Tel *599 416 2819*

The best stone-fired pizza on the island is served here, together with classic grilled meats and local fish, and the ancestral rock oven is used for the occasional hog roast. Nautical and historical memorabilia give a traditional pub-like look, while a rock'n'blues MP3 "juke box" lends a relaxed, friendly vibe. Open 10am–10/11pm daily.

SABA, WINDWARDSIDE Brigadoon [$][$][$][$][$]
Tel *599 416 2380*

This eclectic restaurant in a century-old house serves anything from Creole dishes and *schwarma* (Middle-Eastern non-vegetarian wrap) to lobster, steaks, and fresh seafood. The owners Trish and Michael keep their patrons entertained with a running commentary. Open for dinner only and closed on Tuesday.

SABA, WINDWARDSIDE My Kitchen [V] 🍸 ⛱ [$][$][$][$][$]
Tel *599 416 2539*

This 35-seat casual restaurant near the Mount Scenery Trail serves freshly made sandwiches and salads for lunch, while the menu includes pasta dishes and fresh seafood. Do not miss the home-made desserts such as tiramisu, cheesecake, and chocolate mousse, or anything from the adjacent bakery.

SABA, WINDWARDSIDE Rainforest Restaurant [V] ⛱ [$][$][$][$][$]
Ecolodge Rendezvous ***Tel*** *599 416 3888*

This unique restaurant reflects the eco-sensibility of the Ecolodge *(see p296)*. The setting is rustic and candlelit. The menu uses fresh produce from the hotel's own gardens. Seafood entrées feature what is caught daily from the sea, and steaks and vegetarian entrées are also available. Tuesday nights feature Indonesian cuisine. Closed Monday nights.

Key to Symbols *see back cover flap*

SABA, WINDWARDSIDE Tropics Café

🖼🎵♿ $$$$$

Juliana's Hotel **Tel** *599 416 2469*

This pleasant, breezy restaurant at Juliana's *(see p297)* with a good ocean view stands out for Creole cuisine and its theme nights three evenings a week. On Fridays a movie screen is put up by the pool and burgers are offered; Wednesdays and Sundays are grill nights, with cocktails and kebabs. There is local art on the walls.

ST. EUSTATIUS, ORANJESTAD Superburger

🖼🎵📄 $$$

Tel *599 318 2412*

St. Eustatius' form of fast food is reflected in this casual restaurant on a main corner in Oranjestad. In addition to burgers and great fries, they offer West Indian dishes and ice cream. Owner Skell has added TVs for a sports bar atmosphere on the large patio, as well as an area where live bands perform on weekends.

ST. EUSTATIUS, ORANJESTAD Chinese Restaurant

🅥🖼📄 $$$$

H.M. Queen Beatrixstraat **Tel** *599 318 2389*

If you are looking for Chinese food in St. Eustatius, this is the place to visit. It offers all the standard Chinese dishes done well, some Caribbean extras, and a couple of vegetarian options. The restaurant is set back off the road, so keep an eye out for it.

ST. EUSTATIUS, ORANJESTAD Blue Bead

🖼📄 $$$$$

Lower Town, Gallows Bay **Tel** *599 318 2873*

This bright, Caribbean-style restaurant at the bottom of the hill at Gallows Bay is a favorite with both locals and visitors. The Italian and French cuisine has lots of seafood, including salt cod fritters, mussels, and shrimp. Pizzas are also available. Be sure to taste the great home-made vanilla rum. It is closed on Tuesdays.

ST. EUSTATIUS, ORANJESTAD Golden Era

🖼♿ $$$$$

Lower Town, Golden Era Hotel **Tel** *599 318 2455*

This is one of the few truly waterfront restaurants in St. Eustatius, overlooking Gallows Bay and Oranje Beach. The cuisine is primarily West Indian/Creole, with some good salad and entrée selections. Try to get a table on the patio where the waves crash right below you. Dinner only, unless you're staying at the hotel *(see p297)*.

ST. EUSTATIUS, ORANJESTAD King's Well

🖼 $$$$$

King's Well Resort **Tel** *599 318 2538*

The owner's German background is obvious in this restaurant at the King's Well Resort *(see p297)* which serves excellent German cuisine, including *schnitzel*, *Rostbraten*, and fresh fish. The smoked barbecue ribs are legendary and the eatery boasts the best sunset views on the island. Dinner only.

ST. EUSTATIUS, ORANJESTAD Ocean View Terrace

🖼 $$$$$

Tel *599 318 2934*

This gracious dining area sits on a terrace of the Government House, overlooking historic Fort Oranje and the sea in downtown Oranjestad. The cuisine is West Indian, and seafood, chicken, goat, and even oxtail are served. Lunch offerings include sandwiches and salads.

ST. EUSTATIUS, ORANJESTAD The Old Gin House Restaurant

🖼♿ $$$$$

Lower Town, Oranjebaai 1, Old Gin House **Tel** *599 318 2319*

Often cited as the best restaurant on the island, the place offers great Antillean cuisine. The menu offers interesting seafood and meat dishes, and the restaurant overlooks the hotel pool *(see p292)*. Lunch only, unless you are staying at the hotel. The adjoining Mooshay Pub is a popular evening gathering place.

ST. EUSTATIUS, ORANJESTAD Original Fruit Tree Restaurant

🖼📄 $$$$$

Tel *599 318 2584*

Located near the Mazinga Gift Shop *(see p301)*, this place dishes up authentic West Indian cuisine that involves bull foot soup and heaping plates of chicken, fish or pork with rice, plantain, and salad. It is hearty eating that keeps locals happy and is good for visitors as well.

BARS AND CLUBS

Saba and St. Eustatius are small, peaceful islands where everyone knows each other and there is not a great deal of socializing outside family parties. Visitors should not expect a busy nightlife, although there are a few bar/restaurant combos and some of the hotel-restaurants make an effort to create nightlife through special events.

Bar at The Old Gin House

RECOMMENDED PLACES TO GO

Cool Corner
Oranjestad.
(St. Eustatius' oldest bar.)

The Old Gin House
Lower Town, Oranjestad.
(Barbecue nights on Wednesdays.)

Scout's Place
Windwardside.
(Karaoke nights on Fridays.)

Smoke Alley
Oranjestad.
(Live music or DJs on Friday nights.)

Swinging Door
Center of Windwardside.
(Relaxed bar and eatery.)

Tropics Café
Juliana's, Windwardside.
(Special activities on weekends.)

Practical Information

These charming little islands have been closely affiliated to the Netherlands, so the general appearance, hospitality, and culture are European. The people, who are very proud of their islands, are warm and welcoming to visitors. If lost, visitors just need to stop and ask the locals for directions. A taxi is the best way to get around since the islands are small. Saban lacework makes an especially pretty souvenir.

Office of the Saba Tourist Bureau at Windwardside

WHEN TO GO

The climate on both islands is pleasant year round, and nights can be cool. The summer months are hotter and more humid, and the peak hurricane season is from June through to October. Many people go to Saba in July for the Summer Festival, or in October for the Sea and Learn workshops. In St. Eustatius the special days include Carnival in mid-July, and November 16, the designated Statia-America Day.

GETTING THERE

Winair operates several flights daily from Princess Juliana International Airport (SXM) in St. Martin to Juancho E. Yrausquin Airport (SAB) in Saba. It also has daily flights between St. Eustatius and Saba. Ferries, including the **Dawn II** and **The Edge**, operate on a weekly schedule between Saba and St. Martin.

St. Eustatius can be reached via air transport on Winair, with several daily flights from St. Martin to Franklin D. Roosevelt Airport (EUX), daily flights from Saba, and a weekly flight from Golden Rock Airport (SKB), St. Kitts. There is no ferry service at present, but private boats can be chartered in St. Martin.

DOCUMENTATION

For both islands, travelers need a valid passport and onward/return ticket. Residents of certain countries are required to obtain a visa to enter the Netherlands Antilles; for a list of these countries, it is advisable to consult the website of the tourism bureau. There is a departure fee to be paid just before getting on the plane to return home. The two islands have different departure fees and one can expect a lower fee if the final destination shown on the onward ticket is another Caribbean island.

VISITOR INFORMATION

Information on Saba can be obtained from the office of the **Saba Tourist Bureau** located in Windwardside and on St. Eustatius at the **St. Eustatius Tourism Office** in Fort Oranje. Both have their own tourist websites. There are tourist desks at the airports providing maps and brochures, as well as assistance with transportation.

HEALTH AND SECURITY

Saba and St. Eustatius, being small islands, are relatively crime-free. For health-related emergencies, there are hospitals such as **A M Edwards Medical Center** and **Queen Beatrix Hospital** on both islands which are staffed by local physicians. Both islands have hyperbaric chambers.

BANKING AND CURRENCY

The official currency in both Saba and St. Eustatius is the NAfl (guilder) although the predominant currency is the US dollar. Credit cards and traveler's checks are widely accepted. ATM machines are available at the banks in Windwardside and The Bottom in Saba, and in Oranjestad in St. Eustatius.

COMMUNICATIONS

In Saba, hotels have direct dialing worldwide, and Landsradio has phone booths in Windwardside and The Bottom for international calls. The **St. Eustatius Telephone Company NV (EUTEL)** provides international phone services, and visitors can buy calling cards. Internet connections are available at most of the hotels, as well as at **Island Communication Services**. Internet access is available at the **Public Library** and **Computers and More**.

TRANSPORT

Taxis are the favored way to get around both islands, since there is no public transport. Tourist desks at the airports can connect you with available drivers, and the drivers in their turn give customers

Plane landing at Juancho E. Yrausquin Airport, Saba

their cell phone number so that they can be contacted whenever transport is needed. Saba has only one car rental agency, **Caja's Car Rental**, while in St. Eustatius, there are several, including **ARC Car Rental**, **Brown's Car Rental**, **Schmidt Car Rental**, and **Trep Car Rental**, providing small cars capable of navigating the narrow roads.

SHOPPING

While both islands are duty-free ports, there is not a great deal of shopping, unlike on other Caribbean islands. In Saba, there is a collection of shops in Windwardside that include a gallery, **The Peanut Gallery**, and a gift boutique. Also, there are several sites where Saban lace can be purchased. In St. Eustatius, there are only two small shops – the **Mazinga Gift Shop** and the **Historical Society Museum Shop**.

LANGUAGE

Dutch is the official language on both islands but English is spoken everywhere.

ELECTRICITY

Electricity on both islands is 110 volts. For 220-volt appliances a converter is needed.

TIME

Both islands are in the Atlantic Time Zone, 5 hours behind GMT. When the US is on daylight saving time, the islands follow the time on the US East Coast.

GETTING MARRIED

To marry in Saba, a couple must apply for a wedding date a month in advance by writing to the Lieutenant Governor at the **Census Office**, along with the necessary documents. If getting married at a location other than the Court Room at the Government Building, approval for the venue is also required. For St. Eustatius, the couple needs to submit the documents at least a week in advance but then must wait for the government to approve all documents. Details can be obtained from the websites of Saba Tourist Bureau and St. Eustatius Tourism.

Interior of a gift boutique in Saba

DIRECTORY

GETTING THERE

Dawn II
Fort Bay, Saba.
Tel 599 416 2299.
www.sabactransport.com

The Edge
St. Maarten.
Tel 599 544 2640.
www.stmaarten-activities.com

Winair
Tel 599 545 4237/4230.
www.fly-winair.com

VISITOR INFORMATION

Saba Tourist Bureau
Windwardside, Saba.
www.sabatourism.com

St. Eustatius Tourism Office
Fort Oranje, Oranjestad.
www.statiatourism.com

HEALTH AND SECURITY

A M Edwards Medical Center
The Bottom, Saba.
Tel 599 416 3289/88.

Queen Beatrix Hospital
Oranjestad, St. Eustatius.
Tel 599 318 2211.

COMMUNICATIONS

Computers and More
Oranjestad.
Tel 599 318 2596.

Island Communication Services
Windwardside, Saba.
Tel 599 416 2881.
www.icssaba.com

Public Library
Fort Oranje, Oranjestad.
Tel 599 318 2222.

St. Eustatius Telephone Company NV (EUTEL)
Oranjestad, St. Eustatius.
Tel 599 318 2210.
www.goldenrocknet.com

TRANSPORT

ARC Car Rental
St. Eustatius.
Tel 599 318 2595.

Brown's Car Rental
St. Eustatius.
Tel 599 318 2266.

Caja's Car Rental
Saba. *Tel 599 416 2388.*

Schmidt Car Rental
St. Eustatius.
Tel 599 318 2788.

Trep Car Rental
St. Eustatius.
Tel 599 318 2626.

SHOPPING

Historical Society Museum Shop
Oranjestad, St. Eustatius.
Tel 599 318 2856.

Mazinga Gift Shop
Oranjestad, St. Eustatius.
Tel 599 318 2245.

The Peanut Gallery
Windwardside, Saba.
Tel 599 416 2509.

GETTING MARRIED

Census Office
The Bottom, Saba.
Tel 599 416 3497/3311/3312. www.statia government.com

Exploring St. Kitts and Nevis

St. Kitts divides fairly naturally into two halves. While the north is mountainous with pretty villages and delightful former plantations such as Romney Manor Plantation, the south of the island is more active due to the beach-based tourism. Luxury hotels and hotel chains here are scattered in Frigate Bay. Nevis is a smaller island and is also divided in a similar way but here the beach activities dominate in the north while former plantations, now converted into charming inns, sit higher on the mountainside in the south. A good way to discover Nevis is to go for a drive around the base of Nevis Peak, stopping off at the plantations for lunch or afternoon tea.

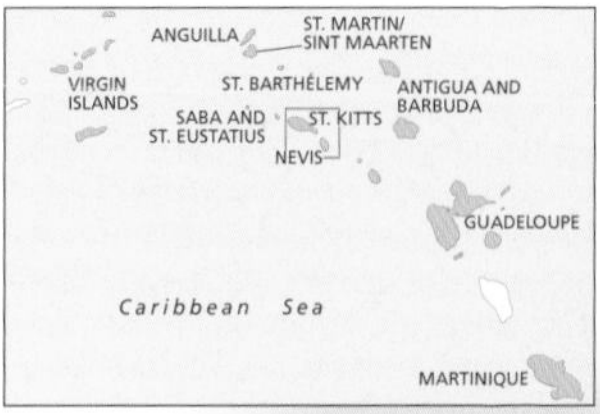

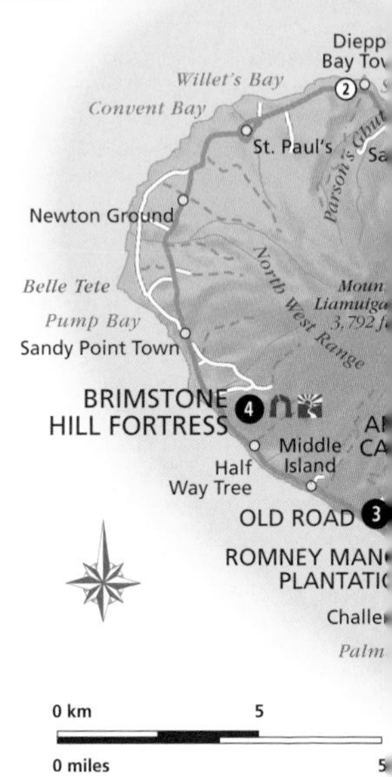

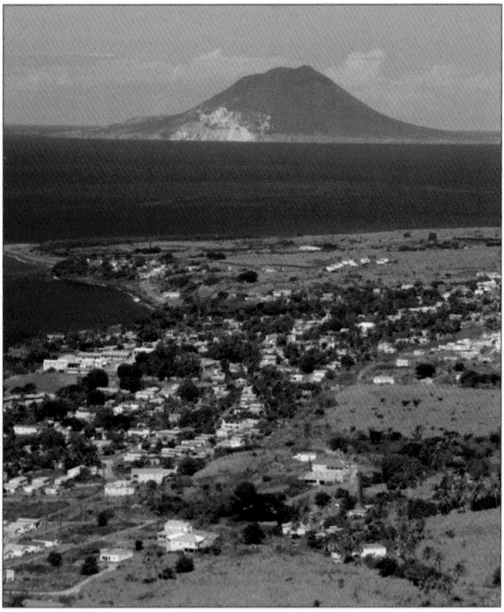
View of St. Kitts and St. Eustatius from the Brimstone Hill Fortress

KEY

- Highway
- Major road
- Minor road
- Ferry route
- ▲ Peak

SIGHTS AT A GLANCE

Arawak Carvings ❺
Basseterre ❶
Botanical Garden of Nevis ⓫
Brimstone Hill Fortress pp304–5 ❹
Charlestown ❾
Fig Tree Church ❿
Frigate Bay Resorts ❻
Nevis Plantation Inns ⓬
Old Road ❸
Oualie Beach ❽
Romney Manor Plantation ❷
Southeastern Peninsula ❼

Hotels and Resorts
Banyan Tree Bed and Breakfast ⑧
Basseterre hotels ①
Four Seasons Resort ⑨
Frigate Bay North hotels ⑤
Frigate Bay South hotels ⑥
Golden Lemon ②
Golden Rock Plantation Inn ⑬
Hart of Nevis ⑦
Hermitage Plantation Inn ⑭
Montpelier Plantation Inn ⑮
Mule House ④
Nisbet Plantation Beach Club ⑫
Ocean View Guest House ⑪
Ottley's Plantation Inn ③
Oualie Bay hotels ⑩

SEE ALSO

• ***Where to Stay*** pp314–15
• ***Where to Eat & Nightlife*** pp316–17

A beach at Frigate Bay South, St. Kitts

GETTING AROUND

Both islands have airports – Robert L. Bradshaw International Airport (St. Kitts) and Vance W. Amory International Airport (Nevis). The ferry is the most commonly used transport between the islands. There are car ferries between Major's Bay in the south of St. Kitts and Cades Bay in Nevis. The trip between Basseterre and Charlestown takes 45 minutes and there are about eight or ten crossings each day. For day visits, the car hire rental agency may allow (with advanced warning) visitors to drop the rented car at the ferry terminal and then pick up another car on arrival in the other island. Buses leave from the two main towns and run in both directions around the islands. There is no schedule, instead buses leave when they are full or on the decision of the driver. There are no bus services to Frigate Bay or the Southeastern Peninsula on St. Kitts.

Ottley's
Ottley's Plantation Inn above Ottley's is unique and surrounded by tropical gardens.

acle
Nicola Town

Grange
Bay
Lodge
Ottley's
Cayon
Key
Hermitage Bay
Barker's Point

t. Kitts
St. Peter's
Upper
Conaree
Conaree Bay
Half Moon Point
Half Moon Bay

BASSETERRE

Frigate
Bay North

FRIGATE
BAY RESORTS
Frigate
Bay South
South Friar's Bay

SOUTHEASTERN
PENINSULA
White House Bay
Guana Point
Ballast Bay
Green Point
Shitten Bay
Nag's head

Sand
Bank Bay

Great
Salt
Pond

Turtle Bay
Booby Island
Cockleshell Bay
Major's
Bay
The Narrows

Frigate Bay
This is the most crowded bay with a few well-known resorts and hotel chains.

Nevis Plantation Inns
Nevis has some of the loveliest plantation inns in the Caribbean including Hermitage, Old Manor, Golden Rock, and Nisbet Plantation.

Lover's
Beach
Newcastle
Bay
Nisbet Beach
 Oualie Bay
Newcastle
Long Haul
Bay

OUALIE BEACH
Round Hill
1,014 ft
Hick's Village
Cades Bay
Cotton
Ground
Fountain

Pinney's
Beach
Vaughans

Nevis

Butlers
Eden Brown
Bay
Huggins Bay
Nevis Peak
3,232 ft

New
River

CHARLESTOWN

NEVIS
PLANTATION INNS
Old Manor
FIG TREE
CHURCH
Taylors Pasture
White Bay
Buck's Hill

BOTANICAL
GARDEN OF NEVIS

Berkeley Memorial clock at
The Circus, Basseterre

Basseterre ❶

S coast of St. Kitts. 🏘 13,000. ✈
🚌 ⛴ ℹ Pelican Mall, Bay Road.
www.stkittstourism.kn
🎵 Annual Music Festival (Jun).

Basseterre sits on the Caribbean, or leeward, coast of St. Kitts – *basse-terre* is French for the sailing term leeward. It is a pretty West Indian town, where many of the original Georgian buildings are still intact.

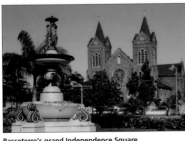

Basseterre's grand Independence Square

A century ago all visitors to the island would arrive by sea, passing through the arch of the old colonial Treasury Building, with its rich volcanic stonework, white frames, and a dome. The Treasury Building houses the **National Museum of St. Kitts**, which displays artifacts from the Amerindian era, including pottery and axe-heads, and colonial military and domestic items such as muskets and irons, as well as maps and prints of plantation life. Nowadays visitors are more likely to arrive via Port Zante, the cruise ship dock with a few duty-free shops such as the Amina Craft Market and the Pelican Mall. West from the

port, and beyond the Treasury Building, is the Nevis ferry dock, the bus station, and the main market building. The waterfront here is a busy area of the town. Inland from the Treasury Building is The Circus. At its center stands the quaint Victorian Berkeley Memorial Clocktower, which dates from 1883. There is a café with a balcony upstairs with a view of the bustle below. Southeast of here is **Independence Square**, a grassy park surrounded by a white picket fence overlooked by stone and wooden buildings. Originally the commercial center of Basseterre, it once held the slave market. At the eastern end of the square is the catholic Co-Cathedral of the Immaculate Conception, which has a barrel-vaulted nave and a distinctive rose window. Next to it is the Court House and, in a pretty wooden Creole building on

Brimstone Hill Fortress ❹

This massive fortress is a vast network of defensive structures. Built in stages between 1690 and 1790, when the wars for a British Empire were at their fiercest, Brimstone Hill stands at 800 ft (243 m) and commands an exceptional view of the islands. Its name is indicative of the hellish smell of sulphur, or brimstone, the result of St. Kitts' volcanic geology.

The remnants of the Infantry Officers' Quarters

The Magazine Bastion was constructed with a paved water catchment.

Prince of Wales Bastion
The first building to be fully restored, this bastion housed the Brigade Office and the main Guard Barracks.

The Orillon Bastion
Once the location of the bomb-proof Ordnance Store and a hospital, the Orillon is also the site of a cemetery, with tombstones still intact.

For hotels and restaurants on these islands see pp314–15 and pp316–17

the north side, the Spencer Cameron Gallery, which exhibits work by Caribbean artists.

Located on Cayon Street is the Anglican St. George's, the main church built by the British in 1706. Fortlands District, on the western edge of the town, has luxurious homes and one hotel, Ocean Terrace Inn *(see p314)*, which hosts a lively streetside grill on Friday nights. The northern outskirts of the town has modern buildings, with supermarkets and light industry. Warner Park, the national stadium, lies on Wellington Road, which runs towards the airport. Built for the Cricket World Cup in 2007, it now hosts cricket matches and the annual music festival.

🏛 National Museum of St. Kitts
Old Treasury Building. **Tel** *869 465 5584.* ☐ *9am–5pm Mon–Fri, 9am–1pm Sat.* 🖉

Manicured gardens of Romney Manor Plantation

Romney Manor Plantation ❷

4 miles (6 km) NW of Basseterre, St. Kitts. **Tel** *869 465 6253.* 📷 ☐ *9am–5pm Mon–Fri.* 🖥 🚻

Set in extensive and attractive gardens, Romney Manor is a restored former plantation estate house. It was originally owned by an ancestor of Thomas Jefferson, third President of the US. The house was then renamed Romney Manor after its acquisition by Earl of Romney in the 17th century. This plantation was the first in St. Kitts to free its slaves in 1834.

Old Road ❸

6 miles (9 km) NW of Basseterre, St. Kitts. 🚗

Situated at the foot of the concave slopes of the main St. Kitts mountain range, Old Road is a simple town of clapboard and stone buildings. Settled in 1624 by Thomas Warner, Old Road was the capital of the English part of St. Kitts when the island was known as the "Mother Colony of the West Indies". It was so called as it was the first permanent intrusion by French and English nationals into the Spanish domain.

The Citadel
Called Fort George, it is the central defensive structure, a fortress within a fortress.

VISITORS' CHECKLIST

10 miles (16 km) NW of Basseterre, St. Kitts. 🚗 **Tel** *869 465 2609.* ☐ *9:30am–5:30pm daily.* 🖉 📷 📷 📷
www.brimstonehillfortress.org

Visitors' Center
Located in the reconstructed Commissariat Building, the visitors' center has displays of the history of the fort and a gift shop.

The Green Tank was the largest cistern of the fortress.

The Artillery Officers' Quarters
The quarters were reputed to be the finest residences of the Fortress with good views.

Royal St. Kitts Golf Course, Frigate Bay resort area

Arawak Carvings ❺

6 miles (9 km) NW of Basseterre, St. Kitts. 🖼️

Before the arrival of the Europeans, St. Kitts, then called Liamuiga, meaning fertile land, was inhabited by the Arawak and subsequently Carib Indians. Inland from Old Road town, in an unassuming setting on a lawn behind a white picket fence, is a small but touching reminder of their life and art. These Arawak carvings, also known as petroglyphs, are depictions of a man and a woman (or possibly male or female gods of fertility), carved in a graphical design into boulders of black volcanic rock. They have been painted white to emphasize their square bodies, waving arms, and antennae.

Frigate Bay Resorts ❻

3 miles (5 km) S of Basseterre, St. Kitts. 🏖️ 🍴 🛏️ 🖼️ 🏨
www.stkittstourism.kn

Frigate Bay is the heartland of tourism in St. Kitts and it has a very different atmosphere from the north of the island. From the top of the hills, there is a panoramic view of Frigate Bay, a low-lying sliver of land between the Atlantic Ocean and Caribbean Sea.

On the Atlantic side is Frigate Bay North where the sandy beach is lined with condominiums and large resort hotels offering an array of entertainment and activities. This is the location of the Marriott hotel *(see p314)* with its casino and several

restaurants and bars. Just inland lie the fairways and bunkers of the Royal St. Kitts Golf Course *(see p313)*. The golf course stretches right up to the coast and the onshore ocean winds can have a considerable effect on play.

On the Caribbean side, Frigate Bay South, also known as "The Strip", has calmer seas, but a livelier atmosphere. Instead of hotels, a string of beach bars and watersports operators stand shoulder to shoulder, giving the beach a partylike, easy-going vibe. It is particularly lively at sundown on Thursday and Friday evenings, when there is a bon-fire and live music at some of the bars, and at weekends, when the locals come to spend the day on the beach.

Southeastern Peninsula ❼

St. Kitts. 🚗 🖼️ 🏨

While the north of St. Kitts is characterized by Kittitian villages dotting the flanks of volcanic, rainforested mountains, the lower-lying hills of the southern part of the island are much less populated and drier. The area is worth visiting because the island's prettiest beaches are situated here, and there are some excellent beach bars as well. Unlike the more

Southeastern Peninsula overlooking the turquoise Caribbean Sea

For hotels and restaurants on these islands see pp314–15 and pp316–17

A beach and bar restaurant in Oualie Beach, Nevis

developed Frigate Bay to the north, the Southeastern Peninsula is only now being built-up. The road along the peninsula leads up and out of Frigate Bay from where, switch-backing several times, it descends into Friar's Bay. The beach at **South Friar's Bay** is probably the best strip of sand on the island. Although it was projected for development, nothing has happened so far. Instead, the beach bars that line the beach continue their laid-back trade as travelers come to spend the day. The road climbs and falls, sashaying over the hills until it reaches the southern tip of the island. En route, visitors are likely to spot green velvet monkeys on the way to White House Bay. East of Great Salt Pond, but on the Atlantic Coast, is the quiet **Sand Bank Bay**.

On the southern coast, there are several beaches with lovely views across the 2-mile (3-km) The Narrows to Nevis. The liveliest are **Turtle Beach**, which tends to get a bit crowded due to cruise ship passengers, and Cockleshell Beach. Both have restaurants, bars, and some watersports and offer stunning views of Nevis. This whole area is under construction with plans to build a number of hotels and a marina here. Farther south, at **Major's Bay**, a roll-on-roll-off car ferry leaves for Cades Bay in Nevis. Offshore, the tiny Booby Island (accessible by boat) has spectacular marine life and is popular with snorkelers and divers.

Oualie Beach ⑧

North coast of Nevis. 🚌 🛥 🍴

Oualie was the original name for Nevis. Pronounced as "oo-wah-lee", meaning beautiful waters, it referred to the freshwater springs on Nevis. Oualie Beach is quite lively with pale yellow sands backed by palms and a great view of St. Kitts across The Narrows. Oualie Bay, formerly known as Mosquito Bay, is well protected, so swimming and other watersports are good here. There is a watersports and mountain biking shop, and a scuba diving outfit. The bay has a small dock, where visitors from St. Kitts can be dropped off by water taxis. The pretty Oualie Beach Resort (see p315) is located on this beach as well. The family who runs this resort has been on the island for nearly 350 years. On the beach is Under the Sea Nevis (see p313), a small marine center run by a marine biologist, who offers excellent introductory and exploratory programs to the reefs and the underwater world. There is also a touch-tank. It is particularly suitable for children but visitors of all ages will find it interesting. Apart from an introduction to the underwater life of the island, the center organizes snorkeling trips to reefs around this area of the island.

Environs

Towards the north, the road swings around Nevis Peak before reaching Nisbet Beach. Facing the Atlantic, Nisbet is a pretty beach dotted with coconut trees strung with hammocks which makes it a pleasant place to relax.

Marine life in the waters of Oualie Bay, Nevis

Portrait of Horatio Nelson

HORATIO NELSON AND FANNY NISBET

As a young captain in the 1780s, Horatio Nelson was based in Antigua on HMS *Boreas*. He had the unpopular job of enforcing the Navigation Laws, which prevented the lucrative trade between the British Leeward Islands and the newly independent United States of America. Horatio visited Nevis frequently and eventually married a native widow, Fanny Nisbet, at Montpelier. At the wedding, she was "given away" by Prince William Henry, later King William IV, who was also based in Antigua at the time. The marriage did not last and when he returned to England Nelson took up with Emma Hamilton, who was the wife of the ambassador to Naples.

Charlestown's Alexander Hamilton House, now the Museum of Nevis History

Charlestown ⑨

4 miles (6.5 km) S of Oualie Beach, Nevis. 🏙 1,500. ✈ 🚌 ⛴
ℹ Nevis Tourism Authority, Main Street, 869 469 7550 ⛴ Tue & Sat.

Charlestown is a classic, pretty West Indian waterfront town, set on the protected Caribbean coast of Nevis. As the small capital of a quiet island, it is never really that busy or crowded, but it is a lovely place to spend an hour wandering around. A small network of streets with attractive stone and wooden buildings sits behind the main esplanade, where many of the buildings have been restored.

The ferry port is located at the southern end of the esplanade, a good place to start any exploration of the small town. Inland from here is the Cotton Ginnery, which now houses local craft vendors. The Charlestown Market has local fruit and vegetables on sale in stalls under a pitched tin roof.

The heart of the town, Main Street, has banks, businesses, and a tourist information office at the Nevis Tourism Authority. Heading south, Main Street cuts diagonally inland, creating two "squares" that are actually triangular and surrounded by some of the town's most attractive wooden and stone buildings. In the smaller of the two squares, D.R. Walwyn Plaza, is the tiny Nevis Sports Museum which has exhibits on famous Nevisian athletes,

cricketers, and other sportsmen and women. Next is the Memorial Square, a small war memorial and a clocktower. The island buses leave from these two squares.

To the north, standing between the esplanade and Main Street, is a pretty stone building called Alexander Hamilton House. Alexander Hamilton, father of the United States' constitution and portrayed on the US$10 bill, was born here in 1757. Known as the "Little Lion", Hamilton was killed in a duel in 1884. Alexander Hamilton House is home to both the Nevis Assembly, the five-member Nevisian Parliament that sits just four or five times a year, and the **Museum of Nevis History**. The museum has displays of Nevis through the ages, with artifacts including

Amerindian pottery and colonial porcelain. North of here, the road out of town leads to the palm-fringed Pinney's Beach. The most manicured parts of this beach belong to the Four Seasons Resort (see p315) but there are access tracks to the rest.

On the southern outskirts of town the road runs on to the Bath Hotel. This large stone building was one of the glories of the island in the late 1700s and one of the first hotels in the Caribbean. Many European visitors came here to treat ailments using the volcanic hot springs nearby. Now the building is used by the Nevis government. Close to Bath Hotel is the **Horatio Nelson Museum**. Dedicated to the British admiral (see p307), it has an excellent series of displays, with maps and models of 18th-century ships, and the largest collection of Nelson memorabilia in the world, including portraits, clay pipes, and statuettes. Some of the porcelain from Nelson and Fanny Nisbet's marriage feast can be seen here.

🏛 **Museum of Nevis History**
Alexander Hamilton House. **Tel** 869 469 5786. ◯ 9am–4pm Mon–Fri, 9am–noon Sat. 🎫 ♿ 🚻
www.nevis-nhcs.org

🏛 **Horatio Nelson Museum**
Belle Vue. **Tel** 869 469 5786. ◯ 9am–4pm Mon–Fri, 9am–noon Sat. 🎫 🚻 www.nevis-nhcs.org/nelsonmuseum.html

Typical "gingerbread trim" building, Charlestown

CHARLESTOWN ARCHITECTURE

The lovely old houses of this small town are outstanding examples of 18th- and 19th-century colonial architecture. Several streets in Charlestown (Nevis) and many in Basseterre (St. Kitts) still have traditional houses embellished with fret-cut woodwork called "gingerbread trim". Most of the structures here are made of the distinct dark volcanic stone found locally. These buildings tend to have massive foundations and walls, often over 4 ft (1.2 m) thick, with a rubble-filled interior space. Also common, the "skirt and blouse" design consists of a stone first floor and a light, wooden second floor. This enables the houses to withstand high winds and earthquakes, common to the region.

Fig Tree Church  ❿

2 miles (3 km) E of Charlestown, Nevis. 🚌

The round-island road that climbs inland from the town of Charlestown passes Fig Tree Church, where Horatio Nelson and Fanny Nisbet were married in 1787 *(see p307)*. The original church was built in the 1680s, but the current building actually dates from 1838. It is a stone structure with a bell tower and a red tin roof. Inside, it is possible to see a copy of the marriage certificate that the Nelsons signed at their marriage. Their wedding celebration took place at Montpelier Plantation, where it is commemorated on a plaque on the gates.

The grand old Hermitage Plantation Inn, Nevis

Botanical Garden of Nevis ⓫

3 miles (5 km) SE of Charlestown, Nevis. *Tel* 869 469 3509. 🚗
🕐 9am–5pm Mon–Sat. 🔴 pub hols.
💳 🖥 🎫 www.botanicalgarden nevis.com

The Botanical Garden of Nevis is spread over 7 acres (3 ha). The attractive gardens display plants from across the tropical world. They are laid out in several areas covering different environments, including the Tropical Vine Garden, the Orchid Terrace, the Rose Garden, and a Rainforest Conservatory. The conservatory has re-created Mayan temple ruins and a few waterfalls. Other delights include fruit trees, cacti, and several flowering shrubs and trees. A café and a gift shop are set in an attractive Creole building.

Nevis Plantation Inns ⓬

Nevis has some of the loveliest plantation inns in the Caribbean. While they are excellent places to stay, it is also possible to just visit for lunch, afternoon tea, or dinner to get a sense of a long bygone era. Dating from the late 1600s, the main house at the **Hermitage Plantation Inn** *(see p315)* is one of the finest wooden buildings in the Caribbean. It has attractive "gingerbread" woodwork, shingle walls and a red tin roof. Montpelier Plantation Inn *(see p315)* was restored in the 1960s and is well worth a stop for lunch or dinner. Other plantation inns include **Old Manor**, in Gingerland, whose old chimney and sugar-crushing gear are on view, and farther ahead, above the Atlantic Coast, the Golden Rock has a spectacular view over the coastline. The only plantation inn with the advantage of being on the beach is in Nisbet Plantation, which has a magnificent view from its great house through tall and slender palms to the sea.

🏛 Old Manor
Gingerland. *Tel* 869 469 3445.
Fax 869 469 3388.
www.oldmanornevis.com

Well-tended flower beds in the Botanical Garden, with Nevis Peak in the background, Nevis

Outdoor Activities and Specialized Holidays

St. Kitts and Nevis have great beaches and visitors can expect to spend much time swimming, snorkeling, sailing, or deep-sea fishing. Both islands also have excellent golf and very good hiking into the rainforested mountains. For a small island, Nevis offers outstanding sport and first-class mountain-biking. Between them, the two islands have an interesting and visible history to explore on organized tours of attractive Creole buildings, plantation houses, inns, and ruins.

Horse-riding along Half Moon Bay, St. Kitts

HIKING

The islands of St. Kitts and Nevis are small but full of stunning scenery, run through by trails of varying difficulties. On Nevis in particular, there are many historic plantation ruins to explore, some set amongst lush rainforest greenery. There are several companies offering guided walks to various places of historical and natural interest on Nevis, two of the most popular being **Sunrise Tours** and **Earla's Eco Tours**. Hikes tailored to different abilities explore the wilder side of the island, ranging from nature walks along old island paths through the rainforest, birdwatching tours, and visits to local villages and plantation ruins, to the challenging climb to the top of Nevis Peak at 3,232 ft (985 m).

St. Kitts also has a number of guided tours. Earl Vanlow of **The Duke of Earl Adventures** leads hikes through old canefields, past plantation ruins and into the rainforest, often above Romney Manor Plantation (see p305). Other trips head for the top of Mount Liamuiga. Tours, by both vehicle and on foot, are also available with **Greg's Safaris**, located in Basseterre.

MOUNTAIN BIKING

Windsurf 'N' Mountainbike Nevis offers tours to mountain bikers of all levels, from simple road excursions through local villages to hard-core single tracks. Owner and operator Winston Crooke takes bikers on rides such as the historic Upper Round Road, which once linked the higher sugar estates. He also offers triathlon training and stages an annual triathlon, which is usually held in March, out of Charlestown.

HORSE-RIDING

Trinity Stables in St. Kitts offer trips along the narrow trails in the rainforest on the flanks of the central mountain range and down to the windswept beaches on the Atlantic Coast. Guides explain local history and the medicinal properties of plants along the way. **Nevis Equestrian Centre** provides both leisurely beach rides on Pinney's Beach and more difficult trail rides in the hills, as well as riding lessons from the owners Erika and John.

BEACHES

Although particularly beautiful, the volcanic nature of St. Kitts and Nevis means that their beaches vary in color between white and jet black, often a mid-brown. There are plenty of good strips of sand though, with classic beach bars and watersports, that are frequented by the islanders. The busiest beach in St. Kitts is Frigate Bay South, which teems with bars such as Mr X's Shiggidy Shack and Monkey Bar (see p317), as well as sports operators. The excellent Reggae Beach bar is located on Cockleshell Bay.

Beaches in the north of the island tend to have dark sand, but along the Southeastern Peninsula (see pp306–7), the sand improves and the bays are also less developed. There are some inviting strips of sand where visitors may enjoy a near Robinson Crusoe experience for a day. Such isolated stretches include South Friar's Bay, which has some facilities now such as the Shipwreck Beach Bar. Major's Bay and Sand Bank Bay are some other remote bays.

By contrast, the beaches in Nevis range from brownish sand to light colored sand. Oualie Beach (see p307), which overlooks St. Kitts, is the most active with several watersports opportunities. The 3.5 miles (6 km) of golden sand on Pinney's Beach is gorgeous with Nevis Peak rising in the background, and is perfect for swimming. It has hotels and bars such as Sunshine's and Chevy's. Lover's Beach, at the northern tip of the island, though hard to get to and sometimes windy, is a lovely remote stretch of light-colored sand.

Shipwreck Beach Bar sign

Hiking on St. Kitts and Nevis

St. Kitts and Nevis have exceptionally good hiking. In addition to the unspoilt landscape, there is an extraordinary variety of fauna and flora, as well as evocative plantation ruins to explore along the trails. The dormant volcano of Mount Liamuiga is, with its height of 3,792 ft (1,156 m), one of the toughest mountains to climb in

Ginger flowers on Nevis Peak

the Caribbean. This tour can start with a horseback-ride from the Belmont plantation, followed by a rigorous hike to the top. Nevis Peak also offers a challenging trek, and both hikes should be attempted only with an experienced guide. Hotels also recommend guides and operators who take visitors for volcanic hikes.

NATURE HIKES

Both St. Kitts and Nevis have a considerable diversity of environment. The dry littoral forests rise from the coasts through immensely fertile, cultivable slopes. But it is the rainforest, where ancient paths criss-cross the gullies and slopes, that is the most captivating.

Informative guides usually relate fascinating botanical and historical facts.

Many plants found in the forest have practical or medicinal uses. Some are even used in *obeah* or black magic.

Volcano hikes *are popular on both islands. On Nevis a steep climb necessitates a scramble near the top. The dormant Mount Liamuiga in St. Kitts has a crater into which hikers descend.*

Bird-watching hikes *are rewarding and a variety of birds can be found in the different habitats on the islands, including wading birds in the remote lagoons of St. Kitts' Southeastern Peninsula.*

HIKES TO THE PAST

At the height of the sugar era, St. Kitts and Nevis were cultivated up to a height of around 1,000 ft (305 m). The plantation ruins, now shrouded in overgrowth, are atmospheric and interesting to explore with a well-informed guide.

Plantation ruins *can include remains of boiling houses, storage areas, stables, dormitories, workshops, and even hospitals, most of which were built in the 18th century.*

Conical shells of old sugar mills *dot the landscapes of St. Kitts and Nevis. Many mills still have their old crushing gear, massive metal rollers between which the cane was crushed to a dry pulp, and are a poignant reminder of those who lived here under harsh conditions.*

Yacht anchored just off Pinney's Beach, Nevis

SAILING

The Narrows, which is the stretch of water separating St. Kitts and Nevis, is very scenic and spending a day aboard a sailing boat is a delightful way of exploring the area. Day sails, leaving from both islands, tend to steer to the isolated bays of the Southeastern Peninsula in St. Kitts, where there is a stop for snorkeling before a sail across The Narrows. Drinks and lunch, often a barbecue on the beach, are included in the rate. Companies that provide day sails include **Leeward Island Charters**, which picks up passengers in both islands, **Blue Water Safaris** in St. Kitts and **Nevis Yacht Charters**.

SCUBA DIVING

While St. Kitts and Nevis might not be known as scuba destinations, there are some spectacular dives that make a worthwhile addition to a holiday on the islands. Dive sites tend to be in The Narrows, and along St. Kitts' Southeastern Peninsula (easily reached by boat from Nevis or from Basseterre), so it actually does not matter which island visitors are based on. Divers can expect to see good reefs, pinnacles, drop-offs, as well as reef fish and occasional pelagic fish. There are also some interesting wrecks

and reefs farther northwest along the Caribbean Coast of St. Kitts. **Scuba Safaris Ltd.**, based in Nevis, and **Kenneth's Dive Centre** in St. Kitts are among the popular diving operators on the islands.

SNORKELING

Besides scuba diving, St. Kitts and Nevis also offer some outstanding snorkeling opportunities. Reefs can be reached from many of the beach hotels, but some of the best reefs are along the undeveloped bays of the Southeastern Peninsula of St. Kitts – to which the day sailing trips head for a snorkeling stop as a part of their itineraries. On Nevis, **Under the Sea Nevis** includes a snorkeling trip as part of their extremely informative program where in

addition to a visual treat, participants can also learn more about the marine species in the reef.

WATERSPORTS

Visitors will find many opportunities for different watersports on the two islands. On St. Kitts, the best bet is to head for Frigate Bay South, where operators, such as **Mr X's Watersports**, hire out equipment for all sorts of watersport activities. These usually include kayaks, windsurfers, small catamarans, and Jet Skis.

On Nevis, outlets including Windsurf 'N' Mountainbike Nevis rent out equipment. The large hotels, such as The Four Seasons Resort in Nevis *(see p315)*, offer water-based activities.

A watersports center on Oualie Beach, Nevis

For hotels and restaurants on these islands see pp314–15 and pp316–17

DEEP-SEA FISHING

Deep-sea fishing is readily available through a handful of captains with their own fishing boats that can be chartered by the day or half-day. Barracuda, mahimahi, and marlin are found in the waters off St. Kitts and Nevis. **Tropical Tours** in St. Kitts organizes daily deep-sea fishing trips. Refreshments are included in the rates. **Speedy 4 Charters** are popular fishing outfitters and offer special packages.

GOLF

Both islands have good 18-hole golf courses, and golfers have been known to fly from St. Barthélemy to play at the 6,766 yards (6,186 m) par 71 Four Seasons Golf Course (see p315), designed by famous golf course architect, Robert Trent Jones II. It is set on the Caribbean Coast and climbs into the hills, providing some challenging holes, with fantastic views over The Narrows and out to the sea. The 6,900 yards (6,310 m) par 71 **Royal St. Kitts Golf Course** is in Frigate Bay and also has

The fabulous Royal St. Kitts Golf Course, Frigate Bay

some spectacular holes along the Atlantic coastline. More golf courses are slated for development on St. Kitts, the Southeastern Peninsula, and in the north of the island.

ISLAND TOURS

An interesting way to explore St. Kitts is on the **St. Kitts Scenic Railway Tour**. The old narrow-gauge railway that formerly brought the cut sugar cane to the main factory near the airport is now used as a tour train. The carriages have large glass windows to enable breathtaking views of the island during this leisurely ride along the Atlantic coast. Tours by minibus are popular and tend to head around the north of the island and take in the major sights such as Brimstone Hill Fortress (see pp304–5), with a stop in Basseterre. In Nevis, tours are generally offered by taxi drivers. For visitors who prefer setting out on foot, there are also ample hiking tours (see p311).

DIRECTORY

HIKING

The Duke of Earl Adventures
St. Kitts.
Tel 869 663 0994.

Earla's Eco Tours
Tel 869 469 2833.

Greg's Safaris
Basseterre, St. Kitts.
Tel 869 465 4121.
www.gregsafaris.com

Sunrise Tours
Gingerland, Nevis.
Tel 869 469 2758.
www.nevis
naturetours.com

MOUNTAIN BIKING

Windsurf 'N' Mountainbike Nevis
Oualie Beach.
Tel 869 469 9682.
www.bikenevis.com

HORSE-RIDING

Nevis Equestrian Centre
Pinney's Beach, Nevis.
Tel 869 662 9118.

Trinity Stables
Basseterre, St. Kitts.
Tel 869 465 3226. **www**.
trinityinnapartments.com

SAILING

Blue Water Safaris
Basseterre, St. Kitts.
Tel 869 466 4933.
www.bluewater
safaris.com

Leeward Island Charters
St. Kitts. *Tel 869 465 7474.*
www.spiritofstkitts.com

Nevis Yacht Charters
Oualie Beach, Nevis.
Tel 869 664 9171.
www.sailnevis.com

SCUBA DIVING

Kenneth's Dive Centre
Basseterre, St.Kitts.
Tel 869 465 2670.
www.kennethsdive
center.com

Scuba Safaris Ltd.
Oualie Beach, Nevis.
Tel 869 469 9518.
www.scubanevis.com

SNORKELING

Under the Sea Nevis
Oualie Beach, Nevis.
Tel 869 469 1291.
www.underthesea
nevis.com

WATERSPORTS

Mr X's Watersports
St. Kitts. *Tel 869 762 3983.* **www**.mrxwater
sports.com

DEEP-SEA FISHING

Speedy 4 Charters
Frigate Bay, Nevis.
Tel 869 662 3453. **www**.
speedy4charters.com

Tropical Tours
Basseterre, St. Kitts.
Tel 869 465 4167.
www.tropicalstkitts-
nevis.com

GOLF

Royal St. Kitts Golf Course
Frigate Bay, St. Kitts.
Tel 869 466 2700. **www**.
royalstkittsgolfclub.com

ISLAND TOURS

St. Kitts Scenic Railway Tour
Basseterre, St. Kitts.
Tel 869 465 7263.
www.stkittsscenic
railway.com

Choosing a Hotel

St. Kitts and Nevis have quite different accommodations from one another. In St. Kitts the hotels are mostly upbeat and lively, whereas in Nevis, hotels are mostly small and privately owned. All hotel bills incur a 9 percent government room tax and usually a 10 percent service charge. Villas are usually rented for a week and prices reflect the weekly rental charge.

PRICE CATEGORIES
The following price ranges are for a standard double room per night and all taxes included.

$ under $100
$$ $100–200
$$$ $200–300
$$$$ $300–400
$$$$$ over $400

ST. KITTS AND NEVIS

Plantation Inns
Between them, Nevis and St. Kitts have a superb collection of plantation inns, set in and around restored 18th-century great houses with traditional Creole architecture. A stay at one of these is characterized by a relaxed yet refined atmosphere, excellent food, thoughtful service, and lots of activities available for those who wish. See also page 309.

Marriott Resort

Ottley's Plantation Inn

ST. KITTS, BASSETERRE Brian Kassab & Associates
PO Box 1588 **Tel** *869 466 6341* **Fax** *869 466 6340*

This villa rental agency based in St. Kitts has a range of dozens of private homes, villa apartments, and condominiums for rent in several locations around the island, particularly around Frigate Bay, Half Moon Bay, and the Southeastern Peninsula. Mostly high-end accommodations. **www.bkassab.com**

ST. KITTS, BASSETERRE Palms All-Suite Hotel
PO Box 64, The Circus **Tel** *869 465 0800* **Fax** *869 465 5889* **Rooms** *12 suites*

Right at the heart of Basseterre, overlooking The Circus itself, Palms All-Suite Hotel is an attractive Creole building with an airy veranda and a bar. It is fairly simple and comfortable, good for business travelers as well as holiday-makers wanting to base themselves in town. **www.palmshotel.com**

ST. KITTS, BASSETERRE Ocean Terrace Inn
PO Box 65, Wigley Av. **Tel** *869 465 2754* **Fax** *869 465 1057* **Rooms** *69*

Set on the prosperous outskirts of Basseterre with a lovely view back over the town and the bay, Ocean Terrace Inn is a part business and part resort hotel. It is set over multiple levels in superb gardens. It has a bar, business facilities, and weekend evening action for all visitors at its restaurant across the road. **www.oceanterraceinn.com**

ST. KITTS, CAYON Mule House
PO Box 6009, Brighton Plantation **Tel** *869 466 8086* **Rooms** *4*

An extremely low-key and homely guesthouse set in attractive gardens, Mule House sits quite remotely on the Atlantic Coast. It has 4 fully equipped apartments and the family atmosphere of a private house and is peaceful. Ideal for independent travelers wanting to explore the island. **www. stkittstourism.kn/WheretoStay/Villas.asp**

ST. KITTS, DIEPPE BAY Golden Lemon
Dieppe Bay **Tel** *869 465 7260* **Fax** *869 465 4019* **Rooms** *26*

A small and very stylish hotel on the north coast of St. Kitts, set around a beautifully restored stone 17th-century building (originally a trading warehouse). There are several rooms in the main house, decorated with antiques, and then more modern suites in villas in the gardens. Children under 18 not allowed. **www.goldenlemon.com**

ST. KITTS, FRIGATE BAY NORTH Rock Haven
PO Box 821 **Tel** *869 465 5503* **Fax** *869 466 6130* **Rooms** *2*

A very personable bed-and-breakfast in a private home, Rock Haven has a fantastic view over the Atlantic side of Frigate Bay. It has a homely feel, with some gingerbread trim on the outside and original Caribbean art and antiques in the brightly painted interior. Spacious rooms, always a friendly reception. **www.rock-haven.com**

ST. KITTS, FRIGATE BAY NORTH St. Kitts Marriott Resort and Casino
Frigate Bay Road **Tel** *869 466 1200* **Fax** *869 466 1201* **Rooms** *648*

St. Kitts Marriott dominates the skyline on the Atlantic beach on Frigate Bay, a vast resort hotel with every facility. There is a lively buzz, with nightly entertainment, a casino, shops, spa, 6 restaurants, 3 pools, children's activities, tennis courts, and golf right at hand. A full service resort, also conference facilities. **www.marriott.com**

ST. KITTS, FRIGATE BAY SOUTH Frigate Bay Resort
PO Box 137 **Tel** *869 465 8935* **Fax** *869 465 7050* **Rooms** *64*

This is a small resort hotel tucked into a hillside just behind the busiest beach in St. Kitts. Its brightly decorated rooms have kitchens and overlook the restaurants and central pool with a swim-up bar. Resort entertainment, and all the action of the beach are nearby. It also has conference and golf facilities. **www.frigatebay.com**

Key to Symbols *see back cover flap*

ST. KITTS, FRIGATE BAY SOUTH Timothy Beach Resort $$

PO Box 81 **Tel** *869 465 8597* **Fax** *869 466 7085* **Rooms** *60*

A friendly hotel with rooms and self-catering apartments set right above the beach. Brightly painted, Timothy Beach Resort has a lively buzz in its open-sided restaurant and bar, golf course, with plenty of watersports and beach action. There is also a secluded pool. **www.timothybeach.com**

ST. KITTS, OTTLEY'S VILLAGE Ottley's Plantation Inn $$$$

PO Box 345, Atlantic Coast **Tel** *869 465 7234* **Fax** *869 465 4760* **Rooms** *24*

A unique plantation house hotel with an exquisite setting in manicured tropical gardens high above the Atlantic. Ottley's offers comfortable rooms and modern cottages, and superb traditional Caribbean hospitality. An ideal setting for a wedding. Spa, pool, Royal Palm restaurant *(see p316)*, bar, tennis, and croquet. **www.ottleys.com**

NEVIS, GINGERLAND Hart of Nevis

PO Box 492, Charlestown **Tel** *869 469 2328* **Fax** *869 469 3262*

Hart of Nevis is an agency that specializes in private villa rentals around the island. It has a small but strong collection of about 20 attractive houses in varying sizes in all areas of the island, both down by the beach and in spectacular settings up in the hills on former plantation estates. **www.nevisvillarentals.com**

NEVIS, GINGERLAND Golden Rock Plantation Inn $$$

PO Box 493, Charlestown **Tel** *869 469 3346* **Fax** *869 469 2113* **Rooms** *15*

A lovely, low-key plantation inn, set on the eastern slopes of Nevis Peak with a superb view of the Atlantic Ocean and other islands from its very attractive restored stone buildings. Golden Rock has rooms set in modern cottages by a pool, but its magic is in the gardens and the elegant atmosphere of the great house. **www.golden-rock.com**

NEVIS, GINGERLAND Hermitage Plantation Inn $$$$

Gingerland, Nevis **Tel** *869 469 3477* **Fax** *869 469 2481* **Rooms** *15*

The Hermitage has a wonderful setting in hillside tropical gardens. Its rooms are in pretty gingerbread cottages centered around a beautiful Creole great house, where afternoon tea is taken. Pool, tennis, horse-riding, and even a farmyard. **www.hermitagenevis.com**

NEVIS, MONTPELIER PLANTATION Montpelier Plantation Inn $$$$$

PO Box 474 **Tel** *869 469 3462* **Fax** *869 469 2932* **Rooms** *19*

The most elegant of the plantation inns, Montpelier is set in lush grounds high above the south coast. Rooms are in cottages scattered around the delightful great house. Pool, tennis court, afternoon tea, and fine dining. It has its own private beach club on Pinney's Beach. **www.montpeliernevis.com**

NEVIS, MORNING STAR Banyan Tree Bed and Breakfast $$

Morning Star **Tel** *869 469 3449* **Fax** *869 469 3449* **Rooms** *3*

A small but charming guesthouse in a residential area above Charlestown, this is an ideal hideaway for independent travelers looking for a friendly base from which to explore Nevis. Guests stay in 2 pretty self-contained Creole cottages in lovely gardens, and breakfast is served in the Main House. **www.banyantreebandb.com**

NEVIS, NEWCASTLE Ocean View Guest House $

Newcastle **Tel** *869 469 9580* **Fax** *869 469 9580* **Rooms** *5*

A simple but friendly bed-and-breakfast set in a modern West Indian home in pretty gardens above Newcastle in the north of Nevis. It has a dining room, bar, and a veranda with a lovely view over the ocean. The helpful resident owners will give advice for exploring the island. **www.oceanviewnevis.com**

NEVIS, NEWCASTLE Nisbet Plantation Beach Club $$$$

PO Box 1461, Newport **Tel** *869 469 9325* **Fax** *869 469 9864* **Rooms** *36*

Nisbet Plantation's lovely traditional estate house looks down an alleyway of tall and slender palms to the sea. Its comfortable rooms, furnished in classic Caribbean style, are set in cottages amid lush grounds. The beach area is more modern, brightly decorated, with a pool and beach bar. It also has a spa. **www.nisbetplantation.com**

NEVIS, OUALIE BAY Hurricane Cove Bungalows $$$

Oualie Beach **Tel** *869 469 9462* **Fax** *869 469 9462* **Rooms** *12*

A series of 12 one- to three-bedroom self-catering bungalows set on a hillside above Oualie Beach, with lovely views of St. Kitts across The Narrows. Simple and comfortable, they are very low-key and ideal for the independent traveler. Central pool, a small shop and some watersports, and bars nearby. **www.hurricanecove.com**

NEVIS, OUALIE BAY Oualie Beach Resort $$$$

Oualie Beach **Tel** *869 469 9735* **Fax** *869 469 9176* **Rooms** *32*

Set on a calm and pretty beach in the north of Nevis, with great views of St. Kitts across The Narrows, this small, casual resort consists of colored Caribbean cottages with gingerbread trim next to a central bar and dining area right on the sand. Lots of sports and watersports, sometimes lively bar. **www.oualiebeach.com**

NEVIS, PINNEY'S BEACH Four Seasons Resort $$$$$

PO Box 565, Charlestown **Tel** *869 469 1111* **Fax** *869 469 1112* **Rooms** *237*

Four Seasons Resort sits right on Pinney's Beach, its two-story buildings of luxurious bedrooms and suites hiding among slender palms and around the fairways of its excellent golf course. It offers elegant dining *(see p317)*, a full service spa, tennis courts, plenty of watersports, and a children's program. **www.fourseasons.com**

Where to Eat & Nightlife

The restaurants of the more visited St. Kitts are lively and upbeat, and range from breezy, busy restaurants to simple local eateries in Basseterre, plantation hotels in the north, and beach bars in the Southeastern Peninsula, offering simple fish dishes to top cuisine. In Nevis, the restaurants of the plantation inns (see p315) serve excellent food in elegant settings at an unhurried pace.

PRICE CATEGORIES
The price ranges are for a two-course meal for one, including tax and service charges and half a bottle of wine.

$ under $10
$$ $10–15
$$$ $15–25
$$$$ $25–35
$$$$$ over $35

RESTAURANTS

Special Evenings
Some restaurants have lively evenings with simple grilled food and a busy crowd. On Thursdays in St. Kitts, Mr X's Shiggidy Shack has a bonfire with live music. On Fridays, there is a special fish fry at Fisherman's Wharf in Basseterre and at Sprat Net in Old Road, there is fish and delicious seafood. On Nevis, the Hermitage Inn holds a pig roast each Wednesday, which is always fun.

Ottley's Plantation Inn

Miss June's

ST. KITTS, BASSETERRE Chef's Garden
TDC Mall, 4th Street **Tel** *869 465 6956* $$$$

Chef's Place is a simple West Indian restaurant at the back of town. Mainly frequented by locals, it serves the best Caribbean cuisine including pumpkin and carrot soup followed by fish, chicken, and mutton with rice and peas, and a mound of staple vegetables such as sweet potato and yam. Local fruit juices are also served. Closed Sundays.

ST. KITTS, BASSETERRE Ballahoo
The Circus, Central Basseterre **Tel** *869 465 4197* $$$$$

Set on an upstairs veranda in The Circus, the very heart of Basseterre, Ballahoo overlooks the clock, passers-by, and the general life of the town. International and Caribbean fare, burgers and salads, and even roti or chilli shrimp are served. Drop in for a drink or a meal. It has bright interior decoration and Caribbean paintings for sale as well.

ST. KITTS, BASSETERRE Fisherman's Wharf
Fortlands **Tel** *869 465 2754* $$$$$

Located on a deck right on the waterfront in uptown Basseterre, with a lovely view back across the bay and town. A very easy atmosphere and a nautical decor with a good crowd of locals and visitors. It serves jerk chicken, fresh fish, lobster, and steaks cooked on an open charcoal grill. Lively during the weekend.

ST. KITTS, BASSETERRE Serendipity
3 Wigley Av., Fortlands **Tel** *869 465 9999* $$$$$

Ever popular with islanders and visitors, Serendipity is set on a breezy terrace with a view back across the waterfront of Basseterre. A nice mix of local dishes – Caribbean *bouillabaisse* or fillet of grouper in tangy lemon butter, and international favorites – lamb loin in a red wine sauce and vegetarian Thai green curry. Closed Mondays.

ST. KITTS, FRIGATE BAY NORTH PJ's Pizza Bar and Restaurant
Frigate Bay North **Tel** *869 465 8373* $$$$

This breezy Italian restaurant is located at the heart of Frigate Bay, and within walking distance of the Atlantic resorts. It offers a hearty Italian fare – bruschetta, pasta, salads, some local fish dishes, and a long list of pizzas, and serves vegetarian food as well. PJ's is also a late-night bar after meals, and has a lively crowd.

ST. KITTS, FRIGATE BAY SOUTH Marshall's
Horizons Villa Complex **Tel** *869 466 8245* $$$$$

Set poolside on a very attractive, open-air terrace with views of Nevis in the distance, Marshall's offers some of the finest food in St. Kitts. The cuisine is French and international, with imported ingredients such as Chilean seabass in a seafood sauce and tuna in spicy sweet chilli. It has a fine wine list.

ST. KITTS, OTTLEY'S VILLAGE Royal Palm
Ottley's Plantation Inn **Tel** *869 465 7234* $$$$$

Nestled within the old stone walls of a former boiling house, Royal Palm has a magnificent setting overlooking the plantation gardens (see p315), and down to the Atlantic Coast. Serves contemporary "New Island" cuisine, including West Indian peanut soup or fresh tomato dill bisque, and great local fish. Renowned for its Sunday Champagne brunch.

ST. KITTS, TURTLE BEACH The Beach House
Turtle Beach, Southeast Peninsula **Tel** *869 469 5299* $$$$$

The Beach House brings elegance to the beach at the southern tip of St. Kitts, with a lovely view across The Narrows to Nevis and out to sea. Cuisine ranges from top-class burgers and panini by day to sophisticated seafood dishes and duck *foie gras* in the evenings. It is an excellent option for a meal out. Closed Sundays.

Key to Symbols *see back cover flap*

NEVIS, CHARLESTOWN Bananas Bistro

Upper Round Trail, Hamilton Estate **Tel** 869 469 1891

An enchanting setting in a classic Creole-style house in a garden with a magnificent view down over the Caribbean Coast of the island and tables set out on a large veranda. Short but satisfying menu with barbecue ribs, Moroccan chicken, and fresh Caribbean fish. There is a live string band occasionally in the evenings.

NEVIS, GINGERLAND Mem's Pizzaria

Prospect Gardens **Tel** 869 469 1390

A pizzeria that offers plenty of other dishes as well, including salads, burgers, and some West Indian cuisine such as roti, goat curry, and goatwater. Best known for their pizzas of course, which come in many flavors, including lobster and Mem's Inferno, with a generous amount of chilli. It is also a popular takeaway.

NEVIS, JONES BAY Miss June's

Midway between Four Seasons Resort and the airport **Tel** 869 469 5330

Miss June's is an institution in Nevis. Enjoy a splendid evening in a private home, with an introduction to the buffet dinner of more than 20 dishes, in four or five courses, cooked by Miss June herself. Much of her food is spicy, as are her stories of Caribbean life. Usually open 3 days a week, strictly by reservation.

NEVIS, OUALIE BAY Gallipot

Jones Estate **Tel** 869 469 8230

Although in a new location, this open-fronted dining room near Oualie Beach continues in the same trusty style. Gallipot specializes in fresh fish, caught on its own boat, the *Sea Brat*, and then served smoked for starters. Other tasty dishes include curries, lasagne, and quiche. Open for lunch and dinner Thu–Sat, and for lunch on Sundays.

NEVIS, PINNEY'S BEACH Lime Café

Behind Chevy's Café, Pinney's Beach **Tel** 869 469 1147

Ocean views and stunning sunsets are on the house at the Lime Café, as are shaded chaise longues and the cooling herbal flannels offered as you arrive. Hearty but health-conscious salads and sandwiches and top-class seafood make up the menu. Jet-ski hire, full-moon beach parties in high season, and a live steel band on Friday nights.

NEVIS, PINNEY'S BEACH Coconut Grove Restaurant and Wine Lounge

Main Island Road, Clifton's Estate **Tel** 869 469 1020

Set among the plams, on an open-fronted wooden deck with a high thatched ceiling and a view to the sea, Coconut Grove offers an elegant evening out in informal tropical style. On the menu are flavors from around the world – Asian, French, and Caribbean including beautifully presented local and imported fish. Closed Mondays.

NEVIS, PINNEY'S BEACH Double Deuce

Southern end **Tel** 869 469 2222

Double Deuce has a classic Caribbean setting, with deck chairs and wooden tables under the palms and parasols, reached by a wooden bridge right onto the sand. It serves a hearty West Indian fare – tannia fritters, fresh fish, and other typical West Indian dishes including stewed oxtail and mutton curry. Karaoke on Thursday.

NEVIS, PINNEY'S BEACH Mango's

Four Seasons **Tel** 869 469 1111

Mango's is located on an attractive covered deck on a rocky outcrop on Pinney's Beach, next to the Four Seasons Resort *(see p315)*, and has a mesmerizing seaside feel. It offers a broad menu with Caribbean and other dishes. A great place for a lazy lunch or a romantic dinner.

BARS AND CLUBS

Much of the entertainment on both St. Kitts and Nevis is centered around the beach bars. While they see a sporadic crowd by day, at sundown they liven up, attracting islanders as well as visitors. The bars stay lively till late into the evening, particularly on their busy "night of the week", most offering music, sometimes live, to dance to. Hotels around Frigate Bay offer some entertainment and there are the two casinos. Nevis has fewer late evening gathering places than the livelier St. Kitts.

Sunshine's on Nevis

RECOMMENDED PLACES TO GO

Bobsy's
Frigate Bay South, St. Kitts. (Sports bar, and DJs at weekends.)

Chevy's
Pinney's Beach, Nevis. (Simple beach bar, hosts reggae nights.)

Eddy's
Charlestown, Nevis.
(Lively bar on the balcony.)

Monkey Bar
Frigate Bay South, St. Kitts.
(Octagonal wooden bar.)

Mr X's Shiggidy Shack
Frigate Bay South, St. Kitts. (Reggae and lobster by night.)

Rumours
Newcastle, Nevis. (Popular with islanders and visitors.)

Shipwreck Beach Bar
Friar's Bay, St. Kitts. (Exuberant with a spectacular sunset view.)

Sprat Net
Old Road, St. Kitts. (Great seafood and Caribbean music.)

Sunshine's
Pinney's Beach, Nevis. (Home of the "Killer Bee" drink.)

Practical Information

St. Kitts and Nevis are relatively undeveloped in terms of tourism but since there is little else to bring in foreign exchange, their economies are directed towards the tourism industry and there is considerable development on the drawing board for both islands. But today, Nevis in particular still has a low-key approach, with charm rather than speed characterizing services. When it comes to banking and communications, the islands are fully in the 21st century, with credit cards widely acceptable and local SIM cards and Internet access easily available.

Inter-island carrier, St. Kitts airport

WHEN TO GO

The best time to go to St. Kitts and Nevis is between mid-December and mid-April, when the weather is cooler although this is also the most expensive time to visit. It is humid during August and September.

GETTING THERE

St. Kitts has direct flights from the US on **American Airlines**, **Delta**, and **US Airways**. From the UK, there is a weekly direct flight on **British Airways**. On other days, the best alternative is to fly via Antigua, which is linked by **LIAT**. Another hub is St. Martin/Sint Maarten, which is served by **Winair**.

Getting to Nevis is not easy. Traveling via St. Kitts is one alternative, from where it is possible to cross via ferry from Basseterre to Charlestown or to take a flight (although these are not frequent). If arrival is too late in the day, a water taxi can make the crossing. From within the Caribbean, there are daily flights from San Juan with American Airlines. From Antigua there is a hopper service that is supposed to meet the North American and European flights that land in the mid–late afternoon.

DOCUMENTATION

All visitors to St. Kitts and Nevis should travel on a valid passport with a valid onward ticket. Citizens of most European countries and the US do not need a visa. Guests have to pay a departure tax when leaving the island.

VISITOR INFORMATION

The **St. Kitts Tourism Authority** has offices in the US, Canada, and the UK. On the island, its main office is in Basseterre. The **Nevis Tourism Authority** has its head office and information office in Charlestown.

HEALTH AND SECURITY

The main hospitals are **Joseph N France General Hospital** in Basseterre and **Alexandra Hospital** in Charlestown. Vaccinations are necessary if you are coming from a yellow-fever infected area. St. Kitts and particularly Nevis are safe islands. There are few problems with personal security (virtually none in Nevis) and theft is very rare, though it is advisable not to leave valuables visible in a car or unattended on the beach.

BANKING AND CURRENCY

Credit cards are accepted in almost all establishments that are accustomed to dealing with tourists in both islands. There are ATMs in Basseterre and Charlestown. The currency of St. Kitts and Nevis is the Eastern Caribbean Dollar. Banks follow regular business hours, 8am–2pm Mon–Thu, 8am–4pm Fri.

COMMUNICATIONS

The international direct dialing code for St. Kitts and Nevis is +1 869, followed by a seven-digit island number. On the islands dial the seven digits. Handsets and SIM-cards with local numbers for rental are available through **Cable and Wireless** and **Digicel**. When phoning out of the islands, dial 011 and the international code. Most of the hotels and some villas have wireless Internet available. There are cyber cafés as well.

TRANSPORT

Car hire companies will deliver to the airport, ferry terminals, hotels, and villas. They will also issue the obligatory local driving license. Car rental companies include **TDC Thrifty** (both islands), **AVIS**, and **Delisle Walwyn** (St. Kitts) and **Nevis Car Rental** at the

Small Internet café in Basseterre, St. Kitts

airport in Nevis. Taxis are available at all hotels and at the airport and ferry terminals. Taxi stands include **Circus Taxi Stand** in Basseterre and **Charlestown Taxi Stand** in Nevis. Bus services are good on both islands, but as they are designed for local people, no buses run to Frigate Bay. They emanate from the main towns, on the waterfront in Basseterre and the two squares in Charlestown.

SHOPPING

As a cruise ship destination, St. Kitts has extensive shopping, around the dock, Port Zante and in Basseterre. There are several duty-free shops and Caribbean chains, including **Driftwood Duty Free**, **Ashbury's**, and **Brinley Gold** for local spice rums. The **Spencer Cameron Art Gallery**, set in a pretty building in Independence Square, is

Batik display at Caribelle Batik in Romney Manor, St. Kitts

well worth a visit, as is **Caribelle Batik**, which sells batik clothing. **Island Fever** in Charlestown is good for beach wear. The Museum of Nevis History *(see p308)* has some great historical material, including maps, for sale.

LANGUAGE

The language of the islands is English, which is spoken with a Caribbean lilt.

ELECTRICITY

There is a mix of three square-pin sockets in UK style and two-pin sockets in US style. The hotel front desk will often have an adapter.

TIME

Both islands are 4 hours behind Greenwich Mean Time and an hour ahead of Eastern Standard Time. The islands do not observe daylight savings.

GETTING MARRIED

Couples may obtain a license once they have been resident in the island for 48 hours. The license then takes 24 hours to produce. Couples must show a photo ID and a birth certificate, with a decree nisi if divorced and the spouse's death certificate if widowed. Many hotels also arrange weddings.

DIRECTORY

GETTING THERE

American Airlines
Tel 869 465 2273.
www.aa.com

British Airways
www.ba.com

Delta
www.delta.com

LIAT
www.liatairline.com

US Airways
Tel 1800 622 1015.
www.usairways.com

Winair
Tel 869 469 5302.
www.fly-winair.com

VISITOR INFORMATION

Nevis Tourism Authority
Main Street, Charlestown, Nevis. *Tel 869 469 7550* (Nevis), *0808 234 2064* (UK), *1866 556 3847* (US & Canada).
www.nevisisland.com

St. Kitts Tourism Authority
Pelican Mall, Bay Road, Basseterre, St. Kitts.
Tel 869 465 4040, 212 535 1234 (NY), 020 7376 0881 (UK).
www.stkittstourism.kn

HEALTH AND SECURITY

Alexandra Hospital
Charlestown, Nevis.
Tel 869 465 5473.

Joseph N France General Hospital
Basseterre, St. Kitts.
Tel 869 465 2551.

COMMUNICATIONS

Cable and Wireless
PO Box 86, Basseterre, St. Kitts.
Tel 869 465 1000.
www.time4lime.com

Digicel
Cable Building, Basseterre, St. Kitts.
Tel 869 466 3400.
www.digicelstkitts andnevis.com

TRANSPORT

1st Choice Car Rental
Shaws Road, Newcastle, Nevis.
Tel 869 469 1131.
www.neviscarrental.com

AVIS
Basseterre, St. Kitts.
Tel 869 465 6507.
www.horsfords.com/horsford/avis

Charlestown Taxi Stand
Nevis. *Tel 869 469 5631.*

Circus Taxi Stand
Basseterre, St. Kitts.
Tel 869 466 6999/869 465 9053.

Delisle Walwyn
Liverpool Row, Basseterre.
Tel 869 465 8449.
www.delislewalwyn.com/rentals.html

TDC Thrifty
Tel 869 465 2511 (St. Kitts), *869 469 1005 (Nevis).*
www.tdclimited.com

SHOPPING

Ashbury's
Pelican Mall, St. Kitts.
Tel 869 465 8175.

Brinley Gold
Port Zante, St. Kitts.
Tel 869 465 7748.
www.brinleygoldrum.com

Caribelle Batik
Romney Manor, St. Kitts.
Tel 869 465 6253.
www.caribellebatik stkitts.com

Driftwood Duty Free
Port Zante, St. Kitts.
Tel 869 466 2432.
www.driftwood dutyfree.net

Island Fever
Henville's Plaza, Charlestown, Nevis.
Tel 869 469 0867.

Spencer Cameron Art Gallery
Basseterre, St. Kitts.
Tel 869 465 1617.
www.spencer cameron.com

Exploring Antigua and Barbuda

Antigua and sister island Barbuda lure cruise ship passengers, yachtsmen, and casual travelers with world-class service and entertainment, gorgeous beaches, luxury resorts, and plenty of historic sights. Antigua is internationally renowned for its sailing festivals, while Barbuda's rare frigate birds colony is a bird-watcher's paradise. A British overseas territory, the neighboring volcanic island of Montserrat offers a true eco-experience.

ANGUILLA   ST. MARTIN/
SINT MAARTEN
VIRGIN
ISLANDS   ST. BARTHÉLEMY   BARBUDA
SABA AND   ANTIGUA
ST. EUSTATIUS
ST. KITTS   MONTSERRAT
AND NEVIS
GUADELOU

Caribbean Sea

MARTINIQUE

Boon Point   Ho

Soldiers Bay   14   13

Dickenson Bay   2 SANDALS
GRANDE AN

Runaway Bay   McKinnon's
Salt Pond

Montserrat   Pillar Rock   Barr
Shipstern Point   Bay
Deep Bay   1   St. John
Guard Point   2   3   Villag
Hawksbill   Five Islands
Bay   Village   ST. JOHN'S

Potter
Hansons   Golden Grove   Village
Maiden   Bay
Island   The Flashes

Creekside

Antig

4   Ebenezer   Emanuel
Jennings
JOLLY HARBOUR   13   Bolans   Bendals   Buc
Lignum Vitae   5
Bay   Valley Church
6   Sawcolts
Darkwood   7
Beach   Boggy Peak   Jo
12   1,5   ft   H
TURNER'S AND   FIG TREE DRIVE
DARKWOOD BEACHES   11
Johnson's Point   Urlings   FIG TREE
Cades Bay   DRIVE
8   Old Road
Carlisle
Bay   Rende
Old Red Bluff

Boats moored at the busy marina at Nelson's Dockyard, Antigua

MONTSERRAT

Antigua
Little Bay   Silver Hill
Sweeney's   1,323 ft
Carr's Bay   16
Brades   Caribbean
Bunkum Bay   St. John's   Sea
St. Peter's
Woodlands   Woodlands
Bay
Old   Salem
Towne   18
Iles Bay   MONTSERRAT
EXCLUSION
Fox's   ZONE
Bay
Plymouth   Soufrière
Hills Volcano
3,180 ft
0 km   5   Guadeloupe Passage
0 miles   5

KEY

— Major road

== Minor road

-- Ferry route

△ Peak

GETTING AROUND

V.C. Bird International Airport in Antigua is a major regional airline hub, while the port of St. John's welcomes large cruise ships on a regular schedule. Antigua and Barbuda are connected by air and sea, with daily flights and ferry service. Antigua has three protected harbors with marinas and immigration checkpoints for yachts wanting to tour the coastline and visit Barbuda. Daily flights from Antigua land at Gerald's Airport in Montserrat. Taxis are readily available on all three islands, while cars can also be hired on Antigua and Montserrat.

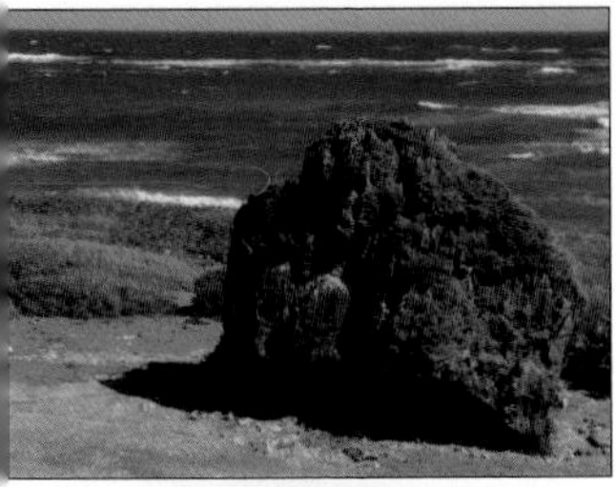

Limestone formation, Two Foot Bay National Park, Barbuda

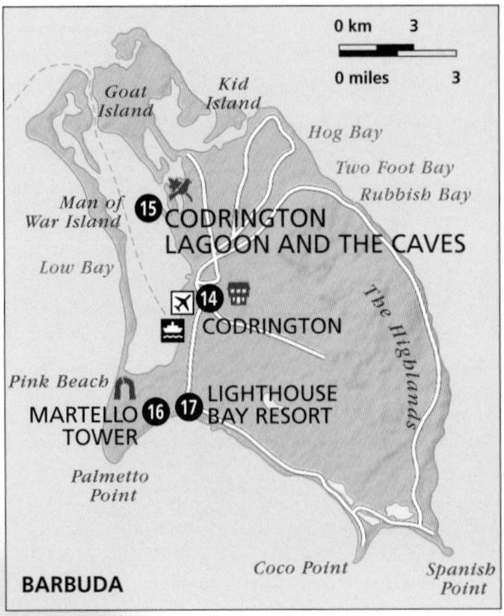

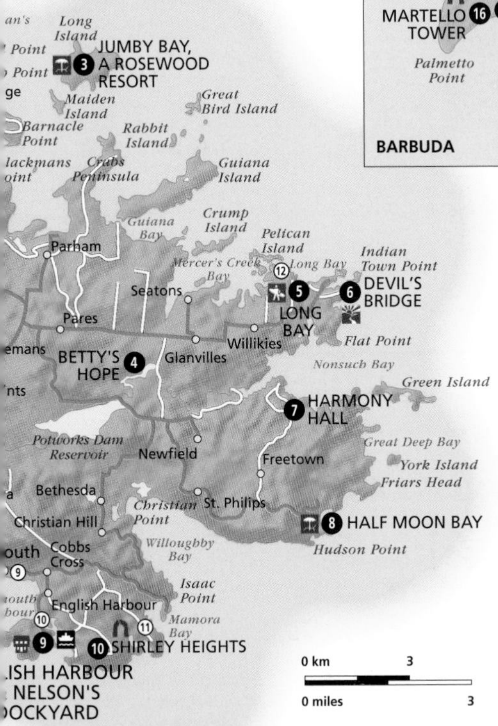

SEE ALSO

• ***Where to Stay*** pp336–7

• ***Where to Eat & Nightlife*** pp338–9

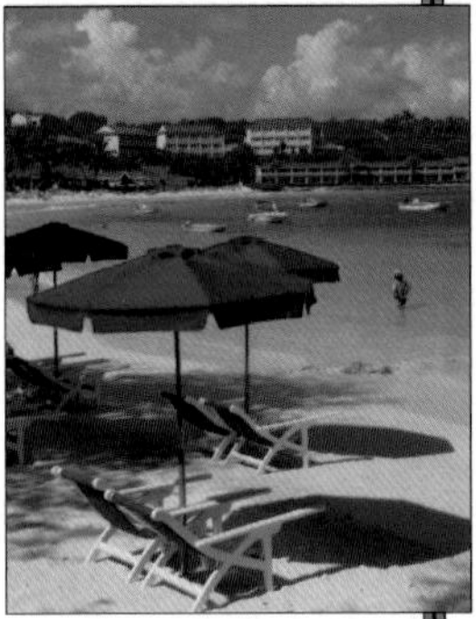

Long Bay Beach with resorts in the background, Antigua

SIGHTS AT A GLANCE

Betty's Hope 4
Codrington 14
Codrington Lagoon and the Caves p326 15
Devil's Bridge 6
English Harbour and Nelson's Dockyard p324 9
Fig Tree Drive 11
Half Moon Bay 8
Harmony Hall 7
Jolly Harbour 13
Long Bay 5
Martello Tower 16
Montserrat 18
Shirley Heights 10
St. John's 1
Turner's and Darkwood Beaches 12

Featured Hotels and Resorts

Jumby Bay, A Rosewood Resort 3
Lighthouse Bay Resort 17
Sandals Grande Antigua 2

Other Hotels and Resorts

Antigua Yacht Club Marina Resort 9
Blue Waters 14
Carlisle Bay 8
Cocobay 7
Coconut Beach Club 1
Coco's 6
English Harbour hotels 10
Five Islands hotels 3
Grand Royal Antiguan 2
Hermitage Bay 4
Hodges Bay hotels 13
Jolly Beach Resort and Spa 5
Long Bay Hotel 12
Siboney Beach Club 15
St. James' Club 11
Tropical Mansion Suites 16

Twin towers of St. John's Anglican Cathedral

St. John's ❶

W coast, Antigua. 🚶 24,500. ✈ 🚌
🚢 🛈 Goverment Complex, Queen
Elizabeth Highway, 268 462 0480.
📋 🍴 Fri–Sat. 🎭 Carnival (early
Aug). www.antigua-barbuda.org

This bustling, historic port city
is the governmental and commercial hub of Antigua. At the
center is the cruise ship dock
at Heritage Quay, lined with
upscale duty-free shops and
restaurants. Next to this area
is the Vendors Mart where
visitors can purchase local
souvenirs, and Redcliffe
Quay, a more quaint shop-
ping and dining area. Other
points of interest include
the twin-steepled **St. John's
Anglican Cathedral**. A wooden
church was first built here in
1681 but after a series of
earthquakes, the present
cathedral was built in 1847.
Church services are held on
Sunday mornings and eve-
nings. Also worth seeing is
the **Museum of Antigua and
Barbuda**, and the Public
Market Complex on Market
Street, where local farmers
sell their produce. Parking is
difficult to find, so it is recommended that visitors use
taxis or buses to come in for
a day of shopping or touring.

Environs
On the eastern outskirts of
St. John's is the legendary
Antigua Recreation Ground,
which has seen many cricket
matches and records since it

opened in 1978. A
new stadium was
built farther east for
the 2007 World Cup,
and named after
local hero Sir Vivian
Richards, a former
West Indies cricket
team captain.

At the far end
of Fort Bay is **Fort
James**, built in the
early 1700s. It was
the primary fortifi-
cation to protect the
harbor of St. John's.
Among the artillery
were ten cannons
that formed part of
the ramparts. When
most of the other
forts on the island
were disassembled, these cannons were left intact. Adjacent
to the fort is Russell's (see
p339), a full-service restaurant
installed in a historic building.

🏠 **St. John's Anglican
Cathedral**
Newgate Street.
Tel 268 462 0820. 🕐 vary.
🏛 **Museum of Antigua
and Barbuda**
Long Street.
Tel 268 462 1469.
🕐 8:30am–4pm Mon–Fri. 📋 🛈
www.antiguamuseums.org

Sandals Grande
Antigua ❷

🛶 Dickenson Bay, Antigua. **Tel** 268
462 0267. **Fax** 268 462 4135.
💲💲💲💲💲 Rooms 373. 🖥
🍴 📋 🍷 W www.sandals.com

This sprawling extravagant
complex on one of the best
beaches on the island was
expanded in 2007 with the

addition of the Mediterranean
Village, a resort within the
resort with its own huge pool,
restaurants and bars, as well
as an all-suite layout. The
original Caribbean Village is
extensive, with 5 restaurants,
5 pools, a fitness center, and
the Red Lane Spa.

Honeymooners love the
rondavels, small round buildings near the beach housing
one-bedroom suites with
private plunge pools. One of
the exclusive Sandals' features
is a personal butler service,
available for the rondavels as
well as for the Mediterranean
penthouse suites. If the entertainment in the all-inclusive
resort is not enough, the Rush
Entertainment complex, with
Madison's Casino, Rush
Nightclub (see p339), and
Conors Sports Bar is just down
the road in Runaway Bay.

Jumby Bay,
A Rosewood
Resort ❸

🛶 Long Island. **Tel** 268 462 6000.
Fax 268 462 6020. 💲💲💲💲💲
40 suites, 12 villas. 🖥 🍴
📋 🏊 W www.jumbybay
resort.com

One of the premiere luxury
resorts of the world, this
elegant all-inclusive gem is
located on its own island off
the north coast of Antigua.
It has been popular with celebrities, such as Oprah Winfrey
and Paul McCartney, as a
place to get away from everything in surroundings that are
uniquely British colonial.

In addition to the hotel
suites, pool, restaurants, bars,

One of the luxurious pools at Sandals Grande Antigua, Dickenson Bay

A section of the popular Long Bay Beach, Antigua

and great beach, the island also offers large luxury villas for rent, many with their own beach and plunge pools.

Betty's Hope ➍

5 miles (7 km) E of St. John's, Antigua. **Tel** 268 462 1469.
🏢 Betty's Hope Visitors' Center, 268 462 1469. ⏲ 10am–4pm Tue–Sat.
🖼 📷 www.antiguamuseums.org

Remains of 17th- and 18th-century sugar plantations are everywhere throughout the Caribbean, but it is unusual to find an actual working windmill of the type used to grind sugarcane on those plantations. Betty's Hope offers that rare find, in one working and one non-working mill surrounded by ruins of a plantation that was a major agricultural contributor to the economy of the island from about 1650 to the 1920s. Exhibits of the island's plantation era are displayed in the visitors' center. An eco-tourism enhancement project aims to continue the conservation of the site.

An old plantation windmill, Betty's Hope

Long Bay ➎

10 miles (16 km) E of St. John's, Antigua. 🏢

The highlights of Long Bay, on the northeast coast (Atlantic side), are the 1,600-ft (488-m) crescent of white sand and the good snorkeling sites on the barrier reef close to shore.

The bay accommodates guests from two adjacent resorts, **Grand Pineapple Resort** and the smaller Long Bay Hotel (see p337) as well as local families with children.

The Grand Pineapple Resort is a luxurious resort with pools, restaurants, tennis courts, spa, and watersports. Rooms are brightly done in white wicker and floral textiles, most with gorgeous ocean views out to the Atlantic. Those that are high up on the hill and the ones down on the beach offer the most spectacular vistas. Visitors on the Long Bay Beach can get lunch from the Beach House restaurant, and colorful trinkets and souvenirs are on sale from the beach vendors.

🛏 **Grand Pineapple Resort**
Long Bay. **Tel** 268 463 2006.
Fax 268 463 2452. $ $ $ $ $
Rooms 180. 🖥 🍴 🖩 🌴 🆆
www.grandpineapple.com

Devil's Bridge ➏

11 miles (17 km) E of St. John's Antigua. 🏢 📷 Kite Festival (Mar–Apr). www.tropikiters.com

This natural formation on the Atlantic Coast draws visitors who want to see the dramatic coastline. The bridge itself is a stone arch over the sea; during high tide the area below becomes a pool with the waves cresting over the top of the bridge. It is said that anyone falling from the bridge is bound to drown, and legend has it that many slaves chose this fate by throwing themselves off the bridge into the sea. The area, designated a national park, is also the site of the annual Kite Festival, because the very strong winds off the ocean are perfect for aerial kite maneuvers.

Environs

Adjacent to Devil's Bridge National Park and sprawling over 30 acres (12 ha) is the grand eco-friendly **Verandah Resort & Spa**. This pretty hotel features two spectacular protected beaches, a spa and fitness center, children's center, tennis court, and three restaurants. The rooms are spacious and easily accommodate small families. Some can be interconnected for larger families. All rooms have air-conditioning, flat-screen satellite TVs, and small kitchens.

🛏 **Verandah Resort & Spa**
Long Bay. **Tel** 268 562 6848.
Fax 268 562 7024. $ $ $ $ $
Rooms 200. 🖥 🍴 🖩 🌴 🆆
www.verandahresortandspa.com

Devil's Bridge rock formation at the eastern end of Antigua

Interior of the art gallery in Harmony Hall

Harmony Hall ❼

8 miles (13 km) SE of St. John's, Antigua. **Tel** 268 460 4120. 🚗 ⏺ 10am–6pm Tue–Sun. **www**.harmonyhall.com

Located on the southeastern coast of Antigua, near Freetown village, Harmony Hall is a charming art gallery in Brown's Bay Mill. Fine paintings, sculptures, jewelry, photographs, and pottery by local artists are on display here. Harmony Hall also holds regular exhibitions from November to April. The complex has a restaurant on a terrace that overlooks Brown's Bay and offers delicious Italian cuisine.

Half Moon Bay ❽

🚢 14 miles (22 km) SE of St. John's, Antigua. 🏊 ⛵ 🏄

One of the most beautiful beaches on Antigua, Half Moon Bay's crescent-shaped strand offers two completely different beach experiences – the rough surf on the Atlantic side and calm, clear waters at the far eastern end.

Snorkeling is a favorite activity along the reef that forms the bay's breakwater, but there are no watersports operators so visitors need to bring their own equipment. There is a small bar at the entrance with limited food service, and bringing a picnic basket and cooler is recommended.

English Harbour and Nelson's Dockyard ❾

On the southern coast of Antigua sits its historic gem: the 15-sq-mile (38-sq-km) Nelson's Dockyard National Park and English Harbour. Some of the main buildings here can be traced to the late 18th century when the British ruled the island. The dockyard park has a museum, restaurants, and an inn *(see p336)*. English Harbour, along with the adjacent Falmouth Harbour, is known as an international yachting center and hosts several regattas and races.

VISITORS' CHECKLIST

11 miles (18 km) S of St. John's. **Tel** 268 481 5022. 🚌 ⏺ 9am–5pm daily. 🅿 🍴 **www**. nationalparksantigua.com

KEY

🚢 Ferry port/Marina

═ Minor road

0 meters   300
0 yards   300

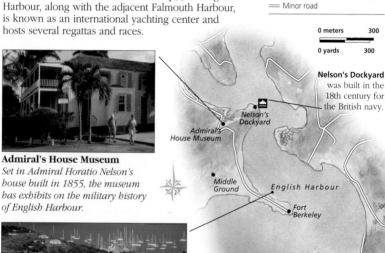

Nelson's Dockyard was built in the 18th century for the British navy.

Nelson's Dockyard

Admiral's House Museum

Admiral's House Museum
Set in Admiral Horatio Nelson's house built in 1855, the museum has exhibits on the military history of English Harbour.

Middle Ground

English Harbour

Fort Berkeley

English Harbour
This protected harbor was a haven for pirates and military fleet alike. It now plays host to the world-renowned Antigua Sailing Week (see p329).

Fort Shir

Shirley Heights 10

12 miles (19 km) S of St. John's, Antigua. ***Tel*** *268 728 0636/764 0389.* 🚗 🎉 🍴 *9am–10pm Tue–Sun, 9am–sunset Mon.*
www.shirleyheightslookout.com

High on the hill above English Harbour sits this renovated historical site, overlooking the sea. It is famous for its panoramic views and on clear days, visitors can see as far as Guadeloupe and Montserrat. It is popular for its Sunday evenings when the place hosts the biggest party on the island, including steel band and soca band entertainment. The complex also has a restaurant and a band plays on Thursday evenings.

Fig Tree Drive 11

8 miles (13 km) SE of St. John's, Antigua. 🚗 🌿 🛍

Heading south from the village of Swetes, the winding road passes through the most thickly forested area on the island – Fig Tree Hill. Ironically there are no fig trees here but banana and mango trees line the road. A lovely stop on the way is the Fig Tree Culture Shop where visitors can buy fresh fruits, juices, jams, and locally-made food products. A favorite stopover is Wallings Dam, a historic park with a picnic area, hiking trails, and canopy tours *(see p331)*. In the heart of the rainforest is also the Fig Tree Studio Art Gallery, that features the art of local artist Sallie Harker as well as crafts from island's artists. Most of the tour operators and taxi drivers offer tours of the area.

Located along Fig Tree Drive at Old Road Village, **Curtain Bluff Resort** is an elegant all-inclusive resort. Owned by Howard and Michelle Hulford, the resort has 73 rooms and suites, pool, spa, 2 beaches, 2 restaurants, and a beautiful garden setting.

Curtain Bluff Resort
Morris Bay. ***Tel*** *268 462 8400.*
Fax *268 462 8409.* $$$$$
Rooms 73. ⛱ 🍴 ▤ 🏊 ♿ [W]
www.curtainbluff.com

Peaceful Turner's Beach, on Antigua's southwestern coast

Turner's and Darkwood Beaches 12

⛱ 3 miles (5 km) SW of St. John's, Antigua. 🚻 🍸 🤿

Along Antigua's southwestern coast lie these two wide, golden-sand beaches. Both offer good restaurants and beach bars with lounge chair rentals, and are perfect for those not staying at the beach resorts. The snorkeling off Turner's Beach is good, but visitors need to bring their own equipment. Cruising yachts often anchor just offshore so passengers can enjoy the beach. Darkwood Beach has a lovely stretch of sand and is a great spot to swim.

Yachts lined up at the Jolly Harbour marina

Jolly Harbour 13

2 miles (3 km) SW to St. John's, Antigua. ***Tel*** *268 462 6042.* 🚌 ⛴
🎉 *Sailing Week (Apr–May).*
www.jolly-harbour-marina.com

North of Darkwood Beach, this marina complex has a little of everything: a great beach, shopping center, elegant casino and nightclub building, an 18-hole golf course, and tennis courts, as well as a number of restaurants and bars. It also offers a world-class marina for visiting yachts and is one of the harbors for the annual Sailing Week. Spreading out alongside the beautiful beach is Jolly Beach Resort *(see p336)*, one of the largest all-inclusives on the island.

Driving through the forested Fig Tree Drive

Codrington ⑭

Eastern edge of the Lagoon,
Barbuda. 🏘 1,500. ✈ 🚢 🚐 ⛵
Caribana Festival (May).
www.barbudaful.net

The small town of Codrington
is Barbuda's capital and the
commercial and government
center. Many of the original
buildings from the 19th
century still exist, and have
been enlisted for other uses:
the former Ginnery now
houses offices and the stables
of the Government House
have been converted into a

Wa Omoni's popular local restaurant, Codrington

school. The town also has
several supermarkets, grocery
stores, bars, bakeries, and
restaurants; lobster lunches
featuring the spiny lobster

caught off Barbuda's
shores, are a favorite
with visitors. On
the outskirts of
Codrington is an
Internet café, a
pharmacy, an ice-
cream parlor, a
souvenir shop,
and the Art Café,
home of local artist
Claire Frank. Here,
visitors can browse
through her collection of
hand-painted silks.
    The town has many small
guesthouses which provide
economical overnight lodging.

Codrington Lagoon and the Caves ⑮

A sheltered waterway separated from the ocean by a
narrow spit of land, Codrington Lagoon is home to
170 species of birds. It serves as a major habitat for
the frigate birds, of which 5,000 make their home
here. The caves nestled into the sea bluffs on the northeastern side of the island are rich in history from the
days when Arawak Indians and later runaway slaves
sought the protection of these underground grottos.

Frigate Birds Colony
*One of the largest colonies in the world, this
is home to the frigate birds. The birds can
be seen nesting in the mangrove
swamps around the lagoon.*

Two Foot Bay is dotted with caves
which feature Amerindian rock
carvings. It is best to go with a guide
since there are no marked trails.

Darby Cave
*This 180-ft (55-m) deep
sinkhole leads to a broad
cavern that ends in five
freshwater pools.*

Codrington Lagoon
*Separated from the Caribbean
Sea by a narrow piece of land,
this lagoon occupies a large
part of this small island.*

Two Foot Bay

Man of War Island

Codrington Lagoon

Rubbish Bay

THE HIGHLANDS

Codrington

BARBUDA

KEY
✈ Airport
═ Road

Martello Tower, rising
to 32 ft (10 m), served
as an observation post.

VISITORS' CHECKLIST
West of Codrington, Barbuda.
🚖 **Note:** *taxi drivers can
arrange boat tours of the
lagoon.* **www**.barbudaful.net

For hotels and restaurants on these islands see pp336–7 and pp338–9

The luxury Lighthouse Bay Resort on the 11 Mile Beach

Martello Tower 16

3 miles (5 km) S of Codrington, Barbuda. 🚌 🕒 *6am–8pm daily.* 🎫 💻 **www**.barbudaful.net

Early attempts at settling upon Barbuda by the English were resisted by the fierce Carib Indians. Barbuda was eventually colonized by John and Christopher Codrington, who came over from Antigua in 1685 to establish a provisioning station and, legend has it, a slave-breeding home for their plantations in Antigua, under a 99-year lease from Queen Anne of England.

Between 1750 and 1800, the British built a fort at a point called River, which included the 52-ft (17-m) high observation tower now known as Martello. It was modeled after a tower built on Cape Mortella in Corsica during the Napoleonic Wars. The fort was equipped with three guns. Apart from defense purposes, the fort was also used as a high vantage point to spot shipwrecks on the reefs surrounding the island.

At the beach's edge adjacent to the Martello Tower is the laid-back **Martello Anchorage Bar and Grill**, the only beach bar on Barbuda. This locally-owned restaurant prepares a variety of seafood including fish and lobster dishes, served with traditional Barbudan vegetables, such as squash, beans, pumpkin, and peppers, as well as cool drinks. With some spectacular ocean views, the bar is a favorite venue for beach parties.

The robust exterior of the Martello Tower

Martello Anchorage Bar and Grill
River Beach. ***Tel*** *268 460 0137.*
🕒 *10am–midnight daily.*

Lighthouse Bay Resort 17

🛥 Low Bay, Barbuda. ***Tel*** *268 562 1481.* $$$$$ *9 rooms.* 🏖 🍴 ☰ 🏃 [W] **www**.lighthousebayresort.com

This small luxury resort, sits on a strip of land at the southeastern edge of Codrington Lagoon, on the spectacular pink-sand 11 Mile Beach. The sense of being out at the end of the world is pervasive, since there are no other resorts or facilities nearby. The property includes the Lighthouse Bay Bar. The hotel concierge can arrange activities such as deep-sea fishing, tours of the Frigate Bird Sanctuary, water-skiing, cave exploring, and diving.

THE SPINY LOBSTER

Grilled spiny lobster

In the Caribbean, when a menu says "lobster" it generally means the spiny lobster, endemic to the warm tropical waters. Unlike the New England-type lobsters that have the fat frontal claws, these creatures have long, straight spikes coming off the head, great for defense, but not very edible. However, the lobster meat is delectable. Fishermen in the waters around Barbuda bring in large quantities of the catch, and visitors can buy them right off the docks, still alive. Those lucky enough to be traveling the islands' waters by boat often buy them fresh, fuel up the grill, cut the lobsters in half and brush with a little butter, then throw them on the heat – a quick and easy meal fit for a king. Land-based visitors can find them already grilled at many of the roadside food vendors' stands, and of course, at all the better restaurants.

Outdoor Activities and Specialized Holidays

Antigua's most outstanding natural resource is its coastline – its numerous coves and bays provide an array of opportunities for water-based activities. Offshore, the island is ringed by reefs providing diving and snorkeling sites, as well as by small islands perfect for day explorations. Antigua is also an island of rolling hills, broad valleys, and in the southernmost area, a rainforest. Hiking or biking through the hill areas, touring off-road and overland, riding a zip line through the rainforest, or golfing are all available to active tourists.

The busy beach at Dickenson Bay

BEACHES

Each beach on Antigua features different types of wave action, wind, sand, and vegetation depending on its location. The Atlantic Coast has rougher surf and sand, while the tame beaches of the Caribbean side offer powdery sand and clear seas.

All beaches are open to the public. Some resorts offer day passes which allow use of their facilities or all-inclusive passes which also include food and drink. On beaches without resorts, bars and restaurants offer beach chair rentals and facilities, and some have watersports equipment for hire.

Among the best Atlantic beaches are Long Bay (see p323), Green Island, and Half Moon Bay (see p324). Popular ones on the west coast are Dickenson, Runaway, Deep, Hawksbill, and Lignum Vitae Bays. Turner's and Darkwood Beaches (see p325) are top spots on the southwest coast, as well as Cades and Rendezvous Bays.

In Barbuda, Pink Beach is well known for its rose-hued sands.

SAILING AND KAYAKING

One of the best ways to explore Antigua is by sea, in a sailboat or catamaran. Depending on the tour operator, these tours can take on a party atmosphere or be an educational trip where passengers learn about ecological efforts to preserve marine life. **Pirates of Antigua** even offers pirate cruises on a beautifully restored schooner. **Adventure Antigua** is run by Eli Fuller, a

A sailboat arriving at Nelson's Dockyard

local who competed in the 1988 Olympics as part of a sailing crew. He and his staff offer eco-tours on traditional yachts built in the Caribbean. Boat trips may include a stop at **Stingray City Antigua**, an offshore habitat where visitors can swim with the friendly stingrays (see also ATV/4X4 Tours, p330).

Day and cruise ship charters are available at **Adventure Caribbean Yacht Charters** and bareboat and crewed charters can be hired from **Antigua Yacht Charters Ltd**. and **Nicholson Yacht Charters**.

Kayak tours are offered by **Paddles Eco Kayak Tours**. Passengers climb into individual crafts and are guided through interesting sections of coastline or waterways. Other operators include **Sailing Antigua** and **Wadadli Cats**.

DIVING AND SNORKELING

The sheltered western and southern coasts are the islands' primary diving areas. Among the best sites are Cades Reef, the Pinnacles of Hercules, Big John's Reef, and Ffryes Shoal.

Most dive operators are PADI certified, own custom-designed dive boats, have equipment and packages, and conduct classes on all levels. Some also have underwater cameras for rent, so divers can return with unique souvenirs of their dives. Tour operators include **Sea Wolf Diving School**, **Dive Antigua**, **Jolly Dive**, and **Indigo Divers**.

KITESURFING AND WINDSURFING

The north coast of Antigua is blessed with perfect conditions for kitesurfing. The wind is constantly high and side-on, the water has enough swells for good bump and jump conditions. Equipment rentals have everything a beginner or advanced surfer may need. Operators include **Kitesurf Antigua**.

Windsurfing equipment and lessons are available at Sunsail Club Colonna (see p337) on the north coast at Hodges Bay.

For hotels and restaurants on these islands see pp336–7 and pp338–9

Sailing in Antigua

An almost circular island with a raggedy coastline of deep bays and harbors sitting between the wild and windy Atlantic Ocean and the more serene Caribbean Sea, Antigua is a yachter's paradise. Among the many offerings of the island are international yachting events, bareboat or crewed charters, and learn-to-sail

Colorful catamaran

schools. Colorful marinas capable of servicing everything from small monohulls and catamarans to super yachts are located at English Harbour, Falmouth Harbour, and Jolly Harbour. Services at these locations include marine engineering, electronics, and rigging, making this a one-stop destination for the yachting industry.

REGATTAS AND RACES

For yachtsmen around the world, Antigua is the place to be in the spring. Among the international yacht racing events held here are the Classic Yacht Regatta in early April, and then the Stanford Sailing Week in late April.

Yachts of all sizes can be seen participating in the various races.

Ondeck Ocean Racing *offers a chance for individuals to become a member of the crew for a day on a Beneteau 40.7 or a Farr 40 or 60 yacht. An ocean race is set up so that participants get a genuine racing experience.*

Stanford Sailing Week *includes several classes ranging from large yachts and monohulls to gunboats. The week is filled with beach parties at locations around the island where locals join in the fun.*

OTHER EVENTS AND ACTIVITIES

Antigua has four yacht clubs and hosts an annual inter-club race in January. English Harbour and Jolly Harbour, with their lively clubs, restaurants, and shops, serve as yachting centers that attract gatherings of yachtsmen year round.

Charters *are available all around Antigua. Several companies offer crewed and bareboat charters on yachts and will provision and set the itinerary according to individual preferences.*

Learn-to-sail *programs at Sunsail Club Colonna (see p337) include the RYA Start Sailing Course for all those who are keen. The resort also has a fleet of Laser 1, Taz, Topper Topaz, and Hobie 15 Club dinghies for practice.*

A breathtaking view of English Harbour from Shirley Heights, Antigua

HIKING

Many of the trails in Antigua are not fully developed, but lead to interesting historic sights or natural wonders. Trails in the English Harbour area *(see p324)* lead from Nelson's Dockyard to Fort Barrington and up to Shirley Heights. A trail starting in the Half Moon Bay National Park leads to a promontory looking out to the neighboring butterfly-shaped island of Guadeloupe. Trails through the beautiful rainforest area start at Wallings Dam and head up Boggy Peak, the highest point on the island, and out to Rendezvous Bay, which is not accessible by road. The **Environmental Awareness Group** and the **Antigua Historical and Archeological Society** occasionally sponsor hikes in these areas.

BIKES AND SCOOTERS

For fresh-air touring, there is nothing like the immediacy of a bicycle or scooter. Most of the roads are flat or on rolling hills, making this form of transportation ideal. **Bikes Plus** in St. John's offers mountain bike rentals and they also have a stock of spare parts and equipment. **Paradise Boat Sales** in Jolly Harbour also rents out mountain bikes with special children's seats, by the day. **Barbuda Bike Tours** on Barbuda provides guided mountain-biking trips and also rents bikes and cycling gear to independent bikers.

For motorized fun, **Cheke's Scooter Rentals**, located in St. John's, has scooters ranging from 50–150cc, for rent by the day. This is inclusive of two helmets, maps, as well as instructions.

RAINFOREST ZIP LINE TOURS

Soaring high above the rainforest canopy is an exhilarating experience. At **Antigua Rainforest Canopy Tour**, the guides, well trained in safety, attach state-of-the-art harnesses and helmets to ensure that everyone arrives in great shape at the end of one of the four available tours. After zooming through the high-altitude lines, participants then end at the "Leap of Faith" (similar to bungee-jumping but safer), and then on to the Challenge Course. The last physical test is then the 400-step climb back to the top. Children can participate, if taller that 4 ft (1.20 m). It is advisable to make reservations.

ATV/4X4 TOURS

The interior of Antigua is hilly, dotted with historical ruins and small villages.

Several tour operators offer trips overland into these oft-unexplored parts of the island. Tour agencies such as **Tropical Adventures** combine inland safaris in open jeeps with kayaking or a visit to Stingray City Antigua.

Happy Trails Tours uses 4x4 off-road vehicles that add a touch of comfort with air conditioning. Some tour operators also offer quad bikes (or ATVs). Adventure Antigua offers a Quad Off-Road Tour that involves only adventure trails and no streets.

A jeep safari at Betty's Hope, Antigua

For hotels and restaurants on these islands see pp336–7 and pp338–9

The sprawling Jolly Harbour Golf Club on the ground of Jolly Beach Resort, Antigua

GOLF

There are two picturesque 18-hole courses on the island, taking advantage of the rolling hills, tropical landscapes and sea views.

Cedar Valley Golf Club, in the northern part of the island, is a par 70, 6,157 yard course for all skill levels, and also offers a 300-yard (274-m) driving range and a resident pro. The place offers panoramic views of the Caribbean coastline. **Jolly Harbour Golf Club**, a par 71, 5,587 yard (5,108 m) course, was designed by well-known golf course architect Karl Litton, and is set next to the Jolly Harbour marina. Its clubhouse has a pro shop, snack bar, showers, and locker rooms. Both are open to the public, and many hotels can arrange for guests to use the courses.

DIRECTORY

SAILING AND KAYAKING

Adventure Antigua
Tel 268 726 6355. www.adventureantigua.com

Adventure Caribbean Yacht Charters
Tel 268 764 0595. www.adventurecaribbean.com

Antigua Yacht Charters Ltd.
Tel 268 463 7101. www.antiguayachtcharters.com

Nicholson Yacht Charters
Tel 268 460 1530. www.nicholson-charters.com

Paddles Eco Kayak Tours
Tel 268 463 1944. www.antiguapaddles.com

Pirates of Antigua
Tel 268 562 7946. www.piratesofantigua.com

Sailing Antigua
Tel 268 726 6355. www.sailing-antigua.com

Stingray City Antigua
Tel 268 562 7297. www.stingraycityantigua.com

Wadadli Cats
Tel 268 462 4792. www.wadadlicats.com

DIVING AND SNORKELING

Dive Antigua
Tel 268 462 3483. www.diveantigua.com

Indigo Divers
Jolly Harbour, Antigua.
Tel 268 562 3483. www.indigo-divers.com

Jolly Dive
Jolly Harbour, Antigua.
Tel 268 462 8305. www.jollydive.com

Sea Wolf Diving School
English Harbour, Antigua.
Tel 268 783 3466. www.seawolfdivingschool.com

KITESURFING AND WINDSURFING

Kitesurf Antigua
Jabberwock Beach, Antigua. Tel 268 720 5483. www.kitesurfantigua.com

HIKING

Antigua Historical and Archeological Society
Tel 268 462 1469. www.antiguamuseums.org

Environmental Awareness Group
Tel 268 462 6236.

BIKES AND SCOOTERS

Barbuda Bike Tours
Barbuda.
Tel 268 460 0539.

Bikes Plus
Independence Drive, St. John's, Antigua.
Tel 268 462 2453. www.bikesplusantigua.com

Cheke's Scooter Rentals
St. John's, Antigua.
Tel 268 562 4646. www.antiguanice.com/chekes

Paradise Boat Sales
Jolly Harbour, Antigua.
Tel 268 460 7125. www.paradiseboats.com

RAINFOREST ZIP LINE TOURS

Antigua Rainforest Canopy Tour
Fig Tree Drive, Antigua.
Tel 268 562 6363. www.antiguarainforest.com

ATV/ 4X4 TOURS

Happy Trails Tours
St. John's, Antigua.
Tel 464 2089. www.happytrailsantigua.com

Tropical Adventures
St. John's, Antigua.
Tel 268 480 1225. www.tropicalad.com

GOLF

Cedar Valley Golf Club
St. John's, Antigua.
Tel 268 462 0161. www.cedarvalleygolf.ag

Jolly Harbour Golf Club
Jolly Harbour, Antigua.
Tel 268 462 7771.

Montserrat ⓲

During the 1990s, the Soufrière Hills Volcano repeatedly roared to life with activity that buried the main town of Plymouth and a significant portion of the southern half of Montserrat in ash. In the years since the tragedy, the island has developed a new role, offering "volcano tourism," with people coming just to see the devastation and the cloud-shrouded mount. A hardened dome covers the active core of hot lava, quieting the major threat, but there is still significant seismic activity as well as gas and steam venting. The island is divided into the Exclusion Zone, covering the southern half, and the northern hills where the locals have rebuilt their governmental center and cultural core at Brades.

Red phone box almost buried in volcanic ash, Plymouth

Lava covering what was once the Golf Club

The Exclusion Zone

Southern part of Montserrat.
⦿ daylight hours. 🚗 **Avalon's Taxi-Tours** Brades. *Tel 664 491 3432 or 664 492 1565.* **Clifford "Shaw-Duck" Ryan** Brades. *Tel 664 492 1849.* **Grant Tours** Brades. *Tel 664 491 9654.* **'JIG' Tours** Brades. *Tel 664 491 2752, 664 492 2752 or 664 496 2752.*
In 1995, the Soufrière Hills Volcano erupted, spewed ash that covered the main town of Plymouth and darkened the sun for 15 minutes. A year later, the town was abandoned, buried under layers of ash and mud deposited by pyroclastic activity. Houses on the hills around the center of the island, as well as the W.H. Bramble Airport on the eastern side of the island, were similarly buried and now stand as a modern-day Pompeii for all to observe. If volcanic activity is at a minimum, people are allowed to go briefly into some areas of the Exclusion Zone to observe the devastation from a closer vantage point. But

nobody can enter the zone without a qualified guide, and must follow the restrictions and safety measures. Since no one is allowed near the town of Plymouth, the best place to view it is from Richmond and Garibaldi Hills, where many of the homes remain half-buried in ash. To arrange a tour, contact the Montserrat Tourist Board or one of the tour operators.

Another interesting way to view the effects of the volcano is on a boat tour starting from Little Bay. From this vantage point, the town of Plymouth and the paths of the volcanic flows are visible.

On the eastern side of the island, the remains of Bramble Airport and the lava dome can be viewed from the

lookout at Jack Boy Hill. From this point, the airport as well as the severely damaged Indian burial grounds and villages can be seen. The specially constructed building offers a viewing platform, a telescope to see the volcanic dome (if the clouds have lifted), and picnic areas.

Montserrat Volcano Observatory

Flemmings, Montserrat. *Tel 664 491 5647.* ⦿ 8:30am–4:30pm Mon–Fri. 🍴 📷 ♿ www.montserrat volcanoobservatory.info
The Montserrat Volcano Observatory, which is responsible for monitoring the volcano and issuing status alerts, has its own headquarters at Flemmings, built in 2003. At the Interpretation Center, posters provide an explanation of the techniques used in monitoring volcanic

View of Montserrat's former airport from Jack Boy Hill

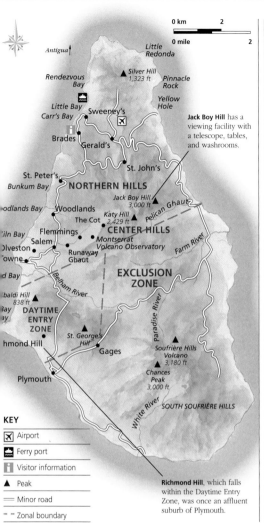

Jack Boy Hill has a viewing facility with a telescope, tables, and washrooms.

Richmond Hill, which falls within the Daytime Entry Zone, was once an affluent suburb of Plymouth.

KEY

⊠	Airport
🛳	Ferry port
ℹ	Visitor information
▲	Peak
═	Minor road
‑ ‑	Zonal boundary

activities and video shows give a synopsis and examples of the volcano's recent activity, along with a touch screen and displays of rocks, ash, and artifacts. Scientists are available to answer questions at sessions held on Tuesdays and Thursdays.

The website gives the most up-to-date information about the volcano through weekly status reports. Those planning to visit the island should check this site before traveling. Also of interest is the photo gallery that is updated weekly and has an archive of photographs taken during the periods when the dome was still growing. For those interested in learning more about volcanos, the site also offers extensive information on volcano-specific events and their monitoring methods. A CD as well as a sample set to aid teaching geology, geography, and science for children aged 11 to 18 are also available.

VISITOR SAFETY

Visitors can pick up a brochure titled *Guide to Volcanic Hazards* at the tourist board office or at the observatory. This gives a brief history of the volcano and the current risk assessments. It outlines the Exclusion Zone, the criteria for entering it, and the safety rules to be observed while traveling through it (such as carrying ash masks and drinking water). It also lists emergency numbers and what to do if the early-warning sirens go off.

View of the volcano from the Montserrat Volcano Observatory

Outdoor Activities and Specialized Holidays

In contrast to the southern part of Montserrat, which resembles a moonscape and is largely inaccessible, the northern area reminds both locals and visitors of what the island used to be. The hills are covered by lush greenery, sparkling creeks in deep ravines (*ghauts*) trickle down to the sea, and winding roads lead to charming villas and guesthouses. It is an ideal place for rest and relaxation. The prime activities here, apart from volcano watching, are sunning on the beaches, hiking through the many trails of the Center Hills rainforest, as well as snorkeling and diving through the offshore reefs.

The black-sand beach of Bunkum Bay, Montserrat

BEACHES

The island is ringed by many beaches, with some dramatically changed by the pyroclastic flows. Rendezvous Bay, accessible only by boat or hiking, is at the northwestern tip of the island. The most popular is Little Bay Beach, a little farther south near the main town of Brades, at the port area. It has some facilities such as a good restaurant and diving operations. Farther down the Caribbean coast are Bunkum Bay and Woodlands Bay, both featuring volcanic black sand. Bunkum is good for snorkeling, and also has a beach bar. Woodlands offers a covered picnic area on a bluff overlooking the sea, but the surf is a little rougher here. Just north of the Exclusion Zone is Old Road Bay, which was extended so far out in the sea by the flows, so that

now Jumping Jack's Beach Bar is a considerable distance away from the beach. During heightened volcanic activity, this beach is often included in the Exclusion Zone.

HIKING AND BIRD-WATCHING

The center of the northern area is filled with a lush rainforest around the Center Hills, noted for its biological diversity. This includes 132 tree species, 13 mammal species, and 117 species of birds including the native Montserrat oriole. The galliwasp lizard and the endangered mountain chicken, a large frog that is a local delicacy, are also found here. The area is host to the Center Hills Project, a British Darwin Initiative-funded project that does ecological assessments and informs the government and public about activities that may have an impact on the protected species here.

The trails leading up into the hills are somewhat challenging in places, so they are not for the casual walker. The Blackwood Allen Trail, for example, offers steep climbs and deep valleys, with a viewing platform to look out over the northern villages and the sea. Bird-watching is a favorite activity on the Oriole Walkway, deceptively named because it too has some steep areas. Among the birds seen on this trail are the rare forest thrush, the bridled quail dove, the mangrove cuckoo, the trembler, and the purple-throated carib. Other popular trails include the one

LEGEND OF THE RUNAWAY GHAUT

The deep ravines, or *ghauts* as they are called in Montserrat, are marked by sparkling clear streams carrying

Sign of the Runaway Ghaut

fresh water from the hills down to the sea. Visitors are invited to taste the water, which is of astonishingly high quality, at an unassuming little tap at the side of the road near Runaway Ghaut. The legend goes that if you drink from this tap you will be drawn back to Montserrat time and again. Since it is not clearly marked, visitors should ask their guide to include it in their tour. Adjacent to the tap is a trail that provides a pleasant and easy walk into a lush picnic and strolling area.

For hotels and restaurants on this island see pp336–7 and pp338–9

The Oriole Walkway, known for its bird-watching opportunities

running from Little Bay to Rendezvous Bay, because of its access to the island's only white-sand beach as well as some excellent snorkeling areas. The trail to The Cot winds through an old banana plantation up to an elevation of 1,000 ft (305 m) with commanding views of the sea and parts of the Exclusion Zone.

Another favorite activity is turtle-watching, since several species of sea turtles – including the green turtle, the hawksbill, and the loggerhead – can be found on the black-sand beaches. The **Montserrat National Trust** sponsors guided turtle treks during the peak months of August and September.

The trust has published detailed road and trail maps, which are available in the Oriole Complex on the Salem Main Road. They can also arrange guided hikes.

Montserrat's famous oriole

DIVING AND SNORKELING

Montserrat has always been known as a good diving area, with reefs teeming with coral, sponges, and tropical fish. However, many experts believe that after the volcano calms down and the reefs off the southern shores are accessible, the diving opportunities will be spectacular because of the changes in the landscape from the volcanic activity.

Right now, the main dive areas are in the northern part of the island, off the western coast and include Carr's Bay, Lime Kiln Bay, Woodlands Bay, Rendezvous Bay, and Bunkum Bay. Other diving spots, such as Little Redonda, the Pinnacles, and Yellow Hole, are on the northeastern side, but high seas sometimes prohibit diving altogether. Dive operators include the **Green Monkey Inn and Dive Shop**, which provides simple accommodations, a beach bar, the full array of lessons and dives, sea scooters, and sea kayaks. They also organize deep-sea excursions and boat tours that allow visitors to get expansive views of the volcano-affected areas.

The other dive operator in Montserrat is **Scuba Montserrat**, located in Little Bay, which offers professional instruction and introductory lessons for beginners and children, and rental equipment. It also organizes fishing trips and boat tours to Plymouth.

Diving through underwater passages, off Montserrat

Choosing a Hotel

The islands' reputation has long been established in the all-inclusive luxury resort category. Every resort sits on a beautiful bay with white- or brown-sand beaches, plenty of watersports, and surrounding tropical gardens for the perfect vacation or honeymoon setting. Visitors can also find some real value in smaller hotels that offer personalized service and comfortable rooms.

PRICE CATEGORIES
The following price ranges are for a standard double room and taxes per night during the high season.

$ under $100
$$ $100–200
$$$ $200–300
$$$$ $300–400
$$$$$ over $400

ANTIGUA AND BARBUDA

Sandals Grande Resort – *p322*
True to the Sandals chain, this large couples-only resort is elegant, fun, and lively.

Jumby Bay, A Rosewood Resort – *p322*
This luxurious property on its own island pampers guests with every amenity imaginable.

Lighthouse Bay Resort – *p327*
This small, luxury resort is the newest hotel in Barbuda.

Sandals Grande Hotel　　　**Jumby Bay, A Rosewood Resort**

ANTIGUA, BOLANS VILLAGE Jolly Beach Resort and Spa　　$$$$

Box W2009, St. John's **Tel** *268 462 0061* **Fax** *268 562 2302* **Rooms** *464*

This all-inclusive is geared to those who want everything in one place – great beach, tennis, spa, pool, fitness center, 5 restaurants, 7 bars, watersports, and a Kids' Club. Rooms range from supersavers to junior suites and beachfront cottages. Live entertainment on most nights. **www.jollybeachresort.com**

ANTIGUA, DEEP BAY Grand Royal Antiguan　　$$

Box 976, St. John's **Tel** *268 462 3733* **Fax** *268 462 3732* **Rooms** *265, plus 12 one-bed cottages*

One of the largest on the island, this high-rise resort is situated on a beautiful beach with great snorkeling, and has 3 restaurants, 6 bars, pool, tennis courts, spa, gym, and an electronic casino. Guests can choose from rooms with mountain views, lagoon views or ocean views. Cottages are available too. **www.grandroyalantiguan.com**

ANTIGUA, DICKENSON BAY Siboney Beach Club　　$$$

Box 222, St. John's **Tel** *268 462 0806* **Fax** *268 462 3356* **Rooms** *13*

A small inn on Dickenson Beach, this place offers personalized service and a lush garden setting. Coconut Grove Restaurant (*see p338*), part of the complex, is great for romantic evening dinners. Choose from standard, superior, deluxe, and deluxe ocean view rooms. There is a pool on-site. **www.siboneybeachclub.com**

ANTIGUA, ENGLISH HARBOUR Copper & Lumber Store　　$$

Box 184, St. John's **Tel** *268 460 1058* **Fax** *268 460 1529* **Rooms** *14*

Housed in an 18th-century Nelson's Dockyard building, this gem offers a sense of history in comfortable studios and suites furnished in antiques and period pieces and with the modern convenience of kitchenettes. Beach access is at Galleon Beach via watertaxi. Dockyard shops and restaurants are steps away. **www.copperandlumberhotel.com**

ANTIGUA, ENGLISH HARBOUR Galleon Beach Club　　$$$

Box 1003, St. John's **Tel** *268 460 1024* **Fax** *268 460 1450* **Rooms** *31*

This laid-back resort is a bargain, since accommodations are in roomy one- or two-bedroom cottages or roundhouses with kitchens, patios, and dining areas. Larger villas up on the hill also available. Snorkeling in the nearby Freeman's Bay is outstanding. There is a ferry service to Nelson's Dockyard and English Harbour. **www.galleonbeach.com**

ANTIGUA, ENGLISH HARBOUR The Inn at English Harbour　　$$$$$

Box 187, St. John's **Tel** *268 460 1014* **Fax** *268 460 1603* **Rooms** *34*

Situated on Freeman's Bay at the entrance to English Harbour, this comfortable hotel offers beautiful views and outstanding service. Room categories include standard beachfront and beachfront junior and deluxe suites. There is a restaurant, a beach bar, and a bar. Gym, tennis courts, and watersports are on the property. **www.theinn.ag**

ANTIGUA, FALMOUTH HARBOUR Antigua Yacht Club Marina Resort　　$$$$$

St. John's **Tel** *268 562 3030* **Fax** *268 562 3031* **Rooms** *49*

A boat-lover's delight, this compact resort sits on a hill overlooking Falmouth Harbour. Decorated with Indonesian wood furnishings and luxury fixtures. Options include one-bedroom suites, garden and sea view studios, and hotel rooms. Rates include breakfast. There is a restaurant, bar, and spa as well. **www.aycmarina.com**

ANTIGUA, FIVE ISLANDS Galley Bay　　$$$$$

Box 305, St. John's **Tel** *268 462 0302* **Fax** *268 462 4551* **Rooms** *98*

This elegant luxury resort has Gauguin cottages with private plunge pools, beachfront rooms, and premium beachfront suites, all with rattan furniture and first-class appointments. It is self-contained, with restaurants, bar, pool, tennis, fitness center, spa, and beauty salon all in one place. **www. galleybayresort.com**

Key to Symbols *see back cover flap*

ANTIGUA, FIVE ISLANDS Hawksbill By Rex Resorts
Box 108, St. John's **Tel** *268 462 0301* **Fax** *268 462 1515* **Rooms** *111*

With 4 beaches (one clothing-optional), this sprawling resort is a delight for both families and couples. The setting is very picturesque, with a historic windmill at the center. Rooms are set around the garden and there are sea view bungalows too. There are 2 restaurants, 2 bars, a tennis court, and a wellness cottage. **www.rexresorts.com**

ANTIGUA, HODGES BAY Colonna Resort
Box W 1892, St. John's **Tel** *00 44 2392 222 222 (UK)* **Rooms** *124*

The windy northern coast is ideal for sailing, and this resort offers specialized sailing instructions *(see p329)*. Good for families, with a sailing club for older children (8+). Large pool, a spa, a fitness center, and tennis courts. Room choices range from double rooms and one-bedroom suites to two- and three-bedroom villas. **www.sunsail.com**

ANTIGUA, HODGES BAY Hodges Bay Club
Box W 1273, St. John's **Tel** *268 462 2300* **Fax** *268 462 1333* **Rooms** *105*

This north-coast luxury property has a wide range of room types from hotel suites to apartments and villas. Elegantly furnished rooms are surrounded by lush gardens; rate includes breakfast. The property houses 3 restaurants, bars, the Pelicanos children's club, a spa, pool facilities, a fitness center, and tennis courts. **www.hodgesbayclub.com**

ANTIGUA, JENNINGS Hermitage Bay
Box 60, St. John's **Tel** *268 562 5500* **Fax** *268 562 5505* **Rooms** *25*

Rated as one of the best on the island, this resort has cottages arranged beachside and hillside, with bedroom, lounge area, large veranda and luxury bath; hillside suites have private plunge pools. There is a spa on-site. Special room features include DVD player, Wi-Fi, and iPod docking station. **www.hermitagebay.com**

ANTIGUA, LONG BAY Long Bay Hotel
Box 442, St. John's **Tel** *268 463 2005* **Fax** *268 463 2439* **Rooms** *25*

This old Caribbean-style hotel is built around a plantation house, and has two waterfronts. Bayfront upper and lower rooms, suites, and cottages with cane furniture and four-poster beds. Larger cottages have kitchens and separate living areas with trundle beds for children. On-site tennis facilities. **www.longbayhotel.com**

ANTIGUA, MAMORA BAY St. James' Club
Box 63, St. John's **Tel** *268 460 5000* **Fax** *268 460 3142* **Rooms** *291*

This sprawling south coast hotel has a great variety of room types from basic rooms to suites and villas. Four restaurants, 5 bars, a casino, 2 beaches, pool facilities, tennis courts, a spa, a fitness center, Children's Club, a deli, and an Internet café are all on-site. **www.stjamesclubantigua.com**

ANTIGUA, SOLDIERS BAY Blue Waters
Box 256, St. John's **Tel** *268 462 0290* **Fax** *268 462 0293* **Rooms** *110*

An elegant, self-contained resort on the north coast, the place features a good beach, pools, gym, tennis courts, golf course, restaurants, a beauty shop and spa. Choices range from superior hillside rooms to villas with either garden or water views, and a five-bedroom Rock Cottage. Rates include breakfast. **www.bluewaters.net**

ANTIGUA, ST. MARY'S Carlisle Bay
Old Road, St.John's **Tel** *268 484 0002* **Fax** *268 484 0003* **Rooms** *82*

With sophisticated luxury on a beautiful southern beach, this resort stresses calm and relaxation. Rooms feature Indonesian themed furnishings. Two restaurants, 3 bars, 9 tennis courts, a library, a screening room and an internationally acclaimed spa are all housed in the property. **www.carlisle-bay.com**

ANTIGUA, VALLEY CHURCH Cocobay
Box 431, St. John's **Tel** *268 562 2400* **Fax** *268 562 2424* **Rooms** *53*

Climbing the hill from Ffryes Bay is a collection of pastel cottages offering luxurious rooms with hammocks, balconies, and king-sized beds. Also includes outdoor showers, 2 beaches, a Wellness Cottage, infinity-edge pool, and 2 restaurants, of which Sheer Restaurant *(see p338)* is open to the public. **www.cocobayresort.com**

ANTIGUA, VALLEY CHURCH Coco's
Box 2024, St. John's **Tel** *268 460 2626* **Fax** *268 460 9707* **Rooms** *26*

These one-bedroom cottages staggered up the hill overlooking Lignum Vitae Bay are for romantics who can climb hillsides comfortably. Room choices are standard, superior, and premium, depending on the elevation; all have outdoor showers and refrigerators. Pool, restaurant, spa, gym, tennis, and beaches on-site. **www.cocoshotel.com**

ANTIGUA, YEPTON ESTATE Coconut Beach Club
Box 1427, St. John's **Tel** *268 462 3239* **Fax** *268 462 3240* **Rooms** *38*

This secluded hotel offers comfortable accommodations, a beach, and lots of relaxation. Choose from deluxe rooms, junior or deluxe suites, all with king-sized beds and ocean views. With a five-day all-inclusive booking guests receive extras such as airport transfers and stocked mini-bar. Tennis and spa on-site. **www.coconutbeachclub.com**

MONTSERRAT Tropical Mansion Suites
Sweeney's **Tel** *664 491 8767* **Fax** *664 491 8275* **Rooms** *16*

One of two hotels on Montserrat, this one is centrally located and includes tropical gardens with a sugar mill, a pool, restaurant, and bar. The rooms are simple and comfortable, and range from standard to deluxe and full-service rooms with kitchenettes. Some are air-conditioned. **www.tropicalmansion.com**

Where to Eat & Nightlife

Although a much smaller island than Barbados or Jamaica, Antigua holds its own with innumerable choices that include sophisticated dining, romantic cafés by the sea, and Creole roadside dens, as well as various styles of entertainment. In Barbuda and Montserrat visitors will find the choices much smaller, more relaxed and homey, and less expensive than in Antigua.

PRICE CATEGORIES
The price ranges are for a two-course meal for one, including tax and service charges and half a bottle of wine.

$ under $10
$$ $10–15
$$$ $15–25
$$$$ $25–35
$$$$$ over $35

RESTAURANTS

Choosing a Cuisine
Antigua has on offer a wide variety of cuisines ranging from French, Asian, and Continental to roadside stands selling delicious food on a budget. Some of the local specialties are the *ducana* (grated sweet potato steamed with coconut and spices in a banana leaf) and *fungi* (pepperpot stew with salt beef, pumpkin, and okra, served with cornmeal pudding).

Coconut Grove

The Cove Antigua

ANTIGUA, COOLIDGE The Pavilion 🍷 📋 $$$$$
No. 7 Pavilion Drive ***Tel*** *268 480 6800*

Easily the most elegant and expensive restaurant on the island, The Pavilion serves Continental cuisine with French Creole influences in a luxurious colonial setting with beautiful fresh rose centerpieces on each table, silver goblets, and fine china. It has an 8,000-bottle wine cellar. Open for dinner only. Closed on Sundays. Reservations required.

ANTIGUA, COOLIDGE The Sticky Wicket 📋 ⛱ $$$$$
No. 20 Pavilion Drive ***Tel*** *268 481 7000*

Located adjacent to the airport, this restaurant features a brightly lit cricket field where the Stanford 20/20 matches take place annually. Displays and photos highlight cricket greats, and TV screens scattered throughout show various matches. Casual dining with American favorites such as ribs, burgers, salads, and soups.

ANTIGUA, DICKENSON BAY Coconut Grove ⛱ $$$$$
Siboney Beach Club ***Tel*** *268 462 1538*

Set in the Siboney Beach Club *(see p336)*, Coconut Grove is often cited as the most romantic restaurant on the island, with elegantly set tables just steps away from the surf of Dickenson Bay. Fresh seafood, pasta, and meat entrées in European-style cuisine, plus local soups and desserts are specialties. Open for breakfast, lunch, and dinner.

ANTIGUA, FFRYES BAY Sheer Restaurant 🍷 ⛱ $$$$$
Cocobay Resort ***Tel*** *268 562 2400*

Its setting in six romantic and intimate dining pavilions atop a cliff over the sea in Cocobay Resort *(see p337)*, and the Pan Asian and South American fusion cuisine, with imaginative combinations and beautiful platings, make for a dining experience unlike any other on the island. Open for dinner only, 5 nights a week. Reservations recommended.

ANTIGUA, HODGES BAY Le Bistro Restaurant 🍷 ⛱ $$$$$
Hodges Bay ***Tel*** *268 462 3881*

The restaurant serves Caribbean and French haute cuisine in a pleasant West Indian setting. Lobster, rack of lamb, and desserts are highly recommended by regulars. It has an extensive wine list with vintages from around the world. Open for dinner only and closed on Mondays. Reservations recommended.

ANTIGUA, RUNAWAY BAY La Bussola [V] 🍷 ⛱ $$$$$
Runaway Bay ***Tel*** *268 562 1545*

Exquisite Italian cuisine in an intimate beachfront setting made perfect with a garden and shaded gazebo on Runaway Bay. Menu includes seafood, meat, and vegetarian entrées as well as fresh pastas. Don't miss the lobster thermidor and saltimbocca. Also prepares the best tiramisu on the island. Reservations recommended.

ANTIGUA, SOLDIERS BAY The Cove Antigua 🍷 ⛱ $$$$$
Boon's Point ***Tel*** *268 562 2683*

On the northwest coast, in a sophisticated open-air setting with torches lighting the way to the entrance, The Cove Antigua's menu celebrates local ingredients, including fresh seafood and highest-quality meats. The classic bar is popular for after-dinner drinks. Open for dinner from Mondays to Saturdays and on Sundays for lunch.

ANTIGUA, ST. JOHN'S Big Banana Pizzas in Paradise ⛱ $$$
Redcliffe Quay, St. John's ***Tel*** *268 480 6985*

Popular pizza place in St. John's, run by the group that also owns The Beach restaurant in Dickenson Bay. Guests enjoy quality pizzas plus salads, subs, appetizers and pasta dishes in an open-air, two-level setting. Take-out and delivery are also available. Open for lunch and dinner from Mondays to Saturdays. Dinner only on Sundays.

Key to Symbols *see back cover flap*

ANTIGUA, ST. JOHN'S Mama Lolly's Vegetarian Café

🟥 ☑ 🖼 📧 $$$

Redcliffe Quay **Tel** *268 562 1552*

This small café's wholesome and tasty all-vegetarian menu includes outstanding lasagne, tofu stir-fry, bean stews, and veggie wraps and burgers. There are fish specials on Tuesdays and Fridays. Selection of fresh salads and juices, and egg- and wheat-free home-made cakes are available. Smoothies are made to order. Closed on Sundays.

ANTIGUA, ST. JOHN'S Café Napoleon

🖼 ♿ $$$$$

Redcliffe Quay **Tel** *268 562 1820*

Charming French café serving breakfast and lunch on the patio in historic Redcliffe Quay, adjacent to cruise ship docks. Its menu offers salads, daily specials, traditional French favorites like salade Niçoise and quiche lorraine, plus Caribbean specials and fresh seafood. The place has a full bar with tropical drinks, wine, and liquors. Closed on Sundays.

ANTIGUA, ST. JOHN'S Hemingway's Caribbean Café

🖼 $$$$$

St. Mary's Street **Tel** *268 462 2763*

A long-time favorite of visitors, this café is set on a second-story terrace overlooking busy Heritage Quay. The menu features Caribbean favorites, daily soup and entrée specials, grilled lobster, and lots of seafood. Tropical bar drinks are well made, and hospitality by owners Lowell and Ann is excellent. Closed on Sundays.

ANTIGUA, ST. JOHN'S Home Restaurant

🍴 $$$$$

Gambles' Terrace **Tel** *268 461 7651*

Local chef Carl Thomas prepares delicious Caribbean fusion cuisine using conch, crab, lobster, and cockles, as well as duck, *filet mignon*, and pork. Desserts such as crème brûlée and bread pudding are not to be missed. Open for dinner only. Closed on Sundays. Reservations are required.

ANTIGUA, ST. JOHN'S Papa Zouk

🖼 $$$$$

Hilda Davis Drive **Tel** *268 464 6044*

This rustic seafood restaurant is hard to find, off a side road to the north of St. John's – but it is worth the search. Fresh seafood is prepared Creole-style or to the guests' taste, and lobster, tuna, and *bouillabaisse* are also served. It has a large rum collection, plus Cuban cigars for after-dinner. Open for dinner only. Closed on Sundays.

ANTIGUA, ST. JOHN'S Russell's

🖼 🎵 $$$$$

Fort James **Tel** *268 462 5479*

Housed in a historic building at the entrance to St. John's Harbour, Russell's offers fantastic views. Caribbean seafood is the specialty, including grilled Antiguan lobster. Guests can sit inside the stone house or out on the expansive patio at the edge of the sea. On Sundays only, dinner is served with live jazz in the background.

BARBUDA, CODRINGTON Wa'omoni Best Restaurant

📄 $$$

Duck Pond Road **Tel** *268 562 1933*

Along with lobster and seafood, Wa'omani Restaurant offers salads, sandwiches, and a wide assortment of baked goods. Local juices, wine, and champagne are also available. It is open for lunch and dinner from Mondays to Saturdays.

MONTSERRAT Tina's Restaurant

📄 🖼 📧 $$$$

Brades **Tel** *664 491 3538*

This local favorite in Montserrat, near the center of business, offers simple, well-prepared food. Local dishes include curries and Creole fare, along with lobster burgers and sandwiches, and home-made desserts are served. Seating indoors with air-conditioning or outdoors on the terrace overlooking Brades. Closed on Sundays.

BARS AND CLUBS

The nightlife scene in Antigua is lively and multifaceted, with casinos, dance halls, and beach bars where locals and visitors mix. Many of the clubs offer special live entertainment, theme nights and contests. The all-inclusive hotels also feature live evening entertainment. For an informal, close-to-local experience, some of the ubiquitous rum shacks that sit by the main roads are perfect. Entertainment offerings are not extensive on Barbuda and Montserrat, where quiet evenings are the norm.

Live music by a steel band, Antigua

RECOMMENDED PLACES TO GO

Abracadabra
Dockyard Drive, English Harbour. (Famous for its costume parties.)

The Coast
Heritage Quay. (Live soca and reggae bands perform.)

Dogwatch Tavern & The Deck
Jolly Harbour. (Widest selection of beers on the island.)

Funky Buddha Bar
St. John's. (Asian-themed bar with karaoke and DJ nights.)

Grand Princess Casino Complex
Jolly Harbour. (Houses a casino, a disco, and a sports bar.)

Mad Mongoose Bar
Falmouth Harbour. (Live music on Fridays, DJ on Wednesdays.)

Miller's by the Sea
Fort James. (Hosts major events; beach barbecue on Sundays.)

Rush Nightclub
Runaway Bay. (Offers special theme nights.)

Sandhaven
Runaway Bay. (Live local bands and DJs on weekends.)

Practical Information

Antigua, Barbuda, and Montserrat, at the farthest eastern edge of the Leeward Islands, offer visitors the perfect tropical vacation with a British accent. Antigua is the most cosmopolitan, with the major transportation hub of V.C. Bird International Airport, and the shopping and historic delights of St. John's. Barbuda is ideal for getting away from the world, and visitors will find that there are few services other than tours of the island. Apart from the ruined city, Plymouth, the island of Montserrat also has a busy commercial center on the non-volcanic side of the island, with new shops and attractions being added continuously.

Visitors alighting at V.C. Bird International Airport, Antigua

WHEN TO GO

While Antigua, Barbuda, and Montserrat are basically warm year round, the heat can get sticky from June to October, which is also the hurricane season. Peak times for visitors to Antigua other than the winter holidays are late April (Sailing Week), August (Carnival), and November (Independence Day); March (St. Patrick's Day – the only one on the islands) in Barbuda; May (Caribana); and July (Calabash) in Montserrat.

GETTING THERE

V.C. Bird International Airport (ANU) in Antigua is served by major airlines such as **British Airways**, **Air Canada**, **Delta**, **United Airlines**, **US Airways**, **American Eagle**, and **Virgin Atlantic** as well as regional airlines such as **LIAT** and **Caribbean Airlines**. The smaller regional airlines, **Winair** and **Carib Aviation**, have flights from Antigua to Barbuda and Montserrat.

Barbuda and Antigua are also linked by a **Barbuda Express Ltd.** daily ferry. **Caribbean Helicopters** operates from Antigua to Montserrat.

DOCUMENTATION

Travelers are required to have a valid passport to enter Antigua, Barbuda, and Montserrat. Visitors also need to have return tickets and confirmed accommodations. Visas are not required for US, some European, and certain other countries. Check with the embassies for details.

VISITOR INFORMATION

For Antigua and Barbuda, visitors can contact the tourism offices located in the US, Canada, and the UK. The **Antigua and Barbuda Ministry of Tourism** also operates an information kiosk at Heritage Quay in downtown St. John's and has information available at the V.C. Bird International Airport. The Montserrat Tourist Board *(see p333)* has its main office at Farara Plaza in Brades, as well as offices in London. Useful information for visitors is also available at the island's Gerald's Airport.

HEALTH AND SECURITY

The primary health facility for Antigua and Barbuda is **Holberton Hospital**, located in St. John's. In Montserrat, **Glendon Hospital** offers emergency services to both locals as well as visitors.

While not idyllically crime-free, these islands are relatively safe for visitors. However, it is advisable to take the normal precautions of keeping valuables guarded, sticking to well-populated areas, and not roaming around alone at night.

BANKING AND CURRENCY

The currency for all three islands is the East Caribbean (EC) dollar. Antigua has a number of banks and cash can be obtained (as EC dollars) at most ATMs. Credit cards are accepted in Antigua and many vendors also accept US dollars (but not euros or British pounds). In Barbuda and Montserrat, credit cards are not as commonly accepted and vendors prefer EC dollars.

COMMUNICATIONS

In Antigua and Barbuda, **Cable & Wireless** and **Digicel** offer inexpensive phones with prepaid minutes and local SIM cards. Cable & Wireless also provides cell services in Montserrat. Some US cell phone services such as Cingular work on Antigua. Montserrat and Antigua have Internet cafés and most hotels in Antigua offer high-speed Internet connections.

TRANSPORT

Car rentals on Antigua and Montserrat are plentiful and easy to arrange either in advance or at the airport but

Entrance of a bank building in Brades, Montserrat

in Barbuda, there are no cars for hire. **AVIS** and **Hertz Rent-A-Car** in Antigua, and **Neville Bradshaw Agencies** and **Equipment & Supplies Ltd.** in Montserrat are popular car rental agencies. In Antigua, vans and minibuses are available. The public bus system runs on an unscheduled basis. In Barbuda, a popular way to get around this flat island is by bike and rentals can be arranged. Taxi drivers on the islands double as tour guides. In Montserrat, drivers can also arrange for a guided trip into the Exclusion Zone if the volcano is not threatening.

SHOPPING

Downtown St. John's in Antigua is a shoppers' delight. Activity centers around the dock area, specifically Heritage Quay and Redcliffe Quay duty-free areas and the adjacent Vendor's Mall. There are also clothing boutiques, bookstores, and shoe stores on St. Mary's Street. For authentic Antiguan food, try the Farmer's Market complex on Market Street. Other supermarkets include the

Popular shopping area of Heritage Quay in St. John's, Antigua

Epicurean in Woods Mall and Jolly Harbour. Barbuda does not have much by way of shopping. Montserrat has a few stores in the Brades area. For souvenirs, visit the Oriole Gift Shop in the Montserrat National Trust complex or the Montserrat Arts and Crafts Association shop in Brades.

LANGUAGE

English is the official language spoken on Antigua, Barbuda, and Montserrat.

ELECTRICITY

The electricity is mainly 220 volts though some hotels have 110 volts as well.

TIME

The islands are on Atlantic Standard Time, 1 hour ahead of US Eastern Standard Time.

GETTING MARRIED

Antigua has emerged as a major destination for couples looking to tie the knot, with several incredibly romantic settings and no residency requirement. The couple need to apply for a license at the **Ministry of Legal Affairs**, show their passports and other appropriate documents (divorce papers or death certificate of spouse), and pay the fees. Many of the hotels also offer wedding coordinators who can assist in getting the necessary documents. In Montserrat, the residency requirement is 3 days. The couple can apply for a marriage license at the **Department of Administration** in Brades.

A PORTRAIT OF
THE FRENCH ANTILLES

*S**t. Barthélemy, Guadeloupe, and Martinique stand out from other Caribbean isles due to their unapologetic Frenchness. While history and geography have left their marks, France influences everything from language to politics and culture. Citizens carry French passports, buy French goods, and enjoy a French lifestyle.*

St. Barthélemy (often called St. Barths or St. Bart) was an elite playground for the rich, and although facilities and services are first-class, the prices are still shockingly high. Guadeloupe, 155 miles (250 km) south, though comparatively larger in area is significantly different, while Martinique, about 100 miles (160 km) to the south of Guadeloupe, is just as sophisticated, yet less opulent than St. Barths.

Karukera rum, Guadeloupe

HISTORY

In the 15th century, when Christopher Columbus and the early explorers encountered the South American Arawak inhabitants, they thought that these islands were inhospitable and of little commercial value. This way of thinking changed, however, when they recognized the favourable agricultural conditions here. Over the next decades, as economic growth soared, several colonial powers fought with each other to establish control of the islands, and African slaves were imported to work the fields. France gained, lost and regained control of St. Barths, Guadeloupe, and Martinique as the Netherlands, England, and Sweden battled for dominance. Pirates and government-sponsored privateers contributed by attacking merchant ships. By 1794, as a result of the French Revolution, slavery was declared illegal, and many wealthy land owners

Hiking through the rainforest at the base of La Soufrière volcano, Guadeloupe

Musée Schoelcher, Guadeloupe, dedicated to the Parisian instrumental in abolition of slavery

petroleum products, rum, sugarcane, and bananas. About 6 percent of the GDP comes from agriculture. Tourism is gaining importance here, however, since the population speaks French, many English-speaking visitors have difficulty communicating, especially in small towns.

were guillotined. Six years later, Napoléon Bonaparte reversed the law, but his decision was opposed by abolitionists and defeated by the French parliament in 1848 due to the influence of leaders such as Victor Schoelcher. In 1946, Guadeloupe, Martinique, St. Martin, and St. Barths became French overseas departments.

ECONOMY

Tourism is the mainstay of St. Barths' healthy economy and a majority of the population speaks English as well as other languages. Guadeloupe's economy is still based on agriculture, with about 25 percent of land under cultivation. The chief exports include sugar, rum, bananas, coffee, and cocoa. About 75 percent of the trade is with France, which is one of the reasons why most residents speak only French or French Créole. However, since the 1980s, Guadeloupe has seen a decline in revenue from the export of agricultural products and depends on France for financial aid. Martinique is also dependent on France for economic shortfalls from exports, which include refined

LIFESTYLE AND CULTURE

In the French Antilles, there is no occasion that does not call for good food, rum, music, and dance. Music and dance are as important as cooking, and all these pleasures feature during Carnival. Parades, fireworks, concerts, and non-stop street parties run continuously. Zouk is the current rhythm of choice, but locals are just as adroit with the waltz, mazurka, and beguine. Zouk, French Creole for party, was started in the 1980s by Jacob Desvarieux and Pierre Eduard Decimus from Guadeloupe who founded the band Kassav', featuring well-known singer Jocelyn Beroard.

The French Antilles have also produced many world-class writers such as the Martinique-born author and politician Aimé Césaire (1913–2008), the Guadeloupe-born Nobel Laureate, Lexis Léger, known as Saint-John Perse (1887–1975), and the novelist Maryse Condé (b.1934).

Men playing drums on the streets at the Carnival held during Lent in Martinique

Exploring St. Barthélemy

With a distinct French flavor, St. Barths is one of the most sophisticated and expensive of the Caribbean islands. For a dry outcrop, it has a surprisingly dramatic and attractive terrain, ranging from rocky peaks to picturesque coves and excellent white-sand beaches. Trendy upscale boutiques line the streets of Gustavia, the main harbor town, while the most luxurious resorts and villas are scattered around the island. The adventurous can hike down to the beaches to escape from the crowds. With French chefs and a good supply of produce via St. Martin, the island is also known for its great cuisine.

ANGUILLA
ST. MARTIN/
SINT MAARTEN
VIRGIN
ISLANDS
ST. BARTHÉLEMY
ANTIGUA AND
BARBUDA
SABA AND
ST. EUSTATIUS
ST. KITTS
AND NEVIS
GUADELOUPE
Caribbean Sea
MARTINIQUE

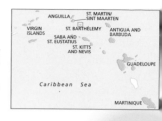

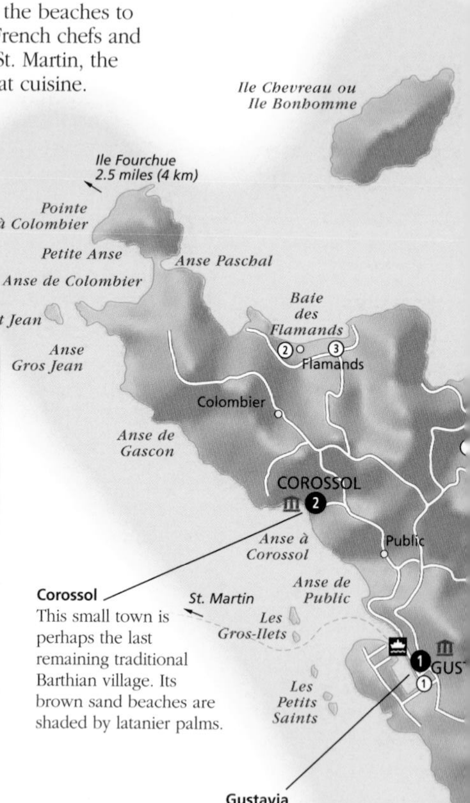

KEY
Minor road
Ferry route
Peak
Ile Chevreau ou
Ile Bonhomme
Ile Fourchue
2.5 miles (4 km)
Pointe
à Colombier
Petite Anse
Anse de Colombier
Anse Paschal
Baie
des
Flamands
Ile Petit Jean
Anse
Gros Jean
Flamands
Colombier
Anse de
Gascon
COROSSOL
Anse à
Corossol
Public
Anse de
Public
St. Martin
Les
Gros-Ilets
Les
Petits
Saints
GUS

Corossol
This small town is perhaps the last remaining traditional Barthian village. Its brown sand beaches are shaded by latanier palms.

Gustavia
The capital of the island, Gustavia is the most developed town and has some excellent Swedish-style architecture.

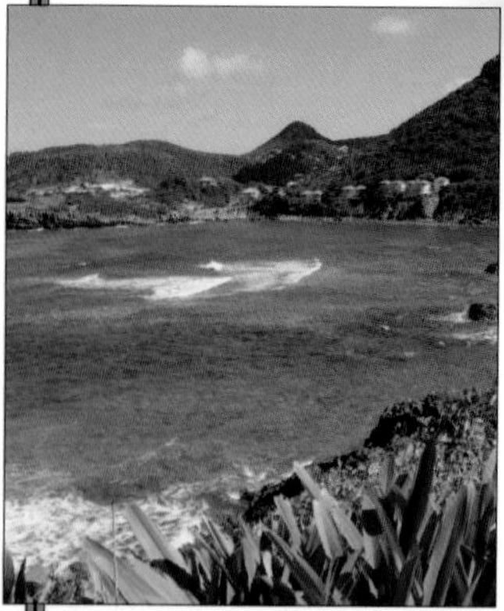

Spectacular view from the hike to Anse de Colombier

SIGHTS AT A GLANCE

Beaches of St. Barthélemy 5
Corossol 2
East End 4
Gustavia 1
St-Jean 3

Hotels and Resorts

Auberge de Terre Neuve 3
Christopher Hotel – St. Barth 8
Flamands hotels 2
Grand Cul-de-Sac hotels 9
Gustavia hotels 1
La Banane 6
Le Toiny 10
Normandie Hotel 7
O'Kaï Beach Residence 4
St-Jean hotels 5

SEE ALSO

• ***Where to Stay*** pp352–3

• ***Where to Eat & Nightlife*** pp354–5

The little village of Flamands overlooking the Baie des Flamands

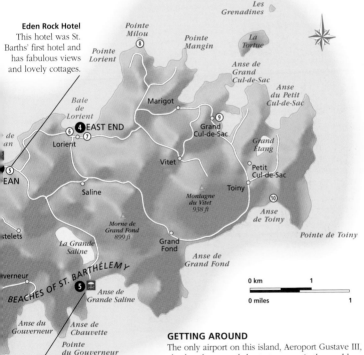

Eden Rock Hotel
This hotel was St. Barths' first hotel and has fabulous views and lovely cottages.

Anse de Grande Saline
This area is known for its large salt pond, which is harvested for salt. The beach here is one of the best in the Caribbean.

GETTING AROUND

The only airport on this island, Aeroport Gustave III, also has the second shortest runway in the world, after Saba. Only small aircraft can land here. There are infrequent ferries from Gustavia to St. Martin, only 15 miles (24 km) to the northeast, but the sea can be a bit rough. Most of the hotels in St. Barths offer a pick-up and drop service on arrival and departure. Although hiring a car can be quite expensive, most visitors opt for this as St. Barths has few taxis and no buses or other public transport.

Red-roofed buildings overlooking Gustavia's harbor

Gustavia ❶

W coast of St. Barthélemy.
🏃 3,500. ✈ 🚢 ℹ Quai General
de Gaulle, 590 278 727. 🚢
🎵 St. Barths Music Festival (Jan).
www.stbartsmusicfestival.org

Gustavia is one of the prettiest harbor towns in the Caribbean. Its steep bay walls tumble to a rectangular waterfront, with attractive red-roofed buildings overlooking the harbor from three sides. Much of the waterfront itself is a boardwalk, where tenders moor at the restaurants and bars, which gives the bay a very pleasant ambience. At Christmas and New Year, Gustavia harbor is one of the most fashionable places in the world. Luxury yachts anchor shoulder to shoulder, sterns to the boardwalk, hosting parties for celebrities.

Onshore, the streets are steep and narrow but full of character. There is often a lively buzz around the many bars and shops, particularly on the boardwalk. The streetfronts are lined with serious names in the world of fashion, Armani, Dolce & Gabbana, and Bulgari (see pp350–51). On the waterfront at the head of the bay is the Anglican church and behind it the Catholic church. Above them, the Swedish clock tower can be seen from several points around the harbor. It can be recognized by its small triangular roof.

At the far point of the bay's outer arm, beneath the fort, are two notable buildings. The

Mairie de St. Barth (town hall) is a modern version of the mayoral buildings that are seen all over France and its dominions. Adjacent to it and housed in the Wall House, an old stone Swedish warehouse, is the **Wall House Museum**. This displays an eclectic series of artifacts, photographs, and paintings illuminating the island's history, including the Swedish period. The exhibits include models of traditional St. Barthian houses (low buildings that face away from the prevailing wind), household items, and articles woven from the local latanier palm.

Just a few elements of Swedish heritage remain in the small town, which took its name from King Gustav III, the Swedish ruler at the time the island became Swedish. Only a handful of the pretty stone buildings date from this era, as sadly most were destroyed in a devastating hurricane and fire in 1850. However, several streets carry Swedish names, including Prinsgatan and Kungsgatan.

🏛 **Wall House Museum**
La Pointe, Gustavia Harbor.
Tel 590 297 155. ⬜ 8:30am–noon
& 2:30–6pm Mon–Fri, 9–11am &
2:30–6pm Sat. 🖼

The diminutive Swedish clock tower with its distinct red roof, Gustavia

SWEDISH HERITAGE IN ST. BARTHS

The island of St. Barths was Swedish for a century. In the late 1700s, King Gustav III of Sweden decided to capitalize on the growing global sea-borne trade and looked for an outpost in the Caribbean. A deal was struck with France and the island was loaned to Sweden in return for a French presence in Gothenburg and trading rights in the Baltics. For a while, as a free port (open to ships of any nationality without tax), St. Barths became a very successful entrepôt and the population rocketed. In the mid-1800s, the trade tailed off and the island gradually went into a decline. Eventually, in 1878 King Oskar II of Sweden put nationality to a referendum and the islanders voted to return to France. There is not a lot of evidence of Swedish interest left in St. Barths, beyond the name of the capital, several street names, and some buildings.

Corossol ❷

1 mile (2 km) N of Gustavia. 🏖️

Corossol, set on a protected bay to the north of Gustavia, is one of the distinctly local areas of St. Barths. It is home to many "Barthéleminois" families and has a slightly more local character. In one of the houses is located the **Inter Oceans Museum**, an eccentric and extraordinary collection of seashells. There are approximately 9,000 different shells on display, of which about 1,600 are from the Caribbean waters. Many are exceptionally beautiful and have intricate patterns.

🏛️ **Inter Oceans Museum**
Along the waterfront. *Tel 590 276 297.* ◻ *9am–12:30pm and 3–5pm Tue–Sun.* 📷

St-Jean ❸

1 mile (2 km) E of Gustavia.
👥 500. ✈️

The second and only other sizable town in St. Barths, St-Jean sits on the island's north shore on Baie de St-Jean, just over the hill from Gustavia, overlooking a spectacular blue bay. The small airport is set at one end, on the aptly named Plaine de la Tourmente (Plain of Torment), a very difficult runway to land on, and there are several hotels and bars along the beach, the most fashionable on the island. At the center of the beach stands the iconic Eden Rock Hotel *(see p353)*, set on its own promontory. Behind the beach is the small town, which has two rows of shops and several restaurants and bars. Roads lead inland past a couple of hotels to many of St. Barths' numerous villas.

East End ❹

2 miles (3 km) E of Gustavia.

The East End is the least developed area of St. Barths. Beyond St-Jean, the settlements of Lorient, Grand Cul-de-Sac, and Petit Cul-de-Sac along the north coast are home to several luxurious resorts. The south of the island, however, is largely untouched by progress. Here, a few of the remaining traditional St. Barthian houses, often a series of *cases* or small square buildings with tin roofs, can still be seen.

Beach terrace of Le Sereno Hotel on Anse de Grand Cul-de-Sac

Beaches of St. Barthélemy ❺

Cut into the extremely rough and steep land along the south coast are two of St. Barths' remote beachs. The first is the unrivalled Anse de Grande Saline, considered one of the best on the island. Just inland, behind the beach is a large salt pond, which was earlier used for salt harvesting. Stilts and other waterbirds can be found at the pond.

Next beach in line, accessed only by a very steep road, is the Anse du Gouverneur, another superb stretch of sand hemmed in by high cliffs. Like Anse de Grande Saline, it is undeveloped and has a good view of other islands to the south.

While most beaches on St. Barths are easily accessible, the white-sand **Anse de Colombier** in the northwest can only be approached by sea or by a steep hiking path overland. This remote strip of sand is a favorite getaway for St. Barthians on holidays and special occasions. The view from Colombier stretches to the northwest, towards the offshore island of Ile Fourchue, which has a good beach in a protected cove. Both these beaches can be reached on a day-sail with one of the watersports companies *(see p349)*. In true St. Barths' style, it is even possible to arrange a gourmet picnic, with foie gras, and chilled champagne on the sand.

Secluded coves of the scenic Anse de Colombier

Outdoor Activities and Specialized Holidays

For a small island, St. Barths boasts a surprising array of day activities. In keeping with the style of the island, there are even lunchtime fashion shows here. Beaches are great, with good snorkeling and diving spots, and a range of watersports are on offer. Several companies organize top-notch sailing trips. On land there are fewer activities, but some hotels have tennis courts and horse-riding is exhilarating on the rough terrain. Two spas cater to visitors who want to unwind here.

in search of complete peace and quiet. Of these, Anse de Grande Saline and Anse du Gouverneur are relatively secluded and have no facilities, though there are restaurants within walking distance of Salines. The third, Anse de Colombier, a lovely stretch of sand on the northwestern coast, can only be reached by boat or on foot.

DEEP-SEA FISHING

The Atlantic waters to the east of St. Barths offer fairly good fishing. Fish that ply the deep include wahoo, tuna, marlin, and kingfish. Day- and half-day trips can be arranged through watersports companies such as **Ocean Must Marina** and **Nautica FWI**.

BOAT TRIPS

St. Barths offers a good variety of offshore day trips by motor yacht and sailing yacht, and these are often the highlights of a holiday here. Trips take visitors to the remoter beaches, particularly Anse de Colombier in the northwest, where there is good snorkeling, but they also head to the smaller islands between St. Barths and St. Martin/Sint Maarten. The closest is Ile Fourchue, which has a protected beach without facilities, but there are also two small islands just off St. Martin/Sint Maarten itself – Pinel and Tintamarre, both with excellent beaches and snorkeling. Some trips also go to Anguilla, 20 miles (32 km) to the northeast. These trips are generally arranged by the watersports

The remote and less-crowded Anse du Gouverneur

BEACHES

Set in extremely attractive, often steep-sided bays, the beaches on St. Barths have bright white and soft sand that descends gently into shallow, often startlingly blue water. Some beaches have activities such as watersports, while others are remote and undeveloped, offering a quiet escape. Going topless is the norm on St. Barths beaches, and on the south coast, Anse de Grande Saline and Anse du Gouverneur also have areas for naturists.

St-Jean is the most popular beach. There are a handful of hotels and beach bars such as the famous Nikki Beach *(see p355)* with its wispy white drapes and bamboo furniture. At Eden Rock, the Sand Bar at Eden Rock Hotel *(see p353)* is stylish too. La Plage in Tom Beach Hotel is less ostentatious, but often lively.

Anse de Grand Cul-de-Sac is set on a shallow lagoon, making it popular with families and the islanders at the weekends. It is also a favorite spot for watersports with excellent wind and kite-surfing. Cocoloba here has

a sweeping view over the lagoon. There is passable sand at Shell Beach outside Gustavia, which has a good beach bar, Do Brasil, a classic Caribbean feel with great music and a fantastic sunset view.

Less-crowded beaches can be found at Flamands, a great stretch of sand with a couple of hotels, and the quieter Lorient. The Hotel Saint-Barth Isle de France *(see p352)* at Flamands has a very attractive setting and an elegant beach-front dining room.

Three of the best beaches on St. Barths have little in the way of amenities, making them ideal for beach-goers

The grand Eden Rock Hotel on the shore of Baie de St-Jean

Yachts anchored in Gustavia harbor

agencies based in Gustavia, including **Marine Service** and **Master Ski Pilou**, both of whom also offer Jet Ski rides and waterskiing trips.

HIKING

There are hiking paths in the northwest of St. Barths, leading down to Anse de Colombier, and around Toiny in the far east of the island, from where the views are spectacular. There are some (self-guided) hikes around Gustavia. Leaflets are available at the tourist office on the waterfront.

Visitors hiking to Anse de Colombier

HORSE-RIDING

Galop des Iles is based at Ranch des Flamands, high above the coast between Anse des Cayes and Flamands in northwestern St. Barths. The stable offers rides through the rough and rocky terrain in this area and along the sand and waves of Anse des Flamands Beach.

SCUBA DIVING AND SNORKELING

There are many underwater reefs in several of the bays, but the best area is in the northwest of St. Barths, in Petite Anse and Colombier. Scuba dive companies such as **Plongée Caraibes**, **St. Barth's Plongee**, **Carib Waterplay**, **Splash**, and **Coté Mer** offer equipment and trips. There are several diving areas; most sites are in the west, protected from Atlantic waves, and off the islands towards St. Martin/Sint Maarten. There is also a marine reserve with sections in the west off Gustavia and in the east towards the Atlantic.

SPAS

For an island as luxurious as St. Barths, there are surprisingly few spas. Hotel Guanahani and Spa *(see p352)* has six treatment rooms. In Flamands, Hotel Saint-Barth Isle de France has two treatment rooms. Both spas offer massages and beauty treatments and are also open to non-guests. There are many independent practitioners in the island's main towns that can be contacted through the tourism office in Gustavia.

Kitesurfing at Anse de Grand Cul-de-Sac

WATERSPORTS

Hotels generally have watersports equipment to offer their guests but visitors staying in villas depend on outside operators for equipment. These are on beaches such as St-Jean and Grand Cul-de-Sac, which is known for its windsurfing and kitesurfing. The main operators are **Wind Wave Power**, **Hookipa Surf Shop**, **Totem Surf Shop**, and **Kitesurf**.

DIRECTORY

DEEP-SEA FISHING

Nautica FWI
Gustavia.
Tel 590 275 650.

Ocean Must Marina
Gustavia.
Tel 590 276 225.

BOAT TRIPS

Marine Service
Gustavia.
Tel 590 277 034.

Master Ski Pilou
Tel 690 613 707.

HORSE-RIDING

Galop des Iles
Ranch des Flamands.
Tel 690 398 701.

SCUBA DIVING AND SNORKELING

Carib Waterplay
St-Jean.
Tel 690 618 081.

Coté Mer
Tel 590 279 179.

Plongée Caraibes
Gustavia.
Tel 590 275 594/ 690 546 614.

Splash
Tel 690 569 024.

St. Barth's Plongee
Gustavia.
Tel 690 419 666.

WATERSPORTS

Hookipa Surf Shop
Tel 590 277 131.

Kitesurf
Grand Cul-de-Sac.
Tel 690 692 690.

Totem Surf Shop
Tel 590 278 372.

Wind Wave Power
St-Jean Beach.
Tel 590 278 257.

Shopping in St. Barthélemy

Cosmetic store
signage, St. Jean

The best place in the Caribbean for luxury tax-free shopping, St. Barths has plenty of options and caters to the whims of the island's wealthy and elegant clientele. It boasts the crème de la crème of international designer labels, with designer clothes well represented, as well as jewelry, watches, and other luxury items, including cigars and excellent wines. The main shopping areas are in Gustavia, on Rue de la République and Rue du Bord de Mer, and St-Jean.

Designer boutiques on Rue de la
République, Gustavia

CLOTHES AND ACCESSORIES

Many major luxury fashion outlets can be found in St. Barths, selling prêt-à-porter clothing, shoes, lingerie, jewelry, perfumes, and leather goods. Labels include Cartier, Hermès, Armani, La Perla, Versace, Ralph Lauren, and even Petit Bateau for children.

Haute-couture shops *are clear indicators of the passion for fashion in Gustavia. There is even a shop called Vintage that sells imported contemporary as well as vintage clothing.*

Le Carré d'Or, *a shopping mall on Rue de la République, has outlets of several leading fashion brands. It is also a good place to linger as there is a restaurant, Caviar Island, serving tapas-sized portions of caviar and foie gras.*

Pati de St. Barth, *a French designer, artist, and resident of St. Barths since the 1980s, has two boutiques here and her own line of tropical clothing for men, women, and children.*

Leatherware, *by international labels such as Louis Vuitton and Hermès, includes bags and shoes. Local St. Barth collections, including Kokon and Elysées Caraïbes, are also available.*

Designer jewelry *can be found at Cartier, Chopard, and Donna del Sol in the Carré d'Or or at Bulgari and Louis Vuitton in Gustavia's Cour Vendôme mall.*

Watchmakers *and jewelry shops, which carry some of the leading brands in the world, are mainly located in Gustavia, close to the waterfront.*

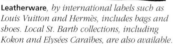

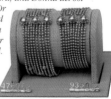

OTHER LUXURY PRODUCTS

In addition to haute couture and jewelry, St. Barths is a treasure trove for furniture, antiques, and other luxury goods that are sought after by the island's wealthy villa-owners and visitors on holiday. Patisseries and delicatessens offer a marvelous range of the finest food, including foie gras and French cheese and wine.

Le Cellier du Gouverneur Gustavia *is a leading liquor shop selling alcohol and wine from all over the world. Wines are imported young so they suffer less damage on the ocean crossing.*

Ligne de St. Barth, *based in Lorient and Gustavia, makes its own line of perfumes as well as face and body care products. Most of the leading brands are also available at this and the other cosmetics outlets on the island.*

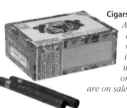

Cigars *from Central America and around the Caribbean, including the world-renowned ones from Cuba, are on sale in St. Barths.*

Balinese furniture *is much in demand among wealthy house-owners. Gustavia's Tek and The House, where many famous French designers have worked, specializes in Oriental tropical furniture.*

LOCAL SHOPPING

Many artists and some skilled craftsmen are based here, and their creations can make for great souvenirs. These can be found in the numerous art galleries and studios around the island and include locally-made jewelry, paintings, and traditional woven straw work.

T-shirts *with the popular "St. Barth French West Indies" logo designed by Pati de St. Barth are available at Villa Créole, a small shopping mall in the village of St-Jean.*

Art galleries *such as the Galerie Bagdad and Pipiri Fine Art Gallery in Gustavia showcase the paintings and sculptures of the island's several talented artists.*

Straw work *made by the islanders can be found in Corossol. The straw of the latanier palm is used to weave hats and bags. Some artisans also make jewelry from shells and corals; however, St. Barths does not have as many handicrafts on sale as the other Caribbean islands.*

Hat

Purse

Basket

Choosing a Hotel

Most St. Barths' hotels are small and offer an intimate and sophisticated ambience rather than a typical "resort" style atmosphere. Many are stylish with impeccable service, while others are low key; there is a good variety of accommodations available, but budget ones are hard to come by. All independent travelers' accommodation bills are supplemented by a 5 percent government room tax.

ST. BARTHS

Villas of St. Barths
Many visitors stay independently in the spectacular array of private villas built by the island's wealthy home-owners. These vary in size from one- to six-bedroom villas. They are located all around the island, but tend to have little beachfront space. There are small villa resorts for couples as well. Villa rental agencies, scattered around the island, can rent out villas on a weekly basis and prices are reflected likewise.

Eden Rock Hotel

Interiors of Le Sereno

ANSE DE TOINY Le Toiny
🍴 🖥 W $$$$$

PO Box 612, Anse de Toiny, 97133 **Tel** *590 278 888* **Fax** *590 278 930* **Rooms** *15*

Exceptionally comfortable private suites secluded at the eastern end of St. Barths, each with their own plunge pool and fantastic views. Large sitting rooms and bedrooms. All modern comforts on offer, including 24-hour room service, a spa, bar, and a superb dining room, Le Gaïac *(see p354)*, at the elegant main house. **www.letoiny.com**

ANSE DES CAYES O'Kaï Beach Residence
🏠 🖥 $$$$$

Anse des Cayes, 97133 **Tel** *590 297 519* **Fax** *590 297 519* **Rooms** *8*

A lovely four-bedroom villa and two gorgeous two-bedroom cottages comprise this small unit in a pretty garden in Anse des Cayes. Built and decorated in Creole style around a private pool, O'Kai Beach Residence offers the best of St. Barths. All eight rooms can be taken together. Family rooms available. **www.okaibeach.com**

FLAMANDS Hotel Baie des Anges
🏠 🍴 🖥 🌴 $$$$

PO Box 162, Baie des Anges, 97133 **Tel** *590 276 361* **Fax** *590 278 344* **Rooms** *10*

A small, friendly family-run inn set right on a fantastic stretch of sand. The 10 rooms have 24-hour room service and are small but comfortable, overlooking the beach or set around the pool and a pretty enclosed courtyard. The complex also has a good restaurant called Le Langouste *(see p354)* and a bar. **www.hotelbaiedesanges.fr**

FLAMANDS Hotel Saint-Barth Isle de France
🏠 🍴 🖥 $$$$$

PO Box 612, Baie des Flamands, 97098 **Tel** *590 276 181* **Fax** *590 278 683* **Rooms** *37*

This elegant and stylish hotel has a pleasant decor matching the colors of sea and sand. Some rooms are located in the main house above the beach, others in a delightful palm garden, where there is a Molton Brown spa. La Case de L'Isle offers fine dining *(see p354)*. Bar, tennis facilities, and 24-hour room service. **www.isle-de-france.com**

GRAND CUL-DE-SAC Hotel Guanahani and Spa
🏠 🍴 🖥 $$$$$

PO Box 609, Anse de Grand Cul-de-Sac, 97133 **Tel** *590 276 660* **Fax** *590 277 070* **Rooms** *75*

Situated on the quiet sports beach of Grand Cul-de-Sac, this is the only large hotel in St. Barths. It is an elegant resort with attractive Creole cottages overlooking two beautiful bays. It has a full service Clarins spa, a bar, and a lovely gourmet restaurant. Family rooms and 24-hour room service available. **www.leguanahani.com**

GRAND CUL-DE-SAC Hotel Les Ondines
🏠 🖥 🌴 W $$$$$

Grand Cul-de-Sac, 97133 **Tel** *590 276 964* **Fax** *590 522 441* **Rooms** *7*

These one- and two-bedroom apartments are set in a building right on the sand, looking out over the shallow bay of Grand Cul-de-Sac. There is a pretty courtyard with a pool hidden by foliage. Family rooms available. Low-key but full self-catering and daily maid service also offered. **www.stbarth-lesondineshotel.com**

GRAND CUL-DE-SAC Le Sereno
🏠 🍴 🖥 W $$$$$

Lagoon de Grand Cul-de-Sac, 97133 **Tel** *590 298 300* **Fax** *590 277 547* **Rooms** *37*

An elegant resort overlooking the calm turquoise waters of Grand Cul-de-Sac. Styled by a French designer (and habitué of St. Barths) Christian Liaigre, Le Sereno is sleekly minimal with suites exquisitely presented in white and polished wood. Spa services, gym, pool, bar, gourmet dining, and 24-hour room service. **www.lesereno.com**

GUSTAVIA Ici et Là

Rue Samuel Fahlberg, PO Box 219, 97096 **Tel** *590 277 878* **Fax** *590 277 828*

A friendly medium-sized villa rental agency based in offices on the waterfront in Gustavia, Ici et Là has more than 180 villas on offer all over the island and in all price ranges. An efficient on-island team greets visitors and helps with all concierge requests. **www.icietlavillas.com**

Key to Symbols *see back cover flap*

GUSTAVIA St. Barth Properties

Rue du Centenaire, 97133 **Tel** *1800 421 3396/1508 528 7727* **Fax** *1508 528 7789*

Based in the center of Gustavia with an overseas office in Franklin, Massachusetts, St. Barth Properties is a villa rental agency with around 150 properties for rent all in desirable locations, from simple cottages with one room to super-luxury with six. Some hotel bookings available too. **www.stbarth.com**

GUSTAVIA Sunset Hotel

Rue de la République, 97133 **Tel** *590 277 721* **Fax** *590 278 159* **Rooms** *10*

A two-star hotel right in the center of Gustavia. Relatively simple rooms with a central balcony that overlooks the harbor and offers a great sunset view. Within walking distance of the town, this hotel is the least expensive option in St. Barths. **www.st-barths.com/sunset-hotel**

GUSTAVIA Hotel Carl Gustaf

PO Box 700, Rue des Normands, 97099 **Tel** *590 297 900* **Fax** *590 278 237* **Rooms** *14*

Set high on a hillside above Gustavia and its harbor, the hotel has comfortable one-and two-bedroom suites with bright sophisticated decor, each with a plunge pool and terrace. Other facilities include 24-hour room service, a gym, spa, bar, and gourmet dining room with truly superb views. **www.hotelcarlgustaf.com**

LORIENT Normandie Hotel

Lorient, 97133 **Tel** *590 276 166* **Fax** *590 279 883* **Rooms** *8*

A small but grand guesthouse hotel tucked away inland, but within easy walking distance of the shops and sands of Lorient Beach. Just nine rooms are set in a small enclave of greenery with a plunge pool – a good and inexpensive escape from the crowded areas of the island. **www.normandiehotelstbarts.com**

LORIENT La Banane

Baie de Lorient, 97133 **Tel** *590 520 300* **Fax** *590 276 844* **Rooms** *9*

A small and attractive hotel with beautiful Creole cottages set in a secluded enclave of sand and palms in Lorient. La Banane is not on the beach, but it has an exceptional ambience, with a minimalist foyer, meandering pools surrounded by a deck and bright interiors. Includes a bar and 24-hour room service. **www.labanane.com**

POINTE MILOU Christopher Hotel – St. Barth

Pointe Milou, 97133 **Tel** *590 276 363* **Fax** *590 279 292* **Rooms** *41*

Situated on the waterfront, this small resort looks west over the calm waters of Baie de Lorient. The rooms, many oceanfront, are arranged around a large infinity pool. Other facilities include a good dining room, family rooms, gym, yoga classes, Wi-Fi access, and 24-hour room service. **www.hotelchristopher.com**

ST-JEAN Hotel Le Village St Jean

Colline de St-Jean, 97133 **Tel** *590 276 139* **Fax** *590 277 796* **Rooms** *30*

A friendly family-run hotel situated on the hillside in St-Jean. Rooms and very comfortable self-catering suites are set in cottages around a pool. Other facilities include an Italian dining room and bar, family rooms, a spa, and gym with a view. Walking distance down to the beach and shops. **www.villagestjeanhotel.com**

ST-JEAN Hotel Tropical

St-Jean, 97133 **Tel** *590 276 487* **Fax** *590 278 174* **Rooms** *21*

Brightly painted and with pretty gingerbread fretwork, this small hotel has 21 air-conditioned rooms, including family rooms, all with private terraces, some with magnificent views and includes a bar. There are restaurants nearby. Within easy walking distance of the fashionable Baie de St-Jean. **www.st-barths.com/tropical-hotel**

ST-JEAN Eden Rock Hotel

Plage de St-Jean, 97133 **Tel** *590 297 999* **Fax** *590 278 837* **Rooms** *34*

This iconic hotel sits astride a rock in the heart of the popular Baie de St-Jean, with its spacious suites set right by the sea offering high style and extreme luxury, and caters to a world-famous clientele. Its restaurant, On the Rocks *(see p355)*, is excellent, as is the Sand Bar. Family rooms offered. **www.edenrockhotel.com**

ST-JEAN Emeraude Plage

Baie de St-Jean, 97133 **Tel** *590 276 478* **Fax** *590 278 308* **Rooms** *28*

Independent living right on Baie de St-Jean, at the center of the action. Emeraude Plage is decorated in minimalist, modern style, its white walls and fittings neatly offset by Caribbean colors. Friendly reception, casual atmosphere, bar, and large rooms, including family rooms, with kitchenettes. **www.emeraudeplage.com**

ST-JEAN Les Ilets de la Plage

Plage de St-Jean, 97133 **Tel** *590 278 857* **Fax** *590 278 858* **Rooms** *11*

A collection of brightly painted one-, two- and three-bedroom cottages located on the hillside and on the glorious sand of a quiet section of the beach. Includes family rooms. There is a central pool and reception, but no restaurant. The cottages have good facilities for cooking if visitors do not want to eat out. **www.lesilets.com**

TERRE NEUVE Auberge de Terre Neuve

Terre Neuve, 97133 **Tel** *590 277 532* **Fax** *590 277 899* **Rooms** *10.*

This is a string of self-catering cottages in Terre Neuve, high above Baie des Flamands. The one- and two-bedroom cottages are small but comfortable and ideal for an independent traveler. The owners also run a car rental company and offer a good combined deal with car hire and accommodation. Includes family rooms.

Where to Eat & Nightlife

An amazing number of restaurants, in lovely settings, dot the island, and the cuisine is usually excellent. With a seamless supply of the finest ingredients arriving from around the world, some top-class chefs, and great service, St. Barths offers a truly unique eating experience. Gourmet takeaway and made-to-order meals prepared by private chefs in the villas are also available.

PRICE CATEGORIES
The price ranges are for a two-course meal for one, including tax and service charges and half a bottle of wine.

Ⓢ under $10
ⓈⓈ $10–15
ⓈⓈⓈ $15–25
ⓈⓈⓈⓈ $25–35
ⓈⓈⓈⓈⓈ over $35

RESTAURANTS

Top Cuisine

St. Barths has some of the finest chefs in the Caribbean, who prepare local cuisine as well as internationally acclaimed dishes. The techniques they use are generally classical French, which have been adapted to suit the demands and tastes of their varying clientele. Sauces are lighter and Caribbean fruits and spices are cooked in unique ways known only to St. Barths chefs.

L'Esprit Saline

Le Tamarin

ANSE DE TOINY Le Gaïac   Ⓥ Ⓟ 🔲 ♿   ⓈⓈⓈⓈⓈ
Le Toiny Hotel, 97133 **Tel** *590 297 747*

The elegant dining room is a fine example of traditional Caribbean decor adapted to modern sensibilities and is located in the secluded Le Toiny *(see p352)*. Tables overlook the pool and the sea, and the menu is based on ingredients from around the world including a selection of caviars. Stylish dining in an exquisite setting.

ANSE PUBLIC Maya's   Ⓥ 🔲   ⓈⓈⓈⓈⓈ
Anse Public, 97133 **Tel** *590 277 573*

A classic informal Caribbean restaurant in a bayfront setting, where simple but pretty tables and safari chairs are set under palms. Overseen by Maya herself, the restaurant has the best in Creole and international fare. This is one of the most popular restaurants on the island. Reservations required in winter.

FLAMANDS La Case de L'Isle   Ⓥ Ⓟ 🗒 🔲 ♿   ⓈⓈⓈⓈⓈ
Hotel Saint-Barth Isle de France, 97133 **Tel** *590 275 868*

Set right above the spectacular sands of Flamands Beach in Hotel Saint-Barth Isle de France *(see p352)*, La Case de L'Isle is an elegant dining room with a tropical feel of natural wood and white seats shaded by palms. Top-quality cuisine, fundamentally French but with tropical flavors and tastes.

FLAMANDS La Langouste   Ⓥ 🔲 ♿   ⓈⓈⓈⓈⓈ
Hotel Baie des Anges, Baie des Flamands, 97133 **Tel** *590 276 361*

The restaurant is set in a Creole courtyard of the family-owned Hotel Baie des Anges *(see p352)* right on the sand of Flamands Beach, overlooking the pool. As the name suggests, La Langouste serves delicious grilled lobster as well as fine French fare; all in a friendly atmosphere.

GUSTAVIA Caviar Island   Ⓥ Ⓟ 🔲 ♿   ⓈⓈⓈⓈⓈ
Rue de la République, 97133 **Tel** *590 524 611*

Set in the courtyard of the Carré d'Or mall in Gustavia surrounded by smart St. Barths shops, Caviar Island is open-air with low tables and sofas. Many champagne varieties are served with the special caviar menu, *foie gras*, sushi, and smoked salmon. French platters are also available. Live entertainment most evenings.

GUSTAVIA Eddy's   Ⓥ 🔲   ⓈⓈⓈⓈⓈ
Rue du Centenaire, 97133 **Tel** *590 275 417*

Located in a pretty setting in the middle of Gustavia, Eddy's is a lovely restaurant. It has fine hefty wooden chairs and tables on a covered teak deck surrounded by golden palms. The cuisine is French with international tinges including Oriental. A laid-back place to spend an evening.

GUSTAVIA La Route des Boucaniers   Ⓥ 🔲   ⓈⓈⓈⓈⓈ
Rue Bord de Mer, 97133 **Tel** *590 277 300*

La Route des Boucaniers is a friendly restaurant set on a deck right on the waterfront at the heart of Gustavia, overlooking the yachts. Decorated in a nautical and buccaneering theme, it serves French and Creole specialties and also has a good bar.

GUSTAVIA Le Pipiri Palace   Ⓥ 🔲   ⓈⓈⓈⓈⓈ
Rue Général-de-Gaulle **Tel** *590 275 320*

A beautiful setting based around a wooden Creole house partly hidden by palms in a courtyard in the middle of Gustavia. The cuisine is French and there is a good team of chefs headed up by Pierre and Regine. Le Pipiri Palace is also known to serve great ribs and grilled fare.

Key to Symbols *see back cover flap*

GUSTAVIA Le Sapotillier

V 🍴 🎫 $$$$$

Rue du Centenaire, 97133 **Tel** *590 276 028*

Set in a restored traditional stone house in Gustavia, Le Sapotillier offers an elegant evening out in a very attractive own setting. Tables are available inside and out in a courtyard under a sapotillier tree. They offer traditional French uisine with some regional French specialties.

GUSTAVIA The Wall House

V 🍴 🗏 $$$$$

Rue de la Presqu'île, 97133 **Tel** *590 277 183*

The Wall House is set on a quiet section of the Gustavia waterfront, in a restored Swedish trading warehouse. The rench owners serve excellent food, prepared using the best of the island's ingredients. The international cuisine as a strong Gallic touch, but also includes a Swedish dish or two.

LORIENT Le Wok

V 🗏 $$$$$

orient **Tel** *590 275 252*

Oriental cooking in the small town of Lorient, a good escape from the buzz of the island and its crowds. Set in a raditional-looking red and gold Chinese dining room, Le Wok is atmospheric and fun. It serves Thai mussels, luck, sautéed shrimp, and delicious spring rolls.

SALINE L'Esprit Saline

V 🍴 🎫 $$$$$

Anse de Grand Saline, 97133 **Tel** *590 524 610*

Set near the beach at Anse de Grand Saline, L'Esprit Saline has an attractive tropical garden and a lovely courtyard etting. It serves fine French cuisine and some Creole dishes in an informal atmosphere and is the perfect place to nger for lunch.

SALINE Le Grain de Sel

V 🎫 $$$$$

Anse de Grande Saline, 97133 **Tel** *590 524 605*

Set on the rocks right near the entrance to the lovely Saline beach, Le Grain de Sel is an ideal retreat in the shade or beachgoers, who can enjoy a leisurely breakfast or lunch here. On the menu is excellent Creole fare and some Oriental specialties such as sushi and sashimi.

SALINE Le Tamarin

V 🍴 🎫 $$$$$

Route de Saline, 97133 **Tel** *590 277 212*

Tables at Le Tamarin are set around an enclosed garden and beneath a huge tamarind tree, making it a very nice spot for a leisurely lunch (or dinner). Gourmet French and international fare – there is a tasting menu – is served in an extremely informal atmosphere. Closed Tuesdays.

ST-JEAN Chez Andy's Hideaway

V 🎫 ♿ $$$$$

The car park, St-Jean, 97133 **Tel** *590 276 362*

An Englishman in St. Barths, Andy the proprietor serves beer, wine, and food at his open-air restaurant. Good oizzas and other international dishes are served with a cheery grin. The casual, always lively atmosphere makes for a fun evening out for diners. Closed Sundays.

ST-JEAN On the Rocks

V 🍴 🎫 $$$$$

Eden Rock Hotel, 97133 **Tel** *590 297 999*

A very stylish tiered dining room with brightly colored bench seats set on the flanks of the rock at Eden Rock Hotel *(see p353)*. The Continental cuisine includes home-made terrine of *foie gras* but the ravioli of mushroom served with crispy parma ham-wrapped jumbo shrimps is also among the house specialties.

BARS AND CLUBS

An early evening drink at any of the island's nightspots is one of the highlights of St. Barths. The lively Eden Rock Hotel is popular, while the harbor in Gustavia, with its pretty waterfront bars, is the best place for an evening out. Beach bars stay open late into the night and restaurants even permit guests to linger after meals. There are a couple of clubs around the island that come alive in the evenings with energetic music and dance.

The popular bar Le Select, Gustavia

RECOMMENDED PLACES TO GO

Bar de L'Oubli
Rue de la Republique, downtown Gustavia. (Outstanding cocktails.)

Do Brazil
Shell Beach, Gustavia. (Sunset views and good music.)

La Bete a Z'Ailes
Gustavia Harbor. (Waterfront setting, popular with locals.)

La Mandala
Rue de la Sous-Prefecture, Gustavia. (Great views of the town.)

Le Select
Rue de la France, downtown Gustavia. (Popular all-day bar.)

Le Ti St. Barth
Pointe Milou (Themed shows, excellent drinks.)

Nikki Beach
St-Jean Beach.
(Lively on the weekends.)

On the Rocks
Eden Rock Hotel, St-Jean.
(Excellent cocktails.)

Yacht Club
Gustavia. (Most popular nightclub on the island.)

Practical Information

Politically, St. Barthélemy is part of France and many of its regulations and services are the same as in metropolitan France and most of the European Union. The standards of service are generally good. In terms of tourism, the facilities on the island are top-notch though often quite informal. Once the initial challenge of getting to St. Barthélemy is dealt with, visitors will find that the island provides excellent amenities and has some of the best, albeit quite expensive, food and shopping *(see pp350–51)* options in the Caribbean.

Revelers at the Mardi Gras Festival, St. Barthélemy

WHEN TO GO

The weather in St. Barths is generally good year round. The dry season lasts from December through May, while heavier rains are expected between June and November during the hurricane season. Most visitors arrange a trip during the winter season from January to April, when there are also a handful of cultural and sporting events.

GETTING THERE

There are no direct flights to St. Barths and a change of planes will be necessary. From neighboring St. Martin/ Sint Maarten, there are island-hopping flights into Aéroport Gustave III on St. Barths itself. Scheduled flights are offered by **WinAir** and **St Barth Commuter**, and **Air Caraïbes**. **Tradewind Aviation** flies from San Juan, Puerto Rico. Visitors can also charter a plane through these companies.

Travelers from Britain may choose to fly via Antigua, from where chartered planes to the island are available.

It is also possible to make the link from St. Martin/Sint Maarten by boat. Daily ferries are also available. However, taking one of these might entail an overnight stay on St. Martin. The **Voyager** offers daily ferry service between St. Martin, Saba, and St. Barths. Though expensive, boats are available for private charter from agencies such as **Marine Service**.

DOCUMENTATION

Entry regulations are the same as in France and the European Union. EU travelers are permitted entry without a visa. US and Canadian citizens can also enter on a passport without a visa. Other nationalities should check with their local French embassy. An onward or return ticket is needed.

VISITOR INFORMATION

There is an efficient tourist office, the **Office du Tourisme**, on the waterfront in Gustavia.

Abroad, the publicity for St. Barths is handled through the various **Maisons de France** around the world. Many publications on St. Barths offer useful information on facilities and activities available here.

HEALTH AND SECURITY

No vaccinations are needed to enter St. Barths. For medical emergencies there is an Accident and Emergency department at the **Hôpital de Bruyn** in Gustavia. However, it does not have enough facilities to handle complicated procedures and patients are transferred either to St. Martin or farther afield to Puerto Rico. There is little likelihood of a security problem on St. Barths.

BANKING AND CURRENCY

The official currency of St. Barths is the euro. Banks are located in Gustavia and St-Jean, while ATMs are found around the island. Some American cards may not work in the local ATMs so visitors must check with their bank beforehand. Credit cards are accepted at all establishments connected with tourism, and some restaurants may offer a choice of either paying in euros or US dollars.

COMMUNICATIONS

The telephone system in St. Barths is overseen by France Telecom and other providers such as **Orange Caraïbe**, which offer good mobile coverage and Internet in addition to

Aircraft taking off from the short runway of Aéroport Gustave III, St-Jean

landlines. Mobile phones can be hired through a handful of shops. St. Barths' International Direct Dialing code is 590. This is followed by a nine-digit number that begins with 590 for landlines and 690 for cell phones. Local calls can be made by dialing 0 before the nine-digit number. Gustavia has the main post office.

TRANSPORT

Hiring a car is the best option in St. Barths. Vehicles can be delivered to the respective hotels and returned at the airport on departure. Most car rental companies such as **Gumbs Car Rental**, **Europcar**, and **Top Loc Car Rental** are at the airport. A local driving license is not required here.

Taxis are not readily available, particularly after dark, and during high season they may have to be booked days in advance. However, many hotels have their own cars that pick up guests arriving at the airport or the ferry dock. There are taxi stands at the airport and at the municipal parking in Gustavia.

LANGUAGE

The language of St. Barths is French. However, most islanders involved with tourism also speak good English.

The post office in Gustavia, part of the French postal system

ELECTRICITY

The St. Barths' electrical system delivers 220 volts at 60 cycles through standard French sockets. British and American appliances will need an adapter and perhaps a transformer as well.

TIME

St. Barths is on Atlantic Standard Time, 4 hours behind Greenwich Mean Time and 1 hour ahead of US Eastern Time during the winter. The island does not observe daylight saving, so when the Northern Hemisphere changes its clocks between March and end of October, the island is the same as Eastern Time.

GETTING MARRIED

Getting married on St. Barths is quite complicated. One party needs to be a resident for a month before the wedding. A number of documents need to be provided, including proof of identity and marital status. **Premium IV St Barts** and **Destination Management Services** provide assistance.

Hired cars lined up at a lookout, Anse de Grande Saline

DIRECTORY

GETTING THERE

Air Caraïbes
Tel 590 277 190.
www.aircaraibes.com

Marine Service
Tel 590 277 034.
www.marine-service.fr

St Barth Commuter
Tel 590 275 454.
www.stbarth commuter.com

Tradewind Aviation
www.tradewind aviation.com

Voyager
Tel 590 871 068.
www. voyager-st-barths.com

WinAir
Tel 590 276 101.
www.fly-winair.com

VISITOR INFORMATION

Maisons de France
Tel 020 7399 3545 (UK).
Tel 1 212 838 7800 (US).
www.franceguide.com

Office du Tourisme
1 Quai Général de Gaulle, Gustavia. *Tel 590 278 727.* **www**.cttsb.or

HEALTH AND SECURITY

Hôpital de Bruyn
Rue Jean-Bart, Gustavia.
Tel 590 276 035.

Police, Fire, and Ambulance
Tel 18.

COMMUNICATIONS

Orange Caraïbe
Espace Neptune, St-Jean.
www.orangecaraibe.com

TRANSPORT

Europcar
Aéroport Gustave III, St-Jean.
Tel 590 277 434.

Gumbs Car Rental
Aéroport Gustave III, St-Jean.
Tel 590 277 532.

Top Loc Car Rental
Aéroport Gustave III, St-Jean.
Tel 590 290 202.

GETTING MARRIED

Destination Management Services
Rue de la Colline, Gustavia.
Tel 590 298 454.
www.destination managementservices.net

Premium IV St Barts
Les Galeries du Commerce, St-Jean.
Tel 590 290 007.
www.premiumiv

Exploring Guadeloupe

Guadeloupe is two islands hinged together like an open oyster shell. Smaller outer islands float nearby like spilled pearls in a turquoise sea. Grande-Terre, the eastern half, is a flat field of sugarcane dotted with colorful towns. Basse-Terre, the western half, is a mountainous forest marked by waterfalls and rivers. The two are joined by bridges over the Rivière-Salée (Salt River). Of the outer islands, Marie-Galante is the most developed. Les Saintes are a cluster of eight islands with Terre-de-Bas the most developed. La Désirade has a minimum of tourist facilities but great natural appeal.

GETTING AROUND

Guadeloupe has a well-maintained network of highways and secondary roads that connect every part of the main island and a rental car is the best way to travel from one point to another. Taxis are easy to find at the airport and boat docks, but rates are high, especially at night and on holidays. Buses run throughout the island. The outer islands, connected to the main islands via ferry, can be navigated on foot or by bicycle. Marie-Galante has a minivan service between towns, but most visitors take group tours or rent a car.

Route de la Traversée
This road cuts across Basse-Terre passing through mountains and rainforest.

KEY

—— Major road

=== Minor road

-- Track

--- Ferry route

△ Peak

ANGUILLA   **ST. MARTIN/ SINT MAARTEN**

VIRGIN ISLANDS   **ST. BARTHÉLEMY**   **ANTIGUA AND BARBUDA**

SABA AND ST. EUSTATIUS

ST. KITTS AND NEVIS

GUADELOUPE

Caribbean Sea

MARTINIQUE

Îlet à Faj

Sainte-Rose ⑦   *Gr Cul-d Ma*

Grande Anse

Deshaies ⑧   D18

D19

Sofaïa   Le Lamentin   B Mah

N2   N2

Basse-Terre   D2

Baille-Argent   Versaill

D1

Pointe-Noire   D17   Acomat   D23

ROUTE DE ⑥   Pet Bou

JACQUES COUSTEAU ⑧   LA TRAVERSÉE

UNDERWATER   *Les Mamelles   Cascade*   Vernou

RESERVE   N2   *2,519 ft   aux Ecrevisses*

Îlets Pigeon   Pigeon   ⑦   G

Malendure   *Pitons de*   PARC NATIONAL DE

Bouillante   *Bouillante   3,569 ft*   LA GUADELOUPE

D14

Mateliane   Sain

Marigot   *4,258 ft*

Vieux-Habitants   *Chutes*

PLANTATIONS ⑨   *du Carbet*   Cap

D13   *La Soufrière*   Be

N2   *1,813 ft*

Baillif   D30   Saint-Sauve

⑨ Saint-Claude   D5

Bana

Basse-Terre   *Monts Caraïbes*   D8   Trois-

2,254 ft   N1   Rivières ⑩

D6

Vieux-Fort

0 km   10

0 miles   10

TERRE-I HA

Grande Anse   ①

Terre-de-Bas   *La Coche*

Les Saintes

The Cascade aux Ecrevisses on Route de la Traversée, Basse-Terre

SIGHTS AT A GLANCE

Gosier 2
Jacques Cousteau Underwater Reserve 8
La Désirade 12
Marie-Galante 11
Morne-à-l'Eau 4
Parc National de la Guadeloupe 7
Plantations 9
Pointe-à-Pitre 1
Porte d'Enfer and Pointe de la Grande Vigie 5
South Coast Beaches 3
Route de la Traversée 6
Terre-de-Haut 10

Hotels and Resorts

Auberge de la Vieille Tour 4
Domaine de la Pointe Batterie 8
Gosier hotels 3
Hotel Bois Joli 11
Hotel Saint-Georges 9
Hotel Saint-John-Perse 1
Le Jardin de Malanga 10
Le Soleil Levant 12
Oualiri Beach Hotel 13
Sainte-Anne hotels 5
Saint-François hotels 6
Sainte-Rose hotels 7
Village Soleil 2

SEE ALSO

• ***Where to Stay*** pp370–71

• ***Where to Eat & Nightlife*** pp372–3

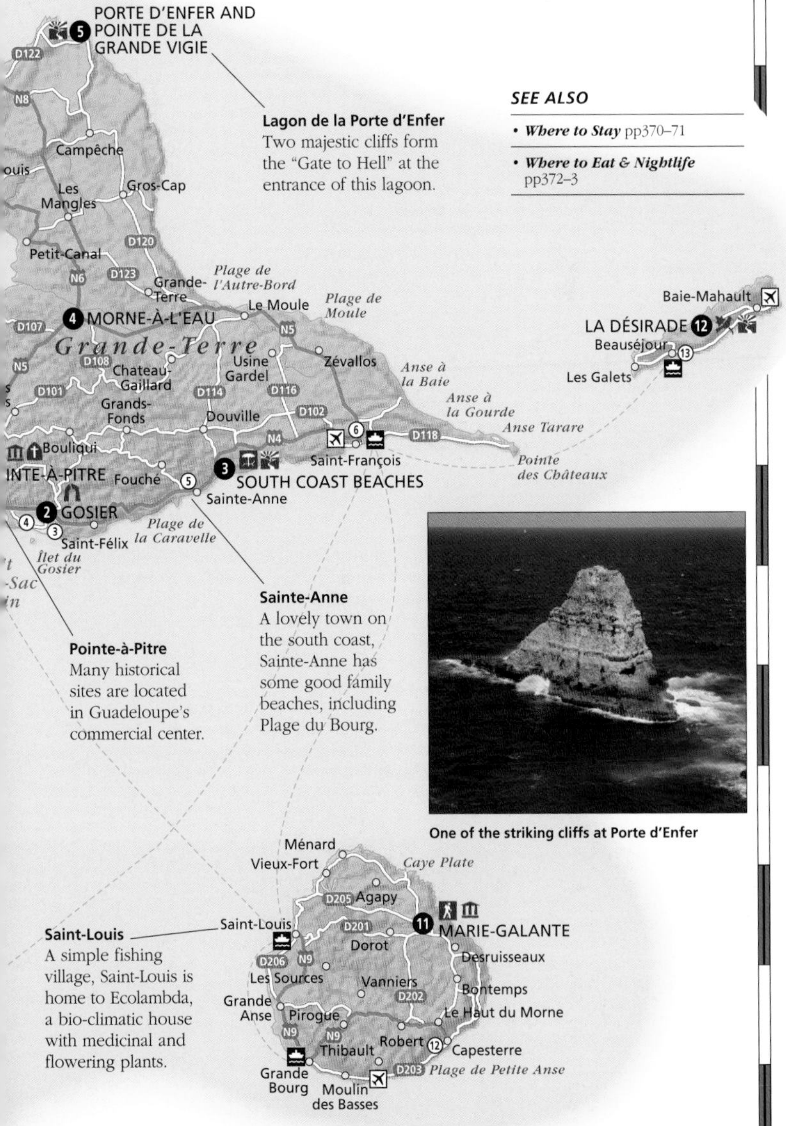

5 PORTE D'ENFER AND POINTE DE LA GRANDE VIGIE
Lagon de la Porte d'Enfer
Two majestic cliffs form the "Gate to Hell" at the entrance of this lagoon.
D122
N8
Campêche
Les Mangles
Gros-Cap
D120
Petit-Canal
N6
D123
Grande-Terre
Plage de l'Autre-Bord
Le Moule
Plage de Moule
4 MORNE-À-L'EAU
Grande-Terre
D107
D108
N5
Chateau-Gaillard
Usine Gardel
Zévallos
D101
D114
D116
Grands-Fonds
Douville
D102
N4
Bouliqui
Fouché
3 SOUTH COAST BEACHES
Saint-François
D118
Anse à la Baie
Anse à la Gourde
Anse Tarare
Pointe des Châteaux
Sainte-Anne
2 GOSIER
Saint-Félix
Plage de la Caravelle
Îlet du Gosier
Baie-Mahault
LA DÉSIRADE 12
Beauséjour
Les Galets
Sainte-Anne
A lovely town on the south coast, Sainte-Anne has some good family beaches, including Plage du Bourg.
Pointe-à-Pitre
Many historical sites are located in Guadeloupe's commercial center.
Ménard
Vieux-Fort
Caye Plate
D205
Agapy
11 MARIE-GALANTE
Saint-Louis
D201
Dorot
Desruisseaux
D206
N9
Les Sources
Vanniers
D202
Bontemps
Grande Anse
Pirogue
Le Haut du Morne
N9
Thibault
Robert
Capesterre
Grande Bourg
Moulin des Basses
D203
Plage de Petite Anse
Saint-Louis
A simple fishing village, Saint-Louis is home to Ecolambda, a bio-climatic house with medicinal and flowering plants.

One of the striking cliffs at Porte d'Enfer

Sculpture of Perse, Musée Saint-John-Perse

Pointe-à-Pitre ❶

W coast of Grande-Terre. 🏚
25,000. ✈️ ☒ 🚌 ⛴ ℹ️ *Office
Départemental du Tourisme de la
Guadeloupe, 5 Square de la Banque,
590 820 930.*

Guadeloupe's commercial
center, and the main town on
Grande-Terre, Pointe-à-Pitre
sits on the eastern shore of
Petit Cul-de-Sac Marin, at
the southern end of Rivière
Galée, the waterway that
separates Grande-Terre
from Basse-Terre.

Though battered by fires
and hurricanes over the years,
Pointe-à-Pitre boasts many
interesting historical sites. One
such highlight is Place de la
Victoire (Victory Square), an
atmospheric site surrounded
by colonial buildings. It once
held the guillotine used to
behead aristocrats who were
opposed to a revolutionary
French government. Now,
ferry boats ply from Quai de
La Darse at one end of this
square, while street vendors
sell fresh produce, fragrant
spices, and colorful dresses.
Place Gourbeyre is dominated
by the Neo-Classical L'Eglise
Saint-Pierre et Saint-Paul. The
spacious interior of this church
is a fine example of the hurri-
cane- and earthquake-resistant
metal-frame construction
made popular by Gustave
Eiffel. Across the square is the
Art Deco courthouse known
as Palais de Justice. A couple
of streets south, **Musée Victor
Schoelcher** has a collection of
art and memorabilia related to

the rich Parisian,
who was instrumen-
tal in the abolition
of slavery in the
French West Indies.
Located near the
museum is the
Sougues-Pagès
House, a lovely
example of French
Caribbean architec-
ture popular during
the 1800s. It houses
the **Musée Saint-
John-Perse**, which
honors the island's
Nobel Laureate
(1960), Alexis de
Saint-Léger, better
known as the poet
Saint-John Perse.

🏛 **Musée Victor Schoelcher**
24 Rue Peynier. *Tel 590 820 804.*
⭕ 9am–5pm Mon–Fri. 🖼

🏛 **Musée Saint-John-Perse**
9 Rue Nozières. *Tel 590 900 192.*
⭕ 9am–5pm Mon–Fri,
8:30am–12:30pm Sat. 🖼 🖼
www.sjperse.org

Gosier ❷

4 miles (6 km) SE of Pointe-à-Pitre,
Grande-Terre. 🏚 25,360. ⛴

Historically, Gosier was an
important defense point for
the island. The ruins of Fort
Louis still sit atop a hill at the
entrance of the waterway that
divides the eastern and western parts of Guadeloupe. Built
in 1695, the fort was renamed
Fort l'Union during the French
Revolution. Another citadel,
Fort Fleur d'Épée, was built
by the English in 1756. Below
the ruins, **Musée Fort Fleur
d'Épée** is located in the trendy
Bas-du-Fort area. It displays a

fine repertoire of objects from
the 18th-century war between
France and England. For
marine life enthusiasts there is
L'Aquarium de la Guadeloupe,
which showcases sea life,
corals, and mangroves of the
French Caribbean region.

The town's beach is lined
with outlets offering trips to
the offshore islands, deep-sea
fishing, sailing, diving, and
motorized watersports.
Vendors sell colorful clothes,
spicy aromas waft from waterfront cafés, and there are
all-budget hotels closeby. The
best strip of sand is along
Pointe de la Verdure, west of
town. Shops, hotels, and
nightclubs fill the area.

🏛 **Musée Fort Fleur d'Épée**
Bas-du-Fort. *Tel 590 909 461.*
⭕ 10am–5pm Mon, 9am–5pm
Tue–Sun.
🐟 **L'Aquarium de la
Guadeloupe**
Place Creole, Bas-du-Fort Marina.
Tel 590 909 238. ⭕ 9am–7pm
daily. 🖼 🖼 🖼 🍴 🖼
www.guadeloupeaquarium.com

South Coast
Beaches ❸

Gosier marks the western
edge of a string of sandy
beaches that run along the
south coast of Grande-Terre
to Saint-François and the
narrow peninsula of Pointe
des Châteaux, together
forming Guadeloupe's most
popular tourist area. Busy
hotels, restaurants, and snack
bars are set on the sand. Dive
shops and watersport centers
offer equipment and guided
trips. The beach at Anse-
Dumant in Saint-Félix is often

A sunny beach lined with deck chairs, Gosier

For hotels and restaurants on these islands see pp370–71 and pp372–3

Trademark checkerboard styled tomb, Morne-à-l'Eau

deserted, while Plage du Bourg in Sainte-Anne is an active family beach. Plage de la Caravelle, and Plage de Bois Jolan are two gorgeous beaches to the east. Between Sainte-Anne and Saint-François, the coast road leads through a rural area dotted with isolated coves. The hills above, known as Les Grands-Fonds, offer a splendid view of the coast. At the end of the main road, Avenue de l'Europe, two beaches called Plage des Hotels provide a wide ribbon of soft sand for some upscale resorts.

The D118 coast road leading to Pointe des Châteaux is flanked by excellent small unnamed beaches, reached by cutting through wild vegetation that grows between the road and the water. On the Atlantic side, Anse à la Gourde is a beach popular with locals while Anse Tarare is a sheltered cove with crystal-clear waters favored by naturists, and good snorkeling. Pointe des Châteaux is a narrow peninsula that juts into the ocean, ending in a line of huge freestanding boulders.

Morne-à-l'Eau ❹

11 miles (18 km) N of Pointe-à-Pitre, Grande-Terre. 🏃 7,800. 🚌 🛈 *Town Hall, Place de la Mairie, 590 242 709.* 🎏 *The Day of Crabs (Easter weekend); All Saints' Day (Nov 1).*

This fishing and agricultural village was once a major sugar-producing town. Today, the only reason to visit is to

see the famous cemetery which sits on a hillside above the intersection of highways N5 and N6. This unique above-ground graveyard has elaborate shrines dedicated to deceased islanders. Originally, the monuments were constructed of black-and-white tiles set in a checkerboard pattern, but other colors and materials have also been added. On All Saints' Day, people come here to honor the dead and thousands of candles illuminate the site.

Porte d'Enfer and Pointe de la Grande Vigie ❺

13 miles (21 km) N of Pointe-à-Pitre, Grande-Terre. 🚌

Two of Guadeloupe's dramatic natural sites lie on the north coast of Grande-Terre. At

land's end, Pointe de la Grande Vigie provides great views. The northern end of Grande-Terre is a series of craggy headlands that soar over the sea. Cliffs along this shoreline tower more than 250 ft (76 m) above the rocky coast. Two extraordinary lookouts reached by driving south down the east coast are Pointe du Piton, a signed viewpoint, and Porte d'Enfer, a sheltered lagoon guarded by two majestic cliffs that form "The Gate of Hell". Nearby is Trou de Madame Coco, a spot where legend says Madame Coco, a lady whose identity is not known, disappeared. Chemin de la Grande Falaise is a 7-mile (11-km) path that runs south along the coastal ridge to Pointe Petit-Nègre and takes a 2-hour hike to complete.

The striking shoreline at Pointe de la Grande Vigie

Bust of Schoelcher, Musée Victor Schoelcher

VICTOR SCHOELCHER

Statues honoring Victor Schoelcher stand in several public plazas throughout the French Antilles. Born in 1804, he began publishing anti-slavery articles in 1833, founded an abolition society in 1834, and led the commission that emancipated slaves in all French colonies in 1848. Guadeloupe and Martinique credit him with beginning the republican political movement on the islands after the abolition of slavery. He served as their representative to the French National Assembly between 1848 and 1851, when he was forced into exile for opposing the coup d'état of Louis Napoléon Bonaparte. He returned in 1871 and was declared senator for life in 1875. He died in 1893, on Christmas night.

Parc Zoologique et Botanique des Mamelles

Route de la Traversée ❻

1 mile (2 km) W of Versailles, eastern Basse-Terre. 🅸 *La Maison de la Forêt, Route de la Traversée, 10am–5pm daily.*

The cross-island roadway D23, known as Route de la Traversée, cuts east-west across Basse-Terre through the mountains and rainforest of the Parc National de la Guadeloupe. While the drive itself is a pleasant shortcut from one coast to the other, the stops along the way are the true appeal. Beginning at the eastern end, the Route leaves Highway N1 near the commune of Versailles. After traveling for approximately 7 miles (11 km), a turn south on a small road leads to the settlement of Vernou and Sault de la Lézarde (Lizard's Leap), a magnificent 45-ft (14-m) waterfall that cascades into a rocky pool which is safe for swimming. Visitors are advised to wear shoes with good traction, and carry a swimsuit for a dip in the waterfall's pool. From the parking lot on the outskirts of Vernou, the hike leads through resplendent green fields and forest for 20 minutes along a groomed, but steep, trail to the falls. West of Vernou, after about 5 miles (8 km), the Route leads to Cascade aux Ecrevisses (Crayfish Waterfall), which is one of the most popular attractions on Basse-Terre, as well as the easiest to reach. The walk from the parking lot takes less than 15 minutes, which explains why visitors flock here. Two paths lead up to the top of the falls, and the one on the left is used as a 20-ft (6-m) slide into the Corossol River. Visitors may stop at the visitors' center – **La Maison de la Forêt** (Forest House), to pick up information and explore the three interpretive trails, then continue along Route de la Traversée through the Col des Deux Mamelles (Pass of Two Breasts), which sits between two lofty peaks, Mamelle de Petit-Bourg at 2,349 ft (716 m) and Mamelle de Pigeon at 2,519 ft (768 m), before sloping back towards sea level.

The final stop is at the **Parc Zoologique et Botanique des Mamelles** (Zoo and Botanical Gardens). Besides the interesting flora and fauna, the park also features an elevated rope bridge and zip line through the tree tops.

> 🅧 **Parc Zoologique et Botanique des Mamelles**
> Route de la Traversée, D23.
> **Tel** 590 988 352. ⏱ 9am–5pm daily. 🅰 🔲 🔲 **www**.parcdes mamelles.com

Parc National de la Guadeloupe ❼

3 miles (5 km) S of Vernou.
🅸 *Habitation Beausoleil, Montéran, 97120 Saint-Claude, 590 808 600.*
🅿 🅶 **www**.guadeloupe-parcnational.com

La Soufrière, a 4,813-ft (1,467-m) high active volcano, towers over the tropical forest at the southern end of Basse-Terre that makes up Guadeloupe's national park. In 1992, UNESCO designated 74,100 acres (30,000 ha) around the volcano as a biosphere reserve because of its importance as a diverse habitat for more than 300 species of trees and bushes.

Most days, the top of the volcano, the highest peak in the Lesser Antilles *(see p368)*, is hidden by clouds and rain, but several maintained hiking trails lead to the summit and other viewpoints. Parc National operates an office in the town of Saint-Claude, which is the base for many guided and independent tours of the park. Visitors can pick up maps, guide recommendations, brochures, and other information from here before heading into the park.

The biosphere reserve extends outside the park to include 9,200 acres (3,723 ha) of coral reefs, mangrove forests, freshwater swamps, and sea-grass beds in and around Grand Cul-de-Sac Marin, the northern lagoon that separates Grande-Terre and Basse-Terre.

Picnic area at Parc National de la Guadeloupe

Glass-bottom boat exploring Jacques Cousteau Underwater Reserve

This sensitive area has turtles, giant sponges, soft corals, sea urchins, and many fish species. The mangrove forest also shelters kingfishers, terns, pelicans, herons, and other migratory and native birds.

Jacques Cousteau Underwater Reserve **8**

West coast of Basse-Terre. **Tel** 590 988 172. ⬛ Office du Tourisme, Plage de Malendure, 590 988 687. ⬛ www.cip-guadeloupe.com

The dark-sand beaches of Malendure and Pigeon, just north of Bouillante, are the gateway to the Jacques Cousteau Underwater Reserve, a protected sea park that pays homage to the legendary "Man-Fish", recognized as the father of underwater exploration. The reserve, which extends from the steep-sided coast to nearby Îlets Pigeon, teems with marine life and shelters two sunken ships that provide excellent conditions for scuba divers. Also available are glass-bottom boats, which skim the water, enabling non-divers to view the tropical fish living along the park's pristine coral reef. In January 2004, the

town of Bouillante honored Jacques-Yves Cousteau, who died in 1997, by commissioning a bust of the underwater pioneer and submerging it 39-ft (12-m) deep in Coral Garden off Îlets Pigeon. Cousteau developed the first scuba and declared the west coast of Guadeloupe as one of the world's ten best dive sites.

Plantations **9**

West coast of Basse-Terre. www.ca-en.franceguide.com

Plantations played a major role in Guadeloupe's development, but today only a few remain as eco-museums, inns,

or restaurants. Coffee lovers will want to visit **Musée du Café** and **Maison du Café**, both in Vieux-Habitants, where coffee, cocoa, and vanilla became important crops as early as the mid-1700s. The Musée du Café presents a historical tour of coffee production, while the House of Coffee, set in a working plantation, has guided tours, a shop, a museum, and restaurant. Farther up the western coast in Pointe-Noire, **Caféière Beauséjour** is a coffee plantation with a carefully restored, splendid 1764 planter's house. It sits 1,000 ft (305 m) above the Caribbean with marvelous views of the surrounding valley. Chocolate lovers will find bliss at **La Bonifierie**, an old sugar plantation and coffee estate in the hills of Saint-Claude, where a small Créole-style house has been converted into a gourmet chocolate factory with an adjoining tasting room.

🏛 **Musée du Café**
Le Bouchu, 97119 Vieux-Habitants. **Tel** 590 985 496. ☐ 9am–5pm daily. ⬛ www.cafechaulet.com

🏛 **Maison du Café**
Vallée de Grand'Rivière, 97119 Vieux-Habitants. **Tel** 590 986 306. ☐ 9am–5pm daily. ⬛ Sep–mid-Oct. ⬛ ⬛ ⬛ ⬛
www.vertevallee-guadeloupe.com

🍫 **La Bonifierie**
Morin, 97120 Saint-Claude. **Tel** 590 800 605. ☐ 9am–4:30pm, Tue–Sun. ⬛ ⬛ ⬛ ⬛

🏛 **Caféière Beauséjour**
Acomat, 97116. **Tel** 590 981 009. ☐ 10am–5pm, Tue–Sun. ⬛ ⬛ ⬛ ⬛
www.cafeierebeausejour.com

Musée du Café, housed in former plantation buildings

Typical houses at the base of a hillock, Terre-de-Haut

Terre-de-Haut ⓾

9 miles (15 km) SW off Basse-Terre's coast. 🏠 *1,750.* ✈ ⛴ 🚌
ⓘ *Tourist Office, 39 Rue Jean Calot, Terre-de-Haut, 590 995 860.*
🎭 *Carnival (last week of Feb).*
www.omtlessaintes.fr

Of the eight islands that make up Les Saintes, only Terre-de-Haut and Terre-de-Bas are populated. Terre-de-Haut attracts more visitors given its harbor, natural beauty, picturesque fort, and easy access. The flat outer island is only 3 miles (5 km) long and 2 miles (3 km) wide, making it ideal for exploring on foot, but group tours by minibus are offered from the harbor.

The main town is Le Bourg, which sits in the curve of a striking bay midway along the western coast and a 5-minute walk from the airstrip. Brightly-painted houses, restaurants, and boutiques line the narrow streets. An old cemetery with graves of the island's first French settlers is located in the center of the town. The fortified summit of Morne du Chameau, at the east end of town, is the island's highest point at 1,014 ft (309 m), and offers stunning views of the sea and nearby islands. A hike up and back takes about 3 hours.

Fort Napoléon, which sits 374 ft (114 m) above La Baie des Saintes, is the biggest tourist attraction on the island and offers spectacular views

in all directions. Though Fort Napoléon was never fired upon or called on to defend the region, a section of the fort houses a museum featuring pictures, maps, drawings, and artifacts attesting to the violent period of Caribbean history during the 17th and 18th centuries. Other parts of the fort have been renovated as a modern art museum exhibiting more than 250 paintings, none with a military theme. A cactus garden surrounds the fort and boasts some of the most exotic and best maintained species in the Caribbean. Directly across the bay, at the top of Îlet à Cabrit, sit the ruins of Fort Joséphine, named in honor of Emperor Napoleon's wife.

Most visitors spend their time on the island's splendid beaches or explore underwater with one of several dive operators *(see p369)*. In town, Baie du Bourg is a UNESCO World Heritage Site and listed as one of the world's most

Entrance of the Fort Napoléon, Terre-de-Haut

beautiful bays. Plage de Pompierre is a popular, palmshaded beach that curves around yet another bay on the northeast shore and is connected by a 2.4-mile (4-km) hiking trail called Trace des Crêtes to Grande Anse, a beautiful but unsafe-for-swimming beach midway down the east coast, a trip that takes over an hour one way. Anse Crawen, near the southern tip of the west coast, allows topless sunbathing and swimming. However, snorkelers prefer the nearby Plage Figuier. Watersports equipment, including Hobie Cats and kayaks, can be rented at Plage de Marigot.

🏛 **Fort Napoléon**
Le Chameau. **Tel** *690 610 151.*
⏱ *9am–4pm daily.*
🎫 *pub hols.* 🎦 *in French only.*

Marie-Galante ⓫

27 miles (44 km) S off the coast of Grande-Terre. 🏠 *13,000.* ✈ ⛴ 🚌
🚌 ⓘ *Office du Tourisme de Marie-Galante, Rue du Fort, 590 975 651.*
🎭 🎭 *Terre de Blues (May).*
www.ot-mariegalante.com

Marie-Galante is called The Island of a Hundred Windmills, though only 72 of the 19th-century stone structures remain, giving the flat isle a nostalgic ambience. Ox-drawn carts, once the chief means of transportation, are not an uncommon sight. On weekends from June through February, islanders and visitors from Guadeloupe turn out for oxen tug-of-war competitions. Sugar production remains an important part of the economy, but tourism is gaining ground due to the island's superb beaches and old-fashioned appeal.

Among the most interesting sights, **Murat Plantation** stands out. Once a huge sugar plantation requiring the labor of more than 200 slaves, its Neo-Classical mansion has been restored to its original state and is now an eco-museum featuring colonial memorabilia. The grounds include a garden, windmill, and sugar refinery. The reconstructed **Moulin de Bézard** (Bézard Windmill), on the southeast coast, is another top attraction. Built in 1814, it was restored in 1994 and is now in working condition. A shop set up in an adjacent former slave cabin offers locally-made products. Three rum distilleries offer tours and tastings. Of these, **Distillerie Bielle** is the largest producer and turns out well-known rums in various flavors, such as the gold-medal winning Shrubb, which tastes of oranges. Close to the simple fishing village of Saint-Louis, the **Ecolambda** is a bio-climatic house with medicinal and flowering plants. The adjacent shop sells Z'Oliv Rum, made on-site. Several hiking trails are maintained by the Office National des Forêts. There are a dozen lovely beaches along the west coast. The best for swimming are the southern reef-protected waters at Plage du Grand-Bourg and Plage de la Feuillère at Capesterre.

🏛 **Murat Plantation**
Section Murat 97112, Grand-Bourg. *Tel* 590 979 441. ◯ 9am–noon & 2:30pm–5:30pm Mon–Fri. ▨

🏭 **Moulin de Bézard**
Section Bezard 97140, Capesterre. *Tel* 590 974 495. ◯ 10am–1pm daily. ▨ ▨ ▨

⚒ **Distillerie Bielle**
Section Bielle 97112, Grand-Bourg. *Tel* 590 979 362. ◯ 10am–12:30pm Mon–Sat, 10am–noon Sun. ▨

🏛 **Ecolambda**
Section Saragot 97134, Saint-Louis. *Tel* 590 973 180. ◯ by reservation. ▨ ▨

Visitors arriving at the main harbor, Marie-Galante

DAY TRIPS TO THE OUTER ISLANDS

A day trip to one of the outer islands is an opportunity to explore a less populated area, scuba or snorkel unspoiled reefs, and enjoy a solitary picnic or dine with the locals. Overnight accommodations are basic, but charming. The islands are accessible from Guadeloupe by air and by sea. Organized guided tours (see p369) are the best way to see the islands on a day trip. Independent travelers can arrange transportation and plan activities through the various tourist board offices.

La Désirade ⑫

6 miles (10 km) off Grande-Terre's east coast. 🏃 1,700. ✈ 🚢 ℹ *Tourist Board of La Désirade, Capitainerie, 590 850 086.*

La Désirade is the most off-the-beaten-track island of Les Saintes. Most visitors consider the 7-mile (11-km) long and 1-mile (2-km) wide isle perfect for a day trip, but there are also many places to stay overnight. Only the south coast is populated and a single road links Beauséjour, the principal town, with smaller settlements that dot the reef-sheltered shore. A bike or motor scooter is ideal for exploring the white-sand beaches, protected by a long strand of pristine coral reefs. The island is home to an astonishing variety of plants and rare animals. Development is catching up as more visitors discover the untouched beauty

The picture-perfect Plage du Souffleur, La Désirade

of the beaches and hiking trails. The main town features a public square, seamen's cemetery, and a small hilltop chapel with splendid views. Plage de Beauséjour or Grande-Anse, at the town's edge, is a popular beach. Inland trails run across the central plateau and hikers are rewarded at the end of a steep climb with panoramic views from the 895-ft (273-m) Grande Montagne. Fine beaches lie off the road, the most beautiful at Souffleur and Petite Rivière near Baie-Mahault, a former lepers' colony. Visitors can see the remains of the colony, explore the ruins of a cotton factory, and stop at the cemetery dedicated to sailors and run by Soeurs de la Charité (Sisters of Charity), before strolling on to the lighthouse.

Moulin de Bézard, restored to former glory, Marie-Galante

Outdoor Activities and Specialized Holidays

Guadeloupe and its nearby outer islands offer an immense choice of outdoor activities, varying from trekking the lush rainforests with gushing waterfalls to diving a marine reserve, which has coral reefs teeming with rainbow-colored fish. For first-time visitors, perhaps the best starting point may be an orientation trip and day sailing around the islands. The islands of Grande-Terre and Basse-Terre offer a wide range of specialized holidays, while the outer islands are less developed. To sample a completely different aspect of Guadeloupe, a tour of a rum distillery is a great choice.

Palm-lined sands of Plage de Pompierre, Terre-de-Haut

BEACHES

The most popular beaches lie along the south coast of Grande-Terre *(see pp360–61)*. Elsewhere on Grande-Terre, surfers flock to Plage du Moule, where waves break on the reefs and reach heights of up to 8 ft (2.5 m). Beginners do best on the northwest coast, around Port-Louis, where the swells roll in low and soft. On Basse-Terre, Grande Anse on the north coast is a beautiful beach. Palm-shaded, golden sands slope steeply to gentle surf, and there are snack bars, watersport huts, and shops nearby. Farther south, Anse Caraïbe is a small, less crowded strip of sand. Divers congregate on the beaches that border Jacques Cousteau Underwater Reserve *(see p363)*. A day trip to Marie-Galante invariably leads to time spent on the beaches near Capesterre – Plage de Petite Anse, and Plage de la Feuillière, one of the most stunning beaches in the

Caribbean. It has a long stretch of sand and a coral reef that tempers the surf, making the water ideal for swimming. On Terre-de-Haut, Plage de Pompierre is a crescent-shaped golden strand situated northeast of Le Bourg. Petite Rivière and Souffleur are two gorgeous white-sand beaches on the southern shore of La Désirade.

BOATING AND SAILING

Internationally known as a prime destination for sailors, Guadeloupe has even amateurs sailing from the marinas of Saint-François, Malendure, Pointe-à-Pitre, and Gourbeyre. **Corail Caraïbes**, **Antilles-Sail**,

and **Privilege Croisières** rent motor and sail boats, and local tour companies run full-day, half-day, and evening cruises that include a variety of activities, typically coastal sightseeing, swimming, snorkeling or diving, with lunch on board or in a secluded cove. Most often, day cruises depart around 8am on a large, modern catamaran that accommodates up to 20 passengers. Trips to the nearby outer islands are also popular. A tour to the Jacques Cousteau Underwater Reserve by the glass-bottom boat, **Le Nautilus**, leaves the beach at Malendure daily and gives passengers a panoramic view of the sea life at a depth of 5 ft (1.5 m) in the Caribbean Sea.

The best way to explore the mangroves is by canoe or kayak, and sea-kayaking is the rage in the Reserve and around the Îlets Pigeon. **Caraibe Kayak**, **Ti-Evasion**, and **Rando Passion** offer kayaking trips.

SURFING

Both amateur and experienced surfers find excellent wave action off the Atlantic Coast near Le Moule, especially during October, November, February, and March. Trade winds blow most of the year causing waves to break over the reefs and the different tide levels vary surfing conditions throughout the day. Skilled surfers enjoy tackling the extraordinary swells during hurricane season from late summer through October. Other areas of the island offer good surfing, and local surfers have identified more than 30 spots with fine waves. **No Comply Surf School** offers lessons. **Karukera Surf Club**, **POYO Surf Club**, and **Arawak Surf Club** are among the popular surfing clubs.

Sea-kayaking on the clear blue waters of the Atlantic Ocean, Grande-Terre

For hotels and restaurants on these islands see pp370–71 and pp372–3

Distillery Tours in Guadeloupe

More than just a drink, rum is an essential part of Guadeloupe's history, economy, and culture. Jean-Baptiste Labat, a French Catholic priest stationed here as a missionary in the late 17th century, is credited with scientifically improving the local method of producing crude spirits from sugarcane. Said to have been miraculously cured of an illness by a bitter, foul-smelling tonic called

Bright rum distillery poster

taffia, a fermented and distilled by-product of sugarcane, he then designed copper stills to produce an agreeable-tasting liquor from the juice. Guadeloupe now produces four types of *rhum agricole* (agricultural rum) at small family-owned distilleries. A visit to rum distilleries such as Rhum du Père Labat, Distillerie Bielle *(see p365)*, and Rhum Damoiseau provides an insight into 300 years of tradition.

Distillerie Reimonenq, Musée du Rhum, in north Basse-Terre, displays farming artifacts, distillery machinery, a sugar mill, and a barrel-making workshop.

THE MAKING OF RUM

Sugarcane juice and molasses are fermented and distilled. The resultant clear liquid is aged with the help of yeast in barrels for different periods of time to produce either light or dark varieties of rum.

Sugarcane fields *cover up to 25 percent of Guadeloupe's landscape. Cane is still cut by hand with machetes.*

Final products *include a 59-proof agricultural rum that is regarded as one of the best in the world, due to its unique taste and fragrance acquired from high-quality cane.*

Distillery machines *in Rhumeries Agricoles de Bellevue grind and press up to nearly 22 lb (10 kg) of cane to obtain 2 pints (1 liter) of rum.*

MAIN DISTILLERIES

Distillerie Reimonenq
www.musee-du-rhum.fr
Domaine de Séverin
www.severinrhum.com
Rhum Damoiseau
www.damoiseau.com
Rhum du Père Labat
www.rhumbielle.com
Rhumeries Agricoles de Bellevue
Tel 590 972 650.

Domaine de Séverin *arranges a train tour that traverses the property of the rum distillery, which includes a fishing pond, sugarcane field, plantation home, and spice and rum factories. Rum and punch tasting follows the tour.*

DIVING AND SNORKELING

With an impressive underwater environment, snorkelers and divers can explore the amazing sea life and thriving reefs in shallow water off most beaches. Dive shops, including **Tropical Sub**, **La Dive Bouteille Plongées des Saintes**, **Pisquettes Club de Plongée des Saintes**, and **Ti'bulles**, provide rental equipment, guided dives, and instruction leading to certification. Some large resorts offer introductory classes in their pools and follow up with guided diving or snorkeling excursions through approved dive shops. In addition, most half- and full-day cruises offer snorkeling stops, and have scuba equipment for certified divers.

WATERSPORTS

Watersport equipment is available for rent, and introductory lessons are offered at watersport huts on many beaches. **Club Nautique Sportif de Basse-Terre** has a full menu of activities for all skill levels. **Club UCPA**, **Jet l'Eponge**, and **Caraibes Evasion** rent jet skis, Hobie Cats, and kayaks. The larger hotels usually have watersport shops open to the public, and small independent operators set up huts with various equipment at the beaches along the south coast of Grande-Terre and the west coast of Basse-Terre.

SPORTFISHING

The waters off Guadeloupe and the outer islands lure anglers with the promise of

Hiker in a forest near Soufrière volcano

grand adventure, gorgeous scenery, and a bounty of bonefish, tarpon, snook, and other indigenous Caribbean species. Several outlets offer instruction, guided saltwater fly fishing, light tackle spin fishing, and day-long deep sea excursions. Tuna and bonito are in season from December until May, and barracuda and kingfish are in season from January through May. Most hotels arrange for private charters and book space on scheduled trips. Outfitters include **Ekwatafly**, **Michel Peche au Gros**, and **Les Hauts de Deshaies**.

HIKING

More than 186 miles (300 km) of marked trails wind through the mountainous rainforest on Basse-Terre and the steep cliffs on Grande-Terre. Maps and information are available from the La Maison de la Forêt *(see p362)*, and professional guides may be contacted

through **Organisation des Guides de Montagne de la Caraibe** in Basse-Terre. Several companies lead hikes or make hiking part of a larger eco-tour, including **Zion Trek**. The most popular hiking routes are on Basse-Terre, including the trek to the top of La Soufrière. The trails leading up the slope of the volcano begin gently, but the difficulty increases with elevation and only avid hikers are able to reach the steaming, sulfurous summit. Easier trails nearby lead to La Citerne, a water-filled crater surrounded by dense vegetation, and Cascade Vauchelet, a waterfall. The most popular hiking routes in Grande-Terre are along the precipices at Pointe des Châteaux and Porte d'Enfer.

On La Désirade, Coulée du Grand Nord runs across the island's central plateau offering some spectacular views. Ardent hikers cannot resist the hour-long trek to the summit of Morne du Chameau *(see p364)*, on Terre-de-Haut. An easier trip along the popular Sentier des Crêtes is a 40-minute hike though the lush countryside.

Marie-Galante is easily explored on foot. Guelle Grand Gouffre offers incredible views of Grande-Terre and the *gouffre* itself is a deep chasm with a rock arch that allows the sea to rush in and spew skyward. The path continues along low cliffs to Caye Plate and Anse du Coq, about 1 mile (2 km) farther along the shore.

CYCLING

Each August, Guadeloupe hosts a ten-day international bike race, Tour de la Guadeloupe, a mini version of the Tour de France with nine strenuous routes. The smooth, flat roads on Grande-Terre are ideal for casual riders, but given the lack of designated bike lanes, most vacationers prefer to pedal the less-traveled back roads through small villages. **Vert Intense** and **Eli Sport** rent equipment and offer cycling excursions around the island.

A watersports center, Plage de la Verdure

For hotels and restaurants on these islands see pp370–71 and pp372–3

HORSE-RIDING

A vigorous horseback ride in the surf or a leisurely canter in the forest are great ways to spend an afternoon in Guadeluope. Stables including **Le Haras de Saint-François**, **Ranch des Deux Îlets Ferne Equestre**, and **La Bellencroupe** offer lessons and guided rides to both skilled and novice riders and even children can participate. The best locations are along the secluded waterfront between Saint-François and Pointe des Châteaux on Grande-Terre, the dirt roads, creek-side paths, and deep forest on Basse-Terre, and anywhere on Marie-Galante.

The spectacular Golf International de Saint-François, Grande-Terre

GOLF

The **Golf International de Saint-François** is a lovely 18-hole golf course, designed by well-known golf course architect Robert Trent Jones II. Golfers enjoy stunning views of the ocean and Grande-Terre from every hole and tee. The par 71 course sprawls across 6,670 acres (2,700 ha) and includes a restaurant, club house, and pro shop. Most of the staff speaks English, equipment rentals are available, and lessons may be arranged.

TENNIS

Most large hotels have at least one tennis court, and many are lighted for night play. Tennis clubs such as the **Marina Tennis Club** welcome non-members when courts are not booked for league play.

DIRECTORY

BOATING AND SAILING

Antilles-Sail
Grande-Terre.
Tel 590 901 681.
www.antilles-sail.com

Caraibe Kayak
Basse-Terre.
Tel 690 743 912.

Corail Caraibes
Grande-Terre.
Tel 590 909 113.
www.corail-caraibes.com

Le Nautilus
Basse-Terre.
Tel 590 988 908.
www.lesnautilus.com

Privilege Croisières
Grande-Terre.
Tel 590 846 636.
www.tip-top-one.com

Rando Passion
Basse-Terre.
Tel 590 289 873.
www.randopassion.fr

Ti-Evasion
Grande-Terre.
Tel 590 828 706.
www.ti-evasion.com

SURFING

Arawak Surf Club
Grande-Terre.
Tel 590 236 068.
www.arawak-surf.gp

Karukera Surf Club
Grande-Terre.
Tel 590 236 615.
www.karukerasurfclub.com

No Comply Surf School
Grande-Terre.
Tel 690 579 747.

POYO Surf Club
Basse-Terre.
Tel 690 764 607.
www.poyosurfclub.com

DIVING AND SNORKELING

La Dive Bouteille Plongées des Saintes
Plage de la Colline, Terre-de-Haut.
Tel 590 995 425.
www.dive-bouteille.com

Pisquettes Club de Plongée des Saintes
Le Mouillage, Terre-de-Haut. *Tel 590 998 880.*
www.pisquettes.com

Ti'bulles
Grand Bourg, Marie-Galante.
Tel 590 975 498. www.tibulles-plongee.com

Tropical Sub
Basse-Terre.
Tel 590 285 267.
www.tropical-sub.com

WATERSPORTS

Caraibes Evasion
Basse-Terre.
Tel 590 953 362.

Club Nautique Sportif de Basse-Terre
Basse-Terre.
Tel 590 813 996.

Club UCPA
Baie de Marigot, Terre-de-Haut. *Tel 590 995 494.*

Jet l'Eponge
Grande-Terre. *Tel 690 325 018.* www.jet-guadeloupe.com

SPORTFISHING

Ekwatafly
Grande-Terre. *Tel 590 218 685.* www.ekwatafly.com

Les Hauts de Deshaies
Deshaies, Basse-Terre.
Tel 690 728 404.

Michel Peche au Gros
Basse-Terre. *Tel 590 991 918.* www.michelpecheaugros.com

HIKING

Organisation des Guides de Montagne de la Caraibe
Tel 590 920 610. www.ogmc-guadeloupe.org

Zion Trek
Basse-Terre. *Tel 690 550 638.* www.ziontrek-guadeloupe.com

CYCLING

Eli Sport
Grande-Terre.
Tel 590 903 750.

Vert Intense
Basse-Terre.
Tel 690 554 047.
www.vert-intense.com

HORSE-RIDING

La Bellencroupe
Centre de Tourism Équestre, Saint-Louis, Marie-Galante.
Tel 590 971 869.

Le Haras de Saint-François
Grande-Terre.
Tel 690 589 992.

Ranch des Deux Îlets Ferne Equestre
Basse-Terre.
Tel 590 285 193.

GOLF

Golf International de Saint-François
Grande-Terre.
Tel 590 884 187.

TENNIS

Marina Tennis Club
Grande-Terre.
Tel 590 908 408.

Choosing a Hotel

Guadeloupe is one of the Caribbean islands that offers the largest choice of accommodations, from simple studios to luxurious resorts. The hotels here have been chosen for good value based on the quality of their facilities and the amenities offered. Rates drop during low season and discounts may be available year-round by booking through travel agencies and Internet sites.

PRICE CATEGORIES
The following price ranges are for a standard double room per night during the high season, including taxes and service charges.

$ under $100
$$ $100–200
$$$ $200–300
$$$$ $300–400
$$$$$ over $400

GUADELOUPE

Private Rentals – Gîtes

French vacationers are fond of furnished and fully-equipped vacation rentals known as *gîtes*. These offer extra space, cooking facilities, and an opportunity to live island-style. Avoid unpleasant surprises by booking through Gîtes de France, a government agency that inspects all properties before granting their seal of approval.
Tel 590 916 433. **www.**gites-de-france.fr

Le Jardin de Malanga

Auberge de la Vieille Tour

BASSE-TERRE, DESHAIES Domaine de la Pointe Batterie $$
Chemin de la Batterie, 97126 **Tel** 590 285 703 **Fax** 590 285 728 **Rooms** 18

This hotel is a real find – a mix of studios, bungalows, and villas near one of the best beaches on Basse-Terre. The landscaped grounds include a full-service spa. Studios have a kitchenette on the terrace, bungalows have private pools, and the villas have pools and ocean views. **www.pointe-batterie.com**

BASSE-TERRE, SAINT-CLAUDE Hotel Saint-Georges $$
Rue Gratien-Parize, 97120 **Tel** 590 801 010 **Fax** 590 803 050 **Rooms** 42

Hotel Saint-Georges has cozy, nicely-decorated rooms with balconies, modern baths, and a European ambience; two suites offer additional space. Guests enjoy a free-form pool, fitness center, an outstanding restaurant, and a good location in the hills near the forest. **www.hotelstgeorges.com**

BASSE-TERRE, SAINTE-ROSE La Marmite Kreyol $
Baie de Nogent, 97115 **Tel** 590 681 010 **Fax** 590 681 015 **Rooms** 8

Tucked into a residential area near the water, each bungalow faces the small swimming pool and has a kitchenette and patio. Breakfast and dinner are available at the restaurant. Evening entertainment is arranged. Friendly owners, Didier and Patricia, offer airport pickup and island information.

BASSE-TERRE, SAINTE-ROSE Villas Aquarelles $$$$$
Domaine de Nogent, 97115 **Tel** 590 686 523 **Fax** 590 683 823

The place offers 15 villas, each with a private pool, furnished living area, well-equipped kitchen, and patio. All the villas have air-conditioning and facilities for disabled guests. Breakfast is delivered to the villa at extra charge. Tours, babysitting, and massage services are also available at additional cost. **www.aquarelles-villas.com**

BASSE-TERRE, TROIS-RIVIÈRES Le Jardin de Malanga $$$$
Hermitage, 97114 **Tel** 590 926 757 **Fax** 590 926 758

This luxurious colonial house is surrounded by tropical trees and flowering plants and has three beautiful cottages, all with three bedrooms, including one for children. There is also a bungalow with suites, some of which have unique features and king-sized beds. **www.jardinmalanga.com**

GRANDE-TERRE, BAS-DU-FORT Village Soleil $
La Marina, 97190 **Tel** 590 908 576 **Fax** 590 909 365 **Rooms** 65

The units here are set above the marina, each with a living-dining area and terrace. The extra-spacious duplexes can accommodate up to four people. Complimentary breakfast is served in the poolside pavilion. The hotel has an excellent location for boating activities. **www.hotel-village-soleil.com**

GRANDE-TERRE, GOSIER Karaibes Hotel $
Pointe de la Verdure, 97190 **Tel** 590 845 151 **Fax** 590 842 374 **Rooms** 66

A well-priced hotel offering good value for economy travelers. The brightly-painted hotel is 300 ft (100 m) from the beach, near shops, restaurants, and the casino in Gosier. Rooms are basic, but colorful and nicely furnished; VIP rooms offer more space and Jacuzzi tubs. **www.karaibeshotel.com**

GRANDE-TERRE, GOSIER Canella Beach Hotel-Residence $$
Pointe de la Verdure, 97190 **Tel** 590 904 400 **Fax** 590 904 444 **Rooms** 143

This hotel, on a great beach, offers all the conveniences of a traditional resort with the independence of apartment accommodations. The 143 units, in luxuriant gardens, all have terraces and kitchenettes. A fine array of free land and water activities, a children's club, and weekly live entertainment make this a family favorite. **www.canellabeach.com**

Key to Symbols *see back cover flap*

GRANDE-TERRE, GOSIER La Maison Créole

Montauban, 97190 **Tel** *590 843 643* **Fax** *590 845 516* **Rooms** *58*

This two-level hotel is laid out around a large landscaped pool and within walking distance of the beach, casino, shops, and restaurants. The on-site restaurant, La Table de Bacchus, serves excellent meals and a buffet breakfast is available at an additional charge. **www.lamaisoncreole.com**

GRANDE-TERRE, GOSIER Karibea Beach Resort Gosier

Pointe de la Verdure, 97190 **Tel** *590 826 464* **Fax** *590 847 272* **Rooms** *270*

This resort is on one of the best beaches; it has 3 restaurants, 2 pools, a full-service bar, and all the rooms open on to a balcony. Superior rooms offer more space and apartments sleep up to four with two bathrooms and a kitchenette. Buffet breakfast is included in the price. A choice of activities is offered. **www.karibea.com**

GRANDE-TERRE, GOSIER Le Creole Beach Resort

Pointe de la Verdure, 97190 **Tel** *590 904 646* **Fax** *590 904 666* **Rooms** *218*

Large rooms and suites, vast landscaped grounds, private beach, big pool, tennis court, and fitness center makes this resort a good choice for families. All rooms are nicely furnished and well equipped. The resort offers organized activities and nightly entertainment. Rates include breakfast. **www.creolebeach.com**

GRANDE-TERRE, MONTAUBAN Auberge de la Vieille Tour

Montauban, 97190 **Tel** *590 842 323* **Fax** *590 843 343* **Rooms** *103*

As part of the luxurious MGallery group, this marvelous hotel is one of the grandest properties on the island. Built around an 18th-century sugar mill and surrounded by landscaped grounds that slope to the sea, every spacious room looks across the water to the outer islands. It has a tennis court and offers watersports. **www.mgallery.com**

GRANDE-TERRE, POINTE-À-PITRE Hotel Saint-John-Perse

Quai des Croisières, 97110 **Tel** *590 825 157* **Fax** *590 825 261* **Rooms** *44*

This two-star hotel is situated in the heart of the old town, within easy walking distance of the museums and markets. A convenient base for travelers wishing to explore Pointe-à-Pitre for a day or two, it also has good access to ferries and airplanes to the outer islands. **www.saint-john-perse.com**

GRANDE-TERRE, SAINTE-ANNE Eden Palm

Le Helleux, 97180 **Tel** *590 884 848* **Fax** *590 884 849* **Rooms** *66*

Luxurious bungalows set around a historical mill within a tropical garden, this hotel is among the most luxurious on the island. Fine woods and fabrics decorate spacious units with plushly furnished patios. The on-site restaurants and bars offer various cuisines and entertainment. Activities include tennis. **www.edenpalm.com**

GRANDE-TERRE, SAINTE-ANNE Le Diwali

Sainte-Anne Beach, 97180 **Tel** *590 853 970* **Fax** *590 885 574* **Rooms** *8*

This intimate, friendly hotel is usually filled with faithful return guests. Steps from the water, all rooms have fancy bathrooms and lovely furnishings. Deluxe rooms open onto a private ocean-view terrace. Breakfast is included in the rate. Reserve early, especially during high season. **www.lediwali.fr**

GRANDE-TERRE, SAINT-FRANÇOIS Hotel Résidence Golf Village

96 Hauts de Saint-François, 97118 **Tel** *590 887 373* **Fax** *590 886 170* **Rooms** *94*

Located on a hill overlooking the sea, this hotel is close to the island's only 18-hole golf course. Each spacious unit is contemporarily furnished, with refrigerators in standard rooms and kitchenettes in the studios and villas. A range of activities are on offer and there is a shuttle service to the town and beach. **www.primeahotels.com**

GRANDE-TERRE, SAINT-FRANÇOIS La Cocoteraie

Avenue Europe, 97118 **Tel** *590 887 981* **Fax** *590 887 833* **Rooms** *50*

A large pool is the centerpiece of this elegant French-colonial hotel situated between the marina and the sea. Each spacious suite has a sitting area, deluxe bathroom with an octagonal tub and a furnished terrace. Shops, clubs, restaurants, and a golf course are nearby. The hotel is close to an excellent beach. **www.lacocoteraie.com**

LA DÉSIRADE, BEAUSÉJOUR Oualiri Beach Hotel

La Désirade, 97127 **Tel** *590 202 008* **Fax** *590 896 850* **Rooms** *6*

This hotel has simple Creole-style architecture with basic rooms opening directly on to the sand. Most guests spend days lounging on the beach. Other activities include hiking the trails that begin just inland or strolling around the island. Cars, scooters, and bikes are available to rent. **www.im-caraibes.com/oualiri/index-gb.htm**

MARIE-GALANTE, CAPESTERRE Le Soleil Levant

42 Rue de la Marine, 97140 **Tel** *590 973 155* **Fax** *590 974 165* **Rooms** *21 plus 2 (village)*

A complex with two locations, one in the village of Capesterre, and the other in the hills above, offering guests a choice of rooms, bungalows, and apartments. Accommodations in the village open directly onto the sea while those in the hills offer great views. **www.im-caraibes.com/soleil-levant/index-gb.htm**

TERRE-DE-HAUT, ANSE PAN-DE-SUCRE Hotel Bois Joli

Le Bourg, 97137 **Tel** *590 995 038* **Fax** *590 995 505* **Rooms** *29*

The hotel has rooms in two hillside buildings, all with balconies and some with ocean views. Stand-alone bungalows sit just above the water and have great sea views. There is an arrangement for shuttle bus pickup and return to airstrip or ferry dock. Rates include breakfast. A lovely bar on-site. **www.hotelboisjoli.fr**

Where to Eat & Nightlife

Every town has small pizzerias, crêperies, and sandwich shops along the main roads, serving simple inexpensive dishes. Basic cafés offer excellent Creole-style dishes at moderate prices, and gastro restaurants are the places to splurge on exquisitely prepared French meals. Nightlife centers around a few after-hours clubs on the south coast of Grande-Terre.

PRICE CATEGORIES
The price ranges are for a two-course meal for one, including tax and service charges and half a bottle of wine.

$ under $10
$$ $10–15
$$$ $15–25
$$$$ $25–35
$$$$$ over $35

RESTAURANTS

Eateries in Guadeloupe
The restaurants serve a variety of cuisines – from classical French to West Indian home cooking. Lunch is often the main meal, and visitors will do well to enjoy a filling *déjeuner*, when prices are lower than those charged in the evening. Most restaurants close for a few hours during the afternoon while snack bars and grills offer continuous service throughout the day.

Outdoor eateries

Iguane Cafè

BASSE-TERRE, MATOUBA Restaurant Chez Paul ≡ ⚑ $$$

Rivière Rouge, 97120 ***Tel*** *590 802 920*

This lunch-only restaurant beside the river right in the center of the village is an ideal stop on the way to or from La Soufrière. Both the fixed-price and à-la-carte menu feature generous portions of traditional island favorites, and a few Indian dishes are also served. There is an upper level too. Open daily.

BASSE-TERRE, BASSE-TERRE TOWN Le Jazzy's ≡ ♫ ⚑ $$$$

Boulevard Félix Eboué, 97100 ***Tel*** *590 255 002*

The restaurant's specialty is Creole-style meats and seafood, such as moules wrapped in pastry with muscadet sauce, but veggie options are also available. The dessert list is longer than the main-course menu, each one very creative and delicious. Open every night for dinner and on weekdays for lunch.

BASSE-TERRE, BAIE-MAHAULT Au Paradis Gourmand 🍷 ⊞ $$$$

Plaisance Convenance, 97122 ***Tel*** *590 387 939*

The eatery has a lovely setting with an outdoor-seating option. Provençal Mediterranean specialties are prepared by chef Audrey; try one of the honey-laced tarts for dessert. The fixed-price lunch served during the week is a bargain. There is a separate menu for children. Dinner only on Friday. Reservations on other days.

BASSE-TERRE, BAIE-MAHAULT Chez Laurent 🍷 ≡ ⚑ $$$$$

Boulevard Marquisat de Houelbourg, 97122 ***Tel*** *590 252 188*

A favorite with locals and visitors, the place is run by husband-wife team of chef Laurent and hostess Nathalie. It is known for its elegant surroundings, exquisite cuisine, and wonderful service. Seafood and traditional French specialties feature on the menu. Open on weekdays for lunch.

BASSE-TERRE, BOUILLANTE Les Tortues ⊞ $$$$

Duché, 97125 ***Tel*** *590 988 283*

Its name means turtles, and is perfect for this feet-in-the-sand waterfront restaurant with spectacular views. The menu is based on seafood including freshwater crayfish, marlin with a choice of cream or Creole sauce, and conch. Watch for the sign on N2 at the road to Anse Duchy. Open for lunch and dinner daily.

BASSE-TERRE, POINTE-NOIRE Caféière Beauséjour [V] ≡ ⚑ $$$$$

Gros Morne, Acomat, 97116 ***Tel*** *590 981 009*

Make a reservation at this unique restaurant in the main house of a coffee plantation dating from 1764. A set menu is made up daily from produce fresh from the garden. Elaborate recipes, gracious surroundings with antique furniture, and the aroma of brewing coffee make it special. Open for lunch from Wednesday to Sunday.

BASSE-TERRE, SAINTE-ROSE Restaurant Chez Clara ⊞ $$$$$

Boulevard Saint–Charles, 97115 ***Tel*** *590 287 299*

Named for the owner who regularly greets guests at the door or as they dine on dishes that meld island recipes with French finesse. Sit on the terrace to sip fruity rum punch, then enjoy a meal of crayfish, conch, crab, or fish tweaked with a dash of spice or a savory sauce. Open for lunch and dinner; closed on Wednesdays.

GRANDE-TERRE, GOSIER Le Pirate Caribéen ≡ ⊞ ⚑ $$$

La Marina de Gosier, 97190 ***Tel*** *590 907 300*

DIners here drop in to watch their favorite sports on the big screen TV or sit out on the bamboo-shaded terrace while enjoying excellent Creole dishes. Wi-Fi is free, and the pirate-motif bar serves unique cocktails and ice-cold beer. Kids' menu and fixed-price meals are a bargain. Open daily for lunch and dinner.

Key to Symbols *see back cover flap*

GRANDE-TERRE, GOSIER Le Negresco

🔲 📋 🔁 $$$$$

36 Boulevard Amédée-Clara, 97190 **Tel** *590 842 941*

French cuisine fills the menu, and Caribbean fish, conch, and lobster are served in various preparations. Braised veal and rare beef filet are also popular, followed by crème brûlée or a warm tart for dessert. Reserve a table with a view of Îlet du Gosier. Open for lunch Tuesday to Friday, and for dinner from Monday to Saturday.

GRANDE-TERRE, MONTAUBAN Restaurant la Vieille Tour

🔲 📋 🔁 👤 $$$$$

Auberge de La Vieille Tour, 97190 **Tel** *590 842 323*

This is the most expensive and elegant of three restaurants at the upscale Auberge de la Vielle Tour *(see p371)*. The gourmet international menu is exquisitely prepared and presented. The place has a surprisingly relaxed atmosphere with friendly service. Closed on Tuesdays. Reservations recommended.

GRANDE-TERRE, POINTE-À-PITRE Maharajah Monty

🅥 📋 🔁 $$$$

47 Rue Achille René Boisneuf, 97110 **Tel** *590 831 260*

A long-time city favorite, the place is popular with visitors and residents from India, which attests to its authentic cuisine. Specialties from East India include vegetarian dishes, tandoori chicken, seafood curry, and fresh-baked naan. Open on evenings and Saturdays; call to check hours.

GRANDE-TERRE, POINTE-À-PITRE La Canne à Sucre

📋 🎵 🔁 $$$$$

Quai #1, Port Autonome, 97110 **Tel** *590 903 883*

The eatery is in the center of town. Seafood dominates the menu, and the chicken breast stuffed with conch is outstanding. The desserts are decadent. There is a Creole buffet lunch on Saturdays and live music on Friday and Saturday evenings. Dinner reservations are recommended. Closed on Sundays.

GRANDE-TERRE, SAINTE-ANNE Kon Tiki

🔁 $$$

Chemin de la Plage Sainte-Anne, 97180 **Tel** *590 235 542*

One of the best of several casual eateries on or near the town beach, Kon Tiki specializes in excellent salads, sandwiches, grilled fish, and meat. Continuous open-air service from 9am–6pm allows lunch and snacks whenever hunger strikes throughout the day. Crêpes and ice cream for dessert.

GRANDE-TERRE, SAINT-FRANÇOIS Iguane Café

🔲 📋 🔁 🔁 👤 $$$$$

Chemin Rural de la Coulée, 97118 **Tel** *590 886 137*

This is the place for beef and lobster, and they are good enough to justify the high prices. Other fine choices include veal and fish. Try and get a seat on the terrace. Ask for suggestions from an extensive wine list. The café serves a Sunday lunch; dinner daily except on Tuesdays. Reservation recommended.

LA DÉSIRADE, PLAGE DE LA PETITE-RIVIÈRE Restaurant la Providence

$$$$

Chez Nounoune, Baie-Mahault, 97127 **Tel** *590 200 359*

Serving perhaps the best food on the island, the eatery specializes in lobster fricassée. Other seafood and Creole dishes are available; the *igname au gratin* (yams) are highly recommended. Open for lunch daily. Reservations recommended. Closed all of September.

MARIE-GALANTE, CAPESTERRE Le Touloulou

🔁 $$$

Petite Anse, 97140 **Tel** *590 973 263*

In his restaurant set right on the beach, proprietor Jose Viator oversees a casual crowd as they are waited on by his amiable staff. Shellfish dishes are superb, and the adventurous may enjoy the *bébélé* made of boiled sheep or cow tripe and green bananas or breadfruit. Closed on Sunday nights and Mondays.

TERRE-DE-HAUT, ANSE MIRRE La Saladerie

🔁 $$$$

Anse Mirre, 97137 **Tel** *590 995 343*

This place offers generous portions of favorites such as salads, pasta, grilled fish, and beef and ham dishes. The fish fondue is a bit different from usual island fare and is served with six freshly made sauces. Open from Wednesday to Sunday for lunch and dinner.

BARS AND CLUBS

People in Guadeloupe gather at restaurants and bars for happy hours and dinner, then linger on with friends, enjoying *zouk* performed by local talent. The best cocktails involve rum and fruit juice. Several of the large hotels host theme-night entertainment, and there is always something going on at the marina bars and clubs in Bas-du-Fort and Saint-François.

Rums produced in Guadeloupe

RECOMMENDED PLACES TO GO

Complexe Le Cheyenne
Quartier Montauban, Grande-Terre.
(No shorts.)

Disco Schiva
La Baie, Le Moule, Grande-Terre.
(Great disco with all the gadgets.)

Fonzy Bar
Mathurin, Poucet, Grande-Terre.
(Rock music most nights.)

La Brise
Deshaies, Plage de Riflet, Grande-Terre. (Beach-bar and restaurant.)

Le Zenith
Route de Bas-du-Fort, Grande-Terre.
(Mix of locals and tourists.)

Zoo Rock Café
Le Gosier, Grande-Terre. (Bar with exotic drinks and tapas.)

Practical Information

As an overseas department of France, Guadeloupe is a tropical destination with a truly French touch when it comes to infrastructure, cuisine, culture and, of course, language (although most people in contact with tourists speak some English). Visitors fly into the international airport near the main city of Pointe-à-Pitre. Once there, getting around is easy by car, taxi, and ferry, and tourist offices are plentiful. Shopping here is rewarding with lots of local crafts and rum on offer.

A pharmacy at the town center in Le Moule, Guadeloupe

WHEN TO GO

While air temperature varies little from one month to another, February through June is the driest period, with rain and humidity picking up in July and lingering through early January. Carnival begins the Friday after Epiphany Sunday and ends on Mardi Gras (Fat Tuesday). Following the French tradition, businesses close for several weeks during August and September.

GETTING THERE

Guadeloupe has only one international airport, Guadeloupe Pôle Caraïbes in Pointe-à-Pitre, and seven regional airstrips, including Marie-Galante Grand-Bourg, Terre-de-Haut Airport and La Désirade Airport. The outer islands of the archipelago may be reached by ferry service. Both air and sea service change seasonally, but **Air Canada**, **American Airlines**, and **Delta** offer flights from North America, at least weekly during high season. **Air France** provides non-stop service from Paris, and **Air Caraïbes** and **LIAT** connect the islands within the Antilles. The ferry companies between these islands are **L'Express des Iles**, **Comatrile**, and **Brudey Frères**.

DOCUMENTATION

Other than the French, the citizens from all countries within the EU must present a valid passport to enter the island. Citizens of France may show a passport, an official identity card, or a valid French residence permit. Immigration officials may ask to see an onward or return ticket, proof of sufficient funds for the planned stay and an address where visitors will be staying.

VISITOR INFORMATION

Tourist information kiosks are located at the arrival area of the airports and other tourist-oriented sites on all islands. **Comité du Tourisme des Îles de la Guadeloupe** maintains tourism offices on each of the Guadeloupen islands.

HEALTH AND SECURITY

Crime is rare in Guadeloupe and the outer islands, but take simple precautions and do not leave valuables in rental cars. Bottled water is sold everywhere, but tap water in main towns is drinkable. There are several modern medical facilities located throughout the islands, including the **Centre Hôpitalier Universitaire de Pointe-à-Pitre** with a 24-hour emergency room.

BANKING AND CURRENCY

Most major credit cards are accepted, but may not be welcome at small cafés, especially on the outer islands. The legal

A tourist office in Pointe-à-Pitre

currency is the euro, and other currencies can be exchanged at 24-hour ATMs and banks, which are open in all the main towns from 8am–4pm Mon–Fri. Some US cards may not work in the local ATMs.

COMMUNICATIONS

The country code for Guadeloupe is 590 followed by the 6-digit local number. Within Guadeloupe, including the outer islands, dial only the 6-digit local number, which begins 690 for mobiles. From France or other French islands, dial 0 plus the 9-digit local number. Calling cards are needed for local phone booths. Cell phones can be purchased from Orange Caraïbe offices. Hotels may offer Internet service, and Wi-Fi hotspots are scattered around the island. Cybercafés are located in larger towns. Post offices may have terminals for public use, but the keyboards are French.

TRANSPORT

Most large international agencies rent cars on the island. Book well ahead during high season. Large hotels may have rental cars on site for daily or weekly rental. Several agencies such as **AVIS**, **EuropCar**, **Quickly**, **Budget**, and **Voitures des Îles** have booths at the airport. Taxis are abundant at the airports, ferry docks, and cruise-ship terminals. They have meters and legally add a hefty surcharge to fares between 9pm and 7am and on Sundays and holidays. The operators for taxis are **Taxi Art**, **Tele-Taxi**, **C.D.L Taxi**, **Taxi Les Saintes Travel**, **Elie Castanet**, **Etienne Leveille**, and **Taxi: La Désirade**. There are frequent bus services throughout the island but it is best to know some French to communicate with the drivers.

SHOPPING

The markets in Pointe-à-Pitre and Basse-Terre town have great souvenirs, locally-made foods, and Caribbean art. This is the place to find Colombo seasoning (a local type of curry powder), fruit punch spiked with island rum, and Madras fabric (the bright check material seen in Creole festive dress). Most markets are open daily, except Sundays, from early morning to noon. In Pointe-à-Pitre, there is Marché de la Darse and Marché Artisanal, and a smaller market in Basse-Terre on Boulevard du Général de Gaulle. For gifts and souvenirs, **Tee Shirt Adventure** is ideal. The largest shopping center on the island is **Centre Commercial Destreland**, with more than 170 stores. **Centre Commercial Milenis** is another big center. Along the south coast of Grande-Terre, stop at **Village Artisanal** to visit shops with unique items, and **Artisan d'Art Aquaverre** to see the hand-painted glass objects.

LANGUAGE

The official language is French, but Creole is widely spoken, and recognized as a language.

ELECTRICITY

Gaudeloupe uses 220 volts AC, 50 cycles and most places have French-style outlets so adaptors might be necessary.

TIME

Guadeloupe is on Atlantic Standard Time (AST), 4 hours behind Greenwich Mean Time (GMT), and does not observe daylight savings time.

GETTING MARRIED

Getting married in the archipelago is quite complicated for non-French citizens; the same rules apply as for Martinique *(see p393)*. Check the website of Comité du Tourisme des Îles de la Guadeloupe for more details regarding the legalities.

DIRECTORY

GETTING THERE

Air Canada
Tel 590 211 277.
www.aircanada.ca

Air Caraïbes
Tel 0820 835 835.
www.aircaraibes.com

Air France
Tel 0820 820 820.
www.airfrance.gp

American Airlines
Tel 590 211 180.
www.aa.com

Brudey Frères
Gare Maritime Pointe-à-Pitre. *Tel 590 900 448.*
www.brudey-freres.fr

Comatrile
Saint-Francois,
Grande-Terre.
Tel 590 222 631.

Delta
Tel 0800 225 630.
www.delta.com

L'Express des Iles
Gare Maritime de Bergevin, Grande-Terre.
Tel 0825 359 000.
www.express-des-iles.com

LIAT
Tel 590 211 393.
www.liatairline.com

VISITOR INFORMATION

Comité du Tourisme des Îles de la Guadeloupe
Pointe-a-Pitre.
Tel 590 820 930 (Grande-Terre), *590 325 101* (Basse-Terre), *590 975 651* (Marie-Galante), *590 995 860* (Terre-de-Haut) *590 850 086* (La Désirade).
www.lesilesde guadeloupe.com

HEALTH AND SECURITY

Centre Hôpitalier Universitaire de Pointe-à-Pitre
Pointe-à-Pitre,
Grande-Terre.
Tel 590 891 010.

Fire
Tel 18.

Medical
Tel 15.

Police
Tel 17.

TRANSPORT

AVIS
Tel 590 836 900.
www.avis.com

Budget
Tel 590 211 349.
www.budget-antilles.com

C.D.L. Taxi
Grande-Terre.
Tel 590 207 474.

Elie Castanet
Marie-Galante.
Tel 590 973 334.

Etienne Leveille
Marie-Galante.
Tel 590 978 783.

EuropCar
Tel 590 387 388.
www.europcar-gpe.com

Quickly
Tel 590 211 360.
www.quickly.fr

Taxi Art
Pointe-à-Pitre,
Grande-Terre.
Tel 590 822 626.

Taxi: La Désirade
La Désirade.
Tel 690 385 408.

Taxi Les Saintes Travel
Terre-de-Haut,
Les Saintes.
Tel 590 995 677.

Tele-Taxi
Guadeloupe.
Tel 590 943 340.

Voitures des Iles
Tel 590 252 432.
www.voituresdesiles.com

SHOPPING

Artisan d'Art Aquaverre
Saint-François,
Grande-Terre.
Tel 590 886 844.

Centre Commercial Destreland
N1, Baie-Mahault,
Basse-Terre.
Tel 590 385 385.
www.destreland.com

Centre Commercial Milenis
N1, Les Abymes,
Grand-Terre.

L'Abeille Creole
Route de la Chapelle,
Gosier,
Grande-Terre.
Tel 590 859 897.

Tee Shirt Adventure
4 Quai Ferdinand de Lesseps, Pointe-à-Pitre.
Tel 590 212 101.

Village Artisanal
N4, west to Sainte-Anne,
Grande-Terre.

Exploring Martinique

With tropical flowers carpeting the countryside, which inspired French artist Paul Gauguin's famous landscapes, Martinique is breathtakingly beautiful all year round. The dormant volcano Mont Pelée and the Pitons du Carbet dominate the island, and Fort-de-France, the capital, lies in proximity of a lush rainforest. The primary tourist area, along the south coast, extends west into the sea forming a beach-lined peninsula. A scenic route cuts through the island's northern forest preserve to the Atlantic Coast, with some of the most spectacular bays in the Antilles.

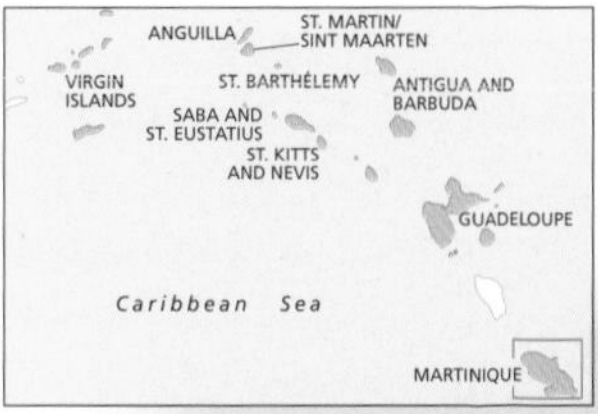

Craft shop in Village de la Poterie, Trois Ilets

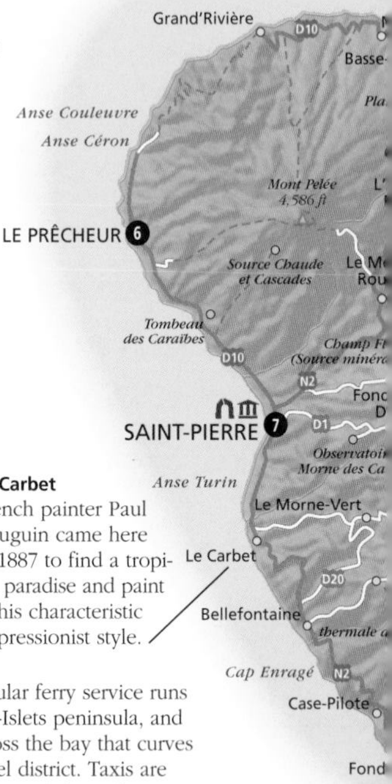

Le Carbet
French painter Paul Gauguin came here in 1887 to find a tropical paradise and paint in his characteristic Impressionist style.

GETTING AROUND

A rental car is the best way to get around the island. Regular ferry service runs between Fort-de-France and the resort areas on the Trois-Islets peninsula, and many visitors use these *vedettes* to go back and forth across the bay that curves deep into the west coast between the capital and the hotel district. Taxis are easy to find and some drivers give private tours. Collective taxis leave from Pointe Simon, near the cruise-ship terminal in Fort-de-France, and travel to most towns on the island but these minivans are often full, and do not follow a reliable schedule.

SIGHTS AT A GLANCE

Caravelle Peninsula 3
Fort-de-France 1
Le Prêcheur 6
Route de la Trace pp380–81 4
Sainte-Marie 5
Saint-Pierre p383 7
Trois-Ilets and Around Pointe du Bout 2

Hotels and Resorts
Chez Julot 8
Club Med Buccaneer's Creek 10
Frégate Bleue 7
Hôtel la Caravelle 5
Hôtel Résidence-Bungalow Tracée 3
La Valmenière 1
Le Domaine de Sainte-Marie 2
Le Domaine Saint Aubin 4
Le François hotels 6
Pierre & Vacances Village 12
Résidence des Iles 11
Résidence Mercure Diamant 13
Sainte-Anne hotels 9
Trois-Ilets hotels 14

SEE ALSO

• ***Where to Stay*** pp388–9
• ***Where to Eat & Nightlife*** pp390–91

KEY

- Major road
- Minor road
- Track
- Ferry route
- ▲ Peak

For additional map symbols *see back flap*

Allée Pécoul, leading to Distillerie Depaz in Saint-Pierre

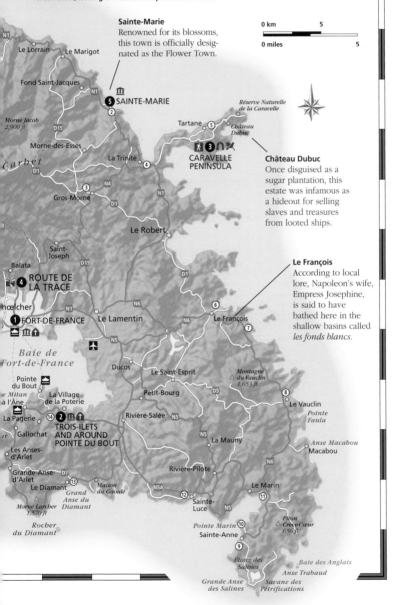

Sainte-Marie
Renowned for its blossoms, this town is officially designated as the Flower Town.

0 km 5

0 miles 5

Le Lorrain
Le Marigot

Fond Saint-Jacques

5 SAINTE-MARIE

Réserve Naturelle de la Caravelle

Tartane 5

Château Dubuc

Morne Jacob 2,900 ft

Morne-des-Esses

La Trinité 4

3 CARAVELLE PENINSULA

Carbet

Château Dubuc
Once disguised as a sugar plantation, this estate was infamous as a hideout for selling slaves and treasures from looted ships.

Gros-Morne 3

Le Robert

Saint-Joseph

Balata

4 ROUTE DE LA TRACE

hœlcher

1 FORT-DE-FRANCE

Le Lamentin

Le François 6

7

Le François
According to local lore, Napoleon's wife, Empress Josephine, is said to have bathed here in the shallow basins called *les fonds blancs.*

Baie de Fort-de-France

Pointe du Bout

e Mitan
à l'Âne

La Village de la Poterie

La Pagerie

Galiochat 14 **2**

TROIS-ILETS AND AROUND POINTE DU BOUT

Les Anses-d'Arlet

Ducos

Le Saint-Esprit

Petit-Bourg

Rivière-Salée

Montagne du Vauclin 1,653 ft

Le Vauclin 8

Pointe Faula

La Mauny

Anse Macabou Macabou

Grande-Anse-d'Arlet 13

Le Diamant

Maison du Gaoulé

Grand Anse du Diamant

Rivière-Pilote

Le Marin 11

Morne Larcher 1,570 ft

Rocher du Diamant

12

Sainte-Luce

Piton Crève-Cœur 656 ft

Pointe Marin 10
Sainte-Anne

Étang des Salines

Baie des Anglais

Anse Trabaud

Grande Anse des Salines

Savane des Pétrifications

Fort-de-France ❶

West coast of Martinique.
🏙 *150,000.* 🛬 🚢 ❼ *Office du Tourisme de Fort-de-France, 76, Rue Lazare Carnot 97200, 596 602 773.* 🛒 *Indoor market 6am–4pm Mon–Sat.* 🎭 *Carnival (Jan/Feb); Cultural Festival (Jul).* **www**.tourismefdf.com

The capital of Martinique is a lively city with French flair wrapped in tropical colors. Next to the harbor in Baie des Flamands, the lovely, green Place de la Savane, full of palm trees and flowers, is an ideal starting point for a walking tour.

Fort Saint-Louis occupies a peninsula on the east side of Place de la Savane. The fortress was built in 1638 during the rule of Louis XIII. Part of the fort is still used by the military, so it is not open to the public, except on special occasions such as Heritage Day in September. East of Fort Saint-Louis is Fort Desaix, which was built from 1768 to 1771, and is now the military headquarters.

On the west side of the park, the two-story **Musée d'Archéologie et de Préhistoire** is set up in a historic building with well-organized relics and exhibits of the island's pre-Columbian inhabitants and its early European colonists. Among the impressive artifacts

The busy indoor market in Fort-de-France

are the ceramics and stone tools used in pre-Columbian times. The museum also has an interesting display of clay figureheads used by the Arawaks to decorate their vases. Just a short distance from Musée d'Archéologie et de Prehistorie is the **Cathédrale Saint-Louis**. Built in the late 1800s on the site of six earlier churches (the first constructed in 1671) and renovated in 1978, this cathedral is the masterpiece of Henri Picq, a renowned French architect. Many of the island's former governors are buried beneath the church's choir gallery, and an enormous pipe organ dominates the interior. The church has a 187-ft (57-m) high steeple and lovely stained-glass windows. The largest market in town is located just north of the cathedral on Rue Antoine Siger. Each morning farmers lay out their produce under the building's metal roof as the city wakes up. Main products on offer are spices, vanilla, peppers, flavored rums, and a vast variety of vegetables and fruits. The most outstanding building in Fort-de-France, also designed by Henri Picq, is the **Bibliothèque Schoelcher**

Statue of Schoelcher

(*see p59*), which pays homage to the French abolitionist writer Victor Schoelcher. The domed coral-and-white library, a mix of architectural styles, was constructed in Paris for the 1889 World Exposition, then dismantled and shipped here, and reassembled in 1893. Today it houses more than 130,000 books, many of which were donated by Schoelcher himself. The collection here ranges from old texts to crime novels. North of La Savane is **Musée Régional d'Histoire et d'Ethnographie**. Housed in a Neo-Classical villa, the museum is elegantly decorated with mahogany furniture and fine latticework. The prime attraction here are the dolls dressed in lace and gold jewelry.

🏛 **Musée d'Archéologie et de Préhistoire**
9 Rue de la Liberté. **Tel** 596 715 705. ⬜ 1–5pm Mon, 8am–5pm Tue–Fri, 9am–noon Sat. 🎫 📷

⛪ **Cathédrale Saint-Louis**
Corner of Rue Victor Schoelcher and Rue Antoine Siger. **Tel** 596 735 978. ⬜ 🕕 6:30–11:30am daily, 2:30–5pm Tue–Thu.

📚 **Bibliothèque Schoelcher**
1 Rue de la Liberté. **Tel** 596 556 830. ⬜ 1–5:30pm Mon, 8:30am–5:30pm Tue–Thu, 8:30am–5pm Fri, 8:30am–noon Sat.

📚 **Musée Régional d'Histoire et d'Ethnographie**
10 Boulevard Général de Gaulle. **Tel** 596 728 187. ⬜ 8:30am–5pm Mon, Wed–Fri, 2–5pm Tue, 8:30am–noon Sat. 🎫 **www**.cr-martinique.fr

Interior of Cathédrale Saint-Louis

Trois-Ilets and Around Pointe du Bout ❷

18 miles (28 km) S of Fort-de-France.
🚢 🛈 *Office du Tourisme des Trois-Ilets, Place Gabriel Hayot, 596 684 763; Marina de la Pointe du Bout, Trois-Ilets, 596 634 879.* **www.**
trois-ilets.com

Located on a peninsula that forms the southern curve of the Baie de Fort-de-France, Martinique's prime tourist district lies just across the water from the capital. Frequent ferries connect Fort-de-France to the marina at Pointe du Bout, on the peninsula's north shore. It is possible to drive between the capital city and the peninsula along the curve of the bay, but traffic on the national highway is usually heavy.

In addition to the large marina and picturesque beaches offering a range of watersports, the district has a golf course, luxury resorts, upscale restaurants, and cafés.

In Trois-Ilets, **L'Eglise Notre Dame de la Bonne Délivrance** (Our Lady of Good Deliverance) dominates the square. This church was where the parents of Empress Josephine, Napoleon's wife, were married in 1761, where the future empress was baptized in 1763, and the site of her mother's funeral in 1807. Now designated a historic monument, the lovely white church is open to visitors who wish to see the baptismal font.

On the outskirts of Trois-Ilets lies **Le Village de la Poterie**, home to potters and

House where Empress Josephine was born, Musée de la Pagerie

other craftspeople who sell their wares here. Nearby, **Domaine Château-Gailliard** is a complex of studios and shops producing and selling primarily pottery, as well as an assortment of art, spices, handmade soaps and candles, and various food products. The shopping complex also houses **Le Musée du Café & Cacao**, which showcases information about the farming and production of coffee and chocolate on the island. Domaine Château-Gailliard also offers helicopter tours of Martinique. Farther west is **La Maison de la Canne**, part of an 18th-century plantation that includes the old Vatable rum distillery.

Located to the east of Trois-Ilets, in La Pagerie, is **Musée de la Pagerie**, which is filled with mementos of Empress Josephine, who was born here in 1763.

Heading south, the drive from Trois-Ilets to the town of Le Diamant on Highway D7 is

one of the most picturesque areas on Martinique. Le Diamant is a charming hamlet of pretty houses with colorful façades. It is also the starting point of the 3-hour hike to Morne Larcher 1,570 ft (478 m), which is the island's highest point. From its base, visitors can get marvelous views of Rocher du Diamant, a 600-ft (183-m) chunk of rock that sits about 2 miles (3 km) offshore. In 1804, during the Napoleonic wars, the British Navy fortified it with cannons and more than 100 sailors, and registered it as the warship HMS *Diamond Rock*. From this unsinkable ship, the English managed to blockade Martinique for 17 months, before the French floated barrels of rum to the rock, got the sailors drunk, and captured the stronghold.

⛪ L'Eglise Notre Dame de la Bonne Délivrance
Town Square (Place Centrale de la Commune), Trois-Ilets.
🕐 9:15–11:45am daily.

Domaine Château-Gailliard
Route des Trois-Ilets. **Tel** 596 681 568. 🕐 9am–6pm daily. 🖥 🛈

🏛 Le Musée du Café & Cacao
Route des Trois-Ilets, Domaine Château-Gaillard. **Tel** 596 482 440
🕐 9am–6pm daily.

La Maison de la Canne
Point Vatable. **Tel** 596 683 204. 🕐 8am–5pm Tue–Sat; 9am–5pm Sun.

🏛 Musée de la Pagerie
La Pagerie, D7, Trois-Ilets.
Tel 596 683 834. 🕐 9am–1pm & 2–5pm Mon–Fri, 9:30am–12:30pm & 3–5pm Sat–Sun. 🖼 🛈

Pottery studio at Le Village de la Poterie, outskirts of Trois-Ilets

Caravelle Peninsula ❸

17 miles (27 km) NE of Fort-de-France. ℹ️ *Office de Tourisme de Trinité, Centre Commercial le Galion,* 596 586 998. **www**.ot-trinite martinique.fr

Jutting 7 miles (11 km) into the Atlantic Ocean off the east coast of Martinique, Caravelle Peninsula, a sheer strip of steep cliffs descending to picturesque beaches, almost looks like an independent islet. The tip of this ragged peninsula is protected within the **Réserve Naturelle de la Caravelle**, which is intersected by several hiking trails. The lighthouse here, rising over Galleon Bay, is the island's oldest working one and has great views over Tartane, a popular beachfront village.

The ruins of **Château Dubuc** lie within the reserve and visitors can explore its grounds and stone relics. Built in about 1770 by the legendary Dubuc de Rivery family, the estate, in the guise of a sugar plantation, was allegedly used for smuggling operations and acquired great wealth from selling slaves and valuables from looted ships. A nature trail begins just outside the château grounds and winds through a mangrove forest.

🥾 **Réserve Naturelle de la Caravelle**
Tel 596 644 259.

🏛 **Château Dubuc**
Caravelle Peninsula.
Tel 596 644 259.
⏱ 8:30am–5:30pm daily. 📷 ♿

Remnants of the Château Dubuc on the Caravelle Peninsula

Route de la Trace ❹

A stained-glass pane

A scenic drive through the interior rainforest, Route de la Trace or N3 climbs from Fort-de-France, on the Caribbean coast, to Le Morne Rouge, the highest village on the island at 1,500 ft (457 m). Flanked by lush vegetation, the route follows an old path laid by Jesuit priests in the 1700s. Visitors now drive on the well-paved road winding through the mountain range and professional guides lead 4WD excursions off-road and through rugged terrain. However, some areas can only be navigated on foot. A popular hiking trail is the Trace des Jésuites, which runs along a ridge above the Route de la Trace and offers sweeping views of Mont Pelée.

Plateau Boucher ④
The route passes a gorge cut by the Rivière Blanché and trailheads at Plateau Boucher, where a network of paths lead up the five *pitons* (peaks).

Jardin de Balata ③
The Garden of Balata is laid out around an old Creole house and features a collection of labeled trees, plants, and tropical flowers. The garden's flora was introduced from around the world by horticulturist Jean-Philippe Thoze.

Eglise de Balata ②
This Balata church was built along the lines of Basilica of Sacré-Coeur (Blessed Heart Basilica) in Montmarte, Paris.

Bellefon

Case-Pilote

Fond Lahaye   Terrev

Schœlcher   Ba

① ②
Fort-de-France

Fort-de-France ①
The capital *(see p378)* has many historic sites, ideal for exploration.

For hotels and restaurants on this island see pp388–9 and pp390–91

Pitons du Carbet ⑤
The Carbet Mountains or the Pitons du Carbet comprise five peaks, the tallest, Piton Lacroix reaching up to 3,925 ft (1,200 m).

KEY

▲ Peak

━━ Route

═══ Other road

– – Trace des Jésuites

Anse Turin
Saint-Pierre
Le Carbet
D1
D20
N2
Mont Pelée
⑦
⑧
Le Morne-Vert
⑥
Champ Flore
(Source minérale)
NS DU CARBET
Piton Lacroix ▲
3,925 ft ⑤
N3
Deux-Choux
Morne Jacob
2,900 ft
Station thermale
l'Absalon
④

0 km 2
0 miles 2

Fonds-Saint-Denis ⑥
From Deux-Choux, a detour on the D1 leads to Fonds-Saint-Denis, a pretty village with abundant flowers, and a church and square named after Jules Pain, the village's former mayor.

Observatoire du Morne des Cadets ⑦
West of Fonds-Saint-Denis, the Observatoire du Morne des Cadets offers exceptional views of Mont Pelée and the Pitons.

Le Morne Rouge ⑧
This village stretches along the slope of the volcanic Mont Pelée and was destroyed on August 30, 1902, by an eruption. Annually, on the anniversary of the devastation in which 1,500 people were killed, islanders gather in Morne Rouge to pay homage to the Virgin Mary while kneeling before her beautiful statue, that was carved in Normandy, France.

Some of the items on display in Musée du Rhum, Sainte-Marie

Sainte-Marie ❺

21 miles (34 km) NE of Fort-de-France. 🏘 20,290. 🚹 Office Samaritain du Tourisme, Town Hall, Coast Road, 596 691 383. 📅 Fête du Rhum (Dec). **www**.ville-sainte marie.fr

The town of Sainte-Marie, an officially-designated Ville Fleurs (Flower Town), is the largest urban area on the Atlantic side of the island, and Martinique's fourth largest city. Most of the daily activity takes place along the lovely waterfront, which faces Ilet de Sainte-Marie, a scrap of land 1,320 ft (400 m) offshore. This is accessible by foot via a *tombolo* (sandbar) when the tide is low, usually from January to April. The island's hiking club organizes guided walks along the *tombolo* via the town's tourism office, when sea and weather conditions permit. The sandbar is also a popular destination for cyclists and ATV riders. While the geological formation is rare and worth seeing and a major highlight of the town, strong ocean currents usually make swimming dangerous in the coves carved into the sediment strip, and hiking on the Ilet can be extremely arduous.

The **Musée du Rhum** is located on the edge of town at Distillerie Saint-James. Tours of the museum feature an overview of rum production in Martinique. Set in a beautiful colonial house on the former Sainte-Marie Sugar Plantation, the museum holds a fine collection of antique machinery, photographs, documents, and a tasting bar.

The **Habitation Fond Saint-Jacques**, 1 mile (1.6 km) north of town, is one of the best preserved estates on Martinique. Self-guided tours include a visit to the renovated chapel, warehouses, kitchen, and ruins of other buildings where Père Jean-Baptiste Labat developed a rum still and oversaw the profitable production of the liquor by Dominican priests in the late 1600s.

🏛 **Musée du Rhum**
Distillerie Saint-James, Le Bourg-Sainte-Marie. **Tel** 596 693 002.
⏰ 9am–5pm Mon–Fri, 9am–1pm Sat. 💳 ♿ 🍴 🛍

⛪ **Habitation Fond Saint-Jacques**
11 rue du Pavé, 97230. **Tel** 596 691 012. ⏰ 9:30am–4:30pm Mon–Fri, 10am–5pm Sat. 💳 with reservations. **www**.fondsaintjacques.com

Le Prêcheur ❻

40 km (25 miles) NW of Fort-de-France. 🏘 2,100. 🚹 Le Syndicat d'Initiative du Prêcheur, Le Bourg, Espace Samboura, Le Prêcheur, 596 529 143. **www**.si-precheur.org

The Caribbean coast at the base of Mont Pelée was the first area of the island to be settled during the 17th century, and the villages of Le Prêcheur and Saint-Pierre became the center of Martinique's thriving sugar and cocoa industries.

Once home to an elite society that included French aristocrats, Le Prêcheur is now a simple fishing village. Just south of town, the coastal road passes steep cliffs known as Tombeau des Caraïbes, where, according to legend, a band of native Caribs jumped to their death to avoid being captured or shamefully defeated by French settlers in the 1600s.

Distillerie Neisson is one of the last producers to grow its own sugarcane, and connoisseurs claim the rum made from this cane is one of the best in the world.

Distillerie Neisson
Domaine Thieubert. **Tel** 596 780 370. ⏰ 8am–5pm Mon–Fri, 8am–noon Sat. **www**.neisson.com

Lithograph of the Mont Pelée eruption by Clement A. Andrieux (1902)

MONT PELÉE ERUPTION 1902

A few days before the 1902 eruption, Mont Pelée emitted large clouds of volcanic ash. Although Saint-Pierre's residents had experienced many natural disasters, including two volcanic explosions, in 1792 and 1851, and frequent earthquakes, they ignored these signs of imminent danger. At 8am on May 8, 1902, Mont Pelée erupted, spewing molten ash over Saint-Pierre city. All but one of the 30,000 residents were killed, the largest number of casualties from a volcanic eruption in the 20th century. The sole survivor, an inmate of the local jail, was rescued 3 days later by French sailors.

Saint-Pierre ❼

Founded in 1635 as the island's first capital, Saint-Pierre was the economic hub of Martinique and a thriving cosmopolitan city when it was devastated by the eruption of Mont Pelée in 1902. The town was rebuilt, and today is a prosperous urban area with modern buildings, shops, and restaurants, all constructed around and into the ruins left by the volcano's fury. The best way to get an overview of the present-day city and the overgrown volcanic remains is to take the Cyparis Express, a mini-train that travels through the narrow, one-way streets, with stops at interesting sites.

VISITORS' CHECKLIST

12 miles (20 km) NW of Fort-de-France. 🚌 ℹ️ *Office Municipal de St. Pierre, Rue Victor-Hugo, 596 783 405.* ⏰ *9am–1pm & 2–5pm Mon–Fri.* 🎫 *Cyparis Express* **Tel** *596 555 092; Oct–Aug: 9:30am–12:30pm, 2:30–4:30pm Mon–Sat.* 🍴 🛍️ 🚻
Musée Vulcanologique *Rue Victor Hugo.* **Tel** *596 781 516.* ⏰ *9am–5pm daily.*

Eglise du Fort
On the morning of the eruption, the fort was filled with residents celebrating Ascension Day and all in attendance died. Overgrown with vegetation, the church's stone remains are still a haunting reminder of that fateful day.

0 metres	50
0 yards	50

Eglise du Fort

Cachot de Cyparis
Built in 1660, these thick prison walls saved inmate Auguste Cyparis, the sole survivor of the catastrophe. The prison was named after him.

Ancien Théatre
The staircases leading to the lobby of the Ancien Théatre still stand as a symbol of the grandeur of the city's 800-seat theater that was built in 1786 to resemble the performance hall in Bordeaux in France.

Musée Vulcanologique
Created by American geologist Franck Perret in the 1930s, the museum displays relics from the disaster – deformed clocks that stopped at 8am, a melted bell, and photographs from when the city was known as the Little Paris of the West Indies.

Outdoor Activities and Specialized Holidays

With more than 100 miles (161 km) of marked trails, hiking is a major highlight on Martinique. Other activities include touring the countryside on horseback or in an all-terrain-vehicle, engaging in watersports, diving along coral reefs or into caves or wrecked ships, and lounging on soft sand in a sheltered cove. Many first-time visitors sign up for a tour of the coast by sail or motorboat, hire a guide for a private land tour, or rent a car for independent exploring. The main tourist areas south of Fort-de-France, between Trois-Ilets and Le Diamant, offer a vast number of options for tours and watersports.

The palm-fringed Anse d'Arlet Beach, western coast of Trois-Ilets

BEACHES

Grande Anse du Diamant, across from Rocher du Diamant on the south shore, is the longest beach on the island with 3 miles (5 km) of soft white sand. Grand Anse d'Arlet, on the western coast of the Trois-Ilets peninsula, is ideal for families. Colorful fishing boats line up on the sand at Anse Noire and Anse Dufour. Grand Anse des Salines, between Sainte-Anne and Pointe d'Enfer on the southern cape, is called the pearl of the Antilles. Wave action picks up at the southern tip of the promontory, where the Atlantic meets the Caribbean, but surfers favor Anse Trabaud and Baie des Anglais, two excellent little beaches. The golden sand at Anse Macabou is almost always deserted, except by land crabs. Among the west coast black-sand beaches, Anse Turin is popular in the Le Carbet area, and Anse Couleuvre, north of Le Prêcheur, offers snorkeling.

DIVING AND SNORKELING

The graveyard of sunken ships off Saint-Pierre interests many experienced divers but Martinique also has caves and tunnels to discover off Rocher du Diamant, and splendid coral gardens near Cap Enragé. Novice divers enjoy shallow-water exploration of coral reefs that are inhabited by an enormous variety of fish. Visitors interested in scuba can take a course given in a hotel pool, then dive with an instructor in the waters near the shore. Among the dive operators that offer bilingual staff, **Espace Plongée** is easily recognized by the orange and blue boat at the marina of Pointe du Bout. Also in the Trois-Ilets tourist area, Laurent and Sophie run **Aliotis Plongée** near Anse Mitan. Diving around Diamond Rock is done best with **Antilles Sub Diamond** or **Okeanos Club**, and Lionel and Françoise Lafont at **Tropicasub** are the people to contact for wreck diving in the bay off Saint-Pierre.

BOATING AND SAILING

One of the largest annual events on Martinique is the Tour des Yoles Rondes, a regatta for traditional canoe-like yawls made of wood and powered by two sails. Locals and visitors turn out to watch the racers maneuver the brilliantly-painted boats around the island from the starting point in Le François.

Charters, both crewed and bareboat, are available from **Autremer Concept** and **Sparkling Charter** at the marina in Le Marin. Full-day, half-day, and multi-day excursions by **A Fleur d'Eau** leave from the marina at Pointe du Bout, across the harbor from Fort-de-France, and include cruises around the coast of Martinique and day trips to St. Lucia. Self-drive motorboat rentals are available at Pointe du Bout from **Turquoise Yachting**.

WATERSPORTS

Many hotels have watersports gear available for registered guests and sports shacks on the beaches rent a variety of equipment. The most popular activities are sea kayaking, Jet Skiing, and windsurfing. Wind conditions are best for surfing of all types on the Atlantic coast and around the southern cape. Kayaking through the lagoons and mangroves is a great eco-adventure, and several outfitters on the Trois-Ilets peninsula offer guided trips. Operators are **Madinina Surf Club, Les Kayaks du Robert, Fun Caraïbes, W.I.N.D Force, Windsurf Club, Alize Fun Dilon, Kayak Nature Evasion**, and **Zagayaks**.

Surfing in the waters of Martinique

For hotels and restaurants on this island see pp388–9 and pp390–91

Wreck-diving off Saint-Pierre

The sea bottom off Saint-Pierre is a graveyard of sunken ships. When Mont Pelée erupted in 1902, at least a dozen ships were in the port and each sank fast to the floor of the deep-water harbor. Only one ship survived the catastrophic

Tiles found in the Teresa Lo Vico

incident. Today, diving to these wrecks is a popular pastime. The wrecks are underwater treasure troves for divers to explore the varieties of colorful fish and corals. There are several tour operators who take visitors to explore these sites.

POPULAR WRECKS

There are at least 10 wrecks resting at varying depths just off the shore. Among these, the ones that attract the most divers are *Roraima*, *Teresa Lo Vico*, and *Raisinier*.

Sea sponges and corals cover the wrecks of sunken ships.

Water scooters are normally used to explore the underwater world. They are available on daily rental basis.

The main hull *of* Raisinier, *a Canadian barge, was overturned by strong oceanic currents. Due to its shallow depth, the 131-ft (40-m) shipwreck is the best dive site for beginners.*

Corals *thrive around the wreck of the* Raisinier, *which has become an ideal habitat for a wide variety of sea flora.*

Tiles and rope *remain stacked on the wrecked* Teresa Lo Vico, *lying 100 ft (30 m) below the surface. Built in 1874, the wooden vessel was carrying building supplies at the time of eruption. Only three crew members survived.*

Roraima *became the best-known shipwreck after it was filmed for television by underwater explorer Jacques Costeau in 1977.*

The engine room *of* Roraima *is still intact after many years. Of its 50 passengers, 35 died when the ship sank with all its cargo.*

Well-marked trails, common in the parks of Martinique

SPORTFISHING

The deep waters surrounding Martinique are a fisherman's paradise. The easiest way to book a fishing trip is through major hotels. Also, the marina offices in Pointe du Bout and Le Marin can suggest operators for fishing charters. Visitors can contact Yves Pélisson at **Centre de Pêche**. Other operators include **Association Coup de Senne**, **Somatras Marina**, **Little Queeny and Maverick Too**, and **Le Marin Pêcheur**.

HIKING AND BIKING

There are more than 100 miles (161 km) of marked trails laid out across the island and an unlimited number of well-worn paths and back roads. Serious hikers welcome the challenge of reaching the Mont Pelée summit or making it through the thick foliage of the rainforest along the north coast. Casual trekkers enjoy shorter walks along nature trails. Visitors can bike or hike the trails that cut through the

Parc Naturel. Official park guides conduct organized outings. Bike rentals are offered at **V.T. Tilt** and at **Aventures Tropicales**.

CANYONING

Guides from the **Bureau de la Randonnée et du Canyoning** and the regional Parc Naturel conduct tours of Martinique's rivers and canyons which include rafting, swimming, and climbing. Itineraries vary from 3-hour excursions to 12-hour technical climbs. One of the most popular circuits is the Gorges de la Falaise, a picturesque gully in the center of the rainforest surrounding Mont Pelée that leads to a waterfall. In the Carbet region, Rivière Mitan and Absalon Falls are favored for their beautiful terrain.

CANOPY TOURS

An exhilarating adventure, canopy tours allow thrill seekers to soar through the treetops, secure in a harness

attached to a zip line, and walk high-wire lines while protected by safety ropes. The main operator is **Mangofil**.

JEEP AND ATV TOURS

Four-wheel-drive vehicles allow visitors to get off the road to explore the island's wildest areas. **Kata Mambo** combines 4WD excursions with catamaran sea adventures. **Evasion Tropicale** has jeep tours of either the southern or northern sections of the island, and **Martinique Quad Explorer** does outback tours by self-drive all-terrain vehicles.

WATER PARKS

Many locals and visitors to Martinique enjoy a day at **Aqualand**, a water park for people from all age groups. Set in 10 acres (4 ha) of lush tropical vegetation, the French-designed park features water slides and a wave pool. A small-scale version of Aqualand is set up for kids at **Maya Beach Club**. Activities here include large trampolines and waterslide toboggans.

GOLF

Designed by Robert Trent Jones Sr and opened in 1976, the **Martinique Golf and Country Club** is a superb course with good landscaping and more than 155 acres (63 ha) of prime land. English-speaking pros offer lessons through the David Leadbetter Golf Academy, and provide assistance with tee times and equipment rental. They have a well-stocked shop as well.

Well-manicured grounds of Martinique Golf and Country Club, Trois-Ilets

For hotels and restaurants on this island see pp388–9 and pp390–91

HORSE-RIDING

Horse-riding along the beach is spectacular, and there is no easier way to see the rainforest. **Black Horse Ranch** offers guided tours and up to 5-day vacation packages. Try a moonlight ride along the ocean with the guides at **Ranch des Caps** on the south coast. Pony rides are suggested for young children without experience.

Horse-riding along the shore, Martinique

TENNIS

Hotels that have at least two tennis courts include Hôtel Carayou and Hotel Bakoua Martinique (*see p389*). The Martinique Golf and Country Club and the **Tennis Club Sainte-Marie** have lighted courts. **La Ligue Régionale de Tennis** and the tourist office in Fort-de-France can also recommend available courts on the island.

DIRECTORY

DIVING AND SNORKELING

Antilles Sub Diamond
Pointe de la Cherry, Le Diamant. *Tel 596 761 065*. www.asdr.fr/

Aliotis Plongée
Anse Marette. *Tel 696 904 025*. http://aliotis.plongee.free.fr/diving_center_martinique.htm

Espace Plongée
Marina Pointe du Bout, Les Trois Ilets. *Tel 596 660 179*. http://espace.plongee.free.fr/

Okeanos Club
Village Pierre & Vacances, Saint-Luce. *Tel 596 625 236*. www.okeanos-club.com/en/presentation.html

Tropicasub
Madi Créoles Resort, Le Carbet. *Tel 696 242 430*. www.tropicasub.com

BOATING AND SAILING

A Fleur d'Eau
Marina de la Pointe du Bout, Trois-Ilets. *Tel 596 660 217*. www.afleurdeau.fr/

Autremer Concept
Tel 596 747 911. www.autremerconcept.com

Sparkling Charter
Tel 596 746 639. www.sparkling-charter.com

Turquoise Yachting
Marina Point du Bout, Trois-Ilets.
Tel 596 661 074. www.turquoise-yachting.com

WATERSPORTS

Alize Fun Dillon
Route de Pérou, Le Marin. *Tel 596 747 158*. www.alizefun.com

Fun Caraïbes
Tel 596 548 834. www.funcaraibes.com

Kayak Nature Evasion
Trois-Ilets. *Tel 596 682 710*. www.kayaknatureevasion.com

Les Kayaks du Robert
Pointe-Savane, Le Robert. *Tel 596 653 389*.

Madinina Surf Club
Tartane. *Tel 596 580 236*. www.madininasurfclub.com

W.I.N.D Force
Pointe-Fort, Le Robert. *Tel 596 655 970*.

Windsurf Club
Hotel Carayou, Pointe-du-Bout, Trois-Ilets. *Tel 596 661 906*.

Zagayaks
Plage de l'Autre-Bord, Caravelle Peninsula, La Trinité. *Tel 596 483 890*.

SPORTFISHING

Association Coup de Senne
Bellefontaine.
Tel 596 551 388.

Centre de Pêche
Port de Plaisance, Le Marin. *Tel 596 762 420*.

Le Marin Pêcheur
Port de Plaisance, Le Marin. *Tel 596 746 754*.

Little Queeny and Maverick Too
Le Diamant.
Tel 596 762 420.

Somatras Marina
Pointe du Bout.
Tel 596 660 774. www.marina3ilets.com

HIKING AND BIKING

Aventures Tropicales
14 Chemin Bois Thibault-Didier, Fort-de-France. *Tel 596 645 849*.

Parc Naturel
Maison du Tourisme Vert, 9 Boulevard du Général-de-Gaulle, Fort-de-France *Tel 596 552 800*.

V.T. Tilt
Pointe du Bout, Trois-Ilets. *Tel 596 660 101*.

CANYONING

Bureau de la Randonnée et du Canyoning
Quartier Jolimont, Morne-Vert.
Tel 596 550 479. www.bureau-rando-martinique.com

CANOPY TOURS

Mangofil
Forêt Rateau, Trois-Ilets. *Tel 596 680 808*.

JEEP AND ATV TOURS

Evasion Tropicale
Mapou, Trois-Rivières, Sainte-Luce.
Tel 696 227 358.

Kata Mambo
Marina Pointe du Bout. *Tel 596 661 183*. www.katamambo.com

Martinique Quad Explorer\Distillerie
Trois-Rivières, Sainte-Luce.X *Tel 696 293 344*. www.mqe.fr

WATER PARKS

Aqualand
Route des Pitons, Carbet. *Tel 596 784 000*.

Maya Beach Club
Plage de l'Hôtel, Anse Caritan, Sainte-Anne. *Tel 596 762 653*.

GOLF

Martinique Golf and Country Club
Quartier Esperance, Trois-Ilets. *Tel 596 683 281*. www.golfmartinique.com

HORSE-RIDING

Black Horse Ranch
La Pagerie, Trois-Ilets. *Tel 596 683 780*.

Ranch des Caps
Cap-Macré, Le Marin. *Tel 596 747 065*. www.ranchdescaps.com

TENNIS

La Ligue Régionale de Tennis
Petit Manoir, Lamentin. *Tel 596 510 800*.

Tennis Club Sainte-Marie
Sainte-Marie.
Tel 596 692 363.

Choosing a Hotel

Martinique has several accommodation options, including beach bungalows, private villas, and friendly family-run inns easily identifiable by the *chez l'habitant* sign. Resorts offer great activities and services, with hotels built around plantation-era ruins. Rates drop by 25–50 percent from mid-April to mid-December, and travel agencies and Internet booking sites provide year-round discounts.

PRICE CATEGORIES
The following price ranges are for a standard double room and taxes per night during the high season.

$ under $100
$$ $100–$200
$$$ $200–$300
$$$$ $300–$400
$$$$$ over $400

MARTINIQUE

An interesting option for accommodations is the fully-furnished and well-equipped rentals known as *gîtes*.

Gîtes de France Martinique
Galerie de la Baie,
30 Rue Ernest Deproge,
Fort-de-France, **Tel** 596 737 474
www.gites972.org.

Le Plein Soleil Resort   Hotel Bakoua Martinique

FORT-DE-FRANCE La Valmenière $$$
Avenue des Arawaks, 97200 **Tel** *596 757 575* **Fax** *596 756 970* **Rooms** *120*

At 3 miles (5 km) from the airport, La Valmenière is ideal for short stays and overnights in transit. Rental cars are available at the front desk. Boasts a pool, hot tub, and roof-top restaurant with great views of the bay. Modern architecture and deluxe furnishings. Rooms have a minibar and daybed. Breakfast included. **www**.karibea.com

---

GROS MORNE Hôtel Résidence-Bungalow Petite Tracée $$
Rue de la Paix, 97213 **Tel** *596 679 002* **Fax** *596 679 003* **Bungalows** *9*

Each little bungalow is a one-bedroom vacation home with a fully-equipped kitchen, living-dining area, modern shower, and patio. The grassy grounds are shaded by mature trees. Guests relax around a small pool, casual bar, and grill. Car rental can be arranged. No English-speaking staff available. **www**.petitetracee.com

---

LE DIAMANT Résidence Mercure Diamant $$
Pointe de la Chery, 97223 **Tel** *596 764 600* **Fax** *596 762 599* **Rooms** *149*

Located about 3 miles (5 km) from Le Diamant, this residence has old-fashioned rooms, but the grounds are lovely. Offers good value. There is no daily maid service, but towels can be exchanged every day. There is also a pool with a waterslide overlooking Diamond Rock. Big breakfast buffet, kitchenette, and balcony. **www**.mercure.com

---

LE FRANÇOIS Frégate Bleue $$
Frégate Est 4, Route de Vauclin (Highway N6), 97220 **Tel** *596 545 466* **Fax** *596 547 848* **Rooms** *7*

This cozy hideaway is perfect for vacationers looking for romance, seclusion, and countryside tranquility. Set on a hill with sea views, each room in the Créole-style house is furnished with antiques and opens on to a private terrace. Breakfast is included and served on the poolside. **www**.fregatebleue.com

---

LE FRANÇOIS Le Plein Soleil Resort $$$
Villa Lagon Sarc, Pointe Thalemont, 97240 **Tel** *596 380 777* **Fax** *596 655 813* **Rooms** *16*

Creole-influenced villas on a hill surrounded by lush gardens have upper level master rooms with air-conditioning and lower level open-air rooms, well-equipped kitchenettes, and a patio/balcony. Guests can rent a car to tour the island. There is an impressive gourmet restaurant *(see p390)*. **www**.pleinsoleil.mq

---

LE FRANÇOIS Le Cap Est Lagoon Resort $$$$$
Domaine de la Prairie, 97240 **Tel** *596 548 080* **Fax** *596 549 600* **Rooms** *50*

Features among the island's top five deluxe resorts and is a member of the prestigious group Relais and Châteaux. Some suites feature a private plunge pool, all have a terrace, king-sized bed, plasma TV, mini-fridge, and espresso maker. Pool, spa, tennis courts, and common areas are elegant and artistically designed. **www**.capest.com

---

LE MARIN Résidence des Iles $$
Quartier Mondésir, 97290 **Tel** *596 740 234* **Fax** *596 749 890* **Rooms** *17*

Set on a hill, Résidence des Iles is only a 10-minute walk from the marina. Basic but clean with patio, kitchenette, and living area. Gorgeous pool and barbecue grills. Air-conditioning only in bedrooms, fans elsewhere. Bikes and cars are available for rent. Breakfast included. **www**.residence-des-iles-martinique.fr

---

LE VAUCLIN Chez Julot $
Rue Gabriel-Péri, 97280 **Tel** *596 744 093* **Fax** *596 744 093* **Rooms** *10*

Julot is on-site to make sure everything runs smoothly at her simple Creole-style hotel and restaurant. Rooms are small but air-conditioned and the bathrooms have showers. Kitchenettes on the terrace are handy for snacks. Some apartments have extra space. There is also a café on-site *(see p390)*. Breakfast is included. **www**.chezjulot.com

---

Key to Symbols *see back cover flap*

SAINTE-ANNE Cap Sud Résidence ❄ [W] $

23 Les Hauts de Beauregard, 97227 ***Tel*** *596 769 903* ***Fax*** *596 769 903* ***Rooms*** *12*

The hotel is a 10-minute walk to Sainte-Anne and a 15-minute walk to the nearest beach. Studios and larger apartments have a terrace with a kitchenette that looks over the pool or gardens. Provides weekly maid service and linen. Rooms are let out for two nights or more. Wi-Fi hotspots available. **www.capsud-hotel.com**

SAINTE-ANNE Domaine de l'Anse Caritan ⛱ 🍴 ❄ 🏊 $$

Route des Caraibes, Anse Caritan, 97227 ***Tel*** *596 769 200* ***Fax*** *596 747 304* ***Rooms*** *228*

This hotel is set on a white-sand beach with watersports. Organized activities and entertainment shows for children and adults are available. Large, active pool area. Rooms have a kitchenette on a covered patio. Bungalows and suites come with extra space. Not a deluxe hotel but offers all basic amenities. **www.anse-caritan.com**

SAINTE-ANNE Club Med Buccaneer's Creek ⛱ ❄ 🏊 [W] $$$$$

Pointe Marin, 97227 ***Tel*** *596 767 272* ***Fax*** *596 765 700* ***Rooms*** *289*

This fabulous resort is set on 55-acres (22-ha) of shaded beachfront. Besides excellent food, there is an impressive spa, top-notch fitness center, tennis courts, infinity pool, and continuous activities and entertainment for all ages. The mid-size rooms have a mini-fridge and flat-screen TV. **www.clubmed.us**

SAINTE-LUCE Pierre & Vacances Village ⛱ ❄ 🏊 ♿ $$

Pointe Philippeau, 97228 ***Tel*** *596 621 262* ***Fax*** *596 621 263* ***Rooms*** *337*

Self-catering apartments with towels, cleaning supplies, maid service, and toiletries available at extra charge. Modern units have double bed, and sofa bed in living area that opens onto a terrace with equipped kitchen. On-site grocery, laundry, café, and kids' club. Ideal for families and budget travelers. **www.pierreetvacances.com**

SAINTE-MARIE Le Domaine de Sainte-Marie ⛱ ❄ [W] $$

Anse Azérot, 97230 ***Tel*** *596 694 040* ***Fax*** *596 690 937* ***Rooms*** *57*

Villas and two-bedroom units are spread out over 30 acres of grounds among mature trees and plants. The large suites have queen beds, a sofa bed in living/dining area, a well-equipped kitchen, and terrace. There is a gift shop and a mini-mart on-site. Bar and tennis courts are also available.

TARTANE Hôtel la Caravelle 🍴 ❄ $$

Route du Château Dubuc, L'Anse l'Etang, 97220 ***Tel*** *596 580 732* ***Fax*** *596 580 790* ***Rooms*** *14*

La Caravelle overlooks the ocean on the Caravelle Peninsula and the beaches and village are only at walking distance but guests can easily rent a car to get around. Spacious two-bedroom and two-bath apartments available. Meals at Mamy Nounou *(see p391)* are priced separately. **www.hotel-la-caravelle-martinique.com**

TRINITÉ Le Domaine Saint Aubin 🍴 ❄ [W] $$$

Petite Rivière Salée, 97220 ***Tel*** *596 693 477* ***Fax*** *596 694 114* ***Rooms*** *30*

This restored colonial plantation house with antique furniture and fabulous gardens has a superb restaurant. Each room has a private bathroom and opens on to a common terrace or private patio. Pool nearby. Trinité is 2 miles (3 km) and the nearest beach is 1 mile (1.6 km) away. Meals at additional cost. **www.ledomainesaintaubin.com**

TROIS-ILETS Hôtel Carayou ⛱ 🍴 ❄ 🏊 ♿ [W] $$

Pointe-du-Bout, 97229 ***Tel*** *596 660 404* ***Fax*** *596 660 057* ***Rooms*** *207*

Families return here year after year for the kids' programs, rooms with daybed and balcony, a huge pool with a waterfall and lots of lounge chairs, and complimentary American-style breakfast buffet. Wi-Fi in lobby, restaurant, spa, and tennis courts. Rooms are basic, but clean and comfortable. Friendly staff. **www.hotel-carayou.com**

TROIS-ILETS Le Bambou ⛱ ❄ 🏊 ♿ $$

Anse-Mitan, 97229 ***Tel*** *596 660 139* ***Fax*** *596 660 505* ***Rooms*** *147*

This is summer camp for families. Individual cabins are rustic with simple furniture and bathroom facilities. Games and entertainment are organized all day and carry on well into the night. Half-board plans including breakfast and dinner are available. Watersports and most activities are accounted for in the basic rates. Good value.

TROIS-ILETS Résidence Le Village Créole ❄ $$

Pointe-du-Bout, 97229 ***Tel*** *596 660 319* ***Fax*** *596 660 706* ***Rooms*** *28*

Located at the edge of Pointe-du-Bout in a village made up of modern Créole-style buildings. Units accommodate two to seven guests and come with equipped kitchens, dining-living area, and one or two bedrooms, with an optional mezzanine. Village includes shops, restaurants, and laundry. **www.village-creole.com**

TROIS-ILETS Hotel Bakoua Martinique 🍴 ⛱ ❄ 🏊 ♿ [W] $$$

Pointe-du-Bout, 97229 ***Tel*** *596 660 202* ***Fax*** *596 660 041* ***Rooms*** *132*

Strives to be the best resort on the island, with remarkable success. Constant updates to rooms and grounds. The main building is set around the ruins of a sugar mill. Includes tennis courts. Freshwater infinity pool seems to merge with sea and secluded beach. A hearty breakfast buffet is also included. **www.mgallery.com**

TROIS-ILETS Club Trois-Ilets ⛱ 🍴 ❄ 🏊 ♿ $$$$

Anse à l'Âne, 97229 ***Tel*** *596 683 167* ***Fax*** *596 683 765* ***Rooms*** *77*

Formerly the Coralia Club, Club Trois-Ilets is family-oriented and all-inclusive. Faces a sandy beach. Rooms are modern and colorful and open onto a small patio. Most guests are French, so the club offers non-stop activities and entertainment geared to French speakers. **www.hotel-club3ilets.com**

Where to Eat & Nightlife

In addition to independent eateries, most hotels and inns have a restaurant open to the public, but call to be sure that space is available for non-guests. The *Ti Gourmet en Martinique* gives details about many places to eat. Although the publication is in French, numbers, restaurant names, and locations are easy to recognize. Call for dinner reservations during high season.

PRICE CATEGORIES
The price ranges are for a two-course meal for one, including tax and service charges and half a bottle of wine.

$ under $10
$$ $10–15
$$$ $15–25
$$$$ $25–35
$$$$$ over $35

RESTAURANTS

Local Cuisines
Meals often begin with Ti Punch, an apéritif made with white rum, sugarcane syrup, and a dash of lemon or lime. The island's exquisite Creole dishes that feature seafood, fresh produce, and spices blended into a gourmet feast inspired by India, Africa, Asia, and France. Other dishes including *foie gras* and *escargots* appear beside *cabri* (young goat) and *accras* (fried cod fritters).

Plein Soleil

La Villa Creole

CARBET Chez les Pecheurs — $$$$
Plage de Grande-Anse, 97221 **Tel** *596 780 572*

Enjoy the catch of the day seated beachside with feet on the sand. Live music most weekends, which draws locals and visitors. The *plat du jour* is a bargain and changes daily, depending on availability of ingredients. It is open daily noon–3pm and 7–11pm and only serves fish. Closed from mid-September to mid-October.

FORT-DE-FRANCE La Cave à Vin — $$$$
118 Rue Victor Hugo, 97200 **Tel** *596 703 302*

Serves southwestern French cuisine and specialties include *foie gras, filet mignon*, fresh fish, and caviar on special occasions. Excellent wine list. Desserts are decadent and include crispy biscuit with cream and raspberry and chocolate cake with sorbet ice cream. Open noon–2pm and 7:30–9:30pm. Closed Sundays and Mondays.

GRAND-RIVIÈRE Chez Tante Arlette — $$$$$
3 Rue Lucy de Fossarieu, 97218 **Tel** *596 557 575*

This casual café is connected with a small hotel. Auntie Arlette and her friendly staff offer traditional island cooking. The home-made Creole sausage is a local favorite and the *marmite du pêcheur* (fisherman's pot) with lobster and three other seafood items is superb. Lunch is served 12:30–3pm. Dinner by reservation only. Fixed price menu.

LAMENTIN Le Torii Sushi — $$$$
Zi La Lézarde, 97232 **Tel** *596 633 441*

This trendy little place is a popular lunch-spot for the business community and a dinner venue for young couples. Japanese dishes are attractively presented. Fish is served sushi style, tempura battered or pan fried. Salads, stir-fry, and other Asian dishes are also served. Lunch on weekdays and dinner Friday to Saturday.

LE FRANÇOIS Plein Soleil — $$$$$
Pointe Thalémont, 97240 **Tel** *596 380 777*

Reservations required at least 24 hours in advance for this chic restaurant located in a colonial house in the Le Plein Soleil Resort *(see p388).* Dine on the terrace facing the sea. Choice of two international meals prepared each day. Special selections for kids under 10. Lunch and dinner daily, closed on Saturday night.

LE VAUCLIN Chez Julot — $$$$
Rue Gabriel-Péri, 97280 **Tel** *596 744 093*

A simple café in a plain hotel *(see p388)* a few steps from the waterfront in the center of town. Excellent Creole specialties including a spicy shrimp in *piquante* (pepper) sauce. Grilled lobster is another good choice, and the daily fixed-price meal is a bargain. Daily lunch and dinner except on Sunday evenings.

MORNE ROUGE La Chaudière — $$$
Quartier Propreté, 97260 **Tel** *596 523 447*

This is a great late-lunch stop when exploring the sites near Mont Pelée or driving the Trace. Award-winning chefs prepare classic Creole dishes with gourmet refinement. Do not miss the dessert. The fixed-price daily special is a bargain and includes fresh fish and seasonal vegetables. It is open daily from 11:30am to 5pm.

SAINTE-ANNE Le Touloulou — $$$$$
Pointe du Marin, 97227 **Tel** *596 767 327*

Follow the locals to this long-time favorite right on the beach. Lunch plates are a bargain. At dinner choose one of the combination seafood meals. Le Touloulou plate includes prawns, clams, lobster, and crab. Ti Loulou is next door offering sandwiches and light meals. Closed Sunday evenings and Mondays.

Key to Symbols *see back cover flap*

SAINTE-MARIE Le Bredas

V 🚗 🍴 $$$$$

Entrée Presqu'île, St. Joseph, 97212 **Tel** *596 576 552*

With a tiled terrace of teak and walnut, this restaurant boasts award-winning chef Jean Charles Bredas. His signature dish is a perfect *mille-feuille* of foie gras and green bananas caramelized with rum and pineapple. Experimental fusion cuisine. Menu is changed every 3 weeks. Food is served on ceramic plates handcrafted by a local potter.

SAINT-PIERRE La Tartine

☰ 🍴 $$$$

Rue Gabriel-Péri, 97250 **Tel** *596 781 839*

Great place for lunch or light dinner. La Tartine means a little piece of bread, and the sandwiches prepared here on a small baguette are delicious. Stuffed crab, sea tartare, and *accras* are available and for dessert, chocolate and coconut treats are great. Open Tuesday–Sunday, noon–2:30pm and 7pm–9:30pm. Closed in October.

TARTANE La Table de Mamy Nounou

🚗 🍴 $$$$

Hôtel la Caravelle, Route du Château-Dubuc, L'Anse l'Etang, 97220 **Tel** *596 580 732*

Member of Euro-toques (exclusive artisan chefs), with great food and French-like dining experience. Reservations required, especially for the candlelit dinners. Savour international dishes with island flavors on the covered terrace with sea views. Daily lunch and dinner. At the Hotel la Caravelle *(see p389)*.

TROIS-ILETS Au Poisson d'Or

V 🚗 🍴 $$$$

Anse Mitan, Pointe du Bout, off D38, 97229 **Tel** *596 660 180*

With an abundance of potted plants at the entrance, this popular place has a lovely setting and reasonable prices. Great selection of dishes featuring fresh fish tweaked with island spices and a splash of wine. Its specialty is a coconut jelly dessert. Lunch and dinner served from Tuesday to Saturday. Only lunch is served on Sundays.

TROIS-ILETS Chez JoJo

🚗 🎵 $$$$

42 Rue du Caret, Anse à l'Âne, 97229 **Tel** *596 683 689*

During tourist season, this place is packed on Friday nights with locals and visitors who know about the live zouk and salsa band. Year-round, open noon–3pm daily, featuring the signature JoJo plate, a selection of Creole favorites. Dinner from 7 to 10pm during high season; music 8pm–2am on Fridays.

TROIS-ILETS La Villa Creole

V 🎵 🍴 $$$$

Anse Mitan, 97229 **Tel** *596 660 553*

Music is as much a part of this legendary open-air garden restaurant as the food. Musician Guy Bruère Dawson entertains on stage. Typical island fare, such as *accras* and grilled red snapper, appear on the menu, along with a few French dishes. Orders are taken noon–2:30pm and 5–10pm Tuesday–Saturday.

TROIS-ILETS Fleur de Sel

🍴 V 🚗 🍴 $$$$$

27 Ave de l'Imperatrice Joséphine, Bourg de Trois-Ilets, 97200 **Tel** *596 684 211*

Reservations are required at this popular restaurant with international, Creole and French cuisine. Specialties include fish tart in coconut milk, smoked fish, *foie gras* with caramelized apples and salted butter, and beef fillet flambéed in green tea. Rare vintage wines. Dinner from Monday to Saturday. Menu changes every three months.

ST. PIERRE Moulin à Cannes

V 🍴 $$$$$

Plantation de la Montagne Pelée, 97250 **Tel** *596 668 047*

Located inside an ancient windmill situated in the midst of fields and overlooking the Caribbean Sea, this restaurant offers great Creole specialties, including lobster and duck breast served over apple chutney with *legumes*, and *aumonière* (exotic fruits with chocolate sauce). Open all week, but only serves lunch.

BARS AND CLUBS

Martinique's active nightlife centers around weekend theme-night dinners held at hotels and restaurants, which usually includes a band or cultural music show. Nightclubs spring to life around midnight with salsa and zouk. A free French-language publication, *Martinique Scoop*, widely available throughout the island, has current information on music shows, festivals, and dancing. Casino Batelière Plaza in Schoelcher and Casino des Trois-Ilets in Pointe du Bout are Martinique's two casinos.

Casino Batelière Plaza

RECOMMENDED PLACES TO GO

Calebasse Cafe
Boulevard Allègre, Le Marin.
(Nightclub, disco, Cuban music.)

Calypso Latino
Les Hauts de Dizac, Le Diamant.
(Salsa and merengue music.)

Casino Batelière Plaza
Rue des Alizés, Schoelcher.
(Open slot machines.)

Casino des Trois-Ilets
Pointe du Bout, Les Trois-Ilets.
(Blue Jack and roulette games.)

Coconuts Club
Rivière Salée 97215. (Live bands
with RnB, zonk, and electronic.)

Karaoke-Café
Pony de Californie, Le Lamentin.
(Chic clientele.)

L'Amphore
Pointe du Bout, Trois-Ilets.
(Nightclub, disco, beach nights.)

Le Milk
20 Blvd Allègre, Fort-de-France.
(Live music and DJ every night.)

Top Night Club
La Trinité.
(Salsa, zonk, dancehall.)

Practical Information

Pleasant most of the year, visitors flock to this beautiful island during summer. Carnival time is busy, so all bookings must be made well in advance if visiting during the festive season. As an overseas province of France, Martinique has excellent infrastructure at par with mainland France and most of the European Union. The standards of service are decent and the island is well-connected with public transport and its friendly people are always eager to help. Shopping is super-lative here and it is also a good wedding destination.

Drummers in their regalia at the Carnival parade

WHEN TO GO

Temperatures vary little from one month to another, but February through June is the driest period, with rain and humidity picking up in July and lingering through to the end of the year. The annual Carnival often begins in January and runs non-stop into late March. Budget trav-elers and students prefer the summer months, when prices are lower and crowds are lighter, but tropical storms regularly pass over the region and sometimes develop into hurricanes. Following the French tradition, some busi-nesses close for several weeks during August and September.

GETTING THERE

Martinique has a modern international airport, Airport Aimé Césaire in Lamentin. Air services change seasonally, but airline companies, including **Delta**, **Air Canada**, and **American Eagle**, offer flights from North America at least weekly during high season. **Air France** has direct flights from Paris and **Air Caraïbes** connects Martinique with several nearby islands. There are no direct flights to Martinique from the UK. The largest ferry companies, with frequent service between Martinique and Guadeloupe, Les Saintes and Marie-Galante, are **Express des Iles** and **Brudey frères**. Martinique's principal port is in Fort-de-France and there is a cruise ship terminal within walking distance of the capital.

DOCUMENTATION

Citizens of countries other than France must present a valid passport to enter Martinique. Citizens of France may show a passport, an official identity card, or a valid French residence permit. In addition, immigration offi-cials may ask to see a return ticket, proof of sufficient funds for the planned stay, and an address where visitors will be staying on the island.

VISITOR INFORMATION

Tourist information kiosks with maps and brochures are found at the airports and near the ferry docks. The **Office de Tourisme** in Fort-de-France and the **Martinique Tourism Authority** offices provide valuable information. Tourism offices are also found in the US, Canada, and UK. Websites run by the official tourism offices have photographs, maps, details about vacation planning, and links to a large number of tourist-oriented businesses. Much of the information is in French.

HEALTH AND SECURITY

Crime is relatively rare on Martinique, with crimes against tourists even more uncommon. However, visitors are advised to take precau-tions, especially against theft from rental cars. Report any crime to the police and request a written report. While tap water in the main towns is potable, avoid drinking tap water in rural areas, and note that the words *eau non potable* mean the water is not drinkable. Medical facilities are modern and conveniently located throughout the island. The main hospital is **Hospital Pierre Zobda Quikman**.

BANKING AND CURRENCY

Most major credit cards are widely accepted, but may not be welcome at small cafés and shops, especially in rural areas. The legal currency is the euro, and other currencies are exchanged at banks in the main towns. Bank hours are Monday to Friday, 8am–4pm. Most major towns have ATMs.

COMMUNICATIONS

The country code is 596. When calling from abroad, dial the access code plus 596 followed by the 9-digit local number.

Aircraft on the runway of the Airport Aimé Césaire, Lamentin

On the island, dial the 9-digit local number, which begins with 596 for landlines and 690 for cell phones. Phone cards, sold at post offices and retail stores, or a major credit card must be inserted into the phones in most public booths to initiate a call. **Orange Caraïbe** provides mobile network on the island. Some hotels have wireless Internet, most large towns have Internet cafés, and Wi-Fi hotspots are scattered around the island.

Souvenir dolls displayed in a street market, Fort-de-France

TRANSPORT

Most large international agencies and many local companies including **AVIS**, **Europcar**, and **Budget Rent-a-Car** rent cars on Martinique. Book well ahead during the high season when rates are higher. Large hotels may have rental cars on site. Agencies either have booths or deliver to the airport. It is advisable to have insurance that covers rentals, especially for theft and damage. Check the vehicle for preexisting damage.

Taxis are abundant at the airports, cruise ship terminals, and ferry docks. Hotels also arrange taxis for guests. Taxis are equipped with meters and legally add a hefty surcharge to fares 8pm–6am and on Sundays and holidays. If the taxi does not have a working meter, a rate and surcharges should be agreed upon beforehand.

SHOPPING

Several street markets located in Fort-de-France offer souvenirs, spices, locally-made food, and Caribbean crafts. The largest market covers a block on Rue Isambert. Shops on Rue Victor Hugo stock French items. Most shops are open Monday to Saturday from 8:30am to 5:30pm. Large shopping malls are on the outskirts of town. **Centre Commercial Le Phare** and **Centre Commercial La Galleria** are popular malls.

Each town has small boutiques filled with island-made goods and imports from France, but do not expect bargains here.

LANGUAGE

French is the official language of Martinique but Creole is also widely spoken. Most residents who work in tourist-related jobs speak many languages, including English.

ELECTRICITY

Martinique uses 220 volts AC, 50 cycles. Most places only have French-style outlets.

TIME

Martinique is on Atlantic Standard Time, 4 hours behind Greenwich Mean Time.

GETTING MARRIED

Getting married in Martinique is complicated for visitors who are not French citizens. Birth certificates, blood test, certificates of good legal status, and proof of single status are needed to obtain a marriage license, which takes about a month. Medical certificates and residency cards need to be presented. All documents must be in French. Having the official rites beforehand, followed by a *faux* ceremony and/or the reception on the island is easier. Contact the Martinique Tourism Authority for details.

DIRECTORY

GETTING THERE

Air Canada
www.aircanada.com

Air Caraïbes
www.aircaraibes.com

Air France
www.airfrance.com

American Eagle
www.aa.com

Brudey frères
Tel 590 900 488.
www.brudey-freres.fr

Delta
www.delta.com

Express des Iles
Tel 596 420 405.
www.express-des-iles.com

VISITOR INFORMATION

Martinique Tourism Authority
Pointe de Jaham, Schoelcher.
Tel 596 616 177.
www.martinique.org

Office de Tourisme
Fort-de-France.
Tel 596 602 773.
www.tourismefdf.com

HEALTH AND SECURITY

Ambulance
Tel 15.

Fire
Tel 18.

Hospital Pierre Zobda Quikman
Fort de France.
Tel 596 552 000.

Police
Tel 17.

COMMUNICATIONS

Orange Caraïbe
www.orangecaraibe.com

TRANSPORT

AVIS
www.avis.com

Budget Rent-a-Car
www.budget-antilles.com

Europcar
www.europcar.com

SHOPPING

Centre Commercial La Galleria
Lamentin.

Centre Commercial Le Phare
Fort-de-France.

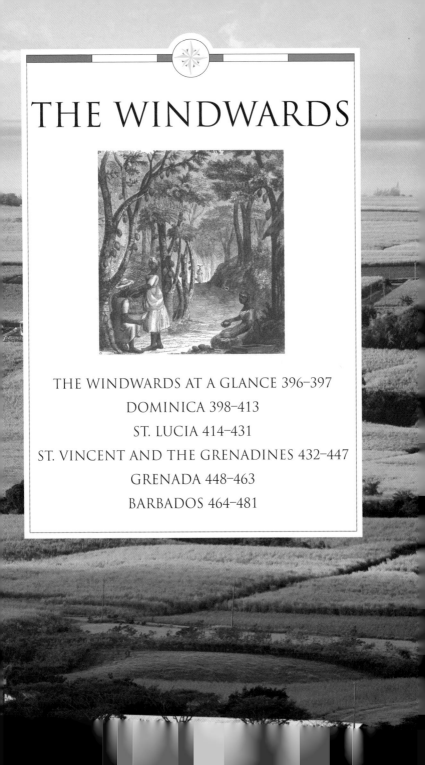

THE WINDWARDS

THE WINDWARDS AT A GLANCE

The Windward Islands, comprising Dominica, St. Lucia, St. Vincent and the Grenadines, Grenada, and Barbados, were once part of the British Windward Islands. Except for Barbados and the Grenadines, the islands are part of a long volcanic arc rising from the eastern edge of the Caribbean Sea, as evidenced by St. Lucia's steaming sulphurous vents. With rainforest-covered mountains, tumbling waterfalls, endless green fields, and a rich diversity of flora and fauna, all are great choices for eco-tourists and adventure seekers.

DOMINICA
(see pp398–413)

Dominica *is popularly known as the nature island. This eco-paradise is covered by tropical forests and abounds in lakes, streams, and waterfalls. Its national parks ensure it remains a great place to explore nature, be it diving or hiking.*

St. Vincent and the Grenadines, *32 islands and cays steeped in old world charm, attract a lot of famous visitors as well as dedicated yachters. The islands' rare flora and fauna are protected by numerous wildlife agencies.*

Grenada's *capital St. George's is one of the most beautiful cities of the Caribbean. The tranquil island with verdant rainforest is well known for its rum and aromatic spices.*

GRENADA
(see pp448–63)

◁ Rolling fields surrounding the parish of St. George, Barbados

LOCATOR MAP

Barbados *boasts a bevy of amazing white sand beaches. The most cosmopolitan of the English islands with a thriving nightlife, this long-time favorite has offerings to fit all budgets as well as natural wonders such as the remarkable Harrison's Cave.*

MARTINIQUE
(The Leewards and French Antilles, see pp376–93)

0 km   50

0 miles   50

ST. LUCIA
(see pp414–31)

T. VINCENT AND HE GRENADINES
(see pp432–47)

BARBADOS
(see pp464–81)

St. Lucia's *most famous landmarks, the Pitons, leave no doubt of the island's volcanic origins. Lushly forested, it is also blessed with unspoilt beaches and seas teeming with tropical fish, along with top-of-the-line resorts, great cuisine, and a renowned jazz festival.*

Exploring Dominica

Dominica is a treasure island of nature which has remained largely undisturbed for thousands of years. Most of the 72,000 islanders live in and around the capital Roseau, which leaves much of the rest of the island unpopulated and an eco-paradise. Tropical forests, such as Cabrits National Park, cover two-thirds of the island's spectacular mountain interior and contain more than 1,200 species of plants and 160 species of birds. There are great unspoilt beaches and reefs, and a growing number of national parks to ensure that Dominica's reputation as the nature island of the Caribbean is protected for future generations.

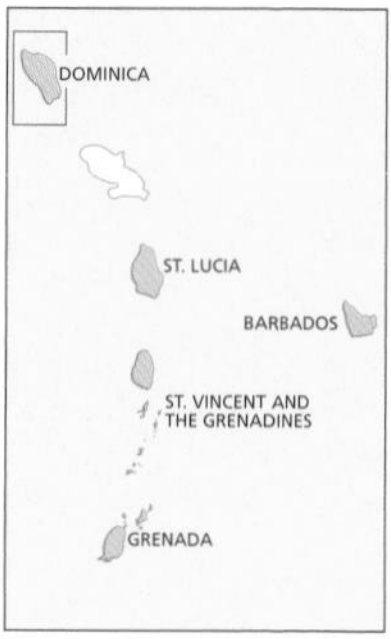

SIGHTS AT A GLANCE

Cabrits National Park ❾
Carib Territory ❼
Emerald Pool and Falls ❻
Massacre Village ❺
Morne Diablotin National Park ❽
Morne Trois Pitons National Park p401 ❹
Roseau ❶
Soufrière ❸
Trafalgar Falls ❷

Hotels and Resorts
Beau Rive Hotel ⑦
Calibishie Lodges ④
Carib Territory Guest House ⑥
Castle Comfort hotels ⑫
Crescent Moon Cabins ⑨
Exotica Cottages ⑪
Marigot hotels ⑤
Papillote ⑭
Picard Beach Cottage Resort ③
Rainforest Shangri-La ⑬
Rosalie Forest Eco Lodge ⑧
Roseau hotels ①
Sunset Bay Club & Dive Centre ②
Zandoli's Inn ⑩

SEE ALSO

• ***Where to Stay*** pp408–9
• ***Where to Eat & Nightlife*** pp410–11

0 km 5
0 miles 5

GETTING AROUND

Getting around Dominica is fun and hiring a car allows visitors to fully explore the island. Most of the roads are paved and much of the island is now accessible by car even if the last leg of the journey may have to be made on foot – to the start of a hiking trail or to a deserted beach. Heavy rains can cause sudden landslides so watch out for potholes. If lost, it is best to ask one of the locals for directions. Buses are also available everywhere and ply dawn to dusk.

KEY

- Major road
- Minor road
- Peak

Boats moored along the Indian River, Portsmouth

For additional map symbols *see back flap*

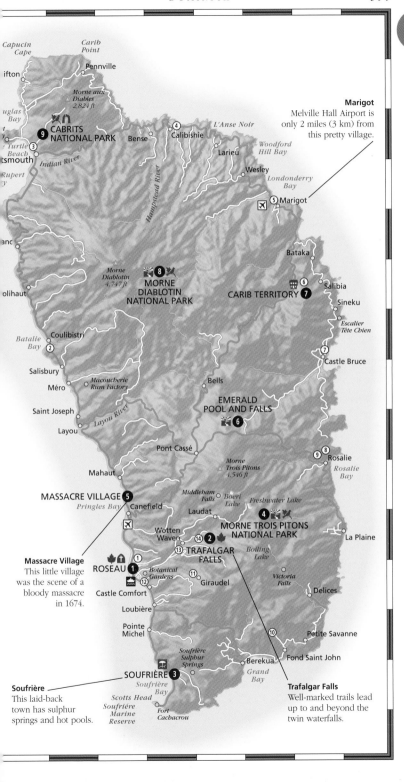

Capucin Cape

Carib Point

Pennville

...ifton

Morne aux Diables 2,824 ft

CABRITS NATIONAL PARK ⑨

...uglas Bay

...y

..e Turtle Beach

...tsmouth ③

Rupert ...y

Indian River

Bense

Calibishie ④

L'Anse Noir

Larieu

Woodford Hill Bay

Wesley

Londonderry Bay

Marigot
Melville Hall Airport is only 2 miles (3 km) from this pretty village.

Marigot ⑤

Batali

Morne Diablotin 4,747 ft

MORNE DIABLOTIN NATIONAL PARK ⑧

...anc

...olihaut

Batalie Bay

Coulibistri ②

Salisbury

Méro

Saint Joseph

Layou

Macoucherie Rum Factory

Layou River

Bells

Pont Cassé

Mahaut

EMERALD POOL AND FALLS ⑥

Batàka

CARIB TERRITORY ⑦ ⑥

Salibia

Sineku

Escalier Tête Chien

Castle Bruce ⑦

Morne Trois Pitons 4,546 ft

Rosalie ⑧ ⑨

Rosalie Bay

MASSACRE VILLAGE ⑤

Pringles Bay

Canefield

Middleham Falls

Boeri Lake

Laudat

Freshwater Lake

MORNE TROIS PITONS NATIONAL PARK ④

Wotten Waven

TRAFALGAR FALLS ⑬ ⑭ ②

Bolling Lake

La Plaine

Massacre Village
This little village was the scene of a bloody massacre in 1674.

ROSEAU ① ①

Botanical Gardens ⑫

Castle Comfort

Giraudel ⑪

Victoria Falls

Delices

Loubière

Pointe Michel

Soufrière Sulphur Springs

⑩

Petite Savanne

Fond Saint John

Soufrière
This laid-back town has sulphur springs and hot pools.

SOUFRIÈRE ③

Soufrière Bay

Scotts Head

Soufrière Marine Reserve

Berekua

Grand Bay

Fort Cachacrou

Trafalgar Falls
Well-marked trails lead up to and beyond the twin waterfalls.

Colorful souvenir dolls in Old Market Square, Roseau

Roseau ❶

36 miles (58 km) SW of Melville Hall Airport. 🏙 *15,000.* ✈ 🚌 ⛴
ℹ *First Floor, Financial Center, 767 448 2045.* 🛍 *daily.* 🎭 *Carnival (Feb) and Independence (Nov 3).*

The capital, Roseau, is a busy, bustling, colorful, and noisy town during the day and very quiet at night. The town is small enough to be easily explored on foot.

The oldest part of town is around Old Market Square, formerly the original slave market, and has several interesting old buildings and many specialty craft stores. Also near the Old Market Square is the Dominica Museum which has a small collection of artifacts tracing the island's history. The newer part, along the southern banks of the Roseau River, has offices, shops, and bazaars where goods of all kinds spill out onto the sidewalks. The New Market on Bay Front is best visited early in the morning when it is at its busiest and liveliest.

Also worth visiting is the **Roman Catholic Cathedral of Our Lady of Fair Haven**, built of volcanic stones gathered from the banks of the river. Its construction started in 1841 but the building was not completed until 1916 when the west steeple was added. The **Botanical Gardens**, on the site of an old sugar planta-tion, cover 40 acres (16 ha), and comprise the largest open space in the city. Freelance guides are available at the

entrance. However, visitors should agree on a price with the guide before the tour starts.

🏛 **Roman Catholic Cathedral of Our Lady of Fair Haven**
Virgin Lane. 🕐 *dawn to dusk.*

🌺 **Botanical Gardens**
Bath Road, Morne Bruce. 🕐 *7am–7pm daily.* 🖥 www.da-academy.org/dagardens.html

Trafalgar Falls ❷

5 miles (8 km) E of Roseau. 🚌 🚗
🕐 *daily.* 📷 🔵 🚻

Trafalgar Falls are the easiest to reach of the island's many waterfalls. They are a short drive from Roseau through Ford Cani to the start of the trail and then a gentle 15-minute walk along a well-marked trail, although the rocks can sometimes be slippery. There are two falls cascading down a gorge into pools littered with huge black rocks and surrounded by lush

vegetation. The larger of the falls, on the left, is known as "father" and the other as "mother". If visitors scramble up the rocks to the left of "father", there is a hot pool to relax in. Close to the falls is the **Papillote Wilderness Retreat and Nature Sanctuary**. The small eco-resort *(see p409)* is set in magnificent tropical gardens with many rare orchids and has its own mineral pools, natural hot springs, and waterfalls. There are long stretches of beautiful hiking trails and at the end of the day visitors can dine on the terrace of the retreat's delightful restaurant.

🌺 **Papillote Wilderness Retreat and Nature Sanctuary**
Papillote Wilderness Retreat, Roseau. **Tel** *767 448 2287.* 🕐 *daily.* 🍴 🔵 🚻 www.papillote.dm

Soufrière ❸

7 miles (11 km) S of Roseau.
🏙 *1,500.* 🚌

Soufrière is a small village noted for its palm-fringed beach, fishing boats, and waterside church with its murals of village life. It was named by early French settlers after the sulphur which belches out from the ground nearby. Visitors can walk up to the sulphur springs and hot pools along the Soufrière river valley through huge stands of towering bamboo. There are a number of small distilleries in the area producing bay oil for the perfume industry.

Trafalgar Falls amid lush vegetation

For hotels and restaurants on this island see pp408–9 and pp410–11

Morne Trois Pitons National Park 4

This national park dominates the southern half of the island and can be accessed by several roads running inland from the coast. The park is named after the mountain which has three peaks, the highest of which is 4,546 ft (1,385 m). In 1975, this 17,000 acre (6,800 ha) park was the first to be designated a nature reserve in the Caribbean and it contains many of Dominica's most spectacular attractions including the Titou Gorge, Boeri and Freshwater Lakes, Boiling Lake, and the Middleham Falls just to the northeast of Laudat.

VISITORS' CHECKLIST

8 miles (13 km) E of Roseau. 🚌
🚲 🛈 ℹ️ *Dominica Forestry and Wildlife Division, 767 266 3817.*
🍴 ⬜ **Note:** *guided walking tours are available and guides are advisable for most hikes except the easiest.*

0 km   2

0 miles   2

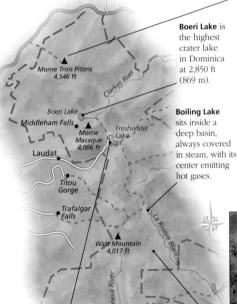

Boeri Lake is the highest crater lake in Dominica at 2,850 ft (869 m).

Boiling Lake sits inside a deep basin, always covered in steam, with its center emitting hot gases.

Morne Trois Pitons 4,546 ft

Clarkes River

Boeri Lake
Middleham Falls
Morne Macaque 4,006 ft
Freshwater Lake
Laudat
Titou Gorge
Trafalgar Falls
Watt Mountain 4,017 ft
La Riviere Blanche
Geneva River

Morne Trois Pitons Peak
A UNESCO-designated World Heritage site and Dominica's second highest mountain, it affords great views of the island.

Valley of Desolation
Hot springs and bubbling mud pools are features of the volcanic land-scape in this valley. Vegetation is sparse because of the sulphur-laden gas from more than 50 vents.

KEY

▲ Peak

▬ Major road

═ Minor road

- - Trail

- - Park boundary

Freshwater Lake
The largest lake in Dominica is located 2,500 ft (762 m) above sea level and supports a wealth of wildlife. According to legend, a giant serpent lurks under its surface.

Massacre Village

4 miles (6 km) N of Roseau. 🚌

Just north of the Canefield
Airport lies Massacre Village.
The little village was the
scene of one of the bloodiest
massacres in the country's
history and hence has a
special place in island lore.
Sir Thomas Warner, governor
of St. Kitts, had a son from a
Carib woman and another
son, Philip, with his English
wife. When the governor
died, the Carib son had no
one to protect him so he
fled to Dominica and became
a powerful chief.

In 1674 Philip was chosen
by the new governor to lead
a military force to Dominica
to quell the Caribs who were
trying to keep Dominica for
themselves. According to
legend, the two half-brothers
met for a feast that Philip
had arranged on board his
ship. But Philip stabbed his
half-brother to death and
his troops then massacred
the remaining Caribs. Shortly
after, the French gave the
village its name – presumably
to embarrass the English.
Later, Jean Rhys set part of
her famous novel *Wild
Sargasso Sea* (1965) in this
small village.

Indigenous souvenirs made by the Caribs on display, Carib Territory

Emerald Pool and Falls ❻

8 miles (14 km) NE of Roseau.
🚌 📷 📖

Located mid-way between
Canefield and Castle Bruce,
Emerald Pool and Falls are
one of the most visited sites
on the island. It is a 5- to 10-
minute walk through wood-
land from the road about 3
miles (5 km) northeast from
Pont Cassé. The pool is a
grotto with its own waterfall
and surrounded by tropical
plants, flowers, and ferns.
Notable are the gommier trees
and the mont blanc trees along
the trail with their buttress

roots, the many varieties of
orchid, giant epiphytes, and
anthuriums. The thick canopy
does not allow too many
ground-hugging plants to
flourish. The rich birdlife
includes hummingbirds, jaco
parrots, and the elusive mountain warbler. A short section
of the trail is paved with slabs
of rocks laid by the Caribs
centuries ago. The pool does
get crowded at times and a
morning visit is best.

Carib Territory ❼

20 miles (32 km) NE of Roseau.
🚌 📷 *guides from Kalinago Barana
Aute.*

Carib Territory occupies 3,700
acres (1,480 ha) with an extensive coastline and agricultural
land behind. The land was
given back by Queen Victoria
of England to the descendants
of the island's original inhabitants in 1903. Today, the
Caribs engage in mostly
agriculture and fishing, still
making their canoes by hand.
They are also expert potters
and weavers – traditions that
have been passed down for
centuries – and their baskets
are so tightly woven they are
watertight. Traditional music,
dance, and herbal medicine
are still practiced here. There
are more than 16 arts and
crafts shops in the territory
selling various handicrafts
made by the locals. Experience the heritage of the
Kalinago people at the Carib
cultural village – **Kalinago
Barana Aute**. It has traditional
buildings by Crayfish River.

Visitors enjoying themselves at the Emerald Pool and Falls

Morne Diablotin National Park ❽

14 miles (23 km) N of Roseau.

Fort Shirley's cannons looking out toward the sea, Cabrits National Park

The Morne Diablotin National Park is home to the "Little Devil" Mountain, Dominica's highest peak at 4,747 ft (1,447 m) and covers 34 sq miles (88 sq km) of oceanic rainforest, including the area known as Syndicate, which is home to the jaco and rare sisserou parrot. Morne Diablotin is not named for the devil but for the devilish call of the black-capped petrel that used to breed on the higher slopes of the mountain. The park is part of the vast Northern Forest Reserve and teems with birdlife and hundreds of species of towering trees, plants, and exotic flowers.

Visitors need to allow themselves six to seven hours to climb the mountain, have a picnic lunch at the top and descend after that. The trail starts at a height of about 1,700 ft (518 m) and gets progressively steeper and can be wet in places. The Syndicate Nature Trail, on the edge of the park, is much easier and ideal for the less adventurous. It takes about 30 minutes but it is best to allow for more time in order to fully enjoy everything there is to see along the way.

A short distance away, the trail runs through a section of forest that contains most of the avian species to be found on the island. There are three lookout points along the trail.

Basket weaver at work in Carib Territory

CARIBS AND MAROONS ON DOMINICA

The Caribs were warlike Indians who migrated north from South America in about AD 1000 and settled the islands, ousting the peaceful Arawaks (Amerindians) who had arrived 1,000 years earlier. Their war canoes, holding more than 100 men, were fast enough to catch a sailing ship. The Caribs built villages and cleared land to farm. They were skilled potters too. About 2,200 Caribs, direct descendants of those early settlers, still live on the island which they call Waitikubuli, which means "tall is her body". In the late 18th century, Dominica became the home for large numbers of slaves who had managed to escape from surrounding islands. They took refuge in the heavily forested, mountainous terrain and were known as Maroons. They developed a system of inland trails that allowed them to travel quickly – many are still used today. They raided settlements, encouraged slaves on the island to join them and fought a running guerrilla war against the British troops until 1814 when they were finally defeated and their leaders executed. After Emancipation in 1848, however, the island again became a refuge for slaves escaping from the surrounding French islands where slavery was still practiced. They were allowed to stay and farm small plots of land and fish.

Cabrits National Park ❾

20 miles (32 km) N of Roseau.

Cabrits National Park covers 1,313 acres (525 ha) of upland and 1,053 acres (421 ha) of the surrounding underwater park, Cabrits Marine Reserve. The site contains the ruins of the 18th-century **Fort Shirley**, the volcanic peaks of East and West Cabrits, tropical forest, the largest swamp on the island, sandy beaches, and coral reefs just offshore to the north. *Cabri* is a French word for young goat. The place got its name from the practice of French sailors to leave goats on the peninsula so that they would have fresh meat when they returned.

Fort Shirley and the garrison was largely built by the British but the French added to it during their years of occupation. Altogether there were more than 50 major buildings although many of them were covered by vegetation after the fort had been abandoned. At its height, the fort had seven gun batteries. Today, cruise ships dock at the pier in Prince Rupert's Bay to visit the park. There are fabulous views from Fort Shirley across the bay and inland to the mountains.

Signage, Cabrits National Park

Outdoor Activities and Specialized Holidays

Dominica, with its fabulous beaches and vast and unexplored wilderness, has everything a visitor could dream of in a tropical island. The beaches are fringed with gently swaying palms overlooking the warm and calm turquoise seas. Many beaches consist of fine volcanic sand which varies from black to grey, while there are golden sand beaches on the northeast coast beyond Melville Hall. The island's flora and fauna is best viewed on guided boat tours or on aerial trams that cross over endless rainforests. Many tour operators take visitors to see the fascinating marine life on the island.

An aerial tram passing through the lush rainforest

BEACHES

The best beaches for swimming are on the sheltered western coast, although there are many fine, unspoilt beaches to be discovered on the north coast. Some pretty beaches to visit are located around Portsmouth, especially Purple Turtle Beach, and near Calibishie, L'Anse Noir and Woodford Hill Bay in the north and northeast of Dominica. On the east coast, beaches are long but usually have choppier seas, making them great places for surfing and windsurfing.

INDIAN RIVER BOAT TRIPS

A trip up the Indian River is memorable in more ways than one. It allows visitors to see many different island habitats and view the flora and fauna up close. Visitors can negotiate the price of the trip at the jetty in Portsmouth or by the bridge at the mouth of the estuary. It is best to take a row boat rather than one with an outboard motor, as the noise scares off the wildlife. The journey takes visitors through swamps and reed beds teeming with fish, crabs, and birdlife. Look out for iguanas basking under the sun on the branch of a tree.

The boatman-guides give running and often very humorous commentaries as the boat meanders upriver. The boats stop at a ramshackle river bar, where they serve a very good coconut punch, before the return trip. If time permits, it is also worth going for a short walk inland through fields of banana, plantain, and pumpkin to the edge of a large marsh which is home to thousands of birds.

CANOPY TOURS

Visitors can soar over the treetops and get a panoramic view of Dominica's plush green rainforests in their full splendor in an aerial tram suspended from cables. **Rainforest Aerial Trams** takes visitors through the Rainforest Sky Ride, with expert guides who talk about the trees, plants, birds, bats, and many other species of animals. The tram leaves from Laudat and it is advisable to check before setting out to ensure the tram is running that day. The service often runs only when a cruise ship is in port.

Boats moored at Scotts Head, where the Atlantic meets the Caribbean

For hotels and restaurants on this island see pp408–9 and pp410–11

DIVING AND WATERSPORTS

Dominica offers great diving with its warm, clear waters and reefs teeming with marine life. Best dive areas are around Cabrits National Park and Cabrits Marine Reserve *(see p403)*, Douglas Bay on the northwest coast, and around Scott's Head in the Soufrière Marine Reserve on the southwestern tip of the island. All dive sites have permanent moorings.

A great variety of watersports ranging from yachting, parasailing, and snorkeling to windsurfing are on offer in Dominica. A day's cruise can be arranged around the island or a yacht can be hired with a crew to spend several days touring the islands.

Most dive operators cater not only to divers but also offer other watersports. The main ones are **Anchorage Dive Center**, which includes whale-watching, **Cabrits Dive Center**, and **Dive Dominica**. **Nature Island Dive** also organizes adventure activities. **Al Dive and Watersports** has interesting packages that include dives and personal guides for surfing lovers.

Apart from these activities, every year Dominica holds Dive Fest. It is an annual scuba diving event hosted by the Dominica Watersports Association, to educate the islanders and visitors about the need to protect the marine environment.

WHALE-WATCHING

Dominica is often called the whale-watching capital of the Caribbean because so many species of whale can be seen year round, although the peak season is between November and June. The west coast is the best place to spot them and most whales and dolphins congregate in the warm waters offshore to feed and breed during the peak season. The most commonly encountered ones are sperm whales; during winter, migrating humpback whales also make an appearance.

Visitors going out for a dive with the help of a guide

Visitors can spot pilot, pygmy, false-killer, and melon-headed whales as well as Atlantic spinner dolphin and spotted dolphin. Altogether 22 species have been recorded. Apart from Anchorage Dive Center, which runs boat tours for whale-watching, other operators are **Antours**, **Dominica Tours**, and **Hibiscus Eco-Tours**.

DEEP-SEA FISHING

Fishing is an island pursuit and Dominicans will fish for hours from harbor walls or jetties. Operators such as **Island Style Fishing Fortune** and Dive Dominica organize deep-sea and game fishing, which is mostly for blue marlin and tuna that can weigh up to 1,000 lbs (450 kg), wahoo, and the fighting sailfish. Snapper, grouper, bonito, dorado, and barracuda can all be caught closer to the shore.

Surfer enjoying the waves of a Dominica beach

Hiking in Dominica

A lobster claw

The best way to see Dominica is on foot, along one of the many hiking trails. In fact, hiking is the only way to reach some of the island's hidden treasures – emerald pools, cascading waterfalls, and bubbling lakes. The island's best hiking trails are found in the magnificent Morne Trois Pitons National Park *(see p401)*. The hikes run from the less-strenuous ones to the spectacular Trafalgar Falls to the more arduous climbs to Boiling Lake. Some trails require an experienced guide's assistance and a local guide will ensure that hikers get much more out of their trip.

The views from Morne Anglais hike

EASY LEVEL

Many of the hiking trails are designated easy, which means they are of short duration and can be tackled by most people. Trails to Emerald Pool and Trafalgar Falls can be very busy on days when cruise ships are in port. The earlier visitors set out on a hike, the greater are their chances of spotting wildlife.

Emerald Pool *is a well signposted, family-friendly 10-minute hike which allows visitors to explore the lush vegetation of the tropical rainforest and wildlife on the way to the pool. Those who bring swimwear can also take a dip in the very cool water.*

Trafalgar Falls *is one of Dominica's most popular natural attractions. The twin falls are only a short hike from the visitors' center just outside Trafalgar. Hikers can swim in the pool below the smaller waterfall to cool off.*

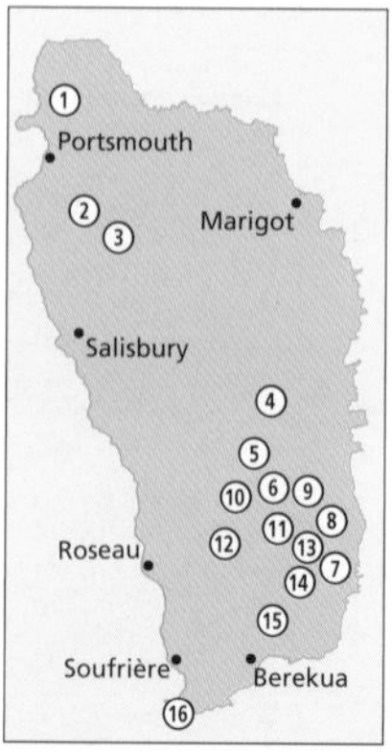

LOCATION OF TRAILS

Boeri Lake 6
Boiling Lake 13
Cabrits 1
Emerald Pool 4
Freshwater Lake 9
Glassy 7
Middleham Falls 10
Morne Anglais 15
Morne Diablotin 3
Morne Trois Pitons 5
Sari Sari Falls 8
Scotts Head 16
Syndicate 2
Titou Gorge 11
Trafalgar Falls 12
Victoria Falls 14

Titou Gorge *can be reached by a short hike and the trail passes through a series of pools, surrounded by solidified lava formations and a canopy of trees. A hot spring, just outside the entrance of the gorge, is ideal for swimming.*

TOUR COMPANIES

Antours
Tel 767 440 5390.
www.antours.dm
Dominica Tours
Tel 767 448 2638.
www.anchoragehotel.dm
Escape Tours
Tel 767 317 0490.
www.canyonspeleo.com
Impression Tours
Tel 767 225 1353.
www.impressiontours.com
Wacky Rollers
www.wackyrollers.com

MODERATE LEVEL

Moderate level walks take longer to hike and involve more difficult terrain that may require some scrambling. It is best to begin the Middleham Falls hike from Laudat. The initial hike is a little steep but the path levels out before descending to the falls.

Middleham Falls *is one of Dominica's highest waterfalls, it takes about an hour to hike through the beautiful, pristine rainforest to reach these high-altitude falls. The forest is home to numerous bird species.*

DIFFICULT LEVEL

There are strenuous but exhilarating hikes for experienced hikers. It takes at least 6 hours for the roundtrip to Boiling Lake and the Valley of Desolation, and about the same time to scramble up to the summit of Morne Diablotin and back.

Sisserou Parrot *is found only on the island. Dominica's national bird is a large, shy creature that can be spotted in the dense rainforests, especially at higher elevations.*

Syndicate *starts at the Syndicate Visitors' Center and the walk passes through spectacular scenery. It takes about 2 hours and follows the gorge of the Picard River, which runs into the sea at Portsmouth. Hikers can arrange a pick-up, if they do not want to hike back.*

Boiling Lake *is the world's second-largest actively boiling lake and is enveloped in a vaporous cloud. The lake seems to disappear as gases fill the center of the crater.*

Choosing a Hotel

Dominica has a wide range of accommodations to suit all tastes and pockets, from a few top-class, though comparatively inexpensive, hotels to delightful guesthouses and self-catering apartments. Many new hotels and resorts have taken special care to make skilful use of natural materials which blend with their unspoiled surroundings. There are also holiday villas, and beach cottages available for rent.

PRICE CATEGORIES
The following price ranges are for a standard double room per night and all taxes included.

(S) under $100
(S)(S) $100–$200
(S)(S)(S) $200–$300
(S)(S)(S)(S) $300–$400
(S)(S)(S)(S)(S) over $400

DOMINICA

Villas and condos of Dominica
Dominica is proud of its reputation as an eco-island and boasts a growing number of eco-resorts. However, these can run the gamut from basic and primitive to pampered luxury so it is advisable to first check what is on offer. Almost all offer total seclusion in beautiful, tropical surroundings and most are genuinely eco-friendly, using solar panels or wind generators to provide electricity, drawing water from their own springs and wells, recycling, and growing their own organic crops.

Rainforest Shangri-La

Fort Young Hotel

BATALIE BAY Sunset Bay Club and Dive Centre   (S)(S)(S)
Tel 767 446 6522 *Fax* 767 446 6523 *Rooms* 13

Located on the west coast, the cozy, great-value Sunset Bay Club and Dive Centre makes a great base for exploring the region. It has its own dive center as well as a sauna. The gardens are delightful. B&B facility is available for those who prefer it. The hotel has a restaurant *(see p410)* as well as a bar. **www.sunsetbayclub.com**

CALIBISHIE Calibishie Lodges   (S)(S)
Main Road **Tel** 767 445 8537 **Fax** 767 445 8074 **Rooms** 6

Surrounded by a working plantation, Calibishie Lodges offers both lodges and apartments, all built in typical Caribbean style and all with sea views. It makes a great base for touring and a wide range of adventure packages are available. The restaurant menu varies from day to day. **www.calibishie-lodges.com**

CARIB TERRITORY Carib Territory Guest House   (S)
Tel/Fax 767 445 7256 *Rooms* 8

Located in the heart of Carib Territory, this small, friendly guesthouse offers excellent guided tours to the nearby forest reserves and national parks. The home-made Carib and Creole dinners are delicious. Carib Territory Guest House offers a great opportunity to discover what real island life is like. **www.caribterritory.wordpress.com**

CASTLE BRUCE Beau Rive Hotel   (S)(S)
Tel 767 445 8992 *Fax* 767 445 8992 *Rooms* 8

Tucked away on a hillside overlooking the Atlantic Ocean, the secluded Beau Rive Hotel is set amidst large, tropical gardens with more than 170 fruit and flowering trees. Solar energy heats the water and powers some of the lighting. All rooms have ocean views. Children below 16 not permitted. Lunch is not served. **www.beaurive.com**

CASTLE COMFORT Castle Comfort Dive Lodge   (S)
Tel 767 448 2188 *Fax* 767 448 6088 *Rooms* 15

A small family-owned and run guesthouse just south of Roseau, Castle Comfort Dive Lodge has a good-value restaurant and bar. It offers great-value honeymoon and dive packages as well as whale-watching, tours, and hikes. Guests can dive straight off the lodge's private dock. **www.theevergreenhotel.com**

CASTLE COMFORT Evergreen   (S)(S)
Tel 767 448 3288 *Fax* 767 448 6800 *Rooms* 16

A charming, family-run, seafront inn, Evergreen has comfortable and good-value rooms and a secluded honeymoon hut in the gardens. It offers a wide range of good-value packages and tours, including whale-watching and horseback riding; there is also a dive center next door. Restaurant on-site. **www.evergreenhoteldominica.com**

GIRAUDEL Exotica Cottages   (S)(S)
Tel 767 448 8839 *Rooms* 8

Built of local wood and stone, Exotica Cottages offers very comfortable cottages featuring typical Caribbean architecture such as high-pitched, multisided roofs, wide verandas, and vented ceilings. Each cottage is named after the native Caribbean tree planted outside its door. The gardens are lovely. **www.exotica-cottages.com**

MARIGOT Hibiscus Valley Inn   (S)
Tel 767 445 8195 *Fax* 767 445 8195 *Rooms* 10

The Swedish-owned eco-guesthouse Hibiscus Valley Inn has 3 "nature" bungalows as well as 2 semi-deluxe rooms with air-conditioning and cable TV. It offers trips and excursions including 2-day hikes into the rainforest. It uses solar cells for electricity, provides fresh spring water, and produces its own organic crops. **www.hibiscusvalley.com**

Key to Symbols *see back cover flap*

MARIGOT Silks
🍴 W 📋 $$$

Hatton Garden **Tel** *767 445 8846* **Fax** *767 445 8049* **Rooms** *9*

This relaxing, luxury boutique hotel is built in the style of a 17th-century mansion. Adding Zen design has enhanced the tranquility of its location amidst stunning gardens between two rivers. The restaurant relies heavily on its kitchen garden and local produce. Spa and restaurant on-site. **www.silkshotel.com**

PORTSMOUTH Picard Beach Cottage Resort
🏨 🍴 $$$

Tel *767 445 5131* **Fax** *767 445 5599* **Rooms** *18*

Set at the foot of Morne Diablotin, the Picard Beach Cottage Resort is spread across tropical gardens along Dominica's longest beach. It offers self-contained tropical hardwood cottages built in 18th-century Dominican style. Wade out from the beach to dive the reefs and then enjoy the Wellness Spa. **www.avirtualdominica.com/picard.htm**

RIVIERE LA CROIX Crescent Moon Cabins
🍴 W $$

Tel *767 449 3449* **Fax** *767 449 3449* **Rooms** *4*

On the foothills of Morne Trois Pitons National Park, the comfortable Crescent Moon Cabins make an ideal base for hiking and exploring. The cabins are built on the site of a former hotel and have beautiful gardens. The restaurant uses home-grown organic produce. Closed from July to October. **www.crescentmooncabins.com**

ROSALIE Rosalie Forest Eco Lodge
🍴 W $

Tel *767 446 1886* **Rooms** *8*

The small, secluded award-winning Rosalie Forest Eco Lodge is set in the rainforest and features bamboo tree houses, natural Carib forest cabins, isolated jungle tents, and dormitories to suit all tastes and pockets. The Sustainable Living Education Center runs renewable energy workshops. **www.rosalieforest.com**

ROSEAU Garraway Hotel
🍴 W $

Bay Front **Tel** *767 449 8800* **Fax** *767 449 8807* **Rooms** *31*

The double room and suite Garraway Hotel is on Roseau's bayfront and a short walk from the city center shops, restaurants, and historic sites. The hotel is run by descendants of James Garraway, a Scottish planter who settled in Dominica in the 1800s. The hotel has a good restaurant and bar. **www.garrawayhotel.com**

ROSEAU Roseau Valley Hotel
🍴 W $

Copt Hall **Tel** *767 449 8176* **Fax** *767 449 8722* **Rooms** *10*

Set high in the lush Roseau Valley, the laid-back two-story Roseau Valley Hotel makes an ideal base for hikers and bird-watchers. Although it is only 2 miles (3 km) from Roseau, it offers peace and tranquility. Some of the rooms have kitchenettes but there is a restaurant also. Meeting facilities are available. **www.roseauvalleyhotel.com**

ROSEAU Cocoa Cottages and Gallery
🍴 W $$

Tel *767 448 0412* **Fax** *767 448 0412* **Rooms** *6*

A tucked-away six-room eco-resort surrounded by tropical gardens and rainforest, Cocoa Cottages and Gallery offers adventure tours including canyoning. The "TV" room has open doors for a screen and the surrounding forest is the ever-changing picture. **www.cocoacottages.com**

ROSEAU Fort Young Hotel
🍴 📋 $$

Victoria Street **Tel** *767 448 5000* **Fax** *767 448 5006* **Rooms** *70*

The waterfront Fort Young Hotel on the outskirts of Roseau is Dominica's main hotel with all rooms and suites having private balconies and most offering fabulous ocean views. It is a great base for both business and leisure travelers. There is a different themed buffet lunch daily and delicious Creole dishes for dinner. **www.fortyounghotel.com**

ROSEAU Sutton Place Hotel
🍴 📋 W $$

Old Street **Tel** *767 449 8700* **Fax** *767 449 3045* **Rooms** *8*

The affordable family-run Sutton Place Hotel, located in the town center, has been rebuilt in traditional Dominican style and has 5 comfortable rooms and 3 suites. The bar is in the original cellar, which was earlier used to store liquor and guests can dine in the open-air courtyard. **www.suttonplacehoteldominica.com**

STOWE Zandoli Inn
🍴 $$

Tel *767 446 3161* **Fax** *767 446 3344* **Rooms** *5*

A small, secluded hideaway, Zandoli Inn offers ocean views and lots of forest trails. This is really the place to get away from it all – there are five delightful rooms and no TVs, radio, or phones. The restaurant serves the freshest fish and the best of locally-grown produce. Only breakfast and dinner. **www.zandoli.com**

TRAFALGAR FALLS Papillote Wilderness Retreat
🍴 W $$

Tel *767 448 2287* **Fax** *767 448 2285* **Rooms** *7*

An idyllic, small, secluded inn with comfortable rooms, Papillote is set in tropical gardens with waterfalls and hot pools, high in the tropical rainforest *(see p400)*. It was Dominica's first eco-resort. The excellent Rainforest Restaurant *(see p411)* is open to the public. Closed in September and 2 weeks in October. **www.papillote.dm**

WOTTEN WAVEN Rainforest Shangri-La
🍴 $$

Tel *767 440 5093* **Rooms** *7*

Nestled 1,000 ft (305 m) above sea level on the edge of a tropical rainforest teeming with wildlife, Rainforest Shangri-La provides a great base to hike the forest trails, soak in the natural steam sauna and hot pools and even indulge in some tai chi or yoga. Good restaurant on-site. **www.rainforestshangrilaresort.com**

Where to Eat & Nightlife

Most of the restaurants in Dominica serve popular local cuisine and also offer dishes made from freshly caught fish. Eating out is not exactly cheap, particularly at hotel restaurants, which tend to be more expensive. It is ideal to book in advance as most restaurants do not stay open late. There are a lot of "snackettes", especially in Roseau and Portsmouth.

PRICE CATEGORIES
The price ranges are for a two-course meal for one, including tax and service charges and half a bottle of wine.

Ⓢ under $10
ⓈⓈ $10–15
ⓈⓈⓈ $15–25
ⓈⓈⓈⓈ $25–35
ⓈⓈⓈⓈⓈ over $35

RESTAURANTS

Seafood Special
Dining out in Dominica allows visitors to be adventurous and taste all sorts of unusual spices, vegetables, and fruits. While many types of cuisine are available, the island cooking is a blend of French and Creole. Try traditional soups such as christophene and coconut or *callaloo* and main dishes like Caribbean *souse* (pickled pork) or *crapaud* (mountain chicken).

Rainforest Restaurant

Purple Turtle Beach Club

BATALIE Four Seasons   Ⓥ 🏠 🎵   ⓈⓈⓈⓈⓈ
Sunset Bay Club and Dive Centre **Tel** *767 446 6522*

Eat inside or out on the terrace of this restaurant set in Sunset Bay Club and Dive Centre *(see p408)* with views of the beach and sea. It is open for lunch and dinner and offers snacks and a menu that combines European and Creole cuisine including great seafood platters and fish dishes. The service is leisurely and friendly.

CALIBISHIE Bamboo   Ⓥ 🍴   ⓈⓈⓈ
Tel *767 445 8537*

Looking out over the tropical gardens, Bamboo also allows guests to enjoy a dip in the hot pools after their meal. It is open for breakfast, lunch, and dinner and specializes in local, home-cooked food using local products and garden produce. The menu reflects what is available on the day.

CASTLE COMFORT The Crazy Coconut   Ⓥ 🏠   ⓈⓈ
Tel *767 235 8752*

This restaurant serves both local cuisine and food from all over the Caribbean. Grilled fish, steamed fish, and mutton curry are some of the dishes on the menu. Grilled fish and coconut punch are recommended. Open from 8am and lunch is served at 1pm. Dinner by reservation only. Sunday only fast food, no à la carte menu.

CASTLE COMFORT Evergreen   Ⓥ   ⓈⓈⓈⓈⓈ
Tel *767 448 3288*

The award-winning Evergreen restaurant and bar is set in tropical gardens overlooking the sea and specializes in local cuisine with French touches. Enjoy a drink on the terrace and watch the divers setting out from the pier or, in the evening, Roseau glowing in the sunset across the water.

PORTSMOUTH BEACH Le Flambeau   Ⓥ 🏠   ⓈⓈⓈⓈ
Portsmouth Beach Hotel **Tel** *767 445 5131*

Portsmouth Beach Hotel is located right on the beach and its all-day beachfront restaurant, bar, and lounge, Le Flambeau, offers friendly, relaxed sunset watching, and dining in a wonderful setting by the water's edge. Lots of snacks are available in addition to hearty, good-value local Creole dishes.

PORTSMOUTH Tomato Café   Ⓥ 🍴   ⓈⓈⓈⓈ
Tel *767 445 3334*

The menu at Tomato Café changes daily because only the freshest ingredients are used. Most of the produce comes from local farmers but deli meats, cheeses, and steaks are flown in. Dishes include subs and specialty wraps, pastas and salads, steaks, seafood, and great desserts. The restaurant has a good wine selection. Closed on Sundays.

PORTSMOUTH Purple Turtle Beach Club   Ⓥ 🏠   ⓈⓈⓈⓈⓈ
Purple Turtle Beach Club **Tel** *767 445 5296*

The Purple Turtle Beach Club is open for breakfast, lunch, and dinner. Great for snacks and a quick lunch if exploring along the coast or a leisurely, romantic alfresco dinner by the sea. Local dishes take pride of place on the menu. It also has a great bar.

ROSEAU Orchard   Ⓥ   ⓈⓈ
King George V Street and Great George Street **Tel** *767 448 3051*

A popular place for a snack or traditional Creole meal with lamb, goat, chicken or fish, Orchard is good value for money. Try the roti and black pudding. Vegetarian dishes are also usually available. Open for breakfast, lunch, and dinner Monday to Friday. Only breakfast and lunch is served on Saturdays.

Key to Symbols *see back cover flap*

ROSEAU Pearl's Cuisine

V $$$

50 King George V Street **Tel** *767 448 8707*

A great eatery in the heart of Roseau for lunch or dinner, Pearl's Cuisine serves local fare particularly delicious crayfish in garlic butter, fresh shrimp, and stewed chicken. Other specialties include freshly made fruit juices. It offers a good-value set three-course lunch. Open for breakfast for both eat-in or take-out. Closes at 6pm.

ROSEAU Ancient Capital

V $$$$

10 Churchhill Street **Tel** *767 448 6628*

This lovely open-air restaurant has unique Chinese decor and offers an extensive menu with delicious Chinese dishes. It specializes in Japanese sushi and Thai dishes as well. The Singapore noodles, and deep-fried chicken with sweet and sour sauce recommended. Fresh local juices also served.

ROSEAU Guiyave

V $$$$

Cork Street **Tel** *767 448 2930*

Dine in style on the lively balcony of Guiyave, an old wooden-frame town house. This popular restaurant serves good local dishes such as goat stew. The buffet lunch, served Monday to Friday, offers exceptional value. Try some of the sensational local fruit juices like soursop, a native Caribbean fruit, and tamarind. Dinner is not served here.

ROSEAU Balisier

V $$$$$

Bay Front **Tel** *767 449 8800*

Open all day for breakfast, lunch, and dinner, Balisier offers great views whether you want a quick snack or to dine off the menu which features international and traditional Creole cuisine. Enjoy an exotic cocktail at the bar watching the sunset, or enjoy an informal dinner overlooking the water.

ROSEAU Fort Young Hotel

V $$$$$

Victoria Street **Tel** *767 448 5000*

A good restaurant offering Creole and international dishes in a historic setting, Fort Young Hotel offers themed buffet lunches daily – from East Indian and Caribbean to Italian and seafood – and the dinner menu features island specialties. The wine list is good and live steel bands perform.

ROSEAU La Robe Creole

V $$$$$

Fort Street **Tel** *767 448 2896*

On the bayfront and serving snacks as well as excellent à la carte Creole dishes, La Robe Creole offers friendly and attentive service by staff dressed in traditional island costume. Try the lobster in creamy curried coconut milk or the steamed chilli shrimp. Vegetarian dishes are available.

SALISBURY Tamarind Tree

V $$$$$

Tamarind Tree Hotel **Tel** *767 449 7395*

This small hotel-restaurant nestles on the cliffs 100 ft (30 m) above the sea and is open to non-guests. It offers great views from the terrace and focuses on good-value, local Creole dishes although there are some international favorites. An American-style brunch is served every Sunday but only on reservation. Open from Wed–Mon.

TRAFALGAR FALLS Rainforest Restaurant

V $$$$$

Tel *767 448 2287*

The eco-resort Papillote's *(see p409)* restaurant is set in tropical gardens beside a natural hot mineral pool in the heart of the rainforest. The place serves Creole as well as Caribbean and Continental dishes. Much of the produce comes from their own or local gardens. It is open for both lunch and dinner but reservations are required for dinner.

WESLEY Randy's Restaurant & Bar

V $$$

Hunt Road **Tel** *767 315 7474*

Randy Williams ensures that his restaurant lives up to its reputation for excellent local Creole cuisine and international dishes. The open-sided dining room is filled with exotic plants, and the atmosphere is friendly; children are welcome and under-10s eat free. Monday is blues night, and there's a popular reggae party on Wednesdays until 3am.

BARS AND CLUBS

Nightlife in Dominica is at its liveliest over the weekend unlike during the week when most islanders like to shut shop early. A few bars in restaurants attract visitors and entertain them with *jing ping* – the traditional local music. Dancing and drinking and almost all the late-night action takes place in or close to Roseau.

The terrace of Fort Young Hotel

RECOMMENDED PLACES TO GO

All Nations Bar and Restaurant
Victoria Stree. 767 449 8339.
(Cozy spot.)

The Cove
Rockaway Beach, Canefield. 767 440 2683. (Live band.)

Fort Young Hotel
Victoria Street. 767 448 5000.
(Entertainment and local bands.)

Garraway Hotel
Bay Front. 767 449 8800.
(Karaoke.)

Pagua Bay Bar & Grill
Marigot. 767 445 8888.
(Spectacular view of the Atlantic.)

Symes Zee's
34 King George V Street. 767 614 2037. (Great jazz on Thursdays.)

Practical Information

Dominica is one of the few countries in the world that does not have an international airport in a deliberate effort to preserve the unspoilt beauty of the island. The Dominicans do not want massive jets roaring in and out of their island, upsetting their own very special brand of eco-tourism. However, this is no great inconvenience for visitors as there are still plenty of options for flying in and it is a relatively small price to pay if it preserves Dominica, as it is, for generations to come.

Duty-free shopping center in Dominica's capital, Roseau

WHEN TO GO

The best time to visit the island is between January and June when it is generally dry. The rainy season is between August and October, when hurricanes can occur.

GETTING THERE

There are no direct international flights from North America or Europe to Dominica. Airlines fly into Puerto Rico, Antigua, St. Martin, Barbados, Martinique, and Guadeloupe. From these islands there are connecting flights on **LIAT** and **American Eagle** to Dominica's two airports: Canefield, and Melville Hall. While Canefield is 15 minutes from Roseau, Melville Hall is a 90-minute drive from the capital.

There is a high-speed catamaran ferry service between Dominica and St. Lucia, Guadeloupe, and Martinique, and cruise ships regularly dock at the island. The main ferry operator is **L'Express des Îles**. It is ideal to check the timetables before traveling.

DOCUMENTATION

Visitors are required to show a valid passport on arrival in Dominica to immigration officials. They need to show a return ticket and have to pay a departure tax when leaving Dominica. Visitors from North America and Europe do not require a visa. Customs officers may ask visitors to open their luggage for a quick inspection. It is a good idea to carry a copy of proof of ownership such as receipts for expensive items.

VISITOR INFORMATION

Discover Dominica Authority in Roseau helps visitors find their way around the island. It guides them on where to stay, activities, and more. There are visitor information centers in the US and UK.

HEALTH AND SECURITY

Dominica has three major hospitals, **Portsmouth Hospital** and **Princess Margaret Hospital**, both of which have intensive care units, and the smaller **Marigot Hospital**. Princess Margaret Hospital has the island's only hyperbaric chamber. Visitors should have adequate personal insurance and medical cover. Most big hotels also have a doctor on call in case of minor medical emergencies. Dominica has a low crime rate but it is better not to wear expensive jewelry or carry large sums of money. It is also sensible not to leave valuables unattended on the beach or in view in parked rental cars. In case of an emergency, contact the police.

BANKING AND CURRENCY

The local currency is the East Caribbean dollar. However, most places on the island accept British pounds, US dollars and euros. All major credit cards are widely accepted although some restaurants take only cash so check in advance. Banks are open from 8am to 2pm from Monday to Thursday and 8am to 5pm on Fridays.

One of the many cruise ships arriving at the Roseau cruise ship terminal

Indigenous crafts from the Carib region on display

COMMUNICATIONS

The island's area code is 767. To call from and to the US dial 1 and then the number. For calls to the UK dial 011 44 and then the number (omitting the first 0). Phone cards are available from the post office, **Cable & Wireless**, and convenience stores.

TRANSPORT

The best way to explore the island is to hire a car and there are several rental agencies such as **Budget Rent-a-Car** and **Best Deal Rent-a-Car**. Most rentals are based in the capital, Roseau. Visitors need to buy a month's valid license and have to be over 25. Public buses can be flagged down on the road. Taxis are also available from the airports and Roseau but are usually expensive.

SHOPPING

Most of the stores are usually open from 8am to 4pm from Monday to Friday and from 9am to 1pm on Saturdays. There are lots of arts and crafts stalls all around the island, perfect for getting souvenirs for friends and family. In Roseau, there are mainly three stalls in the Old Market Square offering a wide range of coconut, straw, and Carib craft specialty products.

TIME

The island is on Atlantic Standard Time, 4 hours behind Greenwich Mean Time. Dominica does not observe daylight saving time.

LANGUAGE

English is the official language although many people speak Kweyol, a sort of Creole based on French and Carib vocabularies.

ELECTRICITY

Dominica operates on 220–240 volts and US visitors need to carry adaptors and transformers for their appliances.

GETTING MARRIED

At least one member of the couple must be in Dominica for at least two days before the wedding. The stamp in the passport will be considered proof.

On arrival, visitors should contact the **Ministry of Social Services, Community Development and Gender Affairs** to obtain Form G, which must be signed by both parties before a magistrate. The couple will also need birth certificates and legal proof that any previous marriage is over. Each of them must then sign a completed declaration form before a Commissioner of Oaths and attach a stamp to both these forms and a marital status form. All these forms should be returned to the ministry which will then issue a marriage license. This is presented to the Registrar before the wedding ceremony.

Many hotels such as **Jungle Bay Resort and Spa** offer wedding and honeymoon packages. There are also several marriage consultants such as **JTAS Weddings** who can make all the arrangements.

DIRECTORY

GETTING THERE

American Eagle
Tel 1800 433 7300.
www.aa.com

L'Express des Îles
www.express-des-iles.com

LIAT
Tel 767 440 2542.
www.liat.com

VISITOR INFORMATION

Discover Dominica Authority
Valley Road, Roseau. *Tel* 767 448 2045. www.dominica.dm

HEALTH AND SECURITY

Ambulance, Police, and Fire
Tel 999.

Marigot Hospital
Marigot. *Tel* 767 445 7091.

Portsmouth Hospital
Portsmouth.
Tel 767 445 5237.

Princess Margaret Hospital
Roseau. *Tel* 767 448 2231.

COMMUNICATIONS

Cable & Wireless
www.cwcaribbean.com

TRANSPORT

Best Deal Rent-a-Car
15 Hanover Street, Roseau.
Tel 767 449 9204.

Budget Rent-a-Car
Canefield Estate, Roseau.
Tel 767 449 2080.

GETTING MARRIED

Ministry of Social Services, Community Development and Gender Affairs
Tel 767 266 3207.

Jungle Bay Resort and Spa
Pointe Mulatre.
Tel 767 446 1789.
www.junglebaydominica.com

JTAS Weddings
PO Box 1528, Roseau.
Tel 767 440 5827.
www.experiencescaribbean.com

Exploring St. Lucia

St. Lucia lies in the eastern Caribbean about 21 miles (34 km) south of Martinique and 26 miles (42 km) northeast of St. Vincent – both of which can be seen on clear days. The island has had a turbulent history and for centuries was fought over because of its strategic position, changing hands 14 times between the English and French. Today, there are few reminders of this troubled past and St. Lucia offers unspoiled beaches such as Marigot Bay and Choc Bay, and turquoise seas teeming with tropical fish, a wealth of watersports and land-based activities, breathtaking scenery with tropical rainforests and a drive-in volcanic area, world-class resorts, and great food.

The well-maintained Derek Walcott Square, in Castries

GETTING AROUND

Hiring a car is the best option here but taxis are cheap and plentiful, and drivers attend special courses so they make excellent guides. Taxis can be hired for a trip, by the hour or by the day, but always negotiate a price first. Privately owned minibuses are the island's chief means of transport and ply along the main routes. There are frequent services between Castries and Gros Islet and less frequent services to Soufrière and Vieux Fort. The southern-bound buses do not run late in the evening. There are boat services between Castries and Soufrière.

SIGHTS AT A GLANCE

The Pitons
A World Heritage Site, the Gros Piton and the Petit Piton lure the adventurous with excellent hiking opportunities.

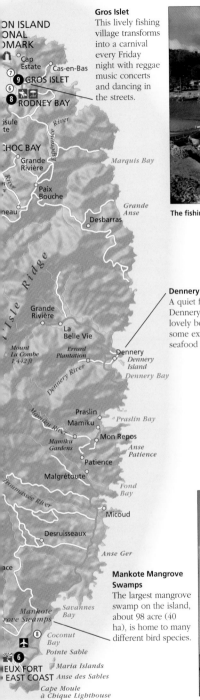

**ON ISLAND
ONAL
OMARK**

Cap
Estate
Cas-en-Bas
⑦
⑨ **GROS ISLET**
⑥
⑧ **RODNEY BAY**

CHOC BAY
Grande
Rivière

Paix
Bouche

Desbarras

Grande
Anse

Marquis Bay

Isle Ridge

Grande
Rivière

La
Belle Vie

*Mount
La Combe
1,442 ft*

*Errard
Plantation*

Dennery

*Dennery
River*

*Dennery
Island*

Dennery Bay

Praslin
Mamiku

Praslin Bay

*Mamiku
Gardens*

Mon Repos

*Anse
Patience*

Patience

Malgrétoute

*Fond
Bay*

Micoud

Desruisseaux

Anse Ger

*Mankote
rove Swamps*

*Savannes
Bay*

⑧ *Coconut
Bay*

Pointe Sable

EUX FORT
EAST COAST

Maria Islands

Anse des Sables

*Cape Moule
à Chique Lighthouse*

Gros Islet
This lively fishing village transforms into a carnival every Friday night with reggae music concerts and dancing in the streets.

The fishing harbor at Choiseul, south of Soufrière

| 0 km | 5 |
| 0 miles | 5 |

Dennery
A quiet fishing village, Dennery has a few lovely beaches and some excellent seafood restaurants.

SEE ALSO

• *Where to Stay* pp426–7

• *Where to Eat & Nightlife*
pp428–9

KEY

—— Major road

== Minor road

---- Ferry route

△ Peak

**Mankote Mangrove
Swamps**
The largest mangrove swamp on the island, about 98 acre (40 ha), is home to many different bird species.

Swaying palms at the popular Marigot Bay

The Roman Catholic Cathedral, Castries

Castries ①

NW coast of St. Lucia. 🏛 66,000.
✈ ⛴ ℹ Pointe Seraphine,
758 452 3036. 🎵 St. Lucia Jazz
Festival (May).

Castries is a bustling little city of gingerbread houses that hug the hillsides surrounding the shops and busy harbor. It has suffered four major fires over the last 200 years, but the last one enabled the planners to rebuild the city on a grid, making it very easy to explore. The colorful market on Peynier Street has interesting local produce, such as straw items, spices, and herbs. A market guide, available for a small tip at the entrance, explains the use of these goods.

Built in 1899, the **Roman Catholic Cathedral of the Immaculate Conception** contains many paintings with biblical scenes in which all the characters are black. The cathedral is located on the eastern side of Derek Walcott Square, named after the island's 1992 Nobel laureate in literature, Derek Walcott. The large samaan tree in the square is thought to be at least 400 years old.

Environs
A short walk north of town, Pointe Seraphine offers world-class duty-free shopping next to the cruise ship terminal. The main tourist information center is located here as well as several good restaurants, cafés, and bars.

A hill to the south of town, The Morne offers a superb aerial view of Castries. Given its strategic position, the French built **Fort Charlotte** near its summit in the late 18th century, which was later added to by the British. The area is now a protected historic sight and has many restored military buildings. However, it is the panoramic views from The Morne that are undoubtedly the most breathtaking.

> 🏛 **Roman Catholic Cathedral of the Immaculate Conception**
> Laborie Street. **Tel** 758 452 2416.
> ⏰ 8am–4pm daily.
> 🏰 **Fort Charlotte**
> The Morne. ⏰ dawn to dusk daily.

Discovery at Marigot Bay ②

⚓ Marigot Bay. **Tel** 758 458 5300.
Fax 758 458 5299. $ $ $ $
124 rooms. 🛗 🍴 🏊 🖥 Ⓦ
www.discoverystlucia.com

A short drive from the main road leading to the water's edge, Marigot Bay is about 7 miles (11 km) south of Castries. Surrounded by lush foliage-covered hills, the bay is considered among the most beautiful anchorages in the Caribbean and has been the setting for several films, including the original *Dr. Dolittle* (1967) and *Firepower* (1979). The busy marina here is full of local craftsmen at work.

Discovery at Marigot Bay is a luxury resort with accommodations nestled in the hillside overlooking the Marigot Bay. Some of the suites have private plunge pools and most units offer fabulous views of the palm-fringed bay. The restaurant *(see p428)* features everything from the finest haute cuisine to casual tropical tastes, and excellent drinks are mixed at the bar. The Lapli Spa provides a wide range of beauty treatments. The hotel's restaurants and spa are open to non-guests too.

La Sikwi ③

8 miles (13 km) SW of Castries.
Tel 753 451 0425. ⛴ ⏰ 8am–4pm
daily. 🎫 🚻 🍴 🏪

This 400-acre (162-ha) working estate, also called Invergoll, is located at Anse La Raye. It used to cultivate sugarcane in the mid-19th century, but now produces bananas, cocoa, and coffee. There is a museum and visitors can tour the old sugar mill with its huge waterwheel fed by an aqueduct. There is a bar and a small theater that hosts local folk music programs every other month.

View of Marigot Bay from the lookout point above

Soufrière

15 miles (24 km) S of Castries.
 7,500.

St. Lucia's first settled town and former capital during French rule, Soufrière is now a picturesque fishing town. During the French Revolution, the Revolutionary Council ordered that all French names must be changed, so Soufrière became La Convention and a guillotine was built in the town square. While most Royalist plantation owners fled, some were executed. The town, which has a beach fringed with coconut palms, is divided into two by the Soufrière River. Most of the shops, craft centers, restaurants, and guesthouses are located in the few streets inland from the jetty. Traditional Creole homes with their ornate filigree friezes and elaborate balconies stand out, and the market is decorated with colorful murals.

Malmaison, situated on the outskirts of town, is where Napoleon Bonaparte's wife Josephine (see p418) spent her childhood.

Environs

Other estates in the area that can be explored include the **Diamond Estate**, famous for its therapeutic mineral baths and gardens. Visitors can see coconuts, copra, and cocoa being processed at the Morne Coubaril Estate (see p421).

The **Soufrière Volcanic Area** is located just south of town. There is a giant crater, formed during an eruption 40,000 years ago that blew the mountain apart. There are 24 cauldrons of bubbling mud that boil at around 340° F (171° C) within the 7-acre (3-ha) site. It is advisable to keep to the marked paths. Guides can be hired at the entrance.

The Pitons

20 miles (32 km) S of Castries.

The island's most famous and most photographed landmark, the volcanic Pitons dominate the landscape as one drives south from Soufrière. Rising

View of Soufrière with the Pitons rising up in the background

like two sugar loafs out of the sea, Petit Piton (the northernmost) is 2,437 ft (743 m) high while Gros Piton reaches 2,529 ft (771 m). The latter is the easier to climb although it is steep towards the summit. It would take about 5 hours to climb and descend either peak. Gros Piton Tours (see p423) offer guided hikes.

Vieux Fort and East Coast

25 miles (40 km) S of Castries.
 16,500.

Vieux Fort is close to the southern tip of the island and commands fine views across to St. Vincent. Once the island's capital and main harbor, and named after a fort built here in the 17th century, Vieux Fort is now the island's windsurfing center. On its outskirts, the **Mankote Mangrove Swamps** is a favorite spot with bird-watchers.

Farther north along the eastern coast is **Savannes Bay**, famous for its bird reserve. While the west coast is sheltered, the rocky east coast is often battered by Atlantic breakers, making it popular with surfers. Farther ahead from Micoud are the **Latille Gardens**, which present a blaze of tropical color, exotic fruits, and waterfalls.

Dennery, farther north, is one of the island's most beautiful villages and has a long tradition of fishing and boatbuilding. Some of the boats are still constructed by hand from trees felled in the rainforest.

Mankote Mangrove Swamps
Tel 758 452 5005. dawn to dusk daily. **Note:** *there are short trails and a wooden viewing tower overlooking the swamp.*

Savannes Bay
dawn to dusk.

Latille Gardens
Tel 758 489 6271.

DEREK WALCOTT

Born in Castries in 1930, Derek Walcott is one of the island's most famous poets. Both his grandfathers were white while his grandmothers were apparently of slave descent. His father, an artist, died when Derek was young and his mother ran the town's Methodist school. All this influenced his works, which are a blend of Caribbean, English, and African traditions. His first poems were published at the age of 18 and he has produced many widely acclaimed volumes of poetry and plays since. Awarded the Nobel Prize for Literature in 1992, he continues to write and teach in the Caribbean and the United States.

Portrait of playwright and poet Derek Walcott

The sweeping Choc Bay on the northwest coast of St. Lucia

Choc Bay ⑦

3 miles (5 km) N of Castries. 🚌

Choc Bay boasts a tree-lined stretch of sand, with gentle waves lapping the shore. A popular tourist area, it is well developed with several classy hotels and all-inclusive resorts, restaurants, and galleries.

Inland from the bay, Union Trail is a short self-guided nature walk. It starts at the Union Agricultural Center's Interpretive Center on Babonneau Road. The herb garden here was used for traditional medicinal practice. The trail is an easy looped walk through the rainforest. The rare multi-hued St. Lucia parrot can be spotted here.

Nearby, **Fond Latisab Creole Park**, in the Fond Assau community, is part of St. Lucia's Heritage Tourism Program. It provides a glimpse of the Creole traditions of preparing cassava bread, cooking on macambou leaves, catching freshwater crayfish, and log sawing to the rhythms of a traditional *chak chak* (musical instrument) band.

Fond Latisab Creole Park
Babonneau. **Tel** 758 450 5461.
⭘ 9am–4pm daily. 📷

Rodney Bay ⑧

6 miles (10 km) N of Castries. 🚌

One of the most popular yachting destinations in the Caribbean, Rodney Bay has a beautifully landscaped marina with restaurants, bars, shops, and galleries. It is also one of the leading charter centers in the Caribbean and many charter companies are based here. The bay is worth visiting during the day to browse through the shops and enjoy a

Yacht moored in Rodney Bay marina

waterside lunch, and at night when it becomes lively thanks to its many nightlife venues.

Gros Islet ⑨

8 miles (13 km) N of Castries.
🚶 19,000. 🚌

Across Rodney Bay is Gros Islet, a small fishing village and home to the famous Friday night "Jump Up". This huge open-air party fills the streets and lasts until the early hours of the morning. Tables and chairs are placed in the narrow streets and loud music booms from huge speakers, as revelers move from one bar to the next, drinking beer and dancing the night away. It is also a great place to try local food specialties from the scores of street vendors.

EMPRESS JOSEPHINE

Empress Josephine was born as Marie-Joseph-Rose de Tascher de la Pagerie on June 23, 1763, at Morne Paix Bouche, in the north of St. Lucia. In 1779, Rose, as she was known, accompanied her father to France and married the wealthy landowner Alexandre Vicomte de Beauharnais. During the Reign of Terror in 1794, both she and her husband were imprisoned. While he was guillotined in Paris, she was freed. She met Napoleon Bonaparte in 1795, when he was still a general in the army, and they married in March 1796. Called Josephine by Bonaparte, who did not like the name Rose, she was crowned empress in 1804. She died on May 29, 1814.

Portrait of Empress Josephine

Pigeon Island National Landmark ⑩

Jutting out into the sea, the Pigeon Island National Landmark is connected to the mainland by a causeway. Covering an area of 44 acres (18 ha), it was first fortified by the French in 1778, who were ousted the following year by a huge British naval force. It was from here that English Admiral Rodney attacked the French fleet in 1782. The ensuing Battle of Saintes ended French domination in the Caribbean. Pigeon Island remained one of the most formidable forts for decades but was eventually abandoned in 1861. Since then it has been a whaling station and served as a US Naval Air Station during World War II.

VISITORS' CHECKLIST

8 miles (13 km) N of Castries. **Tel** 758 452 5005. 🚢 🚌 ℹ️ *Interpretive Center, near the entrance gate.* ◻️ *9am–6pm daily.* 📷 🎫 🍴 🛍️ 🏠

Interpretive Center
The former officers' quarters host the Interpretive Center and museum, which displays items of local historical interest, such as this bust of Admiral Rodney.

KEY

🚢 Ferry port

ℹ️ Visitor information

– – Walking path

Signal Peaks
Pigeon Island is dominated by two small peaks which made excellent observation posts.

Pigeon Island entrance gate

Officer's Kitchen

Gros Islet
2.5 miles (4 km)

Bakery

0 metres 100
0 yards 100

Cemetery

US Signal Station

Lookout

Barrack Ruins
Remnants of military barracks and encampments are scattered about on the eastern side of the island.

Fort Rodney
Once a British stronghold, Fort Rodney is in ruins today. The top of the fort offers sweeping views of Rodney Bay.

Pigeon Island Beaches
A number of excellent, white-sand beaches around the island provide good swimming opportunities.

Outdoor Activities and Specialized Holidays

St. Lucia is an outdoors wonderland with a wealth of land and water activity opportunities. Visitors can hike, go in search of rare and elusive wildlife in the rainforest, ride on horseback along the sand or scuba dive over pristine reefs in warm, crystal-clear water. Farther out to sea, there is deep-sea fishing and year-round whale- and dolphin-watching. Back on land, there is tennis, golf, rock climbing, and cycling.

The all-inclusive Sandals Grande resort at Rodney Bay

BEACHES

The beaches in St. Lucia are fabulous for sunbathing, swimming, and snorkeling. All are open to the public even if some hotels and resorts make it difficult to access them. There will be a public path down to the beach although visitors may have to search a little to find it.

The southwest coast of the island is relatively sheltered and safer for swimming. Anse des Pitons is a fabulous crescent-shaped beach overlooked by the Pitons.

Anse Chastanet, located just north of Soufrière, is a picture postcard beach with 1 mile (1.6 km) of soft, white sand fringed by gently swaying palms and lapped by warm, crystal-clear blue water. Soufrière itself has a stretch of dark sandy beach to the north of town which is a favorite spot with the local residents.

On the northwest coast, the popular Marigot Bay *(see p416)* is home to another spectacular beach. The bay itself is surrounded on three sides by forested hills and

vacationers can find a number of restaurants, bars, cafés, and shops nearby. For those looking for some peace and quiet, there is an inlet closeby with a couple of secluded, sandy coves.

Choc Bay *(see p418)* is a sweeping, sandy bay near Castries. The calm waters make it a good place for families with children and palm trees provide shade during the hottest parts of the day. Farther north, Labrelotte Bay is a small,

Diving preparation at Anse Chastanet, near Soufrière

sandy beach with sparkling blue water, located close to Windjammer Landing.

Reduit Bay and Rodney Bay *(see p418)*, St. Lucia's main beach area, has several bars and watersport activities but can get a bit crowded, especially during the weekends. Pigeon Island *(see p419)* is both a historic landmark and a very popular recreation area, with several small but attractive beaches.

Anse des Sables, on the south coast, is an accessible, sandy but windy beach looking out to the Maria Islands. It is popular with surfers and windsurfers and also a great beach for sunning.

Information about the various beaches and beach activities is available at hotel desks and tourist centers including Pointe Seraphine in Castries *(see p416)*.

RESORT-BASED ACTIVITIES

The different resorts around the island provide the widest range of land and water activities, including canoeing and kayaking, windsurfing, sailing, waterskiing, hydro biking, kneeboarding, snorkeling, and scuba diving – all usually included in the price of the stay or day pass. Land activities include table tennis, shuffleboards, croquet, fitness routines, golf, tennis, beach volleyball, and billiards.

It is also possible to get pampered with a wide range of treatments at the resort spa. Many spas offer special side-by-side treatment programs for couples and will accept reservations from non-guests.

Visitors not staying at luxury all-inclusive resorts can still enjoy the facilities they offer through half-day or one-day passes. Sandals *(see pp426–7)*, which has three fabulous all-inclusive resorts – the Grande, Halcyon, and Regency St. Lucia – offers a day pass. The price includes food, drinks, and watersports, and visitors can also spend the day in the landscaped pool and beach areas. Those who do not want a day pass can use the resort's beach chairs and umbrellas for a small fee.

Plantations of St. Lucia

Plantations are the living history of St. Lucia. They were worked by African slaves whose descendants now populate the island. Several plantations are still working estates with their great houses and the original heavy machinery, imported from Europe to process sugarcane, cotton, and tobacco, intact.

A banana flower

Many estates still bear their French names, often given in anticipation of great things to come, such as L'Espérance (Hope) and Tranquilité (Peace). There are many tours available to working plantations which try to show what life was like for both the owners and the slaves in olden days.

Soufrière Estate, *home to the oldest watermill still operating in the Caribbean, shows how local crops are grown and processed.*

Fond Latisab Creole Park *(see p418)* demonstrates ancient Creole farming practices and traditional cooking methods.

Marquis Estate offers tours and has displays of old agricultural equipment.

Morne Coubaril Estate, *a fully working plantation, allows visitors to experience traditional agricultural activities such as the making of copra (dried coconut kernel), cocoa, and cassava.*

Cap Estate
Gros Islet
Grande Rivière
Castries
Paix Bouche
Babonneau
Marquis Bay
Anse la Raye
La Sikwi Estate
Mount La Combe 1,442 ft
Fond d'Or Estate
Dennery
Barre de l'Isle Ridge
Errard Estate
Soufrière
Soufrière Bay
Morne Gimie 3,118 ft
Mount Grand Magazin 2,022 ft
Micoud
Gros Piton 2,529 ft
Choiseul
Laborie
Vieux Fort

Fond Doux Estate, *a 250-year-old working estate with spectacular views, uses historic cocoa-drying sheds to process cocoa. Visitors can also walk the estate trails.*

0 km ————— 5
0 miles ————— 5

PLANTATIONS

Balenbouche Estate
Tel 758 455 1244.
www.balenbouche.com
Fond Doux Estate
Tel 758 459 7545.
www.fonddouxestate.com
Morne Coubaril Estate
Tel 758 459 7340.
Soufrière Estate
Tel 758 459 7565.

KEY

🍁 Estate

▲ Peak

— Major road

— Minor road

Balenbouche Estate, *a 19th-century estate, is surrounded by a charming garden. Nearby are the remains of an impressive 18th-century sugar factory.*

View of Gros Piton from a hiking trail

HIKING

Hiking is one of the best ways to explore the quieter side of St. Lucia, especially with a guide, who has a good knowledge of the local terrain and wildlife.

Hikers should wear sturdy, non-slip footwear and carry a hat, insect repellent, and drinking water. It is a good idea to pack a pair of binoculars for wildlife spotting; 8x40 are ideal.

St. Lucia's interior is covered in mountainous rainforests rising to almost 1,800 ft (548 m) and there are 29 miles (47 km) of trails. On these, visitors can see rare birds and exotic plants. Walks include the Union Nature Trail, an easy loop walk through lush vegetation rich in wildlife that ends at a mini-zoo, which is home to many local species, such as the rare St. Lucia parrot and the St. Lucia iguana.

Barre de l'Isle Trail, off the highway between Castries and Dennery, is an easy walk through a forest reserve. It gets its name because it divides the eastern and western halves of the island. It takes about an hour to walk this 1-mile (1.6-km) trail and another hour to climb up to the Mount La Combe ridge, but it is worth it for the panoramic views.

The Edmund Forest Reserve Trail starts at the entrance to the reserve. A strenuous walk, it takes about 4 hours to complete and ends at the Des Cartiers Rainforest Trail. Various species of orchids grow along the trail. A side trail leads to Morne Gimie, which at 3,118 ft (950 m) is the highest point on the island.

The trails can only be accessed with the permission of the **Forest and Lands Department**. A list of walks can be obtained from the tourist offices as well as well-known tour operators, such as **Heritage Tours** and **Gros Piton Tours**.

CANOPY TOURS

An aerial tram journey into and over the tropical rainforest offers a bird's-eye view of the forest and its flora and fauna. Gondolas are suspended from cables and guides provide a running commentary during the tour. For more information and guides, contact **Rainforest Aerial Trams**.

DIVING AND SNORKELING

The clear, warm waters off St. Lucia are ideal for scuba divers of all levels and the reefs teem with an amazing variety of plant and marine life. It is possible to swim among nurse sharks, turtles, and shoals of tropical fish. Some of the more spectacular dive sites include Key Hole Pinnacles and Superman's Flight, a drift drive along a wall that drops to 1,600 ft (488 m), situated just off Petit Piton. Just down the coast, off Gros Piton, are the spectacular Coral Gardens, rising from a depth of 15 to 50 ft (5 to 15 m). Well-known operators include **Sunsail**, **Tornado Kite and Surf**, **Scuba Steve's Diving**, **Sailing Let's Go**, and **Mako Watersports**. For diving trips, popular agencies to contact are **Island Divers** and **Frogs Diving**.

Stunning coral reef in the waters off St. Lucia

For hotels and restaurants on this island see pp426–7 and pp428–9

HORSE-RIDING

The **International Riding Stables** and **Trims National Riding Academy** offer an assortment of trail rides to suit all levels of experience, from riding through the forest to a splashing gallop along the water's edge.

GOLF

Visitors can enjoy a round of golf in the most stunning of settings. There are 9- and 18-hole courses that test the most skilled golfer and views are breathtaking. Guests are welcome at the private clubs. The **Sandals Regency Golf Resort and Spa** and **St. Lucia Golf & Country Club** have 18 holes while Jalousie Plantation (*see p427*) has 9 holes.

TENNIS

There are lots of courts but only a few are floodlit. It is better to play early before the sun becomes too hot. Most hotels allow visitors to use their tennis courts for a fee.

CYCLING

Cycling is a great way to get around trails, especially in Anse Mamin, a historic plantation. The island is hilly so fit and experienced cyclists can make the most of it.

SAILING

A major yachting center, St. Lucia is home to many yachting and charter agencies such as **Destination St. Lucia**, **Escape to Paradise**, **Tradewind Yachts**, and **Moorings St. Lucia**. It is possible to charter yachts for a day sail or to tour the islands.

FISHING

World-class charter and deep-sea fishing boats are available for whole and half-day excursions. Reputed fishing concessionaires include Mako Watersports.

WHALE-WATCHING

Over 20 whale species, such as sperm, humpback, and pilot whales, can be spotted off St. Lucia's coast year round.

Mountain biking at Anse Mamin

DIRECTORY

HIKING

Forest and Lands Department
Tel 758 468 5645.

Gros Piton Tours
Soufrière.
Tel 758 489 0136.

Heritage Tours
La Clery,
Castries.
Tel 758 458 1454.
www.heritage
toursstlucia.org

CANOPY TOURS

Rainforest Aerial Trams
Near Fond Asseau.
Tel 758 458 5151.

DIVING AND SNORKELING

Frogs Diving
Rodney Bay.
Tel 758 458 0798.
www.frogsdiving.com

Island Divers
Ti Kaye Village, Anse Cochon. Tel 758 456 8110. www.islanddivers stlucia.com

Mako Watersports
Tel 758 452 0412.

Sailing Let's Go
Rodney Bay.
Tel 758 452 8234.

Scuba Steve's Diving
Tel 758 450 9433.
www.scubasteves diving.com

Sunsail
Rodney Bay Marina.
Tel 758 452 8648.

Tornado Kite and Surf
Tel 758 713 2110.
www.tornado-surf.com

HORSE-RIDING

International Riding Stables
Tel 758 452 8139.

Trims National Riding Academy
Gros Islet.
Tel 758 450 8273.

GOLF

Sandals Regency Golf Resort and Spa
Tel 758 452 3081.
www.sandals.com

St. Lucia Golf & Country Club
Cap Estate, Rodney Bay.
Tel 758 450 8523.
www.stluciagolf.com

SAILING

Destination St. Lucia
Rodney Bay.
Tel 758 452 8531.
www.dsl-yachting.com

Escape to Paradise
Tel 758 452 0344.

Moorings St. Lucia
Marigot Bay.
Tel 758 451 4357.
www.moorings.com

Tradewind Yachts
Rodney Bay.
Tel 758 452 8424.

Palm-fringed beach with the dramatic Pitons forming the backdrop, St. Lucia ▷

Choosing a Hotel

There is a huge choice of accommodations available, from world-class all-inclusive resorts to small hotels, inns, and modest guesthouses. Independent travelers have the option of staying at self-catering apartments and beach cottages. For those who want some pampering, there are luxury villas that include the services of a butler and cook.

PRICE CATEGORIES
The following price ranges are for a standard double room per night and all taxes included.

$ under $100
$$ $100–200
$$$ $200–300
$$$$ $300–400
$$$$$ over $400

ST. LUCIA

Discovery at Marigot Bay – *p416*
This delightful luxury resort is set in the hills with fabulous views of the bay. It combines sustainable, low-impact design with the ultimate in chic. Discovery offers 57 suites and 67 rooms with private plunge pools and has one of the finest restaurants on the island. Other facilities include harborside bars, a spa, and a fitness center.

Discovery at Marigot Bay

Sandals Grande

ANSE CHASTANET Anse Chastanet　　　🏊 🍴 ⚓ W　　$$$$
Tel 758 453 2073　Fax 758 459 7700　Rooms 49

Near the Pitons on the western coast, the Anse Chastanet stands on a 600-acre (243-ha) estate with spacious hillside and beachside accommodations. The villas do not have phones or TVs, making them perfect for a getaway. Restaurants *(see p428)*, bars, and activities are also on offer. **www.ansechastanet.com**

ANSE LA RAYE Ti Kaye Village　　　🏊 🍴 ▤ ⚓ W　　$$$
Tel 758 456 8101　Fax 758 456 8105　Rooms 33

The exquisite Ti Kaye Village has charming traditionally designed cottages and duplexes, dotted along the cliffs and overlooking the sea. Each cottage has its own private garden shower. There are steps down to a small sandy cove and a dive shop on the beach. It also has a pleasant restaurant and bar. **www.tikaye.com**

CASTRIES Auberge Seraphine　　　🍴 ▤ ♿ W　　$$
Vieille Bay, Pointe Seraphine **Tel** *758 453 2073* **Fax** *758 451 7001* **Rooms** *28*

An elegant, intimate getaway, Seraphine overlooks Vigie Cove and the marina and is only 5 minutes from Castries. It has spacious rooms, a fine, creative French restaurant *(see p428)* with an excellent wine list, a pool, and a gift shop. A minibus shuttles guests to and from the nearby beach. **www.aubergeseraphine.com**

CASTRIES Harbour Light Inn　　　🍴 ▤　　$$
Tel 758 452 3506　Fax 758 451 9455　Rooms 24

Close to Vigie Beach and a 10-minute walk from downtown Castries, the Harbour Light Inn is a convenient place for those on a budget or anyone flying out of George Charles airport. It has 16 suites, 8 comfortable rooms, and a kitchen that is accessible around the clock. Restaurants and shops are close by.

CHOC BAY Almond Morgan Bay　　　🏊 🍴 ▤ ⚓ W　　$$$$
Tel 758 450 2511　Fax 758 450 1740　Rooms 340

The four-star Almond Morgan Bay caters to singles, couples, and families. Set in tropical gardens, the resort offers four gourmet restaurants, land and water sports, and a fitness center with personal trainers. There are floodlit tennis courts, a spa, and an 18-hole golf course. **www.almondresorts.com**

CHOC BAY Sandals Halcyon　　　🏊 🍴 ▤ ⚓ ♿ W　　$$$$$
Tel 758 453 0222　Fax 758 451 8435　Rooms 170

The luxury beachfront Sandals Halcyon is exclusively for couples. It has three gourmet restaurants, including the Pier Restaurant which sits over the water. Activities offered include tennis and watersports. Guests can also use all the facilities at the other Sandals properties on the island. **www.sandals.com**

COCONUT BAY Coconut Bay Resort and Spa　　　🏊 🍴 ▤ ⚓ ♿ W　　$$$$$
Tel 758 459 6000　Fax 758 456 9900　Rooms 254

The Coconut Bay Resort and Spa, with luxurious rooms, is set in 85 acres (34 ha) of tropical gardens with three restaurants, beach grill, and bars. It offers a full range of watersports and land-based activities including fully supervised children's programs. **www.coconutbayresortandspa.com**

GROS ISLET Golden Arrow Inn　　　$$
Tel 758 450 1832　Fax 758 450 2459　Rooms 15

The friendly, family-owned and managed Golden Arrow Inn is aimed at the budget traveler. Situated just off the main road in Marisule, it is within easy walking distance of beaches and restaurants. The hotel's balcony offers fabulous sunset views. Facilities include a laundry.

Key to Symbols *see back cover flap*

GROS ISLET The BodyHoliday at LeSport 🅿 🍴 🗔 ⛱ ♿ 🚾 $$$$$

Tel *758 457 7800* **Fax** *758 450 0171* **Rooms** *155*

A beach resort and therapeutic spa, this resort places great emphasis on health, exercise, and relaxation. The extensive range of activities on offer includes yoga, *tai chi*, and fitness classes with personal instruction. The restaurant offers great food with lighter options. **www.thebodyholiday.com**

LABRELOTTE BAY Windjammer Landing 🅿 🍴 🗔 ⛱ ♿ 🚾 $$$

Tel *758 456 9000* **Fax** *758 452 9454* **Rooms** *248*

The luxurious Windjammer Landing features fully-equipped rooms and large villas with private plunge pools. Amenities include five restaurants, bars, pools, a serenity spa, activities, and a health and beauty center. Specially supervised children's activities are also on offer. **www.windjammer-landing.com**

MALABAR BEACH Rendezvous 🅿 🍴 🗔 ⛱ ♿ 🚾 $$$$$

Tel *758 457 7900* **Fax** *758 452 7419* **Rooms** *100*

Set in tropical gardens along a sandy beach, this is a couples-only boutique hotel with luxury cottages, suites, and rooms. Guests can have a romantic candlelit dinner in their room, on the beach, or in the gourmet restaurant. Spa, sauna, and gym services are offered. Sunset cruises are also arranged. **www.theromanticholiday.com**

MARIGOT BAY Oasis Marigot 🅿 🍴 🗔 ⛱ $$

Tel *758 451 4185* **Fax** *758 451 4608* **Rooms** *21*

The small, intimate Oasis Marigot is on the hillside overlooking Marigot Bay. Each unit has stunning views and access to the small palm-fringed beach. There are restaurants, bars, and a dive shop. Watersports, including sailing to Soufrière, Rodney Bay, and Martinique are offered. **www.oasismarigot.com**

REDUIT BAY St. Lucian 🅿 🍴 🗔 ⛱ ♿ 🚾 $$$

Tel *758 452 8351* **Fax** *758 452 8331* **Rooms** *260*

The luxury resort St. Lucian is on the island's best beach. The resort offers a number of options ranging from bed-and-breakfast to all-inclusive. With eight restaurants and bars there is a wide choice of dining. A number of activities such as horse-riding, tennis, and watersports are available. **www.rexresorts.com**

REDUIT BAY Royal 🅿 🍴 🗔 ⛱ ♿ 🚾 $$$$$

Tel *758 452 9999* **Fax** *758 452 0767* **Rooms** *97*

The elegant Royal resort with luxurious suites is located beside the island's most scenic beach. The restaurants L'Epicure and Chic *(see p428)* serve delicious food. Other attractions include bars, a spa, and a shopping mall. It also has a pre-teens club and offers babysitting services. **www.rexresorts.com**

RODNEY BAY Bay Gardens 🍴 🗔 ♿ 🚾 $$

Tel *758 457 8006* **Fax** *758 452 8059* **Rooms** *86*

A modern hotel, within easy reach of Reduit Beach, Bay Gardens comes with comfortable and affordable rooms and suites, some with their own kitchenettes. It has a restaurant, bars, and two pools. The hotel also arranges entertainment programs by local artistes. **www.baygardenshotel.com**

RODNEY BAY The Landings 🅿 🍴 🗔 ⛱ 🚾 $$$$

Tel *758 458 7300* **Fax** *758 458 7392* **Rooms** *62*

Located over 19 acres (8 ha) of oceanfront land, this hotel features suites with full kitchens ideal for families. The luxury resort includes restaurants, a spa, a fitness center, a pool, and a 4-acre (2-ha) private yacht harbor. Relax in The Beach Club, which offers live entertainment and happy hour drinks on Friday evenings. **www.landings.rockresorts.com**

RODNEY BAY Sandals Grande 🅿 🍴 🗔 ⛱ ♿ 🚾 $$$$$

Tel *758 455 2000* **Fax** *758 455 2001* **Rooms** *284*

An ultra-luxurious resort on a peninsula with the Caribbean to the north and Rodney Bay to the south. There are five gourmet restaurants, bars, activities, entertainment, and a spa. Guests can even swim up to the bar as well as to their rooms along the edge of the lagoon pool. No children under 18 allowed. **www.sandals.com**

SOUFRIÈRE Stonefield Estate Villas 🍴 🗔 🚾 $$$

Tel *758 459 5648* **Fax** *758 459 5550* **Rooms** *20*

Set in 26 acres (10 ha) of tropical gardens just south of Soufrière, Stonefield Estate Villas has elegant villas built to maximize the views. Each villa has intimate outdoor garden showers, verandas, and hammocks. The restaurant's menu features local fish and organic, local produce. **www.stonefieldvillas.com**

SOUFRIÈRE The Jalousie Plantation 🅿 🍴 🗔 ⛱ 🚾 $$$$$

Tel *758 456 8000* **Fax** *758 459 7667* **Rooms** *112*

An exclusive resort and spa with deluxe rooms and secluded villas set in 192 acres (78 ha) of tropical grounds nestling between the spectacular Pitons, Jalousie Plantation is noted for its spa and fine dining. The resort also offers an extensive program of activities and sports and caters to children. **www.thejalousieplantation.com**

SOUFRIÈRE Ladera 🍴 🗔 ⛱ ♿ 🚾 $$$$$

Tel *758 459 7323* **Fax** *758 459 5156* **Rooms** *27*

An award-winning small resort with 6 villas and 21 suites with open-air bedrooms and plunge pools, Ladera is nestled in the mountains with stunning views of the Pitons and the rainforest below. Some of the villas have their own waterfalls. The resort has a small spa. No children under 14 allowed. **www.ladera.com**

Where to Eat & Nightlife

Apart from the large hotels and resorts which provide nightly entertainment, most of the action in St. Lucia is concentrated in Castries and Rodney Bay, which are the entertainment hubs of the island. Vacationers will come across a large number of late-night bars and a wide variety of music that ranges from local bands to very entertaining DJs.

PRICE CATEGORIES
The price ranges are for a two-course meal for one, including tax and service charges and half a bottle of wine.

ⓢ under $10
ⓢⓢ $10–15
ⓢⓢⓢ $15–25
ⓢⓢⓢⓢ $25–35
ⓢⓢⓢⓢⓢ over $35

RESTAURANTS

Eateries in St. Lucia
There is a huge choice of restaurants from gourmet to casual in St. Lucia. Lunches are best eaten at beach cafés which usually offer excellent barbecued fish and conch (called *lambi*). Dinner generally features local Creole dishes with heavy French influences such as *pouile dudon* – a chicken stew with coconut and molasses.

Anse Chastanet

The Edge

ANSE CHASTANET Anse Chastanet   Ⓥ🍽🖼🎵 ⓢⓢⓢⓢⓢ
Tel 758 459 7354

The beachfront Anse Chastanet offers laid-back lunches. Trou au Diable serves Indian, while the Treehouse Restaurant perched on the cliff offers "Tropical World" cuisine, blending the best of Caribbean with other world cuisine influences. Much of the produce comes from the namesake hotel's *(see p426)* own gardens.

CASTRIES Auberge Seraphine   Ⓥ🍷🍽🖼 ⓢⓢⓢⓢⓢ
Vieille Bay, Pointe Seraphine **Tel** *758 453 2073*

A very pretty location overlooking Vigie Bay and the busy marina, Auberge Seraphine is located in its namesake hotel *(see p426)* and offers an exciting mix of Continental, French, and island cuisines. There is a well-stocked wine cellar and great-value daily specials. Open daily for breakfast, lunch, and dinner with an extended happy hour.

CASTRIES Caribbean Pirates   Ⓥ🍽 ⓢⓢⓢⓢⓢ
Tel 758 452 2543

Housed within the shopping complex, La Place Carenage, Caribbean Pirates has been styled to resemble the interior of an old ship. Dine on the balcony for the best seats and enjoy good food with fine views of the harbor. Try the jerk chicken and fish stew. Open daily for breakfast, lunch, and dinner.

CASTRIES Green Parrot   Ⓥ🍽🎵♿ ⓢⓢⓢⓢⓢ
Tel 758 452 3399

A St. Lucian institution thanks to the delectable food it serves, this restaurant has attracted numerous celebrities over the years. There is a large fixed-price menu offering deliciously prepared cuisine using the finest local produce from both land and sea. Dinner served daily. Reservations recommended.

MARIGOT BAY Boudreau at Discovery   Ⓥ🍷🍽🖼🎵 ⓢⓢⓢⓢⓢ
Tel 758 458 5300

Named for Walter Boudreau, this restaurant has ample memorabilia on the legendary schooner captain and is owned by the luxurious Discovery at Marigot Bay *(see p416)*. Open daily for casual breakfasts and lunches, and more formal dinners with fine cuisine, good wines, and great views. Dinner reservations are recommended.

MARIGOT BAY Chateau Mygo   Ⓥ🎵 ⓢⓢⓢⓢⓢ
Tel 758 451 4772

Chateau Mygo serves an exciting blend of Caribbean and Indian cuisines. Extensive and interesting menu with generous portions. Local lobster and the freshest of fish served with rice and beans. Try their scrumptious desserts. Happy hour lasts all day with potent cocktails on offer. Open daily for breakfast, lunch, and dinner.

REDUIT BAY Chic   Ⓥ🍷🍽 ⓢⓢⓢⓢⓢ
Tel 758 452 9999

Located in the Royal *(see p427)*, the small but elegant Chic offers an innovative menu for a memorable, and leisurely dinner. The dishes are international with Caribbean infusions. Try the Boudin Noir with caramelized ripe plantain apple and Calvados purée as a starter. Reservations are required. Closed on Sundays.

RODNEY BAY Razmataz   Ⓥ🖼 ⓢⓢⓢⓢ
Tel 758 452 9800

This lively and popular waterside restaurant overlooks the marina and specializes in East Indian and tandoori cuisine. Curries range from mild to explosive. The lamb *vindaloo* and the delicious chicken *tikka masala* stand out but great seafood is also served. Reservations are recommended. Open daily for dinner.

Key to Symbols *see back cover flap*

RODNEY BAY Big Chef Steakhouse [V] ▤ ⛱ $$$$$

***Tel** 758 450 0210*

The local TV celebrity "Big Chef" offers great steaks, seafood, and pasta. All steaks are seasoned with the chef's secret spices and then cut to order. If guests finish the 32 oz (900 gms) rib or strip steak they get a certificate. Try the mussels and save room for the home-made cheesecake. Dinner served daily. **www.bigchefsteakhouse.com**

RODNEY BAY Buzz [V] 🍸 ⛱ $$$$$

***Tel** 758 458 0450*

Known for its great food, wines, ambience, and service, Buzz gives diners the option of eating inside or alfresco. Try the lobster and crab cakes for starters. The fish is always good, as is the lamb, especially the Moroccan spiced lamb shanks. Local dishes include West Indian pepper pot and Creole seafood. Closed on Mondays.

RODNEY BAY Charthouse [V] 🍸 $$$$$

***Tel** 758 452 8115*

Long noted for its seafood and charcoal-broiled steaks, Charthouse offers good food and service in a naturally air-conditioned greenhouse at the water's edge. Try the stuffed crab backs and *callaloo* soup. A large selection of wines and excellent Cuban cigars are also available. Dinner served daily. Reservations recommended.

RODNEY BAY The Edge [V] 🍸 ▤ $$$$$

***Tel** 758 450 3343*

Overlooking the water, The Edge is run by award-winning Swede Bobo Bergström, who combines European and Caribbean cuisines to create some stunning dishes. The five-course dinner menu is a great way to experience these. Open daily for breakfast, lunch, and dinner

RODNEY BAY Lime On The Bay [V] ⛱ $$$$$

***Tel** 758 452 0761*

Good food in generous portions and quality service makes Lime On The Bay great value for money. Dine either inside or out. Try the lobster or Creole steak. After dinner, head upstairs to the Upper Level nightclub or next door to the Late Lime, one of the island's liveliest nightclubs. Open daily for lunch and dinner.

SOUFRIÈRE Camilla's [V] ⛱ $$$$

***Tel** 758 459 5379*

This place specializes in good, flavorsome West Indian and Creole fare, often based around locally caught fresh fish. Casual and friendly ambience. Tables on the balcony overlook the busy market street. Serves breakfast, lunch, and dinner. Closed on Mondays.

SOUFRIÈRE Dasheene [V] 🍸 ⛱ ♫ $$$$$

***Tel** 758 459 7323*

Perched 1,000 ft (300 m) above the Anse de Pitons inlet, the restaurant set in the Ladera *(see p427)* has stunning views. The chef combines New Wave Californian with traditional Caribbean cuisine to create memorable dishes. Fresh farm produce served and the fresh fish is always good. An impressive wine list. Lunch and dinner daily.

VIGIE COVE Jacques Waterfront [V] 🍸 ▤ ⛱ $$$$$

***Tel** 758 458 1900*

This delightful restaurant offers fine dining focusing on fish and seafood, and great views overlooking the marina. Local fishermen often present owner and chef Jacky Rioux with unusual catches, so you never know what might be on the menu. Try octopus and conch in a curried coconut sauce. Excellent wine list. Closed on Sundays.

VIGIE MARINA Coal Pot [V] 🍸 ▤ $$$$$

***Tel** 758 452 5566*

The award-winning Coal Pot, started by the Elliot family over 40 years ago, offers fabulous food – the best Caribbean ingredients and classic French cooking techniques. The fish is excellent, the ambience delightful, and there is an outstanding wine list. Reservations essential.

BARS AND CLUBS

When the sun goes down it is time to "lime", the local word for hanging out and having a good time. Rodney Bay has the largest concentration of restaurants, bars, and nightclubs and some stay open all night. Friday night is "Jump Up" night in Gros Islet with barbecuing, drinking, and dancing in the streets – and very, very loud music.

A view of Rodney Bay

RECOMMENDED PLACES TO GO

Banana Split
St. George's Street, Castries. (Live entertainment.)

Captain's Cellar
Pigeon Island. (Live jazz on weekends.)

Indies
Rodney Bay. (Island's hottest dance club.)

The Late Lime
Rodney Bay. (DJs every night, very popular.)

Rumours
Rodney Bay. (Music played until early hours.)

Shamrock's
Rodney Bay. (Popular and lively Irish pub.)

Practical Information

St. Lucia's attractions make it a year-round tourist destination. The island is fairly accessible with direct flights arriving from the US and UK, and neighboring islands are easily reached by high-speed ferry. The tourist infrastrucure is top-notch and transport and accommodations are easily available. The island's capital, Castries, has some interesting markets to explore and shop for memorable gifts and souvenirs.

Visitors relaxing under the shade on Reduit Beach

WHEN TO GO

St. Lucia has year-round good weather but the high season is between mid-November and March, which are the driest months. Most rain falls between May and October. Average daytime temperatures are around 85° F (29° C). Hurricane season lasts from June to November.

GETTING THERE

The international airport is at Hewanorra just outside Vieux Fort, about 40 miles (64 km) south of Castries. It receives regular scheduled non-stop services from **British Airways** and **Virgin Atlantic** from the UK, **American Eagle**, **Air Jamaica**, and **Delta** from the US, **Air Canada** and **West Jet** from Canada. Visitors from Europe and Australia have to connect with one of these carriers. The smaller George Charles Airport at Vigie, just north of Castries, has some international connections, but mostly serves flights to and from other Caribbean destinations. St. Lucia is visited almost daily by cruise ships, and the main terminal is at Pointe Seraphine, just outside

Castries. **Caribbean Express** is a great way to explore nearby islands, and runs a high-speed ferry service between St. Lucia, Martinique, Guadeloupe, and Dominica.

DOCUMENTATION

A passport is required to visit St. Lucia. An immigration form has to be filled in, one part of which is stamped and returned, and must be handed back at the time of departure. Citizens of the US and of specific Commonwealth nations do not require a visa to enter. Check with the concerned embassies for details. Luggage is often checked, so in case of jewelry or expensive cameras, travel with a copy of the purchase receipt. A departure tax for passengers over the age of 12 is applied at the time of ticket purchase.

VISITOR INFORMATION

The **St. Lucia Tourist Board** has its main office at Castries, and overseas offices in the UK, USA, Canada, France, and Germany. Tourist information centers are located at La Place Carenage, Pointe Seraphine, Soufrière, and at both airports.

HEALTH AND SECURITY

All hotels have doctors on call. **Victoria Hospital**, **St. Jude's Hospital**, **Dennery Hospital**, and **Soufrière Hospital** are the island's main medical facilities. Insect repellent is essential, as mosquitoes can be a problem.

St. Lucia has a low crime rate but stick to well-lit, popular areas, and avoid wearing expensive jewelry or carrying large sums of money. It is a good idea to keep valuables in the hotel safe. Vendors are likely to pester visitors, especially on the beach or in town, but a firm "no thanks" should do the trick.

BANKING AND CURRENCY

Banks are open Monday to Thursday 8am to 2pm, and to 5pm on Fridays. The official currency is the East Caribbean dollar (EC$), but US dollars are accepted almost everywhere. Banks offer a fixed rate of exchange, usually better than the rates offered in hotels and shops. There are ATMs throughout the island and all major credit cards are widely accepted. When arranging for a taxi, guide, or charter, visitors should check which currency they are dealing in.

COMMUNICATIONS

The international dialling code for St. Lucia is 1 758. To call the UK, dial 011-44 and the number, and for the US, dial 1 followed by the number. Card and coin-operated public

Cruise liner viewed from the Morne Lookout, Castries

phones are found easily. Cards can be purchased through **Cable & Wireless** offices which also rent cell phones. Internet access is available at most large hotels, at Pointe Seraphine, and at cyber cafés.

TRANSPORT

Car hire is the best way to explore the island. Renters should be over 25 and have a valid driver's license. If they do not have an international driver's license, a temporary one can be purchased from rental firms such as **AVIS**, **Hertz**, **Budget Rent-a-Car**, and **Island Car Rental**. In St. Lucia driving is on the left side of the road. Road signs are rare and some side roads may be pot-holed. In case of an accident or breakdown in a hired car, call the hire company or the police. An exhilarating means of moving around the island is by helicopter, available at **St. Lucia Helicopters**.

Taxis and island buses are easily available and cheap. Taxi drivers make excellent guides, but negotiate the price beforehand. There are regular bus services between the main towns, but evening services are less frequent, and smaller towns and villages may not be served.

A bustling marketplace, Castries

SHOPPING

Castries Market and beachside vendors offer local arts and crafts. Pointe Seraphine and La Place Carenage are duty-free shopping centers, and there are many galleries and boutiques in Castries. Most large hotels and resorts have mini-shopping malls.

LANGUAGE

English is the official language, although many people speak a French-based patois.

ELECTRICITY

The usual electricity supply is 220 volts, but most hotels also have 110-volt sockets, which are suitable for US appliances.

TIME

St. Lucia is 4 hours behind Greenwich Mean Time (GMT), and 1 hour ahead of Eastern Time in the United States.

GETTING MARRIED

It is possible to marry on the day of arrival at an additional cost. Documents required include birth certificate, passport, deed poll in case of name change, divorce papers if any, and parents' notarized consent if under 18 years. Documents must be in English or have an English translation. Besides the cost of the marriage certificate, a registrar fee is also charged. **A Wedding in St. Lucia**, **Tropic Isle Weddings**, and **Weddings in St. Lucia** have special offers.

DIRECTORY

GETTING THERE

Air Canada
www.aircanada.com

American Eagle
www.aa.com

Air Jamaica
www.airjamaica.com

British Airways
www.ba.com

Caribbean Express
Tel 758 452 2211.

Delta
www.delta.com

Virgin Atlantic
www.virgin
atlantic.com

West Jet
www.westjet.com

VISITOR INFORMATION

St. Lucia Tourist Board
Sureline Building, Vide Bouteille, Castries.
Tel 758 452 4094 (Castries); *1 800 869 0377* (Canada); *020 7431 3675* (UK); *212 867 2950* (USA). www.stlucia.org

HEALTH AND SECURITY

Ambulance and Fire
Tel 911.

Dennery Hospital
Hospital Road.
Tel 758 453 3310.

Police
Tel 999.

Soufrière Hospital
WC Queenland Street.
Tel 758 452 7258.

St. Jude's Hospital
St. Jude's Highway, Vieux Fort.
Tel 758 454 6041.

Victoria Hospital
Hospital Road, Castries.
Tel 758 452 2421.

COMMUNICATIONS

Cable & Wireless
Tel 758 453 9000.

TRANSPORT

AVIS
Tel 758 452 2700.

Budget Rent-a-Car
Tel 758 452 0233.

Hertz
Tel 758 452 0679.

Island Car Rental
Tel 758 450 4840.

St. Lucia Helicopters
Tel 758 453 6950.
www.stlucia
helicopters.com

GETTING MARRIED

A Wedding in St. Lucia
www.awedding
instlucia.com

Tropic Isle Weddings
www.tropicisle
weddings.com

Weddings in St. Lucia
www.weddingsin
stlucia.com

Exploring St. Vincent and the Grenadines

With its lush rainforests, waterfalls, black sand beaches, and spectacularly jagged terrain, topped off by La Soufrière volcano in the north, St. Vincent is a dream haven for eco and adventure travelers. To the south, its capital Kingstown is bustling during the day but towards the evening, the action moves to the nearby Villa and Indian Bay areas, where lively bars and restaurants abound. The Grenadines comprises tiny islands stretching between St. Vincent and Grenada and are politically divided between the two. Thirty-two of these exquisite isles belong to St. Vincent, and offer the quintessential Caribbean holiday experience of shimmering sand beaches, gorgeous cays, and turquoise waters.

Palm-shaded Carenage Bay Beach, Canouan Resort, Canouan

GETTING AROUND

There are no direct international flights to St. Vincent and the Grenadines, but connecting flights from other Caribbean islands land at the E.T. Joshua Airport in St. Vincent. There are airstrips on Canouan, Bequia, Mustique, and Union Island as well. Inter-island ferries are a cheap and popular way to travel. Visitors can get to most places by minibus, taxi, or rental vehicle, and there are a number of reliable tour services for sightseeing trips around the islands. The fit and adventurous can opt for bike and scooter rentals.

KEY

- —— Major road
- === Minor road
- -- Track
- --- Ferry route
- ▲ Peak

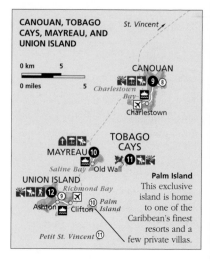

CANOUAN, TOBAGO CAYS, MAYREAU, AND UNION ISLAND

Palm Island
This exclusive island is home to one of the Caribbean's finest resorts and a few private villas.

SIGHTS AT A GLANCE

SEE ALSO

- *Where to Stay* pp442–3

- *Where to Eat & Nightlife*
  pp444–5

Fancy

Owia Bay

OWIA **5**

Falls of Baleine

Sandy Bay

La Soufrière
4,000 ft

Sandy Bay

Larikai Bay

Orange Hill

LA SOUFRIÈRE **6**
HIKE

Chateaubelair   Richmond

Rabacca

Mt Brisbane   Langley Park
3,058 ft

Troumaca

Richmond Peak
3,523 ft

Georgetown

Cumberland   Rose Hall

South
Rivers

Black Point

Illabou Bay

Gordon
Yard

St. Vincent

Colonarie

Barrouallie

Grand Bonhomme
3,181 ft

Colonarie Bay

Peter's Hope   Vermont

North Union

Layou Bay

Layou   *Mt St Andrew*
2,413 ft

Biabou   South Union
Grant's Bay

uccament Bay

Questelles   Green Hill

MESOPOTAMIA **4**
VALLEY

KINGSTOWN **1** **2** BOTANICAL GARDENS

Mesopotamia

Cane
Garden

3 VILLA   Stubbs

Orange Hill
Four-wheel drives to
Bamboo Ridge start
from Orange Hill,
to go to La Soufrière.

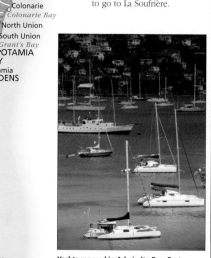

Yachts moored in Admiralty Bay, Port
Elizabeth, Bequia

Man Point

BEQUIA **7**   *Spring Bay*

Admiralty
Bay

Port Elizabeth
Mount Pleasant

West
Cay Adams
Bay

Paget   *Mount Pleasant Bay*

Petit Niévès

Quatre

Bettowia

Baliceaux

Lovell Village

Britannia Bay   *Macaroni Bay*

MUSTIQUE **8**
7

Petit
Mustique

Mustique
Mustique is the hotspot
for the rich and famous.

0 km   5

0 miles   5

Canouan

Arcaded buildings in downtown Kingstown

Kingstown ❶

SW coast of St. Vincent. ⛰ 26,000.
✈ ⛴ 🚌 ℹ️ *Ministry of Tourism,*
Upper Bay Street, 784 457 1502.
🛍 *Fri & Sat.* 🎉 *Vincy Mas (late Jun).*

A busy port city nestled in a
sheltered bay, Kingstown is
known as the City of Arcades,
thanks to the many arched
walkways in its tiny downtown area. The area features
some of the town's main
attractions, including the three
churches on Grenville Street:
the Anglican St. George's, the
more flamboyant St. Mary's
Cathedral, and the Methodist
Church, which was built in
1841 with money raised by
freed slaves. Not far from
downtown is a market area
known as Little Tokyo, so
named because its fish market
was built with Japanese aid.
Situated on a 630-ft (192-m)
ridge, north of the capital,
Fort Charlotte offers great
views of the island's leeward
coast and the Grenadines.
Built in 1805 to repel invasions
from the sea, it had many of
its 34 cannons pointing inland,
as the British felt their greatest
threat came from the Black
Caribs. A few of its cannons
still exist and oil murals
displayed in the fort depict
Black Carib history.

Botanical Gardens ❷

2 miles (4 km) E of Kingstown.
Tel *784 457 1003.* 🚌 ⏱ *6am–6pm*
daily. 🎟 🚻 🅿️

The oldest in the Western
Hemisphere, the Botanical
Gardens were founded in
1762 as a station to propagate
plants from all parts of the
British Empire. The gardens
have a great variety of native
and exotic plants. A famous
specimen is a thriving
descendant of a breadfruit
tree, brought here by the
British naval officer Captain
William Bligh. There is a breeding program for rare plants
and the endangered national
bird, the St. Vincent parrot.

Villa ❸

3 miles (5 km) SE from Kingstown,
St. Vincent. 🚌

The liveliest strip in St. Vincent,
Villa is the place to be for
those looking for great nightlife. Villa and the nearby
Indian Bay boast several good
restaurants, bars, and nightclubs. Some of the best-known
hotels can be found here as
well, both upscale and the
more moderately priced,
while the Young Island Resort
(*see p442*) is just offshore.

Mesopotamia Valley ❹

8 miles (13 km) NE of Kingstown,
St. Vincent. 🚌 �· *HazECO Tours.*

The Mesopotamia Valley or
"Mespo," regarded as the
bread-basket of St. Vincent, is
a luxuriant valley teeming
with cultivated vegetation:
nutmeg, bananas, breadfruit,
and all varieties of root crops.
Encircled by mountains,
including Grand Bonhomme,
the island's highest at 3,181 ft
(970 m), it is a unique sight in
the southern Caribbean.
    Just north of Mesopotamia
Valley, the colorful **Montreal
Gardens** are worth visiting for
the great variety of flowers
and plants grown here.

🌺 **Montreal Gardens**
Near Richland Park, Windward
Highway. **Tel** *784 458 1198.* ⏱
9am–4pm Mon–Fri. 🎟 ♿ *limited.*

Owia ❺

30 miles (48 km) NE of Kingstown,
St. Vincent. ⛰ 2,700. 🚌

On the north side of La
Soufrière, Owia is one of
the few Carib villages on the
island's rugged northeastern
coast. It is known for a
series of beautiful tidal pools
encircled by volcanic rock in
an area called Salt Pond. The
scenery here is quite dramatic
as waves of the feisty Atlantic
dash against the surrounding
volcanic rocks.

**Black Caribs making cassava
breads outside their huts**

BLACK CARIBS
In 1675, a Dutch ship carrying
settlers and African slaves was ship-
wrecked off St. Vincent's southern
coast. The sole survivors, the
Africans, were welcomed by the
native Caribs. They intermarried,
producing the "Black Caribs" or
"Black Calinagos". During the wars
of possession between the British
and French in the 18th century,
they favored the French. When St.
Vincent was ceded to Britain under
the Treaty of Versailles of 1783, the Caribs resisted, leading to
the Carib Wars. Finally defeated in 1797, most Black Caribs
were deported, while the rest were sent to Sandy Bay, where
their descendants have settled.

For hotels and restaurants on these islands see pp442–3 and pp444–5

La Soufrière Hike ❻

Wild flowers, La Soufrière

The hike up the 4,000-ft (1,219-m) high La Soufrière is a moderately strenuous, approximately 4-hour climb. The active volcano can be approached from either side of St. Vincent, though the easier trek is via the Atlantic Coast.

The trail leads through varied vegetation such as arrowroot, banana, and coconut plantations, tropical rainforest, and then cloud forest with its stunted growth. The view from the summit is absolutely breathtaking.

TIPS FOR HIKERS

Starting point: Bamboo Ridge.
Length: 3 miles (5 km).
Getting there: Minibus from Kingstown to Orange Hill; 4-wheel drive from Orange Hill to Bamboo Ridge.
Note: Ideal to go on a guided tour as novices can get lost. Wear sturdy shoes and carry a change of clothes in case of rain. Bring insect repellent.

La Soufrière Crater ④
The highest peak on the island, La Soufrière dominates the northern part of St. Vincent. In 1970, a new island was formed in its crater lake.

Jacobs Well ③
A dry riverbed, Jacobs Well is surrounded by pristine tropical rainforest.

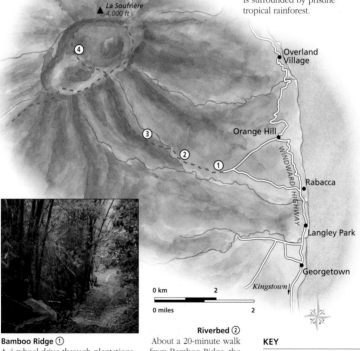

Bamboo Ridge ①
A 4-wheel-drive through plantations ends at Bamboo Ridge, where the foot-trail begins. At 1,300 ft (396 m), this is the point where the mountain climb starts.

Riverbed ②
About a 20-minute walk from Bamboo Ridge, the dry Riverbed is full of lava flow and rocks. A popular picnic spot, it is a good place to rest.

KEY

▲ Peak

═ Highway

– – Trail

Waterfront restaurant in Port Elizabeth, Bequia

Bequia ⑦

9 miles (14 km) S of St. Vincent.
🏠 5,000. ✈ 🚤 🛈 *Bequia
Tourism Association, Port Elizabeth.*
🏆 *Easter Regatta (Mar/ Apr).*
www.bequiatourism.com

The largest of the Grenadine islands at 7 sq miles (18 sq km), Bequia is the northernmost in the Grenadine chain. Its capital, Port Elizabeth, is a picturesque waterfront town set in the natural harbor of the sweeping Admiralty Bay. Lined with hotels, restaurants, bars, and shops, it is a popular stop with visitors and sailors. Bequia's famous model boatbuilders have their workshops here and can be seen crafting their intricate, traditional double-ended whalers as well as other contemporary boats.

Bequia has a long tradition of fishing and whaling. The International Whaling Commission now allows the island to kill a quota of two humpback whales a year. The Whaling Museum at Paget chronicles the island's whaling history. The aptly named Mount Pleasant near the east coast offers panoramic views of Bequia's golden beaches, coves, and sparkling waters, which all make it a popular sailing and snorkeling spot. The Old Hegg Turtle Sanctuary on the far northeastern side of the island is worth visiting. It is

run by conservationist Orton King, who lovingly tends to hawksbill turtles.

Mustique ⑧

7 miles (11 km) SE of Bequia.
🏠 550. ✈ 🚤 🏆 *Mustique Blues
Festival (early Feb).* **www**.mustique-island.com

**Frangipani
flowers, Bequia**

Mustique has long been associated with British royalty and celebrities. The tiny 1,400-acre (565-ha) island was acquired by a single proprietor, Scottish landowner Colin Tennant, in the 1960s. He developed it into a private resort for the rich and famous. Today, apart from private residences, there are villas available for weekly rental. Visitors can explore the island by scooter or car, or go swimming and hiking. Day trips

from St. Vincent to the island are organized by the Mustique Company. The island is best known for the world-famous Basil's Bar *(see p445).*

Canouan ⑨

14 miles (22 km) S of St. Vincent.
🏠 1,200. ✈ 🚤 🏆 *Canouan
Regatta (May).* **www**.canouan.com

Stretching over not more than 5 sq miles (13 sq km), Canouan is home to some of the Caribbean's most spectacular beaches. Its powder-white sands, clear waters, and an impressive coral reef make it excellent for sailing, swimming, and snorkeling. The main town, Charlestown, is in Charlestown Bay, the island's primary anchorage with a long beach. The exclusive Canouan Resort and its 18-hole Trump International Golf Course *(see p440)* and its stylish casinos draw many famous guests.

Mayreau ⑩

6 miles (10 km) SE of Canouan. 🚤
🏠 260.

An essential stop on a sailing day trip, Mayreau is the smallest inhabited island in the Grenadines. Most of its population lives at Station Hill, which has a handful of restaurants and bars. Built of stone in 1929, the old Roman Catholic Church is a short uphill walk from Station Hill. It offers great views of the island, across Salt Whistle Bay with its private resort, and the Tobago Cays.

View across Charlestown Bay, Canouan

Tobago Cays ⑪

Sheltered by the aptly named Horseshoe Reef, the Tobago Cays are a group of uninhabited isles. To protect the delicate reefs, the islands have been declared a marine park by the St. Vincent government. The waters are exceptionally clear, and the diverse marine life includes squirrel fish, angelfish, and groupers.

Horseshoe Reef
Although some of the reef has suffered damage from anchors, over-fishing, and removal of black corals, much of it remains in surprisingly excellent condition.

0 metres 700
0 yards 700

Snorkeling
One of the most remarkable sites for snorkeling in the Caribbean, the Tobago Cays become very busy during the high season (Dec to Apr).

Boat Vendors
Locals on boats paddle between the yachts, selling wares that range from fresh fish to jewelry and clothes.

Union Island ⑫

1 mile (1.6 km) SE of Mayreau.
👥 3,000. ✈ 🚤
🎭 Easterval (Mar or Apr).

In the southern part of the island chain, Union Island is the commercial center of the Grenadines, and also the hub of yachting and airport traffic. Measuring around 3 miles (5 km) long, it is fringed with gorgeous bays, lagoons, and reefs with perfect swimming and sailing waters.

Though many people visit Union Island to catch a yacht charter, there is a lot to do on the island itself. The main town, Clifton, has a few good restaurants, small hotels, main harbor and anchorage, and an open-air market where visitors can buy crafts as well as fresh produce. Mount Taboi, at 1,000 ft (305 m), is the highest point in the Grenadines, and hiking the mountain or any of the island's numerous nature trails is a good way to explore the terrain. The island is also known for its Big Drum dance, a combination of African and French influences, which is performed in times of disaster, but also on joyous occasions such as weddings, or the launching of a new boat.

Yachts anchored at Clifton harbor, Union Island

Outdoor Activities and Specialized Holidays

The tiny islands of St. Vincent and the Grenadines offer visitors a stunning range of activities, including exploring the dramatic terrain, dolphin-watching, and hiking at La Soufrière volcano on St. Vincent. The islands have a good assortment of tour operators, who can organize sightseeing or hiking tours, and are especially well-equipped for sailing, scuba diving, and other watersports. Sports enthusiasts can play tennis, golf, or cycle, and there are some excellent spas for recuperating from the exertion as well.

A beach on Young Island, St. Vincent

BEACHES

The beaches on the calm leeward side of St. Vincent are mostly smooth, black-sand beaches formed from volcanic rock that sparkle in the sun. The palest sand can be found on the beaches to the south, especially in Villa and Indian Bay areas where most of the hotels are located. Calliaqua Bay, Blue Lagoon, and the Young Island Cut are among the beautiful beaches in this area.

The Windward coast is rocky with strong currents, making it unsafe for bathing, but the black-sand beaches are impressive and a number of them are popular, including Argyle, where the surf crashes dramatically on to the sand. The Salt Pond at Owia *(see p434)* is set in a magical landscape and good for a swim while waves break on huge rocks all around the tidal pools. For turquoise sea and dazzling powder-white and golden sands, visitors can head to the Grenadines, where

most spend at least a day to experience life on a postcard-perfect Caribbean island. All beaches, except some on Mustique, are public.

DIVING AND SNORKELING

There are numerous wall diving sites and sunken wrecks in St. Vincent and the Grenadines. Extensive coral reefs with crystal-clear water surround these islands, which makes them among the best for diving and snorkeling in the Caribbean. Rich reef life can usually be found at a depth of 80 ft (25 m), while there is a whole world of marine creatures and abundant tropical fish flourishing at only 25 ft (8 m).

There are several companies that cater to divers. On St. Vincent, **Dive St Vincent** is a popular dive shop. On the Grenadines, diving

and snorkeling gear can be hired from **Mustique Water Sports, Bequia Dive Adventures, Canouan Dive Center,** and **Grenadines Dive.** Divers and snorkelers should take care not to disturb the islands' marine life and corals.

WATERSPORTS

There are facilities for all types of watersports, with kayaking off the calm leeward coast of St. Vincent being a special treat. **SVG Multi-Day Adventures** and **Coreas Caribbean Adventures** arrange kayaking excursions. Other operators organize wind-surfing and Jet Skiing tours including Dive St Vincent, **Sea Breeze Nature Tours,** and **Fantasea Tours.**

FISHING

Both amateur and experienced fishermen enjoy the islands for their rich sea life and excellent sailing conditions. Many options are offered by dive and watersports companies such as Fantasea and Sea Breeze Nature Tours, which include both deep-sea and shallow water fishing. Fishing is not allowed in protected areas such as the northeast coast of Bequia, all of Palm Island, Mustique, Mayreau, and Tobago Cays. Barrouallie on St. Vincent's leeward coast is a popular center for fishing. The village is known for its "black fish", a small whale species, plentiful in the waters.

Clusters of corals in the waters off St. Vincent and the Grenadines

For hotels and restaurants on these island see pp442–3 and pp444–5

A catamaran picking up visitors for a sailing tour

SAILING

St. Vincent and the Grenadines have a long-standing seafaring tradition as well as perfect sailing conditions. The first visitors to notice the holiday potential of St. Vincent and the Grenadines were sailors and yachtsmen.

Privately owned yachts need to clear immigration and customs at one of the several designated entry points. These are Kingstown, Chateaubelair, and Wallilabou in St. Vincent, and Port Elizabeth in Bequia, Mustique, Canouan, and Union Island.

Charter agencies such as **Barefoot Yacht Charters** and **Yannis Sail Private Charters** offer some great exploring and allow people with little know-how of sailing to get a taste of the sea as well as experience the active and luxurious life aboard a crewed yacht.

SEA TOURS

A good way to experience the seafaring side of St. Vincent and the Grenadines is to join a tour to some of the hidden coves and beaches inaccessible by road.

A sea tour of St. Vincent involves a trip on a speedboat along the leeward side of the island. Fort Charlotte *(see p434),* overlooking Kingstown, is the first notable landmark, but as the boat skims along the coast visitors can see black-sand beaches, statuesque cliffs, and forest-covered mountains. The route traces the coast, past several pretty villages, all the way to the

Falls of Baleine. The tour will include a stop at the Falls for a swim at its lovely natural pool. The trip also gives a good idea of the fishing culture of these islands, with its colorful boats and quiet coastal villages.

If the trip includes dolphin-watching, the captain goes farther offshore where dolphins are flipping in the water. For whale-watching the boat will go still farther out. Around 20 species of whales and dolphins, including the humpback whale, are found in the the waters off St. Vincent and the Grenadines. Sea Breeze Nature Tours and **Calypso Tours** are among the reputed operators that offer tours.

HIKING AND BIRD-WATCHING

There are many hiking trails in St. Vincent, ranging from relaxed treks in the Dark View Falls area and through the rolling terrain of the Vermont Nature Trail to challenging hikes to the crater of La Soufrière *(see p435).* **Sailor's Wilderness Tours** and **HazECO Tours** offer hiking trips in St. Vincent and **Ruff and Ready Hiking** on the Grenadine islands. Much of St. Vincent is forested, providing a protected habitat for many bird species, while the Grenadine islands are flatter and drier. This geographical diversity in such a small area makes for a varied terrain that includes birdlife, rainforest, wetland, and garden. Thrushes, warblers, herons, and hummingbirds, are easily spotted. The Vermont Nature Trail is a good place to see the St. Vincent parrot. Other birding sites are the Falls of Baleine, Trinity Falls, Owia Salt Pond, Buccament Valley, Wallilabou Falls, La Soufrière Volcano trail and Richmond Beach. The **Ministry of Agriculture** has a wealth of information on the birdlife. Sailor's Wilderness Tours, HazECO Tours, and **Treasure Tours** organize birding trips.

St. Vincent parrot

Trail to La Soufrière's summit through verdant rainforest, St. Vincent

Treatment room, Canouan Resort, Canouan

SPAS

Seclusion and relaxation can easily be achieved in St. Vincent and the Grenadines. Most major resorts have spas, which offer a range of rejuvenating beauty treatments and relaxing massages to soothe both the body and mind. The spa in the Canouan Resort *(see p443)* and the Spa Kalina, located in the Young Island Resort *(see p442)*, are among the best spas on the islands. Day spas such as the **Oasis Spa and Wellness Center** and **Bamboo Spa** are also popular.

GOLF

One of the Caribbean's most scenic and challenging golf courses is located in the Canouan Resort. The **Trump International Golf Course** has been designed by the well-known golf course architect Jim Fazio. The only 18-hole championship course on St. Vincent and the Grenadine islands, it is widely regarded as one of the best in the world. It stretches over 135 acres (55 ha) of hill and seashore and showcases the stunning scenery of Canouan. The 13th hole is considered to be the supreme spot with its spectacular views of the Grenadines, Atlantic Ocean, and the Caribbean Sea. Though a haven for professional golfers, it offers lessons for amateurs too. There is a fully stocked golf shop and a clubhouse on the premises as well.

Well-manicured grounds of the Trump International Golf Course, Canouan

DIRECTORY

DIVING AND SNORKELING

Bequia Dive Adventures
Belmont Walkway, Bequia.
Tel 784 458 3826. **www.**bequiadiveadventures.com

Canouan Dive Center
Tamarind Beach, Canouan.
Tel 917 796 1100. **www.**canouandivecenter.com

Dive St Vincent
Young Island Dock, St. Vincent. *Tel 784 457 4928.* **www.**divestvincent.com

Grenadines Dive
Clifton, Union Island.
Tel 784 458 8138. **www.**grenadinesdive.com

Mustique Water Sports
1 Watersports Way, Mustique. *Tel 784 488 8486.* **www.**mustique-island.com

WATERSPORTS

Coreas Caribbean Adventures
Kingstown, St. Vincent.
Tel 784 456 2158. **www.**coreascaribbeanadventures.com

Fantasea Tours
Villa Beach, St. Vincent.
Tel 784 457 4477. **www.**fantaseatours.com

Sea Breeze Nature Tours
Kingstown, St. Vincent.
Tel 784 458 4969. **www.**seabreezenaturetours.com

SVG Multi-Day Adventures
Bay Hill, St. Vincent.
Tel 784 456 6452. **www.**svgmultidayadventure.com

SAILING

Barefoot Yacht Charters
Blue Lagoon, St. Vincent.
Tel 784 456 9334. **www.**barefootyachts.com

Yannis Sail Private Charters
Clifton, Union Island.
Tel 784 458 8513. **www.**yannissail.com

SEA TOURS

Calypso Tours
Canash Beach Appartments.
Tel 784 493 3076.

HIKING AND BIRD-WATCHING

HazECO Tours
Gun Hill, Kingstown St. Vincent. *Tel 784 457 8634.* **www.**hazecotours.com

Ministry of Agriculture
Richmond Hill, Kingstown, St. Vincent. *Tel 784 456 1410.* **www.**gov.vc/

Ruff and Ready Hiking
Bequia. *Tel 784 495 2524.*

Sailor's Wilderness Tours
Upper Middle Street, St. Vincent. *Tel 784 457 1712.* **www.**sailortours.com

Treasure Tours
Kingstown, St. Vincent.
Tel 784 456 6432.

SPAS

Bamboo Spa
Caine Hall, St. Vincent.
Tel 784 482 9506.

Oasis Spa and Wellness Center
Villa Flat, St. Vincent.
Tel 784 456 2555.

GOLF

Trump International Golf Course
Canouan Resort, Canouan. *Tel 784 458 8000.* **www.**canouan.com/golf.asp

For hotels and restaurants on these islands see pp442–3 and pp444–5

Sailing the Grenadines

Fishing, sailing, diving, and boat-making are a way of life in St.Vincent and the Grenadines. It is no surprise then that sailors and yachtsmen were the first to discover their tranquil waters, white sand beaches, and extensive reefs. The Grenadines, along with the Virgin Islands, have the best sailing in the Caribbean because of the

Signage of a dive shop, Bequia

many islands at good sailing distance from each other, as well as the infrastructure – the number of marinas, chandlers, anchorages, seaside restaurants, and bars. Sailing here favors seasoned sailors, but there are crewed boats and yacht charters to ensure that amateurs have just as good a time.

Bequia, *the largest of the Grenadines, has secluded beaches, coral reefs, and blue lagoons. Sailors love to visit Port Elizabeth for its many seaside restaurants and bars.*

Man Point

Bequia

Admiralty Bay — Port Elizabeth

Petit Niévès

Quatre

Mustique *attracts royalty and the well-heeled, as well as sailors in small and grand yachts.*

Lovell Village
Britannia Bay — Pasture Bay

Petit Mustique

Canouan *is known by sailing folk for its powder-white sand beaches, turquoise sea, coral reefs teeming with ocean life, and some of the best snorkeling in the world.*

Tobago Cays *are five, uninhabited islands encircled by coral reefs and gorgeous, sparkling water. They are worth a visit even during the busy high season when there are many boats and visitors.*

KEY

🔺 Marina

— Minor Road

Grand Bay

Charlestown

Salt Whistle Bay — Old Wall

0 km	10
0 miles	10

Ashton — Clifton

Palm Island

Union Island *is a port of entry to St. Vincent and the Grenadines and sailing boats have to be checked in by customs on arrival. It is also a good base for sailing trips around the smaller islands.*

Mayreau *is one of the stop-off points for yacht charters. The island is a great spot for a swim, snorkeling, or a barbecue on the beach.*

Choosing a Hotel

Accommodations in St. Vincent and the Grenadines range from the fabulously expensive and exclusive resorts where guests need not see another guest to moderately priced little guesthouses within walking distance of a beach. On St. Vincent itself there are many fine but less pricey options, as well as the exclusive Young Island Resort just offshore.

PRICE CATEGORIES
The following price ranges are for a standard double room per night and all taxes included.

Ⓢ under $100
ⓈⓈ $100–$200
ⓈⓈⓈ $200–$300
ⓈⓈⓈⓈ $300–$400
ⓈⓈⓈⓈⓈ over $400

ST. VINCENT AND THE GRENADINES

Mustique's Exclusive Resorts

Many of the Grenadine islands are known for their stylish resorts, but Mustique, a getaway for British royalty, is still the best known for attracting the rich and famous, many of whom have villas here. Some of the luxurious residences can be rented from the Mustique Company, founded by Colin Tennant, who owns many of the villas. The island is also a hideaway for the glamorous celebrities Mick Jagger and Tommy Hilfiger, who have their own private residences.

Canouan Resort

Young Island Resort

ST. VINCENT, BLUE LAGOON The Lagoon Marina and Hotel 🏊 ▤ 👪 [W] ⓈⓈ

PO Box 133, Blue Lagoon ***Tel*** *784 458 4308* ***Fax*** *784 456 8928* ***Rooms*** *19*

Located on St. Vincent's secluded southern shore, this beautiful hotel is also a good place to charter a yacht and explore around the islands. Rooms are large and breezy with a spacious private balcony and great views of the sea. Conference room available. **www.lagoonmarina.com**

ST. VINCENT, INDIAN BAY Villa Lodge Hotel 🏊 🍴 ▤ 👪 [W] ⓈⓈ

PO Box 1191, Indian Bay ***Tel*** *784 458 4641* ***Fax*** *784 457 4468* ***Rooms*** *10*

Small hotel on a hill conveniently located near the capital and all major attractions, it is also close to Indian Bay Beach and the Villa Strip. Pool with a lovely view. The adjacent Breezeville Apartments are run by the same company and are ideal for a longer stay. **www.villalodgehotel.com**

ST. VINCENT, KINGSTOWN Cobblestone Inn 🍴 ▤ 👪 [W] Ⓢ

PO Box 867, Bay Street, Downtown Kingstown ***Tel*** *784 456 1937* ***Fax*** *784 456 1938* ***Rooms*** *26*

Originally a sugar warehouse, this pleasant hotel stands in the heart of the capital's small business district, overlooking the harbor. It is a 15-minute drive from the airport, close to the beach. Georgian architecture with cobblestone walkways and arches. It has a rooftop restaurant *(see p444)*. **www.thecobblestoneinn.com**

ST. VINCENT, KINGSTOWN Grenadine House 🍴 ▤ [W] ⓈⓈⓈ

PO Box 2523, Kingstown ***Tel*** *784 458 1800* ***Fax*** *784 458 1333* ***Rooms*** *20*

Originally built in 1765 as the residence of the British governor, this is an elegant and luxurious boutique hotel. It sits on a hill in a suburb of Kingstown, with panoramic views of the capital, surrounding hills and Bequia. Room service is from 7am–10:30pm. **www.grenadinehouse.com**

ST. VINCENT, VILLA Beachcombers Hotel 🏊 🍴 ▤ 👪 [W] Ⓢ

PO Box 126, Kingstown ***Tel*** *784 458 4283* ***Fax*** *784 458 4385* ***Rooms*** *31*

Family-run boutique hotel in a garden setting, with an outdoor pool, fitness and business centers. Very picturesque and in an excellent location near Villa's restaurants and bars, with a view of the nearby Young Island and Bequia. **www.beachcombershotel.com**

ST. VINCENT, VILLA Grand View Beach Hotel 🏊 🍴 ▤ 👪 [W] ⓈⓈⓈ

PO Box 173, Villa Point ***Tel*** *784 458 4811* ***Fax*** *784 457 4174* ***Rooms*** *19*

A quiet hotel in a 19th-century mansion, surrounded by a large tropical garden and overlooking the beach on the south coast of St. Vincent. Bright and breezy with spacious rooms and fantastic views. It also offers a fully equipped gym, beach bar, restaurant *(see p444)*, and pool with a swim-up bar. **www.grandviewhotel.com**

ST. VINCENT, VILLA Sunset Shores 🏊 ▤ 👪 [W] ⓈⓈⓈ

PO Box 849, Villa ***Tel*** *784 458 4411* ***Fax*** *784 457 4800* ***Rooms*** *32*

Established in 1973, this beach hotel with Spanish-style accents is set on lush landscaped grounds and has meeting and banquet facilities, including a fully equipped conference room. The bar is famous for its special rum punch. The hotel arranges day tours to other islands. **www.sunsetshores.com**

ST. VINCENT, YOUNG ISLAND Young Island Resort 🏊 🍴 ▤ 👪 [W] ⓈⓈⓈⓈⓈ

1 Young Island Crossing, PO Box 211, Kingstown ***Tel*** *784 458 4826* ***Fax*** *784 457 4567* ***Rooms*** *29*

This is an exclusive self-contained resort on a private island off St. Vincent's southeast coast. There is abundant bird and marine life, white-sand beaches for snorkeling and scuba diving, and a salt water pool. Good restaurant on-site *(see p445)*. Beautiful view of the nearby 18th-century relic, Fort Duvernette. **www.youngisland.com**

Key to Symbols *see back cover flap*

THE GRENADINES, BEQUIA Friendship Bay
🖥 🍴 📋 🐾 W $$
PO Box 9, Bequia **Tel** *784 458 3222* **Fax** *784 458 3840* **Rooms** *26*

Luxurious beachfront hotel on a hillside and in the setting of a large tropical garden, with views of the sea and neighboring islands. Tranquil and relaxing, the rooms and suites are designed in colonial Caribbean style. The hotel has Wi-Fi and a good beach bar. **www.yachtcharterclub.com/friendshipbay.htm**

THE GRENADINES, BEQUIA Gingerbread
🖥 🍴 🐾 W $$
PO Box 191, Port Elizabeth, Bequia **Tel** *784 458 3800* **Fax** *784 458 3907* **Rooms** *10*

Small hotel in a beautiful colonial-era house, near Admiralty Bay and the main town, Port Elizabeth. It is only a 5-minute ride in a water taxi to excellent beaches at Lower Bay and Princess Margaret Beach. Live acoustic music in the restaurant several nights a week. **www.gingerbreadhotel.com**

THE GRENADINES, BEQUIA Bequia Beach Hotel
🖥 🍴 🐾 W $$$
Friendship Bay, Bequia **Tel** *784 458 1600* **Fax** *784 458 1700* **Rooms** *33*

This hotel sits on a hillside above one of Bequia's loveliest beaches at Friendship Bay and very close to the beach. The hotel is designed in breezy Caribbean style, with comfortable spacious suites, rooms and villas. Infinity pool, beach bar and top-class restaurant *(see p445)*. **www.bequiabeach.com**

THE GRENADINES, BEQUIA The Frangipani Hotel
🍴 📋 🐾 W $$$
PO Box 1, Bequia **Tel** *784 458 3255* **Fax** *784 458 3824* **Rooms** *15*

This small, charming hotel overlooking Admiralty Harbor was originally built from local stone and hardwoods by a Bequia sea captain around 100 years ago. It is a well-loved spot for dinner and just passing time, and has a lovely open-air waterfront bar. **www.frangipanibequia.com**

THE GRENADINES, BEQUIA Firefly Plantation Bequia
🖥 🍴 📋 🐾 W $$$$$
Spring, Bequia **Tel** *784 458 3414* **Fax** *784 457 3305* **Rooms** *4*

Built hillside on an old working plantation, Firefly has spacious rooms with great views over the idyllic Spring Bay. It is furnished with four-poster beds and double showers. Relaxed and tranquil atmosphere, along with great food and friendly staff. **www.fireflybequia.com**

THE GRENADINES, CANOUAN ISLAND Canouan Resort
🖥 🍴 📋 🐾 W $$$$$
Grand Bay Street, Canouan **Tel** *784 458 8000* **Fax** *784 458 8885* **Rooms** *156*

Built in the style of a Mediterranean village, this oceanfront golf resort set on an extensive private estate has three beaches and is surrounded by one of the world's largest coral reefs. It has five restaurants, a pool bar, a casino, a spa, and even a chapel. Rooms are arranged in an amphitheater-style around the bay. **www.canouan.com**

THE GRENADINES, MUSTIQUE Cotton House
🖥 🍴 📋 🐾 W $$$$$
PO Box 349, Mustique **Tel** *784 456 4777* **Fax** *784 456 5887* **Rooms** *17*

An 18th-century warehouse and sugar mill restored by late British designer Oliver Messel is the only full-service hotel on this private island. It features lovely cottages, rooms and suites with private outdoor showers. Facilities include tennis courts, a spa, a pool, and fitness center. **www.cottonhouse.net**

THE GRENADINES, PALM ISLAND Palm Island Resort
🖥 📋 🐾 W $$$$$
Palm Island **Tel** *784 458 8824* **Fax** *784 458 8804* **Rooms** *42*

Secluded private island resort that epitomizes the idyllic Grenadines. In this tiny island retreat, the buildings blend beautifully with the natural surroundings and there are no telephones or televisions in rooms. Live entertainment, afternoon tea, weekly cocktail parties, and beach barbecues. **www.palmislandresortgrenadines.com**

THE GRENADINES, PETIT ST. VINCENT Petit St. Vincent Resort
🖥 🍴 🐾 ♿ $$$$$
Tel *784 458 8801* **Fax** *784 458 8428* **Rooms** *22*

Cottages just steps away from the beach affording absolute privacy. Each room has its own wooden sundeck, living room, and bedroom. Instead of a telephone, rooms have flags on a pole: yellow for room service, red for not to be disturbed. No check-in, no keys, no television in rooms. Two staff members to each guest. **www.psvresort.com**

THE GRENADINES, UNION ISLAND Clifton Beach Hotel
🖥 🍴 📋 🐾 $
Clifton Harbor, Union Island **Tel** *784 458 8235* **Fax** *784 485 8313* **Rooms** *28*

An institution on Union Island, the hotel was founded in 1952. It is a popular place to enjoy live entertainment or karaoke at night. The hotel is close to the airport and accessible by boat to a private dock. Arranges speedboat excursions and snorkeling trips. **www.cliftonbeachhotel.org**

THE GRENADINES, UNION ISLAND The Anchorage Yacht Club Hotel
🖥 🍴 📋 🐾 W $$
Clifton Village, Union Island **Tel** *784 458 8221* **Fax** *784 458 8365* **Rooms** *11*

Waterfront hotel, large docking facility, and backyard airstrip. Guest rooms are small and all the rooms have seaviews. It has a lovely open-air restaurant with live music. A unique feature is the shallow pool with sharks. Dockside amenities include an elegant boutique and a pastry shop. **www.anchorage-union.com**

THE GRENADINES, UNION ISLAND Amerindi
🖥 🍴 📋 🐾 W $$$$$
Big Sand Beach, Clifton, Union Island **Tel** *784 485 8447* **Fax** *784 485 8448* **Rooms** *16*

Set on a private beachfront with views of the amazingly turquoise sea, this tranquil hotel is perfect for both those who love the outdoors and those who just want to relax. Fine dining at the Casava restaurant right on the beach, featuring à la carte and daily menu. **www.amerindi.com**

Where to Eat & Nightlife

Most of the restaurants, bars, and clubs are clustered in small strips with Villa on St. Vincent and the harbor-front in Port Elizabeth, Bequia, being the major hotspots. Cuisine tends to be international with French, Italian, and local influences. Chefs make the most of amazing fresh produce and seafood, and there is plenty of variety for vegetarians too.

PRICE CATEGORIES
The price ranges are for a two-course meal for one, including tax and service charges and half bottle of wine.

$ under $10
$$ $10–15
$$$ $15–25
$$$$ $25–35
$$$$$ over $35

RESTAURANTS

Seafood Specialty

The cuisine of St. Vincent and the Grenadines owes much to its fresh fish, shrimp, and lobster. Seafood is the specialty of these islands and it is cooked simply or in exotic sauces such as black pepper and ginger sauce. Vegetarian dishes are delicious, made with the island's vegetables such as breadfruit, avocados, and pumpkin. Hairoun, the local beer, is worth a try.

Café at Gingerbread Restaurant

Young Island Resort

ST. VINCENT, GEORGETOWN Ferdie's Restaurant and Bar [V] $$

Commercial Road, Georgetown ***Tel*** *784 458 6433*

Set within Ferdie's Footsteps, a simple hotel, this restaurant serves local food with no set menu but generous portions. Catering mainly for touring parties and hikers, the highlight of this place is that it offers a tour to the peak of volcano La Soufrière. It is open daily.

ST. VINCENT, KINGSTOWN Aggie's Restaurant and Bar [V] ♫ 🚭 ♿ $$

Town Hill ***Tel*** *784 456 2110*

This informal restaurant and bar is known for its delicious seafood specialties: fresh conch, shrimp, fish, and lobster. It serves a good breakfast, lunch, and dinner, with daily specials, a buffet on Fridays, and local juices. It has an open-air bar with happy hour on Friday evenings. The restaurant also features live music.

ST. VINCENT, KINGSTOWN The Bounty Restaurant and Bar 🚭 $$

Egmont Street ***Tel*** *784 456 1776*

Located in a pretty red brick building in the center of Kingstown, this restaurant is open for breakfast and lunch, serving good American and West Indian cuisine with a refreshing variety of juices, including passion fruit. The restaurant has an on-site gallery and gift shop selling works by local artists.

ST. VINCENT, KINGSTOWN Cobblestone Rooftop Restaurant and Bar [V] ⛱ ♫ 🚭 $$

Kingstown ***Tel*** *784 456 1937*

Located in an elegantly renovated warehouse, the Cobblestone Inn's *(see p442)* rooftop restaurant and bar serves traditional Creole cuisine using fresh fish, chicken, mutton, and beef. The restaurant closes at 3pm and does not serve dinner.

ST. VINCENT, KINGSTOWN Mont Rose Restaurant [V] 🍷 ⛱ ♫ 🚭 $$$$

Kingstown ***Tel*** *784 457 0172*

Situated in the hotel of the same name, this breezy restaurant overlooks the city and the Grenadine islands and serves both local and international cuisine with a Creole Sunday lunch once a month and daily meal plans. The restaurant also has an excellent bar and a buffet lunch every Sunday.

ST. VINCENT, KINGSTOWN The Sapodilla Room [V] 🍷 ☰ ⛱ ♫ 🚭 $$$$$

Kingstown ***Tel*** *784 458 1800*

Set within the grand 18th-century mansion of Grenadine House, this restaurant serves good Creole and international cuisine. Its intimate dining room, seating about 20 people, is perfect for candlelight dinners. Reservations are recommended. Live entertainment on Fridays.

ST. VINCENT, VILLA Grand View Grill [V] ⛱ ♫ $$$

Villa Point ***Tel*** *784 457 5487*

Part of the Grand View Beach Hotel *(see p442)*, this popular restaurant has a relaxed atmosphere. It serves grilled meats, pizzas, baguettes, rotis, cocktails, and divine desserts. Jerk night is every Friday and takeout is available. There is a small art gallery downstairs. Open daily from 3pm, except Mondays.

ST. VINCENT, VILLA French Verandah [V] 🍷 ⛱ $$$$$

Villa Beach ***Tel*** *784 453 1111*

Diners sit at candlelit tables on the waterfront terrace of Mariners Hotel, overlooking Villa Beach and enjoying international cuisine with a blend of regional and French touches. Open every day for breakfast, lunch, and dinner. The service is among the most hospitable on the island.

Key to Symbols *see back cover flap*

ST. VINCENT, VILLA The Lime Restaurant and Pub

Opposite Young Island at Villa Harbor **Tel** *784 458 4227*

Popular waterfront eatery, set on a raised deck with a tropical rain garden theme decor. The cuisine is Caribbean, Indian, and international, with fresh fish and lobster from the pond in the restaurant. Choice of pub food or more formal meals. Open from 9am to midnight.

ST. VINCENT, WALLILABOU BAY Wallilabou Anchorage

Tel *784 458 7270*

Beautiful bay setting where scenes from the first *Pirates of the Caribbean* movie were filmed in 2003. It has great Caribbean cuisine with very good fish, shrimp, and lobster dishes. Breakfast, lunch, and dinner every day. Full cocktail bar with happy hours from 5–6pm.

ST. VINCENT, YOUNG ISLAND Young Island Resort Restaurant

1 Young Island Crossing, Kingstown **Tel** *784 458 4226*

This restaurant, situated in the Young Island Resort *(see p442)*, has Continental to regional Caribbean cuisine. In the evening, meals are served in thatched kiosks off the beach. Famous for offering six loaves of freshly baked bread from the kitchen with each meal: white, coconut, banana, raisin, cinnamon, and wheat.

THE GRENADINES, BEQUIA De Reef Beach Bar

Lower Bay **Tel** *784 458 3958*

Located at water's edge on a beautiful beach, this restaurant offers tasty, reasonably priced lunches and three-course dinners mainly based on seafood. Live entertainment most Sunday afternoons. Barbecue on Wednesdays, and local band performances on Sunday afternoon.

THE GRENADINES, BEQUIA Mac's Pizzeria and Bakeshop

Belmont Walkway, Admiralty Bay **Tel** *784 458 3474*

Informal setting by the sea and very popular with locals and visitors alike. Serves pizzas with a choice of 17 toppings including fish, chicken, and lobster. Serves snacks such as conch fritters and pita bread, and also sumptuous desserts. Takeout available.

THE GRENADINES, BEQUIA The Salty Dog

Port Elizabeth **Tel** *784 457 3443*

The main highlight of this restaurant is its Barbados-style flying fish sandwiches, but the burgers and salads are also good. Steak, fish, and shrimp available in the evenings. Dart board and big-screen TVs on the premises. Open for lunch and dinner. Live entertainment on Saturday nights.

THE GRENADINES, BEQUIA Blue Tropic Café

Bequia Beach Hotel, Friendship Bay **Tel** *784 458 1600*

Situated within the same complex as Bequia Beach Hotel *(see p443)*, this lovely restaurant is located beside the hotel's infinity pool and is truly a great place to dine under the stars. It serves both local and international cuisine, a wide variety of meat dishes, and freshly caught lobster and other seafood.

THE GRENADINES, BEQUIA Gingerbread Restaurant

Belmont Walkway, Admiralty Bay **Tel** *784 458 3800*

Specializing in international and Creole dishes and curry, this restaurant serves breakfast, lunch, and dinner under an elevated roof of South American hardwoods and elaborate fretwork. The ground-floor café has good pastries, breads, and cookies. Live local, string, or folk music on Sunday and Wednesday nights.

THE GRENADINES, UNION ISLAND L'Aquarium Restaurant

Clifton Harbor **Tel** *784 458 8678*

This restaurant, part of the Bougainvillea Hotel in the heart of Clifton, serves both French and Creole cuisines, specializing in fresh fish. There is a large saltwater aquarium and lobster tank on-site. Patrons are allowed to feed the fish in the aquarium. Great ambience and relaxing music.

BARS AND CLUBS

Kingstown has very little nightlife, with the most lively places centered around hotel bars. However, a few new places have opened up in recent years, making the capital more interesting at night. It is much the same in the Grenadines, which features hotel restaurants and bars, rather than clubs, as the main spots to hang out.

Basil's Bar

RECOMMENDED PLACES TO GO

Aquatic Club
Villa. (Features live reggae, soca, and calypso.)

The Attic Nightclub
Kingstown. (Karaoke, music and dance bar.)

Basil's Bar
Mustique. (Named in the top 10 bars in the world by *Newsweek*.)

Club 40/40
Kingstown. (Soca, hip hop, DJ, Saturday live jazz.)

Iguana
Villa Beach. (Lively club; Friday is the big party night.)

Teach Restaurant and Bar
Kingstown. (Popular hang-out in cruise ship complex.)

Practical Information

St. Vincent and the Grenadines have always been a sailor's delight and are gradually becoming a popular tourist destination as well. Visitors to the once British Windwards Islands will find the residents very warm and friendly. Relevant information is available from the Ministry of Tourism and most hotels can also provide useful information for tourists. Taxi drivers are usually knowledgeable and helpful.

E. T. Joshua Airport, Arnos Vale, St. Vincent

WHEN TO GO

The average annual temperature in St. Vincent and the Grenadines is 81° F (27°C). The rainy season lasts from May to November, while the coolest months stretch from November and February. A good time to visit the islands is during the winter months between December and February, when some of the islands' biggest events and festivals take place.

GETTING THERE

The E. T. Joshua Airport in St. Vincent is a 15-minute drive to the capital Kingstown. There are no direct international services, but same-day connecting flights arrive via neighboring islands Puerto Rico, Barbados, St. Lucia, Martinique, Grenada, and Trinidad on **Caribbean Airlines**, **Air Jamaica**, **Air Canada**, **American Eagle**, **British Airways**, and **Virgin Atlantic**. **LIAT** has scheduled services that link these islands to the rest of the Caribbean.

Canouan, Bequia, Mustique, and Union Island also have airstrips, where **SVG Air**, **Mustique Airways**, and

Grenadine Airways operate scheduled flights between St. Vincent and the Grenadine islands. SVG Air and Mustique Airways are also available for charter.

DOCUMENTATION

Visitors must have a valid passport, with the exception of citizens of the Organization of Eastern Caribbean States (OECS) who only need proof of citizenship (driver's license or voter's registration card). Visas are required from citizens of various nations, so check with the respective embassies. All visitors must have an onward or return ticket as well. Jewelry, cameras, and other expensive items are allowed if they are for personal use only. Passengers 18 years and over are allowed free import of 200 cigarettes or 50 cigars and 1 quart of wine or spirits. Drugs, firearms and ammunition and spear fishing equipment are prohibited. A departure tax is to be paid when leaving the island.

VISITOR INFORMATION

St. Vincent and the Grenadines Ministry of Tourism has its main office on Upper Bay Street in Kingstown and there is an information booth at the airport as well. **Bequia Tourism Association** has an office in Port Elizabeth. Overseas, tourist offices are located in the UK, Canada, and USA.

HEALTH AND SECURITY

Milton Cato Memorial Hospital is the largest of the six public hospitals on the islands with smaller ones in Georgetown, Chateaubelair, and Bequia and clinics throughout the islands. **Maryfield Hospital** in St. Vincent is a private hospital. The beaches do not have lifeguards. It is advisable not to leave personal belongings unattended and to avoid walking in unlit areas.

BANKING AND CURRENCY

The official currency is the Eastern Caribbean dollar (EC$). Bank hours are Monday to Thursday 8am to 1pm and Friday 8am to 5pm. The bank at E. T. Joshua Airport opens Monday to Friday 9am to noon and 3pm to 5:30pm. A few ATMs are located in St. Vincent, Bequia, and Union Island. Major credit cards are accepted everywhere.

COMMUNICATIONS

The area code for St. Vincent and the Grenadines is 1 784. Coin and phone card services are found throughout the islands. Cell phone service is available in most places, and visitors can receive and

Vehicle available for hire on St. Vincent and the Grenadines

make calls through their roaming service. Local telephone operators include **LIME**, **Caribbean Cellular**, and **Digicel SVG Ltd**.

TRANSPORT

If visitors do not have an OECS or international driving license, a local one can be obtained. Taxis and minibuses are readily available and vehicles can be hired at rental agencies, including **AVIS**, **B&G Jeep Rental**, **Rent and Drive**, and **Greg's Auto Care and Rental Services**. On St. Vincent, public buses link major towns and villages.

SHOPPING

St. Vincent and the Grenadines might not be huge shopping centers but visitors can browse through Kingstown's small town center, where there are locally-made crafts, batik, hand-painted T-shirts, and the famed Sea Island cotton. Some special craft items, including

hand-made dolls, can be found at the nearby **St. Vincent and the Grenadines Craftsmen's Center**. Bequia's model boat-makers sell their amazing creations at workshops in Port Elizabeth and perhaps the most well-known is the **Sargeant Brothers Model Boat Shop**. Port Elizabeth also has several boutiques and shops including **Noah's Arkade** that sells unusual souvenirs.

Model boats lined up and ready for sale, Bequia

LANGUAGE

English is the official language spoken on St. Vincent and the Grenadines.

ELECTRICITY

Voltage is 220 volts, 50 cycles, but Petit St. Vincent has 110 volts, 60 cycles.

TIME

St. Vincent and the Grenadines are on Atlantic Standard Time (AST), 1 hour ahead of Eastern Standard Time in the US, and 4 hours behind GMT.

GETTING MARRIED

Visitors who wish to get married must be residents in St. Vincent and the Grenadines for a minimum of a day. A special Governor General's license (valid for 3 months) is available from the **Ministry of Legal Affairs** for a minimal fee. **A Caribbean Wedding** are wedding coordinators.

DIRECTORY

GETTING THERE

Air Canada
www.aircanada.com

Air Jamaica
www.airjamaica.com

American Eagle
www.aa.com

British Airways
www.ba.com

Caribbean Airlines
www.caribbean-airlines.com

Grenadine Airways
www.caribbeanjet.com

LIAT
www.liatairline.com

Mustique Airways
www.mustique.com

SVG Air
www.svgair.com

Virgin Atlantic
www.virgin-atlantic.com

VISITOR INFORMATION

Bequia Tourism Association
PO Box 146 BQ, Bequia.
Tel 784 458 3286.
www.bequiatourism.com

St. Vincent and the Grenadines Ministry of Tourism
Upper Bay Street, St. Vincent.
Tel 784 457 1502 (Kingstown).
Tel 212 687 4981 (USA).
Tel 020 7937 6570 (UK).
Tel 416 630 9292 (Canada).
www.svgtourism.com

HEALTH AND SECURITY

Maryfield Hospital
Kingstown, St. Vincent.
Tel 784 457 8991.

Milton Cato Memorial Hospital
Kingstown, St. Vincent.
Tel 784 456 1185.

Police, Fire, and Ambulance
Tel 999/911.

COMMUNICATIONS

Caribbean Cellular
Halifax Street, St. Vincent.
Tel 784 457 4600.

Digicel SVG Ltd
Halifax Street, St. Vincent.
Tel 784 453 3022.

LIME
Halifax Street, St. Vincent.
Tel 784 457 1901.

TRANSPORT

AVIS
E. T. Joshua Airport, St. Vincent.
Tel 784 456 6861.

B&G Jeep Rental
Port Elizabeth, Bequia.
Tel 784 458 3760.

Greg's Auto Care and Rental Services
St. Vincent.
Tel 784 457 9814.

Rent and Drive
St. Vincent.
Tel 784 457 5601.

SHOPPING

Noah's Arkade
Frangipani, Bequia.
Tel 784 458 3424.

Sargeant Brothers Model Boat Shop
O'Car Reform, Bequia.
Tel 784 458 3344.

St. Vincent and the Grenadines Craftsmen's Center
Kingstown, St. Vincent.
Tel 784 457 2516.

GETTING MARRIED

A Caribbean Wedding
Bequia. **Tel** 784 528 7444. **www.**acaribbeanwedding.com

Ministry of Legal Affairs
Granby Street, Kingstown, St. Vincent.
Tel 784 456 1762.

Exploring Grenada

Famously known as the "Isle of Spice," Grenada is a lush, mountainous island carved by deep valleys with beautiful waterfalls and cool freshwater streams. Formed by volcanoes, the island's 132 sq miles (344 sq km) are blessed with both tropical rainforest and a bevy of stunning white- and black-sand beaches. To its northeast are the sister islands of Carriacou and Petite Martinique. Their topography is hilly, rather than mountainous, and much drier. Life on the two islands still moves at a leisurely pace. Seafaring, fishing, and boat-building are the major occupations here. The three islands form part of the Grenadine Islands chain that runs south from St. Vincent to Grenada.

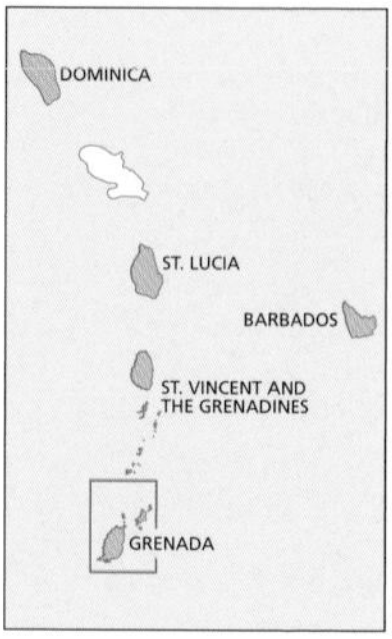

Cruise ships towering over the capital of St. George's, Grenada

KEY

- Major road
- Minor road
- Trail
- Ferry route
- ▲ Peak

SIGHTS AT A GLANCE

Belmont Estate 4
Carriacou 5
Grand Etang Forest Reserve 2
Leapers Hill 3
Petite Martinique 6
St. George's 1

Hotels and Resorts

Ade's Dream 10
Bel Air Plantation 4
Bogles Round House Cottages 11
Grand Anse hotels 1
La Sagesse Nature Center 5
Mango Bay Cottages 2
Monmot Hotel 6
Morne Fendue Plantation House 3
Morne Rouge hotels 9
The Palm Beach Guest House 12
Point Salines hotels 8
True Blue Bay Resort & Villas 7

GETTING AROUND

Island tours are the best way to explore Grenada and its sister isles. On Grenada, visitors can either choose from several tour operators or take a taxi tour. In Carriacou, taxi drivers willing to undertake sightseeing trips await the ferry for prospective customers. Grenada and Carriacou are linked by air (20 minutes), but most visitors prefer taking the ferry. The *Osprey* power-catamaran operates a round-trip passenger service between Grenada and Carriacou. It also plies between Petite Martinique, which is only accessible by boat, and Grenada and Carriacou. Petite Martinique has one taxi service, which offers tours. The *Osprey* runs twice daily during weekdays and once every Saturday and Sunday. Private water taxies are also available.

SEE ALSO

- ***Where to Stay*** pp458–9
- ***Where to Eat & Nightlife*** pp460–61

0 km 5

0 miles 5

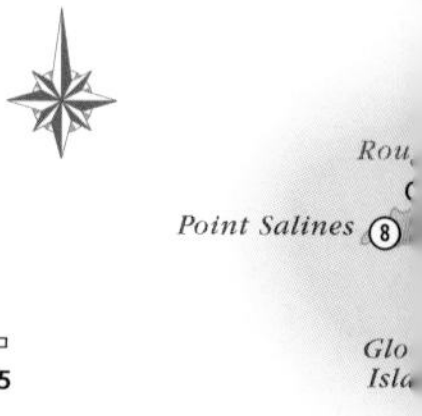

**Mount Carmel Waterfall, Grand Etang
Forest Reserve, Grenada**

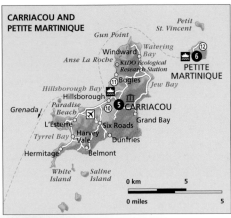

**CARRIACOU AND
PETITE MARTINIQUE**

Petit
St. Vincent

Gun Point

Windward

Watering
Bay

Anse La Roche

KIDO Ecological
Research Station

PETITE
MARTINIQUE

Bogles

Jew Bay

Hillsborough Bay

Hillsborough

Grenada

Paradise
Beach

CARRIACOU

L'Esterre

Grand Bay

Tyrrel Bay

Six Roads

Harvey
Vale

Dunfries

Hermitage

Belmont

White
Island

Saline
Island

0 km 5

0 miles 5

David Bay

Sauters
Bay

Sugar
Loaf

Green
Island

Duquesne Bay

LEAPERS HILL ③

Levera

Sandy
Island

Crayfish Bay

Sauteers

Levera
Pond

St. Mark Bay

Duquesne

ST. PATRICK

Levera Hill
848 ft

Bathway Beach

Waltham

Morne
Fendue ③

R. Salle

Carriacou and
Petite Martinique

Victoria

Victoria Falls

BELMONT ESTATE ④

Lake
Antoine

High Cliff Pt

Maran Bay

Maran

Peggy's Whim

Tivoli

Artiste Pt

Gouyave

Gouyave Bay

Rosemont

Mt. St. Catherine
2,757 ft

Conference

Belmont Estate

Primarily a
cocoa plantation,
this estate has a
chocolate factory
in its vicinity and
offers day visi-
tors an extensive
lunch buffet.

Palmiste Bay

Mt Home

Pearls

Grand Roy

Marigot
Bay

Mt. Granby
2,240 ft

Paradise

Great
River Bay

Marigot

Grenada

Beauregard

Harford
Village

Grenville

Grenville Bay

Telescope Pt

Brizan

Grand Etang
Lake

St. Margaret

Soubise

Marquis Island

Grenville

Founded by the
French in the
1760s, Grenada's
second largest
town boasts the
biggest nutmeg-
processing plant
on the island.

Molinière

Granton

Plaisance

St. Andrews
Bay

Mt. Moritz

Constantine ②

Mt. Carmel

Fontenoy

South East
Mountain
2,348 ft

Munich

Gt Bacolet Pt

La Mode

GRAND ETANG
FOREST RESERVE

Felix Park

Tempé

Mahot

Vincennes

Bellevue

Menere Bay

ST. GEORGE'S ①

Windsor Castle

St. David's

Lower La Tante

Belmont

Laborie

B. Bacolet

Galby Bay

Grand Anse

Marian

Petit Bacaye

La Sagesse
Beach

Requin Bay

Morne
Rouge

Confer

La Sagesse Nature Center

Calvigny

This former plantation is now an idyllic
retreat in proximity to three superlative
beaches, which lure visitors with azure
waters and golden sands.

Hog
Island

Lance
aux Epines

Calvigny
Island

True
Blue Bay

Abundance of flavors for sale at St. George's Spice Market

St. George's ❶

SW coast of Grenada. 🏙 36,000.
✈🚢🚌 ℹ Burns Point (east end
Carenage), 473 440 2279.
www.grenadagrenadines.com

Grenada's capital, St. George's, is renowned for the most picturesque harbor, if not city, in the Caribbean. Rich in West Indian, English, and French history, the city has many architectural gems from the French and British colonial periods. The horse-shoe-shaped harbor is surrounded by pastel warehouses and old Georgian buildings rising up the hills, with distinctive roofs covered with red tiles, which were once the ballasts of ships.

The inner harbor, called the Carenage, is the center of St. George's marine activity, filled with colorful Carriacou sloops, fishing vessels, and tourist boats. Rimming this harbor is Wharf Road, lined with shops and restaurants.

Visitors can stroll along the Carenage waterfront and into the hills to capture stunning views from various angles. Lowther's Lane is the vantage point to watch boats coming into the harbor, especially in the morning.

Fort George is another ideal point from which to photograph the Carenage and the city. Sitting high atop St. George Point with its battery of cannons pointing out to sea, it towers above its surroundings. Built in 1706 by the French, it is now the police headquarters. The site where politician Maurice Bishop and many cabinet members were executed in 1983, this fort was bombed by American troops in the infamous military intervention that followed.

Facing the Carenage are the exquisite Georgian-style Houses of Parliament and three of the city's prominent churches, still roofless after horrific Hurricane Ivan (2004):

St. Andrew's Presbyterian Kirk, St. George's Anglican Church, and St. George's Roman Catholic Cathedral. Built in 1818, the cathedral's Neo-Gothic tower is the city's most visible landmark. The church itself dates to 1884, built on the site of an older church.

Nearby, just off Young Street, is the **Grenada National Museum**. Housed in a former army barracks and prison, this small but interesting museum covers many aspects of the island's history and culture, ranging from the Caribs to Hurricane Ivan.

Built in 1894, the 340-ft (103-m) Sendall Tunnel connects the Carenage to the Esplanade, which is home to the Esplanade duty-free mall, located at the cruise terminal.

Nearby, the Granby Street leads to Market Square (also called Spice Market). Outdoors, women in traditional Grenadian attire sell spices and produce. In the cooler, new indoor market, a range of souvenirs and products made in Grenada are sold. About 5 miles (8 km) to the east of the city along the Eastern Main Road lies La Sagesse Nature Center (see p458), a former manor house built by Lord Brownlow in 1968 that now functions as an inn.

⚓ **Fort George**
St. George Point. 🕘 9am–5pm
Mon–Fri.

🏛 **Grenada National Museum**
Corner Young & Monkton Streets.
Tel 473 440 3725. 🕘 9am–4:30pm
Mon–Fri; 10am–1pm Sat. 📷🚫

Fort George perched above the colonial warehouses of Carenage Harbor, St. George's

For hotels and restaurants on this island see pp458–9 and pp460–61

Grand Etang Lake in a volcanic crater, Grand Etang Forest Reserve

Grand Etang Forest Reserve ❷

7 miles (11 km) NE of St. George's.
🛈 *Grand Etang Visitors' Center, 473 440 6160.* ⭕ *9am–4pm Mon–Fri.* 📷🎥♿🍴🚻 **Note:** *open during weekends if big cruise ships are in port.*

Located high in the central mountains, this reserve protects a lush rainforest and several ecological sub-systems, and is popular for sightseeing and hiking, with trails leading to its many waterfalls *(see p455)*. The forest was greatly damaged by Hurricane Ivan, but has quickly regrown. The visitors' center's walkway is lined with spice vendors and musical entertainers, and visitors may also get a chance to spot mona monkeys. The center has some interpretive displays, and provides a good view of Grand Etang Lake in the extinct volcanic crater.

Leapers Hill ❸

28 miles (45 km) N of St. George's.
Tel *473 444 3222.* ⭕ *10am–4pm daily.* 📷🎥🚻🍴

A historic landmark (also called Carib's Leap), this is where the Carib Indians leapt off a 100-ft (30-m) cliff into the sea, rather than surrender to French colonists in 1650. This site now has a cemetery

and the Interpretive Center, which portrays the history of the place. A short tour takes visitors through Amerindian artifacts and a miniature model Carib village. Just below the center are some recreated petroglyphs on the rocky wall and travelers can enjoy a scenic view of the Grenadine islands.

Belmont Estate ❹

20 miles (32 km) N of St. George's.
Tel *473 442 9524.* ⭕ *8am–4:30pm Sun–Fri.* 📷🎥♿🍴🚻
www.belmontestate.net

It is possible to get a glimpse of traditional Grenadian plantation life at this 400-acre (162-ha) estate dating back to the late 1600s, and owned by the Nyacks since 1944. Originally a coffee plantation, the estate has changed crops over the years; today, primarily cocoa and nutmeg are grown here. Touring the cocoa operation, visitors learn about the traditional processing of a cocoa bean, from its start as a pod on the tree to fermenting to drying on wooden trays in the sun. It is possible to sample delicious cocoa tea and organic dark chocolate, produced by the Grenada Chocolate Company nearby. A small museum documents island history and houses estate memorabilia. The plantation's lunch buffet of

home-cooked Creole dishes, including estate-grown fruits and vegetables, is a feast.

Environs
Other plantations in this area include the 18th-century stone Morne Fendue Plantation House *(see p459)*, with its Victorian museum, guest rooms, and delectable West Indian lunch buffet. Nearby is **Helvellyn House**, a good spot to enjoy an alfresco lunch of authentic Caribbean dishes served in a lovely setting of gardens with a view of the Grenadines. The pottery workshop here also offers lessons.

🏛 **Helvellyn House**
La Fortune, St. Patrick. **Tel** *473 442 9252.* ⭕ *Pottery workshop: 9am–5pm Mon–Sat.*

Women walking on cocoa beans to aerate them, Belmont Estate

Beachside stilt house, the northeast coast of Carriacou

Carriacou 5

23 miles (37 km) N of Grenada. 👥 *5,300.* ✈ ⛴ 🚌 ℹ *Main Street, Hillsborough, 473 443 7948.* **www**.grenadagrenadines.com

Although covering an area of just 13 sq miles (34 sq km), Carriacou is the largest of the Grenadine islands. It is a popular destination for a day trip from Grenada, but also offers overnight budget accommodations in a tranquil setting. The Carib word for Land of Reefs, Carriacou is ringed by some of Caribbean's most exquisite reefs.

The Osprey Lines Ltd. ferry *(see p463)* arrives daily from Grenada to the heart of the main town Hillsborough. In town, the small **Carriacou Museum**, set in a restored cotton gin mill, exhibits Amerindian and African artifacts, and traces the early British and French occupation of the islands. The museum also pays tribute to Canute Calliste (1914–2005), the internationally acclaimed Grenadian artist.

For a sweeping panoramic view of Hillsborough Bay, Carriacou, and the outer islands, visitors can head northeast to the 640-ft (195-m) hilltop site of Princess Royal Hospital in Belair, framed by seaward-pointing cannons.

In the east coast village of Windward, the Carriacou sloops are still built using the highly skilled traditional methods of constructing sturdy wooden boats originally introduced by the Scottish colonial settlers of the island.

On the northern tip, Gun Point is named after the still standing cannon erected here by the British in the 1780s.

Heading south down the west coast, **KIDO Ecological Research Station** arranges guided eco-tours including hiking through High North National Park, the isle's highest point, and turtle-watching.

Nearby, the secluded Anse La Roche, a wonderfully scenic beach with offshore coral reefs, can be reached either by a water taxi or on foot.

South of Hillsborough on L'Esterre Bay is the famous Paradise Beach, an easily accessible, 1-mile (1.6-km) long beach with plenty of amenities. Sandy Island, a lovely islet just offshore, is popular for snorkeling and picnics.

Farther south, Tyrrel Bay is a yachters' haven. Heading east, water-taxis are available in Belmont that ferry visitors to White Island, an islet that has pristine stretches of fine sandy beaches and offers great snorkeling opportunities. It is also relatively uncrowded and is ideal for people who want some solitude.

Carriacou Museum
Paterson Street, Hillsborough. ***Tel*** *473 443 8288.* 🕐 *9:30am–4pm Mon–Fri.* ● *public hols.* 💲 🚫📷 🛍

KIDO Ecological Research Station
Sanctuary, Carriacou. ***Tel*** *473 443 7936.* **www**.kido.optsoftware.com

Petite Martinique 6

3 miles (5 km) NE of Carriacou. 👥 *less than 1,000.* ⛴

Dominated by a 738-ft (225-m) volcanic cone that gives it its conical appearance, the tiny island of Petite Martinique (locally called PM) is roughly 1 mile (1.6 km) in diameter. It is scarcely populated and most residents are acquainted with each other. The sea is the source of livelihood here and boat-building is the main occupation of most islanders.

Travelers arrive at the jetty in Paradise, the sole village on the islet, with basic amenities. There is only one main road, 2-mile (3-km) long, so a taxi tour takes under an hour. The rocky East Coast is uninhabited and unreachable by road. While Paradise has a white-sand beach, Petit St. Vincent, a 5-minute boat ride away, and other surrounding cays have a few good strands and offer excellent snorkeling.

Volcanic peak rising up from Petite Martinique

Spice Isle

More spices are grown in Grenada per square mile than anywhere else in the world. With the fragrant aromas of cinnamon, ginger, and vanilla wafting through the air, the island has been dubbed the "Isle of Spice" as it is the Caribbean's only spice producer. The most important crop is nutmeg,

Souvenir box of spices

coined "black gold" by former Prime Minister George Brizan (1995). Spice estates, including the Gouyave and Grenville Nutmeg Processing Stations and Dougaldston Spice Estate, offer tours highlighting the various stages of spice production, and also sell fresh spices and spice products.

NUTMEG AND MACE

Grenada is the second largest producer of nutmeg in the world. Its production has been the backbone of Grenada's economy and agriculture since 1843, when it was brought here from Banda, India. Along with its twin spice, mace, which grows around the shell of the nutmeg, it is one of the isle's top export crops.

The nutmeg tree *grows up to 75 ft (23 m) in height, bearing a yellow fleshy fruit called the pericarp, which contains two spices – nutmeg and mace. When ripe, the fruit splits open and drops to the ground, from where it is gathered by hand.*

The nutmeg seed *has a dark, thin shell, covered by the lacy, brilliantly scarlet mace.*

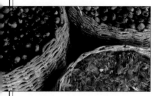

Mace *is separated from nutmeg shells at the processing stations. Cured in wooden bins for four months, the mace gradually assumes a golden tinge.*

Nutmeg syrup, *jams, liqueur, as well as chocolate bars, soaps, perfumes, and candles are some locally-made spice goods.*

Nutmeg shells *are dried indoors for six to eight weeks. Their brittle shells are then removed and the nuts washed, graded, polished, and packaged for export.*

OTHER SPICES

Grenada's famous spices include cloves, ginger, pepper, pimento, cinnamon, bay leaves, and tonka beans. All over the island, there are plantations as well as spice-processing plants.

The cinnamon bark *is peeled during the rainy season. When dried in the sun, it curls to form cinnamon sticks.*

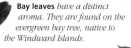

Bay leaves *have a distinct aroma. They are found on the evergreen bay tree, native to the Windward Islands.*

Black pepper *berries grow on creeping vines. Reddish in color when picked, they turn black after drying.*

Clove *buds when picked have a deep red hue. When dried, they turn dark brown.*

Outdoor Activities and Specialized Holidays

Grenada and its sister isles are an ideal getaway for the adventurous and with their varied geographical topography, comprising mountains, volcanoes, rainforests, and waterfalls, the islands lend themselves to a wide range of outdoor activities. Guided hikes are the best way of exploring mainland Grenada and Carriacou. Alternatively, a day-sail or a trip on the *Osprey* catamaran is a great way to see the rugged terrain, jutting shorelines, and beautiful beaches from the sea. The islands also offer popular activities such as scuba diving and snorkeling from its numerous offshore reefs.

A relatively uncrowded stretch of Grand Anse Beach, Grenada

BEACHES

The tri-island nation of Grenada, Carriacou, and Petite Martinique is blessed with 45 white-sand and nine black-sand beaches, which are among some of the best in the Caribbean. The 2-mile (3-km) long Grand Anse, popular with sunbathers, is by far Grenada's most beautiful beach, while the Morne Rouge also on the southwestern side is quieter and attracts relatively fewer visitors. Other choices include Bathway Beach in the northeast and La Sagesse Nature Center with three beaches to explore.

Paradise Beach in Carriacou has a protective reef, which allows visitors the comfort of swimming in its calm waters. Anse La Roche is accessible only by a steep, well-marked trail or a water-taxi.

Paradise village on Petite Martinique is an excellent base to explore the nearby tiny cays and great beaches. Petit St. Vincent is also just a 5-minute boat ride away.

DIVING AND SNORKELING

Although Grenada is not as renowned as some other Caribbean isles for diving, it features a larger variety of marine creatures and less-crowded, more intact reefs, many in its five marine parks. Carriacou, known as the Land of Reefs, is a popular dive center. Together, the two islands boast more than 50 sites, most rated easy (except for a few with strong currents), and quickly reached by a 5-to 15-minute boat ride. There are several walls and wrecks with common marine life, including sharks, turtles, lobsters, giant moray eels, soft coral forests, and sponges. Carriacou is famous for its beautiful coral gardens and small marine creatures such as sea horses.

Wreck enthusiasts will get their fill exploring the many shipwrecks, including *Bianca C*, the largest in the Caribbean Sea. Known as the "*Titanic* of the Caribbean," the sunken 600-ft (183-m) cruise ship is only suitable for experienced wreck divers.

In Grenada, the most convenient snorkeling is south of Grand Anse Beach. La Sagesse is another great spot. A new, unique site for both diving and snorkeling is the **Underwater Sculpture Park** in Grenada's Molinière Bay by artist Jason de Caires Taylor. Several day sails and dive operators, including **Aquanauts Grenada**, offer both diving and guided snorkeling trips to the site.

All the Grenadian islands, including Petite Martinique and its neighboring cays, offer good snorkeling opportunities. Grenada has a few dive shops, most are located on the south coast beaches, and Carriacou has three. For a list, contact the Grenada Board of Tourism (*see p463*) or **Grenada Scuba Diving Association**.

WATERSPORTS

Many resorts, watersports centers, and dive shops, mainly on Grand Anse Beach, offer a full array of watersports and rentals including ocean kayaks, Hobie Cats, windsurfing, parasailing, waterskiing, and wake and knee boarding. **Adventure River Tubing** is a fun, wet activity offered in Grenada. Participants don lifejackets and helmets before boarding a large modified rubber tube with handles. With guides to assist along the way, they "whitewater" tube around rocks and down little drops on Balthazar River, in the depths of the rainforest. Also available are combo adventure jeep/tubing tours.

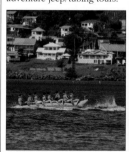

Riding a banana boat at Grand Anse Beach, Grenada

Waterfalls of Grenada

With its mountainous terrain and lush tropical rainforest, Grenada boasts several idyllic waterfalls, some amongst the most beautiful in the Caribbean. Grand Etang Forest Reserve *(see p451)*, has the highest number of falls in any one geographic region. Rosemount Falls, in the western parish

Yellow-eyed thrush found in Grenada

of St. John, is privately owned and only open to visitors lunching at Rosemount Plantation House. Farther north, Victoria Falls (also called Tufton Hall), is the island's tallest waterfall, and is relatively difficult to reach. Visiting one or all of these cataracts is a highlight of a trip to the island.

Tropical plants, including banana, are abundant near the Seven Sisters Falls.

The Seven Sisters range from small cascades to 70-ft (21-m) falls.

Pools, formed at the base of the Seven Sisters, are ideal for a refreshing dip.

WATERFALLS OF GRAND ETANG FOREST RESERVE

Grand Etang harbors five waterfalls within the reserve or on its fringes: Concord, Honeymoon, Annandale, Seven Sisters, and Royal Mt. Carmel. Trails pass through rainforest, citrus groves, and plantations growing fragrant spices and fruits.

Annandale Falls *is one of the easiest to reach. A lovely garden of labeled trees, such as nutmeg and flowering plants, lines the path to the falls.*

Concord Falls *consists of three waterfalls of which the first is the most accessible and popular.*

FLORA AND FAUNA

Trails around the waterfalls are lined with huge mahogany, gommier trees, and endemic plants such as Grand Etang fern. Wildlife includes nine-banded armadillos and iguanas.

The mona monkey, *introduced from Africa three centuries ago, is one of the most easily spotted animals near Rosemount Falls.*

Selaginella and fungi *are widespread in the forest around Victoria Falls.*

Water hyacinths, *among other plants such as balisier, wild fuchsia, and hibiscus, thrive near Grand Etang's waterfalls.*

Day sail boats at the lagoon in St. George's marina

HIKING

Grenada's mountainous terrain, reaching 2,757 ft (840 m) atop Mount St. Catherine, provides one of the Caribbean's loveliest and most varied hiking environments, and a good variety of flora and fauna. To protect its natural environment, the island has set aside one-sixth of its landmass as wildlife sanctuaries and parks.

One of the most popular hiking areas, Grenada's Grand Etang Forest Reserve *(see p451)* has hikes ranging from easy 15-minute jaunts to rigorous expeditions. However, it was severely hit by Hurricane Ivan and some trails remain uncleared. The Forestry Department has not produced any informative material on the trails since the hurricane, but there are plans to start publishing again. Until then, it is best to hire a hiking guide.

Expert **Telfor Bedeau**, who knows the island intimately, assesses visitors' interests and abilities and then creates tailor-made hikes or mountain climbs anywhere on the island. Other popular operators include **Henry's Safari**, **Kennedy Tours**, **K&J Tours**, and **Mandoo Tours**.

Hilly, but not mountainous, Carriacou is ideal for walking. KIDO Ecological Research Station *(see p452)* can arrange a guide for hikers.

DAY-SAILS AND BOAT TRIPS

Thanks to its many bays and sheltered anchorages, Grenada is one of the main yachting centers of the Eastern Caribbean. For a day out on the water, there are some good options. **Carib CATS**, a 60-ft (18-m) sailing catamaran, offers full- and half-day snorkeling and sunset cruises, as does **Shadowfax**. **First Impressions** runs whale and dolphin-watching tours, four sailing tours (minimum six guests), fishing trips, and evening karaoke tours aboard catamarans. **Spice Kayaking & Eco Tours**, launched by the same operator, offers guided eco tours by kayak and pedal-boat in some of Grenada's most untouched spots, including sunset and moonlight trips. **Grenada Seafaris** takes visitors on a high-speed Zodiac tour of Grenada's west coast. The 2-hour tour includes snorkeling at the Underwater Sculpture Park *(see p454)* and fun lessons on the isle's history, ecology, and geography. The UK-based **Carib Tours** is another operator that runs luxury yachts near Grenada. In Carriacou, KIDO runs catamaran trips.

FISHING

Marine life is plentiful in Grenada and a wide range of fish, billfish, **A visitor with her catch**
blue and white marlin, sail-fish, wahoo, yellowfin tuna, and a common dolphin fish, called dorado or mahimahi, populate its waters. Plenty of charters offer half- and full-day deep-sea fishing, including **True Blue Sportfishing** aboard the 31-ft (9-m) *Yes Aye*. The agency believes in conserving billfish stocks and regularly tags and releases all marlin and sailfish. Skipper Stewart's **Wayward Wind Fishing Charters** offers discounts to groups.

Hurricane-damaged forest in the Grand Etang Forest Reserve

For hotels and restaurants on this island see pp458–9 and pp460–61

GARDENS

With such a profusion of tropical flora, it is no surprise that Grenada has some spectacular gardens to tour. On a guided walking tour through pleasant **Laura Herbs and Spice Garden**, visitors can see all the herbs and spices grown on the island, such as thyme, cinnamon, and basil, and learn about their medicinal uses.

Just 15 minutes from St. George's is **Sunnyside Garden**. At this garden, Jean Renwick shares her passion by showing the beautiful 3-acre (1-ha) gardens around her home, which comprise a gorgeous koi pond, native flora, tortoises, a citrus grove, and themed gardens including a Japanese one. The view from here, 600 ft (183 m) above sea level, is stunning.

Hibiscus in Sunnyside Garden

TURTLE-WATCHING

Historically the Grenadians relied upon sea turtles for food and income. **Ocean Spirits**, a non-profit organization that is engaged in protecting the endangered leatherback turtles by demonstrating their higher value as nesting turtles, is the first to offer turtle-watching tours. These are entirely run by two local communities. With a trained turtle guide, visitors witness the spectacle of massive leatherbacks nesting on remote Levera Beach, home to one of the Caribbean's top three largest nesting populations. All profits go to sea turtle or other conservation initiatives in the local communities, providing them with an economic stake in saving turtles. Those interested can book for this program, available from April to July, with **Discover Grenada**.

In Carriacou, leatherbacks and critically endangered hawksbills nest at Petite Carenage Beach from March to October. Guests can join night nesting patrols that protect turtles from illegal hunting and egg poaching. For more information visitors can contact KIDO.

A leatherback turtle laying eggs

DIRECTORY

DIVING AND SNORKELING

Aquanauts Grenada
True Blue Bay Resort and Spice Island Beach Resort, Grenada.
Tel 473 444 1126. www.
aquanautsgrenada.com

Grenada Scuba Diving Association
www.grenadascubadiving
association.com

Underwater Sculpture Park
Tel 776 282 9173.
www.underwater
sculpture.com

WATERSPORTS

Adventure River Tubing
St. George's, Grenada.
Tel 473 444 5337.
www.grenada
jeeptours.com

HIKING

Henry's Safari
Grenada.
Tel 473 444 5313.
www.henrysafari.com

Kennedy Tours
Grenada.
Tel 473 444 1074.
www.kennedy-
grenadatours.com

K&J Tours
St. Pauls, Grenada.
Tel 473 440 4227.
www.grenadaguide.com/
kjtours/hikes.htm

Mandoo Tours
St. George's, Grenada.
Tel 473 440 1428.
www.grenadatours.com

Telfor Bedeau
Grenada.
Tel 473 442 6200.

DAY SAILS AND BOAT TRIPS

Carib CATS
St. George's, Grenada.
Tel 473 444 3222.

Carib Tours
The Point,
210 New Kings Road,
London SW6 4NZ.
Tel 020 7751 0660.
www.caribtours.co.uk

First Impressions
St. George's, Grenada.
Tel 473 440 3678.
www.catamaran
chartering.com

Grenada Seafaris
Grenada.
Tel 473 405 7800.
www.grenada
seafaris.com

Shadowfax
True Blue, St. George's, Grenada.
Tel 473 437 3737.
www.bananaboattours
grenada.com

Spice Kayaking & Eco Tours
Allamanda Hotel, Grand Anse, St. George's, Grenada.
Tel 473 440 3678.
http://spicekayaking.com/

FISHING

True Blue Sportfishing
St. George's, Grenada.
Tel 473 444 2048.
www.yesaye.com

Wayward Wind Fishing Charters
Grenada Yacht Club,
St. George's,
Grenada.
Tel 473 538 9821.
www.grenada
fishing.com

GARDENS

Laura Herbs and Spice Garden
Perdmontemps,
St. David,
Grenada.
Tel 473 443 2604.

Sunnyside Garden
St. Paul's village,
St. George's,
Grenada.
Tel 473 440 2613.

TURTLE-WATCHING

Discover Grenada
Tel 473 435 5958.

Ocean Spirits
St. George,
Grenada.
Tel 473 442 2341.
www.ocean
spirits.org

Choosing a Hotel

From luxury hotels and all-inclusive resorts to small, inviting guesthouses and inns, Grenada offers a wide range of accommodations in all price categories. Most resort hotels are located in the island's southwest corner in Grand Anse, Morne Rouge, Point Salines, and Lance aux Epines. Places to stay on Carriacou and Petite Martinique are, for the most part, smaller and inexpensive.

PRICE CATEGORIES
The following price ranges are for a standard double room per night and all taxes included.

$ under $100
$$ $100–200
$$$ $200–300
$$$$ $300–400
$$$$$ over $400

GRENADA

Homestays Grenada
Visitors can experience the real Grenada with Homestays Grenada, an affordable alternative to hotels. Families can hire their own accommodations – from a simple wooden house with basic amenities to comfortable ones – in a residential community. *Tel 473 444 5845* **www.homestaysgrenada.com.**

Coyaba Beach Resort

True Blue Bay Resort & Villas

GRAND ANSE, ST. GEORGE Allamanda Beach Resort & Spa $$
Grand Anse Beach **Tel** 473 444 0095 **Fax** 473 444 0126 **Rooms** 50

Three-star Allamanda is one of the least expensive resorts on Grand Anse Beach. All 50 suites in the two-story building have a private balcony facing the Caribbean Sea. Executive suites have whirlpools. Other facilities include restaurant and bar, swimming pool, gym, spa, and Grand Anse Scuba. **www.allamandaresort.com**

GRAND ANSE, ST. GEORGE Grenada Grand Beach Resort $$
Grand Anse Beach **Tel** 473 444 4371 **Fax** 473 444 4800 **Rooms** 240

This is the island's largest hotel. Sprawling across 20 acres (8 ha), fronting Grand Anse Beach, its showpiece is a 300-foot (90-m) fantasy pool with waterfalls, swim-up bar, two Jacuzzis, and a sunset pool. A restaurant and bar, fitness center, pool tables, tennis, kayaking, and dive shop keep guests busy. **www.grenadagrand.com**

GRAND ANSE, ST. GEORGE Blue Horizons Garden Resort $$$
Morne Rouge Road **Tel** 473 444 4316 **Fax** 473 444 2815 **Rooms** 32

Surrounded by gardens, this peaceful and informal resort offers spacious rooms with kitchenettes, a tropical bird aviary, pool, whirlpool, a gourmet restaurant *(see p460)*, and a bar. Guests can enjoy the beach and facilities at the nearby sister property Spice Island Beach Resort. **www.grenadabluehorizons.com**

GRAND ANSE, ST. GEORGE Flamboyant Hotel $$$
Morne Rouge Road **Tel** 473 444 4247 **Fax** 473 444 1234 **Rooms** 67

Set in tropical gardens sloping to the south end of Grand Anse Beach, every room in Flamboyant Hotel has a splendid, panoramic view of the bay and St. George's. On the beach guests will find a restaurant, a late-night pub, pool, spa, Jacuzzi, and Dive Grenada. There is a gym and a games room too. **www.flamboyant.com**

GRAND ANSE, ST. GEORGE Coyaba Beach Resort $$$$$
Grand Anse Beach **Tel** 473 444 4129 **Fax** 473 444 4808 **Rooms** 80

This popular resort was redeveloped after Hurricane Ivan. Located on the beach, the guest rooms are spread over eight buildings. The signature restaurant Arawakabana serves gourmet cuisine and there is a bar and spa. Complimentary non-motorized watersports and golf. **www.coyaba.com**

GRAND ANSE, ST. GEORGE Mount Cinnamon Beach Resort $$$$$
Morne Rouge Road **Tel** 473 439 9900 **Fax** 473 439 8800 **Rooms** 21

This luxurious, yet homely resort has million-dollar views of Grand Anse and St. George's from its suites and The Verandah Restaurant *(see p460)*. One-bedroom haciendas and two- and three-bedroom villas are set on the hillside amongst beautiful gardens. Facilities include spa and tennis. **www.mountcinnamongrenada.com**

GRAND ANSE, ST. GEORGE Spice Island Beach Resort $$$$$
Grand Anse Beach **Tel** 473 444 4423 **Fax** 473 444 4807 **Rooms** 64

This redesigned resort is the crème-de-la-crème. Guests are treated like family by owner Sir Royston Hopkin, who extends a weekly invitation to his home for cocktails. Prices are all inclusive, with 24-hour room service. There is a restaurant *(see p460)*, bar, spa, and family rooms. **www.spiceislandbeachresort.com**

LA SAGESSE La Sagesse Nature Center $$$
La Sagesse Beach **Tel** 473 444 6458 **Fax** 473 444 6458 **Rooms** 12

Nature's heaven, La Sagesse Nature Center sits on a tree-shaded beach. The old manor house, once the plantation estate of Lord Brownlow, houses five large guest rooms retaining their original grandeur. There is a restaurant *(see p460)*, bar, room service, and family rooms. **www.lasagesse.com**

Key to Symbols *see back cover flap*

LANCE AUX EPINES, ST. GEORGE Monmot Hotel $$

Samaan Drive **Tel** *473 439 3408* **Fax** *473 444 3407* **Rooms** *20*

Located near Grenada's south coast, Monmot Hotel is a great-value, intimate hotel in a quiet location. The self-contained suites include 14 studios with private shaded patios overlooking the small freshwater pool and Garth's restaurant and bar. Service is excellent. Prickly Bay Beach is a 2-minute walk away. **www.monmothotel.com**

MORNE FENDUE, ST. PATRICK Morne Fendue Plantation House $

Grenville Road **Tel** *473 442 9330* **Fax** *473 442 9294* **Rooms** *13*

Trip back in time at this 18th-century Victorian home, with thick stone walls. Five rooms in the plantation house are furnished with period pieces. The annexe has eight bedrooms. The rooms set within colorful gardens have a view of Mount St. Catherine. Rates include breakfast. Excellent service. **www.mornefendueplantation.com**

MORNE ROUGE, ST. GEORGE Gem Holiday Beach Resort $$

Morne Rouge Beach **Tel** *473 444 4224* **Fax** *473 444 1189* **Rooms** *20*

This great-value resort is the only one on stunning Morne Rouge Beach. Units are self-catering, with air-conditioned bedrooms, satellite TV, kitchenette, and private veranda with ocean or garden view. Good service and family rooms. Optional all-inclusive packages. **www.gembeachresort.com**

MORNE ROUGE, ST. GEORGE Laluna $$$$$

Laluna, Portici Beach **Tel** *473 439 0001* **Fax** *473 439 0600* **Rooms** *16*

A tranquil, romantic hideaway, minimalist chic Laluna blends Italian and Balinese decor. Private cottages have a large veranda with a tiny plunge pool. Includes in-room spa services, meditation, and yoga lessons. Excellent restaurant *(see p460)*. Children under 14 not allowed during high season. **www.laluna.com**

POINT SALINES, ST. GEORGE LaSource $$$$$

Pink Gin Beach **Tel** *473 444 2556* **Fax** *473 444 2561* **Rooms** *100*

The redeveloped LaSource offers a full program of land and watersports on the secluded Pink Gin Beach with personal instruction, from scuba to 9-hole golf. Also includes archery and tennis facilities. Get pampered with a daily spa massage or body treatment. No guests below the age of 16. **www.theamazingholiday.com**

POINT SALINES, ST. GEORGE Maca Bana Villas $$$$$

Magazine Beach **Tel** *473 439 5355* **Fax** *473 439 6429* **Rooms** *7*

On the hill above The Aquarium Restaurant *(see p460)* sit 5 two- and 2 one-bedroom villas. Each is named for the fruit tree in front and the theme is continued inside, with original artworks by owner Rebecca Thompson. Guests will enjoy the sea view from the infinity pool or their private hot tub. **www.macabana.com**

ST. DAVID'S Bel Air Plantation $$$$$

Corinth, St. David's Harbor **Tel** *473 444 6305* **Fax** *473 444 6316* **Rooms** *165*

On a hillside overlooking St. David's Harbor in southeast Grenada, these colorful pastel villas and cottages, built in Caribbean architectural style, are ideal for relaxation and romance. Set in lush gardens, Bel Air has a lovely infinity pool, spa, family rooms, and an excellent bar. Optional all-inclusive packages. **www.belairplantation.com**

TRUE BLUE BAY, ST. GEORGE True Blue Bay Resort & Villas $$$

Old Mill Road **Tel** *473 443 8783* **Fax** *473 444 5929* **Rooms** *42*

On the south coast where the Caribbean and Atlantic meet, this family-owned boutique hotel offers good value. All rooms come with a kitchenette and balcony. Room service and facilities for children. There are 2 pools and a daily complimentary shuttle to beach. Gourmet restaurant *(see p461)*. **www.truebluebay.com**

WOODFORD, ST. JOHN Mango Bay Cottages $$

Woodford **Tel** *473 444 3829* **Fax** *473 444 3829* **Rooms** *4*

On a cliff above a secluded beach on the west coast, this cozy resort gets favorable reviews. The cottages have a kitchenette and large patio, and a view of the sea and tropical garden. Small restaurant serves breakfast and dinner for guests only. Spa facilities. No children under 14 allowed. **www.mangobaygrenada.com**

CARRIACOU Ade's Dream $

Hillsborough **Tel** *473 443 7317* **Fax** *473 443 8435* **Rooms** *23*

Owned and run by a Carriacouan family, Ade's Dream is one of the islands' best budget hotels, located centrally in Hillsborough just 2 minutes from the dock. Studio-rooms include a kitchenette and patio while economy rooms share a large veranda and kitchen. There is a supermarket on the premises. **www.adesdream.com**

CARRIACOU Bogles Round House Cottages $

Bogles **Tel** *473 443 7841* **Rooms** *3*

A casual, laid-back resort set amidst tropical foliage. Three self-contained cottages are just a few steps away from the secluded Sparrow Bay beach, perfect for relaxing with a book. Award-winning chef Roxanne Russell serves Caribbean and European delights *(see p461)*. There is a good bar. **www.boglesroundhouse.com**

PETITE MARTINIQUE The Palm Beach Guest House $

Tel *473 443 9103* **Rooms** *2*

Two fully equipped hillside apartments with kitchens overlooking the bay and the Grenadines. The open floor plan is spacious, with a queen-sized and two single beds in the family apartment and a queen-sized bed in the other. Food is delivered to the rooms from the nearby restaurant *(see p461)* on request. **www.thepalmbeach.net**

Where to Eat & Nightlife

Night-time Grenada, Carriacou, and Petite Martinique are still relatively quiet, although Grenada is attracting a gamut of cosmopolitan international restaurants and clubs, mostly in the busy southwest. Most establishments are open to the warm breezes, the tropical night naturally setting a fun, romantic ambience. Live entertainment livens up the place, especially in high season.

PRICE CATEGORIES
The price ranges are for a two-course meal for one, including tax and service charges. The price excludes any liquor, which is expensive all over the islands.

Ⓢ under $10
ⓈⓈ $10–15
ⓈⓈⓈ $15–25
ⓈⓈⓈⓈ $25–35
ⓈⓈⓈⓈⓈ over $35

RESTAURANTS

Local Cuisine

Distinct Grenadian cuisine blends West Indian and Creole ingredients, with seafood being the specialty. Local dishes include *callaloo* (a vegetable, crab or meat soup) and "oildown", a coconut milk stew. Not surprisingly, aromatic fresh spices enhance most dishes and nutmeg, the principal spice, infuses everything from jam and syrup to ice cream and rum punch.

Plas Manjé

Rhodes Restaurant

BELMONT, ST. PATRICK Plas Manjé   Ⓥ 🍷 📶 ⚡ ♿   ⓈⓈⓈ

Belmont Estate **Tel** *473 442 9524, 473 438 4152*

Belmont Estate makes a great day trip and its restaurant offers an authentic taste of Grenada. The plantation lunch buffet features *callaloo* soup, honey ginger chicken, fish in Creole sauce, and other specialties. Guests can bring their own alcohol for a small corkage. Open noon–3pm, closed on Saturdays.

GRAND ANSE, ST. GEORGE La Boulangerie   Ⓥ 🍷 📶 🍽 ⚡ ♿   ⓈⓈ

Le Marquis Complex, Morne Rouge Road **Tel** *473 444 1131*

For those looking for a taste of Europe, this affordable casual restaurant in Le Marquis Complex is the place to visit. Guests can get their pastry from the French bakery and coffee shop and satisfy their pizza and pasta cravings in the Italian restaurant and pizzeria. Free evening delivery with minimum order.

GRAND ANSE, ST. GEORGE La Belle Créole   Ⓥ 🍷 📶 ⚡ ♿   ⓈⓈⓈⓈ

Blue Horizons Garden Resort **Tel** *473 444 4316*

Featuring creative, gourmet West Indian cuisine, La Belle Créole of the Blue Horizons Garden Resort *(see p458)* is a Grenadian institution. It offers first-class service in a romantic setting with a view of the Caribbean Sea. Try *callaloo* soufflé, sugarcane shrimp, or the daily fish crusted with spicy cornmeal dipped in Creole tomato sauce.

GRAND ANSE, ST. GEORGE The Verandah Restaurant   Ⓥ 🍷 📶 🎵 ⚡ ♿   ⓈⓈⓈⓈ

Mount Cinnamon Beach Resort **Tel** *473 437 2889*

This restaurant has a chic, yet comfortable, ambience with its pleasing decor of bright Caribbean pastels, cozy seating clusters, and archways opening to the skies. The front terrace offers stunning views of Grand Anse Bay and St. George's. It serves Mediterranean dishes with a West Indian twist. Open for breakfast, lunch, and dinner.

GRAND ANSE, ST. GEORGE Oliver's   Ⓥ 🍷 📶 🎵 ⚡ ♿   ⓈⓈⓈⓈⓈ

Spice Island Beach Resort **Tel** *473 444 4423*

A gourmet meal at this AAA four-diamond restaurant in Spice Island Beach Resort *(see p458)* is the most expensive dining option on the island. The five-course international *table d'hôte* menu changes nightly. Extensive wine list. Reservations recommended. Children not allowed for dinner during high season, but an early buffet option available.

LA SAGESSE BEACH, ST. DAVID La Sagesse   Ⓥ 🍷 📶 ⚡ ♿   ⓈⓈⓈ

La Sagesse Nature Centre **Tel** *473 444 6458*

The dining room deck of La Sagesse Nature Center *(see p458)* overlooks the beach and makes a romantic evening setting. Guests enjoy the freshest fish, delivered daily by fishermen, or sample their gourmet version of Grenadian oildown. Signature dishes include beet salad and chocolate mousse.

MORNE ROUGE, ST. GEORGE Laluna   Ⓥ 🍷 🍽 📶 ⚡ ♿   ⓈⓈⓈⓈⓈ

Laluna, Portici Beach **Tel** *473 439 0001*

Laluna's *(see p459)* thatched-roof dining room opens on to the beach. The eclectic Italian-fused menu with a Caribbean twist combines seafood with Italian specialties. Serves well-known Italian wines, as well as ones from small wineries. Open for breakfast, lunch, and dinner. Reservations required. Children under 12 not allowed.

POINT SALINES, ST. GEORGE The Aquarium Restaurant   Ⓥ 🍷 📶 🎵 ⚡ ♿   ⓈⓈⓈⓈ

Magazine Beach, below Maca Bana Villas **Tel** *473 444 1410*

This place has an outstanding setting in tropical gardens fronting Magazine Beach. The dining room is built around a cliff, with a central waterfall and koi ponds. The fused West Indian and European cuisine is beautifully presented. There is an all-day Sunday barbecue with live reggae. Reservations recommended.

Key to Symbols *see back cover flap*

POINT SALINES, ST. GEORGE The Beach House Restaurant & Bar

Portici Beach **Tel** *473 444 4455*

Sharing Portici Beach with Laluna, The Beach House is a tranquil place to have a meal. The Caribbean architecture features shutters that open wide to reveal the beach and sea beyond. Excellent international cuisine includes plenty of fresh fish and seafood. Try chicken or shrimp roti for lunch. Closed on Sundays.

ST. GEORGE'S, ST. GEORGE Victory Bar and Grill II

Port Louis Marina, Lagoon Road **Tel** *473 435 7263*

A fun place for a casual lunch or dinner, the grill dishes out hearty American-style food like burgers, hotdogs, and Caesar salad, served with potato and green salad, coleslaw, and baked beans. The house specialty is the victory burger topped with lettuce, tomato, Gouda cheese, onions, pickles, and pineapple. Happy hours daily.

ST. GEORGE'S, ST. GEORGE The Nutmeg Restaurant and Bar

The Carenage **Tel** *473 440 2539*

One of the isle's oldest restaurants, this simple diner serves local specialties including fish and seafood accompanied by rice and peas with ground provisions, as well as *callaloo* lasagna. Try their famous nutmeg rum punch and nutmeg ice cream. Request a window seat when making reservations. Open for breakfast, lunch, and dinner.

ST. GEORGE'S, ST. GEORGE Patrick's

Lagoon Road **Tel** *473 440 0364*

Patrick's is the place to experience the home-style cooking of Grenada. It is located in a typical Grenadian house overlooking the Lagoon, with lunch and dinner including a feast of 20 local dishes plus soup and dessert. Sample *cou-cou*, Creole *lambie* (conch), tannia cakes with shrimp, and *oildown*.

ST. GEORGE'S, ST. GEORGE BB's Crabback Caribbean Restaurant

Progress House, Carenage **Tel** *473 435 7058*

On the waterfront in St. George's, BB's is the place for great Caribbean food. Signature dishes are lobster calypso and barracuda la port. The restaurant takes its name from crabmeat baked with herbs, wine, and cheese sauce served in a crab shell.

TRUE BLUE BAY, ST. GEORGE True Blue Bay Restaurant & Beach Bar

True Blue Bay Resort & Villas **Tel** *473 443 8783*

The resort's *(see p459)* elegant dining room sits on a deck over the sea. Serves international cuisine with Mexican specials on Fridays and barbecue and live music on Saturdays. Tuesday is Grenadian night, featuring Caribbean specials and live pan music. The casual Dodgy Dock next door has lighter lunch and dinner with weekly specials.

CARRIACOU Bogles Round House Restaurant

Bogles **Tel** *473 443 7841*

The owners of Bogles Round House Cottages *(see p459)*, Roxanne and Phil Russell, describe their restaurant as a piece of art. The food is great – Roxanne was twice Grenada's chef of the year and captained the silver-medal winning team in the Taste of the Caribbean 2007 competition. The restaurant bakes its own bread daily.

PETITE MARTINIQUE The Palm Beach Restaurant

Tel *473 443 9103*

The Palm Beach Guest House *(see p459)* restaurant fronts the palm-shaded beach. Diners relax to the sound of breaking swells in 5 roofed huts in a garden setting, with a panoramic view of the neighboring Grenadine islands. The menu features West Indian and international cuisine, specializing in fresh seafood.

BARS AND CLUBS

Many island bars and rum shops are casual affairs. Most hotels offer live high-season entertainment including dancing and steel bands. Guests should ask their hotel desk for current activities. Do not miss Fish Friday, a lively Friday night street party in Gouyave. Fishermen haul in their fresh catch, which street vendors prepare in a myriad ways along with local favorites, such as plantain chips. Wash it down with rum or Carib beer and "limin" to DJ or live music.

Karma Nightclub, Bar & Grill

RECOMMENDED PLACES TO GO

Club Bananas
True Blue, St. George.
(Fun Fridays. Outdoor sports bar.)

Di Vino Italian Wine Bar
Le Marquis Complex, St. George.
(Only Italian wine bar in Grenada.)

Dodgy Dock
True Blue Bay Resort, St. George.
(Local bands play on Saturdays.)

Fantazia 2001
Gem Holiday Beach Resort,
St. George. (Local favorite.)

Hardwood Bar
Paradise Beach, Carriacou.
(Join locals for weekend "limin".)

Karma Nightclub, Bar & Grill
The Carenage, St. George's, St.
George. (Upscale, state-of-art club.)

Kudos Bar & Grill
Lance aux Epines, St. George.
(Twice-nightly happy hour.)

The Owl
Flamboyant Hotel, Grand Anse.
(Late-night sports bar.)

Victory Bar and Grill
Port Louis Marina, St. George.
(Casual bar; steel pan on Fridays.)

Practical Information

The Western Hemisphere's second smallest independent country, Grenada has had a relatively slower rate of growth in tourism and infrastructure development than its larger Caribbean cousins. After Hurricane Ivan (2004), however, the island rebuilt quickly, attracting several international hotel and vacation property developers. Today, visitors can find luxury accommodations and tourist amenities here. The laid-back tranquil atmosphere makes it a great destination for a relaxed holiday.

WHEN TO GO

Most people visit Grenada between December and April. Year-round temperature ranges from 75 to 85° F (24 to 30° C), with November to February being the coolest and January to May the driest season. June to December is humid, although there are hardly any prolonged spells of rainfall. Hurricane season lasts from June to November, with September the peak month.

GETTING THERE

All flights arrive at Point Salines International Airport (GND). From the UK, **British Airways**, **Virgin Atlantic**, and **Golden Caribbean** have weekly direct flights to Grenada. **Caribbean Airlines** connects London's Heathrow to Antigua, Barbados, and Trinidad with daily direct flights and has connections via **LIAT** that arrive the same day. **Air Jamaica** flies from New York and Montego Bay and **American Eagle** from Puerto Rico. From Toronto, weekly direct flights between December and April are offered by **Air Canada**, which also has year-round flights to Barbados and Trinidad, with

LIAT connections. **Conviasa Airlines** has twice-weekly flights from Venezuela.

DOCUMENTATION

A valid passport for British, and US citizens or a proof of citizenship bearing a photograph for Canadians, and a return ticket are required. The citizens of the USA, Canada, British Commonwealth, Japan, South Korea, most Caribbean and European countries, do not require a visa. A departure tax is mandatory at Point Salines International Airport and there is no ferry service to Grenada. Contact the **Immigration Department** or visit the **Grenada Board of Tourism** website for a list of countries requiring, and those exempt from, visas.

VISITOR INFORMATION

The Grenada Board of Tourism has offices in the US, Canada, UK, and Germany. Its head office is in Grenada and a branch in Carriacou. The **Carriacou and Petite Martinique Tourism Association** also provides information concerning transportation and accommodations on Grenada's sister islands.

HEALTH AND SECURITY

The **General Hospital** in St. George's, **Princess Alice Hospital** in St. Andrew's Parish, and **Princess Royal Hospital** in Carriacou are public hospitals. Visitors should have medical insurance. All hotels have doctors on call. In case of hurricanes and other emergencies, evacuation to a larger center is common.

Grenada is generally safe for traveling. However, muggings and purse snatchings may occur after dark, so it is best to keep valuables in the hotel safe and to exercise caution when walking and traveling in local buses or taxis. Often found on beaches, the tiny green fruit of the manchineel apple trees contains poison, which can blister the skin.

BANKING AND CURRENCY

The official currency is the Eastern Caribbean dollar. Most places accept US dollars, but banks have the best currency exchange rates. Traveler's checks are accepted everywhere, and major credit cards are accepted by most hotels, car rental companies, and shops. Banking hours are usually Monday to Thursday 8am to 3pm, and Friday 8am to 4pm. ATM machines are available on Grenada and Carriacou.

COMMUNICATIONS

Public phones are available throughout the islands. There are coin phones for local calls and prepaid card phones for both local and overseas calls. International Direct Dialing is available from most hotels, but can be expensive. The country code for Grenada is 473, followed by a seven-digit number. Mobile service is available from **Cable & Wireless** and **Digicel**. Roaming service is available to AMPS-compatible cellular owners. Local cell phones can also be rented from the Cable & Wireless and Digicel offices. Most hotels have wireless and/or business centers with Internet. There are a few cyber cafés.

Cruise ships docked at the cruise liner terminal, St. George's, Grenada

TRANSPORT

Taxis and minibuses for hire are readily available and are denoted by an "H" license plate. Between 6pm and 6am, there is an additional charge. Private minibuses provide an inexpensive service. Buses display route numbers, and fares are fixed according to distance. The bus terminus is on Melville Street in St. George's. In Carriacou, buses run from about 7am to 5pm. Water taxis are available in St. George's, Carriacou, and Petite Martinique.

To hire cars, visitors need to be over 21, with a driving license and a local driving permit, issued by car rental firms such as **Dollar Rent-A-Car**, **AVIS** and **Martin & Wayne's Auto Rental**. Grenada has about 650 miles (1,050 km) of paved roads in decent condition. However, most have blind corners, with narrow or no shoulders. Driving is on the left and all occupants must wear seat belts.

Osprey Lines Ltd. has a daily ferry service connecting Grenada, Carriacou, and Petite Martinique. **SVG Air** has a daily 20-minute flight from Grenada to Carriacou's Lauriston Airport.

SHOPPING

The best buys are spices, jellies, jams, syrups (especially nutmeg), rum, batik and screen-printed textiles, locally made handicrafts and art. Most duty-free shops selling jewelry, alcohol, crystal, perfumes, and gift items are on the Carenage and Esplanade Shopping Mall in St. George's, or at Point Salines International Airport.

Souvenir stall displaying locally-made food products

LANGUAGE

Grenada's official language is English but a French-African patois is also spoken.

ELECTRICITY

Grenada operates on 220 volts but 110-volt appliances also work with adaptors.

TIME

Grenada is on Atlantic Standard Time (AST), 4 hours behind Greenwich Mean Time (GMT).

GETTING MARRIED

Visitors need to be on the island three days before applying for a marriage license. On the third day, apply in person at the Prime Minister's office after paying stamp duty and license fees. Generally, the license is ready within two working days, but it may take a little longer if either partner is divorced. View the wedding section on the Grenada Board of Tourism website for details.

DIRECTORY

GETTING THERE

Air Canada
www.aircanada.com

Air Jamaica
www.airjamaica.com

American Eagle
www.aa.com

British Airways
www.ba.com

Caribbean Airlines
www.caribbean-airlines.com

Conviasa Airlines
www.conviasa.aero

Golden Caribbean
www.goldencaribbean.co.uk

LIAT
www.liatairline.com

Virgin Atlantic
www.virgin-atlantic.com

DOCUMENTATION

Grenada Board of Tourism
Tel 473 440 2279 (St. George's),
473 443 7948 (Carriacou),
416 595 1339 (Canada),
800 927 9554 (USA),
020 8877 4516 (UK),
49 611 2676720 (Germany).
www.grenada grenadines.com

Immigration Department
Tel 473 440 2456.

VISITOR INFORMATION

Carriacou and Petite Martinique Tourism Association
Tel 473 443 7882.
www.carriacoupetite martinique.com

HEALTH AND SECURITY

General Hospital
Grand Etang Road, St. George's, Grenada.
Tel 473 440 2051.

Police and Fire
Tel 911.

Princess Alice Hospital
Mirabeau, St. Andrew's, Grenada.
Tel 473 442 7251.

Princess Royal Hospital
Carriacou.
Tel 473 443 7400.

COMMUNICATIONS

Cable & Wireless
Tel 473 440 1000.
www.candw.gd

Digicel
Tel 473 439 4500.
www.digitalgrenada.com

TRANSPORT

AVIS
Corner Paddock and Lagoon Roads, St. George's, Grenada.
Tel 473 440 3936.

Dollar Rent-A-Car
Point Salines International Airport.
Tel 473 444 4786.
www.dollargrenada.com

Martin & Wayne's Auto Rental
Hillsborough gas station, Carriacou.
Tel 473 443 7204.

Osprey Lines Ltd.
Queen's Jetty on the Carenage, St. George's, Grenada.
Tel 473 440 8126.
www.ospreylines.com

SVG Air
Tel 784 457 5124.
www.svgair.com

Exploring Barbados

A tiny island of 166 sq miles (430 sq km), Barbados has beautiful beaches surrounded by clear waters and coral reefs, and year-round good weather. The island has a rich and diverse cultural background with vibrant festivals and fine historic buildings especially in its capital, Bridgetown. The island's biggest asset, however, is its population. The Bajans love to share their island's history, folklore, and traditions. Visitors will have a vast choice of things to do, including exploring the hidden waterfalls and underground rivers in Harrison's Cave. Restaurants serving the island's traditional dishes are found on most beaches.

Brightly colored shops selling local crafts and souvenirs, Holetown

GETTING AROUND

Buses are a great way to get around. They operate throughout the island and there is a set fare irrespective of the distance. It is advisable to carry the exact fare or use tokens which can be bought at bus stations. Taxis are plentiful and reasonably priced. However, they are not metered and it is best to negotiate a price before setting off. Registered taxis have the letter "Z" on their number plate. Taxi drivers also make knowledgeable guides for either a half-day or one-day tour. A hired car is the best way to explore the island independently. A good map can be helpful but many roads are not signposted and secondary ones are often pot-holed.

West Coast
The prime resort area in Barbados, the west coast also has some of the safest beaches for swimming in the Caribbean.

North

Archer's Bay   Flatf
Stroud Bay
Content   ST. LUC
Maycock's Bay   Half Ac
Fustic   1B
Mile And A Quarter   1C
Six Men's Bay
ST. PET
Speightstown   Orar 2A
Mullins Beach   Gibbes
Mount Standfast   ST. JAM
Alleynes Bay   Porters   7

HOLETOWN   11
Paynes Bay Beach   9
Appleby   10   11
12
W.

Black Rock

Bank

BRIDGETOW

St. Vincer
Carlisle
Needham's

KEY

— Major road

═══ Minor road

--- Ferry route

— · Administrative border

0 km   5

0 miles   5

Bridgetown
Cosmopolitan Bridgetown has a wide range of duty-free shops and bars.

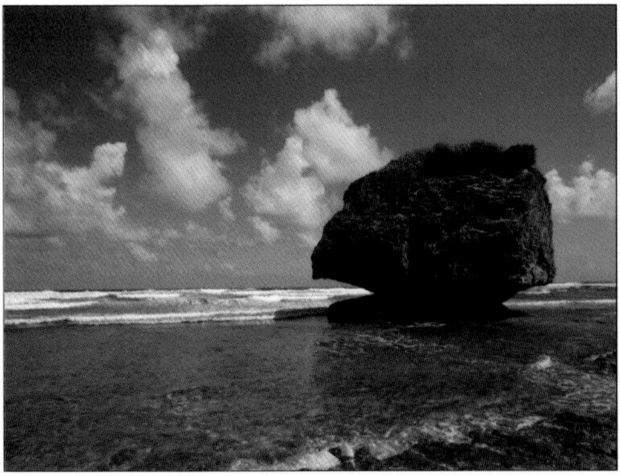

One of the massive boulders dotting the coastline, Bathsheba

SIGHTS AT A GLANCE

Barbados Wildlife Reserve 10
Bathsheba 9
Bridgetown 1
Garrison Historic Area 2
Gun Hill Signal Station 7
Harrison's Cave 8
Holetown 11
Ocean Park 5
Oistins 4
South Coast 3
St. Nicholas Abbey p471 12
Sunbury Plantation House 6

Hotels and Resorts

Accra Beach Hotel (3)
Barbados Hilton (1)
Bougainvillea Beach Resort (6)
Colony Club Hotel (7)
Coral Reef Club (8)
Crystal Cove Hotel (12)
Europa – All Seasons (10)
Hastings hotels (2)
Mango Bay (9)
Paynes Bay hotels (11)
Rockley Beach hotels (4)
St. Lawrence Gap hotels (5)

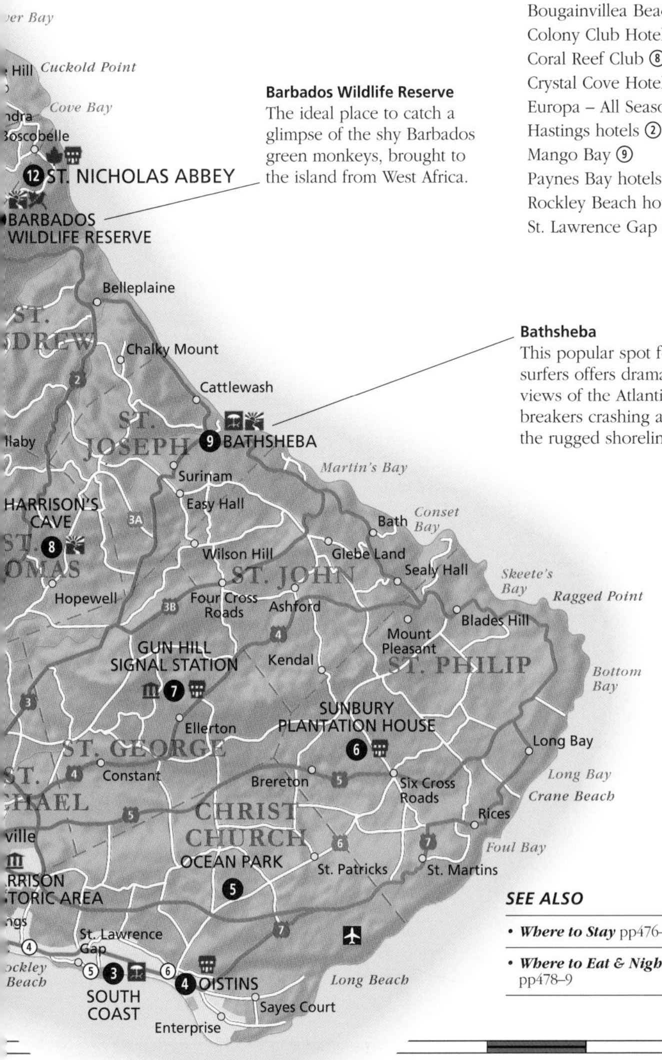

Barbados Wildlife Reserve
The ideal place to catch a glimpse of the shy Barbados green monkeys, brought to the island from West Africa.

Bathsheba
This popular spot for surfers offers dramatic views of the Atlantic breakers crashing against the rugged shoreline.

SEE ALSO

- ***Where to Stay*** pp476–7
- ***Where to Eat & Nightlife*** pp478–9

Parliament Buildings in the capital, Bridgetown

Bridgetown ❶

SW coast of Barbados. 🏛 *96,500.*
✈ 🚌 🚢 ℹ *Barbados Tourist
Office, Bridgetown Harbor Road,
246 427 2623.* 🎭 *Crop Over
Festival (Aug).*

Founded in 1628, Bridgetown
is a fascinating combination
of the old and new. The town
center is compact and any
walking tour typically starts
in the National Heroes Square
with its statue of Lord Nelson.
Adjacent is the colorful
Carenage, where in the
early days ships would be
careened – turned over to
have barnacles scraped off
their sides. A busy marina
today, it is packed with luxury yachts and surrounded by
restaurants, bars, and shops.
   Broad Street has been the
main shopping street in
Barbados for more than
300 years. It is dominated
by the impressive Mutual Life
Assurance building with its
twin white domes.
   At the end of Broad Street
are the Italian-Renaissance-
style **Parliament Buildings**,
the third oldest in the
English-speaking world. The
Parliament was founded in
1637 and has met regularly
since 1639. The west wing
houses the Museum of
Parliament and the National
Heroes Gallery.
   Nearby, in Synagogue Lane,
is the **Bridgetown Synagogue**
and cemetery. The synagogue,
founded in 1654, is the oldest
in the western hemisphere. It
has been restored and is open
to the public, and contains the
Nidhe Israel Museum.

Bridgetown Harbor hosts the
modern cruise ship terminal
and is encircled by upscale
duty-free shops, bars, and restaurants. Along the waterfront
is the Pelican Village, an arts
and crafts center amid beautiful gardens. Visitors can
watch artists at work and buy
their wares.

🏛 **Parliament Buildings**
Broad Street. **Tel** *246 427 2019.*
⏰ *10am–4pm Mon–Fri.* 📷

✡ **Bridgetown Synagogue
and Nidhe Israel Museum**
Synagogue Lane. **Tel** *246 436 6869.*
⏰ *9am–4pm Mon–Fri.* 📷

Garrison Historic
Area ❷

2 miles (3.2 km) SE of Bridgetown.
🚗

The first garrison in the West
Indies was located in the
Garrison Historic Area. More
than 70 original buildings and
forts still stand. Most of the
garrison buildings date from
1789 onwards, when Barbados

became the British army's
headquarters in the Windward
and Leeward Islands. However,
Charles Fort, the first on the
island, was built in the 1650s,
while St. Ann's Fort can be
traced to 1688. The tomb-
stones in the restored Military
Cemetery graphically depict
the history and hardships of
the garrison. Today, Garrison
Savannah is the island's main
horse racing track and is used
for parades and celebrations.
   Barbados Museum is set in
what was the garrison's prison.
Built around 1818 and an
example of West Indies
Georgian architecture, it is a
great place to learn about the
island's history, culture, and
people. The exhibits are
displayed in a series of
galleries, set in former cells.
Different galleries realistically
re-create lifestyles from various
periods in the island's history.

Environs
About 3 miles (5 km)
northwest of the Garrison
Historic Area is **Mount Gay
Distillery**, which has been
officially producing rum since
1703 making it the world's
oldest. A visitors' center is set
in a chattel-style house next
to the warehouses where
aged rums are stored. Guided
tours take visitors through the
process of rum-making and
end in the tasting room.
Nearby, the **West Indies Rum
Distillery** houses the Malibu
Visitors' Center. One of the
most modern refineries in the
Caribbean, its main products
are Cockspur rum and Malibu
Coconut rum. Guests can tour
the distillery, enjoy lunch and
rum cocktails at the Malibu

Display of Arawak artifacts in the Barbados Museum, Garrison Historic Area

For hotels and restaurants on this island see pp476–7 and pp478–9

Beach Club, and then laze away the afternoon on the club's beautiful beach.

Close by, Kensington Oval has been the home of Barbados cricket since 1982 and the venue for international test matches. The islanders are passionate about the sport and matches tend to take on a carnival atmosphere.

🏛 **Barbados Museum**
Tel 246 427 0201. ◯ 9am–5pm Mon–Sat, 2–6pm Sun. 🖼 🅿

⛏ **Mount Gay Distillery**
Spring Garden Highway, St. Michael. **Tel** 246 425 8757.
◯ 9:30am–3:30pm Mon–Fri. 🖼
📷 🅿 www.mountgayrum.com

⛏ **West Indies Rum Distillery**
Black Rock. **Tel** 246 425 9301.
◯ 9am–4pm Mon–Fri. 🖼 📷
www.westindiesrum.com

South Coast ❸

5 miles (8 km) SE of Bridgetown.
🚌

The south coast is built up all the way from Bridgetown to Oistins, but still boasts some marvelous stretches of sand such as the Accra, Rockley, and Dover beaches. A well-signposted detour off the main coast road leads to **St. Lawrence Gap**, which is the party capital of Barbados. It has restaurants offering a wide range of cuisines, but the local Bajan dishes, especially the fresh fish, are superb. Towards the evening, fast-food stalls serving cheap but delicious fare spring up along the road. These are extremely popular with residents. Local vendors also set up stalls selling hand-made jewelry and other arts and crafts. Bars play live music and as the diners finish their meals, the nightlife starts to buzz and continues until the early morning hours. St. Lawrence has a small police post but late-night revelers should still take care and avoid walking in areas with poor lighting.

The Gap is also worth visiting during the daytime, for the impressive Chattel House Village, a collection of shops selling tropical fashions, handicrafts, and souvenirs.

Shops and restaurants in the lively St. Lawrence Gap on the South Coast

Oistins ❹

7 miles (11 km) SE of Bridgetown.
🚌 🖼 Fish Festival (Mar or Apr).

Named after Austin, the area's first landowner, Oistins is the island's main fishing port and boasts a modern jetty and busy fish market. It has a long history, and in 1652, a treaty was signed at its Mermaid Tavern which led to Barbados accepting the authority of Oliver Cromwell, Britain's military commander and Lord Protector.

The village is well worth a visit as it has many interesting historic buildings that are now protected, as well as several rum shops. Visitors can also watch the bright and colorful fishing boats return at the end of the day and unload their catch. Oistins is renowned for its annual Fish Festival which celebrates the local fishing industry. During the festival, stalls are set up on the streets selling salt fish cakes and fried fish, drinks, and local goods amid much music and dancing.

Ocean Park ❺

10 miles (16 km) E of Bridgetown.
Tel 246 420 7405. 🚐 🚗 ◯ 10am–5pm Nov–Apr, 10am–6pm May–Oct.
🖼 🅿 📷 www.oceanpark barbados.com

Set in beautifully landscaped tropical gardens, Ocean Park is an aquarium and marine adventure park, and makes for a great family day out. Scattered throughout the park are 26 displays of tropical fish and marine life from around the world. Visitors can feed the fish, pet the rays, and even get close to a reef shark. There is a kids' playground, adventure mini-golf course, restaurant, and a gift shop. It is also home to the Clean Up Barbados Project, which works with local organizations and schools to protect and maintain the island's natural environment. It undertakes a number of conservation protects which inculcate a better understanding of the threats faced by the island's coral reefs.

Fascinating marine life exhibits, Ocean Park

Classic interiors and exquisite furnishings in the lounge area, Sunbury Plantation House

Sunbury Plantation House 6

10 miles (16 km) NE of Bridgetown.
Tel 246 423 6270. ▣ ◯ 10am–5pm daily. 🖼 🅿 🍴 ⟦⟧

Built around 1660 by one of the island's first settlers, Matthew Chapman, Sunbury Plantation House is among the oldest and grandest of the great houses in Barbados. Chapman was apparently granted lands on the island because he was related to the Earl of Carlisle. The house was built to withstand hurricanes with walls more than 30 inches (76 cm) thick.

Restored after a fire in 1995, the Great House recreates the lifestyle and ambience of the 18th and 19th centuries. Its original furnishings have been replaced by antiques from other houses on the island. Look out for the Barbados mahogany furniture, some of which has been made from trees grown on the plantation. It is the only great house with all rooms open for viewing. A unique collection of horse-drawn carriages is displayed in the cellars, and plantation vehicles and machinery are scattered around the land-scaped grounds. There is also a bar, restaurant, and gift shop in the plantation complex. The Planter's Candlelit Dinner is a five-course feast around the 19th-century mahogany table where the

notorious pirate Samuel Hall Lord is said to have dined. After dinner, guests are taken on a tour around the house.

Environs
About 2 miles (3 km) south from Sunbury Plantation House, the **Four Square Rum Factory and Heritage Park** is located on the site of a former sugar plantation. The island's most modern distillery offers tours and tastings. There are a number of shops, galleries, and eateries as well as a small theme park, pet farm, children's park, and sugar machinery museum.

Farther east, **Crane Beach** nestles beneath cliffs that overlook the fabulous white and pink coral sands. This isolated stretch of sand along

Entrance of the Gun Hill Signal Station

the south coast is among the most stunning beaches on the island. In olden times, ships would anchor in the bay and a crane set on top of the cliff would load or unload their cargo. Protected by a coral reef, Crane Beach provides for safe swimming inshore.

Gun Hill Signal Station 7

5 miles (8 km) NE of Bridgetown.
🚗 ◯ 9am–5pm Mon–Sat.

Gun Hill Signal Station is part of a chain of signal stations built across the island by the British in 1818. Signaling mirrors were used to flash warnings about approaching enemy ships from one station to the next. Standing at 700 ft (213 m) above sea level, the station has been carefully restored by the Barbados National Trust *(see p474)*. It offers great views over most of the island and has a small museum housing military memorabilia. From its tower, the statue of a large white lion is visible below the station. This British military emblem was carved from a single boulder in 1868 by Henry Wilkinson, a British officer.

Harrison's Cave ❽

7 miles (11 km) NE of Bridgetown.
Tel 246 438 6640. 🚌 ℹ️ *Welchman Hall, St. Thomas, 246 438 6640.*
🕘 *9am–3:45pm Wed–Sun.* 🎫 ✓
📷 📁 **www**.harrisonscave.com

A magnificent attraction, this cave was carved out over millions of years by seeping surface water. It comprises a series of crystallized limestone subterranean caverns with underground rivers, waterfalls, and uniquely shaped stalagmites, stalactites, and columns. The cave is named after Thomas Harrison, who owned the land in the 1770s. Although several expeditions ventured into the caves, it took almost 200 years before it was fully explored and mapped by Danish engineer and cave adventurer, Ole Sorensen. Conducted tours through the floodlit caverns aboard small electric trams are available.

Environs
About 3 miles (5 km) north of Harrison's cave, the Old Richmond Plantation is the setting for the 50-acre (20-ha) **Flower Forest**. It was planted by a group of islanders who wanted to preserve an area of tropical beauty for future generations. A map available at the visitors' center provides information about the tropical fruit trees, exotic plants, and flowers. The area is also rich in wildlife and includes green monkeys and chattering birds. There is wheelchair access throughout although some of the nature trails are uneven. There is an information center and refreshments are available.

Home to 200 species of tropical plants, flowers, and fruits, the **Welchman Hall Gully**, 2 miles (3 km) north of Harrison's Cave, is owned by the Barbados National Trust. It is named after General William Asygell, a Welshman whose plantation included the gully. The remnants of a colossal cave whose roof collapsed thousands of years ago are still visible. There used to be an entrance from the gully into Harrison's Cave. Asygell introduced tropical plants from around the world in

Lilypond and palm trees in Andromeda Gardens, near Bathsheba

1860, and today there are mature trees and towering bamboo groves. The grapefruit, once called the forbidden fruit of Barbados, is said to have originated here. The aim is to introduce more native plants so that the Gully's flora and fauna resembles that of the island in the 18th century.

Bathsheba ❾

11 miles (18 km) NE of Bridgetown.
🚗

As travelers approach this small, pretty fishing village on the rugged Atlantic coast, they are met with spectacular views of the huge boulders offshore that line its dramatic landscape. The crashing waves makes Bathsheba a popular spot for surfers and it hosts many international surfing events. Swimmers must be wary of the powerful waves and undercurrents.

Environs
On the outskirts of Bathsheba is **Andromeda Gardens**, one of the most remarkable and varied botanical gardens in the Caribbean. Created by Iris Bannochie in 1954, it was bequeathed by her to the Barbados National Trust. The gardens showcase spectacular botanical displays including hibiscus, orchids, bougainvillea, and heliconia.

Bottles of locally produced white rum

RUM PRODUCTION

Barbados has been a rum producer for at least 350 years and continues to manufacture many of the world's finest rums. By the end of the 17th century, rum had become an important commodity and figured prominently in the infamous Triangle Trade in which slaves from Africa were sold for rum in the West Indies, which was then sold in Europe to raise more money to buy more slaves. Rum is produced from sugarcane which is grown throughout the island. The cane is crushed to extract sugar which is boiled to obtain the sticky molasses. This is then fermented and distilled into a clear liquid. Light or white rums can be bottled immediately or aged for only a few months until they are smooth, while dark or gold rums are usually aged for many years in oak barrels as they develop their color, richness, and flavor. Two of the world's best gold rums found on Barbados are Mount Gay Eclipse and Mount Gay Extra Old.

Trail through the mahogany forest, Barbados Wildlife Reserve

Barbados Wildlife Reserve ❿

14 miles (22 km) N of Bridgetown. **Tel** 246 422 8826. 🚌 ⬛ *10am–5pm daily, monkey feeding at 2pm.* 🖼 ✅ 🛒 🏪 www.barbados.org

The Barbados Wildlife Reserve is a wonderful place to see the island's wildlife in its natural surroundings. The reserve was founded in 1985 by Canadian primatologist Jean Baulu to protect the Barbados green monkey. These monkeys originally came from West Africa about 350 years ago, but are now found

Agouti inside an enclosure, Barbados Wildlife Reserve

throughout the island. Over time, other Caribbean animals such as iguanas, agoutis, deer, armadillos, and the rare red-footed tortoise, have also been introduced into the reserve's mahogany woods.

There are several imported animal species, a walk-through aviary, and also a collection of snakes. The reserve has an information and education center, built from coral stone gathered from the nearby fields, while the pathway bricks come from 17th- and 18th-century sugar mills.

Environs
Nearby, a delightful 3-mile (5-km) trail gently winds through a natural forest to the restored 19th-century **Grenade Hall Signal Station**. The signal tower was one of six straddling the island, designed to get news back to the Garrison in Bridgetown as quickly as possible. During the restoration of the tower, more than 6,000 artifacts were found, including pre-Columbian tools. Many of these are now on display in the tower alongside old military equipment, including the semaphore flags once used to signal messages from tower to tower. These were in use until 1883 when telephones were introduced in Barbados. The tower offers stunning views over the island.

There are interesting signs along the nature trail explaining the medicinal, culinary, and other uses of the various trees, herbs, and shrubs growing in the forest.

Holetown ⓫

6 miles (10 km) N of Bridgetown. 🏃 *35,000.* 🚌 📷 *Holetown Festival (Feb).*

Located on the west coast, Holetown was first named Jamestown (after the British monarch, James I) by Captain John Powell who led a band of English sailors ashore in 1625. Two years later, the first English settlers arrived here and began calling the place Holetown; the inlet where they anchored reminded them of a stretch of the Thames in London called the Limehouse Hole. A memorial in the center of town marks the first British landing on Barbados.

A short distance away from the town center, **St. James Parish Church** is one of the oldest churches on the island and parts of its lower levels are believed to be from the original stone structure built in 1660. The south entrance and porch are over 300 years old.

Today, Holetown is a busy center with a few good restaurants, bars, and shops. During the Holetown Festival, the place comes alive with street parades and entertainment such as sporting events, exhibitions, and concerts.

Environs
Driving out of Holetown, visitors will see long stretches of palm-fringed, white sand beaches along the west coast.

Impressive façade of St. James Parish Church, Holetown

The safe, shallow turquoise Caribbean waters are in sharp contrast to the crashing Atlantic surf on the eastern side of the island. The extensively developed coastline is home to many of the island's high-end resorts and private homes, and is dotted with bays, most with cafés and bars for refreshment.

Just north of Holetown, the **Folkstone Marine Park** was officially designated a marine reserve and park in 1981. It was created in 1976 when the Greek freighter *Stavronikita*, previously destroyed by fire, was deliberately sunk to create an artificial reef. The ship lies at a depth of 120 ft (37 m), making this site suitable only for experienced divers. However, the shallow waters off Folkstone Beach feature a marked underwater trail through the Dottins Reef, suitable for all levels of experience. A wide range of fish and other oceanic creatures can be spotted. A small aquarium and interpretive center onshore has exhibits on the reef and its marine life.

Lifeguard station on Folkstone Beach, near Holetown

St. Nicholas Abbey ⑫

Set in a former sugar plantation, St. Nicholas Abbey is a magnificent stone great house built in the mid-17th century by a wealthy planter, Colonel Berringer. The grounds are spectacular and feature several labeled plants and a herb garden. A film shot in 1935 by Colonel Cave, another former owner of the Abbey, is screened daily and vividly depicts the house and plantation life at that time.

VISITORS' CHECKLIST

17 miles (27 km) NE of Bridgetown. *Tel* 246 422 5357. 🚌 ⬤ *10am–3:30pm Sun–Fri.* 🏞 ✓ **Note:** *the film is shown every two hours daily.* www.stnicholasabbey.com

Old sugar factory and rum distillery

Great House
The Jacobean great house is the oldest building in Barbados.

Interiors
The house has some classic porcelain and china, as well as antique pieces of furniture, some of which were made with local Barbados mahogany.

Windmill
The old windmill and other out-buildings including the sugar syrup factory have been restored.

Outdoor Activities and Specialized Holidays

White and pink coral sands, palm tree-fringed beaches and warm, clear turquoise waters make Barbados a fabulous destination for those who want to sun, swim or enjoy a host of watersports ranging from scuba to water skiing. Cricket is the national game and there are scores of teams throughout the island. It is a great spectator sport, but for visitors seeking something more energetic there is no shortage of opportunities from cycling to golf and hiking to horseback riding.

Coastline at Bathsheba, eastern Barbados

BEACHES

There are more than 70 miles (112 km) of beautiful beaches around Barbados. The west coast beaches have warmer waters and safer swimming. Mullins Beach is a superb white-sand strip close to Speightstown. The popular Paynes Bay Beach has all amenities including cafés, restaurants, and watersports outlets. The east coast beaches are great for sunbathing but the strong Atlantic rollers can be dangerous for young and inexperienced swimmers. The island's southern coast has a few good beaches too. The lively Accra Beach, also known as Rockley Beach, attracts both locals and visitors. On the southeast coast, the reef-protected Crane Beach is good for body-surfing. All beaches are public with free access although visitors have to pay to use facilities such as beach chairs and umbrellas.

YACHTING AND DAY SAILS

The island's offshore waters attract yachts from around the world and there are a number of international regattas including the annual Mount Gay Regatta every December. Many hotels and watersports centers offer day cruises – either bareboard or crewed. The best sailing is off the west and south coasts. Some of the reputed concessionaires that offer yachting and sailing services are **Outdoors Barbados**, **Small Cats**, **Shasa**, **Shamon Too**, **El Tigre Catamaran Cruises**, and **Jolly Roger**.

PIRATE SHIP CRUISES

Pirate ship cruises are fun, noisy, and an opportunity, for those who wish, to consume large quantities of free rum. Organized by agencies, such as Jolly Roger, they offer a chance to see what the west coast of Barbados looks like from the sea, though there are usually lots of distractions such as walking the plank and a pirate wedding.

RECREATIONAL SUBMARINE

Visitors can join the tender at Bridgetown for the 15-minute journey out to the *Atlantis 11*, the world's first recreational submarine which dives to 130 ft (40 m). Organized by **Atlantis Adventures**, the underwater trip over reefs and shipwrecks lasts almost an hour. It is possible to get eye-to-eye with the fishes through the large portholes.

GLASS BOTTOM BOATS

For those who are not good swimmers, glass bottom boats are a great way to safely explore the wonderful world of reefs, especially with a good guide to point things out. Many companies offer glass-bottom boat tours and most will pick up visitors from their hotels and drop them back.

WATERSPORTS

There are opportunities for watersports all around the island. Jet Skis are provided by the many hotels and resorts on the west coast. The best surfing, both body and board, is off the east coast although the waves can be rough. Rental and surfing lessons are available through

Hobie Cats for hire lined on a beach, western coast of Barbados

For hotels and restaurants on this island see pp476–7 and pp478–9

Windsurfing at Silver Sands Beach on the south coast

agencies such as **Surf Barbados** and **Zed's Surfing Adventures**. International events are held at Bathsheba's Soup Bowl (*see p469*), named after the foaming water. There is good parasailing along the west coast and excellent wind-surfing as well, especially in Little Bay near South Point. The best water skiing is along the west coast, particularly early or late in the day when there are fewer people in the water. Many companies such as **Good Times Barbados** and **The Boatyard** specialize in watersports and offer a large number of activities.

SCUBA

The shallow, warm, clear waters, pristine reefs with teeming marine life, and many shipwrecks make Barbados a world-class diving site with dives to suit all levels of experience. Carlisle Bay, on the west coast, is one of the most popular sites because of the many wrecks, but it also has caves, deep trenches and drop-offs for the more adventurous. It is estimated that since 1666 more than 200 ships have foundered offshore. Others have been deliberately scuttled to create artificial reefs. Popular dive sites include Bright Ledge, Clarkes Reef, Fisherman's Reef, and Speightstown Reef. There are several licensed dive centers offering certification, equip-ment rental, as well as diving trips. The popular outfits offering scuba diving activities include **Reefers and Wreckers**, **Barbados Blue**, and **Hightide**.

FISHING

There is great deep-sea fishing for world-record breaking fish in Barbados. The best fishing is off the north and south coasts because of the stronger currents. Local records include blue marlin (505 lbs/230 kg), yellow fin tuna (167.5 lbs/76 kg), and wahoo (74 lbs/33 kg). Most hotels and resorts offer fishing trips and there are many boats available for half- or full-day charters. **Cannon Charters**, **IOU Charters**, **Blue Marlin Barbados**, and Outdoors Barbados can be contacted for organizing fishing trips.

GUIDED WALKS

There are many trails and a number of organizations offer guided walks, many of which are free. Most of the trails are along the coast but there are some inland hikes. The **Welchman Hall Gully** (*see p469*) is another place where

visitors can walk through a tropical forest with innu-merable exotic plants. It is advisable to walk very early in the morning before the sun gets too high. The **Barbados National Trust** organizes short rural walks on Sundays from January to March. These walks attract a large number of people, making for a very convivial amble. **Hike Barbados** also offers free walks but these are longer – around three hours. The degree of difficulty is captured in their names – such as Stop 'n Stare and Grin 'n Bare.

Fishing boat at Oistins on the south coast of Barbados

OFF-ROAD TOURS

Many operators such as **Adventure 4x4**, **Out Back 4x4**, and **Island Safari** offer off-road tours in specially equipped, four-wheel drive vehicles. The tours take visitors to parts of the island that they may not visit on their own and include a stop for lunch or a dip in the sea. Knowledgeable guides make the trips more enjoyable.

Visitors enjoying a special jeep safari tour of Barbados

Riding tour through the Bajan countryside

HORSE-RIDING

There are several stables and riding is available in all the resort areas with scenic trails. Those with little or no experience can take a gentle trot while adventure rides are available inland for those with more experience. Stables such as the **Caribbean International Riding Center** and **Ocean Echo Stables** normally pick up visitors from the hotel and drop them back.

MOUNTAIN BIKING

Mountain bikes are available at several locations and there are long stretches of side roads and trails to explore. Although not mountainous, some of the hills are very steep. The views are magnificent and there is always a bar, restaurant or beach to stop at. **Highland Adventure Center** and **Flex Bicycle Tours** provide equipment and assistance. Insurance is also available.

SPAS

After all that physical activity a little pampering is welcome. Most large resorts and hotels have spas such as The Spa at Sandy Lane *(see p477)*, Yin Yang at the Savannah hotel, and the spa at **Sea Breeze** hotel. **Suga Suga Spa** offers a range of beauty treatments.

DIRECTORY

YACHTING AND DAY SAILS

El Tigre Catamaran Cruises
Tel 246 417 7245.
www.eltigrecruises.com

Jolly Roger
Tel 246 430 0900.
www.tallshipcruises.com

Outdoors Barbados
Tel 246 262 7960.
www.outdoors
barbados.com

Shamon Too
Tel 246 233 6089.
www.westwater-
adventures-barbados.com

Shasa
Tel 246 433 8274.
www.shasacatamaran
cruises.com

Small Cats
Tel 246 421 6419.
www.smallcats
cruises.com

RECREATIONAL SUBMARINE

Atlantis Adventures
Tel 246 436 8929.
www.atlantis
adventures.com

WATERSPORTS

The Boatyard
Tel 246 436 2622.
www.theboatyard.com

Good Times Barbados
Tel 246 422 1900.
www.goodtimes
barbados.com

Surf Barbados
Tel 246 256 3906.
www.surfing-
barbados.com

Zed's Surfing Adventures
Tel 246 428 7873.
www.barbadossurf.com

SCUBA

Barbados Blue
Tel 246 434 5764.
www.divebarbados
blue.com

Hightide
Tel 246 432 0931.
www.divehigh
tide.com

Reefers and Wreckers
Tel 246 422 5450.
www.scuba
diving.bb

FISHING

Blue Marlin Barbados
Tel 246 234 1688.
www.bluemarlin
barbados.com

Cannon Charters
Tel 246 424 6107.
www.fishing
barbados.com

IOU Charters
Tel 246 429 1050.
www.ioucharters
barbados.net

GUIDED WALKS

Barbados National Trust
Tel 246 426 2421.
www.trust.fun
barbados.com

Hike Barbados
Tel 246 228 8027.
www.hikebarbados.com

Welchman Hall Gully
Tel 246 438 6671.
www.welchmanhall
gullybarbados.com

OFF-ROAD TOURS

Adventure 4x4
Tel 246 418 3687.
www.adventure
landbarbados.com

Island Safari
Tel 246 429 5337.
www.islandsafari.bb

Out Back 4x4
Tel 246 231 5642.
www.outback4x4
tours.com

MOUNTAIN BIKING

Flex Bicycle Tours
Tel 246 419 2453.

Highland Adventure Center
Tel 246 438 8069.

HORSE-RIDING

Caribbean International Riding Centre
Tel 246 422 7343.
www.funbarbados.com

Ocean Echo Stables
Tel 246 433 6772.
www.barbados
horseriding.com

SPAS

Sea Breeze
Tel 246 428 2825.
www.sea-breeze.
com/spa

Suga Suga Spa
Tel 246 419 4507.

For hotels and restaurants on this island see pp476–7 and pp478–9

Golf Courses of Barbados

There are six golf courses on Barbados, more than on any other Caribbean island of comparable size. The island's first course, the 9-hole Rockley Golf Club, was laid out as early as 1946. Sandy Lane Resort has three courses – Old Nine, Green Monkey, and Country Club, all of which

Golf ball placed on a tee

are different in style and difficulty, while Royal Westmoreland is set within a gated luxury community. Barbados Golf Club is located inland from Oistins. Most of these are private clubs, so tee time for outsiders is limited. Many of the resorts offer special non-member deals for their guests.

Old Nine Course *at the Sandy Lane estate was constructed in the early 1960s. This is where world-renowned golfer Tiger Woods got married in 2004. At 3,345 yards (3,059 m) and par 36, the Old Nine has small greens and tight fairways providing a real challenge to golfers.*

The Country Club Restaurant *is welcoming after a round of golf at the Country Club, designed by Tom Fazio. The club hosted the 2006 World Golf Championships World Cup.*

Barbados Golf Club *has a par 72 course stretching over 6,805 yards (6,222 m). Restyled in 2000 by Ron Kirby, the 18-hole championship course has a challenging "Amen corner" on holes 15 and 16.*

Green Monkey Course *is an exclusive par 72 course spread over 7,343 yards (6,715 m). It is aptly named after the monkeys that can be seen around, though they can occasionally be a hazard.*

Royal Westmoreland *championship course was designed by Robert Trent Jones Jr. The par 72 course has magnificent ocean views from every hole. Some of the holes can be challenging, with one green bordering a ravine.*

GOLF

Barbados Golf Club
Tel 246 428 8463.
www.barbadosgolfclub.com

Rockley Golf Club
Tel 246 435 7873.
www.rockleygolfclub.com

Royal Westmoreland
Tel 246 422 4653.
www.royal-westmoreland.com

Sandy Lane
Tel 246 444 2000.
www.sandylane.com/golf

Choosing a Hotel

A huge choice of accommodations is available, ranging from extremely expensive and all-inclusive hotels to budget guesthouses and specialist properties, some offering inclusive packages. Many properties offer rooms with kitchen facilities for those who wish to self-cater. Hotels generally add a 10 percent service charge to the 7.5 percent Value Added Tax (VAT).

PRICE CATEGORIES
The following price ranges are for a standard double room per night and all taxes included.

$ under $100
$$ $100–$200
$$$ $200–$300
$$$$ $300–$400
$$$$$ over $400

BARBADOS

Hotels In Barbados
Barbados hotels are very friendly and go out of their way to make their guests feel welcome. Most have complimentary cocktail parties at least one night a week, as well as special themed evenings such as barbecues, Bajan music nights, and calypso. They all provide a great way to meet fellow guests and have fun.

Escape at the Gap

Accra Beach Hotel

CHRIST CHURCH Dover Beach
$$
St. Lawrence Gap **Tel** *246 428 8076* **Fax** *246 428 2122* **Rooms** *39*

A good-value hotel whose guests return year after year. The rooms are comfortable and most have balconies with ocean views. There is a pool and a wide range of activities such as tennis, horseback riding, and golf are available. All the restaurants, bars, and nightlife of the Gap are nearby. Children are welcome. **www.doverbeach.com**

CHRIST CHURCH Accra Beach Hotel
$$$
Rockley Beach **Tel** *246 435 8920* **Fax** *246 435 6794* **Rooms** *224*

Close to the airport and the capital, this beachside hotel offers a wide range of amenities including a spa, Chakra. The Wytukai, one of its three restaurants, is the only Polynesian restaurant on the island. There is a barbecue and floor show every Thursday night on the pool deck. **www.accrabeachhotel.com**

CHRIST CHURCH Allamanda Beach Hotel
$$$
Hastings **Tel** *246 438 1000* **Fax** *246 435 9211* **Rooms** *48*

The hotel is close to some of the island's best beaches, with restaurants and nightclubs all within walking distance. Guests can use the snorkeling and watersports facilities at the sister hotel, the Amaryllis Beach Resort on Palm Beach, a three-minute drive away. Amenities include spa services and family rooms. **www.allamandabeach.com**

CHRIST CHURCH Blue Horizon
$$$
Rockley Beach **Tel** *246 435 8916* **Fax** *246 435 8613* **Rooms** *87*

Located across the road from Rockley Beach, this good-value hotel is great as a touring base or for families with children. Some rooms have fully equipped kitchens if guests want to self-cater. There is a poolside restaurant, and other eateries are only a short stroll away. Rockley golf course is nearby. **www.gemsbarbados.com**

CHRIST CHURCH Savannah
$$$
Hastings **Tel** *246 435 9473* **Fax** *246 435 8822* **Rooms** *98*

Part of the Gems of Barbados Resorts group, this boutique hotel offers good value accommodation. The immediate beach is rocky but there is safe swimming a short walk away. The hotel has 2 pools, a spa, and nearby golf club. Families are welcome and wedding and honeymoon packages are also available. **www.gemsbarbados.com**

CHRIST CHURCH South Beach
$$$
Rockley Beach **Tel** *246 435 8561* **Fax** *246 435 8954* **Rooms** *47*

A modern boutique hotel across the road from popular Rockley Beach, it is known for personalized service. All suites have self-catering facilities. The large pool has a special laps section in the middle and a safe area for children. Special packages are available for golf and honeymoons. **www.southbeachbarbados.com**

CHRIST CHURCH Barbados Beach Club
$$$$
Maxwell Coast Road **Tel** *246 428 9900* **Fax** *246 428 8905* **Rooms** *112*

All-inclusive with a wide range of land and water activities for adults. Nightly live entertainment. Families can be accommodated in the family resort, near the main hotel, with a special program of children's activities. Excellent golfing and tennis, as well as wedding and honeymoon packages. **www.barbadosbeachclub.com**

CHRIST CHURCH Bougainvillea Beach Resort
$$$$
Maxwell Coast Road **Tel** *246 418 0990* **Fax** *246 428 2524* **Rooms** *138*

A friendly four-star hotel where families are welcome, set on beautiful Maxwell Beach on the south coast. The pools and tropical gardens are delightful. There is a floodlit tennis court, fitness center, beauty salon, and spa. The resort offers golfing and special wedding and honeymoon packages. **www.bougainvillearesort.com**

Key to Symbols *see back cover flap*

CHRIST CHURCH Divi Southwinds
🚗 🍴 🗐 🏌 🖵 $$$$

St. Lawrence Main Road **Tel** *246 428 7181* **Fax** *246 428 4674* **Rooms** *161*

This sprawling all-suite resort borders a great swimming beach and is a short walk from all the attractions of the Gap. The resort is ideal for families and children under the age of 15 stay free. There is a bar and activities offered include tennis. There is also a small market for guests who want to self-cater. **www.divisouthwinds.com**

CHRIST CHURCH Escape at the Gap
🚗 🍴 🗐 🏌 $$$$

St. Lawrence Gap **Tel** *246 428 6131* **Fax** *246 428 7722* **Rooms** *66*

A family resort hotel in the heart of the Gap, set amid manicured lawns on a wide, sandy, shallow water beach. The price includes most watersports and basic diving instruction in the pool for those who want to learn to scuba. Offers golfing packages. There is live entertainment every night. **www.escapehotels.co.uk**

CHRIST CHURCH Turtle Beach
🚗 🍴 🗐 $$$$$

St. Lawrence, Dover **Tel** *246 428 7131* **Fax** *246 428 6089* **Rooms** *164*

A four-star, luxury contemporary resort with an emphasis on fun for the family. It offers lush, tropical gardens, 2 pools, tennis, Tommy Turtle Kids Club, and complimentary watersports. It has 3 restaurants including the acclaimed Italian eatery, Asiagos. Afternoon tea is served daily. **www.turtlebeachresortbarbados.com**

ST. JAMES Europa – All Seasons
🚗 🍴 🗐 🏌 🖵 $$

Sunset Crest **Tel** *246 432 5046* **Fax** *246 432 0893* **Rooms** *48*

A west coast *en-suite* resort noted for its friendly staff and children-friendly atmosphere. Fully equipped kitchenettes are great for families and others who want to self-cater. A free shuttle bus is available to local amenities and to their beach house. **www.europaresort.com**

ST. JAMES Colony Club Hotel
🚗 🍴 🗐 🏌 🖵 $$$$$

Porters **Tel** *246 422 2335* **Fax** *246 422 0667* **Rooms** *96*

A remarkable, luxury property set in 7 acres (3 ha) of tropical gardens. All rooms and suites have private balconies or patios. There are four freshwater swimming lagoons and concierge service at the pools and on the beach. Spa services as well as tennis and golf available. Complimentary watersports offered. **www.eleganthotels.com**

ST. JAMES Coral Reef Club
🚗 🍴 🗐 🏌 ♿ 🖵 $$$$$

Holetown **Tel** *246 422 2372* **Fax** *246 422 1776* **Rooms** *80*

A family-owned luxury hotel with a reputation for its style and elegance. The rooms, suites, and cottages are all individually designed. Stroll through landscaped tropical gardens to the pristine beach. Relax in the spa and dine alfresco from an à la carte menu *(see p479)*. Children are welcome. **www.coralreefbarbados.com**

ST. JAMES Crystal Cove Hotel
🚗 🍴 🗐 🏌 $$$$$

Appleby **Tel** *246 432 2683* **Fax** *246 432 8290* **Rooms** *88*

An all-inclusive, luxury tropical getaway, Crystal Cove Hotel has great gardens, multi-tiered lagoon swimming pools, and a fabulous beach in its own cove. It also offers different water and land sports, and activities for children. A Dine Around program lets guests eat at the resort's three sister hotels. **www.crystalcovehotelbarbados.com**

ST. JAMES The House
🚗 🍴 🗐 🏌 🖵 $$$$$

Paynes Bay **Tel** *246 432 5525* **Fax** *246 432 5255* **Rooms** *34*

A luxury, all-suite hotel that offers peace and serenity in a gorgeous beachside setting. Start the day with a champagne breakfast. A host of complimentary services on the beach and in the hotel add that extra bit of pampering. There is also a 24-hour bar, a spa, and round-the-clock room service. **www.thehouse-barbados.com**

ST. JAMES Mango Bay
🚗 🍴 🗐 🏌 $$$$$

Holetown **Tel** *246 432 1384* **Fax** *246 432 5297* **Rooms** *76*

A spectacular family-owned, luxury property along a splendid safe beach. Guests can pamper themselves at the Elements Spa and dine on the beach with live entertainment. Families are welcome and there are a wide range of activities including golf and island tours. Watersports are complimentary. **www.mangobaybarbados.com**

ST. JAMES Sandy Lane
🚗 🍴 🗐 🏌 🖵 $$$$$

Paynes Bay **Tel** *246 444 2000* **Fax** *246 444 2222* **Rooms** *112*

Favored by the rich and famous, this luxury resort is ideal for both a romantic retreat and a fun-packed family holiday. The state-of-the-art rooms and suites are colossal and all feature private verandas. There is a spa and several activities including watersports, tennis, and golf. Live entertainment most nights. **www.sandylane.com**

ST. JAMES Treasure Beach
🚗 🍴 🗐 🏌 🖵 $$$$$

Paynes Bay **Tel** *246 419 4200* **Fax** *246 432 1094* **Rooms** *38*

All-suite, intimate luxury hotel with a superb, white-sand beach. The suites form a horseshoe shape around the pool with spectacular views over the beach and water. Deluxe suites have their own plunge pool. Alfresco dining in the award-winning restaurant. Family rooms, bars, and watersports. **www.treasurebeachhotel.com**

ST. MICHAEL Barbados Hilton
🚗 🍴 🗐 🏌 ♿ 🖵 $$$$$

Needham's Point **Tel** *246 426 0200* **Fax** *246 434 5770* **Rooms** *350*

This is a five-star hotel nestled between two great swimming beaches. All rooms have ocean views. There is a huge landscaped pool area, tennis courts, a fitness room, and conference room facilities. Families are well catered for with the Kidz Paradise Club offering ample activities and entertainment. **www.hiltoncaribbean.com**

Where to Eat & Nightlife

Restaurants in Barbados vary from casual, laid-back beach bars offering freshly caught fish to upscale gourmet establishments that feature international cuisine on their à la carte menus. Popular Bajan-Creole dishes include *cou-cou* (cornmeal and okra pudding), salt-fish cakes, and the spicy pepperpot stew. In general, eating out is more expensive than on most other Caribbean islands.

PRICE CATEGORIES
The price ranges are for a two-course meal for one, including tax and service charges. Price does not include wine.

$ under $10
$$ $10–15
$$$ $15–25
$$$$ $25–35
$$$$$ over $35

RESTAURANTS

Fresh Seafood
Restaurants and beach cafés throughout Barbados offer some of the freshest fish visitors might have ever tasted. Guests can savor delicious and innovative preparations of daily caught seafood. There is an extensive choice ranging from flying fish – the national emblem – to mahimahi, dorado, red snapper, and barracuda among other local varieties.

Daphne's

The Fish Pot

AQUATIC GAP Brown Sugar · $$$$$

Bay Street **Tel** *246 426 7684*

Casual, elegant dining in a beautiful heritage Barbadian home. The menu features Bajan and Caribbean specialties including flying fish, pepperpot, and souse, which are served as part of the four-course Planter's Buffet Lunch. Dinner entrées include succulent stuffed roast pork Caribe and curried lamb. Open nightly for dinner.

CHRIST CHURCH Aqua · $$$$$

Hastings **Tel** *246 420 2995*

Guests can sink into comfortable sofas or dine alfresco on the terrace overlooking the ocean. Great tasting dishes combine international cuisine with traditional Bajan fare. Service is good and the bar is open until the early morning hours. Dinner is served every night. Reservation required.

CHRIST CHURCH Champers · $$$$$

Skeetes Hill **Tel** *246 434 3463*

This place has a gorgeous waterside location and excellent food. Overlooking Accra Beach, the restaurant is set in an old Barbadian building. Casual dining at its best. The sesame crusted shrimp with ginger and sugarcane rum sauce served with fried green plantain is delicious, as is the popular roasted lamb.

CHRIST CHURCH Harlequin · $$$$$

St. Lawrence Gap **Tel** *246 420 7677*

In the heart of the Gap, Harlequin offers a mix of international and local cuisine on its dinner menu in a casual atmosphere. Visitors can try the Ocean's Harvest (three types of local fish prepared in three different ways, shrimp, scallops, and lobster) or the fresh catch, cooked to order. An affordable children's menu. Live jazz nightly.

ST. JAMES Angry Annie's · $$$$

Holetown **Tel** *246 432 2119*

Nobody is sure how the restaurant got its name, but its owners Annie and Paul Matthews always seem to be enjoying themselves. This small, cozy, and friendly place offers a mix of American and Bajan dishes bursting with flavor, including really fresh fish, great ribs, and home-made pasta. Dinner is served every night.

ST. JAMES Beach House · $$$$$

Holetown **Tel** *246 432 1163*

Splendid beachfront location with superb food and cheerful, attentive service. The buffet lunch offers traditional Caribbean dishes, and the dinner menu features a blend of Mediterranean and Bajan cuisines. Excellent crab cakes and *panko* (breadcrumb) and horseradish crusted shrimp. There is live jazz on Fridays.

ST. JAMES Calabaza · $$$$$

Prospect **Tel** *246 424 4557*

Moroccan architecture, vibrant colors, and a unique Caribbean style of cuisines make this dining experience special. Calabaza perches on a small cliff overlooking the sea. Guests can try the delectable pork and shrimp – crispy Bajan pork with tiger shrimps, and the tasty pineapple ravioli for dessert. Open nightly for dinner.

ST. JAMES The Cliff · $$$$$

Derricks **Tel** *246 432 1922*

One of the island's best restaurants, it is perched on a cliff with panoramic views. Chef Paul Owens and his team continue to win accolades for their creative gourmet dishes. The service is exceptional and the wine list impressive. Cigars can be enjoyed in the lounge upstairs. Reservations are required. Open nightly for dinner.

Key to Symbols *see back cover flap*

ST. JAMES Coral Reef Club

Holetown **Tel** *246 422 2372*

Delightful, elegant alfresco dining with excellent Bajan cuisine at the hotel of the same name *(see p477)*. The à la carte menu changes daily. The grilled Caribbean rock lobster with garlic and lemon butter is delectable. There is live entertainment every night during the winter and most nights during the summer. Reservations required.

ST. JAMES Daphne's

Paynes Bay **Tel** *246 432 2731*

Modern Italian food is served in an elegant beachside setting. The emphasis is on the freshest ingredients and careful preparation that results in some delicious dishes. Try the smoked marlin *carpaccio* with fennel, capers, and tuna dressing for starters or the great home-made pasta dishes. It is open daily for lunch and dinner.

ST. JAMES Lone Star

Mount Standfast **Tel** *246 419 0599*

A very popular contemporary restaurant in a spectacular setting overlooking the ocean. It is open for lunch and dinner and offers European and Continental fine dining with an outstanding wine list. It has great weekend brunches with a special English three-course roast on Sundays. Celebrities are often among the guests.

ST. JAMES The Tides

Holetown **Tel** *246 432 8356*

Set on the water's edge, this award-winning restaurant offers remarkable food, wine, and service. A large range of innovative and memorable dishes, with chilled yellow fin tuna, watermelon tartare, and the Jamaican jerk pork tenderloin among the favorites. Open Monday to Sunday for dinner and Sunday to Friday for lunch.

ST. PETER The Fish Pot

Shermans **Tel** *246 439 2604*

This tucked-away waterside restaurant in a small fishing community serves excellent food and offers good service at great prices. The restaurant and small hotel are built on the site of a 17th-century fort. The sweet grilled lobster and the West Indian masaman curry are scrumptious. Guests can also share a seafood platter for two.

ST. PETER Mango's By The Sea

Speightstown **Tel** *246 422 0704*

An award-winning intimate and romantic restaurant set among a palm tree-fringed terrace with waterside views across the beach. Guests can relish delectable Bajan dishes, fabulous lobster, great steaks and seafood, knockout cocktails, and an outstanding wine list. Open for dinner nightly from 6pm. Reservations recommended.

ST. PETER The Terrace Restaurant

Cobblers Cove hotel, Road View **Tel** *246 422 2291*

Set in the Cobblers Cove hotel, this seafront restaurant features an award-winning cuisine that combines various international influences. Try the Angus beef *carpaccio* or the pan-fried barracuda. Home-made sorbets are served in a brandy snap basket. Live music Tuesdays and Thursdays. Reservations required.

ST. PHILIP L'Azure at the Crane

Crane Bay **Tel** *246 423 6220*

The Crane has three restaurants but its flagship L'Azure offers remarkable seafood, steaks, and pasta. Guests can enjoy the fabulous views in very elegant surroundings. Open for lunch daily, and the traditional Barbadian Sunday brunch accompanied by live gospel music is not to be missed. Reservations required.

ST. THOMAS Bagatelle Great House

Bagatelle **Tel** *246 421 6767*

Built in 1645, The Bagatelle Great House is the third oldest house on the island. When the owner lost it during a card game, he said it was a *"mere bagatelle"* and hence the restaurant's name. It offers good-value buffet lunches and delicious set three-course dinners. Service is excellent. Open daily for lunch and dinner.

BARS AND CLUBS

Barbados is a fun place at night, bursting with action. St. Lawrence Gap is the island's main nightspot with a wide choice of restaurants, clubs, and bars. Here the music continues until the early hours. Bridgetown has some very popular beachside, open-air night clubs, while Holetown is fast becoming the place to be on the west coast.

Live band performance at Harbour Lights

RECOMMENDED PLACES TO GO

Harbour Lights
Bridgetown. (Popular, open-air, breachfront club.)

Jumbies
St. Lawrence Gap. (Lively night-spot, live bands, and a busy bar.)

McBrides
St. Lawrence Gap. (Irish pub offering live music and karaoke.)

Mojo
Worthing Main Road. (Lively hangout with eclectic music.)

Red Rooster
Hastings. (Always fun with live music Friday and Saturday.)

Ship Inn
St. Lawrence Gap. (Music nightly from either live bands or DJs.)

Practical Information

With good weather year round and small enough to explore easily, Barbados is the perfect place for an effortless holiday. It is well connected to both North America and Europe, has a well developed infrastructure and generally excellent service, although prices can be on the expensive side. Rental cars are widely available and the local buses are also a great way to see the island.

Grantley Adams International Airport, near Bridgetown

WHEN TO GO

The high season is from December to April but Barbados has year-round good weather with an annual average temperature of 27°C (80°F). The best time to visit is from January to April which are the coolest months. It tends to get very hot between July and September. There are lots of activities throughout the year but the Holetown Festival in February and Crop Over Festivals in July and August are always exciting times to visit.

GETTING THERE

Grantley Adams International Airport is 8 miles (13 km) east of Bridgetown and is served by several major airlines from the US and Europe, including **American Airlines**, **Air Canada**, **Air Jamaica**, **British Airways**, **LIAT**, **Virgin Atlantic**, and **Caribbean Airlines**.

DOCUMENTATION

All visitors need a valid passport and a return ticket to enter Barbados. A visa is not required from citizens of the US, Canada, UK, most Caribbean and European countries, and Japan. Travelers should contact the **Immigration Department** for a list of countries requiring, and exempted from, visas. Officials may also ask travelers to show adequate funds to cover their visit.

VISITOR INFORMATION

All tourist information, including brochures and maps, is available from the **Barbados Tourism Authority**, which has an office at Bridgetown as well as a kiosk at the airport.

HEALTH AND SECURITY

There are no serious health problems but visitors should protect themselves from the sun and insects. The main hospital is **Queen Elizabeth's** on the outskirts of Bridgetown. The island also has a number of private, modern health centers such as **Bayview Hospital** and **Sandy Crest Medical Center**.

Barbados has a low crime rate but it still pays to take sensible precautions. It is advisable not to wear expensive jewelry or flash large sums of money. Keep valuables out of sight in parked cars or when on the beach and avoid straying into unfamiliar areas late at night. In case of theft or any crime, report to the police.

BANKING AND CURRENCY

Most major credit cards are widely accepted in all the island's cities but may not be welcomed in small places such as cafés. Bridgetown, Holetown, and Speightstown have many banks and they also have branches scattered across the island. There are 24-hour ATM facilities at a number of locations around the island. However, ATM machines dispense only local currency. Banks are open from 8am to 3pm Monday to Thursday and from 8am to 1pm and 3 to 5pm on Friday. The airport bank is open from 8am to midnight daily.

The official currency is the Barbados dollar (BDS$) which is tied to the US dollar at US$1=Bds$2. It comes in bills of 2 (blue), 5 (green), 10 (brown), 20 (purple), 50 (orange), and 100 (gray) dollars.

Building of the Barbados National Bank in Holetown

COMMUNICATIONS

The international dialling code for Barbados is 246. There is direct international dialling from hotels and pay phones, which also accept phone cards. **Digicel** and **Cable & Wireless** are popular phone operators. Cell phones can also be rented from the Cable & Wireless centers.

Most major US and European newspapers and magazines are available. Satellite television is widely accessible and most large hotels offer Internet. Cyber cafés are found in most towns.

TRANSPORT

Visitors must have a valid driver's license or international license and purchase a temporary Barbados one. The license is valid for a year. There is a government tax of 12.5 percent on all rentals. Rental cars have an H on the number plate. Check the condition of the car, especially the tyres, before accepting it and make sure there is a good spare. Cars drive on the left and the speed limit is 25 mph (40 kph) in towns, 40 mph (60 kph) on rural roads, and 50mph (80 kph) on signposted highways. Many service stations only accept cash. The main operators are **ABC Rentals**, **National Car Rentals**, **Courtesy Car Rentals**, and **Double J Car and Moke Rentals**. Buses are the cheapest mode of transport and ply everywhere. They are also a good way to meet the locals. Taxis are easily available as well and they are identifiable by Z on their number plates. There are no meters so visitors are advised to agree on a fare before the trip.

SHOPPING

Broad Street is the main shopping district in Bridgetown but there are small shopping malls throughout the island and many hotels have gift shops selling local arts, crafts and souvenirs. Outside the capital there is the Vista Complex in Worthing, the West Coast Mall and Chattel Village in Holetown, and Sheraton Center at Sergeant's Village. Most shops are open from 8am to 4pm Monday to Friday but open only for half a day on Saturday.

LANGUAGE

The official language is English, but a local Bajan patois – a combination of old English and West African languages – is widely spoken.

ELECTRICITY

The electricity supply is generally 110 volts/50 cycles; All European appliances will need adapters.

TIME

Barbados is on Atlantic Standard Time (AST), 4 hours behind Greenwich Mean Time (GMT). Daylight savings is not observed.

GETTING MARRIED

New laws make it even easier to get married in Barbados. Couples can get married on the day they arrive. Apply to the **Ministry of Home Affairs** in person to get a marriage license. Visitors will need to present a valid passport or birth certificate, proof of divorce or death, return tickets, and money for the license and revenue stamp. Many hotels have their own wedding consultants who can make all the arrangements and most offer special honeymoon packages.

Crafts and souvenirs shopping area in Holetown

DIRECTORY

THE SOUTHERN CARIBBEAN

THE SOUTHERN CARIBBEAN AT A GLANCE

The Southern Caribbean has lovely coastlines, diverse landscapes, and stunning underwater reefs with abundant marine life. Each island, from the ABC Islands to Trinidad and Tobago, has developed its own unique personality since settlement by various European nations about 500 years ago. Islanders place high value on music, art, fine cuisine, and jubilant celebrations, and visitors quickly fall into the sensual style and leisurely pace of the region.

A blue gray tanager found in Trinidad and Tobago

Aruba's *entire eastern coast is a stretch of picture-perfect white-sand beaches. High-rise resorts line up along Palm Beach and low-rise accommodations pepper Eagle Beach.*

ABC ISLANDS
(see pp508–35)

Bonaire *is still the Caribbean of old and strives to remain so with restrictions in its underwater parks and reluctance to court land developers.*

Curaçao's *charming capital, Willemstad, is a UNESCO World Heritage Site and serves as the seat of government for the entire Netherlands Antilles.*

LOCATOR MAP

Trinidad *is a highly industrialized island with a population of approximately one million people, mostly of African or East Indian descent. The island is known for its vibrant nightlife, unparalleled in the pre-Lenten Carnival, and its thrilling soca music.*

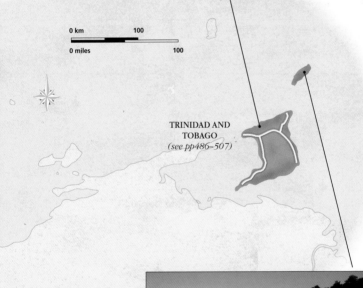

TRINIDAD AND
TOBAGO
(see pp486–507)

Tobago *is an eco-paradise for nature lovers who spend their time hiking through the Forest Reserve, driving back roads that wind through craggy hills, climbing to picturesque waterfalls and seeking hidden bays with white-sand beaches.*

A PORTRAIT OF TRINIDAD AND TOBAGO

As culturally diverse as it is physically varied, the twin-island republic of Trinidad and Tobago makes for a fascinating place to visit. The most southerly of the Caribbean chain, Trinidad and Tobago have wild Atlantic beaches as well as calm Caribbean shorelines and an incredibly rich array of flora and fauna.

As holiday destinations, Trinidad and Tobago are not as developed as some of their regional neighbors, which makes a refreshing change. In Trinidad, particularly, the beaches and attractions are equally shared by locals and visitors. Tobago, on the other hand, is well geared up for holidaymakers, with a host of hotels, restaurants, and places to drink and dance, but even here, the beaches away from the busy Crown Point are either completely undeveloped or have a few pleasantly laid-back places to stay and eat. Its central forest reserve is the oldest protected rainforest in the Western Hemisphere.

Trinidad is more industrialized, its southern half characterized by the trappings of the oil and natural gas industries that have long ensured the country's thriving economy. Central Trinidad has a gorgeous palm-fringed beach along much of its east coast, while the north is dominated by the Northern Range rainforest, peppered with hiking trails and waterfalls and the habitat of more than 400 bird species.

Motmot, found in the rainforest

PEOPLE AND HISTORY

Many of the festivals of Trinidad and Tobago are rooted in the ethnic traditions of the two islands' residents, collectively known as "Trinbagonians". Forty percent of the population are of East Indian origin, 38 percent African, and the rest a mix of Syrian, white European, and Chinese, a result of the influx of slaves and immigration that took place after the original inhabitants, the Carib Indians, were wiped out when the

Maracas Bay surrounded by lush green mountains, Trinidad

Stiltwalkers on parade, Trinidad Carnival

Spanish settled in Trinidad in 1592. Encouraged by land grants, French settlers followed, and a nascent plantation economy developed, dependent on African slave labor. Between 1592 and 1814, when it was ceded to the British, Tobago ricocheted between Dutch, French, and British control, changing hands 31 times. In the late 1950s calls for independence from Britain began in earnest; it was finally granted in 1962, with the nation led by the charismatic Dr. Eric Williams, who remains an iconic political figure.

The discovery of vast oil reserves in the 1970s boosted the economy, which remains one of the most stable in the region. Over the last few decades, political power has oscillated between the two main parties, the United National Congress (UNC) and the People's National Movement. In May 2010 the country elected its first female Prime Minister, Kamla Persad-Bissessar, who contested the general election with a UNC-led coalition, the People's Partnership.

CULTURE AND FESTIVALS

Trinidad and Tobago have many occasions to celebrate throughout the year. The original home of the West Indian Carnival, the islands' dedication to good times can seem exhausting to even the most determined of party animals. Swinging into action just before Lent, but with a couple of months of pre-event parties, the Carnival is the highlight of the festival calendar. It starts with the pre-dawn Jouvert – in which revellers slink through the streets covered in mud and body paint – and culminates in the Parade of the Bands, with up to 3,000 costumed masqueraders dancing to pounding soca. Hindus celebrate Phagwa, in which participants color each other with dye, called *abir*, and Diwali, when thousands of oil lamps and electric displays light up the nation. In Tobago, crab and goat races are held after Easter, while in summer a number of parties take place from the Great Race to the Fishermen's Festivals.

Dusk view of the Hindu Temple in the Sea, Waterloo, Trinidad

Exploring Trinidad and Tobago

Trinidad, the largest island of the Lesser Antilles, was named by Christopher Columbus in honor of the three peaks, crowning the southeastern coast, now known as Trinity Hills. While Trinidad's capital, Port of Spain, bustles and throbs with city life, the island's quiet interior is a haven for turtle- and bird-watchers. The much-smaller Tobago is best known for its long stretches of powdery white beaches, excellent diving spots, and lush rainforests.

GETTING AROUND

Apart from a reliable bus service connecting the major towns on both islands, transport is run privately. Trinidad has maxi taxis (color-coded minibuses) and route taxis (cars running on short, set routes). Tobago has only buses and route taxis. The best way to get around the islands is to take a tour or rent a car. The two islands are also linked by air and ferry. Airports are at Piarco and Crown Point, while ferries run between Port of Spain and Scarborough.

Trees lining the lagoon at Blanchisseuse, on Trinidad's north coast

Blanchisseuse
This peaceful village is a favorite retreat for local people.

0 km   15

0 miles   15

Port of Spain
The Laventille area in Trinidad's thriving capital is believed to be the birthplace of the steel pan.

Central Trinidad
This is the heartland of the Indian population, with great beaches, bird-watching sites, and hiking along the east coast.

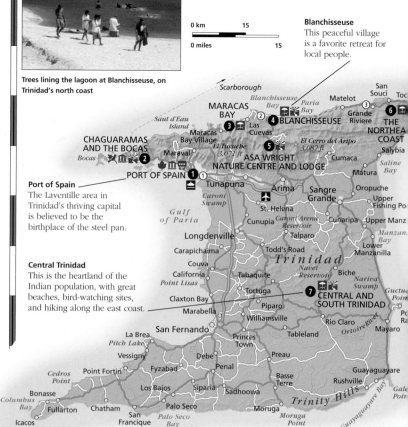

Scarborough

Blanchisseuse Bay   Paria Bay   Matelot   San Souci   Toc

MARACAS BAY   Las Cuevas   BLANCHISSEUSE   Grande Riviere   THE NORTHEA COAST

Saut d'Eau Island

CHAGUARAMAS AND THE BOCAS

Bocas

Maracas Bay Village   El Tucuche 3,073 ft

Maraval

ASA WRIGHT NATURE CENTRE AND LODGE

El Cerro del Aripo 3,087 ft

Cumaca   Salybia   Saline Bay

PORT OF SPAIN   Tunapuna

Arima   Sangre Grande

Matura   Oropuche   Upper Fishing Po

Caroni Swamp

St. Helena

Cunupia   Caroni Arena Reservoir   Cunaripa   Upper Manz

Gulf of Paria

Longdenville

Talparo   Manzan Bay   Lower Manzanilla

Carapichaima   Couva   Todd's Road

Trinidad

California Point Lisas   Tabaquite   Navet Reservoir   Biche   Nariva Swamp   Guctu Poin

Claxton Bay   Tortuga

Marabella   Piparo

CENTRAL AND SOUTH TRINIDAD

Williamsville   Rio Claro   Po Ra

La Brea   San Fernando   Princes Town   Tableland   Ortoire River   Mayaro

Pitch Lake

Vessigny   Debe   Preau

Point Fortin   Fyzabad   Penal   Basse Terre   Guayaguayare

Cedros Point   Los Bajos   Siparia   Sadhoowa   Rushville   Gale Poin

Bonasse   Palo Seco   Trinity Hills

Columbus Bay   Fullarton   Chatham   San Francique   Palo Seco Bay   Moruga   Moruga Point   Guayaguayare Bay

Icacos

For additional map symbols *see back flap*

Sprite
BUSTA

A typical grocery shop near Castara, Tobago

0 km 6
0 miles 6

Charlotteville
Located at the tip of Tobago, this small town has a remote feel, pretty beaches, and some lovely places to stay and dine.

Castara
Known for its yellow-sand beaches, this is a charming laid-back little village.

St. Giles Islands
Pirate's Bay
Man O' War Bay
11
19 CHARLOTTEVILLE
Cambleton
L'Anse Fourmi
Bloody Bay
Parlatuvier
SPEYSIDE 18
12
Little Tobago/ Bird of Paradise Island
ENGLISHMAN'S BAY TO BLOODY BAY 14
Parrot Hall
CASTARA 13
17
TOBAGO FOREST RESERVE
Delaford
10
King Peter's Bay
16
THE WINDWARD COAST
Culloden Bay
Moriah
Tobago
Roxborough
Arnos Vale Bay
8
9
Mason Hall
Glamorgan
Belle Garden
Arnos Vale
Turtle Beach
Plymouth
Goodwood
Pembroke
Goldsborough Bay
7
12 KIMME MUSEUM
MOUNT IRVINE 11
6
Mount St George
Bethel
15
SCARBOROUGH
BUCCOO 10
No Man's Land
PIGEON POINT BEACH 9
4
Bacolet Point
Lambeau
Rockly Bay
Little Rockly Bay
Lowlands
8
5
CROWN POINT
Canoe Bay
Port of Spain

The Blue Haven Hotel in Scarborough, Tobago

SIGHTS AT A GLANCE

Blanchisseuse 4
Buccoo 10
Castara 13
Central and South Trinidad 7
Chaguaramas and the Bocas 2
Charlotteville 19
Crown Point 8
Englishman's Bay to Bloody Bay 14
Kimme Museum 12
Maracas Bay 3
Mount Irvine 11
The Northeast Coast 6
Pigeon Point Beach 9
Port of Spain 1
Scarborough 15
Speyside pp494–5 18
Tobago Forest Reserve 17
The Windward Coast 16

Featured Hotels and Resorts
Asa Wright Nature Centre and Lodge 5

Other Hotels and Resorts
Arnos Vale 9
Blue Haven 4
Castara hotels 10
Charlotteville hotels 11
Crown Point hotels 5
Laguna Mar 2
Mont Plaisir Estate 3
Mount Irvine Golf and Beach Resort 6
Port of Spain hotels 1
Seahorse Inn 7
Speyside hotels 12
Turtle Beach 8

SEE ALSO

- ***Where to Stay*** pp502–3
- ***Where to Eat & Nightlife*** pp504–5

KEY

Highway
Major road
Minor road
Track
Ferry route
Peak

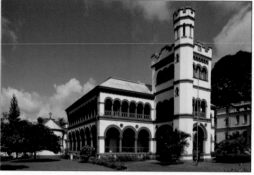

Old planters' mansions along the Queen's Park Savannah, Port of Spain

Port of Spain ❶

NW coast of Trinidad. 🏠 35,000.
✈ ⛴ 🛈 *Tourism Development
Company, 29 Tenth Avenue,
Barataria, 868 675 7034.* 🎭 *Carnival
(pre-Lent), Diwali (Oct/Nov).*

Gridlocked with traffic but seething with life, Trinidad's capital is home to the island's best restaurants and nightlife, as well as a vibrant cultural scene. The centerpiece of downtown Port of Spain is Independence Square, a shop-lined boulevard with the Brian Lara Promenade in the middle. To the north, Frederick Street is busy with shoppers, and threads up past Woodford Square, a grassy little park, home to an impromptu speakers' corner known as the University, where locals debate current affairs. On the square's western side is the Red House, the imposing Neo-Renaissance parliament building. At the northern end of Frederick Street, the **National Museum and Art Gallery** houses a collection on local history and geology, plus an excellent art gallery upstairs.

Past the museum are the wide open spaces of the **Queen's Park Savannah**, the city's largest open area and the focal point of the annual Carnival parade. Dotted with cricket pitches, the Savannah is busiest during late afternoons. At the northern edge of the Savannah, the **Botanical Gardens** are home to some 700 trees and many exotic plants. Next door, the **Emperor Valley Zoo** is one of the largest in the Caribbean and a good

place to view local species such as red howler monkeys and scarlet ibises.

🏛 National Museum and Art Gallery
Corner Frederick & Keate Streets.
Tel 868 623 5941. 🕙 *10am–6pm
Tue–Sat, 2–6pm Sun.* 📷

🌿 Botanical Gardens
Circular Road. *Tel 868 622 1221.*
🕕 *6am–6pm daily.* ♿

🐾 Emperor Valley Zoo
Circular Road. *Tel 868 622 3530.*
🕘 *9am–6pm daily.* 📷 ♿ 💻

Chaguaramas and the Bocas ❷

6 miles (10 km) W of Port of Spain,
Trinidad. *Tel 868 634 4227.* 🚌
🛈 *Chaguaramas Development
Authority (CDA), off Western Main
Road.* 💻 www.chagdev.com

Port of Spain's playground and a haven for yacht owners, the Chaguaramas area occupies the island's western tip. To the north is a national

Yachts moored at Crews Inn Marina, Chaguaramas

park centered around Tucker Valley, with its bamboo groves, rainforests, and hiking trails. On the southern coast, where US troops had built a base during World War II, the **Military History and Aerospace Museum** chronicles the island's military history. Spreading into the Gulf of Paria, the Bocas islands are a favored spot for palatial holiday homes. Gaspar Grande holds the **Gasparee Cave**, a huge cavern with a few impressive stalactites and a pool at its base.

🏛 Military History and Aerospace Museum
Western Main Road, Chaguaramas.
Tel 868 634 4391. 🕘 *9am–5pm
daily.* 📷 💳 🚻 💻 🛈

🏞 Gasparee Cave
Gasparee Island. 📷 💻 *with CDA.*

View of Maracas Bay on the north coast of Trinidad

Maracas Bay ❸

🚗 *7 miles (11 km) NE of Port of
Spain, Trinidad.* 🏊 👫 🍴

The closest beach with amenities from Port of Spain, Maracas Bay is a sweep of fine yellow sand, pounded by waves, lined with palms, and backed by forested hills. Quiet during the week, Maracas becomes the place to be on weekends, when locals set up camp under beach umbrellas and enjoy drinks and food. Vendors in the car park sell bake and shark, a delicious fish sandwich slathered with local sauces, and salads.

Environs
Around 4 miles (6 km) east of Maracas, is another lovely spot for swimming at **Las Cuevas**,

For hotels and restaurants on these islands see pp502–3 and pp504–5

the north coast's longest beach. Quieter than Maracas, with gentler surf but the same facilities, its only downside is the sandfly population.

Blanchisseuse ❹

17 miles (27 km) NE of Port of Spain, Trinidad. 👥 *800.* 🚌

The closest thing to a resort on the northern coast is Blanchisseuse. With its upper and lower villages, this quiet, rural area is backed by a string of wild beaches that are favored by surfers. It offers peace and quiet, a few appealing places to stay and dine, and swimming in the sea and the sparklingly clean Marianne River. The river also has a number of waterfalls upstream, reached by an easy 30-minute walk. It possible to hike from Blanchisseuse along the undeveloped coastline to the east, toward spectacular Paria Bay and waterfall without a guide.

Asa Wright Nature Centre and Lodge ❺

🛏 Arima Valley, Arima–Blanchisseuse Road, Trinidad. ***Tel*** *868 667 5162.* $$ *24 rooms.* 🍴 ♿ [W] **www**.asawright.org

High in the rainforested hills of the Northern Range, the Asa Wright Nature Centre is a renowned eco-lodge that offers some of the best bird-watching

Bird-watching at the Asa Wright Nature Centre

in the Caribbean. Spread out around a colonial great house, the 2-sq-mile (5-sq-km) pristine forest is home to a multitude of birds and animals. Bird-watchers can see up to 159 species of birds, some with stunning plumages. Non-guests can visit during the day to tour the immediate grounds and for lunch.

The Northeast Coast ❻

🚌 *to Arima, then taxi to Sangre Grande and to the coast.*

The northeast coastline is among Trinidad's most beautiful. Matura, a windswept sretch of beach, is favored by leatherbacks as an egg-laying site; it is a great spot for beachcombing, but the waters are too rough to swim. Visitors can take a dip some 2 miles (3 km) north at Salybia, where Rio Seco Waterfall, surrounded by greenery, tumbles about 26 ft (8 m) down into a wide and deep pool. For proper beachlife, it is best to head another 12 miles (19 km) along the main road to Toco, a peaceful fishing village with a white-sand beach, whose calm waters are protected by a reef.

The only good resort area along the northeast coast is Grande Riviere, a wonderfully laid-back spot around the rugged beach with a few staying and eating options. To the west, Shark River offers freshwater bathing.

Central and South Trinidad ❼

🚌

Home to the majority of the island's East Indian population, Central and South Trinidad have some stunning natural attractions. Lining the east coast is the spectacular 14-mile (22-km) Manzanilla Beach, backed with a dense coconut plantation that gives the area its name, The Cocal. Southern Trinidad is oil country, and roadside derricks and offshore rigs are part of the scenery. The geological richness bubbles up to the surface at La Brea, site of the largest **Pitch Lake** in the world, covering an area of 10 acres (4 ha).

On the northern outskirts of Trinidad's second city, San Fernando, visitors can observe rare birdlife at the **Point-a-Pierre Wildfowl Trust**. There is more fabulous bird-watching farther north at the **Caroni Swamp Bird Sanctuary**, a dense network of mangroves providing shelter for the scarlet ibis.

Pitch Lake
Southern Trunk Road. ***Tel*** *868 648 7697.* 🕘 *9am–5pm daily.* 🎫 ℹ

🐦 Point-a-Pierre Wildfowl Trust
Off the Southern Main Road. ***Tel*** *868 658 4200.*
🕘 *8am–5pm Mon–Fri, 10am–5pm Sat & Sun.* 🎫 ℹ ♿ *limited.*
🛍 **www**.pointeapierrewildfowltrust.org

🐦 Caroni Swamp Bird Sanctuary
Uriah Butler Highway. ***Tel*** *868 645 1305.* 🕘 *9am–4pm daily.* 🎫 ℹ

Stunning view of the coastline, northeast coast of Trinidad

Crown Point ⑧

SE coast of Tobago. ✈ 🚌
ℹ *Crown Point International Airport, 868 639 0509.*

Tobago's most touristy area, Crown Point holds a wealth of restaurants and hotels, as well as some great beaches. Within walking distance of the airport, **Store Bay Beach** is a compact stretch of white sand with gentle surf, clear waters and several craft shops; there is also a line of restaurants that serve some delicious takeaway lunches and breakfasts.

🏖 **Store Bay Beach**
Store Bay Local Road. 🍴 🚻 🛍
Note: *lifeguards and changing facilities available from 10am–6pm daily.*

Pigeon Point Beach ⑨

🏖 Pigeon Point Road, Crown Point.
👥 👫 🍴 ⛵ 🏄 🚿 ⛱ 🛟 🎣

Hyped as Tobago's best beach, Pigeon Point is certainly the island's most quintessentially Caribbean seashore, its white sand overhung by palm trees and lapped by turquoise water; controversially, it is also the only one in the island to charge an entrance fee. It is a great place to spend the day, especially for families with kids, as there is a playground and the calm waters remain shallow almost up to the distant reef. There are places selling food and drinks, while Jet Skis and Hobie Cats buzz around offshore.

Houses in the fishing village of Buccoo, Tobago

Buccoo ⑩

4 miles (6 km) NE of Crown Point, Tobago. 🚌 🚤 *glass-bottom boat tours to the reef from Buccoo, Pigeon Point, and Store Bay.*

Northeast of Crown Point, Shirvan Road shoots off the main Milford Road toward Buccoo, a faded fishing village that plays host to the Sunday School outdoor party each Sunday night. Just offshore, Buccoo Reef is the island's most heavily visited patch of coral, with double-decker glass-bottom boats making regular sorties from all the beaches in the area. Though the 40-odd species of coral have suffered a lot of damage from storms and human encroachment, there is still some color to be seen alongside a host of gorgeous tropical fish such as butterfly and parrot fish. To the south of the reef is the crystal-clear water of the Nylon Pool sandbar where swimming is a refreshing treat.

Mount Irvine ⑪

5 miles (8 km) NE of Crown Point, Tobago. 🚌

The next coastal village after Buccoo is Mount Irvine, home to Tobago's first golf course. Past Buccoo, Shirvan Road cuts through the middle of the 18-hole **Mount Irvine Golf Course** and swings on past **Mount Irvine Bay Beach**, a stretch of yellow sand overhung by sea grape and palm trees, and with covered gazebos for picnicking. The waves here are some of the best in Tobago, making it a surfer's paradise. At the other side of the beach is a sandy area that offers lovely swimming and good snorkeling over the rocks and coral. Beyond Mount Irvine, the coast road sweeps past two more excellent places to swim, Grafton and Turtle Beaches. Both are wide and long and are perfect for a day by the sea.

⛳ **Mount Irvine Golf Course**
Shirvan Road. **Tel** *868 639 8871.*
🍴 🚻 www.mtirvine.com

🏖 **Mount Irvine Bay Beach**
♿ 🍴 **Note:** *changing facilities are available on-site.*

Kimme Museum ⑫

5 miles (8 km) NE of Crown Point, Tobago. **Tel** *868 639 0257.* 🚌
🕙 *10am–2pm Sun; at other times, call to arrange a viewing.* 🎟 📷
www.luisekimme.com

Just past the Mount Irvine Golf Course, the right-hand turnoff on to Orange Hill

The palm-fringed powdery white sand of Pigeon Point Beach, Tobago

For hotels and restaurants on these islands see pp502–3 and pp504–5

View of Parlatuvier Bay, on the north coast of Tobago

Road leads up into the hills and to the intriguing Kimme Museum, the turreted, mural-decorated home and studio of German sculptor Luise Kimme, who has been living in Tobago for some 30 years. Inspired by local life and folklore, her stunning pieces are each sculpted from a whole oak trunk, and depict everything from the mythical character La Diablesse to Nijinski dancers, and dancing couples.

Castara ❸

18 miles (29 km) NE of Crown Point, Tobago.

Past the diminutive town of Plymouth, the coast is paralleled by the Northside Road, a twisting and picturesque route that affords some lovely glimpses of interior villages and inaccessible coastline.

The first point of interest is Castara, a beautiful mini-resort that has grown up around a placid fishing village and a gorgeous curve of beach. It is a laid-back and attractive spot, and is ideal to spend some time relaxing, with a couple of great places to eat right on the beach and a sprinkling of low-key guesthouses overlooking the bay. There is enough space so it rarely feels crowded, however, if need be, it is possible to head for the adjoining Little Bay for some solitude. Castara is also one of the points from which boat tours (see p498) are available for the various excellent beaches and snorkeling spots located nearby.

Englishman's Bay to Bloody Bay ❹

20 miles (32 km) NE of Crown Point, Tobago.

The countryside beyond Castara becomes noticeably less developed, with the Northside Road twisting through jungle-smothered hillsides with hardly a building in sight. The first place to stop is Englishman's Bay, a delightful and stunning horseshoe of yellow sand that lies between untouched rainforest on one side and deep emerald waters on the other. The offshore reef here offers good snorkeling opportunities.

Just above the fishing village of Parlatuvier, some 2 miles (3 km) farther along the coastal road, people can stop off at a roadside parking spot for some pretty views of the bay below, with fishing boats bobbing in the turquoise waters and terraced small-holdings rolling up the hillside.

About 2 miles (3 km) from the village is Bloody Bay, offering some fine coastal views, with the spectacular Sisters Rocks lying just offshore. At the bay's rough, yellow-sand beach, a turnoff swings inland leading to the Tobago Forest Reserve (see p495). Moving east along the coast, visitors pass through the pretty village of L'Anse Fourmi and finally reach Charlotteville (see p495) at the island's northeast tip.

SUNDAY SCHOOL

An enduring Tobago tradition that remains popular with both locals and visitors, Sunday School is a huge outdoor party that overtakes Buccoo each Sunday evening. From around 8pm, the Bucconeers steel band play under the covered section of the beach facilities for a predominantly older crowd, who take to the dance floor to display some killer moves. After the live music, DJs take over, playing dancehall, hip-hop, and R&B for a younger crowd – the drinks flow and everyone lets their hair down. The sandy "dance floor" in front of the beach facilities becomes a great place to dance and mingle. Vendors sell crafts and jewelry, all night long, along the roadside leading to Buccoo. Dinner options include a full-fledged fish menu as well as lighter snacks such as corn soup. If not driving, it is best to arrange for a taxi pickup at the end of the night.

Steel pan band playing at Sunday School, Buccoo, Tobago

Scarborough ⑮

7 miles (11 km) NE of Crown Point, Tobago. 🏠 20,000. 🚢 🛳 Cruise ship complex, 868 635 0934. **www**.gotrinidadandtobago.com

Tobago's capital, Scarborough is a hotbed of activity compared to the rest of the island, with taxis and shoppers crowding the streets, vendors setting up their stalls at the roadside, and plenty of traffic to and from the busy ferry port. The best place for shopping is the market, set back from the seafront and accessed from Gardenside Street. It is busiest on Fridays and Saturdays, but visitors will always find piles of exotic fruits and vegetables and other assorted general goods. On the other side of

Signage at Fort King George, Scarborough

Gardenside Street is the 18-acre (7-ha) Botanical Gardens, its smooth lawns and fishponds offering quiet respite from the clamor. It is open on all days.

Scarborough's other main draw is Fort King George. A collection of handsome restored colonial-era brick buildings surrounding the modern lighthouse, the complex features many cannons and offers sweeping views down the windward coast and Scarborough. The fort is also home to the small but interesting **Tobago Museum**, which has some absorbing exhibits on the island's local history.

🏛 **Tobago Museum**
Fort King George. **Tel** 868 639 3970. ◯ 9am–4:30pm Mon–Fri. 📷

The Windward Coast ⑯

9 miles (14 km) NE of Scarborough, Toabgo. 🚌

In comparison to the tranquil leeward side of the island, bordered by the calm Caribbean Sea, the windward coast is a lot more rugged, washed by pounding Atlantic waves and with strong currents that make some beaches out of bounds for swimmers. The best place to experience the sea is King's Bay, bordered by a forest of palms and with calm water and fine volcanic sand. To the southwest there is another chance to get wet at Argyle Waterfall, the island's highest three-tiered 177-ft (54-m) cascade with several pools. Otherwise, the windward coast is best appreciated as a scenic – if winding – drive, its pretty villages with board houses teetering at the edge

Speyside ⑱

A short drive from Charlotteville, over the island's central spine and onto the east coast, Speyside offers some of Tobago's best diving and snorkeling. The viewing area above town on the Scarborough road gives a bird's-eye view of the brightly-painted village and the offshore islands, including Little Tobago rising from the blue seas. Glass-bottom boats make regular trips out to the reef from the beach; visitors can also don a mask and flippers and just swim out themselves.

Jemma's Sea View Kitchen, built around a tree at the Speyside seashore

Diving *is great in Speyside with several wonderful scuba sites nearby and a teeming reef just offshore between the mainland and the nearby Goat and Little Tobago Islands.*

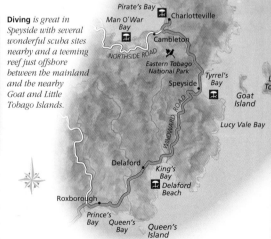

KEY

🏖 Beach

🦌 Nature reserve

▬ Major road

═ Minor road

For hotels and restaurants on these islands see pp502–3 and pp504–5

of the cliffs or spreading out on either side of the road running along the coast.

🪶 Argyle Waterfall

Windward Road. ⏰ *9am–5pm daily; last tour 4pm.* 🏝️ 📷 ▭
Note: *changing facilities are available on-site.*

Tobago Forest Reserve ⑰

17 miles (27 km) NE of Scarborough, Tobago. 🚗 📷

The oldest protected rainforest in the Western Hemisphere, the Tobago Forest Reserve comprises 22 sq miles (57 sq km) of densely forested land in the northern half of the island, accessible via a scenic road. Much of the area is inaccessible, but from Gilpin Trace – marked by a huge rock by the roadside – visitors can follow a trail into the dense forest, with its towering

A gazebo at Cambleton Battery, Charlotteville

trees and greenish light filtering through the thick canopy. Guides are available at the entrance to the reserve.

Charlotteville ⑲

27 miles (43 km) NE of Scarborough, Tobago. 🚌

Tucked into a protected bay at Tobago's extreme northeast tip, Charlotteville is a slow-paced place, with tourism and

fishing co-existing easily as the main industries. Tumbling down a steep hillside, the village meets the sea at the yellow sands and calm waters of Man O'War Bay. Overlooking the Man O'War Bay to the west is the British-built Cambleton Battery, while to the east, via a rough track around the headland, is Pirate's Bay, perhaps Tobago's prettiest beach, completely undeveloped and with excellent snorkeling spots.

Panoramic view *of Speyside from the lookout, with the village to the left, Goat Island in the lee of the larger Little Tobago, and a craft stall in the foreground. This is among the most photographed spots on the island.*

VISITORS' CHECKLIST

Around 20 miles (32 km) NE of Scarborough. 🚌 *from Scarborough.* 🚤 *glass-bottom boat tours with snorkeling are available from Frank's at Blue Waters Inn (868 660 5438), and from Fear Not at Jemma's Sea View Kitchen (868 660 4654).*
🍴 🖥️ ♻️

```
0 km          2
0 miles       2
```

Speyside's Beach *is best at the village's western end, around the Blue Waters Inn hotel (see p503), and to the east, where there are changing facilities adjacent to the football field.*

SPEYSIDE'S WILDLIFE

Enriched by nutrients from Venezuela's Orinoco River, the reefs around Speyside are some of Tobago's best. It is possible to see incredibly diverse marine life and corals, including, at the Kelleston Drain site, one of the largest brain corals in the world, measuring 13-ft (4-m) high and 20-ft (6-m) wide. The island's position at the con-fluence of the Caribbean Sea

Two divers approaching a gigantic brain coral

and Atlantic Ocean also makes it a great place to spot deep-water pelagic species, most notably the huge, graceful manta rays that are a common sight here. Above ground, there is also some great bird-watching on Little Tobago, a protected sanctuary since 1924 and a good place to spot species such as boobies, frigates, and the red-billed tropic-bird. Specialist guides *(see p498)* lead trips to the island.

Outdoor Activities and Specialized Holidays

Trinidad and Tobago offer plenty of activities that take place beyond their beaches. With a wide range of habitats, ranging from swamp to savannah to rainforest, they provide some of the Caribbean's best hiking and bird-watching. Tour operators arrange trips or entire holidays based around birding or diving. Along with guided hikes or mountain-bike rides, visitors can watch millions of bats exit from their daytime roost in a cave, kayak through the swamps in search of manatees, and take in the unforgettable sight of a huge leatherback turtle hauling herself up a beach to lay eggs in the sand.

One of the secluded beaches at Blanchisseuse, north coast of Trinidad

BEACHES

Of the two islands, Tobago boasts of better beaches. However, the north coast of Trinidad with its wide curves of yellow sand and clean waters, features some great spots for swimming. Maracas Bay *(see pp490–91)* has excellent facilities and cool green waters. Popular with both locals and visitors, it tends to get crowded during weekends. For quieter alternatives to the buzzing northeast coast, it is best to head to the secluded One Thousand Steps at La Filette or the deserted and wild Yarra. Accessible only on foot or by boat from Blanchisseuse, Paria Bay has a waterfall with a deep pool and a generous stretch of untouched yellow sand.

Tobago's leeward coast boasts a couple of sublime beaches. Pigeon Point Beach *(see p492)* lures visitors with its soft white sand and azure waters. A boat trip around the island allows access to beaches that might not be reached on foot or by car. These include the picture-perfect No Man's Land and the lovely Stingray Beach, where people can swim with the friendly rays.

DIVING AND SNORKELING

Trinidad and Tobago's reefs are impressively rich and diverse, as they are fed by sediments from the great South American rivers. In Trinidad, visibility ranges from just 6 ft (2 m) to a depth of 50 ft (15 m). Though there is some interesting diving around the Bocas islands, most prefer Tobago's waters, where the visibility is better and the Guyana Current makes for some exciting drift diving. Tobago is also one of the few places in the world where divers can swim alongside manta rays and spot the unusual toadfish and short-nose batfish. The best dive sites are around Speyside *(see pp494–5)*, but there are some prime spots along the north coast, at Man O' War Bay in Charlotteville and the St. Giles Islands off the northwest tip. Buccoo Reef, Arnos Vale Bay Beach, Pirate's Bay, and Speyside also have good snorkeling. Diving and snorkeling gear can be hired from dive shops such as **R & Sea Divers**, **Aquamarine Dive**, and **Tobago Dive Experience**.

WATERSPORTS

The more visited Tobago has the bulk of the available watersports, with most outlets in Crown Point, with a particular concentration at Pigeon Point Beach, including **Radical Sports**. From there visitors

Diver approaching a cluster of stunning corals in the waters around Tobago

A watersports center at Pigeon Point Beach, Tobago

can enjoy banana boat rides, kitesurfing, waterskiing, and parasailing. Jet Skis and Hobie Cat catamarans can also be rented. Watersports agencies also include **World of Watersports** in Scarborough.

BOAT TOURS

With its jungle-covered hillsides tumbling down to deserted, inaccessible beaches and a host of offshore islands, Tobago's coastline is best seen by boat. Many operators such as **Frankie's Tours** and **Alibaba Tours** offer trips that include lunch, drinks, and stops for snorkeling and swimming, along with a bit of line fishing. Trips from the western end of the island tend to go up to Englishman's Bay for snorkeling and then head back for lunch at the gorgeous No Man's Land Beach. From places such as Castara, it is possible to reach secluded hard-to-reach shores, while spotting dolphins, turtles, and flying fish along the way. **Sail Tobago** has crafts that accommodate up to 30 passengers and offer freshwater showers and a buffet lunch.

In Trinidad, boat tours around the Bocas islands give an insight into the fascinating local history. Tourists can enjoy swimming at secluded beaches or in a cave on Gasparee Island, and hiking through dry scrub forest as part of the tour. **In-Joy Tours**, located in Petit Valley, also organizes boat trips.

FISHING

The waters of Trinidad and Tobago promise some good game fishing, with the main catches being marlin, tuna, and wahoo. Chartering an entire sportfishing boat to head out to the deep-sea waters might make for an expensive day out. It may be a better idea to hire a local fishing pirogue and try line fishing for kingfish, mahimahi, barracuda, and jack. **Hard Play Fishing Charters** and **Alpha Lime** on Tobago are reputed fishing charters.

KAYAKING

With just a few inland rivers, kayaking in Tobago is mostly restricted to the sea. **Tobago Sea Kayak Experience** in Charlotteville offer guided paddles that provide a gentle

and unique way to see the undeveloped coastline. They also offer a trip from Pigeon Point that includes lunch and snorkeling at No Man's Land.

In Trinidad, **Chaguaramas Kayak Centre** is a kayak rental outlet. From here visitors can paddle around the sheltered waters of Williams Bay, or take a guided tour around the Bocas islands. It is also possible to paddle up the Marianne River from Blanchisseuse. On the east coast, the protected wetland of Nariva Swamp at No Man's Land is a habitat for birds and animals, and offers some fantastic kayaking through calm waters choked with water hyacinth and lilies. Kayaking trips on Trinidad are arranged by companies such as Caribbean Discovery Tours and Paria Springs Eco Community *(see p499)*.

MOUNTAIN BIKING

Though mountain biking is a relatively new sport in Trinidad and Tobago, there are several operators on both islands who take visitors on exciting trails and can provide excellent guided rides for amateurs and aficionados. It is better to ride early in the morning and stick to shaded forest trails to avoid the tropical sun. However, many trails end with a cool dip in the sea or at a waterfall. Interested visitors can contact **Mountain Biking Tobago** in Tobago and Paria Springs Eco Community in Trinidad.

Kayaking in the calm waters of Williams Bay, Trinidad

Hiking through the verdant trails of the Tobago Forest Reserve

HIKING

Although Tobago has plenty of splendid trails, particularly through the Tobago Forest Reserve (see p495) and along undeveloped portions of the leeward coast, it is Trinidad that offers the nation's best hiking. The Northern Range mountains are laced with trails that take in waterfalls, rivers, gorges, and lush rainforest. Climbs up Trinidad's highest peaks, El Tucuche at 3,071 ft (936 m) and El Cerro del Aripo at 3,087 ft (941 m), are challenging. Others may prefer the short trek up Mount Tamana to watch the spectacular dusk exit of a

colony of resident bats. Paria Springs Eco Community and Caribbean Discovery Tours arrange guided hikes. **Harris' Jungle Tours** and Peter Cox Nature Tours (see p499) offer excursions in Tobago.

BIRD-WATCHING

Ranking among the world's top ten destinations in terms of the number of species, with around 460 recorded, Trinidad and Tobago are a bird-watchers' paradise. Alongside the common cowbirds and bananaquits, it is possible to spot bay-headed tanagers, channel-billed toucans, and the very rare nocturnal oil-birds. The islands boast the full spectrum of iridescent hummingbirds. In fact, the Taíno name for Trinidad was *Iere*, or "land of the humming-birds." The Northern Range is home to the birders' mecca – the Asa Wright Nature Centre and Lodge (see p491). Other great places for birding include the Caroni Swamp, where flocks of scarlet ibis roost each evening, and the Cocal at Manzanilla, which serves as a nesting site for red-bellied

macaws. Birding trips are arranged by Paria Springs Eco Community and Caribbean Discovery Tours in Trinidad, and **Nature Lovers** and Peter Cox Nature Tours in Tobago.

GOLF

The islands have a few great golf clubs. In Tobago, the 18-hole Mount Irvine course (see p492) offers sea views from every hole. The Plantations course is another 18-hole option. In Trinidad, the 9-hole Chaguaramas Golf Club, the 18-hole St. Andrew's, and Millennium Lakes have fine courses. The **Trinidad and Tobago Golf Association** provides all details.

Golfers at the Mount Irvine Golf Course, Tobago

DIRECTORY

DIVING AND SNORKELING

Aquamarine Dive
Speyside, Tobago.
Tel 868 639 4416.
www.aquamarine
dive.com

R & Sea Divers
Crown Point, Tobago.
Tel 868 639 8120.
www.rseadivers.com

Tobago Dive Experience
Speyside, Tobago.
Tel 868 660 4888.
www.tobagodive
experience.com

WATERSPORTS

Radical Sports
Pigeon Point Heritage Park, Tobago.
Tel 868 631 5150.
www.radical
sportstobago.com

World of Watersports
Scarborough, Tobago.
Tel 868 660 7234.
www.worldof
watersports.com

BOAT TOURS

Alibaba Tours
Castara, Tobago.
Tel 868 635 1017.
www.alibaba-tours.com

Frankie's Tours
Mount Irvine Bay Beach, Tobago. *Tel 868 639 4527.* www.frankietours-tobago.com

In-Joy Tours
Petit Valley, Trinidad.
Tel 868 633 4733.
www.injoytours.com

Sail Tobago
Bon Accord, Tobago.
Tel 868 639 7245.
www.sailtobago.com

FISHING

Alpha Lime
Mount Irvine, Tobago.
Tel 868 639 9386.

Hard Play Fishing Charters
Tobago. *Tel 868 639 7108.* www.hardplay.net

KAYAKING

Chaguaramas Kayak Centre
Williams Bay, Trinidad.
Tel 868 633 7871.

Tobago Sea Kayak Experience
Tobago. *Tel 868 660 6186.* www.
seakayaktobago.com

MOUNTAIN BIKING

Mountain Biking Tobago
Tobago. *Tel 868 639 9709.* www.mountain
bikingtobago.com

HIKING

Harris' Jungle Tours
Crown Point, Tobago.
Tel 868 639 0513.
www.harris-jungle-tours.
com

BIRD-WATCHING

Nature Lovers
Tobago.
Tel 868 639 4559.
www.tobagobirding.com

GOLF

Trinidad and Tobago Golf Association
St. Andrew's Golf Club, Moka, Trinidad.
Tel 868 629 7127.
www.trinidadandtobago
golfassociation.com

For hotels and restaurants on these islands see pp502–3 and pp504–5

Turtle-Watching

A turtle hatchling

Each year during the March–July season, thousands of turtles draw themselves up onto the beaches of Trinidad and Tobago to lay their eggs. The most common species in local waters is the leatherback turtle, with up to 50 visiting the more well-known beaches on a good night. There are several places where environmental groups have set up turtle watches to protect the animals from human and animal predators, and at many of these, visitors too can take in the amazing spectacle. In Trinidad, the main beaches for turtle-watching are at Matura and Grande Riviere, while in Tobago there are occasional nestings at Turtle Beach.

A hole, *slightly larger than her own body, is dug by the female. Decoy nests are also made to confuse predators.*

The eggs, *laid over a period of approximately two hours, number between 80 to 100. The leatherback turtle sheds tears to protect her eyes against the sand. After depositing the eggs, she covers the nest with sand and returns to the sea.*

THE NESTING PROCESS

Female leatherbacks may lay up to nine times during the season. They usually come ashore at night during the high tide to lay their eggs, which are deposited well beyond the waterline. This is done to ensure that tides do not erode the nests and uncover the eggs.

Powerful flippers are used to remove the surface sand and dig the nest.

Visitors can observe the turtle at close quarters due to the trance-like state she enters while laying eggs.

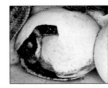

Hatchlings, *fully-formed but tiny, emerge from the eggs after an incubation period of around 60 days. The eggs usually hatch during the night.*

Newborn turtles *head for the sea upon hatching. During the early stages, hatchling populations are very vulnerable and most fall prey to large fish, birds, and crabs. Once in the sea, the males never return to shore, while the female turtles visit the same beach where they hatched to lay their own eggs.*

TOUR OPERATORS

Caribbean Discovery Tours
Trinidad. **Tel** *868 624 7281.*
www.caribbeandiscovery
tours.com
Grande Riviere Nature Tour Guide Association
Trinidad. **Tel** *868 670 4257.*
Nature Seekers
Trinidad. **Tel** *868 668 7337.*
Paria Springs Eco Community
Trinidad. **Tel** *868 622 8826.*
www.pariasprings.com
Peter Cox Nature Tours
Tobago. **Tel** *868 751 5822.*
www.tobagonaturetours.com

Choosing a Hotel

On Trinidad, it is feasible to stay based in Port of Spain and sightsee by way of day trips, but there are some good hotels on the beaches as well. Tobago has a lot more variety, with everything from palatial all-inclusives to basic B&Bs. Much of Tobago's accommodations are in Crown Point, but there also are some great places to stay in quieter corners such as Mount Irvine and Castara.

PRICE CATEGORIES
The following price ranges are for a standard double room per night and all taxes included.

$ under $100
$$ $100–200
$$$ $200–300
$$$$ $300–400
$$$$$ over $400

TRINIDAD AND TOBAGO

Asa Wright Nature Centre and Lodge
(see p491)
A favorite destination with bird-watchers, this lovely lodge in the midst of the rainforest has simple rooms with mahogany floors, antique furniture, and a balcony. The huge grounds are laced with walking trails. There is a waterfall nearby to swim in and a cave with resident oilbirds.

Coblentz Inn

Blue Haven

BLANCHISSEUSE, TRINIDAD Laguna Mar $
North Coast Road **Tel** 868 628 3731 **Fax** 868 628 3737 **Rooms** 16

Just steps from the main beach in Blanchisseuse, this is the most "hotel-like" place to stay in a village of small guesthouses. Across the road from the sand, this family-friendly hotel has simple clean rooms with a shared balcony. The rooms upstairs are airy and there is an excellent restaurant and bar too. **www.lagunamar.com**

GRANDE RIVIERE, TRINIDAD Mont Plaisir Estate $$
Main Street **Tel** 868 670 2216 **Fax** 868 670 0057 **Rooms** 13

Trinidad's loveliest beach hotel has rooms decorated with furniture made by local craftsmen, and driftwood sculptures on the walls. The restaurant serves delicious food grown organically on-site. Some rooms are on the beach and in season there is a chance of seeing leatherback turtles right outside the door. **www.mtplaisir.com**

PORT OF SPAIN, TRINIDAD Alicia's House $
7 Coblentz Gardens, St. Ann's **Tel** 868 623 2802 **Fax** 868 623 8560 **Rooms** 25

Tucked away in a quiet residential street, walking distance from the north side of the Savannah, this is a busy little place. It has neat, appealing rooms with fridge and cable TV, a pool, Jacuzzi, and sundeck, bar, as well as wireless Internet. Babysitting and meals are available. **www.aliciashouse.com**

PORT OF SPAIN, TRINIDAD Coblentz Inn $$
44 Coblentz Avenue, Cascade **Tel** 868 621 0541 **Fax** 868 624 7566 **Rooms** 16

This gorgeous little boutique hotel has regular rooms as well as others decorated on themes ranging from rum to cricket. All have facilities such as DVD and CD players, minibar, and iron and board. There is a renowned restaurant, Battimamzelle *(see p504)* on-site. Rates include breakfast. **www.coblentzinn.com**

PORT OF SPAIN, TRINIDAD Trinidad Hilton $$
Lady Young Road, St. Ann's **Tel** 868 624 3211 **Fax** 868 624 4485 **Rooms** 412

Grand old Port of Spain hotel, recently refurbished and with all the facilities of this chain, including a large pool and a children's pool, a play area, several restaurants and bars, gym, spa facilities, games room, and shops. Its terrace provides lovely views over the Savannah. **www.hiltoncaribbean.com**

PORT OF SPAIN, TRINIDAD Kapok $$$
16–18 Cotton Hill, St. Clair **Tel** 868 622 5675 **Fax** 868 622 9677 **Rooms** 94

Just off the Savannah and perfectly located for Carnival, this hotel has stylish rooms and suites with all facilities, including iron and board and coffeemaker. The two restaurants/bars are popular with guests and non-guests. There's a pool, shops, gym, sundeck, 24-hour computer room, and self-service laundry. **www.kapokhotel.com**

ARNOS VALE ESTATE, TOBAGO Arnos Vale $$
Arnos Vale Road **Tel** 868 639 2881 **Fax** 868 639 4629 **Rooms** 29

Set amid lush grounds teeming with birdlife and with a private white-sand beach and one of the island's best reefs just offshore, Arnos Vale is perfect for relaxation. Afternoon tea is served each day at 4pm, and there is a lovely pool overlooking the sea. **www.arnosvalehotel.com**

BACOLET, TOBAGO Blue Haven $$$
Bacolet Bay **Tel** 868 660 7400 **Fax** 868 660 7900 **Rooms** 51

This stylish, upscale, and family-friendly hotel has fabulous views of Bacolet Bay, where a hotel-run bar is located on the sand. The rooms have a romantic feel with elegant four-poster beds. There is a gym and a pool overlooking the sea. **www.bluehavenhotel.com**

Key to Symbols *see back cover flap*

BLACK ROCK, TOBAGO Seahorse Inn

Stone Haven Bay **Tel** *868 639 0686* **Fax** *868 639 0057* **Rooms** *4*

This intimate little hotel is on the beach and is run by an English chef, who cooks in the on-site restaurant *(see p504)*. Rooms have teak floors, pleasant decor, and arched windows that have lovely views out over the waters. The owners also rent several villas nearby. Rates include breakfast. **www.seahorseinntobago.com**

CASTARA, TOBAGO Alibaba's Sea Breeze

Little Bay **Tel** *868 635 1017* **Fax** *868 635 1017* **Rooms** *4*

A fabulous location just above Little Bay and overlooking the whole of Castara, the apartments in this handsome wooden house have hammocks on private balconies, wood furnishings, and well-equipped kitchens. The owners run a tour company and are a gold mine of information. **www.alibaba-tours.com**

CASTARA, TOBAGO The Naturalist

Castara Village **Tel** *868 639 5901* **Fax** *868 660 7166* **Rooms** *6*

Just above Castara's main beach, The Naturalist has clean and neatly decorated apartments, all equipped with kitchenettes. There is a balcony that overlooks the beach. The hotel also has an air-conditioned restaurant and bar on the beach, as well as an Internet café. **www.naturalist-tobago.com**

CHARLOTTEVILLE, TOBAGO Cholson Chalets

Man O'War Bay **Tel** *868 639 8553* **Fax** *868 639 8553* **Rooms** *12*

Right on the bay and overlooking the pier, these pretty green-and-white painted buildings hold different apartments, all with a homely feel. Pirate's Bay is only a walk away. Better units are located upstairs although they might cost a little more. There is also a basic studio on the ground floor. **www.cholsonchalets.com**

CHARLOTTEVILLE, TOBAGO Man O'War Bay Cottages

Man O'War Bay **Tel** *868 660 4327* **Fax** *868 660 4328* **Rooms** *10*

Right on the beach in Charlotteville's main bay, these basic cottages with kitchens are set in shady gardens and offer plenty of peace and quiet. Bird-watching and nature tours are arranged by the hotel. Other activities such as scuba diving, fishing, and snorkeling are on offer. Service is excellent. **www.man-o-warbaycottages.com**

CROWN POINT, TOBAGO Crown Point Beach Hotel

Store Bay Road **Tel** *868 639 8781* **Fax** *868 639 8731* **Rooms** *62*

Overlooking Store Bay Beach, these studios and one-bedroom apartments, ranged around grassy lawns, are simply decorated but have everything required for a beach holiday. All have cooking facilities and there is a convenience store on-site, as well as a pool, shuffleboard court, and beach access. **www.crownpointbeachhotel.com**

CROWN POINT, TOBAGO Kariwak Village

Store Bay Local Road, Bon Accord **Tel** *868 639 8442* **Rooms** *24*

Set in lush landscaped gardens dotted with hammocks, and a decent-sized pool, this is a family-friendly and holistic retreat offering massage, yoga, and meditation classes in the thatch-roofed studio. Located around the pool, the rooms are stylish and simple, and there is a great restaurant and bar as well. **www.kariwak.com**

CROWN POINT, TOBAGO Toucan Inn

Store Bay Local Road, Bon Accord **Tel** *868 639 7173* **Fax** *868 639 8933* **Rooms** *20*

This friendly and lively English-run hotel has octagonal teak cabins that are set around the pool or in the beautiful gardens. The rooms have a pleasant decor. Bonkers *(see p505)*, the on-site restaurant, is very popular and features live entertainment. There is a bar as well. **www.toucan-inn.com**

MOUNT IRVINE, TOBAGO Mount Irvine Golf and Beach Resort

Orange Hill Road **Tel** *868 639 8871* **Fax** *868 639 8800* **Rooms** *105*

This grand old hotel, at the edge of its own golf course *(see p492)*, is popular with those who spend their time on the greens. Rooms are clean and decent, and there is a lovely stretch of private beach across the road for guests' use. Highlights include a huge pool and tennis court. **www.mtirvine.com**

PLYMOUTH, TOBAGO Turtle Beach

Stone Haven Bay **Tel** *868 639 2851* **Fax** *868 639 1495* **Rooms** *125*

Popular with package visitors, many of whom are on all-inclusive plans, this long-established place is showing some signs of wear and tear, but the location on Stone Haven Bay amid tropical gardens is fantastic. All the rooms, in two-story blocks, are on the sand. Facilities include a bar and restaurant. **www.rexresorts.com**

SPEYSIDE, TOBAGO Blue Waters Inn

Bateaux Bay **Tel** *868 660 4341* **Fax** *868 660 5195* **Rooms** *38*

Located on a gorgeous yellow-sand beach that far eclipses Speyside's public one, this is the largest hotel in the village, with excellent facilities and bright rooms. There is a PADI dive center and a variety of watersports are available. Other activities include tennis and bird-watching. **www.bluewatersinn.com**

SPEYSIDE, TOBAGO Speyside Inn

Windward Road **Tel** *868 660 4852* **Fax** *868 660 4852* **Rooms** *21*

Across from Speyside's beach and with fabulous views out to Little Tobago and Goat Islands, the inn has stylish rooms that get lovely sea breezes and have large balconies overlooking the ocean. Family rooms available. There is a pool and dive center on the premises. The food is reliably good. **www.speysideinn.com**

Where to Eat & Nightlife

Eating out is one of the great highlights of a visit to Trinidad and Tobago. Trinidad has a thriving restaurant culture, while Tobago offers a wide choice of places to eat serving Italian and Chinese food alongside Indian and Creole cuisine and even sushi. There is plenty to do after dark, including live entertainment at many of Tobago's hotels and restaurants.

PRICE CATEGORIES
The price ranges are for a two-course meal for one, including tax and service charges and half a bottle of wine.

$ under $10
$$ $10–15
$$$ $15–25
$$$$ $25–35
$$$$$ over $35

RESTAURANTS

Local Cuisine

Other than tasty seafood, local staples include roti, a split-pea infused bread wrapped around curried meat, shrimp, or vegetables; and *pelau* (classic Creole cook-up of rice), chicken and pigeon peas stewed with coconut milk. Street food is great, from doubles (fried breads filled with chickpea curry) to *pholourie* (split-pea doughballs with tamarind sauce).

The Lure

Seahorse Inn

PORT OF SPAIN, TRINIDAD Femmes du Chalet (Breakfast Shed) 🅥 📷 📧 ♿ $

Wrightson Road, opposite Independence Square

Originally established to provide dockworkers with inexpensive lunches, this collection of stalls, with views over the Gulf of Paria, is one of the best places to sample Creole breakfasts and lunches from coconut bake with saltfish salad with *callaloo*, and macaroni pie.

PORT OF SPAIN, TRINIDAD Sails 📷 🎵 $$$$

Power Boats Marina, Western Main Road, Chaguaramas **Tel** *868 634 1712*

Laid-back place popular with the yachting fraternity, with tables in a covered area and on a deck by the water. The menu ranges from stuffed jalapeños or fried wontons to shepherd's pie, steak, or the catch of the day. There are pool tables in the air-conditioned bar. DJs play later in the evening on Wednesdays.

PORT OF SPAIN, TRINIDAD Battimamzelle 🅟 📋 📷 ♒ ♿ $$$$$

Coblentz Inn, 44 Coblentz Av., Cascade **Tel** *868 621 0591*

This upmarket restaurant, in Coblentz Inn *(see p502)*, serves nouvelle-style Caribbean cuisine in an indoor dining room or in the patio garden. The menu changes weekly, but might include Kobe beef *buljol* for starters, and grilled lamb with bacon and lentils or oxtail pepperpot. Try the seamoss crème brulée with *cassava pone* for dessert.

PORT OF SPAIN, TRINIDAD The Lure 📋 📷 🎵 ♿ $$$$$

Sweetwater Marina, 2 Stella Maris Drive, Western Main Road, Chaguaramas **Tel** *868 634 2783*

Great for a romantic dinner with tables at the water's edge, and an eclectic menu. Starters include seafood chowder or shrimp rolls, while main courses range from a succulent seafood lasagne to sushi platters and lamb loin with tamarind sauce. Guests can view sharks, turtles, and cruising kingfish in the fenced-off seawater pen.

PORT OF SPAIN, TRINIDAD Veni Mange 🅥 $$$$$

67 Ariapita Av., Woodbrook **Tel** *868 624 4597*

Set in a lovely board house bedecked with Caribbean art, Veni Mange is a popular and stylish lunch spot, serving Creole cuisine with an imaginative twist. Try the steamed shrimp-stuffed snapper with coconut tomato sauce or grilled chicken with pineapple, raisin, and tamarind salsa. Dinner served only on Wednesday and Friday.

BLACK ROCK, TOBAGO Seahorse Inn 🅟 📷 🎵 $$$$$

Old Grafton Beach Road **Tel** *868 639 0686*

In an attractive setting overlooking the beach, Seahorse Inn *(see p503)* has reliable good food. There is plenty of seafood on the menu, including lobster thermidor or seared tuna with garlic mash and spicy tomato sauce. Meat dishes include Creole pork chops stuffed with pine nuts or duck breast with pineapple sauce and potato rosti.

BUCCOO, TOBAGO La Tartaruga 🅥 🅟 📋 ♿ $$$$$

Buccoo Bay Road **Tel** *868 639 0940*

Just above the main road with tables on the patio and indoors, this is one of the best Italian restaurants on the island. Food is well-cooked with authentic ingredients. The home-made pasta with rock lobster, fish, shrimp, and squid is excellent. The delicious and decadent desserts are worth a try.

CASTARA, TOBAGO Cascreole 📷 $$$$

Big Bay **Tel** *868 639 5291*

The location is the main attraction here with tables on a wooden platform overlooking the water. The food is tasty with plenty of seafood made in Creole style. The seafood is fresh and cooked with vegetables and rice. Delectable lamb and shrimp concoctions are served as well.

Key to Symbols *see back cover flap*

CROWN POINT, TOBAGO Store Bay Kiosks

Store Bay beach facility, Milford Road

This row of huts set just back from Store Bay's sand is an institution, serving some of the best Tobagonian cooking on the island. Along with staples such as Creole fish or chicken with all the trimmings, there is roti or the specialty dish of curried crab with dumplings. There are long queues, so it is best to arrive early.

CROWN POINT, TOBAGO Bonkers

Toucan Inn, Store Bay Local Road **Tel** *868 639 7173*

Located in Toucan Inn (*see p503*), and popular both for its food and nightly entertainment, Bonkers has tables set around the pool area. Well-executed favorites include forest paté or shrimp cocktail with a lamb curry. Chicken breast stuffed with mushrooms, tuna in a green peppercorn sauce, and the lobster creations are great.

CROWN POINT, TOBAGO La Cantina

Off Pigeon Point Beach **Tel** *868 639 8242*

La Cantina is one of the best Italian restaurants in Tobago. Baked in an authentic wood-fired brick oven, the pizzas are straight out of Italy, with great sauce and toppings. There are a few pasta and meat dishes, served alongside salads and starters, as well as daily specials.

CROWN POINT, TOBAGO Café Iguana

Corner of Store Bay Local Road and Milford Road **Tel** *868 631 8205*

A softly lit place with regular live jazz and good cocktails from the bar, Café Iguana is popular. The international menu is strong on seafood, including crab backs, spaghetti with shrimp, and fish or lobster in garlic butter or white wine sauce. There are good choices of meat dishes too, including coconut chicken and rib-eye steak.

CROWN POINT, TOBAGO Kariwak

Kariwak Village Hotel, Store Bay Local Road **Tel** *868 639 8442*

Made with fresh local ingredients, many organic, and seasoned with fresh herbs, the set-menu meals here are invariably delicious. The offerings change daily but dinner highlights include pumpkin soup with dill, and blackened fish or grilled mushrooms with herbs, accompanied by basmati rice and stuffed *christophene* (vegetable pear).

MOUNT PLEASANT, TOBAGO Shirvan Watermill

Shirvan Road **Tel** *868 639 0000*

This is a fine dining restaurant with a lovely open-air setting surrounding an old cut-stone watermill, with waterfalls, fishponds and lots of lights. The menu ranges from seafood crêpes and shrimp tempura to baby snapper stuffed with crab and honey breast of duck. Desserts include pineapple and ginger cheesecake.

SCARBOROUGH, TOBAGO Blue Crab

Corner of Robinson and Main Streets, Upper Scarborough **Tel** *868 639 2737*

This place is an excellent choice for an inexpensive lunch and extremely popular with locals. Tables are set out on a breezy patio, and the Creole cooking is invariably excellent, from fresh fish to curried crab served with green fig salad, macaroni pie, and vegetable rice. Unsweetened natural juices served too.

SPEYSIDE, TOBAGO Jemma's Sea View Kitchen

Main Street **Tel** *868 660 4066*

A staple tour-bus stop, with an unusual location built around the branches of an almond tree, and with fabulous views out to the nearby islands, Jemma's lives up to its hype. The seafood, including lobster, is excellent, as are the side dishes, from breadfruit pie to aubergine casserole. However, this place does not serve alcohol.

BARS AND CLUBS

Trinidad and Tobago's party-hard attitude ensures a lively nightlife, from sedate jazz bars to tiny rum shops or raucous drinking holes playing loud music. Tobago offers some great open-air venues, while Port of Spain's state-of-the-art nightclubs are world class. Trinidad offers countless buzzing bars along Ariapita Avenue and Western Main Road in St. James, and though the selection is more limited in Tobago, the weekly Sunday School party provides some entertainment.

Sunday School, Tobago

RECOMMENDED PLACES TO GO

51 Degrees
51 Cipriani Blvd, Port of Spain, Trinidad. (Busy indoor club.)

Bar Code
Milford Rd, Scarborough, Tobago. (The capital's best bar.)

CroBar
Ariapita Av., Port of Spain, Trinidad. (Open-air bar.)

Golden Star
Crown Point, Tobago. (Hosts talent shows.)

G-Spot (Girls Spot)
Sun Spree Hotel, Old Store Bay Road, Tobago. (Upscale dance club.)

The Shade
Mt Pleasant Blvd, Bon Accord, Tobago. (Tobago's best nightclub.)

Shakers
Ariapita Av., Port of Spain, Trinidad. (Indoor and outdoor seating.)

Smokey and Bunty's
97 Western Main Rd, St. James, Trinidad. (Brilliant bar.)

Zen Nightclub
9–11 Keate Street, Trinidad. (Four floors of clubbing glamor.)

Practical Information

Trinidad and Tobago are easy islands to travel to. Public transport is relatively reliable, with several options to choose from, including maxi taxis, which are unique to the two islands. The infrastructure is also quite good. The two islands are comparatively less expensive than the others in the region. This is particularly true for Trinidad, where restaurant prices and the like are geared more to locals than to tourists. Shopping is a pleasant experience on both islands as there are a variety of places to visit, each selling interesting souvenirs.

WHEN TO GO

The best time to visit is between January and May, when the weather is most pleasant. By May, the dry season has parched the landscape. June to December is the rainy season. Visitors also come during September when there is a dry spell known as the Indian summer and the air fares dip.

GETTING THERE

The islands are served by international flights which land at Piarco International Airport and Crown Point International Airport in Trinidad and Tobago respectively. The main airlines are **American Airlines**, **Caribbean Airlines**, **Continental**, **Delta**, **Condor**, **British Airways**, and **Virgin Atlantic**. Ferries and cruise ships dock at King's Wharf in Trinidad, and Scarborough in Tobago.

DOCUMENTATION

Citizens of the European Union (plus Switzerland and Norway), the US, and Canada do not need a visa for stays of less than three months. Citizens of other countries must apply for a visa from the nearest Trinidad and Tobago embassy or consulate. Visitors are allowed to import 200 cigarettes, 50 cigars, or 9 oz (250g) of tobacco, 3 pints (1.5 l) of spirits, and gifts worth TT$1,200.

VISITOR INFORMATION

The **Tourism Development Company**, Trinidad and Tobago's tourist board, operates booths at both international airports.

HEALTH AND SECURITY

There are no major health hazards on the islands. Tap water is safe to drink. Both islands have good hospitals such as the **Port of Spain General Hospital** and **Tobago County Hospital**.

Crime is a problem in inner city areas of Port of Spain, and visitors have been victims of robberies in both Trinidad and Tobago. Be especially alert if leaving Piarco International Airport after dark, as travelers have been accosted in the airport parking lot, on the highway, and outside residences on arrival. Avoid maxi taxis and arrange a taxi pick-up through your hotel. To stay safe, avoid walking alone at night in deserted areas, and lonely beaches.

One of the many ATMs located on Trinidad

BANKING AND CURRENCY

The local currency is the TT dollar (TT$). Banks, found in all towns and cities, offer the best exchange rates. ATMs are widespread; those at Crown Point and Piarco airports dispense US dollars and local currency. Credit cards are widely accepted.

COMMUNICATIONS

Both islands' code is 1 868. There are card phones dotted around the two islands, but many are out of service. Phone cards are available from supermarkets and small stores, which sell cheap-rate international calling cards. These cards can be used from any landline. Tri-band mobiles will work in the two islands, and local pay-as-you-go SIM cards are also widely available.

TRANSPORT

All buses in Trinidad leave from the City Gate terminus in downtown Port of Spain, as do maxi taxis (20-seater buses), color-coded yellow (Port of Spain and the west), red (east-west corridor), green (central and south), black (around Princes Town), and brown (San Fernando). In Tobago, buses depart from

Passengers boarding a plane at Crown Point International Airport, Tobago

Maxi taxi, Port Of Spain, Trinidad

the depot on Sangster Hill Road in Scarborough. Route taxis running on set routes are great for short trips. It is best to ask locals for help with the routes.

There are numerous car rental companies on both islands as well. Visitors renting a car need to be over 25 and should hold a valid driving license. Major international companies such as **Thrifty** and **Hertz** have franchises on both islands. Other car rental companies include **Econo-Car**, **Auto Rentals**, **Rattan's**, and **Sheppy's**. It is advisable to check the condition of the vehicle before hiring it.

SHOPPING

Both the islands offer a wide variety of souvenirs and crafts. Specialties include pretty woven palm hats, local handicrafts such as fine carvings from driftwood, and jewelry made from shells and beads. Both islands also have a rich musical tradition and music CDs are available at most shops. A good selection of fabric can be bought in Port of Spain on Charlotte Street.

Shops are open from around 8am to 5:30pm on weekdays, and from 8am to 5pm on Saturdays. Large shopping malls tend to stay open until 9pm Monday to Saturday. On Sundays, they remain open from 1pm to 5pm.

LANGUAGE

English is the main language spoken on both islands but French Creole (or patois) is still spoken among elders in Trinidad.

ELECTRICITY

The electric current is 110 or 220 volts, 60 cycles. Plug sockets take two flat prongs.

TIME

Both islands are 4 hours behind GMT (5 behind British Summer Time) and 1 hour ahead of EST.

GETTING MARRIED

To get married in Trinidad and Tobago, both parties must have been on the island for three or more days before the ceremony; on the fourth day one can apply for a marriage license for which the person will need ID, Decree Absolute or death certificate if divorced or widowed, and proof of any name change. There are many companies, such as **Tobago Weddings**, who can sort out the formalities for the couple.

Souvenir stall on the Northside Road, Tobago

DIRECTORY

GETTING THERE

American Airlines
www.aa.com

British Airways
www.ba.com

Caribbean Airlines
www.caribbean-airlines.com

Condor
www.condor.com

Continental
www.continental.com

Delta
www.delta.com

Virgin Atlantic
www.virgin-atlantic.com

VISITOR INFORMATION

Tourism Development Company
29 Tenth Avenue, Barataria, Trinidad.
Tel 868 675 7034. **www.** gotrinidadandtobago.com

HEALTH AND SECURITY

Fire and Ambulance
Tel 990.

Police
Tel 999.

Port of Spain General Hospital
Port of Spain, Trinidad.
Tel 868 623 2951.

Tobago County Hospital
Scarborough, Tobago.
Tel 868 639 2551.

TRANSPORT

Auto Rentals
Tel 868 675 7368 (Trinidad); 868 639 0644 (Tobago).

Econo-Car
www.econocarrentalstt.com

Hertz
www.hertz.com

Rattan's
Tobago.
Tel 868 639 8271.

Sheppy's
www.tobagocarrental.com

Thrifty
www.thrifty.com

GETTING MARRIED

Tobago Weddings
www.tobagoweddings.com

A PORTRAIT OF ABC ISLANDS

The ABC islands line up along the north coast of Venezuela, well outside the Atlantic hurricane belt. These Dutch isles provide an amazing mix of desert landscapes, awesome beaches and coves, spectacular underwater reefs brimming with marine life, and heritage architecture, as well as world-class shops and casinos.

Each of the islands – Aruba, Bonaire, and Curaçao – is a jagged scrap of rocky land that broke away from South America before dinosaurs roamed the earth. Over time, reefs began growing around the islands' stone cores. Today, the underwater coral acts as a protective barrier for the numerous beaches, as well as a habitat for marine creatures and a playground for divers.

Former slave huts at Oranje Pan, Bonaire

HISTORY

The Caiquetio tribe, a subtribe of the Arawaks, were the inhabitants of these islands when Christopher Columbus and subsequent European explorers arrived in the late 15th century. The Spanish had expected to find gold on the islands, but when they discovered that there was none and that fresh water was scarce, they captured the natives and sent them to work on their plantations in Hispaniola and abandoned their claim to these islands.

The Dutch West India Company took over the islands in the 1630s, established successful plantations and began a thriving export business that included importing African slaves, training them for domestic and farm labor, then reselling them throughout the Caribbean and the Americas. During these years, the Papiamento language began to evolve, incorporating Dutch, Spanish, Portuguese, and several African dialects. Today, it is the preferred language, even though the official language is Dutch. In the

Dutch-style buildings with outdoor cafés lining the waterfront in Willemstad, Curaçao

Landscape of cactus and shrubs, typical of Aruba

early 18th century, the islands' ports and favorable location attracted European settlers who were interested in valuable trade routes and military strongholds. Ownership of the islands changed regularly in the early 1800s, but the Dutch regained control by mid-century. When Venezuela discovered oil off its northern coast in 1920, Aruba and Curaçao became distilling centers, and immigrant workers arrived from around the world. The Dutch developed Curaçao into one of the Caribbean's most important ports, bred horses on Aruba, and produced salt from the saline pits of Bonaire. After World War II, the islands were granted partial autonomy.

THE ISLANDS TODAY

The official status of the ABC Islands is complicated, even to its residents. All are part of the Netherlands, which is a Commonwealth and includes Holland, the Netherlands Antilles (Bonaire, Saba, and St. Eustatius), and Aruba, Curaçao, and Sint Maarten. Aruba was part of the Antilles group until 1986, and Curaçao until 2008, when they became autonomous countries within the Commonwealth. About 75 percent of the islands' GDP comes from tourism-related businesses, though oil transport, local construction, and financial services also contribute a significant income. Unemployment is low and the people enjoy a standard of living that is relatively higher than in many other Caribbean islands, mainly because of good education, steady employment, and a stable government.

CULTURE AND THE ARTS

Music, dance, and the visual arts are a vital part of island life. The Dutch heritage is a strong presence, but well mixed with English, Spanish, and African influences. Local artists draw international attention with dramatic sculptures, often depicting African and Dutch characters, and paintings splashed with the vivid Caribbean colors. All the islands hold annual carnivals showcasing their music, a combination of traditional calypso and drum-pounding tumba that produces unique spirit-lifting beats, as well as street dances called jump-ups.

Children dressed in colorful, traditional costumes at the Carnival, Curaçao

Exploring the ABC Islands

Aruba, Bonaire, and Curaçao are all part of the Kingdom of the Netherlands, and have been since the Dutch took them from the Spanish in 1634. While there is non-stop action in glamorous resorts and casinos on the beaches along Aruba's coast, world-class scuba diving thrives in the unspoiled waters surrounding Bonaire. The quietest of the three, Curaçao, is famous for its UNESCO World Heritage Site, Willemstad, lined with pretty old Dutch buildings.

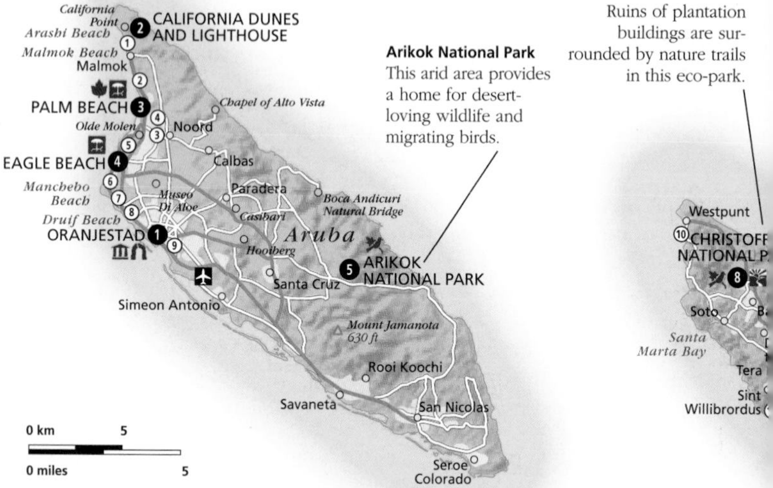

Christoffel National Park
Ruins of plantation buildings are surrounded by nature trails in this eco-park.

Arikok National Park
This arid area provides a home for desert-loving wildlife and migrating birds.

California Point
California Point
Arashi Beach ② **CALIFORNIA DUNES AND LIGHTHOUSE**
Malmok Beach ①
Malmok
PALM BEACH ③ Chapel of Alto Vista
Olde Molen Noord
EAGLE BEACH ④
Manchebo Beach ⑥ Museo Di Aloe Paradera
Druif Beach ⑦ Casibari Boca Andicuri Natural Bridge
ORANJESTAD ① Hooiberg *A r u b a*
Simeon Antonio Santa Cruz **ARIKOK NATIONAL PARK** ⑤
Mount Jamanota 630 ft
Rooi Koochi
Savaneta San Nicolas
Seroe Colorado

Westpunt
CHRISTOFF NATIONAL P. ⑩ ⑧
Soto B.
Santa Marta Bay
Tera
Sint Willibrordus ( )

0 km 5
0 miles 5

SIGHTS AT A GLANCE

Footpath leading to Kunuku Arikok, Arikok National Park

The wide Queen Emma Bridge in Willemstad, Curaçao

Washington Slagbaai National Park
This is the oldest nature sanctuary of the Netherlands Antilles and comprises two of the largest plantations on the island – Washington and Slagbaai.

0 km   10

0 miles   10

WASHINGTON SLAGBAAI
NATIONAL PARK
Playa Funchi ⑪ *Boca Cocolishi*
Boca Slagbaai
KAMINDA GOTO ⑫ ⑩ RINCÓN
Lake Goto

Bonaire

Playa Kanoa
Curaçao
t Michiel
⑳
Turtle Beach
Antriol
⑥ WILLEMSTAD
Klein Bonaire
⑨ KRALENDIJK
⑬ ⑭ ⑮
Mambo Beach
⑦ CURAÇAO SEA AQUARIUM
⑰ ⑱ ⑲ *Fuikbaai*
⑳ ② ①
②
③
Jan Thiel Bay
Oostpunt (Punt Kanon)
②
④
Lac Bay
② *Sorobon Beach*
Pink Beach
⑬ PEKELMEER

Lacre Pt.

Curaçao Sea Aquarium
The Curaçao Sea Aquarium is a large complex featuring at least 400 saltwater species.

0 km   10

0 miles   10

Pekelmeer
Located on the south end of Bonaire, Pekelmeer is a protected sanctuary for flamingos. These birds fly in from Venezuela to lay eggs and hatch them.

SEE ALSO

• *Where to Stay* pp526–9

• *Where to Eat & Nightlife*
  pp530–33

KEY

— Major road

= Minor road

△ Peak

GETTING AROUND
Aruba's Reina Beatrix International Airport and Curaçao's Hato International Airport are large while Bonaire's Flamingo Airport is small with daily flights to and from other Caribbean islands, including Aruba and Curaçao, and less frequent international service. Ferries are not practical due to the long distances between the islands, and unpredictable sea conditions. Aruba has a good bus service that connects the airport, Oranjestad, and resorts along the west coast beaches. Bonaire has no public transportation, and Curaçao has limited bus and van service. Visitors must rely on tours or rental cars to explore the countryside. Taxis are also available on all three islands.

Cannons at Fort Zoutman, Oranjestad, Aruba

Oranjestad ❶

W coast of Aruba. 🏛 30,000. ✈
🚌 ⚓ cruise ship port. ℹ L.G.
Smith Boulevard, 297 582 3777.
🎭 daily along waterfront. 🎉 Bonbini
Festival (Thu). **www**.aruba.com

At the center of Aruba's
capital, Oranjestad, lies the
Yacht Basin and cruise ship
port fronted by brightly
painted shops and restaurants
built in Dutch colonial style.
Lloyd G. Smith Boulevard, the
main roadway, runs along the
waterfront and connects the
town to the popular tourist
areas along the northwest
coast. Although the town
lacks major attractions, it
offers a pleasant diversion
from the beach.
    At the south end of the
town lies Fort Zoutman, constructed in 1796 and named
for an admiral in the Dutch
navy. Adjoining the fort is
Willem III Tower, which was
built in 1868. It is the best-
preserved part and used to
serve as a lighthouse. Across
from the fort, on the

waterfront, is the Renaissance
Mall and marketplace, with
more than 100 upscale shops.
A couple of blocks inland, the
small **Archaeological Museum**
displays stone tools from
4,500 years ago found at
Arikok and Sero Muskita,
and human bones unearthed
from the ruins of the island's
first Arawak inhabitants, the
Caiquetio. The **Numismatic
Museum** of Aruba houses a
coin collection that is far
more interesting than it
sounds. There are approximately 40,000 pieces from
400 countries in this treasury
owned by the Mario Odor
family, who were avid coin
collectors, and each piece is
displayed with a written
account of its significance.

🏛 **Archaeological Museum**
Schelpstraat 42. **Tel** 297 582
8979. ⏰ 8am–noon & 1–4pm
Mon–Fri. 🚫

🏛 **Numismatic Museum**
Weststraat 7. **Tel** 297 582 8831.
⏰ 9am–4pm Mon–Thu,
9am–1pm Fri, 9am–noon
Sat. 📷 🚫

California Dunes and Lighthouse ❷

7 miles (11 km) N of Oranjestad,
Aruba. 📷 🍴

The main west coast highway
leads north to the California
Lighthouse at the tip of the
island. Just past the town of
Malmok is an elevated stretch
of isolated land known locally
as *hudishibana* (in the native
language once spoken by the
Caiquetio), but often called
the California Dunes. Here,
rolling mounds of white sand
spread across a desert landscape, surrounding the lighthouse which was designed by
a French architect in 1910 and
constructed on the island
between 1914 and 1916. The
name comes from the S.S.
California, a wooden-hulled
ship with five masts that sank
just offshore in the late 1800s
and now is a popular dive
site. The lighthouse is closed
to visitors, but the views from
its elevated base are spectacular and include the dunes,
beaches, and the greens of
Tierra del Sol Country Club
(*see p524*). Late in the afternoon, the view gets even
more breathtaking as the
sun sets.

Palm Beach ❸

🚌 4 miles (6 km) NW of Oranjestad,
Aruba. 👥 🍸 🏄 🎣 🚤

Ranked among the best in the
world, Palm Beach is a long
stretch of white sand lined
with luxurious upscale resorts,
restaurants, beach bars, and
watersports operators. Among

The California Lighthouse, surrounded by rolling dunes

For hotels and restaurants on these islands see pp526–9 and pp530–33

The immaculate Palm Beach, Aruba

the extravagant resorts, three Marriott complexes *(see p527)* anchor the north end of the beach and sprawl across the landscaped grounds, which provide a flowering habitat for tropical birds. At the southern end, Divi Aruba Phoenix Beach Resort *(see p527)* occupies the last bit of sand before a rocky outcrop that separates Palm from Eagle Beach.

Just opposite the resort is the **Butterfly Farm** featuring 40 species of butterflies *(see p518)*. There are interesting guided walks exploring the lifecycle of a butterfly. Just south of the high-rise Palm Beach hotels is an open marsh where birds are protected in Bubali Bird Sanctuary. The sanctuary attracts hundreds of migratory birds and bird-watchers.

Butterfly Farm
J. Irausquin Boulevard, Oranjestad.
Tel 297 586 3656. 9am–4pm daily. **www**.thebutterfly farm.com

Eagle Beach ❹

2 miles (3.2 km) NW of Oranjestad, Aruba.

Eagle Beach is separated from Palm Beach by a rocky over-grown stretch of coastline.

While Palm Beach is known for non-stop action, Eagle Beach is more relaxed; motorized water-sports are not allowed offshore and shaded picnic tables draw many local families as well as guests from nearby low-rise resorts. The white-sand beach is wide and the water is calm and perfect for swimming. There are fewer bars and restaurants than on Palm Beach and the hotels reach no higher than the shady palm trees. Many properties participate in the Green Globe Program signifying that they adhere to environmental-friendly policies and sustainable tourism standards.

Arikok National Park ❺

8 miles (12 km) E of Oranjestad, Aruba. *National Park Office, Santa Cruz, 297 585 1234.* 7am–5pm daily (entrance hut); park open 24 hr daily. at the entrance to caves.

The entrance to this ecological park is off Highway 7 A/B, east of the town of Santa Cruz. The park protects a large portion of land bordered on the east by the sea. Within its boundaries are 21 miles (33 km) of marked hiking trails that wind through native flora, including divi-divi trees, rare cacti, aloe plants, and flowering bushes. Wildlife includes *conejos* (rabbits), indigenous *kododo blauw* (whiptail lizards), and the *cascabel* (rattlesnake).

A walking path beyond the entrance leads to Cunucu Arikok, a semi-restored farm at the foot of Cero Arikok, a 500-ft (150-m) tall hill that is the base of the airport's radar station. The farm has a typical country house made of mud-and-grass adobe and protected by the remains of a cactus fence and stone wall.

Heading east from the road at the entrance is a 2-mile (4-km) trail that leads to the highest point on the island, Mount Jamanota at 630 ft (189 m). The same road also leads visitors to the coastline which begins with sand dunes. The Dos Playa beach here is not ideal for swimming due to strong currents, but photographers will enjoy snapping shots of the unique landscape and sea vistas. There is a small snack bar here for a picnic.

From the snack bar, a road takes people to the Fontein Caves, where beautiful Indian rock paintings decorate the walls and ceilings. Near the caves is the Fontein Garden, which has a 19th-century plantation house. It is also the site for a museum displaying old tools.

Gigantic cacti growing in Arikok National Park

Street-by-Street: Willemstad ●

Designated a UNESCO World Heritage Site in 1997,
historic Willemstad is the capital of Curaçao. Its older
area is made up of distinct districts, with their architectural styles reflecting the 17th-century Dutch colonization of the ABC islands. Sint Annabaai, a channel
linking the sea to the inner harbor, divides the central city
into Otrobanda, a primarily residential area, and Punda,
the commercial hub. The much photographed floating
pontoon bridge, Queen Emma Bridge, spans the channel
and swings open to allow passage for ships.

**Centuries-old Dutch style
buildings, Punda**

Philatelic Museum, located in
a restored colonial building,
displays a large collection of
Netherlands Antilles stamps.

★ Queen Emma Bridge
*One of the major landmarks
in Willemstad, the bridge
was designed by US
businessman Leonard
B. Smith in 1888.*

| 0 meters | 50 |
| 0 yards | 50 |

HANDELS KADE

HEERENST

KEUKENSTRA

BREEDESTRAAT

WATERFORTSTRA

★ Fort Amsterdam
*Dating from 1635, Fort Amsterdam now houses a
government complex. It is painted in traditional bright
colors of Dutch colonial architecture. A small museum,
set in the old fort church, still has an English cannon-
ball embedded in its southwestern wall.*

STAR SIGHTS

- ★ Queen Emma Bridge

- ★ Fort Amsterdam

- ★ Mikve Israel-Emanuel
  Synagogue

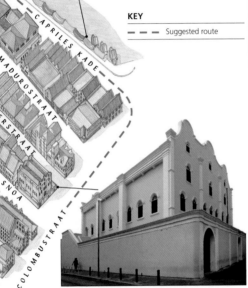

Floating Market

*Merchants from Venezuela sell
various products including
fresh fish, meat, tropical fruits,
vegetables, and spices from their
boats at the Floating Market.*

KEY

- - - Suggested route

★ **Mikve Israel-Emanuel Synagogue**
*The 350-years-old Mikve Israel-Emanuel
Synagogue is the oldest synagogue to be in
continuous use in the New World. It is sand-
floored and its courtyard houses the Jewish
Cultural Historical Museum.*

Waterfort
*Built in 1634 and renovated in 1827, the Waterfort
is now a lively area with shops and restaurants overlooking the sea. Many of the fort's original turrets
and vaults are still visible.*

Curaçao Sea Aquarium ❼

3 miles (5 km) SE of Willemstad,
Curaçao. **Tel** 599 9461 6666.
🕐 8:30am–5:30pm daily. 🖼 ✓
🔵 ☐ 🖬 **www**.curacao-sea-
aquarium.com

Located on a large beach, this
complex includes exhibits of
more than 400 saltwater
species in their natural
environment. Touch tanks
allow direct contact with sea
stars, conchs, and urchins.
Participants of all ages can
snorkel or dive with rays,
sharks, and turtles in the
Animal Encounter program.
Visitors can also touch, feed,
and swim with dolphins and
sea lions. The kids' programs
include instruction on pre-
serving reefs, and allow contact with endangered species.
The adjoining Seaquarium
Beach has sports outlets that
rent watersports gear.

Christoffel National Park ❽

25 miles (40 km) NW of Willemstad,
Curaçao. **Tel** 599 9864 0363.
🕐 7am–4pm Mon–Sat,
6am–3pm Sun. 🖼 ☑ ☐ ☐ 🖬
www.carmabi.org

Spread over what was once
three plantations, Christoffel
National Park now serves as
Curaçao's prized eco-preserve.
At the entrance, the Savonet
Museum showcases the
island's natural features and
history through geological
and archaeological exhibits.
Four marked hiking trails
wind through the 4,500-acre
(1,821-ha) park. Hikers take
on the challenge of the 1,240-ft
(370-m) Mount Christoffel,
that offers views of the rugged
countryside. Color-coded
driving routes lead to various
areas of the sprawling park
including the windward coast,
noted for its ancient rock
drawings and cave-riddled
cliffs. Another route begins
at Piedra de Monton, from
where it winds past hillsides
covered with wild orchids, to
the coves of Santa Marta Bay
and Seru Bientu.

Waterfront of Kralendijk, capital of Bonaire

Kralendijk ⑨

W coast of Bonaire. 🏠 12,000. ✈
🚢 cruise ship port. ℹ Tourism
Corporation Kaya Grandi 2, 599 717
8322. 🛍 produce market at the pier
& crafts market at Wilhelmina Park.
www.infobonaire.com

Bonaire's capital, Kralendijk,
is a large, easygoing village
about midway along the
island's sharply-curved leeward coast. The town's main
road runs parallel to the sea,
so orientation and navigating
is simple. The best way to get
around is on foot. When a
cruise ship is in port, the
narrow streets transform into
an outdoor marketplace and
mini-festival. Artists, craftsmen,
and cooks set up booths
offering West Indian specialties
and performers put their heart
into island-style dance and
cultural shows backed by
local musicians. A daily produce market takes place in
an open-air building near the
town pier. Most of the permanent shops and restaurants line
the two main roads, Kaya
Craane, with a pretty waterfront promenade, and Kaya
Grandi, a block inland.

Fort Oranje stands guard at
the southern end of the town
center. It is one of the oldest
structures on Bonaire, built by
the Dutch in 1639 and allotted
four cannons to defend against
the English, Spanish, and
French. The stone tower was
added in 1932, and the fort
now houses government
offices. Next door, the lovely
two-story white-trimmed
golden-yellow building also
dates from the 19th century

and is a fine example of
Dutch-Caribbean architecture.
The raised front porch and
staircase is particularly
attractive. Various government
offices are located in the
building, known as the
Bestuurskantoor (government
office). Neither of these two
historic buildings is open to
the public, but the
Museo Boneriano,
located a short walk
from the town center,
welcomes visitors.
This beautifully restored
plantation home was
built at the end of the
19th century and has
the original architec-
tural plans on display
inside. Other exhibits
include a shell collection,
ancient maps, and bits
of island memorabilia,
but the most interest-
ing display is the
building itself.

🏛 **Museo Boneriano**
Kaya J.C. van der Ree 7, at the
junction of Kaya Sabana. **Tel** 599
717 8868. 🕐 8am–noon, 1:30–
5pm Mon–Fri. 🖼

**Signage,
Kralendijk, Bonaire**

Rincón ⑩

11 miles (18 km) NW of Kralendijk,
Bonaire. 🏠 1,800. 🛍 first Sat
of the month. 🎉 Dia de Rincón
(Apr 30).

The oldest town on the
island, Rincón (Spanish for
corner), is rich in local flavor.
It was founded by the
Spanish late in the 1500s as
an inland safe haven hidden
from view of pirate ships.
Later, the village became a
community of former slaves
and is the birthplace of many
of the island's political and
business leaders. There is
little to see here, except on
festival days, which occur
with amazing frequency.
Tradition and culture are
important to the residents,
and the town annually hosts
a jubilant Dia de Rincón
(Rincón Day) to celebrate
the official birthday of the
Queen of the Netherlands.

At the center of the town,
the impressive San
Luis Bertran Church
is considered a
historical monument,
even though the
present structure
was completed as
recently as 1984.
Originally built in
1861, the church
was destroyed by a
hurricane in October
1907. The present
church was rebuilt
around the ruins
beginning in 1977.

On Market Day (Marshe
Rincón), dozens of booths
are set up along the main
road to sell fresh fruits,
plants, colorful handicrafts,
and locally made foods.

San Lodovico Bertran Catholic Church in Rincón, Bonaire

Renovated aloe oven, Washington Slagbaai National Park

Washington Slagbaai National Park ⓫

16 miles (26 km) NW of Kralendijk, Bonaire. 🚗 🛈 *park entrance, 599 717 8444.* ⏰ *8am–5pm daily.* 🎄 *Christmas & New Year's Day.* 🖐 📷 📄 📷 **www**.washington parkbonaire.org

Extending over 16,358 acres (6,620 ha), the Washington Slagbaai National Park covers about 20 percent of the northern part of the island. Dive sites, hiking trails, salt pans, a lake, and driving routes are within the boundaries of what originally comprised two of the largest plantations on the island, Washington and Slagbaai. The plantations, called *kunukus* in the local Papiamento language, grew the distinctive divi-divi trees for their pods, which were processed into tannin for use in tanning animal hides, and aloe plants for their sap, which was used as a laxative.

The Washington *kunuku* became a public park in 1969, and when the Slagbaai property was added in 1979, the area became the first nature sanctuary in the Netherlands Antilles. Parrots, flamingos, iguanas, and parakeets are a few of the many endemic species that live within the park. The beaches provide nesting grounds for all four species of Caribbean sea turtles, and the park is part of the Ramsar Convention, an international treaty that protects wetlands and their inhabitants. The Visitors' Center, located at the park entrance, has many of the original plantation-era structures still intact and is a good place to pick up maps and information. A museum, set in the former main house, displays historical, archaeological, and geological information about the island and its native plants and wildlife. Highlights of the park include the 784-ft (238-m) Brandaris Hill, the highest point on the island; Pos di Mangel, a key area for bird-watching; Boca Chikitu, a rocky cove backed by sand dunes; Playa Funchi and Boca Slagbaai, the prime snorkeling beaches. Two dirt driving tracks wind through the park: Yellow, making a 21-mile (33-km) sweep along the north coast and Green, a 14-mile (24-km) stretch connecting sites in the middle of the park. Nature lovers will want to spend time on the walking paths starting at the Visitors' Center and the hiking-biking trails up to Brandaris and Pos di Mangel. The fresh water lake at Pos di Mangel attracts large flocks of birds.

Kaminda Goto ⓬

9 miles (15 km) NW of Kralendijk, Bonaire.

Kaminda Goto is a road that follows the shores of Lake Goto (Gotomeer), on the southwest border of the national park. The road up to the landlocked saltwater Lake Goto offers excellent close-up views of flocks of flamingos that nest and feed around the water. The birds are shy, but are most interested in food and preening, so patient watchers have a good chance of getting a proper look at these fascinating creatures. Benches at the paved and bricked Salina Grande viewing area provide a good place to sit and watch the birds.

Pekelmeer ⓭

13 miles (21 km) S of Kralendijk, Bonaire.

At the far south end of Bonaire, Pekelmeer is a protected sanctuary for Southern Caribbean flamingos. Many of them come from Venezuela, 50 miles (18 km) away, to breed and tend their young. During hatching season, as many as 2,500 chicks are born. The nests are easy to spot, as they are 1 ft (0.3 m) tall and about 2 ft (0.6 m) wide.

Other birds also nest and feed here, including heron, osprey and other marine birds. Morning and late afternoon are the best times to see the birds in flight, but visitors are advised to stay in their cars to avoid disturbing the birds.

The rocky coastline at Boka Chikitu, Washington Slagbaai National Park, Bonaire

Driving on the ABC Islands

Aruba, Bonaire, and Curaçao are each small enough to tour by car in a single day. Cruise-ship passengers can see all the highlights and make it back to the ship in time for dinner, but visitors with more time benefit from a leisurely drive with stops at key attractions. Tour operators offer a variety of around-the-island excursions and many taxi drivers are knowledgeable guides. First-time visitors may want to get oriented with a guided tour but the best way to discover the islands' unique features is on a self-guided driving tour. The main roads are paved but secondary roads may be rough and some pass through rugged terrain.

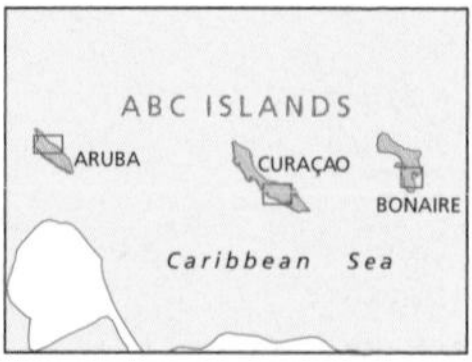
ABC ISLANDS
ARUBA
CURAÇAO
BONAIRE
Caribbean Sea

The mysterious Casibari Rock Formations, Aruba ⑦

ARUBA

Aruba is a two-faced beauty with glamorous west coast beaches and a high-energy downtown area while its sunburned interior is strewn with curious rock formations. About 3 miles (5 km) from Oranjestad lies **Butterfly Farm** ①, a mesh-enclosed garden teeming with butterflies from all over the world *(see p513)*. A visit in the morning is best as the butterflies are most active and newborns emerge.

Another 2 miles (3 km) away is Noord village, inland from Palm Beach. Its little **Santa Anna Church** ② is where brides often choose to be married. The solid oak altar was carved in Neo-Gothic style by Dutch craftsman Hendrik van der Geld in the 1870s. Some 2 miles (3 km) from Noord stands the **Chapel of Alto Vista** ③. Known as the pilgrim's church, this tiny yellow chapel is one of the most photographed buildings on the island. Constructed by native Indians and Spanish settlers, it was rebuilt in 1952. The tranquil site is on a spectacular bluff above the sea with white crosses lining its narrow paved road. At 6 miles (10 km) from Noord are the **Bushiribana Gold Mine Ruins** ④. A rock heap and a crumbling stone wall is all that remains of the Aruba Island Gold Mining Company, but the views from here are great. **Boca Andicuri Natural Bridge** ⑤ is 2 miles (3 km) east of Bushiribana. The famous long stretch of limestone at Boca Andicuri unexpectedly collapsed in 2005 but still holds the curiosity of visitors. Another natural bridge is still standing on the southern curve of Andicuri Bay. About 2 miles (3 km) inland from Andicuri are the **Ayo Rock Formations** ⑥. These boulders resemble images from a space fantasy and geologists cannot explain how they came to be on the otherwise flat island. Nearby caves have pictographs left by native inhabitants. Similar boulders are also found at **Casibari Rock Formations** ⑦, locates about 2 miles (3 km) farther inland.

The charming Chapel of Alto Vista, overlooking the north coast ③

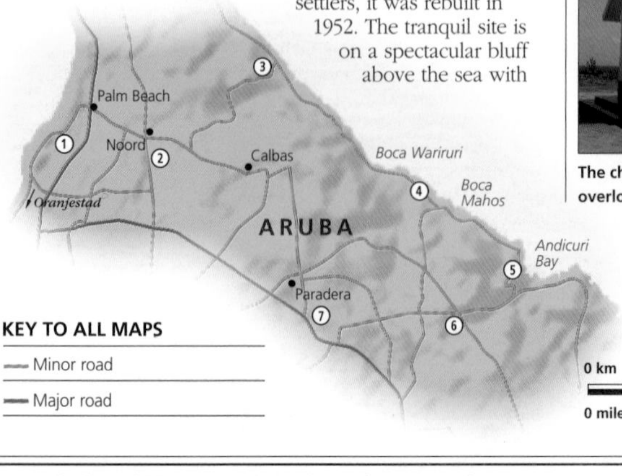
Palm Beach
Noord
Calbas
Oranjestad
Boca Wariruri
Boca Mahos
ARUBA
Andicuri Bay
Paradera
KEY TO ALL MAPS
Minor road
Major road
0 km 2
0 miles 2

For more details on driving tours, visit the visitor information websites on p535

CURAÇAO

Locals call the eastern part of Curaçao Banda Riba, which means upwind. The countryside is dotted with developments, yacht-filled harbors, and a few tourist sites. About 70 *landhuizen* (old plantation homes), with Dutch colonial architecture, sit on hill tops. In Salina Ariba, 2 miles (3 km) east of the capital, Willemstad, is the **Senior Curaçao Liqueur Distillery** ①. Housed in the 17th-century Landhuis Chobolobo, this distillery still uses 19th-century equipment to make the famous cordial from dried orange skins. Guided tours include an overview of the production process. The liqueur is sold in quaint bottles at the adjacent gift shop. About 3 miles (5 km) from the capital are **Spanish Water and Caracasbaai** ②. These trendy developments are popular with young locals and yacht owners. Visitors can enjoy a meal at the Landhuis Brakkeput Mei Mei in Spanish Water and a tour of Fort Beekenburg at Caracasbaai. **Dinah's Botanic and Historic Garden (Den Paradara)** ③ lies 6 miles (10 km) east of the capital. The scent of herbs lures visitors to this garden featuring local plants that have been used for centuries as folk medicines. It has a model village and lodge built by Amazon Indians and the owner Dinah Veeris tells visitors about it. The largest farm of its type outside Africa, the **Ostrich and Game Farm** ④ is 7 miles (11 km) from Willemstad. Tours on zebra-striped jeeps let visitors watch the world's largest birds closely and feed them. Hand-crafted products from Africa are on sale at the African Art Shop. To the north of the capital lie the **Hato Caves** ⑤, 4 miles (7 km) away. These caves were formed millions of years ago, when Curaçao was underwater. There are underground waterfalls, a lake, and chambers with stalagmites, stalactites, and hundreds of bats.

Dinah Veeris in her Botanic and Historic Garden ③

Curaçao liqueur bottle

BONAIRE

Bonaire's sun-drenched, quiet countryside has many natural attractions. Eco-tourists treasure the protected areas and a drive around the island reveals long stretches of desert landscape punctuated by surprising beauty. **Paradise Safari Park** ① lies 2 miles (4 km) south of Kralendijk. When donkeys become old, injured, or orphaned, they find refuge at the Safari Park and live along with an assortment of iguanas, turtles, and birds. About 4 miles (7 km) east of Kralendijk is **Rooi Lamoenchi Kunuku Park** ②. Plantation estates are called *kunuku* in Bonaire, and this is one of the best preserved. Guided tours include a visit to the historic plantation house, aloe fields, and gardens filled with native plants and wildlife. On Lac Bay the **Mangrove Information Center** ③, 4 miles (7 km) southeast of the capital, works with The Netherlands's Rotterdam Zoo to investigate the endangered environment of mangrove forests. Guided kayak or boat tours take visitors through this site. Small stone huts that once served as quarters for slaves are located at **Witte Pan** ④, 7 miles (11 km) south of the main coastal road from Kralendijk. During the 1800s, Dutch companies depended on slave labor to process and export the island's salt to Europe. The workers were housed in the tiny huts where five or six slept on the floor.

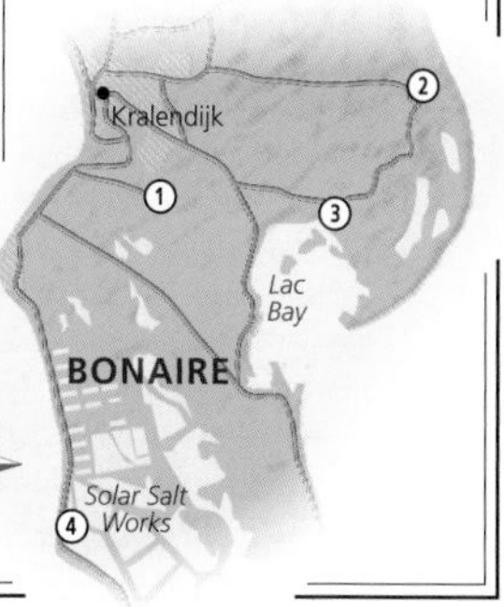

Outdoor Activities and Specialized Holidays

Visitors to the ABC islands often plan their holiday around specific outdoor activities. While Aruba draws people who prefer to just lie on the beach with a good book, Curaçao appeals to those who love sightseeing and exploring the island to break up the beach time. Bonaire attracts adventurous scuba divers and snorkelers. The tour operators on the three islands also offer thrilling inventive eco-tour packages such as night kayaking through mangroves or snorkeling through coastal caves, and sightseeing on a motorcycle.

Palm Beach, Aruba, one of the busiest beaches on the three islands

BEACHES

Among the ABC islands, Aruba has the best beaches and liveliest beach life. Palm and Eagle Beaches *(see pp512–13)* are the most well-known. To the north, Arashi and Malmok are less crowded while Hadicurari, between Malmok and Palm, is the site of an annual windsurfing competition. In the south, Sereo Colorado is popular with families. On the windward side of the island, most of the beaches are rocky and strong currents make it risky for swimming.

Curaçao's beaches on the windward side also have strong tides, making swimming dangerous. On the leeward side, the sand is often mixed with coral. Mambo Beach, near Willemstad, has a long stretch of white sand while Jan Thiel Beach has little sand but people can relax on the cement quays along the bay. At the

Signage on Palm Beach, Aruba

far northwest end of the island, Westpunt Beach is well-known for its towering cliffs. The area is dramatic but better sand is found to the south at Knip Bay Beach.

Bonaire is known for fantastic diving, though the beaches are not-so-fantastic as most are rocky. Boca Cocolishi has lovely black sand, and is ideal for snorkeling. Playa Funchi has a strong current far out from the shore, but a shallow shelf closer in has fine coral that draws hundreds of fish. Lac Cai is piled high with conch shells and is popular with locals on weekends, while Pink Beach is often named as one of the most spectacular of the Caribbean due to its pink hue in the late-afternoon sunlight, which comes from its sand being mixed with bits of red coral. Out on Klein Bonaire, an island off Kralendijk, is a pleasant palm-shaded beach called Turtle Beach. The beach can be reached by water taxis.

DIVING AND SNORKELING

Bonaire is recognized as the best scuba and snorkeling destination in the Southern Antilles, mainly due to its protected marine parks. Beaches slope steeply and drop off into deeper waters, which makes it easy for divers to enter the ocean from the shore. Curaçao also has protected virgin sites with large coral formations sheltering an abundance of marine life, and some of its most popular dive locations feature shallow reefs that slope to magnificent walls. Aruba is known for its sunken wrecks that include several ships which were torpedoed during World War II and two airplanes that were deliberately sunk to create artificial reefs.

Each island has various programs to sustain and improve the growth of their coral reefs and protect underwater wildlife. Visitors are told to avoid stepping on the coral or anchoring boats in protected waters. In addition, all marine life is protected, so fishing and shell collecting is not allowed. Visibility is routinely high throughout the area, and snorkelers can often see underwater reefs and fish at depths of 50 ft (15 m). Divers report visibility of 100 ft (30 m) or more, except during and right after a storm. All three islands offer snorkeling and scuba excursions. Rental operators are **Bonaire Dive & Adventure, Ocean Encounters, Red Sail Sports,** and **Dive Aruba.**

Scuba divers getting ready to explore the waters off Aruba

For hotels and restaurants on these islands see pp526–9 and pp530–33

Diving Off Bonaire

Bonaire's National Marine Park protects some of the healthiest reefs in the world, and scuba divers enjoy exploring more than 80 named sites, many accessible after a short boat ride. Water off the leeward side is sheltered by the island's reverse-C-curve shape, providing excellent conditions for learners and novice divers, while the more exposed sites

Yellow seahorse, Bonaire

near the north and south coasts present plenty of challenges for experienced divers. With little rainfall and virtually no tropical storms to stir up the sea, underwater visibility is consistently 100 ft (30 m) or more. Several sites have pretty reefs that extend to depths of about 200 ft (60 m), making Bonaire a popular destination for experienced divers.

UNDER THE SEA

Thriving coral formations grow close to the shore in fairly shallow water, which allows snorkelers fabulous opportunities to observe a wide variety of tropical fish, rays, and other marine life.

Caribbean reef octopuses *are easy to spot at night as their blue-green skin is reflective, and they feed in shallow coastal seagrass beds.*

Elkhorn coral *gets its name from antler-like branches that grow up to 4 inches (10 cm) per year; one of the fastest growing corals.*

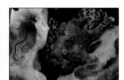

BONAIRE

KLEIN BONAIRE

Caribbean Sea

SITE MAP

■ Novice divers

■ Experienced divers

Frog fish *which changes colors to camouflage itself crawls along the sea floor using its bottom fins as feet.*

Yellow goatfish are night feeders.   **Scuba divers** use flashlight to observe fish.   **Brain coral** grows in a spherical shape.

DIVING RESORTS

Diving resorts serve as one-stop destinations for vacationers who want to spend most of their time in or under water.

Diving lessons *begin in shallow water near the shore. Even beginners may dive with an instructor during a discovery class.*

Buddy Dive Resort (see p527) *is one of the several hotels in Bonaire that cater to divers with packaged vacations.*

Windsurfing in Aruba

SPORTFISHING

The islands of Aruba, Bonaire, and Curaçao offer many choices to the fishing enthusiasts. Charter boats locate large schools of tuna, dolphin, and bonito, while fishermen catch tarpon and snook using squid and sardines for bait. Most charter fishing is on a catch-and-release basis. Fresh fish cannot be brought back into most countries and the islands prohibit visitors from selling their catch. On Aruba and Curaçao, charter boats have fishing licenses that cover their clients, so individuals need not apply for their own non-commercial license. Everyone who uses the waters of Bonaire's National Marine Park must pay a nature fee and receive a usage tag, which also allows complimentary admission to Washington Slagbaai National Park. The tags are available through watersports operators, marinas, and most hotels. The main operators are **Mahi Mahi**, **Piscatur Fishing Charters**, **Multifish Charters**, **Curaçao Activities**, and **Let's Fish**.

WINDSURFING

Bonaire is a popular vacation destination for surfers, with windsurfing as the dominant sport followed by kiteboarding. Lightweight kites and sails, safety release systems and high-tech boards make surfing sports fun for all skill levels. While Curaçao is still in a nascent stage, Aruba is rapidly gaining recognition as a world-class surfing destination. All three islands have full-service operators that

offer expert advice and top-of-the-line equipment rentals. Aruba's Hi-Winds Pro Am Windsurfing Competition is a windsurfing event for all skill levels held at Hadikurari Beach each summer, with contestants coming from more than 30 countries. On Bonaire, Lac Bay is one of the best-known spots among international windsurfing and kiteboarding enthusiasts due to its clear water, consistent on-shore breezes, and excellent facilities.

Curaçao has a loosely organized surfing club and a couple of shops that set up events, give lessons, and rent equipment. Locals usually meet at secluded coves on the eastern end of the island, while surfing operators are located at Caracas Bay on the south shore and St. Joris Bay on the north shore. The operators are **Jibe City**, **Aruba Active Vacations**, **Kitesurfing Aruba**, and **Windsurfing Curaçao**.

Windsurfing sign at Sorobon Beach, Bonaire

WATERSPORTS

Jet Ski rentals, parasailing, waterskiing, and wakeboarding are all centered on Palm Beach in Aruba. On Curaçao, outfitters specialize in providing the latest water-based activities. On Bonaire, motorized watersports are almost nonexistent, due to restrictions within the marine park and visitors tend to be interested in underwater and wind-powered sports.

The islands have ideal conditions for kayaking in the swampy mangroves, and various operators lead eco trips. Instruction is also available for sea kayaking. Operators are **Pelican Watersports**, **Aruba Watersport Center**, and **Caribbean Sea Sports**.

BOATING AND SAILING

There is no better way to see the coastal areas than by boat. Day sails and theme cruises give visitors a chance to explore sites that are inaccessible from land. Day-sail tours include **Jolly Pirates**, **Bounty Adventures**, and **Samur Sailing Charters**. Long-term private charters are possible and when booking a trip, ask how many passengers will be on board as the difference between a good and a fantastic cruise is the amount of open space on the boat. Party boats are popular on Aruba, and all three islands offer sunset cruises.

Motorboats, Hobie Cat sailboats, and other small watercraft may be rented for sightseeing. The rental agencies are **Cat Sailing**, **Insulinde**, **Tattoo Party Cruises and Mi Dushi Sailing** and **Woodwing Sailing**.

Watersport equipment for hire on Palm Beach, Aruba

For hotels and restaurants on these islands see pp526–9 and pp530–33

Sailing Trips off ABC Islands

Aruba, Bonaire, and Curaçao have been a safe harbor for sailors for more than 500 years. The islands are outside the hurricane belt and rarely experience tropical storms, so the calm seas surrounding the coasts are perfect for day sails that include snorkeling off remote islands, such as Klein Curaçao, and sunset cruises offering

Charter boat, Curaçao

elaborate snacks and drinks. Some outfitters also offer an adventure aboard a pirate ship, Asian junk, or multi-mast schooner. Crews often dress to match the ship's design or the sailing theme and even add themed music and entertainment to fit the occasion. Night cruises are also a wonderful experience not to be missed.

Themed cruises *with Jolly Pirates include one-day sailing tour. It is a day of fun aboard a finely-crafted 85-ft (26-m) gaff-rigged sailing yacht, designed like a pirate ship.*

Activities such as snorkeling *are common on day-sails. Visitors are assisted by knowledgeable crew members who point out amazing underwater sights.*

Night cruises *are a unique experience. Diving or snorkeling after dark is fantastic as sea creatures slumber, graze, and hunt in secret after the sun goes down.*

Passengers aboard Samur *wait to watch the green flash, a phenomenon that sometimes appears in the sky at sundown in Bonaire.*

Shipwrecks *along the shore of Klein Curaçao are a fascinating sight. Many leading tour operators offers day trips to see the wrecks.*

Fantastic buffets *are usually served to day-trippers on private charters, either aboard the boat or at a private beach. Some of these are included in the price.*

Cyclists taking a break on the northwest coast of Bonaire

HIKING

With national parks and good hiking conditions on all three islands, hiking and related activities such as climbing, rappelling, and caving are becoming more common. On Aruba, Arikok National Park *(see p513)* is great for hiking, and trail maps for self-guided hikes are available at the visitors' center. On the eastern point of the island, the cliffs in the Grapefield area are popular with climbers and explorers. Curaçao has more than three dozen marked trails and outfitters such as **Curaçao Actief** offer guided hikes. Christoffel National Park *(see p515)* provides information on all activities available in the park, such as hiking and climbing. On Bonaire, Washington Slagbaai National Park *(see p517)* has 21 miles (33 km) of dirt road and three signed trails, including a moderately rigorous trek up Brandaris, the highest point on the island. Hiking companies are **Sensitive Hikers**, **Bonaire Dive & Adventure**, and **Outdoor Bonaire**.

CYCLING

Mountain bikers often use the same trails as hikers on the ABC islands, and guided tours are available through operators such as **Pablito's Bike Rental**, and **Wanna Bike**. Washington Slagbaai Park on Bonaire does not have any rental facilities for bikes, but visitors may bring their own gear rented from operators such as **De Freewieler**. All biking begins early morning as the park staff recommends it. Christoffel on Curaçao has several moderate to difficult

bike routes that go past secluded coves, caves with ancient drawings on the walls, and the island's highest peak, Christoffelberg. Rangers at Arikok on Aruba provide information about touring the dirt trails by mountain bike. The routes start near the entrance and go on to Kunuku Arikok and Cero Arikok.

JEEP AND ATV TOURS

Jeeps and All Terrain Vehicles (ATVs) can reach remote places where cars and buses cannot. Group and private excursions offer trips into the countryside and along the windward coasts on all three islands. Those who want to let someone else do the driving can sign on for a jeep tour while joining a guided ATV tour offers a bigger thrill. On Aruba, Four Wheelin't at **Rancho Daimari**, **Aruba Jeep Safari**, and **ABC Tours** schedules jeep excursions. There are 4-hour and full-day trips on Curaçao arranged by **Eric's ATV Adventures** which includes trips to caves. Contact **Rento Fun Drive** for exciting tours to remote sites on Bonaire.

Visitors on ATVs near Bushiribana Gold Mine Ruins, Aruba

GOLF

Bonaire does not have a golf course, but Curaçao and Aruba have lovely 18-hole courses. On Curaçao, the **Blue Bay Golf** course is laid out on the grounds of a plantation, and the views are fantastic from greens located on cliffs overlooking the sea. At **Tierra del Sol Country Club** on Aruba, the 18-hole golf course, designed by owner Robert Trent Jones II highlights the dramatic contrast between desert landscapes and ocean vistas.

Horseback-riding at a ranch in Aruba

HORSE-RIDING

Guided tours through the countryside and along the coasts are offered on all three islands. Hotels and multi-activity operators, **The Riding Academy Club** and **Criadero El Hijo de David**, make arrangements, and the stables also may be contacted directly. Some rides include a seaside picnic or trips along secluded beaches.

TENNIS

Many resorts on the ABC islands have tennis courts for use by registered guests, and some allow non-guests for a fee. On Aruba, the best courts are found on Palm Beach at resorts such as Marriott's Surf Club, Holiday Inn SunSpree, and the Hyatt Regency *(see p527)*, **Aruba Tennis Academy** also welcomes visitors. On Bonaire, the best courts are at **Harbor Village Beach Club Tennis Center**. **Sport and Country Club** and most of the upscale resorts have courts for visitors on Curaçao.

DIRECTORY

DIVING AND SNORKELING

Bonaire Dive & Adventure
Kaya Gobernador N Debrot 77A, Kralendijk, Bonaire. **Tel** 599 717 2229. **www**.bonairedive andadventure.com

Dive Aruba
Renaissance Marina, Oranjestad, Aruba. **Tel** 297 582 7337. **www**.divearuba.com

Ocean Encounters
Seaquarium – Mambo Beach, Curaçao. **Tel** 599 9461 8131. **www**.oceanencounters. com

Red Sail Sports
L.G. Smith Boulevard 17, Oranjestad, Aruba. **Tel** 297 586 1603. **www**.aruba-redsail.com

SPORTFISHING

Curaçao Activities
Willemstad, Curaçao. **Tel** 599 9465 1664. **www**.curacaoactivities. com

Let's Fish
Brakkeput Abou K 92, Curaçao. **Tel** 599 9747 4489. **www**.letsfish.net

Mahi Mahi
Seaport Marina, Oranjestad, Aruba. **Tel** 297 587 0538. **www**.aruba-mahimahi. com

Multifish Charters
Harbor Village Marina, Bonaire. **Tel** 599 786 1228. **www**.multifish. com

Piscatur Fishing Charters
Kaya J. Pop 4, Kralendijk, Bonaire. **Tel** 599 717 8774. **www**.bonaire fishing.com/piscatur

WINDSURFING

Aruba Active Vacations
Fisherman's Huts, Hadikurari Beach, Aruba. **Tel** 297 586 0989. **www**.aruba-active-vacations.com

Jibe City
Lac Bay, Bonaire. **Tel** 599 717 5233. **www**.jibecity.com

Kitesurfing Aruba
Fisherman's Huts, Hadikurari Beach, Aruba. **Tel** 297 733 1515. **www**.kitesurfingaruba. com

Windsurfing Curaçao
Caracasbaai, Curaçao. **Tel** 599 9738 4555. **www**.windsurfing curacao.com

WATERSPORTS

Aruba Watersport Center
J.E. Irausquin Boulevard 81b, Palm Beach, Aruba. **Tel** 297 586 6613. **www**.arubawatersport center.com

Caribbean Sea Sports
John F. Kennedy Boulevard, Marriott Resort, Curaçao. **Tel** 599 9462 2620. **www**.caribsea sports.com

Pelican Watersports
J.E. Irausquin Blvd 232, Oranjestad, Aruba. **Tel** 297 587 2302. **www**.pelican-aruba.com

BOATING AND SAILING

Bounty Adventures
www.bountyadventures. com

Cat Sailing
Jan Thiel Beach, Curaçao. **Tel** 599 9747 5830. **www**.catcuracao.com

Insulinde
Punda, Curaçao. **Tel** 599 9560 1340. **www**.insulinde.com

Jolly Pirates
www.jolly-pirates.com

Samur Sailing Charters
www.samursailing.com

Tattoo Party Cruises and Mi Dushi Sailing
Noord, 128p, Aruba. **Tel** 297 586 2010. **www**.arubaadventures. com/tattoo

Woodwind Sailing
Kaya Seminole 3, Bonaire. **Tel** 599 786 7055. **www**.woodwind bonaire.com

HIKING

Bonaire Dive & Adventure
Kaya Gobernador N. Debrot 77A, Kralendijk, Bonaire. **Tel** 599 717 2229. **www**.bonairedive andadventure.com

Curaçao Actief
Willemstad, Curaçao. **Tel** 599 9433 8858. **www**.curacao-actief.com

Outdoor Bonaire
Road to Lac Bay Kralendijk, Bonaire. **Tel** 599 791 6272. **www**.outdoorbonaire. com

Sensitive Hikers
Oranjestad, Aruba. **Tel** 297 594 5017. **www**.sensitivehikers

CYCLING

De Freewieler
Kaya Grandi 61, Kralendijk, Bonaire. **Tel** 599 717 8545.

Pablito's Bike Rental
L. G. Smith Boulevard, Oranjestad, Aruba. **Tel** 297 587 8655.

Wanna Bike
www.wannabike.com

JEEP AND ATV TOURS

ABC Tours
Tel 297 582 5600. **www**.abc-aruba.com

Aruba Jeep Safari
Oranjestad, Aruba. **Tel** 297 582 5600. **www**.abc-aruba.com

Eric's ATV Adventures
Kaya Serafin 63, Willemstad, Curaçao. **Tel** 599 9524 7418. **www**.curacaoatv.com

Rancho Daimari
Noord, Aruba. **Tel** 297 748 4559. **www**.visitaruba.com/ ranchodaimari/

Rento Fun Drive
Kaya Grandi 47, Kralendijk, Bonaire. **Tel** 599 717 2408. **www**.rentofunbonaire. com

GOLF

Blue Bay Golf
Landhuis Blauw, Curaçao. **Tel** 599 9868 1755. **www**.bluebaygolf.com

Tierra del Sol Country Club
Tel 297 586 0978. **www**.tierradelsol.com

HORSE-RIDING

Criadero El Hijo de David
Seru Lora Weg 175, Curaçao. **Tel** 599 9465 1166.

The Riding Academy Club
Kunuku Warahama, Bonaire. **Tel** 599 560 7949. **www**.infobonaire. com/ridingacademy/

TENNIS

Aruba Tennis Academy
Oranjestad, Aruba. **Tel** 297 583 7074. **www**.tennisaruba.com

Harbor Village Beach Club Tennis Center
www.harbourvillage.com

Sport and Country Club
Santa Catharina, Curaçao. **Tel** 599 9767 7030.

Choosing a Hotel

Aruba, Bonaire, and Curaçao have quite varied accommodations. Glitz best describes the resorts in Aruba while hotels with a casual ambience appeal to Bonaire's divers and eco-tourists. Curaçao features a mix of luxurious resorts, lovely historical establishments, and casual beach hotels. Rates peak during the winter high-season and fall by 25–50 percent during the summer.

PRICE CATEGORIES
The following price ranges are for a standard double room per night and all taxes included.

$ under $100
$$ $100–200
$$$ $200–300
$$$$ $300–400
$$$$$ over $400

ABC ISLANDS

Heritage Hotels of Curaçao
Among the three islands, Curaçao has some of the loveliest old-world hotels. Some buildings, with their Dutch-influenced architecture, have been turned into resorts, and well-known hotel chains claim prime ocean-front property. These resorts are often surrounded by exotic gardens and pretty courtyards. Most of the buildings are painted brightly and tastefully furnished to retain their elegance and charm.

Kura Hulanda Beach Club

Bucuti Beach Resort

ARUBA, DRUIF BEACH Tamarijn Aruba All-Inclusive
👪 ☰ 🏊 ♿ [W] $$$$$

J.E. Irausquin Boulevard 41 ***Tel*** *297 525 5200* ***Fax*** *297 525 5203* ***Rooms*** *236*

There are plans to upgrade to a mega package, which allows use of the facilities at Divi Aruba, where the beach is better. Rooms here are oceanfront, but the shore is rocky. All units are spacious and open onto a patio or balcony. Extensive activity list, though the resort presents a slow-paced ambience. **www.tamarijnaruba.com**

ARUBA, EAGLE-DRUIF BEACH Divi Aruba All-Inclusive Resort
👪 ☰ 🏊 ♿ [W] $$$$$

J.E. Irausquin Boulevard 45 ***Tel*** *297 525 5200* ***Fax*** *297 525 5203* ***Rooms*** *201*

Choose from several packages and accommodations, then forget about the cost. Everything is included, except extra luxuries, such as spa treatments and motorized watersports. All units are well maintained, the food is good, and the facilities and activities are extensive. **www.diviaruba.com**

ARUBA, EAGLE BEACH Amsterdam Manor Beach Club
🍴 ☰ 🏊 ♿ [W] $$$

J.E. Irausquin Boulevard 252 ***Tel*** *297 587 1492* ***Fax*** *297 587 1493* ***Rooms*** *72*

Across the road from the beach, just before the high-rise resorts begin to the north, this small hotel has a European flavor. Some rooms have sea views, and guests may order lunch in their rooms. While they do not cater specifically for kids, families are welcome. Best rooms are suites on the top floor. **www.amsterdammanor.com**

ARUBA, EAGLE BEACH Bucuti Beach Resort
🍴 ☰ 🏊 ♿ [W] $$$

L.G. Smith Boulevard 55B, PO Box 1347 ***Tel*** *297 583 1100* ***Fax*** *297 582 5272* ***Rooms*** *104*

Upgrade to the top-floor Tara Beach Penthouse Suite for the ultimate romantic experience. All rooms are beautifully decorated and suites have kitchenettes. Eagle Beach spreads out around this friendly Euro-style boutique resort. Rates include Continental breakfast. The resort also has a lovely spa. **www.bucuti.com**

ARUBA, MANCHEBO BEACH Aruba Beach Club
⛱ 🍴 ☰ 🏊 ♿ [W] $$$

J.E. Irausquin Boulevard 53 ***Tel*** *297 587 1100* ***Fax*** *297 587 1112* ***Rooms*** *131*

These spacious studios and suites have kitchens, living areas, and balconies. High ceilings characterize the top-floor units, and the best suites include dining tables and an extra bathroom. The club is run as a timeshare, with a choice of activities, and guests may also use the facilities at the adjacent Casa del Mar. **www.arubabeachclub.net**

ARUBA, MANCHEBO BEACH Manchebo Beach Resort and Spa
👪 ⛱ ☰ 🏊 ♿ [W] $$$

J.E. Irausquin Boulevard 55 ***Tel*** *297 582 3444* ***Fax*** *297 583 2446* ***Rooms*** *71*

This hotel was one of the first hotels on this beach and is a good choice in this area. The lobby is tastefully decorated with Indonesian furniture and there is an elegant beachfront spa. Each room has a private patio with fantastic views of the ocean or garden. **www.manchebo.com**

ARUBA, MANCHEBO BEACH Casa del Mar Beach Resort
⛱ 🍴 ☰ 🏊 ♿ [W] $$$$

J.E. Irausquin Boulevard 51 ***Tel*** *297 582 7000* ***Fax*** *297 582 9044* ***Rooms*** *147*

This is the more deluxe sister resort to Aruba Beach Club and offers an extensive list of planned activities and watersports. The newer wing has no ocean view, but balconies overlook one of the two pools. All units have a kitchen, living area, and a patio or balcony. It is ideal for families. **www.casadelmar-aruba.com**

ARUBA, NOORD Coconut Inn
☰ [W] $

Noord 31 ***Tel*** *297 586 6288* ***Fax*** *297 586 5433* ***Rooms*** *40*

Coconut palms shade this little budget hotel located about a 20-minute walk inland from Palm Beach. Each tidy room has simple furniture, cable TV, tiled floors, and kitchenette. An outdoor bar and grill serves poolside in high season, and breakfast is included in the rates year round. **www.coconutinn.com**

Key to Symbols *see back cover flap*

ARUBA, NORTH END Tierra del Sol Resort & Country Club 🍴📋 W $$$$$$$

Malmok Road **Tel** *297 586 0405* **Fax** *297 586 0941* **Rooms** *114*

Golfers consider this resort paradise with the big draw of a gorgeous golf course. Guests stay in privately-owned villas and condos which have spacious living areas, full kitchens, and shady patios. Facilities include an excellent spa and health center, tennis courts, and two restaurants *(see p530)*. **www.tierradelsol.com**

ARUBA, OFF PALM BEACH Boardwalk Boutique Hotel 📋 W $$

Bakval 20 **Tel** *297 586 6654* **Fax** *297 586 1836* **Rooms** *13*

Across the road from the Marriott complex on Palm Beach, this small hotel is an ideal alternative to the big resorts. Guests may use the adjacent racquet club with fitness center, pool, and playground. Towels, lounge chairs, and umbrellas are supplied for the beach. Units have a kitchen and living area. **www.arubaboardwalk.com**

ARUBA, ORANJESTAD Talk of the Town Hotel and Beach Club 🛏🍴📋💪 W $$

L.G. Smith Boulevard 2 **Tel** *297 582 3380* **Fax** *297 582 0327* **Rooms** *51*

This small hotel is ideal for visitors who want to be near Oranjestad and the airport. Basic rooms have two double or one king-sized bed. Some king-sized bedrooms have a sofa bed as well. Apartments have one or two bedrooms and a kitchenette. Surfside Beach is across the street. **www.tottaruba.com**

ARUBA, ORANJESTAD Renaissance Aruba Resort & Casino 🍴📋💪♿ W $$$$

L.G. Smith Boulevard 82 **Tel** *297 583 6000* **Fax** *297 582 5317* **Rooms** *556*

This resort is based in the town, but has a private island with access by free water taxi and an upscale open-air shopping mall. The Ocean Suites adjoin a small man-made beach, and units feature a living area, large bathroom, and large balcony. Two casinos are on-site. **www.renaissancearuba.com**

ARUBA, PALM BEACH Divi Aruba Phoenix Beach Resort 🛏🍴📋💪♿ $$$

J.E. Irausquin Boulevard 75 **Tel** *297 586 6066* **Fax** *297 586 1165* **Rooms** *101*

This resort is located at the south end of Palm Beach which is often windy – great on a hot day and for windsurfing. Rooms are fitted with kitchenettes or full kitchens, and the balconies have great ocean views. Villas offer additional space and extended balconies. Excellent fitness center. **www.diviarubaphoenix.com**

ARUBA, PALM BEACH Aruba Marriott Resort & Stellaris Casino 🛏🍴📋💪♿ W $$$$

L.G. Smith Boulevard 101 **Tel** *297 586 9000* **Fax** *297 586 8000* **Rooms** *413*

Large rooms and balconies, with big beds and luxurious down pillows. The bathrooms have two sinks and each room also has a sofa bed. Great waterfall-pool and all the standard amenities expected of a Marriott hotel. The south tower has non-smoking rooms. **www.arubamarriott.com**

ARUBA, PALM BEACH Hotel RIU Palace Aruba 🛏🍴📋💪♿ W $$$$

J.E. Irausquin Boulevard 79 **Tel** *297 586 3900* **Fax** *297 586 1941* **Rooms** *450*

This large complex offers almost every amenity and comfort, all-inclusive, right on the beach. Rooms are spacious and the suites have Jacuzzi tubs, a large step-down sitting area and king-sized beds. Meals are included; the buffets are average to good, while the theme restaurants are much better. **www.riu.com**

ARUBA, PALM BEACH Hyatt Regency Aruba Resort & Casino 🛏🍴📋💪♿ W $$$$

J.E. Irausquin Boulevard 85 **Tel** *297 586 1234* **Fax** *297 586 1682* **Rooms** *360*

Rooms are on the small side but excellent amenities make up for lack of space. Book a suite for a larger room and decent-sized balcony. The multi-level pool is magnificently landscaped and the spa is excellent. Ideal for families. Fine dining at the Ruinas del Mar *(see p531)*. Watersports and other activities on-site. **www.aruba.hyatt.com**

ARUBA, PALM BEACH Marriott Surf Club 🛏🍴📋💪♿ W $$$$

L.G. Smith Boulevard 103 **Tel** *297 586 9000* **Fax** *297 586 8000* **Rooms** *900*

The lazy river is the hot feature at this timeshare resort. It gets crowded during school holidays, but there is always plenty of room at the beach. Villas feature one to three bedrooms with king-sized beds, luxury linen, soaking tubs, full kitchens, and large balconies. **www.marriott-vacationclub.com**

ARUBA, PALM BEACH Marriott Aruba Ocean Club 🛏🍴📋💪♿ W $$$$$

L.G. Smith Boulevard 101 **Tel** *297 586 9000* **Fax** *297 586 8000* **Rooms** *311*

Marriott resorts take up a long stretch of Palm Beach and offer every amenity. Visitors might find the beach and facilities a bit crowded, but if high-energy non-stop action is appealing, this is vacation heaven. Suites are spacious and have a kitchen, dining and living areas, and king-sized beds. **www.marriott-vacationclub.com**

BONAIRE, KRALENDIJK Buddy Dive Resort 🛏🍴📋💪 W $$

Kaya Governador Nicholaas Debrot 85 **Tel** *599 717 5080* **Fax** *599 717 8647* **Rooms** *46*

This family-run resort has superb facilities and has drawn divers for many years. The hotel rooms are small and basic, but have a TV and mini-refrigerator. Apartments are spacious with furnished patios, and it is a short walk to three pools. There is also a stairway down to the beach. **www.buddydive.com**

BONAIRE, KRALENDIJK Sand Dollar 🛏🍴📋💪 W $$

Kaya Governador Nicholaas Debrot 79 **Tel** *599 717 8738* **Fax** *599 717 8760* **Rooms** *76*

This resort complex is focused on diving and offers a vast selection of other sports activities. All the condos face the beach and have full kitchens, living-dining areas, and big balconies. The beach is a small stretch of sand and divers enter from the pier. Great children's program. **www.divesanddollar.com**

BONAIRE, KRALENDIJK Captain Don's Habitat
Kaya Governador Nicholaas Debrot 103 **Tel** *599 717 8290* **Fax** *599 717 8240* **Rooms** *72*

Habitat is run by Don Stewart, a well-known reef conservationist, who believes a diver should be able to grab a tank and hit the water 24/7. Cottage-style villas with kitchens and patios are near the sea, there are well-priced dive packages and activities for non-divers too, including a swimming pool. **www.habitatbonaire.com**

BONAIRE, KRALENDIJK Divi Flamingo Beach Resort & Casino
J.A. Abraham Boulevard 40 **Tel** *599 717 8285* **Fax** *599 717 8238* **Rooms** *129*

A short walk to Kralendijk, the standard rooms here are fresh and colorful, and have patios. Studios are clustered in a complex with a private pool and have kitchenettes and double beds. On-site facilities include dive center, casino, fitness center with spa services, and business center. **www.diviflamingo.com**

BONAIRE, KRALENDIJK Harbour Village Beach Club
Kaya Governador N. Debrot 71, Playa Lechi **Tel** *599 717 7500* **Fax** *599 717 7507* **Rooms** *40*

The hotel is located on a beach and has a dive shop and full-service spa. It is only a 15-minute walk to Kralendijk. Standard rooms are small but comfortable. Beachfront suites are large, and have a terrace with hammock, refrigerator, and microwave. Landscaped grounds wrap around the white-sand beach. **www.harbourvillage.com**

BONAIRE, SOROBON Sorobon Beach Resort
Lac Bay **Tel** *599 717 8080* **Fax** *599 717 6080* **Rooms** *30*

This clothing-optional eco-inn is in a nature reserve and has the only naturist beach on the island. Guests can relax in total privacy behind palm shelters. Villas are at the water's edge and have one, two or three bedrooms, kitchen, and hammocks on a covered patio. Windsurf centers are farther along the beach. **www.sorobonbeach.com**

BONAIRE, SOUTH OF KRALENDIJK Coco Palm Garden & Casa Oleander
Kaya van Eps 9 **Tel** *599 717 2108* **Fax** *599 717 8193* **Rooms** *22*

Set in a residential area near the southwest beaches, this two-property complex has a small swimming pool, private restaurant, and bar. Accommodations include houses, studios, and apartments with kitchens, porches, landscaped grounds with hammocks, and lounges. **www.cocopalmgarden.org**

BONAIRE, SOUTH OF KRALENDIJK Bellafonte Chateau de la Mer
E.E.G. Boulevard 10 **Tel** *599 717 3333* **Fax** *599 717 8581* **Rooms** *20*

Set at the water's edge above a rock breakwater, this castle-like hotel is sleek, modern, and luxurious. The studios have king-sized beds, balcony, and kitchenette. Larger units have 2 bedrooms, 2 baths, full kitchen, and living area with sea views. Diver and surfer storage lockers and freshwater showers. **www.bellafontebonaire.com**

BONAIRE, SOUTH OF KRALENDIJK Plaza Resort Bonaire
J.A. Abraham Boulevard 80 **Tel** *599 717 2500* **Fax** *599 717 7133* **Rooms** *74*

This resort has gorgeous grounds with lots of plants and trees. Suites are one room, but spacious. Villas have a living area, separate bedroom, and mini or full kitchen. All baths are good size. Three restaurants, large pool, casino, 4 tennis courts, fitness center, and watersports. **www.plazaresortbonaire.com**

CURAÇAO, BAPOR KIBRA Lions Dive & Beach Resort
Bapor Kibra **Tel** *599 9434 8888* **Fax** *599 9434 8889* **Rooms** *139*

This is one of the top dive resorts on the island. It is located next to Underwater Park, and the resort's private beach connects to Mambo Beach. Rooms are basic, but comfortable, and some have sea views. Dive packages and meal plans are popular with guests who spend most of their time underwater. **www.lionsdive.com**

CURAÇAO, BAPOR KIBRA The Royal Sea Aquarium Resort
Bapor Kibra **Tel** *599 9465 6699* **Fax** *599 9465 6689* **Rooms** *29*

Admission to the Curaçao Sea Aquarium is free for guests at this resort. Each villa has 2 bedrooms, 2 baths, full kitchen, living-dining areas, and a patio. Two pools, Jacuzzi, restaurant, and activities center are on-site. Full facilities are available on the beach. Willemstad is just 10 minutes away by car. **www.royalresorts.com**

CURAÇAO, BLUE BAY Blue Bay Village
47 C Blue Bay **Tel** *599 9888 8800* **Fax** *599 9888 9090* **Rooms** *52*

Previously a plantation, this plush facility has many extras: 18-hole golf course, dive center, kids club, large beach with a pool, children's pool, playground, showers, volleyball, and shade huts. The three-bedroom villas have kitchen, living area, kitchen, covered veranda, two baths, and Wi-Fi. **www.bluebay-village.com**

CURAÇAO, BOCA SANTA MARIA Habitat Curaçao
Coral Estate, Rif St. Marie **Tel** *599 9864 8304* **Fax** *599 9864 8464* **Rooms** *70*

Unlimited shore freedom sums it up. Guests can dive 24/7, and the house reef is thriving. Book an ocean view room with balcony close to the surf. All rooms have a kitchenette and patio. Spacious villas are set around a salt water lagoon. Great spa treatments, infinity pool, and art gallery. **www.habitatcuracaoresort.com**

CURAÇAO, JAN THIEL BEACH Livingstone Jan Thiel Resort
Jan Thiel Bay **Tel** *599 9747 0332* **Fax** *599 9767 9600* **Rooms** *130*

Lovely villas in Mediterranean style with modern kitchen, living areas, cable TV, and large furnished patios. Caters to families who enjoy the landscaped pool, playground, open-air bar, well-priced restaurant, and nearby beach with watersports, clubs, and shops. **www.janthielresort.com**

Key to Symbols *see back cover flap*

CURAÇAO, JAN THIEL BEACH Papagayo Beach Resort $$$
Jan Thiel Bay **Tel** *599 9747 4333* **Fax** *599 9747 4322* **Rooms** *80*

Beautifully designed and decorated villas have a wrap-around veranda overlooking the lovely gardens, and kitchen, living area and one or two bedrooms, each with a bathroom. There is a large pool with thatch shade huts; the beach is a short walk away. The full-service restaurant is open for all meals. **www.papagayo-beach.com**

CURAÇAO, MAMBO-SEAQUARIUM BEACH Breezes Curaçao $$$
8 Dr. Martin Luther King Boulevard **Tel** *599 9736 7888* **Fax** *599 9461 7205* **Rooms** *339*

Caters to couples, but has a good kids' program and everything is included in the room rate. It shares the beach with Curaçao Sea Aquarium, and has three pools, several Jacuzzis, nightclub, casino. Four theme restaurants serve a good variety of food. All rooms have balconies; the best have ocean views. **www.breezes.com/resorts/curacao**

CURAÇAO, PISCADERA BAY Clarion Hotel & Suites $$
World Trade Center **Tel** *599 9433 6666* **Fax** *599 9433 6602* **Rooms** *98*

Connected to the island's World Trade Center and across the street from the beach, this basic chain hotel has well decorated rooms, friendly staff, and a business center. Ideal for guests who want to mix work with fun. Cable TV and free Internet are a plus. Continental breakfast is included. **www.clarionhotel.com**

CURAÇAO, PISCADERA BAY Floris Suite Hotel $$$
J.F. Kennedy Boulevard **Tel** *599 9462 6111* **Fax** *599 9462 6211* **Rooms** *71*

Modern, yet colonial, European, yet Caribbean, this hotel is almost too unique to describe. This level of luxury usually comes at a higher price, and while the spa, watersports, and beach are not part of the property, they are just across the street. It has a great restaurant *(see p352)* and a gorgeous pool. **www.florissuitehotel.com**

CURAÇAO, PISCADERA BAY Hilton Curaçao Resort $$$
J.F. Kennedy Boulevard **Tel** *599 9462 5000* **Fax** *599 9462 5846* **Rooms** *190*

The rooms here are typical Hilton, but the bathrooms are spacious and the amenities and location are superb. Executive floor rooms have access to a gorgeous lounge. Facilities include a pool, in-house dive center, luxury spa, tennis courts, and a wellness program. **http://hiltoncaribbean.com**

CURAÇAO, PISCADERA BAY Marriott Beach Resort & Emerald Casino $$$
6603 Piscadera Bay **Tel** *599 9736 8800* **Fax** *599 9462 7502* **Rooms** *247*

Marriott quality shines throughout this elegantly casual resort. Beach with a dive center, big pool with swim-up bar, fitness center with spa services, kids' clubhouse with playground. Rooms are spacious and bright with Wi-Fi and balconies. Four restaurants *(see p352)*; all-inclusive available. **www.marriott.com**

CURAÇAO, SPANISH WATER Limestone Holiday $$
Spanish Water **Tel** *599 9767 3007* **Fax** *599 9747 2091* **Rooms** *11*

Beach cottages at this tiny resort have kitchens and a car for getting around to the nearest heritage town, Willemstad. Each unit is different, but well outfitted with TV, DVD player, and Wi-Fi access. The sandy beach slopes to calm water for swimming. **www.limestoneholiday.com**

CURAÇAO, WESTPUNT Lodge Kura Hulanda Beach Club $$$
1 Playa Kalki **Tel** *599 9839 3600* **Fax** *599 9839 3601* **Rooms** *74*

A sister resort to Kura Hulanda in Willemstad, this luxury beachfront property features stunning views of the island's dramatic northwest coast. All spacious units are beautifully decorated with furnished patios. A dive shop is on the beach and a pristine reef offshore. It has a fitness center and a free shuttle into town. **www.kurahulanda.com**

CURAÇAO, WILLEMSTAD Otrobanda Hotel and Casino $$
Breedestraat, Otrobanda **Tel** *599 9462 7400* **Fax** *599 9462 7299* **Rooms** *45*

European-style hotel on the waterfront overlooking the Queen Emma Bridge, Bionplein Square, floating market and all the activity of Willemstad. Rooms are basic but clean and well appointed with queen-sized beds; some may be interconnected. Gorgeous pool and restaurant. Buffet breakfast is included. **www.otrobandahotel.com**

CURAÇAO, WILLEMSTAD Avila Beach Hotel $$$
130 Penstraat **Tel** *599 9461 4377* **Fax** *599 9461 1493* **Rooms** *137*

This historic family-run hotel, which has been hosting royalty for generations, is better than ever following modernization. The original structure, a 19th-century mansion, has access to two beaches and is a 10-minute walk from the Willemstad town center. It has a fine restaurant *(see p532)*, pool, and fitness center. **www.avilahotel.com**

CURAÇAO, WILLEMSTAD Kura Hulanda $$$
Langestraat 8, Otrobanda **Tel** *599 9434 7700* **Fax** *599 9434 7701* **Rooms** *80*

This is the most unique resort on the island, perhaps in the Caribbean. An eight-block, 65-building historic district has been converted into a luxurious village with every modern convenience. Walk to town, shuttle to beach. Spa, casino, 2 pools, 5 restaurants *(see p533)*, and a museum are on-site. **www.kurahulanda.com**

CURAÇAO, WILLEMSTAD Renaissance Curacao Resort & Casino $$$$
Baden Powellweg 1 **Tel** *599 9435 5000* **Rooms** *237*

International levels of service and stylish, colorful contemporary decor characterize this modern hotel in the historic center of the capital. Guests can relax and enjoy its large private beach (with bar and grill), infinity pool, casino, and spa facilities, or stroll out to explore this smart, lively shopping and dining district. **www.renaissancecuracao.com**

Where to Eat & Nightlife

Aruba has a Dine Around Program where visitors can purchase a card valid at select restaurants, for up to seven three-course dinners. Bonaire's restaurants on the waterfront have fabulous views, and specialize in Asian, Indonesian, Dutch, and American-style meals. Curaçao has several specialty restaurants that serve authentic dishes from all over the world.

RESTAURANTS

Special Cuisines
Krioyo (local fare) includes fresh seafood and meat, along with *funchi* (boiled cornmeal) and fried plantains, *kabritu* (goat stew), *aros moro* (rice and peas), *tutu* (sweet cornmeal and bean dish), and stewed iguana. These are best eaten at small roadside stands in villages. Many places serve a Dutch dish, *keshi yená*, baked Gouda cheese.

Matilde Island Chic, Aruba   **Jaipur, Curaçao**

ARUBA, EAGLE BEACH Madame Janette   Ⓥ🍷▤▦🍴&   ⓈⓈⓈⓈ
Cunucu Abao 37 **Tel** *297 587 0184*

Named for a pepper used throughout the island, this restaurant boasts award-winning chefs that turn out creative international dishes with an Austrian flair and Caribbean twist, and there is a fine wine list. The small menu includes mahimahi, veggie strudel, and Chilean sea bass in a wine butter sauce. Closed on Tuesdays. Only dinner.

ARUBA, EAGLE BEACH Screaming Eagle   🍷▤▦   ⓈⓈⓈⓈⓈ
J.E. Irausquin Boulevard 228 **Tel** *297 587 8021*

The decor of this restaurant alone makes it worth a visit. The setting includes draped bedlike lounges which invite cozy chats over champagne. Fish and beef tenderloin dominate the menu. The restaurant also has a well-stocked wine cellar and an impressive list of cocktails from around the world.

ARUBA, NOORD Papiamento   Ⓥ▤▦   ⓈⓈⓈⓈ
Washington 61 **Tel** *297 586 4544*

Located inside one of the island's well-preserved manor houses, this family-run restaurant serves seafood dishes, such as the popular Clay Pot for two, a mix of vegetables, seafood, and herbs steamed in a hand-made clay pot. Guests can ask for a table in the garden where fairy lights glitter among the trees. Dinner only. Closed on Mondays.

ARUBA, NOORD Wacky Wahoo's   Ⓥ🍷▤▦🍴🏃   ⓈⓈⓈⓈ
33B Palm Beach **Tel** *297 586 7333*

A welcoming, popular restaurant and bar in a lively area, owned by German-born chef Harald Rudel and his Aruban wife Rossanna. Specialties include Aruban *ceviche*, Argentine steak, and Caribbean conch and shrimp stew. Family-friendly, and although there is no wheelchair access, staff are happy to assist disabled guests. Closed on Sundays.

ARUBA, NORTH END Ventanas del Mar   🍷▤▦🍴&   ⓈⓈⓈⓈ
Tierra del Sol Resort **Tel** *297 586 0879*

The *ventanas* (windows) at this restaurant, at the Tierra del Sol *(see p527)*, open onto sea views broken by a golf course and a historic lighthouse. Food is excellently prepared. Highlights include the Angus beef *carpaccio* and New Zealand rack of lamb or duck breast finished with roasted pineapple, and bananas over ice cream.

ARUBA, ORANJESTAD Cuba's Cookin'   Ⓥ▤♫&   ⓈⓈⓈⓈ
Wilhelminastraat 27 **Tel** *297 588 0627*

This little place is set in an 1877 colonial home across from the police station. Cuban food is the specialty and steaks and seafood are also available. Order one of the icy drink specials to quench the sting of the fiery hot salsa served with yucca chips. The lobster enchiladas are outstanding. There is live music in the restaurant as well. Closed on Sundays.

ARUBA, ORANJESTAD El Gaucho   🍷▤🍴♫&   ⓈⓈⓈⓈ
Wilhelminastraat 80 **Tel** *297 582 3677*

El Gaucho offers a variety of dishes on its menu including the delicious Argentine beef. A Torro Client is a huge shish kebab, while the Gaucho steak weighs about 16 oz (450 g). They serve Aruban delicacies as well. Argentine wines are present on the wine list, and there is live music too. Closed on Sundays.

ARUBA, ORANJESTAD Marandi   Ⓥ▦   ⓈⓈⓈⓈ
Bucutiweg 50 **Tel** *297 582 0157*

This restaurant is a short drive from the airport. Marandi means "on the water," and tables are set under a *palapa* (thatched-roof) hut and along the Laguna Pier. Fish is the specialty, but the menu also includes meat and vegetarian dishes, all tweaked a bit with Caribbean spices and delicate sauces. Dinner only and closed on Sundays.

Key to Symbols *see back cover flap*

ARUBA, ORANJESTAD Tatami Sushi Bar

V 🍽 🏠 ♿ $$$$

L.G. Smith Boulevard 123 **Tel** *297 582 9945*

This restaurant, in a shopping mall, is popular for its authentic sushi and its warm, cosy atmosphere; it's very small, and tables are in demand, so reservations are recommended. The chef uses fresh seafood caught off Aruba for sashimi and other specialties including crispy crab, "Spicy Dragon", and wahoo rolls. Closed on Mondays.

ARUBA, ORANJESTAD Driftwood

🍽 🏠 ♿ $$$$$

Klipstraat 12 **Tel** *297 583 2515*

An extremely popular seafood restaurant, Driftwood is usually a busy joint. Aruban-style recipes tend to be spicy, but orders are customized to suit individual taste. The fish is so fresh that it requires no embellishment, and the sauces are absolutely suberb, tantalizing the palate. Closed on Tuesdays.

ARUBA, ORANJESTAD Matilde Island Chic

V 🍽 🍽 $$$$$

Havenstraat 23 **Tel** *297 583 9200*

Long an island tradition, the well-loved Chez Mathilde has been reinvented and renamed. The redesigned bar serves food and cocktails to a trendy crowd, and a large stroll-through wine cellar holds the island's largest selection. Traditional and creative gourmet dishes are served in two elegant dining areas. Also serves vegetarian fare.

ARUBA, PALM BEACH Moomba Beach Bar & Grill

V 🍽 🎵 $$$

J.E. Irausquin 230 **Tel** *297 586 5365*

Located on the sand between the Holiday Inn and Marriott Surf Club, this lively place serves delicious favorites, such as pasta, fajitas, and grilled meats. Full-moon parties are popular, and live music or DJ sounds are featured most days. Open morning until late at night with Internet and pool tables.

ARUBA, PALM BEACH Ruinas del Mar

🍽 🍽 🏠 ♿ $$$$$

Hyatt Regency **Tel** *297 586 1234*

In the Hyatt Regency (see p527), this restaurant has an elegant atmosphere and tables set on the stone faux-ruined terrace overlooking the sea. Food is delicious and aesthetically presented and the Sunday brunch is fabulous. The menu features mixed seafood platter, surf-and-turf with lobster, and steaks. It tends to get busy during high season.

ARUBA, SAN NICOLAS Charlie's Bar

🍽 $$$

Zeppenveldstraat 56, Main Street **Tel** *297 584 5086*

Customers have been pinning personal mementos to the walls and ceiling of this popular bar for more than 60 years, just to be a part of the fun and tradition. The owner behind the bar is now Charlie III, who entertains guests with stories about his family. The steamed jumbo shrimp with Honeymoon sauce is a prize-winner.

ARUBA, SAVANETA Brisas del Mar

🍽 🎵 $$$$

Savaneta 222A **Tel** *297 584 7718*

Classy and casual with cushioned wicker furniture, this restaurant is set on the beach and offers lunch and dinner daily, and brunch on Sunday. Catch of the day is always a good choice, but other options include pasta, chicken, and beef, and various side dishes. Guests can also enjoy the live music performed here. Closed on Mondays.

ARUBA, SAVANETA Flying Fishbone

🍽 🍽 $$$$$

Savaneta 344 **Tel** *297 584 2506*

The food served is excellent, the wine selection is good and well-priced, but the secluded beach setting is the main attraction of this feet-in-the-sand restaurant. There are tables right at the water's edge. The grilled seafood is always superb, and the peppers, sauces, herbs, and nuts do wonders for the taste buds. Dinner only.

BONAIRE, KRALENDIJK City Café & City Restaurant

V 🍽 🍽 🎵 🏠 $$$

Kaya J.N.E. Craane 7 **Tel** *599 717 8286*

This two-in-one eatery has an outdoor café and indoor restaurant. The café is known for its good bar drinks and live music on weekends. The restaurant is popular for its large varied menu. Great choices include the three-egg breakfasts, French-bread sandwiches, vegetarian lasagne, and the Dutch and Mexican specialties.

BONAIRE, KRALENDIJK It Rains Fishes

🍽 🍽 🍽 🏠 ♿ $$$

Kaya J.N.E. Craane 24 **Tel** *599 717 8780*

Fantastic views of the bay from the open-air dining pavilion. Salads are large, creative, and filling. Main courses served include seafood, pasta, Asian-style chicken, pork ribs, and beef tenderloin. A range of excellent desserts on offer, as well as specialty coffee or liqueur.

BONAIRE, KRALENDIJK Bistro de Paris

🍽 🍽 🍽 🏠 $$$$

Kaya Governor 46 **Tel** *599 717 7070*

French-owned and operated, this place serves superb authentic French dishes in a cozy house with tables both inside and out on the terrace. Lunch and dinner served daily. The classic croque-monsieur is a popular lunch option, while the grilled fish topped with artichoke and roasted tomato sauce makes a great dinner dish.

BONAIRE, KRALENDIJK Richard's Waterfront Dining

V 🍽 🍽 $$$$

J.A. Abraham Boulevard 60 **Tel** *599 717 5263*

For a special treat book the single table for a maximum of four people, on the pier across the street. This is the only spot in town directly on the water. The main dining area is across the road, where regulars gather for happy hours at 5:30pm. Blackboard menu changes daily. Vegetarian fare, pastas, grilled seafood, and steaks.

BONAIRE, KRALENDIJK Zeezicht Seaside 📋 🍴 🎵 ☀ $$$$

Kaya J.N.E. Craane 12 ***Tel*** *599 717 8434*

The name means "sea view" in Dutch and perfectly describes this downtown landmark. Dine inside or out in the open. A great variety of salads, main courses, and home-made soups are available. Their seafood is the star, but other choices include sushi, and a small selection of Indonesian rice-table dishes.

BONAIRE, NORTH OF KRALENDIJK Vespucci's 🍷 📋 🍴 $$$

Kaya Gobernador N. Debrot 69, Harbor Village Marina ***Tel*** *599 717 2596*

Located on the marina with open-air seating and a view of the water, this Mediterranean restaurant serves lunch and dinner Monday to Saturday, with happy hour running from 4 to 6pm. Guests can choose from a menu that includes pastas, salads, fish, and other seafood. Popular with the boating crowd.

BONAIRE, SOROBON Kontiki Beach Club 🍴 🎵 $$$$

Kaminda 64 ***Tel*** *599 717 5369*

Breakfast buffet, lunch, and dinner are served daily. The club has Wi-Fi, beach chairs, live jazz, and an outstanding mango rum shake. Lunch includes fish soup, and Philly sandwiches; favorite dinner choices are Thai specialties, Creole-sauced fish, and grilled shrimp. Chef specials feature daily. The Dutch apple-pie is mouthwatering.

BONAIRE, SOUTH OF KRALENDIJK Banana Tree 🍴 🎵 $$$

J.A. Abraham Boulevard 80, Plaza Resort ***Tel*** *599 717 2500*

This open-air garden restaurant has an excellent setting, just off the beach. Caribbean and international favorites are served daily at dinner. Meal-sized salads and fresh fish are dependably delicious. Live island music plays several times a week. It is advisable to call for reservation.

BONAIRE, SOUTH OF KRALENDIJK Chibi Chibi 🍷 🍴 $$$

J.A. Abraham Boulevard 40, Divi Flamingo Resort ***Tel*** *599 717 8285*

This trendy two-level restaurant has lovely views of the sea from the terrace. Ask for a waterside table on the terrace to see the fish in the water below. Lunch and dinner served daily. While salads and sandwiches dominate lunch, guests tend to prefer Asian specialties, seafood, and steaks for dinner. A fine wine list.

CURAÇAO, NEAR JORIS BAY Zambezi [V] 🍷 🍴 ☀ ♿ $$$

Groot Sint Foris West, Ostrich Farm ***Tel*** *599 9747 2766*

The menu here includes exotic cuisine – ostrich steak with raspberry or mustard sauce. Less experimental guests may want to try dishes like the vegetarian stir fry. Children have their own menu with choices such as a burger with pumpkin pancake. South African wines are a specialty here.

CURAÇAO, WILLEMSTAD Belle Terrace 🍷 📋 🍴 $$$$

Avila Beach Hotel, Penstraat 130 ***Tel*** *599 9461 4377*

On the waterfront, Belle Terrace is set in a 19th-century plantation house *(see p529)*, and accustomed to serving the Dutch royal family. Breakfast and lunch are beachy affairs, but guests must dress for dinner and make a reservation. Dutch, Danish, and Antillean cuisine is served, and the wine is excellent. Also has theme nights.

CURAÇAO, WILLEMSTAD Blues 📋 🍴 🎵 ☀ $$$$

Avila Beach Hotel, Penstraat 130 ***Tel*** *599 9461 4377*

Built over the water at the end of a pier, this casual place is named for the music and not the color of the sea. Live performances on Thursdays/Saturdays, but drop in any time for great sunsets, icy drinks, lobster dinner or a lunch of Dutch *keshi yena*, baked Gouda cheese. Closed on Mondays.

CURAÇAO, PISCADERA BAY Sjalotte 🍷 🍴 ☀ $$$

Floris Suite Hotel ***Tel*** *599 9462 6111*

In the Floris Suite Hotel *(see p529)*, this is one of the island's best dining experiences due to the expertise of the kitchen crew that specializes in regional cuisine and artistic presentation. The dining patio is in a garden with an open kitchen. It opens for all meals daily and has a great wine list. Lighter meals are served at the beach grill.

CURAÇAO, PISCADERA BAY Portofino 🍷 📋 🍴 ☀ ♿ $$$$

John F. Boulevard, Marriott Resort ***Tel*** *599 9736 8800*

Italian chef Sylvia Nicolini oversees the kitchen that turns out exquisite dishes from her homeland, with half portions available for light eaters. Located in the Marriott Resort *(see p529)*, with seating outdoors on a garden patio and inside a Mediterranean-style dining room. Spectacular wine selection and a popular Sunday brunch.

CURAÇAO, SALINJA Sawasdee Thai Restaurant [V] 📋 ☀ ♿ $$$$

Mercuriusstraat 13, near Avila Beach Hotel ***Tel*** *599 9462 6361*

One of the most interesting meals on the island is the Indonesian rice-table, called *rijsttafel* in Dutch, served here daily at lunch and dinner. Individual dishes are available, but the rice-table offers 16 to 25 selections, which can be spiced to taste. Traditional Thai also on the menu. Vegetarians have many choices. Closed on Mondays.

CURAÇAO, SPANISH WATER Landhuis Brakkeput Mei-Mei [V] 📋 🍴 🎵 ☀ ♿ $$$$

Jan Sofat Spaanse Water ***Tel*** *599 9767 1500*

Dine under the stars at a table on one of the porches of this historic plantation house restaurant which serves excellent grilled steaks, seafood and some vegetarian options. Specialty paella on Wednesday nights and lobster on Thursdays. Island music and dancing on the side terrace. Children are welcome.

Key to Symbols *see back cover flap*

CURAÇAO, WESTPUNT Jaanchies Restaurant

Westpunt 15 **Tel** *599 9864 0126*

Named for the friendly owner, this café at the far northwest end of the island has become a dining tradition. Jaanchi himself may very well recite the daily menu choices and suggest filet of snake or iguana. Other options usually include fish, chicken, and goat. Lunch and dinner are served daily.

CURAÇAO, WESTPUNT Watamula

Playa Kalki 1 **Tel** *599 9839 3600*

Set in an open-air pavilion with views of the sea, this informal restaurant serves local favorites and international specialties from morning until night. Menu includes pasta, stir fries, pizzas, jerk pork loin, and grilled mahimahi as well as an excellent wine selection.

CURAÇAO, WILLEMSTAD La Pergola

Waterfront Bougies 47, Punda **Tel** *599 9461 3482*

Set in the historical Waterfort complex guarding the bay, this restaurant has fabulous views and serves great Italian meals. The Caribbean-Italian fare includes crab-stuffed ravioli and pasta tossed with island-herb-infused olive oil. Open daily.

CURAÇAO, WILLEMSTAD Scampis Eetcafé

Waterfort Boug 7, Punda **Tel** *599 9465 0769*

Perhaps the best seafood on an island teeming with such restaurants. The views are outstanding, with music on most nights and, theme nights weekly. Get adventurous with the choices, which include octopus and grilled conch. Scampis also has well-prepared steaks and delicious pastas. Dinner only. Open daily.

CURAÇAO, WILLEMSTAD Jaipur

Hotel Kurá Hulanda, Otrobanda **Tel** *599 9434 7700*

Jaipur's outdoor setting overlooking the pool's waterfall is romantic and tranquil, and guests can ask for a table perched on the rocks. The open-kitchen turns out excellent Indian dishes, especially the tandoori. Dinner is served daily. A snack menu is available daily from noon to 6pm beside the eco-pond pool. Closed on Tuesdays.

CURAÇAO, WILLEMSTAD Astrolab Observatory Restaurant

Hotel Kurá Hulanda, Otrobanda **Tel** *599 9434 7700*

This restaurant is located next to the Indian Marble Garden in this unique resort complex (*see p529*), and is named for the collection of astrolabes (early astronomical instruments) on display. The food is exquisite, the wine cellar is stocked with excellent international vintages. Dine indoors or alfresco on tender beef and inspired seafood dishes.

CURAÇAO, WILLEMSTAD Bistro le Clochard

The Rif Fort, Otrobanda **Tel** *599 9462 5666*

Popular upscale restaurant with a faithful local clientele. Overlooking Punda and the bay, Bistro le Clochard is especially spectacular at night. Serves lunch and dinner daily, with a non-stop service on the terrace. There are creative appetizers, fondue and crêpes, and the seafood, steaks, and wine meet all expectations.

CURAÇAO, WILLEMSTAD Fort Nassau

Schottegatweg 82, near Point Juliana. **Tel** *599 9461 3450*

Set in a national monument fort built in 1779 by the Dutch, this restaurant is recognized as one of the best on the island. Views are fantastic from the hillside site overlooking the city and harbor. Main courses focus on steaks and seafood jazzed up with innovative sauces. Outstanding appetizers, wine, and desserts.

BARS AND CLUBS

Aruba has the best nightlife, followed by Curaçao. Most hotspots are casual, open-air bars and clubs that offer live bands or DJ-hosted music till late. Most resorts on Aruba have nighttime entertainment, and tour operators run evening bar-hopping excursions by party bus. On Curaçao, nightlife revolves around major resorts, casinos, and restaurants that feature music and dancing. Bonaire's tourists are mostly divers, so few people stay up late. Some spots in Kralendijk play live music on weekends.

Brightly painted Banana Bus, Aruba

RECOMMENDED PLACES TO GO

Banana Bus
Oranjestad, Aruba. (Party bus stopping at three bars per nightly tour.)

Club Façade
Salinja, Curaçao. (Popular club with 3 dance floors.)

Garufa
Oranjestad, Aruba. (Jazz musicians play nightly, premium liquor.)

Karel's Beach Bar
Kralendijk, Bonaire. (Upbeat music, live bands on weekends.)

K-OZ
Salinja, Curaçao. (Outdoor rooftop, trendy retro club inside.)

The Paddock
Oranjestad, Aruba. (Live music several nights per week.)

Sopranos Piano Bar
Palm Beach, Aruba. (Piano music by entertainer Casey Hayes.)

Wet & Wild Beach Club
Seaquarium Beach, Curaçao. (Beach-front dance floor.)

Zen
Salinja, Curaçao. (Dance floor on Thursday and Saturday.)

Practical Information

The three islands – Aruba, Bonaire, and Curaçao – are linked by location and politics, both past and present, but each one is fiercely independent and unique. Accommodations are varied with Aruba being the most expensive, Bonaire catering to divers, and Curaçao, with the most number of budget hotels. The tourist organizations on each island have a friendly staff willing to help organize and promote comforts, entertainment, and attractions for visitors. An immense amount of information is available at tourist offices including maps and magazines, for those planning a trip to the region.

Terminal of the Curaçao International Airport, Hato

WHEN TO GO

The ABC Islands are well out of the hurricane belt, and though storms can occur, warm temperatures and cool breezes can be found all year round. Summer and fall are the best time to visit the three islands, when many cultural events are held.

GETTING THERE

Aruba and Curaçao have daily direct air service from North America and Amsterdam. Bonaire has weekly non-stop service from North America and Amsterdam and one-stop daily service from North America. Flights land at the international airports of Queen Beatrix on Aruba, Flamingo on Bonaire, and Hato on Curaçao. **Delta** flies non-stop to all islands from Atlanta. **American Eagle** flies to Aruba and Curaçao from the US, and to Bonaire from Puerto Rico. **US Airways** and **United Airlines** have flights to Aruba from the US. Flights from Amsterdam to all three islands are on **KLM**. Regional airlines

such as **Dutch Antilles Express** and **Divi Divi** fly within the ABCs, and **Air Jamaica** connects Curaçao with Jamaica. There is no scheduled ferry service to the ABC Islands.

DOCUMENTATION

Citizens of the EU nations as well as all other nationalities, including Canadians and Americans must show a passport to enter the ABC Islands. Visits may extend to three months without a visa. In addition, immigration officials may ask for an onward or return ticket, proof of sufficient funds for the planned stay, and an address where travelers plan to reside on the islands. Visitors can also check with their concerned embassies.

VISITOR INFORMATION

Tourist information kiosks are located at the airports on all three islands. Government Tourist Boards including the **Aruba Tourism Authority**, **Tourism Corporation Bonaire**, and **Curaçao Tourist Board**

have offices on each island as well as public relations agents overseas. Websites run by the official tourism offices give all the details about planning a vacation and provide links to a number of tourist-oriented businesses.

HEALTH AND SECURITY

Crime is rare on the three islands, with crimes against tourists among the lowest in the Caribbean. Still, precautions should be taken, especially against theft from rental cars. Visitors should also avoid leaving valuables unattended. Drug-related crimes occur occasionally, so avoid secluded roads and alleys after dark. Any crime must be reported with a request for a written report. Tap water here is safe to drink. **Dr. Horacio Oduber Hospital** in Aruba, **San Francisco Hospital** in Bonaire, and **St. Elizabeth Hospital** in Curaçao are among the best hospitals.

BANKING AND CURRENCY

US dollars and major credit cards are widely accepted on the ABC islands. The official currency on Aruba is the Aruban Florin (AF or Afl), which is divided into 100 cents. Bonaire and Curaçao use the Netherlands Antillean Florin (NAFl or Fl). The NAFl is also known as the Netherlands Antillean Guilder (ANG). Banks and ATMs are located throughout the islands. Banking hours are Monday to Friday from 8am to 3:30pm.

COMMUNICATIONS

The country codes for Aruba, Bonaire, and Curaçao are 297, 599, and 5999 respectively followed by the seven-digit local number. To call from outside the Caribbean, dial the international code (011 from the US) plus the area code, and the local number. For example, dial 011, then area code 297, and the seven-digit number for Aruba. Internet access is provided at major resorts and airports, and there are many Wi-Fi hotspots. Local SIM cards are available at **Digicel** offices.

TRANSPORT

Taxis are easily found at the airports, cruise ship terminals, hotels, and major tourist attractions. The international airports have car rental agencies on-site. A valid driver's license and major credit card are needed to hire a car. Driving is on the right side, and all the islands have a network of paved roads connecting the main towns. Dirt roads run through the countryside, and a four-wheel drive vehicle is practical for independent travelers touring outside major tourist areas. **AVIS**, **Hertz**, **AB Carrental**, **Amigo Rent-A-Car**, and **Michel Car Rental** are popular car rental companies. Aruba and Curaçao also have public bus systems.

SHOPPING

Curaçao offers the best shopping experience. Cheese, chocolates, and Delftware are popular items. The goods in Aruba and Curaçao are cheap

Market stalls awaiting cruise ship passengers in Brionplein, Willemstad

due to a low import duty. Dutch goods are of particular interest on these two islands. On Bonaire, Kralendijk offers art, jewelry, and beachwear. Look out for Aruba's **Strada complex**, **Island Fashions** in Bonaire, and **Riffort Village** in Curaçao.

LANGUAGE

Dutch is the official language, but locals speak a dialect called Papiamento, as well as English, and Spanish.

ELECTRICITY

On Aruba, the voltage is 110 AC, 127/120 AC on Bonaire, and 110/130 AC on Curaçao. Most outlets accept US plugs.

TIME

The ABC islands are on Atlantic Standard Time, 4 hours behind Greenwich Mean Time.

GETTING MARRIED

On Aruba, couples need to submit their documents at the **Office of Civil Registry** at least 14 days prior to the wedding date. On Bonaire, either party needs to become a temporary resident of the island. Check the Bonaire tourism website for details. Paperwork on Curaçao begins two months in advance, and both the bride and groom must be temporary residents for at least 3 days. Contact **Wedding Services Curaçao** for assistance.

DIRECTORY

GETTING THERE

Air Jamaica
www.airjamaica.com

American Eagle
www.aa.com

Delta
www.delta.com

Divi Divi
Tel 599 9839 1515.
www.flydivi.com

Dutch Antilles Express
Tel 599 717 0808.
www.flydae.com

KLM
www.klm.com

United Airlines
www.united.com

US Airways
www.usair.com

VISITOR INFORMATION

Aruba Tourism Authority
www.aruba.com

Curaçao Tourist Board
www.curacao.com

Tourism Corporation Bonaire
www.infobonaire.com

HEALTH AND SECURITY

Ambulance
Tel 911 (Aruba), 119 (Bonaire), 912 (Curaçao).

Dr. Horacio Oduber Hospital
Tel 297 587 4300.

Police
Tel 100 (Aruba), 911 (Bonaire), 911 (Curaçao).

San Francisco Hospital
Tel 599 717 8900.

St. Elizabeth Hospital
Tel 599 9462 5100.

COMMUNICATIONS

Digicel
www.digicelaruba.com
www.digicelbonaire.com
www.digicelcuracao.com

TRANSPORT

AB Carrental
www.abcarrental.com

Amigo Rent-A-Car
www.amigocar.com

AVIS
www.avis.com

Hertz
Tel 297 588 7570 (Aruba), 599 717 7221 (Bonaire), 599 9888 0188 (Curaçao).

Michel Car Rental
www.michelcarrental.com

SHOPPING

Island Fashions
5 Kaya Grandi, Kralendijk.

Riffort Village
Otrobanda, Willemstad.

Strada Complex
Caya G.F. Betico Croes, Oranjestad, Aruba.

GETTING MARRIED

Office of Civil Registry
Oranjestad, Aruba.
Tel 297 583 4400.

Wedding Services Curaçao
Piscadera Bay, Curaçao.
Tel 599 9463 6207.
www.weddings curacao.com

General Index

Acknowledgments

Dorling Kindersley would like to thank the many people whose help and assistance contributed to the preparation of this book.

Contributors

Christopher P. Baker, winner of the 2008 Lowell Thomas Award as the Travel Journalist of the Year, is a Caribbean specialist and an authority on Cuba travel. He has contributed to more than 200 publications worldwide, including Caribbean Travel & Life, Islands, Maxim, and National Geographic Traveler. He has been named Travel Writer of the Year by the Caribbean Tourism Organization and the Jamaican Tourist Board.

James Henderson has been visiting the Caribbean for more than 20 years, contributing words and images to travel guides and the press. He has written for many leading UK publications and magazines and is the founder-editor of definitivecaribbean.com, an on-line guide to the islands.

Skye Hernandez is a writer and editor living in Trinidad and Tobago. She has traveled widely in the Caribbean and is a former editor of Caribbean Beat and MACO Caribbean Living magazine.

Lynda Lohr moved to the Caribbean seeking an adventure 25 years back. A resident of St. John (US Virgin Islands), she regularly writes articles for many news organizations, travel publications, and has contributed to many guidebooks on the Caribbean.

KC Nash, an American freelance writer who has been visiting the Caribbean for over 20 years, now lives in Antigua. A former editor of a daily newspaper, she has also written for many regional magazines and publications.

Don Philpott, a writer for more than 40 years, has authored about 90 books on many subjects including travel. More than 5,000 of his articles have been published in US and UK newspapers and magazines.

Theresa Storm, a Canadian freelance travel journalist, author, and photographer, has contributed to well-known magazines such as Reader's Digest, Islands, and Caribbean Escapes. She has also won several awards for her travel writing.

Lynne Sullivan, an American freelance journalist, writes extensively about Caribbean destinations. She is a member of the Society of American Travel Writers and the American Society of Journalists and Authors.

Polly Thomas lives in Trinidad and is a freelance writer and editor who first visited the Caribbean aged 17, when she traveled around Jamaica. Since then, she has explored most of the islands, and is the author of guidebooks to Jamaica, Trinidad and Tobago, St. Lucia, and Antigua.

Fact Checkers

Lynda Lohr, Textosdom (Santo Domingo), Rukmini Tilara

Proofreader
Stewart Wild

Indexer
Cyber Media Services Ltd.

Design and Editorial

Publisher Douglas Amrine
List Manager Vivien Antwi
Managing Art Editor Jane Ewart
Project Editor Alastair Laing
Project Art Editor Kate Leonard, Shahid Mahmood
Editorial Assistance Vicki Allen
Senior Cartographic Editor Casper Morris
Managing Art Editor (Jackets) Karen Constanti
Jacket Designer Tessa Bindloss
Senior DTP Designer Jason Little
DTP Designer Natasha Lu
Picture Researcher Ellen Root
Production Controller Liz Cherry

Design and Editorial Assistance
Emma Anacootee, Christopher Baker, Cobalt Id, Jane Ellis, Fay Franklin, Skye Hernandez, Priya Kukadia, Alison McGill, Anna Streiffert, Rukmini Tilara, Janis Utton

DK Picture Library
Romaine Werblow

Additional Photography
Max Alexander, Andy Crawford, Ian Cummings, Mike Dunning, Lydia Evans, Neil Fletcher and Matthew Ward, Trish Gant, Heidi Grassley, Frank Greenaway, Dave King, Cyril Laubscher, Martin Norris, Ian O'Leary, Gary Ombler, Martin Richardson, Tim Ridley, Lucio Rossi, Karl Shone, Tony Souter, Jon Spaull.

Photography Permissions
Dorling Kindersley would like to thank the following for their assistance and kind permission to photograph at their establishments:

Ajili Mójili, Puerto Rico; Altar de la Patria, Santo Domingo; Anse Chastanet, St. Lucia; Apple Bay, British Virgin Islands; Barbados Golf Club; Cindy Corbin at Barbados Museum;

Resort Hotel, Sint Maarten; Caribelle Batik, St. Kitts; Catedral Primada de América; Craighton Estate Coffee Farm and Great House; Daphne's, Barbados; Decker's Grille & Lounge; Diamond Casino; Discovery at Marigot Bay; Firefly; Grace Bay Club, Turks & Caicos; Mr Bob Betton at Greenwood Great House; Half Moon Club, Jamaica; Harbour Lights, Barbados; Annabella Proudlock at Harmony Hall; Hotel El Convento, Puerto Rico; Jobean's Hot Glass Studio; Jump Up Casino; La Cathédrale Saint-Louis, Martinique; Le Plein Soleil, Martinique; Le Sereno; Grand Cul-de-Sac, St Barthélemy; Matilde Restaurant & Historic Monument, Guadeloupe; Carlos I. Ayala at Museo de Arte de Puerto Rico; Museo de Arte e Historia de San Juan; Old Gin House; St. Eustatius; Parque de Bombas; Pati de St. Barth; Pedro St. James National Historic Site; Pyrat Rum Factory, Anguilla; Raffles Canouan; Rainforest Restaurant at Papillote, Dominica; Rawlins Plantation Inn; RockHouse; Negril; Royal Westmoreland; Sacred Heart Church, a Roman Catholic Church; Frank Costin at Savannah Gallery, Anguilla; Marietta Norville at St. Nicholas Abbey, Barbados; Sunbury Plantation House; The Blue Haven Hotel, Tobago; The Cove, Antigua; The Edge, St. Lucia; The Fort Young Hotel, Dominica; The Grenadines Resort; The Hermitage Plantation Inn, Nevis; The Jaipur Restaurant; The Rhodes Restaurant; The Roman Catholic Cathedral, St. Lucia; Westin Dawn Beach Resort Casino, St. Martin; Young Island Resort, St. Vincent & the Grenadines; Zurra, Anguilla.

Picture Credits

Placement Key- t=top; tc=top centre; tr=top right; cla=centre left above; ca=centre above; cra=centre right above; cl=centre left; c=centre; cr=centre right; clb=centre left below; cb=centre below; crb=centre right below; bl=bottom left; bc=bottom centre; br=bottom right; ftl=far top left; ftr=far top right; fcla=far centre left above; fcra=far centre right above; fcl=far centre left; fcr=far centre right; fclb=far centre left below; fcrb=far centre right below; fbl=far bottom left; fbr= far bottom right.

Every effort has been made to trace the copyright holders, and we apologize in advance for any unintentional omissions. We would be pleased to insert the appropriate acknowledgments in any subsequent edition of this publication.

The publisher would like to thank the following individuals, companies, and picture libraries for their kind permission to reproduce their photographs:

Works of art have been reproduced with the kind permission of the following copyright holders:

Figura Ecuestre in Plaza de la Revolución © Alberto Lescay Merencio 87c; Sam Sharpe Monument in Montego Bay © Kay Sullivan 137tl; Maternity at the Galeria de Arte Cándido Bidó © Cándido Bidó 166bl; Girafo in San Juan © Jorge Zeno 194c; The Resurrection and Ascension mural in the Sacred Heart Church, a Roman Catholic Church, Saba © Heleen Cornet 288bl

4CORNERS IMAGES: Larsen Collinge 54tr; Devaux Danielle 406-407c; Cozzi Guido 347br, 523crb, 524tl; SIME /Biscaro Alberto 184-185, / Dutton Colin 365cr, /Romiti Fabrizio 116br, / Damm Fridmar 509br, /Gräfenhain Günter 25crb, 26-27c, 245tr, 484cl, 509tl, 523br, / Kaos03 524cr, /Mehlig Manfred 42cr, /Ripani Massimo 270b, /Schmid Reinhard 5tr, 25br, 36bc, 69br, 80tl, 86bl, 88tr, 98cla,132b, 133tl, 152br, 489tl, /Bertsch Werner 22-23

ABACUS RESTAURANT LOUNGE & PIANO BAR: 112ca

ALAMY IMAGES: Rolf Adlercreutz 350cl; John Anderson 521c; Arco Images GmbH 10cl, 83cra, 181cla, 335c; Bill Bachmann 254cr; Mark Bassett 27br, 145clb, 160ca; Henry Beeker 523bl; Henry George Beeker 515tl; John Bentley 48clb; Blickwinkel 27bl; Tibor Bognar 13tl; Brandon Cole Marine Photography 44clb; George Brewin 54br; George Brice 451t; Caribbean 131tr; Maria Grazia Casella 50tr; Robert Clay 457tr; Thornton Cohen 30-31c; Content Mine International 51cb, 305br; Dennis Cox 453tc; Chris A Crumley 128cra, 351tr; Stuart Crump 54crb; CuboImages srl 78tl, 155br; Tim Cuff 40crb, 118bc, 130tr; Richard Cummins 410cra; Danita Delimont 3c, 102clb, 106bc, 119tr, 125tl, 128ca, 130clb, 311bc, 363br, 367cl, 401bl, 406tl, 515c, 524bc; Susan E. Degginger 244cl, 421cla; Delfini Int Ltd (UK) 245tl; Reinhard Dirscherl 44tr, 180br; Alissa Everett 37br; Eye Ubiquitous 471clb; Fabian Gonzales Editorial 421clb, 421br; FAN travelstock 121tc; Waldhaeusl Franz 192br; Robert Fried 44cla, 137cl, 161br, 207tr; Dan Galic 33bl; geogphotos 108br, 109cl; Oliver Gerhard 10br; Jeff Greenberg 40tr, 124tl, 124b; Guillen Photography/UW/Bonaire 521cl; Nick Hanna 40bl, 183cl; Blaine Harrington III 50cr; Headline Photo Agency 147br; Bill Heinsohn 100bl; Gavin Hellier 45tl, 303t, 474tl; Hemis 80br; John Henshall 74bl; Wesley Hitt 140b; Peter Horree 350clb; Iconotec 367tc; ImageGap 156ca; ImageState 57tr; Imagestate Media Partners Limited - Impact Photos 51bl; Ingolf Pompe 480crb; Ingolf Pompe-8 363tl; 367br, 372ca; Ingolf Pompe-32 48cla, 492tc;

Isifa Image Service s.r.o 83tc, 85cl; James Davis Photography 329cla; Andre Jenny 244bl, 254c; Matthew Johnston 455clb; Jon Arnold Images Ltd 75tl, 304cr; JTB Photo Communications, Inc 82clb; Kim Karpeles 200cla; David Kilpatrick 473br; Dan Leeth 27tr; Yadid Levy 505br; Mark Lewis 33tl, 119tl, 237cl; LH Images 304bl, 305crb; Randy Lincks 291bc; Melvyn Longhurst 74cla; Lordprice Collection 48tr; Iain Lowson 484tr; Ilene MacDonald 11br; MagicSea.com/Carlos Villoch 241br, 245bl, 286br; Stephen Mallaby 82cl; Mary Evans Picture Library 418br; mediacolor's 30bl; Michael DeFreitas Caribbean 32crb, 125cr; MJ Photography 507cr; Mountain Light/ Galen Rowell 261bl; Steve Murray 37cr; nagelestock.com 136bl; Martin Norris 82tr; Brian North 455bc; North Wind Picture Archives 143crb; M. Timothy O'Keefe 36cb, 36br, 44bl, 105br, 122cl, 179c, 179br, 192cla, 308tl, 401crb, 407br; Papilio 455tc; Paul Thompson Images 463c; Peter Arnold, Inc. 203br; Photov.com/Hisham Ibrahim 138t; David Pick 54cr, 322br, 336ca; Walter Pietsch 360br, 367clb, 373br; Kristjan Porm 350br; Reimar 275br; Robert Harding Picture Library Ltd 71b, 493br; Helene Rogers 340tr, 506cra, 507tl; Grant Rooney 50cl; Rough Guides 325bl; Kevin Schafer 213c, 455bl; James Schwabel 237clb; SCPhotos 228c; Alex Segre 74cb, 75crb; Ramona Settle 129br; Linda Sikes 181tc; Stephen Frink Collection 13tr, 28cr, 123br, 248ca, 438br; Karen & Ian Stewart 29cr, 45cr; Stock Connection Blue 49tr; Stockfolio 367cr; Lee Karen Stow 179tr; Rick Strange 236tl; Mark Summerfield 232bl, 232br, 233crb; Mark Sykes 350bc; terry harris just greece photo library 41tl; Terry Smith Images Turks and Caicos Collection 122crb; Topcris 162tr, 163bl; Travelib Asia 43br; Travelshots.com 317br, 323br, 456cr; Kirk Treakle 237bl; Bob Turner 506bl; Tom Uhlman 27cra, 35tr; V1 50crb; Michael Ventura 447c; Visual&Written SL 29crb; Nik Wheeler 35tl; Poelzer Wolfgang 453ca; Andrew Woodley 38cl, 326cl, 332tr, 350tl, 350tr; World Pictures 467bc, 470br; WorldFoto 107cl; Worldspec/NASA 14bl; www. rekindlephoto.com/Don Despain 102tr; XSPhoto 458ca; Rüçhan Ziya 45br

ARDEA.COM: Masahiro Iijima 499tc

AXIOM PHOTOGRAPHIC AGENCY: 407bl; Axiom Raffles/Chris Caldicott 36-37c; Ian Cumming 133br, 145tl, 151tl, 153tl; Hemis 31tl, 342b

CHRISTOPHER BAKER: 89cra

LOUIS N BATIDES: 41tr

BLISS SINT MAARTEN: 283br

BLUE BUBBLES WATERSPORTS & DIVE CENTRE: 278tl

BOATSWAIN'S BEACH: 103tl

CAYMAN BRACK LOST CITY OF ATLANTIS: Elisa Buller 107bc

ANNE CHOPIN: 383br

CHUKKA CARIBBEAN ADVENTURES: 155c, 155cra

PHILIP CHUNG: 59cl

CORBIS: 434bc; C.I. Aguera 273tc; Tony Arruza 63br; Yann Arthus-Bertrand 435cla, 437cla; Atlantide Phototravel 11t, 54bl, 67br, 194b, 486b; Tom Bean 34br, 195br; Bettmann 36tr, 63tr; Tibor Bognar 84tl; Gary Braasch 499br; Diane Cook & Len Jenshel 181br; Reinhard Eisele 145bl; Epa/Alejandro Ernesto 16bl; Macduff Everton 55br, 441br; Ales Fevzer 37bl; Stephen Frink 107crb, 291cl, 495br; Goodlook/Philippe Giraud 34-35c, 59br, 381br, 397br; Blaine Harrington III 5crb, 487tl; Rose Hartman 37crb; Gavin Hellier 396bl; Hemis/ Bertrand Gardel 165br; Dave G. Houser 49cra, 50br, 261t, 262bc, 293crb, 453cla; George H.H. Huey 401cra; image100 484cr; Catherine Karnow 34tr; Layne Kennedy 153br; Bob Krist 12tl, 31bl, 232cl, 243cr, 311cla, 403clb, 453clb, 495c; Buddy Mays 233bl; Joe McDonald 43cr; MedioImages 121clb, 406cl; Amos Nachoum 291tc, 523cl; NewSport/Troy Wayrynen 39tr; Mark Peterson 139bc; photocuisine/J.Garcia 453cb; Robert Harding World Imagery/Neil Emmerson 324bl; Bill Ross 25cra; Rykoff Collection 63bl; Bob Sacha 48-49c; Paul Souders 107tc; Sygma/Philippe Giraud 346t; Liba Taylor 39br; Onne van der Wal 32cl; Michele Westmorland 118t; Nik Wheeler 287t; Xinhua Press/Liu Dawei 39bl; zefa/Fridmar Damm 12b, /Hein van den Heuvel 32clb

DANITA DELIMONT STOCK PHOTOGRAPHY: Bill Bachmann 521br; Walter Bibikow 5clb, 343tl, 508ca, 516tl, 521bl; Robin Hill 41cr; Greg Johnston 310cl; Jon Arnold Images 24br; Scott T. Smith 343br, 381tl, 392cla; Nik Wheeler 311clb

DIRK DIJKHUIZEN: 515bl

DK IMAGES: courtesy of the Exmoor Zoo, Devon/Gary Ombler 47c; courtesy of the Museo De Arte Colonial, Havana, Cuba/Heidi Grassley 58cr; courtesy of the Museo De Artes Decorativas, Havana, Cuba/Lucio Rossi 81c; courtesy of the Museo Provincial De Historia, Cuba/Lucio Rossi 86c

DUFFY'S LOVE SHACK: 255br

FISH TRAP RESTAURANT: 253ca

FLPA: SA TEAM/FN/Minden 499cl

GETTY IMAGES: AFP/Juan Barreto 39cra, /Adrian Dennis 38cl, /Jacques Demarthon 39clb, /Jewel Samad 38crb, /Stringer/Philippe Merle 49crb; Aurora/Christophe Launay 329bl; Axiom Photographic Agency/Ian Cumming 141tr; Shaun Botterill 38-39c; Gustavo Caballero 49bl; David Cannon 36cla; Digital Vision/Stephen Frink 28crb; Herve Hughes 1c; Hulton Archive/Horst Tappe 417br; Darrell Jones 28bl; Ross Kinnaird 36clb; Michael Ochs Archives/Handout 151clb; Donald Miralle 33cr; Photodisc/Stuart Gregory 397tr, /Medioimages 25tl; Photographer's Choice/Jeff Hunter 107c; Photonica/Daniel Allan 37bc; Premium Archive/Alan Oxley 81bc; Riser/Jeff Hunter 89cl; Robert Harding World Imagery/Richard Cummins 484bc, /Gavin Hellier 68c; Roger Viollet/Harlingue 361bc; Stringer/Brian Kersey 39crb, /Phil Inglis 475bl; Taxi/Richard Bradbury 53tl; The Image Bank/Michele Westmorland 52cl; Vision/Cosulich 64-65

GRAND OLD HOUSE : 112cra

HOUSERSTOCK: Ellen Barone 27cr, 441cb; Dave G. Houser 441cla

ISLAND EXPOSURE INC: 335br

ISTOCKPHOTO.COM: Susanna Pershern 237cr

JACOBSON ASSOCIATES, INC: 123cl, 123clb, 123cr

JOLLY HARBOUR GOLF AND COUNTRY CLUB: 331t

JUPITERIMAGES: Don Hebert 233tr

MIKKO KARVONEN: 51tr

LONELY PLANET IMAGES: Jerry Alexander 519cl; Richard Cummins 132c, 519c; Richard I'Anson 30tr, 350c; John Elk III 213cla; Wayne Walton 327crb

MALLIOUHANA HOTEL & SPA: 40clb

MARY EVANS PICTURE LIBRARY: 65c, 307bc; MARY EVANS ILN PICTURES 23c

MASTERFILE: Jean-Yves Bruel 356cl; Mark Downey 145cb; Steve Fitzpatrick 32cra; Greg Stott 50bl

CHRISTOPHER MAZZ: 291crb, 291br

MIKE MESSINA: 213clb

NATIONAL GEOGRAPHIC STOCK: Cotton Coulson 437cl; Melissa Farlow 42cb; George Grall 521tc; Michael Melford 47bl; Minden Pictures/Gerry Ellis 441cl, /Laus Meyer 47cr, /Mike Parry 89crb; Joel Sartore 213bc; Rex Stucky 4br, 31c; Steve Winter 46cla, 46cr, 46clb

NATUREPL.COM: Nigel Bean 42tl, 46crb; Brandon Cole 120br; Jurgen Freund 123tc; George McCarthy 311cb; Rolf Nussbaumer

42crb, 43cra, 121tc, 144tr, 213bl, 213br; Pete Oxford 46bl, 121bc, 295cla; Doug Perrine 46tr, 210bc, 211tl; Mike Potts 43cla, 46c, 46cl; Jean E. Roche 43bl; Shattil & Rozinski 43tr; Lynn M. Stone 43c; Kim Taylor 42bl; Doug Wechsler 42cl, 121ca; Rod Williams 121cla

PAUL F. NEUMANN: 237cra

NORTH WIND PICTURE ARCHIVES: 9c

ODYSSEY PRODUCTIONS, INC.: Robert Frerck 195tl; James Quine 68b

ONDECK GROUP: 30tl, 30cl, 329cl, 329cr 329br

OTTLEY'S PLANTATION INN: 55crb, 56cl, 56bl, 314cra, 316ca

PHOTOGRAPHER'S DIRECT: Alan Weaver Photography 42clb

PHOTOLIBRARY: age fotostock/Gonzalo Azumendi 382tl, /Walter Bibikow 110ca, 365bl, 516br, /Angelo Cavalli 245br, /Georgie Holland 32tl, 102br, /Terrance Klassen 271cr, / Alvaro Leiva 407cr, /Morales Morales 11c, /P Narayan 360tl, 523clb; Animals Animals/ Hamman/Heldring 499cr; Bill Bachmann 135tl; Dan Barba 66br; Bibikow Bibikow 117bl; Joyce & Frank Burek 45tr; Digital Vision 2-3, / Philip Coblentz 482-483; Imagestate/Greg Johnston 29cl; Japack Photo Library 42tr; John Warburton-Lee Photography/Paul Harris 406bl; Jon Arnold Travel/Walter Bibikow 30br, 222-223, 394-395; JTB Photo 66clb, 246-247, 500-501; Alvaro Leiva 453cl; Mark M Lawrence 67tl; Mauritius/Walter Bibikow 516c; Wendell Metzen 67cr; Moodboard 499cla; Roberta Parkin 453cr; PhotoLink/T OKeefe 135br; Photononstop 368tc; Ingolf Pompe 479br; J-C&D. Pratt 386b; PureStock 272b; Alex Quesada 33tr; Robert Harding Travel/Richard Cummins 398b, 468bc, 508b, 511t, /J Lightfoot 24tr, /Ellen Rooney 24bl; Lothar Schulz 69tl; The Travel Library Limited 424-425; Paul Thompson 31br; WaterFrame – Underwater Images/Reinhard Dirscherl 28tr; 28cl, 521clb, 521crb, /Manuela Kirschner 88bl, 496br

PHOTOSHOT: Authors Images 380c; Eye Ubiquitous 38tr; NHPA/Jany Sauvanet 499cb; World Pictures 24clb, /Bruce Hemming 437cr/ Jean-Marc Lecerf 369tc, 381cr, 384br, 387tc, 390cra, 391br, 392br, /Colin Sinclair 38bl; WPN 51tc

PICTURES COLOUR LIBRARY: PCL Travel/ Terry Harris 455crb; Spain Pix 33clb

RARE SPECIES CONSERVATORY FOUNDATION: Dr Paul Reillo 407cb

REDFERNS: 49tl; Dickson 48bc; JM International 49br; David Redfern 49bc; David Sinclair 48br

REFLEXSTOCK: 461crb; PhotoNonStop/Van Osaka 51cl

REUTERS: Jorge Silva 50cb, 485tr

ROBERT HARDING PICTURE LIBRARY: Bruno Morandi 53c; Angelo Tondini 336cra

LUCIO ROSSI: 55tr, 85bl, 87tr, 88cr, 277clb

SANDY LANE: 475tc, 475cl, 475cr, 475crb

STEVE SIMONSEN/ MARINE SCENES: 8-9, 55cl, 55bl, 105tl, 224cl, 294cla, 307crb, 311bl, 312t, 422tl, 422b, 423cr; Spain Pix 55tl

SONESTA MAHO BEACH RESORT & CASINO, SINT MAARTEN: 40br

SOUTH WEST REGIONAL DEVELOPMENT AGENCY: Grete Howard 155clb

SUPERSTOCK: Angelo Cavalli 119br; Hemis.fr 41crb

THE BRIDGEMAN ART LIBRARY: Plan of Drake's attack on Santo Domingo, c.1595 (engraving) by British Library, London, UK/ © British Library Board. All Rights Reserved 61tr, Sir Henry Morgan (c.1635-88) (coloured engraving) by English School, (17th century)Private Collection/Peter Newark Historical Pictures 61bc, Eruption of a Volcano on Martinique, from 'Le Petit Parisien', 15th May 1902 (colour litho), Andrieux, Clement Auguste (1829-1910)/Musee de La Presse, Paris, France/ Lauros/Giraudon 382crb, BAL42746 Cocoa Plantation in the Isle of Grenada (print from an original sketch); O'Shea Gallery, London, UK; copyright unknown 395c, "XTD75537 Credit: Sir Walter Raleigh's conquest of St. Joseph, Trinidad in 1595, engraved for the Universal Magazine, 1750 (engraving) by British Museum, London, UK 483c

THE CASINO ROYALE AT SONESTA MAHO BEACH RESORT & CASINO: 277cl

THE GRANGER COLLECTION, New York: 60cr, 60bl, 60br, 61cb, 62tl, 62bc, 63cb, 223c

THE MANGROVE INFORMATION CENTER: 32br

THE OCEAN ADVENTURE: 2008 Wayne & Karen Brown/Brown & Co. Photography 385cla

THE SUGAR MILL HOTEL: 251tc

TOPFOTO.CO.UK: The Image Works 367crb

THE TRAVEL LIBRARY: Erik Schaffer 59tl

TRAVEL-IMAGES.COM: 2006 David Smith 276bc; P. Baldwin 51tl; G. Friedman 58clb; M Torres 171br, 177br; R. Ziff 445br

TROPIC ISLE WEDDINGS: 56tr, 57clb

TROPICAL TIES: Celia Sorhaindo 406tr

TROPICASUB PLONGEE: 385tc, 385cl, 385cr, 385clb, 385bl, 385br

BAHAR ZAKER: 253cra

Front Endpaper: GETTY: Vision/Cosulich tl; PHOTOLIBRARY: Digital Vision/ Philip Coblentz bl; Jon Arnold Travel/Walter Bibikow tc, bc.

Jacket images: Front: GETTY IMAGES: Photographer's choice/Sylvain Sonnet. Back: ALAMY IMAGES: Carolyn Clarke tl; Dennis Cox clb; John Arnold Images Ltd/Doug Pearson cla; Stephen Frink Collection bl. Spine: GETTY IMAGES: Photographer's Choice/Sylvain Sonnet t.

SPECIAL EDITIONS OF DK TRAVEL GUIDES

DK Travel Guides can be purchased in bulk quantities at discounted prices for use in promotions or as premiums. We are also able to offer special editions and personalized jackets, corporate imprints, and excerpts from all of our books, tailored specifically to meet your own needs.

To find out more, please contact:
(in the United States) **SpecialSales@dk.com**
(in the UK) **travelspecialsales@uk.dk.com**
(in Canada) DK Special Sales at **general@ tourmaline.ca**
(in Australia)
business.development@pearson.com.au

Caribbean Inter-island Air Routes

UNITED STATES
OF AMERICA

BAHAMAS

ATLA

Gulf of Mexico

Havana

Cayo Coco

CUBA

Providenciales

T'

Nueva
Gerona

Cayo
Largo

Camaguey

Bayamo

Santiago
de Cuba

HAITI

CAYMAN
ISLANDS

George
Town

Montego
Bay

JAMAICA

Kingston

0 km   200

0 miles   200

Caribb

KEY

— Air Antilles
— Air Caraibes
— Air Jamaica
— American Eagle
— Caribbean Airlines
— Cayman Airways
— Cubana
— Dutch Antilles Express
— LIAT
— Turks and Caicos
— Winair

COLOMBIA